THE WORLDWIDE HISTORY OF BEADS

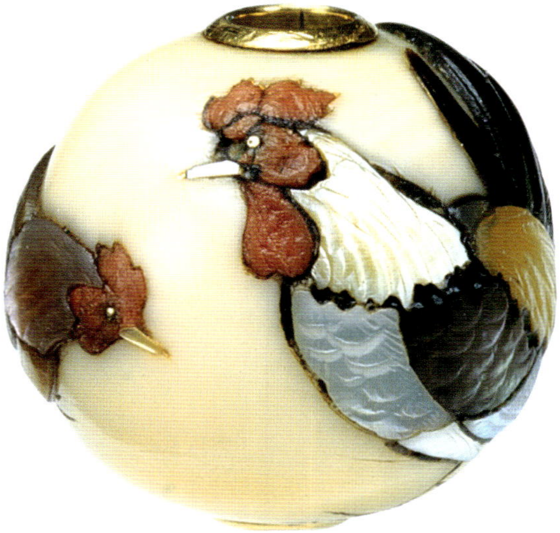

THE WORLDWIDE HISTORY OF BEADS

ANCIENT • ETHNIC • CONTEMPORARY

LOIS SHERR DUBIN

ORIGINAL PHOTOGRAPHY BY KIYOSHI TOGASHI

Thames & Hudson

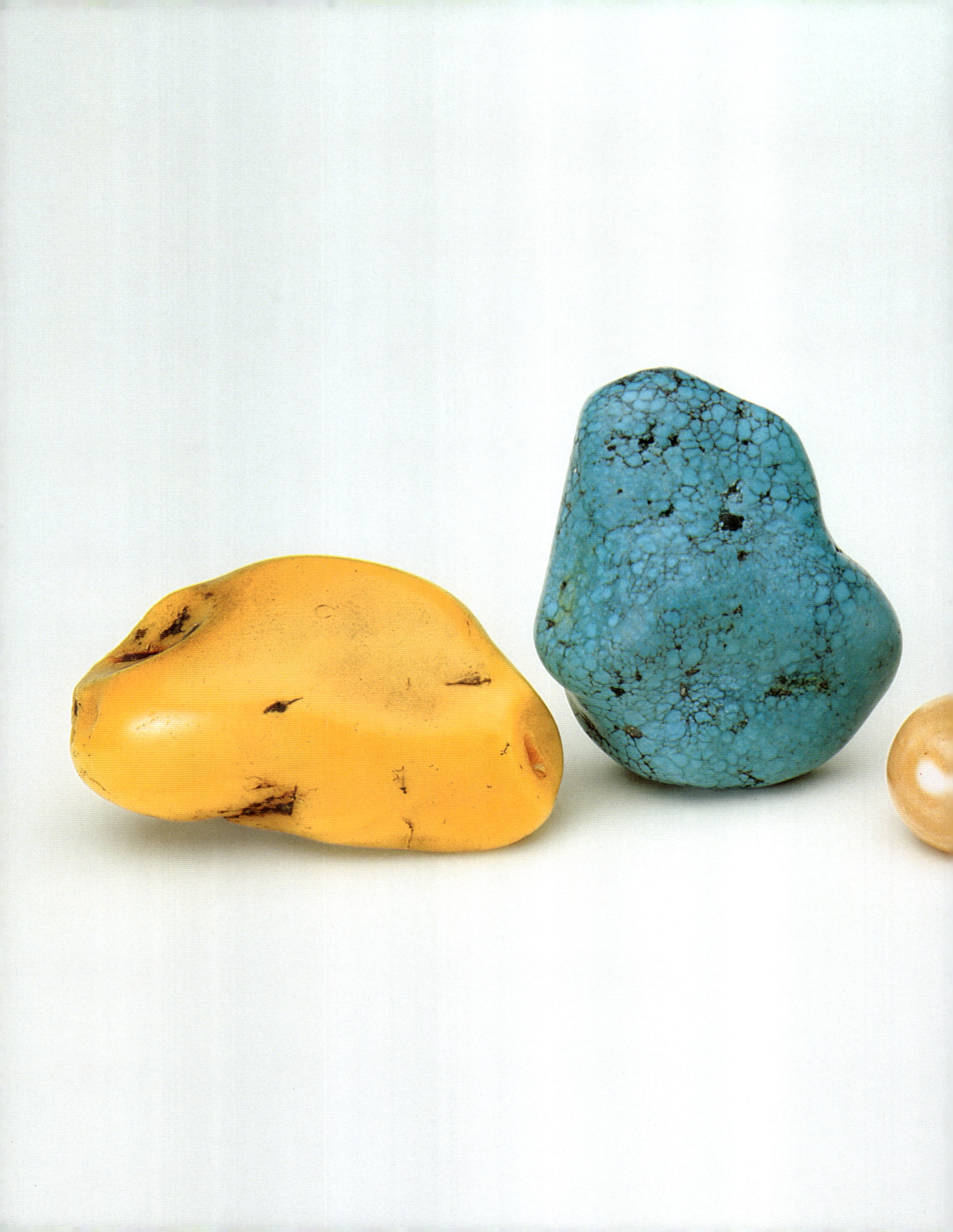

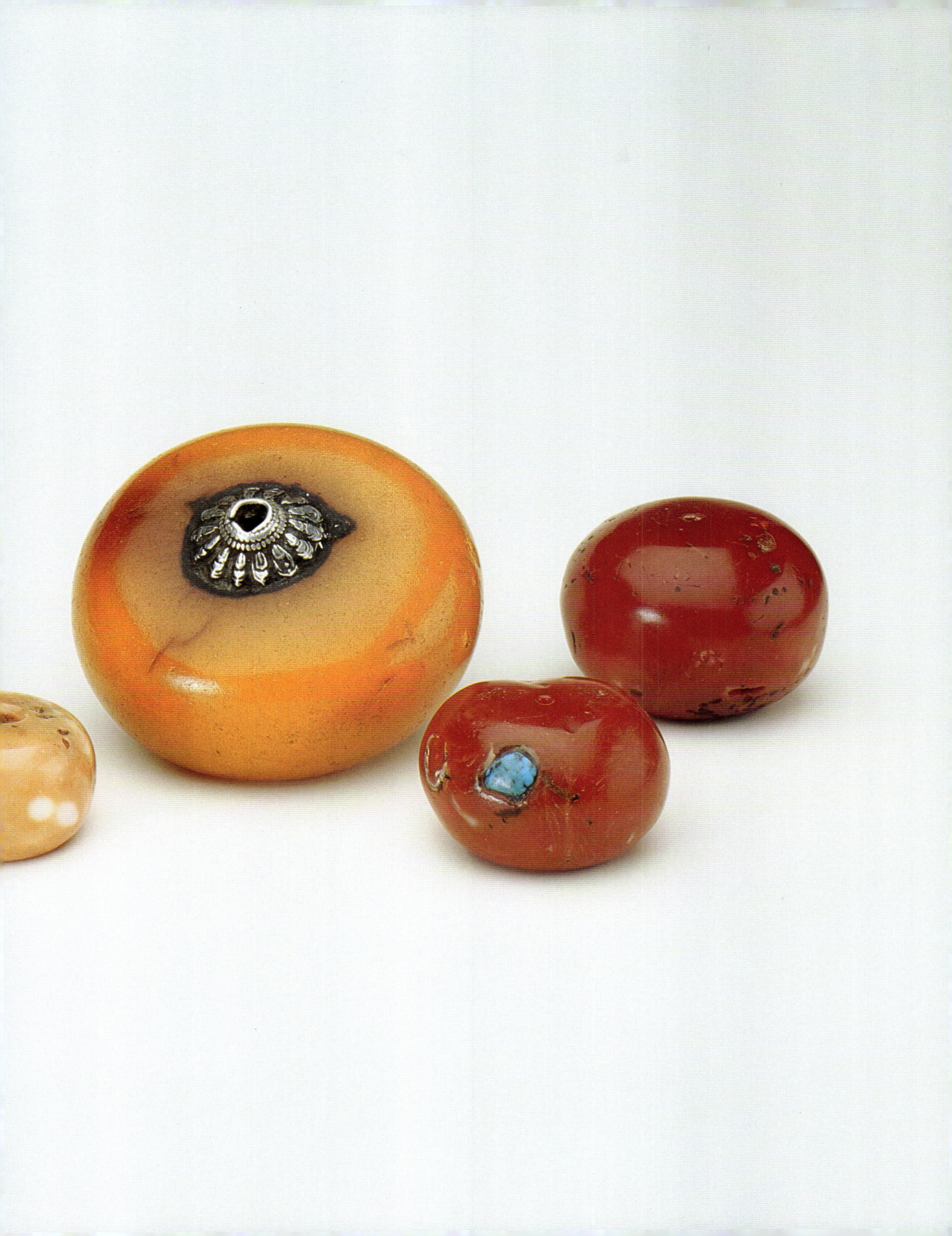

For Ted
who understood
And David
who understands

First published in the United Kingdom in 1987 by
Thames & Hudson Ltd, 181A High Holborn,
London WC1V 7QX

Revised edition first published in 2009
This paperback edition first published in 2015

British Library Cataloguing-in-Publication Data
A catalogue record for this book is available from the British Library

ISBN 978-0-500-29177-1

Printed and bound in China

Measurements: a bead's length is given as the length of the perforation; its diameter is the bead's width measured perpendicular to the perforation.

Maps appear on pages 21, 35, 50, 58, 67, 94, 103, 128, 148, 155, 183, 203, 228, 255, and 272.

COVER: Original photograph by Kiyoshi Togashi. Indonesian glass beads from southeast Kalimantan, thought to date c. A.D. 600-800. The beads were most likely inspired by post-Roman, Middle Eastern beads and were created just prior to Islamic times. Made by mosaic and combed techniques, the beads vary in size, typically from .9 to 1.6 cm. The Bead Museum, Glendale, Arizona
HALF-TITLE PAGE: An ivory shibayama-technique ojime (slide fastener) from nineteenth-century Japan, depicting a proud cockerel and his hen. Inlaid with mother-of-pearl, horn, and lacquer. Diameter, 1.7 cm. The Bead Museum, Glendale, Arizona
PAGES 4–5: Tibetan beads, typical of the shapes and materials worn by most Himalayan peoples. Turquoise, amber, and coral are believed to be imbued with protective powers. Turquoise bead: length, 5.1 cm. Collection Ivory Freidus and Tambaran Gallery, New York

Contents

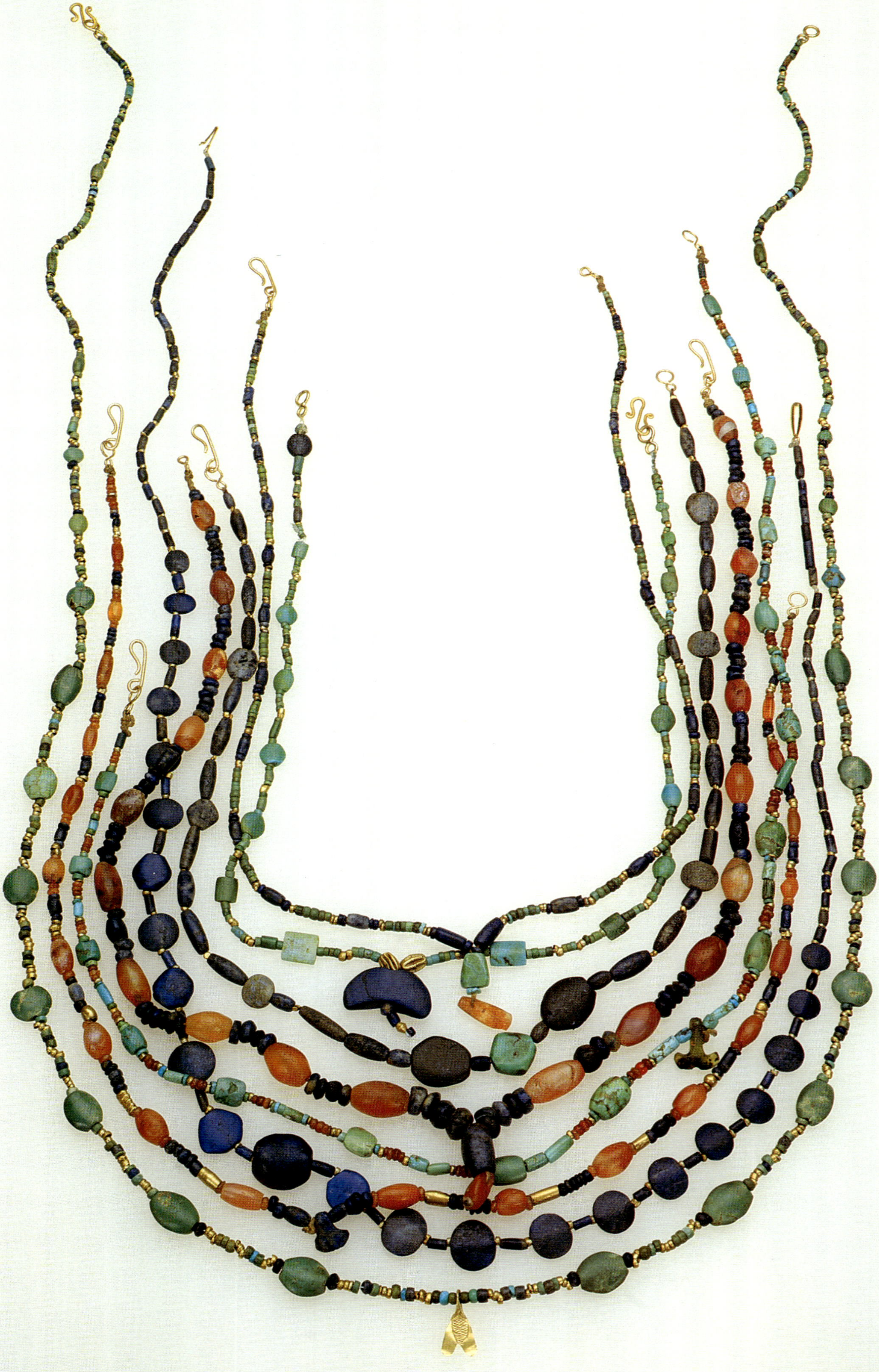

Foreword

Beads were probably the first durable ornaments humans possessed, and the intimate relationship they had to their owners is reflected in the fact that they are among the most common items unearthed from ancient graves. In the past, as today, men, women, and children adorned themselves with beads. In tribal cultures still, certain beads are often worn from birth until death and then are buried with their owner for the afterlife. Abrasion due to daily wear alters the surface features of beads, and if they are buried for long the effects of corrosion can further change their appearance. Thus, beauty is imparted to the bead both by use and the effects of time. When one looks at a bead, it is hard not to think about who previously owned it and how far through time and distance it has traveled to reach its current destination.

Besides their wearability, either as jewelry or incorporated into articles of attire, beads possess the desirable characteristics of every collectible: they are durable, portable, available in infinite variety, and often valuable in their original cultural context as well as in today's market. Pleasing to look at and touch, beads come in shapes, colors, and materials that almost compel one to handle them and to sort them.

Beads are such intriguing objects that one must ask the basic questions of what, where, when, and how whenever an interesting bead is encountered. They are miniature bundles of secrets waiting to be revealed: their history, technology, cultural context, economic role, and ornamental use are all points of information one hopes to unravel. Even the most mundane beads may have traveled great distances and been exposed to many human experiences. For example, in the eighteenth and nineteenth centuries many glass beads were shipped from Venetian and Bohemian factories to African destinations and then were traded through middlemen before reaching their tribal owners.

A collection of lapis lazuli, turquoise, carnelian, agate, and gold beads recently recovered from archaeological sites in northern Afghanistan, believed to date between 2200 and 1600 B.C. These beads resemble in quality, form, and materials those of the same period from Mesopotamia. Their minute scale—as many as forty to an inch have been recorded—is associated with wealth, since it was necessary to waste considerable raw material in their fabrication.

The gold fly amulet (at center of the bottom necklace) has both Sumerian and Egyptian origins, appearing in burials at Ur and in royal Egyptian jewelry of the Twelfth Dynasty (1991–1786 B.C.). Gold fly: Length, 1.5 cm. Private collection

A Nepalese woman holding her prayer beads. Photograph taken in 1983.

During the past two to three decades they have been sold again to bead traders for reexport to the Western world. They were always treated as valued personal adornments, until economic conditions and changing cultures caused them to be sold to a new, appreciative market of Western museums and collectors.

These special attractions of beads contribute to the uniqueness of bead research. While often regarded as the "small change of civilizations," beads are a part of every culture, and they can often be used to date sites and to designate the degree of mercantile, technological, and cultural sophistication. While beads have been and are studied by scholars trained in many different academic fields, the bead expert is often self-trained and sometimes without formal schooling. (This is a trend that is perhaps more pronounced today, although Horace C. Beck and W. G. N. van der Sleen, the spiritual fathers of contemporary bead researchers, were both self-trained.)

The bead researcher concentrates on a single category of artifacts, regardless of their origins in time or space. Yet, like the ethologist, the researcher of beads must gather information from many diverse fields. In addition to having to be a generalist while specializing in what many regard as a very narrow field, the researcher is faced with the problem of primary materials that have little or no documentation. Many ancient beads are from looted sites, and beads of ethnographic interest often are separated from their original cultural context. Furthermore, the bead enthusiast is also a missionary of knowledge, trying to enlighten the vast majority of people who are ignorant of the beauty, charm, and fascinating history that characterize these small, perforated artifacts.

Until now, there has been no comprehensive book on beads that adequately presents all aspects of their story. This book, a five-year labor of love and frustration for the author, who enlisted the cooperation of over thirty-five museums and numerous individuals, covers the cultures of the world in which beads proliferated. Richly illustrated with specially commissioned photographs, the volume also contains a unique time line of bead history. Over two thousand individual specimens are shown in their chronological and geographic contexts. Such an ambitious undertaking has never been attempted before. This feature alone will be of immense aid and interest to both amateur and expert bead connoisseurs. Cognizant of the enormity of the field and the constant flow of new information on beads, the author has presented this work in the hope of generating discussion and feedback from readers around the world. She encourages comments, corrections, and additions that she might incorporate into future editions.

Since beads have been a constant and primary part of jewelry throughout history, those with an interest in personal adornment will find Lois Dubin's book rewarding, not only for her history of tribal and ancient ornaments, but also for her coverage of the exciting renaissance of beads in contemporary jewelry. Today, beads are being combined and shaped into aesthetically dynamic jewelry and are being made of materials and techniques that are in themselves expressing new artistic and technological dimensions. As was the case in so many ancient and tribal cultures, the ordinary is again being used in extraordinary ways by artists and craftsmen.

—Robert K. Liu

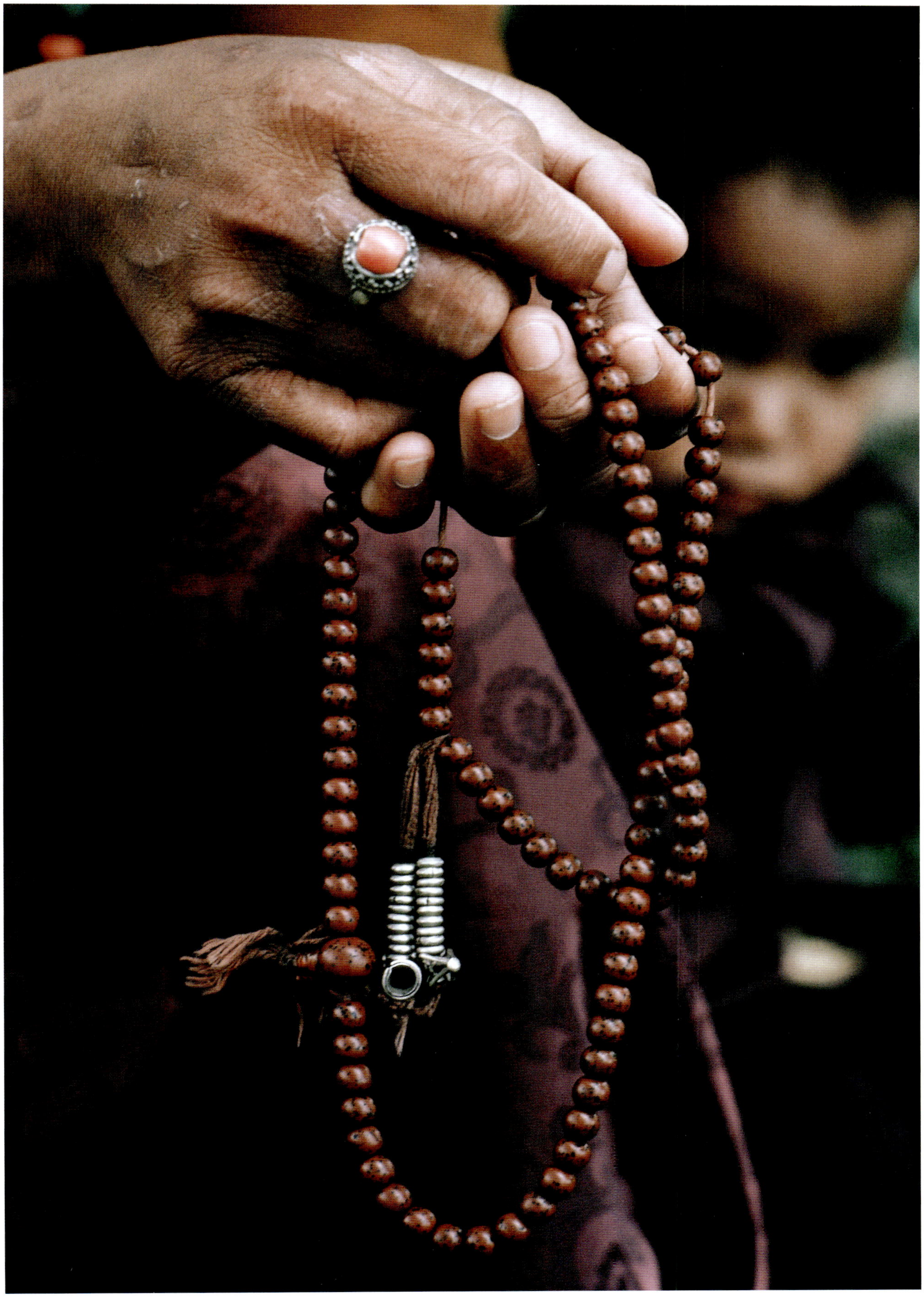

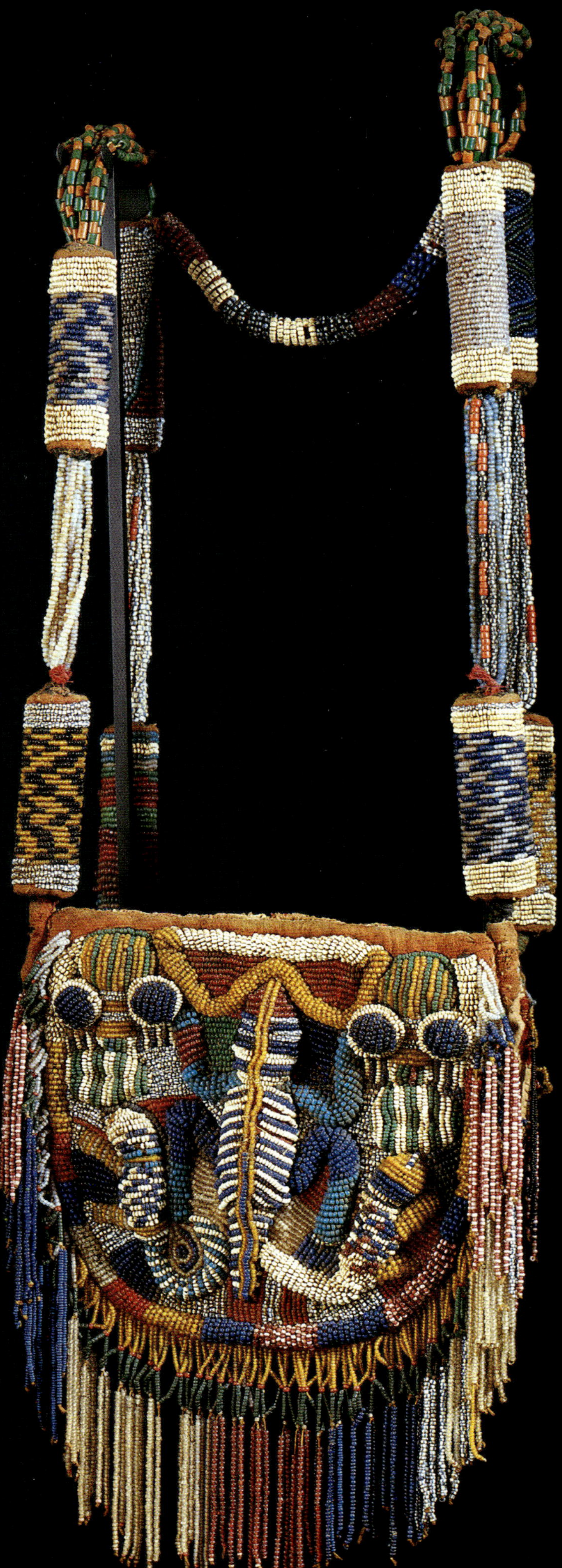

Acknowledgments

It has been twenty-two years since the original edition of *The History of Beads* was published. And, although much has changed in our world, what has remained constant is a universal love of beads and all the history and humanity that they embody.

The number of bead and beadwork artists, collectors and scholars has greatly increased. Anthropologists and archaeologists now study beads as primary components of social systems. Contemporary glass beads have become their own art form. There are significant bead publications, societies, conferences, exhibitions, specialty bead stores, and specialty bead museums.

The major additions to this edition of the book that occur in the first chapter (The Beginnings) and the final chapter (Contemporary) reflect the important broad trends during these past two decades. I have also included new and important bead finds from major archaeological sites—Sipan in Peru and Mission Santa Catalina de Guale in Georgia—as well as updating and correcting information throughout the entire book. It should be noted that although pages could be added to the end of the book, the previous page layout had to remain the same. Therefore, to increase the Beginnings chapter by several pages we eliminated the original Acknowledgements. (Please refer to the 1987 edition of *The History of Beads* for the original acknowledgements.)

For supplying information, beads and images for this edition, I wish to thank: Dr. Walter Alva, Museo Tumbas Reales de Sipan; Nick Barton, the Institute of Archaeology, Oxford; Dr. Christopher Donnan; Karlis Karklins; Dr. Mark Kenoyer; Dr. Daniella Bar-Yosef Mayer; Dave Mort; Lori Pendleton; Marie-Jose and Howard Opper; Norma and Bill Roth; Billy Steinberg and Brian Walls; as well as the contemporary artists (credited with their dazzling beads and beadwork), their galleries and photographers who typically responded to my requests for images with the comment: "It would be an honor to be included in the new edition of *The History of Beads*."

A very special thank you to Dr. Randall White at the Center for the Study of Human Origins, New York University, for his generous guidance with revisions and images for The Beginnings chapter. For allowing us to photograph their treasured beads on the cover, I thank: Henry Anavian, Toby Bowlby, Frederick Bourguet Chavez, Rachel Fox, David Freda, Stuart Golder, Valerie Hector, Gabrielle Liese, Kristina Logan, Walter Seifried, Billy Steinberg, and the family of Albert Summerfield. The updating of the Eye Beads chapter is from the work-in-progress on the evil eye with Dr. Martine Reid.

Toby and Bob Bowlby are friends extraordinaire. Toby's contemporary glass bead collection set the direction for the Contemporary chapter. Daniel Joseph Goldberg was a helpful advisor for the selection of contemporary glass beads. Bravo to Carolyn Benesh and Robert Liu for maintaing *Ornament Magazine* as a vital resource. At the Bead Museum in Glendale, Arizona, I thank Katie Anderson, Karen Karns, and Gabrielle Liese, whose spirit and strength is an inspiration to us all.

A huge thank you to Valerie Hector who was exceedingly gracious with information and contacts regarding contemporary beadworkers. My deepest appreciation to Jamey D. Allen who worked with me on text corrections and additions, coloration of the maps, the glossary, and helped me with all aspects of updating and supplying images for the Timeline.

At Harry N. Abrams, I thank Andrea Danese, senior editor, and Caitlin Kenney, editorial assistant, for superbly guiding the project from beginning to end; art director Michelle Ishay, for the new cover, and gifted designer Shawn Dahl. Margaret Kaplan, the book's original editor during the 1980s, continues to make helpful suggestions, and has become a treasured friend. I am grateful to David Goldberg for his support in every way. Kiyoshi Togashi, as evidenced by his latest photography, is the best. In truth, most books, particularly one of this complexity, require a dedicated team effort. My heartfelt thanks to all.

A Yoruba diviner's bag from late nineteenth- or early twentieth-century Nigeria, used to carry ritual accessories. The six cylinders in the strap are bead-covered corncobs. Height, 125.7 cm. Collection Ruth and Paul Tishman, New York

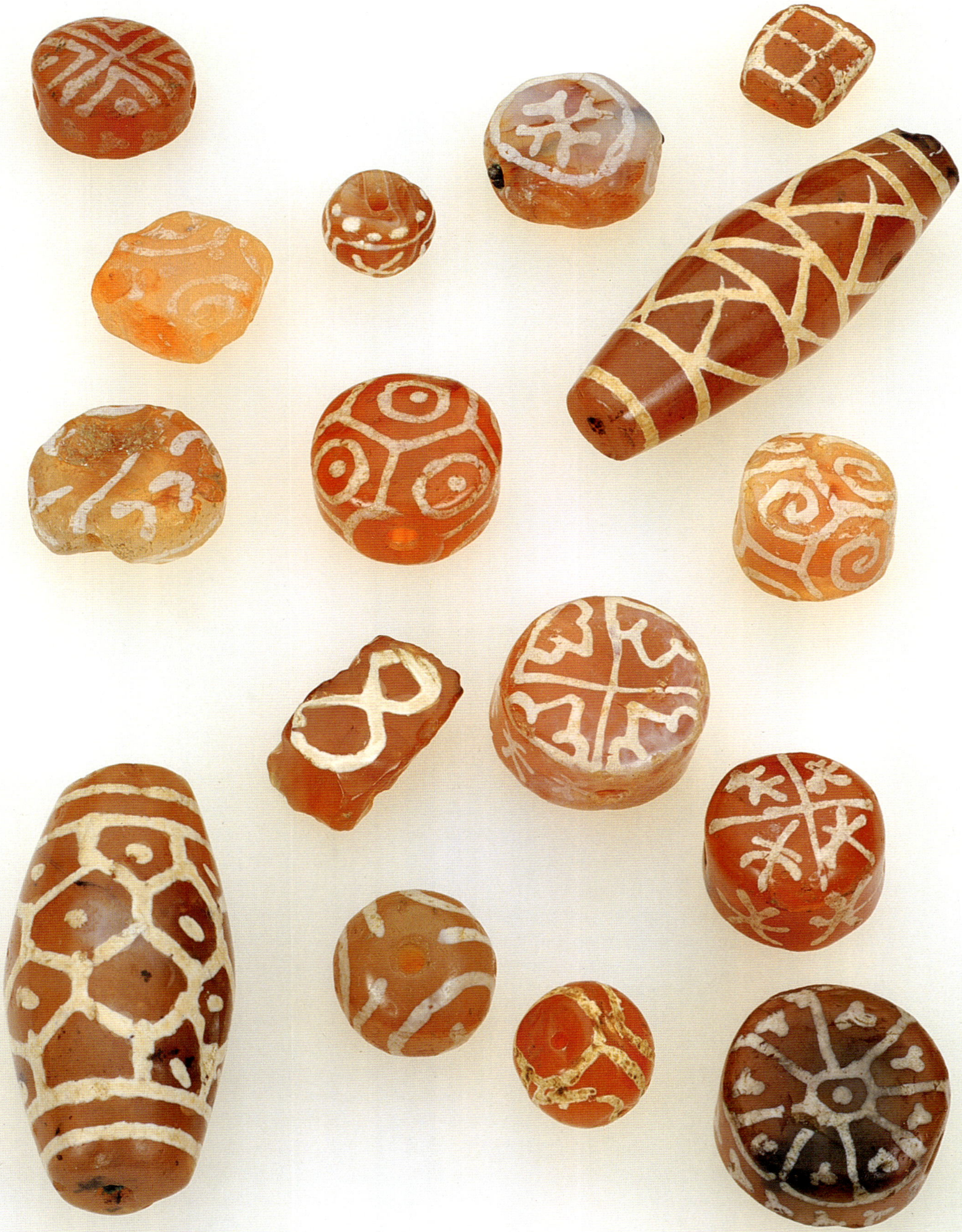

Introduction: Why a Book on Beads

Westerners tend to think of beads as adornment. In fact, we confine ourselves for the most part to draping them around our necks. Yet, through the centuries, beads have functioned as more than jewelry. They are kaleidoscopic, combined and recombined in an astonishingly wide range of materials; they express social circumstances, political history, and religious beliefs.

A collection of etched carnelian beads from Parthian to Sasanian period sites in Iran, dating from 249 B.C. to A.D. 642. The bead with rectangular patterns in the upper right corner may be older. Lower left bead: length, 3.2 cm. Collection Derek Content, Houlton, Maine

Beads are small, colorful, symmetrical, and often quite beautiful. They are frequently standardized, inexpensive units that can be arranged in almost endless configurations. They can be seen not only in the familiar forms of necklaces and bracelets but also on anklets, headbands, and headdresses. Beadwork is used in West Africa on altar mantles, garments for royal statues, and coverings for kingly stools. In ancient Asia, beads were scattered like seeds beneath temples to induce bountiful harvests, and among the Kogi of Colombia beads are part of ritual offerings to insure the future of newly built houses. In the Philippines, the practice of placing two beads in a cup at wedding ceremonies still binds marriages. Beads are worn to communicate status almost everywhere and were even used in North America to cement political alliances.

Beads have frequently been enlisted as symbolic repositories of sacred knowledge, been deemed to have curative powers, served as the fee for passage to the afterlife, and used as prompters to insure the proper conduct of ritual and prayer. Beads have been the medium of exchange in barter and the standard units of value in market systems. From the seventeenth to the nineteenth century, Europeans exchanged glass beads for beaver pelts in North America, for spices in Indonesia, and for gold, ivory, and slaves in Africa. Beads so often mirror the culture of which they are a part that they tell us a great deal about the social, political, economic, and religious lives of the people who have made and worn them.

The ways in which beads are used helps to define a particular group's concept of beauty. Both the selection of individual beads and the combinations and assemblages are informative. In some societies, beauty can even be rewarded by beads: an attractive East African Maasai woman will be courted with beads, and the accumulation of beads in itself will enhance her beauty.

The History of Beads: From 100,000 B.C. to the Present examines beads in twelve areas, not in an attempt to be encyclopedic but rather to identify certain features and patterns that are important to the story of beads. Different facets of the bead story are emphasized in each area. In North America, for example, the impact of European trade on the indigenous bead culture of the Great Lakes and Plains Indians is stressed. By contrast, in the chapter on India the pervasive role beads play in all aspects of life, secular and sacred, and the extraordinary continuity in beadmaking technology over the past four thousand years are the overriding concepts.

There are several perspectives from which beads might be looked at, but this book attempts to observe them primarily from cultural and historical viewpoints, to understand their importance in the lives of people through the history of a region and to account for the striking similarities and differences in bead culture between geographic areas and historical eras.

A combination of qualities makes beads especially interesting artifacts to study. They first appear with the advent of modern man, *Homo sapiens*, at least one hundred thousand years ago, and probably have been made and used by every culture in the world since then. Because beads are often made of durable materials, and because they have always been treated as important personal possessions and therefore not infrequently taken to the grave with their owners, they are well represented in the archaeological record. The great variety of materials, forms, and technology used to create finished beads, together with their portability and their natural prominence as adornment, renders them ideal vehicles for conveying a complex range of cultural information.

Beads and the raw materials to make them have been important trade items for millennia. Discovering the origins of finished beads, as well as bead styles and technologies, and tracing their subsequent travels provides an interesting picture of intercultural relations. The movements of beadmakers, bead technology, bead styles, and beads themselves are each complicated stories. A major task in bead research is identifying which combination of these processes accounts for the spread of bead knowledge at a particular time and place.

An important issue that recurs throughout bead history is the impact of trade on indigenous decorative styles. Over the centuries, cultures have expressed their own decorative styles in locally made beads. However, the sudden importation of quantities of inexpensive finished beads through newly created trade partnerships frequently changed both the role beads played in the recipient culture and the decorative styles produced thereafter.

Almost every society has had the minimum technology necessary to produce beads of one raw material or another. In fact, the technical sophistication of bead manufacturing often mirrors the general technological level of the society. Throughout history, beads have frequently been one of the first items produced by societies experimenting with new technologies. When bronze and iron were first worked by craftsmen, for example, they were often employed to make weapons, tools, and beads at the same time. As soon as glass was invented, it was used to make beads. Moreover, beads were always popular trade items, and more technologically sophisticated cultures traded their finished products to less advanced peoples. Tracing the diffusion of beads thus affords us a view of the broader history of technology.

While this book seeks to explain similarities and differences in bead culture in terms of historical factors, it also recognizes certain universal features of beads and the handling of them that appear to cut across cultural differences. In the chapters that follow, broad commonalities in the creation of beaded adornment are identified that express certain basic human needs.

Although beads are typically described as small balls perforated for stringing, the earliest beads were generally tubular, barrel-, and disk-shaped, reflecting the limitations of technology and availability of raw materials. Once the technical capacity developed to make spheres, they became the most common bead shape for thousands of years thereafter. The appeal of spheres supersedes cultural differences. Moreover, sphere-shaped beads should be thought of as small sculptures: they are whole and perfect. In a perplexing world, this simple, familiar shape has visual and tactile completeness, which is reinforced when several beads are joined together to form a circlet. It is perhaps through the use of rosaries, circlets of prayer beads, that people have achieved their most profound and complete relationship with beads.

We must look for primal causes in the wearing of beads. Some psychiatrists trace bead adornment to feelings of security connected with the eye and sight. Joan Mowat Erikson, author of *The Universal Bead*, suggests:

> The eyes may be a basic clue to the elemental power of rounded objects.... It is with the eyes that mother and child communicate before speech develops, and the meeting of the eyes serves as an adjunct to speech whenever language fails....We begin life with this relatedness to eyes; we are protected by seeing, we feel secure when there is light. Eyes have been described as shining, laughing, dancing, glowing, glaring, gleaming—like beads—and are, like beads, colored blue, green, gray, brown, and golden.[1]

The "eye bead," a common bead type that resembles the form of an eye, was created in many early cultures and continues to be made today. Eye beads were used to meet people's age-old need for protection against malevolence—the "evil eye." Eye beads became "eyes that can see in all directions" and thereby served as protective amulets against the evil eye.[2] Inexorably, the viewer is drawn to look at eye beads, but because of their realism, they disturb rather than charm, and therefore encourage the viewer to look away from them and the vulnerable throats they encircle.

Psychiatrist Robert Bross, on the other hand, believes that touch, not sight, is the primary sense for an infant. He suggests that the passion for beads may be connected to the longing for the tactile pleasures associated with breast-feeding and the nipple. Whether or not we accept his arguments, the power of beads is such that there must be hidden within them some meaning essential to us all.

This volume will give the reader only an idea of the range of human creativity that has been applied to beads. It is a sampling of what people have done with this universal object, but it is hoped that the reader will come away with a sense of how deeply embedded the manufacture and use of beads have become in human society. Beads are tools by which people convey information to other people, while reminding the wearer of his or her own commitment to a set of beliefs and principles. They have been significant to people from Neolithic Asia to twentieth-century New York. They are and have always been used to state basic relationships to life and the supernatural. People have used beads to organize and symbolize their world. They have been guideposts in human relationships and expressions of innermost feelings. Perhaps the reader will identify with a particular segment of the bead story, thus prompting an exploration of the meaning of beads, not only in history, but in his or her life as well.

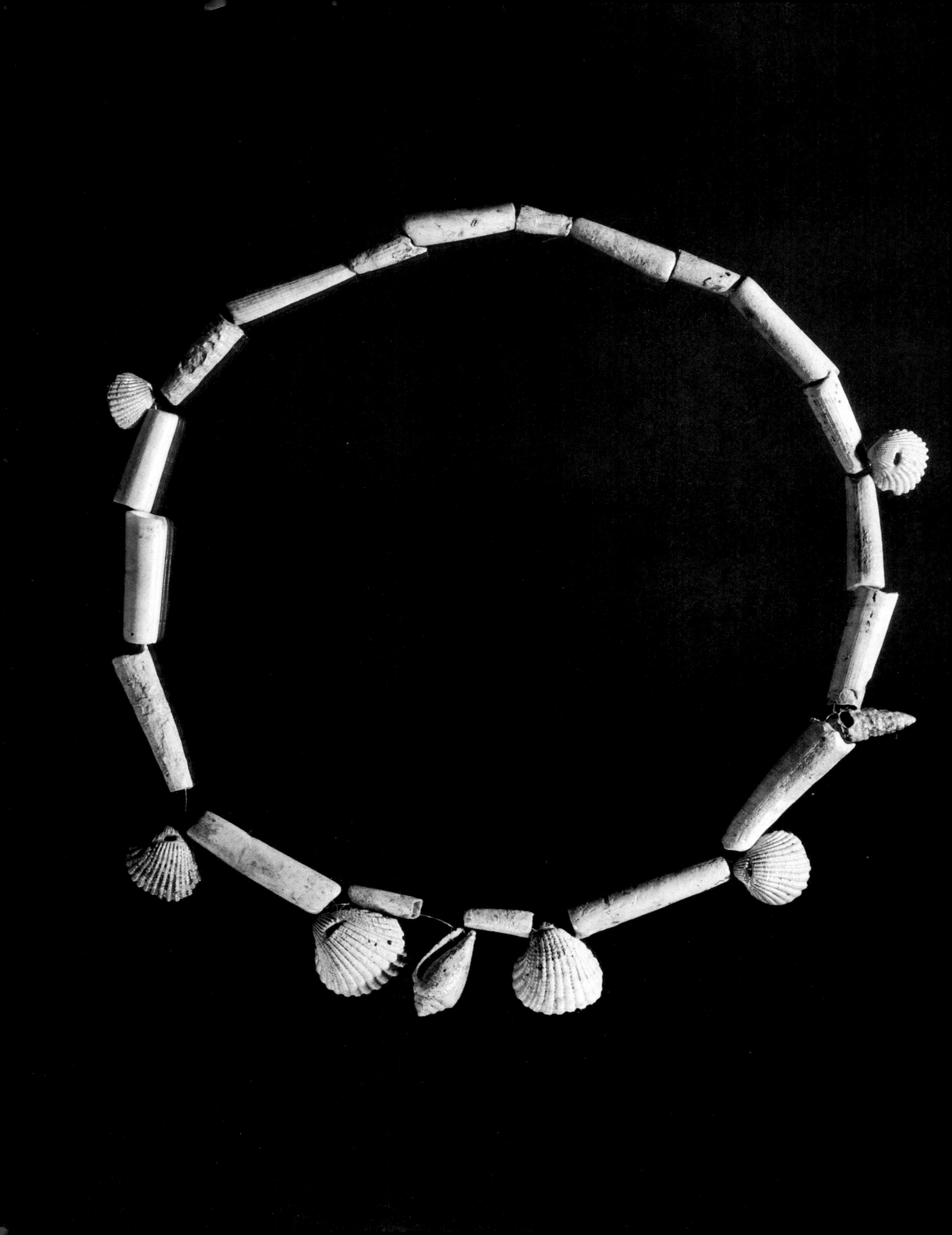

The Beginnings

As I visualize the [prehistoric] artisans sitting around the campfire carefully polishing their beads, I experience a profound sense of shared humanity.

—Dr. Randall White, 2007[1]

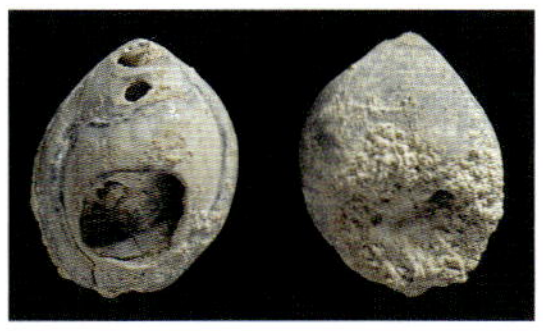

OPPOSITE: 1. *An extraordinary assemblage of Upper Paleolithic beads of various fossilized shell species from the East Gravettian site of Pavlov in the present-day Czech Republic, c. 24,000* B.C. *Length, 35 cm. Moravske Muzeum Brno, Czech Republic*

ABOVE: 2. *Beads of Nassarius shell excavated between 2003 and 2008 at Grotte des Pigeons, a large limestone cave in Taforalt, eastern Morocco. Dated to c. 82,000* B.C.*, the beads (from a group of 32) showed traces of red ocher, and appear to have been intentionally perforated and worn. Typical bead length varies from 1.74 cm to 1.45 cm. Courtesy Institute of Archaeology, Oxford*

While the first evidence of culture is manifested in simple stone choppers and cutting tools that were made in East Africa 2.5 million years ago, the earliest known beads are associated with Middle Paleolithic people. They were discovered at Skhul Cave on Mount Carmel and have been dated to approximately 108,000 B.C., at about the time *Homo sapiens* populations were replacing the Neanderthals and developing new and more complex cultures. The Skhul Cave beads, which predate the earliest known figurative art (engravings on mammoth tusks) by about 75,000 years, are varieties of Cardium, Nassarius, and Pecten shell.[2] Although few in number, other shell beads of a similar age have been documented within Africa and throughout the eastern Mediterranean—the area called the Levant. At Qafzeh Cave (located near Skhul Cave), five Glycemeris shell beads, dating 92,000 B.C., were recovered, the interior one having been stained with red ocher and showing signs of wear. None of these shells had human-made perforations. All were either naturally perforated or pieced by predators: "ready-to-use" explains archaeologist Daniella Bar-Yosef Mayer.[3] A group of thirty-two Nassarius shells from Grotte des Pigeons in eastern Morocco, and dated to approximately 82,000 B.C., does include beads that are argued to have been intentionally perforated.[4] (plate 2)

Increasing quantities of beads begin to appear in Africa and the Levant during the transition into the Upper Paleolithic era (41,000–10,000 B.C.). Ostrich eggshell beads from a Kenyan cave, Enkapune Ya Muto located in the Rift Valley, are at least 39,000 years old. Enkapune was a place for bead-making since worked ostrich shell was abundant.[5] Two sites in the Levant—Üçağizli Cave in Turkey and Ksar 'Akil in Lebanon, both of which were occupied for thousands of years—have yielded numerous marine shell beads that date 41,000–39,000 B.C. As archaeologists have pointed out, "the Paleolithic inhabitants of the caves were selective in their choices of shells for ornament-making, preferring rare varieties with luminous white or brightly colored shells, some with arresting patterns." That the shells were adornment rather than sources of food is known from their very small size (the shellfish used for food are larger), and distinct human-made modifications and/or perforations.[6]

The shell beads are particularly interesting when connected to current scholarship on the origins of modern humans. It is now believed that by at least 100,000 B.C., *Homo sapiens* evolved in Africa and started expanding into other regions. Their expansion into Western Europe and Asia began about 38,000 B.C. The Levant is one likely route of their movement from North Africa into Western Asia and Europe. Some scholars believe that this far-ranging (in both time and geography) wearing of shell beads was a form of symbolic communication—perhaps the earliest system for widely shared information.[7] Others disagree, suggesting that the quantities of beads are too small and random to imply a consciously organized system.

Indeed, it is the systematic production of standardized elements in quantity—embodying forms that are repeated at multiple locations for long periods of time—rather than the dates of the earliest beads that is today's cutting-edge issue for those researching prehistoric adornment.

Although beads have been found with fossil bones and other cultural remains in archaeological discoveries throughout the world (including India, China, Korea, Africa, and Australia), most of these finds involve no more than a few, simply made bead forms.[8]

It is only in the early phases of the European and Russian Upper Paleolithic—the Aurignacian and Châtelperronian periods (c. 38,000–26,000 B.C.)—that beads are found in greater numbers as creations of modern humans.

The European and Russian sites are concentrated in five major regions, including western Europe (southern France and northern Spain), the Mediterranean (Italy and eastern Spain), central Europe (the Czech Republic, Slovakia, Germany, and Austria), and Russia (the upper Ukraine and central Siberia)—where the evidence suggests that beads really made their appearance as part of a significant evolutionary development in culture some 35,000 years ago.[9]

What caused the proliferation of adornment at this time? The archaeologist Dr. Randall White has a compelling concept. He believes that as modern humans dispersed out of Africa and into Eurasia, it was during encounters (and competition with) existing Neanderthal populations and other groups of strangers that the elaborate systems of social cohesion, solidarity, and visual communication—including personal ornamentation—appeared.[10]

Social mechanisms developed that organized people into large multiband groups held together by the bonds of kinship and marriage and the shared requirements of large-scale hunting. Rituals developed to define and reinforce cohesive relationships among the larger groups of individuals and to teach and sanctify the many more complex rules of behavior required by increased group size. This led to even more densely settled communities with greater populations. It is within this context that clearly identifiable systems of art and adornment—and beads—had their beginnings.

Concurrent with the appearance of *Homo sapiens* populations is the arrival of an elaborate structure of symbolism. The most spectacular expressions of this development are the famous ritualistic cave paintings of southwestern France and northern Spain, as well as a few remarkably sophisticated assemblage of carvings used in ceremonies and

THE BEGINNINGS:
Archaeological Discoveries of Beads,
100,000 B.C. to 10,000 B.C.

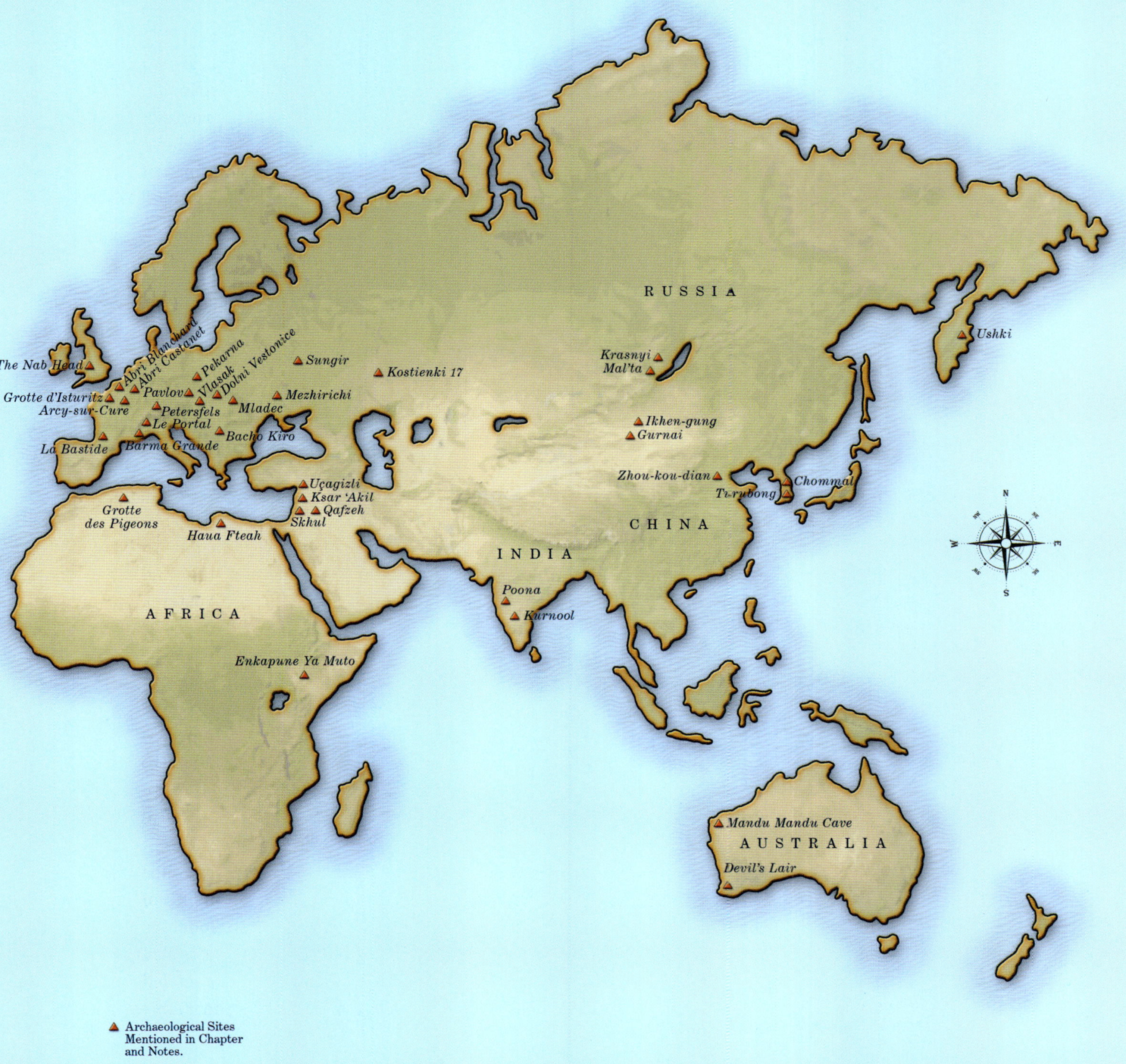

3. *Early Upper Paleolithic Beads: Aurignacian Age (40,000–25,000 B.C.) (1) A soapstone or talc pendant from Grotte de'Isturitz, France, dating 36,000 B.C., is the oldest formed ornament in Europe. Length, 5.5 cm. Excavation repository; (2) Amber pendant from Grotte de'Isturitz. c. 34,000 B.C. This site has yielded the oldest known evidence for amber jewelry in the world in the form of amber pendants, production debris, and raw chunks of amber. The amber was obtained from Cretaceous sources in the Pyrenean forelands. Length, 3.75 cm. Excavation repository; (3) Perforated bear canine from Grotte de'Isturitz, France. 31,000 B.C. Length, 5 cm. Excavation repository; (4) Bird bone beads, Grotte de'Isturitz, France. c. 31,000 B.C. Average length, 4 mm. Excavation repository; (5) Basket-shaped beads from Abri Blanchard, Dordogne, France, c. 31,000 B.C. Unique to the early Aurignacian era, these tiny and uniform basket-shaped beads, averaging 6 mm in length with a range from 2 to 12 mm, were most likely worn not as single elements but rather as part of larger arrangements such as necklaces or sewn onto clothing. Recent excavations at this important site point to intense bead production with a complex chain of operation. (See appendix 1) Musée National de Préhistoire; (6) Basket-shaped ivory bead from Abri Blanchard, Dordogne, France. c. 31,000 B.C. Two qualities of the bead are especially notable at this very early date: the highly polished surface luster (produced by techniques of grinding and polishing with a metallic abrasive—i.e. powdered red ocher [hematite])—and the intentional polishing of the ivory by the ancient artisan to possibly represent other shiny natural textures such as teeth and mother of pearl. Length, 1.1 cm. Musée di Castel-Merle; (7) A bead of a translucent belemnite fossil, an extinct marine mollusk that was abundant during the Jurassic and Cretaceous periods. Kostienki 17, Russia. c. 38,000 B.C. Length, c. 2 cm. Collection Institute of Prehistory, Russian Academy of Sciences, St. Petersburg, Russia; (8) Animal pendant (possibly a horse) of bone/ivory painted and decorated with drilled dots. Sungir, Russia. 22,000 B.C. Width, 5 cm. Collection Vladimir Suzdal Museum Reserve, Russia; (9) A segment of a strand of beads and pierced fox teeth from a man's burial. Sungir, Russia. 22,000 B.C. Length of segment, 6 cm. Collection Vladimir Suzdal Museum Reserve, Russia.*

OPPOSITE: 3.10. *The five main production stages for the manufacture of Aurignacian basket-shaped beads, c. 31,000 B.C. Those pictured are from Abri Blanchard, the type-site for such objects. From top, stage 1: creation of cylindrical, pencil-like rods of talc/chlorite or of ivory. Stage 2: circumcision of these rods into segments of 1 to 2 cm long, which are then snapped off the longer rod. Stage 3: bifacial thinning of one end of the detached cylinders to create a kind of stem at one end and a bulb at the other. Stage 4: perforation by bifacial*

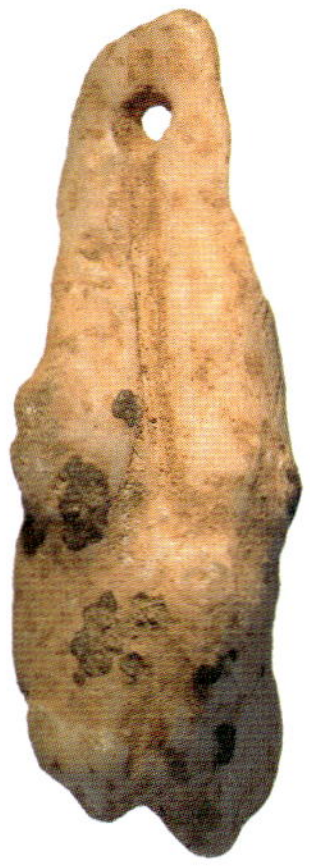
1

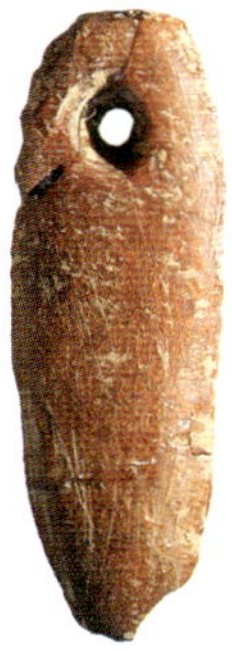
2

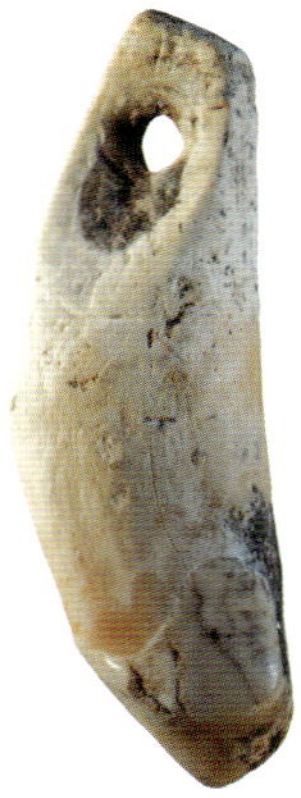
3

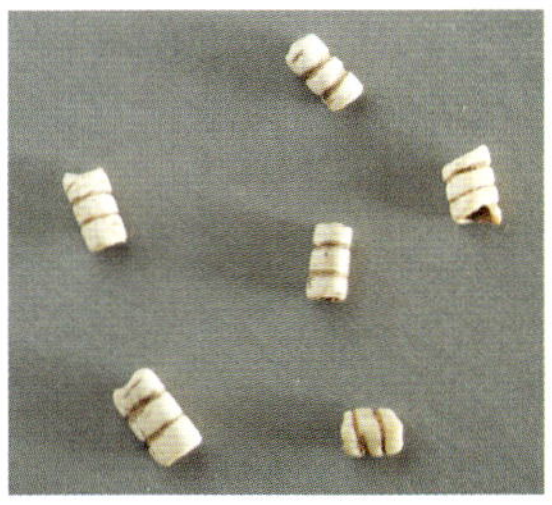
4

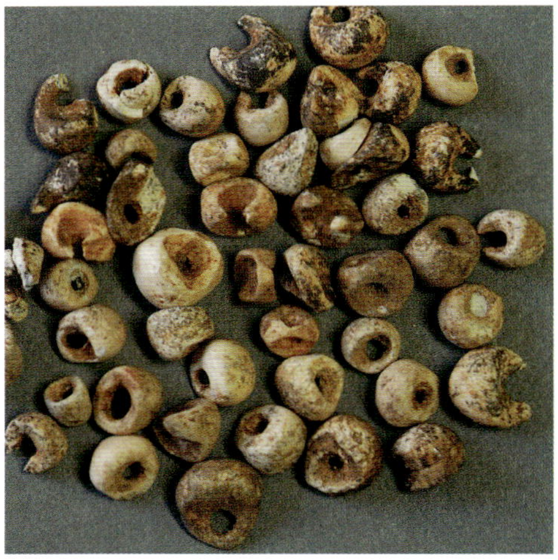
5

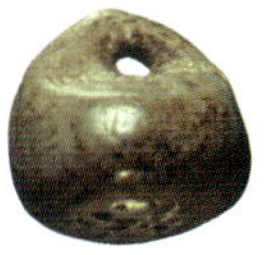
6

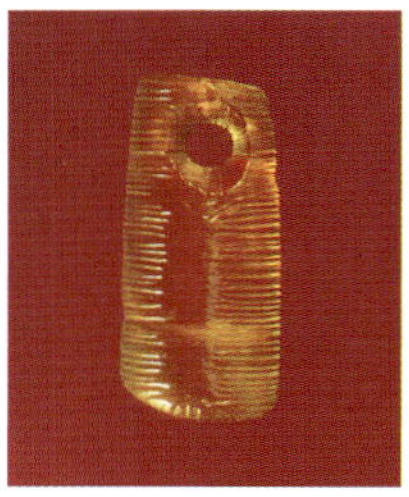
7

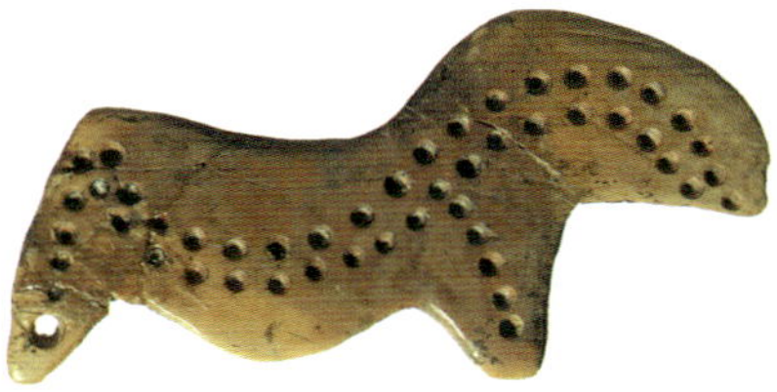
8

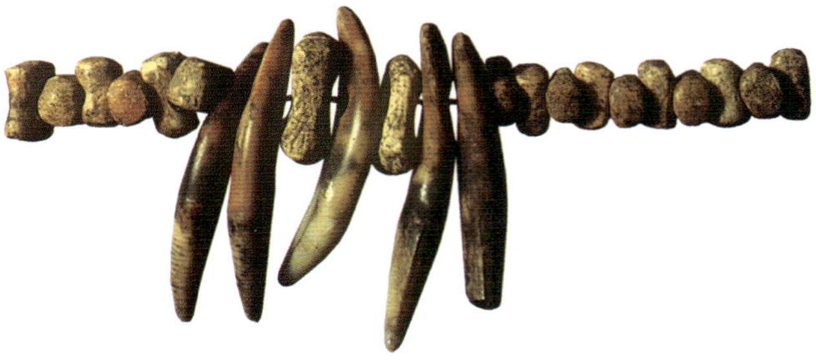
9

adornment. Nonethless, it is the study of personal adornment that is providing today's researchers with much of the essential information on the origins of symbolic thinking. As Dr. White has written, "the presence or absence of personal adornment has become one of the key measures of modernity in the culture-evolutionary record."[11]

The work of Dr. White, who has meticulously studied, excavated, and written about Upper Paleolithic adornment for over thirty years—with a focus on the Aurignacian period—has been central to this effort. His current excavation is the adornment-rich site of Abri Castanet (32,000–29,000 B.C.) in southwestern France, an area of intense bead production. Dr. White emphasizes that what is most important about Upper Paleolithic beads is their systematic production and use, their developed aesthetic choices regarding form, materials, and finishes, and the use of adornment as a symbolic language. Symbolic thought is the capacity to allow one thing to represent another. Beads became the visual represntation—the language—of these thoughts.

Adornment was made from a variety of materials—marine shells, teeth, ivory, talc, amber, stone—exotic to the sites where they were found. That these materials were only obtainable by travel or long distance exchange networks of several hundred kilometers speaks of organizational skills. The transformation of these exotic materials into body adornment rather than tools or weapons further implies that their main function was visual. The adornment was meant to be seen and was worn to communicate social identity such as group membership, gender, age, or marital status. And the materials used had little or no relation to foods consumed by humans.[12]

More sophisticated bead craftsmanship developed during the Gravettian, Souletarian, and Magdalenian periods (26,000–10,000 B.C.), at about the same time the first European cave paintings and carvings appeared. Pieces of bone and ivory were ground into definite bead shapes, grooved or perforated, and decorated with incisions. Important bead discoveries from this period have been made at the sites of Dolni Vestonice and Pavlov in the Czech Republic. These beads were part of the material possessions of a culturally complex, mammoth-hunting society that produced a rich array of bone tools, as well as strands of animal teeth, shells, and pebbles. Some of the beads were carved in the shape of female breasts and torsos and were probably somehow related to the symbolic representation of the value of women (plates 4, 5a). Fired-clay animal figurines, dating to 23,500 B.C.—the oldest ceramic objects known—were also excavated at Dolni Vestonice.[13]

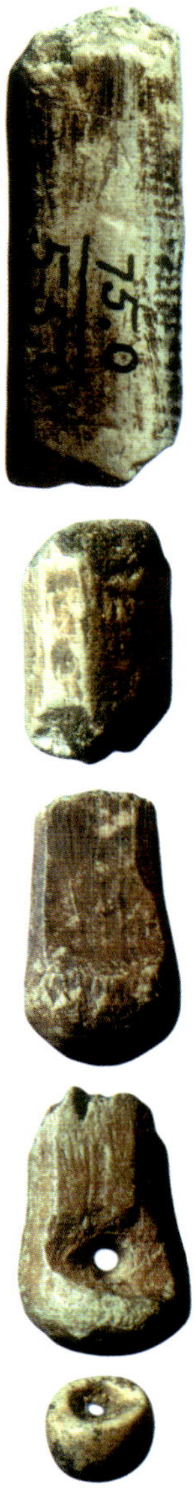

10

gouging or rotational drilling at the junction of the stem and the bulb. Stage 5: reduction of the stage 4 rough-out by coarse abrasion and eventually by fine polishing in order to obtain the characteristic basket shape. Courtesy Dr. Randall White

The early beads reflect the intellect of Upper Paleolithic people, who were able to develop abstract forms and symbols that increased their capacity to cope with an often hazardous environment. Beads were self-conscious expressions of achievement and symbolized people's need for spiritual assistance (and protection) in obtaining resources that they found difficult but necessary to have. They were amuletic, made from parts of the animal: bone, teeth, tusks, and shells. The appearance of jewelry can also be associated with the growing need for personal identity when the human population expanded and large-scale communities evolved 30,000 to 20,000 years ago.

The late Upper Paleolithic era (18,000–10,000 B.C.) witnessed an elaborate development both in the design of individual beads and in the ways in which beads were combined. In France, the Magdalenian culture, which produced some of the most famous cave paintings, is known also for beautifully crafted beads. In southern France, for example, a human burial at Barma Grande, near Grimaldi, was found with three parallel rows of fish vertebrae, Nassus shells, and stag canine teeth arranged symmetrically. The layout was somewhat consistent with rows of beads sewn onto clothing.[14]

Beads were used as grave offerings in Russia at this time. The grave of a young girl and boy excavated at Sungir, 130 miles northeast of Moscow, "suggests that either they were very important, or that the peoples of Sungir 23,000 years ago had very elaborate ideas of an afterlife," wrote anthropologist Bernard Campbell. "The children—one seven to nine years old, the other twelve or thirteen—were laid out in a line, skull to skull. Both had been dressed from head to toe in clothing decorated with ivory beads carved from mammoth tusks and they wore bracelets and rings of the same materials."[15] In another ocher-covered grave at Sungir, a roughly sixty-year-old man was buried "laden with beads, a headband of carved mammoth ivory and the teeth of Arctic foxes."[16] (Plate 3.9)

In Siberia, a number of spectacular late Upper Paleolithic bead finds have been made. At the Ushki Lake site in Kamchatka, graves from 12,000 to 11,000 B.C. were discovered containing pendants and numerous stone beads that evidently had been sewn onto the clothing of the deceased. Ostrich eggshell beads dating to the same period were found at Krasnyi, near Irkutsk. And at Mal'ta, also near Irkutsk, an infant burial dated 18,000 B.C. yielded spatula-shaped, engraved bone beads.[17] Late Upper Paleolithic beads have been found at several localities in India,[18] China,[19] and Korea.[20] Included are beads of bird bone, shell, and polished and perforated stone recovered from the Upper Cave of Zhou-kou-dian in China, dating from 18,000 to 8,000 years ago. At Devil's Lair, a small limestone cave in southwestern Australia, three beads of kangaroo bone were found that were made between 13,000 and 10,000 B.C. The beads have rounded edges and were strung on kangaroo sinew less than one millimeter in diameter.[21] In the Americas, the only bead contemporary with the European and Asian Upper Paleolithic is a single bead of hardened calcium carbonate found at Tule Springs, Nevada, and estimated to have been made in 11,000 B.C. There is possibly one bone bead and several decorated bone disks (though without holes for suspension) recovered from the Folsom culture at the Lindenmeirs site in Colorado, dating c. 9,000 B.C.[22]

This wide-ranging evidence suggests there was an explosion of symbolic expression rendered in ceremonial paraphernalia and personal adornment, including beads, between 35,000 and 12,000 years ago, immediately following the emergence of modern human's increased cognitive powers and his or her new capacities for making cultural objects. It corresponds also with *Homo sapiens*'s emergence throughout the world, often in environments previously uninhabited, and with the development of new and more complex modes of human organization, including ritual behavior, which were an essential part of people's increasingly successful strategies for coping with the natural world.

The use of symbols in ritual activity and in personal adornment began when burials were sprinkled with red ocher and accompanied by offerings of food and tools. The idea of an afterlife, that something human lives on, required symbols of permanence that would remain intact at the grave after the completion of the rituals. The first adornment was possibly made of perishable berries and seeds, but with the discovery of more durable materials, such as bone, shell, and stone, and ways of working with them, beads became one of these symbols.

Something began among the Neanderthals and their anatomically modern contemporaries in Africa and dramatically increased to bring about an increasing self-consciousness and desire for adornment. Early *Homo sapiens* quite possibly used cosmetics (such as red ocher for rouge) and wore great quantities of jewelry, including clothes decorated with rows of beads, jet pendants, ivory bracelets, and multiple strands of pierced animal teeth, vertebrae, and shells.[23]

Beads are therefore among the earliest evidence of abstract thinking. They could not kill an animal or provide warmth, but they could render in material form concepts of prestige, prowess, protection, and beauty. Beads were a conscious effort at self-beautification, reflecting modern human's ability to visualize oneself and enhance his or her appearance through the creation of relatively uniform, valued, and displayable forms. Man's concern with his effectiveness as a hunter had a particularly important influence on adornment. Ornaments made from parts of the animal became metaphors for imbuing the wearer with the animal's courage and strength, among other qualities. To be effective, certain of these transformed objects had to be attached to the owner. Tying them together probably seemed the most obvious solution. Thus, the wearing of pendants and beads was conceived.

The decorating of clothing with numerous beads (a precursor of beadwork), or the stringing together of many beads, as opposed to wearing a single one, occurred at a very early date (at least 32,000 B.C.)[24] and may suggest a deep primal belief that "more is better." If one bead provided protection against life's real or imagined threats or helped to identify the status of individuals associating in groups too large to know everyone by sight, a bead necklace accomplished the task tenfold.

The elaborate ibex-bone necklace composed of head-shaped beads shown in plate 5c, dated to between 11,000 and 10,000 B.C., speaks of a flourishing hunting and gathering society that prized beautifully decorated artifacts and enjoyed rich symbolism. Both miniature animal sculptures and grand cave art had sacred significance connected with the seasons of game and the chase. They were associated with rituals that organized the hunter's life.[25]

The fine quality of the carved ibex beads shows the technological skill of late Paleolithic artists. Working with ivory and bone required highly specialized tools, and their availability predetermined the complexity and often the shape of crafted objects people could conceive and make. Central to understanding human cultural development is the knowledge of how artisans used tools to extend their thinking and dexterity.

To work flexible, organic materials such as bone, antler, and ivory—raw materials readily available as by-products of the hunt—a special kind of tool was required. That tool was the burin. Its strong, sharply beveled edge or point was well-adapted to cut, incise, and shape other materials. It differed from most other Paleolithic stone tools in that it was not used to kill animals or cut meat, but rather to manufacture other tools. It was also used to carve miniature sculptures that served as ritual paraphernalia and items of adornment, such as the ibex beads.

Beads were shaped by chipping, grinding, and polishing, then perforated by turning a sharp-pointed stone tool. The earliest beads were comparatively thin-walled shells or teeth, easy to pierce. The proliferation of disk-shaped beads in early cultures probably indicates that they were easy to form and perforate. A stone tool can engrave, but it cannot gouge for any length of time before its point becomes dull. By the early Aurignacian period (c. 36,000–28,000 B.C.), metallic abrasives were already in use for the demi-rotational drilling of pebbles, fossils, and other hard materials. Drilling thin stones was probably accomplished with bits of flint or chert and palm-rotated hand drills. For thicker stones, bow drills were made of hollow bone and filled with an abrasive of sand or crushed stone. Later, craftsmen developed a technique to bore larger beads by drilling halfway through from opposite ends, with the holes meeting at the center of the bead. Their awareness that it was actually the abrasive and not the drill that effectively ground away the stone marked an important cognitive advance.

Polishing as well as shaping mammoth ivory beads to replicate the luster of teeth of an important animal was a speciality of French Aurignacian artisans (plates 3.2, 3.3,

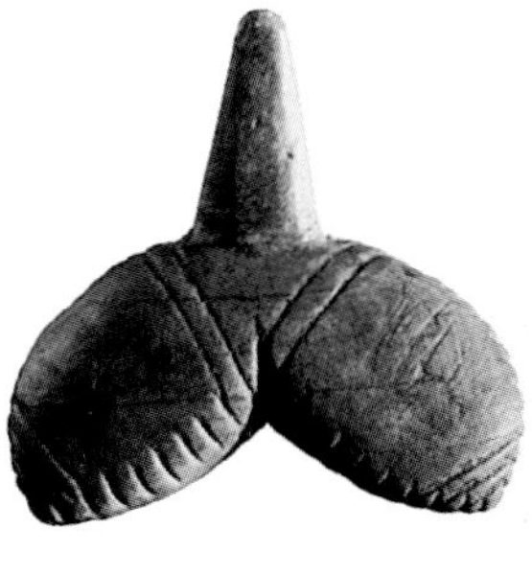

4. *Breast-shaped ivory bead of the East Gravettian culture from Dolni Vestonice, the Czech Republic, c. 24,000 B.C. The Gravettian culture also produced bone, ivory, and stone "Venus" figurines with oversize breasts, belly, buttocks, and thighs. Both the Venus figurines and this bead speak to the symbolic value of women. Length, 3.2 cm. Moravske Muzeum, Brno, the Czech Republic*

5. *Late Upper Paleolithic Beads: The Magdalenian culture*

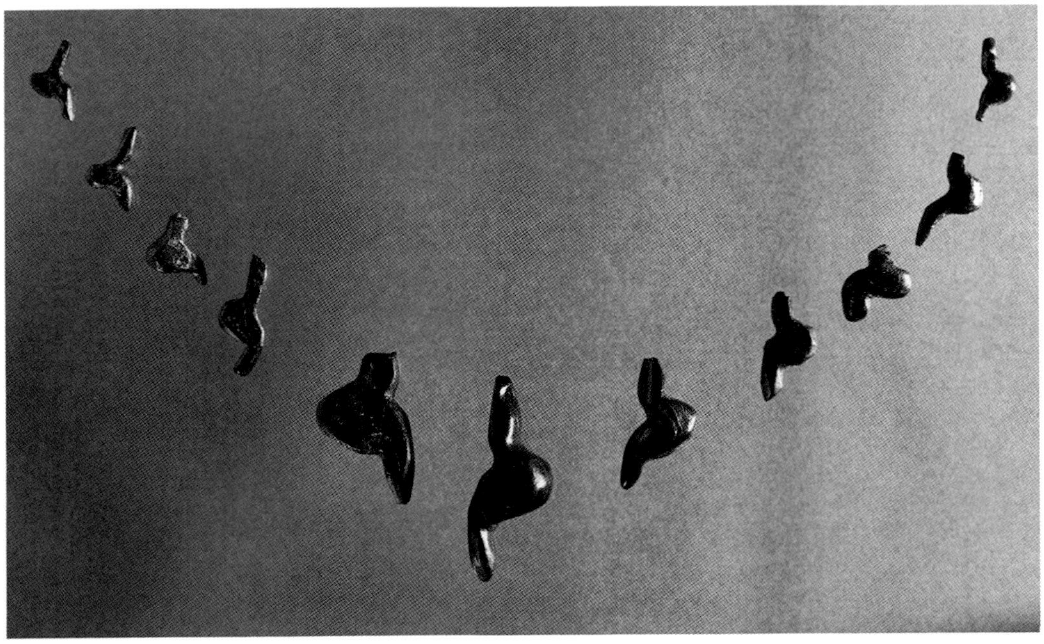

ABOVE RIGHT: 5a. *Necklace of lignite or jet (a hard form of coal) beads shaped as female buttocks, made by Magdalenian craftsmen, from Petersfels, Germany, c. 13,000 B.C. Similar abstract shapes were also engraved on stones. Center bead: length, 4.4 cm. Hegau Museum, Singen, Germany*

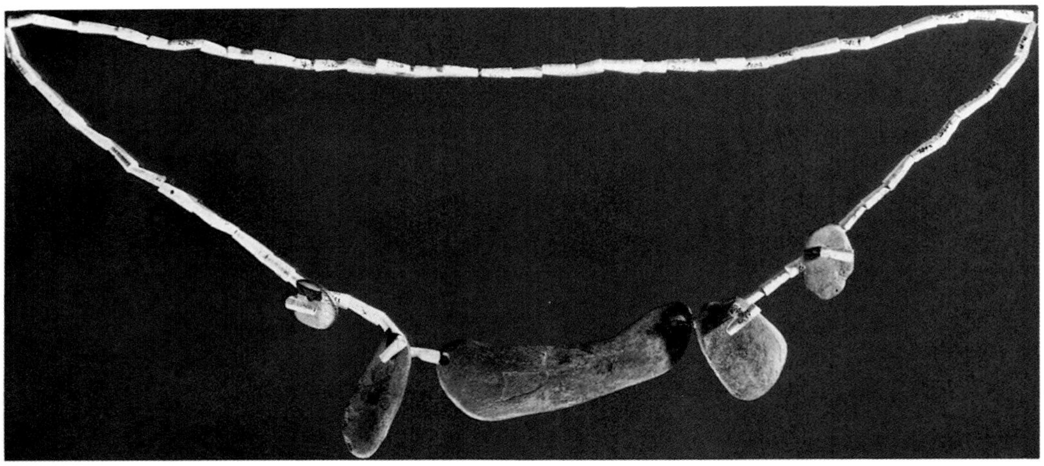

BELOW: 5b. *Late Upper Paleolithic beads of the Magdalenian culture, from Pekarna, the Czech Republic; c. 13,000 B.C. They are made of animal teeth and waterworn pebbles. By this period, bow drills and abrasives were used to perforate stone. Necklace: diameter, 30 cm. Moravske Muzeum, Brno, the Czech Republic*

3.10). The conceptual leap from piercing thin-walled shells to the elaborated processes necessary for working with mammoth ivory and creating intentional imagery had "profound implications...the transfer of qualities from one context to another is an essential part of the construction of metaphors," says Dr. White. The ability of the Aurignacians to think abstractly and create material metaphors through tiny beads went hand in hand with the monumental range of social and technological advances that occurred at this time.[26]

Although archeological evidence is lacking, the earliest materials used for beads may have come from the immediate environment and included seeds, berries, and coal, as well as shells and animal bone. The creation of Upper Paleolithic stone beads was the beginning of the search through the mineral world for variously colored materials that could be shaped and drilled for beads. Early investigations for potential materials anticipate the established trade patterns of later cultures. Indeed, there is evidence of trade in bead materials at the cave site of Patne in India. In a context dating to 23,000 B.C., a bead made of marine shell was found at least 367 miles from its ocean source.[27] In

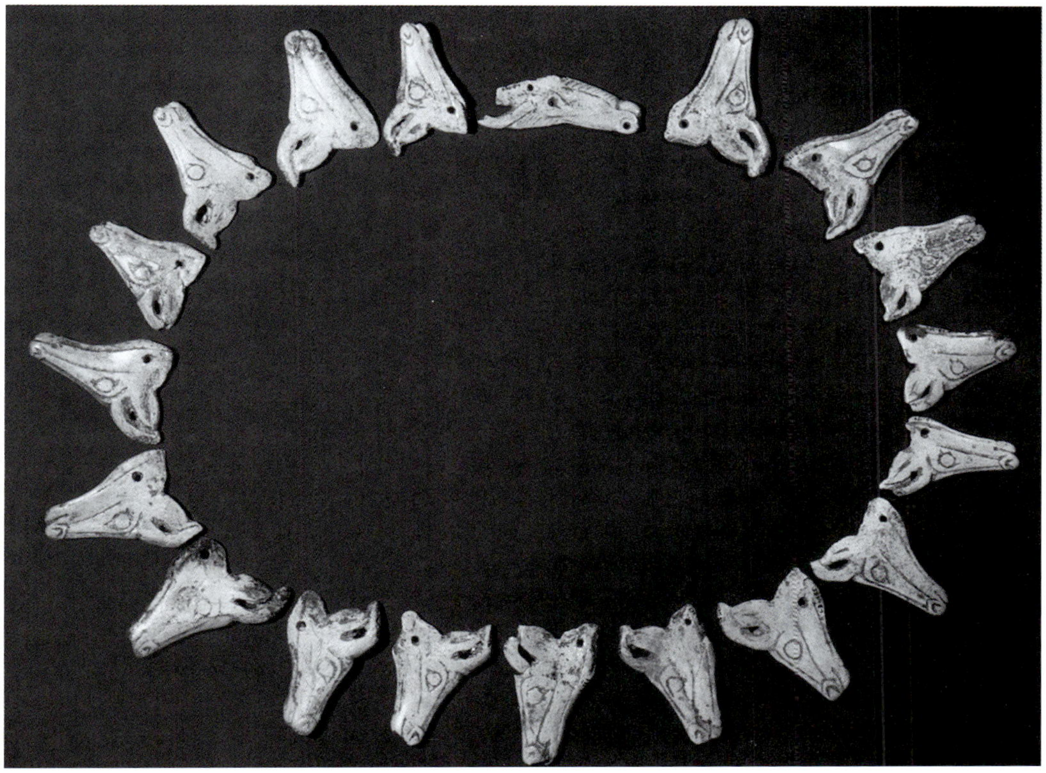

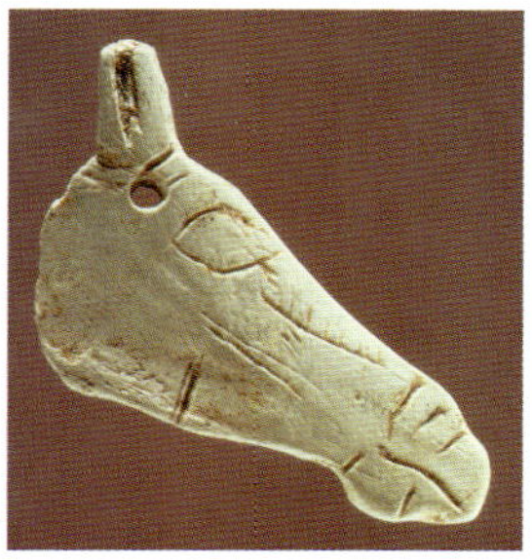

LEFT: 5c. *A necklace of head-shaped ibex beads made from ibex bone with a bison head back-piece. This masterpiece of design and crafts-manship demonstrates the conceptual powers of the recently evolved* sapiens *populations. The necklace has a unique context as all the beads were found together and were thus segments of a unified whole.*[IV] *It is associated with the late French Magdalenian culture, was found at La Bastide, France, and dates between 11,000 and 10,000 B.C. Center bead: length, 6.5 cm. Simonnet Collection*

ABOVE RIGHT: 5d. *Horse's Head. Bone, Le Portel, France, 10,000 B.C. Length, c. 6.99 cm*

the excavation of dwellings at Mezhirichi, southeast of Kiev in western Russia, Soviet archaeologists uncovered seashells of 15,000 years ago that were imported from 400 to 500 miles away, as well as amber that is believed to have been traded in from distant sources.[28] Marine shells used in beadmaking were brought to the Upper Cave of Zhou-kou-dian in about 16,000 B.C. from sources between 93 and 218 miles away.[29]

As the climate warmed up and temperate forests replaced the glaciers, there was a shift to a new way of life known as the Mesolithic era. This transitional period broadly dates between the end of the last glaciations and the adoption of farming, which varied within each geographic region.

Mesolithic people had adornment of a totally different character. Their more simply formed beads were frequently of materials such as shale stone and local shell. An important collection of 690 perforated shale beads, dating 9,200–7,500 B.C., was found at The Nab Head, a Mesolithic seasonal camp in Pembrokeshire, Wales. Similar beads have been recovered from Mesolithic sites throughout Britain.[30] (Timeline 12). At the Mesolithic to early Neolithic site of Vlasac in the Danube Gorge of the north-central Balkans (a site of the Lepenski Vir culture) recent excavations uncovered almost one hundred burials dating c. 6,700–5,900 B.C. Among the excavated adornments were locally available pierced carp teeth, as well as imported beads of a marine snail shell that came from the Black Sea or the Mediterranean Sea, red and white limestone beads, and Spondylus shell beads. The beads are the earliest known examples in southeastern Europe of contact and exchange between the Mesolithic forage-fishers of the Danube and the first Neolithic farming groups. The Spondylus shell is the earliest known example in Europe obtained through trade networks.[31] The use of exotic materials for beads and adornment became increasingly more prevalent with the succeeding Neolithic farming societies.

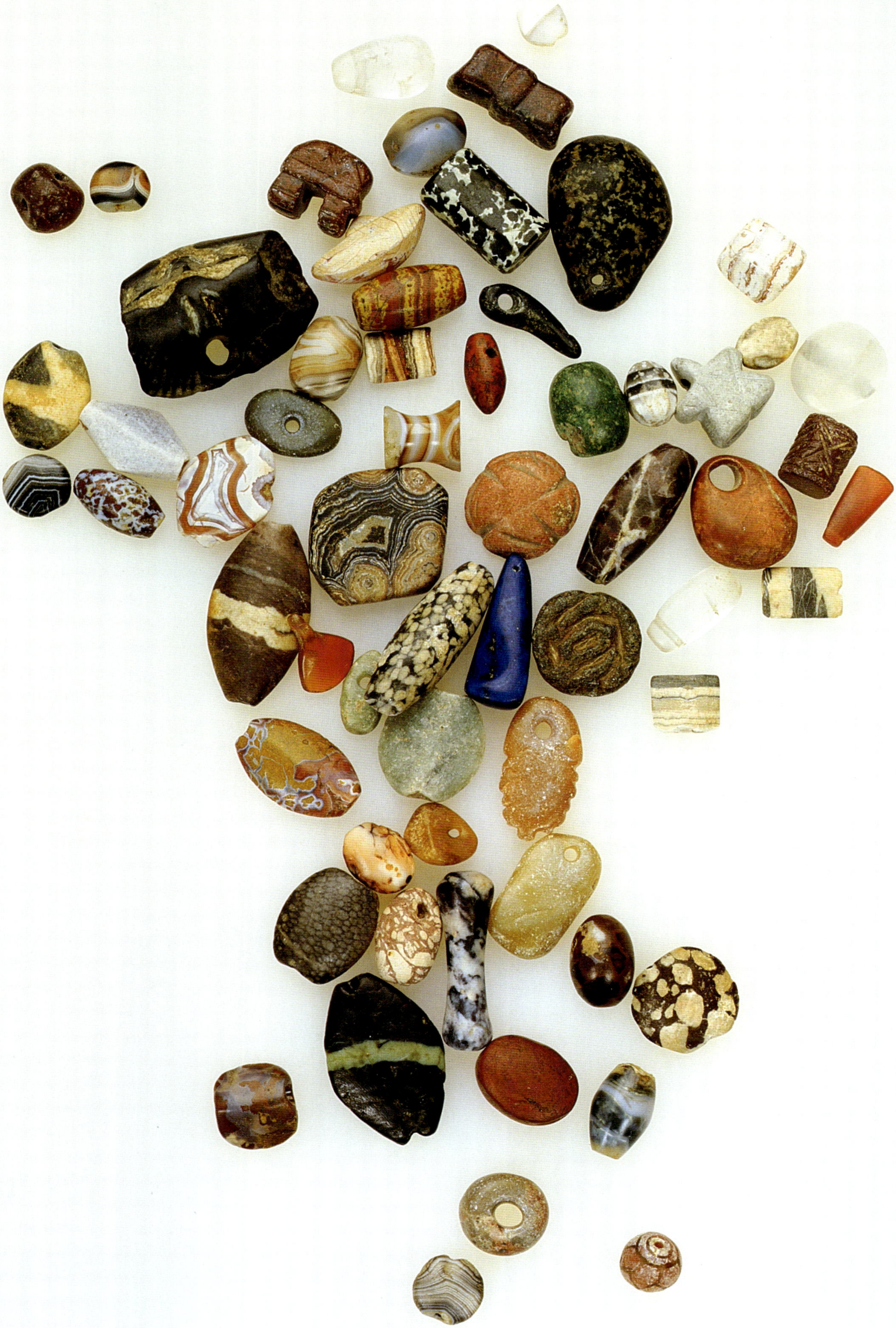

Antiquity: From Neolithic Times to the Roman Empire

In western Asia between 8000 and 6500 B.C., the foundations were laid for what is known as the Neolithic Revolution. It was during this period that people first made the transition from nomadic food-gatherers to settled food-producers—an extremely important advance that led to the establishment of permanent settlements. Village life, in turn, encouraged the accumulation of material possessions and stimulated trade. Moreover, the ability to store surplus food allowed time for craft specialization.

Civilization did not develop in one specific area in western Asia: at least three (and possibly more) centers are now known to have existed in Turkey, Iraq, and Iran. The wild ancestors of some of the modern world's most important agricultural staples—including wheat, barley, pigs, sheep, and goats—thrived on the hilly flanks of the Taurus Mountains of southern Turkey and the Zagros Mountains northeast of the Tigris River, in present-day Iraq and Iran. During the eighth millennium B.C., human populations gradually domesticated these plants and animals. The Neolithic Revolution then spread from these regions into the Levant and northern Greece.

Villages sprang up where people were harvesting plants and raising animals. Realizing the limited agricultural potential of growing crops in the rocky hills, people gradually introduced domesticated plants into the lower floodplains, where the soil was rich, but the rainfall scanty. It was with the invention of irrigation systems that river valley societies in Mesopotamia (present-day northern Syria and Iraq), India, and Egypt evolved into sophisticated, complex city-states.

Settled village life was one of the predominant characteristics of Neolithic society. Stone and mud-brick dwellings were built, providing the first permanent forms of architecture. An unprecedented level of craftsmanship also flourished: the first examples

6. A group of early western Asian stone beads made of hard stones (predominantly quartz minerals), including agate, rock crystal, sard, carnelian, and jasper, c. 4000–2000 B.C. Also shown are beads of lapis lazuli, breccia, steatite, fossilized shell (top left), and fossilized coral (middle left).

During this period, beads were often made with the same techniques employed to create stone weapons and tools—flaking or rough grinding on abrasive blocks. Final shaping and polishing was done with abrasives made of flint chips, sand, or clay slurry. The similarity of shapes between all early beads in the region probably reflects the use of similar technologies. Fossilized shell: length, 4.9 cm. Collection Derek Content, Houlton, Maine

of weaving and pottery and a proliferation of bead forms are associated with Neolithic times. In the later phases of the period, as of 3500 B.C., metal weapons and tools came into use alongside traditional stone implements. (This was a technological advance that led to man's next phase of development, the Bronze Age.) Of great significance for the study of beads was the expansion of long-distance trade between the rapidly evolving, agriculturally intensive civilizations of the Mediterranean and the mountain cultures of western Asia. The uneven distribution of the regions' resources created networks of commercial relations that united these societies and encouraged the exchange of cultural artifacts.

Made of scarce, durable, and easily recognizable raw materials to which commercial value could be easily assigned, and produced in small, standardized, and readily portable sizes, beads became a major commodity for traders. The demand for exotic and rare materials to be used for adornment helped to establish trade networks in western Asia and the Mediterranean at a very early date. By 6500 B.C., there were strong and far-reaching interchanges. Butterfly-shaped beads of imported agate and serpentine as well as other forms of beads made of Sinai turquoise and Mediterranean cowrie shells are recorded at Abu Hureyra, in today's Syria.[1] At Çatal Hüyük, one of the world's first towns and a prosperous Anatolian trading center on the central plains of Turkey, beads of Mediterranean coral dating to 6000 B.C. have been discovered. In the Mediterranean, necklaces of carnelian beads imported from the Levant were worn by Neolithic people on the island of Cyprus.[2]

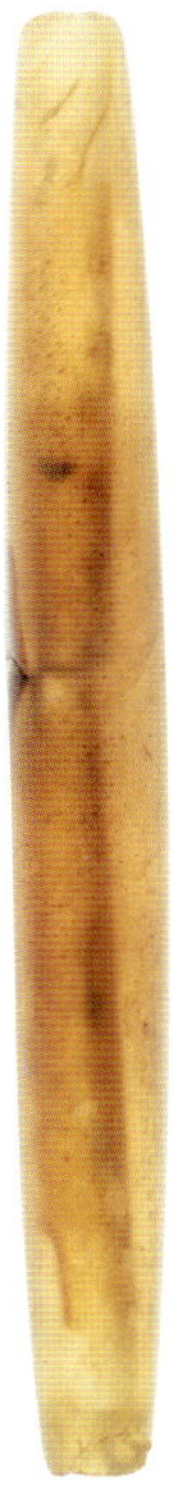

ABOVE: 7. *The most difficult step in stone beadmaking was drilling the holes for suspension, since rough beads fractured easily. The practice of double drilling—piercing the bead from both ends—used for this bead from western Asia, c. 2000 B.C., reduced the stress by enabling the holes to meet in the middle of the bead. Flint drills were used with a powdered quartz abrasive paste. Length, 12.5 cm. Collection Derek Content*

OPPOSITE LEFT: 8. *A necklace of dentalium (a mollusk with a thinly pointed shell) and breast-shaped beads of deer bone, made by the Natufians, the original inhabitants of the Jordan River valley. One of the earliest examples of Neolithic beadmaking, this is from the site of El-Wad, c. 10,000–8000 B.C. Length, 18 cm. Israel Department of Antiquities, Israel Museum, Jerusalem*

Sophisticated systems of commerce evolved by the fourth millennium B.C. in which beads and bead materials often played an important role. Beads of lapis lazuli, a beautiful blue stone with numerous amuletic properties attributed to it, were a great favorite of the Sumerians of southern Mesopotamia during the third millennium B.C. Lapis was mined in the ancient Afghan region Badakhshan, fifteen hundred miles away. While the Sumerians exercised no political control over Afghanistan's production centers or the trade routes traversing the rugged Iranian plateau, supplies of lapis were guaranteed by independent middlemen located at centers on the plateau, such as Shahr-i Sokhta and Tepe Hissar.

At Shahr-i Sokhta, large numbers of finished and unfinished beads and beadmakers' tools, dating from 2600 to 2400 B.C., have been found by archaeologists. A great amount of lapis lazuli waste was also discovered. It has been determined, however, that this was not a beadmaking center for Sumer but primarily an intermediate stop where pure lapis was separated from the worthless limestone cortex. The lapis was then shipped from Persia (Iran) to Mesopotamia in the form of small blocks. This pre-processing of the raw material at a midway point allowed significant savings in transportation costs and also shows how trade stimulated technology.[3]

The early Greeks of Mycenae, who established trading contacts with the Bronze Age cultures in the Baltic, exchanged copper and bronze implements for rare amber with which they made beads. In effect, they extended their technical expertise to the less developed European regions while absorbing new materials and forms of adornment. Eventually, large quantities of glass beads would be carried thousands of miles by the ancient Phoenician and Roman seafaring civilizations.

Throughout antiquity, raw materials were traded more often than finished beads. A system developed in rural areas of Europe and western Asia supplying luxury materials to the urban centers; where craftsmen congregated under the aegis of wealthy patrons. Using the most advanced technology, they created beads in the latest styles. A corollary to this pattern is that finished beads were traded usually by more technically advanced cultures to less advanced ones.

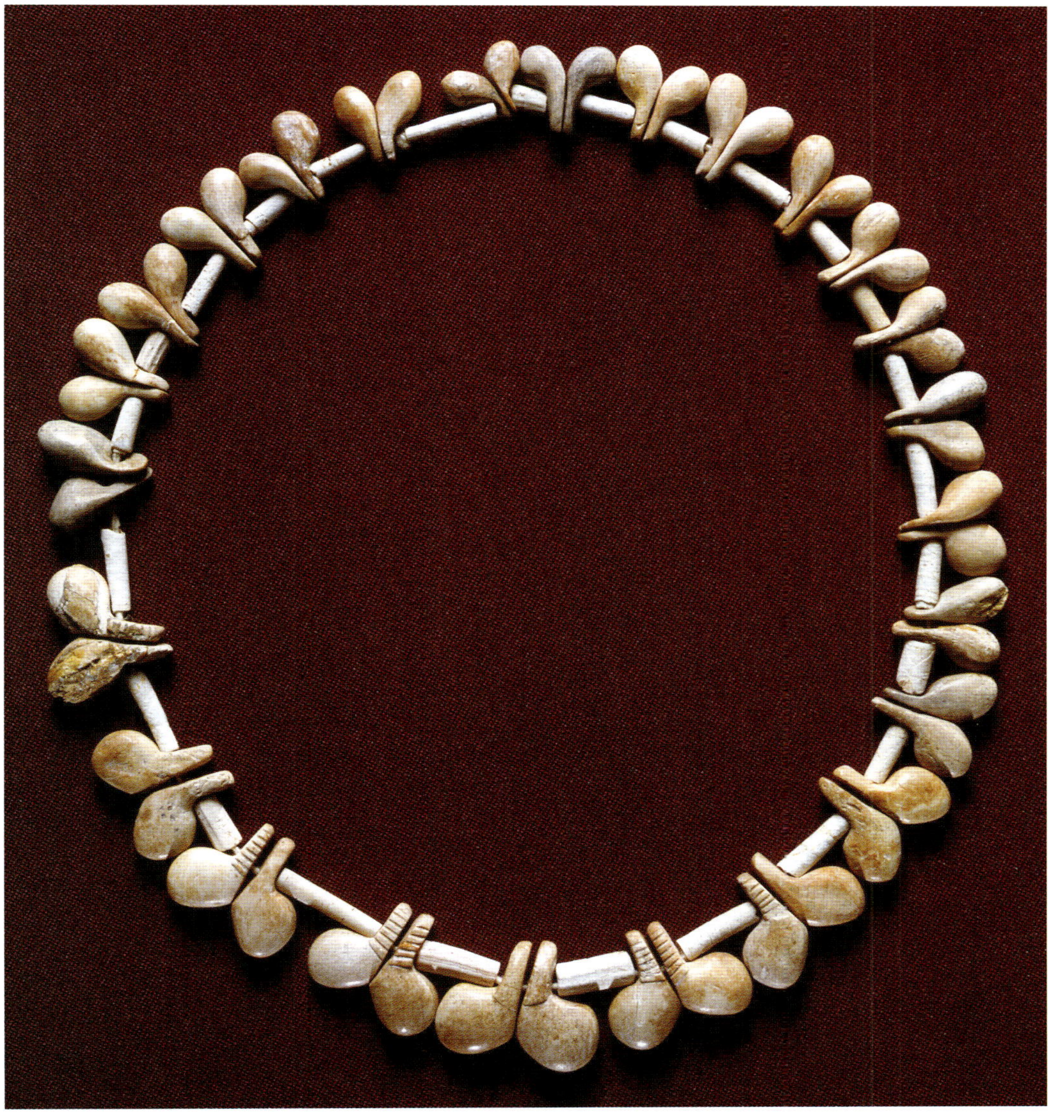

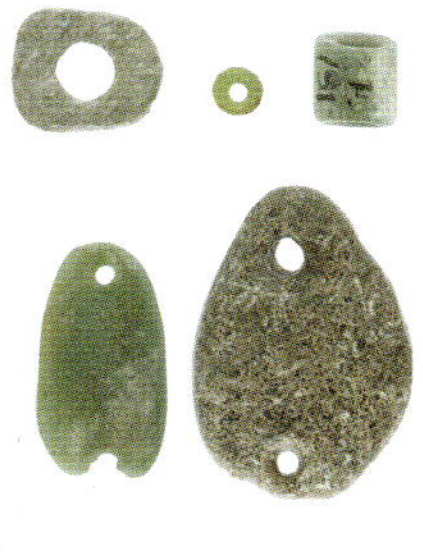

TOP RIGHT: 9. *Greenstone beads and pendants from Gigal II, a late Natufian site. During the transition from hunting and gathering to agriculture in the Near Eastern Levant, a wide variety of green stones were used for the first time to make adornment. It has been suggested that the occurrence of green stone beads is directly related to the emergence of agriculture, with the green color signifying new growth and fertility, and embodying the wish for successful crops. It is likely, wrote archeologists Daniella E. Bar-Yosef Mayer and Naomi Porat, that the same green beads that were "in charge" of improving crops were also responsible for keeping the well-being of the farmers that raised these crops.*

The nearest sources of these stones (either serpentine or amazonite) was at least a 15 km distance.[11] *9600–8500 B.C. Actual size. Courtesy National Academy of Sciences, USA*

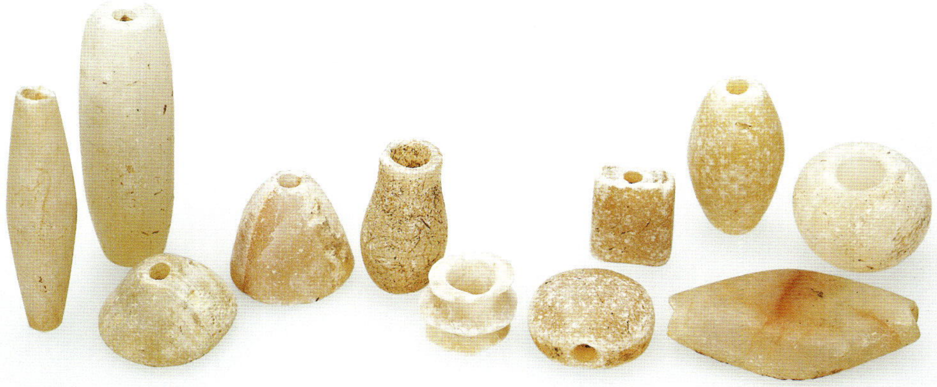

BOTTOM: 10. *Beads of alabaster (gypsum), a soft mineral easily carved with tools of flint, wood, and bone. Although this collection is from northern Syria, the shapes and wide perforations are typical of western Asian and Egyptian beads from the fifth to the third millennium B.C. Far left bead: length, 5 cm. Collection Henry Anavian, New York*

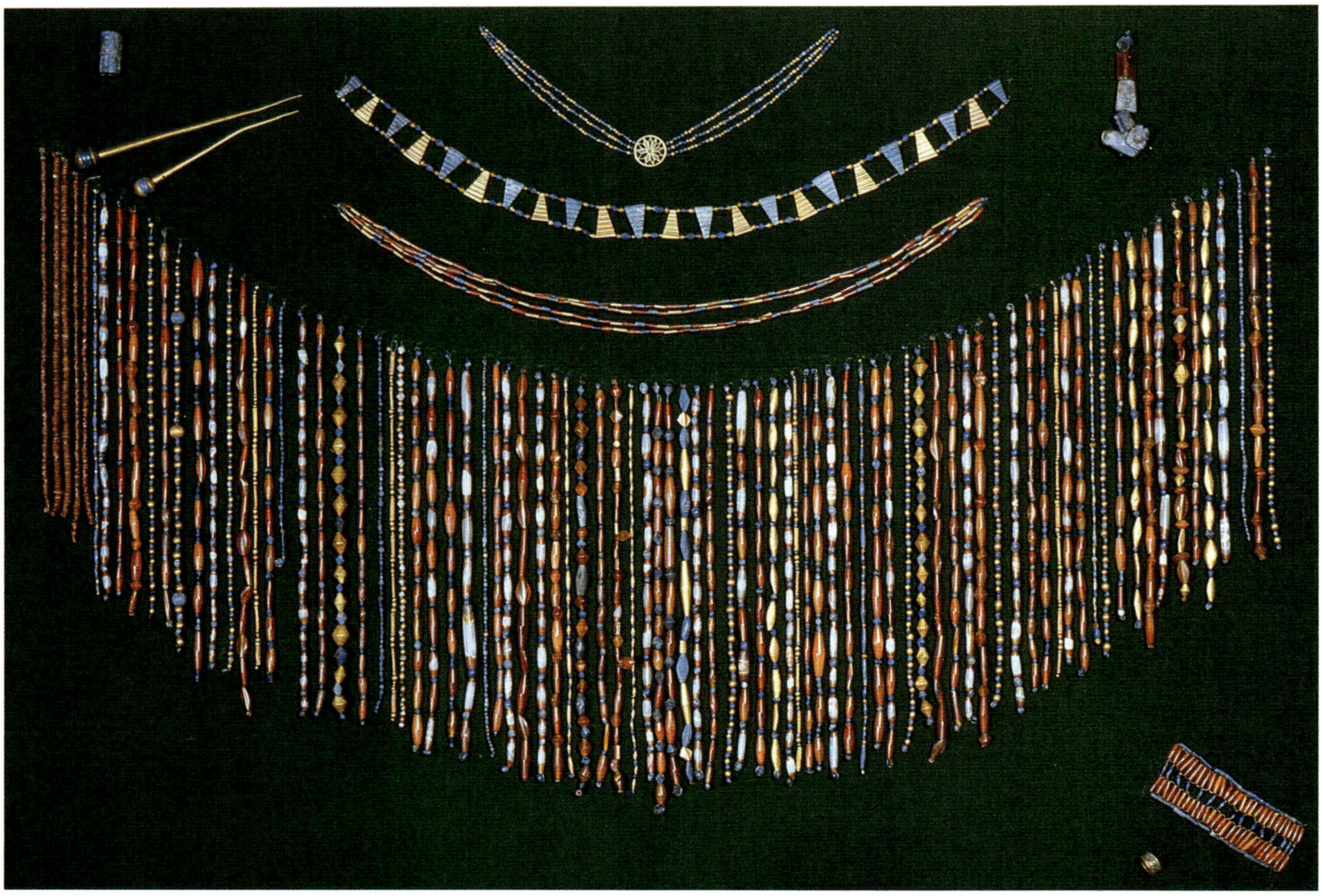

ABOVE: 11. *Bead cloak of Queen Pu-abi, from the royal Sumerian graves at Ur, 2500 B.C. Length of longest strand, 36.2 cm. University Museum, University of Pennsylvania, Philadelphia*

RIGHT: 11a. *Detail of the bead cloak of Queen Pu-abi, showing carnelian, lapis lazuli, agate, silver, and gold loop-in-loop chain beads.*

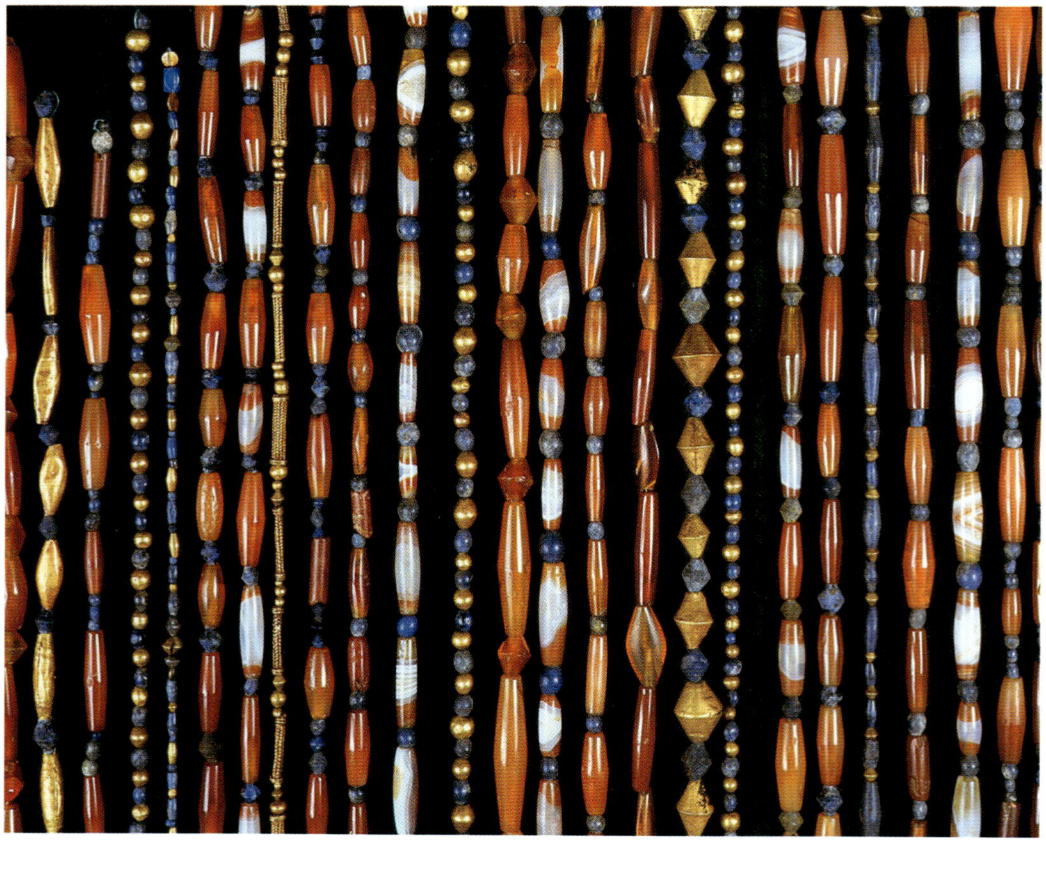

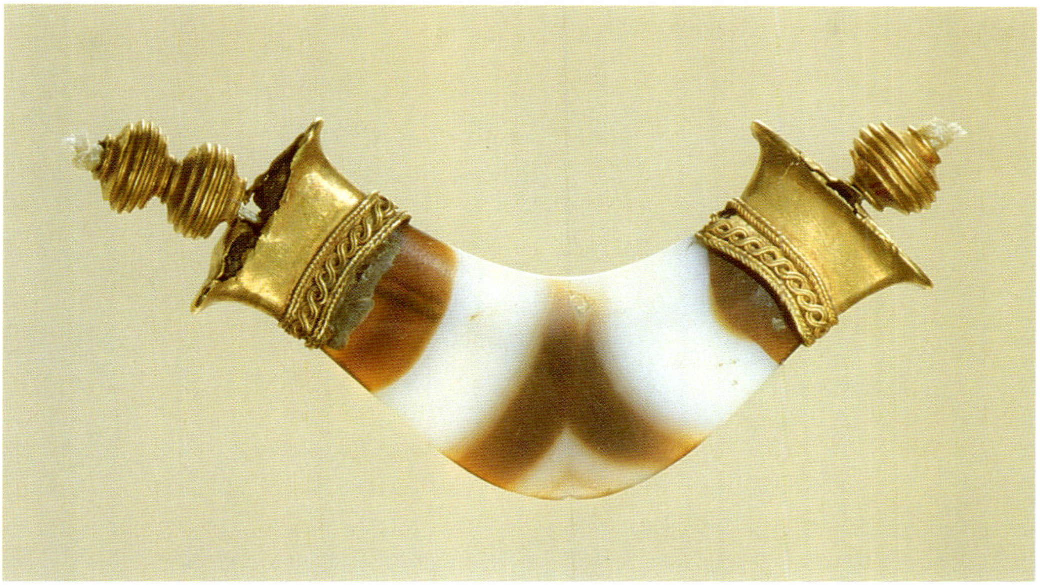

TOP: 12. *Gold-capped agate bead from Uruk in Mesopotamia, 2113–2006 B.C. Length, 6.04 cm. Metropolitan Museum of Art, New York*

BOTTOM: 13. *This "etched" carnelian bead from Ur dates to about 2500 B.C. The process involved painting a natron (white alkalai) design on the bead surface, then heating the object so that the design was absorbed into the crystalline lattice and became part of the stone's material composition. Similar etched beads, made with similar material and techniques, were found in quantity at Ur, as well as in the Indus Valley and Afghanistan, dating from 2500 to 1600 B.C. Their place of manufacture was at the city of Harrapa in the Indus Valley. Their existence is evidence of contact between the three regions at this time. Width, 1.65 cm. British Museum, London*

Beads from the Royal Tombs at Ur

A royal graveyard—the tomb of Queen Pu-abi, in particular—in the Sumerian city of Ur contained some of the most remarkable beads in the ancient world. In the graves, several of which were mass burials that included one noble person and a retinue of attendants, all the women and many of the men were interred with beads. Numerous skeletons were found with the beads in their original arrangements.[III]

The Ur cemetery contained graves spanning five hundred years (2600–2100 B.C.) and three periods: Early Dynastic III, Akkadian, and Post-Akkadian, each of which had its own distinctive group of beads. Queen Pu-abi's beads date from the Early Dynastic III period (2500 B.C.), when Ur was the most powerful city-state in Mesopotamia. The beads are principally of five materials: carnelian, lapis lazuli, agate, gold, and silver. The sophisticated goldsmithing techniques of the Ur beads and the mastery of polishing and precision-cutting of stones show how quickly technology, craftsmanship, and artistry accelerated in the hands of full-time artisans (compare with plates 6 and 10).

All materials used in these beads were imported, testifying to the power of the rulers to protect trade routes and establish foreign alliances. The largest beads using the finest colored stones were recovered consistently from royal graves, another expression of the supreme power of royalty.

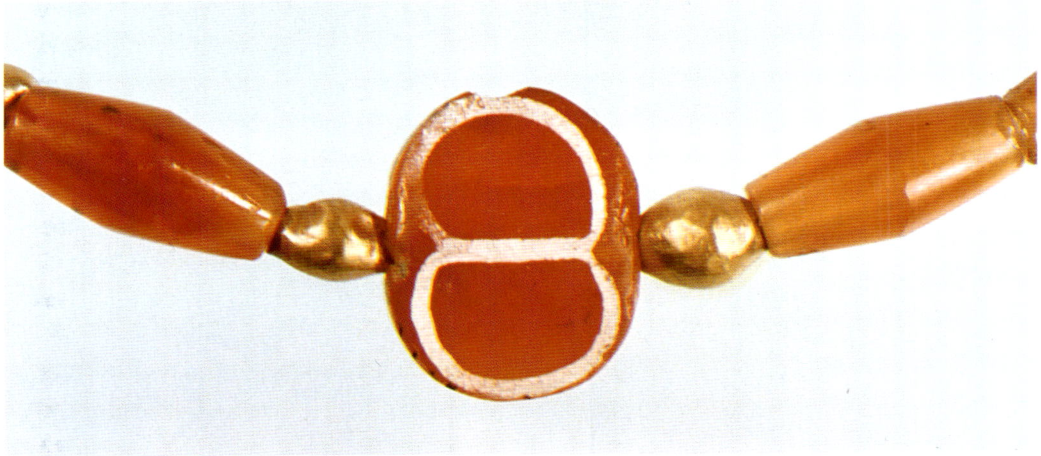

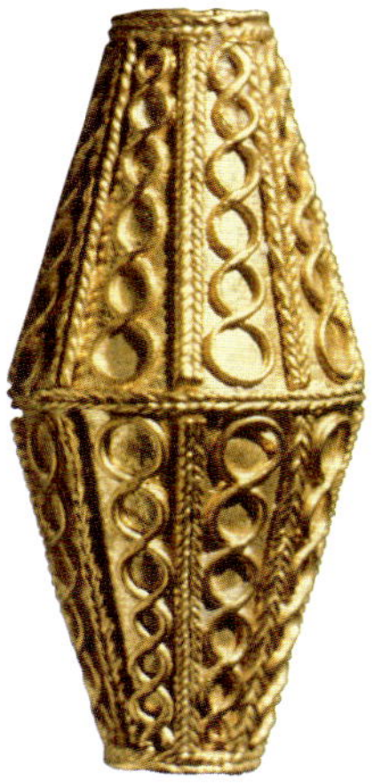

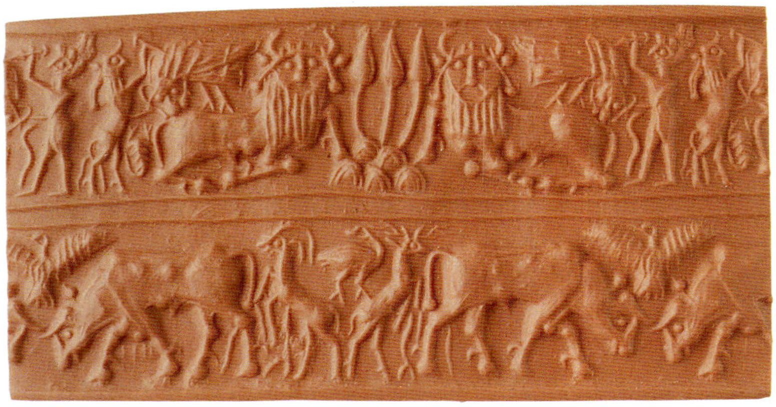

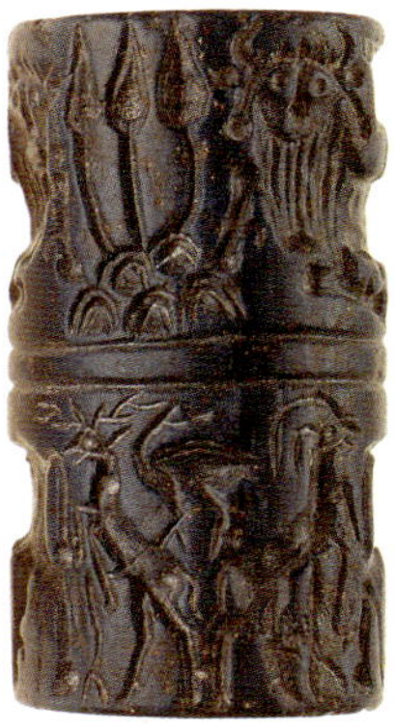

ABOVE LEFT: 14. *A gold filigree bead from the Ur cemeteries, c. 2500 B.C. Many of the common techniques used by goldsmiths today, including granulation, filigree, and cloisonné, were practiced by the Sumerians. Length, 3.37 cm. British Museum, London*

ABOVE RIGHT: 15. *Cylinder seal beads were first made in Mesopotamia about 3500 B.C., although steatite amulets with primitive linear markings, apparently used as seals, have been excavated from Arpachiyah, Iraq, dating to the Halaf period (6000–5000 B.C.). The use of these engraved stone beads to make ownership impressions on clay is one indication of the evolution from village agriculture to urban society. Preceding writing, the seal developed as a means of documenting business transactions.[IV] This lapis lazuli cylinder seal with plaster impression was found at Ur and dates to c. 2400 B.C. Length, 4.1 cm. British Museum, London*

Moving easily through the cultural landscape, beads transmitted stylistic concepts as well as production techniques from one society to the next. Beads demonstrating intricate craftsmanship were particularly prized. This is true, for example, of the complex mosaic, or "millefiori," glass forms invented in Mesopotamia or Egypt about 1500 B.C.[4] Mosaic-glass beads were refined by the Syrians and Egyptians during Roman times and traded as far north as Scandinavia. Over the seven to eight thousand years between the rise of the Neolithic village and the fall of the Roman Empire (A.D. 476), the strong political and cultural relationships between the peoples of western Asia, Egypt, and the Mediterranean were maintained. Hubs of power frequently shifted, as city-states and empires flourished and declined. During moments of prominence, however, each civilization sustained an artistic center that influenced the surrounding region. When a town's political fortunes veered downward, the craftsmen relocated, either willingly or by force, and took their styles, techniques, and secrets with them.

Neolithic Beads in Western Asia

Beads are among the commonest objects recovered from Neolithic sites in western Asia. Since people were interred with valued possessions, the inclusion of large quantities of beads in numerous burials points to their importance within ancient societies. Archaeological evidence also indicates that beads were produced in all shapes and sizes from a very early date. Between 10,000 and 8000 B.C., the Natufians of the Jordan River valley had made beads from stone, shell, and bone (plate 8 and 9). Beads of native copper, serpentine, and malachite have been excavated at Çatal Hüyük, Anatolia, which was founded in 6250 B.C. Seventh- and sixth-millennium B.C. sites in Afghanistan, Iran, Syria, and Mesopotamia have yielded beads made of basalt, limestone, steatite, obsidian, ivory, and occasional examples of the harder agates and carnelian.

Neolithic western Asian craftsmanship was generally quite primitive. Typical bead forms included disks, cylinders, barrels, and flattened rhomboids, shapes that were easily created with available tools and limited technology. Irregularly shaped shell and stone beads were often little more than lumps of raw material pierced for suspension.

Most Neolithic bead materials were locally available, while some shells and obsidian were imported. The early use of Anatolian obsidian for western Asian beads occurred during a period when trade was largely confined to utilitarian materials and objects. Most imported obsidian was used to make knife blades. Its employment in bead-making was

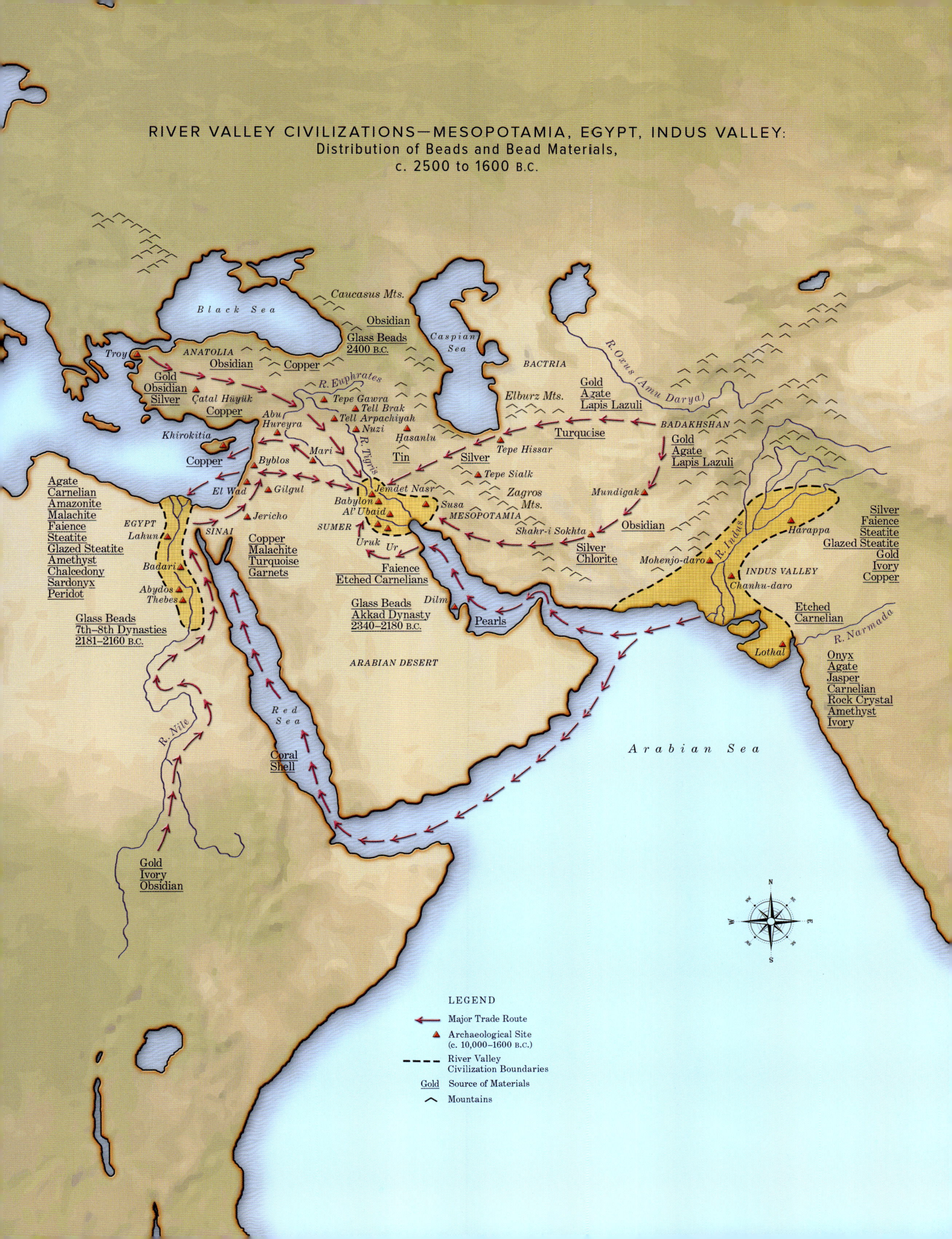
RIVER VALLEY CIVILIZATIONS—MESOPOTAMIA, EGYPT, INDUS VALLEY:
Distribution of Beads and Bead Materials,
c. 2500 to 1600 B.C.
Black Sea
Caucasus Mts.
Obsidian
Glass Beads 2400 B.C.
Caspian Sea
BACTRIA
R. Oxus (Amu Darya)
Troy
ANATOLIA
Obsidian
Copper
Gold
Obsidian
Silver
Çatal Hüyük
Copper
R. Euphrates
Tepe Gawra
Tell Brak
Tell Arpachiyah
Nuzi
Hasanlu
Elburz Mts.
Gold
Agate
Lapis Lazuli
BADAKHSHAN
Turquoise
Tepe Hissar
Gold
Agate
Lapis Lazuli
Khirokitia
Abu Hureyra
Mari
R. Tigris
Tin
Silver
Copper
Byblos
Tepe Sialk
Zagros Mts.
Mundigak
El Wad
Gilgul
Jemdet Nasr
Agate
Carnelian
Amazonite
Malachite
Faience
Steatite
Glazed Steatite
Amethyst
Chalcedony
Sardonyx
Peridot
EGYPT
Lahun
Jericho
Babylon
Al'Ubaid
Susa
MESOPOTAMIA
SUMER
Shahr-i Sokhta
Obsidian
SINAI
Copper
Malachite
Turquoise
Garnets
Uruk
Ur
Silver
Chlorite
Badari
Faience
Etched Carnelians
Mohenjo-daro
R. Indus
Harappa
INDUS VALLEY
Chanhu-daro
Silver
Faience
Steatite
Glazed Steatite
Gold
Ivory
Copper
Abydos
Thebes
Glass Beads 7th–8th Dynasties 2181–2160 B.C.
Glass Beads Akkad Dynasty 2340–2180 B.C.
Dilmun
Pearls
Etched Carnelian
R. Narmada
Lothal
ARABIAN DESERT
Onyx
Agate
Jasper
Carnelian
Rock Crystal
Amethyst
Ivory
Red Sea
R. Nile
Coral
Shell
Arabian Sea
Gold
Ivory
Obsidian
N
E
S
W
LEGEND
Major Trade Route
Archaeological Site (c. 10,000–1600 B.C.)
River Valley Civilization Boundaries
Gold Source of Materials
Mountains

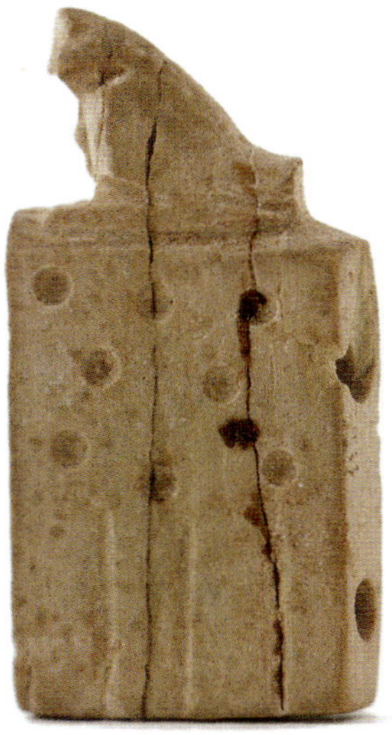

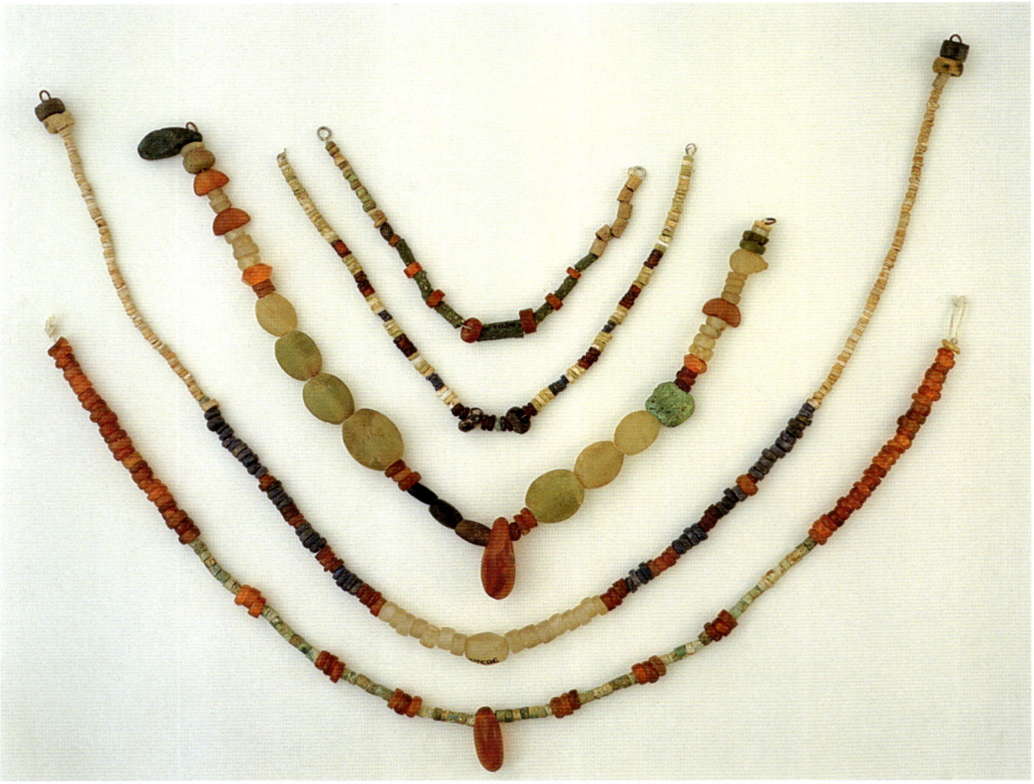

ABOVE: 16. *A First Dynasty ivory bead in the shape of a* serekh, *a rectangular frame with bottom paneling similar to the decorative features on Old Kingdom doors and the facades of early brick tombs. The falcon, Horus, sits atop the* serekh. *Excavated at Abydos in Egypt and dated to about 3000 B.C. Length, 1.6 cm. British Museum, London*

ABOVE RIGHT: 17. *Egyptian beads from the Pre-dynastic and Early Dynastic periods, 3200–2700 B.C. Top to bottom: (1) copper, carnelian, glazed steatite, and shell beads; (2) steatite, lapis lazuli, garnet, shell, and carnelian beads; (3) mixed stone beads, including carnelian, turquoise, and steatite; (4) quartz, lapis lazuli, carnelian, and shell beads; (5) glazed green steatite and carnelian beads with carnelian drop pendant. The use of glazed steatite was a way of producing less expensive colored stones. Bottom pendant: length, 2 cm. British Museum, London*

secondary and probably occurred only when there were enough flakes left over from the knife-manufacturing process. A black, glassy volcanic substance, obsidian was durable, decorative, and rare—ideal properties for beads.

In wealthy societies, however, there was a wide-ranging luxury trade by 4200 B.C. At Tepe Gawra, an important northern outpost of the Mesopotamian 'Ubaid culture that was closely connected with the early trading, beads of turquoise, amethyst, beryl, gold, electrum, and lapis lazuli have been found.[5] While the beads were fashioned at Tepe Gawra, the gold and electrum came from Iran or Anatolia, the turquoise from Iran, and the lapis lazuli from Afghanistan.

Beads played an important role in early organized religion. At the temple site of Tell Brak in eastern Syria (Jemdet Nasr period, c. 3000 B.C.), over one hundred thousand beads, mostly tiny disks of glazed faience, steatite, and shell, were embedded in gray mud bricks used to construct the sacred Eye Temple platform (the temple was named after numerous female figurines with exaggerated eyes excavated there). Neolithic people customarily consecrated a temple area by sowing it with beads or mixing beads into the mud used for foundation bricks. This ritual, symbolically analogous to sowing a field with seed, was intended to bring prosperity to the temple, which was also a repository of the city's wealth.[6]

One can only speculate on the circumstances that produced the earliest western Asian beads. While Neolithic agriculture involved the whole community in subsistence activities for most of the year, the winter months provided some leisure time for farmers to make crafts. Later, more complex societies supported non-food-producing specialists, including full-time craftsmen. The appearance of specialists is one of the distinguishing characteristics of the transition from autonomous local villages of the Neolithic period to large-scale, regional cultures with towns and cities.

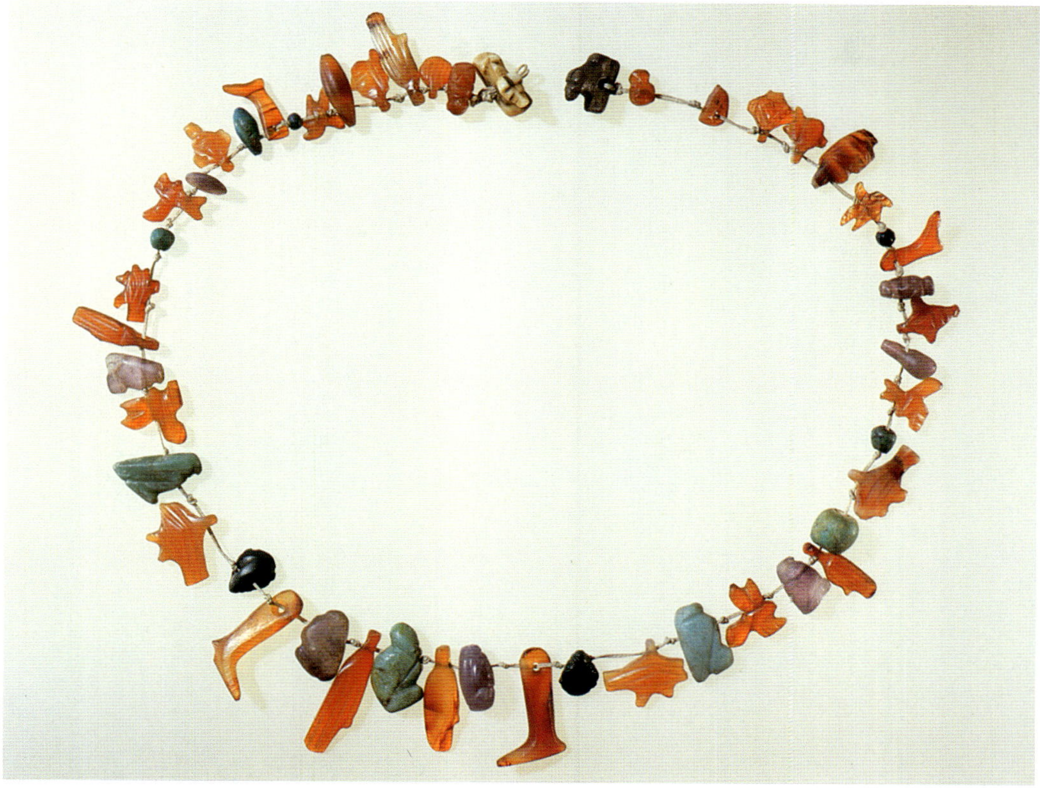

18. *Amuletic beads of carnelian, feldspar, amethyst, faience, jasper, and ivory, from Egypt, during the First Intermediate Period (2181–2130 B.C.).*

Amulets were very important throughout Egyptian history. The common word for amulet in the dynastic periods was mk-t, *or "protector," and* udjat, *"the thing which keeps safe" and "the strengthener."*[V] *Each shape was believed to help the wearer in specific circumstances encountered in life and the afterlife. Amulets were widely used in personal jewelry from the Fifth to the Twelfth Dynasty (2494–1786 B.C.).*

Some amulets represent particular gods and were believed to impart the special qualities associated with those gods. The frog goddess, Heqet, for example, was considered the patroness of birth; the udjat, *also known as the Eye of Horus, had strong amuletic powers; while the* djed *pillar stood for endurance. Amulets in the forms of human anatomical parts were thought to protect those body parts in the living. Furthermore, some beads were made of materials considered especially protective; in particular, garnet, carnelian, and crystal. Longest amulet: length, 3 cm. British Museum, London*

Mesopotamia

Between 4000 and 3000 B.C., three of the earliest centers of civilization based on intensive agriculture developed in the river valleys of Mesopotamia, Egypt, and India. These were hierarchical societies with an upper strata of merchant, priestly, military, and royal classes in whose collective hands wealth was concentrated. One way in which social differences were reflected was the display of adornment, including beads. Indeed, for the first time, the role of beads as status symbols equaled or surpassed their ritual or magical functions. The dual function of beads as amulets and status symbols is a prevailing theme of their history throughout most of western Asia, Egypt, and the Mediterranean in ancient times.

Mesopotamian and Egyptian priests and kings employed full-time jewelers, and through their patronage beadmaking technology developed rapidly. The degree of prestige attached to a necklace depended not only on its craftsmanship, but on the use of rare and precious materials. To obtain not only the basic necessities of life, but these scarce minerals, metals, and marine products as well, trade routes spanning great distances developed into an important part of these civilizations' commercial activities.

Egypt had within its boundaries most of the natural resources used in beadmaking; Mesopotamia, however, had none of the appropriate materials. Gold probably came to the Tigris and Euphrates valleys from the mountains of Anatolia or Iran, carnelian and agate from India and Afghanistan, and lapis lazuli from Afghanistan. Lapis, the one stone important to Egyptian jewelry not found inside its borders, reached the Nile Delta via Mesopotamia.

By 2500 B.C., beads produced for Sumerian royalty in the city-state of Ur in southern Mesopotamia were of superb craftsmanship, employing sophisticated goldsmithing techniques for filigree and cloisonné (plates 11–12 and 14). Fluted melon beads were crafted in gold and lapis lazuli. The products of Sumerian jewelers spread into the less-developed

TOP: 19. *A broad wesekh collar with five rows of beads, semicircular terminal spacers, and pendants, all of faience. The introduction of spacers, to keep multiple-layered necklaces hanging properly, became an important component of Middle Kingdom (2133–1786 B.C.) jewelry. Excavated at Deir-el-Bahari (near Thebes), Egypt. Length (outer row), 41.6 cm. British Museum, London*

BOTTOM: 20. *A girdle of cast gold cowrie shell effigy beads and carnelian, lapis lazuli, and green feldspar beads simulating acacia seeds. Each hollow gold shell effigy contains a pellet, making the girdle sound like a rattle when the wearer moves.*

Dating to the Twelfth Dynasty (1991–1786 B.C.), the girdle belonged to Princess Si-Hathor-Yunet from Lahun. The Middle Kingdom was a period of sophisticated aesthetics in Egyptian history, and jewelry produced then has an elegant, unified style. Length, 84 cm. Metropolitan Museum of Art, New York

OVERLEAF: 21. *Lunar pectoral with necklace of carnelian, lapis lazuli, feldspar, and gold beads and a lotus blossom counterpoise. This is a striking example of the three basic components in Egyptian jewelry—pectoral, beaded necklace, and counterpoise—unified into a single design. Even the beaded tassels hanging from the counterpoise acted as amulets, protecting the wearer from behind. This piece was worn by King Tutankhamen and was buried in his tomb at Thebes, c. 1352 B.C. Pectoral: width, 11.8 cm. Cairo Museum*

cultures of western Asia and into Anatolia, the probable source of the jewelers' gold. Sumerian jewelry techniques also traveled to southern Greece and Crete, where gold beads in related styles appear at slightly later dates.[7] The path of a distinctive four-spiraled bead style can be traced from its origin in Sumer or Iran about 2500 B.C. through its metamorphosis (of materials and form) along this same Mediterranean route (plate 29).

By c. 2500 B.C. beadwork was an art form in Sumeria, as demonstrated on the diadem (headband) of Queen Pu-abi, which was recovered at Ur and is composed of hundreds of tiny lapis lazuli beads.

The importance of Sumerian and Mesopotamian jewelry and beadmaking and its direct or indirect influence on the adornment of subsequent cultures in western Asia and the Mediterranean cannot be overemphasized. Indeed, most techniques practiced by jewelers today were known to the ancient Sumerian goldsmiths. With the dissolution of the Sumerian Empire in about 1600 B.C., the techniques developed by Sumerian smiths were passed on to Babylonian craftsmen in northern Mesopotamia.

Glass and glass beads also appear to have a western Asian and possibly Sumerian origin. The earliest examples are from Mesopotamia, dating to the Akkad dynasty (2340–2180 B.C.),[8] and from the Caucasus region in present-day Russia.[9] Large numbers (over eleven thousand) of artistically beautiful glass beads, made by a wide range of manufacturing methods and dating before the site's destruction in 1400 B.C., have been excavated from the Hurrian settlement of Nuzi, part of the Mittani Kingdom located 130 miles north of Baghdad in present-day Iraq.[10] (Timeline 311 and 312)

Egypt

One of the most stable civilizations of antiquity established itself along the Nile shortly after the emergence of Mesopotamia. While the economic and social organization of dynastic Egypt generally resembled that of Sumer, geography created important differences. Egypt, unlike Mesopotamia, had relatively clear-cut, defensible borders. In addition, the Nile, Egypt's major transportation route, was easily navigated, allowing its rulers to control shipping. By regulating all major movements of goods and people, the Egyptian kings possessed the means for effective rule.[11] Furthermore, Egypt was rich in the precious metals and minerals needed for subsistence and luxury items. These factors provided security and insulated Egyptian life from foreign influences. Consequently, there is a marked conservatism to Egyptian art and jewelry. The styles and techniques developed in early Egypt changed relatively little from early dynastic to Ptolemaic times (c. 3100–30 B.C.) and seem particularly consistent when compared with the variations in western Asian adornment.

No other civilization, however, manufactured such an enormous variety of beads in so many different materials. They were not only used for necklaces but were also attached to linen and papyrus backings to make belts, aprons, and sandals. A spectacular example of Old Kingdom beadwork, dating c. 2200 B.C., is the belt of Prince Ptah-Shepses, which was covered with a beadwork band. The beads were made of gold and semiprecious stones and were threaded with a gold wire. During the Middle Kingdom (2133–1786 B.C.), ceremonial beaded aprons contained multicolored faience and white shell beads. In the New Kingdom (1650–1085 B.C.), a great variety of beadwork objects was put in the tomb of King Tutankhamen (d. 1352 B.C.)—included were broad collars, sandals decorated with a beadwork flower pattern, and a ceremonial garment of bead bands and bead netting. Some of the objects seemed to have been used during the king's lifetime. During the Late Period (1085–332 B.C.), however, beadwork materials were prepared mainly for funerary purposes (plate 26). Egyptian beadwork was produced by a special netted technique that threaded single beads together, rather than using a bead loom. Beadwork bands and figures were the main products made by this method.[12]

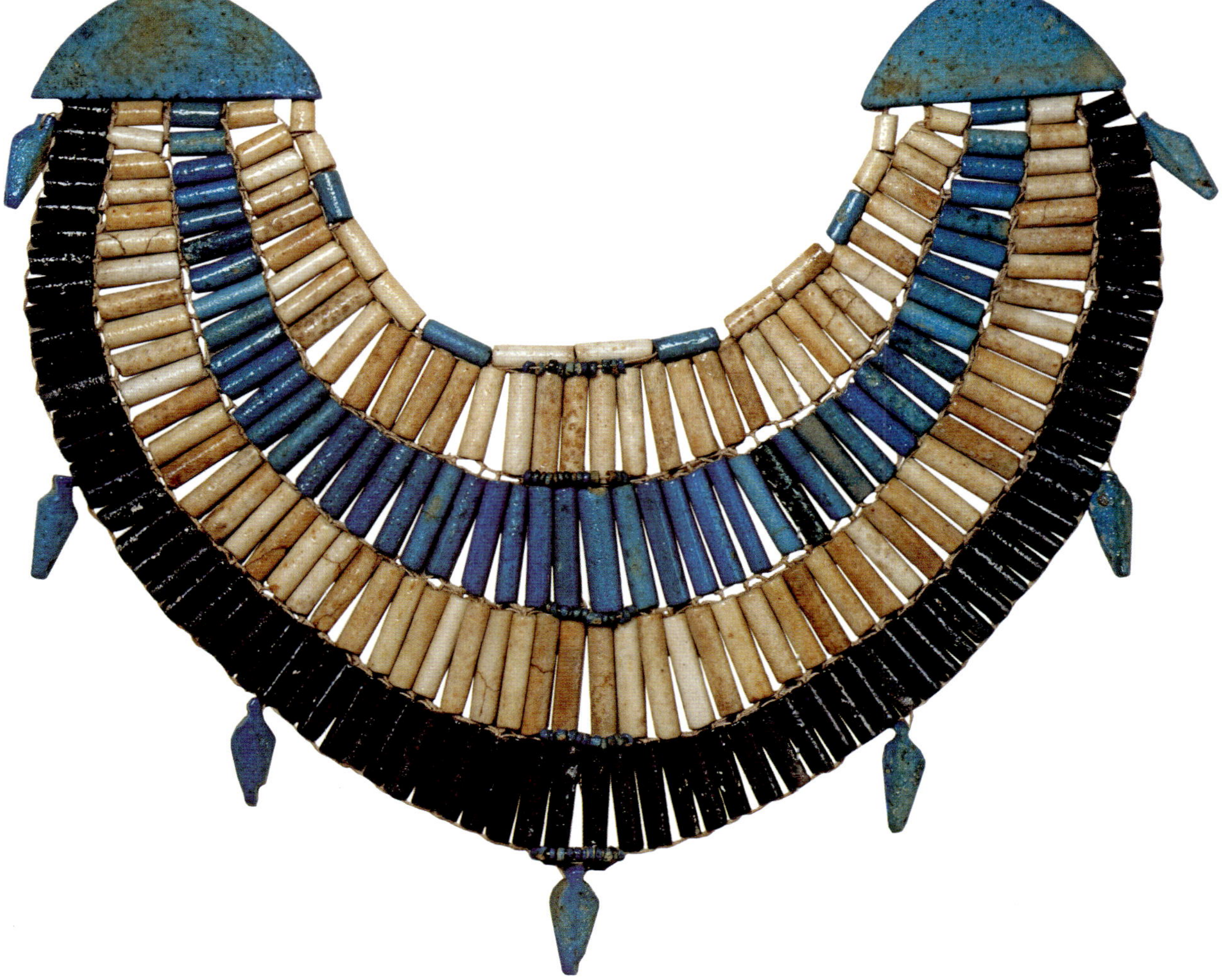

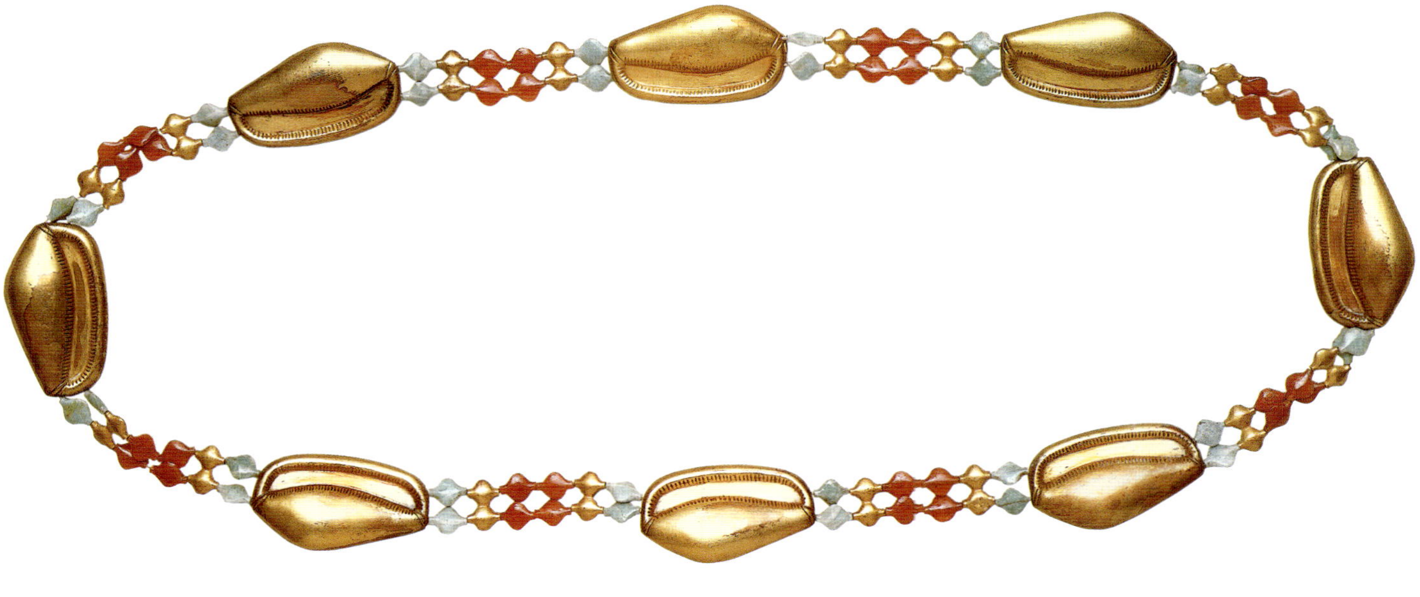

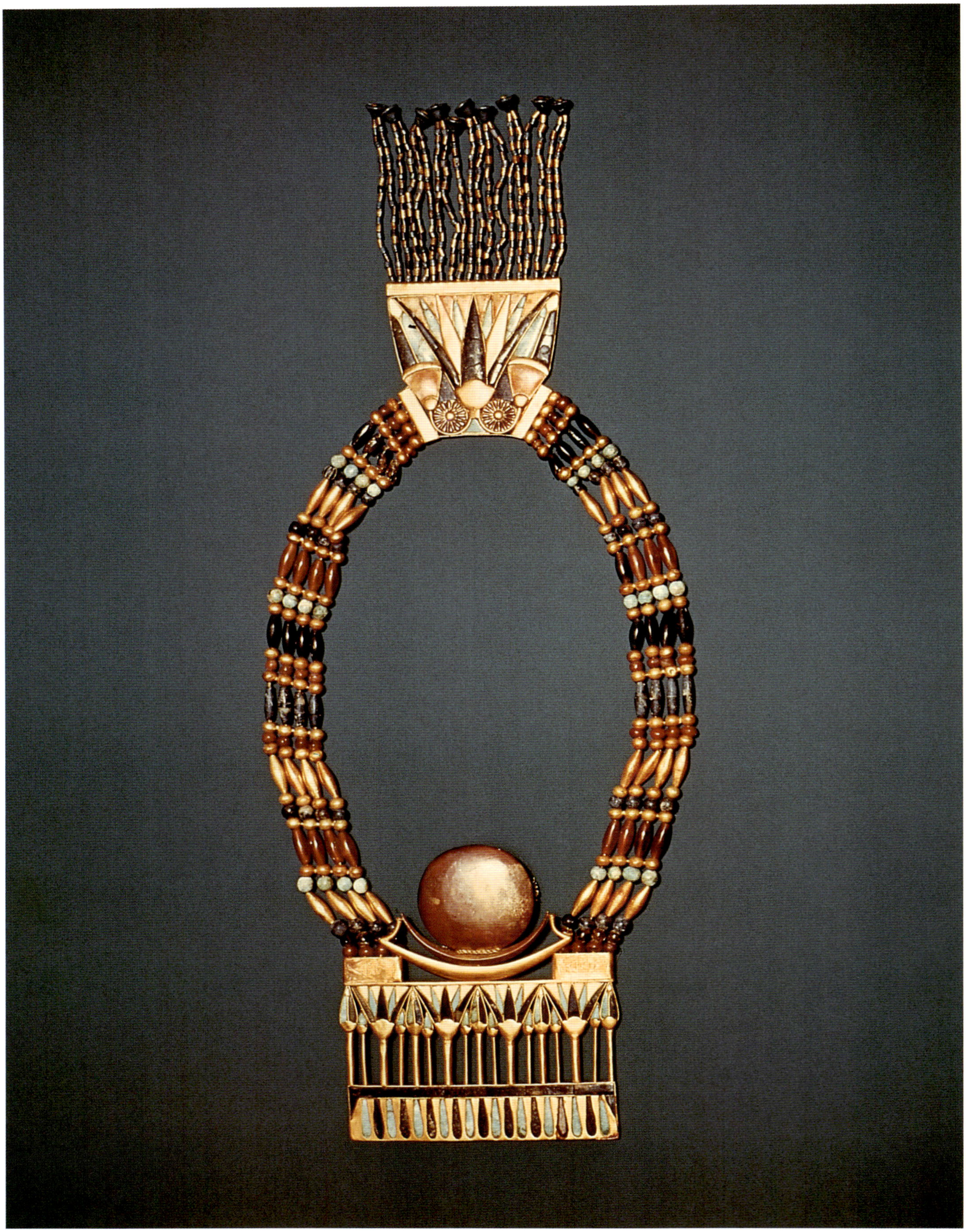

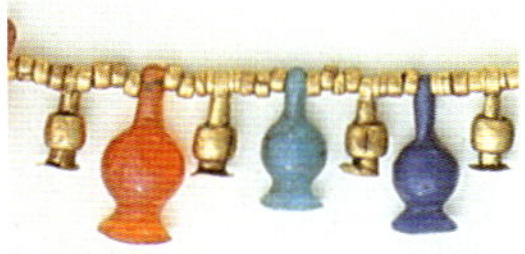

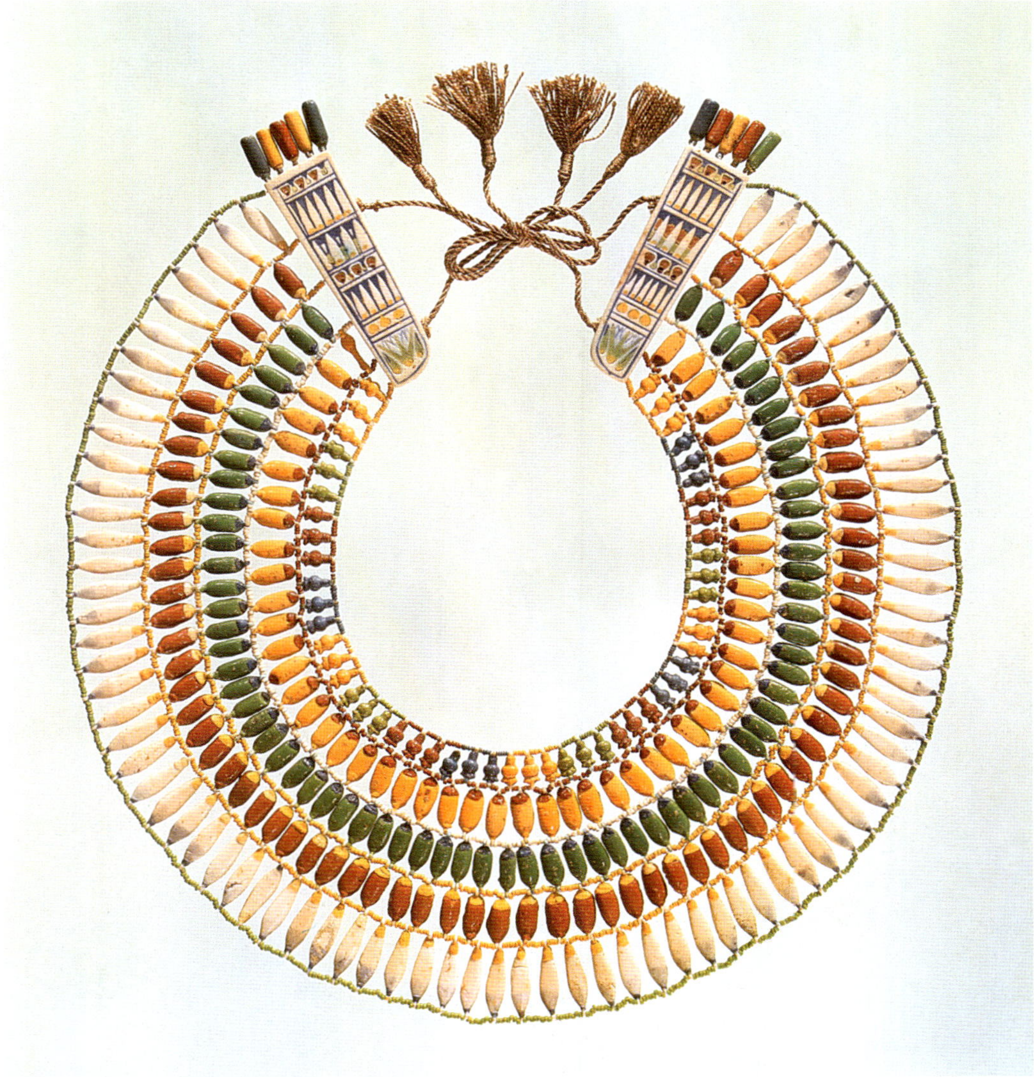

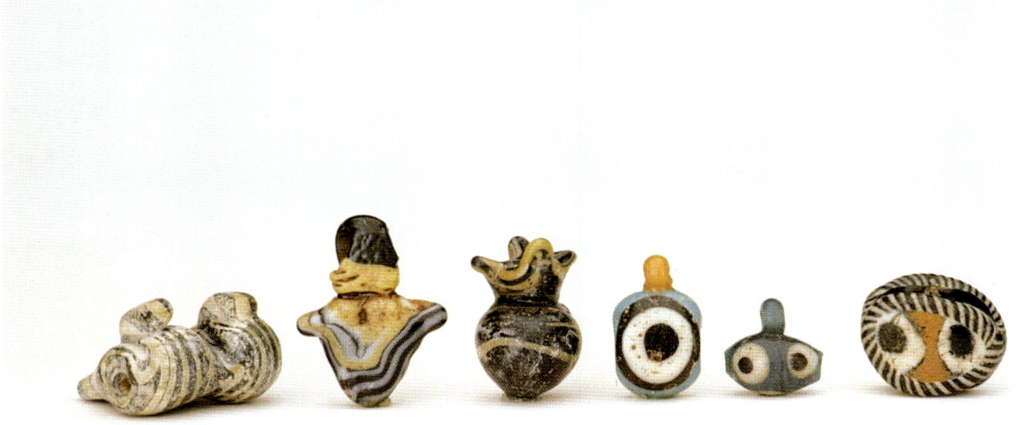

ABOVE: 22. *An example of New Kingdom bead production. Effigy poppy seed pods are of carnelian, gold, lapis lazuli, and feldspar, with tiny carnelian and gold spacer beads. Typical carnelian poppy pod: length, 1.5 cm. British Museum, London*

LEFT: 23. *Collar of faience beads depicting cornflowers, dates, lotus seedpods, and petals in a pattern derived from garlands of real flowers. Faience bead collars were frequently supplied as favors to guests at banquets. This necklace typifies the technical brilliance of the faience and glass jewelry of the Amarna period (1379–1362 B.C.). It has been suggested that the uniquely gay and joyful quality of Amarna period art and jewelry reflects the sudden appearance of outside influences—possibly attributable to Minoan artists who may have fled to Egypt after the fall of Crete. Excavated from the tomb of Tutankhamen at Thebes. Diameter, 31 cm. Metropolitan Museum of Art, New York. Rogers Fund*

BOTTOM: 24. *A collection of New Kingdom core-formed or wound glass beads from the Amarna period. Far right eye bead: diameter, 1.5 cm. Collection Henry Anavian, New York*

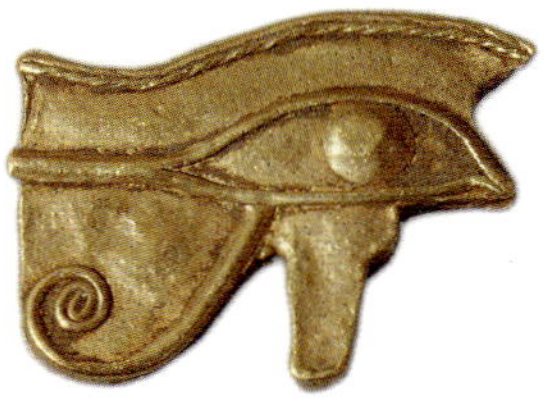

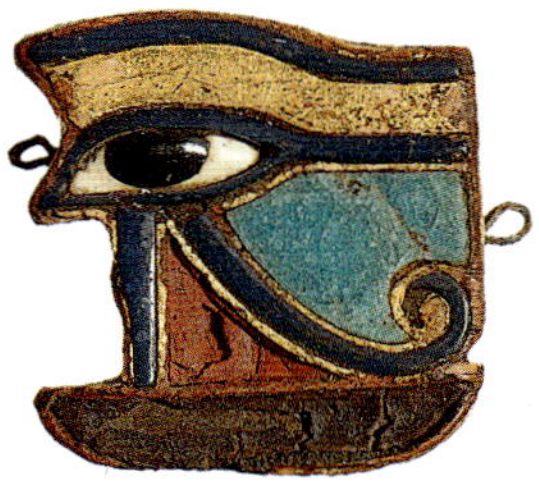

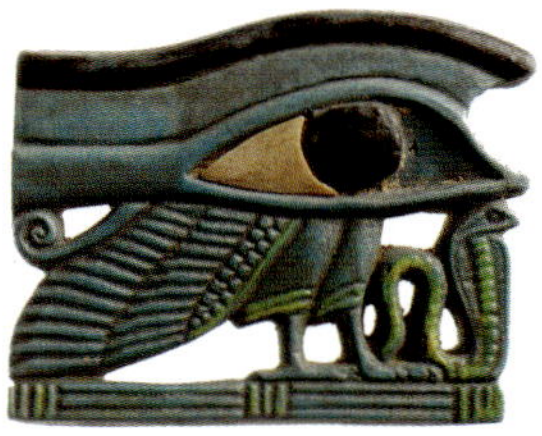

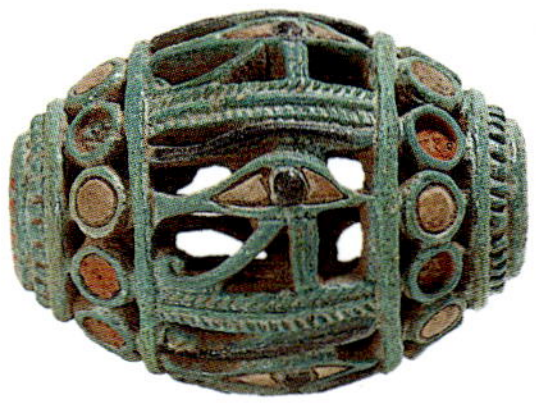

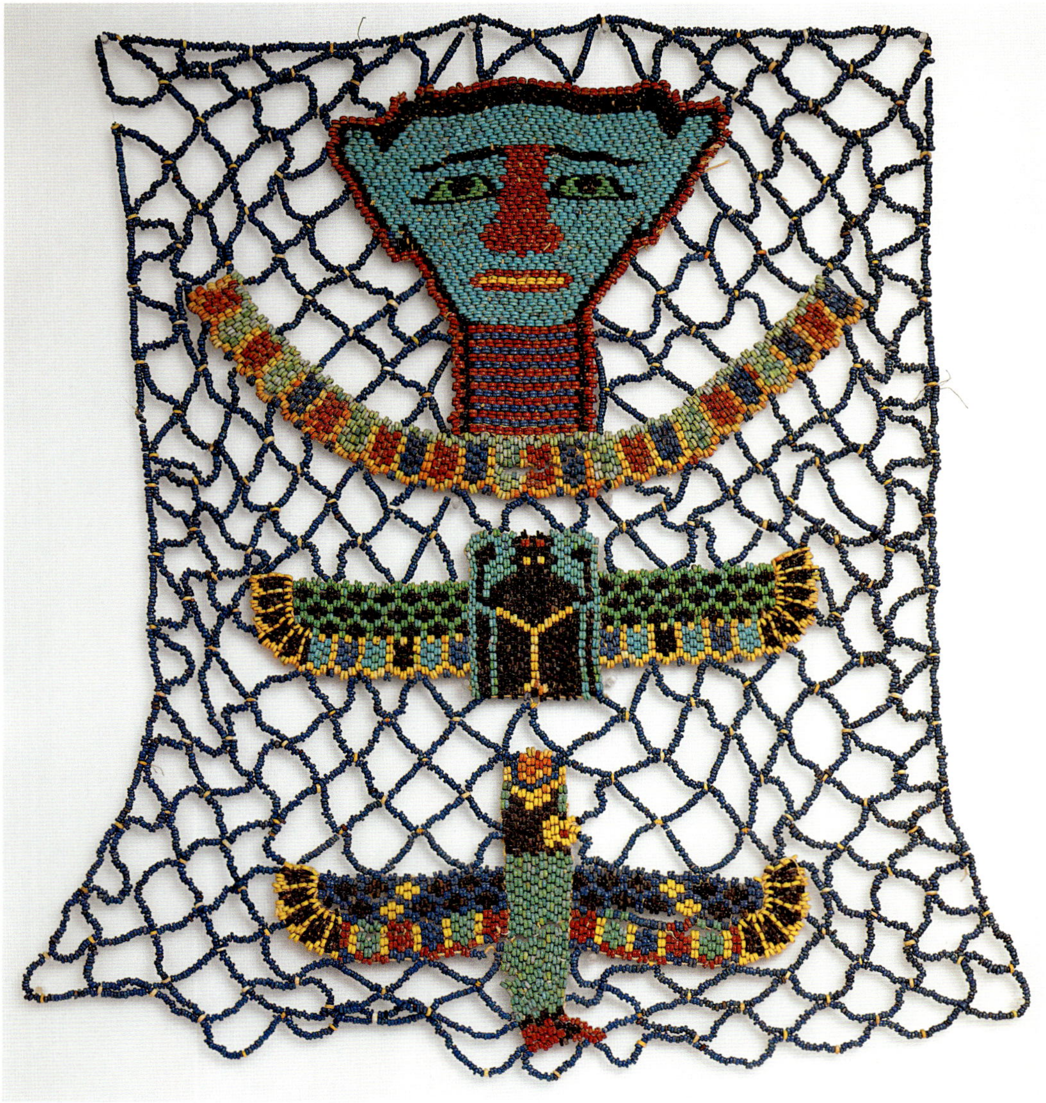

ABOVE: 25 a–d. *Eye of Horus Beads. From the Old Kingdom to Roman times, the Eye of Horus, also known as a wedjat, was a popular amuletic symbol. The earliest known dates from the Vth Dynasty, c. 2495 B.C. Although there are countless variations on the theme in numerous materials, the basic design—representing the all-seeing eye of the powerful falcon-headed god, Horus—remained the same*

a. *Gold Wedjet. Egyptian, Late Period, 664–380 B.C. Height, 3.2cm; The Metropolitan Museum of Art, Rogers Fund, 1923 (23.2.68)*

b. *Wedjet amulet. Egyptian, Late-Period-Ptolemaic Period, 664–30 B.C. Wood, glass, plaster, gold, copper or copper alloy. Width: 2.8 cm. The*

Virtually everyone in ancient Egypt, from predynastic to Ptolemaic times, wore beads. While the famous treasures of Tutankhamen include dazzling examples of the beads of Egyptian royalty, simple strings of shell, stone, and faience have been found in even the poorest of burial sites. The Egyptian word *sha* means "luck" and *sha-sha* means "bead," suggesting that beads were thought to have amuletic or protective properties, which explains the Egyptian custom of using beads to cover almost every article of clothing and every part of the body. The Egyptians also believed that to insure comfort in the afterlife, the dead must be surrounded with the paraphernalia of daily life. Quantities of beads were buried with their owner, the choice of materials depending on the family's wealth. Occasionally, delicately beaded funereal pieces were also included.

As in Mesopotamia, beads were worn by both men and women in Egypt and were depicted on statues of the gods. Although numerous stones were available to the Egyptians (amethyst became very popular in the Middle Kingdom), certain metals and stones were favored, especially gold, carnelian, lapis lazuli, and turquoise. A stone's color almost certainly had particular amuletic value to the Egyptian lapidary and his clients and therefore determined its popularity. Green turquoise or feldspar symbolized the earth's fertility and was considered the color of new life; red carnelian was the color of blood, symbolizing life; while lapis lazuli, the "heavenly stone," resembled the sky.[13] The use of other stones often reflected recent discoveries. The popularity of garnet beads in the Middle Kingdom may have been due to abundant sources of the mineral in Sinai during that period. Since garnets occur in nature in the form of dodecahedral crystals and are frequently detached from their matrix, after which they weather into rounded stones, it required very little work to turn them into beads.[14]

In reliefs and paintings, lapidaries and metalsmiths are shown working side by side in ateliers under the supervision of a chief jeweler. The various materials and phases of beadmaking were divided into specialties according to skill. Separate guilds existed for goldsmiths, faience workers, stone carvers, bead threaders, and eventually glassworkers. The art of beadmaking reached a high point during the Middle Kingdom, when extraordinarily fine stone beads were made in minute sizes and in large sizes with very long perforations. In both types, it is theorized that the holes were drilled first, and afterward the beads were ground down to the desired thickness.[15]

Egyptian jewelers frequently used large numbers of beads of one stone to form blocks of color. Opaque stones were preferred, and repetitious patterns employing multiple strands of a small variety of stone beads were common. The *wesekh*—a broad collar with many beaded strands separated by spacer beads to keep multilayered necklaces hanging properly—was in use by the Fourth Dynasty (2613–2494 B.C.).[16] From the beginning of the Middle Kingdom, the *wesekh* became a characteristic form and almost an essential item of dress. Its visually impressive size and large quantities of precious materials undoubtedly indicated the power and prestige of its wearer. The Egyptians understood that spacers—perforated bars of bone, ivory, wood covered with gold leaf, faience, glass, or metal placed at intervals along the strands—were flexible ornamental bands that kept the beads in position. The integration of spacers as part of a necklace's total design concept was frequently masterful. At first simple in execution, they later became elaborate individual units (plate 19).

The greatest number of Egyptian beads were made of faience, an inexpensive substance generally considered to be the forerunner of true glass, although glass was used earlier in glazed steatite beads of Badarian-period Egypt (5500–3800 B.C.; Timeline 435). Invented in either Mesopotamia or Egypt by 4000 B.C., faience was the first mass-produced synthetic material to simulate precious stones such as turquoise and lapis lazuli. The development of faience and eventually glass satisfied the desire of the general populace to wear beads that emulated the precious stones of the wealthy.

Although glass beads are known by the Seventh and Eighth Dynasties (c. 2181–c. 2160 B.C.), they were first manufactured for a large commercial market beginning in Egypt about 1400 B.C.[17] The New Kingdom, especially the later phases of the Eighteenth Dynasty (c. 1350 B.C.), is generally considered to be the world's first great glassmaking epoch. The earliest glass, an exotic material, was made for use by the pharaohs and their courts, although it eventually became available to wealthier commoners. The proximity of Egyptian glass factories to the palaces at Thebes, Amarna, and Shurak attests to the royal patronage of glassmaking.

During the New Kingdom, glass beads began to replace precious and semiprecious stones. The Egyptians favored deeply colored opaque glass, since it more closely resembled lapis lazuli and turquoise. Early Egyptian glass beads are carefully finished and have luminous colors. Frequently, they were made by quite complex techniques (plate 24).

The elegance and restraint of Middle Kingdom designs gave way in the New

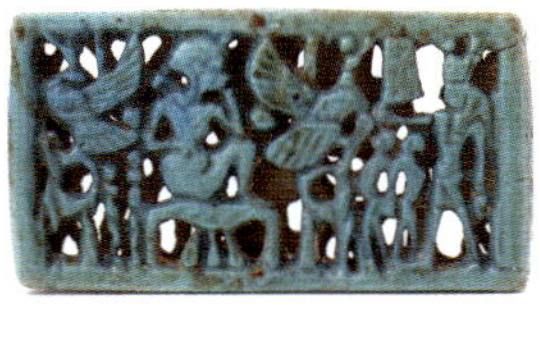

Metropolitan Museum of Art, Gift of Miss Lily S. Place 1923 (23.6.49)

c. *Wedjet-eye and a uraeus. First Persian Period-Late Period, 525–332 B.C. Faience, width, 6.4 cm. The Metropolitan Museum of Art, Gift of J.Pierpont Morgan, 1917 (17.190,1639)*

d. *Openwork bead, Egyptian, Ptolemaic or Roman Period, 304 B.C.–A.D. 364. Faience, Length 5.8 cm. The Metropolitan Museum of Art, Purchase, Rogers Fund, 1944 (44.4.22)*

OPPOSITE RIGHT: 26. *Egyptian beaded mummy shroud made of faience disk-shaped beads. The amuletic images under the face and necklace collar are a winged scarab and a winged son of Horus. Dynasty XXVI, c. 656–525 B.C. There is some original linen stringing. 22.9 × 34.3 cm. Collection The Mingei International Museum, San Diego, California*

ABOVE: 27. *Glazed spacer beads were developed to spread out the layers of beads in collar necklaces. At first simple in design, they later became elaborately designed individual units. This Egyptian spacer bead, c. 1050–750 B.C., depicts the figures of the god Horus the child and Horus the warrior with prisoners. Length, 4.5 cm. British Museum, London*

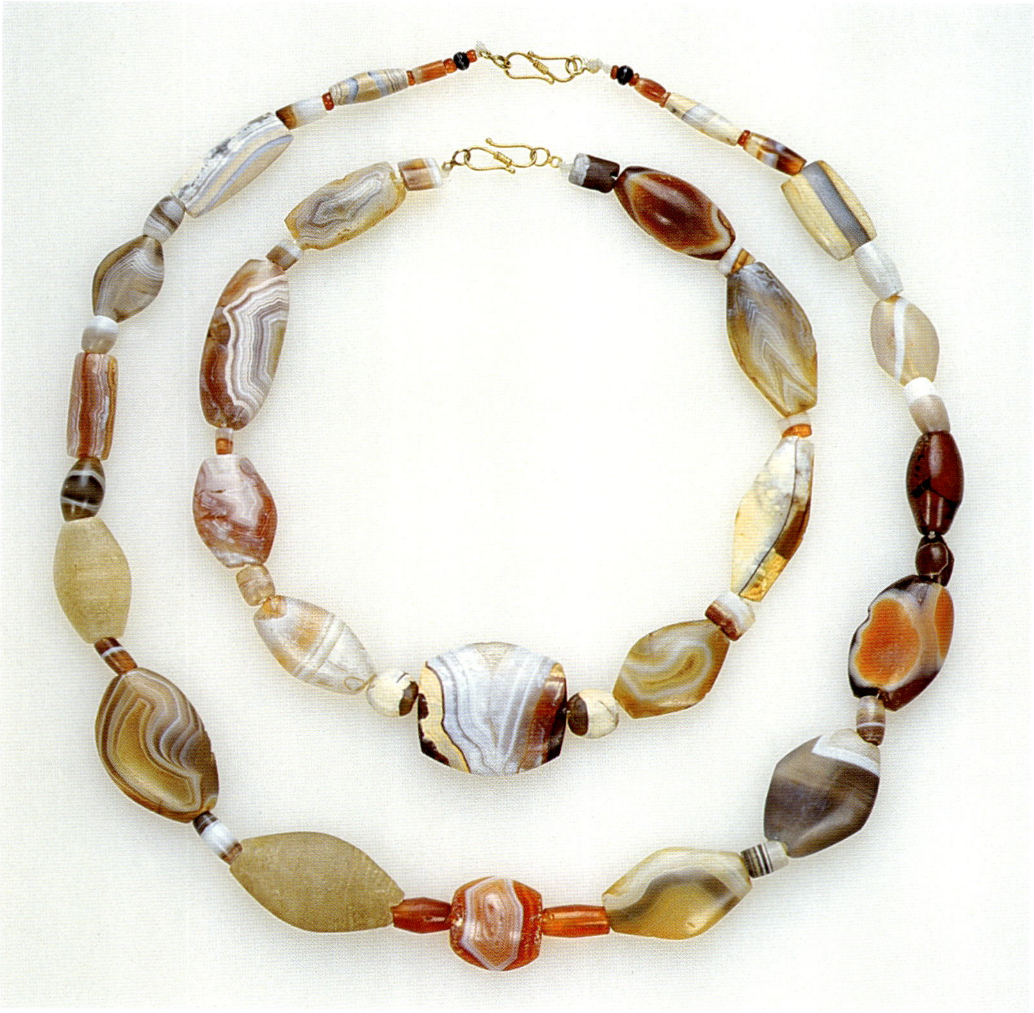

28. *Agate, jasper, and carnelian beads purported to have been excavated near the Amu Darya River, the legendary "Oxus of empires," in northeastern Afghanistan. All the beads of this group, particularly the rhomboidal or lenticular agates, are of the finest quality. Note that the bead forms are beautifully shaped according to the natural banding of the stone. These beads have almost exact counterparts among artifacts discovered in the royal tombs at Ur (2600–2100 B.C.).*

Rhomboidal beads date to 7000 B.C. at Çatal Hüyük, Anatolia. Agates of this fine quality, however, are documented at only a few archaeological sites: Ur (Mesopotamia), Tepe Hissar (Iran), and Mundigak (Afghanistan). Their distribution may be related to the far-reaching third millennium trade in lapis lazuli or to trade in etched beads between Mesopotamia and the Indus Valley.[VI] *Inside necklace, center bead: length, 3.5 cm. Private collection*

Kingdom to a more exuberant style. Forms such as flowers, leaves, and buds were directly copied from nature in both glass and faience. Faience, which had originated as simple tubes and disks in limited colors, became particularly plentiful. Complex shapes were developed and new colors supplemented the familiar blues and greens. Collars of faience beads, imitating woven floral garlands, were particularly popular at Amarna, the capital city of Akhenaten and Nefertiti from 1379 to 1362 B.C. (plate 23).

A decline in glassmaking skills occurred in Egypt after the Nineteenth Dynasty ended (c. 1200 B.C.), and glass virtually disappeared after the fall of the New Kingdom (1085 B.C.). It was revived in Ptolemaic times, during the fourth century B.C., when Alexander the Great founded Alexandria, a cosmopolitan center with international trading links. Glass reputedly produced in Alexandria through the early Roman period included some of the most beautiful and complex beads ever made.

The Indus Valley

Two great cities, Mohenjo-daro and Harappa, and numerous smaller towns prospered on the banks of the Indus River and its tributaries between 2500 and 1500 B.C. Although some aspects of this civilization paralleled those of Mesopotamia and Egypt, notably the architecture and jewelry, little is known of its historical development or why it disappeared. Contact existed between the Indus Valley civilization and Mesopotamia, as seen

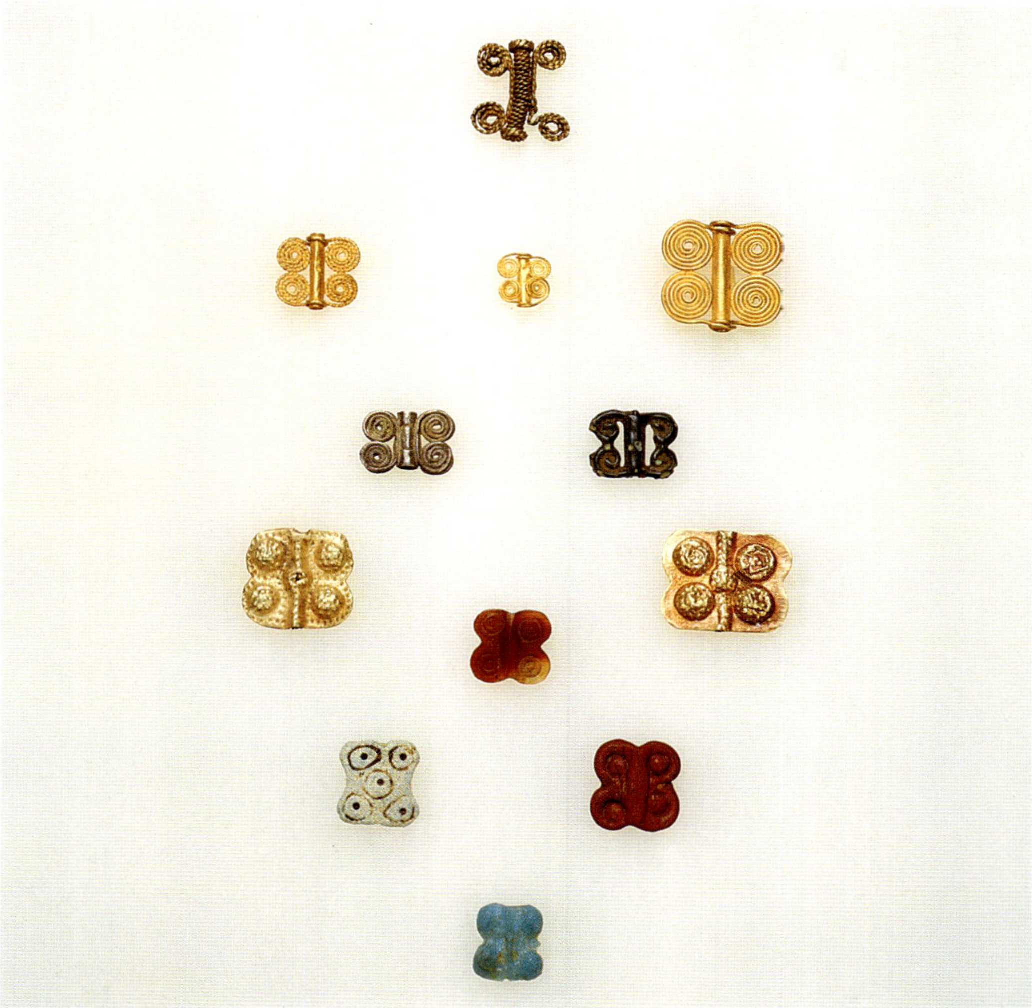

29. *These quadruple spiral beads are interesting examples of a form that originated in Sumer or Iran in the early third millennium* B.C. *and was imitated thereafter over a wide area for two thousand years.*

The motif spread westward as part of the expansion of Mesopotamian culture. After Ur, the bead form appeared at Tell Brak (Syria) by 2200 B.C., *at Troy (Anatolia) by 2100* B.C., *and reached Mycenae and the Caucasus by 1500* B.C. *Examples were excavated at Mari (Syria) dating to 1000* B.C.[VII]

The spread of the quadruple-spiral beads through so many cultures over such a long time span suggests that the motif retained important (though currently unknown) symbolic meaning. The significance of this symbol to the general populace is indicated by the manufacture of these beads in an array of inexpensive materials.

The beads' original form was created by twisting gold wires into a quadruple spiral. They were eventually mass-produced in cast lead, stamped sheet gold, glass, and faience, reflecting the fact that form, supported by symbolism, often changes more slowly than technology.

Beads shown: Twisted gold wire, 2000–1800 B.C.; *gold wire and tube (Mari type), 1300–800* B.C.; *silver and cast lead, c. 800* B.C.; *stamped sheet gold; carved stone; faience; glass. Cast bead (third row, right): length, 1.8 cm. Collection Henry Anavian, New York*

in the quantities of "etched" carnelian beads with similar shapes and white patterns found at both Ur and Mohenjo-daro. The source of manufacture was the city of Harappa in the Indus Valley (plate 13).[18]

Afghanistan

Ancient Afghanistan was a major supplier of both raw materials and beautifully made stone beads, a fact as much related to the mineral wealth of its mountains as to its geographic location. Surrounded by Iran, India, China, and Russia, trade routes between these countries passed through Afghanistan, making it an important transmitter of materials and culture and a strategic intermediary between East and West.[19]

Historically underrated as a source of bead craftsmanship, Afghanistan was considerably more than a source of raw materials. Many beads excavated there and attributed to the third and second millennia B.C. have exact counterparts among the artifacts recovered from the royal tombs of Ur (plates 11, 11a, and 28). Because these beads are found in such quantity in Afghanistan, it is reasonable to assume they were manufactured locally.[20]

The great beadmaking era in Afghanistan ended about 1600 B.C., a date synchronous with the decline of the Babylonian Empire. As trade to the south dwindled, both the incentives and the economic structures supporting beadmaking seem to have disappeared.

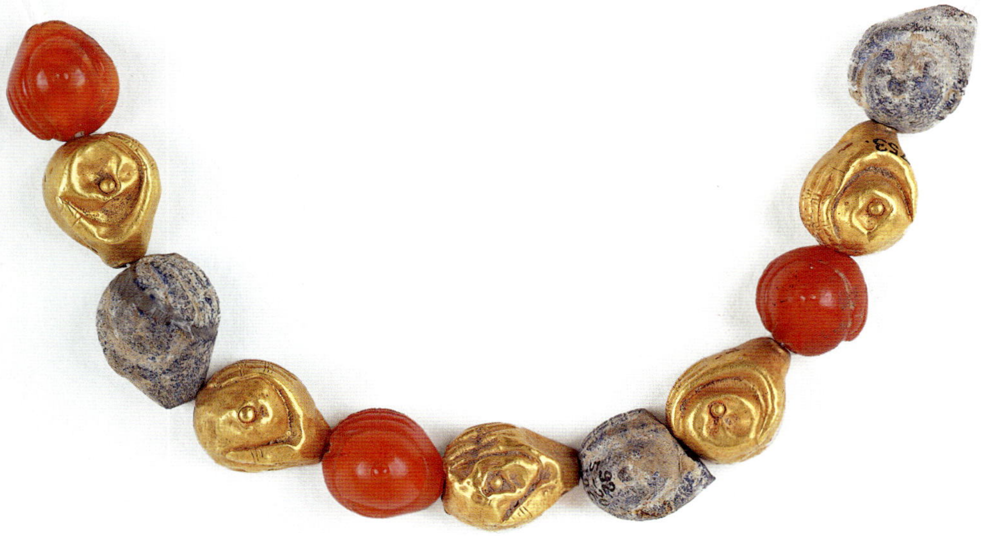

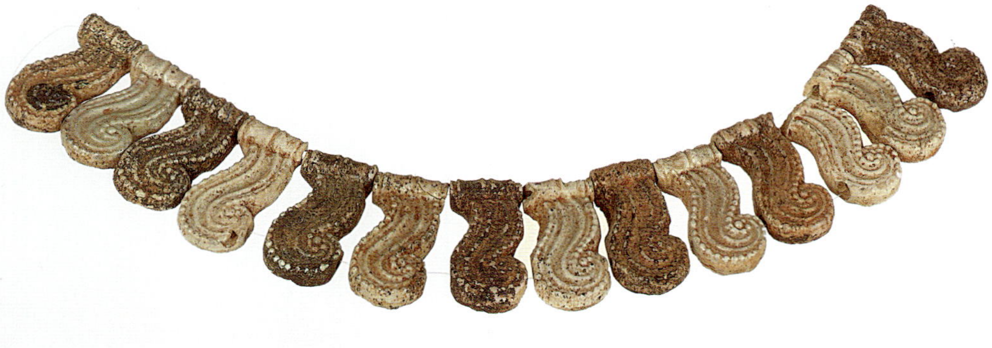

TOP: 30. *Breast beads from Aegina, 1700–1600 B.C. These beads, in the form of a right hand holding a woman's breast, are of Minoan workmanship and were found in a tomb of Cretans who presumably had lived on the island of Aegina. The image of a naked woman holding her breast had a long history in western Asia, where it was associated with fertility goddesses. Mesopotamian and Egyptian influences are evidenced in the combination of gold, carnelian, and lapis lazuli beads of homogeneous shapes and sizes within a single necklace. Typical bead: length, 1.5 cm. British Museum, London*

RIGHT: 31. *To the Mycenaeans, glass was an exotic, treasured material. Flat, molded blue glass relief beads like these were mass-produced in the region of Mycenae from 1400 to 1150 B.C. They were identical to gold relief beads that were made in the same steatite molds. As gold became scarce, glass was used with increasing frequency. In addition to the architectural volute motif shown in relief on these beads, countless stylized designs inherited from the Minoans were used, including shapes of plants, flowers, fish, shells, and animals. Typical bead: length, 2.6 cm. Corning Museum of Glass, Corning, New York*

Crete, Mycenae, and Cyprus

By 2000 B.C., a lively commerce was established between western Asia, Egypt, and the Mediterranean. Sea travel developed as an alternative to hazardous and expensive land journeys. Along with grain, tin, copper, and precious stones, stylistic concepts and technical knowledge were also transmitted from culture to culture.

On the island of Crete, Minoan beads show the influence of both Egypt and the western Asian civilizations. Granulation, filigree, and repoussé techniques were introduced to Crete from western Asia by 2000 B.C. By 1700 B.C., all three methods had been mastered and effectively adapted to Minoan tastes. The Minoans were inspired by the forms of plants, animals, and sea creatures, which they interpreted in their art with enormous originality.[21]

With the fall of Knossos, the capital of Crete, about 1400 B.C., the center of Minoan culture moved to Mycenae on mainland Greece, a transition that is clearly reflected in Mycenaean beads. A variety of pendants and beads made of gold, stone, and glass, often identical to those from Crete, were commonly found in excavated Mycenaean sites. "Relief" beads are the most characteristic ornament of Minoan-Mycenaean jewelry (plate 31). Consisting primarily of stylized representations in shallow relief of marine and plant life, as well as occasional architectural and religious subjects, the beads were initially stamped out of sheet gold. The finest examples were decorated additionally with granulation and enamel. Using the same steatite molds, counterparts of these beads were also made in dark blue glass to imitate lapis lazuli. The early glass relief beads were possibly valued equally with the gold beads, as glass was a rare and exotic material. With the

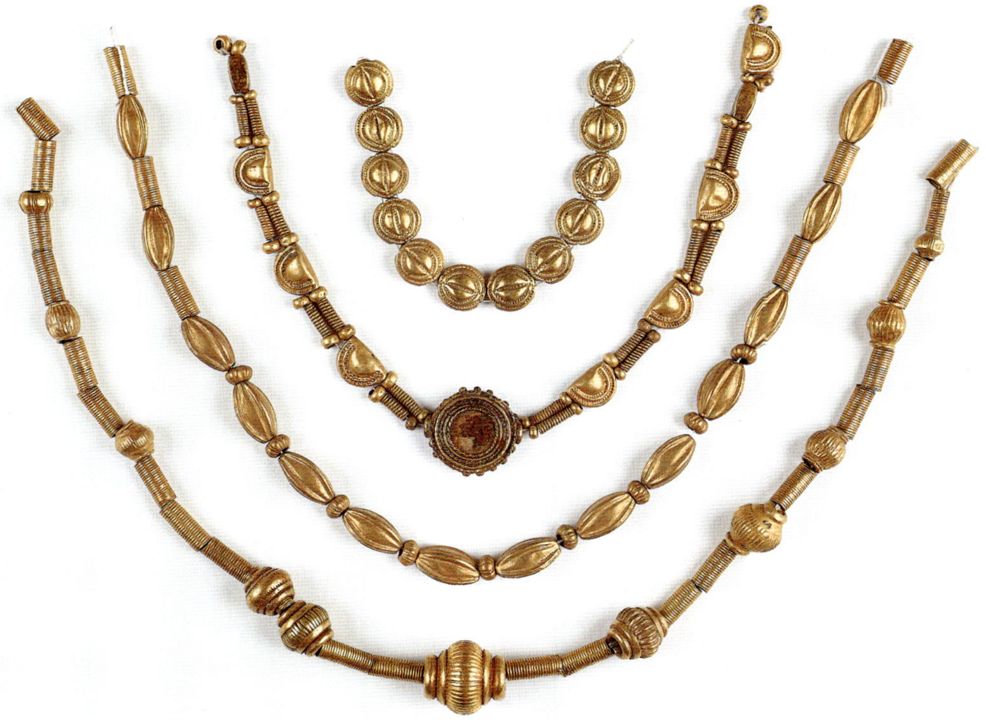

32. *By the late Bronze Age (1300–1200 B.C.), the wealth garnered from the copper trade enabled Cyprus to prosper, a fact reflected in its elaborate gold jewelry. Minoan and Mycenaean influences are evident in the figure-eight shield motif depicted in the first and second necklaces from the top.*

This group of gold bead necklaces was excavated from a townhouse courtyard in the ancient harbor town of Enkomi, Cyprus, and dates to about 1250 B.C. Second necklace from top: length, 25 cm. British Museum, London

decline of the Mycenaean civilization (c. 1150 B.C.), the manufacture of relief beads only in glass appears to reflect the dwindling supply of gold.[22]

The Mycenaeans, who wore large quantities of beads made from a variety of materials, were famed sailors and traders. The presence of amber beads in seventeenth-century B.C. Mycenaean shaft graves indicates they traded with the Baltic region. The source of this amber has been identified as Jutland, the Danish peninsula. It reached Mycenae via the famed amber routes that crossed Europe from the Baltic to the northern coast of the Adriatic Sea. Greek ships were used for the final stage of the southern voyage, possibly accounting for the great concentration of amber beads along the west coast of the Peloponnisos.[23] The dispersion throughout Spain, England, southern France, and Hungary of the segmented faience bead, manufactured in Egypt around 1400 B.C., has also been attributed to Mycenaean enterprise and is considered indicative of their far-reaching importance as major bead traders (Timeline 15).[24]

It is not surprising that beads from Cyprus are a mixture of Minoan-Mycenaean, Syrian, and Egyptian elements,[25] since Cyprus was a convenient halfway point for traders sailing between the Aegean countries and western Asia. Another factor that contributed to the importance of Cyprus in Mediterranean history was its wealth of copper (the Latin word is *cuprius)*. Mycenaeans, attracted to Cyprus for the copper, used harbor towns on the eastern and southern coasts of the island to trade with western Asia.

A developed civilization had evolved in Cyprus between 7000 and 6000 B.C. Most information from that period is derived from Khirokitia, a settlement of approximately 4,500 inhabitants, who practiced weaving and made beads from dentalium shells and imported carnelian as early as 5800 B.C. By 1900 B.C., faience beads were found along with pottery of various origins, suggesting overseas trade with Egypt and the Levant. The design of Cypriot gold beads of the late Bronze Age (1300–1200 B.C.) was strongly influenced by the trade relationship between Cyprus and Mycenae, clearly seen in a jewelry cache uncovered at Enkomi (plate 32). These foreign exchanges had lasting effects on the people and their adornment.

TOP LEFT: 33.
The Phoenicians created distinctive three-dimensional glass head beads and pendants, many of which were manufactured in Carthage. Head beads were popular trade items as early as 700 B.C. and were widely distributed throughout the Mediterranean area.[VIII] *They may have been viewed as a more developed form of the eye bead, with greater protective powers derived from rendering the whole head rather than just the eye. The beads were made by a winding or core-formed technique. Glass was shaped over a core of a friable material, then worked in successive layers of colored glass fired separately in a kiln. When the bead was completed, the core was removed with a pointed tool. This ram's head is dated 300 to 200 B.C. Length, 5.15 cm. Plates 33–36: Corning Museum of Glass, Corning, New York*

TOP RIGHT: 34.
Pendant bead, 450–300 B.C. Length, 5.7 cm

BOTTOM LEFT: 35.
Head bead, 400–200 B.C. Length, 3.4 cm

BOTTOM RIGHT: 36.
Eye bead, 400–200 B.C. Length, 3.1 cm

OPPOSITE: 37. *A necklace of Etruscan gold and Phoenician glass beads. These well-made granulated and filigree gold beads represent the pinnacle of technical excellence for ancient goldsmiths. This necklace was probably created in the early sixth century B.C. when the Phoenicians and Etruscans were political allies, living and trading in relative harmony. Pendant: length, 3.1 cm. British Museum, London*

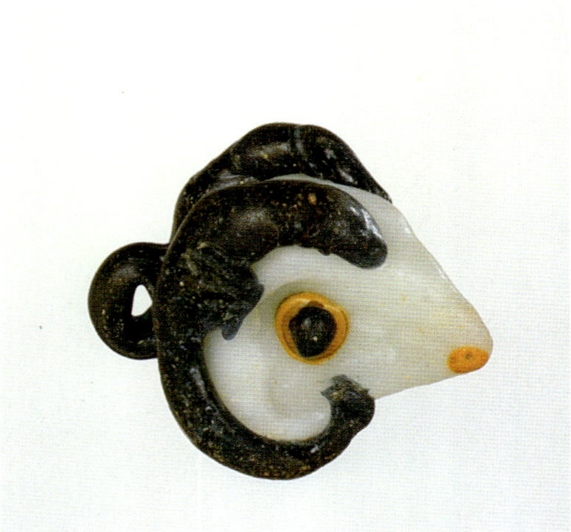

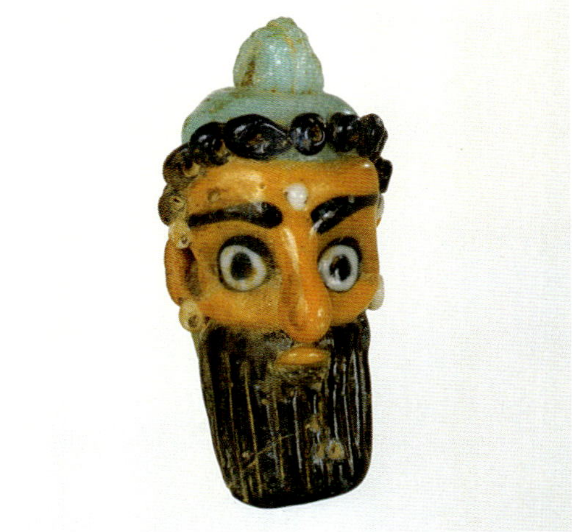

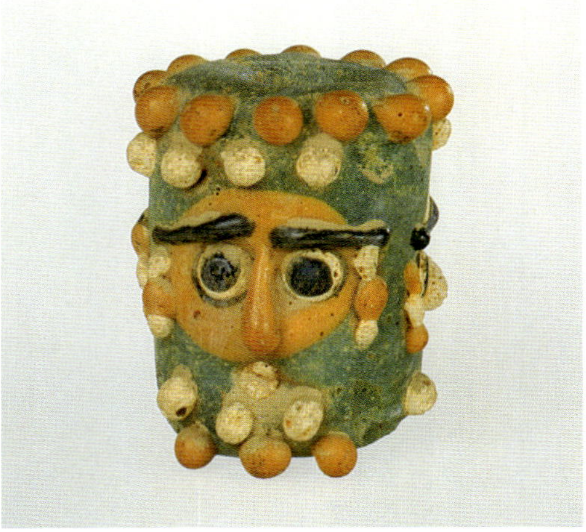

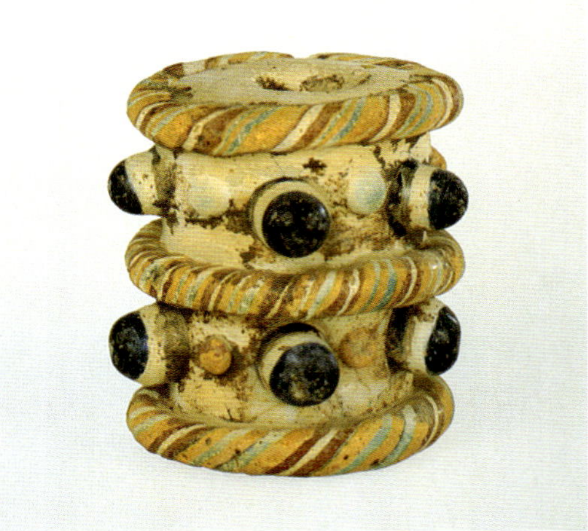

Phoenicia

By 1200 B.C., the Phoenicians (who were centered in present-day Lebanon) had become the leading navigators and traders of their time. From a small group of city-states (Sidon, Tyre, Beirut, and Byblos) located along the eastern coast of the Mediterranean, the Phoenicians sailed great distances, possibly even reaching the southern tip of Africa. Despite their daring explorations, however, Phoenician trade routes essentially duplicated those of the earlier Minoans and Mycenaeans. Phoenician commerce was based on timber—the famed cedars of Lebanon—which was exchanged for Cypriot copper and African gold, precious stones, ivory, and spices. Cloth of Tyrian purple (a dye made from murex shells) and glass beads were also staple exports.

The Phoenicians were highly skilled glass beadmakers, borrowing many stylistic concepts from those with whom they traded, while developing their own technologies. Like the Babylonians (who succeeded the Sumerians as the dominant force in western Asia from 1760 to 1600 B.C.), Egyptians, and Greeks, the Phoenicians buried their dead with great care, interring unique core-formed glass pendants and beads with the deceased.

By 800 B.C., Carthage, originally a colonial Phoenician outpost on the North African coast, became a great international seaport famed for its glass beads and pendants. They were distributed by Phoenician traders throughout the Mediterranean (plates 33–37) until the second century B.C.

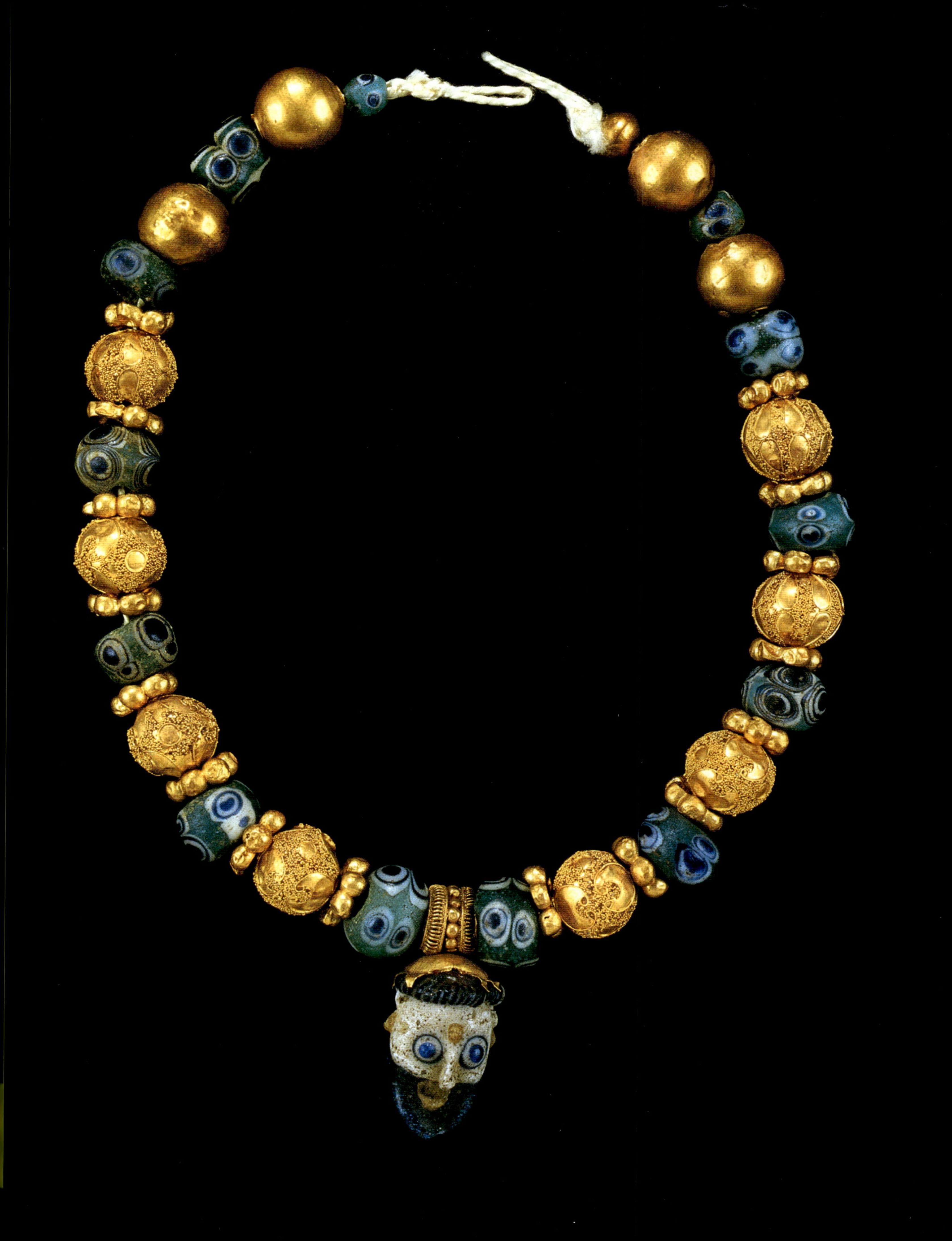

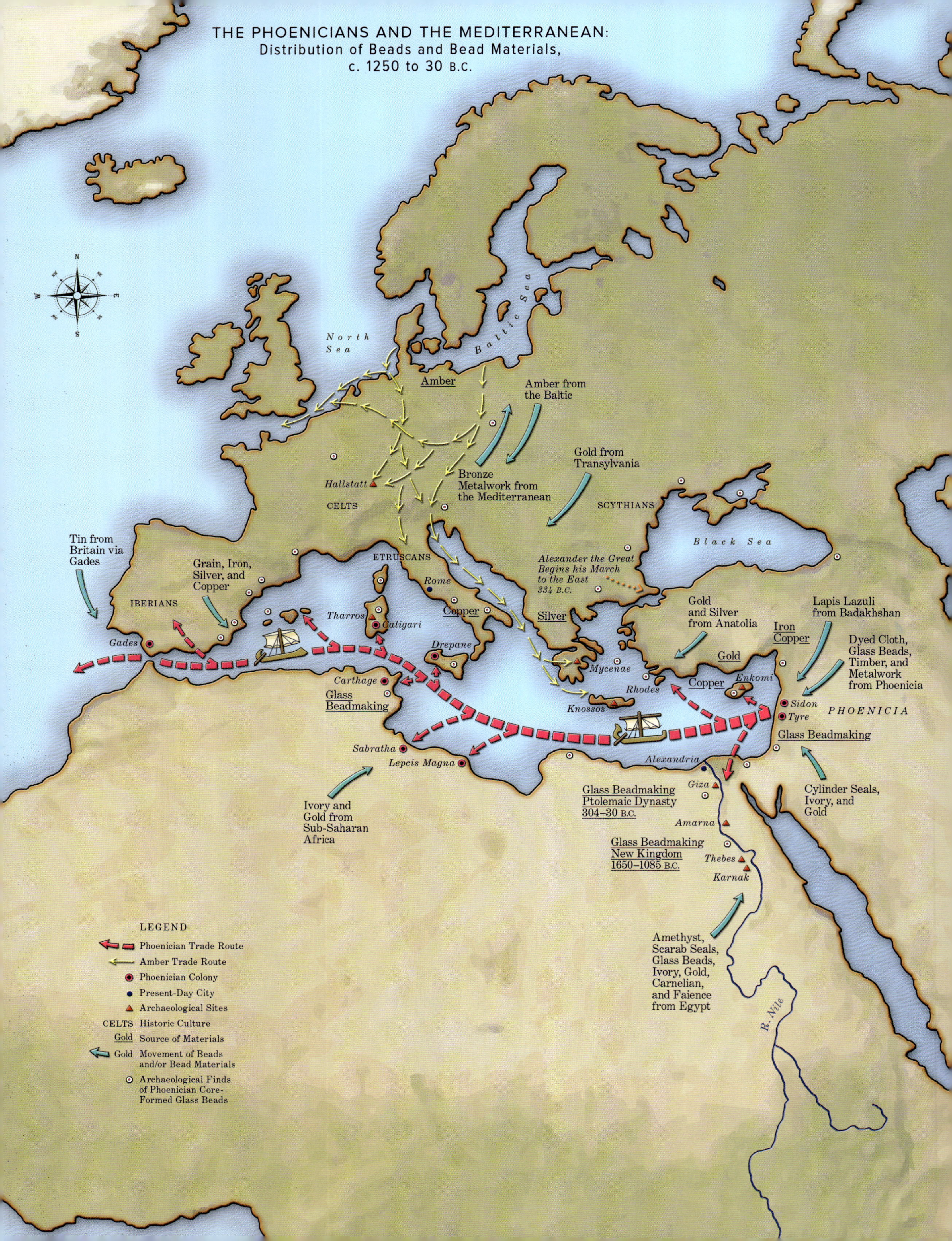
THE PHOENICIANS AND THE MEDITERRANEAN:
Distribution of Beads and Bead Materials,
c. 1250 to 30 B.C.
North Sea
Baltic Sea
Amber
Amber from the Baltic
Gold from Transylvania
Hallstatt
CELTS
Bronze Metalwork from the Mediterranean
SCYTHIANS
Black Sea
Tin from Britain via Gades
Grain, Iron, Silver, and Copper
ETRUSCANS
Alexander the Great Begins his March to the East 334 B.C.
IBERIANS
Rome
Tharros
Caligari
Copper
Silver
Gold and Silver from Anatolia
Lapis Lazuli from Badakhshan
Iron
Copper
Dyed Cloth, Glass Beads, Timber, and Metalwork from Phoenicia
Gades
Drepane
Gold
Mycenae
Enkomi
Carthage
Rhodes
Copper
Sidon
Glass Beadmaking
Knossos
Tyre
PHOENICIA
Glass Beadmaking
Sabratha
Alexandria
Lepcis Magna
Giza
Cylinder Seals, Ivory, and Gold
Glass Beadmaking Ptolemaic Dynasty 304–30 B.C.
Ivory and Gold from Sub-Saharan Africa
Amarna
Glass Beadmaking New Kingdom 1650–1085 B.C.
Thebes
Karnak
LEGEND
Phoenician Trade Route
Amber Trade Route
Phoenician Colony
Present-Day City
Archaeological Sites
CELTS Historic Culture
Gold Source of Materials
Gold Movement of Beads and/or Bead Materials
Archaeological Finds of Phoenician Core-Formed Glass Beads
Amethyst, Scarab Seals, Glass Beads, Ivory, Gold, Carnelian, and Faience from Egypt
R. Nile

Etruria

The exact origin of the Etruscans has long been an enigma. It is likely their ancestors entered Italy from Asia Minor in the ninth century B.C.; by the third century B.C., they were assimilated into the Roman Empire.

Etruria's intensive commercial activities and affluent society were based on its ready access to iron, copper, zinc, and tin ores. Together with manufactured metal objects, their raw materials were exchanged for Eastern luxury products made of gold, silver, and ivory. Trade with western Asia and Greece brought the Etruscans into contact with important Orientalizing influences in the eighth and seventh centuries B.C., resulting in the formation of a distinctive Etruscan style that incorporated Syrian, Phoenician, Iranian, and Greek elements. Etruscan tomb frescoes illustrate a thriving aristocratic class whose noblewomen dressed elegantly and sported the famed Etruscan jewelry—among the finest in the ancient world.

Etruscan beads are known for technical perfection. While some of their technical knowledge came from the Phoenicians, the Etruscans were jewelry innovators in their own right. They developed, for example, a technique of granulation using amber to affix tiny droplets of gold on a piece of jewelry to enhance its beauty.[26] To satisfy their love of color, the Etruscans often combined Phoenician polychrome glass beads with gold beads (plate 37).

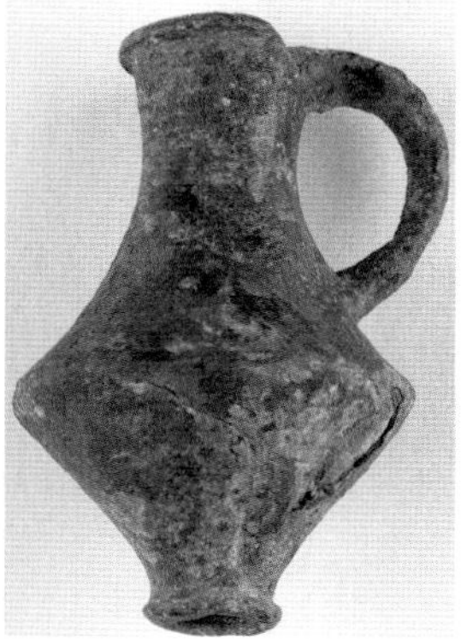

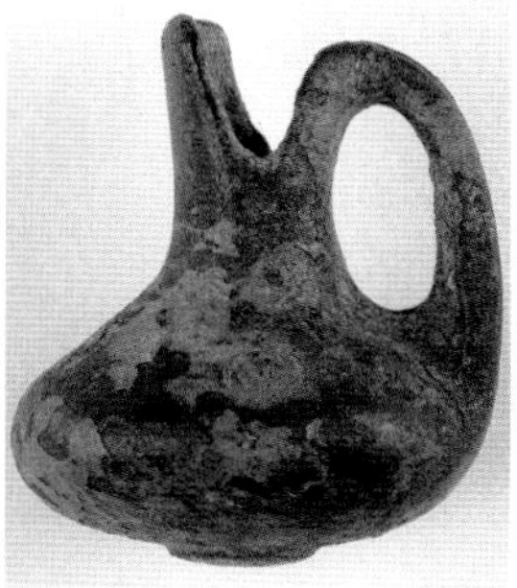

TOP: 38. *Bronze wine jug bead, representing a sacred Minoan motif, recovered from tombs near Potidaea, Macedonia, c. 800–700 B.C. These beads have also been found made of gold in early Minoan sites (2000–1700 B.C.). Length, 3.8 cm. British Museum, London*

ABOVE: 39. *Bronze wine jug bead, from Potidaea, Macedonia, c. 800–700 B.C. Length, 2.6 cm. British Museum, London*

Iran

Ancient Iran was home to one of the most geographically expansive civilizations of the ancient Near East. Unlike the Egyptian and Mesopotamian civilizations, which retained a relatively consistent artistic unity throughout their histories, Iran hosted a mixture of artistic styles; the result of a wide range of political and geographic influences. Caravans crossing the highlands from Badakhshan to Sumer not only brought lapis lazuli, but kept Iranian craftsmen in touch with the latest technical achievements of Mesopotamian and Babylonian goldsmiths and Indian and Afghan beadmakers. The resulting stylistic diversity is illustrated in the variously shaped beads of glazed frit, antimony, copper, bronze, amber, carnelian, shell, stone, glass, and incised bone found at one site—Ḫasanlū—in northwest Iran. (The beads date from 1350 to 800 B.C.) Exquisite granulated gold beads were made in Iran by at least 1000 B.C. (plate 40), and a wide variety of stone beads, particularly the banded agates, enjoyed great popularity in all periods of Iranian history.

Greece and Persia

For three hundred years after the decline of Mycenae in 1150 B.C., Greece was a poor region, and little jewelry was produced. By 850 B.C., Greek contacts with western Asia and the East resumed. Once again, beautifully crafted gold jewelry was made in Greece at Knossos and the great city-states of Corinth and Athens. Although some beads created at this time resemble earlier Mycenaean styles, their presence appears not to reflect a continuity of tradition among Greek craftsmen but instead was due to a reintroduction of Greek designs and techniques by immigrant Phoenician goldsmiths.[27] By 550 B.C., many Greeks had settled in Syria, Egypt, and Palestine and brought with them ideas that were absorbed by the local populace. However, in the next century, the Achaemenids in Iran established themselves as a military and commercial power under Cyrus II (589–525 B.C.). He built an obscure tribe into a major power—the legendary Persian Empire, which stretched from Libya to northern Afghanistan and the Indus Valley.

By 480 B.C., the Persians and Greeks began to compete for the same territories, but dissension among the Greek states allowed the Persians to conquer most of Asia Minor and Egypt. During the mid-fourth century B.C., the Greek ruler Philip II of Macedonia reunited some of the land lost to the Persians. The Achaemenid leadership, weakened by internal strife, was slow to respond, and by 334 B.C., at the age of twenty-two, Philip's

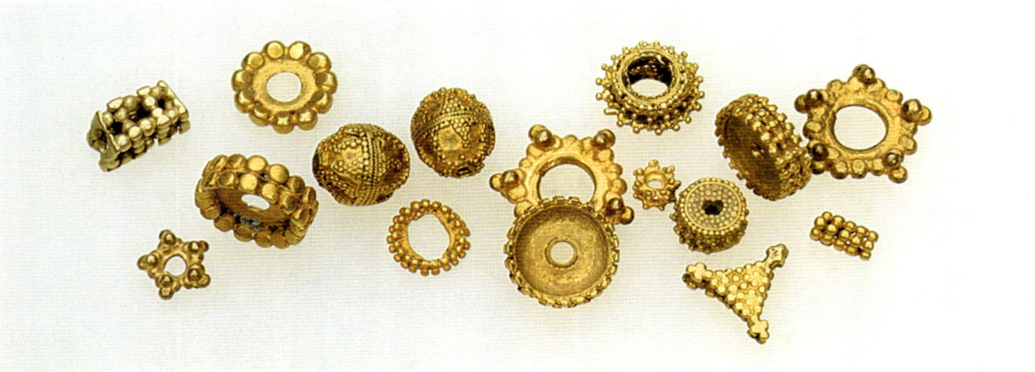

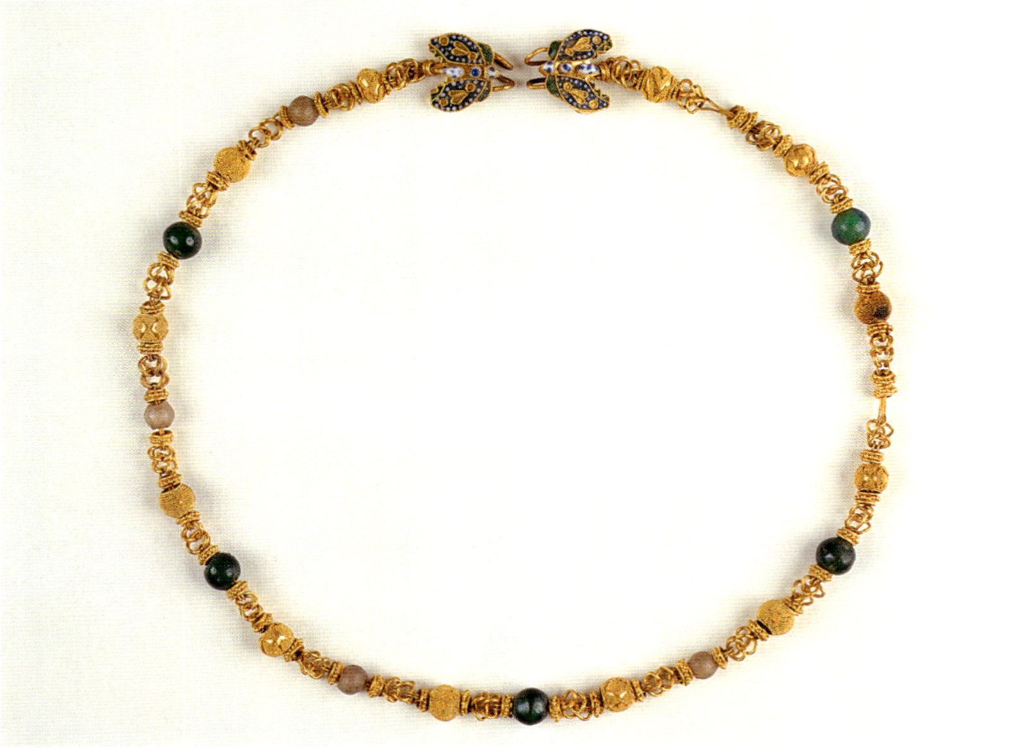

TOP: 40. *Granulated gold beads from Iran, c. 1000 B.C. Although these beads precede the Achaemenid Dynasty (550–330 B.C.), the period of major Greek-Persian contact, they show the superb quality of ancient Iranian goldwork, which later had an impact on Hellenistic jewelry.*

The fine granulation techniques illustrated here reveal influences from neighboring Assyrian, Babylonian, or Elamite goldsmiths. It is also possible that knowledge of granulation was derived from Egypt via Hurrian or Phoenician workshops on the Syrian coasts.[IX] *Upper right bead: diameter; 1.3 cm. Collection Henry Anavian, New York*

RIGHT: 41. *A Hellenistic Greek necklace, c. 300–200 B.C., in the polychrome style. The combination of gold, enameling, and colored glass beads shows the influence of the East. Length, 39 cm. Castellani Collection, British Museum, London*

OPPOSITE: 42. *Banded agates were imitated so perfectly by ancient glassmakers that it is often difficult to determine if a bead is stone or glass. The beads in the left column of this plate are stone, while those on the right are glass. Most of the stone beads date to the Parthian and Roman periods (249 B.C.–A.D. 300), although some rows (third from the top down, for example) date to the early first millennium B.C. The glass beads are from the Roman Period (except for the third row, which may date to 800 B.C.). All beads shown were found in Iran. Bottom left bead: length, 4.5 cm. Collection Henry Anavian, New York*

son, Alexander the Great, began his march through Asia. His campaigns extended into Persia, Bactria, India, and Egypt. Alexander's eastern conquests transformed both the Persian and Greek worlds, as he captured vast territories of the former Persian Empire. In turn, Greece was increasingly exposed to Egyptian, western Asiatic, and northern Indian cultural influences.

The cultural cross-fertilization had a particularly strong impact on Greek adornment. The Persian treasure of Emperor Darius III, captured by Alexander's soldiers, included remarkable jewelry that proved to be a rich source of new design motifs and increased the Greeks' use of inlaid stones, glass, enamel, and pearls. Furthermore, gold, in short supply in Greece after the collapse of Mycenae and during the great age of the city-states (500–400 B.C.), flowed back into the country. Alexander's wars brought his armies into contact with all of the world's known gold mines, and thereafter gold was widely used in Grecian coinage, jewelry, and tomb furnishings. Alexander's empire also brought Mediterranean civilization into direct contact with Near Eastern artistic

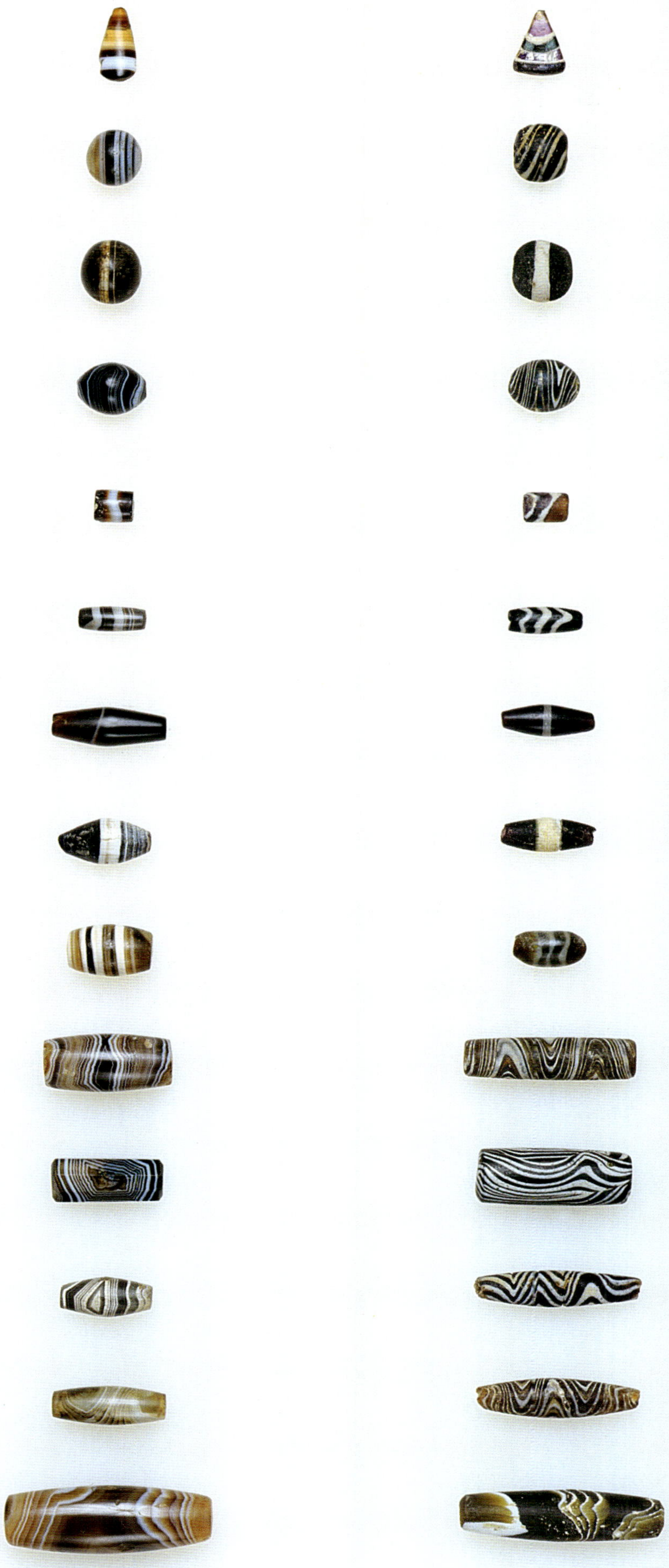

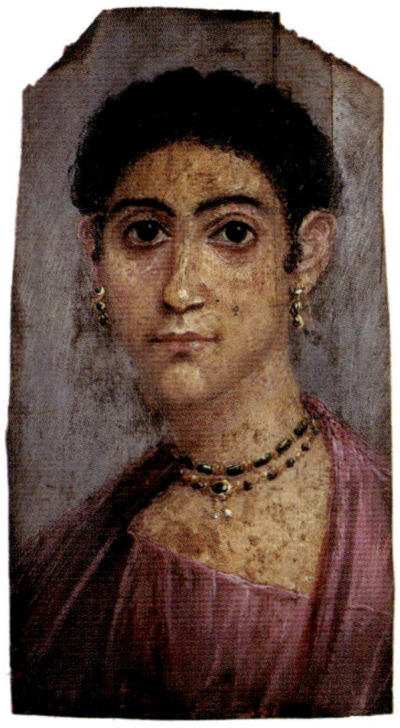

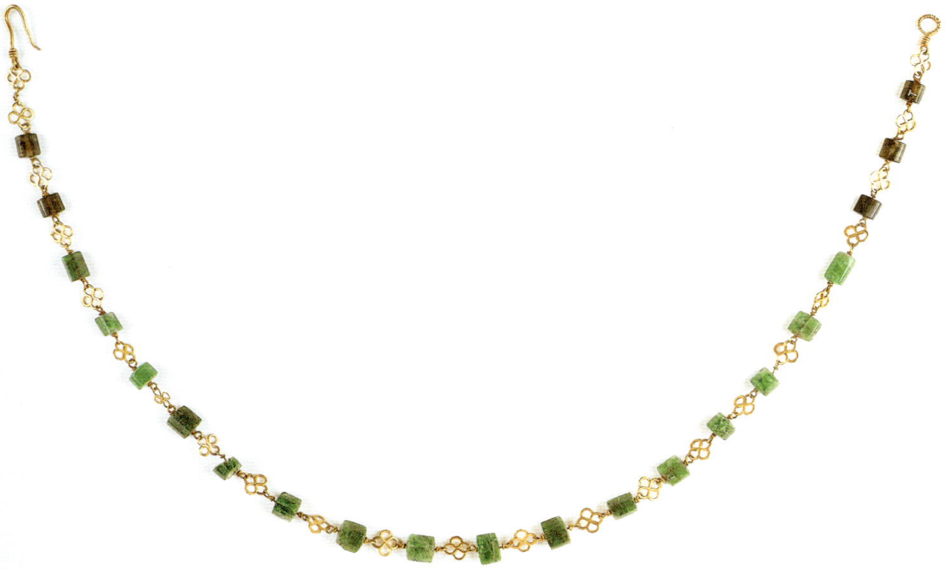

ABOVE LEFT: 43. *Funerary portrait of a young woman wearing jewelry typical of examples found in Roman tombs. The upper necklace is composed of emerald crystal beads separated by gold spacers. The lower one is a chain of garnet and gold beads with an emerald medallion and two pearl pendants. From Hawara, Egypt; Egypto-Roman period (A.D. 100–200). British Museum, London*

ABOVE RIGHT: 44. *Natural hexagonal emerald crystals were popular for beads in Roman times, usually alternated with cut-out gold loops. Linking beads together, rather than stringing them, was a practice derived from the preceding Hellenistic period and is typical of Roman jewelry during the second and first centuries B.C. Length, 41.6 cm. British Museum, London*

traditions, and a period of extraordinarily beautiful Greek jewelry followed. The richness of their beads is indicative of the prosperity that Hellenistic Greece enjoyed (plate 41).

In Persia, the Achaemenid dynasty was followed by the rule of the Parthians (249 B.C.–A.D. 226), who traded with both the Roman Empire and the Chinese Han dynasty, earning a fortune as middlemen in the silk trade. Many Western motifs were incorporated into their culture, and large quantities of Roman and Parthian stone and glass beads have been found throughout present-day Iran (plate 42).

Stone beads of hard and rare materials were time-consuming to make, expensive, and available only to the wealthy. Yet, the continuing spread of civilization invited an interest in fashion and adornment among increasing numbers of people. Attractive and affordable beads were in demand. The glazing of steatite and rock crystal in fourth-millennium B.C. Egypt was an early solution, but only with the invention of faience and the subsequent manufacture of glass was it possible to imitate precious stones in quantity and at low cost. While the manufacturing and trading of glass beads on a truly global scale commenced with the Romans, a major production site for Hellenistic glass beads was recently uncovered on the island of Rhodes. The discovery of debris from a glass factory there proved the island was an important manufacturer of beads during the late third or early second century B.C. Over ten thousand glass beads were excavated. Made by folded, drawn, pressed, wound, and ground techniques, they included melon, heart, biconical, bipyramidal, spherical, and cylindrical shapes and pendants (Timeline 426). Also found were about two hundred gold-in-glass beads in long and short cylinders and spherical forms, providing a very early provenance for these beads. Additionally, there were large quantities of eye beads and numerous more unusual varieties, including dolphin shapes, spacers, spools, and cubes, in opaque and translucent colors, and in polychrome mosaic-glass.[28]

The Roman Empire

The Romans emerged from a small second-millennium B.C. enclave near Rome to become the dominant power in the Mediterranean and Europe until their empire's collapse in A.D. 476. By A.D. 100, Rome's territories extended from Armenia and Assyria in the east to Germany and Britain in the north and Mauritania and Egypt in the south.

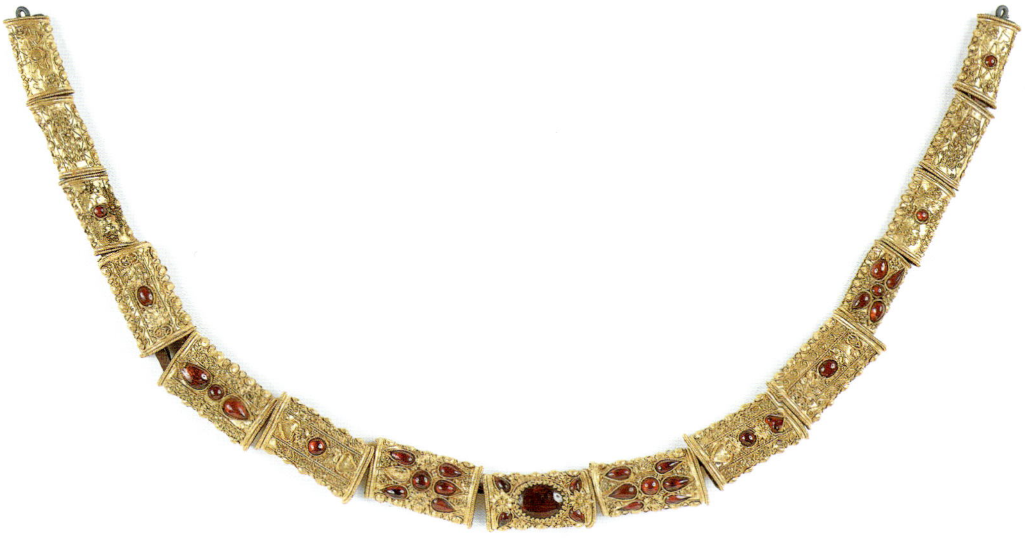

45. *Gold and garnet beads made with filigree, embossing, and twisted wire. The beads are a blend of Hellenistic and Etruscan concepts. Eastern influences are apparent in the combination of gold and garnets, although the lavish use of garnets is specifically Roman. The beads are from Olbia, Sardinia, A.D. 1–100. Center bead: length, 3.6 cm. Castellani, British Museum, London*

Rome's artistic language was largely derived from the preceding Hellenistic period. Its jewelry melded the Eastern taste for colored stones with the Etruscan use of surface-decorated gold, favoring colors and gold that enhanced one another. Originally, jewelry was a luxury disapproved of in Rome, but by the first century B.C., this penchant for austerity had disappeared, and for hundreds of years thereafter, rings, necklaces, and other jewelry commonly adorned Romans.

The vastness of the empire and its extensive trade networks accommodated the wealthy with a wide variety of beads made from precious materials. Pearls and coral from the Persian Gulf and emeralds from Egyptian mines near the Red Sea were made into necklaces and earrings (plates 43 and 44). Trade with northern Europe brought Whitby jet from England and amber from the Baltic. With improved navigational methods, Roman mariners surpassed their Mediterranean predecessors, reaching India, Burma, and Sri Lanka (Ceylon): major sources for rubies, sapphires, and garnets.[29] The old Hellenistic workshops of Alexandria and Antioch, and Rome itself, were the primary centers of production for imperial Roman jewelry, while glass beads were made in numerous locations throughout the empire. Moreover, most craftsmen working within Rome had emigrated from the Eastern provinces.[30]

Roman Glass Beads

The Roman period, New Kingdom Egypt, and the era of Islamic dominance in the Mediterranean (c. A.D. 600–1400) are generally considered the three great periods of ancient glassmaking. The terms "Roman" and "Roman-period" glass are used to describe glass production from 100 B.C. to A.D. 400 within the boundaries of the Roman Empire, including factories in Syria, Egypt, Italy, Switzerland, the Rhineland, France, and England. Everywhere the Romans went they brought glass beads to trade. Produced in a large range of colors, patterns, and frequently complex techniques, Roman-period glass beads were widely coveted (plates 50–53). Exchanged as far north as Scandinavia, and as far east and south as China, Korea, Iran, Syria, Mali, and Ethiopia, quantities of Roman-period glass beads have been found in each of these countries, frequently raising the question of where they were originally manufactured because of their similar patterns and manufacturing techniques.

46. *Iridescent green, blue, and gold pre-Roman and Roman-period glass beads, c. 500 B.C.–A.D. 200. Glass of this period has less color and more transparency than earlier varieties, due to the contemporary taste for translucent precious stones. The second necklace from the bottom is Egypto-Roman and is made of faience disk beads with a glass Eye of Horus, the important Egyptian funerary amulet. The overall greenish blue tinge of pre-Roman and Roman-period glass comes from iron impurities in the sand used in making the glass. Bottom necklace, center bead: diameter, 2 cm. Private collection*

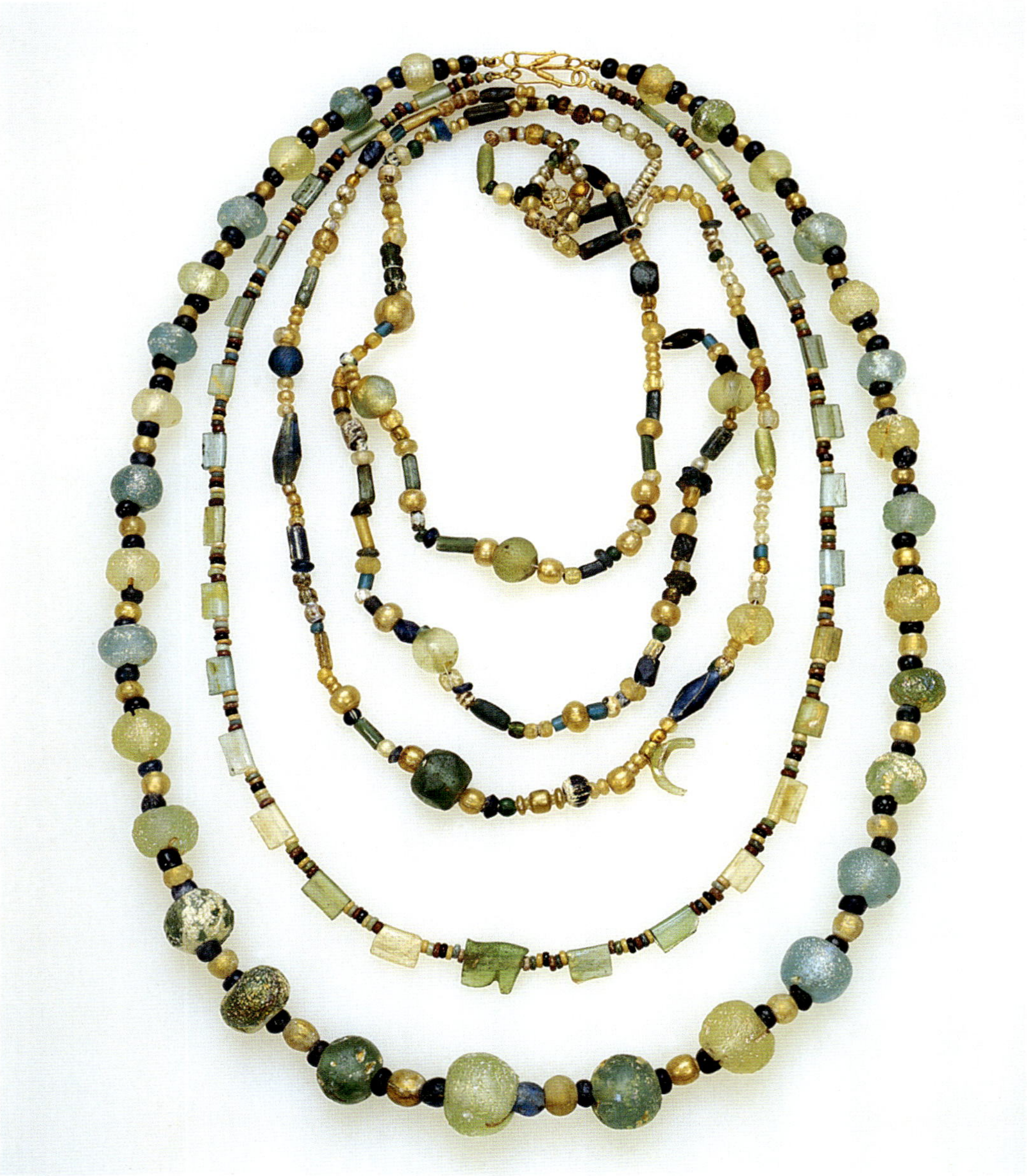

After Alexander's conquests, the practice of glassworking possibly moved from the interior of Egypt to Hellenistic Alexandria, where exquisite mosaic-glass was reputedly manufactured from 300 B.C. to A.D. 100. (Yet despite the city's reputation as the ancient center of the luxury glass industry, no glassmaking factory has ever been found in Alexandria.) About 100 B.C., glassmakers in Sidon and Tyre on the Lebanese coast (descendants of the earlier Phoenican glass bead masters) produced beautiful glass beads. Eventually, craftsmen from both centers migrated to new locations within the Roman provinces, setting up factories and disseminating techniques and forms.

During the first century B.C. newly invented larger furnaces with hotter fires were capable of creating a more fluid glass, affecting bead shapes and their patterns. Furthermore, glass's constituents (sand, alkali, and coloring agents) were refined, subsequently producing purer glass. The invention of the blowpipe, reputedly in Sidon, completely modernized the glass industry by increasing the level of production and opening the way

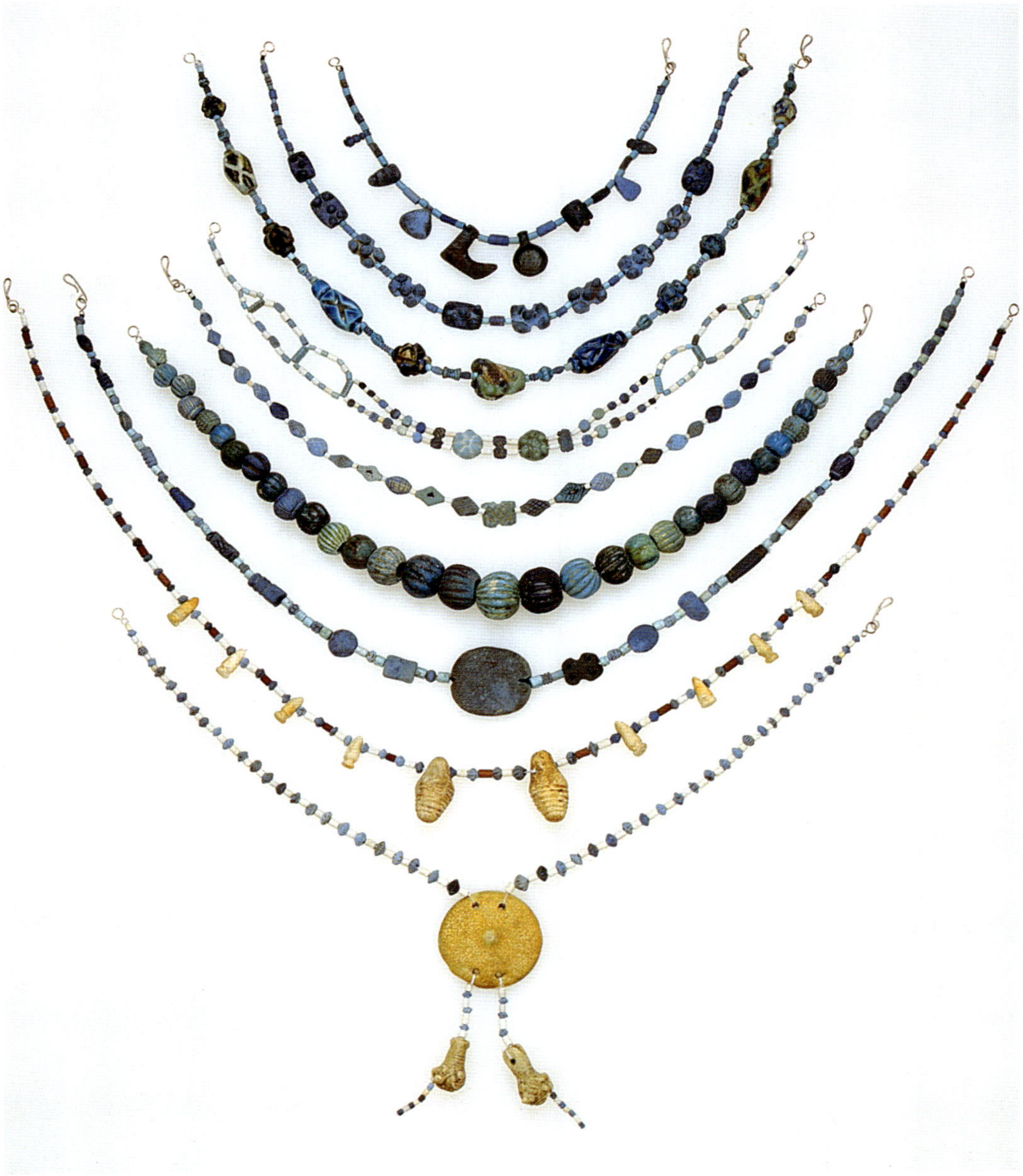

47. *A representative Persian faience bead collection from the Achaemenid, Parthian, and Sasanian periods (550 B.C.–A.D. 642). In addition to Egypt, Iran, the Aegean, and the Indus Valley were important faience manufacturing centers. The Iranian faience industry began early; faience beads dating from the fourth millennium B.C. have been excavated at Susa and Tepe Hissar.*

Persian faience was made in limited colors—blue, green, brown, yellow, and white. Glazes also differed from Egypt: they were thinner, not as brilliant, and had a matte finish.[x] *Bottom row, central white pendant: diameter, 4.15 cm. Collection Henry Anavian, New York*

for still further new techniques, forms, and decorative styles. Although the blowpipe was not directly relevant to glass beadmaking, since few beads were blown (the great majority were still produced by winding and the newly introduced drawn techniques), the combined result of all these innovations under Roman guidance was the growth of glassmaking into a large-scale industry. More glass was made in the first century A.D. than in the previous fifteen hundred years.[31] Because the material was widely obtainable, relatively inexpensive, and no longer reserved for the elite, everyone could now afford to wear beads.

While beads manufactured in the European provinces during the late Roman period were generally of poorer quality than those of earlier times, glassworks along the east coast of the Mediterranean and within the Byzantine and Sasanian empires continued to produce finely crafted and styled beads, providing a link between Rome and the Islamic era, the last great period of ancient glass beadmaking.

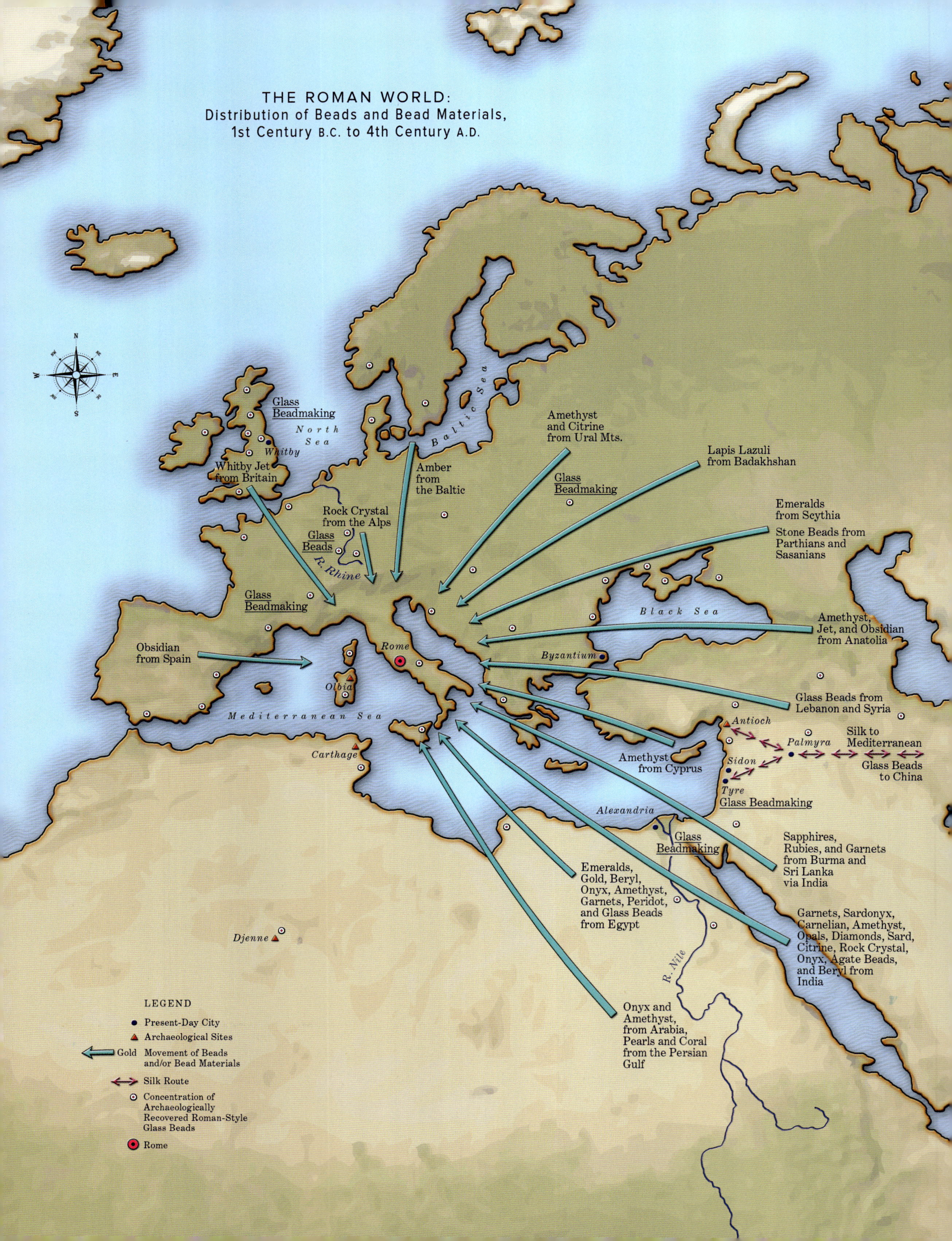

THE ROMAN WORLD:
Distribution of Beads and Bead Materials,
1st Century B.C. to 4th Century A.D.
Glass Beadmaking
North Sea
Whitby
Whitby Jet from Britain
Baltic Sea
Amber from the Baltic
Amethyst and Citrine from Ural Mts.
Glass Beadmaking
Lapis Lazuli from Badakhshan
Rock Crystal from the Alps
Glass Beads
R. Rhine
Emeralds from Scythia
Stone Beads from Parthians and Sasanians
Glass Beadmaking
Black Sea
Amethyst, Jet, and Obsidian from Anatolia
Obsidian from Spain
Rome
Byzantium
Olbia
Glass Beads from Lebanon and Syria
Mediterranean Sea
Antioch
Palmyra
Silk to Mediterranean
Carthage
Amethyst from Cyprus
Sidon
Glass Beads to China
Tyre
Glass Beadmaking
Alexandria
Glass Beadmaking
Sapphires, Rubies, and Garnets from Burma and Sri Lanka via India
Emeralds, Gold, Beryl, Onyx, Amethyst, Garnets, Peridot, and Glass Beads from Egypt
Garnets, Sardonyx, Carnelian, Amethyst, Opals, Diamonds, Sard, Citrine, Rock Crystal, Onyx, Agate Beads, and Beryl from India
Djenne
R. Nile
Onyx and Amethyst, from Arabia, Pearls and Coral from the Persian Gulf
LEGEND
Present-Day City
Archaeological Sites
Gold Movement of Beads and/or Bead Materials
Silk Route
Concentration of Archaeologically Recovered Roman-Style Glass Beads
Rome

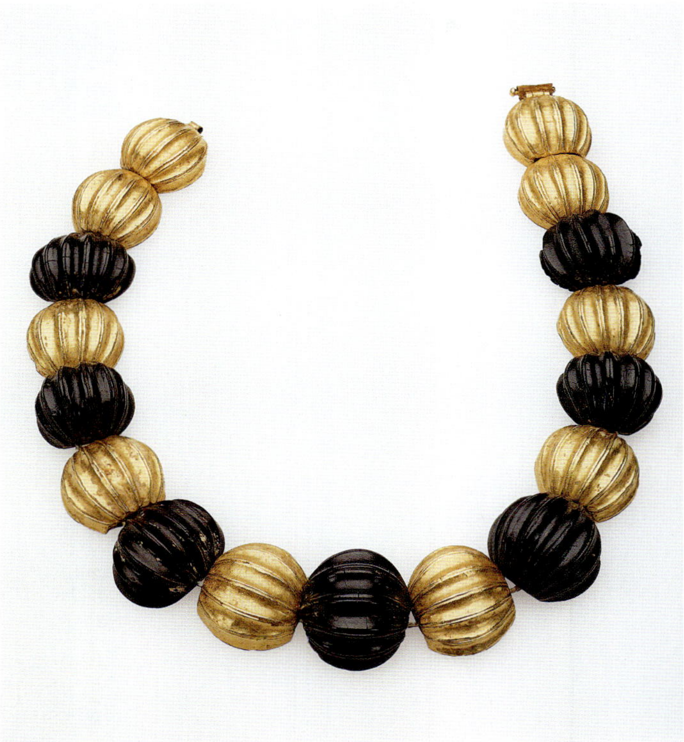

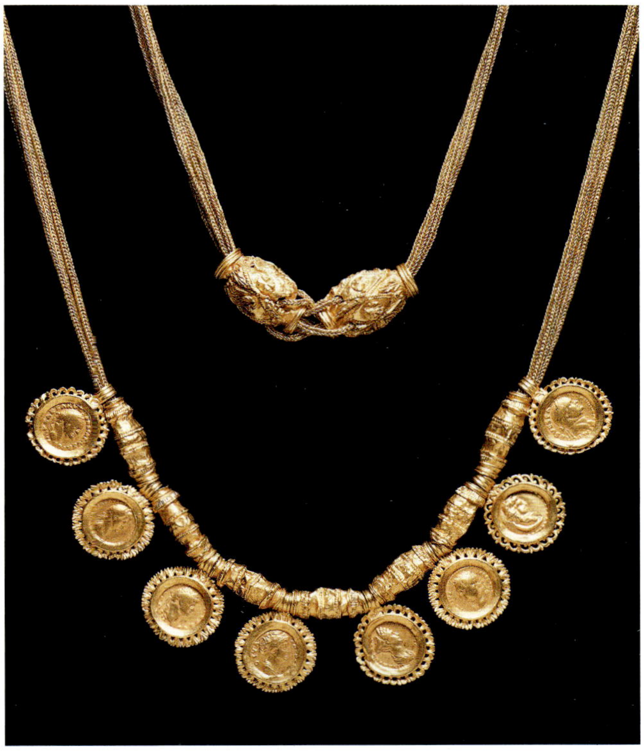

ABOVE LEFT: 48. *Necklace of hollow, hemispherical, half-melon (i.e., only one side is rounded—the back side is flat) beads of gold and jet. The jet, from Whitby, England, reached Italy via the Roman-British tin trade. The pairing of gold and jet may indicate their comparable worth. Roman, A.D. 1–100. Typical jet bead: diameter, 3.5 cm. Collection Derek Content*

ABOVE RIGHT: 49. *A Roman necklace, c. A.D. 200, of gold coins, gold beads, and terminal beads. Four braided gold chains loop through two large gold terminal beads, enabling the wearer to adjust the length of the necklace. Most Roman jewelry is of very pure, refined gold, often made from melted-down gold coinage.[XI] Coin: diameter, 2.6 cm. Walters Art Gallery, Baltimore*

Northern, Central, and Western Europe from Neolithic Times to the Bronze Age

Farming developed in temperate Europe several thousand years after its origins in western Asia. Agriculture spread into Europe from Anatolia, reaching Scandinavia and the British Isles about 4000 B.C. A tin-bronze metallurgy industry emerged in the Balkans by 3000 B.C., giving rise to increased trade and the beginnings of wealth. Burial sites of wealthy chieftains have yielded metal weapons and tools, as well as beads of copper, bronze, faience, and amber. Disk beads made from the copper carbonate minerals azurite and malachite have been found at the site of Lepenski Vir in southeast Serbia dating from 6000 to 4500 B.C.[32]

The European Bronze Age is contemporaneous with the Minoan-Mycenaean civilization (1800–1150 B.C.). The exchange of finished copper and bronze implements from the southern Mediterranean for Baltic amber was an integral part of the cultural growth of Europe's northern regions.

Bronze Age beads from western and northern Europe are frequently of imported materials, including Egyptian faience and glass and Baltic amber. In Wessex, a center of early Britain, blue and green faience beads, possibly from New Kingdom Egypt, have been excavated from more than thirty graves (Timeline 15).[33] Beads from Gilchorn in Scotland and Lough Gur in Ireland resemble those of the Egyptian Eighteenth Dynasty (1567–1320 B.C.).[34] It is not a coincidence that Egyptian faience bead production reached its peak at the same time that faience beads were being widely dispersed throughout Europe. Irish gold copies of segmented faience beads were found as far east as central Germany.[35] Faience may also have been produced locally.

Baltic amber collars with trapezoidal plaques used as spacers to separate rows of spheres are found in excavations in Denmark and Wiltshire in England, and similarly

Mosaic-Glass Beads

Mosaic-glass beads of the Hellenistic and Roman periods (300 B.C.–A.D. 1400) were made with techniques initially used in the earliest days of glassmaking. Archaeological evidence points to the invention of mosaic-glass in western Asia.[XII] *Mosaic-glass reappeared in Egypt and Syria only after the fourth century B.C. It continued to be made in the Byzantine and Islamic periods, with a major renaissance in Venice c. 1500 A.D.*

Artistically crafted mosaic-glass beads, also called millefiori ("thousand flowers"), are the product of great technical expertise. One method for achieving the fine detail of the beads was to lay a bundle of preformed colored glass rods in parallel rows so that the cross-section of the bundle had a pattern. The glass was then heat-softened and stretched, fusing the canes together. This miniaturized the design, but the cross-sectional pattern remained unchanged.

BOTTOM: 50. *Mosaic face beads—miniature masterpieces of ancient glassmaking. The fine detail achieved on beads typically less than one-half inch in diameter was astonishing. Note the eyes with pupils and women wearing tiny bead necklaces. Top left bead: diameter, 1.2 cm. Private collection.* RIGHT: 51. *A mosaic-glass bead of remarkable complexity—identified with the skills of Alexandrian glassmakers. The bead was constructed by fusing eighteen plaques involving four different designs (a lion and three views of a lotus blossom). Each plaque is formed from eighteen to twenty-five separate rods of glass, thus the bead represents the assemblage of nearly 350 individual parts. Length, 1.7 cm. Private collection.* ABOVE RIGHT: 52. *Mosaic-glass bars from which beads could be easily manufactured were an important trade commodity in the Roman world. Thin slices of a bar, as shown here, were cut with a metal blade and abrasive sand. These slices were then pierced for beads. By distributing the bars, complex mosaic-glass was made available to less sophisticated glass industries. It was not unusual for merchants separated by thousands of miles to order the pre-formed units from a common supplier. As a result, mosaic-glass beads of similar patterns were found throughout the empire. 100 B.C.–A.D. 100. Length, 3.7 cm. Corning Museum of Glass, Corning, New York.* NECKLACE: 53. *A wide variety of mosaic and other patterned glass beads interspersed with small carnelians and blue glass cornerless cubes. Beads shown date from the Phoenician through Islamic periods (c. 400 B.C.–A.D. 1400). Center bead: diameter, 1.9 cm. Private collection*

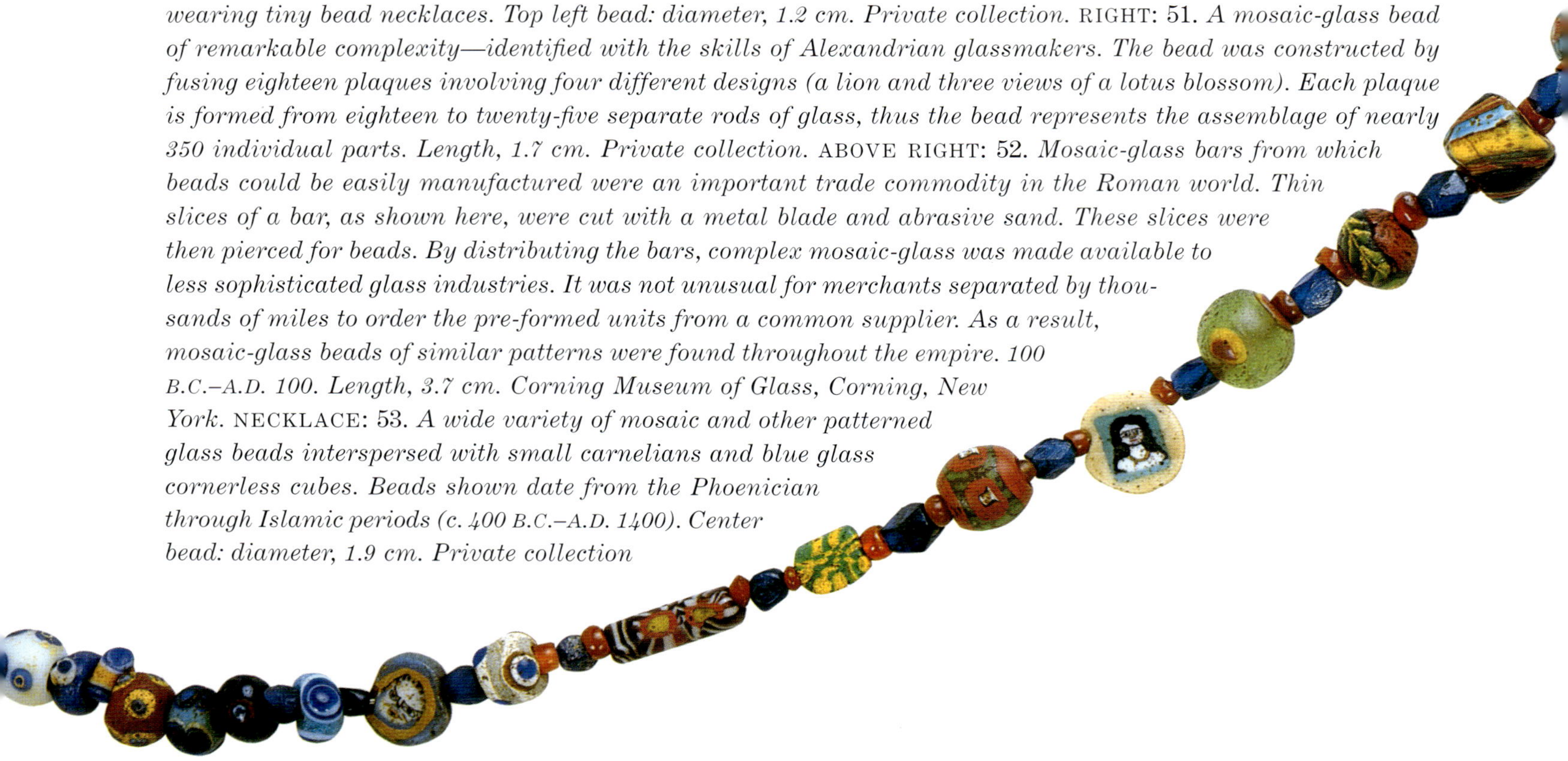

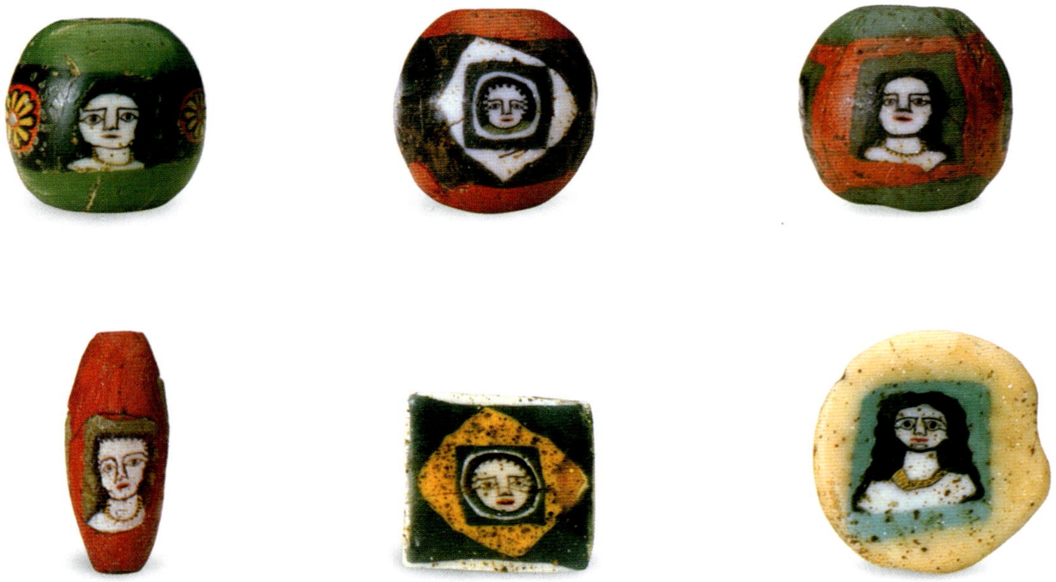

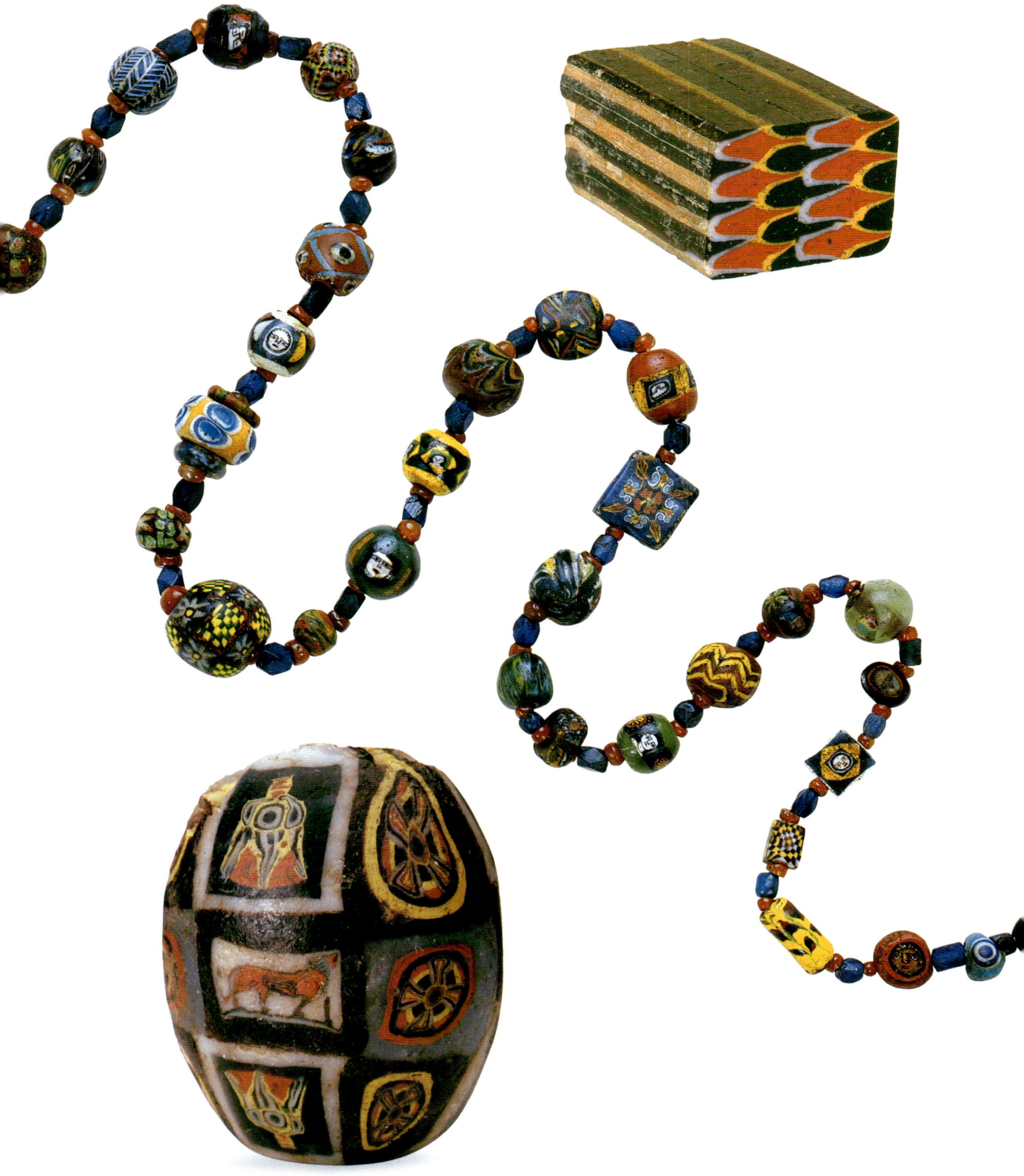

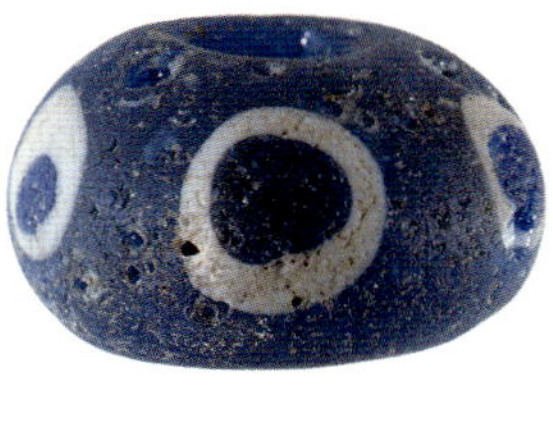

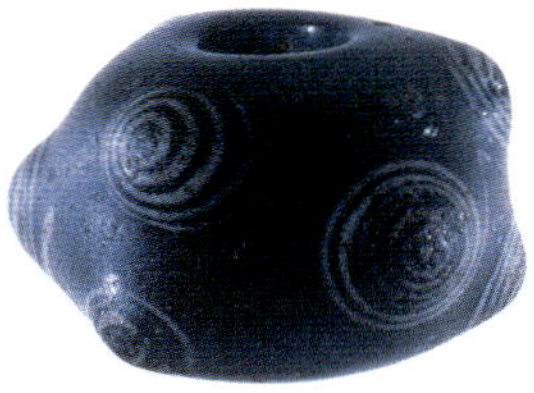

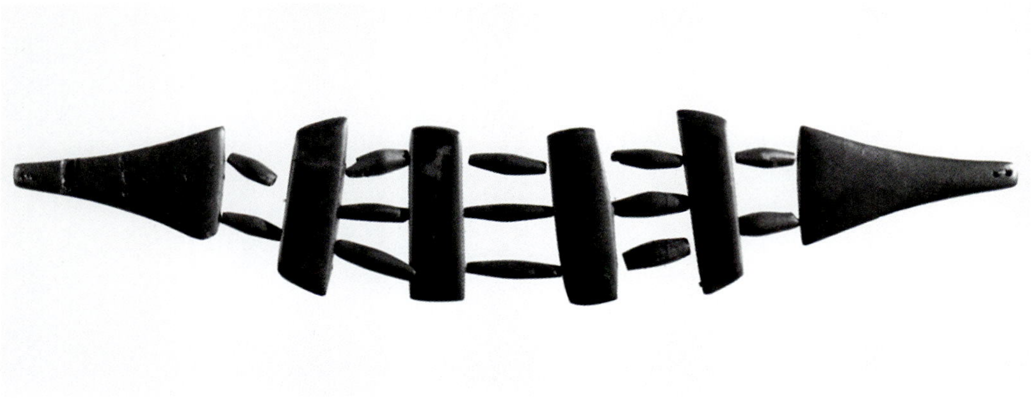

TOP: 54. *Glass eye beads with amuletic properties were the earliest decorated glass beads to appear in western and northern Europe from western Asia. The beads frequently had a dark blue background with white rings encircling blue eyes. In continental Europe, this particular form originated in eighth-century* B.C. *Phoenician sites. It was copied in central Europe, found in France, and introduced into England.*[XIII] *Diameter, 3.6 cm. British Museum, London*

ABOVE: 55. *A well-known continental Celtic bead type found in Iron Age sites that had a close relationship with the torque, a neckring that was the classic item of Celtic jewelry. The bead is dark blue with white spirals on protruding knobs. From Eastbourne, England, 600–500* B.C. *Diameter, 3.1 cm. British Museum, London*

ABOVE RIGHT: 56. *By the early Bronze Age (c. 2000* B.C.*), chieftains in the British Isles became wealthy by controlling trade in tin and other products. Their jewelry involved many new and unusual materials. Jet,*

designed necklaces made of jet are frequently found in Scottish cist burials. The best-known source for jet in the ancient world was located near Whitby in England, and Whitby jet was highly praised. Quantities of it found their way to Italy via the tin trade routes during the days of the Roman Empire (plate 56).

The Iron Age to the Roman Empire

The late Bronze Age peoples of central Europe cremated their dead, placing the ashes in pottery vessels that were buried in "urnfields." Out of these communities, which have been characterized by their urnfield cemeteries, emerged Europe's first iron-using culture, the Hallstatt (700–450 B.C.), who are recognized as the forerunners of the Celts. The Hallstatt, named by archaeologists for an Austrian site near Salzburg, was a culture whose wealth derived from local salt and copper deposits. Over one thousand graves have been excavated at Hallstatt, many rich in amber, bronze, and glass beads. They also contain examples of the torque, the most characteristic item of Celtic adornment.

From the time of their emergence about 600 B.C., the Celts, identified as a culture rather than with a particular region, were important international traders. By 200 B.C., they established manufacturing and distribution centers called *oppida* (after the Latin for "towns"), where specialized products, including Roman amphorae and amber and glass beads, were merchandised. The first century B.C. seems to have been the most active period in the oppida, and many different beads were imported into Britain at this time.[36]

The manufacture—or perhaps just the importation—of glass beads in Europe dates to the late second or early first millennium B.C. The first glass beads were undecorated, but thereafter quantities were produced within various centers throughout the Mediterranean, central Europe, and Russia that had decorative eyes and spirals believed to possess magical or protective properties (plates 54 and 55). It is thought that the beads with raised spiral eyes were produced in Celtic workshops between 200 and 1 B.C.

In Britain, the earliest glass beads were imported by the late second millennium. Between 500 and 100 B.C., Iron Age beads, associated on the Continent with the Celts, appear in large numbers. Between 300 B.C. and A.D. 1, glass beads were probably manufactured in Britain from reused glass imported from Europe. By A.D. 100, most of the typical Roman-period beads are found in Britain, including those of gold-in-glass, cornerless cubes, and melons (Timeline 26).[37]

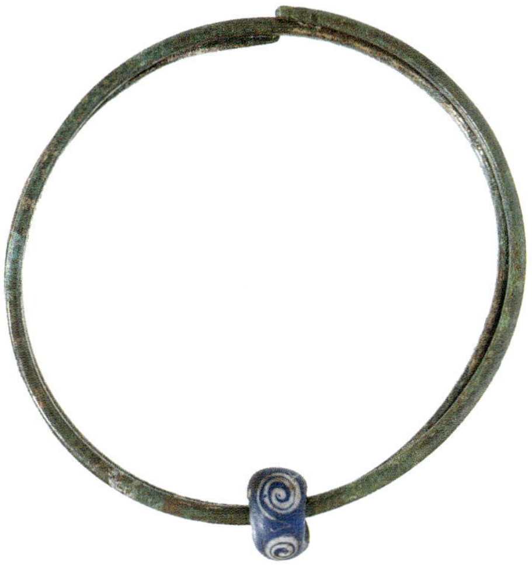

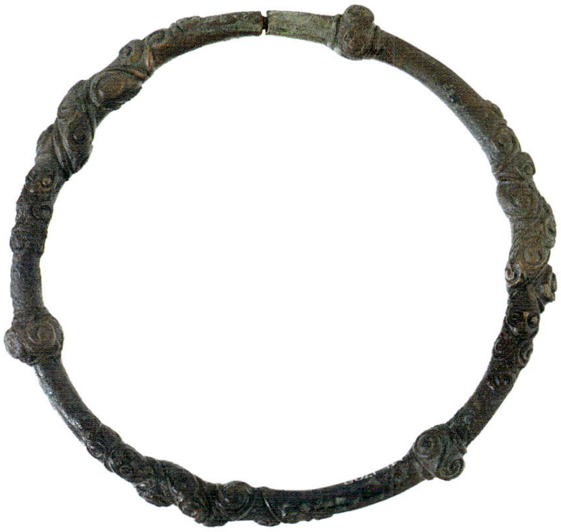

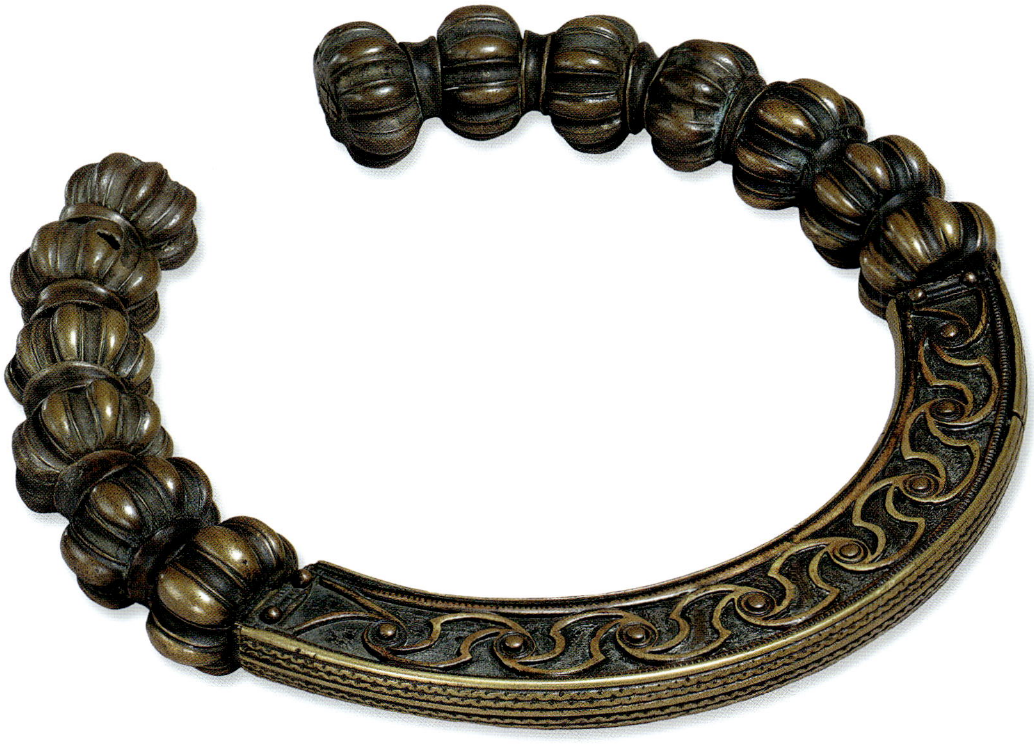

a form of black fossil wood that could be given a high polish, was greatly treasured.

This jet bracelet of platelike spacer beads separating elongated barrel forms has parallels with amber beads of the same date in England, Denmark, and Mycenae. The bracelet is from Pen-y-Bonc, Scotland, 1800–1400 B.C. British Museum, London

TOP LEFT: 57. *A bronze bracelet with a classic Celtic blue glass and white spiral bead. The torque, or neckring, is considered the most identifiable item of Celtic jewelry. Most torques were made of locally produced bronze. The Celts loved beads, which they used for bracelets and torques. This bracelet is from the Hallstatt site, 400–300 B.C. Bead: diameter, 1.2 cm. British Museum, London*

TOP RIGHT: 58. *Bronze torque with spiral-engraved bead elements designed into it. These bead derivations are traceable to actual blue-and-white glass beads used on earlier neckrings. This type of torque was worn by noblewomen in Champagne. From Avon Fontenay, France, 300–200 B.C. Diameter, 15.5 cm. British Museum, London*

LEFT: 59. *A bronze torque incorporating cast melon beads. An outstanding example of British decorative design, this collar represents the final integration of torque and bead in Celtic art. From Lochar Moss, Dumfriesshire, Scotland, A.D. 1–100. Diameter, 16.5 cm. British Museum, London*

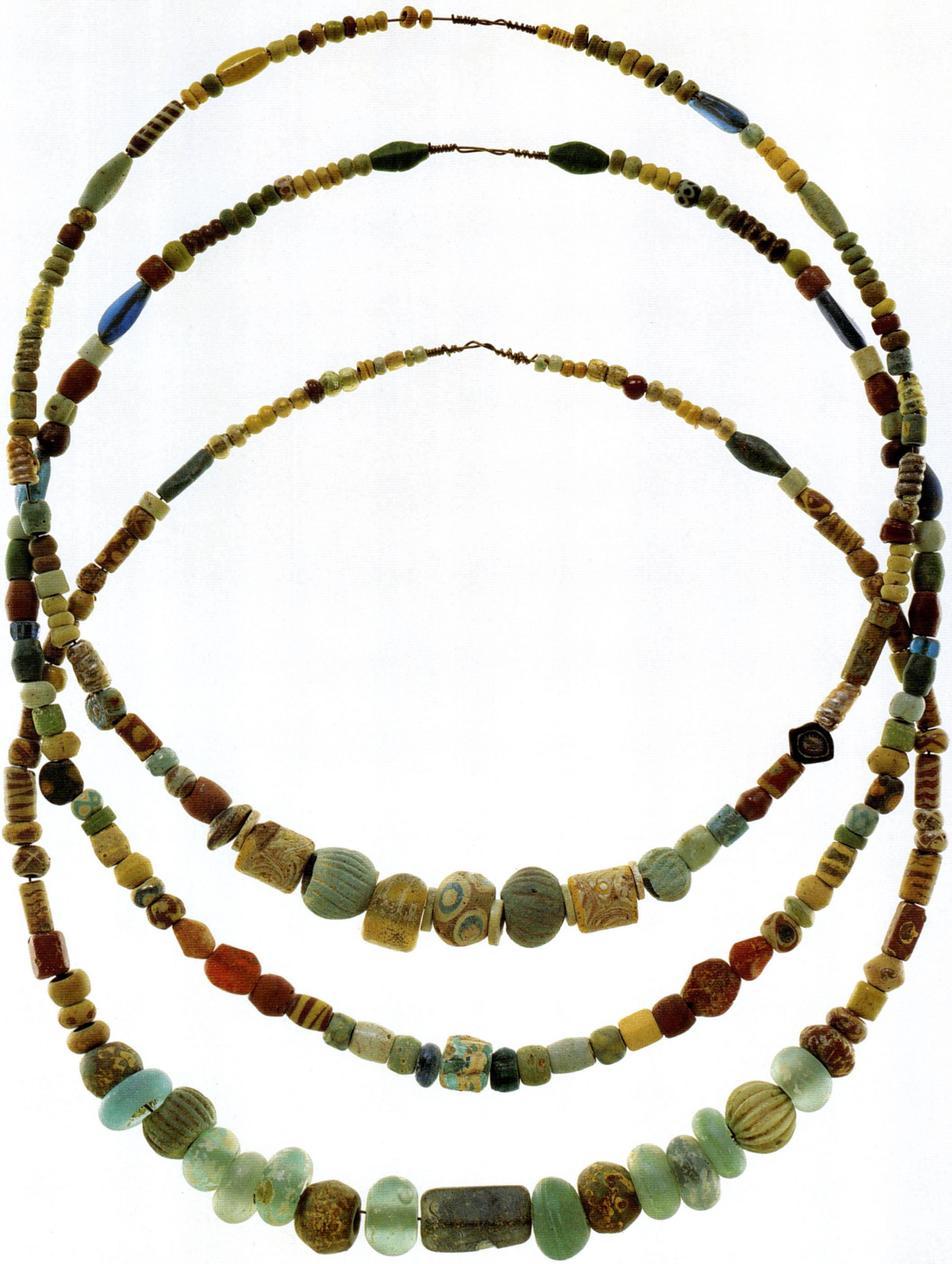

Europe: The Late Roman Empire to the Renaissance

A network of bead manufacturers who shared stylistic and technical methods existed in Europe, western Asia, and the Mediterranean while the Roman Empire flourished. With the dissolution of the empire, however, the major centers of beadmaking were replaced by numerous smaller, local workshops that obtained their ideas and primary materials from a variety of sources, including Persia, Egypt, and regions of Europe settled by the Celts. As traditional beadmaking links were severed, beads with highly localized characteristics developed.

Throughout the history of the Roman Empire, its frontiers were almost continuously assailed by marauding bands seeking booty from the wealthy, civilized world. In addition, there was the constant pressure of groups from central and western Asia who were forced from their own lands by tribes farther east and gradually migrated to the fertile regions of Europe. Asian tribes who invaded western Europe during the fourth century A.D., a time known as the Migrations Period, found a fragmented society with internal political and social problems, neither strong enough to hold them at bay nor flexible enough to absorb them into the Roman system. In the next century, the overwhelming numbers of these nomadic people finally brought about the collapse of imperial power in the West. The remaining power of the Roman Empire was then vested entirely in its eastern capital, Constantinople.

European beads from the late Roman Empire to the beginning of the Renaissance reflect the wide social and historical divisions of the period. Beads of gold and precious or semiprecious stone adorned the elite, Byzantine nobility, Europe's feudal rulers, and officials of the Christian church. Clay, amber, stone, and glass beads were worn by migratory and settled tribal people and by common folk of the indigenous populations.

60. *Necklaces made from stone and glass beads excavated about 1900 from a large Frankish burial field in the German village of Niederbreisig, located on the west bank of the Rhine. Found with a number of other Roman artifacts in a series of tombs, the beads have been dated to the fourth to the seventh century A.D. Although some of the beads were probably produced locally, the face bead on the top necklace (right side) was from the Roman period, made in Syria or Egypt. The turquoise green melon beads, Frankish favorites, were inspired by Roman prototypes. Typical necklace length, 75 cm. Metropolitan Museum of Art, New York. Gift of J. Pierpont Morgan, 1917*

Wealthy, urban Romans did not favor glass beads, which they considered "barbaric" decorations. This was particularly true after the beginning of the Christian Era, when quantities of glass beads made through newly discovered mass-production techniques became affordable to the populace at large. As artistic activity was transferred to Constantinople from Rome, the Empire's jewelers continued to make beads primarily from precious metals and stones, usually in styles characteristic of earlier Roman jewelry.

However, in numerous central and northern European regions that had once been provincial Roman glassmaking centers, glass beads never ceased being made and worn. During the era of the great migrations, colorful and eye-catching beads of gold and garnet or amber and glass were donned by tribesmen. As the tribes settled and in some cases forged their own empires, regional styles of beadmaking developed, particularly in areas that already had a glassmaking tradition.

The Byzantine Empire

By A.D. 330, Emperor Constantine I (306–337) moved his capital from Rome to the city of Constantinople (present-day Istanbul), an action that eventually divided the empire into eastern and western realms. Located on the site of Byzantium, a former Greek colony, Constantinople subsequently grew into a political, cultural, and religious center of international importance from the fourth through the eleventh century.

A geographic meeting point of the Occident and the Orient, Constantinople's ideal location helped it to become a major trading and artistic center. The Byzantine Empire reached its political and economic zenith during the sixth century A.D International commerce prospered: fleets of ships sailed to Cornwall in England, while beautiful gold coins minted by Emperor Justinian I (483–565) and his successors found their way as far afield as Sweden, China, and Zanzibar.[1] A wealth of materials, including gold, garnets, rubies, emeralds, sapphires, pearls, and ivory flowed into Constantinople from India, Burma, southern Russia, and Africa.

The luxurious jewelry of Constantinople was famous and admired throughout the world. The Byzantine emperors had inherited not only the great historic lands of Greece, western Asia, Egypt, parts of Russia, and North Africa, but also the finely developed skills of their artists and artisans, many of whom were drawn to Constantinople by its wealth and concentration of patrons. Consequently, art and jewelry of the period reflected two major styles: one based on the classical Greek and Roman legacy, which epitomized formal elegance; the other derived from the more abstract and robust two-dimensional forms of western Asia and the Far East. Neither style ever completely dominated Byzantine jewelry; they coexisted or reemerged in new configurations.[2] By the sixth century, Byzantine adornment was rich, ornate, and colorfully intricate, a distinctive synthesis of both Hellenistic and Persian elements.

The most complete record of the Byzantine royal court wearing luxurious beaded jewelry is found on mosaics that decorate the church of San Vitale in Ravenna. (In 402, Ravenna officially became the capital of the western Roman Empire. From the late sixth century to 751, it was the seat of the governor of Byzantine Italy. Its capture by the Lombards in 751 finished Byzantine power in Italy.) The portraits of the prosperous, "apostle-like" Emperor Justinian and the Empress Theodora made in 547 convey the regal, highly stylized splendor of their court:

> The imperial diadem, the sign of the ruler's dignity in the time of Constantine was then still a ring of jewels. Under Justinian, elaborate strings of beads were added. This can be seen in the portrait of his wife, Theodora, in

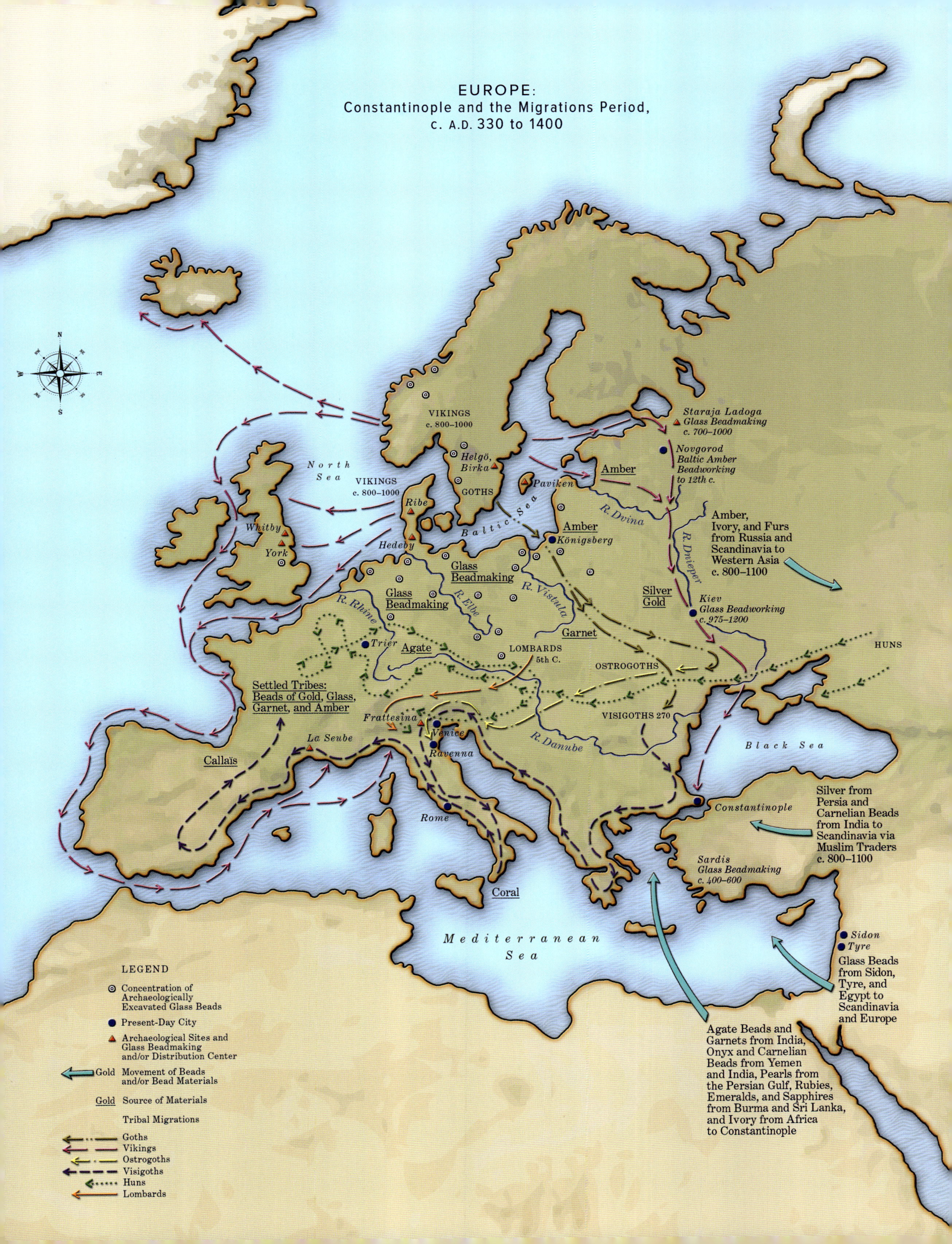

EUROPE:
Constantinople and the Migrations Period,
c. A.D. 330 to 1400
VIKINGS
c. 800–1000
Helgö,
Birka
GOTHS
North
Sea
VIKINGS
c. 800–1000
Ribe
Hedeby
Whitby
York
Paviken
Baltic Sea
Staraja Ladoga
Glass Beadmaking
c. 700–1000
Novgorod
Baltic Amber
Beadworking
to 12th c.
Amber
R. Dvina
Amber
Königsberg
Amber,
Ivory, and Furs
from Russia and
Scandinavia to
Western Asia
c. 800–1100
R. Dnieper
Glass
Beadmaking
Glass
Beadmaking
R. Elbe
R. Vistula
R. Rhine
Silver
Gold
Kiev
Glass Beadworking
c. 975–1200
Trier
Agate
LOMBARDS
5th C.
Garnet
HUNS
OSTROGOTHS
Settled Tribes:
Beads of Gold, Glass,
Garnet, and Amber
Frattesina
Venice
Ravenna
VISIGOTHS 270
R. Danube
La Seube
Callaïs
Black Sea
Rome
Constantinople
Silver from
Persia and
Carnelian Beads
from India to
Scandinavia via
Muslim Traders
c. 800–1100
Sardis
Glass Beadmaking
c. 400–600
Coral
Mediterranean
Sea
Sidon
Tyre
Glass Beads
from Sidon,
Tyre, and
Egypt to
Scandinavia
and Europe
Agate Beads and
Garnets from India,
Onyx and Carnelian
Beads from Yemen
and India, Pearls from
the Persian Gulf, Rubies,
Emeralds, and Sapphires
from Burma and Sri Lanka,
and Ivory from Africa
to Constantinople
LEGEND
Concentration of
Archaeologically
Excavated Glass Beads
Present-Day City
Archaeological Sites and
Glass Beadmaking
and/or Distribution Center
Gold Movement of Beads
and/or Bead Materials
Gold Source of Materials
Tribal Migrations
Goths
Vikings
Ostrogoths
Visigoths
Huns
Lombards

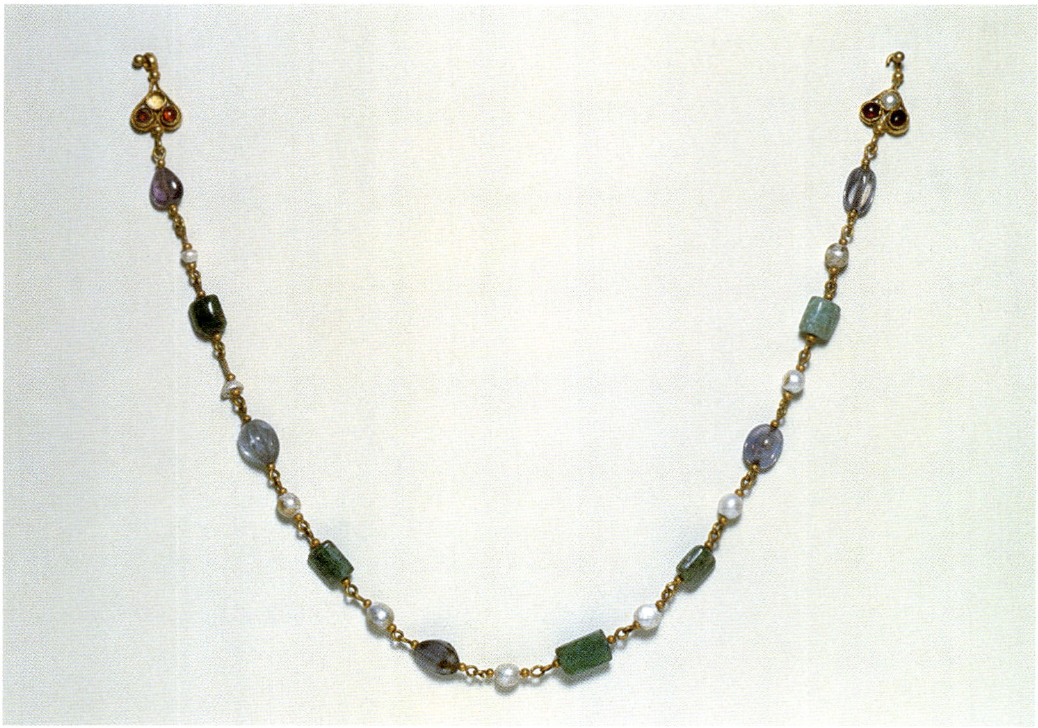

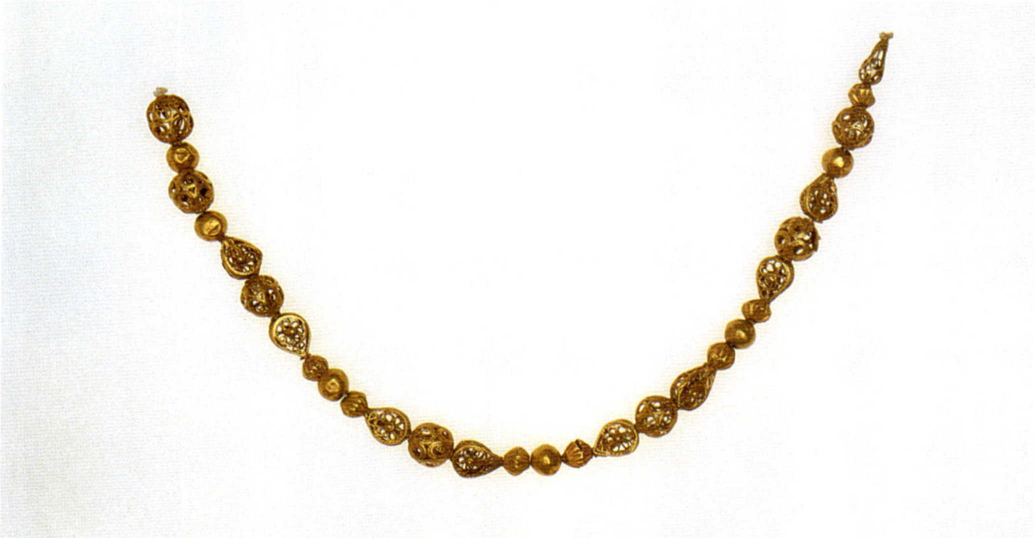

TOP: 61. *Byzantine beads reflect artistic styles inherited from Rome and western Asia. Precious stones cut in cabochon style, emerald crystals, and pearls joined on gold links are typical of the period.*

This necklace of pearls, emeralds, and sapphires—gemstones decreed by Justinian I to be "solely reserved for the splendor and adornment of the sovereign" (with the exception of ornaments usually worn by women)—dates to the fifth century A.D. It is from the Piazza della Consolazione Treasure in Rome, an important find of Byzantine jewelry uncovered during restoration of the piazza in 1910. Length, 40 cm. Dumbarton Oaks Collection, Washington, D.C.

RIGHT: 62. *Openwork filigree beads, representative of Byzantine jewelry of the eighth and ninth centuries A.D. Length, 24 cm. Indiana University Art Museum, Bloomington. Burton Y. Berry Collection*

the mosaics at San Vitale in Ravenna. She wore a magnificent ring of precious stones and beads round her head, from which several strings of beads hung right down to her chest, resembling strands of hair which had been frozen miraculously into precious jewels.[3]

The mosaics are an important source of information, especially since the custom of burying jewelry with the dead was banned by the church. In practice, however, the edicts were not strictly enforced: the Merovingians, among other tribes, continued to place beads in graves even after their conversion to Christianity.

There is no clear separation in technique between late Roman and early Byzantine jewelry beadmaking following the division of the empire in 395. Polychrome jewelry continued to be popular. Beads made from precious stones, such as sapphires and ame-

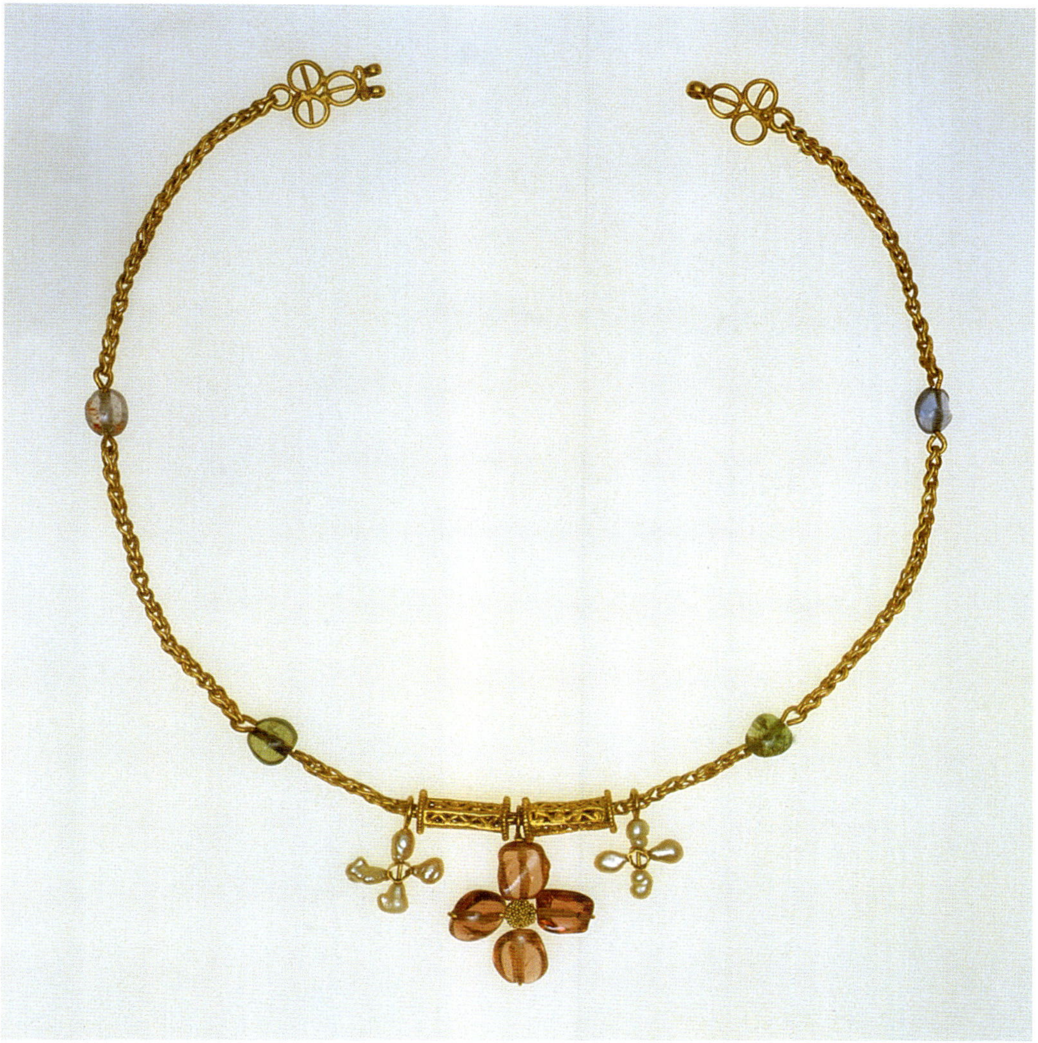

63. *By the seventh century* A.D., *Byzantine jewelry had synthesized Christian symbolism and Eastern forms, and the cross was a popular motif. In this necklace, gold, emerald, and sapphire beads are linked with a loop-in-loop chain, while four rounded ruby beads and eight pearls form the crosses. Rounded stones that "glow" rather than faceted stones that "sparkle" were the preferred aesthetic in Asia (I.). The two openwork tubular beads demonstrate a technique known as* opus interrasile, *an openwork pattern cut from a sheet of metal. Length, 39.85 cm. Indiana University Art Museum, Bloomington. Burton Y. Berry Collection*

thysts, were round in shape rather than faceted, frequently tumble-polished, and strung on gold links with naturally cut emerald crystals and pearls (plate 61). Beads of metal or glass were frequently used as fillers to separate gold coins, for example, that had been mounted as pendants.[4] (Such as plate 49.) Filigree and granulation, techniques used by the Romans, continued to be practiced. A new technique, *Opus interrasile*—cutting through a thin sheet of metal in order to produce an openwork pattern—grew in use (plate 63).

Byzantine and Migrations Period jewelers had many techniques and design motifs in common, but their work also differed in several major ways. Craftsmen from both traditions shared a love for color, best expressed in their combination of metals, colored stones, and glass. Migrations Period artisans tended to employ sturdy forms, perhaps because beads were worn abundantly by every member of the tribal societies. In contrast, Byzantine jewelry was worn primarily by the elite. Pieces were designed for a more sedentary lifestyle and employed a greater use of precious metals and stones, rarely using glass. Tribal jewelers were more dependent than their Byzantine counterparts on whatever raw materials happened to be locally available. Constantinople, on the other hand, was the hub of a vast trade network that allowed access to a very wide range of raw materials, even if only a few specific materials were selected for jewelry. Although the tribal cultures also developed influential lapidary approaches, in-

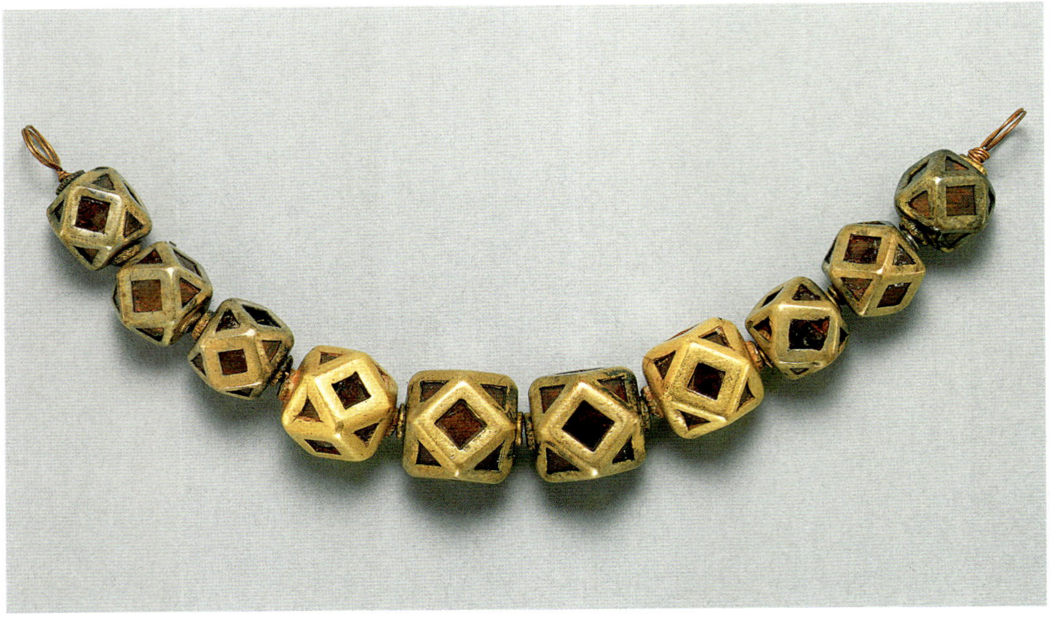

64. *A fifth-century* A.D. *necklace of gold and inlaid garnet polyhedral (ten-faceted) beads found near Olbia in southern Russia and undoubtedly worn by a high-ranking tribal aristocrat. The technique of inlaying garnet in complex cloison cells was perfected in western Europe during the Migrations Period. The garnet was probably imported from India, suggesting that even nomadic horsemen engaged in long-distance trade for luxury goods. Center bead: diameter, 0.95 cm. Walters Art Gallery, Baltimore*

laying garnet-with-gold (the origin of the technique was probably India, via Persia and Egypt), for example, Byzantine goldsmiths preferred enamel cloisonné (the fusing of multicolored enamels within small cells, or cloisons, to produce a mosaiclike effect). Whereas inlaid garnet-and-gold beads were frequently worn by the elite among the settled and migratory tribes, enamel cloisonné was in fact rarely used for Byzantine beads (plate 64).

Byzantine beads typically were made of precious metals and stones. Along with goldsmiths and other artists, glassmakers had moved to Constantinople from the former Roman provinces, but no definite records exist of their having made beads; only their mosaic tiles and vessels remain. Glass historian Gustavus Eisen mentions that Roman-style gold-in-glass beads were manufactured there in the fourth and fifth centuries, and he also describes a necklace of mosaic-glass disks set in gold that he attributes to Constantinople craftsmen.[5] Most glass beads used in early Byzantine jewelry were probably imported from the beadmaking centers of Egypt and Syria. Closer to home, Sardis, in western Turkey, was a glass beadmaking site during early Byzantine times.[6]

By the fourth century, a glass bead industry also existed in Europe. During the first centuries of the Christian Era, immigrant glassmakers from the East (Alexandria and Syria) had established glass workshops in the western Roman provinces of Italy, France, and the Rhineland. Local industries grew out of these early Roman glassworks and supplied beads to their provincial rulers and the export market from at least A.D 200 to 800. It is quite possible that some beads produced in the European provinces reached Constantinople. Later Byzantine glass beads (made both in the East and West) had similar shapes and patterns to earlier Syrian and Egyptian glass but were often less technically accomplished (Timeline 519).[7]

Early in the fourth century, Emperor Constantine allied himself with Christianity, thus paving the way for it to become the empire's official religion. The toleration of Christianity was accompanied by the manufacture of a variety of religious symbols. During the fourth century, the cross and molded-glass amulets representing drops of sacred blood, fish, doves, and faces of Christ were incorporated into necklaces as "amulets in the round." Although later burials rarely included Christian adornment, in the early days of imperial Christianity religious amulets and beads were still interred with the deceased. Two distinctive types of glass beads, called the "Vision of Constantine" and the "Road to Golgotha," were generally found in tombs in Syria and near Jerusalem, the spiritual center that gained increasing importance with the spread of Christianity.[8] By the seventh century, Byzantine jewelry was almost a complete synthesis of Christian symbols and Eastern forms, and the cross had become a popular motif (plate 63).

As the age of classical antiquity came to an end, and its aesthetic values were increasingly rejected by the Christian church's "low opinion of the sensual world," new religious attitudes influenced the wearing of jewelry. Although warned that they should love "not precious stones but the sacred," Byzantine nobility continued to adorn themselves with jewels.[9] They incorporated Christian symbols into their adornment but otherwise generally ignored the church's dictum, apparently heeding the call of materialism over spirituality.

The successful tribal (or "barbarian") invasions of the fifth century and the settlement of Germanic and Slavic peoples within the Roman Empire open a new chapter in Western history. By the seventh century, Muslim Arab conquests of western Asia and North Africa and the eventual migration of the Slavs into the Balkans severed the last links between Constantinople and the West.

Between the eleventh and the fourteenth century, a series of wars known as the Crusades were undertaken by European Christians to recover the Holy Land from the Muslims. In 1204, the knights of the Fourth Crusade, under pressure from the rulers of Venice, who had been eyeing Byzantine riches for centuries, were diverted from their original course and conquered Constantinople, which had been ruled by Macedonian emperors since 864. In the years that followed, the city's wealth was plundered and its jewelry was often melted down; consequently, few examples of Byzantine goldsmiths' work can still be seen.

After the fall of Constantinople to the Turks in 1453, and its incorporation into the Ottoman Empire, the influence of Byzantine jewelers continued only in pockets of the former empire, namely Greece and southern Russia.[10] Byzantine traditions, however, did not entirely die out. A necklace made in sixteenth-century Venice (and currently at the Museo Poldi-Pezzoli in Milan) is composed of enameled gold and filigree beads and shows that Byzantine practices were continued in Europe.[11]

The Migrations Period and the United Tribes

As the Mediterranean framework of the Roman world dissolved, power and influence shifted north of the Alps. Europe began to develop new "Romano-Germanic" civilizations, whose peoples had been on the continent's periphery only a few centuries earlier.[12] The Migrations Period commenced with the rise of the Huns, led by Attila (c. 406–453). The Huns entered eastern Europe from central Asia, crossing the Volga River about 370 and expanding their borders to the south and west until they were defeated in France by the Romans in 451. In their wake, they had unsettled the Teutonic tribes that lived in the regions through which they passed, causing a series of migrations and subsequent wars among tribes north of the Black Sea, in western Russia and eastern Europe, which continued until the tenth century.

From the fourth to the eighth century, powerful seminomadic tribes occupied most of southwest Europe, forming feudal societies that ruled a divided continent. The major tribes were the Visigoths in Spain, the Ostrogoths in eastern Germany and Aus-

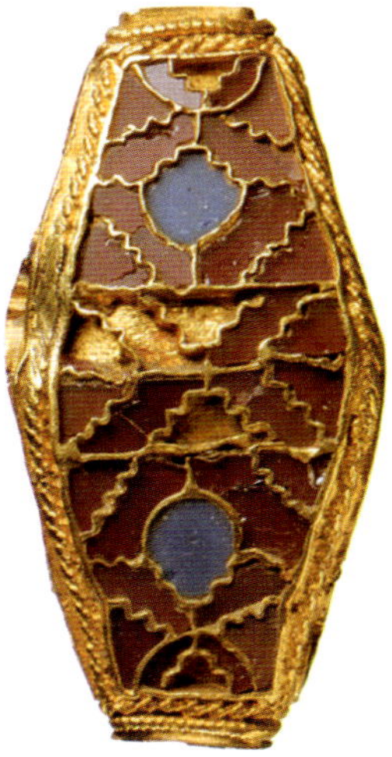

ABOVE: 65. *A unique sixth- to seventh-century A.D. inlaid garnet and lapis lazuli bead, made in two parts by a master Anglo-Saxon jeweler. Length, 3.3 cm. Ashmolean Museum, Oxford, England*

RIGHT: 66. *Gold filigree and finely granulated beads made in Denmark about A.D. 100–200, using techniques probably introduced by the Romans. The beads were found in a peat bog in 1783. Typical biconical bead: length, 2.4 cm. National Museum of Copenhagen*

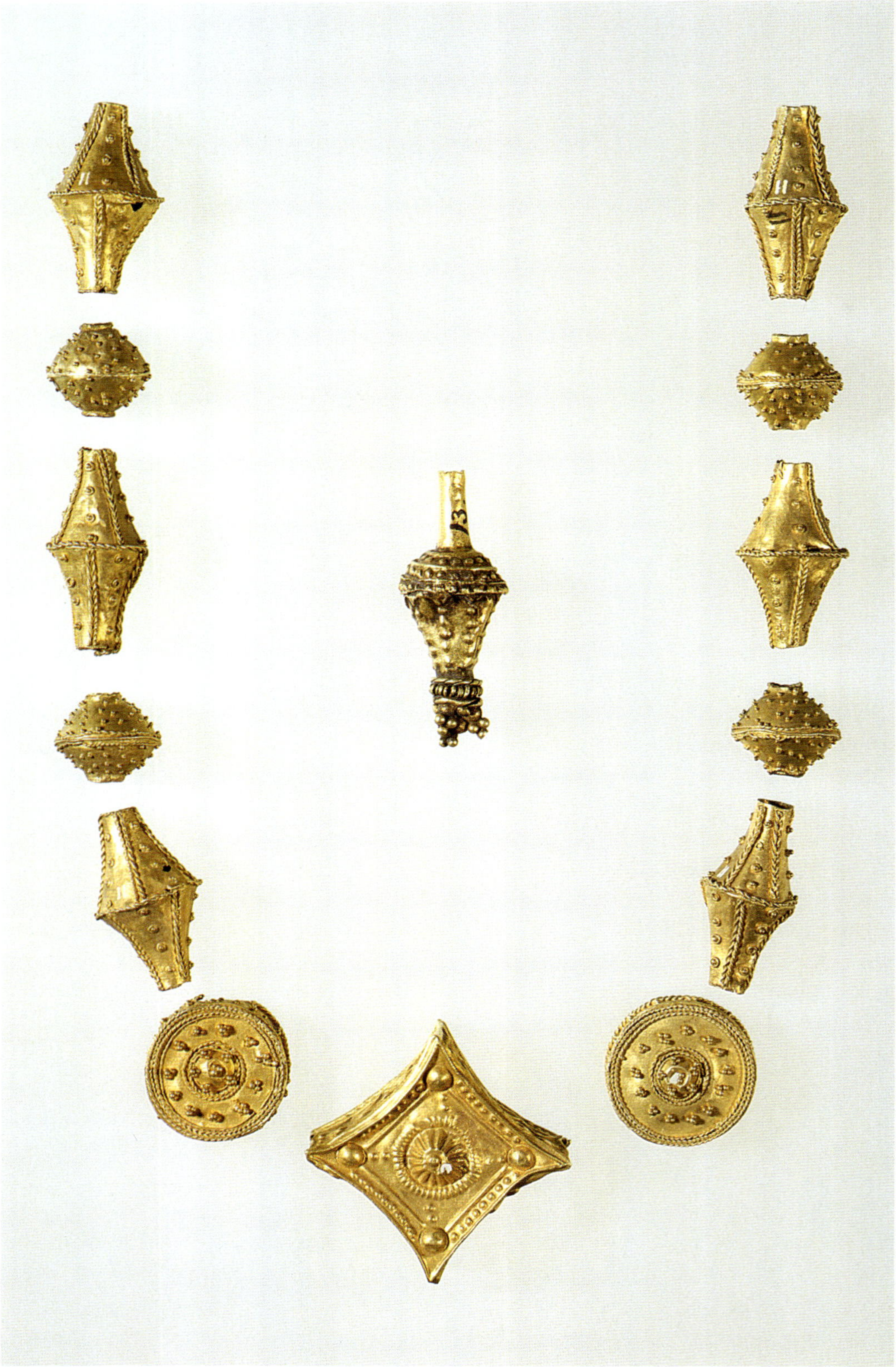

tria, the Vandals in North Africa, the Franks in western Germany, the Lombards in northern Italy, and the Angles and Saxons in England.

Adornment was very important to these people. Although each group produced their own styles of jewelry, reflecting specific tribal traditions, their adornment shared several common characteristics. Due to a long history of nomadic life, few possessions other than jewelry accompanied their journeys. Personal adornment was therefore portable wealth and a "badge of rank" used for decorating themselves as well as their horses.[13] The migratory life meant that jewelry had to be practical, well-constructed, and compact, without too many protruding ends that could catch onto woolen tunics or capes. To be seen, it had to be bold in design, large, and colorful. For these reasons, beads, worn by both men and women, played an important role in their jewelry.

Color was a dominant factor in most decoration of the Migrations Period. The inlaying of shaped garnets in gold cloisons—*verroterie cloisonné*—was a specialty of the period, often giving the finished bead the brilliant and mysterious appearance of a miniature stained glass window whose supports were made of gold rather than lead.[14] Inlaying was also practiced with lapis lazuli, glass, and enamel, and the techniques of filigree and granulation were sometimes used (plates 64 and 65). The intensive use of color and the extensive covering of surfaces with ornamental detail were designed to reflect light and to call attention to the wearer—priorities for jewelry meant to be noticed.

Migrations Period adornment evolved from many cultures, and the tendency to absorb and transform the styles and techniques of other cultures was a continuing feature of this jewelry.[15] A polychrome style was developed in the fourth century by Ostrogoth and Visigoth goldsmiths who worked near the Black Sea and were influenced by Greco-Roman and Eastern jewelry techniques and styles. In this region, as early as the fourth century B.C., Greek methods had been synthesized with the art of the Scythians and Sarmatians, migrant tribes with remarkable aesthetic traditions who lived between the Danube and the Don rivers from the fourth century B.C. to the second century A.D. Trade with Roman colonies north of the Black Sea also allowed the tribes to organize trading connections with India, through which they acquired garnets and other stones needed for their adornment. By the time of the Hun attacks, in the mid-fifth century A.D., most Germanic tribes had a rich and established jewelry tradition characterized by sophisticated geometries and abstract designs.[16] During the seventh century, the polychrome technique was refined into exquisite forms by the Anglo-Saxon jewelers in Britain (plate 65).

Beads of clay, amethyst, amber, and glass were worn by all of the tribes, generally in combinations that were strung or linked with pendants. Bead materials varied as new territories were conquered. The production of colorful glass beads flourished under the Merovingians (500–751), a Frankish dynasty, whose territories encompassed the Rhineland, where numerous glass workshops previously had been established by the Romans (plate 60). Merovingian jewelry was marked by the decline of classical traditions, and by the rise of the new abstract and brilliantly ornamental style of the tribes.[17]

The Franks, the first migrant people to accept Christianity, were the most powerful and important of all the successors of Rome, and their kingdom dominated western Europe from the late fifth to the early ninth century. Frankish glassmakers, although basically inspired by Roman period designs, also developed their own styles, some of which imitated Phoenician-style and Celtic beads known from La Tène and Hallstatt fifteen hundred years earlier. The Franks not only copied Celtic patterns but also wore Celtic beads on their necklaces and carried slivers of La Tène glass.[18] Having recovered these objects from ancient Celtic burial grounds, the Franks probably regarded them as protective amulets. Other beads were distinctively Merovingian, including ones with

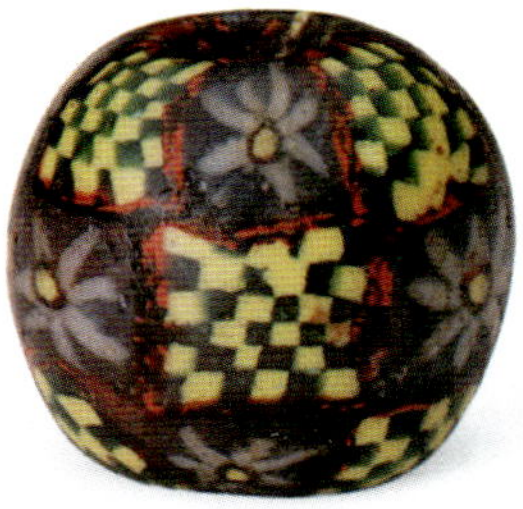

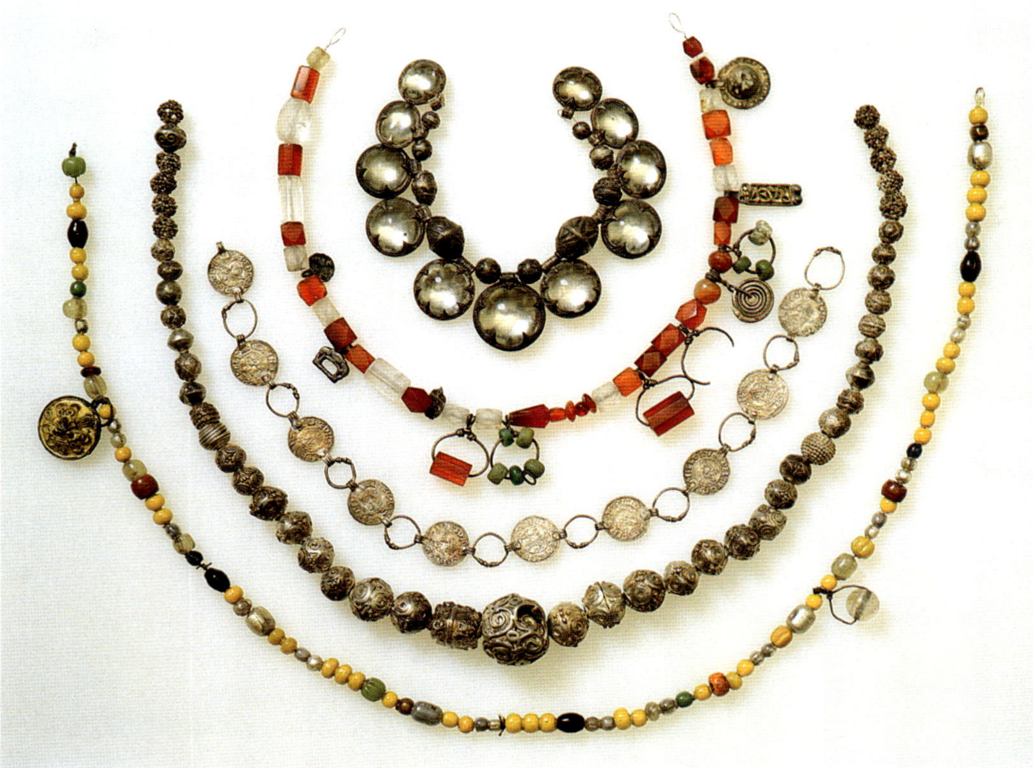

ABOVE: 67. *A distinctive mosaic-glass bead with checker and star panels. Found primarily north of the Alps and in concentrations in Scandinavia, similar beads have been excavated in archaeological contexts dating from A.D. 300 to 400 and have also been found in later Viking sites (A.D. 800–1000). Diameter, 1.95 cm. Private collection*

RIGHT: 68. *Beads of glass, silver, amber, crystal, and carnelian worn by wealthy Viking women. Some beads were made locally, others were obtained as loot and displayed by women to advertise the success of their men in raiding ventures abroad. National Museum of Antiquities, Stockholm*

OPPOSITE: 69. *A richly patterned necklace of glass beads from the Viking period (A.D. 800–1000) excavated at Eidem in Norway. Most of the beads were imported (probably from several locales, including former Roman territories in western Europe and western Asia, as well as eastern and central Europe), although some may have been made with imported glass scrap and glass mosaic ingots, a technique inherited from the Middle Eastern beadmakers (II). Third bead from right center: diameter, 1.95 cm. Trondheim Royal Norwegian Scientific Society Museum*

bright yellow lines embedded in a terra-cotta red background (Timeline 38).[19] Due to their acceptance of Christianity and the church's edicts forbidding grave deposits, beads slowly disappeared from Frankish burials during the seventh and eighth centuries.[20]

The history of glass beads in medieval Europe (800–1400) following the decline of the Merovingian dynasty is not clear. Archaeologists and historians continue to fill in the gaps, but the evidence is slim and is still not very well understood.[21] Glass beadmaking in the Roman tradition did survive, however, in various parts of Europe despite the destruction of the western empire and the subsequent turmoil of the Migrations and early medieval periods. Production continued in pockets of the Rhineland, Italy, and France, and gradually spread into central, eastern, and northern Europe, including Russia, and the Balkans.[22] Potash lime glass, made from local wood ashes rather than imported soda, is characteristic of central European glass and started to replace Roman and western Asian soda glass by the late eleventh century.[23]

During the European Dark Ages (c. 476–1000), glassmaking and working was in the hands of monks at some monestaries who made interesting, unique beads and kept the art alive. As early as 1000, a glass industry existed in Frattesina, Italy, near Venice.[24] By the fifteenth century, Venice became the glassmaking center of the Western world.

The Vikings

The final phase of European migrations involved the Vikings. The region constituting the present-day countries of Denmark, Sweden, and Norway was among the most stable in Europe. Located so far north that they escaped invasions, these countries, however, were not isolated. During the second millennium B.C., Scandinavians were actively involved in the Baltic amber trade, manufacturing beads as well as exporting the raw material in exchange for metal ores not locally available. Although outside the Roman sphere, the Scandinavians traded with the Romans for metal, pottery, and glass. Gold collars found in Scandinavia dating to the

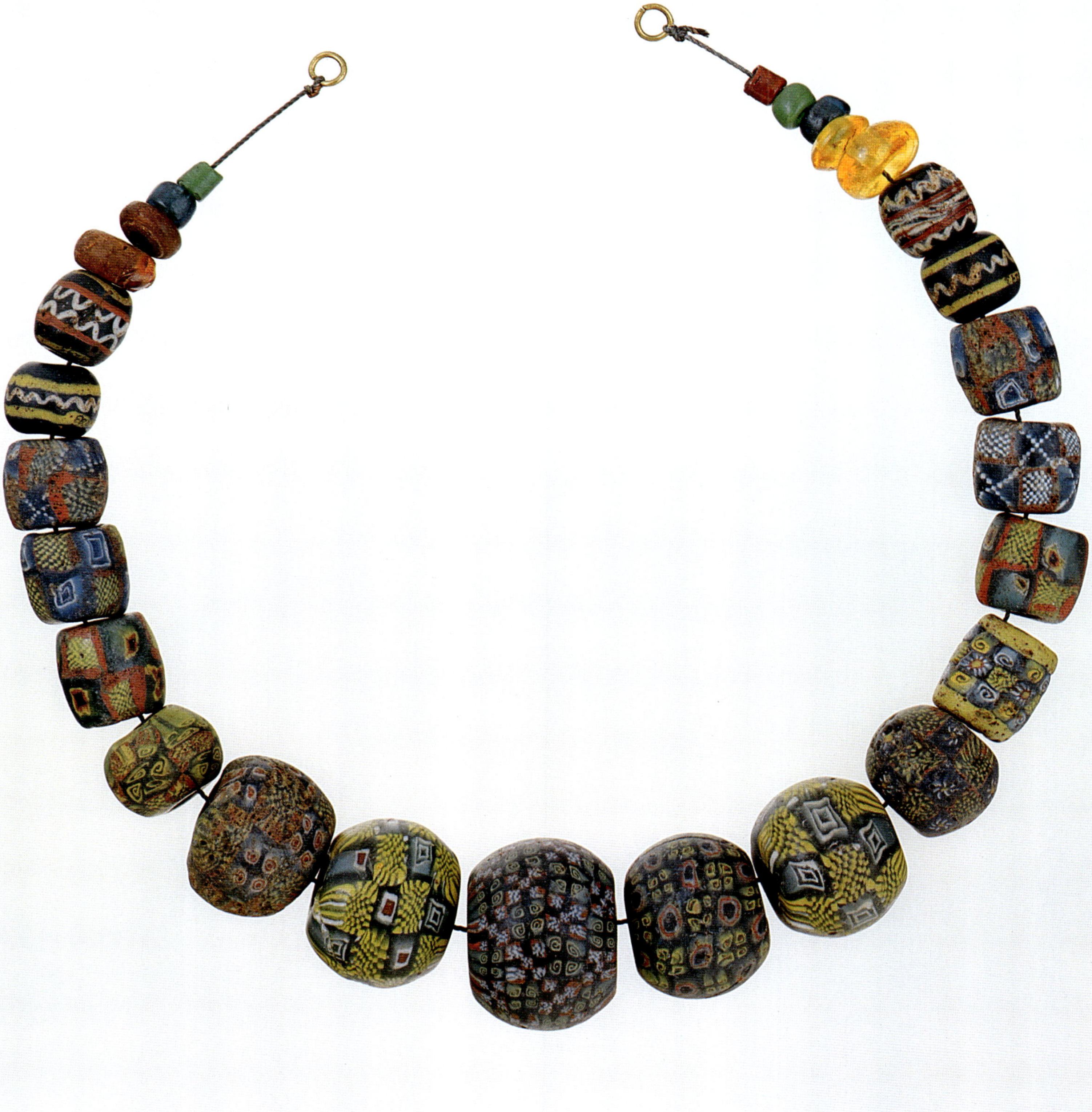

fourth century B.C. show decorative motifs influenced by Scythian, Etruscan, and Celtic art. Techniques of filigree and granulation seen in gold beads that date from the second and third centuries were probably introduced by Roman intermediaries during the first century A.D.

By A.D. 800, the Scandinavians were a seafaring people who raided and traded in northern, western, and eastern Europe. They acquired riches from the Eastern world, settled in Greenland, discovered America, and served as mercenaries at the court of Byzantium.[25]

A major impetus for the Viking raids and commerce was the acquisition of precious materials for adornment. Silver was particularly coveted; a major supply was garnered in the form of coins from the East when contact was established with Arab traders. Great quantities of silver were exported to western and northern Europe by the Vikings to replace the exhausted supplies of Byzantine gold.[26] Indian carnelian beads also entered Scandinavia via Islamic traders, while etched carnelians from Iran went north into Russia in exchange for furs and wax. Amber apparently traveled south along this same route.[27] Ivory walrus tusks and furs from the arctic regions of Scandinavia and Russia were staples the Vikings exchanged for precious materials.

Beads, along with pottery, nails, and knives, are the most common objects found in pre-Christian Viking graves. This has caused bead historian Johan Callmer to observe that Viking beads were directly related to social status, since almost without exception, they occur in the graves of wealthier Vikings. Typically, the beads are silver, amber, carnelian, rock crystal, and glass (plate 68). Some of the beads were made locally; others were imported.[28]

Beadmaking workshops have been excavated in southwest Scandinavia at several sites where flourishing towns existed in the ninth and tenth centuries and served as international marketplaces and import-export centers. Carnelian and crystal may have been imported to the town of Hedeby both as raw materials for manufacturing into beads and as finished products. There is also evidence of specialized amber workshops, where the amber debris shows that it was cut, carved, and turned using many of the techniques for working jet and bone.

Glass beads were made at the towns of Helgö and Paviken. Glass shards at Helgö as well as monochrome and mosaic-glass rods found at nearby Birka and Ribe were all imported, suggesting that beadmakers on the southwestern periphery of Scandinavia worked at least in part with glass brought in from other areas.[29] Most Viking glass beads, however, were imported. Glass beads have been uncovered from graves in a variety of shapes, including spheres, tubes, melons, and cornerless cubes. The techniques they used include gold-in-glass, or gold sandwich, and mosaic, or millefiori, glass in both opaque and translucent colors.[30] It appears that glass beads found in Scandinavian Viking sites have many origins, which is not unexpected, given the far-ranging activities of the Viking sailors and warriors. Some possibly were passed down as heirlooms or obtained as loot; others may have been manufactured in distant western Asia and entered Scandinavia either during the days of trade with the Romans or in the ninth century, when contact was established with Arab traders along the Volga River in Russia.

The Vikings forged strong links between themselves and northern and eastern Europe. Their remarkable ships and nautical abilities took them into many distant waterways, including the rivers of France and the British Isles. Glass beadmaking occurred in most of the regions they traveled to, and it seems logical to assume that beads accompanied the Vikings on their homeward voyages. The Vikings frequently settled where they traded. Beads have been excavated at York, in England, and other Viking colonial outposts, indicating their far-flung trading activities.

Beads from the Coppergate excavation at York include amber, jet, and glass examples. The glass beads range from large, multicolored objects to small seedbeads that were probably sewn onto clothing.[31] A cowrie shell bead from the Red Sea may show there was contact between the Vikings at York and western Asians or Egyptians.[32]

Some glass bead types that were widely distributed throughout Scandinavia suggest production areas existed close to northwest Europe, in Marseilles, northern Italy, or the Rhine Valley. Other Viking beads closely resemble eastern European products, particularly Merovingian and Frankish beads. The Vikings had direct contacts with all of these areas.[33]

A distinctive mosaic-glass bead found outside the Roman Empire and concentrated in Scandinavia is of particular interest. This bead (plate 67), examples of which have been found in Scandinavian archaeological contexts dating from A.D. 300 to 400, is also known from Viking sites that date from 800 to 1000. Some of the beads recovered from the earlier period include unique mosaic-glass faces with Byzantine-style royal helmets. The technical complexity of the beads suggests they were originally manufactured in workshops somewhere within the Roman Empire.[34]

The Middle Ages

During the Middle Ages (A.D. 600–1400), the use of jewelry was considered a pagan custom and was discouraged by the church. The simplicity of medieval dress was generally accompanied only by a brooch at the neck, a belt buckle, and finger rings. Beads of ivory, jet, coral, wood, gemstones, and precious metals were used primarily for rosaries. By the late fourteenth century, however, as rosaries and cruciforms became more popular and ornate, they were worn as necklaces, and their decorative function apparently rivaled their religious significance.

Medieval jewels, including beads, were amuletic and intended to bring supernatural benefits to the wearer. Paganism was generally abandoned in the regions as Christianity spread, although superstitions persisted for a long time and many magical practices were incorporated into Christianity. Materials were selected for their amuletic value, and stones were used that were considered to have protective powers: amethyst prevented drunkenness, coral strengthened the heart, and emeralds combated epilepsy. Crystal was regarded as the symbol of purity.

Certain areas were famed for working specific materials into beads. Novgorod, in Russia, was an important trading city that, until the Mongolian invasions of the twelfth century, produced most of the Baltic amber beads. Trebnitz, in Bohemia, was known for garnets cut into beads. Venice, according to Columbus's later descriptions, was a pearl-processing center.[35] The agates of southern Germany (which would eventually result in the establishment of a famed bead industry at Idar-Oberstein) were beginning to be exploited: the first written notice of them was in 1375, and there were already bead-making guilds by 1451.[36]

With few exceptions, European beadmaking was a decentralized cottage industry from the Roman period until the end of the Middle Ages. With rising prosperity in fifteenth-century Europe—due to sophisticated banking and trading networks, and the beginning of global exploration—glass beadmaking reappeared as an important art and industry. In Venice, many of the old Roman glass techniques were rediscovered, and beadmaking took its place alongside the great arts of the Renaissance.

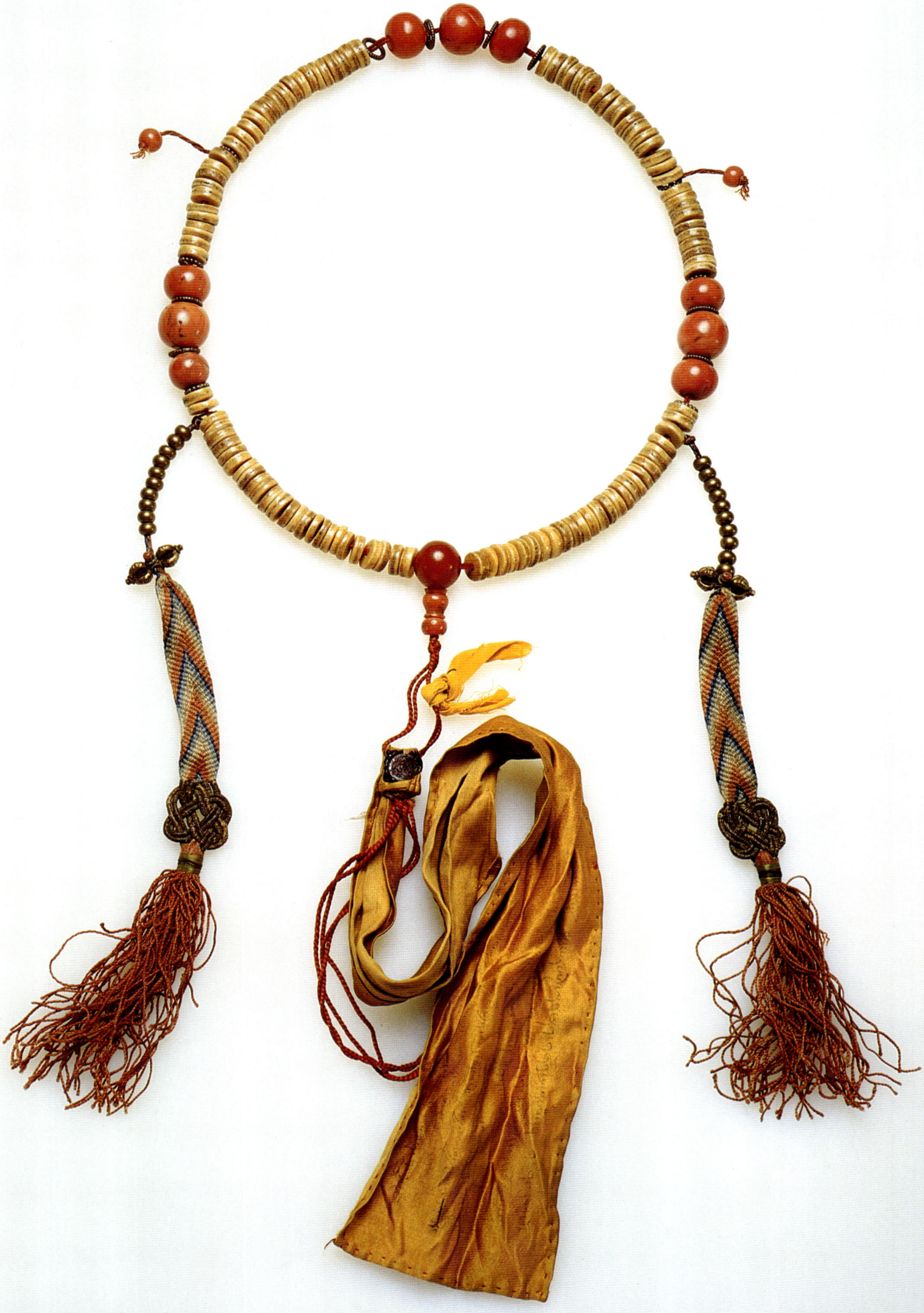

Prayer Beads

All night she spent in bidding of her bedes,
And all the day in doing good and Godly deeds.
—Edmund Spenser
The Faerie Queene

Prayer beads are commonly associated with the Middle Ages (A.D. 600–1400) and Roman Catholicism. Their use, however, is universal and predates the Christian Era. Christianity, in fact, was the last of the major religions to employ prayer beads in an important ritualistic role. Even today, the religions of nearly two-thirds of the world's population utilize some form of prayer beads.

The word *bead* is derived from the Anglo-Saxon *bidden* ("to pray") and *bede* ("prayer"). During the medieval period, when jewelry was discouraged by the church, rosaries were acceptable as convenient portable devices for counting prayers. Their purpose was to assist the worshiper in accurately repeating from memory the correct number of prayers and incantations required by his faith.

The rosary is only one of several ancient ways used to count prayers. The earliest means involved counting on fingers or shifting pebbles from one pile to another as the prayers were recited. These unwieldy methods were replaced by tying knots on a cord: the strings of prayer beads probably evolved from strings of knots. The Greek Orthodox church still employs a knotted rosary, the *kombologion.* One of the oldest forms of the rosary in Europe is a thong of leather sewn into a circlet, with bone rings attached like scales to the spine of a fish. The rings were turned over as prayers were counted. This form of rosary, known from eighth-century graves, was still in use in southern Germany in the nineteenth century.[1]

70. *A Buddhist* mala. *The 108 disk-shaped prayer beads are made from the bones of a lama (holy man). The dividers and retaining beads are coral, and the tassels are silk. The satin ribbon is partially covered with Tibetan writing. The two counters, each with ten silver beads, terminate in thunderbolt pendants (*djore*). Several hundred years old, this* mala *belonged to Lama Kunga Rinpoche of the Ngor monastery. Length (side to top center bead), 40 cm. Collection Ivory Freidus*

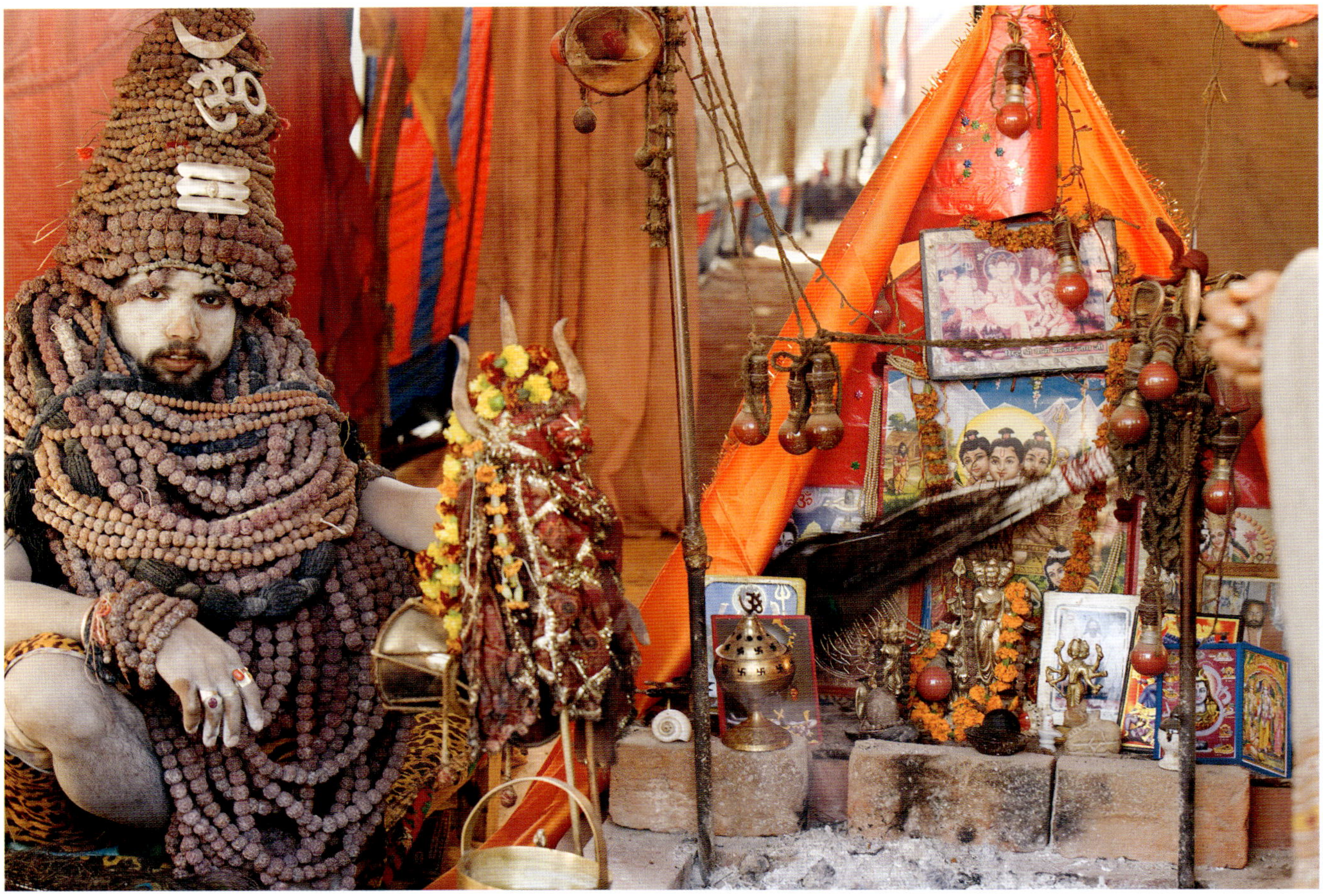

71. *An Indian Sadhu (holy man) sits within his personal altar wrapped in layers of* rudraksha *beads during the festival of Kumbh Mela in Allahabad, India. A devotee stands to the right.*

The use of beads to count prayers appears to have originated with the Hindus in India. Sandstone sculptures of the Sunga and Kushan periods (185 B.C.–A.D. 320) portray Hindu sages holding rosaries.[2] It is possible, however, they were used even earlier by the Hindu cult of Siva or, according to legend, by Sakyamuni (c. 563–483 B.C.), the founder of Buddhism. One account places the rosary's origin in the sixth century B.C. when Sakyamuni paid a visit to King Vaidurya, a recent Buddhist convert. Assisting the king in his new faith, "Sakya directed him to thread 108 seeds of the Bodhi tree [*Ficus religiosa*] on a string, and while passing seed by seed between his fingers to repeat a certain formula meaning 'Hail to the Buddha, the Law, and the Congregation' at least two thousand times a day."[3] Later, Buddhists in Tibet, China, and Japan used rosaries, as did Muslim Persians and Arabs.

Christians may have first learned about the concept of the rosary from the Arabs, either as a result of the Crusaders' experiences in the Holy Land or through its introduction into Spain by eighth-century Muslim invaders. More likely, the Christian rosary evolved independently in western Europe (first, possibly in Ireland) as the church developed more sophisticated rituals and its practitioners had an increasing number of prayers to count. Many church members were illiterate; using beads as a counting device insured that each prayer was repeated the prescribed number of times.

Although the number, arrangement, and materials of prayer beads are different with each religion, there are shared concepts that link the beads of the major faiths. Symbolic associations are frequently made between flowers (particularly the rose) and gardens and prayer beads. The name for prayer beads in Tibet and India is the Sanskrit word *mala*: it means "garden," "garland of flowers," and "necklace of beads." The oldest name for Hindu prayer beads is *japamala*: "muttering chaplet." But *japamala* also means "rose chaplet," presumably because the beads were made of rolled petals from the flower rose of Sharon (*Hibiscus syriacus*).[4] The Roman Catholic rosary has a rich historical relationship with rose garlands and rose gardens. In contemporary Italy, a *coronario* makes both flower wreaths for funerals and prayer beads.

While the quantities of beads used in rosaries differ from religion to religion (and even between various sects of a single faith), multiples of three predominate the numerology of rosaries, reflecting the significance of the number in prayers and even fundamental doctrines—the Buddhist triad (Buddha, the doctrine, and the community), for example, or the Roman Catholic Trinity (the Father, Son, and Holy Ghost). The Buddhist rosary, and the Hindu rosary from which it was derived, have 108 beads; the Muslim, 99; and the Roman Catholic, 150.[5] In addition to their practical purpose, rosaries have intellectual, social, psychological, and aesthetic significance. Highly sensual, inviting continual handling, they were sometimes an ascetic's only material possession. Healing powers have been attributed to rosaries, as well as the power to exorcise evil spirits and ward off lightning. Certain materials, such as agate, were almost universally amuletic; their use as religious beads provided double protection. Coral beads were associated with the prevention of ailments of the blood. In many medieval paintings, the Christ Child is shown wearing or holding a coral rosary, while the child-god Eros (Cupid) sometimes wears a necklace of red coral beads.[6]

Beginning in ancient times, prayers have been recited in cycles. Countless ceremonies exist in which a circle is used to join people together, to create a sense of place, and to "protect what is within; to keep out what is dangerous or to concentrate force."[7] There are also ageless associations with the cycles of life, as well as annual, seasonal, and daily cycles. Symbolizing cycles of prayer, rosaries form closed circlets or chaplets. Whether the circle is large or small, it usually has either a terminal bead or tassel marking the beginning and end of the prayer cycle. Markers of a different shape or size occur at intervals among the counting beads, providing the user with a place to pause and rest.

The rosary's circular form has different levels of religious and psychological meanings. In meditation, the circle centers the mind in contemplation: "One uses prayer beads, ringing oneself in." Meditation involves establishing a space, a circle, and focusing attention within it, thus concentrating energy. Writing about introspection, Saint Augustine admonished the faithful: "God is a circle whose center is everywhere." He prescribed "[returning] within yourself, for it is in the inward man that truth dwells." The solitary, thoughtful manipulation of prayer beads enhances this contemplative state of mind, and the repetitious handling of the beads helps the worshiper concentrate on spiritual needs. As prayers are said, a closed circuit is created: words are spoken, fingers move, and ears listen.[8]

The meditative state induced by repeating prayers while holding beads plays a great role in Eastern religions. The Eastern worshiper suspends thinking during meditation in contrast to the Westerner, who is encouraged to think while reciting prayers. Another difference between the beads' role in Eastern and Western religions is in the handling of the actual rosaries. In the East, prayers are counted by moving the string in one hand; in the West, rosaries are usually held in both hands.[9] This has an interesting parallel with the frequent use of asymmetry in the aesthetics of the East, while the West so often stresses symmetrical balance.

Throughout the centuries, the elaborate craftsmanship of prayer beads often stands in stark contrast to the concepts of simplicity they were meant to enhance. Attempting

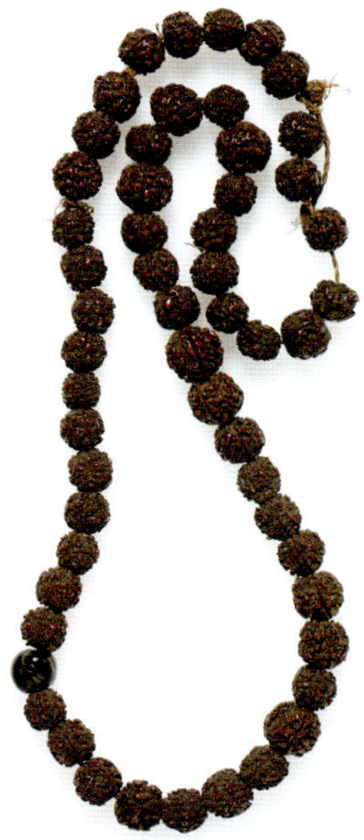

ABOVE: 72. *A* mala *(strand) of fifty-four* rudraksha *beads and one Bodhi bead (lower left). Rudraksha are seeds from a small tree unique to Java. Bodhi are seeds from the Bodhi tree (*ficus religiosa*). Often worn as a necklace by followers of the Hindu god Shiva,* rudraksha *are perhaps the earliest form of prayer beads. The natural surface of each seed is rough with grooves, symbolizing the austere life required for the worship of Siva. The five lines typically on each seed represent Siva's five faces. Largest bead diameter, 1.6 cm, 1990. The Bead Museum, Glendale, Arizona*

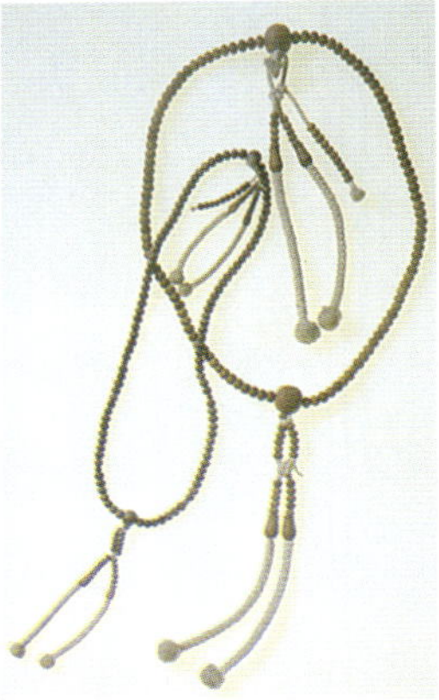

ABOVE: 73. *The* sho-zoiki jiu-dzu *are prayer beads used by all Japanese Buddhist sects. Each composed of 112 plum wood beads of equal size, these two rosaries are split into two groups of larger parent beads called the "father" and "mother" beads. Length (either), 180 cm. National Museum of Natural History, Smithsonian Institution, Washington,* D.C.

RIGHT: 74. *A Buddhist* mala *composed of 108 disk-shaped beads of human bone, inlaid with turquoise, coral, amber, pearl, and lapis lazuli. One retaining bead and three large divider beads of jade, turquoise, carnelian, and coral separate the* mala *into four sections of 27 beads each. The circlet ends in a* djore, *indicating the beginning and the end of the prayer cycle. There are no counters. Skull beads, like other Tibetan ritualistic objects of human bone, were meant to impress upon the devotee the transient nature of human existence.*[1] *Length, 72.4 cm. Collection Franyo Schindler, New York*

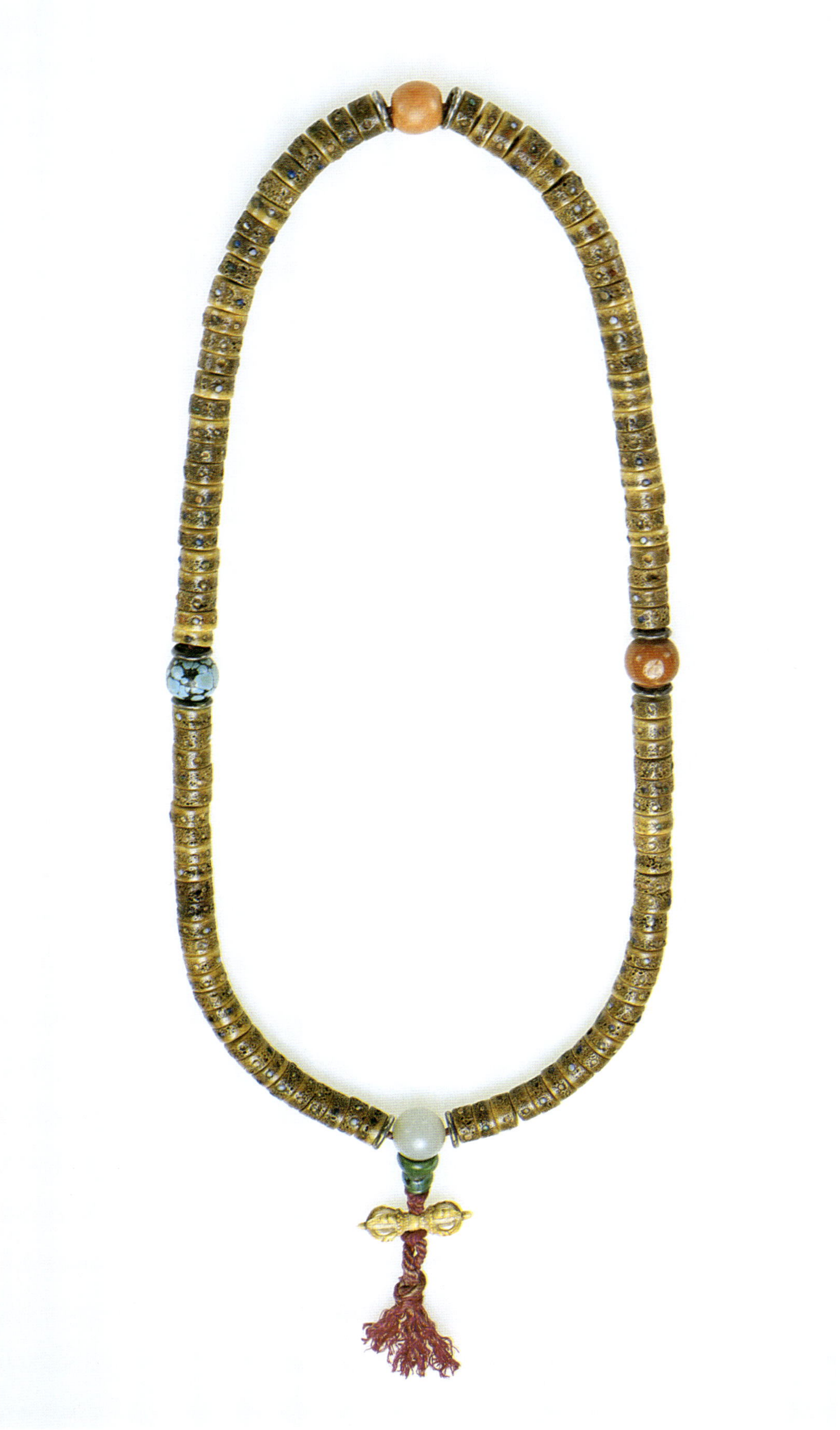

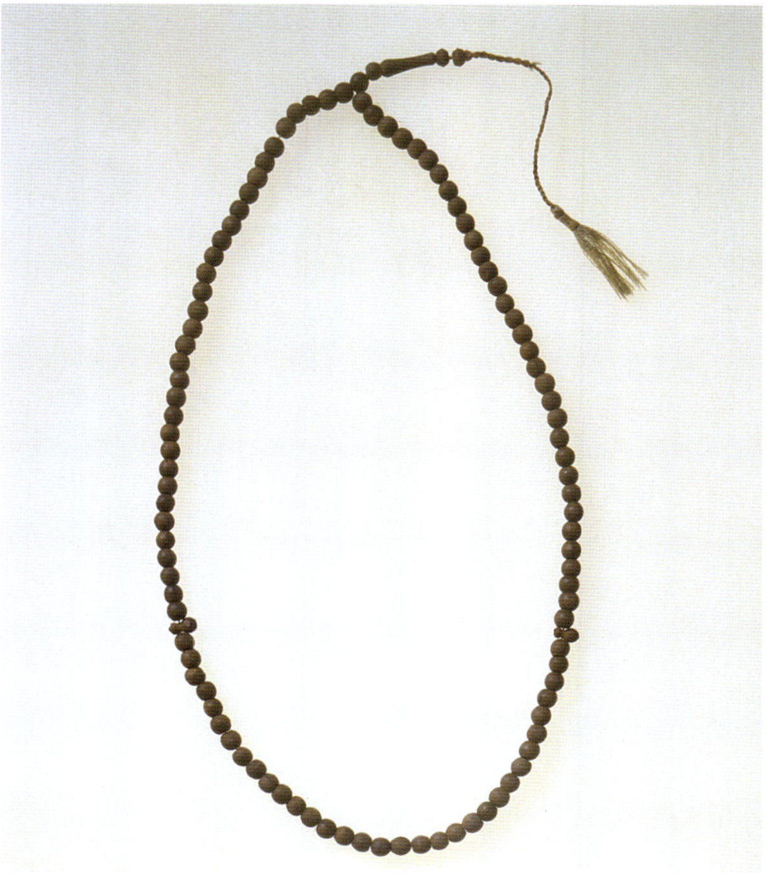

TOP: 75. *Islamic prayer beads (*subha*) from Cairo, consisting of ninety-nine round olivewood beads divided into three sections by two vase-shaped marker beads. The marker beads, placed after the thirty-third and sixty-sixth beads, allow the devotee a respite from counting prayers. The ends of the cord pass through a spindle-shaped terminal bead, known as the "leader," which indicates that one has "come into" the circle of prayer. The cords finally go through two smaller beads, terminating in a tassel. Because evil spirits are believed to dislike fringed objects, the tassel keeps away the evil eye. Length, 101.6 cm. National Museum of Natural History, Smithsonian Institution, Washington,* D.C.

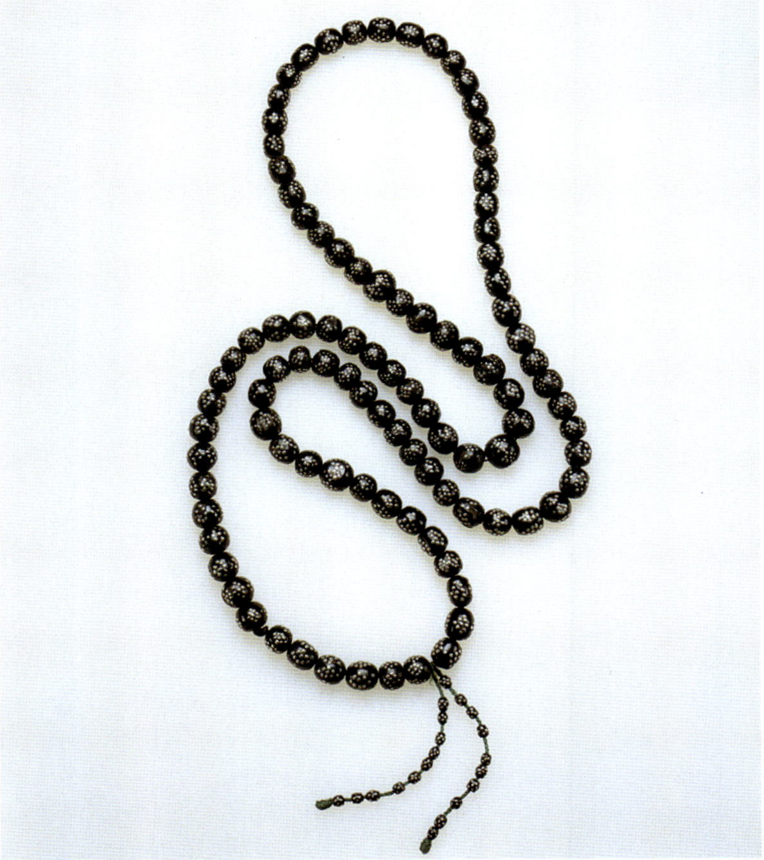

LEFT: 76. *Islamic coral prayer beads inlaid with silver, probably made in Istanbul during the nineteenth century. Length, 146 cm. Collection Franyo Schindler, New York*

to make the beads' appearance conform with spiritual values has led to interesting interpretations. A bead authority notes: "One may feel, as Lady Godiva did in the eleventh century, that it is fitting to count one's prayers on jewels for they are being offered to God. Or one may feel that a wretched sinner like oneself should not presume to offer prayers on any but the plainest beads."[10] It has been difficult to keep luxury out of religion. The custom of prominently displaying prayer beads led to their elevation as objects of social status as well as piety. Rarely does the village priest carry the same beads as an archbishop, or a poor devotee the same as a wealthy one. The most common materials for rosaries throughout the world are wood, glass, and plastic. But museums display examples made of every known precious material, including gold, silver, emeralds, rubies, diamonds, coral, jet, crystal, alabaster, pearls, and lapis lazuli. There are also rosaries of amber, ebony, marble, ivory, jade, mother-of-pearl, enamel, and porcelain. French royal inventories in 1380 listed rosaries of enameled gold encrusted with jewels, and medieval Cordoba was famous for its prayer beads made of gold.

Primarily in reaction to these excesses, Protestants do not use prayer beads. The leaders of the Reformation protested the self-indulgence and blatant materialism of the medieval church. As a result, Protestant doctrines stress moderation, minimize ritual, and tend to reject what are considered displays of material extravagance, including prayer beads. The founders of Protestantism stressed literacy and encouraged individual interpretation of the Scriptures. John Calvin, the great Reformation theologian, said that each person in the reformed church should be able to read the creed for himself. This meant that prayers were not to be memorized in set circular formulas, and therefore aids, such as beads, were not needed.

Judaism also excludes prayer beads. Its history emphasizes the rejection of paganism. Beads were considered magical and therefore pagan. Amuletic beads are generally considered a device to win the beneficence of the gods, and traditionally Jews do not speak to God through intermediaries. Furthermore, since counting prayers on beads served no ethical purpose, Judaism never accorded the custom any significance.[11]

Hindu Beads

Prayer beads are central to the life of many Hindus. Prayers are repeated along with the names of favorite gods for hours daily, causing one nineteenth-century observer to note that "the pious Hindu...computes his daily prayers as if they were so many rupees added to his capital stock in the bank of heaven."[12] Two basic types of prayer beads (*mala*) correspond to the two major Hindu cults of Siva and Vishnu. For at least a thousand years, the devotees of Siva have carried rosaries of *rudraksha*, beads made from the seeds of the tree *Eleaocarpus ganitrus* (plate 72). Vishnu rosaries consist of 108 beads made from tulsi, the holy basil *Ocimum sanctum*. It has been suggested that the continued importance of wooden prayer beads in India parallels a preference for wood in the construction of religious buildings.[13]

Buddhist Beads

Originating in India about 500 B.C., Buddhism reached China in the first century A.D., Korea about the beginning of the fourth century, Japan in the sixth, and Tibet in the eighth. As Buddhism became the established religion in these countries, it was influenced by the diverse cultures with which it came into contact. Unlimited tolerance is an essential principle of Buddhism, a concept reflected in the various forms and materials of its prayer beads. This can be seen, for example, by comparing Tibetan Buddhist beads (plates 70 and 74) with those from Japan (plate 73). Differences exist in the elaboration of form, the number and types of pendants and tassels, the dividing beads, and the materials—the Japanese, regardless of their social status, have tended to use wood, while wealthy Tibetans preferred amber and coral or human bone.

Buddhism adopted rosaries from the Hindus. The rosary, an important part of a Buddhist monk's attire, usually consists of 108 smooth beads, corresponding to the number of mental conditions or sinful desires that can be overcome by recitation with the beads. Although monks use full chains of 108 beads, rosaries carried by lay people often consist of only thirty or forty beads.

Favored beads are from the seed of the sacred bo tree, a species of fig (*Ficus religiosa*). The use of beads for meditation and attainment of a mystical state through repetition of prayer has its widest application in Buddhism, particularly in the Himalayan region, where they are still a familiar part of life.

Tibet

In old Tibet, nearly everyone carried or wore prayer beads of wood, shell, amber, semiprecious, or precious stones. The materials differed according to the owner's taste and wealth, and depended too on the devotee's sect and the deity worshiped. The most highly prized beads were made from the bones of a lama (plate 74).

In old Tibetan rosaries, three beads of different sizes and materials were used to divide the full rosary of 108 round or disk beads into four groups of twenty-seven each. At the point where the two ends of the string came together, three large retaining beads were included to indicate the completion of a round or circuit of prayer. These last beads symbolize the triad of Buddha, the doctrine, and the community.[14] Attached to the main string were usually two strands of ten smaller beads. Known as the "number keepers" or counters, these act like a miniature abacus, keeping track of the number of times the user recites his prayers or mantra. The counter strings generally terminate with two small pendants, called the *djore* and *drilbu*. The *djore* (a representation of the conventionalized thunderbolt of Indra) is the single circuit string, while the *drilbu* (a tiny bell) marks every ten repetitions. In addition to these conventions, it is common to find personal odds and ends, such as tweezers or keys, attached to the rosaries.[15]

China, Korea, and Japan

Prayer beads were less widespread in China. Under Manchu rule (1644–1912), however, Buddhist prayer beads, modeled after those from Tibet, became fashionable with the ruling hierarchy and quite elaborate. Called "court chains," they were used in China primarily for status symbols rather than prayer. In Korea, where Buddhism was the official state religion until banned by the Yi dynasty (1392–1910), rosaries were quite an important part of religious rituals. Korean rosaries typically have 110 beads, whereas most Buddhist rosaries use 108. The two extra beads are large: one is decorated with a swastika and located at the beginning of the strand; the other is plain and placed in the middle. A devotional treatise entitled "The Classic of the Rosary" is displayed as a poster on the walls of Korean Buddhist temples. "The Classic" shows a rosary and explains its numerous uses.[16]

Among the Japanese, prayer beads were also an important component of both social and religious life. The beads were carried by monks and lay citizens to funerals and other ceremonial events. All teahouses had a hook on the wall for hanging the beads; an important or unusual set gave prestige to the teahouse.[17]

The Buddhist rosary took on unique forms in Japan, with different sects exhibiting various numbers and arrangements of beads. The most widely used was the *shozoiki jiu-*

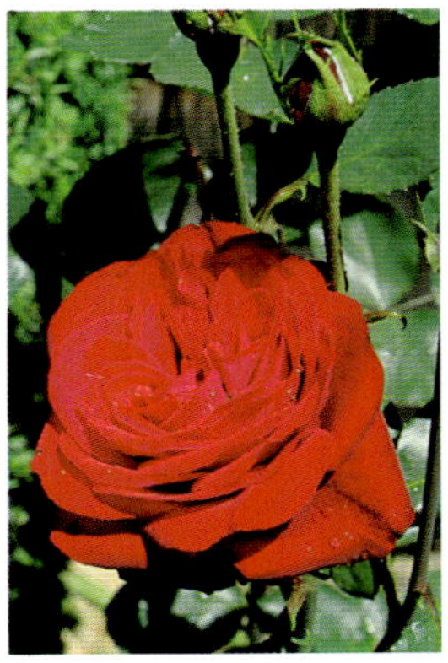

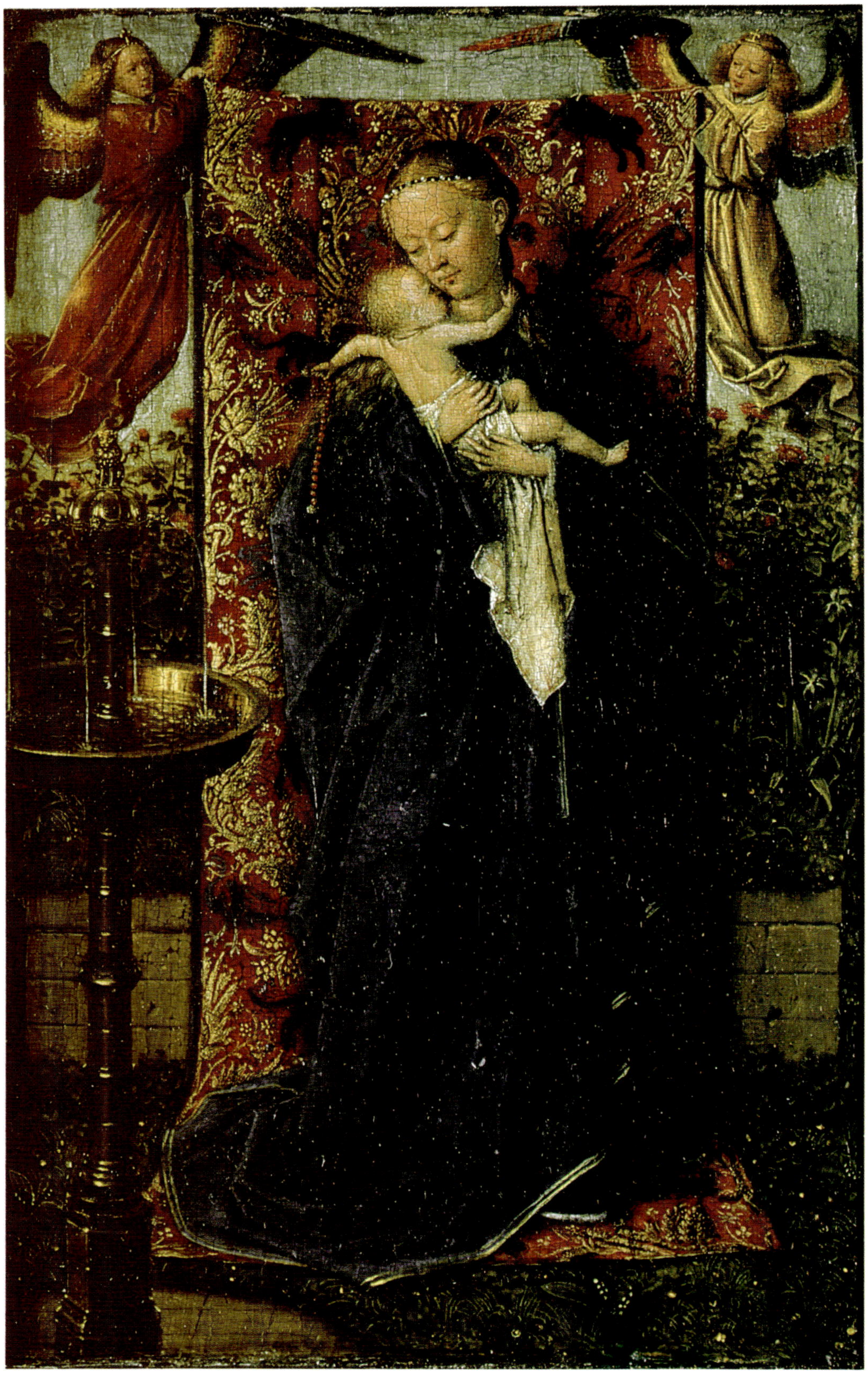

ABOVE: 77. *The rose, the embodiment of beauty, mystery, and perfection in Roman times, became a spectacular Christian symbol. "Rosary" is derived from* rosarium, *meaning "rose garden."*

RIGHT: 78. *Jan van Eyck.* The Virgin of the Fountain. *1439.*

In an enclosed rose garden with a fountain (the "water of life"), the Virgin cradles the Christ Child, who is holding coral prayer beads. The matching color of the coral beads and the roses establishes their connection. This is perhaps the earliest known work showing the relationship between prayer beads and rose gardens. Although the scene was painted at least fifty years before the term "rosary" was officially in use by the church, the association between beads and roses was obviously recognized in Flanders.[11] *Koninklijk Museum voor Schöne Kunsten, Antwerp*

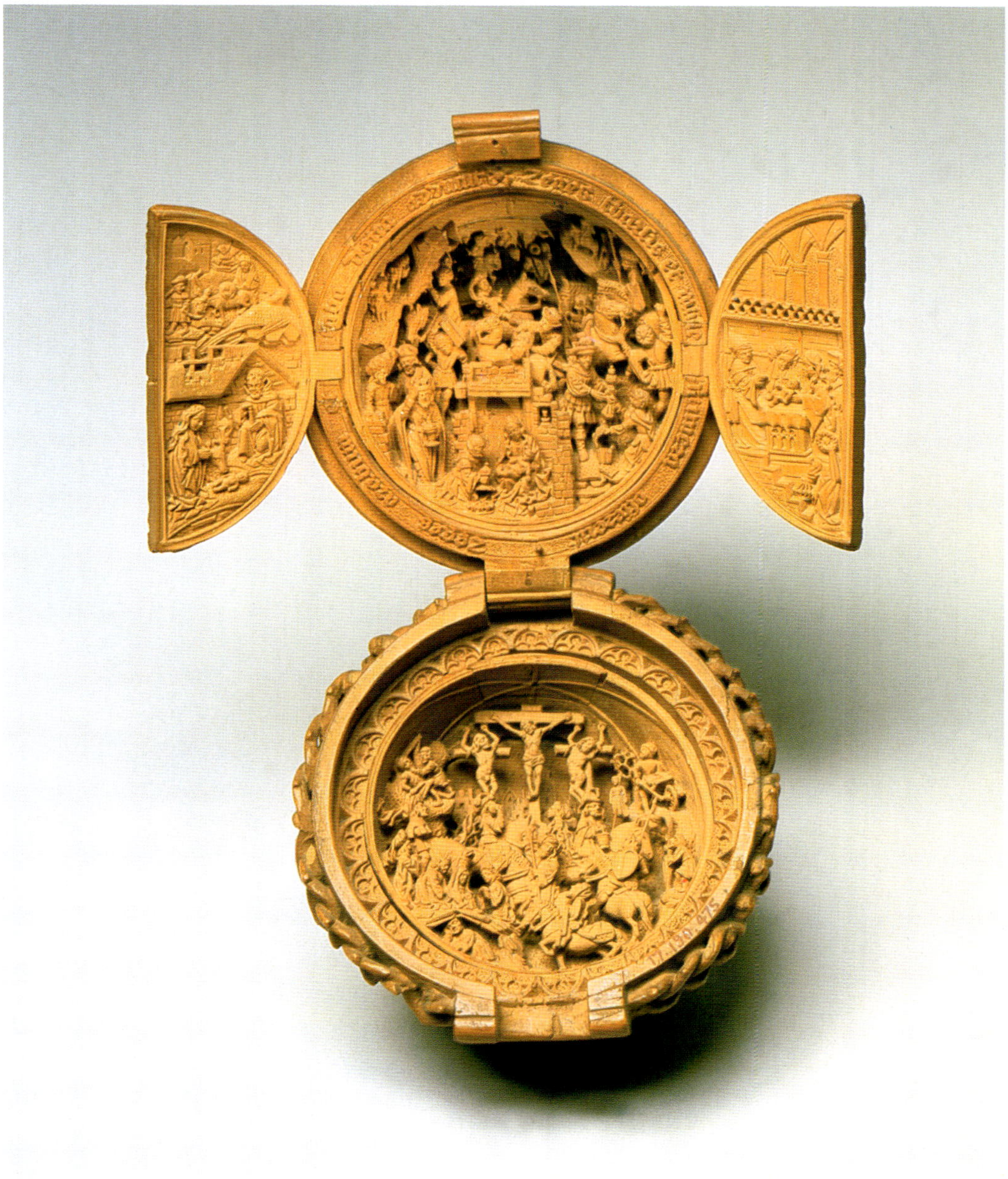

TOP: 79. *A carved boxwood prayer bead made in Flanders about 1500. It usually served as a terminal bead to a one-decade paternoster. The exquisite carving juxtaposes scenes from the life and death of Christ. In the upper sphere, the Nativity, the Adoration of the Magi, and the Annunciation of the Shepherds; in the lower sphere, the Crucifixion. Diameter, 5.4 cm. Metropolitan Museum of Art, New York*

BOTTOM: 80. *A fifteenth-century "thumb" rosary of hollow agate beads, each of which opens, revealing a scene in enameled gold. (The loop is draped over the thumb, and the rosary is thus suspended to count the prayers.) The rosary illustrates the elaborate materialism of the late medieval period, a source of controversy within the church. Length, 51 cm. Musée National du Louvre, Paris*

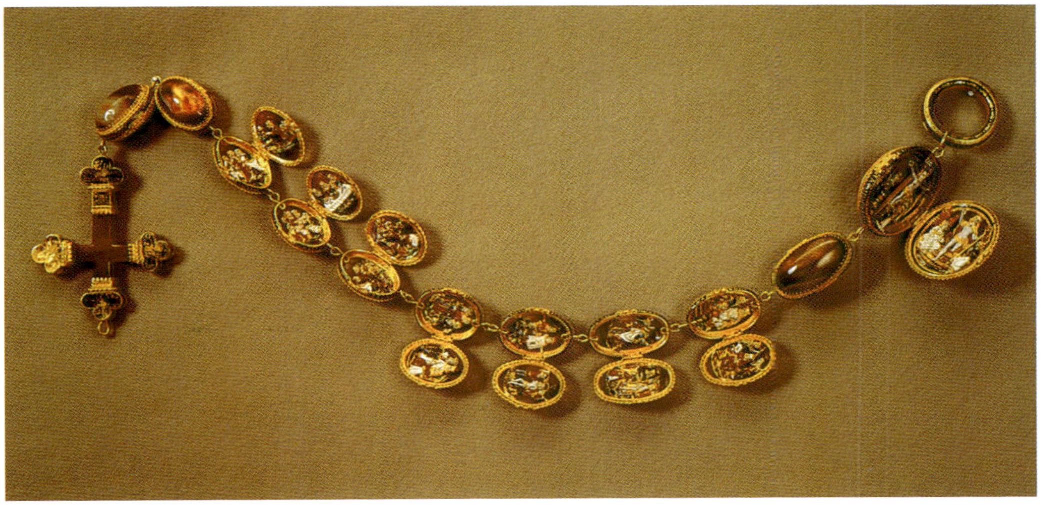

81. *The Langdale Rosary, a fifteenth-century enameled gold English rosary consisting of fifty "Ave beads," six lozenge-shaped paternoster beads, and a suspended gold pendant. Each bead is hollow and decorated with depictions of saints in enamel. The rosary belonged to the Yorkshire family of Langdale. It is possibly the oldest existing rosary in Protestant Europe, since most rosaries were destroyed during the Reformation. Typical bead: length, 1.25 cm. Victoria and Albert Museum, London*

dzu, a strand of 112 beads (plate 73). *Jiu-dzu* shops, often located at pilgrimage stops, advertised their sacred wares by hanging huge wooden rosaries outside the store. A set of prayer beads that had been blessed over the incense smoke of a respected temple was highly valued by its owner.

Wood was the preferred material for Japanese Buddhist rosaries. Cherry, rose, plum, carved and smoothed peach, ebony, and mahogany were all used. Walnut shells, cherry pits, and the nuts of the bead tree (*Melia azedarach*) were also popular.

Islamic Beads

The Muslims probably derived the concept of prayer beads from the Buddhists. When this happened, however, is uncertain. Called *subha,* meaning "to exalt," the Islamic rosary has ninety-nine counting beads in addition to an elongated terminal one, known as the *Iman* or "Leader," "pillar," or "minaret" (plate 75).

The counting beads are used to recite the ninety-nine attributes of God the Holy, the Mighty, the Forgiver, and so forth. The one hundredth bead is reserved for saying the name of God, *Allah.* Devotional phrases recited on the prayer beads include the *tahmid,* "God be praised," and the *tahlit,* "There is no deity but God." Great stock is put into uttering the one hundred names of God and chanting the formulas. A prophet said, "There are ninety-nine names of God, and whoever recites them shall enter into Paradise," and "Whoever recites the *tasbih* and the *tahmid,* a hundred times morning and evening, will have all his sins forgiven."[18] Ultraorthodox, conservative Muslims were, at the time of the prayer beads' appearance, opposed to them. During the thirteenth century Ibn al-Hajj complained that the exaggerated use and esteem of the *subha* was contrary to the primitive simplicity of Islam.[19] Islamic beads are often made of wood, including acacia, olivewood, ebony, sycamore, and sandalwood. Materials such as bone, ivory, coral, amber, carnelian, agate, lapis lazuli, and glass have also been used. In Mogul India (1526–1756), pearls, rubies, emeralds, and sapphires were the beads of the court.[20] Beads of date pits from the sacred cities of Mecca and Medina are revered. Mecca is a huge bead emporium, and a vast array of beads imported from all over the world are sold there. Wooden beads that have been dyed red and immersed in water from the holy well of Zemzem are taken away from Mecca by pilgrims who have made the *hajj,* or pilgrimage, to the sacred Muslim city.[21]

Roman Catholic Rosaries

Different theories exist about the origin of the Christian rosary. Seventh-century graves have disclosed strings of beads twisted around the deceased's hands, a custom still followed in parts of Italy and Japan. Saint Rosalia (742–814), a relative of Emperor Charlemagne's, was reported to have been found buried with a string of little beads that ended in a cross. These beads were probably amuletic rather than counting devices.[22]

The use of beads for saying prayers began in medieval European monasteries almost a thousand years ago. Often illiterate and unable to understand Latin, Christian laity were unable to sing or recite the psalms. Instead, they were given a set of 150 prayers to say, and they used beads to aid in counting.

Most information on European rosaries comes from medieval wills. The earliest mention of a string of beads being used to count prayers occurs in England. The eleventh-century bequest of Lady Godiva to the Monastery of Coventry involves "a circlet of gems which she had threaded on a string in order that by fingering them one by one, as she successively recited her prayers, she might not fall short of the exact number."[23]

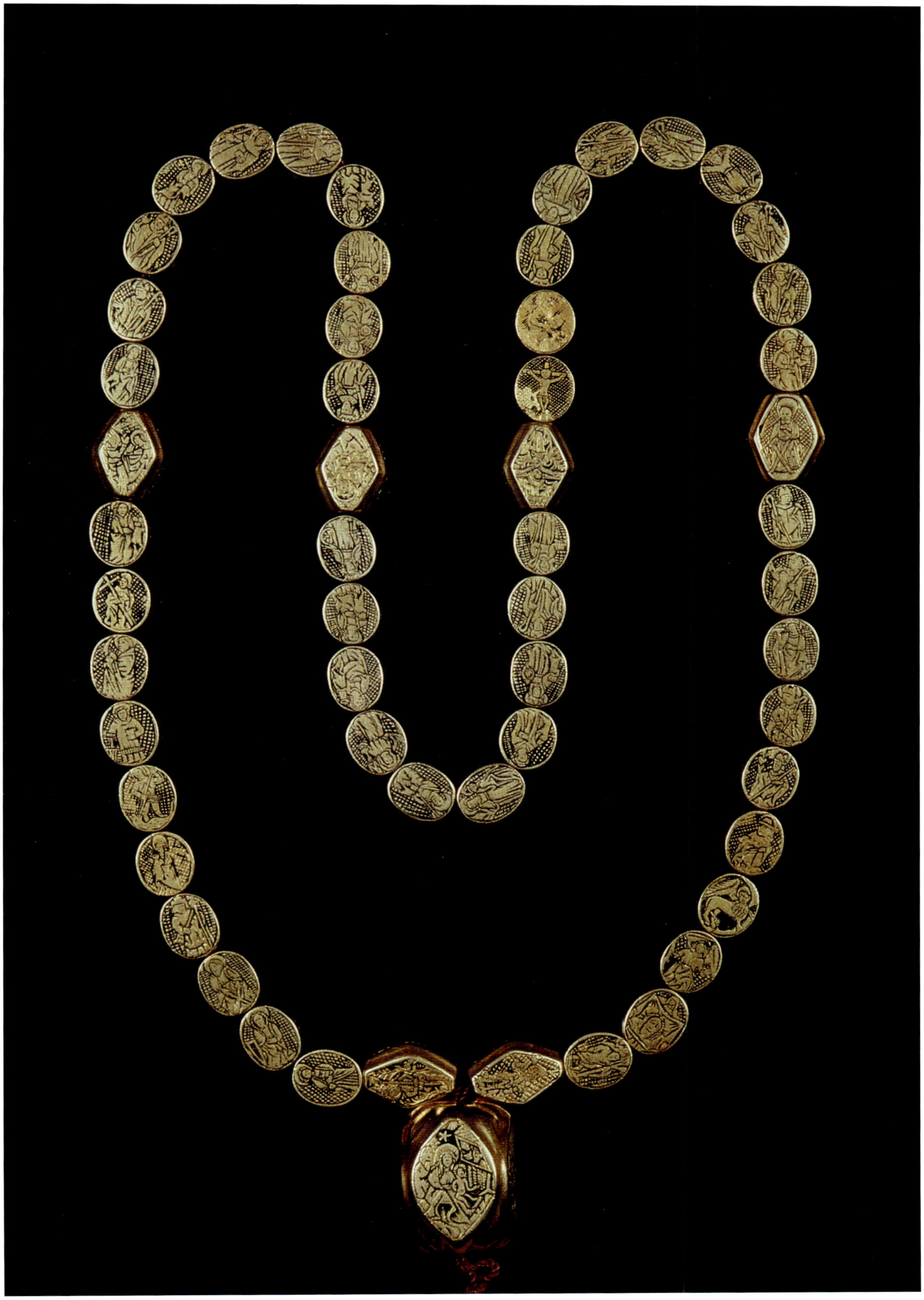

In the mid-sixteenth century, however, Pope Pius V decreed that the rosary had been invented by Saint Dominic (1170–1231). While there is little historical evidence supporting the claim, a series of popes have approved the tradition, and today the Dominicans are officially in charge of making rosaries.[24] The number of beads in a typical Catholic rosary has remained constant since the middle of the sixteenth century. A chaplet of 150 small beads is divided into "decades" (groups of ten beads) by fifteen larger beads. The decade system corresponds to the ten fingers, the original method of counting. A pendant, comprised of one large and three small beads and terminating in a cross, is usually attached to the chaplet.

The 150 beads, known as the "Ave beads," correspond to the number of psalms and are used for reciting the Hail Mary prayer. A decade of Aves, counted on the small beads, is followed by a Paternoster (the Lord's Prayer), for which a larger bead is used. This is followed by the Gloria ("Glory be to God"). The fifteenth Paternoster is counted on the retaining bead, used to close the loop or chaplet. Each of the fifteen decades represents a subject, or "mystery," in the lives of Christ and Mary, which are divided into five joyful, five sorrowful, and five glorious mysteries. The division of the rosary into three sets of five decades, known as "The Three Fifties," allows prayers to be recited on the more commonly used smaller chaplets. The number three, which is a basic component of rosary numerology , has a complex history dating back to early Ireland. It is related to the trefoil of the shamrock, the national symbol of Ireland.[25]

By the late Middle Ages, men and women wore rosaries around their necks, like bandoliers across their chests, or on belts. Rosaries were often clasped in the hands or twisted around the forearm. By the fourteenth century, they were essential possessions as objects of both devotion and adornment. A chronicle of the city of Biberach, dated 1530 to 1540, relates that everyone "carried a paternoster or else was taken not to be a Christian. It was a badge of religion, and therefore of respectability."[26]

By the thirteenth century, makers of rosaries, called "paternoster-makers," had formed guilds that specialized in beads of a particular material. There were paternosters who worked only in amber, and others who specialized in precious stones, metal, or glass. The most common rosaries were those of wood and glass, while beads of amber, agate, and particularly coral were valued for their protective attributes. In the Mediterranean region, the coral of southern Italy and the Tunisian coast was extremely popular for rosary beads. The wealthy owned beads of gold, silver, and precious stones. The elaborate quality of many rosaries became an ongoing subject of controversy. As early as 1261, the Dominicans were forbidding lay brothers to "give themselves airs by using excessively grand beads." In the middle of the fourteenth century, an Augustinian canon of Osnabrück outlawed the wearing of coral rosaries around the neck.[27]

Royalty was not impeded by such limitations. In 1380, a listing of the jewelry of King Charles V of France records nineteen rosaries made of "rose-tinted amber, coral with pearls for markers, gold beads, jet beads with eleven gold crosses, black coral and pearls, coral alternating with beads of silver, and gold beads of Damascus work which were filled with musk." The widow of Cesare Borgia, Charlotte d'Alhret, who died in 1514, had rosaries interspersed with enameled pierced-gold beads for holding scent. It has also been recorded that Mary, Queen of Scots, was beheaded in 1587 while wearing a necklace of pomander beads.[28]

The first descriptions of musk-filled pomanders in the shape of rosary beads stem from inventories of the fourteenth century. Pomanders, often of enameled gold and set with precious stones, were shaped as balls, hearts, or pomegranates. The fashion for wearing scented rosaries was utilitarian as well as aesthetic. In late medieval Europe, musk, cloves, and myrrh, which were commonly placed in the pomanders, were considered to offer protection against the plague.[29]

To control the extravagances, a series of monastic and municipal laws were enacted in which monks were not permitted to wear beads around their neck. Carrying certain beads was permitted, and wearing beads in the belt denoted membership in certain religious orders.

One of the most interesting aspects of the Christian rosary is the history of its name, derived from rosarium ("rose garden").[30] Since classical times, the rose has been universally adored. Its form, fragrance, and color symbolize beauty, mystery, love, and perfection. Aphrodite wore rose perfume and a crown of roses, while the Muses wore garlands of roses and thyme. The ancient Romans associated roses with success and festivity: victorious warriors returning from battle were greeted with roses. In Christianity, the red rose symbolizes Christ's blood and the purity of the Virgin Mary. Originating in the concept of the Paradise Gardens of Persia (with obvious biblical roots in the Old Testament's Garden of Eden), the cloistered rose garden became an essential part of medieval architecture: a secluded, high-walled courtyard filled with fragrant roses. The rose garden was an ideal place for meditation and prayer. Collections of medieval prayers and hymns were bound into books called rosaria ("flower gardens").

By the middle of the fifteenth century, rose gardens, rose garlands, and rosaries were associated with the Virgin Mary and the Christ Child in paintings and in the illustrations of rosary books (plate 78). Religious paintings of the period are often set in rose gardens, under rose arbors, or near a rosebush. Angels and the Christ Child are seen wearing or holding rosaries.

It is unclear at what point the word meaning "a garden of roses" was transformed into "a string of beads used to count prayers." Nonetheless, the spiritual identity of roses was extended to beads, which came to symbolize a permanent garden of prayer called the rosary.

Worry Beads

Visitors to present-day Greece, Turkey, or the Middle East see men and women holding "worry beads." At business meetings in Saudi Arabia, businessmen discuss transactions involving millions of dollars while fingering strings of beads. If questioned, people will deny the beads have any special meaning. However, since there are usually thirty-three beads on the string with a vase-shaped retaining bead ending in a tassel, they are probably derived from Islamic prayer beads. Worry beads, like prayer beads, are made in a great many materials—plastic, glass, olive pits, wood, amber, ivory, and semiprecious stones—catering to various owners' wealth and status. Their primary function as a release for tension provides a security that may, in fact, be subconsciously spiritual.

The secularization of worry beads demonstrates the range of religious and social values associated with rosaries. The arrangement and number of beads, their size and materials, and the way they are worn communicate a great deal of historical, spiritual, and social information. Above all, prayer beads articulate the universal human need for personal adornment. Religious beads, symbolizing piety and fulfilling a practical purpose, could be made of the simplest materials. Yet to fulfill the apparently necessary expressions of social status, prayer beads have been made from a variety of rare and precious materials. However, they are primarily an organizing device, coordinating the fingers, voice, and ears. If used in the prescribed manner, they offer "something to hold onto."[31]

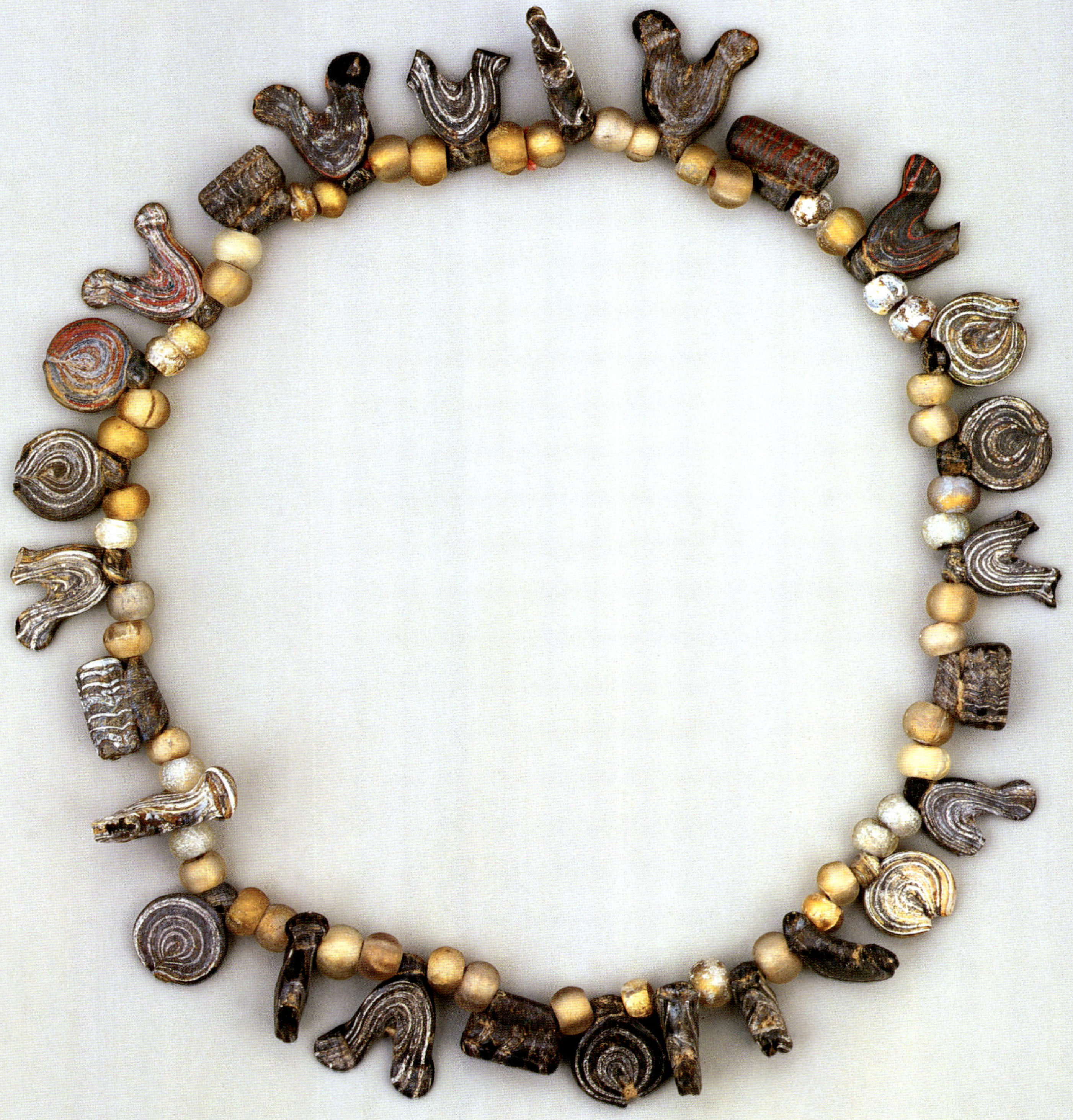

The World of Islam

The art of Islam spans nearly fourteen centuries, three continents, and a wide range of cultures. The Islamic faith originated in seventh-century Arabia with the teachings and revelations of the Prophet Muhammad and quickly spread to Africa, Asia, southeastern Europe, and China.

Despite this vast geographic expanse, a long, tumultuous history, and the significant cultural differences that Islam encompasses, its art has retained a distinct identity. In each area to which Islam spread, local traditions were integrated with Islamic motifs to create new modes of expression. Although great differences exist from region to region, strong underlying iconographic concepts unify much of the artistic output. As craftsmen were able to move freely through Islam's many countries, they concentrated in regions or urban centers with important intellectual communities and politically powerful patrons—in cities such as Damascus, Baghdad, Isfahan, Constantinople, Córdoba, Timbuktu, and Cairo. New styles and techniques were constantly integrated into existing regional traditions, thus creating the overriding characteristic of Islamic art—a unity in diversity.[1]

This dynamic was reinforced by vigorous commercial activity. Islamic merchants became a vital force in international trade. Caravan routes and maritime networks linked Islam's mercantile centers with Scandinavia, Africa, China, and India, resulting in a remarkable diffusion of Islamic styles, techniques, materials, and products. Mosaic-glass beads found in ninth- to eleventh-century Viking sites in Sweden and Denmark, for example, strongly suggest Syrian or Egyptian influence and perhaps even origin (Timeline 384).

Many regions that became part of the Islamic world already had long histories of

82. *Glass beadmaking flourished in the Islamic world—the regional homeland of ancient glassmaking—from A.D. 700 to 1400. Building upon manufacturing techniques from earlier Egyptian and Roman period practices and using traditional Islamic designs, Egyptian and western Asian craftsmen fashioned great quantities of glass beads. Theirs was the last great phase of ancient glassmaking. This early Islamic necklace of combed, marvered, and gold-in-glass beads has concentric circular beads (proto-folded beads) resembling designs of Christian amulets from Syria that appeared after A.D. 400.[1] Length, 51 cm. Metropolitan Museum of Art, New York*

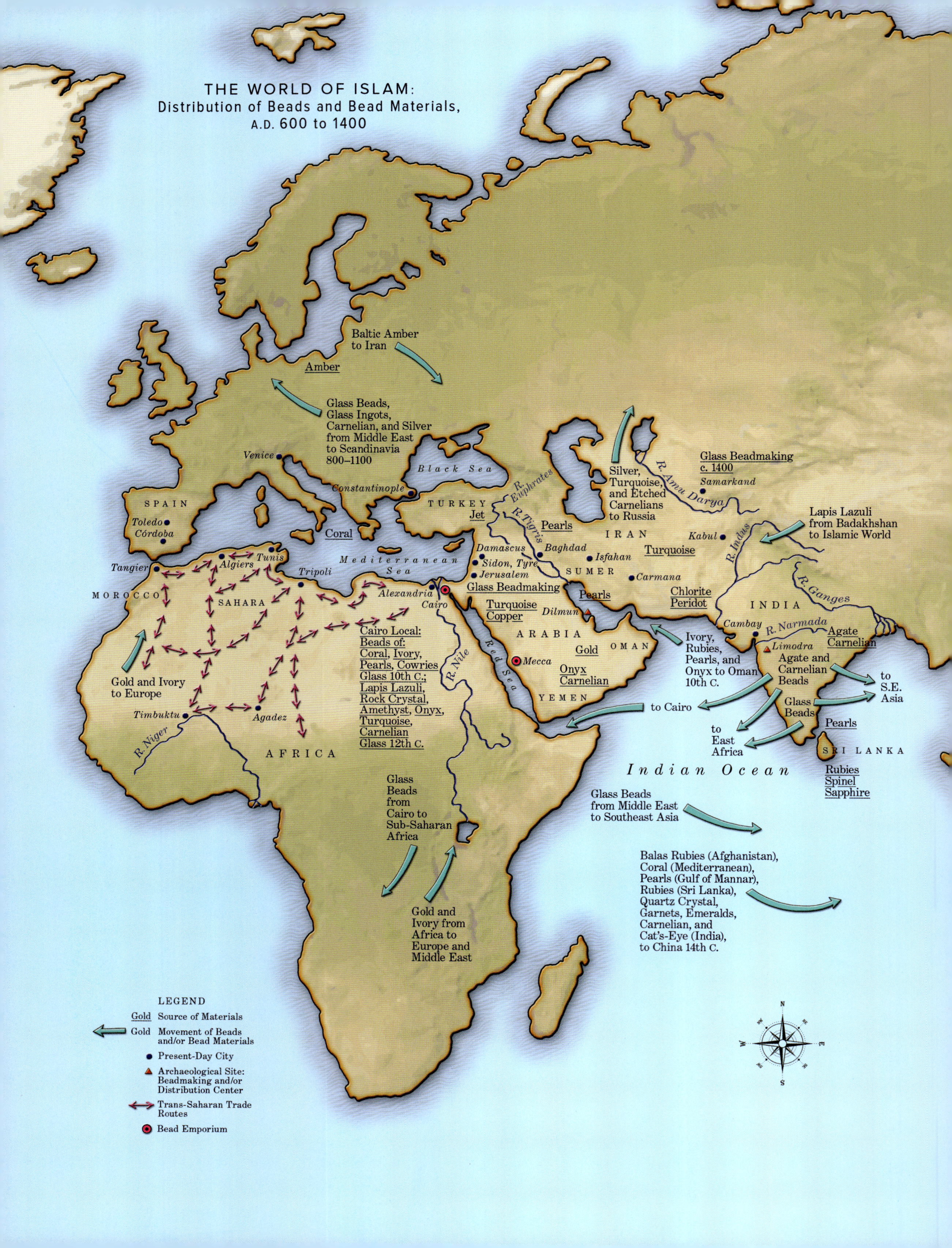
THE WORLD OF ISLAM:
Distribution of Beads and Bead Materials,
A.D. 600 to 1400
Baltic Amber to Iran
Amber
Glass Beads, Glass Ingots, Carnelian, and Silver from Middle East to Scandinavia 800–1100
Venice
Black Sea
Constantinople
SPAIN
Toledo
Córdoba
Coral
TURKEY
Jet
R. Euphrates
R. Tigris
Pearls
Silver, Turquoise, and Etched Carnelians to Russia
R. Amu Darya
Glass Beadmaking c. 1400
Samarkand
Lapis Lazuli from Badakhshan to Islamic World
IRAN
Kabul
R. Indus
Baghdad
Isfahan
Turquoise
Damascus
Sidon, Tyre
Jerusalem
SUMER
Carmana
Mediterranean Sea
Tangier
Algiers
Tunis
Tripoli
Alexandria
Cairo
Glass Beadmaking
Pearls
Chlorite
Peridot
R. Ganges
INDIA
MOROCCO
SAHARA
Turquoise
Copper
Dilmun
Cambay
R. Narmada
Agate
Carnelian
ARABIA
OMAN
Ivory, Rubies, Pearls, and Onyx to Oman 10th C.
Limodra
Cairo Local: Beads of: Coral, Ivory, Pearls, Cowries Glass 10th C.; Lapis Lazuli, Rock Crystal, Amethyst, Onyx, Turquoise, Carnelian Glass 12th C.
Gold
Mecca
Onyx
Carnelian
Red Sea
R. Nile
Agate and Carnelian Beads
to S.E. Asia
Gold and Ivory to Europe
YEMEN
to Cairo
Glass Beads
Pearls
Timbuktu
Agadez
to East Africa
SRI LANKA
R. Niger
AFRICA
Indian Ocean
Rubies
Spinel
Sapphire
Glass Beads from Cairo to Sub-Saharan Africa
Glass Beads from Middle East to Southeast Asia
Balas Rubies (Afghanistan), Coral (Mediterranean), Pearls (Gulf of Mannar), Rubies (Sri Lanka), Quartz Crystal, Garnets, Emeralds, Carnelian, and Cat's-Eye (India), to China 14th C.
Gold and Ivory from Africa to Europe and Middle East
LEGEND
Gold Source of Materials
Gold Movement of Beads and/or Bead Materials
Present-Day City
Archaeological Site: Beadmaking and/or Distribution Center
Trans-Saharan Trade Routes
Bead Emporium
N
S
E
W

trading and cultural exchange. For millennia, finished beads and their raw materials had moved over sea and caravan routes into the Arabian peninsula, home to some of the earliest western Asian civilizations. In the Arabian Gulf, Bahrain served as a trading post between the cities of Mesopotamia and the Indus Valley. Quantities of beads have been found on the island of Bahrain, the site of the ancient city of Dilmun, which had established trade links with the Sumerians of southern Mesopotamia by 2500 B.C.[2]

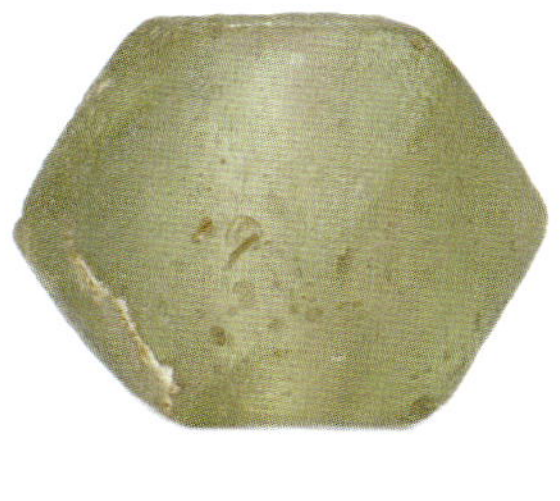

83. *A faceted glass cornerless-cube bead ground or cut by lapidary methods in the seventh-century A.D. Length, 2.7 cm. Private collection*

A vast array of bead materials was traded within Islamic lands, particularly from the tenth through the fourteenth century. Between A.D. 900 and 1000, Cairo became an important center for beadmakers, who imported, processed, and traded coral, pearls, cowrie shells, and African ivory. Cairene artisans also made and exported silver, bronze, and glass ornaments, including beads. A significant Islamic Period glass beadmaking industry was located at Fustat, near Cairo.[3] By the twelfth century, beads of lapis lazuli from Badakhshan, turquoise from Kirman and Nishapur, as well as rock crystal, amethyst, carnelian, and glass, were all so common in Cairo that they suffered price cuts. Only fine onyx from India and Yemen maintained its value at this time. Mecca was also a great center for buying and selling prayer beads of materials from around the world.[4]

The medieval Arab traders were accomplished mariners. From the tenth to the fourteenth century, they shipped agates from western Asia to Mecca, Cairo, and Alexandria, from where they were dispersed throughout the Islamic world. Traders carried agate and glass beads from the Red Sea to the east coast of Africa, establishing permanent outposts in which beads were traded for ivory. At this time, Islamic ships carried Ceylonese rubies, Indian carnelian, emeralds, garnets, pearls, coral, and cat's-eye to China, where they were fabricated into beads. Marco Polo recorded that at Baghdad, pearls from India (and presumably the Arabian Gulf) were drilled and exported to Europe in great numbers.[5]

The manufacture of Islamic glass beads was the last important phase of traditional western Asian glass beadmaking. The Islamic world included many regions in which significant artistic styles and glass manufacturing techniques had already evolved, notably Egypt, Mesopotamia, Syria, the Levant, and Sasanian Persia. Although Islamic craftsmen developed their own glassmaking aesthetics, their repertory was built upon the pre-Islamic traditions. Recalling technical and stylistic concepts that originated nearly four thousand years earlier in Mesopotamia and Egypt, fine Islamic glass beads were primarily derived from Roman period beads made after the division of the empire in the late fourth century A.D. Islamic glass beads developed their own distinctive dragged and trailed, feathered, festooned, and folded patterns. The most original development was the polychrome folded bead. Glass beadmaking centers of note were in Egypt, Syria, and the Levant. Recent archaeological excavations in the Jewish quarter of the Old City of Jerusalem uncovered evidence of a glass workshop that produced vessels at various times between A.D. 661 and 1250, but it is not clear if beads were also part of their production.[6]

Islam is an all-encompassing religion: faith is the center of a Muslim's life, and religious principles guide all endeavors, including art and design. To prevent idolatry, Islamic art has remained primarily abstract and symbolic, consistently avoiding pictorial representations of the divine. Four basic patterns of decoration are used: geometric, floral, and calligraphic designs, and stylized animal and human figures. This "language of decoration" provided a unified framework of imagery within which Islamic craftsmen have had considerable freedom of expression. Islamic design is rich and intricate, but details were rarely isolated ends in themselves. The artists' highest priorities, whether in carpets, tiles, furniture, or beads, are the beauty of overall design and harmony of color.[7]

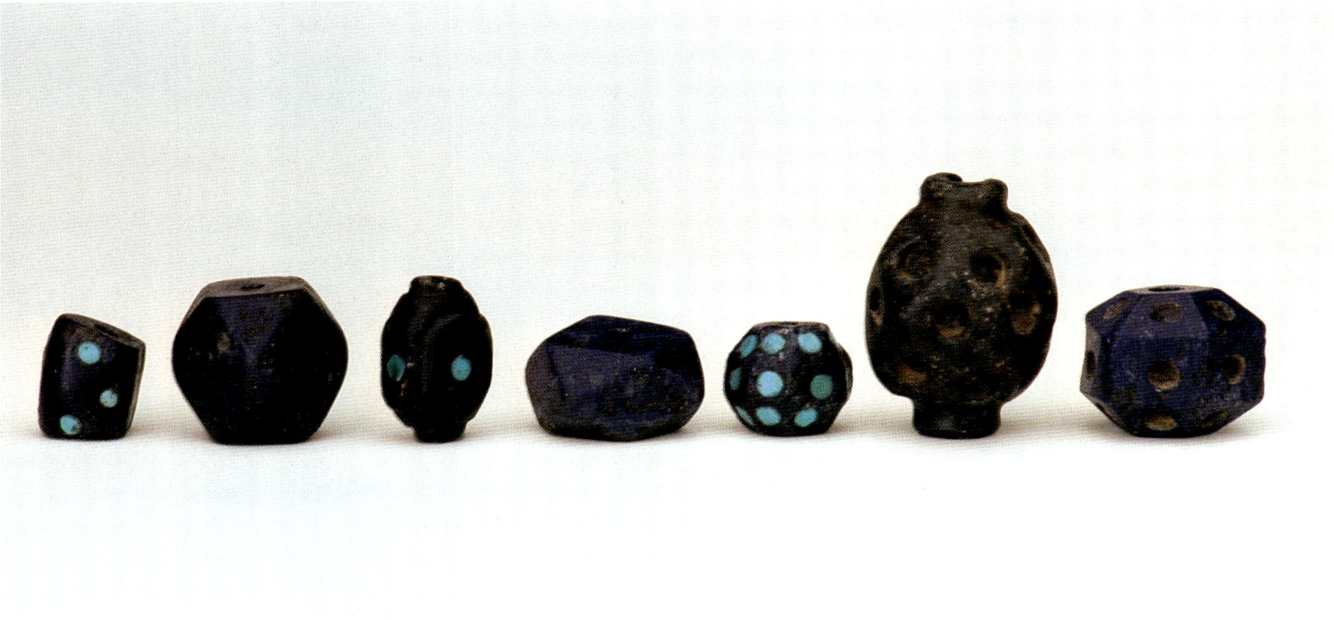

ABOVE: 84. *Faceted lapis lazuli beads made in Iran between the ninth and the sixteenth century A.D. Craftsmen in Islamic countries, especially Iran, developed faceting in tandem with their interest in polyhedral forms. Mathematics was considered an integral part of art, reflecting the underlying geometric patterns in nature. Faceting stones into polyhedral forms articulated that relationship. Second bead from right: length, 2.1 cm. Collection Henry Anavian, New York*

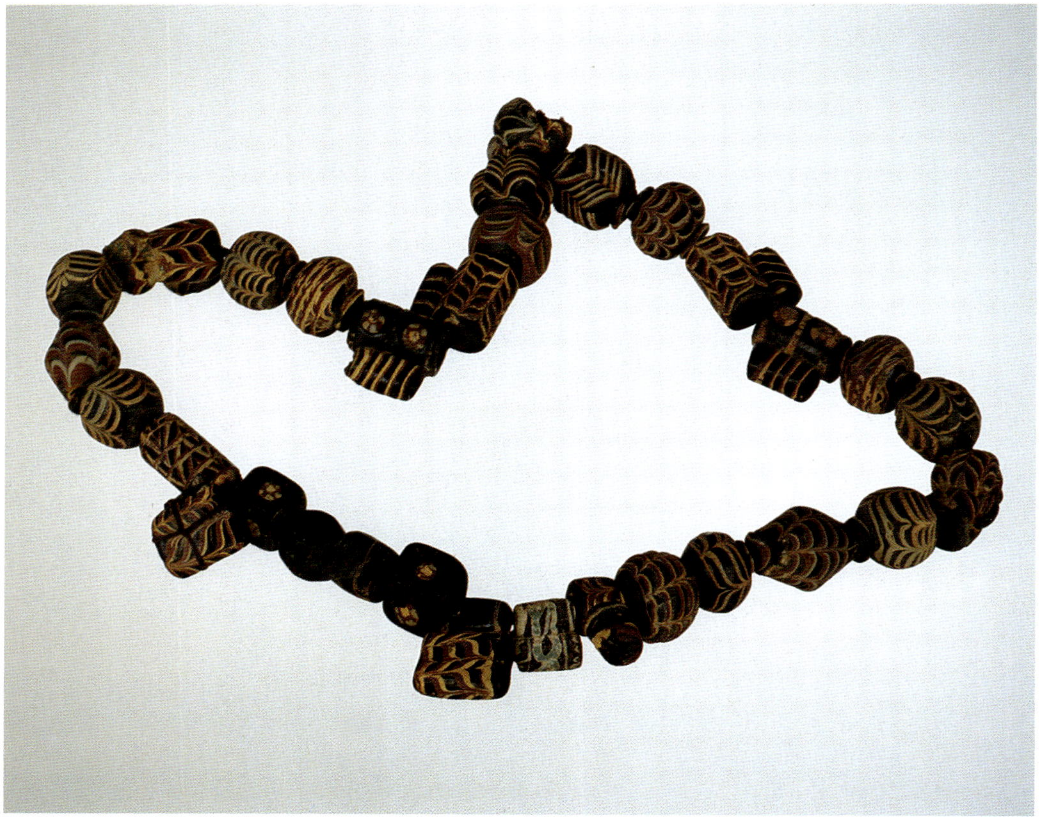

RIGHT: 85. *A necklace of opaque black wound-glass beads, probably made in Iran or Syria between A.D. 900 and 1300, with typical geometric and arabesque lines in repetitive patterns. Largest bead: diameter, 3.2 cm. Corning Museum of Glass, Corning, New York*

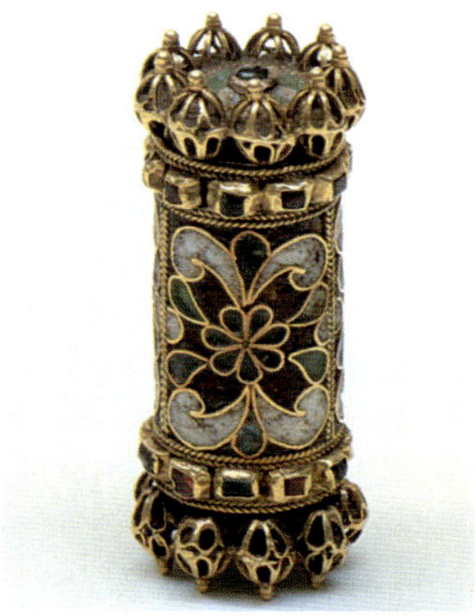 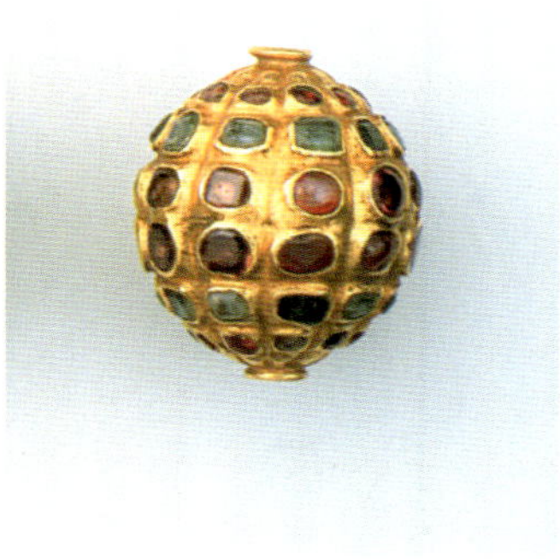 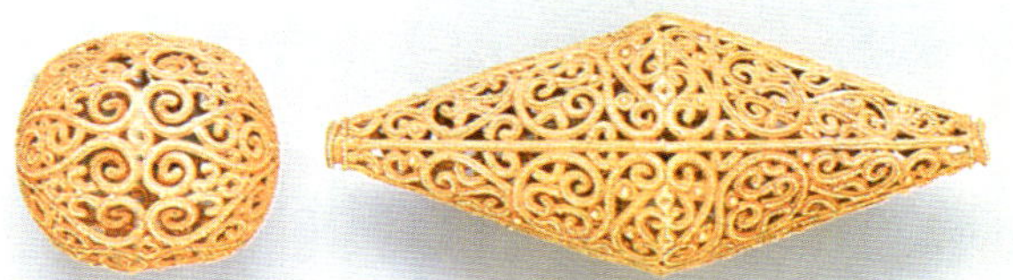

Within the Islamic world, beads serve as status symbols, portable wealth, and amulets. Amulets were worn primarily by women and children, who were thought to require more protection than men: nowhere is the eye bead worn more often to avert the evil eye than in the Middle East. Men wear the *subha*, a strand of thirty-three or ninety-nine prayer beads corresponding to the ninety-nine "beautiful names" of *Allah*. The Koran refers to stars as "beads of the sky."[8] Stars (like beads) are bright and shining "heavenly eyes" that offer protection by lighting up the darkened skies.[9]

It has generally been true throughout Islamic history that an individual's wealth determines which materials will be used for his or her beads. In Islamic lands today, the choice of jewelry usually distinguishes townspeople from poorer villagers and nomads. Urban women tend to wear gold and precious stones, while women who live in the countryside, such as the Bedouin, wear chain and beaded necklaces of brass, silver, copper, and glass. In the past, wood, ivory, amber, and semiprecious and precious stones like carnelian, lapis lazuli, turquoise, and agate were all expensive and equally favored for their amuletic value. Turquoise, *fayruz* in Arabic, means "lucky stone" and is believed to protect the wearer from poison, reptile bites, and diseases of the eye; by changing color—after exposure to heat and sunlight, turquoise sometimes changes color—it warns of the approach of death.[10] Throughout western Asia, wearing carnelian jewelry is thought to repel evil and offer protection against the envious. Its great popularity among Muslims is said to stem from the fact that Muhammad himself wore a ring set with carnelian that he used as a seal.[11] Lapis lazuli beads were common in children's jewelry. Fashions have also governed the choice of beads: in Iran during the eleventh and twelfth centuries, glazed white quartz was particularly in demand.[12]

The role of beads in Islamic cultures may well have been enhanced by the importance accorded to circles and spheres in medieval Islamic thought. The Quran (Koran), Islam's holy book, emphasizes the relationship between the visible world and underlying reality, a philosophy that encouraged the exploration of relationships between design principles and mathematics. Muslims consider mathematics an integral part of art and believe that geometric patterns underlie all natural phenomena. For the Muslim, "The circle is the primary cosmological symbol, one of wholeness and unity."[13] By the twelfth century, Arab mathematicians, exploring theoretical geometry and the philosophy of Platonic solids, discovered that all regular and semiregular forms are based on the sphere. From the basic circle and a hexagonal arrangement of tangential circles of the same radius surrounding it, three primary shapes emerge: the triangle, the hexagon, and the square. During the tenth, eleventh, and twelfth centuries, artisans, particularly Iranians,

ABOVE LEFT: 86. *Similar in design to a Moorish architectural column, this cylindrical gold bead from sixteenth-century Spain is set with emeralds and rubies. Gold filigree scrolls serve as cloisons for white, green, blue, and violet enamel. Openwork filigree balls decorate the ends. This bead possibly served as a cassolette for scent.[11] Length, 5.2 cm. Hispanic Society of America, New York*

ABOVE MIDDLE: 87. *An unusual late Islamic gold bead from eighteenth-century Morocco, set with emeralds and rubies (or garnets). Length, 2.49 cm. Metropolitan Museum of Art, New York*

ABOVE RIGHT: 88. *Gold openwork filigree beads with granulation, a combination of techniques perfected by Syrian and Egyptian artisans in the tenth and eleventh centuries A.D. The openwork filigree has been constructed without additional support. These beads exemplify the Islamic artistic ideal of balancing pure geometry with flowing, organic forms. Biconical bead: length, 5 cm. Metropolitan Museum of Art, New York*

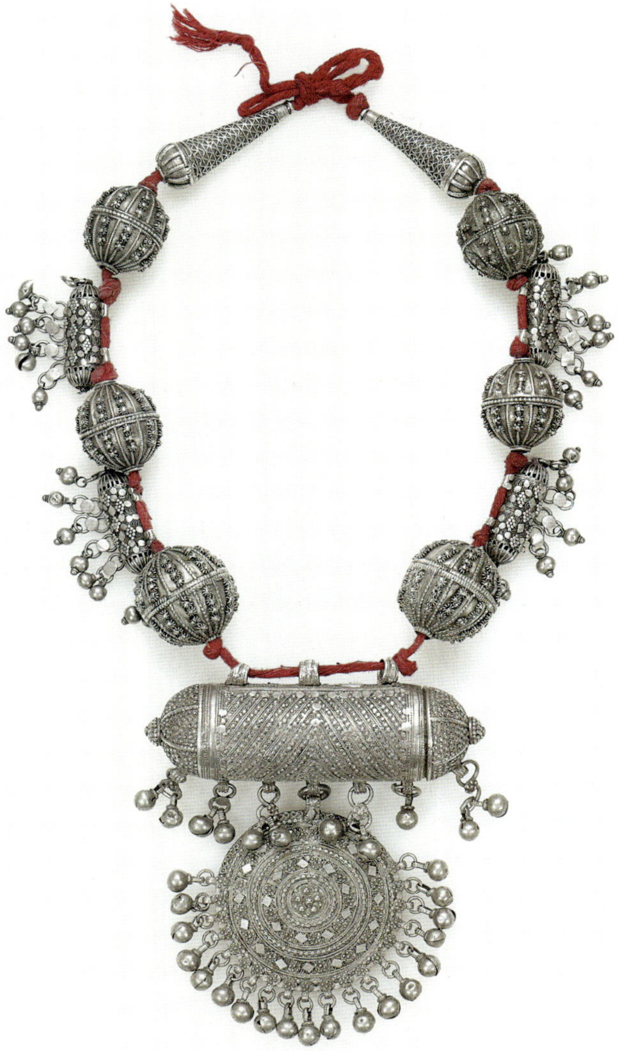

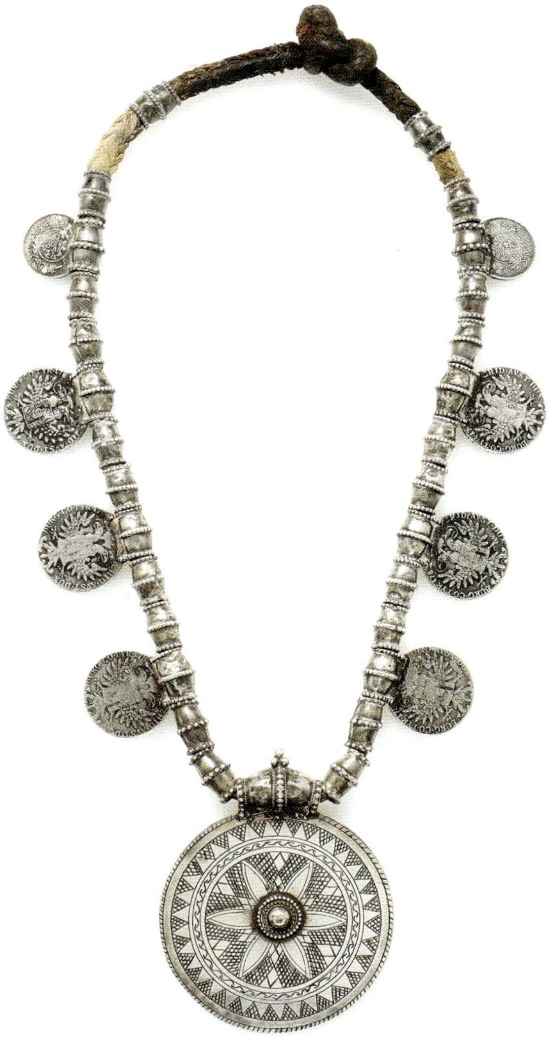

ABOVE LEFT: 89. *Silver beads from the late nineteenth or the early twentieth century showing various embossing styles and silver "shots" (larger-scale granulation) found only in Yemeni jewelry. Unlike Oman, Yemen, at the southern tip of the Arabian peninsula, remained relatively isolated for centuries, and its jewelry developed strong indigenous features, including heavily ornate compositions with considerable granulation.[III] Typical bead diameter, 3.7 cm. Collection Ivory Freidus*

fascinated by the ideas of the sphere as the minimal unit of design, developed a whole family of patterns based on a five- and ten-part division of the circle. In accordance with these principles, polyhedral beads were developed by faceting spheres into hexagons and octagons. The practice of grinding stones into complex geometric forms also indicates that bead craftsmen had learned of the natural crystalline structure of the stones they were working.[14]

The use of gold and silver filigree patterns superimposed over spherical beads was another technique used by Islamic artisans to make complex geometric forms. The art of filigree reached a high level of technical and aesthetic perfection among medieval Islamic smiths, which permitted the manufacture of lightweight hollow forms that required less gold. Gold polyhedral beads were often "filigree illusions," in that wires and tiny granulated balls were adhered to the surface of a hollow gold or silver bead, so that the edges of the resulting polygons hid an underlying spherical form.[15]

There may be an intriguing link between astronomy and these filigree techniques in medieval Islamic beads. Islamic craftsmen mastered filigree beadmaking just as mathematicians and Moorish navigators were recording that astrological patterns in the sky had correlations in the contours of the land and channels of the seas. Their findings were mapped with intricate linear constructions. These patterns, which were often drawn on globes, may well have served as prototypes for the first Islamic filigree beads.[16]

Not many gold beads remain from the early and medieval periods of Islam. Items of openwork filigree are typically very fragile, and jewelry made of precious metals was often melted down later into more fashionable shapes. Furthermore, there were probably never great quantities of filigree beads. Islam used gold sparingly, since the Quran calls for moderation in adornment, as in other things.

However, silver jewelry, including silver beads, was considered less ostentatious than gold and was worn in abundance throughout the Islamic world. In Tunisia, for example, silver was considered a symbol of truth and purity, while gold was associated with vice. Arabic euphemisms express the financial importance of jewelry, noting that "metals are for hard times," and "jewelry is for adornment and investment."[17]

In early nomadic and seminomadic Islamic cultures, craftspeople were often despised because their work did not contribute directly to the livelihood of the tribe. Silversmiths and goldsmiths were therefore often outsiders; frequently, they were Christians, Sabittes, or Jews rather than Muslims. The Jewish smiths of Sana in Yemen were famed throughout the Arab world for their craftsmanship.[18] Most of the Jewish Yemenite community emigrated in the 1950s, and their silversmithing traditions are now practiced in Israel.

Dating Islamic stone beads is often difficult. One reason for this is that Islam prohibits the burial of worldly goods. Even when this law was ignored, the stone beads found in burials are generally spherical or barrel-shaped forms, which were produced prolifically over the centuries and are not easily datable. There are exceptions, including the amulet-case (Timeline 561) and faceted beads, which can occasionally be dated by quality, material, and technical complexity. For reasons of finance and fashion, the majority of Islamic gold and silver beads have been melted down over the centuries. The relatively few surviving metal beads are dated primarily by their manufacturing techniques, since design patterns have changed little through time. Bead necklaces were also regularly restrung and recombined from generation to generation, further eliminating historical clues.

Thanks to the profusion of glass vessels and objects created during the golden age of glassmaking under Islamic rule, glass beads are less difficult to date. Most of the Islamic beads preserved from the seventh to the fourteenth centuries are made of glass and have distinctive geometric, combed, feathered, festooned, and folded patterns with stylistic and technical parallels in Islamic glassware of the period. Also, it may soon be possible to assign Islamic glass beads accurate dates, as well as manufacturing locations, by studying the color of glass. Archaeological finds are not only revealing that patterns of distinctive colors changed over time, but that most glassmaking centers seemed to specialize in certain colors.[19] That specialization probably reflects not only the vagaries of taste, but also the availability of minerals and coloring agents that were obtained through trade.

Mongol conquests of western Asia in the fourteenth century ended major glass manufacturing in the region, a tradition that had lasted more than thirty-five hundred years. When Tamerlane captured Damascus in 1401, many craftsmen were removed to Samarkand. This included beadmakers from Tyre, where glass beads had been continuously produced since Phoenician times.

Although isolated glassmaking continued in regions of Egypt, Iran, Syria, Jordan, and Turkey, activity now centered on the West. By the fifteenth century, Venice had become the bead-producing capital of the world.

OPPOSITE, RIGHT:
90. *Nineteenth-century necklace from Oman made of Austro-Hungarian Maria Theresa silver dollars (thalers) and silver beads. Oman was a prosperous international commercial center renowned over the centuries for its silverwork. From the mid-1700s until the 1930s, the chief source of silver for Omani artisans was the thaler, which had a consistently high silver content. The quality of silver was important because jewelry was bought both for adornment and investment.*

The form of this necklace is traditional: thalers are linked by silver beads to a decorated medallion. The geometric and floral patterns are characteristically Islamic. Original pieces of this quality are rare, as silver was often melted down to make new, more fashionable jewelry.[IV] *Central medallion: diameter, 9.8 cm. Private collection*

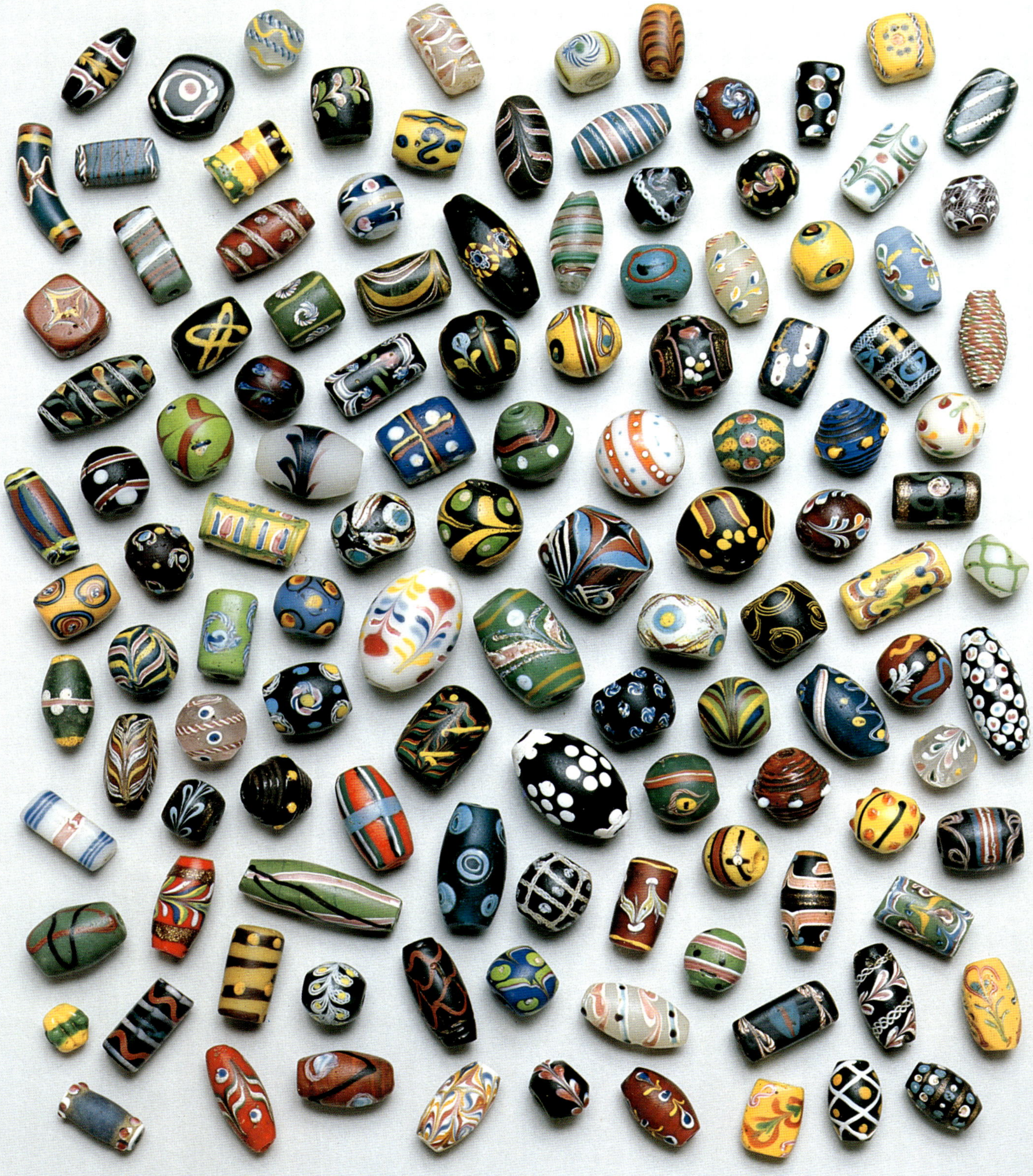

The Age of European Expansion

From the Renaissance until the Industrial Revolution, beads occupied a minor place in European adornment. Lavish jewelry, reflecting the abundance of precious stones and metal flowing into Europe from colonies in the Americas and the East, dominated courtly and aristocratic fashion. Although beads were not greatly coveted by Europeans after the Renaissance, European glassmakers nevertheless mass-produced huge quantities of beads, which were then carried by explorers and traders to non-European peoples around the globe. Selling for great profits in the foreign markets, beads were an important component in the newly developed global trading networks. By the nineteenth century, new materials and manufacturing techniques enabled most Europeans to own jewelry, and as social mores discouraged ostentatious displays of precious jewels, beads once again came into style and were worn by all classes of people.

Shortly before 1500, technical improvements in ship building and navigation gave Europeans the ability and confidence to sail great distances. In rapid succession, bold captains ventured into previously unknown seas: Columbus landed in the Americas in 1492; Vasco da Gama reached India in 1498; and by 1519 Magellan had sailed around the tip of South America. Europe was now linked by sea to most of the earth's shores.

Prior to 1500, the Islamic world, India, and China had far wealthier and more sophisticated civilizations than Europe. Yet within three hundred and fifty years, the balance was reversed. By 1850, Europeans controlled the oceans, had established colonies in Africa, Asia, and the Americas, and were running organized, immensely profitable worldwide commercial transactions. The expansion of European civilization was preceded by a period of significant change within Europe itself. In western Europe, during the late 1300s, there were secular challenges to church doctrine. Intellectual cu-

91. *One hundred and twenty decorated wound-glass beads, most of which are from the nineteenth century. Beads of this type were made in vast quantities: distinct varieties number in the thousands. Illustrated here are a few of the less common types found in West Africa in recent years.*[1]

From the late fifteenth to the twentieth century, explorers and traders carried European glass beads throughout the world. The beads were enormously popular in Africa and North America in particular. The result of this seemingly inexhaustible demand led to a proliferation of bead types, designs, and manufacturing techniques. Sizes ranged from micro (less than 1 millimeter) to macro

(13 centimeters long). Worked over a flame, these beads were produced by first winding filaments of glass on a wire or mandrel (metal rod). While still viscid, the crude bead was then paddled or rolled over a flat, grooved, or contoured form to produce various shapes. Again worked over a flame, thin canes of glass were then trailed or thin cross sections of canes were applied to the surface. The bead was again paddled or shaped, forcing the applied layered design into the background glass and yielding a smooth, finished product. Beads shown 7/8 of actual size. Picard Trade Bead Museum, Carmel, California

riosity focused on understanding and exploring the natural world. Through translations of Islamic works on medicine, mathematics, and astronomy, Westerners discovered that the Muslims possessed sophisticated scientific knowledge far surpassing what was available in Latin.[1] By the mid-fifteenth century a resurgence of interest in the classical arts and sciences, known as the Renaissance, started in Italy. More than a thousand years had elapsed since the decline of the Roman Empire, but Italians now looked to their magnificent past for philosophical and artistic inspiration. Latin and Greek classics opened up a vision of life unencumbered by church doctrine, in which individual expression was of central concern. With the intensified interest in ancient Greek and Roman culture, aesthetic standards embodied in their writings, sculpture, and architecture became ideal norms. In painting and sculpture, systems of perspective, effects of color, and realistic treatments of nature and the human form—expressed, for example, in the works of Michelangelo and Leonardo da Vinci—were investigated.[2] The Renaissance spread throughout the Continent, profoundly affecting every aspect of European life, including adornment. In contrast to medieval proscriptions, the wearing of jewelry was embraced as an important component of dress.

By the mid-fifteenth century, necklines of women's clothing began to fall, and for a brief period during the early Italian Renaissance jewelry ceased to convey status and rank, serving instead simply to enhance female beauty. The new fashion was inspired by the aesthetics of classical art and the study of human anatomy. In the late fifteenth century, Sandro Botticelli portrayed Simonetta Vespucci with pearls entwined in her flowing hair. Portraits by Piero della Francesca, for example, show simple bead necklaces of coral, garnets, and pearls setting off the sitter's slender neck or emphasizing the soft beauty of the breast.[3] This short interlude of harmony between body, dress, and ornament was soon replaced, however, by more aggressive jewelry styles that relegated beads to a minor place in European adornment until the nineteenth century.

Jewelry of the late Renaissance and baroque periods (c. 1550–1750) reflected the plentiful supplies of precious stones and metals that began to pour into Europe from the Americas and the East (particularly India), a result of the new overseas colonies. The fashion was to display wealth and power. Introduced by the Spanish court, whose territories in the New World provided an abundance of gold, pearls, and emeralds, lavish, autocratic standards in dress and jewelry soon spread to other European courts profiting from colonial resources.

The restraint shown in the early Renaissance disappeared. Court adornment typically included heavy gold chains, enameled and jeweled pendants, rings on every finger, and precious stones and pearls sewn into clothing. The treasures of Europe's royal families epitomized this display of riches: the crown jewels of a country, a significant concentration of treasure, were not only symbols of status but were even pledged as surety against loans and frequently used to underwrite the payroll for armies and governments. A heavy, ninety-eight-ounce gold chain worn by Henry VIII, for example, served a dual purpose. Beyond its regal appearance, each link represented a unit of currency; in times of fiscal emergency, the links could be removed and used for payments.[4] Thus, the weight and intrinsic value of these particular metals and gems were of prime political importance.

As a result of the access to great supplies of precious stones—emeralds from South America, colored gems from the East, diamonds from India and eventually Brazil—the cutting and polishing of stones was admired as a new science. Soft, rounded cabochon forms were almost entirely replaced by the sharper geometric style of the lapidary.[5] By the baroque period, jewelry was designed primarily to display stones, par-

THE AGE OF EUROPEAN EXPANSION: 1500 to 1850 A.D.

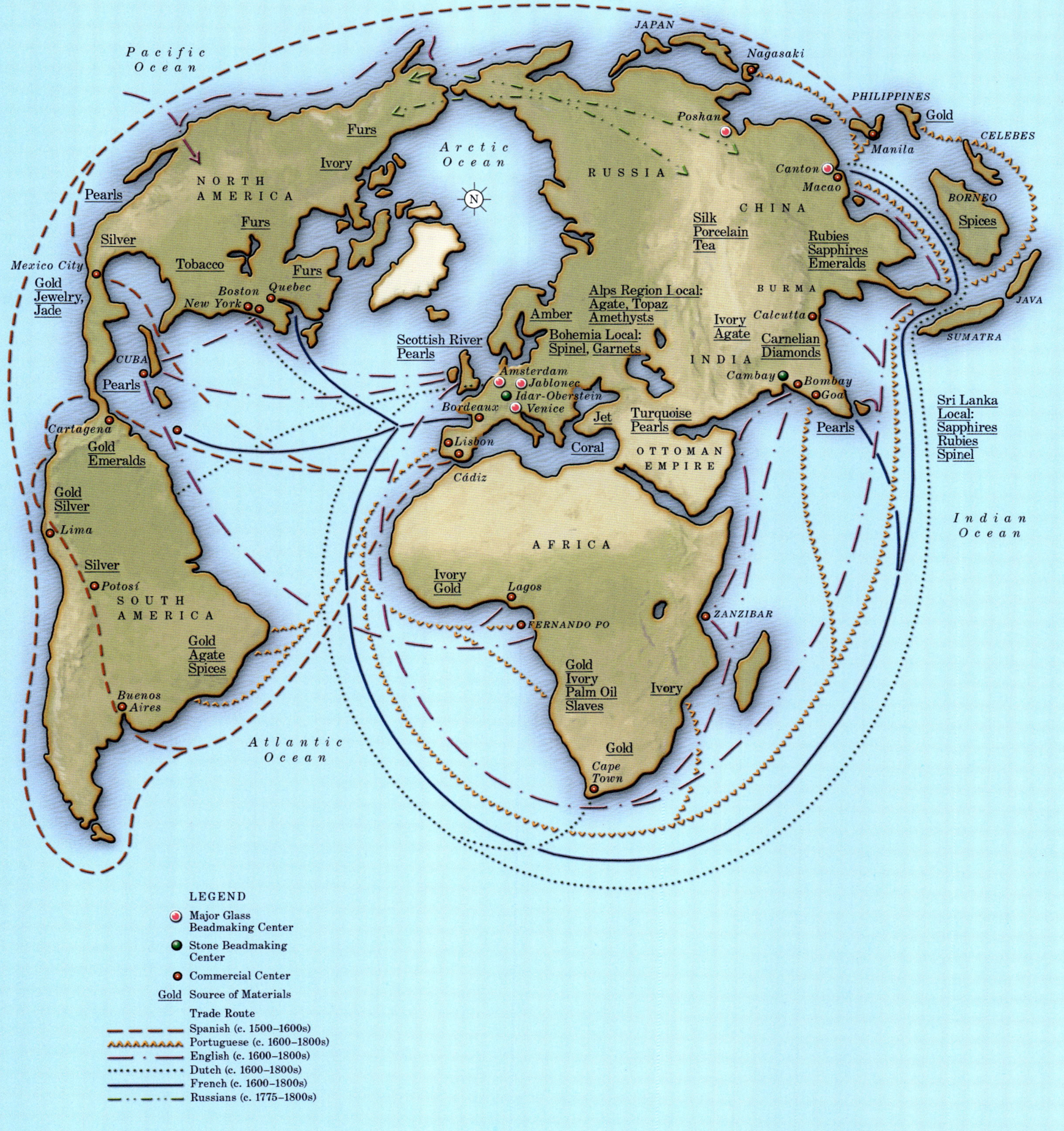

ticularly faceted diamonds, to their best advantage.

There were, nonetheless, some beads worthy of being worn by the elite. Queen Isabella, who ruled Spain with King Ferdinand from 1474 to 1516, and whose jewels backed Columbus's voyages to the New World, ordered her merchants to bring her beads. Inventory records kept for Isabella include bead necklaces of twenty-two-karat gold, amber, coral, jasper, and crystalline (possibly glass) beads, as well as jet beads shaped like crosses. Pearls were also gathered for her in enormous quantities: an inventory of 1499 notes she had strings with more than two hundred pearls on them.[6]

Moorish jewelry of the fifteenth and sixteenth centuries included thinly pierced gold beads from the province of Almería and hollow, enameled gold beads that contained scent.[7] In Venice, fine filigree came back into fashion toward the end of the sixteenth century. The best example of this is known from a necklace of beads in the Museo Poldi Pezzoli in Milan. Each bead is constructed of fine openwork gold filigree decorated with stylized flowers in green and blue enamel. Faceted amber beads were sometimes capped with gold filigree.[8]

From the late sixteenth to the early eighteenth century elaborate pearl necklaces and bracelets accompanied extravagant displays of pearls embroidered onto clothing. The pearls were obtained from the Persian Gulf, the East Indies, and freshwater mountain streams in Saxony, Bohemia, and Bavaria. After 1675, when demand outstripped supply, Parisian craftsmen perfected imitation pearls (which had first been made in the 1400s). They lined the interiors of hollow glass beads with a nacreous solution of ground-up blackfish scales (found in the Seine), which was stabilized with wax.[9]

A new phase of jewelry design began with the Industrial Revolution, which was under way in England by the mid-eighteenth century and in full swing throughout the Continent by the nineteenth century. The emergence of a large middle class changed demands and customs. New materials and manufacturing techniques brought great quantities of fine jewelry within the reach of a mass audience. In earlier times, faience and glass beads had essentially fulfilled the same purpose, working with the available technology of their eras.

Before the nineteenth century, precious ornaments directly reflected the social rank of the wearer. This relationship was altered by the Industrial Revolution as well as by political events. The French Revolution and the revolutions of 1848 were generally followed by periods of austerity in reaction to court excesses: these were not times of luxury or display. As a result, the aristocracy altered their tastes. Beads of coral, amber, rock crystal, and glass were worn not only by the middle class, but also by the nobility for daytime jewelry. Cut-steel beads and cast-iron jewelry were substituted for precious stones and metal. The recessions that reigned over Europe after the Napoleonic Wars contributed to the rapid development of cast-iron jewelry after 1815. Cast-iron jewelry was already known in Paris by the time of the French Revolution, and there was a saying "I gave gold for iron." Garnet beads, made by town craftsmen and traded at marketplaces, were popular with rural people.[10]

Parures (sets) of Mediterranean coral and English jet beads were worn by wealthy European women during the 1830s.[11] After 1827, jet was used as "mourning" jewelry, a practice that continued throughout the century after Prince Albert's death in 1861 led his widow, Queen Victoria, to keep mourning almost constantly fashionable in England.[12] Mourning jewelry reached morbid depths when human hair from the deceased was knotted or braided into beaded necklaces.[13]

Nineteenth-century design was eclectic. The evolving mass-production techniques of the industrial age produced considerable concern that fine craftsmanship would disappear; thus, a demand developed for the styles of the past. Stimulated by archaeological

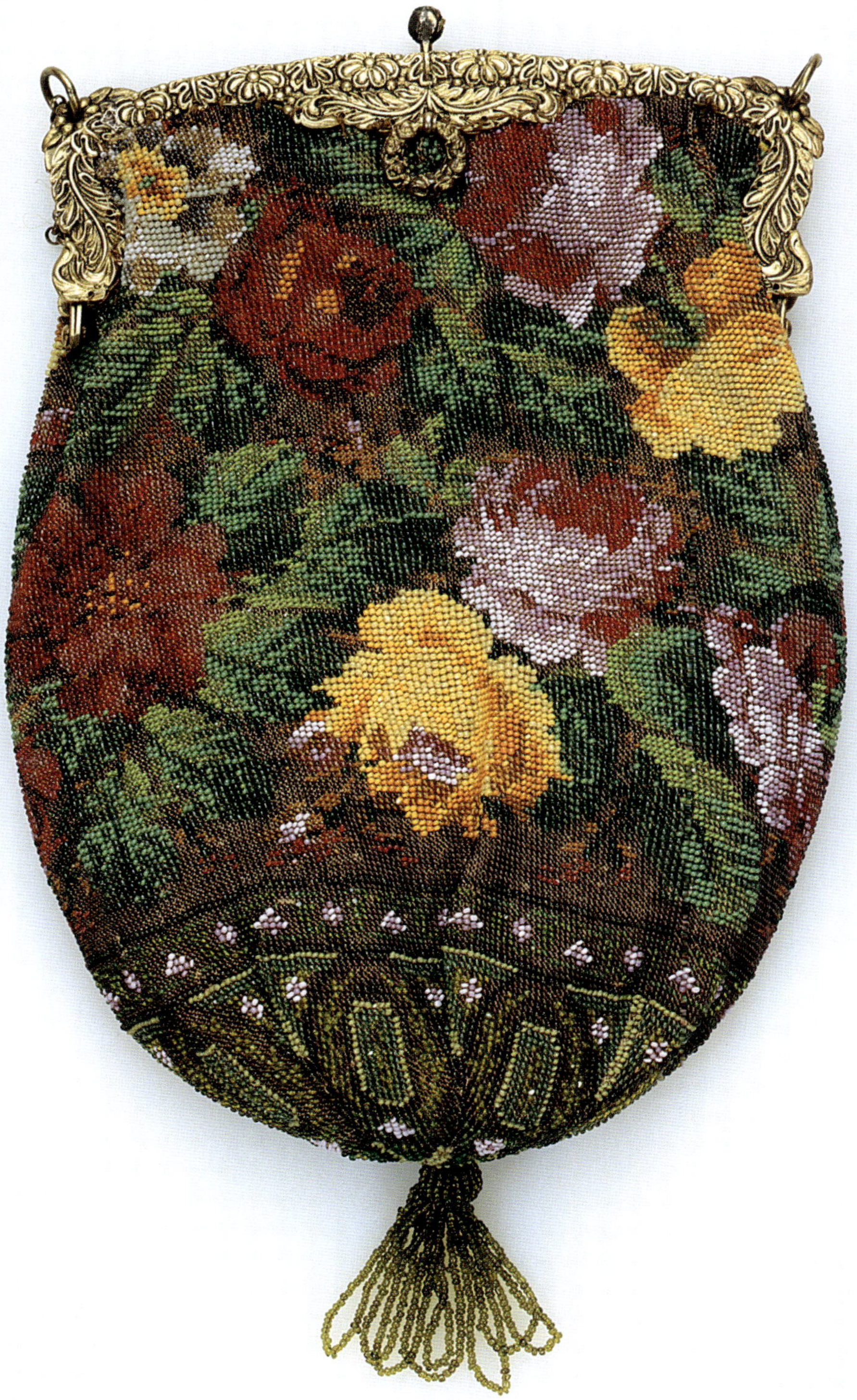

92. *An 1850s beaded bag from France. (The metal frame closure was added c. 1920.) Tiny glass "seedbeads" (one-half millimeter to one millimeter long) crocheted with silk thread form the floral pattern. Although most European glass beads were exported, small, round seed and tubular "bugle" beads were used for embroidering clothing and accessories, a custom fashionable since the Renaissance. Length (top of frame to bottom of fringe), 28 cm. Private collection*

explorations in Egypt, Greece, Italy, Africa, and western Asia (most notably, German classicist Heinrich Schliemann's wonderful gold finds at Troy), jewelers revived the techniques and styles of ancient adornment. The excavations uncovered examples of English Celtic and Etruscan and Greek gold filigree beads that served as excellent prototypes for new jewelry styles.

Two of the most famous neoclassical goldsmiths, Italians Fortunato Pio Castellani in Rome and Carlo Joseph Giuliano in England, rarely set stones but often included beads in their work. The prevailing interest in antiquities meant jewelers returned to polished rather than faceted stones, which they chose from a select range of carnelian, onyx, and lapis lazuli and interspersed with granulated gold beads.[14] Castellani had an important collection of ancient bead necklaces that he studied in great detail. Some of these pieces, which are now owned by the British Museum, obviously had direct influence on his work (plate 45).

It was only with the introduction of the Art Nouveau style at the end of the nineteenth century that imitations of ancient jewelry styles ceased, and a contemporary, modern aesthetic developed that affected beads as well as all forms of adornment.

The Glass Bead Industry

The most important chapter in the story of beads from the Renaissance to the twentieth century belongs to the European glass bead industry. During this period, most explorers, traders, and missionaries carried glass beads with them as gifts or objects of barter. Their activities created considerable markets, and the result was an enormous increase in the volume of bead production, accompanied by a proliferation of bead varieties as well as continual improvements and refinements in manufacturing techniques.[15]

When Europeans set sail, their hosts accepted beads for a variety of reasons. Indonesians and Filipinos coveted stone and glass beads, which they had obtained from Indian, Middle Eastern, and possibly Chinese traders. In the New World, however, glass was completely unknown and was treasured as a rare substance when it was introduced by the Europeans. The introduction of tiny, colorful glass seedbeads was frequently welcomed as a replacement for more labor-intensive adornment techniques. Woodland and Great Lakes tribes in North America, for example, greatly expanded the range of decorative forms and colors that could be produced on clothing and other objects, using glass seedbeads rather than traditional porcupine quills.

For Europeans, whose aim was to maintain maximum profits with a minimum commitment of manpower and resources, glass beads, exchanged for American furs or African ivory, gold, and slaves, yielded enormous margins—1,000 percent was the return on investment, according to a report in 1632—and thus became a central part of international trade patterns.[16] Beads, of course, were only a part of a complex trading cycle: rum, cloth, guns, and beads were sent from Europe to Africa; slaves from Africa were taken to the New World; and sugar, tobacco, and silver and gold bullion from the New World went to Europe.[17]

An important dimension of the European commercial expansion was the ability to integrate their efforts with preexisting trade networks. As a lively bead trade had existed in most of the world for millennia, European traders frequently used the same routes, where their further success depended on identifying local bead tastes and responding with appropriate goods. The prosperity enjoyed by major glass factories in Venice, Holland, Bohemia and Moravia (present-day Czech Republic) was often a result of providing specifically shaped beads in desired colors and patterns. Since tastes varied widely between countries as well as neighboring villages, the variety and quantity of beads produced was enormous.

Beads traveled circuitous routes, and unraveling the workings of the bead trade is quite complex. Carnelian beads excavated from slaves' graves in Barbados were probably from India (but possibly Venice), and accompanied tribesmen from Africa. Other stone beads found in Louisiana (dated 1731–63), Florida, Tennessee, Mississippi, and Venezuela may well have been sold in the New World by the Spanish, who obtained them from English, French, Dutch, Portuguese, or Venetian traders.

The glass bead trade was equally complicated. It is often difficult to know whether a bead was made in Venice or Holland, the date of its manufacture, or the exact route by which it arrived at a particular site. Not only did Venetians set up glass bead workshops in Holland, France, Bohemia, Moravia, and England (thus dispersing Venetian techniques and styles), but many middlemen carried beads throughout the trading cycles. Nevertheless, as a result of intensive archaeological and historical research during the past decade that has focused on the glass bead trade, accurate data and chronologies are emerging.[19]

Venetian Glass Beadmaking

The earliest and most renowned European glass beadmaking centers were in Venice, Holland, Bohemia and Moravia. Although glass factories existed in Italy, France, Switzerland, Spain, Belgium, England, Germany, and the Baltic, Venetian glassmakers dominated the world market in volume, quality, and diversity until the twentieth century.[20]

Venice's rise to glassmaking supremacy corresponded with the decline of the western Asian industries. After Tamerlane's Mongol armies overran Damascus, Tyre, Aleppo, and Sidon in 1401, glass beadmaking practices that had lasted over three thousand years were effectively ended, and quality glass was no longer produced in the region. The Venetians filled this void, successfully inheriting the role of glass beadmaker for the Western world and subsequently taking over markets in Africa and Southeast Asia that had been supplied by India for centuries.[21]

While it is not possible to trace a continuous tradition of glassmaking from Rome to Renaissance Venice, there is much evidence to suggest that the exceptionally strong reemergence and growth of the industry during the Middle Ages was made possible by Venice's cultural and maritime ties with Byzantium and the eastern Mediterranean. It is also believed that after the Ottomans sacked Sidon and Tyre and then captured Constantinople in 1453, glassmakers from these ancient centers went to Venice.[22]

The beginnings of Venetian glass manufacture are not clear, but the discovery of glassmaking furnaces, vessel fragments, and mosaic cubes, dating from A.D. 600 to 650, on the island of Torcello in the Venetian lagoon implies glass production occurred in the vicinity from an early point in Venice's history.[23] Venice itself was founded by the Lombards in A.D. 568.

Although glassmaking is recorded at Venetian monasteries in 882, the foundations of their great glass industry were established primarily from 1200 to 1400.[24] In 1292, all glass factories were relocated from Venice to the island of Murano, a fifteen-minute boat ride across the lagoon, to protect Venice from the risk of fires (always a possibility from the constantly burning furnaces) and to keep glassmaking procedures secret.

The production and export of beads were always important to the Venetian glass industry, even though beadmaking can be traced only to the early 1300s. At that time, Venetian galleys carried beads to the Black Sea, Flanders, and England.[25] It is known, however, that in 1279 German peddlers in Venice were restricted to buying ten lires' worth of glass rods (which were presumably for making beads); by 1280, Venice had established a glass trade with the eastern parts of the old Roman Empire; and Venetian glass was shipped to Rhodes by 1345.[26]

PLATES 93–96: *Glass beads used in the Africa trade. This important collection of glass trade beads was acquired by the British Museum in 1865 from Moses Lewin Levin, a London bead merchant whose import-export business operated from 1830 to 1913. Manufacturer's sample cards or catalogues, such as these examples, are extremely useful for documenting what was being produced and sold at a specific time and place. It is, however, possible that the handwritten notes were added at a later date and some of the information may not be totally accurate.*

Most of these beads appear to be Venetian, although in 1898 the Levin Company was listed as an importer of Venetian, Bohemian, and German beads. (The beads on plate 96, for example, are mostly Bohemian, as are the two bottom right beads on plate 94.) While it is recorded that the beads were used for barter in Africa, many were also traded into North America.[11] Collection of the British Museum at the Museum of Mankind, London

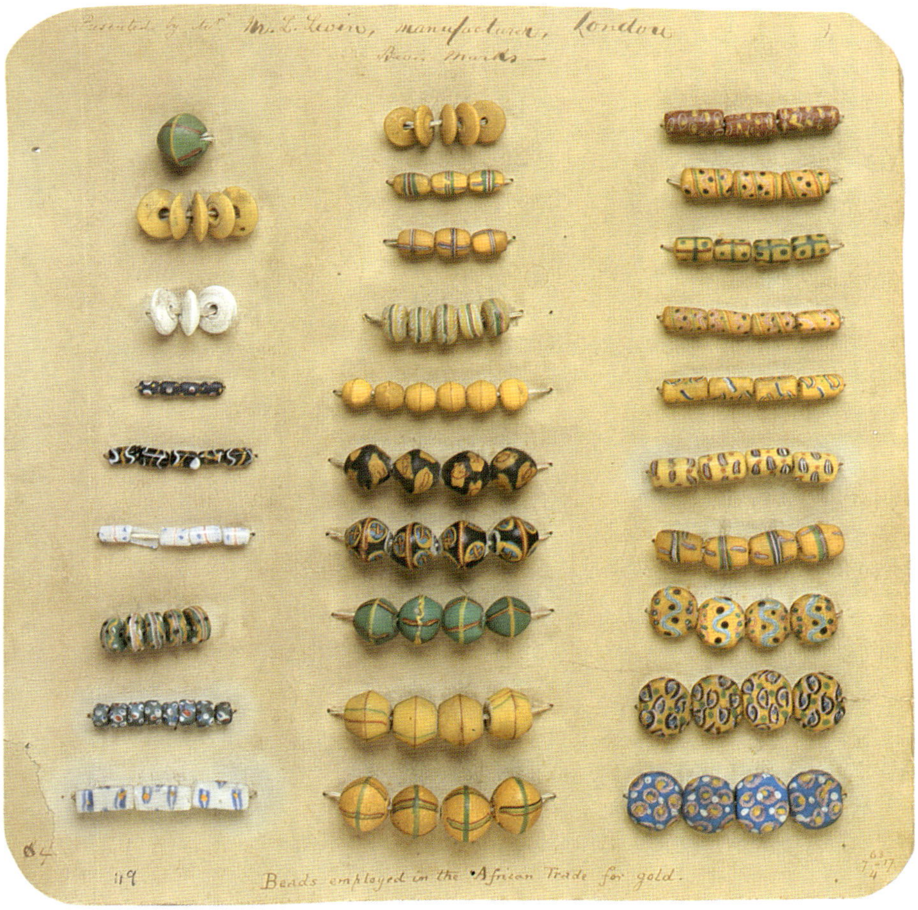

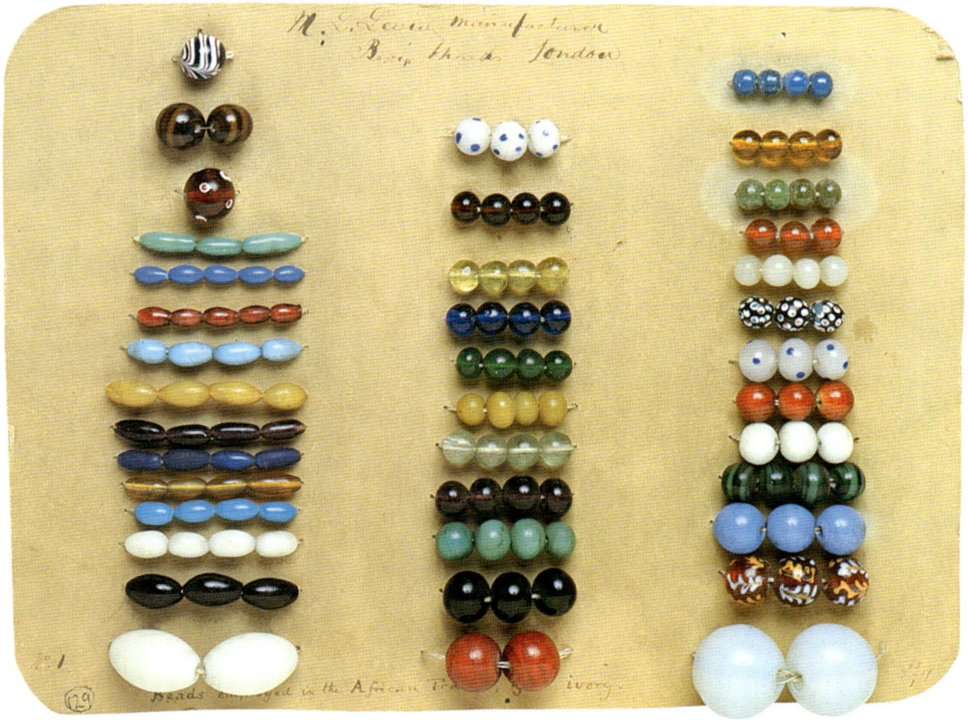

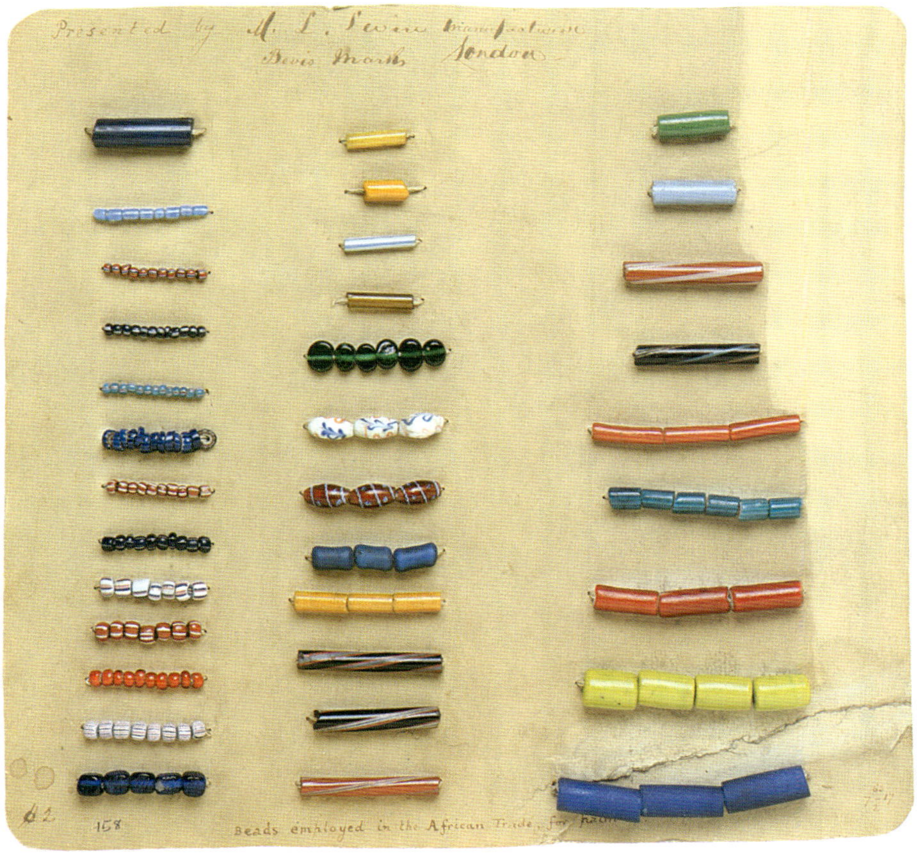

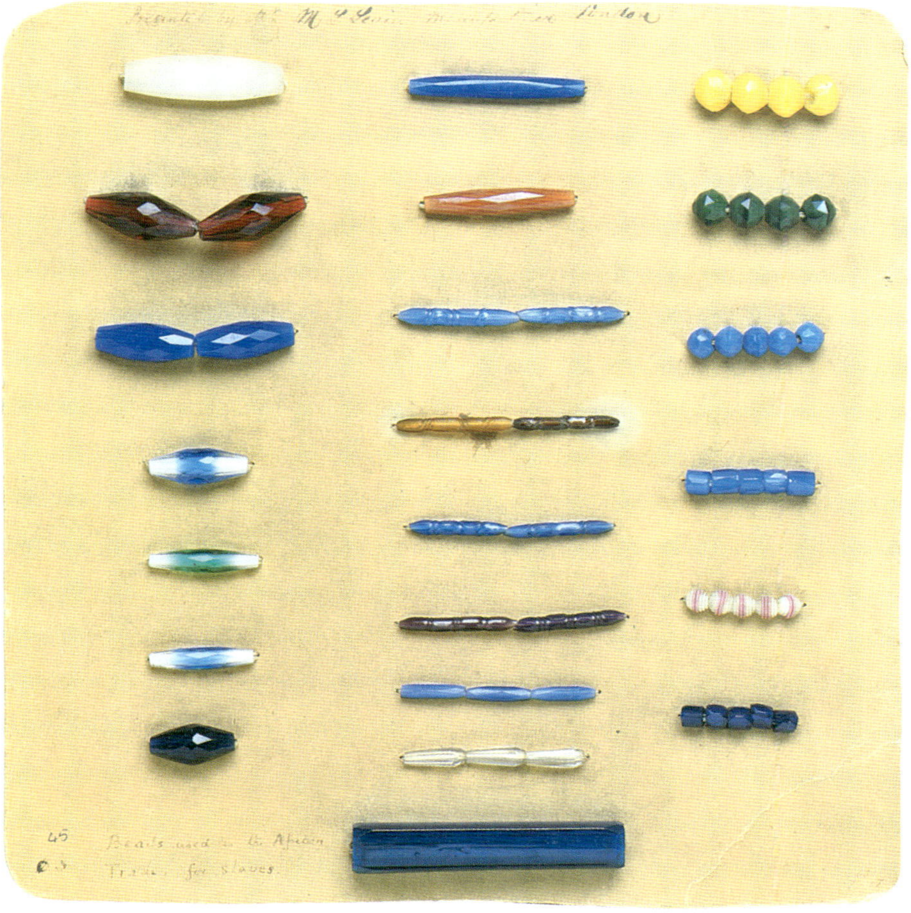

OPPOSITE, TOP: 93. *Beads traded in Africa for gold. Top left bead: diameter, 1.69 cm.*

OPPOSITE, BOTTOM: 94. *Beads traded in Africa for ivory. Top left bead: diameter, 1.48 cm.*

TOP: 95. *Beads traded in Africa for palm oil. Top left bead: length, 3.2 cm.*

BOTTOM: 96. *Beads traded in Africa for slaves. Top left bead: length, 5.2 cm.*

Although Venice could offer its glass industry enormous advantages over its competitors—it had a sophisticated network of commercial relationships and a powerful mercantile trading fleet with links to the Black Sea, the Mediterranean, and northwestern Europe—the authorities feared competition. To establish and maintain their monopoly, laws were enacted in 1490 that placed the glassmakers' guild under the direct jurisdiction of the Council of Ten—the highest governing body in the Venetian Republic. For the next fifty years, Murano glassmakers were forbidden, upon penalty of death, to divulge glassmaking secrets or to leave and set up competitive establishments elsewhere.[27]

After the move to Murano, beadmaking greatly increased in volume due to important changes in glassmaking techniques. Furthermore, Venetian glassmakers of the period were strongly influenced by highly complex ancient Egyptian and Roman glass artifacts, which they were inspired to reproduce. By at least 1468, the process of drawing hollow cane beads had been reinvented and introduced to Murano. Quickly outnumbering the quantities of beads produced by the slower winding method, drawn canes permitted the mass-production of beads in a range of sizes and made new types possible, including seedbeads, rosetta beads, and layered beads such as the *cornaline d'Aleppo*.[28]

Glass beads are classified by their technique of manufacture: wound, drawn, wound-on-drawn, molded, mold-pressed, and blown. Different beadmaking centers generally emphasized the use of certain techniques. For this reason, it is helpful to understand how a bead was made when trying to assign its origin and its date.

Wound glass, a labor-intensive process, involves the winding of molten glass around a metallic rod or wire, similar to the way thread is wound around a spool. By forming molten material in this manner, there is no need to drill or perforate the bead as a separate step. In the manufacture of drawn-glass beads, however, drawn canes with a central hole are produced as a raw material from which great numbers of nearly identical beads can be created in a short time. In contrast to wound-glass beads, which are individually made and therefore expensive, drawn beads are made in great numbers and are relatively cheap. At the same time, the process allows for a great diversity of pattern, color, and finished shapes.

Murano and Venetian beads typically were made by drawn or wound techniques. Although a great deal of secrecy has always surrounded the drawn-glass beadmaking operations at Murano, descriptions written in 1834 and 1917 apparently represent procedures unchanged for centuries. Fifteen separate steps—from the initial fusing of raw materials to the packing of the beads for shipment—were rigorously followed. One of the most interesting stages was the stretching of the glass into hollow tubes. A hollow globe of molten glass was attached to two metal plates with rods. Two men, each holding one of the rods, walked in opposite directions, drawing out a tube of glass at least fifty feet long. (If the gather was for seedbeads, it might be about one hundred feet.) The original bubble of air remained as an orifice or tunnel running the entire length of the tube. The tube was then divided by fracturing into canes, the canes were made into beads, and the beads were finished by methods known as "*a spedo*, a ferrazza (stirred in a pan), tumbling, or grinding (the lapidary technique)."[29]

Depending on stylistic variations, the glass globe could be composed of several differently colored layers, for example, or twisted during the drawing process to create a spiral of colors. Drawn-cane bead types varied from small monochrome seedbeads (typically used for embroidery) to striped beads, Nueva Cádiz, and *cornaline d'Aleppo* (Timeline 49, 52, 54, and 57).

By 1592, beadmaking was permitted again in Venice, and lamp-wound beads became an important Venetian industry. Unlike the drawn-glass techniques, which required large furnaces, extremely hot fires, and an industrial organization, wound beads—made by winding molten glass over oil lamps—were produced in small cottage industries. Essentially a handcrafted art, lamp-wound beads were first made about 1615 in a seemingly endless variety of designs, including floral sprays, combed beads, eye beads, and mosaic-glass (Timeline 63, 81, and 84). These were not secret processes, and they are continued today in Venice.[30]

It is estimated that there were more than one hundred thousand varieties of bead types and designs produced in Venice and Murano.[31] Particularly important types for commercial trade were glass seed and chevron beads (plate 102). Chevron (also called "star" or "rosetta") beads were sophisticated beads made from an early date with a complex manufacturing sequence that included compounding layers of materials and molding, drawing, dividing, and hand-finishing the beads.

The Venetians also reinvented mosaic-glass beads using drawn techniques of compound and composite canes, similar to ancient Roman methods. They simplified the production of intricate designs and patterns by inventing molding techniques. Although these methods were known by the late 1400s, they were not widely used until the 1800s, when cottage industries producing lamp-wound beads flourished.[32]

By 1817, new processes introduced into the beadmaking industry included machinery to make perfectly round beads and the development of an extremely tiny microbead, frequently less than one millimeter in diameter. As their minuscule holes made them nearly impossible to thread, they quickly went out of circulation.[33]

An indication of the volume of Venice's bead production can be seen in the number of glassworks that were established. Between 1500 and 1525 there were twenty-four glass factories in Murano; by 1606, 251 bead firms were recorded in Venice alone. In 1764, forty-four thousand pounds of beads were produced weekly at twenty-two Venetian manufacturers—numerous smaller houses appear to have merged into several larger ones. After the Republic of Venice fell to Napoleon in 1797, the industry suffered a setback as many workmen were taken to France. The number of establishments on Murano decreased to twelve by 1836. When Venice recovered from the Napoleonic Wars, however, large quantities of beads were produced once again. Venetian shipments to the United States alone during the 1880s amounted to six million pounds of beads yearly.[34]

By the eighteenth century, Venice had a near-monopoly on the glass bead market. It was not possible, however, to maintain this position indefinitely. Local industries and markets had existed within Europe—in Germany, the Baltic, Bohemia, and Moravia—since the early Middle Ages, frequently supplying glass beads for rosaries. With help from immigrating Venetians, the Bohemians, Moravians, and Dutch developed their own thriving bead industries.

Bohemian and Moravian Beadmaking

Glass beads are known to have been made in Bohemia and Moravia (today, the Czech Republic) as early as the tenth century. In comparison to Venice, the area was at a marketing disadvantage, located far from populous European districts. Yet vast northern hardwood (beech and oak) forests provided adequate supplies of fuel for glass-making furnaces and ash for alkali (materials absent in Venice), compensating for the cost of transporting beads great distances.[35]

By the seventeenth century, the Bohemians wanted greater quantities of beads than were available to them, and at lower prices. Rather than continue to import Venetian beads at premium prices, they decided to make their own. The Bohemians and Moravians

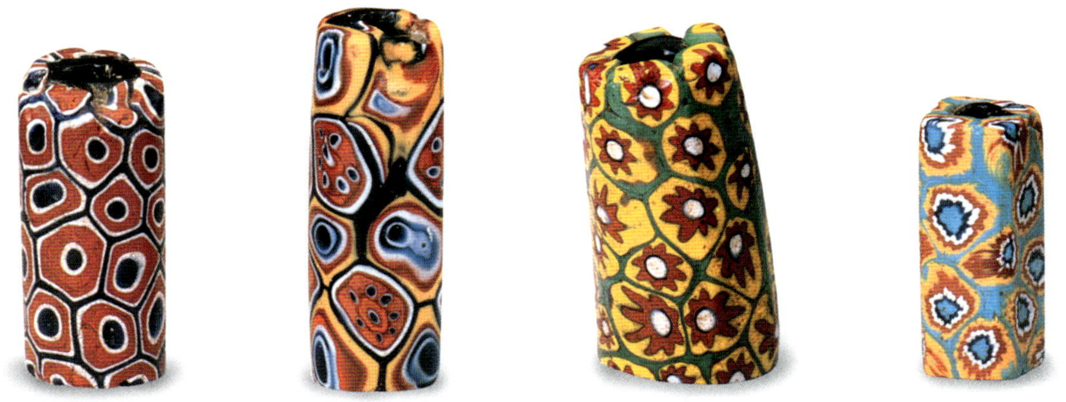

97. *Nineteenth-century mosaic (millefiori) glass beads. Made by an ancient technique invented in western Asia during the first millennium* B.C., *beads such as these were reintroduced by Venetian glassmakers.*

The glass is built up through the use of many small cross sections of multicolored canes fused together or embedded onto a matrix. The canes (elongated gathers of glass) may be simple or compound in composition. A recent study has organized them into four major types of construction (simple, cased, composite, and molded).[III] *Patterns are formed within their structures, generally most apparent in cross-sectional views. Left to right: (1) cased cane, composed of surrounding layers of glass; (2) composite cased cane, composed of a number of preformed cased units fused together; (3) molded flower cane; composite canes; (4) composed of concentric rings of rods. Far left bead: length, 1.25 cm. Private collection*

learned Venetian beadmaking secrets and developed quicker production methods with molded beads. By the end of the century, they were sufficiently organized to trade their beads abroad, in particular to the Baltic, Russia, Scandinavia, Holland, France, England, Spain, and the Ottoman Empire. After the mid-eighteenth century, their beads were found in all parts of the world.[36]

While there are often similarities between Venetian and Bohemian beads (the Bohemians copied some Venetian types, such as *cornaline d'Aleppo* and chevron), a distinct group of beads was made by the Bohemians, including those of blown and molded techniques (Timeline 132–150). Bohemian beads can be recognized by seam lines that run around the bead, a result of the molding process, their use of faceting (a holdover from the Bohemian garnet beadmaking industry), and unique designs.[37]

The Bohemians and Moravians specialized in imitating beads and bead materials used in other areas of the world. During the nineteenth century, Indian agates and carnelians and beads from African cowrie shells, bone, and bauxite were copied in glass and traded into Africa (plate 99). The economics of this are fascinating, since the glass reproductions could apparently be manufactured and distributed more cheaply than beads made of the original and sometimes inexpensive, natural materials.[38]

Dutch Beadmaking

Archaeological excavations in the old parts of Amsterdam suggest the existence of glass beadmaking by the late sixteenth century. At a landfill site in Waterlooplein, the old Jewish quarter, several glass beads as well as glass chunks and glass rods were found dating to 1580, the earliest evidence of beadmaking yet uncovered in Amsterdam. Excavations at the Keizergracht canal produced more than fifty thousand whole and fragmentary drawn-glass beads with the finds including production wasters and crucible fragments, thus providing definite proof of a beadmaking factory in the area during the first decade of the seventeenth century.[39]

Dutch beadmaking appears to have had a relatively short but active life. By 1550, Venetian glassmakers from Murano were working in Holland. From at least 1600 to 1750, beads manufactured in Holland were carried by Dutch, English, and French explorers

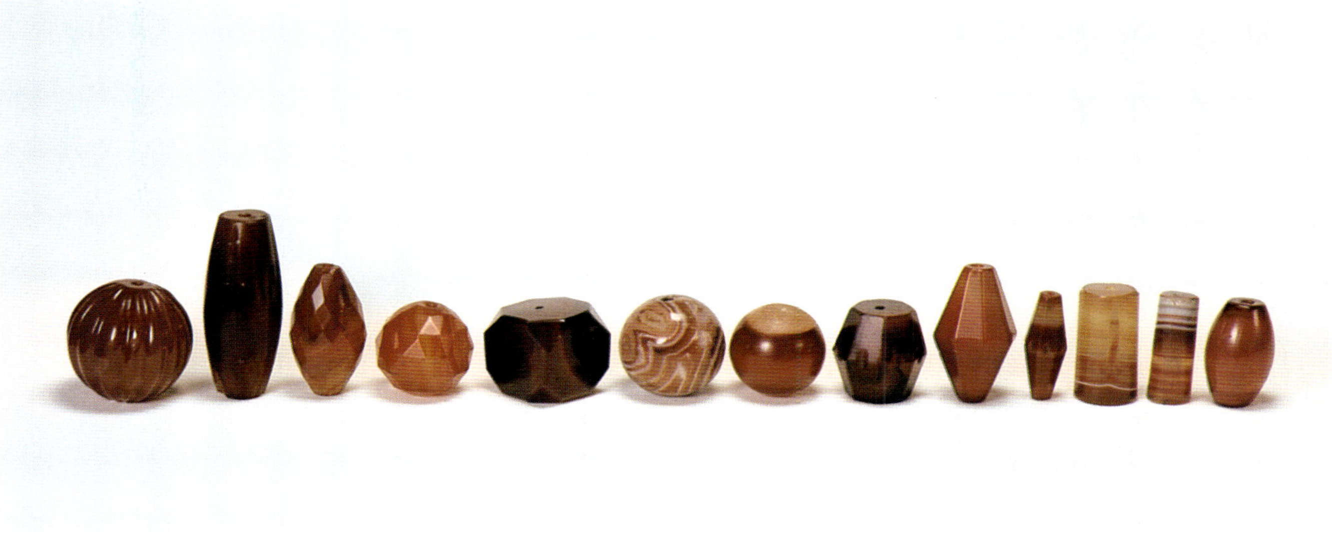

and merchants to North America, South and West Africa, and Indonesia. The Englishman Henry Hudson, who reached North America in 1609 and sailed up the river now bearing his name, is known to have traded "beades, knives, and hatchets" to local Indians during his journey. It seems likely that Hudson bartered Dutch beads, since his employer, the Dutch East India Company, included as one of its founders Jan Jansz Carel, owner of an Amsterdam glassworks.[40]

Large numbers of Dutch-made beads are found in early North American Iroquois and Susquehannock sites, concentrated in sites from western Massachusetts to southeastern Pennsylvania and possibly West Virginia. Dutch beads dating from the late 1500s are scattered in archaeological sites from southeastern Ontario to Florida. Many of these probably moved inland via intertribal trade.[41]

Drawing techniques were practiced in Dutch glass factories. However, archaeologist Karlis Karklins, who has studied Dutch beads for thirty-five years, notes that: "Although wound beads were traded by the Dutch, there is no definite proof for their production in Holland."[42] Since the wound method of beadmaking does not generate waste glass to be recovered archaeologically. The range of confirmed Dutch beads is therefore limited to drawn, stripped, and rosetta beads (Timeline 114–127).

At present, it is difficult to identify positively which beads found outside Holland were definitely manufactured there. Studies are underway to determine differences in forms, decoration, manufacturing techniques, and chemical composition of beads from different production centers that might help to identify Dutch beads in archaeological collections. This situation has become even more problematic with the finding of a number of large drawn beads at the Hammersmith Embankment in London that are identical in appearance to those produced by the Dutch. These date to the early seventeenth century and so are contemporaneous with those from the Keizersgracht site.[43]

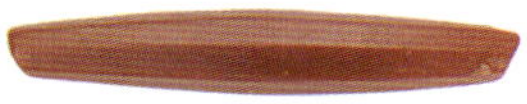

TOP: 98. *Europeans competed with Indian beadmakers for control of the lucrative African market. During the 1800s, these German carnelian and agate beads made in Idar-Oberstein (from Brazilian agate) were traded into Africa, rivaling Indian Cambay products. Second bead from left: length, 5.4 cm. Collection Ruth and John Picard, Carmel, California*

ABOVE: 99. *A Bohemian glass bead made to imitate a stone example. Glass beads, such as this molded glass simulation of carnelian, were cheaper to make and thus undercut both the Indian and German agate industries.*[IV] *Length, 12 cm. Collection Craft Caravan, New York*

German Beadmaking

The manufacture of glass beads in Germany began in the latter days of the Roman Empire and continued through medieval times. During the fifteenth century, Bavarian communities sent men to Venice to purchase glass canes, presumably for paternoster

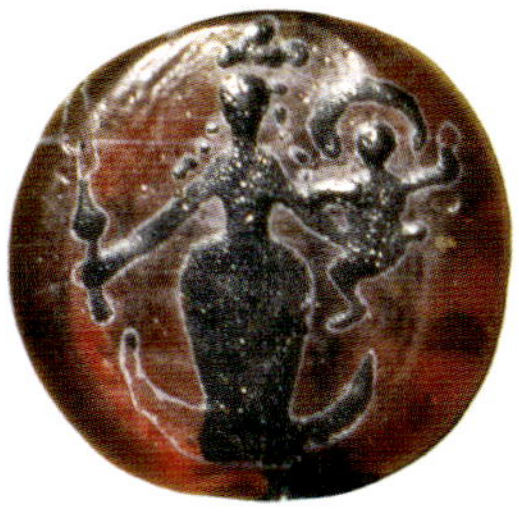

100. *There are still mysteries in the bead world. This wound glass bead was one of a group of similar beads that was recovered from a historic midden within a sewerage pit in Amsterdam, Holland. There are several versions, but all have enameled religious images of Mary and/or Jesus on them. As seen in this example, most depict Mary standing on a crescent moon (like a pagan goddess) holding the baby Jesus in one arm, and a spear (or scepter?) in the other. She is apparently crying, since tears seem to be streaming down her face. She is crowned and Jesus has a halo. All this appears on a bead that is about the size of a quarter. Jamey D. Allen, who is currently researching the beads and their iconography, dates them to the early eighteenth century. Diameter, approximately 2.5 cm. Private collection*

beads for rosaries. By 1630, the wire-winding process was learned through one Abraham Fino, who went from Amsterdam to Nuremberg.[44]

In the district of Fichtelgebirge in the province of Franconia, a heavily wooded region near the Bohemian border, unique iridescent and translucent glass beads in yellow, green, and lavender were produced from 1500 to 1700. Coveted treasures, the beads were exported to royal courts in Europe, India, and Africa. When the industry declined, these beadmakers moved to Bohemia, integrating their secrets and artistic techniques into the processes of the Bohemian and Moravian glassworks.[45]

The agate bead industry of Idar-Oberstein in Germany was a major nineteenth- and twentieth-century beadmaking center, particularly for the African trade. From 1830 to 1980, more than one hundred million stone beads were created in Idar-Oberstein and transported to Africa. Additional beads were also produced for Europeans and the Americas.[46] Although the Idar-Oberstein agate industry goes back to Roman time and local material was used until the mid-nineteenth century, the boom in beadmaking occurred after 1834, when agates were shipped back to Germany from Brazil. Brazilian agate was imported because it was inexpensive and took their coloring treatments easily. The subsequent success of the industry was due to fine craftsmanship combined with clever, aggressive marketing. All operations, including cutting, coloring, drilling, and trading of the agates, were tightly controlled by the same families for generations.[47]

Idar-Oberstein beads had elegant, smooth geometric forms, precisely drilled holes, and finished details, such as slightly larger holes at the end, so that threads holding the beads would not be chafed. Other than the extremely long, olive-shaped agates, which were drilled from two sides, all Idar-Oberstein beads are drilled through from one side (plate 98).[48]

The hues of the beads were particularly notable and had much to do with their popularity. Although the beads were artificially colored—nondescript gray agates were changed through a variety of techniques into stones of intense black, brown and white, red orange, and blue and green—the methods used at Idar-Oberstein resulted in permanent and stronger colors. The stronger colors were apparently desirable in many parts of Africa, as tribesmen believed that the stronger the color, the more protective powers were passed on to the wearer. Apparently, it was not important if the color was natural or artificial.[49]

Flexibility to make a wide variety of shapes in a number of patterns and colors and the ability of the German merchants to identify the needs of specific African markets contributed greatly to sales volumes. Idar-Oberstein beads significantly undermined the Indian agate and carnelian industry, which had been supplying stone beads to Africa for centuries.

Beadmaking in France, England, and Spain

Although Roman glassmaking traditions continued in France during the early Middle Ages, there is no obvious proof that bead manufacturing continued up to the Renaissance. The paternosters, however, had their own guild to make rosaries, dating from 1593. By 1750, glass beads were made in many cities, including Nevers, Dangu, Aubermesnil, and Villers. It is probable that beads of French manufacture were traded to the Americas and Africa.[50]

It was recently determined that an early seventeenth century factory in London,

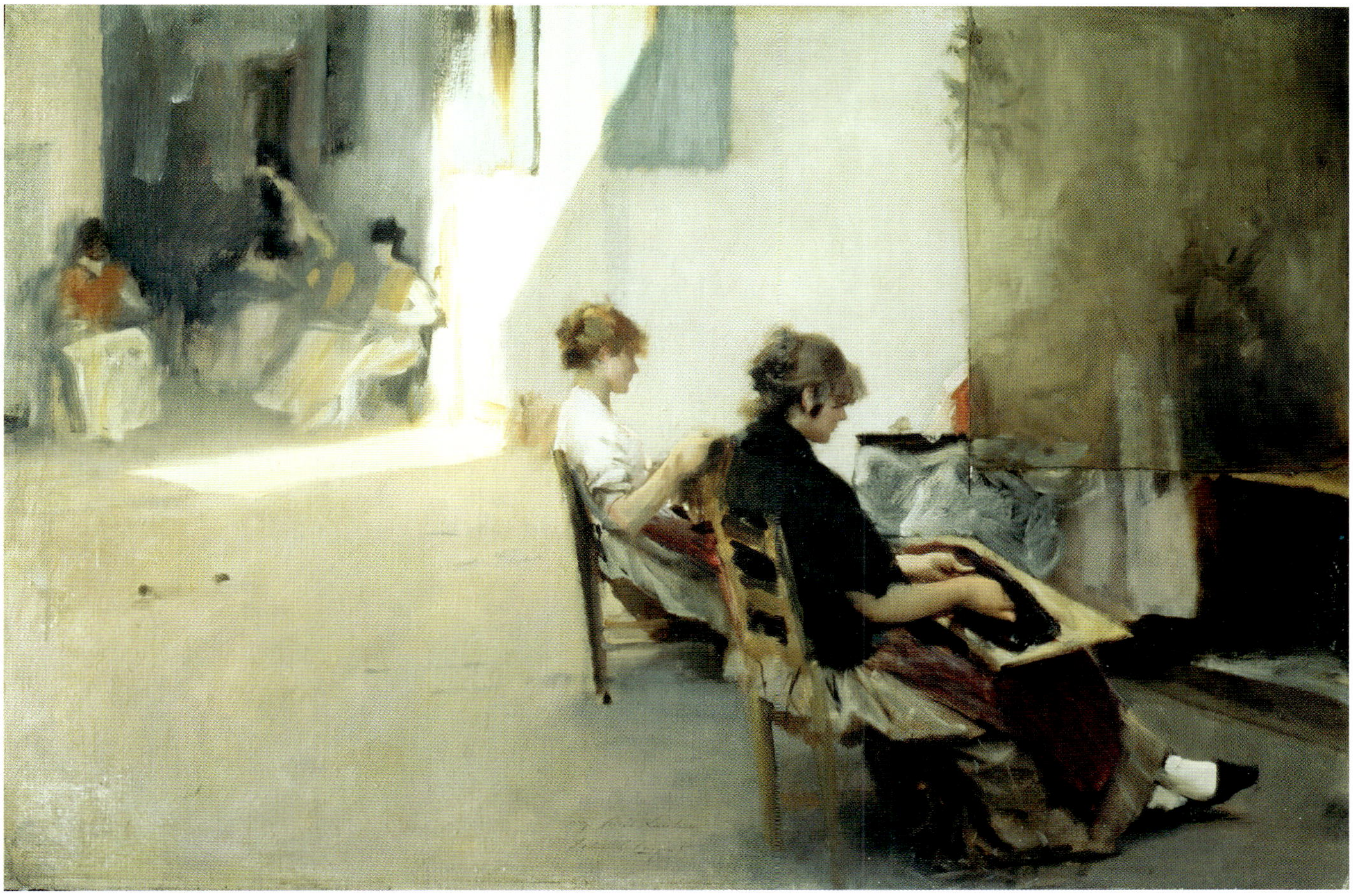

101. The Bead Stringers of Venice, *painted by John Singer Sargent, 1880–1882. Oil on canvas. 56 × 82 cm. Courtesy of the National Gallery of Ireland, Dublin*

England, produced glass beads that strongly resemble Dutch and Venetian beads of this period. Therefore, beads brought to the Americas, India, and Africa by English merchants could have been obtained from their own factories as well as other European sources and, by the 1800s, from China.[51]

Spanish traders brought a variety of beads to the New World in the early sixteenth and seventeenth centuries. Beads distributed in the earlier days of their trade included Nueva Cádiz varieties, faceted chevrons, eye beads, and compound beads (some with three layers of color). There were also monochrome beads in a variety of sizes, ranging from seedbeads in yellow, green, and blue to larger, predominantly blue spheres. By the mid-1600s, most of the complex, more ornate beads had disappeared.[52] Oblate-shaped turquoise blue beads (the "padre" bead; Timeline 1035) continued as one of the most popular types.[53] While the Spanish are reported to have made glass beads, all evidence suggests they were primarily carriers and traders of Venetian products.

The rise of the Venetian, Dutch, and Bohemian and Moravian bead industries and their domination of the world's bead market for over three hundred years had particularly profound consequences for India. German stone and European glass bead production seriously undercut Indian bead manufacturers, who had been trading with Africa and Southeast Asia since before the Christian Era.

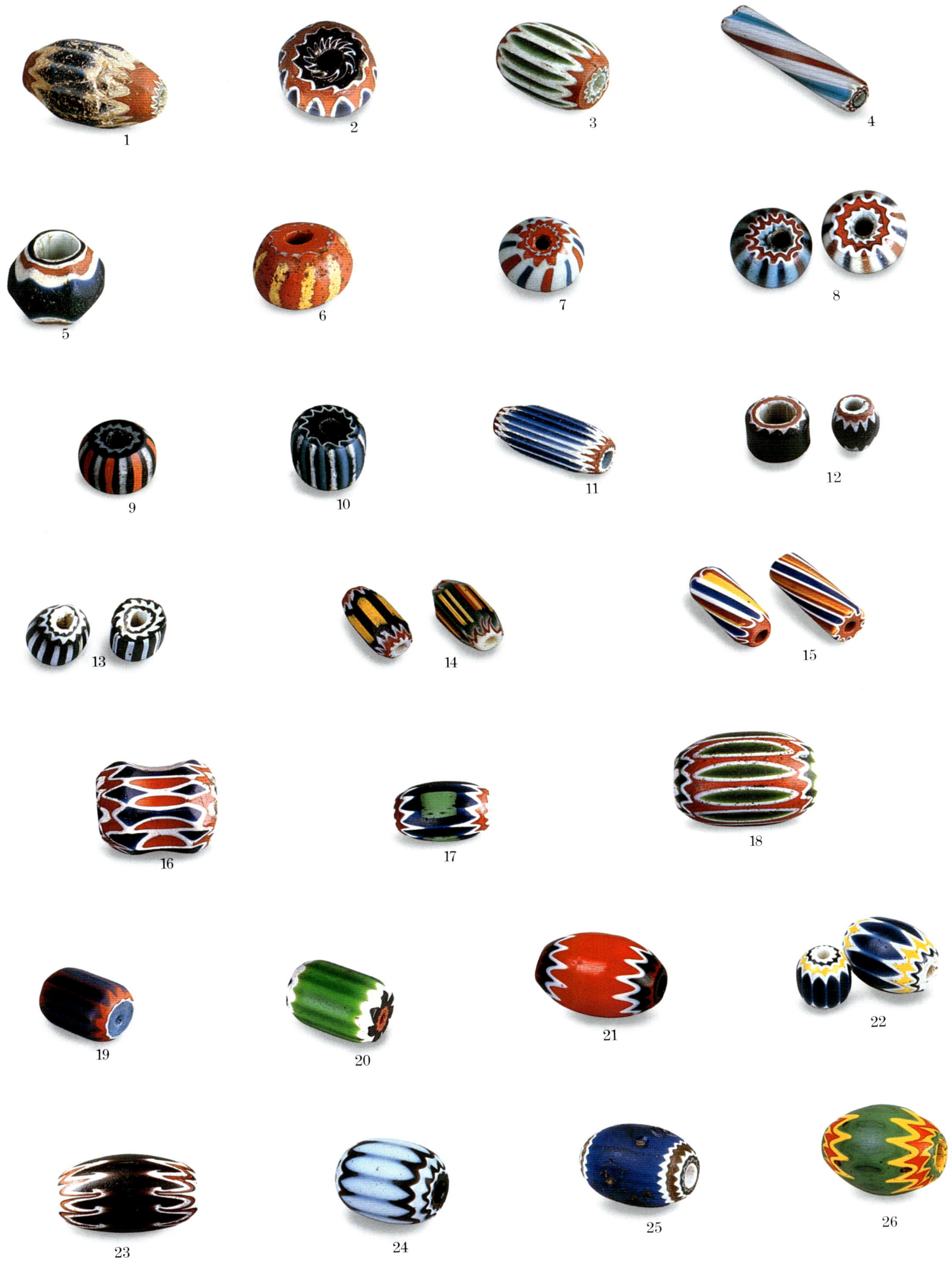
1
2
3
4
5
6
7
8
9
10
11
12
13
14
15
16
17
18
19
20
21
22
23
24
25
26

Chevron Beads

Perhaps no other bead has been as popular as the chevron. First invented in about 1500 by the Venetians, they continue to be produced up to the present time.[V] *(Throughout the seventeenth century, the Dutch manufactured a speo star beads—somewhat similar in appearance to chevrons but made with a different technique as the Dutch did not facet or cut star beads.)*[VI] *For almost five hundred years, chevrons have been produced in the many millions and in several hundred varieties. The examples here are from a special group collected in West Africa—the greatest repository of antique European trade beads—from 1968 to 1985.*

Chevrons are a specialized cane or drawn glass bead. They are formed by forcing or blowing a single- or multiple-layered gather of glass into a tapered mold with corrugated sides, thus producing points on its outer surface.[VII] *This pleated gather is subsequently encased with additional glass layers of various colors, which may again be molded to produce further outer layers with points. Finally, stripes may be applied to the surface. Still viscid, this multilayered, hollow gather is then quickly drawn into a cane (hence the terms "drawn" or "cane") of at least six feet, cooled, and finally sectioned into beads. These sections are often reheated or ground to produce a more finished product in various new shapes. The illustrations here include chevrons with from two to eight layers and a variety of points; twelve was the most common.*

Figures 1–3 and 5 of plate 102 are examples of the first chevrons produced by the Venetians from 1500 to perhaps as late as the early 1600s.[VIII] *All of these beads have seven layers, with the first and third layers (core to surface) a transparent or translucent light green (fig. 9). Although the outer layer is typically a translucent cobalt blue, figure 3 demonstrates black and green were used as well.*

Figure 4 is a rare star bead traded into the Spanish New World (especially Peru) in the early 1500s.[IX] *Who manufactured it is unknown, although the Venetians are considered the most likely contenders. (This bead, in fact, was found in Africa.)*

The beads illustrated in figures 6–8 and 10 were apparently produced by the Dutch during the late 1590s and over the next hundred years. Figure 9 also seems to fit best into this group. However, all of these beads may be Venetian.

Little is known about chevron production in Venice during the 1700s, and it appears relatively few were produced. Figure 11 may be an example from this period.[X] *In the 1800s, the Venetians again produced chevrons in large numbers with a great variety of colors, shapes, sizes, layers, and points. The vast majority have four or six layers, in red, white, and blue. Some of the more unusual examples from this period are represented in figures 9–26.*

The red chevron (fig. 21) is an exception and was not found in West Africa. It is probably Venetian, from the early 1900s, and is one of several matched chevrons from a graduated string discovered in the 1980s in the United States.[XI]

102. *Figures 1 to 26. All of these chevrons are uncommon and several are unique. (For sizes and further bead information, see note XII) Picard Trade Bead Museum, Carmel California*

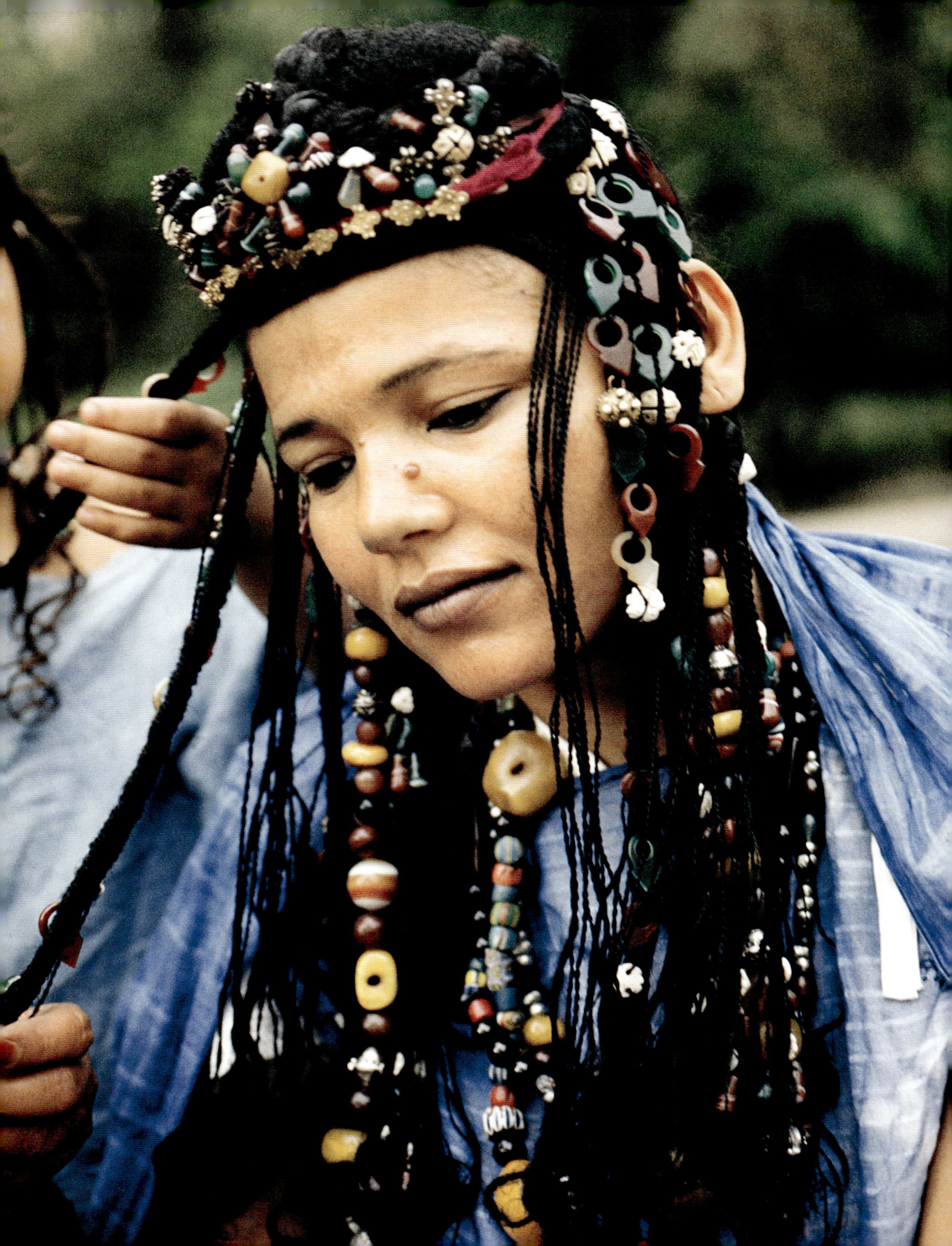

Africa

The story of African beads—perhaps more than the beads of any other part of the world—is also the story of the many contrasting life-styles that have developed in Africa. Beadmaking has been influenced by environmental factors, the availability and distribution of raw materials, and exposure to Islamic and European culture and technology during the past fourteen hundred years.

To understand the beads of Africa it is crucial to appreciate the influence of geography on African societies. The continent is home to several distinct environments: deserts, tropical rain forests, woodlands, savannas, and fertile river valleys. Natural resources are distributed unevenly within these regions, and the structure of different economic, political, and religious systems reflects variations in the natural, setting. Adornment, as an expression of peoples' values and their social and economic organizations, mirrors the wide-ranging contrasts that are the essence of this continent.

When power was concentrated in a ruler who controlled valuable resources—marketable commodities like gold and ivory, for example—he generally encouraged the development of arts and crafts, both to express his power visually and to have offerings to give to the gods out of gratitude for his privileged position. Beaded objects also served to distinguish rulers from ordinary people. Thus, the ornate beadwork produced for the Yoruba king, or *oba*, and his royal court by specialized craftsmen is much more complex than that produced by the pastoral East African Pokot and Samburu for themselves (plates 113 and 137). Nevertheless, for the latter, beads are an essential component of everyday dress, worn to signify their age grade, marital status, and station in society.

Beads are an integral part of a multilayered communication system in all Afri-

103. *In preparation for the Guedra—a traditional courtship dance performed by the Hassania women of Mauritania to honor the loves, lives, and hardships of the Hassania people—a Hassania dancer's hair is painstakingly braided and adorned with triangular glass amulets, carved shell disks, glass, amber and copal beads, and tiny gold pendants. The triangular shape of the beads symbolizes fertility and protection, and their colors represent specific virtues: blue beads stand for purity of the sky; white, the health of Hassania servants; and violet, the dove, a symbol of love and gentleness. The large frontal hair bun studded with jewelry is also a style favored by Hassania brides from wealthy families.*[1] *1994.*

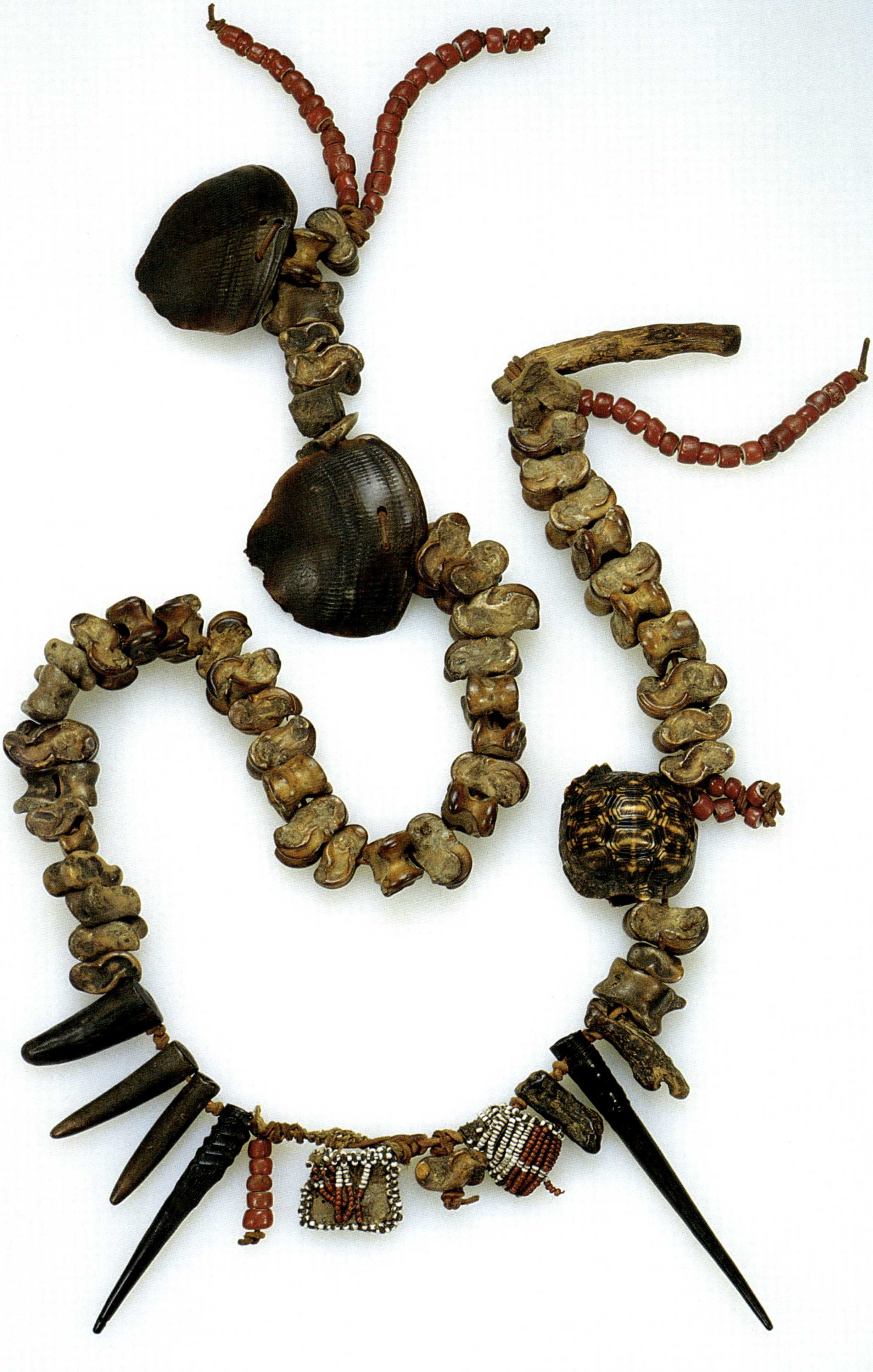

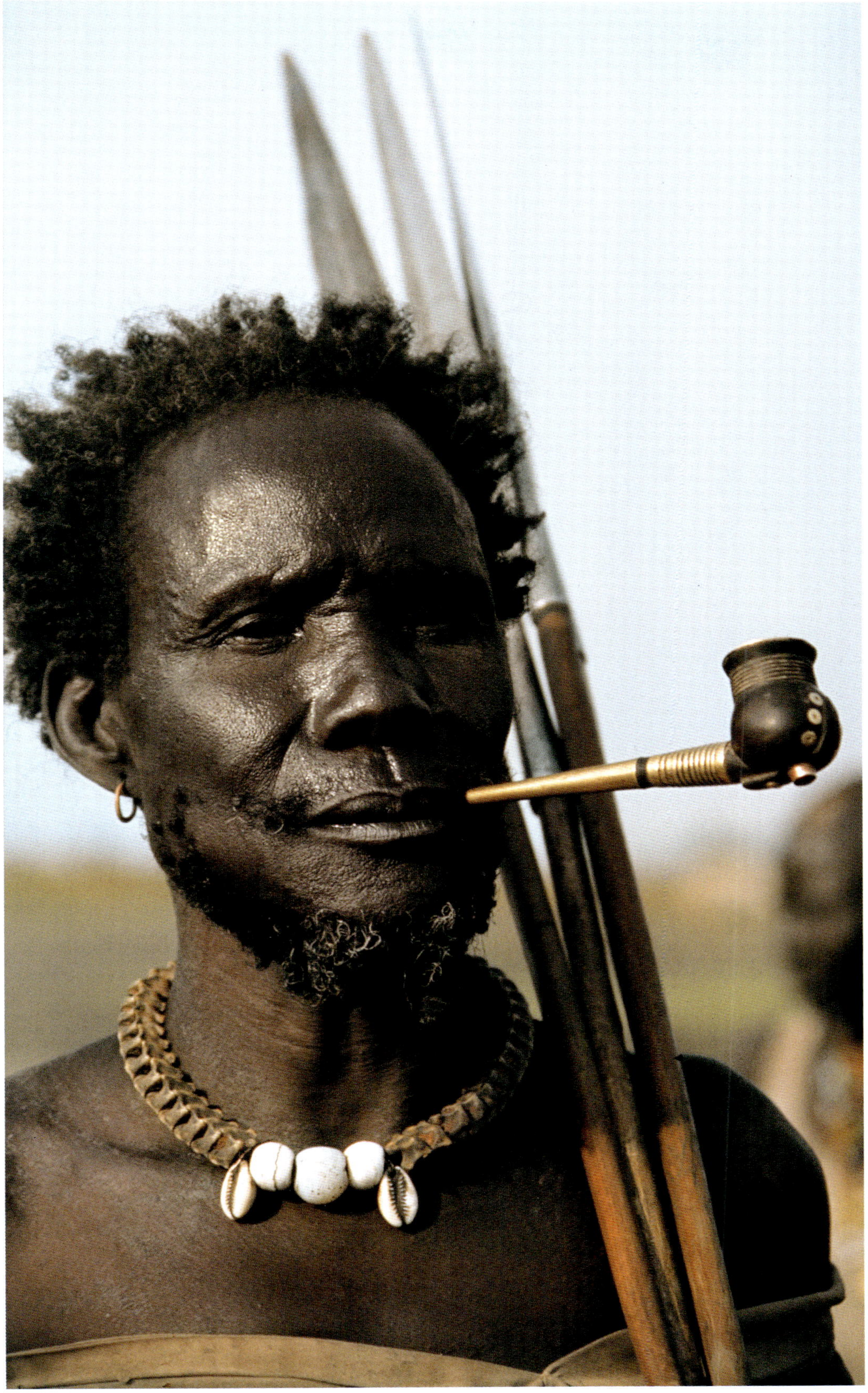

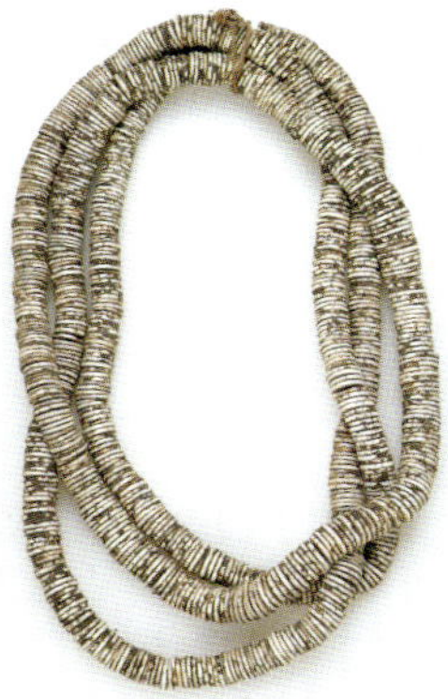

OPPOSITE: 104. *A Zulu shaman's necklace from South Africa made of twigs, tortoiseshell, seeds, animal knuckle bone and horn, teeth, glass beads, and leather and glass beaded amulets. It is a striking example of the African capacity to combine a variety of objects into a powerful item of adornment. Length, 132 cm. Collection Ivory Freidus*

ABOVE: 105. *A necklace of ostrich eggshell disk beads made by the Turkana tribe of Kenya. Length, 66 cm. Collection Jill and Roger Caras, New York*

LEFT: 106. *A snake vertebrae and cowrie shell necklace, known as a "gift from God" and worn by an elder from the Dinka tribe of Sudan*[11]

OVERLEAF, TOP LEFT: 107. *A necklace of elongated granite beads made by the Dogon of Mali. Beads of hard stone have not been worked extensively in Africa, except in a few regions such as Mali and Nigeria. The round pottery beads are a contemporary creation of the Baoule people of the Ivory Coast. Center granite bead: length, 1.6 cm. Collection Craft Caravan, New York*

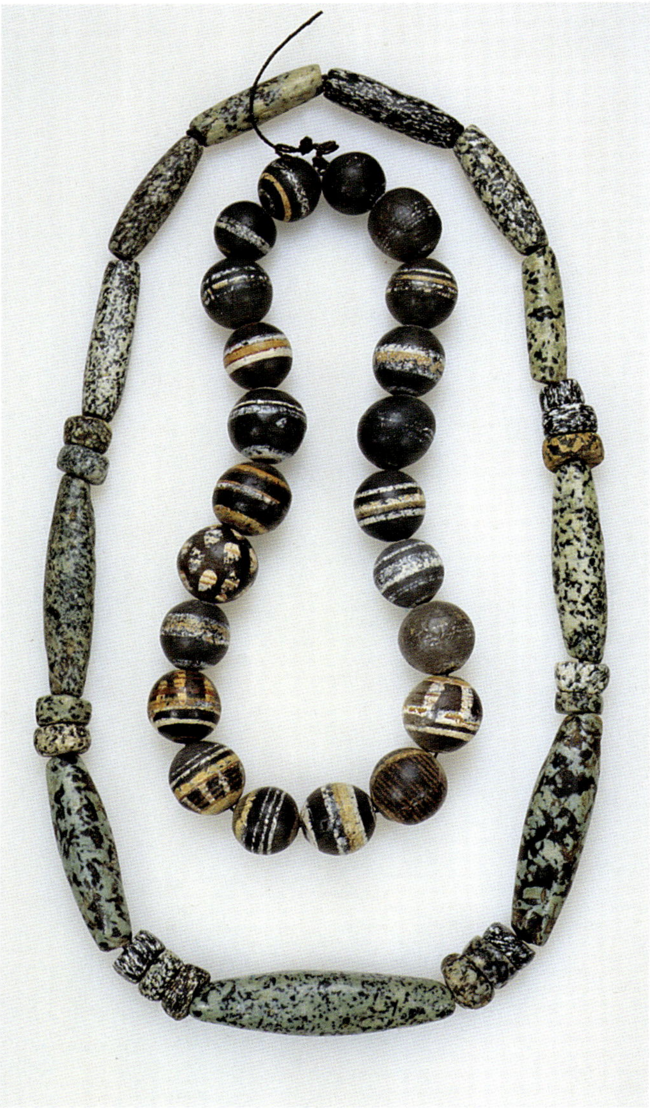

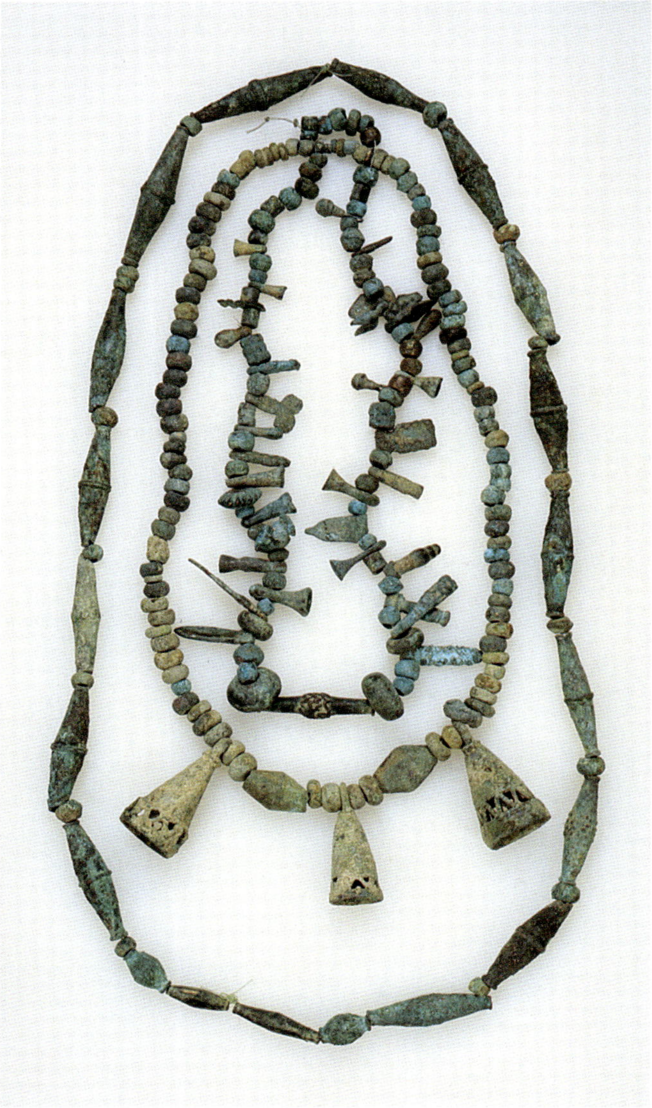

ABOVE RIGHT: 108. *Bronze necklaces recovered near Djenne, Mali. Associated bronze and terra-cotta sculptures indicate that the beads may date to the late Middle Ages (c. A.D. 1200), when western Sudanese kingdoms flourished and cities such as Djenne and Timbuktu were important centers of learning and trade. It is not clear whether the beads were imported or made in Djenne. Typical biconical bead (outer necklace): length, 5.7 cm. Collection Craft Caravan, New York*

can societies. Adornment, particularly with beads, communicates cultural values in a symbolic language that expresses rank, religion, politics, and artistic attitudes. Beads are central to the lives of all Africans—from hunting-and-gathering peoples of the southern Kalahari Desert to wealthy Nigerian and Ghanaian villagers—and their ability to reflect their cultural heritage is still more pronounced in Africa than in any other part of the world.

Bead Materials

An enormous range of beads and raw materials for beads has been available to Africans for centuries. Throughout the continent, there has always been widespread use of organic materials for adornment—including seeds, nuts, shells, bones, tusks, and teeth. The earliest known African beads are a group of Nassarius shell beads from eastern Morocco that date to 82,000 B.C. (plate 2). Disk-shaped forms made of ostrich eggshells have been recovered from an Upper Paleolithic (37,000 B.C.) site in Kenya, a site dating 10,000 B.C. in Libya, and slightly later Neolithic sites in the Sudan. Today, ostrich eggshell is still used for some beadmaking in East Africa, and large quantities of beads are made from this durable

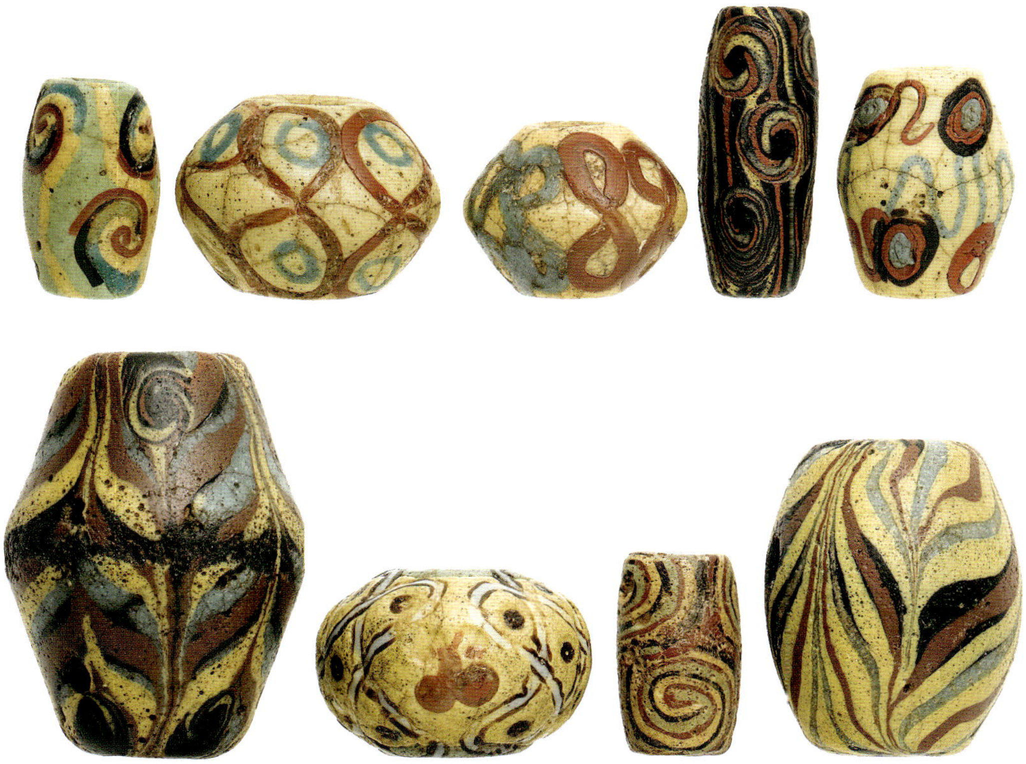

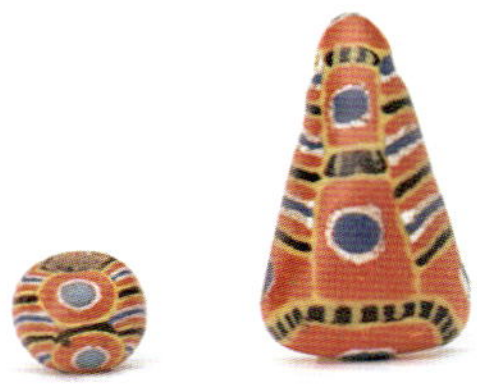

ABOVE: 109. *Polychrome, powder-glass eye beads from Kiffa, Mauritania, probably dating to the 1980s. The devoutly Muslim Mauritanians treasure these beads and developed a specific vocabulary that describes each bead according to its material, size, shape, decoration, and color. Length (largest bead), 1.3 cm. Collection Anita Gumpert, Washington, D.C.*

ABOVE LEFT: 110. *A remarkable collection of* bodom *from Ghana, all dating to the late nineteenth century. Each bead is handmade and one of a kind. They are "close in spirit to the African masks that inspired abstract modern art," remarks the collector, Billy Steinberg. Fig. 6 (bottom row, left): length, 5.08 cm. Collection Billy Steinberg*

Bodom Beads

Bodom*—the name by which old powder-glass beads of a certain age and design are generally known—are called* kpo *by their makers, the Krobo. They are greatly treasured and believed to have magical or medicinal powers. Though produced in various colors,* bodom *are frequently yellow and often have a black or dark gray inner core. Visible signs of use, such as the erosion and chipping of the outer surface and the exposure of a dark inner core, add significantly to their value.*[III] *The date for the advent of powder-glass techniques in Africa—and therefore the appearance of* bodom*—is probably the mid-nineteenth-century.*[III]

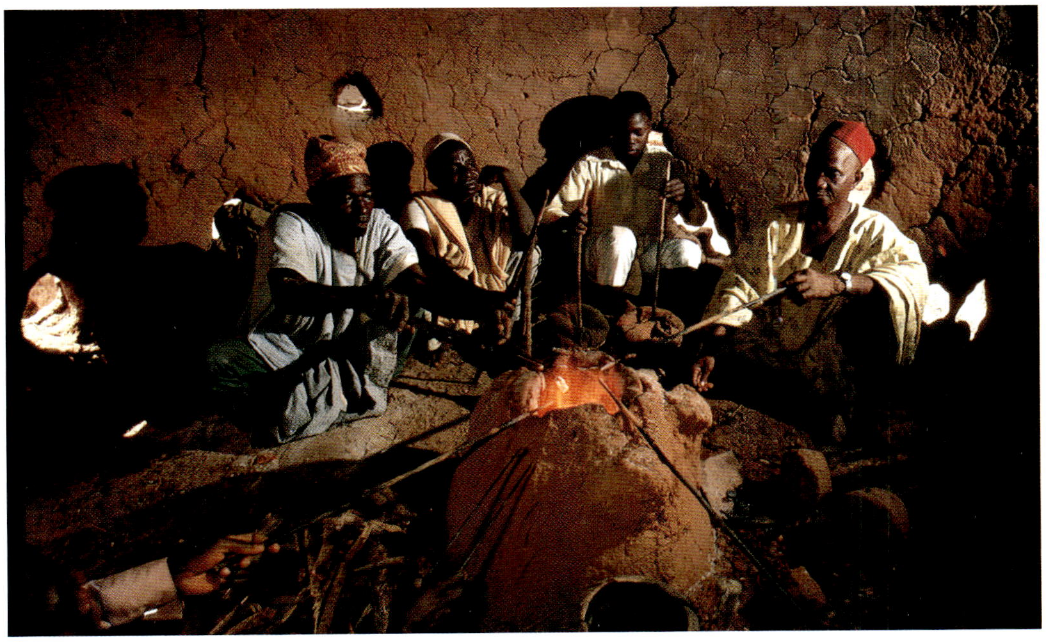

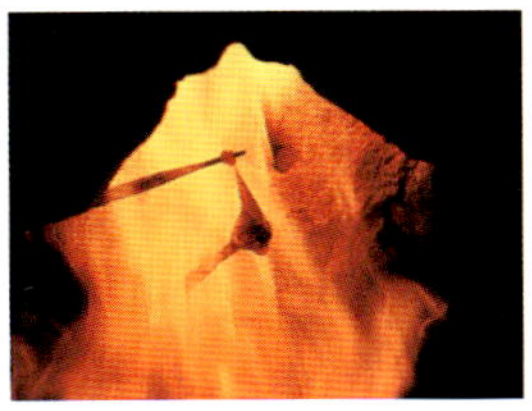

ABOVE: 111a. *Glass on an iron rod (pontil) being mandrel-wound in a furnace.*

LEFT: 111b. *Glass bead-making at Bida, Nigeria. Glassmakers manufacture their beads by winding molten glass over an open fire in a forced-fire furnace. Several families, who constitute a glass-making guild, make all the beads at Bida.*

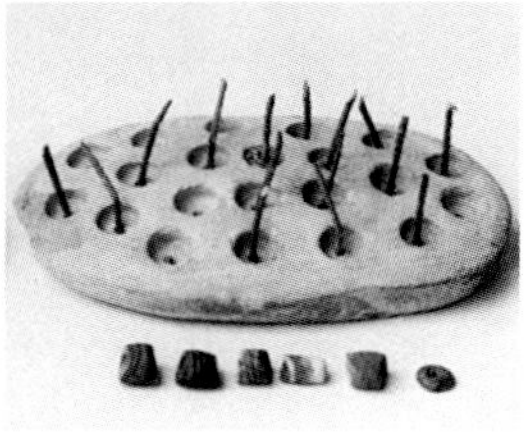

112. *This baked clay mold was used by the Krobo of Ghana to make powder-glass beads around 1930. A stick was set in the center of each bead's mold to form a hole. The beadmaker then placed horizontal layers of variously colored glass powders made from pulverized glass scrap into the mold. The mold was subsequently placed in a furnace and heated until the glass particles congealed into a granular mass without actually melting. Examples of the resulting beads appear in the lower half of the illustration. British Museum, London*

and accessible material in the Kalahari Desert by the !Kung San.[1] Cowrie shells, valued for their durability and their shape (symbolizing female fertility when vertical and the eye when horizontal), also have an ancient history in Africa. Over ten thousand years ago, cowries were used as burial offerings; more recently, they have been considered legal tender. Most cowrie shells in Africa come from India.[2]

The manufacture of stone beads in sub-Saharan Africa was limited to a few localities. A variety of cylindrical and double-drilled stone beads were made by the Nok culture of Nigeria in the first millennium B.C.[3] (Timeline 1201) A Nok terra-cotta male figurine wearing necklaces of what appear to be stone beads has been discovered. The tradition persisted, evidenced by bead-laden bronze king figures of the Ife culture that date to the fourteenth century A.D.[4] Beads recently recovered from ancient sites at Djenne in Mali are almost entirely from India, though some stone may have been worked there at least by medieval times.

During the fifteenth century, stone beadmaking developed in the kingdom of Benin (in present-day Nigeria) with the encouragement of Oba Eware the Great. Benin craftsmen became experts at carving stone beads coveted by the royal court. Beads were considered so important in old Benin that a member of the house of Iwebo (the keepers of the royal wardrobe) was sent by the *oba* to invest a worthy subject with beads. No titled chief was allowed audience with the *oba* unless he wore his necklaces, and if he lost them, he could be punished by death.[5] The beaded regalia of the *oba* became increasingly elaborate until, by the seventeenth century, entire costumes of coral beads, including skirts, shirts, crowns, and staffs, became the official royal dress (plates 132 and 133). (Coral had been introduced by the Portuguese in the early 1500s.)

A stone beadmaking industry is also known to have existed at Ilorin in Nigeria. Nodules of agate, carnelian, red jasper, and even old stone beads were brought to Ilorin by Arab and Sudanic traders. They were then worked or reworked by local craftsmen into beads. Most agate and carnelian beads found throughout Africa today, however, are either of Indian origin or are copies designed to imitate Indian beads that were made in the nineteenth and twentieth centuries by German manufacturers at Idar-Oberstein. Today, the Dogon of Mali continue to make large granite beads (plate 107).

The history of metal beads in Africa is somewhat obscure. It is known that most African societies have tended to develop beads based on indigenous materials, including locally available metals. Africans have used iron for tools and weapons since at least 300 B.C., but only more recently for adornment. Tin beads, however, in the shape of cowries, have been reported from a Nok site dating to the first millennium B.C.[6] In Kenya, where locally made iron was plentiful, large faceted iron beads have been manufactured by the Turkana for generations (plate 119). Today, Kenyan craftsmen make faceted aluminum beads from pans that are cut into strips and hammered.[7] Major deposits of silver are found in Ethiopia, and Ethiopian silversmiths are among the finest in Africa. For centuries, they have hammered or cast beads into a variety of shapes, often using the silver from melted-down coins.

European explorers and traders arriving in West Africa in the early fifteenth century noted an abundance of gold jewelry, including beaded necklaces and bracelets. Many West African gold beads described by Europeans were made by the Asante using a "lost-wax" casting process. This process, known in West Africa since the ninth century, is thought to have been introduced from the north via trans-Saharan traders.[8] It has been acknowledged for millennia that Africa was well endowed with gold. Sudanese mines supplied Old Kingdom Egyptian jewelers, and by the New Kingdom era gold was brought from sources farther south. Throughout the Middle Ages, Islamic Asia and much of Christian Europe depended on African gold.

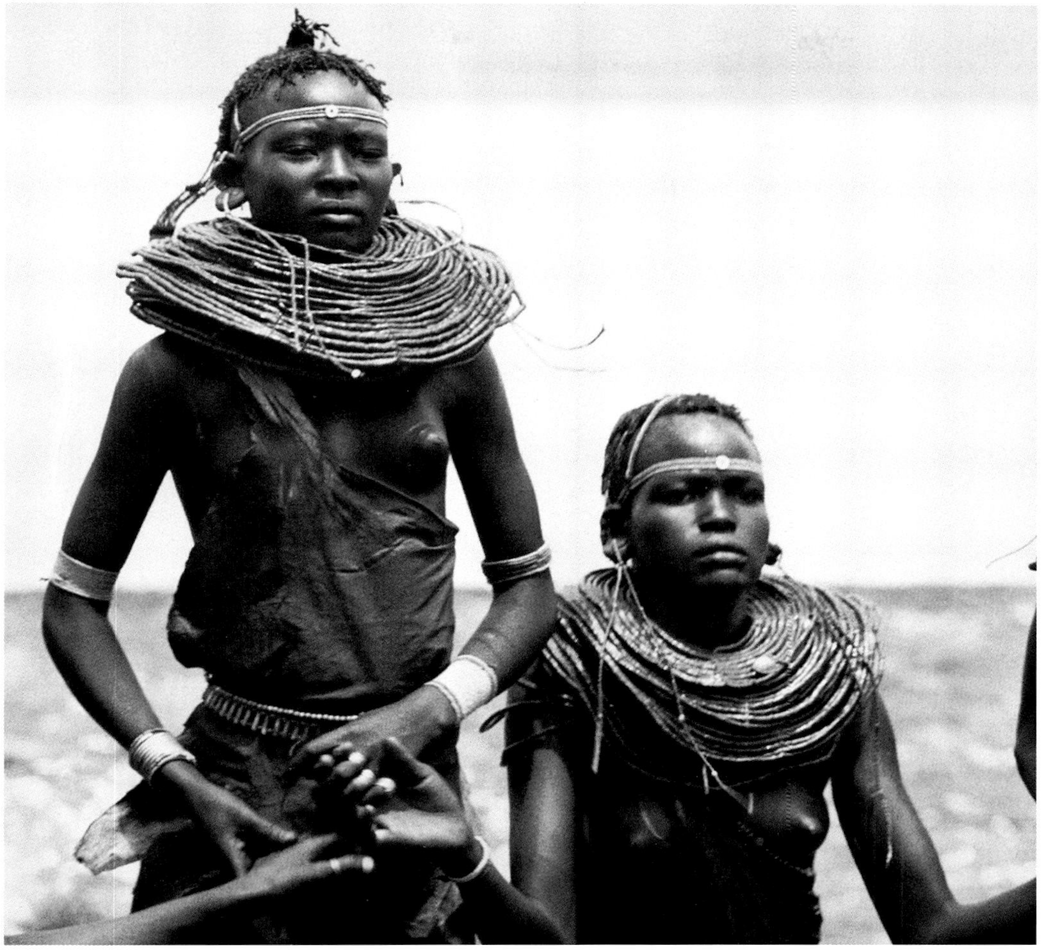

113. *Young girls of Kenya's Pokot tribe wearing wooden beads they made. When the girls reach marrying age, these will be replaced by imported glass seedbeads.*[IV]

OVERLEAF: 114. *Turkana girl with many layers of necklaces, representing her wealth.*

The Turkana are nomadic pastoralists living in a harsh environment, yet they create superb beadwork from leather, metals, wood, glass, and shells.

Turkana are well known for their ostrich eggshell beads, although today the collecting of ostrich eggshells is strictly controlled. If the Turkana men manage to avoid the mother ostrich and the game warden, they bring the eggs to their women, who chip the tough shell into rough shapes using stones or their teeth. Holes are then drilled in the center, and the edges are smoothed on a stone. Ostrich eggshell beads have been made this way in East Africa since at least 7000 B.C.

By the fifteenth century, European observations of West African gold jewelry inspired explorers to search for the sources of the metal and other precious commodities, including ivory. Over the next several hundred years, sub-Saharan Africa was embroiled in a struggle between the European powers for control of its people, land, and riches. Beads—particularly ones of European glass—played an important role in this story.

Indeed, glass beads are the most common feature of African adornment and were not imported into sub-Saharan Africa until early Islamic times. All the glass beads excavated from Djenne in Mali date to the later phases of the Islamic period, c. A.D. 1000–1400.[9]

However, most archaeologically recovered beads were probably manufactured in India. Small, opaque glass beads found along the East and South African coasts were produced in India as early as 100 B.C., and have been found in African sites dating to about A.D. 200, suggesting that trade relations existed between the two continents.[10]

The history of glassworking south of the Sahara has been the focus of much research for several decades. Although some of the world's earliest known glass beads come from Egypt (faience, considered the forerunner of glass, was invented either in Mesopotamia or Egypt about 3400 B.C., and wound-glass beads appear in Egypt between 2181 and 2133 B.C.), the influence of Egyptian glassmaking on the cultures of sub-Saharan Africa appears minimal.[11] Glass beads were traded south from Egypt, but the beadmaking technology does not seem to have accompanied them. One of the earliest sources of indigenous glass beads is thought to be Mapungubwe in South Africa, where beads were made from A.D. 600 to 1200.

African glass beads—except for those produced in Egypt—have always been and

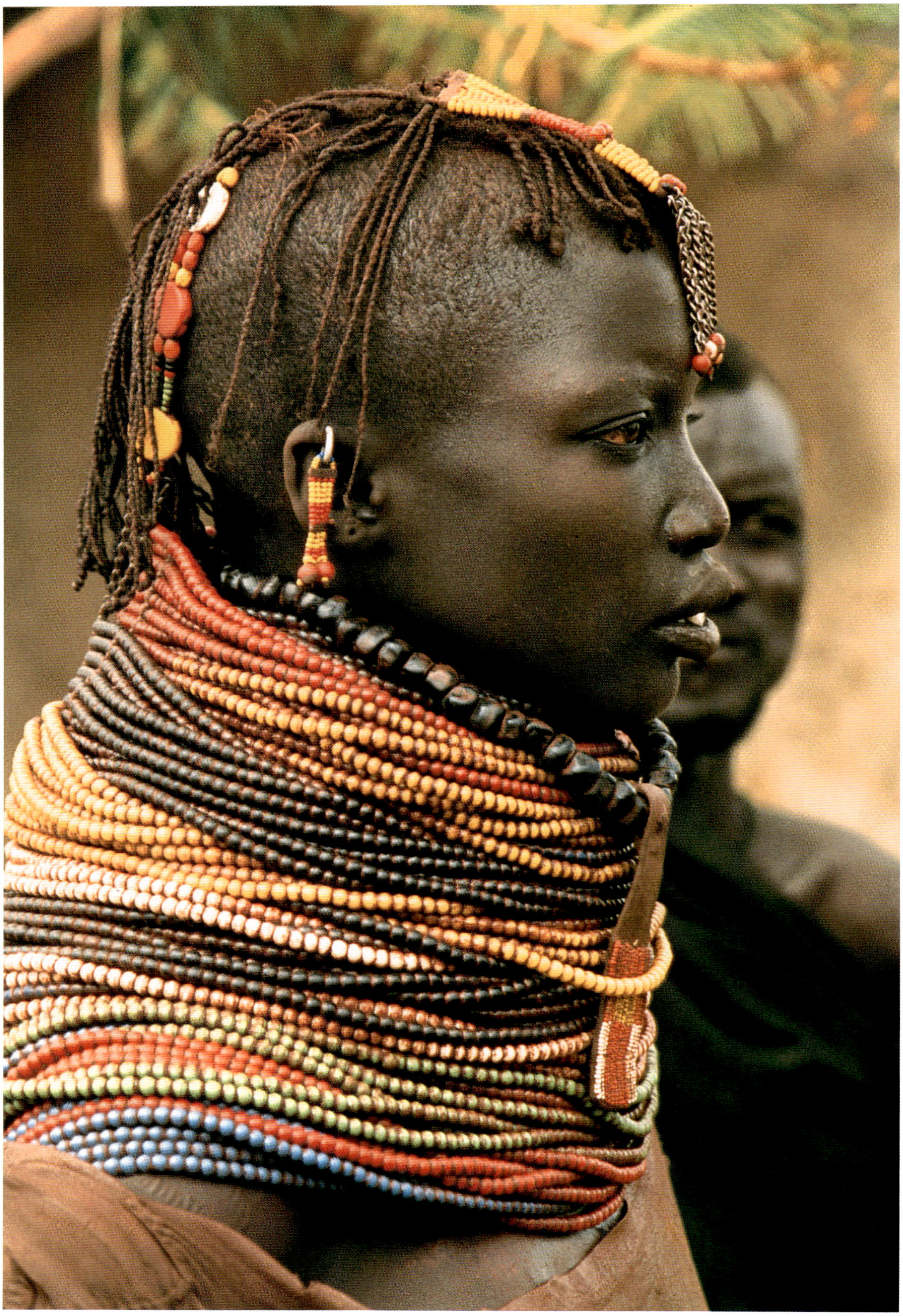

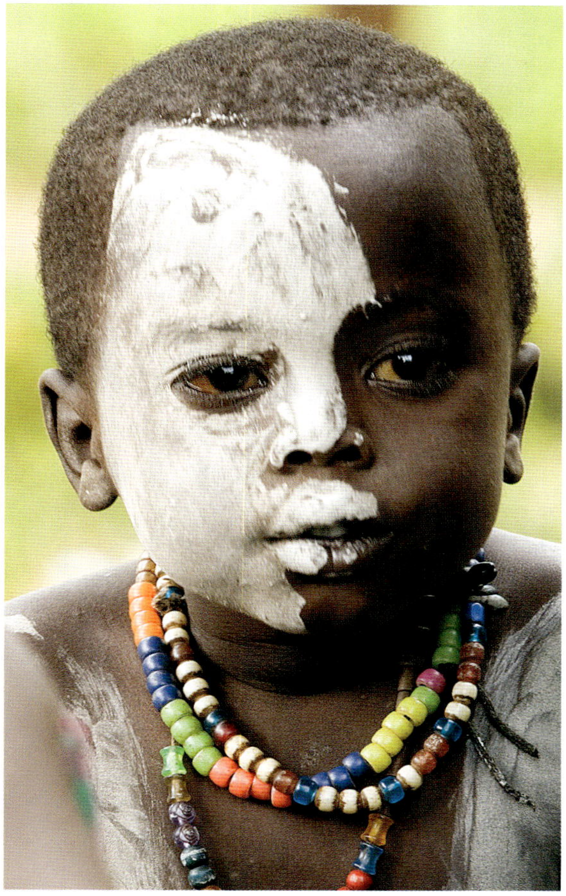

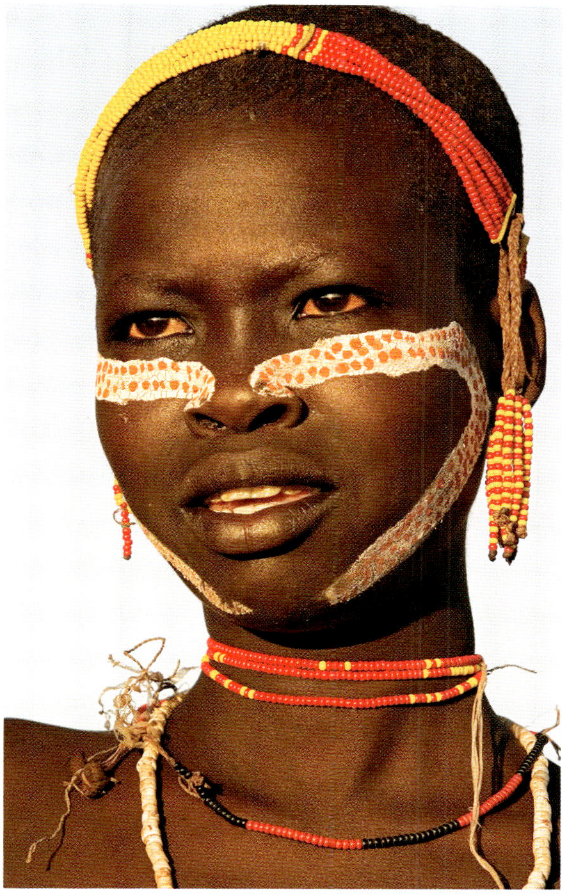

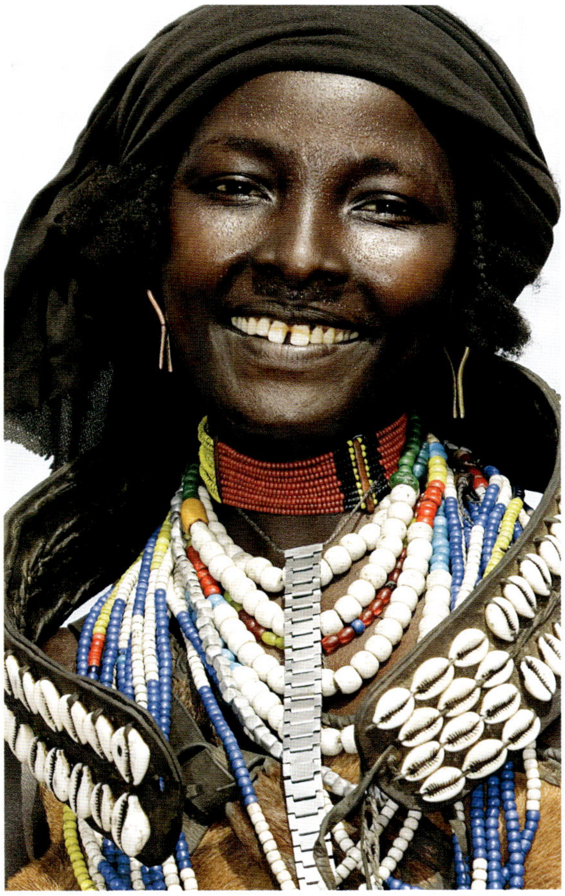

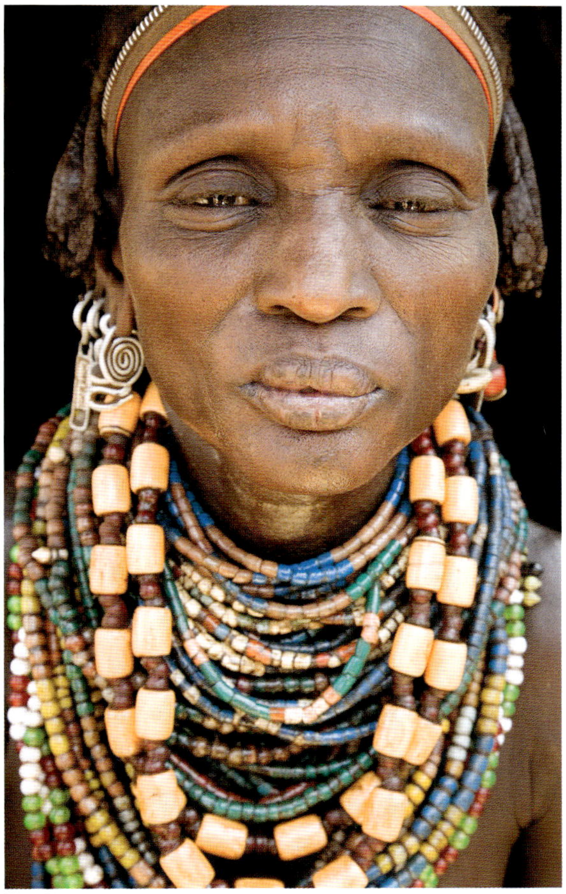

LEFT: *A multitude of beads—made of seedpods, wood, shell, and glass—are part of highly creative body assemblages worn by all the semi-nomadic pastoralist tribespeople living in the arid environment of southern Ethiopia. Although many of the tribes are closely related, the assemblages are nonetheless a visual language identifying specific groups, ages, and gender. (plates 115–118)*

TOP LEFT: 115. *A five-year-old Surma boy with colorful glass beads. The Surma (or Suri) live in the plains of Southwestern Ethiopia where they herd their highly prized cattle. 2006.*

TOP RIGHT: 116. *A young (perhaps thirteen-year-old) Hamar girl from Turmi displays her elegantly designed and masterfully coordinated body paint and glass bead adornment. 2006.*

BOTTOM LEFT: 117. *An Erbore girl from the Rift Valley wears layers of beads, including a baby-carrying strap of cowrie shells and leather. 2006.*

BOTTOM RIGHT: 118. *A Galeb tribeswoman from the Lower Omo Valley in her multi-strand necklaces of wood, seedpod, shell, and colorful glass beads.*

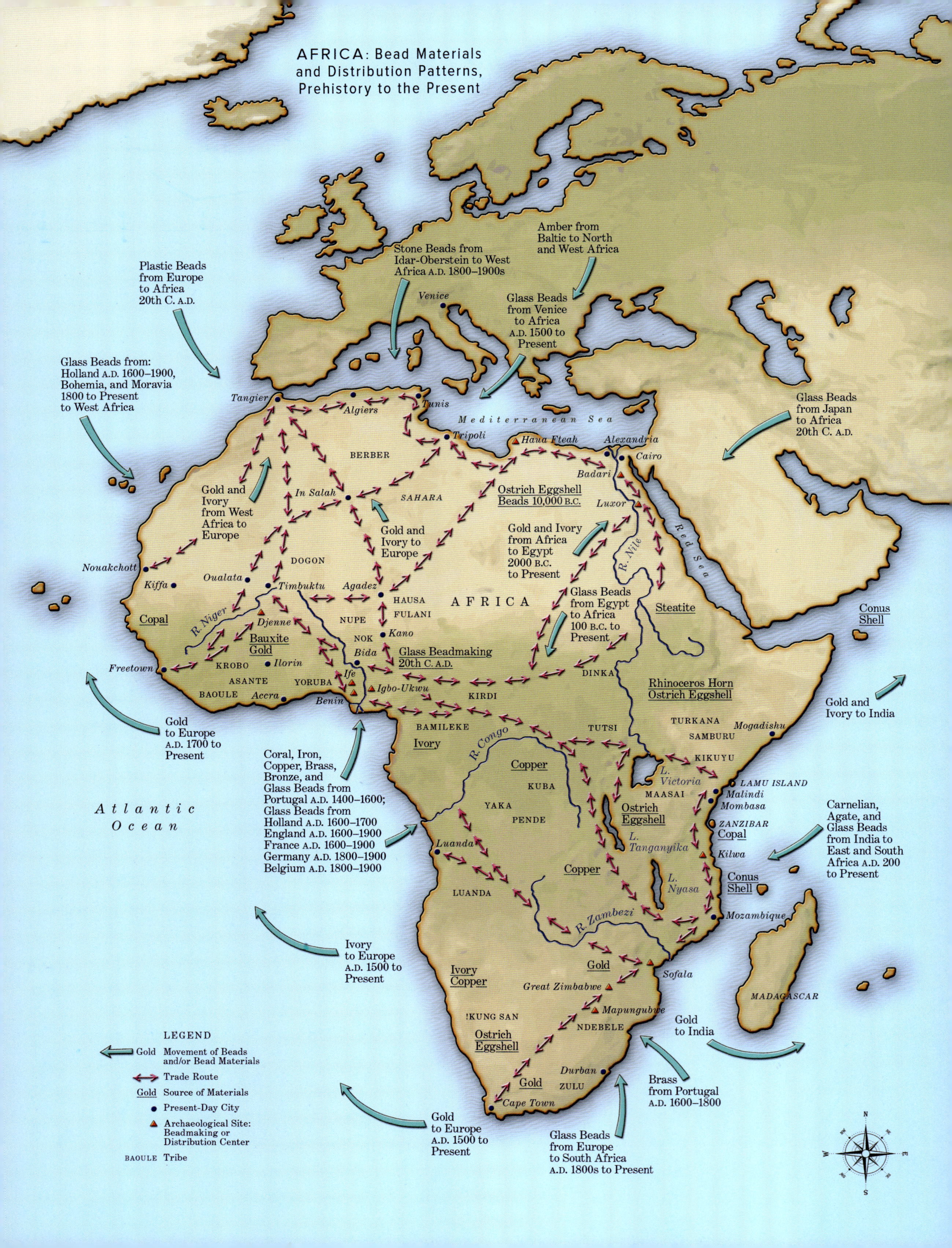
AFRICA: Bead Materials and Distribution Patterns, Prehistory to the Present
Plastic Beads from Europe to Africa 20th C. A.D.
Stone Beads from Idar-Oberstein to West Africa A.D. 1800–1900s
Amber from Baltic to North and West Africa
Glass Beads from Venice to Africa A.D. 1500 to Present
Venice
Glass Beads from: Holland A.D. 1600–1900, Bohemia, and Moravia 1800 to Present to West Africa
Glass Beads from Japan to Africa 20th C. A.D.
Tangier
Algiers
Tunis
Mediterranean Sea
Tripoli
Haua Fteah
Alexandria
Cairo
Badari
BERBER
SAHARA
In Salah
Gold and Ivory from West Africa to Europe
Gold and Ivory to Europe
Ostrich Eggshell Beads 10,000 B.C.
Luxor
Gold and Ivory from Africa to Egypt 2000 B.C. to Present
R. Nile
Red Sea
Nouakchott
Kiffa
Oualata
Timbuktu
DOGON
Agadez
HAUSA
FULANI
AFRICA
Glass Beads from Egypt to Africa 100 B.C. to Present
Steatite
Conus Shell
Copal
R. Niger
Djenne
Bauxite
Gold
NUPE
NOK
Kano
Bida
Glass Beadmaking 20th C. A.D.
KROBO
Ilorin
Freetown
ASANTE
YORUBA
Ife
BAOULE
Accra
Igbo-Ukwu
Benin
KIRDI
DINKA
Rhinoceros Horn Ostrich Eggshell
Gold and Ivory to India
Gold to Europe A.D. 1700 to Present
BAMILEKE
TUTSI
TURKANA
SAMBURU
Mogadishu
Ivory
R. Congo
Copper
KUBA
KIKUYU
L. Victoria
LAMU ISLAND
Malindi
Mombasa
MAASAI
Coral, Iron, Copper, Brass, Bronze, and Glass Beads from Portugal A.D. 1400–1600; Glass Beads from Holland A.D. 1600–1700 England A.D. 1600–1900 France A.D. 1600–1900 Germany A.D. 1800–1900 Belgium A.D. 1800–1900
Atlantic Ocean
YAKA
PENDE
Ostrich Eggshell
ZANZIBAR
Copal
Carnelian, Agate, and Glass Beads from India to East and South Africa A.D. 200 to Present
Luanda
L. Tanganyika
Kilwa
LUANDA
Copper
L. Nyasa
Conus Shell
R. Zambezi
Mozambique
Ivory to Europe A.D. 1500 to Present
Gold
Sofala
Ivory Copper
Great Zimbabwe
Mapungubwe
MADAGASCAR
!KUNG SAN
NDEBELE
Gold to India
Ostrich Eggshell
Gold
Durban
ZULU
Cape Town
Brass from Portugal A.D. 1600–1800
Gold to Europe A.D. 1500 to Present
Glass Beads from Europe to South Africa A.D. 1800s to Present
LEGEND
Gold Movement of Beads and/or Bead Materials
Trade Route
Gold Source of Materials
Present-Day City
Archaeological Site: Beadmaking or Distribution Center
BAOULE Tribe
N
S
E
W

continue to be made from recycled glass using pulverized bottles, or imported glass beads as their raw materials.[12]

By the ninth century, more than 165,000 stone and glass beads were used in ceremonies at Igbo-Ukwu to adorn bronze sculptures and staffs. The large quantity of these beads indicates their importance to the local population. Among the stone beads were carnelians from India. Most of the glass beads are of blue/yellow and blue/green dichroic drawn glass, probably of western Asian manufacture. Several hundred years later, glass beads were made at Ife in western Yorubaland from imported glass. One crucible held nearly two thousand blue glass beads, known as *segi* or *popi*, widely used at the time.[13]

Since the sixteenth century, glass beadmaking in sub-Saharan Africa has been concentrated in today's Nigeria and Ghana. This tradition remains intact, and today the Bida of Nigeria and the Krobo of Ghana are two of the most important African glass manufacturers. There are pockets of glassworking elsewhere on the continent, including the Mauritanian towns of Kiffa and Oualata, where craftswomen have developed exquisite polychrome glass beads (plate 108). Beads from imported glass scrap continue to be made in both West Africa and Mauritania using two basic techniques: traditional winding and drawing, and using ground powder glass. Powder-glass beadmaking is not unique to Africa, but has become a marvelous and sophisticated African art form (plates 109, Timeline 1209–1214, 1220).[14]

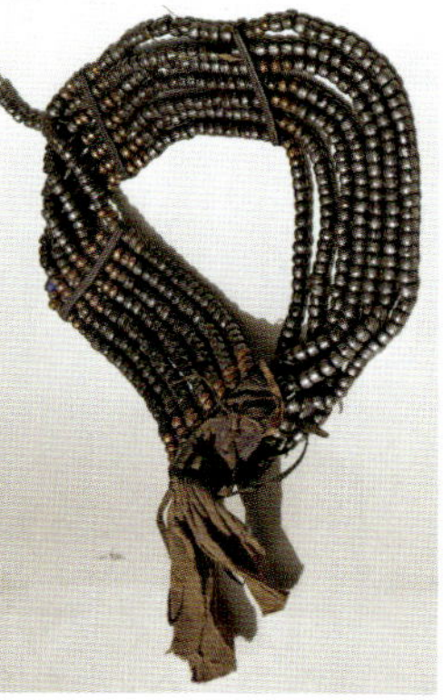

119. *Turkana belt of copper and iron beads, c. 1960. With the exception of the Turkana, East African tribes ignore metalwork. These beads, made and worn by married women, indicate the clan to which their husbands belong. Iron beads indicate that the wearer's husband belongs to the Stone clan; a predominance of copper would symbolize his membership in the Leopard clan. The belt is worn every day.*[IV] *n.s. National Museums of Kenya, Nairobi*

OVERLEAF: 120. *Men's beaded corsets are among the most fascinating articles of adornment. This photograph shows Dinka cowherders of southern Sudan with beaded corsets fitted tightly to their bodies. The colors of the corset indicate the wearer's age group: red and white are for ages fifteen to twenty-five; pink and purple for twenty-five to thirty; and yellow for those past thirty.*[VI]

Empires, Kingdoms, and Trade

Beads were favored trade items with Indian, Middle Eastern, and European merchants. Shipments of beads began arriving in Africa by at least the fourth century A.D. While a few Arab traders penetrated the interior of Africa using established trans-Saharan trade routes, most Indians and Europeans were confined to coastal trading posts until the middle of the nineteenth century. From these commercial outposts, foreigners dealt with African middlemen who moved beads inland along the trade networks. It is not surprising that the early trading centers including Kilwa, Zanzibar, Sofala, Djenne, and Timbuktu—cities that today have archaeological sites rich in imported stone and glass beads.

Trade became a focal point for organizing human affairs: empires grew out of markets. The control of raw materials and their exchange for finished products led to an accumulation of wealth in favored areas, sometimes laying the foundations for the emergence of indigenous African states. During the seventh century A.D., Muslim Arabs conquered Mediterranean Africa and began to exchange brass, cloth, stone, glass beads, and Baltic amber for West African gold, ivory, and slaves. From A.D. 900 to 1500, they created important trade relationships aided by the development of Islamic empires within North and West Africa. Two of the most powerful states were Ghana, which prevailed from the eighth to the eleventh century, and Mali, a huge empire during the twelfth and thirteenth centuries that stretched from the Atlantic to the great bend of the Niger River. The empire of Mali was eclipsed by that of Songhai, centered in the flourishing cities of Gao and Timbuktu. Archaeological finds suggest that beads were a significant part of these empires' trade and their people's adornment.

To the south of the Sahara, Sudanic merchants traded among peoples who lived at the edge of the tropical forests that border the low-lying Guinea coast from Sierra Leone to Nigeria. Trade with the gold-producing region of West Africa was extremely active. By 1500, partly as a result of commercial contacts with the north, the foundations were laid for the development of the great forest states, notably the Benin and Akan kingdoms. At the same time, the first Europeans, mostly Portuguese sailors, reached these coastal

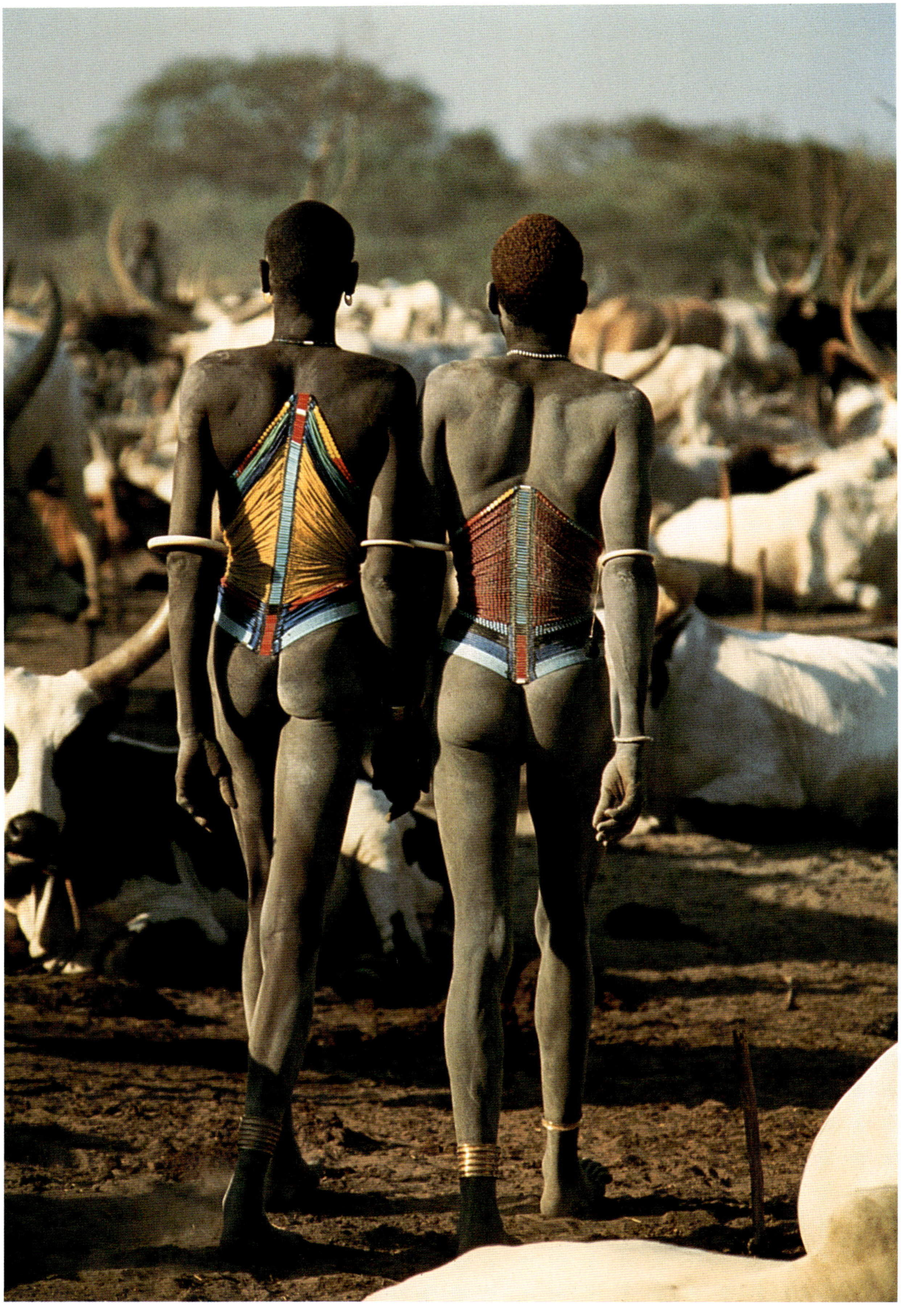

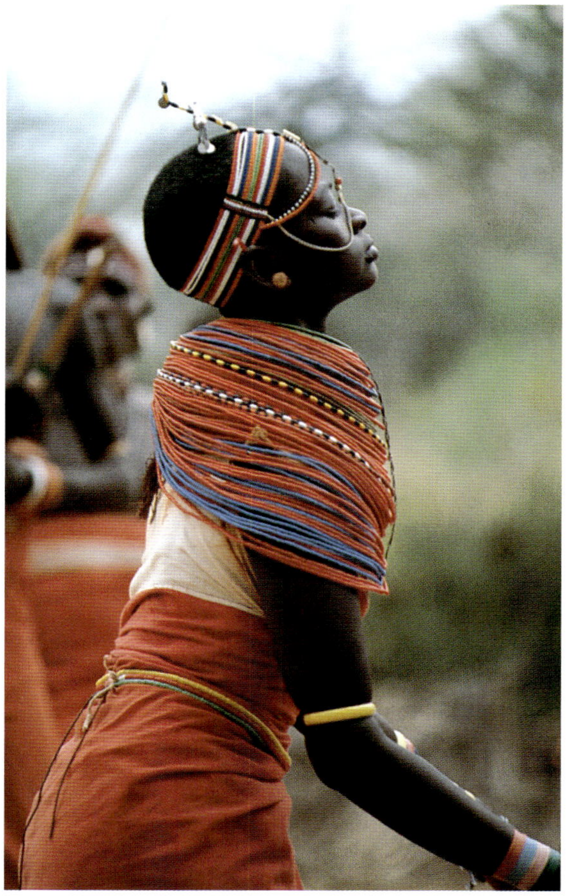

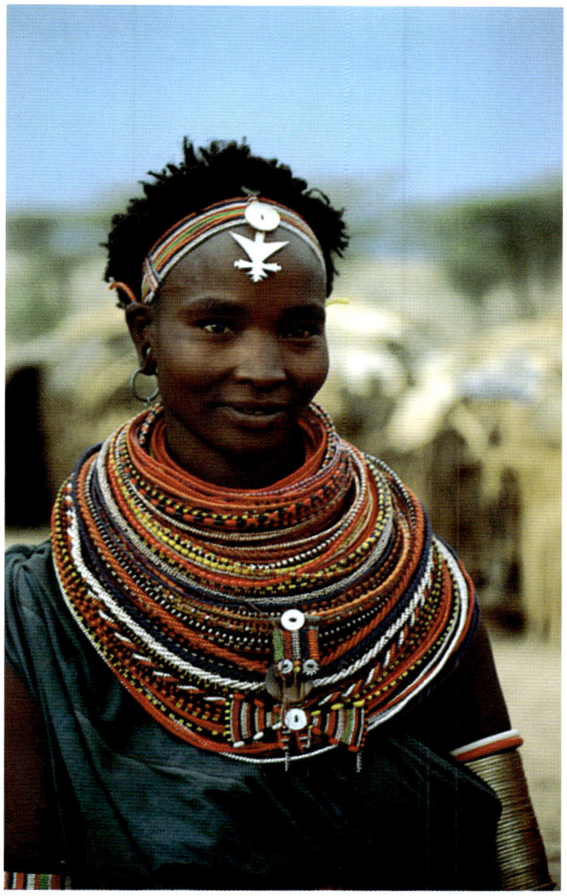

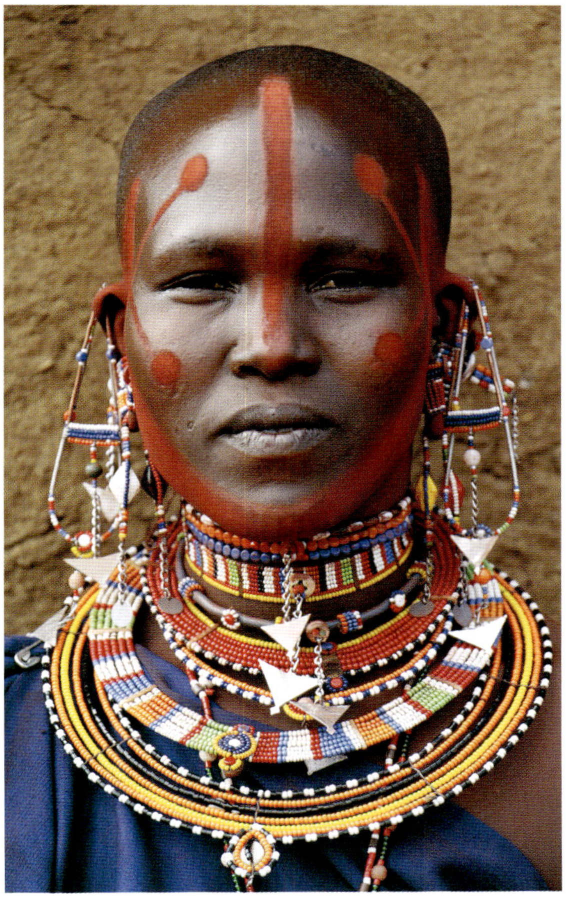

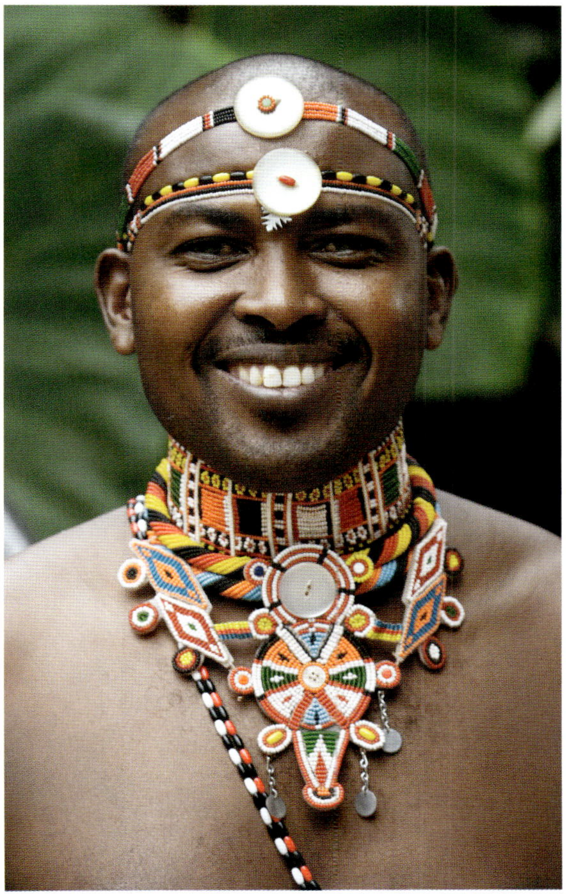

TOP LEFT: 121. *A young, unmarried Samburu girl dancing.*

Beads communicate social status for both Samburu women and men. A Samburu warrior describes a beautiful girl as follows: "She will have many beads right up to her chin; this is what makes her beautiful."[VII] A beautiful girl has many admirers, who make gifts of beads, which both define and reinforce her beauty. By age sixteen, a girl will often have a substantial collection of necklaces, indicating her great desirability and thereby helping to secure a proposal of marriage.

TOP RIGHT: 122. *Married Samburu woman. The beaded necklaces worn by the woman were obtained by the author while visiting a Samburu village in 1983. Although this woman sold the necklace to obtain money to educate her children, it was painful for her to part with it. Such necklaces are symbols of prestige, representing years of gifts.*

BOTTOM LEFT: 123. *A Samburu tribeswoman in a regal display of beaded earrings and necklaces.*

BOTTOM RIGHT: 124. *A Samburu warrior displays a marvelous array of contemporary bead necklaces and headbands. Bachelor warriors devote much time to decorating themselves to attract young women. "Young men accent and highlight their well-muscled, shining bodies with narrow bands, circlets, and bandoliers of beads around the neck, chest, waist, arms, and legs. Such effects give warriors their distinctive and proud appearance."[VIII] Beads are worn by men in most African pastoral societies, although the number of beads they use decreases once they become elders in the tribe.*

kingdoms, thereby establishing their own direct source of African ivory and gold and connecting West Africa to European markets.

Along the east coast of Africa, a string of Muslim city-states, notably Mogadishu and Kilwa on the mainland and the island of Zanzibar, emerged as part of an Indian Ocean trading complex. Especially important to this network was the gold of Zimbabwe, which was shipped from the port of Sofala. In 1498, Vasco da Gama sailed from Portugal around the southern tip of Africa and visited some of these East African ports on his way to India. His journey marks the beginning of European intrusion into the highly lucrative Muslim trading preserve. It is known that Vasco da Gama bartered with beads in the town of Mozambique.[13]

Peoples on the West African coast began to trade with Europe in the late fifteenth century. First were the Portuguese, followed over the next four hundred years by the Dutch, English, French, Belgians, and Germans. They brought millions of Venetian, Dutch, and Bohemian glass beads to Africa. Exactly what happened to most of these beads is unclear. Over the years a variety of uses other than ornamentation has been suggested. Richard Burton, the explorer who searched for the source of the Nile, had his own theory about the ultimate fate of large quantities of imported beads:

> It is difficult to divine what becomes of these ornaments: for centuries ton after ton has been imported into the country. They are by no means perishable substances and the people, like Indians, carry their wealth upon their persons. Yet not a third of the population was observed to wear any considerable quantity; possibly the excessive demand in the lands outlying direct intercourse with the coast tends to disperse them throughout the vast terra incognita of the central African basin.[14]

A consideration of the uses of beads may shed light on the mystery of their apparent disappearance. Henry Morton Stanley, in his book *How I Found Livingstone*, related that when he arrived at the northern stream of the Rugufu River, he distinctly heard the sound of "distant thunder in the west." His interpreters explained:

> It is the great mountain on the other side of the Tanganyika, full of deep holes, into which the water rolls; and when there is a wind on the Tanganyika there is a sound like thunder. Many boats have been lost there, and it is a custom with Arabs and natives alike to throw cloth and especially white beads, to appease the God of the lake. Those who throw beads generally get past without trouble, but those who do not...are drowned.[15]

The beds of lakes, rivers, streams, and coastal waters may well be the resting places of some of those tons of lost beads to which Burton referred. Every year, thousands of beads of every vintage are washed up on the beaches of East Africa and its islands. Some of these without doubt are from shipwrecks, but others must surely be the offerings made by Arabs and Africans through the centuries.[16]

The importation of beads had important consequences for African history. Glass beads were bartered by Africans for incense, ivory, tortoiseshell, rhinoceros horn, palm and coconut oils, timber, pig iron, and gold. The same tightly structured trade networks that for centuries moved gold and ivory from the interior to West African ports, bringing beads back on the return trips, later served the slave trade. Between the 1500s and 1867, slavers shipped perhaps fifteen million Africans to the Americas, routinely exchanging European-made glass beads for their human cargo. One of the many records of this exchange came from a German priest visiting South Africa in 1653. "East of the Cape," he wrote, "nearly halfway to Mozambique, much gold, slaves, and other commodities were to be had at cheap rates for soft goods and glass beads of all sorts."[17]

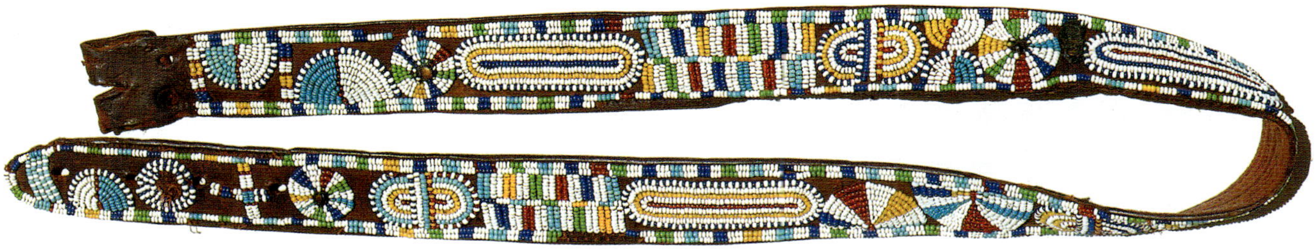

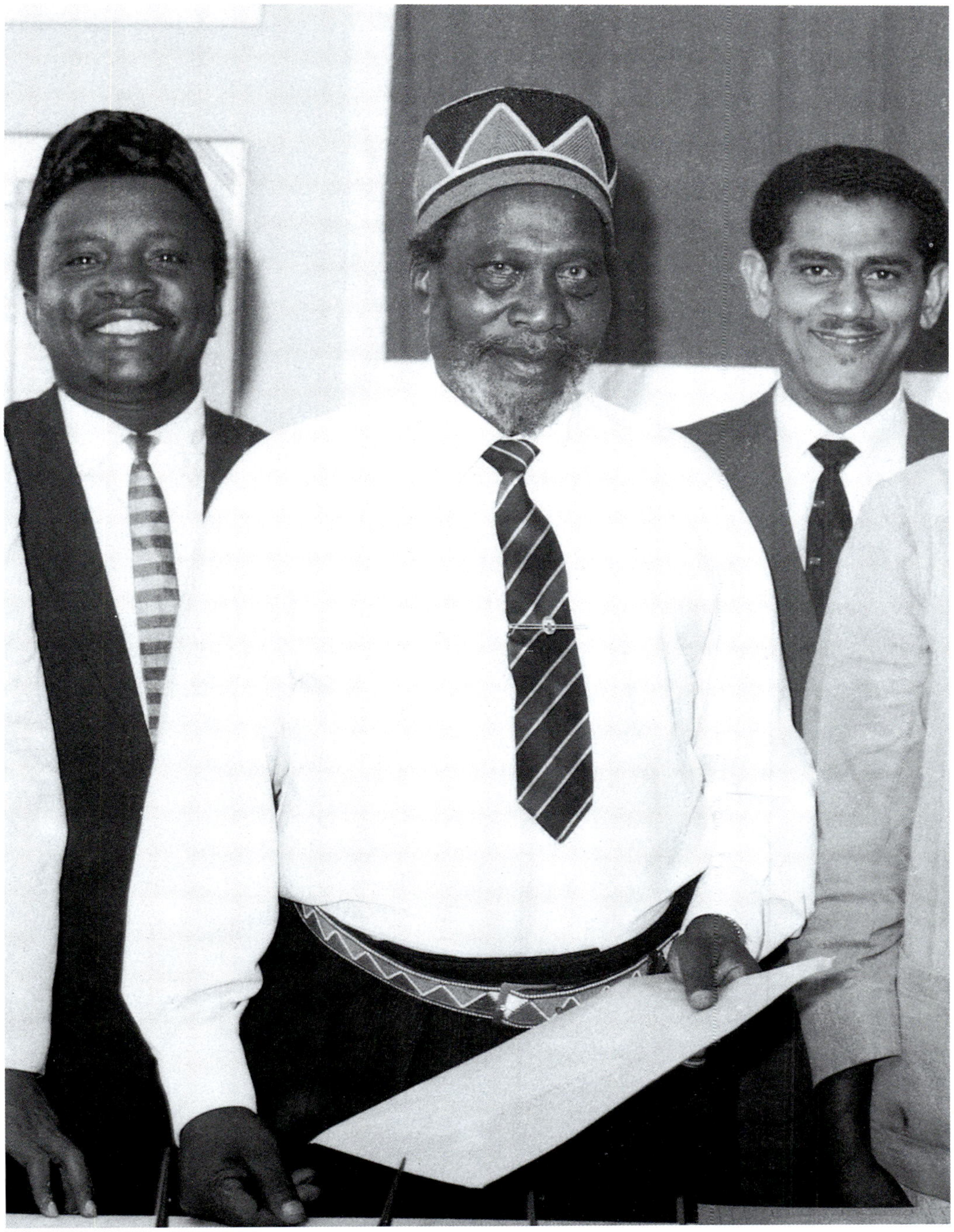

ABOVE: 125. *Circumcised men of the Kikuyu tribe in Kenya wear this type of glass and leather beaded belt until they become elders; thereafter, they wear them only on special occasions. The beadwork pattern on this belt, made about 1969, is called* Kenyatta. *Width, 4.9 cm. National Museums of Kenya, Nairobi*

LEFT: 126. *The late Mzee Jomo Kenyatta wearing the* Kenyatta *style of beaded belt for which he was named. (Photograph undated.) National Museums of Kenya, Nairobi*

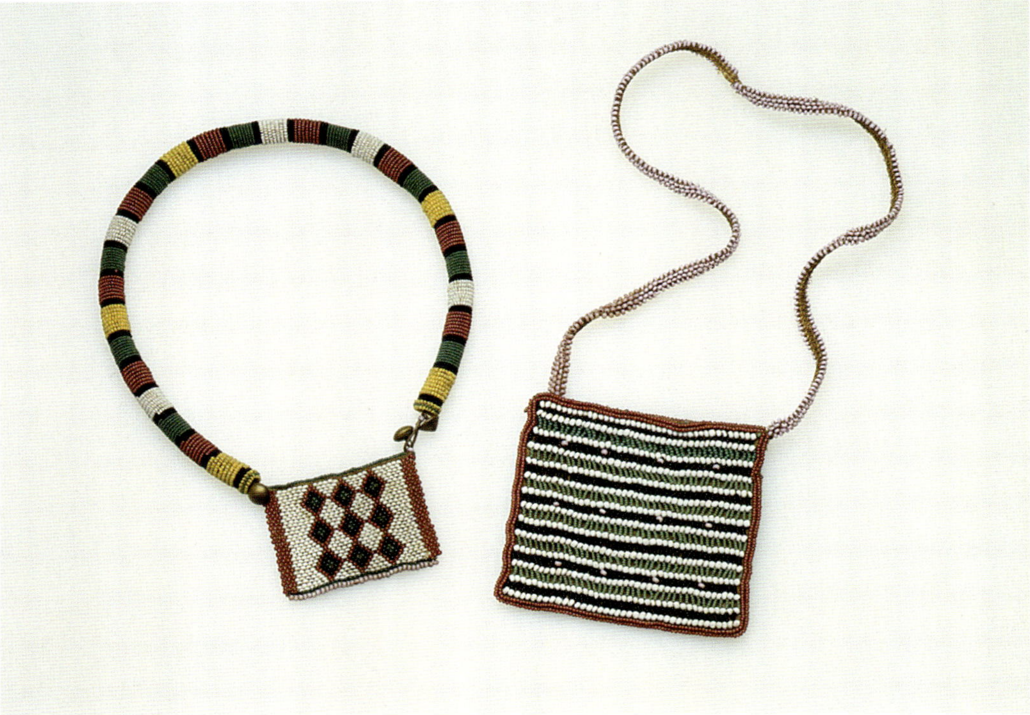

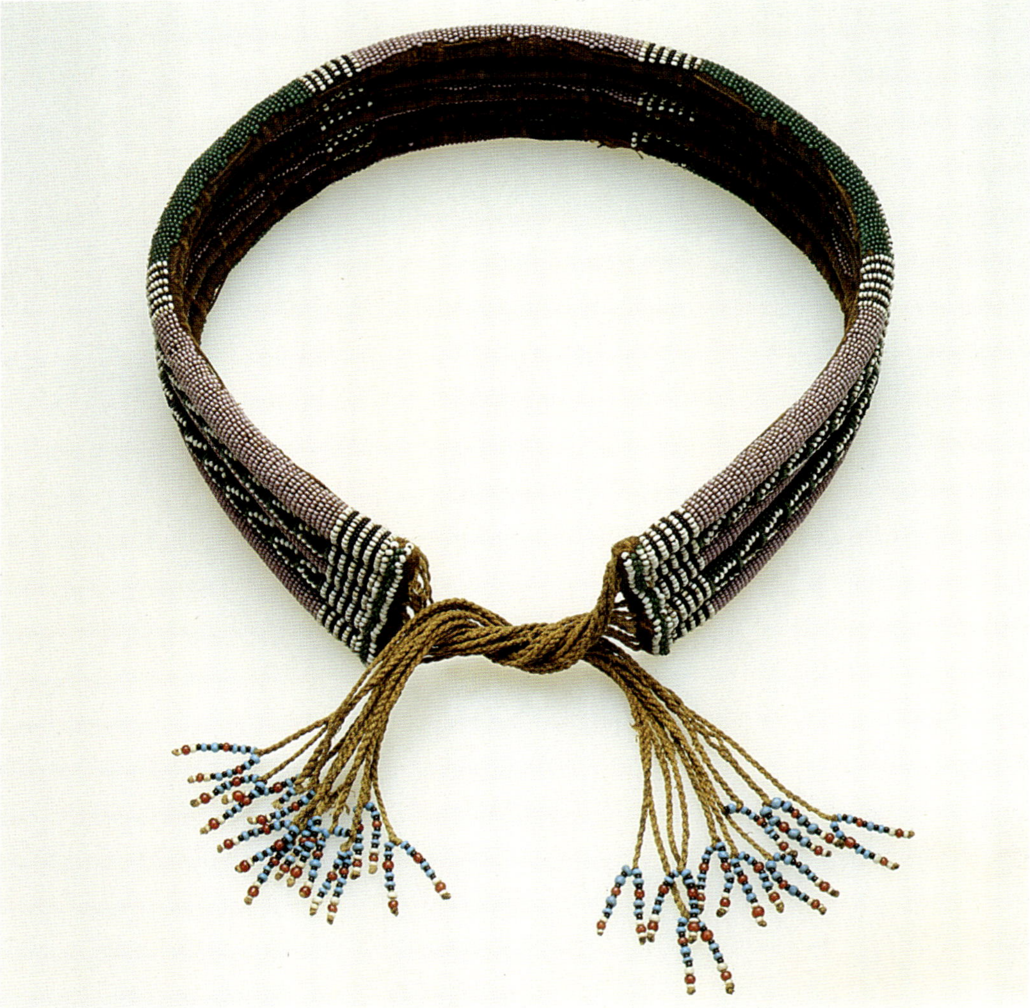

TOP: 127. *On the left is a beaded collar to which is attached a small patterned panel, known as a "love letter." Zulu girls convey to their suitors, and wives to their husbands, feelings of courtship, love, hope, yearning, and sadness through the choice of colors and patterns woven into these flat beadwork panels. Blue may represent gossip, thought, or sky; red can symbolize "eyes red with weeping" from "seeking one's lover in vain," or can symbolize blood or fire; yellow can be for riches or poverty; white always means love and purity.*

Juxtaposed colors take on special meanings: a pink and white panel might say: "You are poor...but I love you." Such messages are part of the private dialogue in a couple's relationship and are rarely understood by outsiders.[IX]

On the right is a beadwork bag similar to those worn by young unmarried Zulu men in the early twentieth century, the time when Zulu men began wearing beads. Collar: length, 36 cm. Collection Tambaran Gallery, New York

RIGHT: 128. *An* umutsha, *a late nineteenth- or early twentieth-century Zulu belt made of several beaded ropes sewn together. It was worn by both young men and unmarried women. This is an example of a beadwork technique that developed at a time when beads became available in great quantities. Length, 80 cm. Collection Tambaran Gallery, New York*

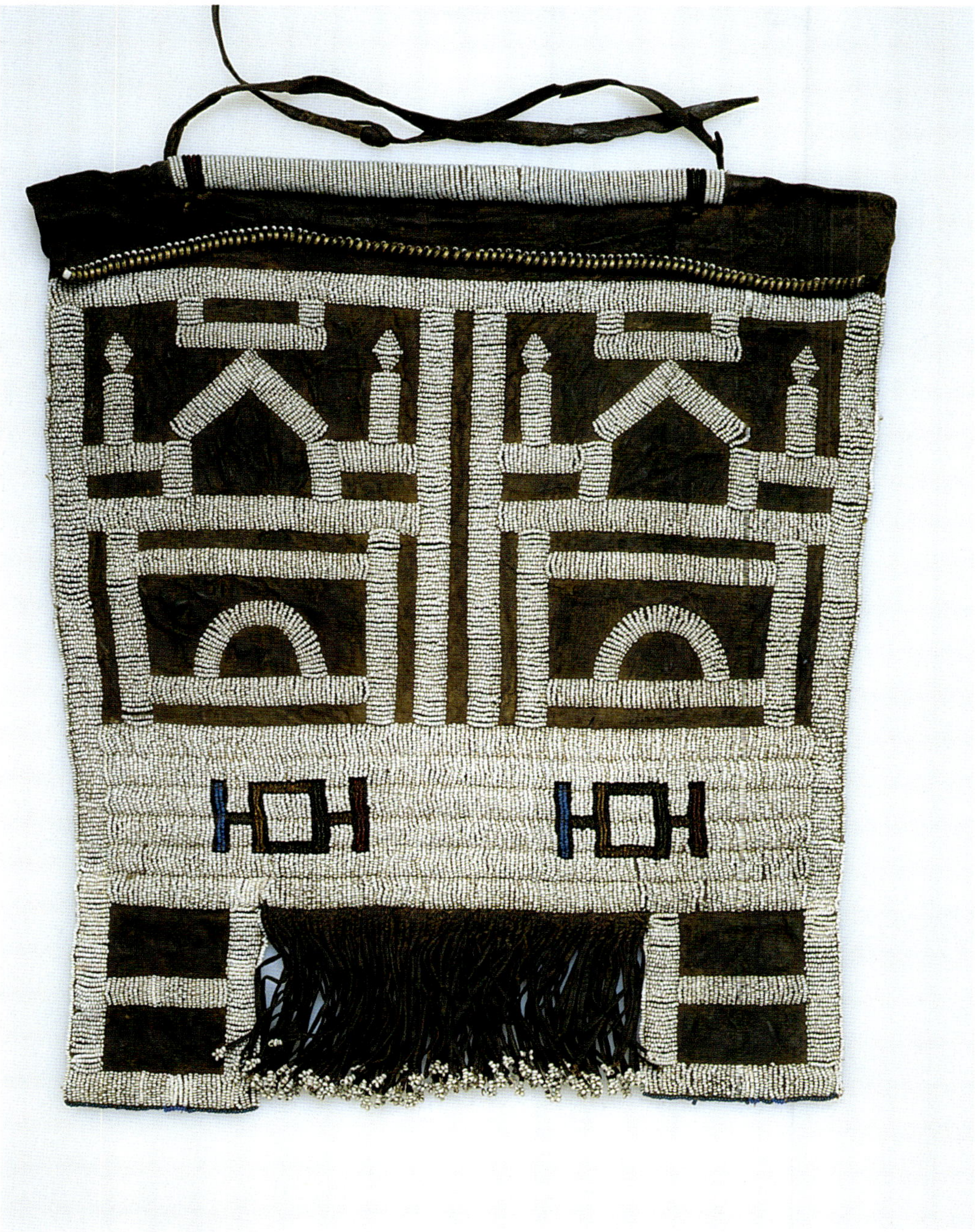

LEFT: 129. *This* mapoto, *a beaded apron worn by married Ndebele women, was made of glass beads sewn on beaten goatskin. It is at least fifty years old. Architectural symbols of houses appear on the top panel, with abstract designs resembling aerial views of the kraal (homestead) below it. Ndebele beadwork designs frequently mirror the tribe's painted murals. Width, 45.72 cm. Private collection*

BOTTOM: 130. *The mural art of Ndebele villages is strongly tied to their beadwork tradition. Both murals and beadwork use geometric patterns and incorporate elements from everyday surroundings, such as telephone poles, airplanes, and electric lightbulbs. The murals dissolve during the rainy season and are repainted annually, while the more permanent beadwork allows for the historical study of Ndebele symbols that have disappeared from the walls.*

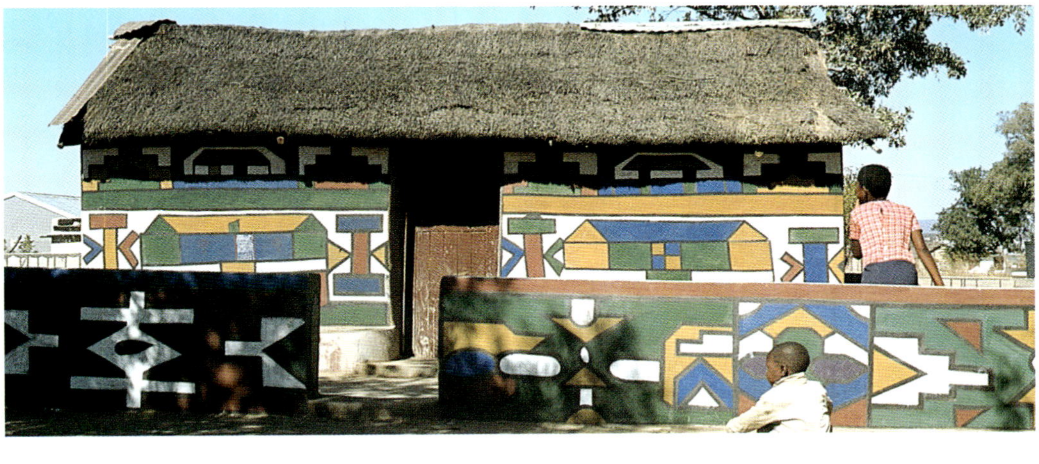

131. *The* nyoga, *a long, beaded train, is an important part of the Ndebele bridal outfit.* Nyogas *have different widths and can be up to eight feet long. Attached to a blanket, the* nyoga *hangs from the wearer's shoulders and trails on the ground like a snake as she dances.* Nyoga *means "snake tail" and may be a fertility symbol. This example of a fine, early twentieth-century* nyoga *has a central abstract motif of woven red, green, and black beads set in a field of white beads.*X *Length, 176 cm. Collection Colette and Jean-Pierre Ghysels, Brussels*

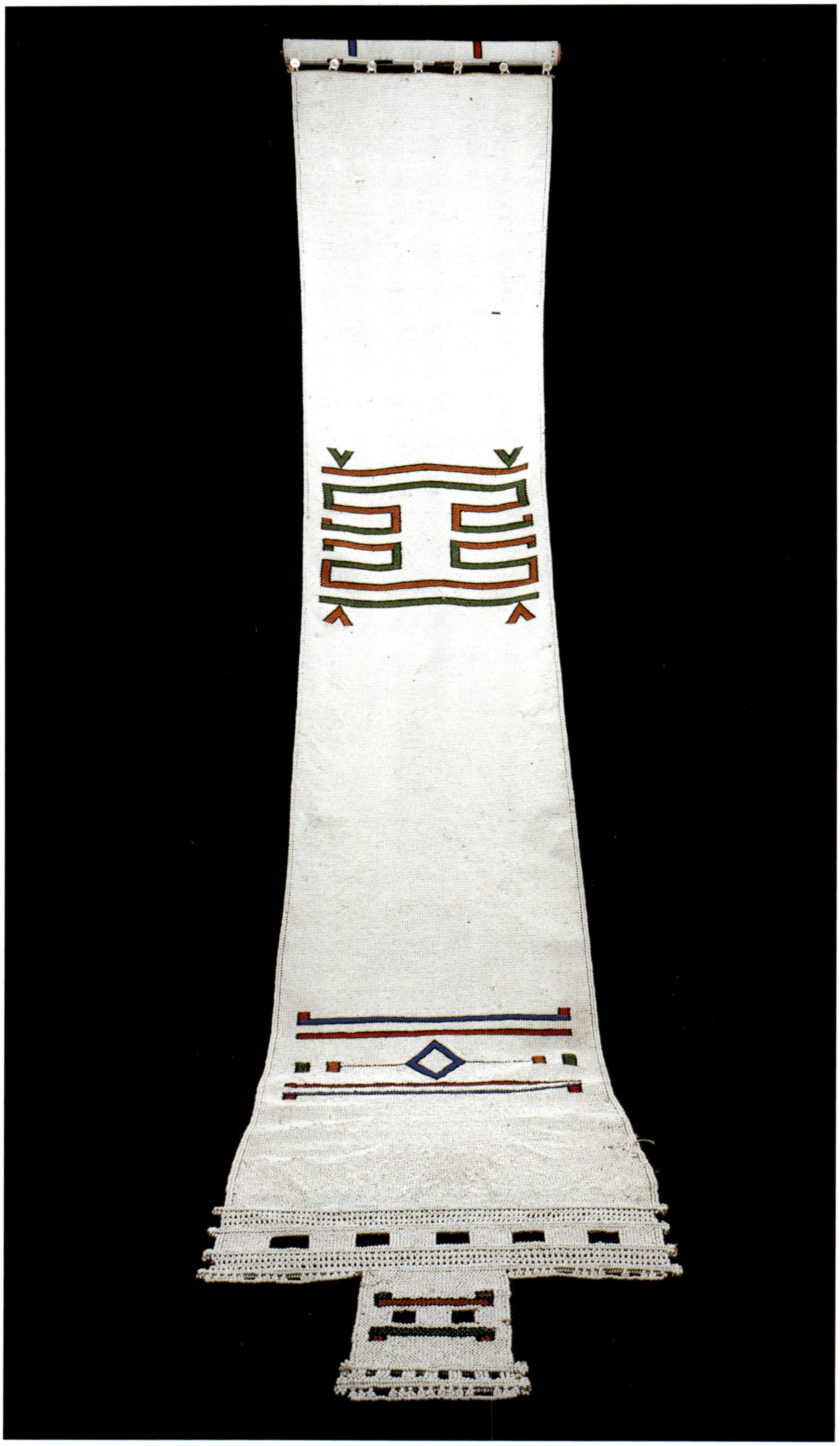

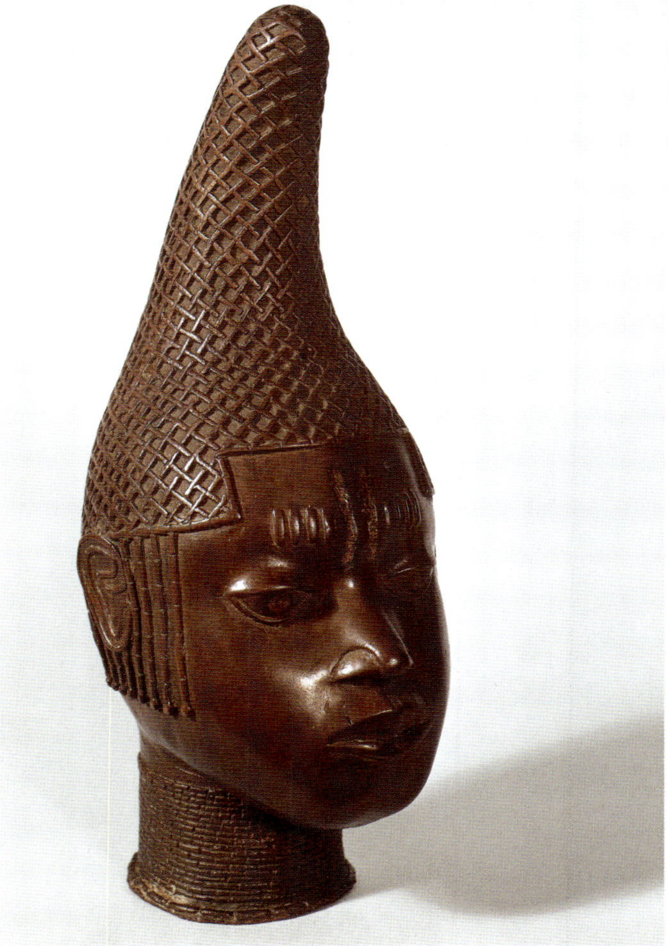

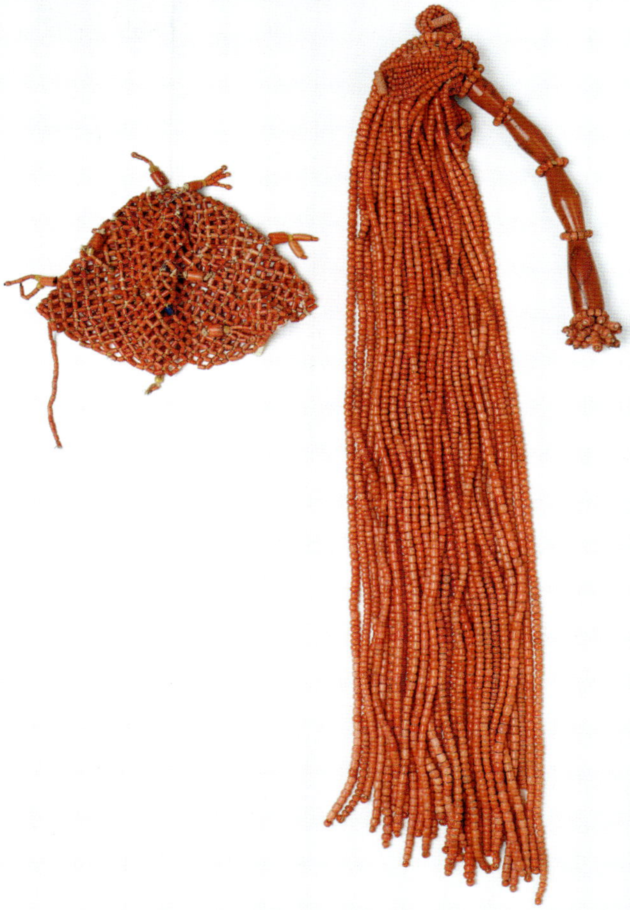

The Many Uses of Beads in African Societies

Beads became essential elements of personal adornment in almost every African society; but how they were (and still are) obtained and used depended on the group's social, political, and economic structure and on its role in the trade system.[18] For example, the Turkana, Samburu, and Dinka are subsistence-level herders occupying the arid grasslands and deserts of Kenya and the Sudan. Because they are constantly seeking fresh supplies of food and water for their livestock, bulky material possessions are impractical. Artistic expression therefore focuses on ornamenting the body rather than the homestead. In these tribes, both men and women wear beads as an essential part of everyday and ceremonial dress that communicates their ethnic affiliation, age grade, marital status, and wealth. The societies are organized according to age sets, a series of clearly defined levels through which each member of the group passes: childhood, warriorhood, and old age for men; childhood, womanhood, and marriage for women. Passage from one age set to the next is signaled by changes in clothing and adornment, including beads whose styles, colors, and assemblages beautify their wearers and communicate important information about them (plates 113–125).

Until this century, artisans in East Africa made beads of local, organic materials, such as shell, roots, seeds, and bone, strung with palm fibers or giraffe hair. When foreign trade invited contact with the Europeans, glass beads frequently replaced or augmented those made locally.

ABOVE LEFT: 132. *A sixteenth-century Benin bronze casting of the queen mother's head, showing a coral beaded headdress and coral bead collar. The beaded headdress covers the unusual hairstyle, called "chicken's beak." The casting was done by the lost-wax process. n.s. British Museum, London*

ABOVE RIGHT: 133. *A coral beaded cap, similar to the one shown on the bronze casting in plate 132, and a coral and jasper (lantana) bead flywhisk. Both belonged to a sixteenth-century* oba. *n.s. British Museum, London*

TOP: 134. *Yoruba face panel or mask for a late nineteenth-century* egungun, *a masquerade cult dancer. Cowrie shells, once the means of economic exchange among the Yoruba, still signify prosperity. The cowries surrounding the face of the dancer symbolize the affluence and power of the lineage that the masquerade honors. The abundant use of beads and the bird motifs suggest the mask belonged to a royal household.*[XI] *Length, 39.3 cm. Mingei International Museum, San Diego*

BOTTOM: 135. *A pair of Yoruba beaded boots, worn only by an* oba *(the ruler). Decorated along the front with a row of beaded birds, the interlaced and zigzag patterns represent royalty. Nineteenth–Twentieth century. Height, 44.4 cm. British Museum, London*

OPPOSITE: 136. *One of a pair of nineteenth-century dance panels, worn by a Yoruba priest or priestess at the time of an annual festival and made of locally woven cotton cloth and imported European glass seed-beads. The faces that appear on many beaded bags or panels are conceived as images of the spiritual power of the worshiper.*[XII] *Length, 34.9 cm. Private collection*

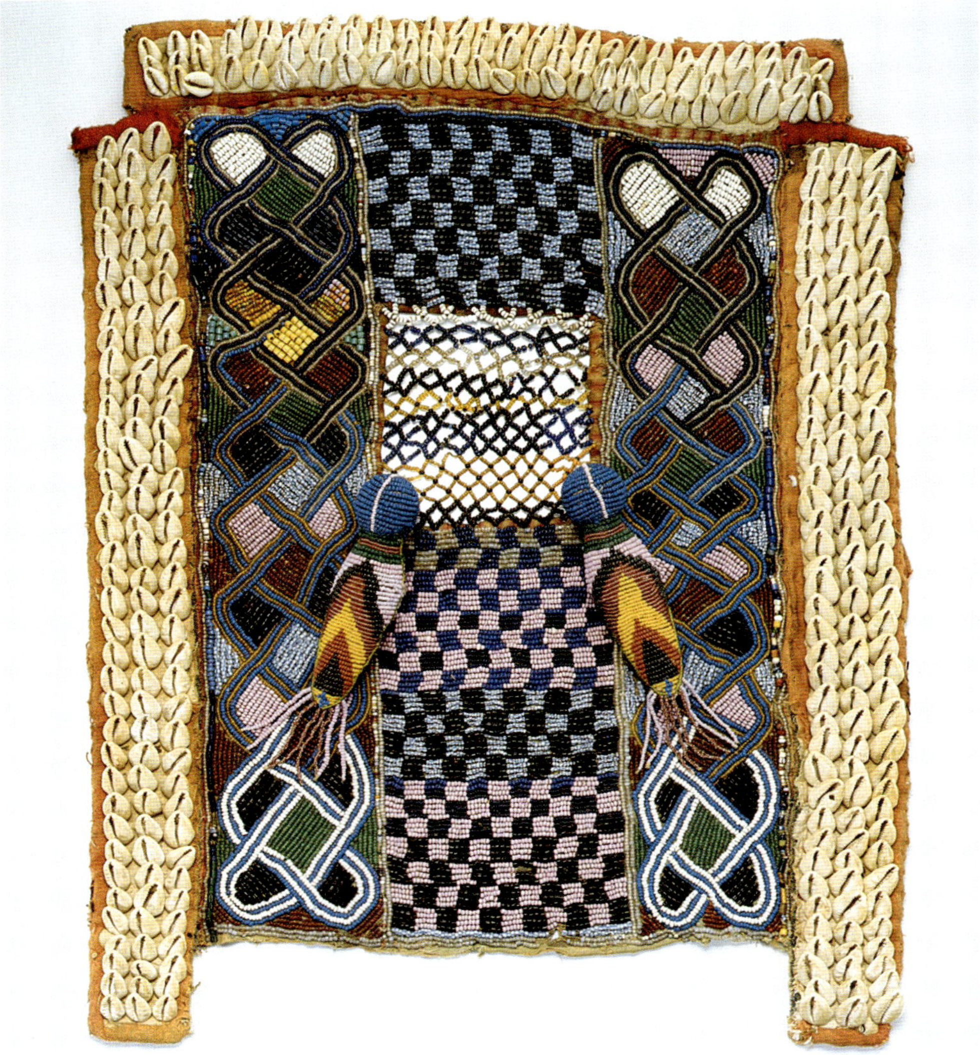

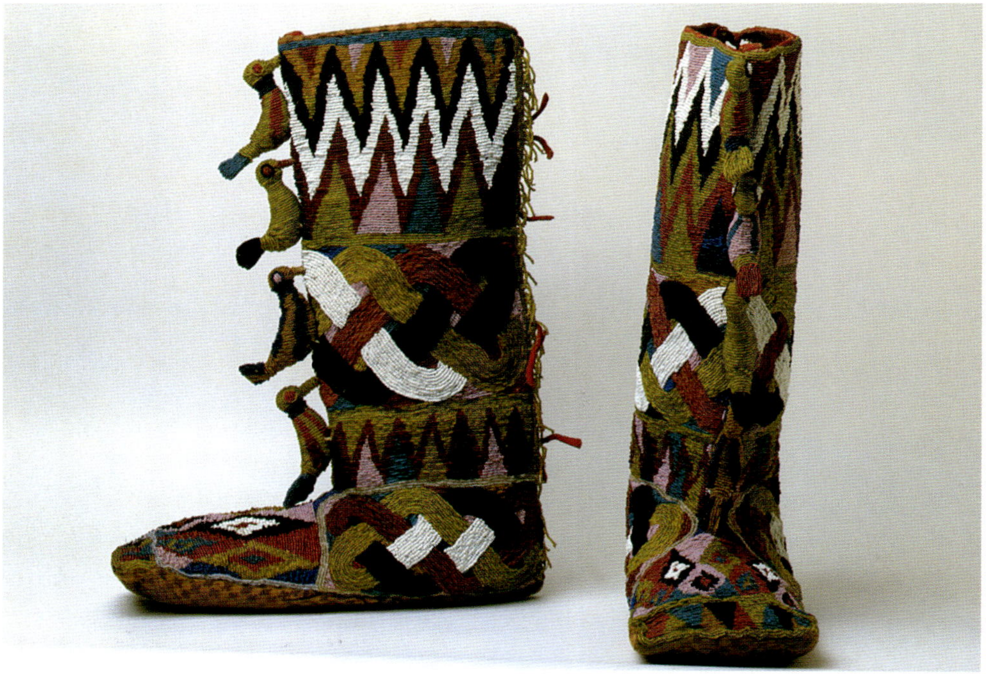

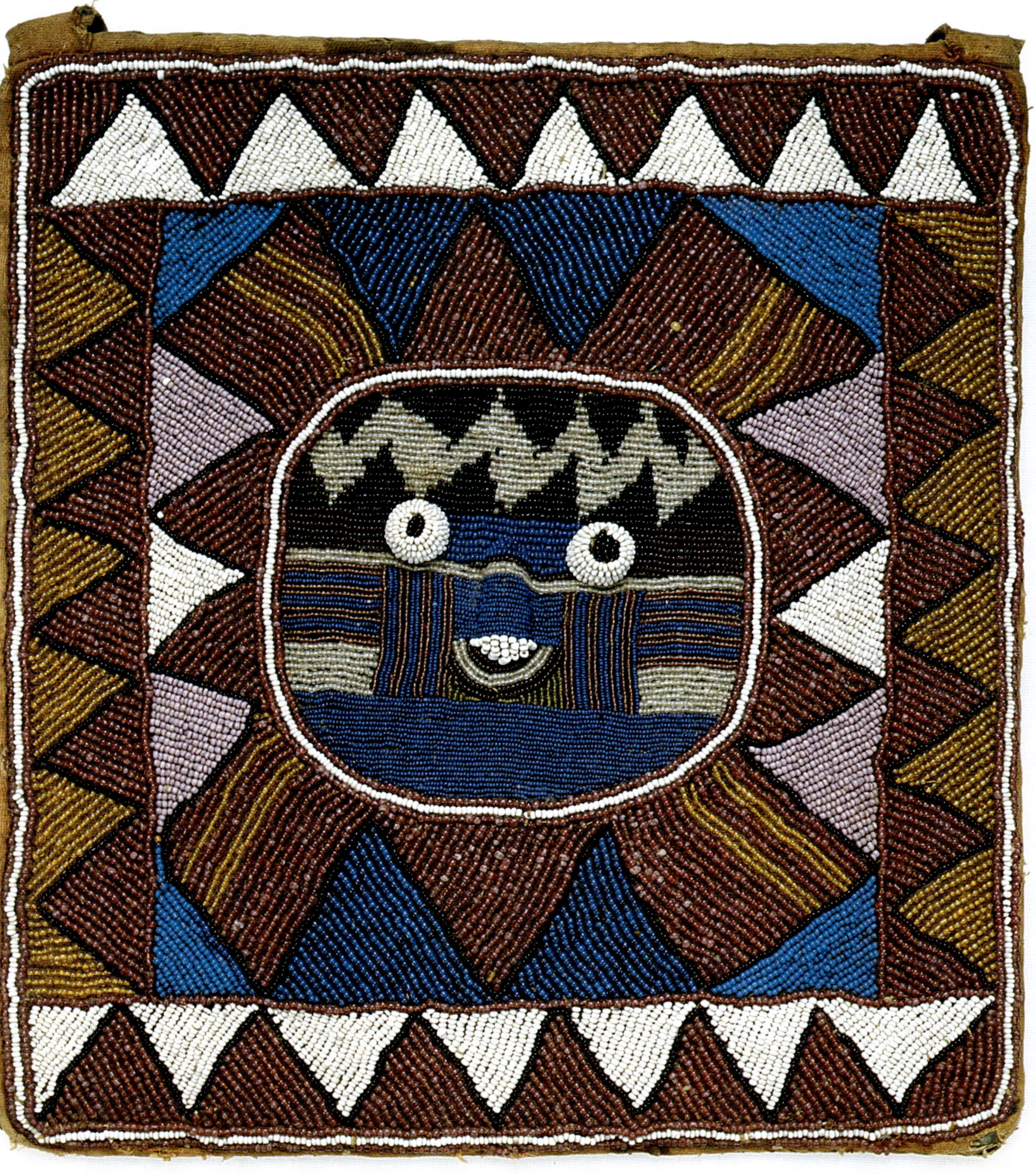

Personal and domestic adornments have long been the predominant modes of artistic expression in South Africa, and beadwork specifically is an important art form in the region. For centuries, small quantities of glass beads originating in India were imported into South and East Africa, where they served as status symbols. By the end of the nineteenth century, trade in the more uniformly shaped and smaller glass seedbeads was fully established, and much greater quantities of beads were now available.

The southern African Zulu and Ndebele tribes used these more plentiful beads to create distinct and elaborate beadwork. Embellishments became more extensive, and the tribes developed beading techniques that made unusual use of the greater quantities of available beads (plates 127–131).

The earliest Ndebele beadwork dates to the beginning of the twentieth century. The oldest examples involve fields of predominantly white beads, sewn onto leather and articulated by sparse, geometric designs of tiny colored beads. The beaded ceremonial dress, worn exclusively by Ndebele women, marks the transition to womanhood.[19]

In contrast, beads are worn by peoples of the fertile river valleys of central and western Africa essentially to indicate social rank. Status was frequently expressed in material wealth, so that the amount, size, and weight of beads became important in the design of beaded adornment.

Benin

Complex, sedentary, food-producing societies that used the rivers as avenues of trade emerged throughout Africa in the Middle Ages. Rivers supplied dependable water sources, allowing farmers, fishermen, and herds to prosper. On the banks of the Congo and Niger rivers, important centralized kingdoms evolved with control of trade networks along overland and river routes. Local products, including foodstuff, gold, ivory, and palm oil, were exchanged originally with the Arabs and later with the Europeans for amber, coral, and glass beads. In the Benin, Asante, Yoruba, and Cameroon kingdoms, all of which grew rich through commercial activities, elaborate beaded necklaces as well as intricate glass beadwork were produced by specialized craftsmen. The cultures of West Africa have created remarkably beautiful sculptural beadwork, which in some instances are the beaded equivalents of the region's great wood sculptures.

The Benin dynasty in southeastern Nigeria began to emerge about A.D. 1000. The *oba* built great wealth through tribute and through control of trade. Benin monopolized trade with the Europeans, first with the Portuguese, who arrived in 1485, and later with other European nations. The king maintained a guild of bronze casters, who produced bronze sculpture of great sophistication and verisimilitude. The quality of Benin bronzes stunned early European explorers.

For centuries, the ceremonial regalia of the *oba*, his warlords, chiefs, and other attendants displayed the wealth of the Benin court. An important feature of this regalia was the *oba*'s coral beads. The number of coral beads worn by an attendant of the *oba* indicated his rank. Once a year, the *oba* rode through old Benin and personally conferred upon his officials the "honor of beads," an honor comparable to knighthood. If the title was not hereditary, the beads might have to be returned upon the owner's death.[20]

The Yoruba

The mythology of the Yoruba, heirs to the rich traditions of Benin, is splendidly reflected in their glass beadwork (plates 134–7). Hundreds of Yoruba *orisha* (spirits) are honored in beadwork: every family or clan has its own spirit, and every event in life—birth, sickness, or death—is related to an *orisha*.

The Yoruba myth of creation relates that the holy city of Ife was the center of the world, the city in which their kingship originated. At Ife, on terra-cottas and bronzes nearly one thousand years old, the *onis* ("priest-kings") are shown wearing large quantities of beads. Ife was a beadmaking center where artisans melted down beads and other glass obtained from medieval Europe and the Islamic world, reworking the material into their own designs.

Waist beads are of great significance to the Yoruba. Traditionally, a bride wraps her waist with numerous strands of beads, signifying that she is a virgin. With a nuptial chant, "*Ekun Iyawo*," the bride then presents herself to her husband's family:

A secret river
That flows in the jungle...
I, Ayoki, reach there and wash
my face
At once, I change into a lovely virgin.
My waist is full of lovely beads.
Count the beads, O my dear friends.
If any are missing, strip me naked.[21]

Cameroon and Ghana

Elephant masks, distinctive beaded sculpture of the Bamileke, who live in the grassland region of western Cameroon, are superb examples of the ability of beads to convey rank, wealth, and artistry (plates 138–40). In Bamileke society, elephants symbolize force and strength, and beads represent wealth. The right to wear a beaded elephant mask is a mark of privilege and status. Adding artistic merit to this combination of qualities results in one of the most beautiful beadwork creations in all of Africa.

Worn by members of an elite secret society at royal dances and funeral ceremonies, the masks have a three-dimensional quality that expresses the most prominent features of the elephant: the soft, oversize ears and the prominent trunk (represented by the elongated front and back panels). The power of the masks is reinforced by a lavish use of beads, in themselves an important display of wealth.

When the mask is worn for dancing, the seemingly static patterns of beaded circles and straight lines on the head, ears, and panels are transformed into one of the most exciting of all African art forms. As the cloth panels whirl about, the rows of beads become kaleidoscopic images that heighten the intensity of the dance.[22]

Beautifully crafted gold beads made by the lost-wax casting technique are still worn in Ghana (plates 142 and 149). The kingdom of Asante, in the modern state of Ghana (formerly the Gold Coast), rose to power in the early eighteenth century. Because this area of West Africa is a gold-producing region, gold ornaments abound in Asante art. Gold beads, called "soul money," are used in rites of passage, such as children's naming ceremonies, puberty rites, and funerals. Wealthy Asante accumulate gold ornaments, wearing them at ceremonies. Large, individually identifiable glass beads, including Venetian millefiori, were often interspersed with those of gold.[23]

North Africa

The Berbers of North Africa live in the rugged Atlas, Rif, and Kabylia mountains and in arid lands at the edge of the Sahara. Perhaps as a reaction to their difficult environment, Berber women wear enormous amounts of colorful beads (plates 145 and 146). Beads bring color into a monotonous existence and also provide the amuletic protection associated with coral and amber. For their men, beads also represent a marketable asset: they may be sold when harvests or

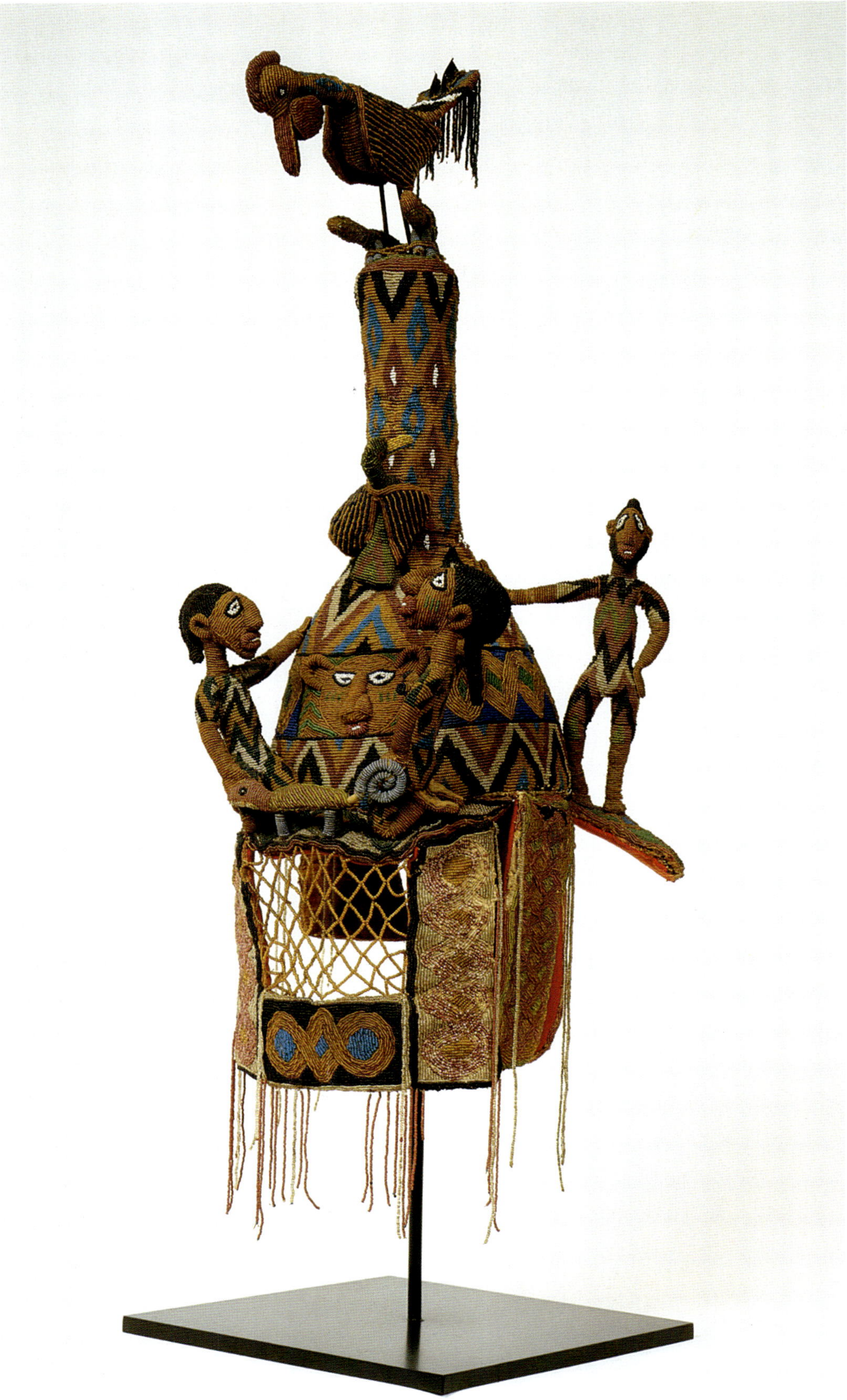

137. *Early twentieth-century Yoruba beaded crown. Beaded royal crowns are revered objects in Yorubaland. According to Yoruba myths, all* obas *who have the right to wear a beaded crown—there are currently about fifty—claim to be descended from Odudua, the first king of Ife.*

The crown shown here is from Ikere, and is considered one of the most beautiful in existence. It was probably created by the famous crownmaker and carver Olowe of Ise, whose trademark was the crafting of free-standing figures—a masterful achievement in beadwork sculpture unsupported by wood. As in all Yoruba crowns, a beaded veil hangs over the face of the divine king, emphasizing his separation from the common people, who are not permitted to gaze on his face. The small figures at the top of the crown (at the feet of the standing bird) mean luck and wealth, blessings thought to accompany the birth of twins: the Yoruba have the highest per capita rate of twin births in the world.

Royal symbolism is connected with the kneeling couple. The bird at the crown's summit, which may represent some abstract link with the divine, peers down at the king's face, centering further attention on his powerful being.[XIII] *Height, 63.5 cm. Collection Ruth and Paul Tishman, New York*

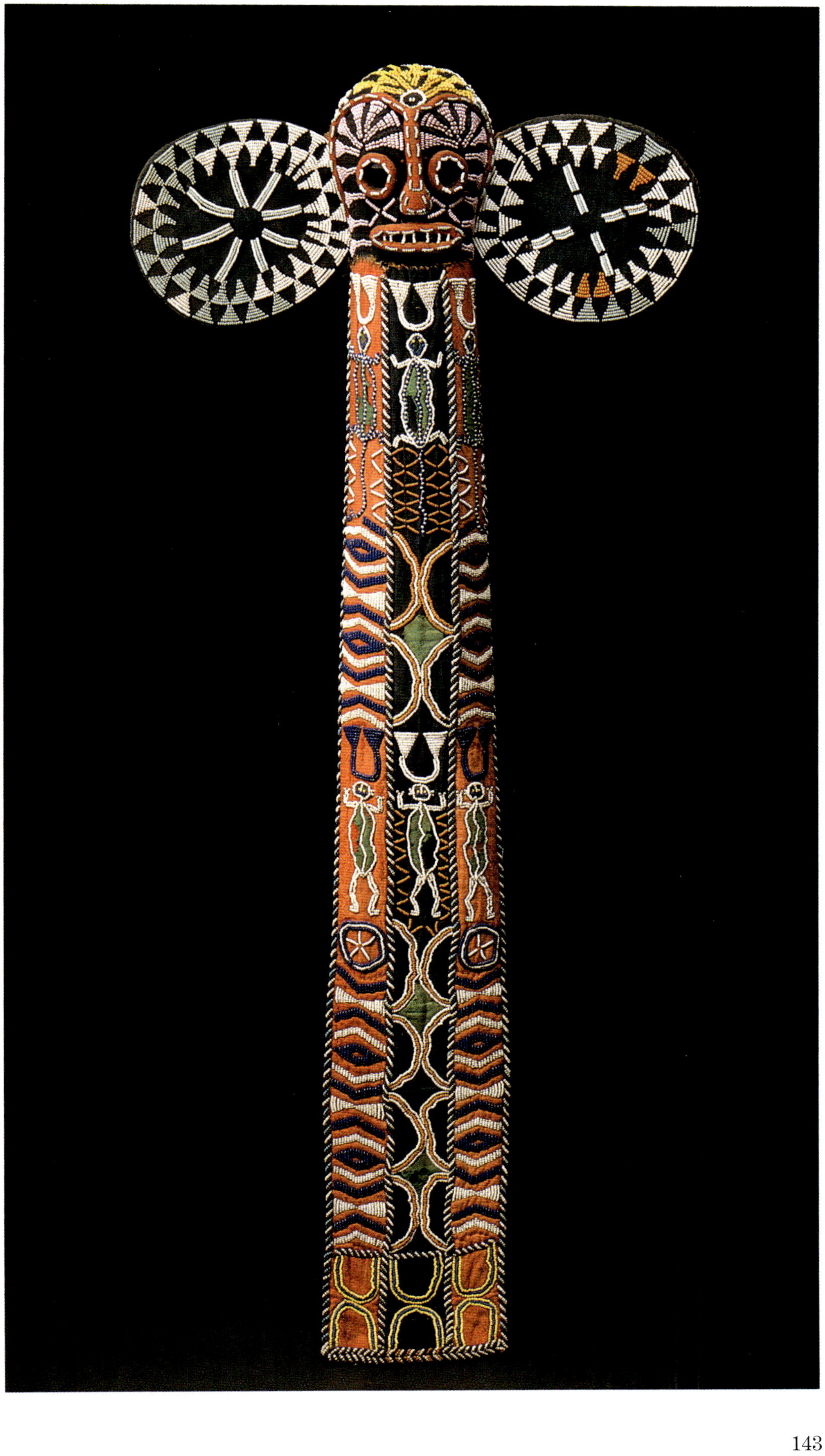

138. *A twentieth-century elephant mask. The combination of symbolic beadwork design and well-balanced proportions of head, ears, and trunk identifies this mask as a masterpiece. Height, 135 cm. Collection Marc Rabun, New York*

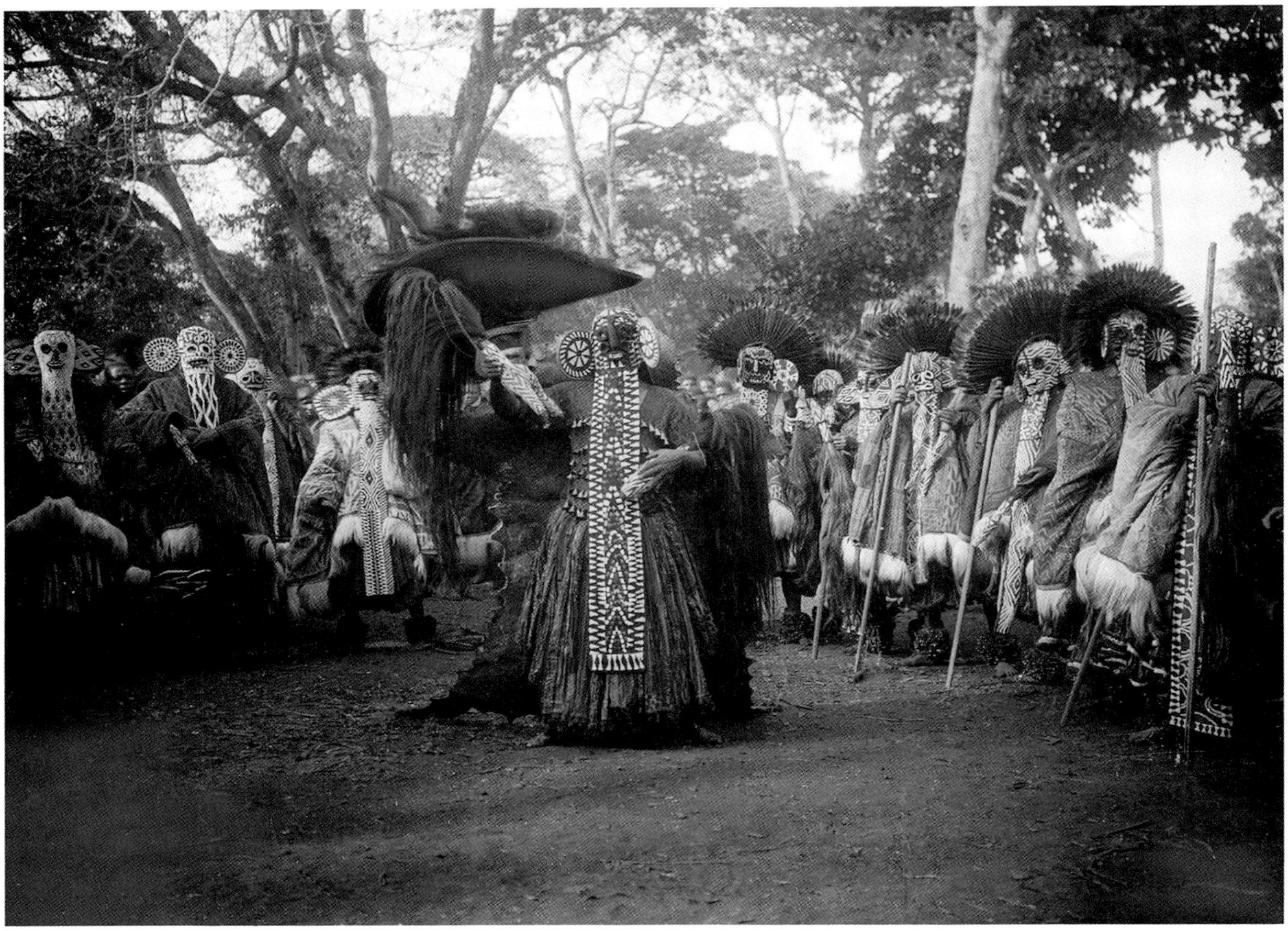

139. *Members of the Elephant Society from Bandjoun, a Bamileke village in Cameroon, parade with beaded elephant masks. In the center is the chief. Photographed in 1930. Musée de l'Homme, Paris*

OPPOSITE: 140. *A Bamileke elephant mask symbolizing strength and power. The triangle, a geometric abstraction of a leopard's spot, frequently appears on elephant masks. Actual leopard pelts are worn with elephant masks but only by the chief. This nineteenth-century mask is made of cloth and imported glass seedbeads. Height, 76.2 cm. Private collection*

flocks are poor. A bead's value is based on weight, especially if it is made of silver. Silversmiths often melt down and rework beads because the Berber prefer new beads to those worn by someone else.

The Berber aesthetic is predominantly Islamic rather than African. As late as the fifteenth century, Jewish gold- and silversmiths fleeing the Spanish Inquisition settled in the Maghreb (the Arabic name for the horn-shaped region of North Africa, including Morocco, Algeria, Tunisia, and the western part of Libya) and introduced filigree, enameling, cloisonné, and niello techniques. Today, Berber smiths are still primarily Jewish.[24]

The Choice of Beads

The way African bead materials are combined varies according to the tastes, hierarchies, traditions, and trade patterns of the region. For example, the Berber of North Africa wear necklaces made of large, variously shaped beads from amber, coral, amazonite, silver, and glass. Each bead is valued individually and carries a specific message. Golden amber protects against disease, while coral and silver beads are associated with ancient amuletic beliefs. The Samburu, on the other hand, prefer multiple strands of uniformly small glass seedbeads. Colors "refer indirectly to valued parts of their world: green to the grass which sustains the cattle, and through the sacred cattle, life itself; blue to the sky and the high God; white for milk and other pure things; red for blood, especially that of cattle which is mixed with milk for food."[25]

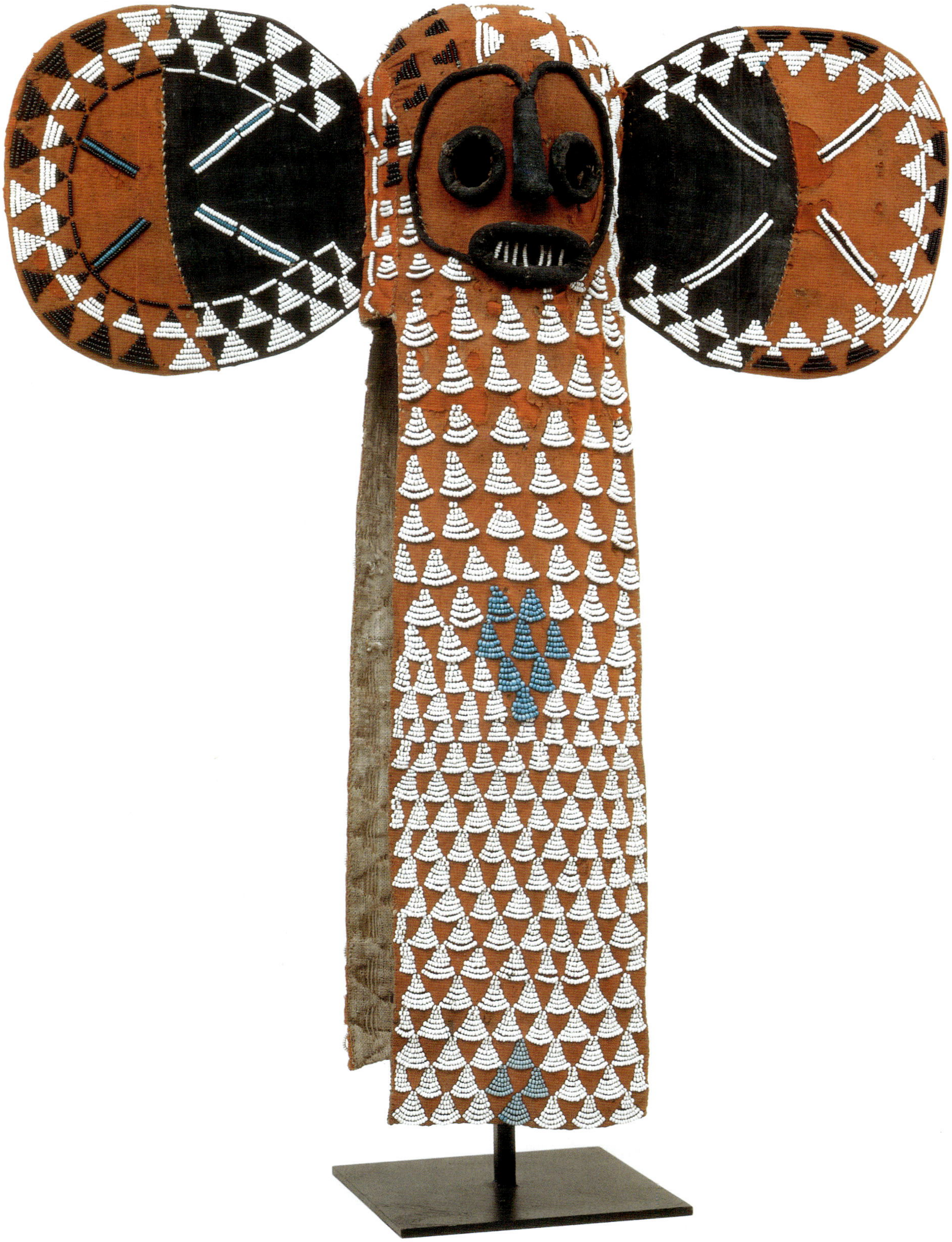

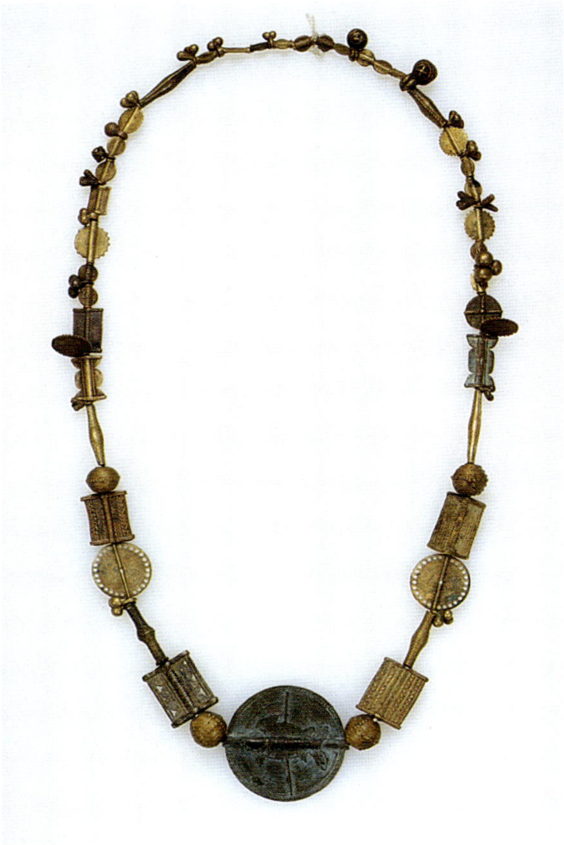

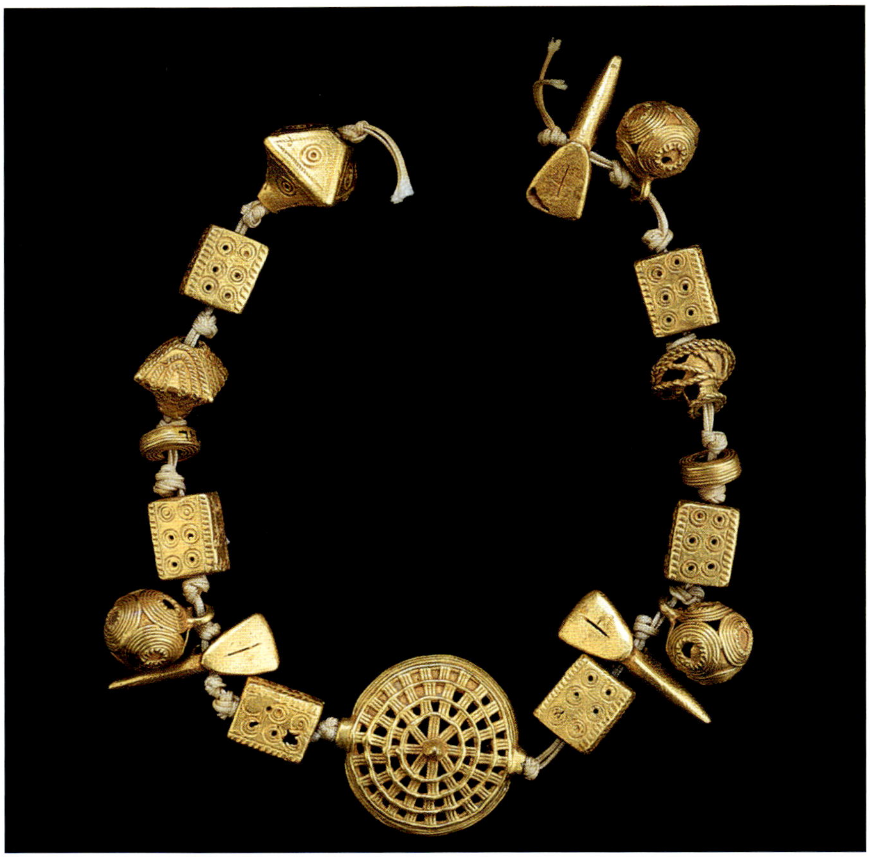

TOP LEFT: 141. *The Baoule of the Ivory Coast share a common history and culture with the Asante. In both cultures, gold was generally available only to royal household members. Thus, goldsmiths created beads for most people in bronze, shown here, matching the styles of gold beads. Center bead: diameter, 5.7 cm. Collection Craft Caravan, New York*

TOP RIGHT: 142. *A collection of gold beads from Kumasi, Ghana, cast by goldsmiths using trade secrets passed from father to son. Made in the 1930s, the beads follow the traditional forms of the royal treasures of Asante chiefs. The lost-wax process, known in West Africa since the ninth century, probably came from the north via the trans-Saharan*

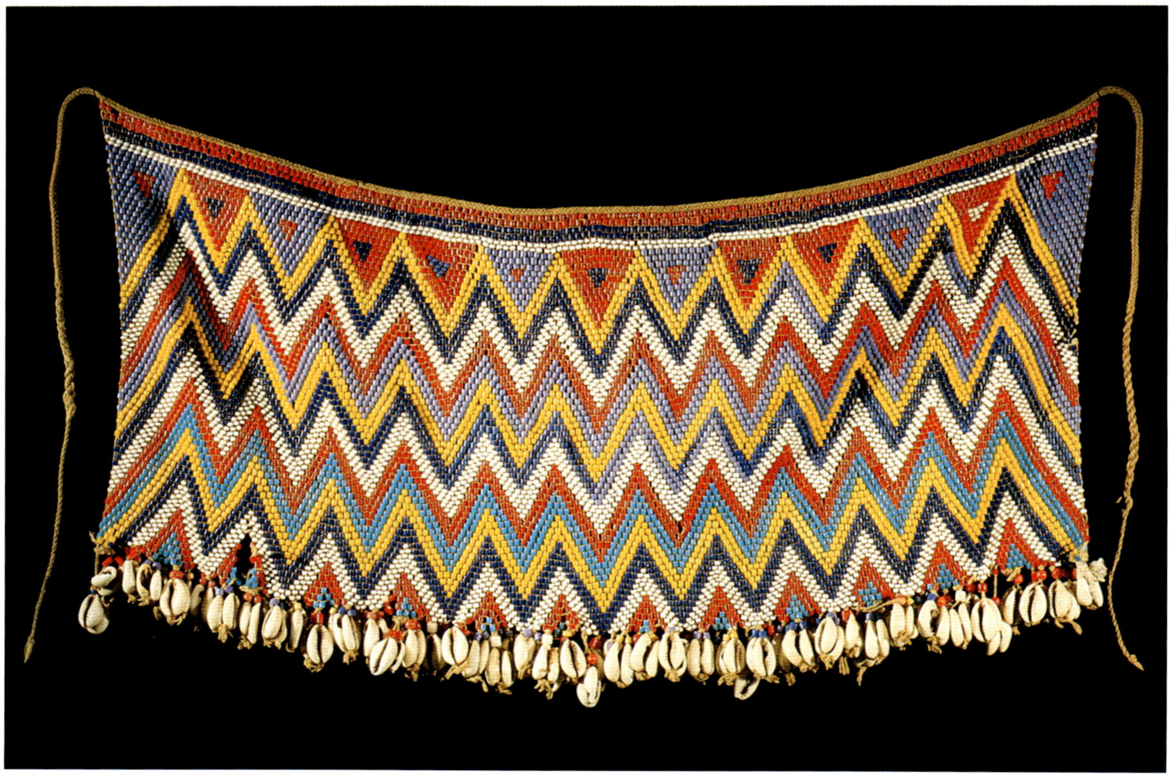

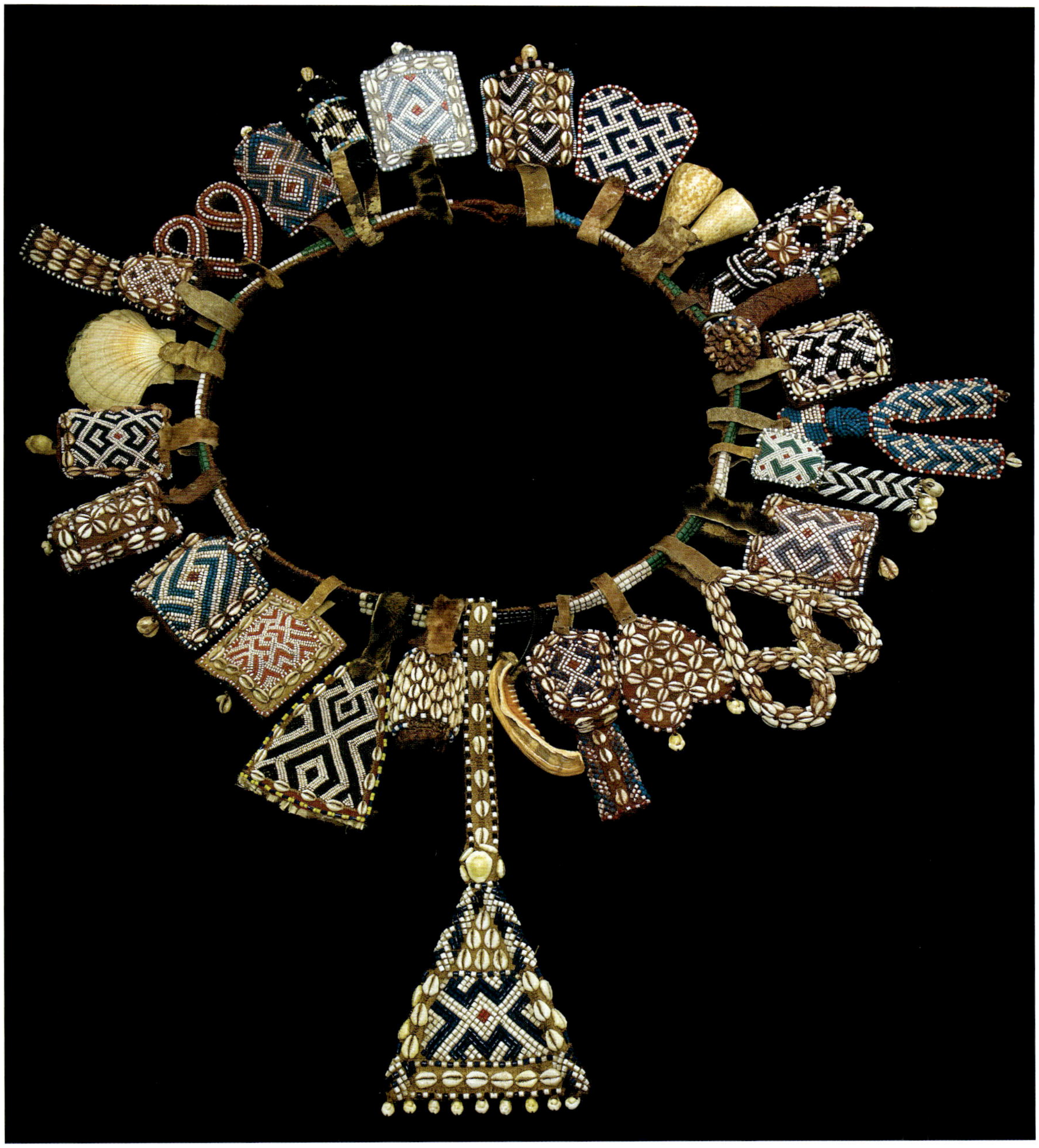

trade routes. Center bead: diameter, 3.17 cm. University Museum, University of Pennsylvania, Philadelphia

OPPOSITE BOTTOM: 143. *The Kirdi, from the Cameroons, create* cache-sexes, *or loincloths, worn by women and girls for protection and to attract attention. Different* cache-sexe *styles identify group affiliations, age grades, and special conditions such as puberty, marriage, and widowhood.*

The Cameroon government has long outlawed the wearing of cache-sexes, *but the practice continues under the cover of long robes. The glass-beaded aprons reveal a variety of chevron and triangular patterns. Cowrie shells are usually hung at the bottom of the apron. It is claimed that the lower portion of the apron is deliberately cut on a wedding night to symbolize the consummation of the marriage.*[XIV] *Length, 43 cm. Private collection*

LEFT: 144. *A Kuba Yet Belt, worn only by the king, the Bwami, or persons of very high status. The more components there are on a belt, the greater the significance. Each element of the belt, although often depicted in abstract form, represents a specific object of importance to the Kuba. Typical design elements—shown within a complex geometric vocabulary that are recognizable within the Kuba design system—might include the horns of a ram, bells, musical instruments, a calabash, and powder horns. Pre-1950. Length, 129.5 cm. Longest component length, 40 cm. Collection Norma Canelas and William Roth*

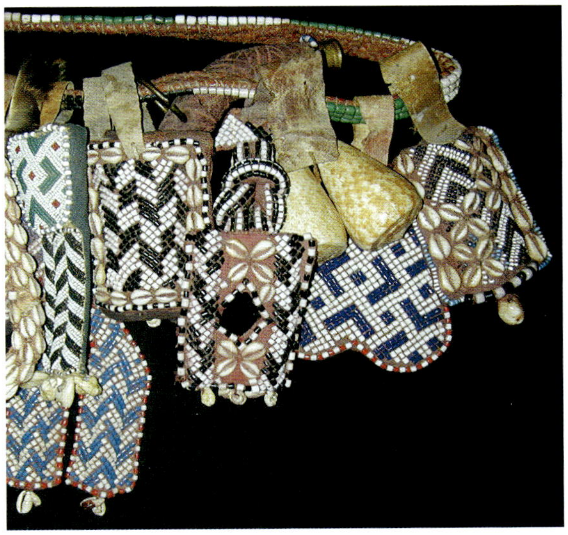

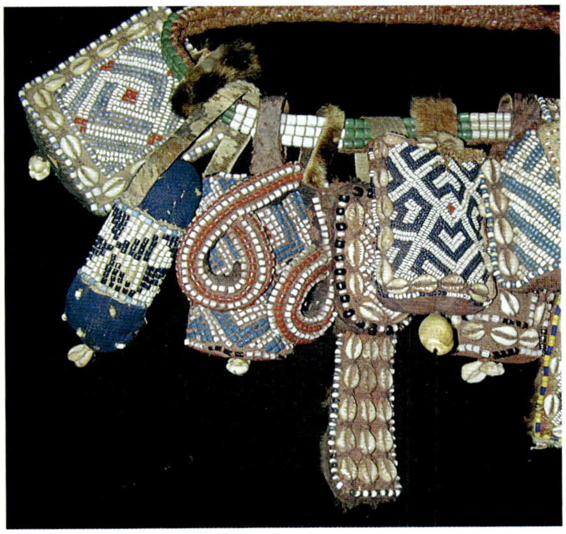

AFRICA 2009

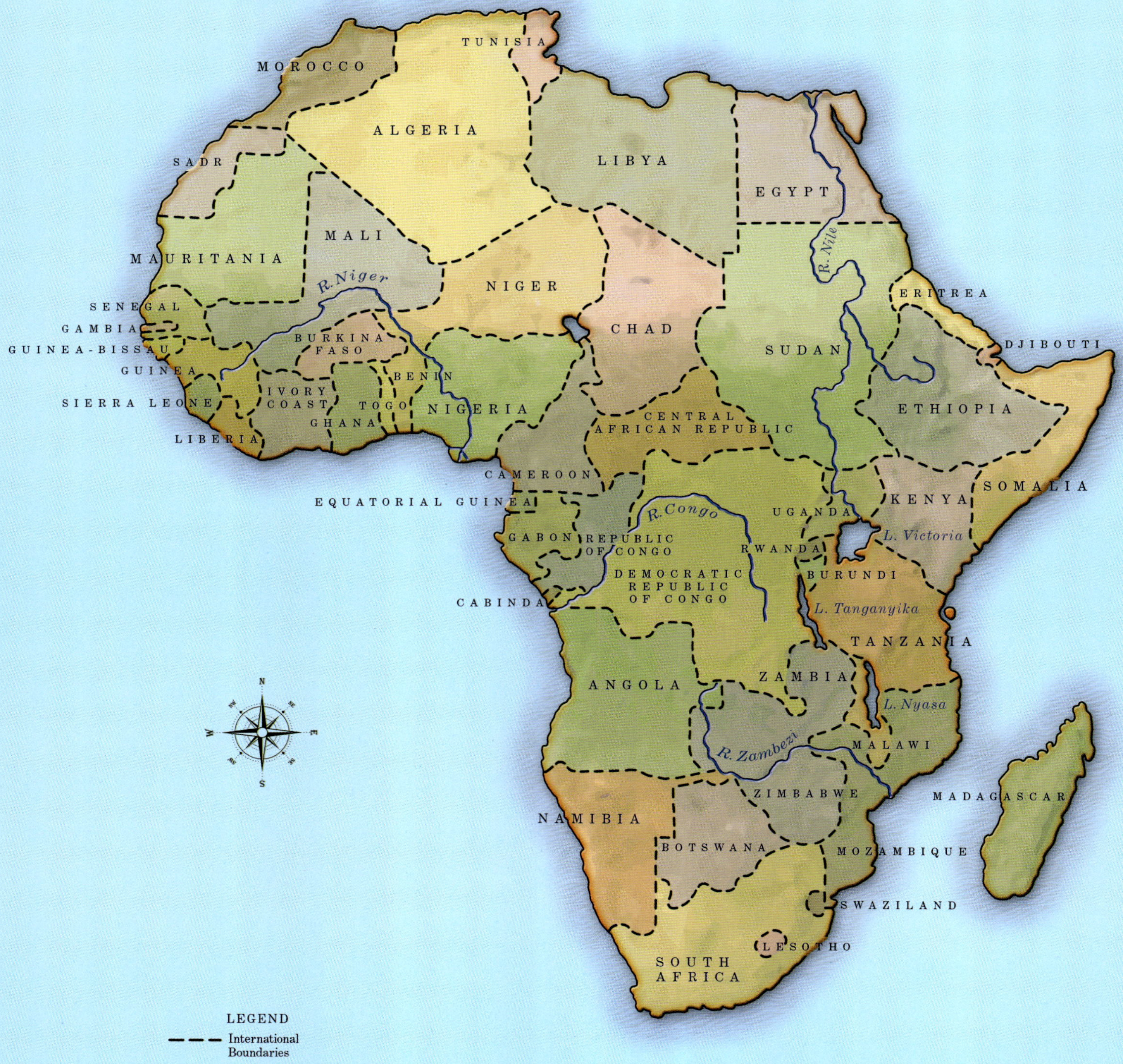
MOROCCO
TUNISIA
ALGERIA
LIBYA
EGYPT
SADR
MAURITANIA
MALI
NIGER
CHAD
SUDAN
ERITREA
DJIBOUTI
ETHIOPIA
SOMALIA
SENEGAL
GAMBIA
GUINEA-BISSAU
GUINEA
SIERRA LEONE
LIBERIA
IVORY COAST
BURKINA FASO
GHANA
TOGO
BENIN
NIGERIA
CAMEROON
CENTRAL AFRICAN REPUBLIC
EQUATORIAL GUINEA
GABON
REPUBLIC OF CONGO
CABINDA
DEMOCRATIC REPUBLIC OF CONGO
UGANDA
KENYA
RWANDA
BURUNDI
TANZANIA
ANGOLA
ZAMBIA
MALAWI
ZIMBABWE
MOZAMBIQUE
MADAGASCAR
NAMIBIA
BOTSWANA
SWAZILAND
LESOTHO
SOUTH AFRICA
R. Niger
R. Nile
R. Congo
R. Zambezi
L. Victoria
L. Tanganyika
L. Nyasa
N
S
E
W
LEGEND
International Boundaries

The forms and colors of beads that people sought changed constantly and varied from region to region. It was not unusual for European traders to arrive in port with large quantities of a bead greatly coveted in the last transaction only to discover that these particular beads were no longer desired. Certain beads, however, were quite popular for long periods of time. *Cornaline d'Aleppo* was popular in different forms. The cornerless, hexagonal dark blue glass beads were known to the Ndebele as "ambassador beads," because they were worn by shamans who "went into the Matopo Hills to ask advice from the great god of the Matabele." The complex millefiori and wound blue glass annular beads were worn by the chiefs who met David Livingstone, the British missionary, at Victoria Falls in 1855 (Timeline 63, 132, and 155).[26]

Special mention should be made of the predominantly blue "aggrey" bead, in use on the west coast of Africa before the European traders arrived. For five hundred years, scholars have disagreed on the source and appearance of this mysterious bead, described as "blue coral" and "produced by thunder" or "created by a supernatural power." According to local legend, the aggrey bead comes from the rivers and the earth.

It is now generally agreed that the aggrey was a blue glass bead. Blue glass beads called *akori* and later aggrey were recorded in Benin as early as 1568. It is believed by one specialist that the aggrey bead was made of silicate slag produced on the Guinea Coast by smelting iron from local ores. As the slag was deposited in rivers, the bead's legendary source is frequently connected with water. The bead's blue or green color may simply reflect mineral impurities in the glass. As people were—and are still—often buried with their treasured possessions, it is not surprising that many aggrey beads have been found in the ground, perhaps after a rainstorm has eroded a local cemetery.[27]

The Unity of African Beads

Although each African culture has evolved distinctive patterns of bead use, several unifying themes apply throughout the continent. Basic to the animism that pervades life in sub-Saharan Africa is the spiritual energy a fine bead necklace or beadwork piece imparts. Although both Islam and Christianity are practiced in Africa, they have been shaped to accommodate animistic beliefs in inanimate objects that, whether created by nature or man, have spiritual force. This is why African artifacts often have such a strong aesthetic presence, even if they are not necessarily technically sophisticated. It is also why we often respond strongly to an African necklace, independently of any knowledge about its origins, use, or imparted meaning.

African beadwork is meant to be noticed. As Angela Fisher has written in *Africa Adorned*, beads say, "Look at me!" They range from the layers of colorful necklaces worn in Kenya to a minimal beaded *cache-sexe* in Cameroon (plates 114 and 143). In Africa, as elsewhere, "One can find superior taste demonstrated through either restraint or abundance. A minimal costume may carry for some group the same prestige as an accumulative one does for another."[28] To draw further attention, the beads are often accompanied by sound effects: the rattling of cowrie shells, for example.

African beads are commonly part of an assemblage, a mixture of materials—twigs, shells, glass, and bones—put on a necklace or article of jewelry in a seemingly haphazard way, so that the object may not appear to have been designed. A marvelous example is the Zulu necklace shown in plate 104.

The concept of assemblage also extends to the layered necklaces worn, for example, by the Turkana, Samburu, Galeb, and Berber women (plates 114, 118, and 123). Multiple necklaces worn by an individual draw attention and create an "altered and expanded image with the head held proudly high as if lifted by the mass of beads."[29] In

OVERLEAF, TOP LEFT: 145. *A silk-tasseled amber necklace typically worn by Berber women of the Moyen (Middle) Atlas region. The red felt fillers protect each bead. Length, 85 cm. Collection Ivory Freidus*

OVERLEAF, TOP RIGHT: 146. *An assembled necklace of both traditional and non-traditional elements. The egg-shaped central bead (*taguemout*) of enameled silver, was made in Tiznit, south of Marakech, in the heart of the Anti-Atlas Mountains. Center bead: diameter, 5.08 cm. Collection Ivory Freidus*

OVERLEAF, BOTTOM LEFT: 147. *A chaplet (*tasbir*) worn by dancers of the* guedra, *the ritual love dance performed by Moorish women for men. The beads are twisted around the wrist or worn around the neck. The wooden beads are inlaid with silver wire. On the tassel are glass and carnelian beads. This object is from Goulimine on the southern Moroccan-Mauritanian border. Length (including the tassel), 52 cm. Collection Colette and Jean-Pierre Ghysels, Brussels*

OVERLEAF, BOTTOM RIGHT: 148. *A necklace of filigree silver and heart-shaped, scented beads called* shab. *Made by Tunisian women according to an old Egyptian method, a* shab *contains ambergris, rose petals, saffron, cloves, nutmeg, and musk. The extraordinarily sensuous fragrance is accentuated by body heat and is said to last a lifetime.*[XV] *Length, 96.5 cm. Collection Ivory Freidus*

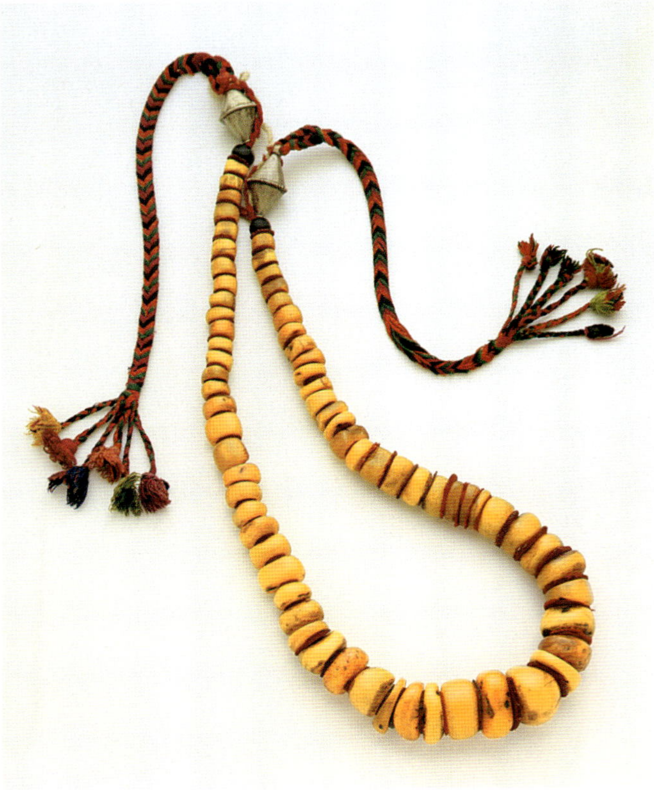
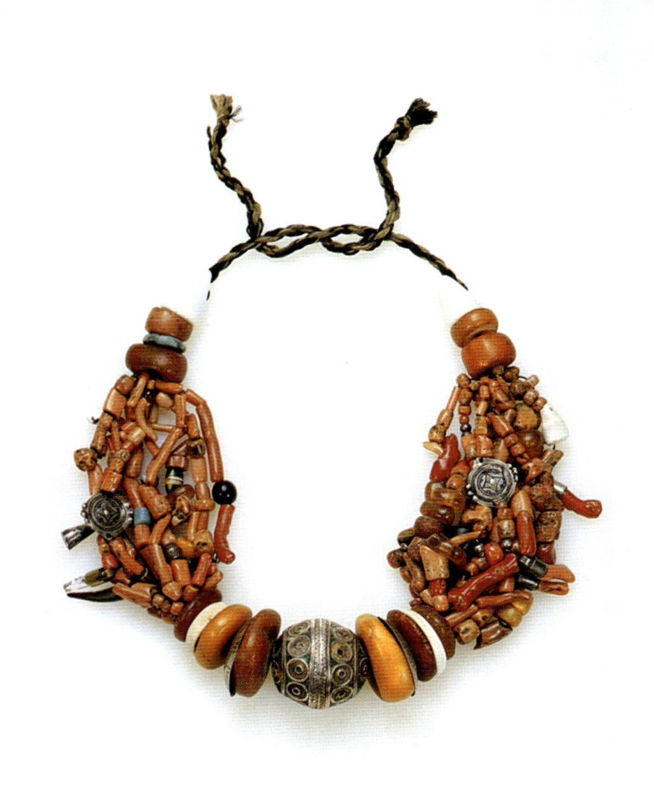
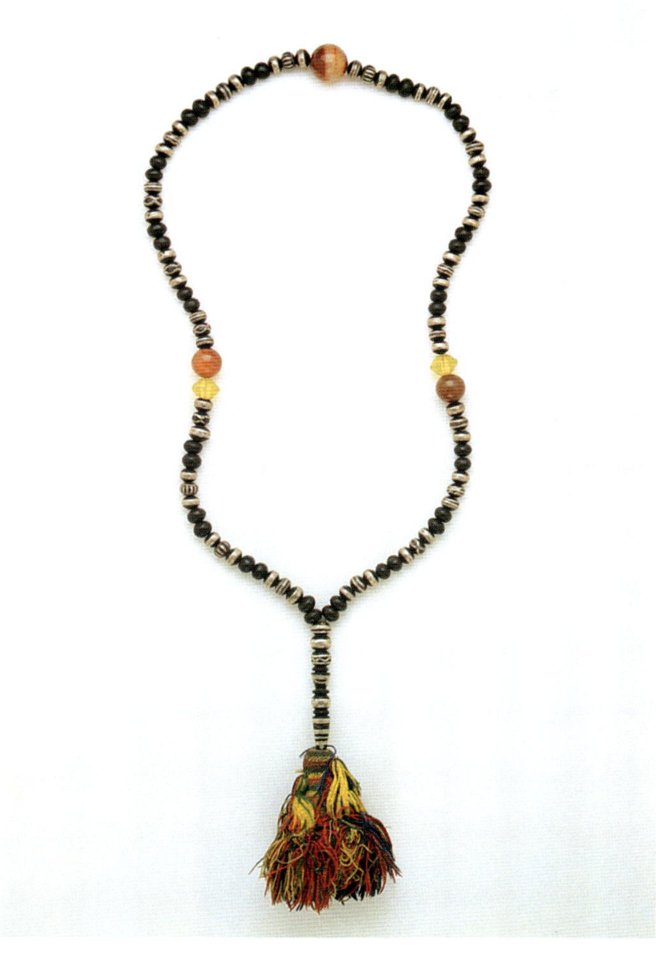
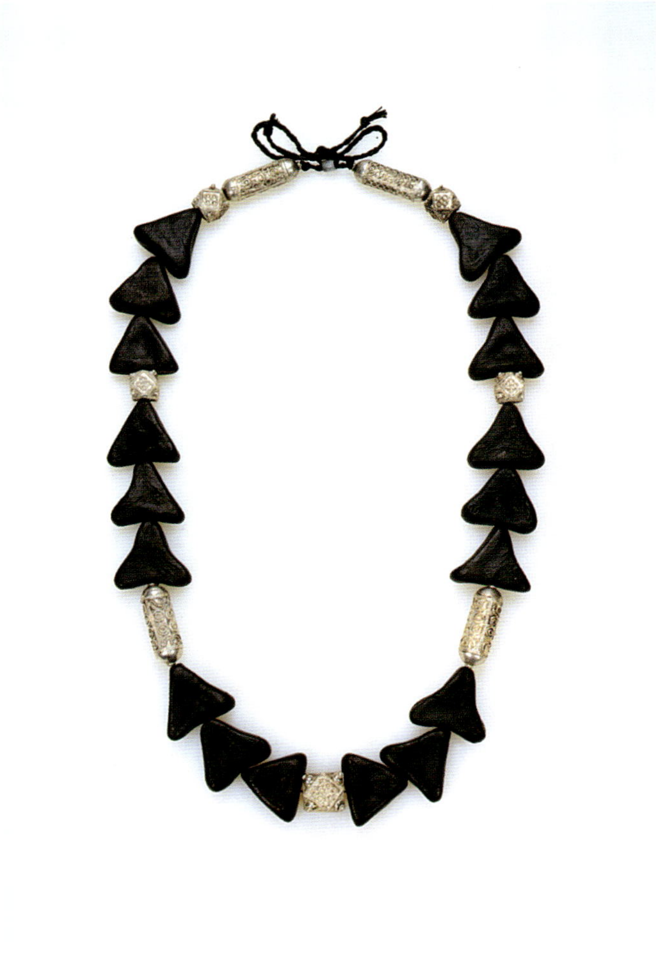

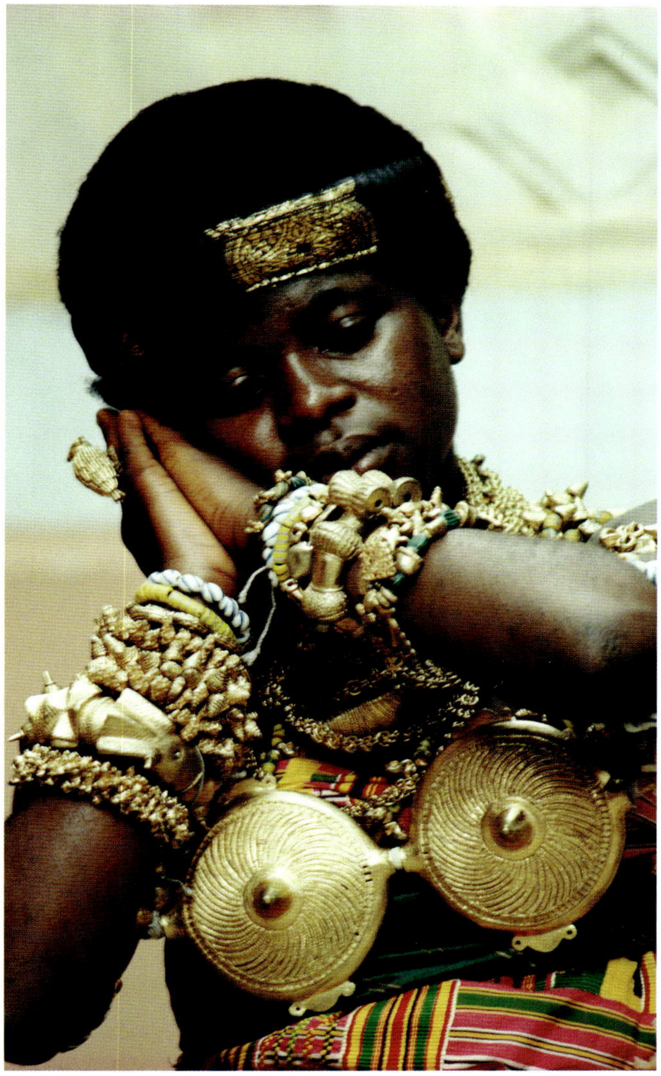 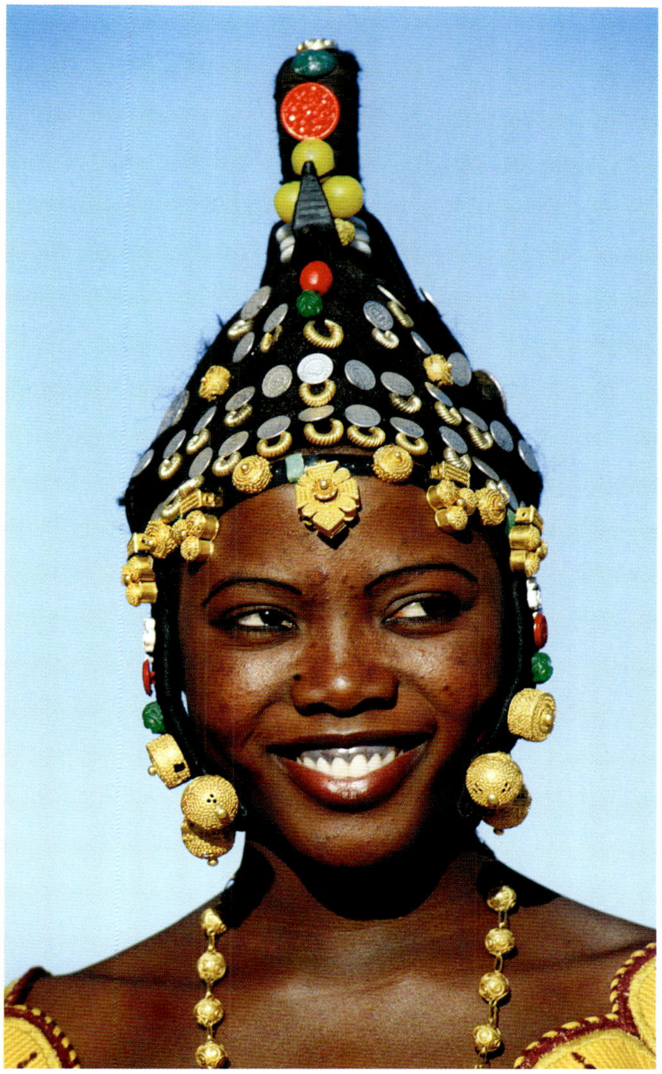

much of sub-Saharan Africa, it is important to recognize not only the internal complexity of the individual beaded necklace, but also how an assemblage of necklaces creates an ensemble.

Finally, African adornment has been and is essentially a community art. The forms taken by beadwork, necklaces, bracelets, hats, and aprons are usually determined by a set of commonly held standards. For the most part, artist and wearer are not expressing their private feelings or inspiration. Rather, personal touches are executed within generally accepted limitations, so that beaded adornment, like all African art, unifies the community by conveying and reinforcing common understandings.

Beads were, and still are, used in Africa to create objects representing spiritual values basic to the survival of the community. These objects play a major role in rituals insuring continuity of the group: birth, circumcision, marriage, warriorhood, kingship, death. Susan Vogel's discussion of African art in *For Spirits and Kings* can be extrapolated to include the significance of much of African beaded adornment: "In societies without writing, art objects can acquire extraordinary importance as visual records.... On a deeper level, works of art are endowed with complex meaning and serve as repositories of traditional knowledge. They are dense concentrations of ancestral wisdom that must be preserved and transmitted to succeeding generations."[30]

ABOVE LEFT: 149. *A young Ashante court dancer performs the Adowa, a traditional dance, for the royal assembly. She is adorned with gold belonging to the royal treasury, including bracelets made with hollow cast gold beads and old glass beads, some of which are valued even more than gold. Kumasi, Ghana. 1995*

ABOVE RIGHT: 150. *A Songhai bride from Mali is adorned with gold filigree amulets and a variety of gold and glass beads reflecting her high status.*

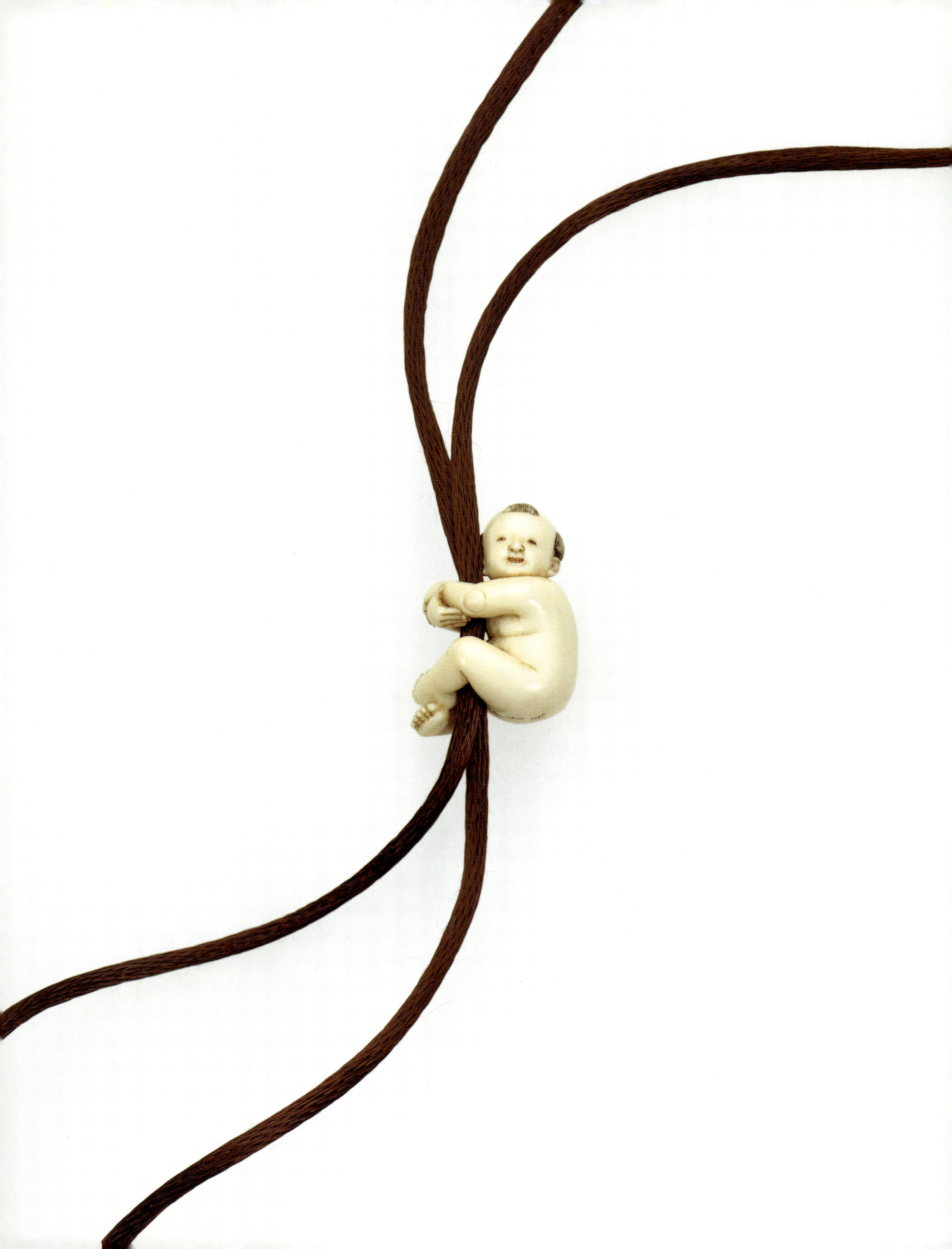

The Far East: China, Korea, and Japan

151. *An example of Japanese* ojime, *carved in the form of a clinging baby boy by the renowned nineteenth-century* netsuke *carver Ono Ryomin. Length, 1.9 cm. Collection Midori Gallery, Coconut Grove, Florida*

The use of jewelry in the Far Eastern civilizations of China, Korea, and Japan contrasts sharply with its role in Western culture and most tribal societies. Necklaces—a seemingly ubiquitous article of adornment elsewhere—were not typically worn in the Far East. Instead jewelry took the form of belt hooks and buckles, plaques, hairpins, bracelets, and other less prominent accessories. Beads often played both functional and decorative roles as attachments to headdresses, hats, and *inro* (small, ornamented containers).

Although beads were not common attire in the Far East, they were consistently manufactured for limited domestic use and for export. Quantities of beads made of precious or semiprecious materials and glass have been uncovered in the ancient tombs of royal or elite households. In antiquity, glass beads were highly valued treasures and were often combined with jade beads and gilded bronze elements, such as belt hooks. Glass beads were also made for export at various times in both China and Japan.[1] Jade beads were revered in China, Korea, and Japan: the character for "jade" and "bead" (玉) is the same in each of the three languages.

Far Eastern beads often demonstrate exquisite craftsmanship. Chinese eye beads dating from the fourth to the first century B.C. (plates 154 and 330) and Japanese ivory and metal *ojime* (slide fasteners for a personal carrying case) from the eighteenth and nineteenth centuries A.D. (plates 170–90) are among the most complex and beautiful beads ever made.

The atypical use of beads in Far Eastern societies has its origins in ancient cultural history. Archaeological evidence indicates that China, Korea, and Japan began their development as separate prehistoric entities. By the second century B.C., China had established the colony of Lo-lang in northern Korea, and a century later Japan was in close contact with China and Korea.[2] Chinese exports, including raw materials, finished beads, craftsmen, and even a philosophy of adornment, soon flowed into Korea and from there to Japan.

By the sixth century, China was the major presence in the Far East, exerting influence over her neighbors in everything from political and religious systems to precepts for the forms and uses of jewelry. Chinese writing, governmental organization, technology, and art were the models for the region. Her influence ebbed and flowed in relation to the fluctuating fortunes of her power and trade.[3] At the same time, Korea and Japan developed independent and distinctive cultures, transforming China's cultural tenets into unique local expressions.

China, followed by Korea and Japan, was among the first societies to become literate. To be literate certified a man as civilized. Such a man did not find it crucial to appeal to a single supreme deity to define, stabilize, and insure his place in the world. (He might, however, consult a variety of ancestral and natural spirits.) Jewelry, therefore, was not worn to influence spirits. Almost without exception, beads seem to have been valued in the Far East more as status symbols than as protective amulets. Moreover, the use of such status symbols was rigorously controlled by civil law and by the precepts and taboos of the indigenous religions of Confucianism, Taoism, and Shintoism. Confucianism, the key to Chinese thought, was extremely influential in the development of Korean and Japanese philosophies (particularly among the ruling classes). It is a system of ethics rather than a religion of magic and superstition and is not given to the production of art, much less to ornament. (Aside from Buddhist prayer beads, the few examples of beads with ritual significance in the Far East are known primarily from earlier, pre-Confucianist times.) Chinese Taoism also advocates naturalness, contemplation, and the disavowal of worldly goods, and Japanese Shintoism stresses respect for the elements of nature—rocks, trees, waterfalls, and plants. Furthermore, Confucianism is based on social responsibility, respect for age and authority, and faith in a patriarchal government founded on moral virtues. These codes kept a rigid class system intact: displays of wealth, particularly the wearing of jewelry, were reserved strictly for the elite.

Buddhism entered the Far East about the first century A.D. and was adapted to the traditional religious philosophies of each country. Differences in Chinese, Korean, and Japanese Buddhist prayer beads demonstrate the integration of Buddhism into indigenous beliefs. Interestingly, it was when Buddhism was at its height (about A.D. 400–900) that beads as items of adornment made their strongest impression on Far Eastern cultures, demonstrating the influence of this religion on all levels of society. By contrast, Confucianism was the religion of the intelligentsia, whose adherence to rationalism and strict social ethics did not allow for beads in ritual practices.

Unfortunately, most of the available information on ancient beads is gleaned from discoveries at royal and wealthy tombs, so that we know little of the possibly perishable adornment of ordinary citizens. It may be that the growth of trade by land and sea, which also helped to spread Buddhism, injected cosmopolitan attitudes about jewelry into Far Eastern society and gave greater access to beads and luxury materials to all classes of people.

Far Eastern history, however, is punctuated by periods of trade and cultural exchange followed by years of self-imposed cultural isolation. Active contact with India and Iran, for example, frequently coincided with important periods of bead development and use in Far Eastern societies.[4] The spectacular beaded crowns, necklaces, and girdles of Korea's fifth- and sixth-century royal tombs, and the glass beads produced during the Nara period (A.D. 645–794) in Japan, are examples of the importance of beads during

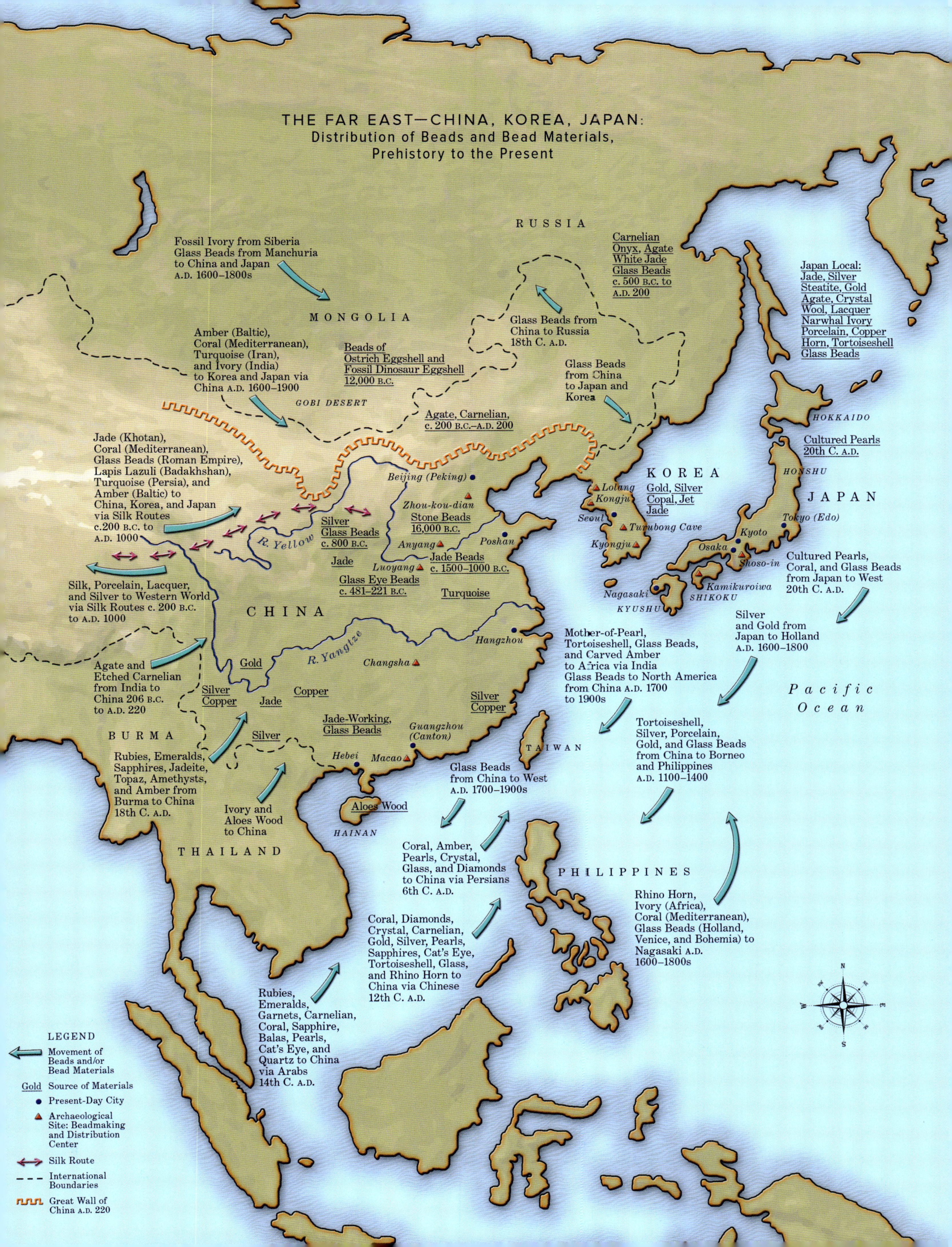

THE FAR EAST—CHINA, KOREA, JAPAN:
Distribution of Beads and Bead Materials, Prehistory to the Present
RUSSIA
Fossil Ivory from Siberia Glass Beads from Manchuria to China and Japan A.D. 1600–1800s
Carnelian Onyx, Agate White Jade Glass Beads c. 500 B.C. to A.D. 200
Japan Local: Jade, Silver Steatite, Gold Agate, Crystal Wool, Lacquer Narwhal Ivory Porcelain, Copper Horn, Tortoiseshell Glass Beads
MONGOLIA
Glass Beads from China to Russia 18th C. A.D.
Amber (Baltic), Coral (Mediterranean), Turquoise (Iran), and Ivory (India) to Korea and Japan via China A.D. 1600–1900
Beads of Ostrich Eggshell and Fossil Dinosaur Eggshell 12,000 B.C.
Glass Beads from China to Japan and Korea
GOBI DESERT
Agate, Carnelian, c. 200 B.C.–A.D. 200
HOKKAIDO
Cultured Pearls 20th C. A.D.
Jade (Khotan), Coral (Mediterranean), Glass Beads (Roman Empire), Lapis Lazuli (Badakhshan), Turquoise (Persia), and Amber (Baltic) to China, Korea, and Japan via Silk Routes c.200 B.C. to A.D. 1000
Beijing (Peking)
KOREA
HONSHU
Lolang
Kongju
Gold, Silver Copal, Jet Jade
JAPAN
Zhou-kou-dian Stone Beads 16,000 B.C.
Seoul
Tokyo (Edo)
Silver Glass Beads c. 800 B.C.
Turubong Cave
Kyoto
R. Yellow
Poshan
Kyongju
Osaka
Anyang
Shoso-in
Cultured Pearls, Coral, and Glass Beads from Japan to West 20th C. A.D.
Jade
Jade Beads c. 1500–1000 B.C.
Luoyang
Glass Eye Beads c. 481–221 B.C.
Kamikuroiwa
Nagasaki
SHIKOKU
Silk, Porcelain, Lacquer, and Silver to Western World via Silk Routes c. 200 B.C. to A.D. 1000
Turquoise
KYUSHU
CHINA
Silver and Gold from Japan to Holland A.D. 1600–1800
Hangzhou
Mother-of-Pearl, Tortoiseshell, Glass Beads, and Carved Amber to Africa via India Glass Beads to North America from China A.D. 1700 to 1900s
R. Yangtze
Agate and Etched Carnelian from India to China 206 B.C. to A.D. 220
Gold
Changsha
Pacific Ocean
Silver Copper
Copper
Jade
Silver Copper
BURMA
Jade-Working, Glass Beads
Guangzhou (Canton)
Tortoiseshell, Silver, Porcelain, Gold, and Glass Beads from China to Borneo and Philippines A.D. 1100–1400
Silver
Rubies, Emeralds, Sapphires, Jadeite, Topaz, Amethysts, and Amber from Burma to China 18th C. A.D.
Hebei
Macao
TAIWAN
Glass Beads from China to West A.D. 1700–1900s
Ivory and Aloes Wood to China
Aloes Wood
HAINAN
THAILAND
Coral, Amber, Pearls, Crystal, Glass, and Diamonds to China via Persians 6th C. A.D.
PHILIPPINES
Rhino Horn, Ivory (Africa), Coral (Mediterranean), Glass Beads (Holland, Venice, and Bohemia) to Nagasaki A.D. 1600–1800s
Coral, Diamonds, Crystal, Carnelian, Gold, Silver, Pearls, Sapphires, Cat's Eye, Tortoiseshell, Glass, and Rhino Horn to China via Chinese 12th C. A.D.
Rubies, Emeralds, Garnets, Carnelian, Coral, Sapphire, Balas, Pearls, Cat's Eye, and Quartz to China via Arabs 14th C. A.D.
N
E
S
W
LEGEND
Movement of Beads and/or Bead Materials
Gold Source of Materials
Present-Day City
Archaeological Site: Beadmaking and Distribution Center
Silk Route
International Boundaries
Great Wall of China A.D. 220

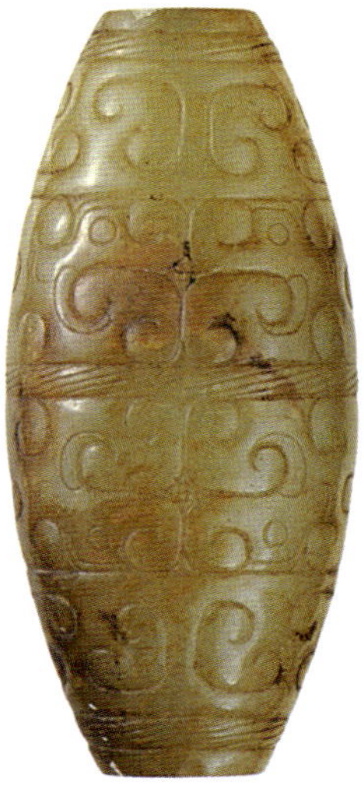

ABOVE: 152. *Probably owned by an aristocrat, this carved and polished barrel-shaped bead of pale green nephrite was fashioned during the middle of the Eastern Zhou period, c. 500 B.C. By this time, jade craftsmanship had reached a high level of technical skill. The back-to-back spirals, derived from bronze designs, are typical Eastern Zhou motifs. Length, 4.1 cm. Royal Ontario Museum, Toronto*

RIGHT: 153. *A bronze tomb figure of a kneeling attendant from the fifth or fourth century B.C., accompanied by a contemporary (or slightly later) miniature bead version of the same bronze bearer made of turquoise faience and perforated lengthwise. Comparable figures were also carved in jade. Bead: length, 1.85 cm. Royal Ontario Museum, Toronto*

OPPOSITE: 154. *This remarkable group of seven Chinese eye beads from the "Warring States" period (481–221 B.C.) are some of the most technically complex glass beads ever created. Clearly derived from Mediterranean beads of Phoenician times (from Egypt and the Fertile Crescent)*

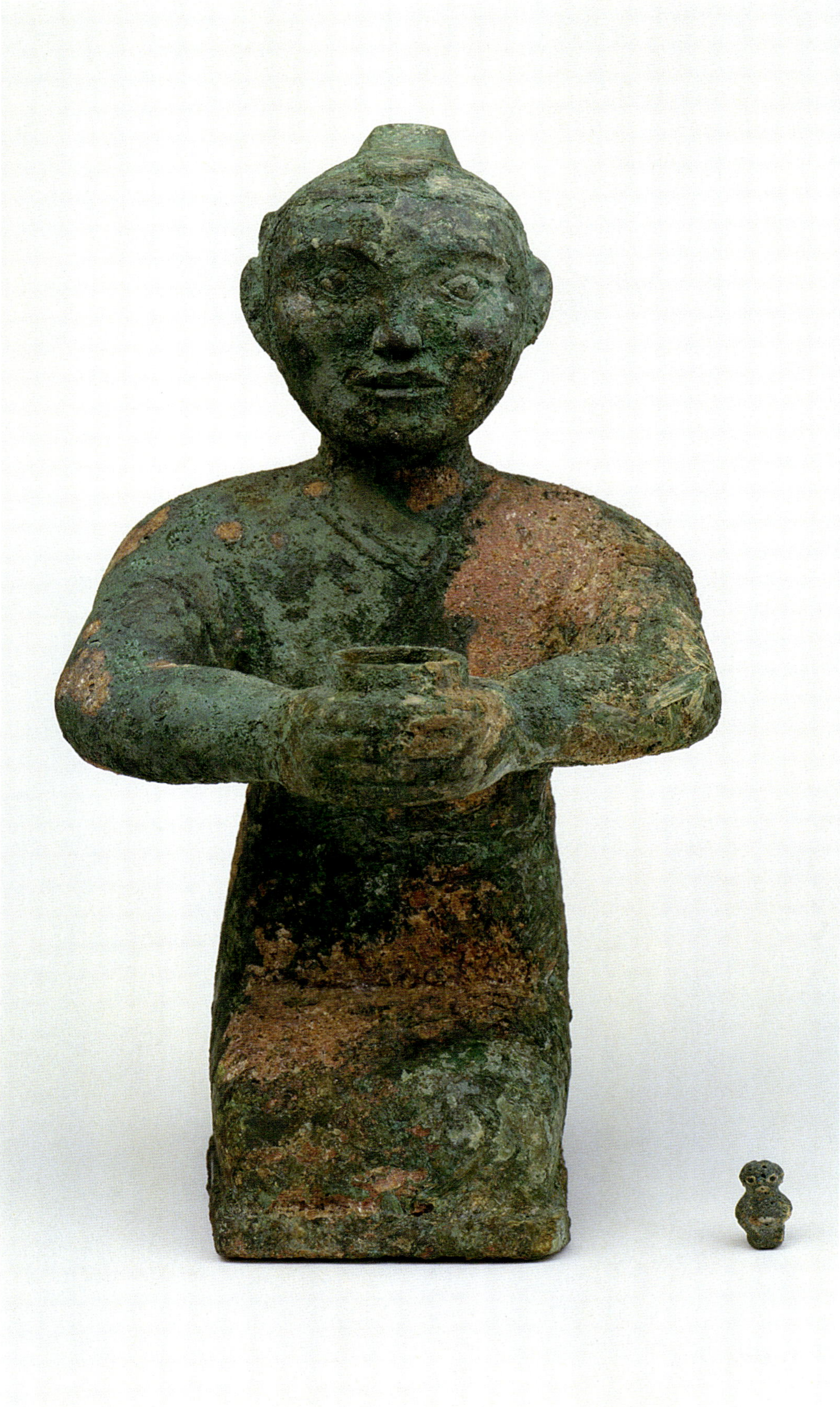

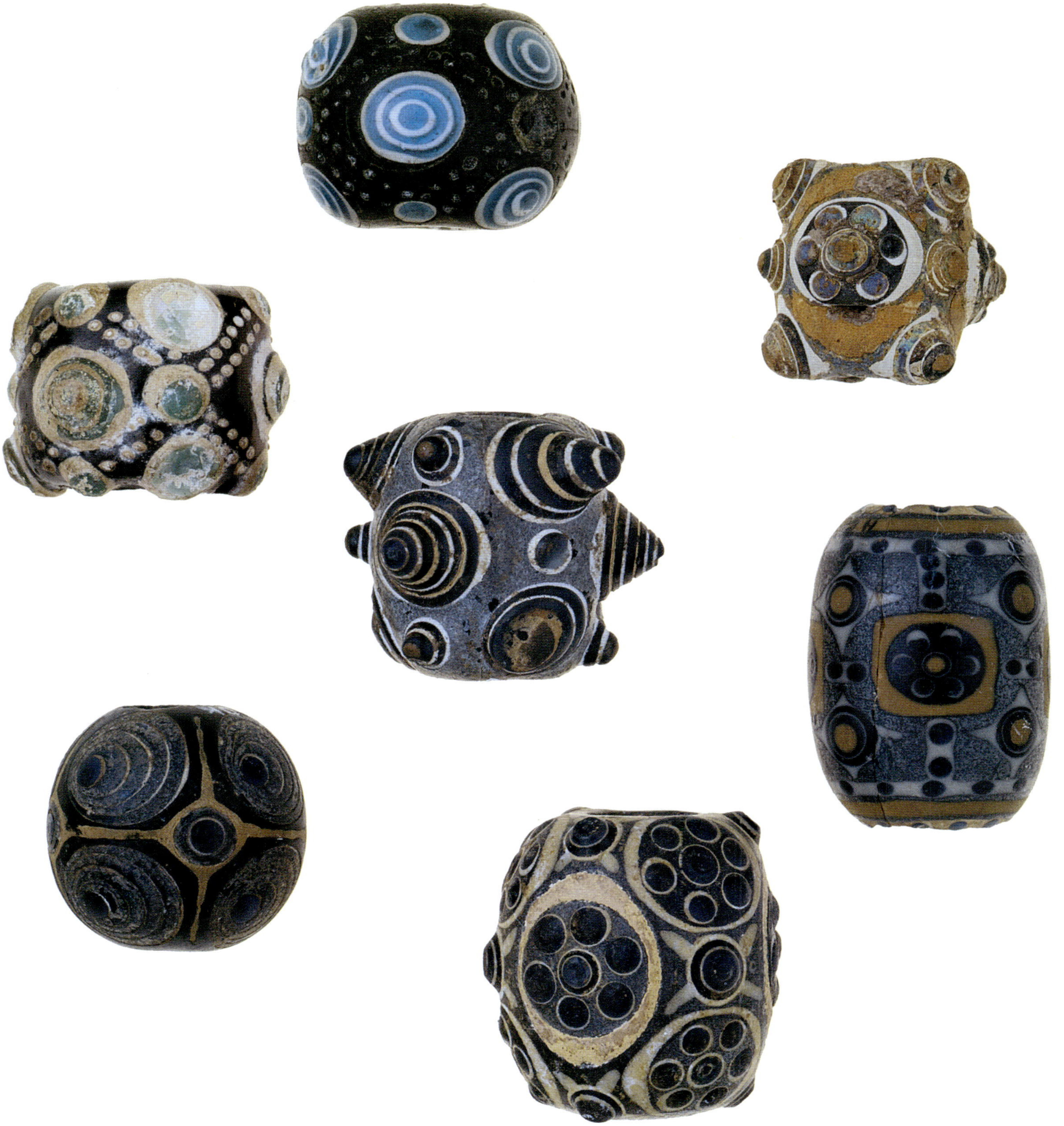

imported into China at this time (Timeline 493), these heavy beads are distinguished by their lead-barium content. The layered-glass technique, often with geometric patterns formed of dotted lines and sometimes demonstrated with more protruding "horned" eyes than are seen here, is a Chinese contribution to the bead type.[1]

These beads were collected by Bishop William Charles White, a Canadian missionary who became the first Anglican bishop of Henan Province. Top bead: diameter, 1.9 cm. Royal Ontario Museum, Toronto

times of cultural interchange. Indeed, many Korean and Japanese tombs have yielded a variety of imported beads.

Conversely, beads do not appear to have been generally available or important in most isolationist periods. The reasons for isolation were complex and varied in each country throughout the centuries. Frequently, isolationism was brought about by rulers attempting to avoid alliances between competing leaders (or enemies) in their own countries and outside powers. During the seventeenth century, when neo-Confucianism spread throughout the Far East, isolationism was a policy to save the country from European colonialism and the influence of Christian missionaries.

During times of isolation, which were often accompanied by a return to the tenets of strict Confucianism, cultural separation led to a decline in the use and manufacture of beads. In these periods, particularly from the seventeenth to the nineteenth century, isolationism was reinforced by sumptuary laws that mandated the styles of clothing, jewelry, and possessions appropriate to each social class. Since beads, which symbolized wealth and status, were restricted even among the elite, the importing, making, and wearing of them in quantity ceased to be an important practice. (An exception was the Japanese *ojime*.) The clothes of the elite, moreover, were often richly patterned and heavily embroidered, providing a substitute for jewelry. Nevertheless, glass beadmaking for export existed as a minor industry in nineteenth-century China and Japan, when their ports were closed to foreign goods; and glass beads were occasionally used for *ojime* in Japan.

China

Some of the earliest ornaments in the world are Chinese. These include beads of stone, animal teeth, marine shells, and fish bone that have been recovered from the Upper Cave of Zhou-kou-dian, south of Beijing, dating to 16,000 B.C.[5] The stone beads were drilled and painted with red hematite powder—perhaps the first decorated artifacts in Chinese history.[6]

In the Gobi Desert, archaeologists have found beads, 12,000 years old, fashioned of ostrich and dinosaur eggshell. By the sixth millennium B.C., strings of cowrie shells existed, although it is not known if, as in Bronze Age China, these were used as adornment or currency (or both).[7]

Jade beads (Bead Chart 800) attributed to Anyang craftsmen of the Shang dynasty (thirteenth to eleventh century B.C.) have been discovered in association with China's earliest known wheel-made pottery, silk-weaving, and bronze-casting. It is surprising that no bronze beads are known, since Shang bronze-casting was well developed, and metal beads were frequently part of metallurgical industries in other areas. The Chinese, unlike peoples of other cultures, do not seem to have had a fondness for gold either.

Possibly the earliest Chinese glass beads—small, pale green forms imitating jade—have been found in ninth- and eighth-century B.C. tombs of the Western Zhou dynasty. Historically, the Chinese preferred to use bronze, lacquer, ceramic, and stone; glass was only a substitute for jade and precious stones. Nevertheless, by the fifth century B.C. they made remarkable glass beads, using lapidary (grinding), metallurgical (casting and molding), and ceramic methods (glazing and sandcore)—techniques not generally associated with glassmaking.

The last three centuries of the Zhou dynasty, known as the "Warring States" period (481–221 B.C.), were marked by artistic inventiveness in many areas. Artisans concentrated on secular objects for personal pleasure and adornment, including the famous Chinese eye beads (plates 154 and 330). First reported from princely tombs near Luoyang (Henan Province), and now excavated from other late Zhou burials as well, these masterpieces of the beadmaker's art employ layered glass to create protruding eyelike motifs, often in complex geometric patterns. While it is possible that these beads were inspired by contemporary western Asian or Phoenician prototypes, their manufacture and chemical composition (lead-barium glass, rather than the soda-lime glass known in the West) strongly suggest they were made in China. Why such remarkable glass beadmaking flourished in China for several hundred years, only to disappear suddenly in the early Han period, remains an important unanswered question.[8]

Jadework also reached high levels of artistry during the later Zhou dynasty. Some of the finest jade jewelry and beads have been recovered from the Luoyang and other Warring States period tombs (plate 152). Faience and pottery beads from late Zhou times were made by ceramic techniques. They feature white, gray, or red cores overlaid with a glazed or slipped decoration that frequently is derived from the design of the glass eye beads (plates 155 and 159).[9]

The Qin dynasty (221–206 B.C.) unified China under a central government, and under the succeeding Han house (206 B.C.–A.D. 220) the country was exposed to contact with the West. Beads from different countries appear in China, while Chinese-made glass beads are now found in both Korea and Japan.[10]

To halt foreign intrusion, China extended her power in central Asia during the second century B.C., gaining control of the caravan routes that cross the Asian deserts. The most famous of these were the silk routes, a series of routes (some dating back to 1500 B.C.) over which Chinese silks and pottery were transported as far west as Rome, while horses, jade, and melon and eye beads—common to ancient western Asia and the Mediterranean—appeared in China. Baltic and Burmese amber were also imported into China at this time.[11]

In Han dynasty times, China also established relations with the Kushan dynasty in Afghanistan and northern India, and built outposts along the silk routes in central Asia that served as commercial centers. Agate and carnelian beads (including etched carnelians) excavated from western Han tombs in Hebei Province in north China are similar to beads of the same date from India, Persia, and Afghanistan.[12] At this time also, Buddhism was introduced to China by the people of Kashmir and by sects along the silk routes. For centuries thereafter, Buddhist missionaries and Asian traders traveled the same routes, both transporting beads.

During the seventh and eighth centuries, emperors of the Tang dynasty (A.D. 618–907) presided over one of the greatest periods in Chinese civilization. China, along with Korea and Japan, was receptive to foreign contact; Buddhism flourished, as did artistic achievement. Unfortunately, only a limited number of Tang beads are extant, although a stunning gold and pearl necklace dating A.D. 608 was excavated from a Sui dynasty noble child's burial, and five gold beads, beautifully decorated with granulation and attributed to the Tang dynasty, are displayed at the British Museum.[13]

After An Lu-shan's rebellion of 755, the central government in China was weakened considerably. As a result, links with central Asia were disrupted, and subsequently overland trade with the West declined. As Tang rule faltered, a period of isolation set in, marked by intense nationalism: import controls were tightened, foreigners banned, and the "alien" Buddhists were persecuted.[14]

During the Tang, "Five Dynasties" (618–960), and Song (960–1279) periods, evidence of glass beadmaking is primarily available from literary references. The few known Tang glass beads are chemically similar to those made in the West; the lead glass of the earlier Zhou period was no longer used exclusively.[15]

The Song period, despite the self-imposed isolation of China, saw new levels of trade and cultural achievement. With the old land routes to central Asia and the West no longer under its control, China turned to the sea, slowly developing maritime trade relations

TOP: 155. *Faience beads, c. 400–100* B.C. *Top bead: diameter, 1.3 cm. Royal Ontario Museum, Toronto*

MIDDLE ROW, LEFT: 156. *A bead of reddish brown opaque glass, possibly imitating carnelian, c. 400–100* B.C. *Length, 2.6 cm. Royal Ontario Museum, Toronto*

MIDDLE ROW, RIGHT: 157. *Glass beads, c. 500* B.C., *strongly resembling Phoenician and Egyptian eye beads of the period. Although the revolving, asymmetrical eyes are said to be Chinese, they may also have been Egyptian imports into China. Upper left bead: diameter, 1.4 cm. Royal Ontario Museum, Toronto*

BOTTOM LEFT: 158. *A hexagonal bead of transparent green glass. The Chinese often substituted glass for jade and other precious stones, working the glass by lapidary methods. The hexagonal faceting on this bead was achieved by grinding; thereafter, the form was drilled and polished. This bead was probably excavated at Changsha, Hunan Province, and dates to the late Zhou dynasty, fifth to third century* B.C. *Length, 8.1 cm. Corning Museum of Glass, Corning, New York*

BOTTOM RIGHT: 159. *A glazed pottery bead, possibly an ancient copy of a glass original, c. 400–100* B.C. *n.s. Royal Ontario Museum, Toronto*

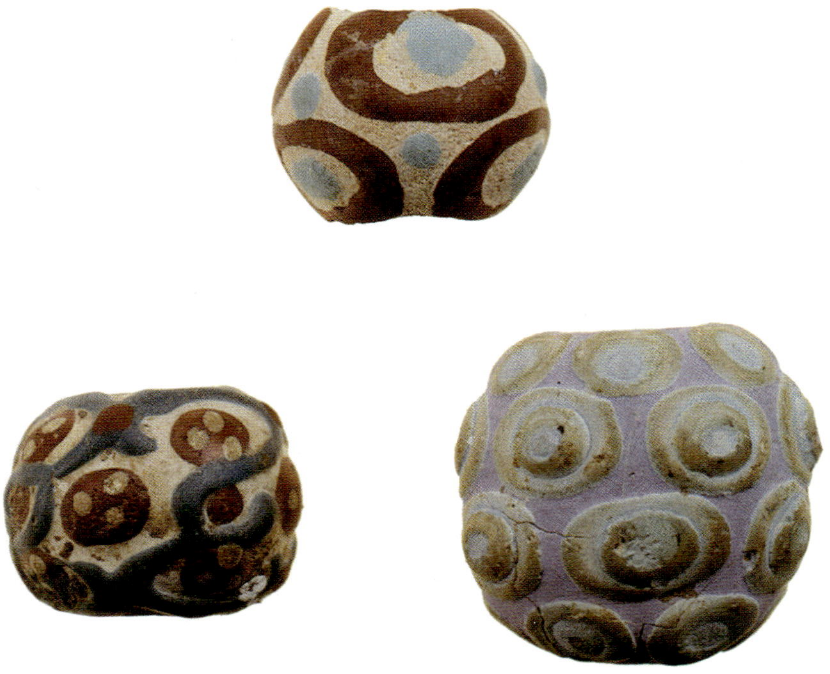

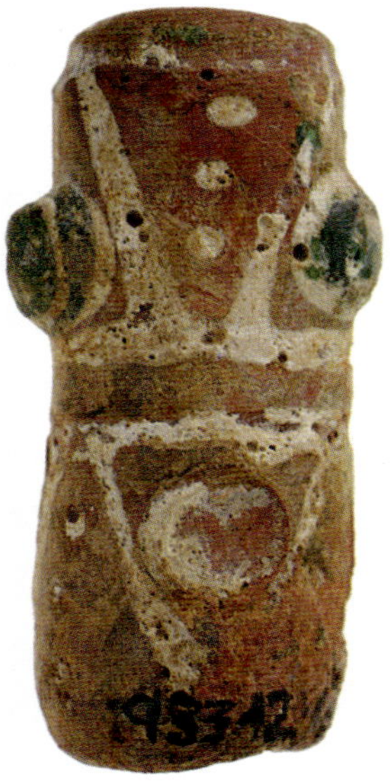

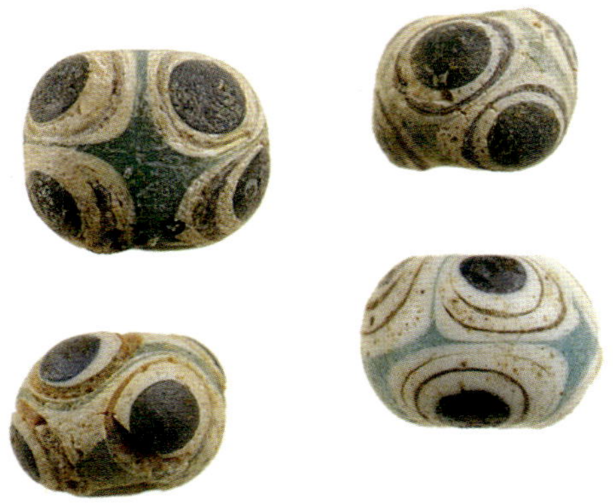

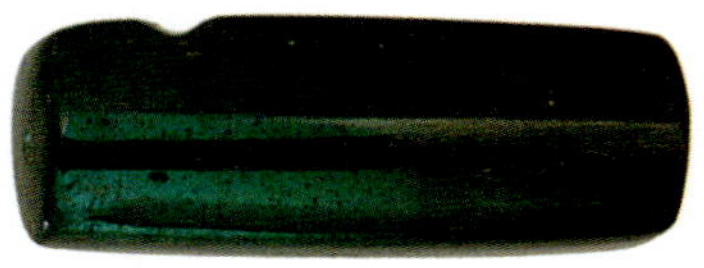

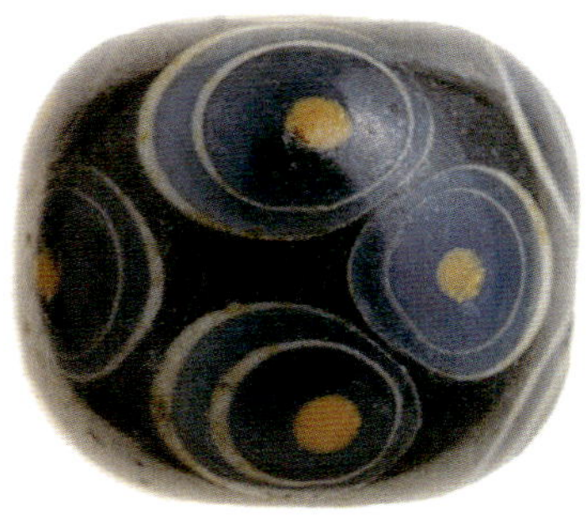

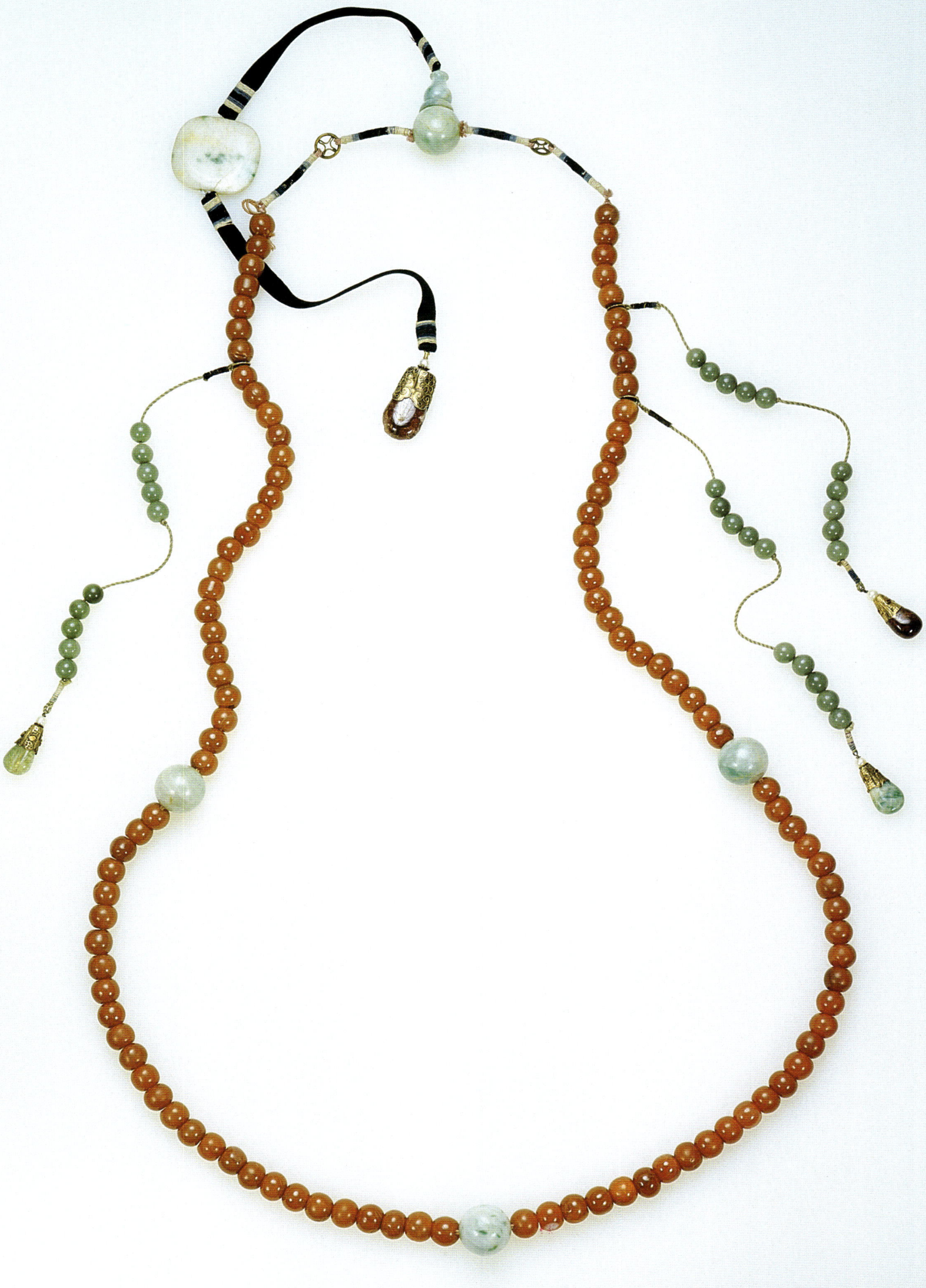

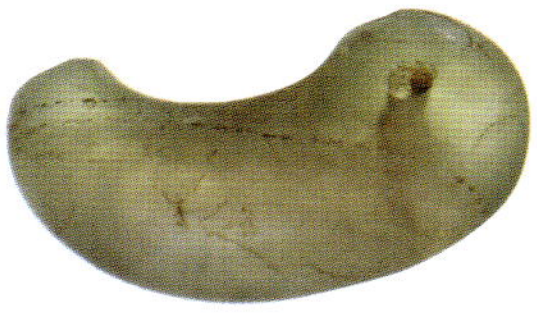

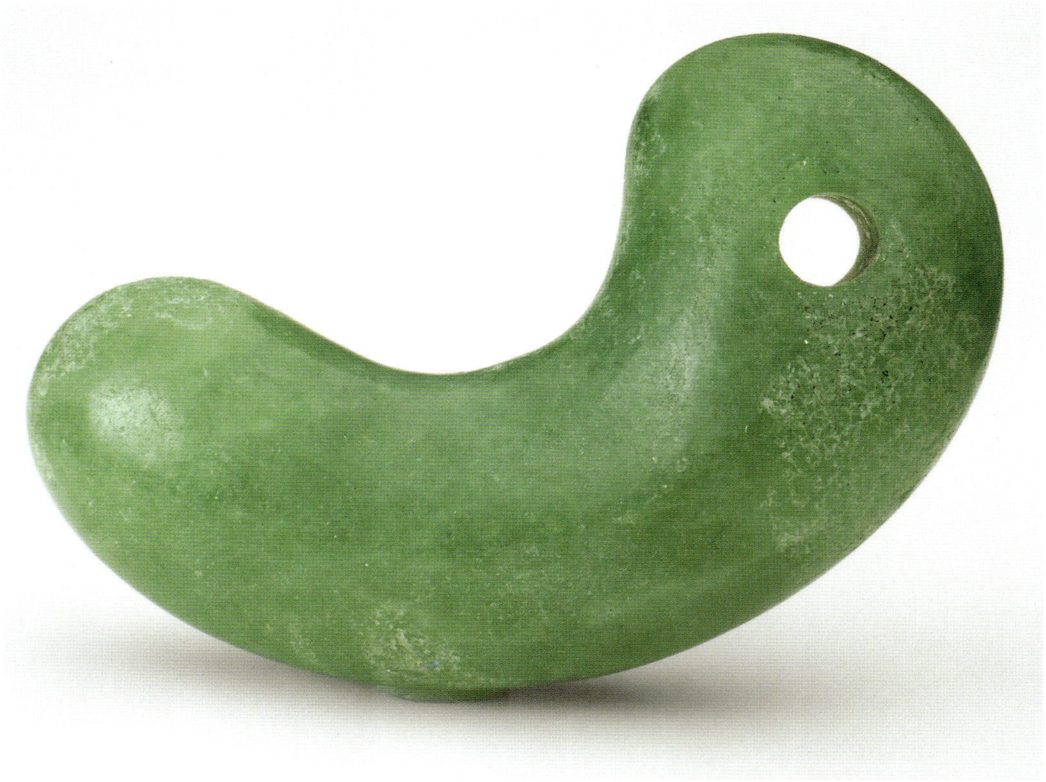

PREVIOUS PAGE: 160. *Official court beads or "Mandarin chain" worn by the emperor and the nobility during the period of Manchurian rule in China (1644–1912). Although the form of the chains was influenced by Tibetan Buddhist rosaries, they were used in China primarily as status symbols rather than prayer aids. This necklace is composed of 108 red Chinese glass beads, four jade dividers ("Buddha heads"), a flat jade plaque, counting beads, and tourmaline dewdrop pendants. The beads on the silk cord and terminal dewdrop pendant attached to the jade plaque were draped on the wearer's back, acting as a counterweight to the necklace. Mandarin officials fingered their beads, handling them like worry beads. They also used them as abacuses for business calculations. Length, 41.3 cm. Collection Ivory Freidus*

ABOVE LEFT: 161. Magatama *("sacred jewel") of blue glass from the Nara period (A.D. 645–794). Shaped by grinding, this bead has been bore-drilled from one side. Length, 2.9 cm. Corning Museum of Glass, Corning, New York*

ABOVE RIGHT: 162. *Jade kogok from Korea, date unknown. Length, 5 cm. Collection Albert Summerfield, Seattle*

with Southeast Asia, India, and the countries of the Persian Gulf. By the Yuan dynasty (1279–1368), trade with central Asia, Sri Lanka, and Russia resumed. The Venetian traveler Marco Polo, visiting China at this time, commented on the number of foreign ships and traders, predominantly Indians, in Chinese ports.[16]

Documentary sources for the Song and Yuan periods note that glass beads, presumably from China, were being exported with porcelain, gold, silver, tin, and silk.[17] Furthermore, many Chinese artisans settled in the foreign communities with which they traded, particularly Southeast Asia and India. By the seventeenth century, Chinese glass beadmakers living in Java were exporting their products to Borneo.[18] During the Qing (Manchu) dynasty (1644–1912), trade in porcelain, lacquerware, tea, and silver continued from a limited number of ports. Chinese craftsmanship was renowned for its elaboration and technical proficiency and enjoyed immense popularity in the West during the late seventeenth and eighteenth centuries.

Quantities of glass beads were manufactured during Qing rule. Most of these were sold to Russians and the Ainu of Hokkaido, Japan, during the eighteenth century, and to Indians, East Africans, and Americans in the nineteenth century. During the 1790s, Russians were so anxious to buy Chinese glass beads that they eliminated all import duties along their border.[19]

As Chinese beads were distributed through a variety of trade networks and through many transactions, knowledge of the origin of particular beads has often been lost. Chinese glass beads sent to Bombay in the mid-nineteenth century were resold to Africans for ivory.[20] Glass beads carried by Europeans during the early days of trade among Indians in the American Southwest and Northwest may have been of Chinese origin, including the well-known "padre" beads (Timeline 1035).[21] Clearer historical evidence and richer archaeological data on Chinese glass beads may help answer questions about a number of Asian bead types, including examples from Taiwan and Indonesia.

Trade with the West expanded in the 1840s, and within ten years China became a

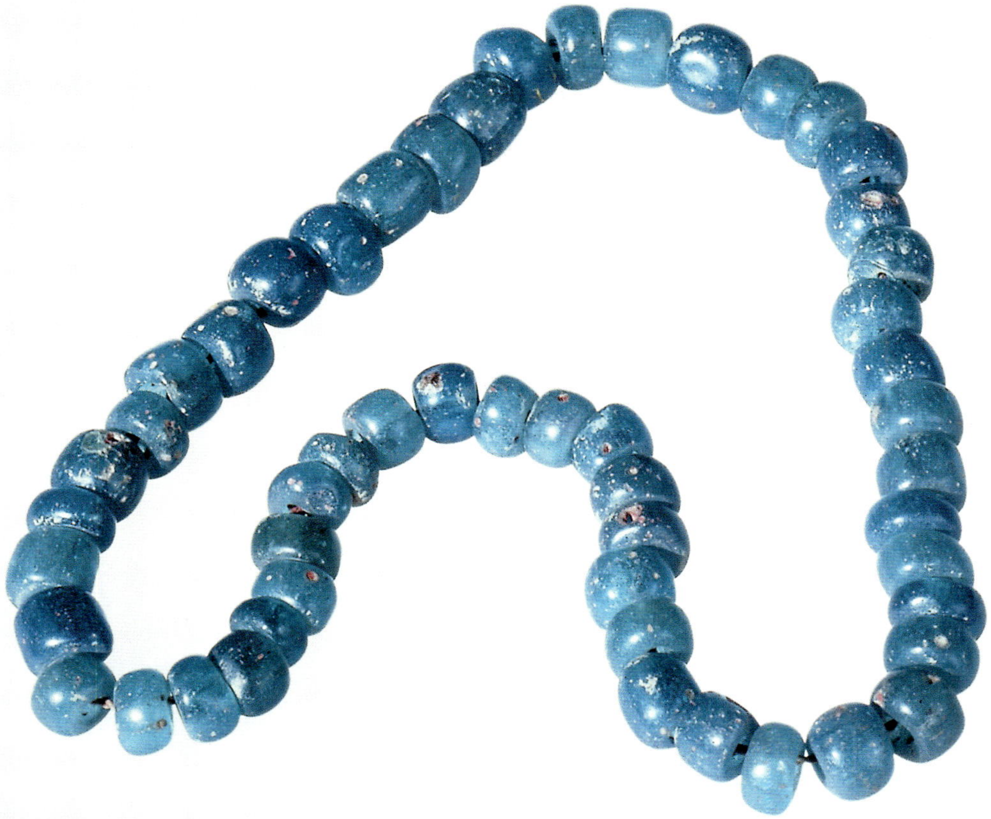

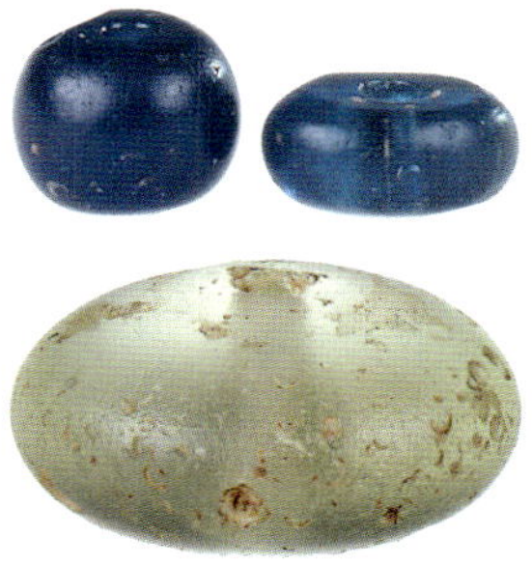

large-scale exporter of beads. These beads were the product of cottage industries located in several centers, notably in Canton in the south and Poshan in northeastern China. The beads commonly referred to as "Peking glass" were probably made in Poshan (Timeline 823–33). Glass beads continue to be made in China even today, frequently involving techniques reported over a hundred years ago.[22]

Chinese Court Beads

In 1644, the Manchu captured Beijing and established the Qing dynasty (1644–1912). Beads of precious and semiprecious stones and glass were produced for necklaces called "court beads" or "Mandarin chains" by foreign observers. Worn by the Manchurian emperors and their court, these distinctive necklaces (plate 160) resembled Tibetan Buddhist prayer beads (plate 70) but differed from those of Tibet in both form and content. The Chinese beads expressed status and were permitted to be worn only by people of high rank. Sumptuary laws of the period established a complex set of rules determining acceptable materials for the beads, as well as identifying those who were allowed to wear them.[23]

Important symbolism was imbedded in the overall form as well as the separate components or "accessories" of the necklaces. Like their Tibetan prototypes, they had 108 principal beads. Four large additional beads, called "Buddha heads," set off four groups of twenty-seven beads each. This division also expressed multiples of three, a sacred number associated with Yang and heaven in old Chinese philosophy.[24]

It was during certain yearly rites, such as the annual sacrifices to heaven and earth conducted by the emperor in Beijing, that sumptuary laws regarding the wearing of court beads became quite important. The extensive regulations were followed by all court

TOP: 163. *Quantities of beads like these have been found in Japanese Old Tomb period graves (A.D. 250–552), often thousands in a single tomb.* Marudama *and* kodama *are round beads made by winding or by drawn, cut-tube methods. The distinguishing difference is size:* marudama *beads are 0.5 cm or larger;* kodama *is any smaller bead. Shown here are opaque, dark blue* marudama. *All are imported Indo-Pacific beads, possibly from Indonesia. Left bead: diameter, 0.7 cm. Plates 163–165: Corning Museum of Glass, Corning, New York*

ABOVE: 164. *Wound transparent* marudama. *Diameter, 2.3 cm*

ABOVE LEFT: 165. *Translucent, gray blue* kodama. *Traces of clay and red pigment remain on the beads. Diameters, 0.2 to 0.4 cm*

OVERLEAF, TOP LEFT: 166. *A glass bead made by inserting one or more tiny red goldfish forms into transparent glass. Spiraled dark blue threads are added to the bead's interior or exterior. This Meiji period bead was made for the Ainu women of Hokkaido. The Ainu were one of the few Japanese groups to wear large quantities of beads. Diameter, 9 cm. Corning Museum of Glass, Corning, New York*

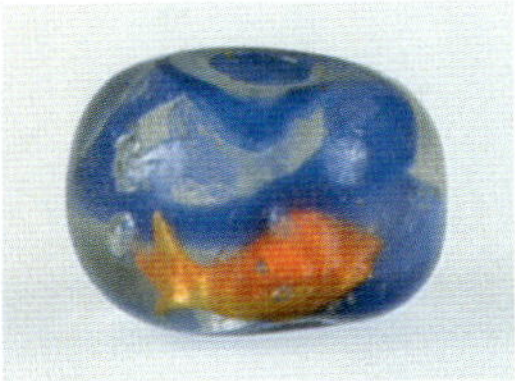

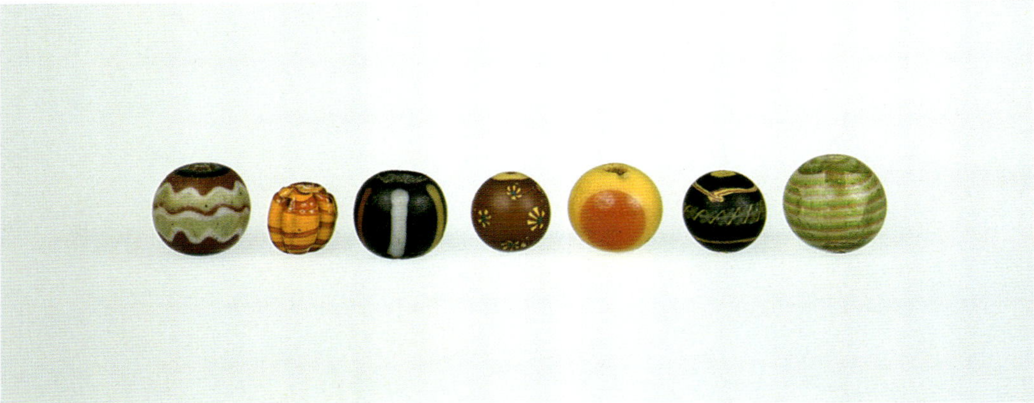

TOP RIGHT: 167. *Edo period glass beads. Left to right:* gangidama, *or "zigzag bead." Diameter, 1.8 cm;* kuchinashi-dama, *which derives its name from the seed of the gardenia (*kuchinashi*), whose form it resembles. In the West it is known as a melon bead;* sujidama, *or "line bead," possibly of Venetian origin or at least made in the Venetian style;* sarasadama, *a delicately patterned nineteenth-century bead that derives its name from imported Indian cottons;* marudama, *or "round bead," found in Japan but possibly made in China;* tombodama, *a "complex glass bead";* tombodama, *possibly of Venetian origin. Corning Museum of Glass, Corning, New York*

The Edo period beads shown on this page were probably ojime, *as their perforations are large enough to accommodate a double cord.*[11]

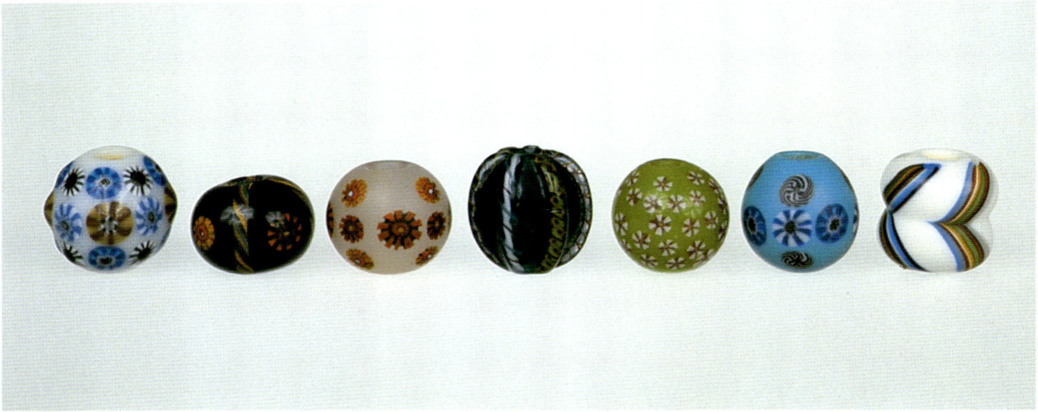

MIDDLE RIGHT: 168. *Glass beads made in Osaka during the 1970s by the late master beadmaker Kyoyo Asao (1918–1985). The beads incorporate traditional manufacturing techniques, including those used in the Nara and Edo periods. Far right bead: length, 2.1 cm. Corning Museum of Glass, Corning, New York*

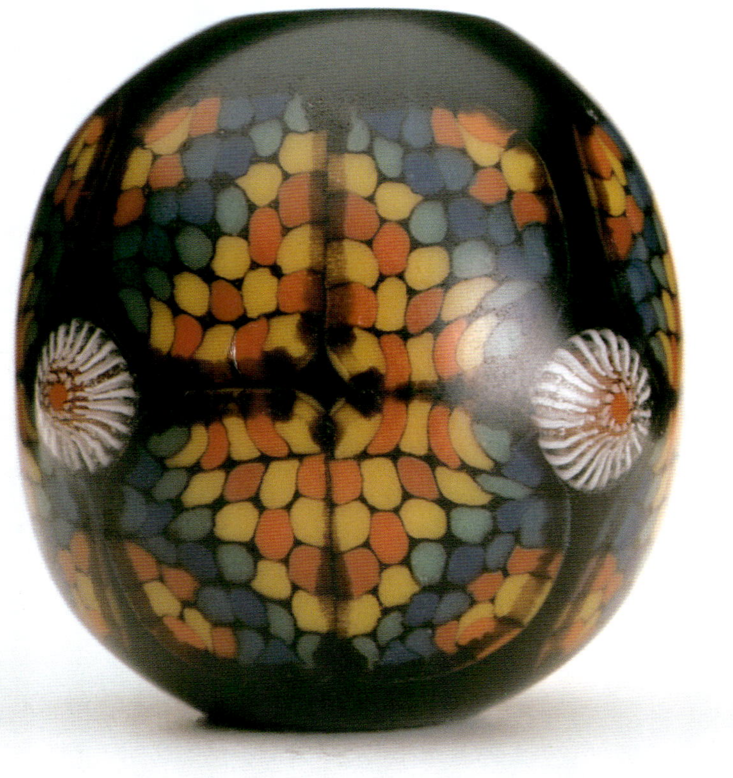

BOTTOM RIGHT: 169. *A glass bead produced in 1984 by Kyoyo Asao. Length, 2.4 cm. Collection Lease Waldron, Lexington, Massachusetts*

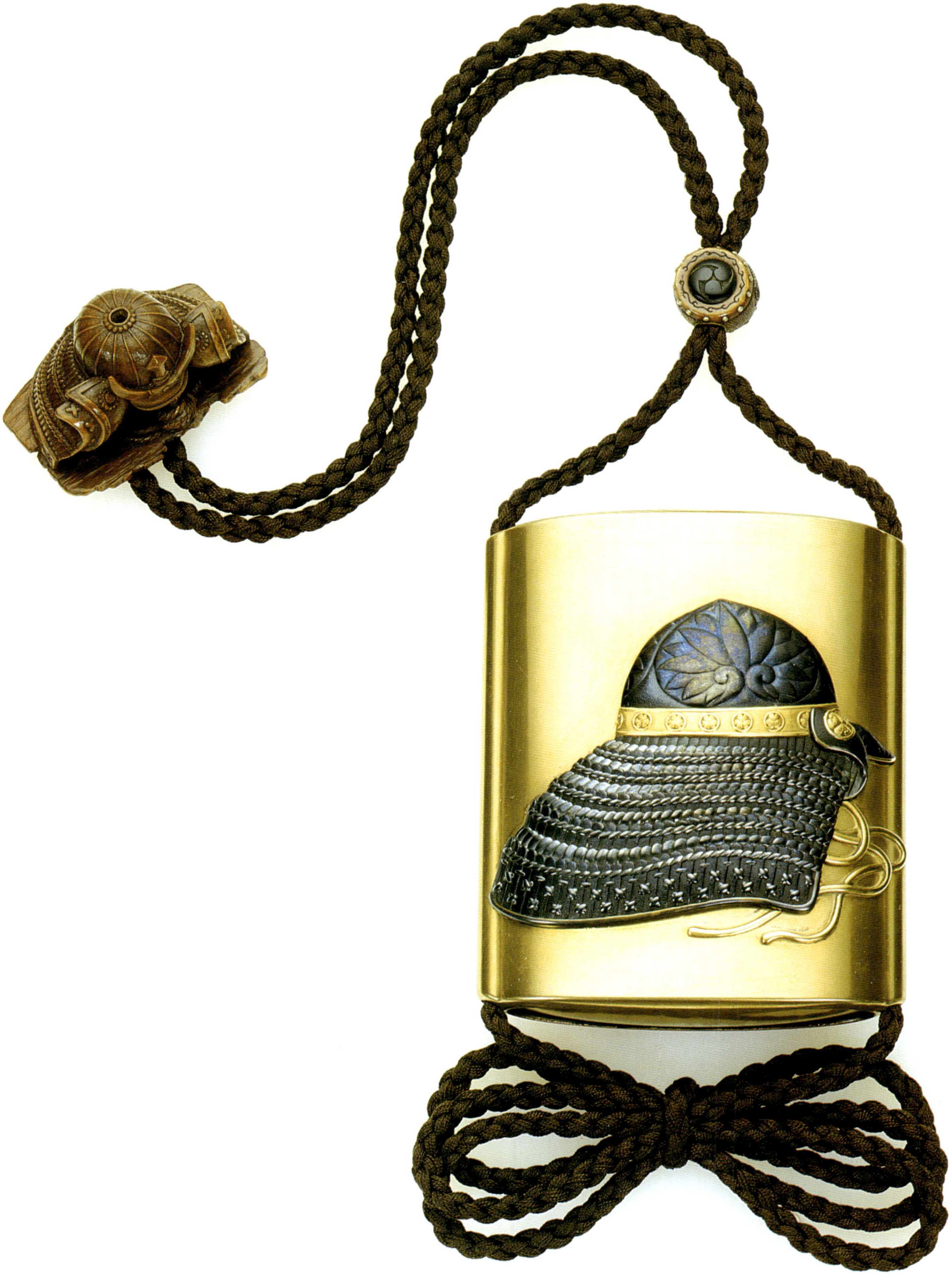

PREVIOUS PAGE: 170. *A nineteenth-century* inro, netsuke, *and* ojime *ensemble, typically worn with a kimono. Private collection. This lacquered wood* inro *was made for a powerful member of the Tokugawa shogunate, Japan's ruling military dynasty between 1615 and 1868. The helmet depicted on the* inro *is inlaid with the crest of the Tokugawa family. The boxwood and ebony* ojime *is inlaid with ivory and shaped in the form of a war drum used to assemble troops. The* netsuke *is also helmet-shaped.*[III] *Length of* inro, *9.9 cm. Collection Dave and Sandy Swedlow, Los Angeles*

members and extended to high-ranking military officers and to civil servants and their wives.[25] Although most aristocratic Chinese women refused to wear Manchurian dress and court beads because they represented the hated foreign rulers, the bead materials of certain court women, such as the emperor's concubines, were exactly prescribed.

All the materials of the court beads mentioned in the Chinese dynastic laws—pearls, coral, honey amber, lapis lazuli, and turquoise—were imported, often from great distances. Understandably, they were highly treasured. Coral came from Italy or the Persian Gulf, amber from Burma and the Baltic area, sky-blue turquoise from Persia (a greener shade of turquoise is native to China), and lapis lazuli from Afghanistan. All of the jade, frequently used for the Buddha's-head divider beads, came from Burma or the Khotan region of central Asia (Chinese Turkmenistan). Noblemen of lower rank and their wives wore glass beads. Fine glass was highly valued and sometimes was used to imitate precious stones. Ivory beads were also worn, including some with intricate cutout patterns. Elephant ivory came from India or Africa, walrus ivory from the North Pacific, and fossil mammoth ivory from Siberia. Beads of rare woods, such as fragrant aloes wood, came from southern China. Aloes wood and rosewood were used for incense, and sometimes a small amount of ambergris (sperm-whale secretion used for perfumes) was added to the incense and compressed into beads. When the beads were held, the warmth of the hand released their fragrance.

With the fall of the Qing dynasty in 1912, the Chinese were eager to break up the necklaces and sell off the various parts. The chains were a reminder of alien rulers, and the foreign costumes and jewelry were best forgotten. Few original Mandarin necklaces still exist.

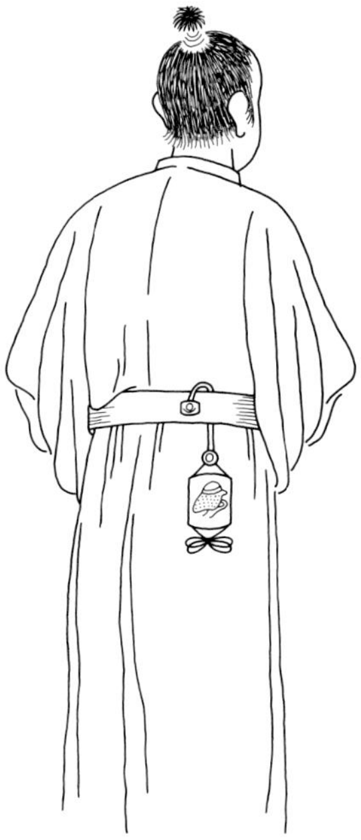

FIG. 1. Inro, netsuke, *and* ojime *ensemble as worn from the* obi *sash.*

Jade Beads

The Chinese have venerated and worn jade for over five thousand years. The character for "king" (⁝) may have symbolized a string of jade beads. The character *pao,* signifying "precious," originally was the outline of a house enclosing symbols for cowrie shells and jade beads.[25] The Chinese were so fond of jade that those who could afford to carried small pieces with them at all times. When handled, jade supposedly passed some of its subtle virtue on to its owner; Chinese poets called it the "concentrated essence of love."[27]

For centuries, the riverbeds of the Khotan region of central Asia were the chief source of ancient jade (nephrite), although some jade may have also come from the region of Lake Baikal in Siberia. Throughout their history, the Chinese prized nephrite rather than jadeite (the two minerals are both called "jade").[28] However, when a source of brilliant emerald-green jadeite ("imperial jade") was discovered in Burma during the eighteenth century, it was highly coveted, and it is from this jadeite that the most expensive modern beads and jewelry are made.

Despite its hardness, jade can be worked with only a bamboo drill if the right abrasives are used. Jade cannot be cut by steel, but only by stones harder than itself. By the late Shang times (Anyang period, 1300–1045 B.C.), the surfaces of flat jade beads, or plaques and pendants, were incised with complex designs. It has been suggested that bronze drill points were used along with abrasives made of crushed quartz.[29]

Korea

The geographic proximity of China and Korea has led casual observers to believe that there must have been close interaction between them, when in fact history shows their border frequently acted as both a physical and cultural barrier. This is probably the result of a combination of the rugged border topography and the Koreans' deeply rooted resistance to foreign control. Nevertheless, their adornment does reflect some outside stimuli.

Elements of culture were introduced early to Korea by nomadic peoples from distant northern Asia. It is not surprising, therefore, that ancient Korean art incorporates shamanistic symbolism associated with cultures from Siberia, Manchuria, and the Asian steppes. China was also a major source of influences, which were reinterpreted in uniquely Korean ways. These sources of ideas also played a role in the development of Korean beads.

Perforated bone beads from deer toes from Turubong Cave No. 2 near Seoul date to 18,000 B.C., while jade beads are known from Neolithic sites (5000–2000 B.C.). The best-known Korean bead, the *kogok*, was developed during the first millennium B.C. (plate 161).[30]

Called *kogok* in Korea and *magatama* in Japan, the crescent- or comma-shaped bead is found exclusively in Korea and Japan, each country claiming to have produced the earliest examples. In both countries, it is a sacred symbol: Korea combines a blue and red *kogok*-shaped figure, the yin-yang symbol, in its national emblem, while in Japan, the *magatama* is combined with the sword and mirror as one of the three emblems of royalty.[31]

Kogok beads are made of jade, lapis lazuli, carnelian, and glass. They were used on crowns and other jewelry in Korea's Old Silla dynasty (57 B.C.–A.D. 668). *Magatama* found in graves of the Japanese Yayoi and Kofun (Old Tomb period; 250 B.C.–A.D. 552) were molded in glass and carved from jade, carnelian, and other semiprecious stones.[32] Both *kogok* and *magatama* are directly related to the beginnings of glass production in each country. The earliest evidence of glassworking in Japan is a Yayoi period mold used to cast *magatama*.[33] In Korea, a glass industry was established during the Three Kingdoms period (57 B.C.–A.D. 668) for the sole purpose of making *kogok*.[34]

Over the course of the Three Kingdoms period the Chinese were ousted from their colonies and three Korean states were formed—Paekche, Koguryo, and Silla. Royal tombs excavated in Paekche and Silla disclose quantities of both imported and locally made beads. Skilled goldsmiths produced dazzling crowns, girdles, and necklaces decorated with beads of gold, jade, and glass. Especially notable were the gold crowns of Silla, with jade and glass *kogok*. Paekche tombs in Kongju (A.D. 526–529) contained beads of gold, silver, jade, glass, and many other materials. Most of these beads were sewn onto clothing, and many were of the small drawn-glass variety in monochrome blue, violet, green, yellow, and orange. Several gold-in-glass beads, similar to those made in the Mediterranean region, were also found.[35]

A great variety of beads was discovered at the royal tombs at Kyongju in Silla, including faceted quartz crystal forms and a mosaic-glass face bead from the fourth or fifth century A.D.[36] This "face bead"—a national treasure of Korea—as well as a similar one in the Liese Collection of the Bead Museum in Glendale, Arizona (plate 171), are Indonesian jatim.[37] Most glass beads found in the Silla tombs were imported, with India, the Roman Empire, and China being possible sources. The *kogok* used in the crowns are the only known beads of this period made of Korean glass. Jade beads (both nephrite and jadeite) in the tombs probably came from sources in Turkmenistan, Korea, and Japan, while amber found there may actually be copal from native Korean pine trees. The jet, pearls, gold, and silver all came from Korea.[38]

Most of Korea's imported beads and materials came over the silk routes into China from the Middle East, central Asia, India, and the West. This pattern of Korean trade conducted via China with the outside world continued for centuries.

The Yi dynasty (A.D. 1392–1910) was the last to rule Korea before its annexation by Japan in 1910. Yi rulers banned Buddhism and molded the nation's social and spiritual life according to neo-Confucianist principles derived from China's Ming dynasty. This meant

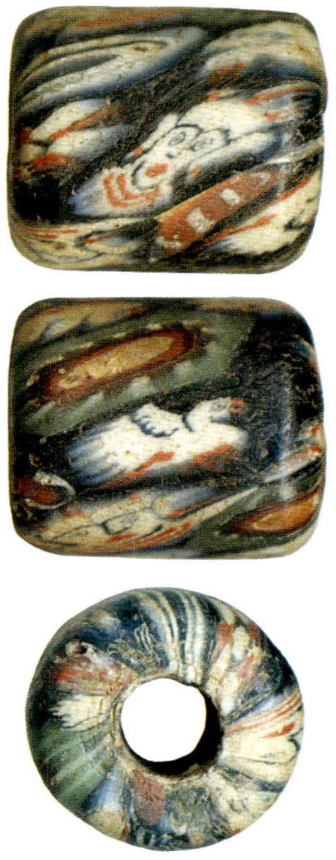

171. *Jatim face bead, three views. This millefiori mosaic bead, similar to several others excavated from fifth to sixth century A.D. high-status Korean (Silla) tombs, is thought to have been produced in eastern Java. The portrait image shown in the top view, upper left side of the bead, may be a representation of Buddha. On the other side, center view, is a bird possibly representing the heavenly goose,* hamsa. *Not visible is a tree, perhaps the Bodhi tree under which Buddha sat while achieving enlightenment.*[IV] *During those early centuries, international trade and travel was strongly linked to the spread of Buddhism throughout Asia. This bead was perhaps brought to Korea by wandering monks to aid in religious teachings. Length, 2 cm. Liese Collection, the Bead Museum, Glendale, Arizona*

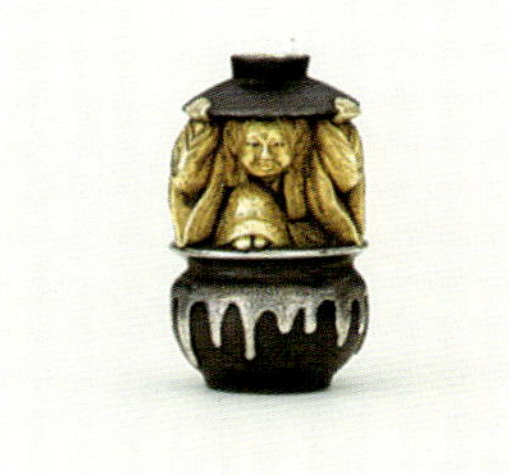

ABOVE: 172. *An* ojime *was made by Somin, a master metallurgist in the nineteenth century. It depicts a* shojo *carved in solid gold emerging from a sake jar. The eyeball, iris, and pupil are inlaid with iron and silver.* Shojo *are mythical creatures living by the sea, who love to drink sake, sing, and dance. These joyous creatures are a symbol of universal happiness. Length, 2.3 cm. (Reproduced actual size.) Collection Dave and Sandy Swedlow, Los Angeles*

RIGHT: 172a. Ojime *in plate 172 enlarged eight times.*

173. *Lacquer, made from the sap of the lacquer tree, can be layered on a wooden bead. Here, red, black, and silver lacquer on ivory creates a dramatic portrayal of a hunting falcon encircling the* ojime *as it swoops to catch a dragonfly. Diameter, 1.6 cm. Private collection*

174. *A lacquer* ojime *made of at least nineteen yellow, black, and red layers of lacquer. Carved in relief, it depicts symbols of Japan's aesthetic life, including tea ceremony implements, musical instruments, and a basket of fruit called "citron Buddha's fingers" or "Buddha's hand." Diameter, 1.65 cm. Collection Dr. Ralph Maercks, Miami*

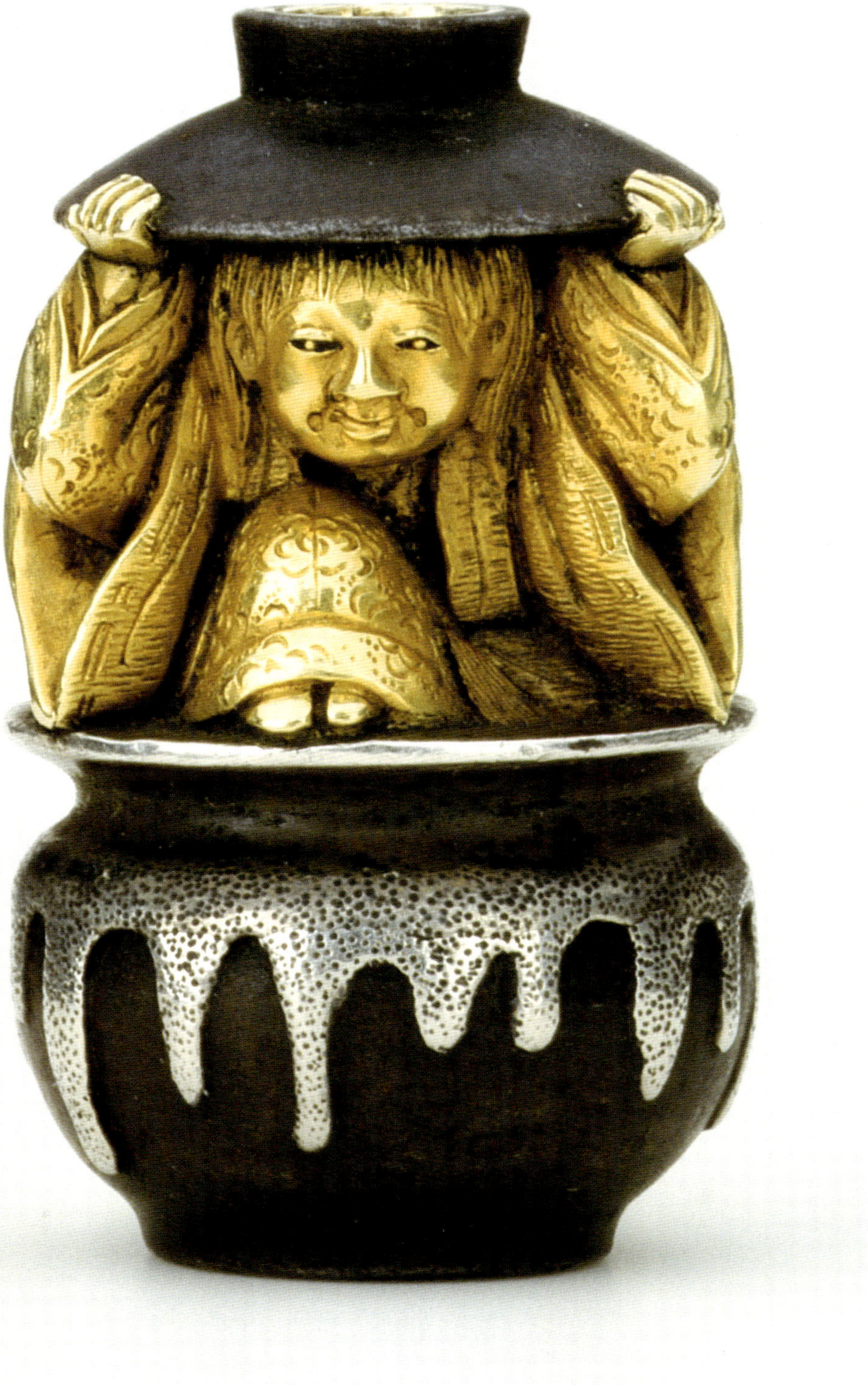

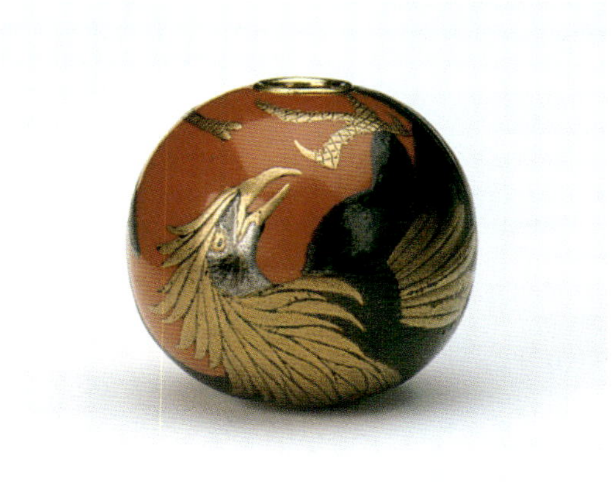

173

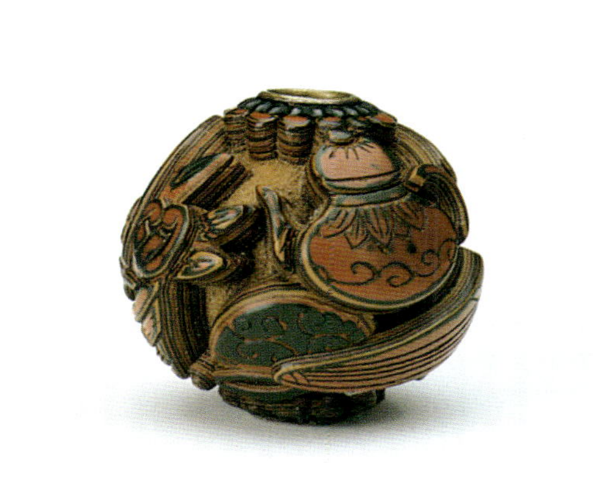

174

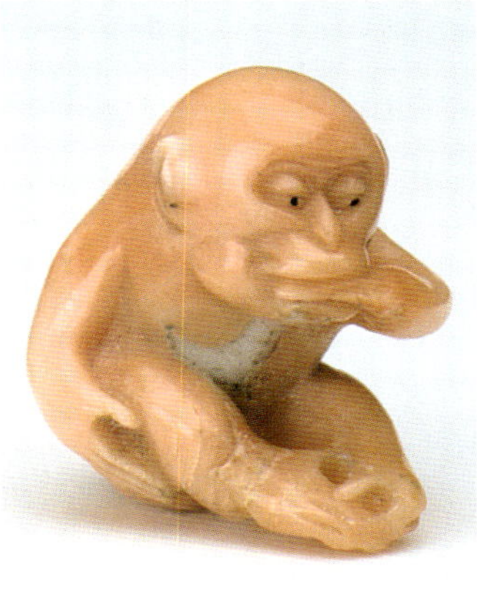

175

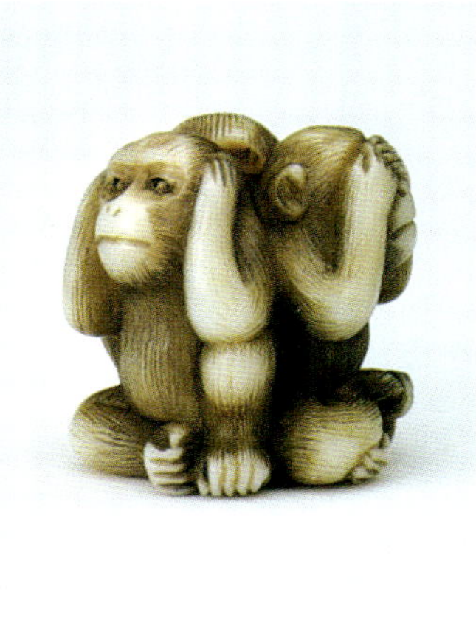

176

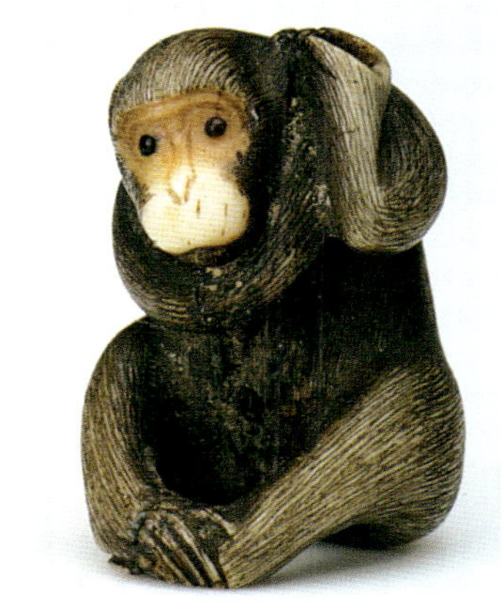

177

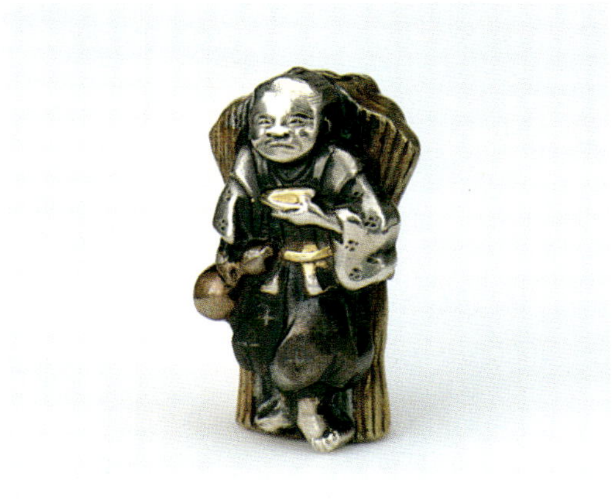

178

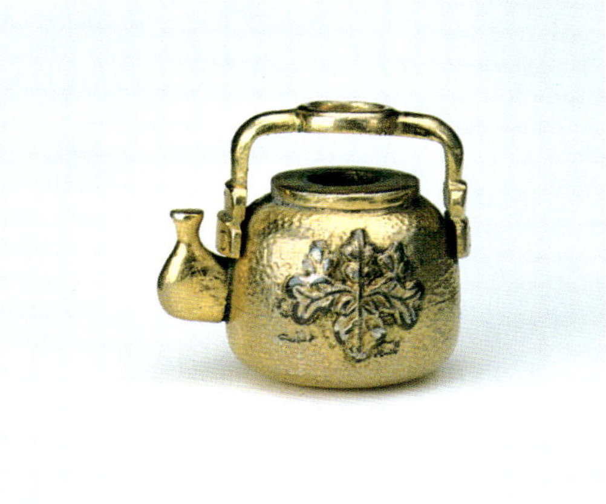

179

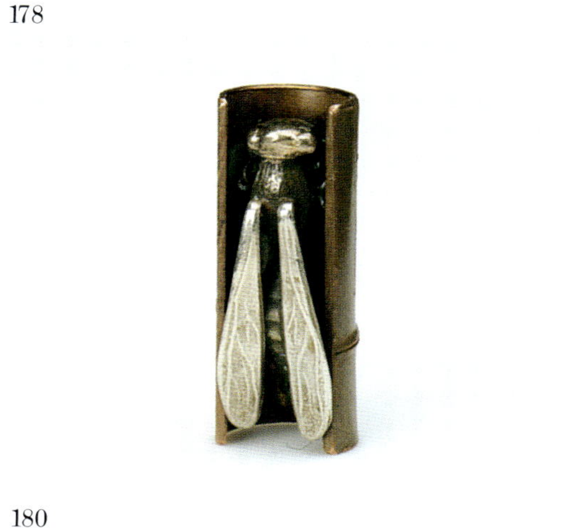

180

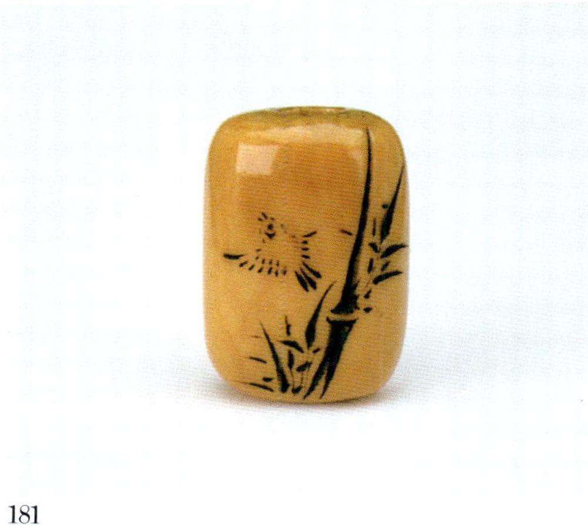

181

175. A rare coral ojime beautifully carved into a seated monkey. Length, 2 cm. Private collection

176. A stained ivory version of "Hear no evil, speak no evil, see no evil." Length, 1.4 cm. Private collection

177. An ojime of stained stag antler carved as a monkey climbing the inro cord. Length, 2.5 cm. Private collection

178. An ojime showing a wood-gatherer pouring himself a bowl of sake. An example of "married" metalwork (the joining of different metals; in this case, gold, silver, and copper). Length, 1.82 cm. Collection Dr. Ralph Maercks, Miami

179. A gold teakettle with a paulownia tree, emblem of the imperial family. Length, 0.4 cm. Collection Dave and Sandy Swedlow, Los Angeles

180. A "married" metalwork ojime of an open strip of bamboo with a finely detailed wasp inside. Length, 2 cm. Private collection

181. An engraved ivory ojime of bamboo and a sparrow. Length, 1.45 cm. Collection Ann Meselson, Los Angeles

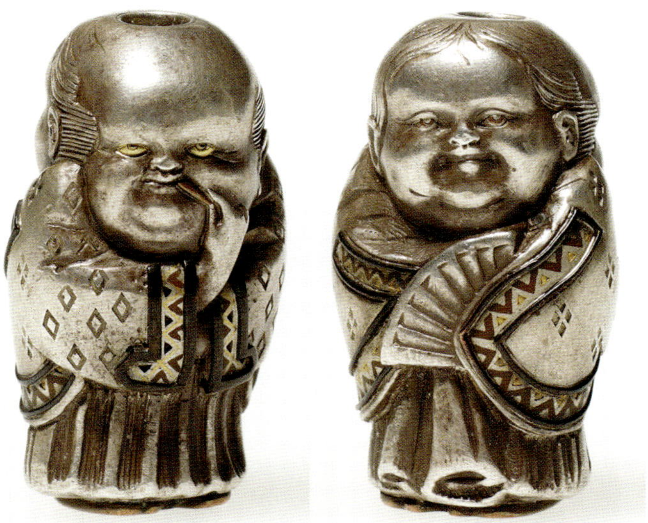

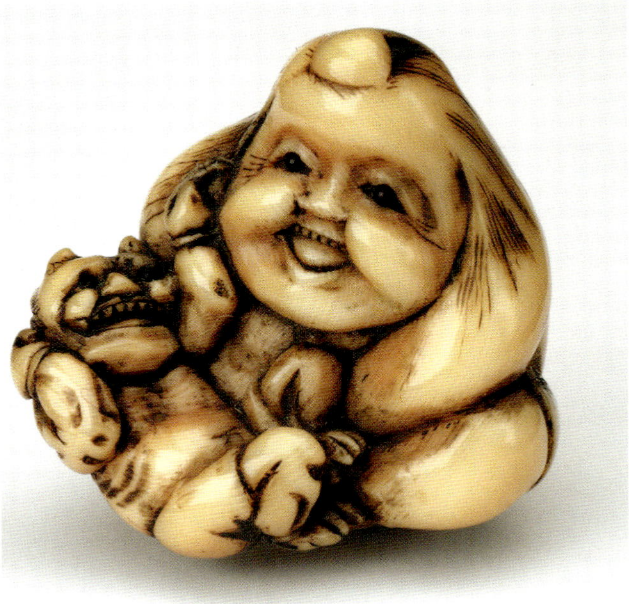

182. *Okame, the Goddess of Mirth. Two views. Silver* ojime. *Length, 2.4 cm. Collection Gabrielle Liese.*

RIGHT: 183. *An ivory* ojime *depicting Okame, the lusty goddess of mirth, fondling a baby* oni. *Length, 2.6 cm. Collection Ann Meselson, Los Angeles*

Ojime

Creating ojime *(slide fasteners) challenged the artisan to work within severe restrictions of space and form.* Ojime *had to be diminutive but sturdy, with a smooth, round shapes. Sharp projections could easily break off or catch on the kimono. Thus,* ojime *had to be finished on all sides, with the cord holes positioned to maintain the harmony of the overall design.*

During the eighteenth and nineteenth centuries, new classes of wealthy merchants commissioned ojime *of extreme fragility and intricacy. Four types of "artistic"* ojime *can be recognized: three-dimensional, miniature sculptural forms resembling* netsuke *(plate 184); engraved* ojime *(plate 181); cameo-style or high-relief carving across a solid surface, including deeply cut, openwork pieces (plate 185); and beads with lacquered and inlaid surfaces (plate 173).*

Sculptural ojime *presented a major design problem: how to carve an artistic opening in a small object while maintaining a precise tension in the double cord. Two solutions were found: running a straight perforation through the carved body or creating a form, such as a monkey, mystic, coiled snake, or child, that would appear to be climbing up the cords (plate 151).*

The other three forms of ojime *use the same technique to accommodate a double cord: a straight perforation through the center. Beads with a wide perforation (typically 4.5 to 5 millimeters in diameter) are distinguishable as* ojime.

One hallmark of the best Japanese design is restraint. This quality is seen in the positioning of a simple coral ojime *between an elaborate* inro *and* netsuke *in many Edo period ensembles. These early* ojime *were simple spheres that, on their cords, created space between the decorated* inro *and* netsuke. *By the late Edo period and throughout the Meiji period, however, the plain, globular forms were eclipsed by beautifully sculpted, complex designs that can be appreciated as individual sculptures in their own right. Most of the* ojime *shown in plates 170–190 are from these later periods.*

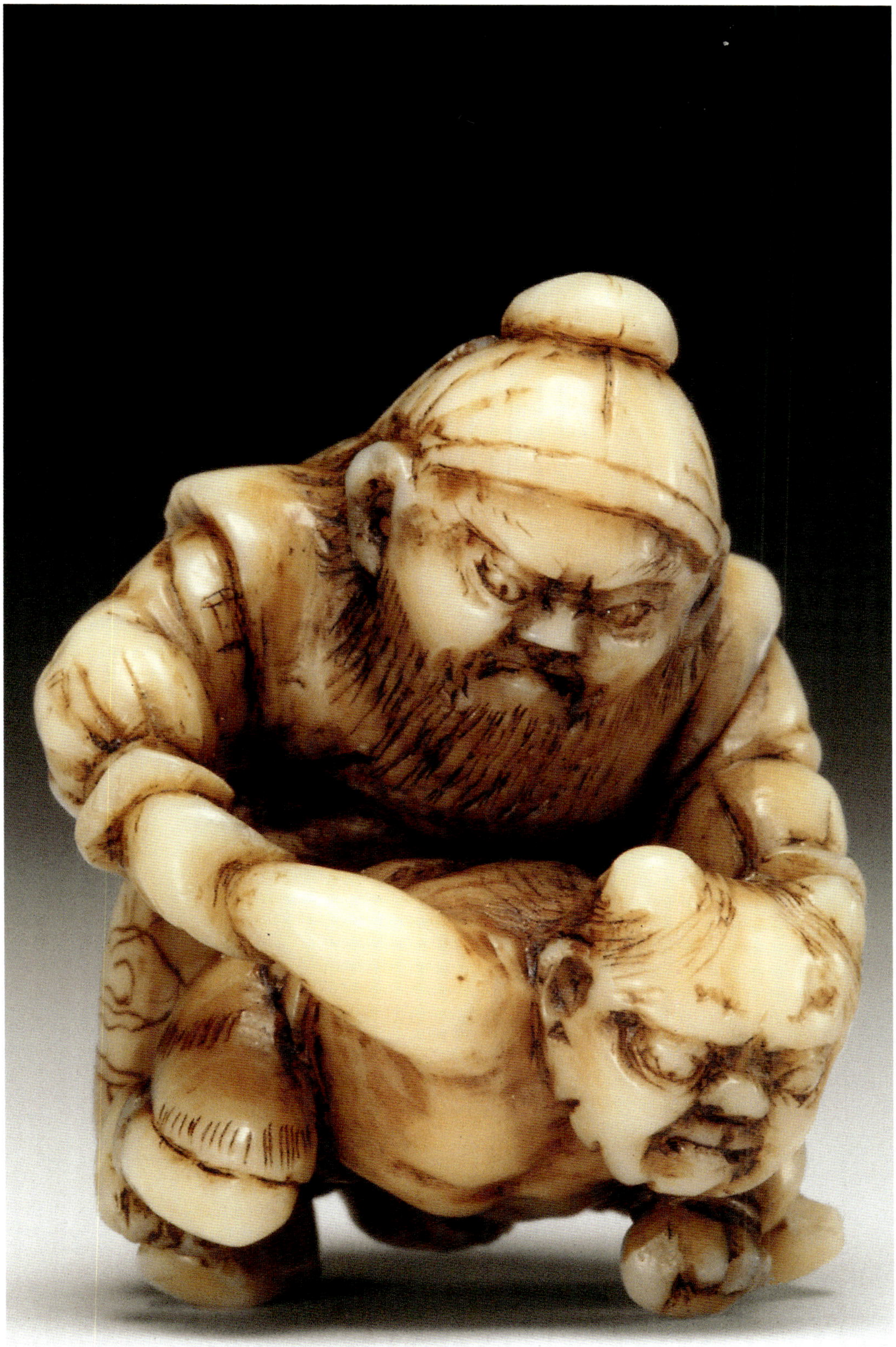

184. *The legendary General Shoki pursues his eternal task of taming a mischievous demon (*oni*). An excellent example of two figures carved in the round within the ivory* ojime*'s limited format. Length, 2.1 cm. Private collection*

OVERLEAF: 185. *Flowers. (1) an eighteenth-century ivory* ojime *in the form of two peony blossoms, the symbol of wealth and feminine beauty. Length, 2.4 cm, Private collection; (2) a silver and red copper* hozuki, *or winter cherry. Length, 1.82 cm. Collection Dave and Sandy Swedlow, Los Angeles; (3) a silver Fuji chrysanthemum on a gold background. Diameter, 2 cm. Private collection; (4) a gold butterfly and silver chrysanthemum on a silver bead. Butterflies were popular in the Far East as emblems of the soul and of womanhood. Length 1.4 cm. Collection Midori Gallery, Coconut Grove, Florida; (5) peony cast and cut from patinated iron with a gold* himotoshi *(the metal lining in the bead). Length, 1.8 cm. Collection Ann Meselson, Los Angeles*

BOTTOM: 186. *Animals. (1) spotted ivory Japanese pug. Length, 1.4 cm. Collection Dave and Sandy Swedlow, Los Angeles; (2) coiled bronze snake. Length, 1.3 cm. Collection Judith Feinberg, Miami; (3) bat, symbol of prosperity, happiness, and good luck, made of bronze with inlaid gold eyes. Length, 2.1 cm. Collection Dave and Sandy Swedlow, Los Angeles. Bottom row, left to right: (4) nest of rats made in ivory. Diameter, 1.5 cm. Private collection; (5) an exceptionally realistic white rat, reclining with its tail wrapped around its body. The eyes have been drilled completely through the ivory head and inlaid in transparent horn, giving them a lifelike appearance. Diameter, 2.2 cm. Collection Norma Canelas and William D. Roth; (6) hare among horsetail plants (*equiseta*), an allusion to the moon hare, the Japanese equivalent of the West's man-in-the-moon. Length, 2.25 cm. Private collection*

187. *Legends. (1) Yoshisada, a fourteenth-century hero, exemplified the samurai code of honor. When he was finally defeated at the battle of Fujishima, his head was publicly displayed in Kyoto. Length, 2 cm. Collection Judith Feinberg, Miami; (2) an ivory* ojime *depicting the falconer's story. As the holder rotates the* ojime, *in this case three times, a story unfolds in the round. The first view shows a daimyo inspecting his fiefdom with his prize falcon on his arm. As the* ojime *is turned, his retriever appears; with another turn, a villager is seen running across a bridge to receive him.* [IV] *Diameter, 1.75 cm. Collection Midori Gallery, Coconut Grove,*

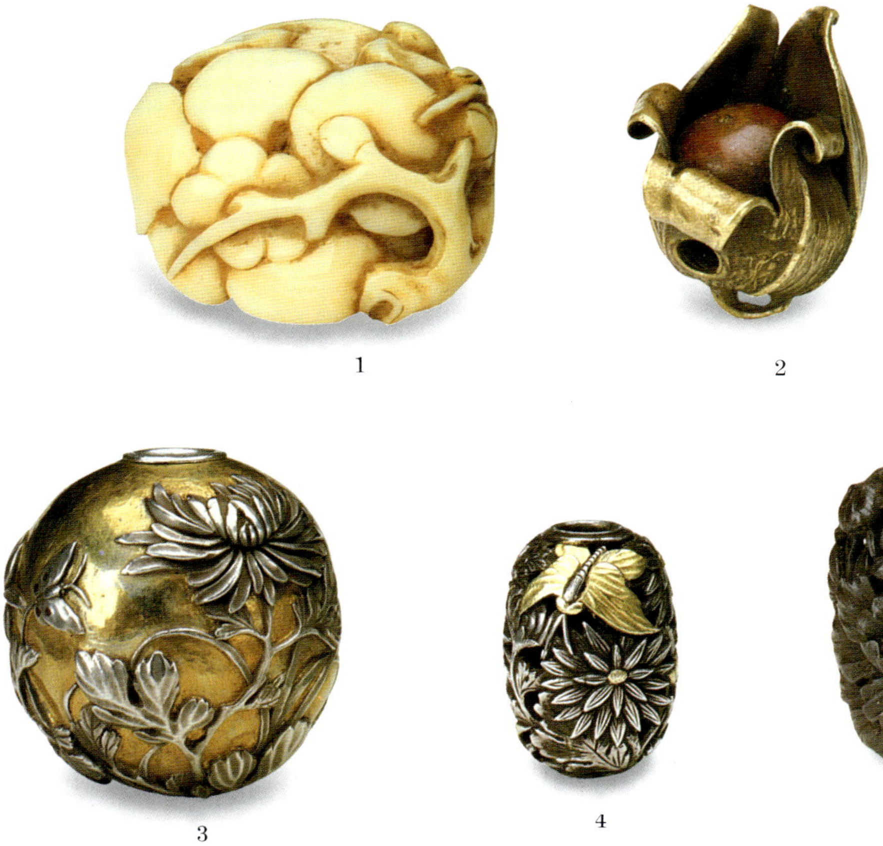

Flowers

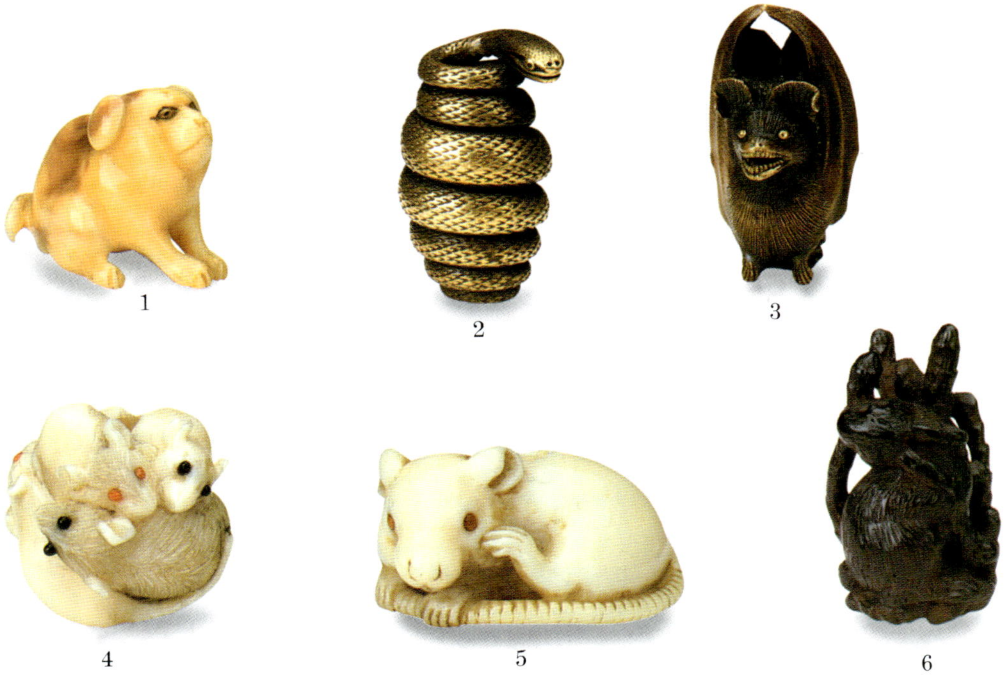

Animals

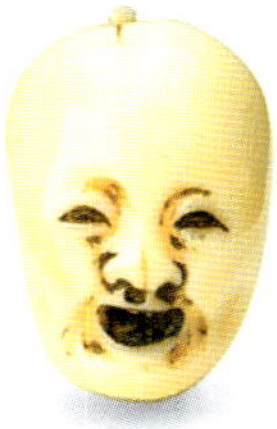
1

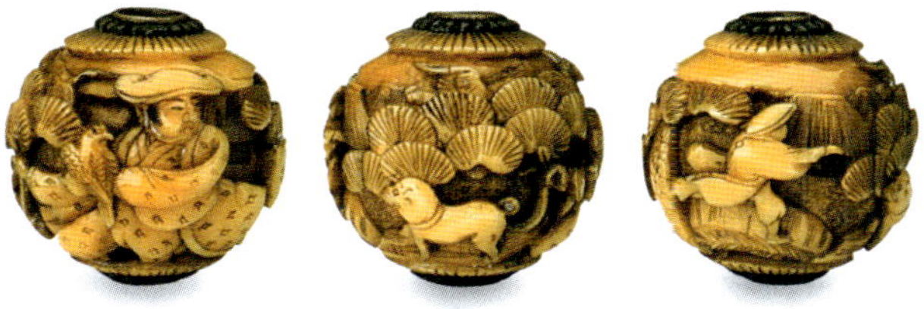
2

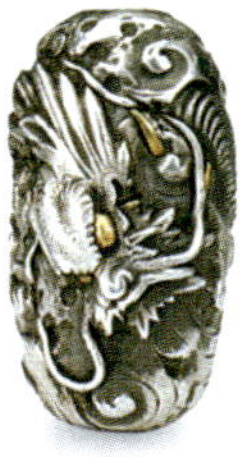
3

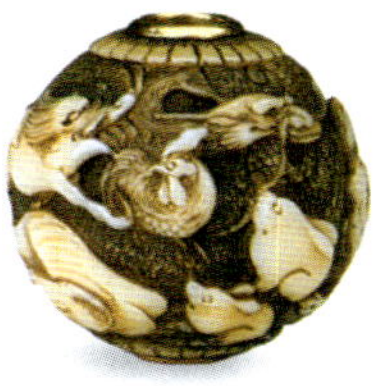
4

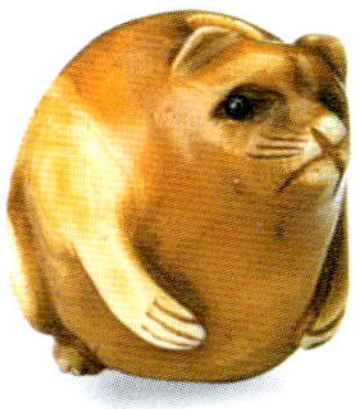
5

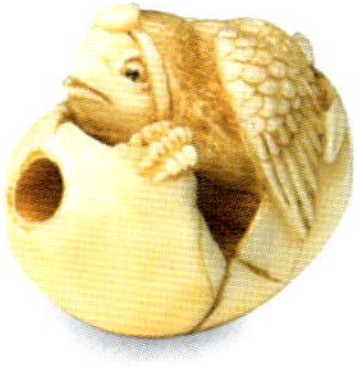
6

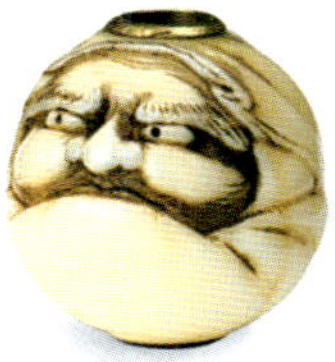
7

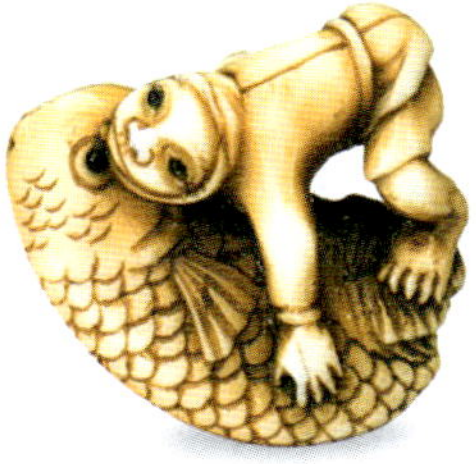
8

Legends

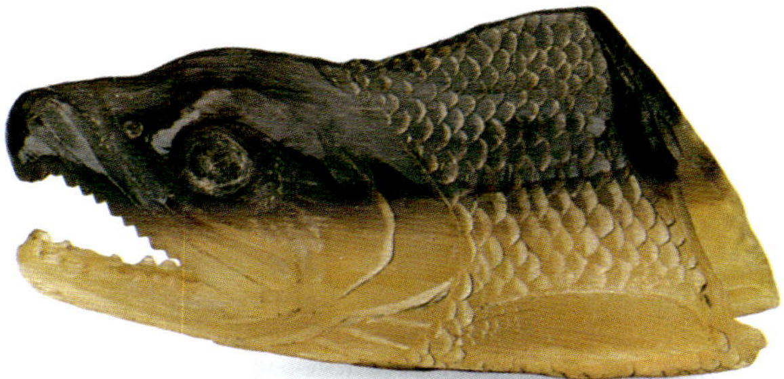
1

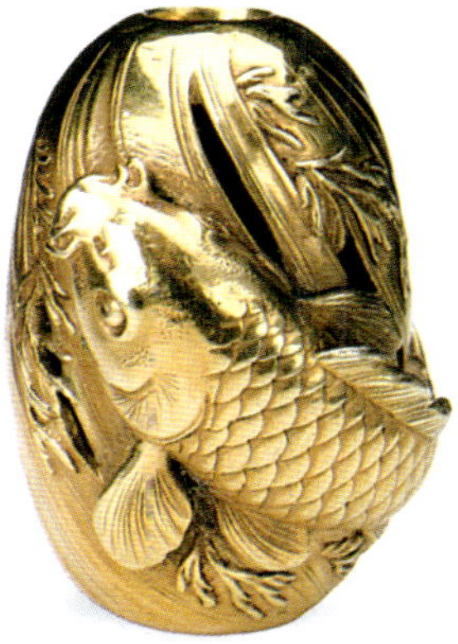
2

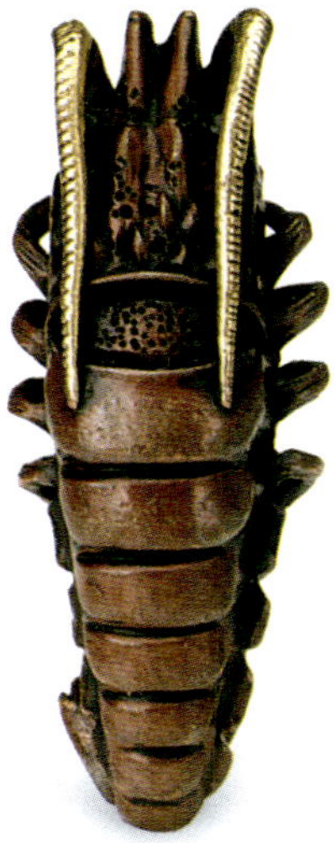
3

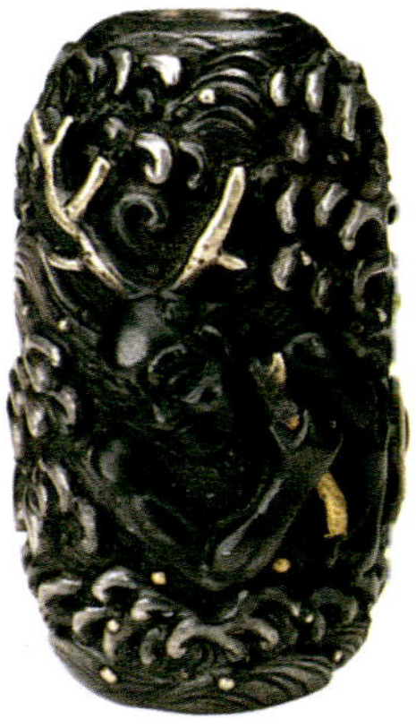
4

Tales of the Sea

Florida; (3) a dragon in swirling clouds, the only mythological creature among the twelve zodiac animals. Length, 2.1 cm. Collection Midori Gallery, Coconut Grove, Florida. Bottom row, left to right: (4) an ivory zodiac, represented by twelve creatures in cyclical order: rat, ox, tiger, hare or rabbit, dragon, snake, horse, sheep or goat, monkey, cock, dog, and pig. It was popular to wear an ojime *depicting the creature of the owner's year of birth. Length, 2.1 cm. Collection Midori Gallery, Coconut Grove, Florida; (5) a badger of stained ivory. Beloved in Japanese folklore as a trickster. Length, 1.9 cm. Private collection; (6) an ivory* tengu *emerging from its egg. This mythical creature has an eagle's beak, wings, and claws, with a humanoid body. Length, 1.85 cm. Private collection; (7) an ivory Daruma. As the founder of Zen Buddhism, Daruma sat meditating for nine years and his legs atrophied, thus he is always depicted legless. Daruma is an adored Japanese subject Height, 1.6 cm. Private collection;*

(8) Kintoki, the boy, who stands for health, strength, and loyalty, struggling with a giant carp. Carved in ivory with eyes of inlaid petrified sea pine. Length, 2.5 cm. Private collection

PREVIOUS PAGE: 188. *Tales of the Sea. (1) a dried fish head made of horn. An overland traveler always took along a piece of dried fish for food, but also as a token of good luck and health. Length, 2.4 cm. Collection Ann Meselson, Los Angeles; (2)* koi, *the personification of perseverance and the will to win, made of gold. The fish strives, the Japanese say, against the stream and conquers rapids and waterfalls. Length, 2 cm. Collection Dave and Sandy Swedlow, Los Angeles; (3) crayfish of "married" metal (bronze and gold). Length, 2.4 cm. Collection Judith Feinberg, Miami; (4) a beautiful example of "married" metalwork: a coral fisherman from the South Sea Islands sails among silver waves holding a coral branch of gold. The fisherman is made of* shakudo, *an alloy of copper and gold turned bluish black by the application of chemicals. Length, 1.9 cm. Collection Dave and Sandy Swedlow, Los Angeles*

a return to sumptuary laws and a limited use of beads.[39] Strings of beads were allowed to tie down hats but were not to be worn as necklaces. Men's topknots and ponytails were held in place by long barrel-shaped beads, while women wore beads sewn onto headdresses and attached to a tasseled ornamental knot *(maedup)* or a pendant (*norigae*).[40] The elite used beads of amber, jade, coral, turquoise, and carnelian for these purposes, while glass served those of lower rank.[41]

In the eighteenth and nineteenth centuries, Koreans wore "perfume beads" made of aromatic spices and gums. Blue, white, green, or red in color, they were strung on white horsehair, and often dangled from fans.[42]

Today, Koreans cut semiprecious stones (amethyst, quartz, carnelian, crystal, and agate) into beads and export pearls from Cheju Island. Glass beads are made by lamp-winding techniques learned from the Japanese in the 1920s. There is also a special type of necklace bead made by hand from a mixture of flour and glue.[43]

Japan

Over the centuries, the Japanese have been the recipients of cultural influences from China, Korea, and the West. Rather than being overwhelmed and transformed by foreign influences, however, they have selectively integrated new ideas into their distinctive culture.

The Japanese are known for the intimate rather than the heroic in design. Surrounded by water, resources, including space, are scarce in Japan, so economy has always been practiced in all things, including design. This is best expressed in the art of miniaturization—the economizing of everything material, cultural, and natural. The concept of artistic microcosms—self-contained worlds within a confined space—was developed by the Japanese and employed in activities from gardening and flower arrangement to personal adornment. No item was too small or unimportant to be designed as a totality in which function and aesthetics were integrated.

The earliest Japanese beads were made from perforated shells, bones, and stones found in Initial Jomon sites (dating about 10,000 B.C.) on Shikoku, Hokkaido, and Honshu.[44] By Middle Jomon times (3600–2500 B.C.) adornment was abundant and made in a variety of stone, including jade.[45] The Yayoi period (200 B.C.–A.D. 200) witnessed development of the potter's wheel, metal forging and casting, and the first glass beads. Unlike the Chinese, the Japanese valued glass beads as "jewels," leaving a profusion of them in sites dating from almost every period of their history.

After 50 B.C., Yayoi people were in regular contact with China via Korea. It is believed that most early Japanese glass beads—small, round, translucent forms in limited shades of green and blue—were made from either imported glass ingots or Chinese glass objects that had been melted down.[46] From the Yayoi period until at least the eighteenth century, China and Japan traded glass beads and shared bead technology. An important bead style that manifests Korean-Japanese relationships found in Yayoi tombs was *magatama*, comma-shaped beads closely resembling the Korean *kogok*, made in both stone and glass (plates 161–2).

The Old Tomb period (A.D. 250–552) is marked by the appearance of large, conspicuous burial mounds containing tombs in which beads were the most numerous artifact. It is believed that the hundreds of thousands of beads found throughout the country and dating to this period held spiritual significance. Bead shapes of the Old Tomb period were spherical (plates 163–5), cylindrical, and faceted, and materials included glass, quartz, green jasper, agate, jadeite, and steatite. *Tombodama*, complex multicolored glass beads, appeared for the first time, as did opaque, reddish glass beads similar to—or perhaps the same bead as—the *mutisalah* found in India, East Africa, and Southeast Asia.[47] Clay figures (*haniwa*) wearing glass bead necklaces, bracelets, and anklets have been excavated from Old Tomb period sites. Gold, silver, and bronze crowns, horse trappings, and earrings were also ornamented with glass beads.

An influx of Chinese and Korean craftsmen occurred during the Old Tomb Period, and most Japanese glass beads were made by Chinese immigrants or by Japanese glass-makers working under the guidance of foreign craftsmen.[48] There were also many imported Chinese glass beads, yet no examples of China's remarkable Warring State eye beads have ever been found in Japan.

Japanese beadmaking was primarily a part-time cottage industry, with glass probably made at a central place and distributed as rods to individual artisans working at home and using clay cooking stoves. Glass beads from this period were formed by winding and cut-tube methods, although some were molded or even shaped by lapidary (grinding) techniques.[49]

Buddhism entered Japan at the beginning of the Asuka period (A.D. 552–645), a time when the Chinese and Koreans deeply influenced the Japanese. Glass beads continued to have spiritual significance, serving in Buddhist rituals. At this time, beads were strung in complex arrangements using a variety of bead styles.[50]

During the Nara period (A.D. 645–794), new ideas, including those associated with Buddhism, were introduced to Japan from Byzantium, Syria, Persia, India, and central Asia through active trade along the silk routes. Nara beads show the impact of this trade. Japanese craftsmen were stimulated by the many imported objects made within the Sasanian Persian empire (A.D. 226–651), a region famed at this time for its beautiful glass and agate beads, most likely produced by the Syrians under Persian control. Japan and Sasanian Persia were in direct contact, and the Sasanian beads appear to have had an important influence on the newly refined designs and techniques characteristic of Nara beads.

Most beads known from the period are preserved, not as mortuary goods, but in the *Shoso-in*, the imperial treasure-house, a unique monument to the Emperor Shomu, who was buried with all his possessions in A.D. 765. These beads are of superb technical quality and of great variety in shape and raw materials.[51] The large number of glass beads stored in the *Shoso-in* is particularly striking: approximately 75,000 beads in 250 strings of 100 to 300 beads each.

By the Nara period, the spiritual role of beads gave way to largely decorative functions. Beads were used primarily to decorate furniture, sword handles and sheaths, clothing, and crowns. One headdress was described as inset with twenty-six thousand beads of pearl, rock crystal, coral, jade, and multicolored glass.[52]

The great age of Nara-period beadmaking lasted less than a century in all, and it was followed by a steady decline in glass beadmaking over the next eight hundred years—although glass beads were still used for sacred purposes, including adornment of portable Shinto shrines, Buddhist rosaries, and the decoration of Buddhist images. There are records of stone beads during the Heian period (897–1185), and these are described as cut from "cold agates," jaspers, and crystal.[53]

The sheaths of Heian swords were wrapped in beads, and at the shrine of the Sun Goddess at Ise a listing of sacred treasures in 1037–39 included a sword "wrapped with three hundred beads."[54] In 1869, while excavating for a sacred enclosure north of the shrine, three swords of exquisite craftsmanship were uncovered, one with a string of three hundred beads of precious stones wrapped around the sheath.

Extensive trade with China characterized the Muromachi period (1392–1573), and imports flooded the country. Portuguese and Spanish merchants began visiting the island of Kyushu in southern Japan, accompanied by missionaries. On the west coast, Nagasaki was opened to the Portuguese in 1570. Although Europeans presumably introduced their

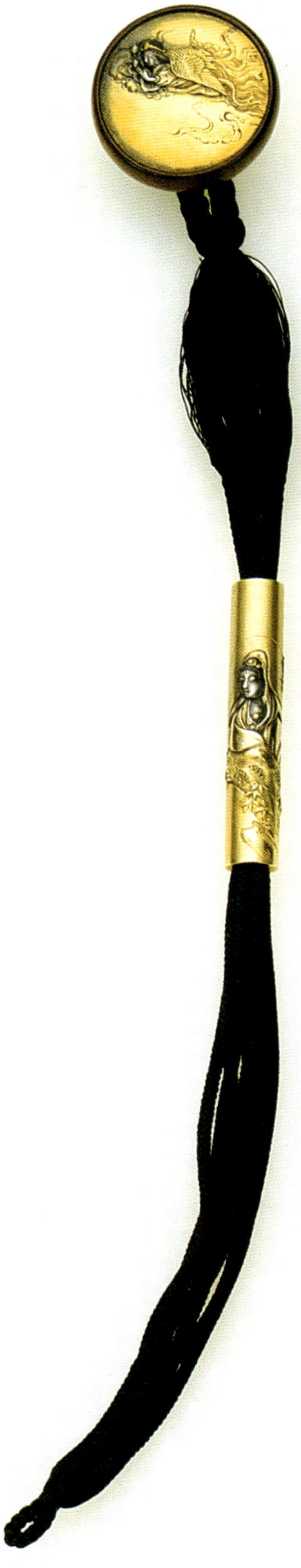

189. *A* kagamibuta *(*kagami *means "mirrored plate";* buta *means "bowl") form of* netsuke, *made of gold, silver, and* shakudo, *depicting a Buddhist angel. The accompanying metalwork* ojime *is a reverent portrayal of the goddess Kannon, who symbolizes the resolution of a man, the graciousness of a woman, and the purity of a sexless being. These types of large metalwork* netsuke *and* ojime *were usually made to accompany a large pouch. Length of* ojime, *5.4 cm. Collection Dave and Sandy Swedlow, Los Angeles*

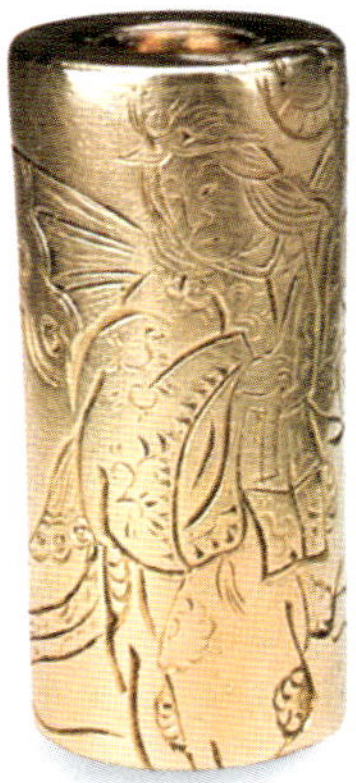

1

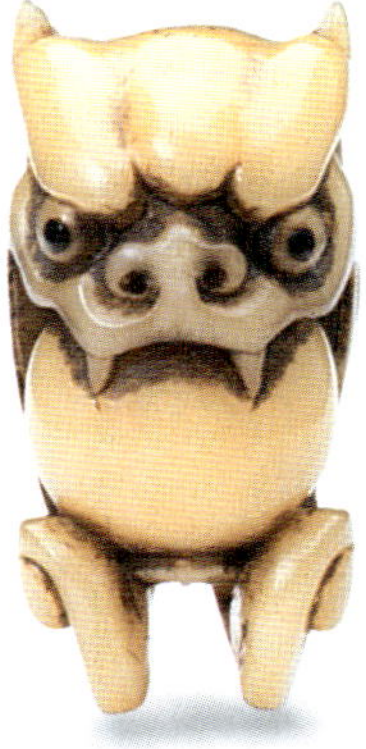

2

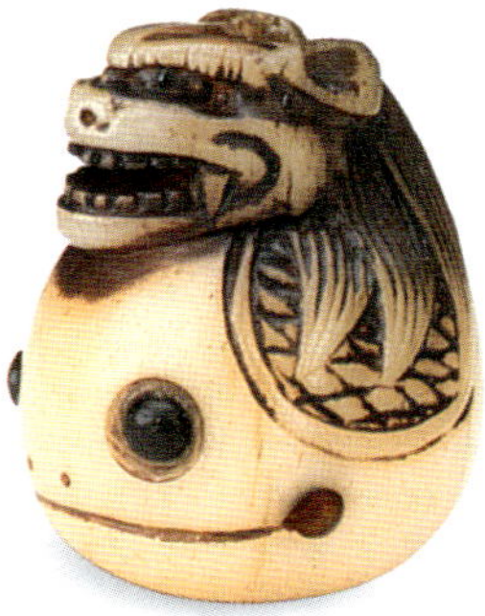

3

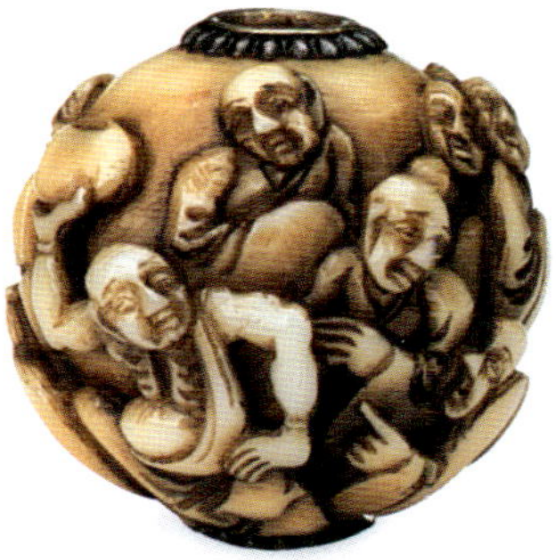

4

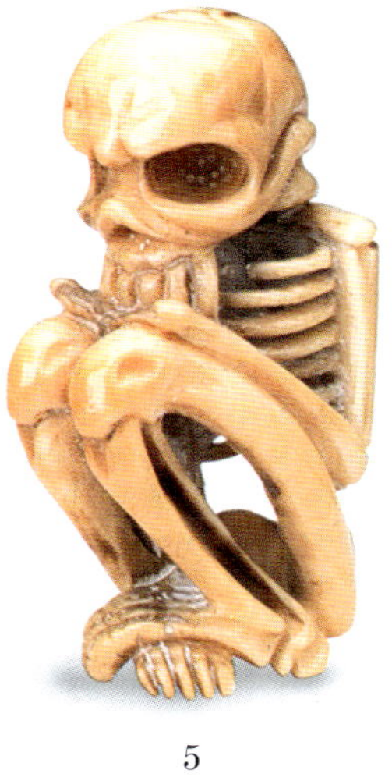

5

190. *(1) A solid gold* ojime *deeply engraved with a butterfly dancer. Length, 2 cm. Collection Dr. Ralph Maercks, Miami; (2) an unusual ivory* ojime *of a stylized dragonlike gargoyle. The object in its jaws is possibly the pearl of wisdom, whose attainment is sought by the dragon as a symbol of heavenly power. Length, 2.2 cm. Private collection; (3) a humorous interpretation of a hollow, wood temple bell used by priests during meditation. Made of stag antler, with inlaid petrified sea pine eyes. Length, 2.3 cm. Private collection; (4) a cameo-style ivory* ojime *depicting* rakan, *sages who descended from Buddha's first disciple. Signed by the carver Komin. Length, 1.8 cm. Private collection; (5) an ivory* ojime *in the form of a skeleton. The posture may reflect the practice of burying the dead in large jars. Skeletons in Buddhist art were not meant to be morbid symbols; rather, they had philosophical overtones. Length, 2.5 cm. Collection Dave and Sandy Swedlow, Los Angeles*

beads, most surviving examples from this period are Chinese.[55] During the Momoyama period (1573–1615), Chinese and possibly Venetian beads were imported into Japan. While some foreign stimulation of Momoyama beadmakers is apparent, it was not until the succeeding Edo period that Japanese glass beadmaking began to flourish.

The Edo period (1615–1867) brought an end to several centuries of civil war as Japan was unified under the Tokugawa shogunate. The arts, including beadmaking, thrived. New designs and techniques from abroad helped to inspire an outpouring of locally made glass and other beads. In fact, it was during this period that most Japanese glass beads were made. Frequently, it is unclear whether an Edo bead is a Venetian import or made by a Japanese or Chinese craftsman imitating foreign styles. Although Japanese artisans were stimulated by seventeenth- and eighteenth-century European glass beads, most learned from Chinese beadmakers residing in Nagasaki or indirectly from European books. By the nineteenth century, when European beads were readily available, Japanese glassmakers had essentially developed their own craft.[56]

Like China, Japan remained for the most part closed to the West until the nineteenth century, except for limited entry of Dutch and Chinese ships at the port of Nagasaki. Nonetheless, quantities of Bohemian, Dutch, and Venetian glass beads were brought in by Dutch traders, and Chinese glass beads were either imported or the products of Chinese glass beadmakers established in the Nagasaki area.

During the years of isolation, when trade was restricted to Nagasaki, merchants in this area not only circulated goods between Japan and Europe but also obtained products from Southeast Asian countries. Dutch traders gave prized glass beads to Japanese provincial lords and important government officials, thus providing Japanese beadmakers with examples of a wide range of glass bead technologies in use at the time in other nations. During this period, most beads, including those made of gold, silver, iron, copper, ivory, coral, glass, crystal, and wood, served as *ojime*, slide fasteners, used to hold *inro*, personal carrying cases, in place. *Ojime* became status symbols and the focus of enormous creative attention.

Ojime

The Japanese say, "Nothing is beautiful that is not also useful, and nothing is useful that is not also beautiful." *Ojime* fully express this precept: they were meant to be worn not merely as ornaments but as fasteners for small cases in which an individual carried items of everyday necessity on his person. The traditional Japanese costume, the kimono, has no pockets; while women kept small articles in their sleeves, men carried personal possessions such as medicine, seals, tobacco, and coins in containers suspended by cords from the *obi*, a wide sash binding the kimono at the waist.

These containers ranged from simple leather pouches to elaborately lacquered wooden *inro*. The *inro* were divided into compartments held in place by two cords that joined at the top where they passed through a bead, called an *ojime*. The cords were finally attached at their far end to a *netsuke*, a counterweight placed under the *obi* to insure that the *inro* would not slip out (plate 170).

The elevation of the *inro*, *netsuke*, and *ojime* ensemble into an art form reflects social, political, and economic circumstances in Tokugawa Japan, which was strictly divided into social classes: nobility, samurai, merchant, farmer, or artisan. Edicts prescribed the appropriate dress for each class, forbidding jewelry to all, including the nobility. In the early days, farmers, merchants, and artisans carried pouches; gentlemen wore *inro*. With peace and stability, merchants prospered, becoming patrons of the arts. *Inro* ensembles were their means of discreetly displaying wealth and taste. Probably considered insignificant, *inro* were not restricted by sumptuary laws.

Chronicles indicate that by A.D. 700 the Japanese wore pouches containing flints to make fire, but there is no record of beads being used in this context. The earliest reference to *ojime* dates from the beginning of the seventeenth century: "There is the fashionable, pleasure-loving young priest of today....A flat silk sash patterned with gold dust, is wrapped around his waist....Suspended from his sash are a yellow dyed *kinchaku* [coin purse], and an *inro* of *maki-e* [gold sprinkled over lacquer]....The cord for these is secured by an *otome* [cord cinch] with bull's eye design."[57]

Early *ojime* in no way resembled the beautifully sculpted beads collected today. They were simple devices of stone, coral, bone, and other materials thought to have magical or curative powers. Jade promoted longevity; the disintegration of coral warned of poison; stag antler assured virility.

By the late eighteenth century, *inro* became less functional but were used instead to display status. The *Shikigusa*, a work published in 1777, relates: "These days, even common people wear *inro* suspended from the sash, but do not use them for carrying medicine. They just like the exotic effect such articles have. These objects have become nothing more than ornaments to show off to other people."[58]

By the early nineteenth century, matched sets of increasingly elaborate *inro*, *netsuke*, and *ojime* were commissioned and collected, and the subject matter of the three parts was carefully coordinated.[59] The *ojime* as an art object reached its zenith between the late eighteenth century and the reign of Emperor Meiji (1868–1912), the period following reestablishment of contact with the West.

Most artistic *ojime* are of ivory, although they were made of many organic materials found in Japan, including horn, bone, wood, seeds, and tortoiseshell. Ivory was imported from India and Africa or obtained from arctic dolphins. Indigenous woods included cypress, cherry, ebony, boxwood, persimmon, camellia, and yew. *Ojime* were also made of native gold, silver, and copper—copper-tin and copper-silver being frequently used alloys. Glass *ojime* were frequently worn by the less affluent classes.[60]

Most *ojime* artists came from two closely related disciplines: *netsuke* carving and metallurgy. The *ojime* was a natural extension of the *netsuke* artist's craft of carving miniature works of art. Metallurgists created *ojime* using the same detailed metalwork techniques they formerly employed in making elaborate accessories for prestigious samurai swords.[61]

Ojime captured the full spectrum of Japanese life: history, religion, flora, fauna, people, and daily events. Hardly a subject was omitted, and the rounded *ojime* form lent itself to depicting narratives, too (plate 187.2).[62] As Japan was opened to trade after 1854, Western dress began to replace the kimono and its accessories. By the turn of the century, the Japanese industrial revolution was in full swing, and few *netsuke*, *ojime*, and *inro* were made. Today, *netsuke* and *ojime* are again being created for decorative purposes and collectors.

Following Admiral Perry's arrival in 1853, traffic in glass beads expanded as part of a general increase in Japanese export manufacturing. By the 1870s, Japanese beadmakers were traveling to Austria, Italy, and India to learn modern manufacturing techniques. Today, mass-production of glass beads thrives alongside the work of a growing number of accomplished beadmakers, such as the late Kyoyo Asao, who revived old techniques in order to understand and reproduce Warring States beads. But it was with pearls that the Japanese made their greatest impact on twentieth-century adornment. By 1913, Mikimoto had perfected the cultivation of pearls, making it possible for almost anyone to own them. The Japanese excelled in pearl farming and controlled the industry worldwide through most of the 1980s. Today, however, pearl production is led by the Chinese.

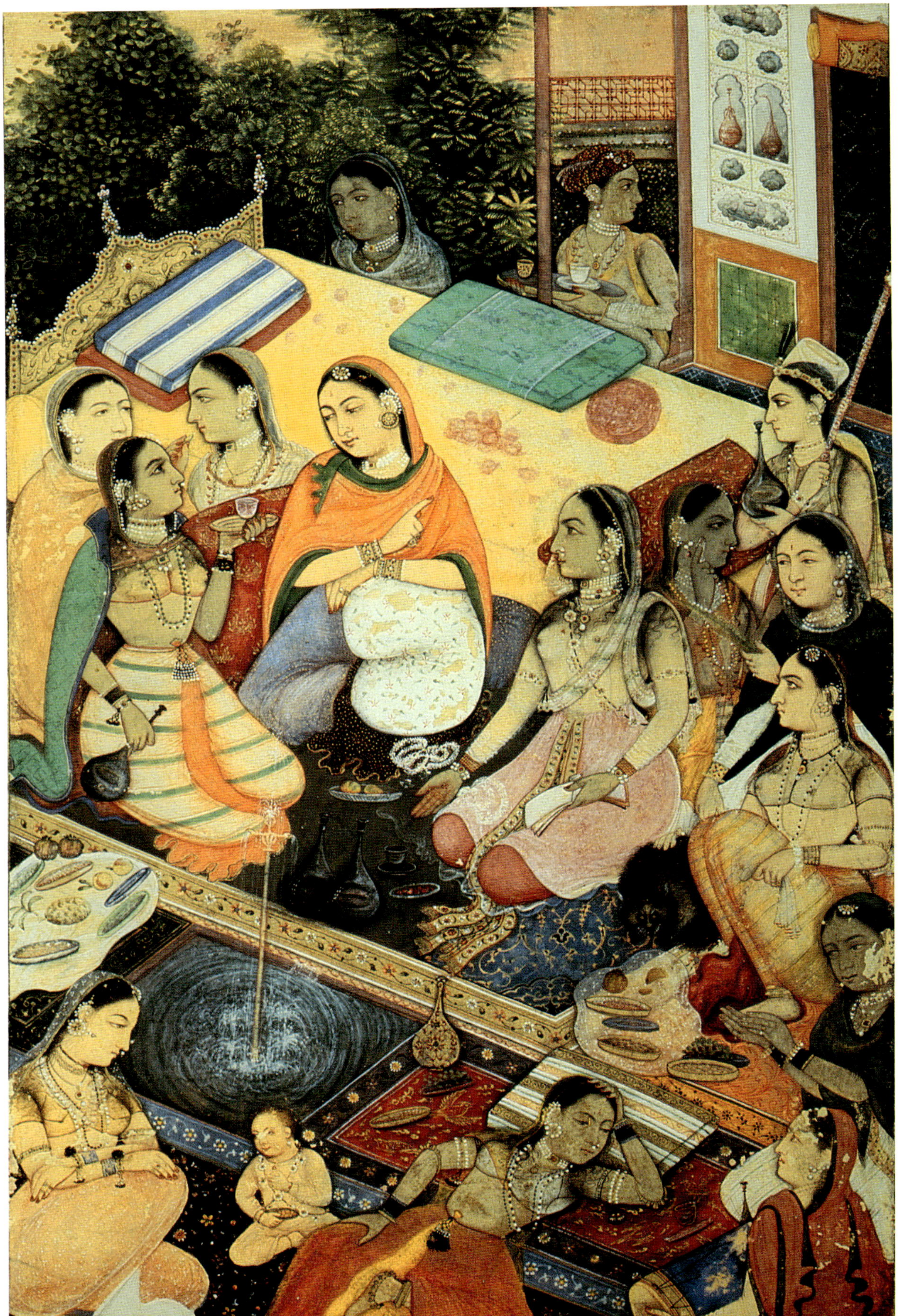

India

From the days of the Indus Valley civilization (2600–1600 B.C.) to the present, Indian craftsmen have produced exquisite bead jewelry, often using precious or semiprecious stones. It is the continuity of the stone bead industry, whose materials, techniques, and styles have remained essentially unchanged for thousands of years, that is the central story of Indian beads.

Quantities of beads from archaeological sites, as well as early icons, reliefs on friezes, and literary texts, affirm that bead jewelry has always been important to all classes of Indian society: rich and poor, sacred and secular. Ancient clay figures, often representing the gods of the common people, were depicted in typical daily dress wearing bead necklaces, earrings, girdles, bracelets, and anklets. Sculptures of Buddha from seventh- to tenth-century Himalayan monasteries are carved or cast with bead necklaces, as are images of the Buddha as the princely bodhisattva before his enlightenment.

Jewelry traditionally marks every stage in an Indian's life. The Hindu code of Manu ("The Law Giver") specifies certain jewelry is to be worn on designated occasions, making adornment a necessity for even the poorest believers. The parents of a bride are obliged to include gifts of jewelry in their daughter's dowry. Even if they can afford only one piece, it symbolizes her marital status and is worn at the time of her wedding, to be removed only when she is widowed or dies.[1]

This strong relationship between beads and religion still exists today. Worshipers of certain Hindu gods wear special beads to differentiate themselves from members of other branches of the faith as well as from non-Hindus. Followers of Siva, for example, have worn *Rudraksha*, beads made from seeds of the *Eleaocarpus ganitrus* tree, since at least A.D. 1000 (plate 71), while Vishnu worshippers wear little wooden beads made

191. *A harem* (zenana) *scene from an early seventeenth-century Mogul painting showing the profusion of jewelry—particularly beads—worn by Mogul court women. The concubines are adorned with pearls and emerald, sapphire, and ruby beads. Even the baby is bejeweled. Multistrand pearl chokers worn with necklaces have a long history in India: clay figures from c. 2000 B.C. are represented wearing them.*

During the Mogul period, both men and women were renowned for wearing magnificent jewels. The quality of a woman's clothing and jewelry represented a man's earning power and how well he cared for his dependents. 12.7 × 20.3 cm. Metropolitan Museum of Art, New York. Gift of Alexander Smith Cochran

192. *"Etched" carnelian beads. A technique of painting the surface of a finished carnelian bead with a calcium carbonate and then baking the mineral on appears to have been invented about 2500 B.C. by craftsmen of the Indus Valley, possibly to imitate banded agates. It was a technique later adopted by the Persians. Etched beads are thought to have been traded from the Indus Valley to Sumer as early as 2500 B.C.*[1] *Illustrated here are beads from the Sumerian royal graves at Ur that are similar to patterns on etched carnelian beads excavated from Indus Valley sites. Typical bead: length, 0.7 cm. British Museum, London*

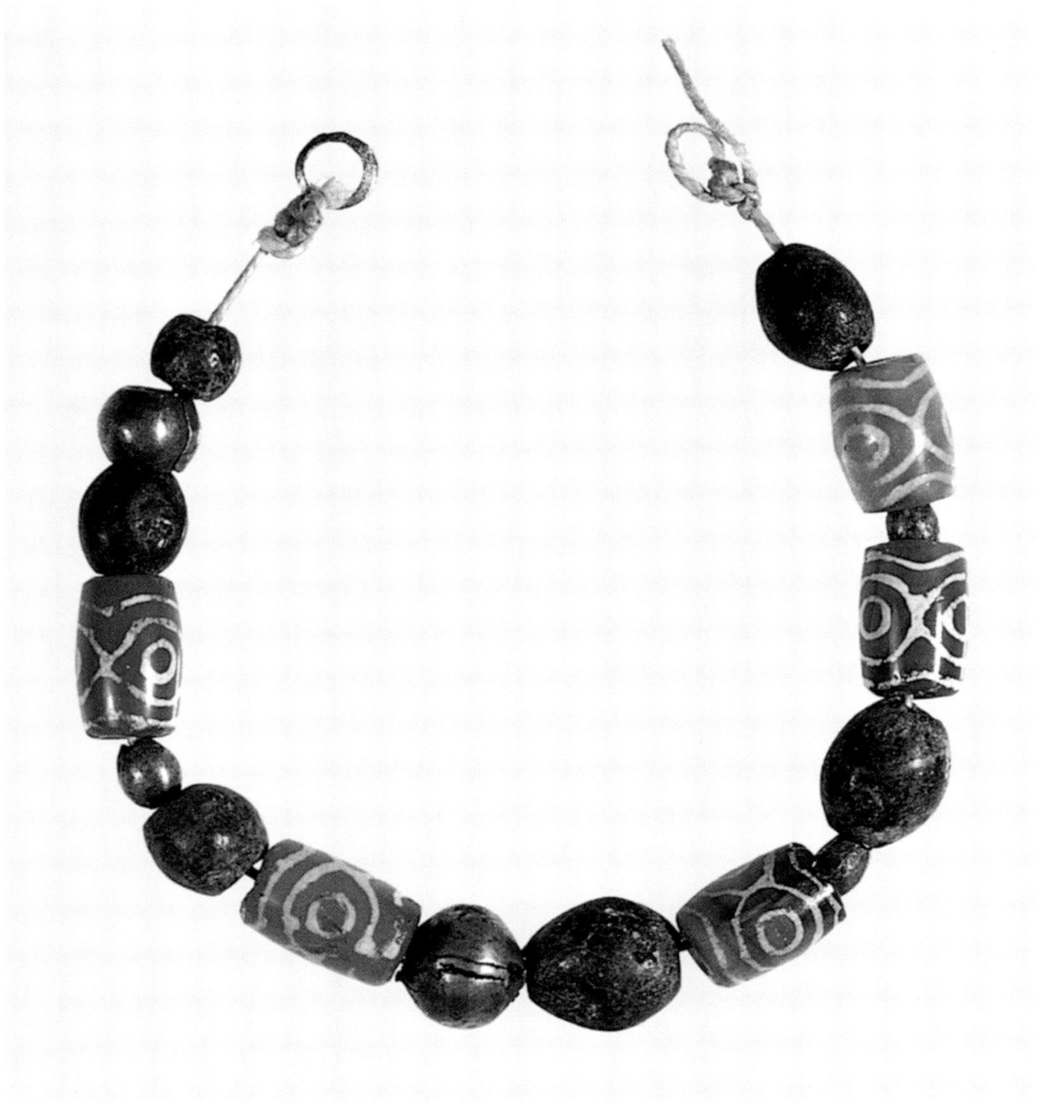

of tulsi, the holy basil *Ocimum sanctum*.[2] The continued importance of wooden beads in India for religious purposes may reflect parallel preferences for wood, clay, and stone—in that order—for the construction of religious buildings.[3]

In India, the poor have traditionally worn beads made from seeds, clay, copper, and silver, while the rich have preferred gold and precious stones. However, beyond displaying wealth and status, precious stones and metals were considered almost holy and believed to have protective powers.[4] Gems were also offered to deities as a means of gaining divine assistance.

The earliest Indian religious text, the Rig Veda, describes the jewels of the gods, and later Sanskrit treatises state that even the gods pray to images studded with precious stones: Vishnu worships sapphires; Indra, the ruby; Agni, diamonds. "It is by constantly worshiping a goddess studded with pearls that the moon attained his 'divine effulgence,' and by worshiping one made of crystal that Varuna gained mastery of all the waters."[5] Each month, a different precious stone (relating to the planets of the Indian astrological system) carries religious or amuletic significance for Indians. Gold and silver represent the sun and the moon, respectively, and the sacred river Ganges.[6]

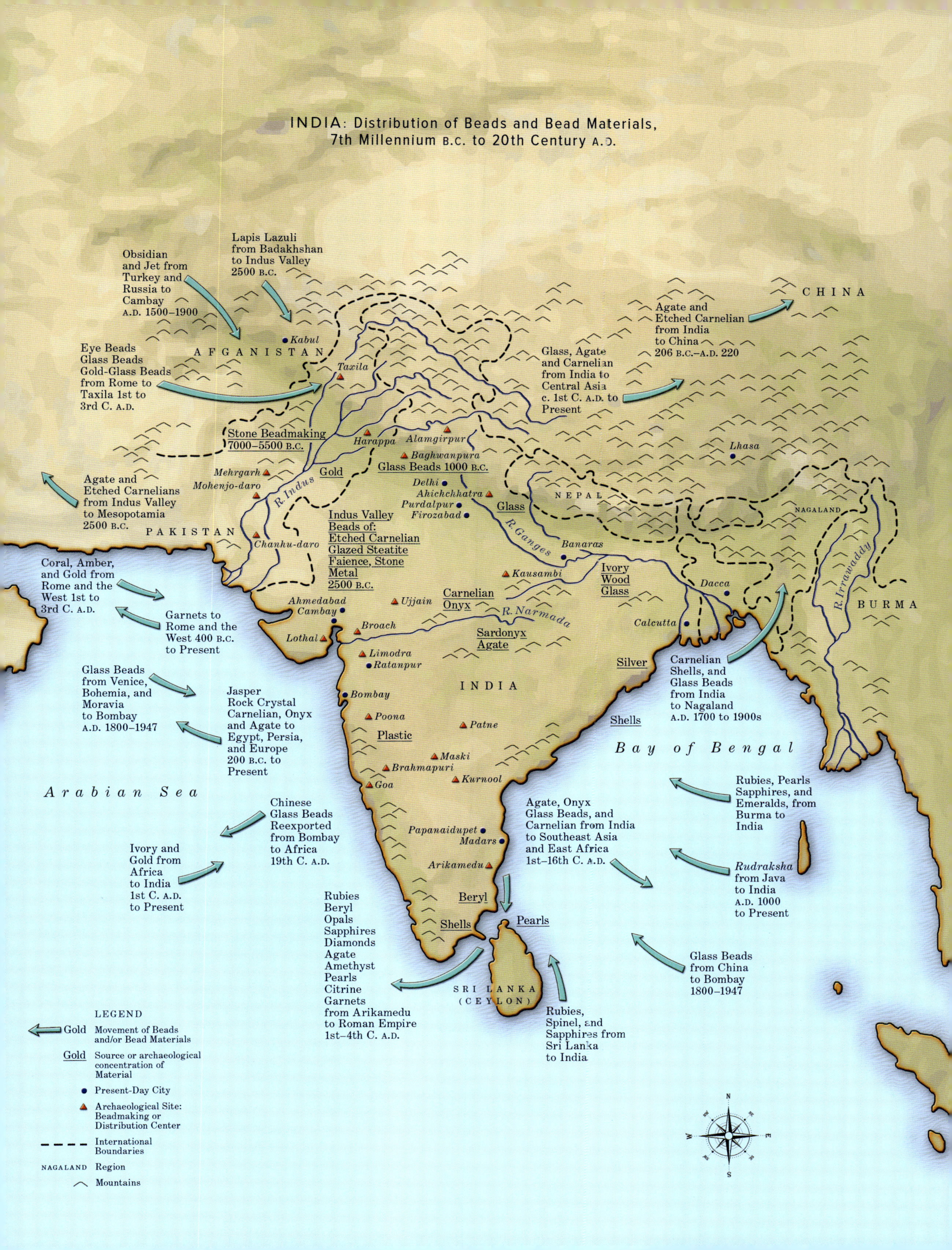
INDIA: Distribution of Beads and Bead Materials,
7th Millennium B.C. to 20th Century A.D.
Obsidian and Jet from Turkey and Russia to Cambay A.D. 1500–1900
Lapis Lazuli from Badakhshan to Indus Valley 2500 B.C.
Kabul
AFGANISTAN
Eye Beads Glass Beads Gold-Glass Beads from Rome to Taxila 1st to 3rd C. A.D.
Taxila
Stone Beadmaking 7000–5500 B.C.
Harappa
Alamgirpur
Baghwanpura
Glass Beads 1000 B.C.
Mehrgarh
Mohenjo-daro
R. Indus
Gold
Agate and Etched Carnelians from Indus Valley to Mesopotamia 2500 B.C.
PAKISTAN
Chanhu-daro
Indus Valley Beads of: Etched Carnelian Glazed Steatite Faience, Stone Metal 2500 B.C.
Delhi
Ahichchhatra
Purdalpur
Firozabad
Glass
R. Ganges
Banaras
Kausambi
Ivory Wood Glass
Coral, Amber, and Gold from Rome and the West 1st to 3rd C. A.D.
Garnets to Rome and the West 400 B.C. to Present
Ahmedabad
Cambay
Lothal
Broach
Ujjain
Carnelian Onyx
R. Narmada
Sardonyx Agate
Limodra
Ratanpur
Glass Beads from Venice, Bohemia, and Moravia to Bombay A.D. 1800–1947
Jasper Rock Crystal Carnelian, Onyx and Agate to Egypt, Persia, and Europe 200 B.C. to Present
Bombay
INDIA
Poona
Plastic
Patne
Maski
Brahmapuri
Goa
Kurnool
Arabian Sea
Chinese Glass Beads Reexported from Bombay to Africa 19th C. A.D.
Ivory and Gold from Africa to India 1st C. A.D. to Present
Papanaidupet
Madars
Arikamedu
Beryl
Shells
Pearls
Rubies Beryl Opals Sapphires Diamonds Agate Amethyst Pearls Citrine Garnets from Arikamedu to Roman Empire 1st–4th C. A.D.
SRI LANKA (CEYLON)
Rubies, Spinel, and Sapphires from Sri Lanka to India
Agate, Onyx Glass Beads, and Carnelian from India to Southeast Asia and East Africa 1st–16th C. A.D.
Glass Beads from China to Bombay 1800–1947
Rudraksha from Java to India A.D. 1000 to Present
Rubies, Pearls Sapphires, and Emeralds, from Burma to India
Bay of Bengal
Shells
Silver
Carnelian Shells, and Glass Beads from India to Nagaland A.D. 1700 to 1900s
Calcutta
Dacca
BURMA
R. Irrawaddy
NAGALAND
NEPAL
Lhasa
Glass, Agate and Carnelian from India to Central Asia c. 1st C. A.D. to Present
Agate and Etched Carnelian from India to China 206 B.C.–A.D. 220
CHINA
LEGEND
Gold Movement of Beads and/or Bead Materials
Gold Source or archaeological concentration of Material
Present-Day City
Archaeological Site: Beadmaking or Distribution Center
International Boundaries
NAGALAND Region
Mountains
N
E
S
W

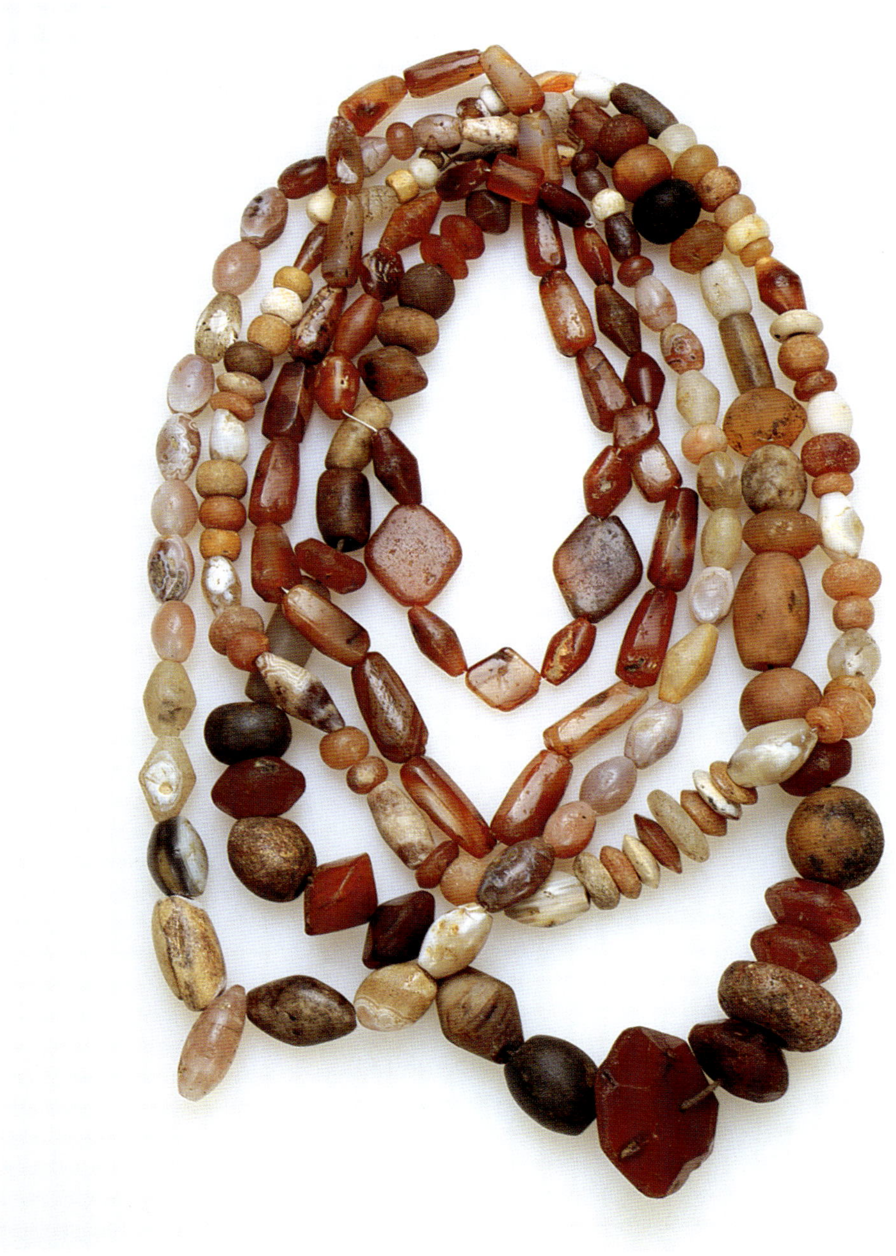

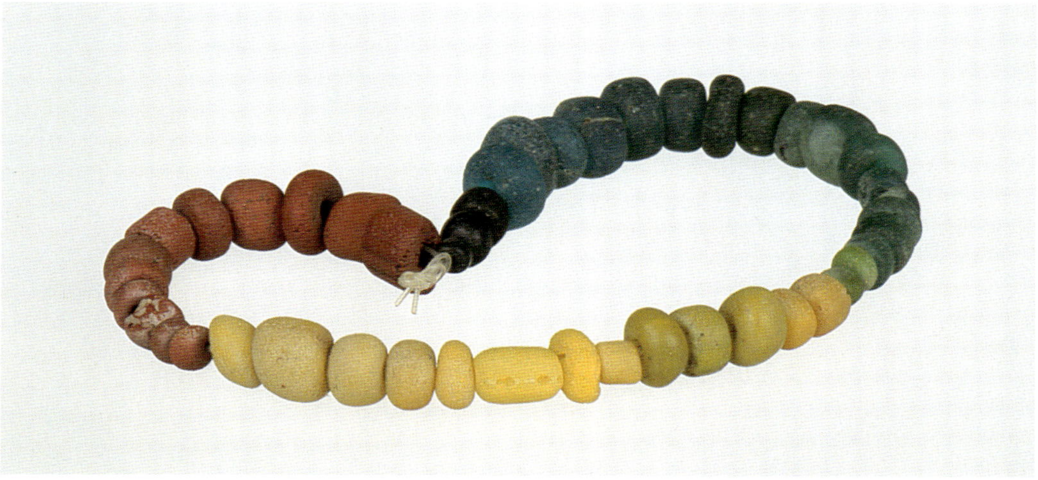

TOP: 193. *Agate, carnelian, and other stone beads, some possibly more than a thousand years old, from excavations at Djenne, Mali. The shapes and raw materials are representative of stone beads that were exported from India to western Asia and Africa, beginning before the Christian Era. A few of these beads may be African-made. Indian stone beadmaking originated about 6500* B.C. *While some manufacturing processes have been modernized, most stone beadmaking techniques in India remain unchanged. Lower necklace, large faceted carnelian bead: length, 5.2 cm. Collection Craft Caravan, New York*

BOTTOM: 194. *Indo-Pacific beads of brick red, yellow, green, and black opaque glass, probably dating to the fifteenth century* A.D.[II] *These distinctive beads were made in India by a drawn-glass technique. Many similar beads were exported, beginning in 200* B.C. *and continuing up to the seventeenth century. They were once labeled trade wind beads because they are found in archaeological sites by the Indian Ocean in East and South Africa and are believed to have arrived there in the ships of Arab, Indian, and Chinese traders, who sailed with the monsoon winds and ocean currents.*[III] *The beads are also found throughout Southeast Asia, including Thailand, Java, Malaysia, and Sumatra. Of particular interest are the brick red beads, known as "Indian reds" in Africa and as* mutisalah *in Indonesia. Largest bead: Diameter, 0.9 cm. Corning Museum of Glass, Corning, New York*

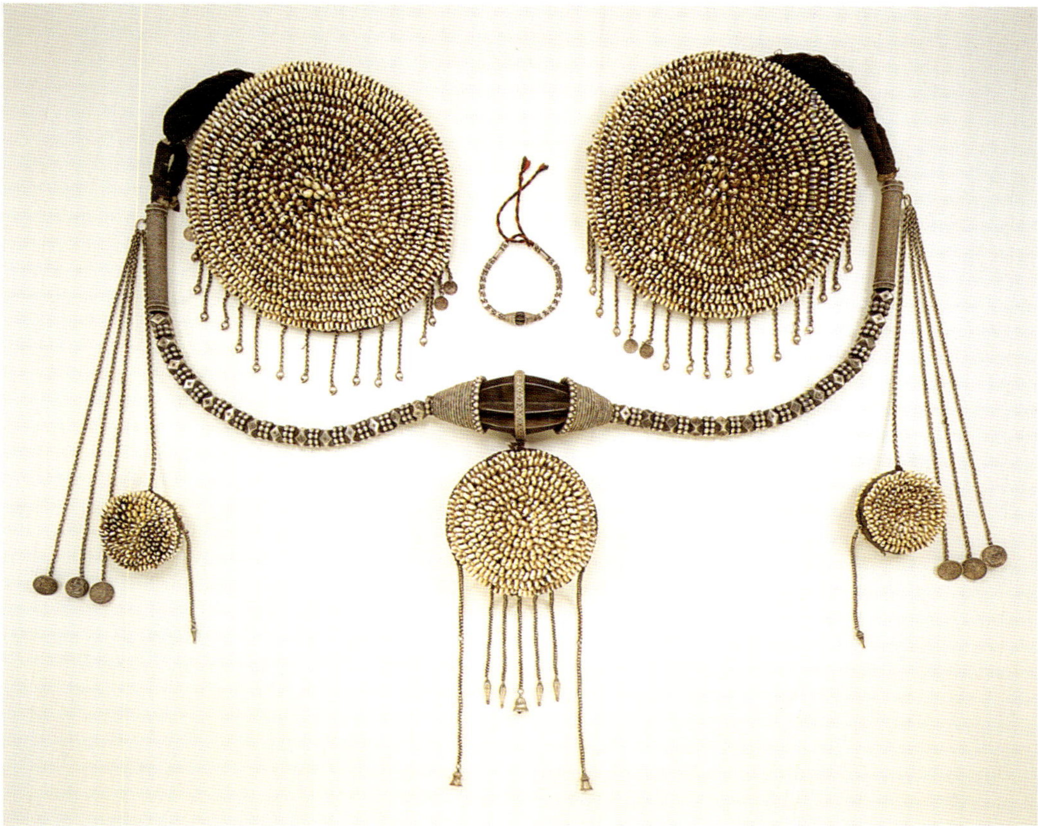

TOP: 195. *A pair of twentieth-century necklaces from the Toda tribes in the Nilgi Hills, southern India. Meant to be worn by sacred bulls, the large necklace is made of cowrie shells, leather, and silver beads and has a prayer-wheel bead (rotated during the chanting of prayers) at the center. The small necklace, made of the same materials and similar in design to the larger one, is worn by shepherdesses who guide the bulls. Bull necklace: length, 259 cm. Small shepherdess necklace: length, 24.5 cm. Collection Colette and Jean-Pierre Ghysels, Brussels*

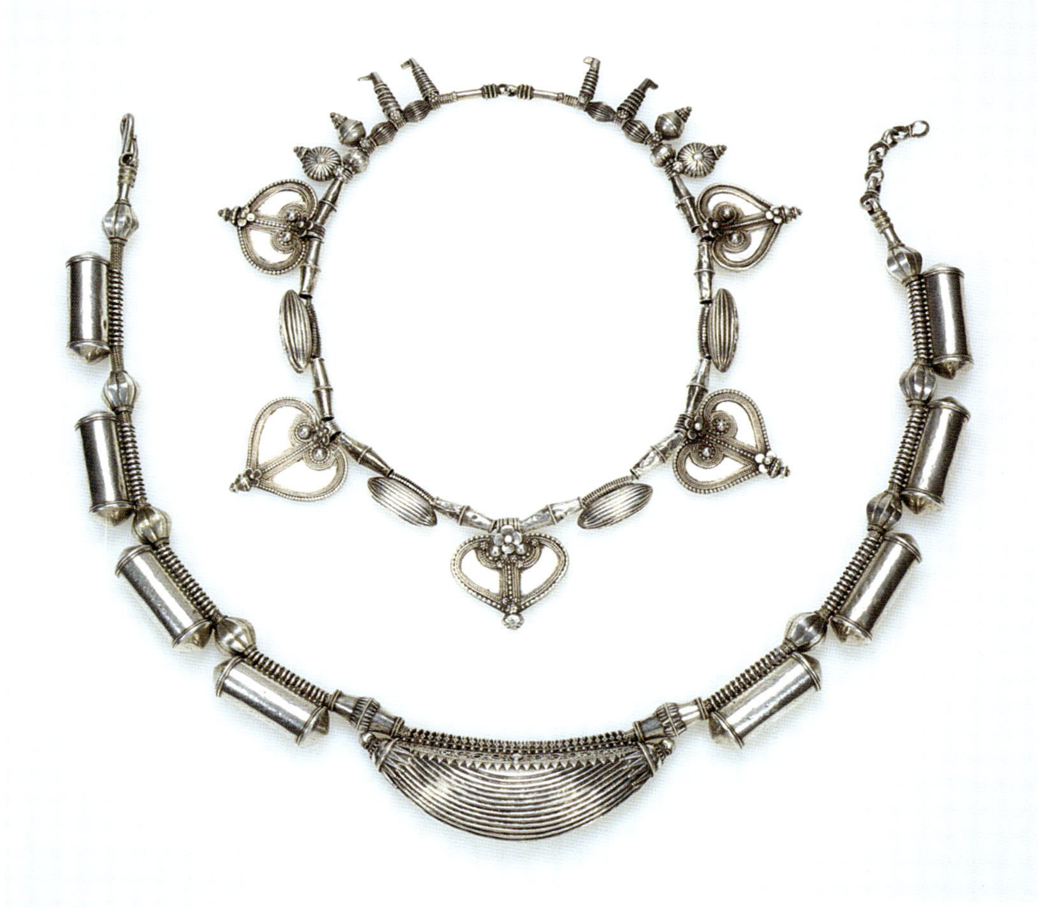

BOTTOM: 196. *Twentieth-century silver necklaces from the Tamil Nadu and Kerala districts. Layers of heavy silver are still worn, both as adornment and as portable wealth. In difficult times, the necklace is always worth at least its weight in silver. Center "heart" in Tamil necklace: diameter, 5.3 cm. Collection Ivory Freidus*

Although religious significance was associated with precious metals and jewels, wearing them obviously added to the owner's prestige, prominently declaring the ability to afford additional protection. Because most people did not own precious stones themselves, they worshiped bejeweled temple deities to gain the stones' protective powers.

However, beads of humbler materials—seeds, glass, carnelian—were of equal importance to a number of India's tribal cultures. The jewelry of Nagaland, now made by only a handful of the Naga tribes, evolved into a complex bead iconography tied to ritualistic ceremonies. Naga beads, combined in highly imaginative and powerful designs with specific meanings assigned to colors, forms, and materials, express remarkable creativity (plates 199–205).

Prehistoric India

Some of the oldest beads in the world have been found in India. Disk beads of ostrich eggshell and an olivia shell bead from Patne in Maharashtra date to 23,000 B.C., and a bone bead and several cattle incisor teeth grooved for stringing, found at the Kurnool Cave,[7] date to 17,000 B.C.

India's great fame as a beadmaking center stems from the country's abundant and accessible supplies of a wide range of semiprecious quartz minerals: chalcedony, agate, onyx, jasper, and rock crystal. Gravels in some Indian rivers yield agate nodules, and shallow underground bedrock agate sources are easily mined. This abundance of high-quality raw materials gave rise to the ancient Indian agate bead industry. (Some of the best-known Indian stone beads, often grouped together as agate, are more accurately described as carnelian and onyx.)

By the early Neolithic period (7000–5500 B.C.), beadmaking technology was sufficiently developed for beads to be shaped and not just simply grooved or pierced. Beads of softer stones, such as steatite, turquoise, lapis lazuli, and alabaster, were produced and traded in the early Indus Valley site of Mehrgarh. The Mehrgarh excavations also revealed that pump or bow drills with a chert bit were used to perforate stone beads.[8] The discoveries are the first examples of an uninterrupted industry of stone beadmaking within India that remains important even today.

Beadmakers in the Chalcolithic period (c. 4500 B.C.) became increasingly specialized, employing longer cylindrical stone drills made of chert or jasper. The new drills were more efficient for perforating long agate and carnelian beads, a necessary development as patrons demanded larger beads as their wealth and status grew. Used with water, the ground dust acted as a natural abrasive.[9]

The Indus had nourished one of the great ancient civilizations by the third millennium B.C., whose effect on later Indian cultures has been considerable. Mixed agriculture, planned towns with elaborate drainage systems, monumental buildings, a hieroglyphic script, and long-distance trade attest to the sophistication of this highly complex society. Beadmakers of Harappa, which alongside Mohenjo-daro was one of the twin capitals of the Indus civilization, mastered stone bead-cutting by 2600 B.C., and they probably traded carnelian and agate beads to Sumer, 1,600 miles to the west.

Harappan beadmaking technology is well understood, due to the discovery of large beadmaking facilities at two other Indus Valley sites, Lothal and Chanhu-daro. Basically, a two-phase chipping operation was required to form beads into their rough shape. The bead was then ground to a smooth outline, and the perforation hole was drilled. Beadmakers thereafter chipped a small cup in both sides of the bead. This indentation was used as a starting hole to steady the drill and act as a reservoir for the cutting abrasive (probably a hard stone grit suspended in liquid). Finally, the beads were polished with a fine abrasive slurry. This technology is surprisingly similar to practices used today in the manufacturing center at Cambay.[10] The Harappans also invented the technique for "etching" carnelian subsequently used in Iran (plate 192).

From 2600 to 1600 B.C., Indus Valley craftsmen at Mohenjo-daro, Harappa, Lothal, and Chanhu-daro created a vast array of bead shapes, many of which are identical to those found in Mesopotamia, Anatolia, Iran, Afghanistan, Crete, and Egypt from the same era. Carnelians and agates were highly prized, but there were also beads of bone, shell, pottery, faience, steatite (including glazed steatite), onyx, amethyst, feldspar, turquoise, lapis lazuli, copper, bronze, silver, and gold. The discovery of many terminal spacer beads shows that, as in Egypt, multiple strings of beads were combined into necklaces, bracelets, and girdles.[11]

Typical Indus Valley beads include disk, spherical, biconical, cylindrical, barrel, and lentoid shapes, as well as more elaborate gold-capped agates. Red-painted clay figurines depicting the contemporary women of Mohenjo-daro show them wearing three necklaces: a choker, a necklace descending to the collarbone, and a third one falling over the breasts. This custom persisted into the Mogul period, four thousand years later (plate 191).

Direct contact between Mesopotamian, Egyptian, and Indus Valley civilizations appears certain. A third-millennium B.C. clay tablet from the Mesopotamian site of Nippur documents the presence of Indian merchants in Babylonia. Indus merchants are known to have visited foreign lands to sell beads and pots and to collect raw materials.[12] Lapis lazuli from the Badakhshan district of Afghanistan has been identified in early dynastic Egypt, and it is believed that Harappan traders acted as middlemen in the lapis trade between Afghanistan, Mesopotamia, and Egypt. Bead-shaped stone weights found at Harappa and Mohenjo-daro suggest that the value of beads was calculated using a system of weights common to both Sumer and the Indus Valley, thereby simplifying the exchange of goods between them.[13] Furthermore, many Mesopotamian and Indus Valley beads—the long, biconical carnelians and gold-capped agates, for example (Timeline 245 and 257)—closely resemble one another. The faceting of stone beads also occurs in both the Indus Valley and Sumer, although it is rarer in the Indus culture.

Perhaps the best evidence for trade between the two civilizations are the etched carnelian beads that were made with similar techniques and sometimes display identical etched patterns (plate 192). These beads have been found in Indus Valley sites from 2500 B.C. and in the contemporaneous royal Sumerian graves of Ur.[14]

With the collapse of the Indus Valley civilizations about 1600 B.C., long-distance trade in Indian beads diminished for the next thousand years. Although beads appear to have been made in quantity, they were primarily for local use. Bead historian Peter Francis has observed: "Many agate localities exist in India and many villages made beads. It is important to recognize that the Indian agate bead industry was mostly decentralized, yet simultaneously supported key centers.... Villages supported an industry for local markets while large centers were big business geared to the export trade."[15] This relationship existed in prehistoric times, and when the great centers collapsed, bead production and consumption continued at the village level. It was not until trade with the Romans started in the second century B.C. that raw agate and agate beads once again were moved on a large scale.

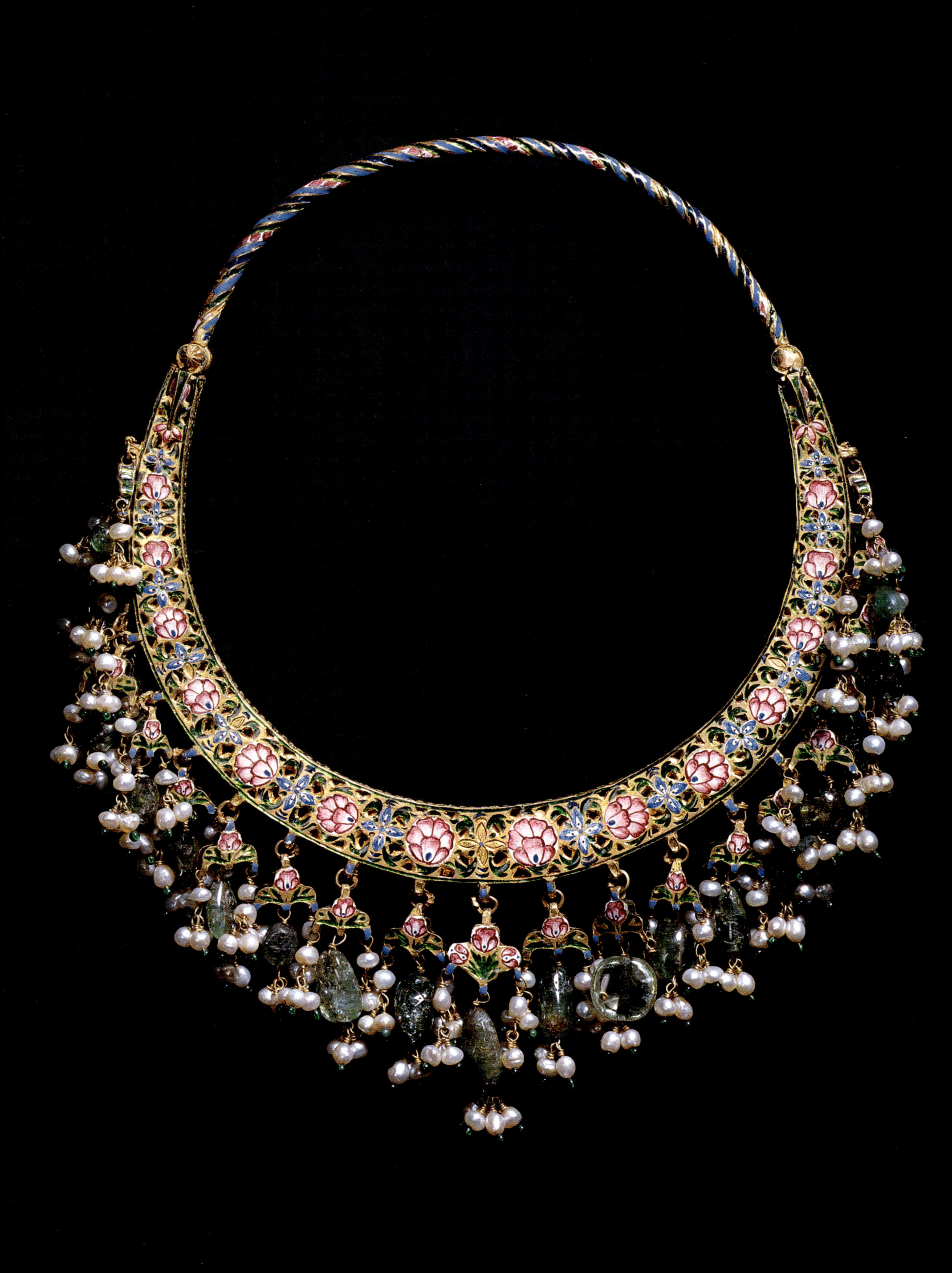

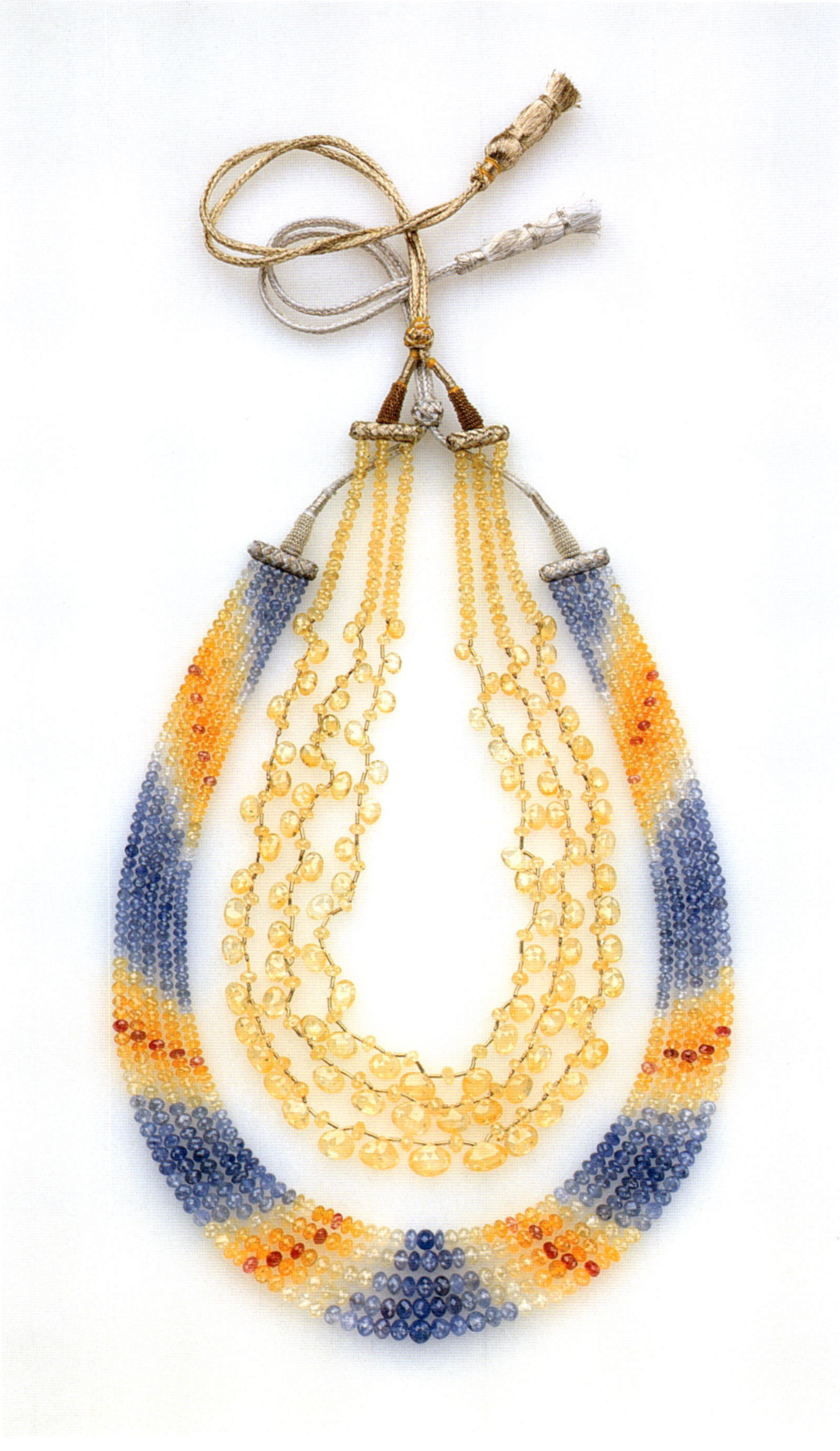

OPPOSITE: 197. *Eighteenth-century Mogul enameled gold necklace with pearls and emerald beads. Once precious stones were pierced, they lost some of their intrinsic value, thus such necklaces conveyed their owners' great wealth. The necklaces of gems and metals created by jewelers of the Mogul court are among the most elaborate ever made, yet their designs are unusually well integrated and not overwhelmed by details. Length, 42.5 cm. Collection Tambaran Gallery, New York*

LEFT: 198. *Sapphire beads in shades of blue, yellow, and pink. These contemporary Indian beads were faceted and pierced by craftsmen on a dirt floor with a bow drill, a method practiced since Mogul days. The shapes of the pure yellow sapphires are similar to motifs in very early Mogul jewelry. The carefully matched and graded stones of the five-strand necklace weigh 530 carats. Necklace: length, 67.5 cm. Collection Dr. Stephen Paul Adler/Collector's Edition, New York*

The Beads of Nagaland

Nagaland, a tribal territory that gained statehood within India in 1977, is located in a rugged, mountainous region bordering southwest Burma (now Myanmar). Divided into sixteen main tribes (with some subtribes), the Naga peoples are of Mongolian descent and many remained isolated until the twentieth century, partly due to their remote location and partly because of their reputation as headhunters. Beaded jewelry was an important part of Naga attire.

The traditional Naga people were farmers who lived in villages. The tribes shared an animistic religion. Like many events in Naga life, agricultural seasons were marked by ceremonies to drive away evil spirits and to insure the harvest. Because the Naga lived in a world they perceived as threatened by malevolent spirits, they believed only those with personal power could survive. This power is concentrated in the head; by taking a man's head, the hunter could possess the victim's power and enhance his own prestige in the community.[IV]

Their isolation notwithstanding, much Naga jewelry is made from traded objects: shells from the Bay of Bengal, carnelian, brass bells, and brass face pendants from India, and glass beads from India and occasionally from Venice. (Some metal elements were Naga-crafted, such as the trumpet-shaped pendants, plates 202, 203.) Beads from Venice and many varieties of glass beads made in India were traded to Nagaland, with certain tribes, such as the Angami, probably controlling much of the trade. Carnelian beads from India and imported shells represented wealth.

A people without notable painting (but some wood carving) traditions, the Naga created exceptionally beautiful beaded jewelry, which was endowed with social symbolism. The Naga wore very little clothing, so beaded jewelry (and tattooing) represented most of their adornment: the degree of ornateness indicated the wearer's exact rank. Their beads were frequently worn during festivals and ceremonies to celebrate plantings, harvests, and successful headhunting.[V]

After a victorious raid, bead necklaces, passed down through the family and stored in baskets at home, were taken out. The heads seized in the raid were distributed, and the dancers adorned themselves with as many as ten necklaces each and danced all night. The necklaces were then stored, awaiting the next ceremony. Certain necklaces were never worn by day.[VI]

As the Naga culture started to disintegrate through increasing contact with the modern world and converstion to Christianity, beads and shells were no longer traded and jewelry-making almost disappeared. With traditions eroding and adornment no longer functioning in a ritual context, the craft lost its meaning. During the 1970s and 80s, many beaded family heirlooms were traded for items considered useful—penicillin, down parkas, and transistor radios. The necklaces illustrated in plates 199–204 probably date to the early 1900s; the necklace in plate 205 was created in the 1980s. There has recently been a return of some traditional ceremonies. A family will display what traditional adornment it still owns, though most must now wear contemporary replicas.[VI]

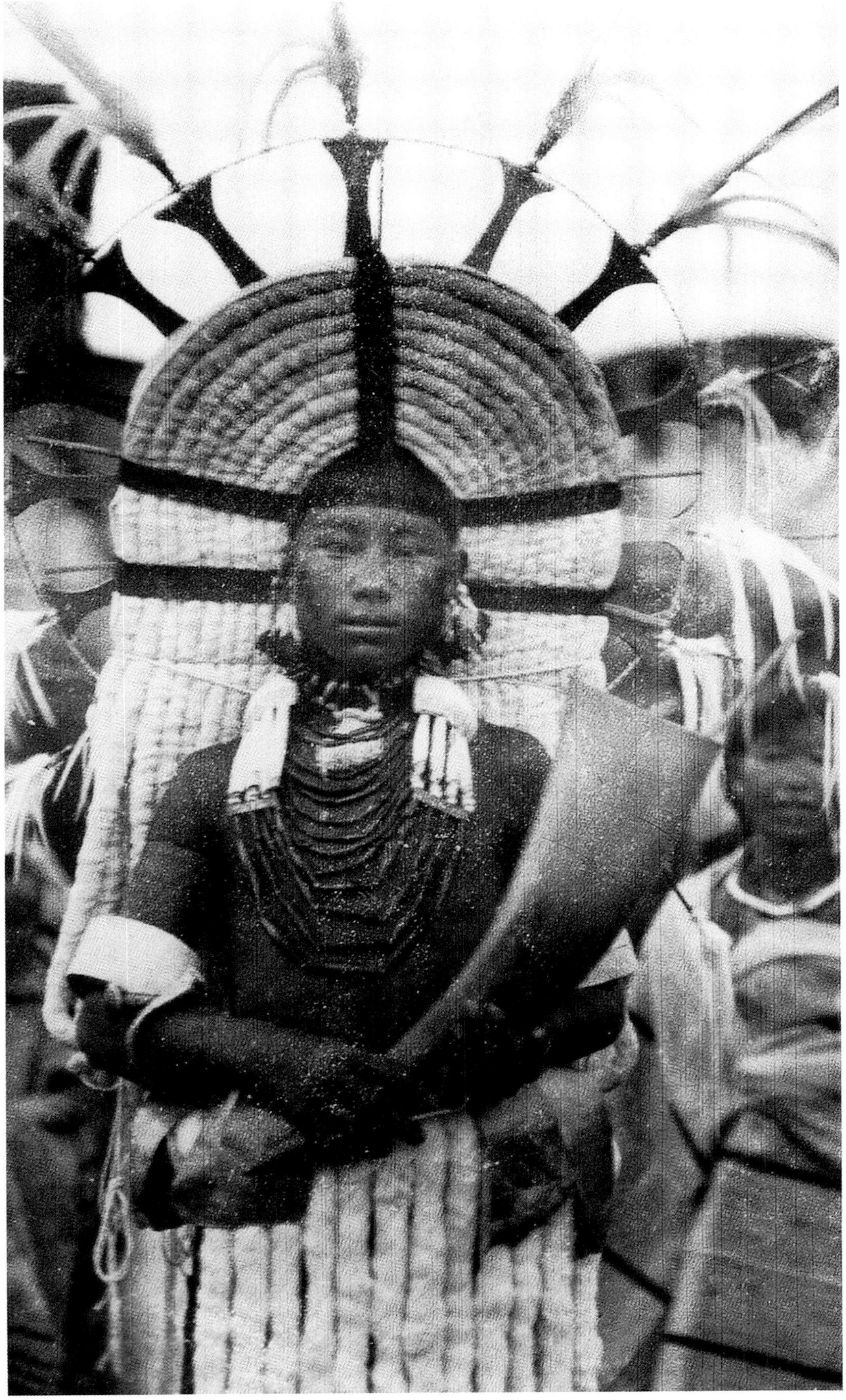

199. *An Angami Naga warrior wearing a necklace of the type shown in plate 201. This is an early twentieth-century photograph. Courtesy of the Smithsonian Institution, Washington, D.C.*

OVERLEAF, TOP LEFT:
200. *The necklace of a successful Naga headhunter. Such assemblies of brass heads and spirals, tiger teeth, and glass trade beads were worn only by men who had actually taken heads. The brass heads (comparable to a shrunken-head trophy) symbolize the number of kills credited to the owner. The marigold yellow beads from India were highly prized. Row of brass heads: length, 22.5 cm. Collection Mimi Lipton and Hansjiirg Mayer, London*

OVERLEAF, BOTTOM:
201. *An Angami necklace from southern Nagaland composed of rare, imported items, including shells, blue and yellow glass, and faceted carnelian beads from India. Bone spacers separate the strands. The two shells symbolize two horns; these may have religious significance, since horns represent fertility. Cut sections of chank shell are characteristic of Angami jewelry. They are worn on the shoulders and back, resembling the huge stone monoliths that surround this tribe's religious buildings. Back shell: length, 14 cm. Private collection*

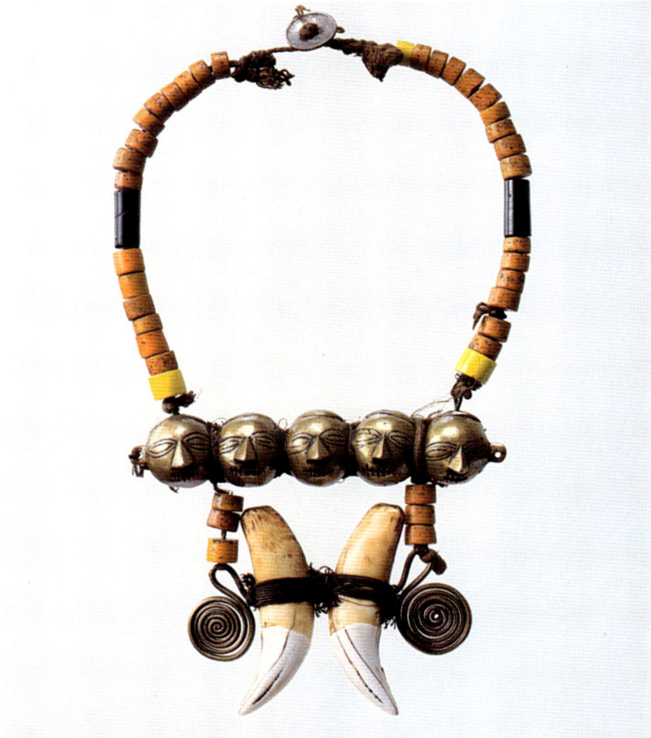

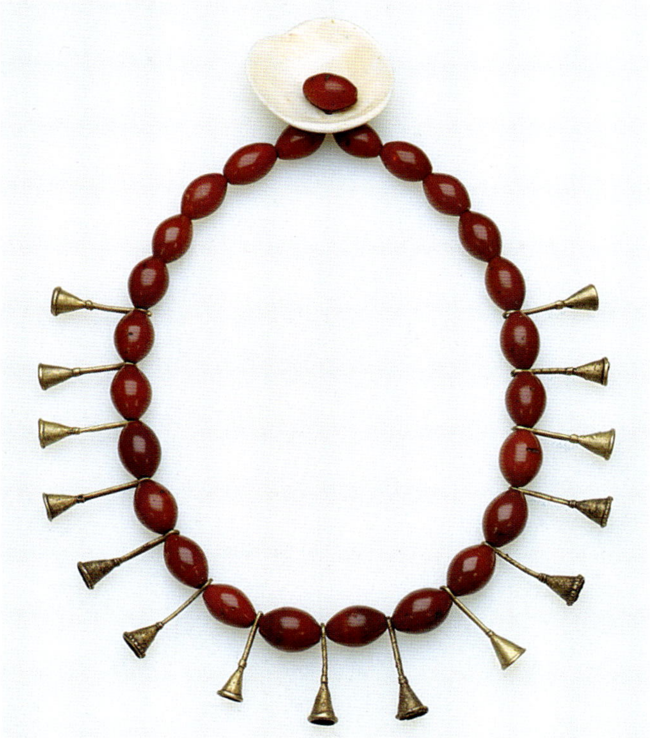

TOP RIGHT: 202. *A commoner's necklace of red glass beads (imitating carnelian) with brass trumpet-shaped pendants. Typical bead: length, 2.8 cm. Private collection*

OPPOSITE: 203. *A chief of the Ao tribe owned this impressive five-strand carnelian bead necklace with bone spacers and brass trumpets. Carnelian beads represented wealth to the Naga; therefore, this necklace, which weighed more than five pounds, had considerable value. Naga used the lost-wax casting technique to make the brass trumpet-shaped pendants. Largest carnelian bead: length, 4.2 cm. Collection Norma Canelas and William D. Roth*

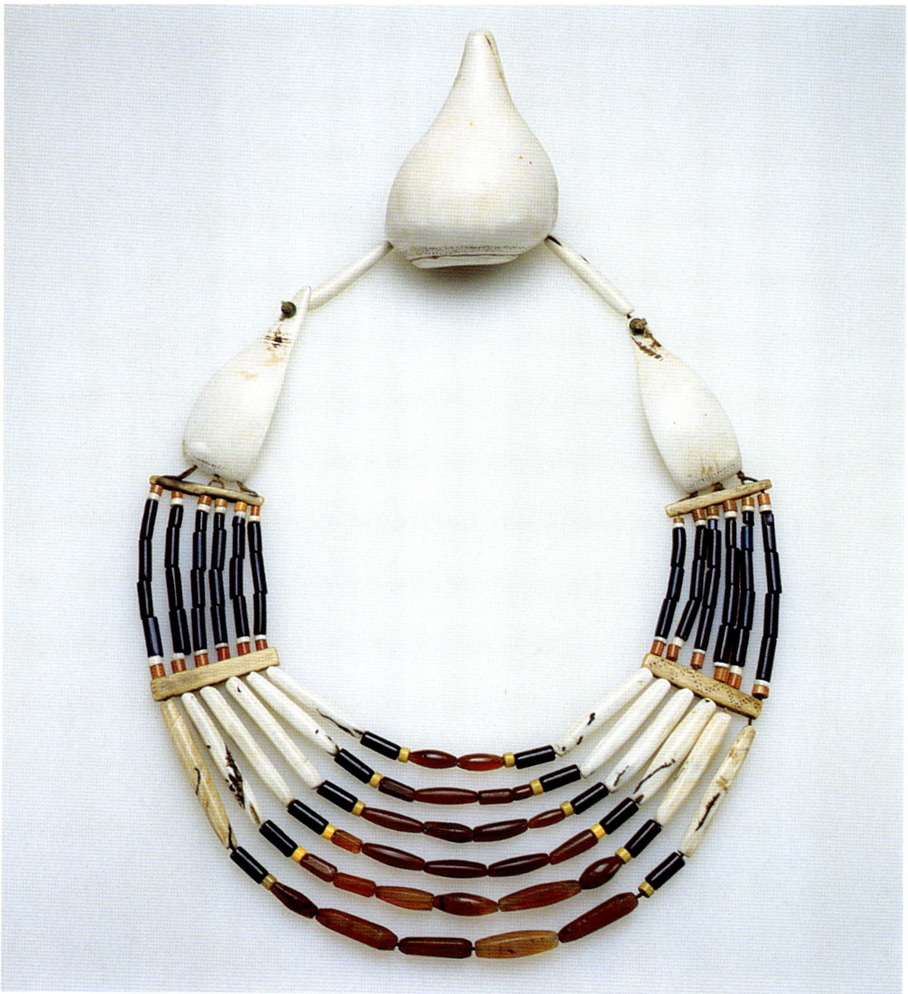

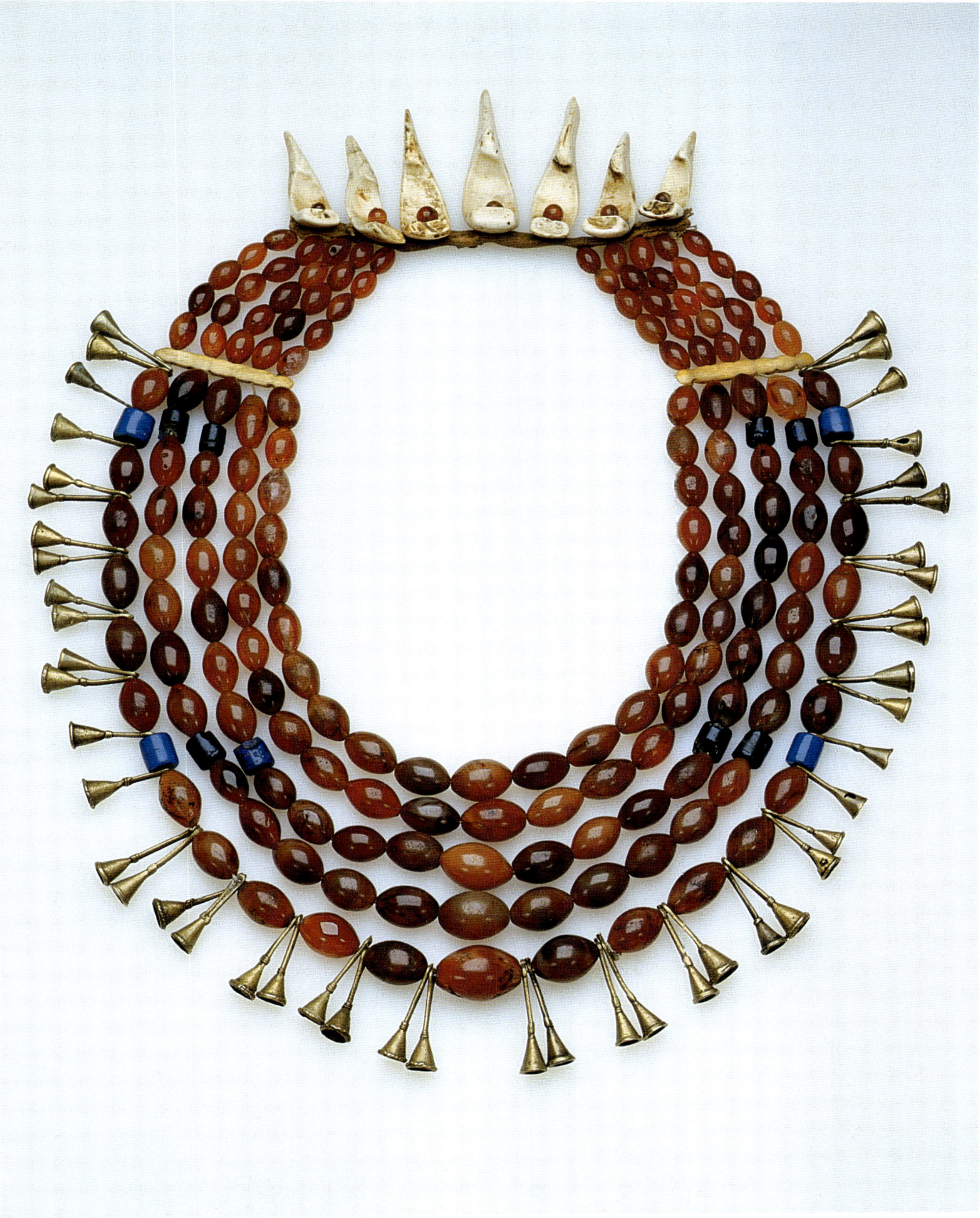

Indo-Hellenistic to Medieval Beads

Following Alexander the Great's invasion of the Indian subcontinent in the late fourth century B.C., Greeks ruled Bactria (eastern Iran) for over a hundred years and influenced the rise of an important Indo-Hellenistic jewelry style. The Greeks provided Indian craftsmen with new motifs: acanthus leaves, palmettes, eglantine flowers, animals, and figures of Eros and the sphinx. They also introduced the technique of granulation into Indian beadmaking. Another technique developed at this time was the faceting of beads, a practice seen only rarely in the earlier Indus Valley and Sumerian civilizations. Beads were fluted, collared, and elaborately decorated in all the familiar spherical, cylindrical, barrel, and disk shapes, using quartz, carnelian, lapis lazuli, faience, and glass. Animal effigy beads and amulets, especially lions, also appeared, a concept perhaps derived from Crete, Egypt, or Iran.[16]

By the beginning of the Christian Era, India was once again involved in long-distance bead trade. Beads of onyx, sardonyx, and other valued stones flowed west to the Romans and Persians, and east to the Chinese. The Romans learned from the Arabs how to navigate the monsoons to their advantage, which helped accelerate trade between Rome and India. Roman mariners now had direct access to the rich gem fields of southern India and Sri Lanka.[17] Pliny, the Roman historian (A.D. 23–79), wrote that Indian beads were not greatly esteemed in his time, although they had been earlier.[18] Evidence of their great worth in Rome, however, is noted in the *Periplus of the Erythraean Sea,* written about A.D. 88, in which it was observed that "the beads so popular in Rome were sold from the port of Broach at the mouth of the Narmada after being cut at Ujjain and floated down the river."[19] This account is believable, since it is known that Broach was an important trading port during this period, and archaeologists have excavated a bead workshop at Ujjain dating to the even earlier Mauryan period (322–185 B.C.).[20]

The source of the stones cut at Ujjain and exported from Broach to Rome was probably Ratanpur, a village near Ujjain where raw agate is still dug with primitive tools. The Ratanpur area is also a possible source for the carnelian exported to Sumer about 2500 B.C. Mining stones at Ratanpur, cutting them into beads at Ujjain, and exporting them from Broach became a system that lasted from the early Christian Era for nearly one thousand years. It was not until the business-minded Solankinors shifted the center of beadmaking to Limodra, closer to the Ratanpur mines, in the twelfth century and eventually to Cambay at the head of the Gulf of Cambay in the sixteenth that the Ratanpur-Ujjain-Broach manufacturing-export system finally broke down.[21] Cambay is still known for its stone beads, particularly carnelians.

Indian Glass Beads

Glass beads appear about five hundred to a thousand years later in India than in Mesopotamia and Egypt. Glass beads occur in Baghwanpura about 1000 B.C. and in the north at Alamgirpur and the south at Maski in approximately 800 B.C. Quantities of glass beads have been found at the trading center of Taxila dating to the sixth century B.C. and later. It is speculated that the abundance of beads at Taxila indicates they were also made there, although no waste glass has been found.[22]

Roman gold-glass and eye beads were imported between A.D. 1 and 200. Despite this and other evidence of trade in Roman glass beads, the Roman Empire appears to have had little influence on the Indian glass bead industry.[23] Beginning in the second century B.C., glass beads were made at different locations throughout India using indigenous techniques, the most important of which was the drawing of glass.

In the north of India, quantities of glass beads, some made to imitate agate, onyx, and etched carnelian, have been found at the sites of Kausambi and Ahichchhatra (250 B.C.–A.D. 450).[24] In the south, glass beads and bead material excavated at Arikamedu range from opaque red to hues of black, green, yellow, translucent blue, green, and violet. These beads, three to five millimeters in diameter, were made by cutting drawn glass tubes into segments, then heating them and rounding off the ends. Some tubes were pressed into molds.[25]

There was a western beadmaking center at Brahmapuri between 200 B.C. and A.D. 200. Small beads made by the drawn technique, similar to those from Arikamedu, were most common; melons and square blue tubes with white center-lines occur in great numbers. Beads with gold foil between two layers of glass are rare, and they most probably were Egyptian imports. Small, orange drawn-glass beads are common from 100 B.C. onward at Taxila and are found at many other Indian sites. The small drawn-glass beads were likely used for centuries in beadwork and may have originated in India, although they were made in several locations.[26] Indian glass traveled both to the East and the West, following the same routes to the same destinations as agate and carnelian beads. The beads appear in East Africa between A.D. 200 and 1600, in Malaysia and Vietnam about A.D. 1000, and in Sumatra beginning in the first century A.D.[27] Although now known as Indo-Pacific beads, they have been referred to as "trade wind beads," since they were carried by ship via routes determined by the seasonal ocean currents and monsoon patterns (plate 194).[28] In medieval India, glass beads appear to have been manufactured at Arikamedu until perhaps the twelfth century and in Brahmapuri through the sixteenth century.[29]

Medieval Period

By A.D. 330, Constantine had created his new capital, Constantinople, in the eastern Roman Empire. With this de facto division of the empire and weakening of central authority, beadmaking in the West—particularly of glass beads—was dispersed among small, localized industries usually situated in former Roman territories. Beads from Byzantium, heir to Roman traditions, were made of precious stones. With the rise of Christianity in the West, the church discouraged the wearing of jewelry, and beads were increasingly limited to rosaries. Beadmaking continued on a limited scale in the formerly great manufacturing centers of Syria, Egypt, and Persia. As the Islamic religion spread from Spain to India between the seventh and tenth century, Muslim craftsmen within these countries, working with techniques passed down from Egyptian and Roman jewelers, still created beautiful and distinctive beads.

The decline in Western beadmaking provided India with the opportunity to become a major manufacturer of both stone and glass beads. Between A.D. 500 and 1500, Indian merchants greatly expanded their efforts to trade beads, shipping quantities of agate and glass beads into East and West Africa, the Middle East, Egypt, and Southeast Asia.[30]

Indian agate beads from antiquity have been identified at Kilwa in East Africa and in the West African countries of Senegal and Mali (plate 193). Indian carnelian and onyx were traded by the Persians to China and Oman respectively. Duarte Barbosa, a sixteenth-century Portuguese traveler to India, noted that Indian agates were sold to Arabia, Persia, Egypt, and Europe.[31] Indian agate beads are also common in the Philippines and throughout Southeast Asia, reflecting a trade relationship that reached its zenith between A.D. 1300 and 1800. Carnelian beads also traveled great distances and have been found in graves of slaves in the West Indian island of Barbados. The beads were most probably brought by their owners from Africa to the New World.[32]

RIGHT: 204. *A Naga sash worn over the shoulder and across the chest, made from strands of Indian glass beads, large shell disks, and dyed goat-hair tassels. The dyed goat hair symbolizes the flames that have ravaged enemy villages. Length, 132 cm. Collection Tambaran Gallery, New York*

OPPOSITE: 205. *A necklace made to be worn by an important man of the Konyak tribe, with orange, marigold yellow, brown, and white glass trade beads, shell beads, brass bells, and incised conch shell sections. The fastenings are crocheted grass or palm fibers. More than any other Naga tribe, the Konyak have withstood modernization, retaining the jewelry and customs of the past. They are considered the best craftsmen among the Naga. Necklace length (from top bone divider to center of necklace), 60 cm. Typical orange bead: length, 1.3 cm. Collection Tambaran Gallery, New York*

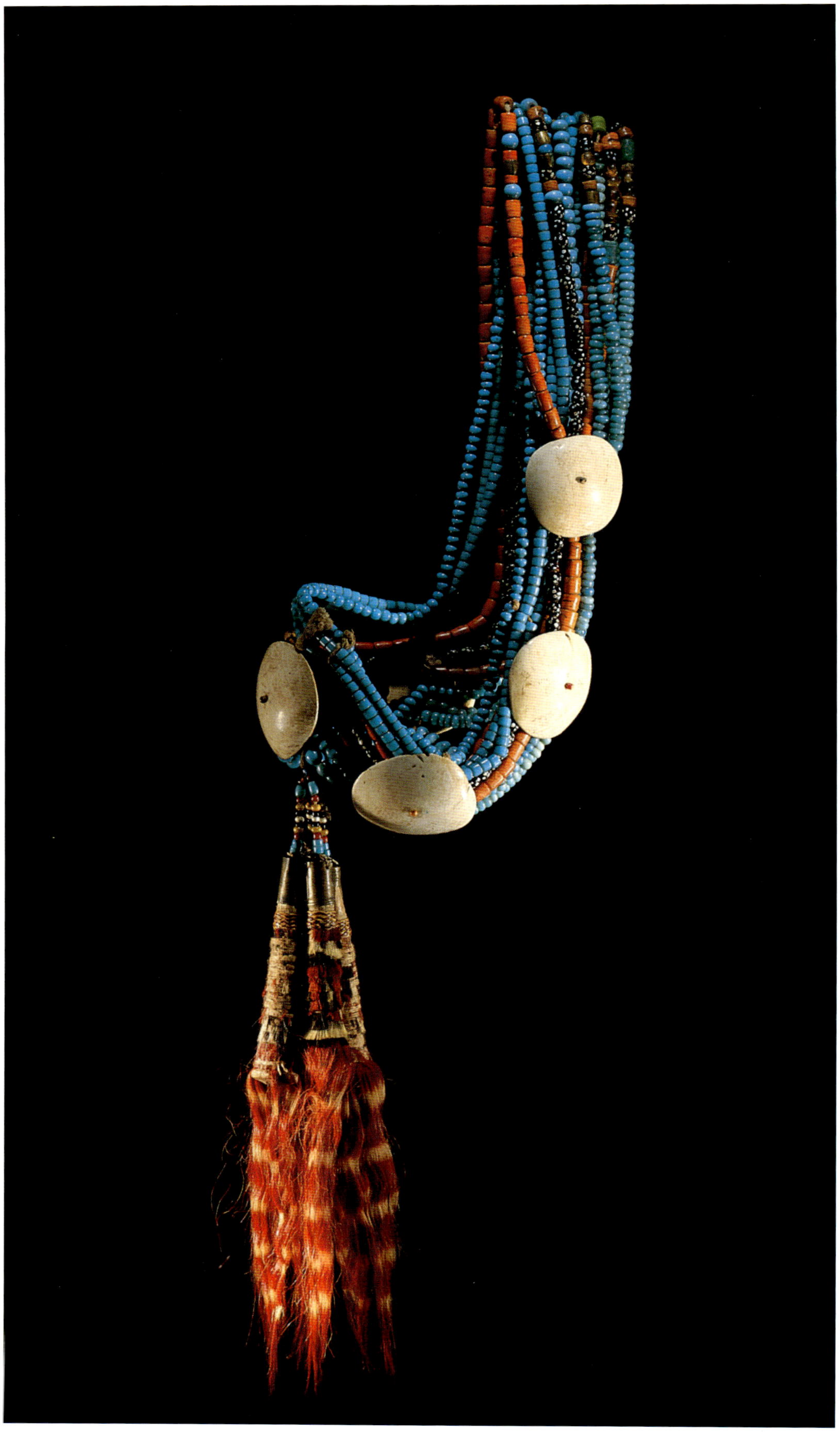

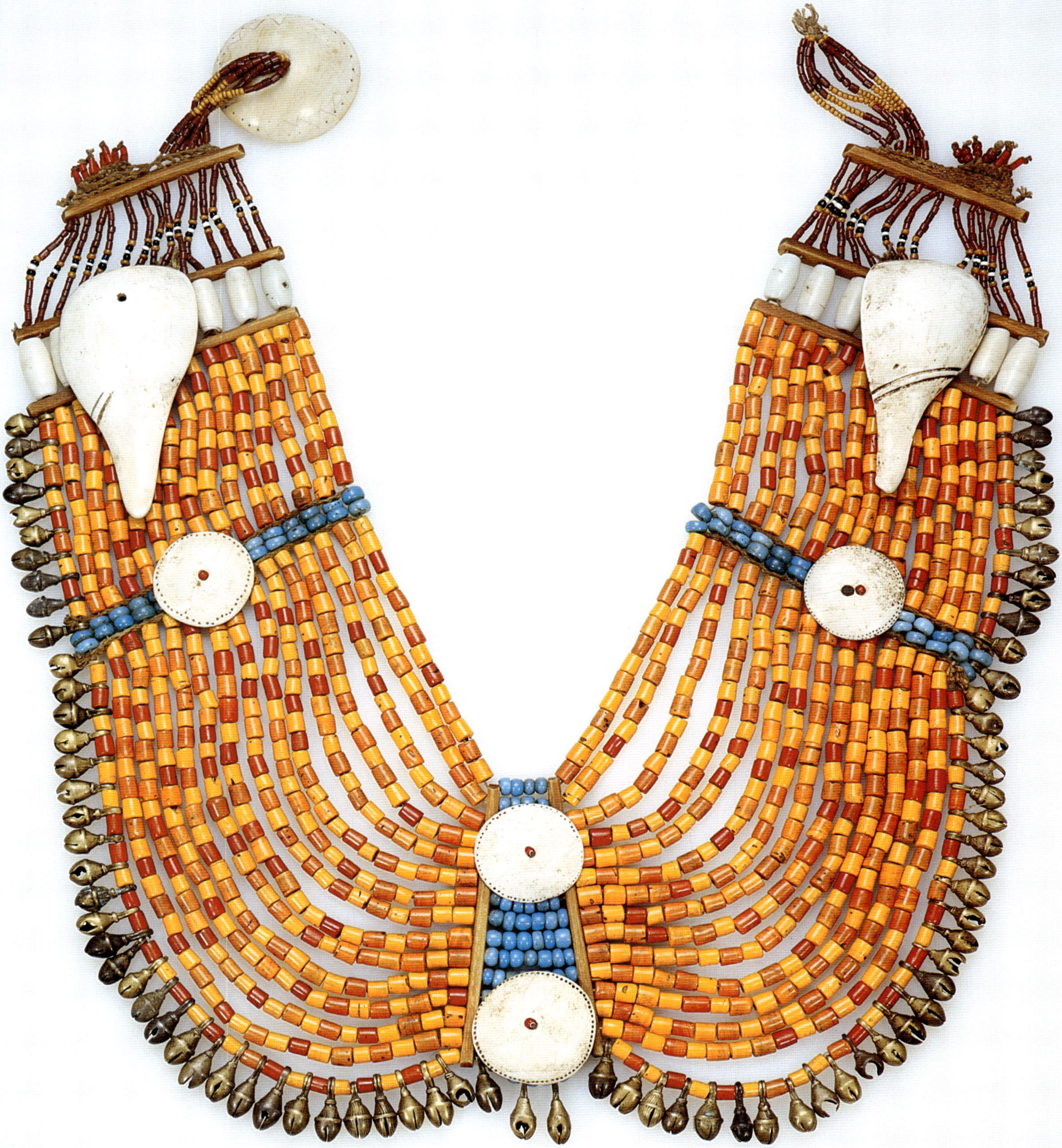

The Mogul Period

Under the Moguls, the Muslim rulers of northern India from the early sixteenth to the eighteenth century, jewelry became very sophisticated. The Mogul dynasty was founded by Babur (1485–1530), great-grandson of both Tamerlane and Genghis Khan. Babur overran Agra and Delhi, and he eventually captured all of northern India. Under strong central rule and free from most internal warfare, the new empire's trade and creativity flourished. Great wealth was concentrated in the hands of the Mogul rulers and their courts, and they desired elaborate personal ornamentation. Exquisite craftsmanship, with lavish displays of precious metals and stones, were hallmarks of imperial Mogul jewelry. Persian jewelers, known for their fine detailing, were invited to establish workshops in India, and they evolved an Indo-Persian style that even today remains unique.[33]

The Moguls epitomized the idea that "the glory of a prince is made more tangible by his buildings, his library, and his jewels."[34] With this motto, they presided over one of the great creative ages of Indian civilization, patronizing painters, architects, and jewelers. The Mogul emperors used their economic power to subsidize mining operations for rare minerals, then encouraged artisans to create new forms of jewelry utilizing these materials. Beadmaking with precious stones flourished. Even the most valuable stones—emeralds, rubies, and sapphires—were made into beads, despite the risk of diminishing their value by piercing them (plate 197).

The size of gems was considered all-important, and it was unthinkable for an artisan to cut a stone to one-third its original size simply to add brilliance.[35] Mogul beads made of precious stones were usually cabochon-cut, accentuating color rather than light (making faceted jewelry seem excessively flamboyant by comparison). This may also explain why using gemstones as beads is rare; only a few examples from Rome, Byzantium, and China are known outside of India.

The Moguls were not shy about displaying their jewels and the vast quantities of pearls they obtained from the Persian Gulf. In 1658, the Frenchman François Bernier observed that even the orthodox and puritanical Emperor Aurangzeb was bedizened on state occasions, wearing a "necklace of immense pearls suspended from his neck which reached his stomach in the same manner as many of the Gentiles wear their beads," an apparent reference to the European manner of wearing rosaries.[36]

The clothes and jewels of Mogul women also reflected the status of their men. Manucci, the Venetian physician at the court of Aurangzeb, noted: "Generally, they [the women] had four or five rows of pearls hanging from their necks, in a chain coming down to the lower part of their stomach. Upon the middle of the head was a bunch of pearls which hung down the center of the forehead with a valuable ornament of costly stones formed into shapes of the sun, the moon or stars, or, at times, even of flowers.... They girded their waists with gold belts set with precious stones and even the strings with which they tied their trousers had pearls at the ends. On their legs they wore metal ornaments or strings of costly pearls while the shoulders were covered with necklaces like scarves."[37] As Mogul power declined toward the end of the eighteenth century, much of their jewelry was broken up for sale as separate items or taken to other countries. Today, only a fraction of the Mogul court jewelry remains intact in India.

Experimentation with new designs and fine craftsmanship was essentially reserved for the rich in Mogul India. By contrast, jewelry for ordinary people tended to remain simple and traditional. In times of economic crisis, it was often melted down and the stones sold; so it was important that there be no loss in the intrinsic value of the metal and stone, making ordinary jewelry more valued for its material than its workmanship.

The Decline of Indian Beadmaking

While the Moguls of northern India were rewarding themselves with the riches of the continent, the rest of India and her beadmaking industries were in decline. Venice and the German city of Idar-Oberstein established themselves as beadmaking centers by the fifteenth century and began to encroach upon India's market. As Europeans colonized the globe, India's role as a major exporting bead producer was steadily destroyed.

Initially, both Venice and Idar-Oberstein copied the popular and successful Indian beads. The German center concentrated on agates, while the Venetian glassmakers, using drawn-glass techniques, began manufacturing the small seedbeads that Indians had been supplying to international markets for centuries.[38] Furthermore, the New World market, with its immense demand for glass beads, which had not been previously available to Indian beadmakers and traders, greatly strengthened the European bead industry. By 1805, the British government formulated economic policies obliging Indians to buy European goods. By the end of the nineteenth century, India herself was importing vast quantities of beads.[40] British policies virtually crippled and ended the glassworking industries of India, which did not recover until the 1970s.

Craftsmen, Tools, and Techniques

Beadmaking in India has always been considered a full-time, specialized craft. For centuries, it was divided among experts in a specific raw material: gold-, silver-, and coppersmiths, as well as specialists in faience, steatite, shell, ivory, and pottery, worked in the industry. Other specialized contributors included the refiner, enameler, precious-stone merchant, cutter, polisher, and even the stringer.[41] Crafts and trades tended to be hereditary and based largely on the caste system. However, the making of carnelian and agate beads at Cambay, an important traditional center of the Indian stone bead industry, has been controlled since the country's independence by those with enough money to buy stones and finance the operation.[42] Cambay stone beads have a limited range of shapes (they come in spheres, cones, bicones, faceted bicones, and long rectangulars) and are created with the same primitive tools and techniques that have been employed for centuries.[43] The rough bead forms are smoothed by finer chipping, then ground smooth, drilled, and polished. Today, grinding and polishing are done mechanically. The faceting of beads, a common practice in India by the third century B.C., is used to enhance the brilliance and luster of the stone, while hiding minor defects. Cambay carnelians are practically always heat-treated to alter chemically the stone's iron compound, thereby accentuating its orange color.[44]

Indian Beadmaking Today

The Indian beadmaking industry remains strong. The mining of agate in Ratanpur and stone beadmaking in Cambay are important industries, while glass beadmaking has grown stronger since the 1970s (Timeline 646–659). By 1980, India had revived mosaic-glass manufacture. There are four major glass beadmaking centers today: Firozabad produces glass for India's beadmakers; Purdalpur is known for copies of Venetian millefiori beads; Papanaidupet is recognized for a unique drawn-glass technique; and Banaras makes glass beads in the Czech style.[45] Even rubies, emeralds, and sapphires, pierced and strung as beads, enjoy renewed popularity.

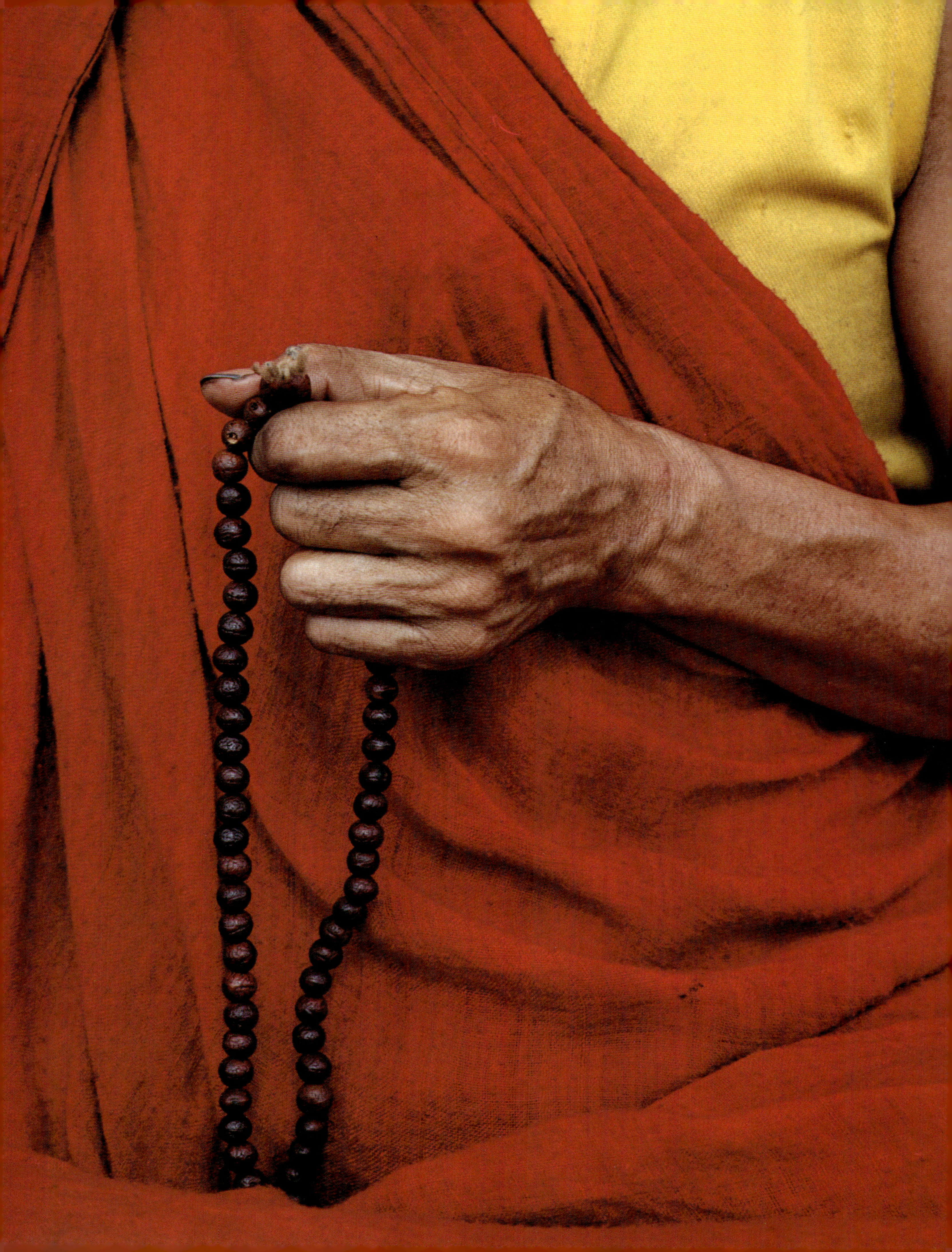

Central Asia

Central Asia is a hybrid of peoples and cultures. It includes the area from Siberia in the north to Iran, Afghanistan, Pakistan, and northern India in the south; from the Caspian Sea in the west to Mongolia in the northeast and China in the east. Today's northern Afghanistan, Soviet Central Asia (Turkmenistan, Uzbekistan, and Kazakhstan), and the Himalayan lands of Tibet, Nepal, Ladakh, Sikkim, and Bhutan are all part of this historic region.

206. *Prayer beads held by a Buddhist monk in Nepal, 1983. All photographs of people in this chapter were taken from 1983 to 1986, unless otherwise noted.*

Glancing at its location and geography, one would not expect central Asia to have been a major hub of cultural interaction. On the contrary, one might well imagine its great land mass, lack of access to the sea, and forbidding terrain of precipitous mountain ranges and formidable steppes—open, semiarid grassland stretching from eastern Europe to the heart of Asia—would have made its peoples isolated and their societies impenetrable. Yet, through the ages, central Asia has been one of the world's great melting pots.

Passing between the great civilizations of the Mediterranean and western Asia to the west and India and China to the east, overland trade routes crisscrossed central Asia, interconnecting the nomadic pastoralists and sedentary agriculturalists of the high, outlying plateaus. Local buyers and sellers converged at centers along the routes, in oases or river valleys. In time, these centers became towns and cities, closely linked to the growth of internal and international trade. With the merchants came new concepts—visibly expressed in their religious, political, and social customs and in their adornment—that were absorbed into the local practices of central Asia's societies. Refugees from Burma, India, and possibly China, facing religious and political persecution at home, found the Himalayans to be especially tolerant of their diverse beliefs. Indeed, the strongest cultural transfusions were injected by Indian and Chinese travelers, particularly those who frequented the eastern parts of central Asia and the Himalayas. Afghanistan and Turkmenistan, on the other hand, were influenced more by the cultures of northern Iran and the Mediterranean. Each ethnic group therefore developed distinct characteristics.

Despite their geographic remoteness and their receptiveness to various foreign ideas, the peoples of central Asia shared common historic and economic circumstances that frequently led to strong cultural similarities. Jewelry is an excellent indicator of these likenesses. The inhabitants of Turkmenistan, Mongolia, and the Himalayas, for example, wear turquoise beads because they share ancient beliefs about the material's amuletic properties. In a region where the networks of cultural interaction are immensely complex, beads, bartered for centuries, not surprisingly reflect the history.

For millennia, almost every person in this part of Asia has worn substantial quantities of beads and always prominently displayed them. Whether as objects of wealth and social status or as amulets, beads were and are part of the daily spiritual and secular life of the people. Beads were usually imported. In finished form or as raw materials, they have always been a major component of central Asian trade. Italian coral, Burmese and Baltic amber, Chinese turquoise and silver, and precious gems from India have passed through the region. The elaborate trade routes—involving nomadic herdsmen, local merchants, and international brokers—that carried goods from Asia and to the West also served to distribute beads to people along the way.

Adornment is one manifestation of the divisions in wealth and circumstances between the pastoral nomads, village agriculturalists, and city dwellers. Each group wore jewelry that was appropriate to its social standing and development. There are frequently greater similarities between beads worn by nomads from Turkmenistan, Nepal, and Mongolia than between the Nepalese nomads and Nepalese urban dwellers, or even between different social classes in Nepalese cities. This is partly because the wealthy could create elaborate ensembles of foreign imports that were not readily affordable to others. Yet despite differences in materials, jewelry from central Asia has a common purpose: to endow the owner with the bead's or jewel's spiritual and protective properties. Given this unifying premise—a continuation of ancient shamanistic beliefs overlaid with Buddhist, Hindu, or Islamic tenets—each ethnic and economic group has chosen distinctive ways to articulate its adornment.

Trade Routes

Dating earlier than the Roman Empire, the silk routes became the most famous of Asia's trading channels. By the second century A.D., demand for Chinese silk in the Mediterranean greatly increased the importance of the active East-West routes, even though some journeys were nine thousand miles long, took as much as a year to complete, and were often dangerous. The overland routes were divided into regional segments, each requiring merchants to know different languages and to have elaborate social connections and means of protection. Rarely did a trader who began a journey in China see the Mediterranean, although Indian and Chinese traders may have traveled between their respective countries. The fame of the Venetian Marco Polo, who traveled the silk routes into China during the thirteenth century, is due not only to the uniqueness and length of his odyssey, but also to the fact that he lived to tell about it.[2]

A dazzling array of finished beads and bead raw materials, including silver, coral, amber, glass, and lapis lazuli, was transported eastward along the silk routes, while caravans originating in China arrived at the emporiums of Samarkand, Balkh, Kabul, and Antioch laden with silk, porcelain, lacquer, and vermilion. The international bead trade helped link the extreme ends of the ancient world from the earliest days of the silk

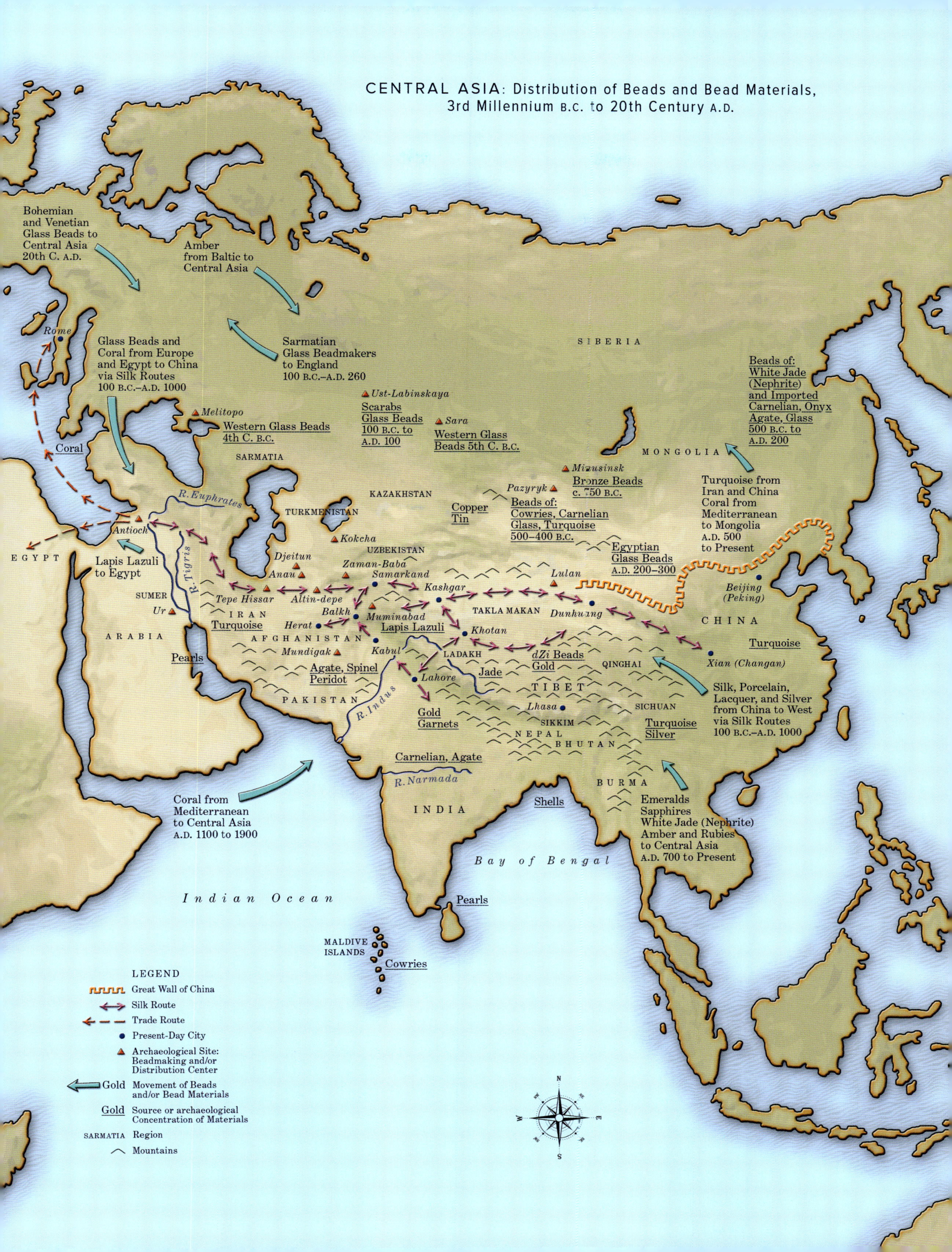
CENTRAL ASIA: Distribution of Beads and Bead Materials, 3rd Millennium B.C. to 20th Century A.D.
Bohemian and Venetian Glass Beads to Central Asia 20th C. A.D.
Amber from Baltic to Central Asia
Rome
Glass Beads and Coral from Europe and Egypt to China via Silk Routes 100 B.C.–A.D. 1000
Sarmatian Glass Beadmakers to England 100 B.C.–A.D. 260
SIBERIA
Beads of: White Jade (Nephrite) and Imported Carnelian, Onyx Agate, Glass 500 B.C. to A.D. 200
Ust-Labinskaya
Scarabs Glass Beads 100 B.C. to A.D. 100
Melitopo
Western Glass Beads 4th C. B.C.
Sara
Western Glass Beads 5th C. B.C.
MONGOLIA
Coral
SARMATIA
Minusinsk
Bronze Beads c. 750 B.C.
Turquoise from Iran and China Coral from Mediterranean to Mongolia A.D. 500 to Present
R. Euphrates
KAZAKHSTAN
Pazyryk
Beads of: Cowries, Carnelian Glass, Turquoise 500–400 B.C.
Copper Tin
TURKMENISTAN
Antioch
Kokcha
UZBEKISTAN
Egyptian Glass Beads A.D. 200–300
EGYPT
Lapis Lazuli to Egypt
Djeitun
Anau
Zaman-Baba
Samarkand
Lulan
R. Tigris
SUMER
Tepe Hissar
Altin-depe
Kashgar
Beijing (Peking)
Ur
IRAN
Balkh
Muminabad
TAKLA MAKAN
Dunhuang
CHINA
Turquoise
Herat
Lapis Lazuli
Khotan
ARABIA
AFGHANISTAN
Kabul
Turquoise
Mundigak
LADAKH
dZi Beads Gold
QINGHAI
Xian (Changan)
Pearls
Agate, Spinel Peridot
Lahore
Jade
TIBET
Silk, Porcelain, Lacquer, and Silver from China to West via Silk Routes 100 B.C.–A.D. 1000
PAKISTAN
R. Indus
Lhasa
SICHUAN
Gold Garnets
SIKKIM
Turquoise Silver
NEPAL
BHUTAN
Carnelian, Agate
R. Narmada
BURMA
Coral from Mediterranean to Central Asia A.D. 1100 to 1900
INDIA
Shells
Emeralds Sapphires White Jade (Nephrite) Amber and Rubies to Central Asia A.D. 700 to Present
Bay of Bengal
Indian Ocean
Pearls
MALDIVE ISLANDS
Cowries
LEGEND
Great Wall of China
Silk Route
Trade Route
Present-Day City
Archaeological Site: Beadmaking and/or Distribution Center
Gold Movement of Beads and/or Bead Materials
Gold Source or archaeological Concentration of Materials
SARMATIA Region
Mountains
N
S
E
W

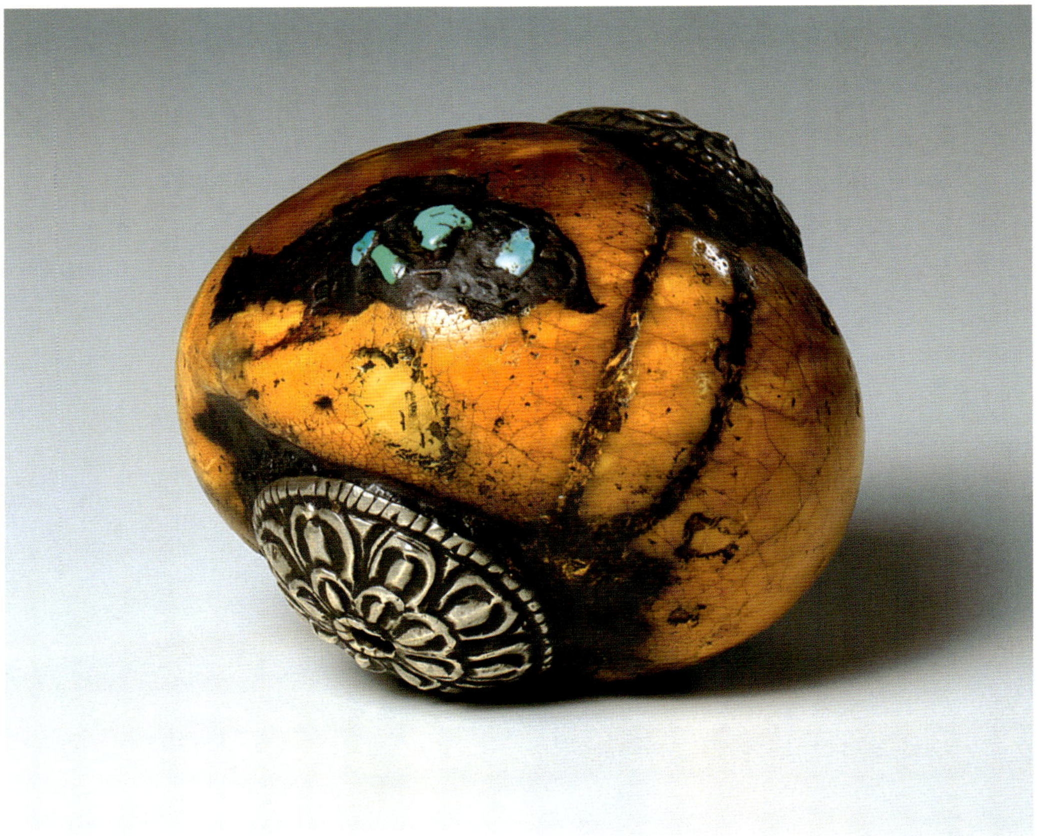

207. *A Tibetan amber bead capped with silver and inlaid with turquoise. The embellishment of surfaces is seen frequently in Himalayan adornment. The larger the bead, the greater its amuletic and status value. Diameter, 9.5 cm. Collection Mimi Lipton, London*

OPPOSITE: 208. *Necklace worn by the great-great-grandmother of Lama Kinga Rinpoche. A note from the lama (a monk or holy man) translated from Tibetan reads: "We don't know how old the actual ambers are, but we do know that this necklace has been with our* labrang *("family") for more than one hundred years. The design of the vase-shaped* dZi *beads is prehistoric."[1]*

This necklace includes coral, amber, lapis lazuli, and dZi *beads, including two barrel-shaped* dZi *with very rare "lotus" patterns and two less precious* dZi *on the upper part of the necklace with designs resembling the "horse tooth" pattern. The satin ribbon has the wax seal of the lama. Center amber bead: length, 9 cm. Collection Ivory Freidus*

routes. Phoenician and Egyptian glass beads have been excavated in the Warring States period (481–221 B.C.) and Han dynasty (206 B.C.–A.D. 220) tombs.[3] Under the Kushan dynasty, which controlled territories from northern India to central Asia during the second century A.D., there was intensive trade between India and the eastern provinces of the Roman Empire. This is seen in the discovery at Kara Bulak, near Ferghana in Turkmenistan, of beads made of carnelian, agate, lapis lazuli, rock crystal, faience, gold-in-glass, and millefiori glass. They were all imported from India, Afghanistan, and the Roman Mediterranean world and can be dated, for the most part, to between the first and second centuries A.D.[4]

With the end of the Kushan period in the fourth century, the main silk routes came under the control of nomadic Turkish tribes who arrived in central Asia as part of the great movement of populations during the Migrations Period. Under tribal rule, the silk routes were extended into the Himalayan kingdoms of Tibet and Nepal, while international trade flourished between Byzantium, Sasanian Persia, India, Samarkand, and the Far East. Beads from the West are found in China, Korea, and Japan through the eighth century. However, following the establishment of more economic sea routes by the tenth century and periods of Chinese isolationism, East-West trade via the silk routes greatly diminished.

Buddhism and Beads

From A.D. 100 to 700, the expansion of trade routes through central Asia was accompanied by the introduction of Hinduism and the spread of Buddhism. Although Islam eventually dominated western central Asia, and Hinduism and Christianity developed some followers, Buddhism made the greatest impact on the region as a whole.[5]

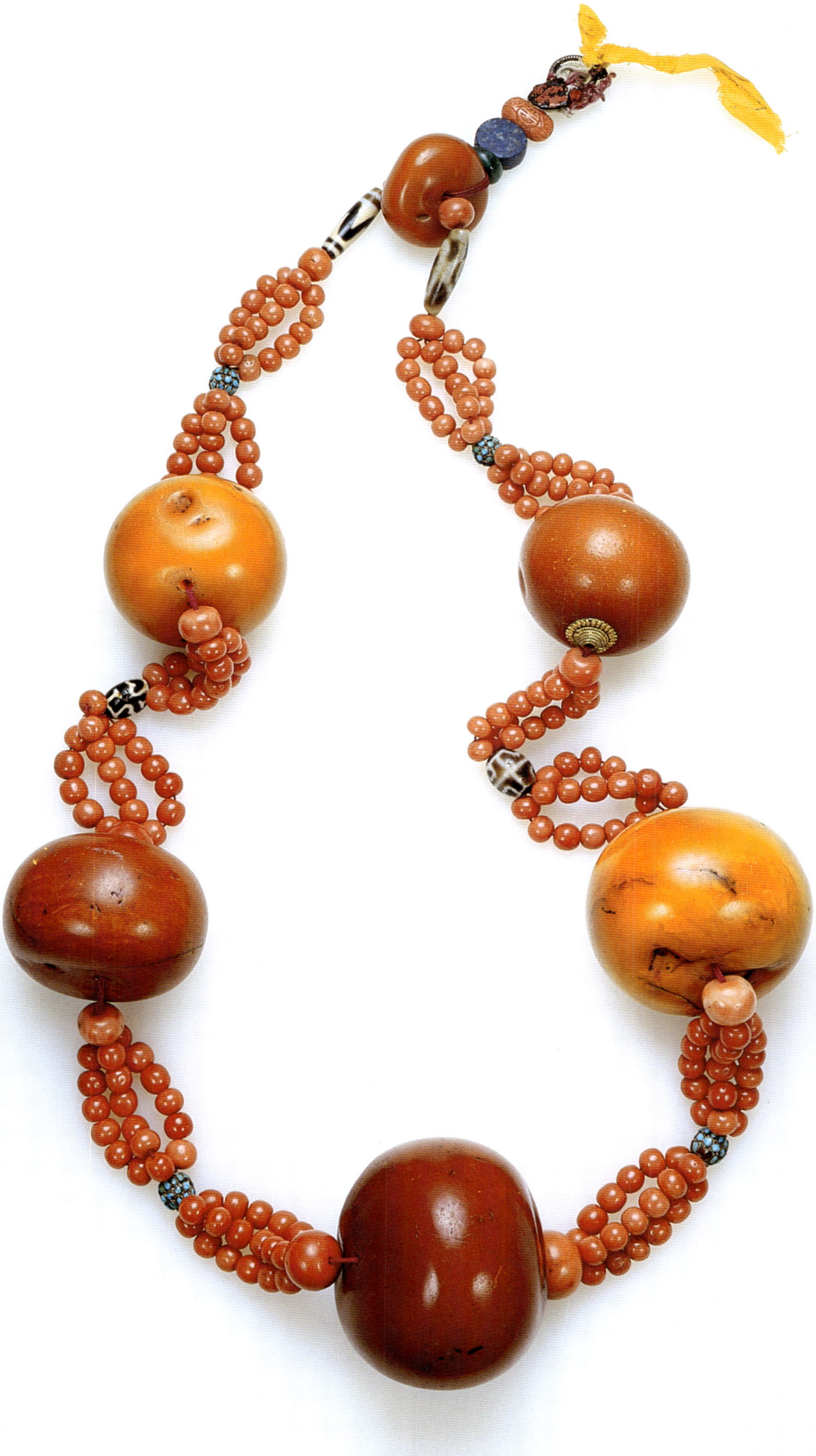

Central Asian Buddhism, rooted in Tibet, was a blend of orthodox Buddhist teachings adapted to indigenous folk practices as well as the ancient Bon religion. (Bon, in its early phases, shared many similarities with animism and shamanistic thought.)[6] This complex set of beliefs profoundly influenced adornment. Living in rugged and sometimes treacherous country, Tibetans attributed numerous misfortunes to evil spirits that resided in the environment, their animal herds, and even in their own bodies. By wearing amulets in the form of prayer boxes or beads, they believed dangerous spirits could be appeased or suppressed. Jewelry was therefore an important part of people's daily dress, and in most Himalayan countries even the humblest citizens owned a few amuletic turquoise beads.[7]

Turquoise and coral, both thought to have significant protective powers, were applied to religious images and used in many ritual objects. Most sculptures of Buddhist and Hindu gods in central Asia display beads and are often inlaid with semiprecious stones.[8] The beads are archetypal and mirror the colors of primal substances: red (coral) represents blood, fire, and light; blue (turquoise) is for water, sky, and air; yellow (amber) is for earth. By wearing beads made from these precious or semiprecious stones, people affirmed their connections to the spiritual realm. By serving as a daily reminder, jewels put people in touch with spirits and deities. Jewels were offered to be set into statues as an act of devotion and also as a way to impart the powers of these stones to the image itself. This gave the image further amuletic power that in turn could help the worshiper.

Tibet

Despite its awesome physical barriers, Tibet was a closed country for only limited periods. Tibetan records from before the seventh century A.D. are rare, but there is evidence that relations existed between tribes of the central Tibetan valleys and both the Chinese and Greco-Roman civilizations. Ties with India were also important and eventually led to the adoption of Buddhism in the eighth century. The Mongolians on several occasions played important roles in Tibetan political affairs, and they adopted Tibetan Buddhism toward the end of the sixteenth century. European Christian missionaries were also active in Tibet during the seventeenth and eighteenth centuries. China, Tibet's great neighbor, saw her influence wax and wane, but relations between the two countries extend from prehistory to the present.[9] Formal ties were established during the Tang dynasty (A.D. 618–907).

Until it was absorbed into China in 1959, Tibet was a Buddhist theocracy ruled jointly by a powerful hierarchy of lamas (monks) and lay nobility that recognized the Dalai Lama as their spiritual and temporal leader. It was by far the most influential country in the eastern regions of central Asia, with Ladakh, Bhutan, Sikkim, Nepal, Mongolia, and the Chinese provinces of Qinghai and Sichuan functioning to varying degrees as cultural outposts of Tibet.[10]

Jewelry in these countries shared important similarities with the jewelry of Tibet. All personal adornment had religious significance, and rosaries were used widely for both counting prayers and making numerical calculations. "Court beads" worn in China by the ruling Manchurian nobles and high officials during the Qing dynasty (A.D. 1644–1912) were in fact elaborate Tibetan rosaries.[11]

Since Tibet's subsistence needs, except for tea, were met from within the country, most trade in the region involved importing luxury goods, including beads and bead materials.[12] Tibetan jewelry is often monumental in scale, to express the rank of the owner, and sturdy enough to withstand life on the road. It is characterized by decorative surface designs, bold handling of precious and semiprecious stones, and the liberal use of turquoise, coral, and amber beads. Tibetan beads are simple and well proportioned. There

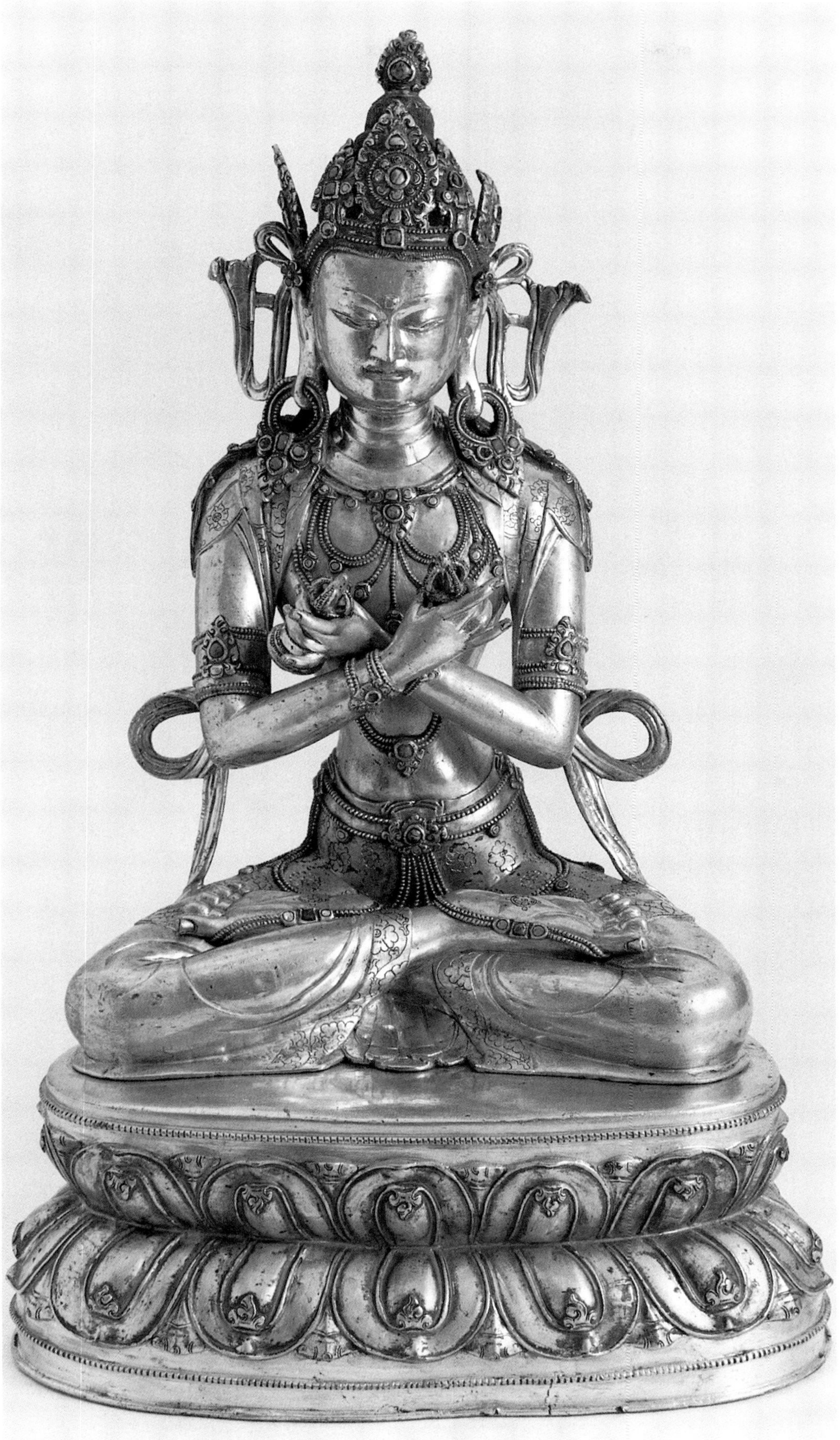

209. *A gilded copper representation of the Buddha, richly ornamented with turquoise and coral beads. Central Asian religious statues are frequently adorned with semiprecious stones, which have their own spiritual powers, thereby enhancing the spiritual power of the image itself. Height, 47.7 cm. Collection the Newark Museum, New Jersey*

OVERLEAF: 210. *This necklace from Ladakh combines an extremely unusual variety of beads, including silver-disked amber inlaid with turquoise, coral, agates, pearls, wood, and silver. The four silver-capped, cream-colored beads are of an unidentified material, probably stone or stained bone. The center bead is a* dZi *bead. Two* phum *("lesser* dZi*") beads are near the top of the necklace, and there is one imitation* phum*. Among the appliances hanging from the chain is an ear cleaner. The safety chains dangling from the bottom fasten the necklace to the wearer's robe. Length, 106 cm. Collection Ivory Freidus*

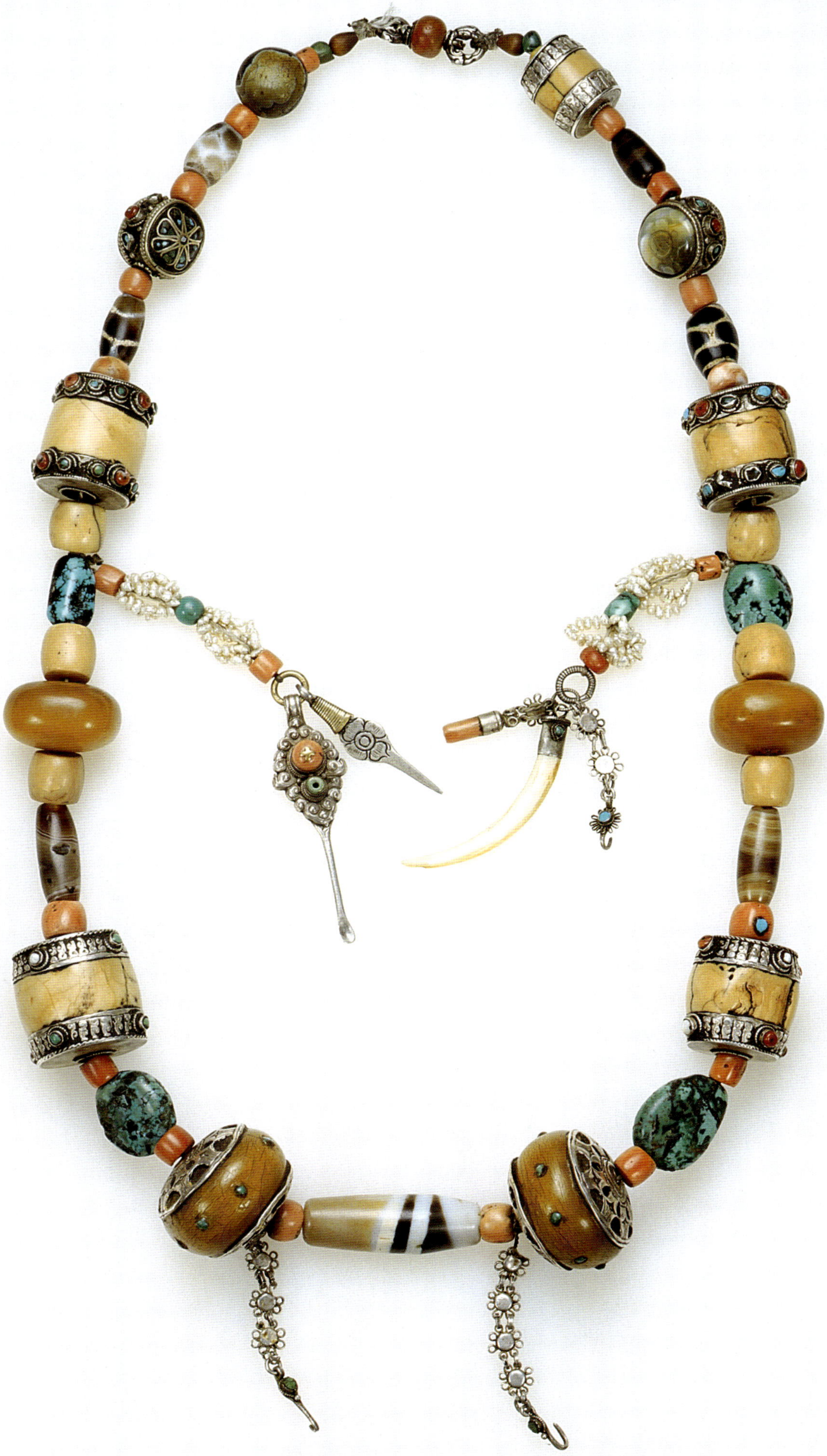

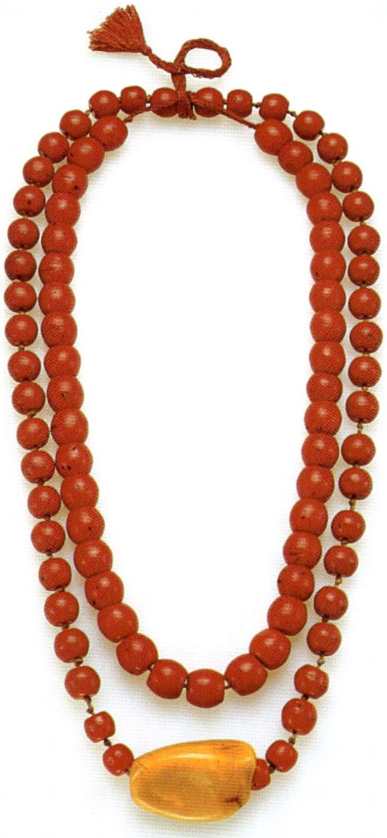

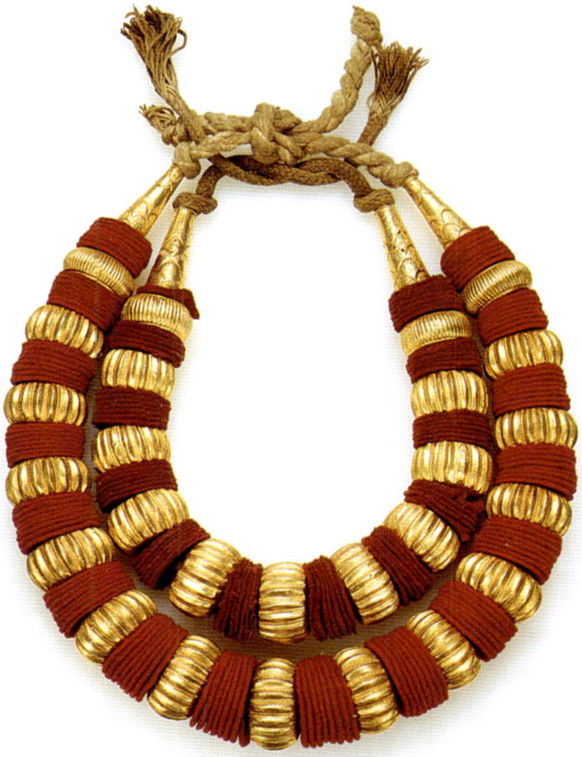

is an exuberance of color in the jewelry, which almost acts as an antidote to the stark landscape, and its sophisticated designs are derived primarily from India and China.[13]

Large quantities of beads were worn by all Tibetans. They were made from the richest materials a family could afford. Thus, Tibet's wealthier urban and village inhabitants generally wore more refined and intricate jewelry than the nomadic peoples, who constituted three-quarters of the country's population. Noblewomen wore necklaces of huge amber and coral beads, sometimes almost long enough to reach the ground.[14] Strings of seed pearls were attached to gold prayer boxes inlaid with turquoise and precious stones (plate 214). The actual value of the jewelry lay not in the precious stones, which were sometimes glass simulants, but in the specific components: the intensity of blue in the turquoise set into the face of the charm box; the gold weight of the box; and the size of the red coral and *dZi* beads of the necklace on which the box was strung. Glass simulants were accepted as colorful and affordable exotic imports. Furthermore, since most Tibetans were not familiar with cut gems, they did not know (or care) about their value. Their main concern was that necklaces look good; whether glass or real stones were used was almost secondary.[15]

Beads were also worn by Tibetan women in their hair and on headdresses, serving as examples of wealth and emblems of tribal or communal identity. Designs varied widely from one locality to another. The following description of a wealthy woman's headdress at a village festival gives an idea of its elaborate character:

> The prevailing form consisted of two, or sometimes three, circular bands of plaited hair placed across the head and richly studded with pearls.... Corals

ABOVE LEFT: 211. *Necklaces from Nepal; the bottom one made of an amber bead flanked by red glass beads from the 1970–80s (a substitute for the more precious coral); the top strand contains only the glass beads. Typical bead: diameter, 2 cm. Collection Tambaran Gallery, New York*

ABOVE RIGHT: 212. *Contemporary gold melon beads with protective red velvet fillers, from eastern Nepal. Nepalese, particularly the Hindus, consider gold a sacred metal. Beads of this type are still frequently worn. Typical bead: diameter, 3.5 cm. Collection Ivory Freidus*

> and turquoise beads as large as hens' eggs, pearl drops, and various sorts of amber and jade encircled their heads like halos of light over the heads of goddesses. These circles were attached to a circular headband, from which six or eight strings of pearls and regularly shaped pieces of turquoise and other precious stones hung down over the forehead.[16]

Turquoise, coral, and amber beads had protective value. Coral, imported from Italy, was generally reserved for the wealthy; the less affluent used coral-colored glass beads. Marco Polo, writing in the thirteenth century, described the esteem accorded coral beads in Tibet: "Coral...is very dear, because they place it round the neck of their women and their idols, and hold it as precious stone."[17]

Turquoise was worn extensively, and even the poorest Tibetan owned a few turquoise beads. The early history and legends of Tibet include many references to turquoise beads. One historian relates the following anecdote:

> In the seventh century, the powerful Tibetan King Songtsan Gampo married a Chinese princess. According to the Tibetan story of his wooing, he was required, in order to win the hand of his bride, to pass a silk thread through a coil of perforated turquoise beads arranged in concentric circles; the problem was solved by tying the thread to a queen ant which he placed in the perforation of the first turquoise, gently blowing into the hole, till to the amazement of the lookers-on, the ant came out at the other end of the coil, dragging the thread along.[18]

Turquoise beads also functioned as barter currency in parts of Tibet. A European visitor gave the following advice in 1891: "No traveler going from China into Tibet should omit laying in a supply of turquoise beads, for with them he can buy better than with money all the necessities of life."[19]

Only the finest *dZi* beads were more valued than beads of coral and turquoise. A black-and-white or brown bead of etched or treated agate, found in a limited variety of shapes but with a wide range of patterns, the *dZi* bead is revered in Tibet; it is considered a "precious jewel of supernatural origin" (plate 216). Few beads have provoked more scholarly controversy: their origin, method of manufacture, and even the precise definition of *dZi* beads are hotly debated. A prime reason for this controversy is that Tibetan religious laws do not permit archaeological excavations, so all information on them is from written, often vague descriptions and orally transmitted folktales. The mysterious and apparently ancient patterns found on most *dZi* beads suggest connections with the shamanism and sorcery of Tibet's pre-Buddhist, animist religion.

The same philosophies that prevent archaeological excavations have been responsible for Tibet's active international trade in beads and bead materials. Despite plentiful natural resources, especially gold, most minerals were imported because mining was discouraged in the belief that the metals would disappear if their "roots" were extracted from the soil. Earth spirits, it was believed, would resent the miners' intrusion and might wreak havoc on the country.[20]

For centuries, Newari craftsmen of Nepal made metal jewelry for Tibetans, using metalworking processes that included repoussé, damascene, engraving, and occasionally granulation. Newari metalsmiths traveled among villages and tribes, at times settling among them and thereby joining the Chinese and Mongolians in influencing Tibetan art. The Newars settled permanently in Lhasa, where their services were always in demand, not only for jewelry, but also for providing ritual items used by the Buddhist clergy.

Although metalsmithing was mostly the work of specialists or village blacksmiths, stone beadmaking required fewer specialized skills, and quantities of beads in softer materials were made by local Tibetan artisans working at home. It was frequently an off-season occupation for farmers and villagers. Nomads also made beads by drilling, smoothing, and polishing traded-in chunks of amber or nodules of turquoise.

Since the annexation of Tibet by China in 1959 and the subsequent elimination of the nobility from Tibetan society, most jewelry, particularly that of the elite in the cities, has disappeared. The use of all adornment, including beads, was further outlawed during the Cultural Revolution and the Chinese repression of Buddhism in the 1960s. Even the carrying of prayer beads (*malas*) was forbidden. In the past few years, however, jewelry is reemerging, although it remains to be seen to what degree this will be permitted to continue.

Tibetan beads continue to be worn primarily by those living in exile within the southern Himalayan borderlands. An important exception, however, is found in the beads of the nomads (plate 218). Isolated in the vast uplands of Tibet and China, various nomadic groups, difficult for the Communist government to control and monitor, continue to wear traditional beaded necklaces.

Nepal

Nepal has a long history of cultural ties with India, China, and Tibet, which is reflected in Nepalese jewelry. Tradition relates that Buddha was born in 567 B.C., a prince of the Sakya clan on the southern frontier of Nepal. His teachings developed into a national religion in India by the third century B.C. Legend also has it that Buddhism arrived in Nepal via China during the middle of the seventh century A.D. when the first king of Tibet, Songtsan Gampo, married a Nepalese and a Chinese princess who were both Buddhists.

Buddhism became the predominant faith in Nepal, although never the country's sole religion. Due to the country's close association with India, many Nepalese rulers were Hindus and the social organization was based on a Hindu caste system. Essentially, the two religions were supportive of each other, as symbolized in the combinations of Buddhist and Hindu elements in most religious artifacts. Like the statues of Tibet, most Nepalese sculptures of gods and goddesses are depicted with quantities of beads.[21]

The Kathmandu Valley, the most populous region in Nepal, has long been an important center for trade and for the shelter of political refugees. The resulting mélange of peoples and cultures is mirrored in adornment. For many years, migrant groups have arrived in Kathmandu with their "portable banks"—jewelry and beads. Since 1959, Kathmandu has been one of the principal centers for Tibetan Buddhists outside of Tibet, and consequently it is a major repository for fine Tibetan beads. During religious festivals, when Buddhists from throughout Nepal and neighboring Sikkim, Bhutan, and Ladakh gather in Kathmandu wearing their turquoise and coral necklaces, the full splendor of Tibetan beads can be seen.

While the ethnic origins of Nepalese jewelry are complex and owe much to other cultures, the Himalayan kingdom has its own ancient traditions. For centuries, Nepalese craftsmanship influenced the arts of Tibet and China. Chinese travelers visiting Nepal in the seventh century A.D. were awed by its architecture and adornment. The palace, said Yuan Chwang, was "seven stories tall and ornamented with gems and pearls.... The King... wore beads of pearls, rock crystal, coral, jade, and amber."[22]

The Newars, the original inhabitants of the Kathmandu Valley, were responsible for creating most Nepalese and Tibetan metal jewelry. For the Nepalese, particularly Hindus, gold has always been a very important, even sacred metal. Thus, in religious images, metals were preferred to stone. Goldsmiths, silversmiths, and bronzeworkers developed their skills to a fine degree. Gold was coveted for jewelry in Nepal, and working with it

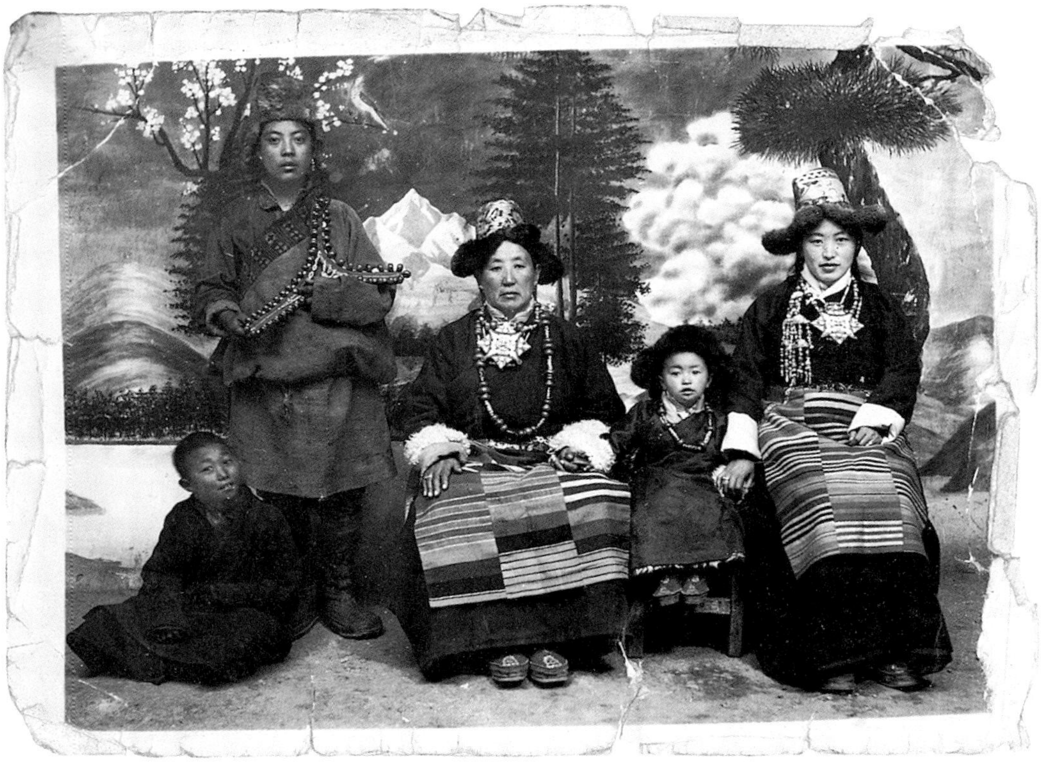

213. *A noblewoman (far right) from Lhasa, the capital of Tibet, with her mother and young daughter, c. 1949. A servant (standing) holds her headdress, which identifies her as a resident of Lhasa. Her beads and jeweled prayer box, similar to the one in plate 214, reflect her status and wealth. Before the Communist Chinese invasion in 1950, a complex ranking system characterized the Lhasa aristocracy. Prescribed styles of clothing and jewelry conveyed the wearer's status.*[11]

OPPOSITE: 214. *A gold prayer box (*gahu*), containing a written prayer to appease the evil spirits, set with turquoise, emeralds, rubies, and diamonds and suspended from a necklace of pearls, coral, emeralds, naturally banded agate, and two types of* dZi *beads. Here, the gems are real, but they were often glass simulations. The lavish shoulder ornament on the left, called a* tru tru, *consists of jade plaques and pearls, as well as* dZi, *coral, jade, tourmaline, sapphire, emerald, ruby, and citron beads. It is derived in form from an earlier silver version thought to have originated in Mongolia.*

Two jeweled straps with hooks anchor the gahu *to the wearer's clothing. To compensate for the* tru tru*'s weight on the neck (it sometimes reaches to the waist), it also hooks onto clothing at the shoulder. Cascading down the torso, it appears to be part of the necklace. Prayer box: width, 15.5 cm. Collection Ivory Freidus*

became a specialty of Newari craftsmen. Although gold beads are used in specific types of necklaces, the most popular bead materials are still the familiar Himalayan combination of imported turquoise, coral, and amber, in addition to shell, bone, and glass. Customers ask for widely recognized designs for their made-to-order jewelry, often supplying craftsmen with the stones and metals to be used.[23]

A distinctive beaded necklace unique to Nepal is the *tilari*, composed of multiple strands of red glass beads joined by a cylinder formed from seven gold or silver beads. Worn by most Nepalese women, the *tilari*, combined with vermilion powder applied to the hair, indicates the wearer is married. A Nepalese man gives a *tilari* to his bride on their wedding day, and the wearing of a *tilari* expresses a wife's wish for her husband's longevity.[24]

Western Central Asia: Ancient Turkmenistan and Afghanistan

Archaeologists have worked in the western lands since the nineteenth century and have been able to create a chronology for many bead forms. Turkmenistan and Afghanistan are famous for beautiful stone beads, many of which were traded south to Mesopotamia, Iran, and the Mediterranean as early as the third millennium B.C.

The first beads documented in Turkmenistan and Afghanistan are from the Neolithic site of Djeitun in Turkmenistan, the earliest agricultural community in central Asia. Beads excavated at Djeitun, dating to 5000 B.C., include crudely shaped disks, plaques, and tubes of bone, marine shell, stone (including turquoise), and clay. There were also zoomorphic pendants.[25]

By the late fifth millennium B.C., southern Turkmenistan was a prosperous region of agricultural oases and developed towns. Brightly colored pottery and quantities of beads,

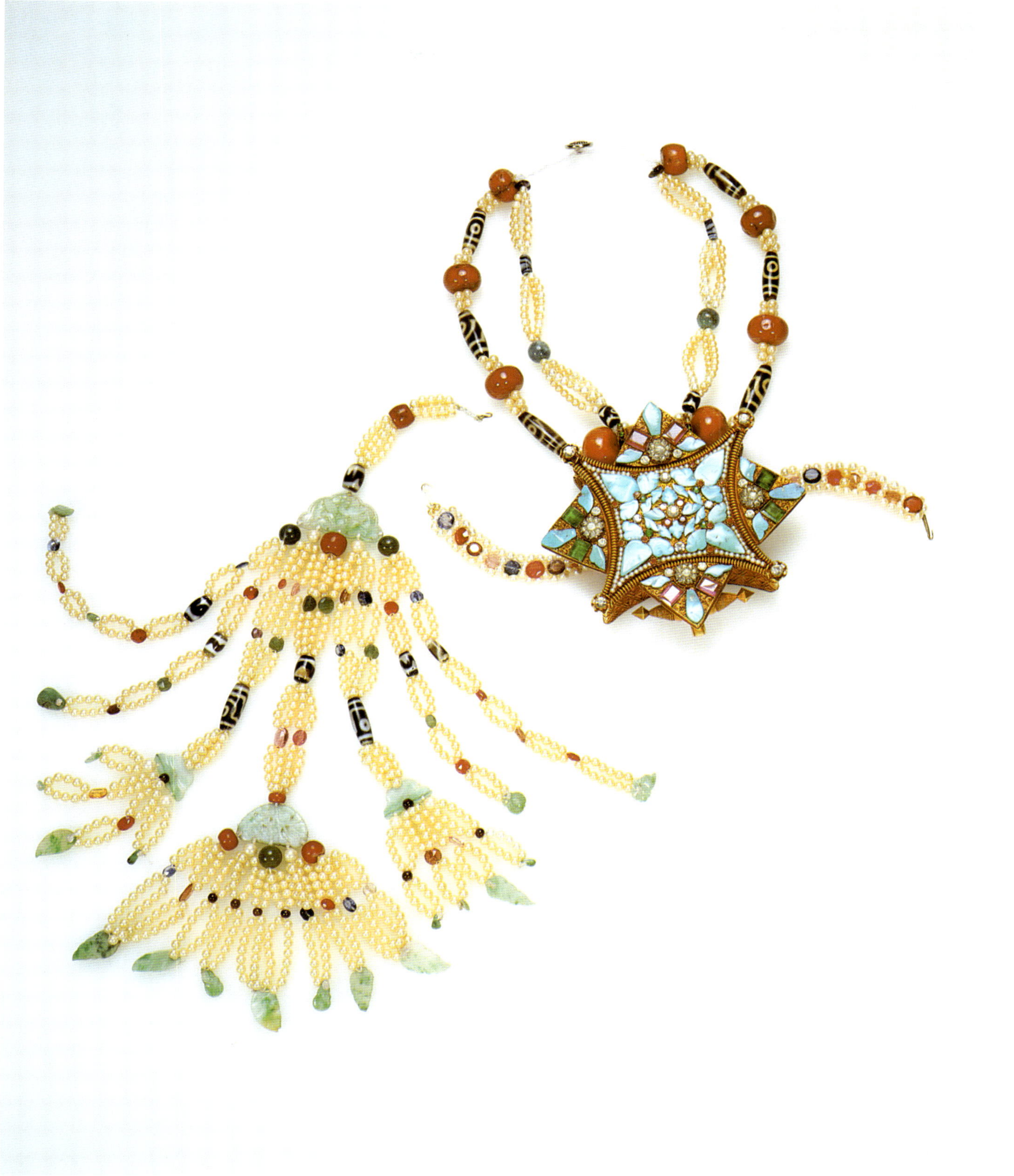

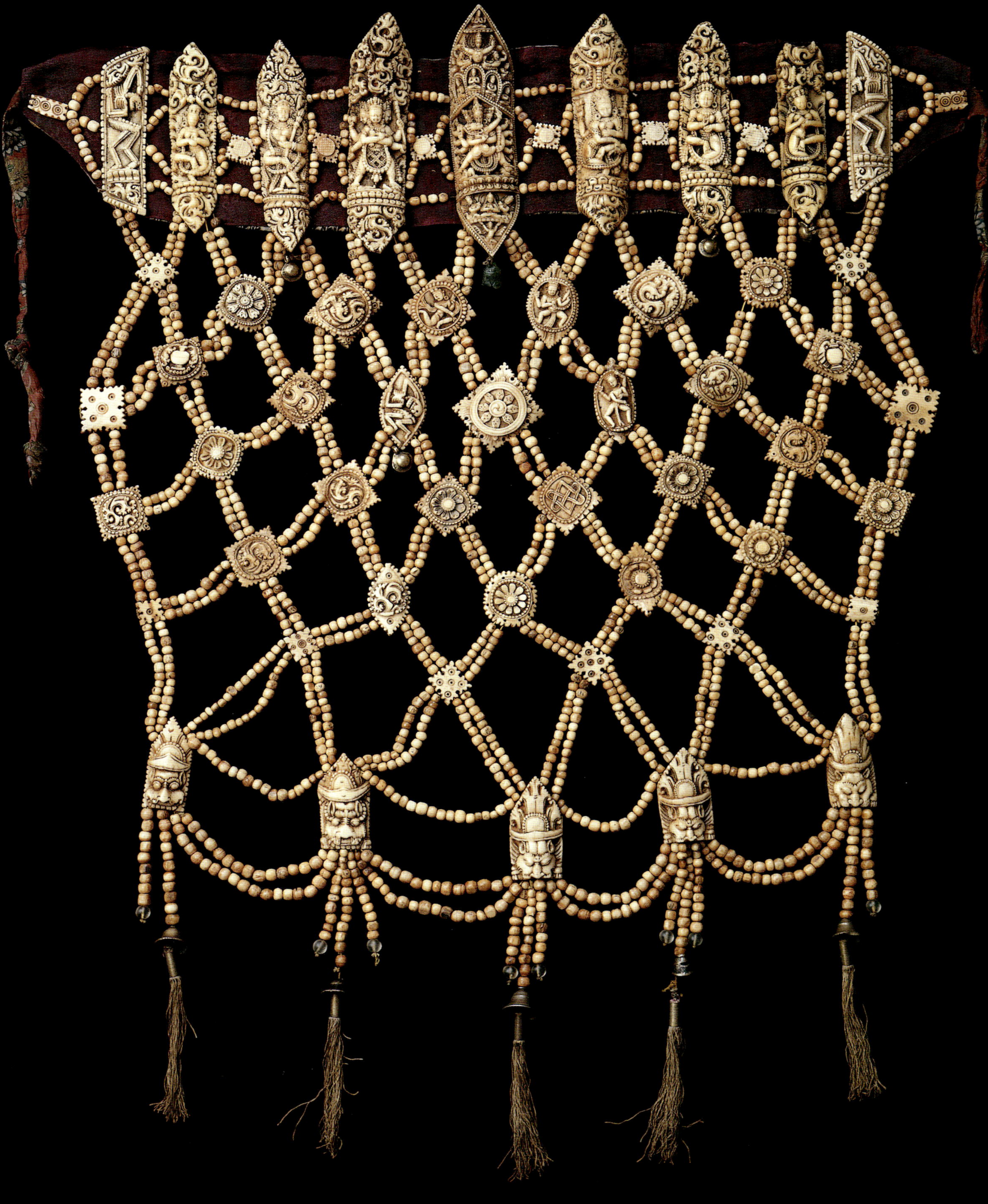

many of which resemble contemporaneous forms in northern Iran, were made. In fact, archaeological evidence suggests that most people in southern Turkmenistan and northeastern Iran belonged at this time to a single culture with local variations. By 4000 B.C., beads of carnelian and other semiprecious stones began to appear in Turkmenistan.[26]

215. *A beautiful apron of beads made from human bones. Such aprons were worn by Tibetan tantric priests during ceremonies to drive away evil spirits. The use of human bones for ritual objects symbolizes the transient nature of earthly life.[III] Length, 72 cm. Collection Mimi Lipton, London*

The Anau and Namazga cultures used beads by the fourth millennium. Turquoise beads, in particular, are known from every phase of the Anau culture, including cylindrical, barrel, annular, disk, and bean-shaped forms. Children's bodies were often buried with turquoise and other beads under the earthen floors of dwellings.[27]

By 3000 to 2500 B.C., many beads in western regions of central Asia were made of white alabaster (gypsum) with incised geometric designs, but others were made of turquoise, azurite, quartz, agate, or chalcedony. During this period, the peoples of southern Turkmenistan carried on active trade relations with the communities of Sialk and Hissar in northern Iran and were probably in contact with Sumerian Mesopotamia via the trade routes that carried lapis lazuli from Afghanistan.[28]

Between 2300 and 1800 B.C., graves of elite people in southern Turkmenistan included clay and stone seals and quantities of well-made semiprecious stone beads. A woman's grave at Altin-depe, dating to about 2100 B.C., contained one hundred agate, carnelian, and lapis lazuli beads, some capped with gold.[29]

This richness in grave goods marks the beginning of urban life in central Asia and accompanies higher levels of agricultural productivity, monumental architecture (resembling the ziggurats of southern Mesopotamia), and specialized craftsmanship. The increase in cultural sophistication paralleled and was obviously brought about by a significant expansion in trade with Iran, the Indus Valley, and Mesopotamia.[30]

Archaeological sites in Afghanistan have recently yielded quantities of exquisitely made stone beads, many of which appear to have been traded to the great civilizations of western Asia and India. Many etched carnelian beads, for example, have been found in Afghanistan, Mesopotamia, and the Indus Valley. A remarkably sophisticated culture developed in Afghanistan by 3000 B.C., due in part to wealth attained through the export of mineral resources. By the fourth millennium, the finest deep blue lapis lazuli was quarried in the Badakhshan region of northeastern Afghanistan. Trade routes from many directions intersected in eastern and northern Afghanistan and formed the lapis routes, which not only carried lapis lazuli to Egypt, the Near East, and the Indus Valley, but also brought finished beads of agate and rock crystal to the Mediterranean region.[31]

Remarkably beautiful beads of identical shapes, craftsmanship, and materials (lapis lazuli, carnelian, agate, gold, and silver) occur in aristocratic burials at the royal tombs of Ur, dating between 2500 and 1800 B.C., and in contemporaneous sites in Turkmenistan and Afghanistan. Since these beads (particularly the distinctive agates) occur in the greatest quantity in Afghanistan, and the finest examples are frequently excavated there, this country was thought to be their place of origin. However, several scholars have recently challenged the concept of local Afghanistan manufacture of large hardstone beads including those of lenticular shape associated with the Namazga culture (Time Line 263, 264, 267). They instead suggest that these beads were imported, and most probably made in India.[32]

Both the quality and quantity of beads appear to have declined in southern Turkmenistan and Afghanistan by 1600 B.C., perhaps the result of the collapse of the Sumerian and Indus Valley civilizations. The decline of these first important societies of central Asia may also be associated with the emigration of Bronze Age tribes from the northern Mongolian steppes to western Asia in the mid-second millennium B.C.[33]

As trade with the western Asian states ended, the primary stimulus for making beads disappeared. Continued contact with northern Iran is suggested, however, by large, biconical steatite beads decorated with incised concentric circles from first-millennium sites in Turkmenistan that appear in identical forms in Iran.[34]

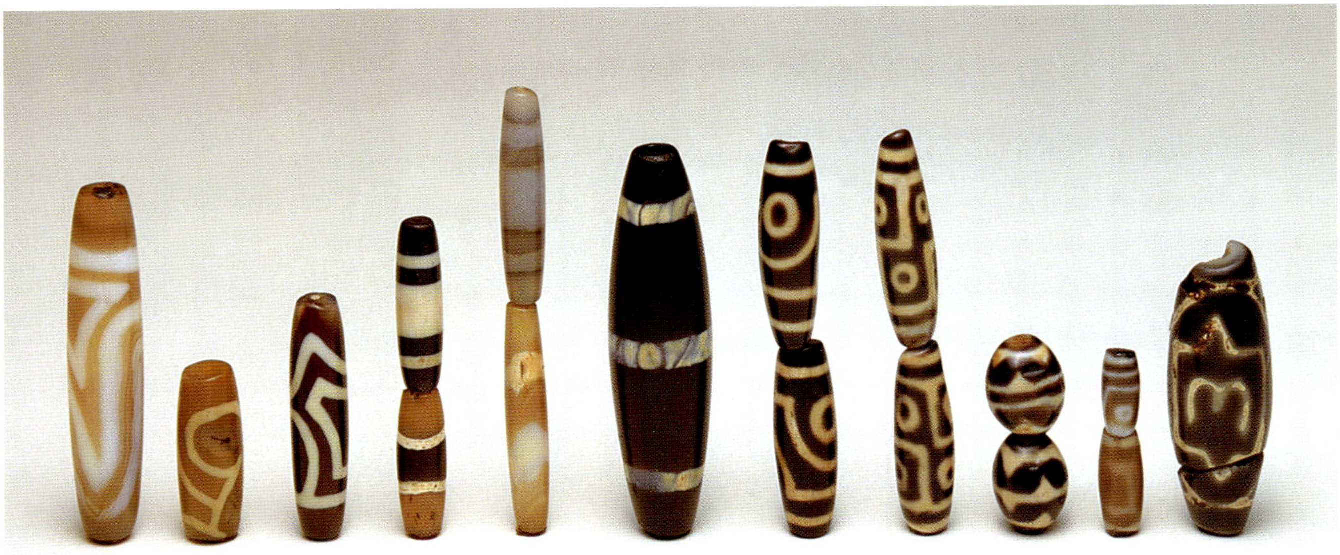

ABOVE: 216. *A collection of* dZi *beads.*[IV] *Left to right: (first two beads) asymmetrical pattern of white lines on tan background; asymmetrical pattern of white lines on blackened background; two blackened beads with applied white stripes; two beads with applied stripes and shapes characteristic of Indus Valley beads; blackened bead with applied white stripes; two-eyed* dZi*; six-eyed* dZi *showing circles ("eyes") and stylized eye and framing line patterns; round* dZi *with tiger stripes; two-eyed* dZi *(top) and "Earth Door, Sky Door" pattern; unusual* phum dZi *with a* W *in a cartouche. Far left bead: length, 3.7 cm. Collection David Ebbinghouse, Bloomington, Indiana*

RIGHT: 217. *Top to bottom: rare, "pure" nine-eyed* dZi*, considered the most precious type;* dZi *with stripes but no eyes; unusually shaped* dZi*, recalling bead forms of ancient Mesopotamia and Iran;*[V] *an unusual (heat-treated) agate bead. Second from top bead: length, 11.5 cm. Collection Ivory Freidus*

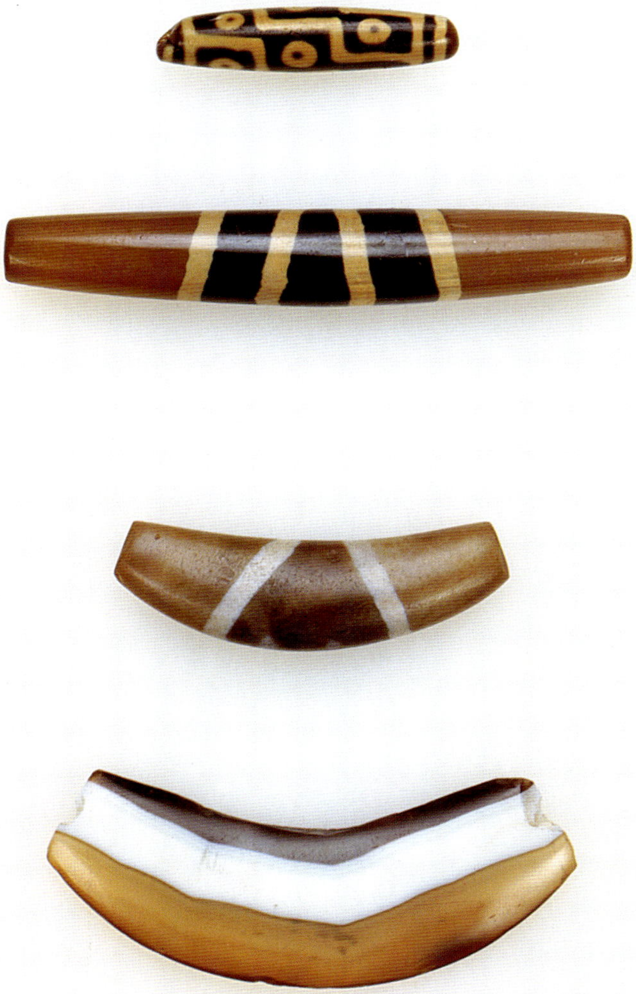

dZi Beads

The unique dZi *bead, a black-and-white (or dark brown) bead of "etched" or treated agate, is revered in Tibet. To Tibetans and other Himalayan peoples, the* dZi *is a "precious jewel of supernatural origin" with great power to protect its wearer from disaster.*[VI]

There is little precise information available on dZi *beads. They are found primarily in Tibet, but also in neighboring Bhutan, Ladakh, and Sikkim. Shepherds and farmers pick them up in the grasslands or while cultivating fields. Because* dZi *are found in the earth, Tibetans cannot conceive of them as man-made. Since knowledge of the bead is derived from oral traditions, few beads have provoked more controversy concerning their source, method of manufacture, and even precise definition.*

Mythical stories are usually told to explain the origin of dZi. *In ancient times, it is said* dZi *adorned the gods, who discarded them when they became blemished, thus explaining why they are seldom found in perfect condition. Another story is that* dZi *were originally insects that moved around like worms and became petrified.*[VII] *One Tibetan gave the following version: "There is a legend of a man on a horse who saw the bead move. If you don't cover it with dust, it will disappear. The man threw dust over the bead and caught it, and it petrified. But* dZi *beads do not remain with unlucky people. The same man traded the bead for so many yak. The point is, the bead was not meant to be with him—the animals were."*[VIII] *Other Tibetan tales concern unfortunates who sell a valuable* dZi, *only to become ill or die soon after.*[IX] *Tibetans are loath to sell prized* dZi *even for the highest prices.*

In some ways dZi *resemble etched carnelian beads traded between Mesopotamia, Afghanistan, and the Indus Valley during the third millennium* B.C. *(Bead Chart 600). Indian and Iranian craftsmen continued making these beads into the first millennium* A.D. *The techniques for making* dZi *beads may be derived from ancient Indian craftsmen; they are also found in India, Pakistan, and Turkmenistan.*[X]

The actual etching of the dZi *agate is accomplished by several methods, and scholars have classified all etched beads, including* dZi, *into several major types and subdivisions based upon their technique of manufacture.*[XI]

The exact origins and dates of dZi *remain elusive. Because Tibetans do not bury their dead and religious beliefs have long prevented archaeological excavations, no beads have been recovered in Tibet under controlled research circumstances. Chinese texts, however, mention* dZi *beads as early as the seventh century* A.D. *Legend suggests the beads (or the technical knowledge for making them) came to Tibet in very ancient times from Iran where the Bon faith, Tibet's pre-Buddhist religion, possibly originated as well.*[XII] *The antiquity of* dZi *beads has been suggested as a major reason for their great value throughout the Himalayan region.*

"Pure" dZi *beads (in the traditional Tibetan system for evaluating* dZi*) are regarded as the most valuable and desirable variety. To qualify as pure, a bead must be genuine etched agate and lie within a certain range of styles. It should also have a sharply delineated pattern, symmetrical shape, strong color, glossy surface, and no flaws. The nine-eyed* dZi *illustrated in plate 217 (top) is a pure* dZi *with the most highly desired pattern. Etched agate beads not considered pure are called* chung dZi, *or "less important* dZi."[XIII]

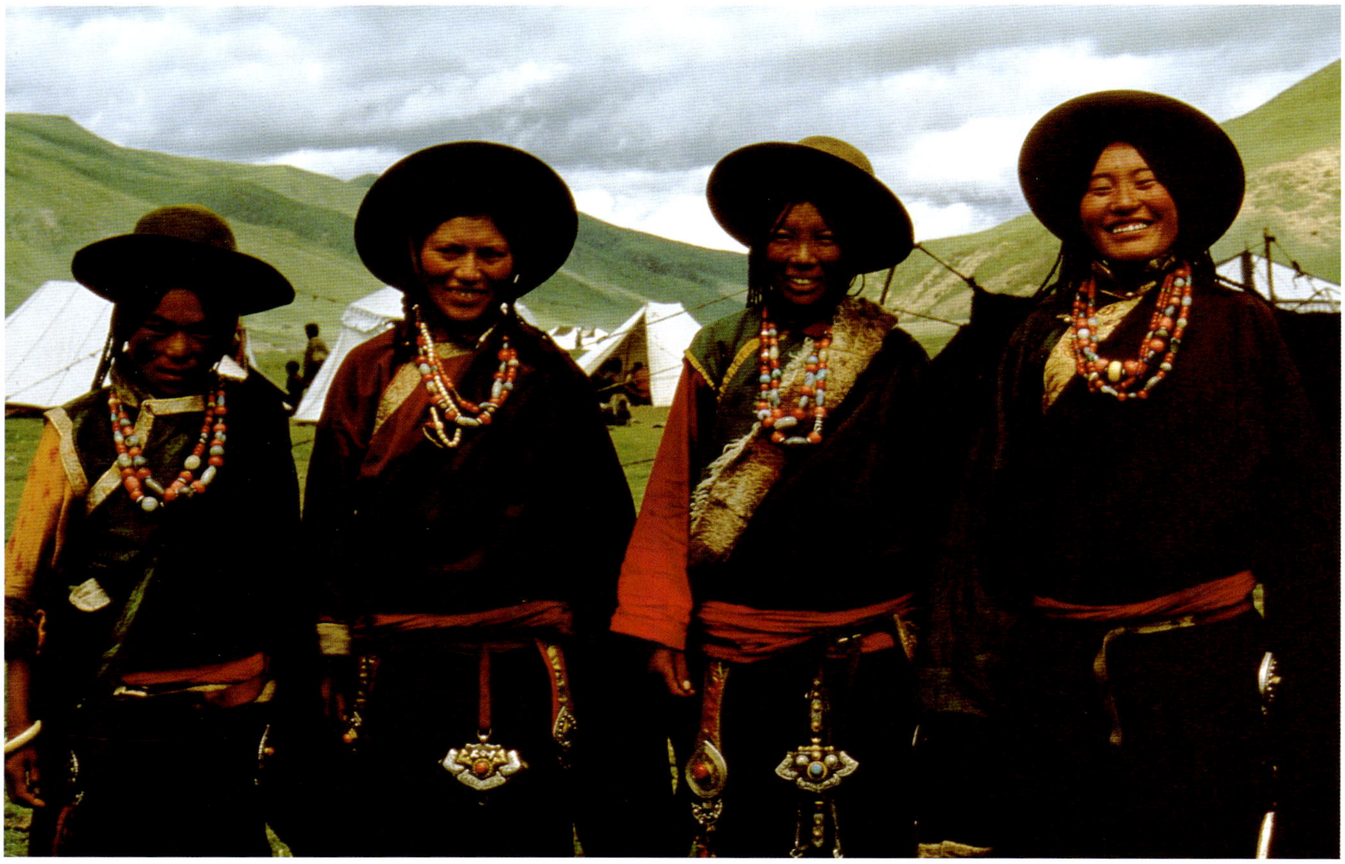
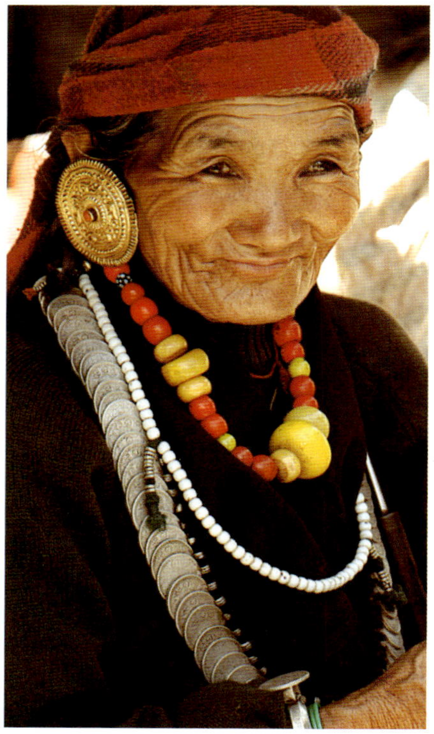
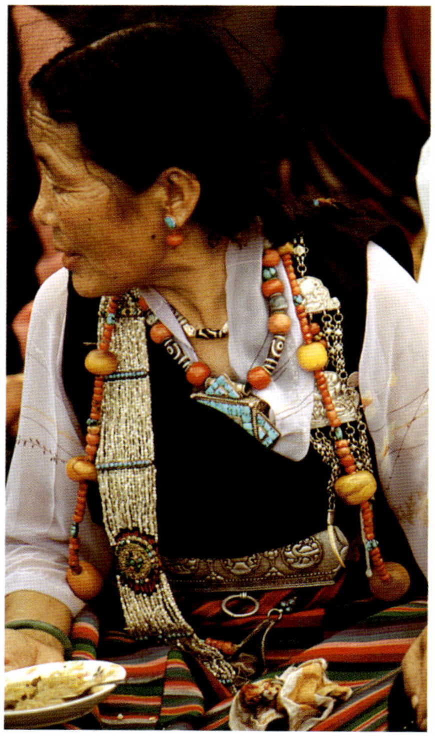
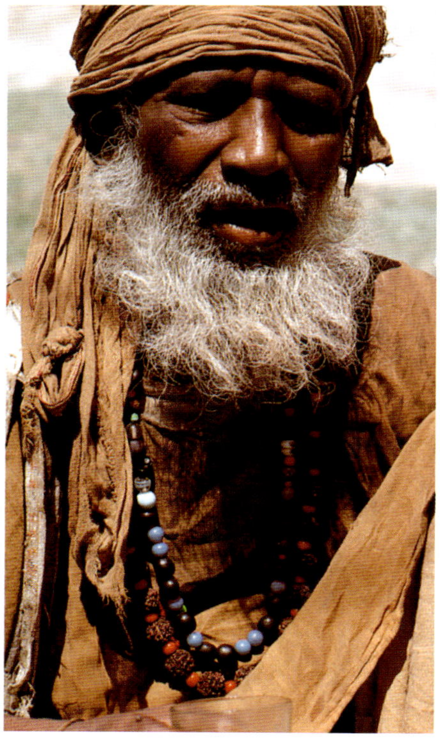

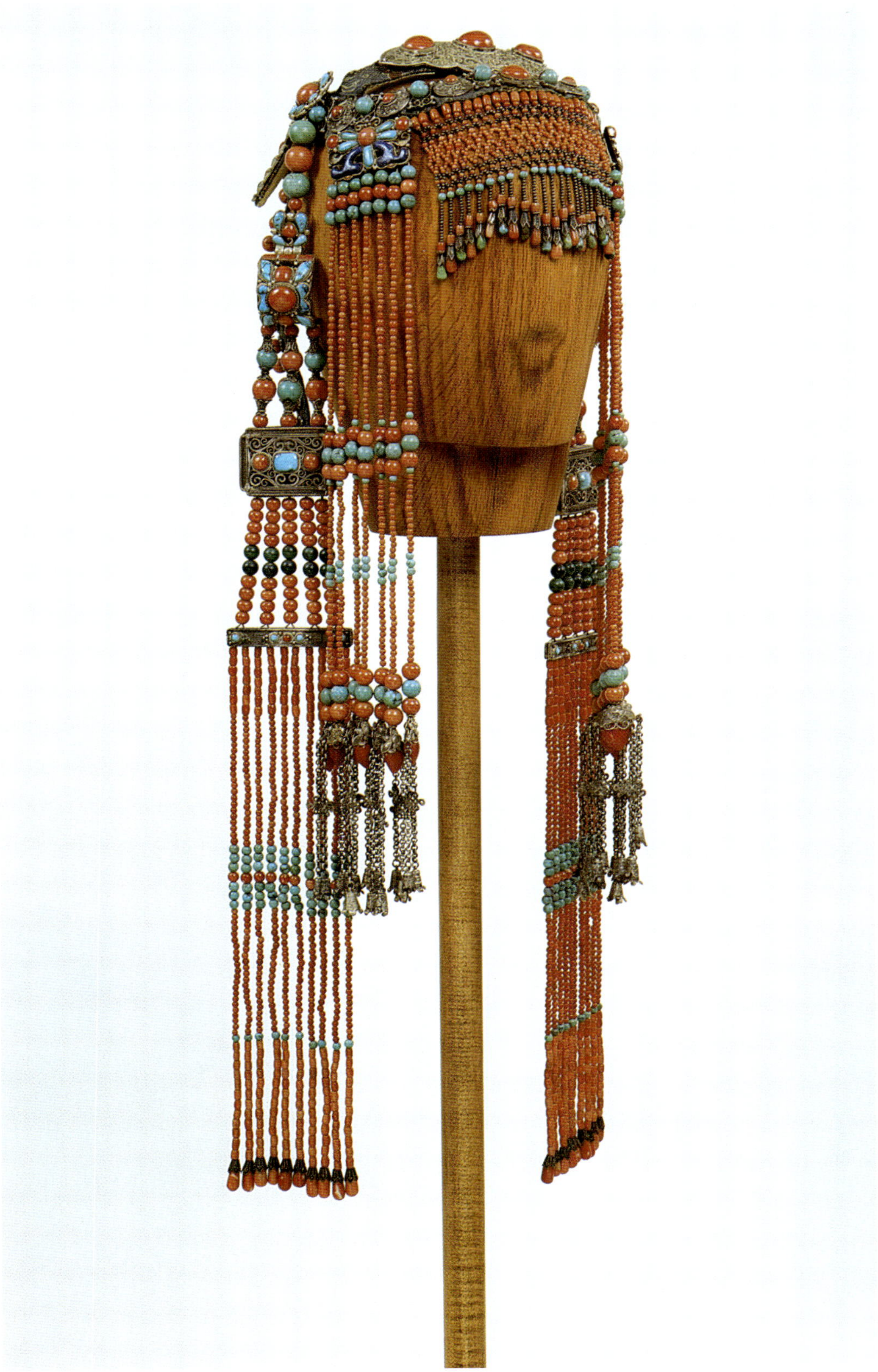

OPPOSITE TOP: 218. *Khampa women in eastern Tibet wearing typical coral and turquoise necklaces.*

OPPOSITE, BOTTOM LEFT: 219. *Sherpa woman wearing Nepalese gold earrings, a necklace made of Indian silver coins, simulated red coral and amber beads (made of glass and plastic or resin), and a Buddhist rosary of beads cut from chank shell. The silver beads dangling to her side help her keep count of thousands of mantras (sacred chants or prayers).*

OPPOSITE, BOTTOM CENTER: 220. *Tibetan woman wearing an aristocratic jewelry ensemble. A small gold charm box is suspended from her necklace of coral and turquoise beads with a matched pair of two-eyed* dZi *beads near its apex. On her throat, she wears three more two-eyed* dZi *strung with multiple strands of pearls.*

OPPOSITE, BOTTOM RIGHT: 221. *A wandering merchant, or* saddhu, *in Nepal, identifiable by his necklace of* rudraksha *seeds spaced with red coral (or glass simulations), which symbolize the red eyes of the Hindu god Siva, the deity of Yogis. He also wears glass simulations of black onyx and turquoise beads.*

LEFT: 222. *Mongolian tribal headdress. Throughout central Asia, the most spectacular part of a woman's ensemble was often her massive headdress, which varied in style from region to region and served to identify kinship groups or tribes. It was both an emblem of rank and a family's portable bank of coins, silver, and semiprecious and precious stones. Much wealth was concentrated in such showy adornment, particularly among the women of nomadic groups.*

In this very beautiful tribal headdress, the silver headband is inlaid with coral and turquoise and draped with coral, turquoise, and malachite beads. As in Tibet and Nepal, the combination of coral and turquoise occurs repeatedly throughout Mongolia. Length, 61 cm. Collection Ivory Freidus

RIGHT: 223. *A Nepalese woman wearing a necklace of turquoise, coral, and granulated silver beads with a center* dZi *bead. All Himalayan peoples love to collect and display their beads. They are worn daily to exorcise evil spirits while laboring in the fields, marketing, or attending a special gathering. Festivals are occasions to wear everything one owns. Many Nepalese wear the popular combination of turquoise, coral, and amber beads. When these are unaffordable, glass and plastic beads are substituted.*

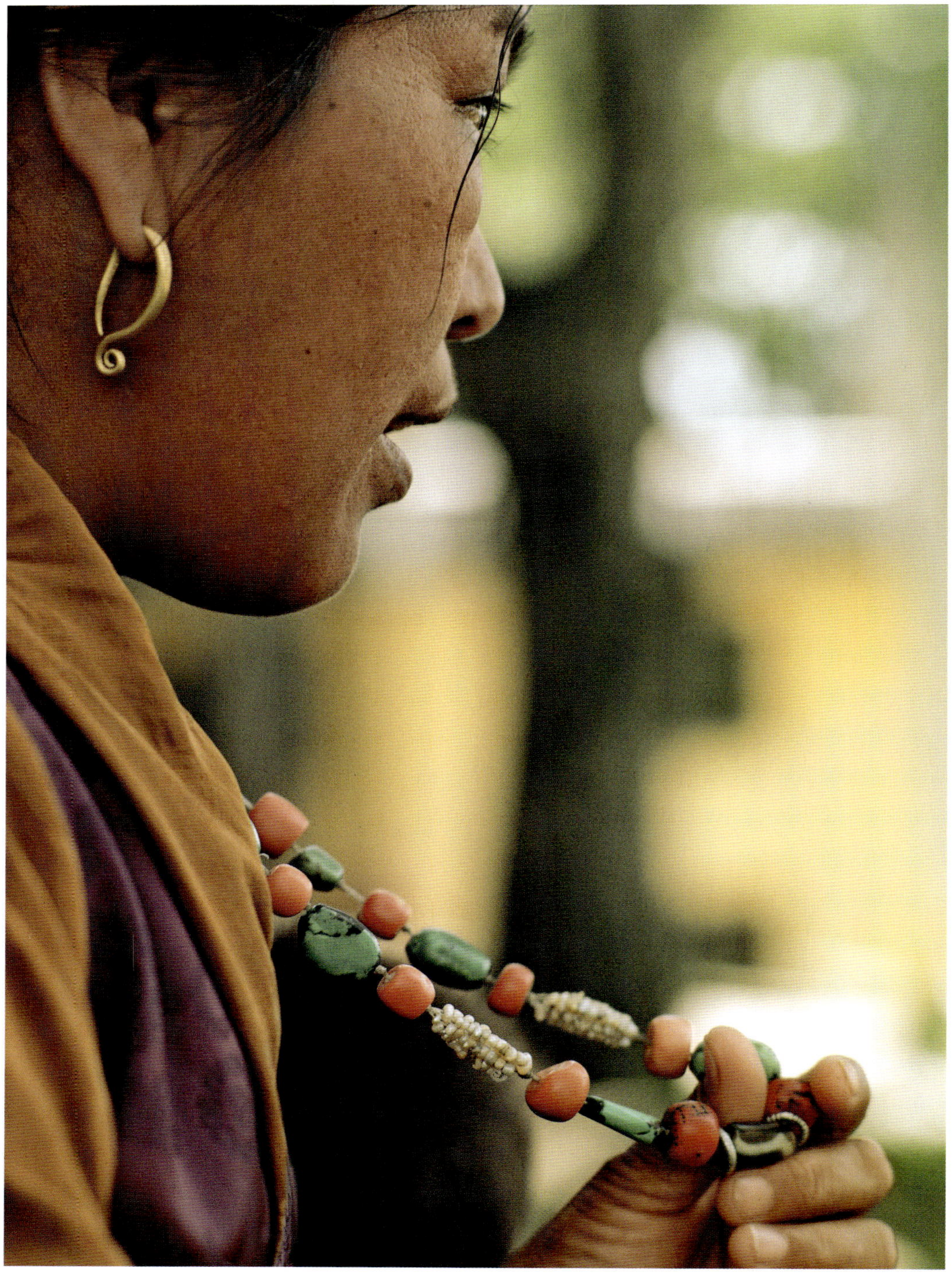

The Steppes

Life on the steppes depended on mobility and taking advantage of scattered, seasonal pastures. As early as 3000 B.C., the horse, ass, and camel were domesticated and had adapted to the semidesert conditions.[35] With the development of horseback riding by 1400 B.C., nomadic pastoralism as a way of life spread rapidly through the area.[36]

Ranging widely in search of grazing lands, the nomads frequently came into conflict with their settled neighbors, and from time to time they threatened the established civilizations in China, the Near East, and Europe: the Great Wall of China remains a powerful symbol of the efforts to defeat this threat. Many nomads were excellent merchants, and their traveling lifestyle encouraged the spread of ideas and culture. Stone, glass, and metal beads were distributed between Mongolia, China, Siberia, central Asia, and Europe through their extensive trade networks.

Adornment for both themselves and their animals was of prime importance to the peoples of the steppes, among whom were Scythians, Sarmatians, Mongols, and Turks. Burials from several regions illustrate their material wealth.[37] In the Altai Mountains, southwest of Minusinsk in Siberia, some of the richest graves have been found in valley pastures used by tribes during the summer months. The Altai were an important source of copper and tin ores. Bronze metallurgy was well established there by 1500 B.C., and people of the seminomadic Altai Karasuk culture wore quantities of distinctive bronze beads and pendants.[38]

Between 600 B.C. and A.D. 100, wide-ranging trade in beads and metals was conducted throughout the steppes. Glass beads, for example, from La Tène in Celtic Europe, arrived in China via the northern steppes by 500 B.C.[39]

In the Altai region, evidence of the wealth attained through trading metal ores is seen in the size and richness of treasures in their tombs. Six of the largest tombs, excavated near Pazyryk, belonged to chieftains of an eastern nomadic tribe related to the Scythians. Dating between 500 and 400 B.C., the tombs, though looted of most gold artifacts, still contained beads of bone, Persian turquoise, and Indian cowrie shells, glass, and carnelian. Women's leather boots were elaborately decorated with embroidery, and glass beads were sewn to their soles.[38]

At Sara, Western-style glass beads were found from the fifth century B.C., while at Ust-Labinskaya, glass beads (probably Western-made) and Egyptian scarabs are reported in sites dating between 100 B.C. and A.D. 100. At the same time, the Sarmatians, at the western edge of the steppes, made distinctive glass beads, some of which found their way to Britain.[39] Coptic glass beads from Egypt, dated between A.D. 200 and 300, were excavated at the Lulan and Niya sites in the Takla Makan basin.[40] About A.D. 1402, glass beads were made in Samarkand, the result of Tamerlane's occupation of Syria and the subsequent arrival of many glassmakers in Samarkand.[41]

Mongolian populations of the eastern steppes wore large numbers of turquoise and coral beads, introduced by their contacts with Tibetan and Turkish tribes. Noble Mongolian women displayed elaborate headdresses of gold and gilded silver, incorporating strands of coral and turquoise beads (plate 222). Most Mongolian jewelry was obtained from Tibet, either through trade or pilgrimages. China supplied Mongolia directly with turquoise beads, and greenish blue stones were the preferred color.[42]

Along the Amur River, at the eastern edge of the steppes, beads were made of local white jade, while glass, Indian agate, carnelian, and onyx were imported (via China) from the first millennium B.C. to A.D. 100.

Contemporary Beads

Today, jewelry worn by the nomadic and village women of the western regions of central Asia often resembles the adornment of their ancient steppes ancestors. In Afghanistan, bridal necklaces with multiple strands of coral and silver amulets, interspersed with intricate melon-shaped silver beads, are family heirlooms.[43] Turkmenistan brides display elaborate headdresses of repoussé silver, chains, and carnelian beads. Carnelian and silver jewelry worn by Turkmenistan women frequently constitutes a substantial part of the family wealth. In hard times, jewelry can always be sold for at least the value of the precious metals and stones. Kirgiz and Uzbek women string necklaces with beads of coral, silver, and shell, and fashion multicolored neck collars of glass beads.[44] Stone beads still have amuletic value. Amber is tied around a baby's neck to prevent skin diseases, while coral and carnelian are said to protect sight, and blue stones (lapis lazuli and turquoise) or blue glass divert the evil eye.[45]

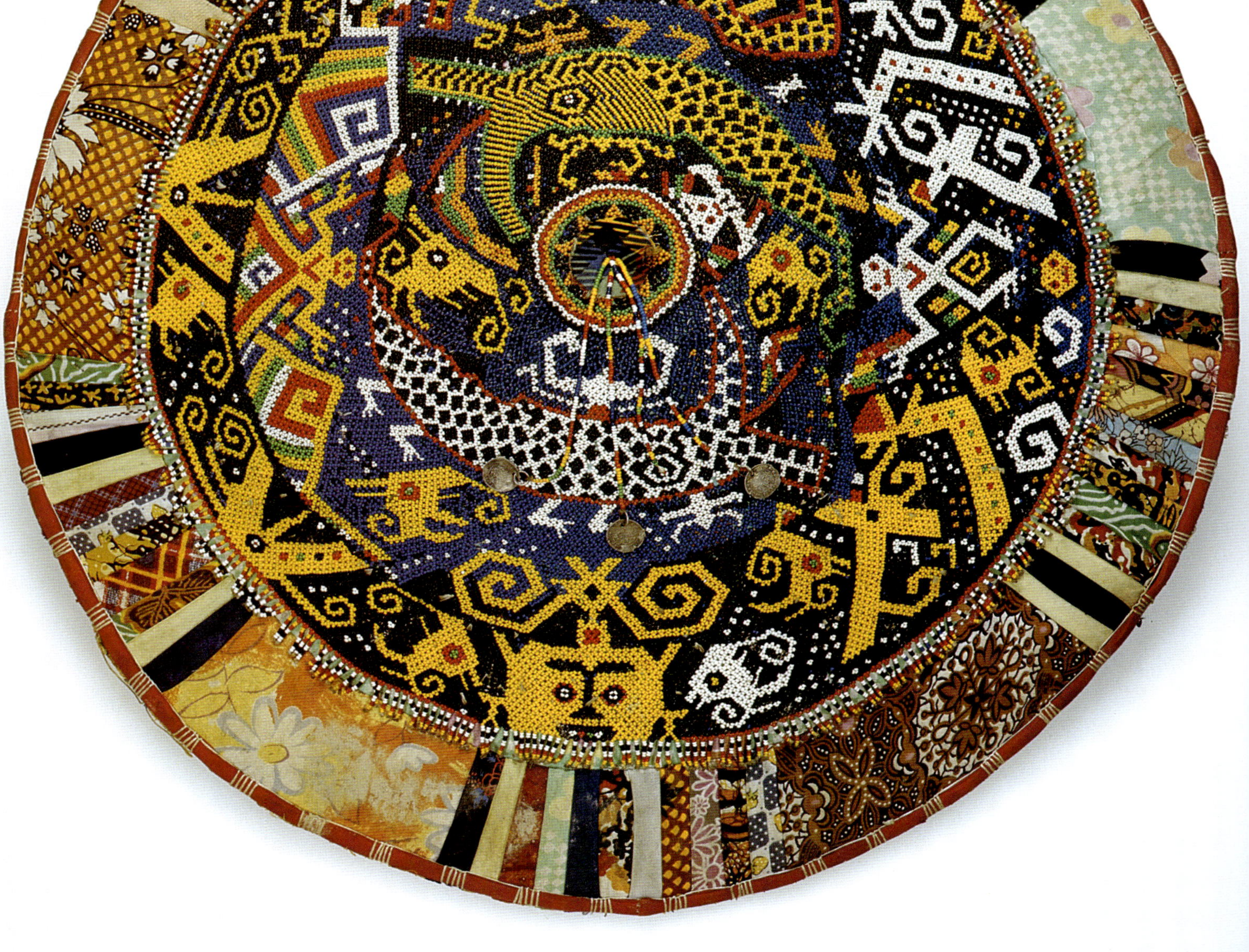

Southeast Asia and the South Pacific

Southeast Asia is a mosaic of large and small land masses scattered over an enormous area of the South Pacific. Throughout history most of the region has been accessible to seaborne traders. Beads have been an important element in the region's trade for thousands of years.

Mainland Southeast Asia is a tropical subcontinent with rugged, forested highlands intersected by rivers. The fractured landscape has fostered cultural diversity: highland forest tribes, cut off by mountain ranges, have lived in isolation for centuries: people of the plains and river valleys, on the other hand, have maintained contact with the coast and participated in regional trade systems. Some of the lowland cultures evolved into sophisticated states whose cultures were influenced either by China or by India (depending upon their proximity). This interchange was reflected in the name "Indochina," which now refers to Laos, Cambodia, and Vietnam but prior to World War II referred to the entire region.

An array of Southeast Asian islands, including Taiwan, Indonesia, and the Philippines, lie at the crossroads of sea routes linking India, China, western Asia, and Europe. Throughout this vast area, merchant seamen forged cultural links, carrying artistic styles from island to island and to the mainland. Their routes were determined by ocean currents and two monsoons (southwest from June through September, northeast from late October through late March). In this way, the peoples of Taiwan, Indonesia, and the Philippines were significantly influenced by the cultures of India, China, and the Southeast Asian mainland.

Southeast Asian beads are as varied and fascinating as any in the world. As necklaces, beaded textiles, or even as individual objects, they were immensely important to all the region's peoples. Among the earliest beads found in Southeast Asia were those

224. *Hats are worn everywhere in Sarawak. One of the most elaborate is this* sa'ong *of the Kenyan Dayak group. It is embellished with appliqué designs in cloth and beadwork, and used by a woman as a sunshade on ceremonial occasions. Diameter, 51.4 cm. Collection Ivory Freidus*

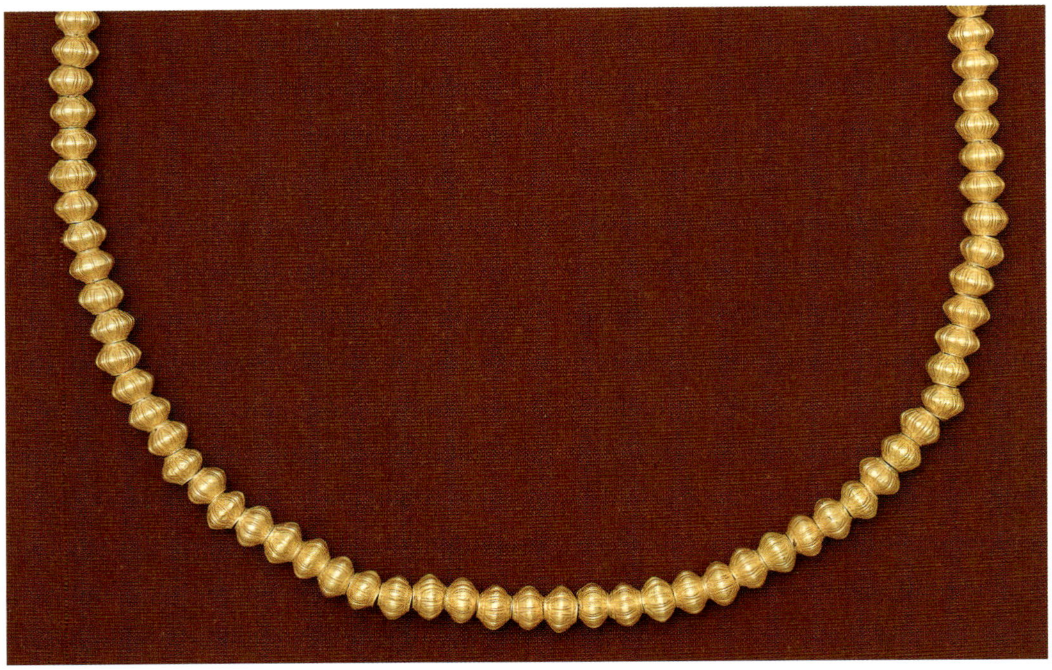

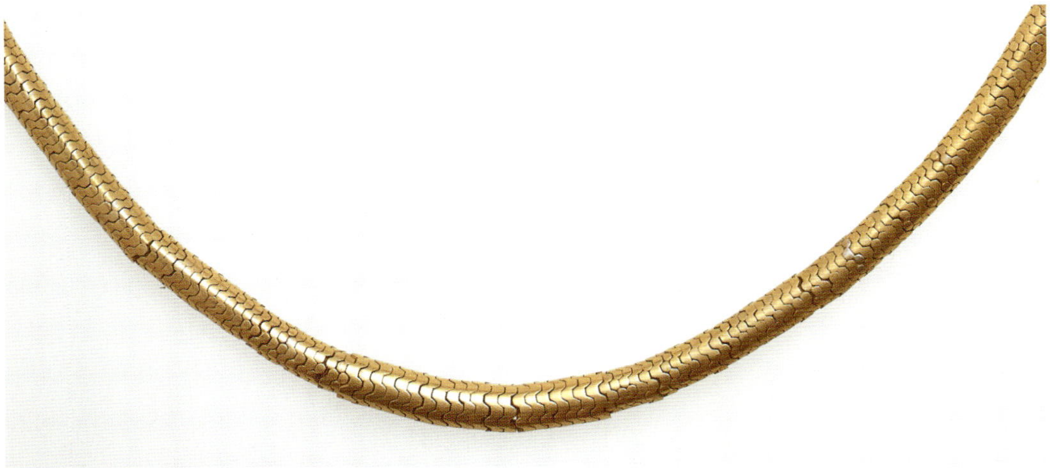

225. *Gold melon beads, believed to be from the Angkor period, c.* A.D. *900–1200 (the classical age of Khmer art). These beads reflect artistic influences from India prevalent in Southeast Asia at the time. Typical bead: diameter, 0.79 cm. Collection Kronos*

226. *Detail from a necklace containing 325 perfectly interlocked gold disk beads that was excavated from a late pre-Hispanic site (c.* A.D. *1500) in the Philippines. Length, 40.6 cm. Collection J. Camp Gallery, New York*

excavated from Neolithic caves (2500–1000 B.C.) at Sarawak in Borneo. Included in the find were necklaces of clay beads alternated with bored shell and animal teeth.[1] Archaeological evidence also indicates that beads were traded into Southeast Asia long before the arrival of Europeans. The "Indian red," or *mutisalah*, beads, made in south India, were sold in Sumatra by at least the first century B.C. (plate 228). Early sites also contain beads of agate, carnelian, crystal, and amethyst, stones found in substantial deposits in India and Sri Lanka. The beads themselves are made in a range of shapes and by various manufacturing techniques that closely resemble Indian styles. Although some early scholarship on ancient glass beads made in Southeast Asia suggested that the beads were manufactured from glass scrap imported from the Middle East or the Mediterranean area, this theory is questionable. It is more likely that the beads were made in India and exported into Southeast Asia. They were later produced by East Indians who transferred the technology to Thailand, Vietnam, and Indonesia.[2]

Jewelry had a number of functions in the lives of premodern Southeast Asian island people, serving as personal adornment, protective amulets, and political badges of rank,

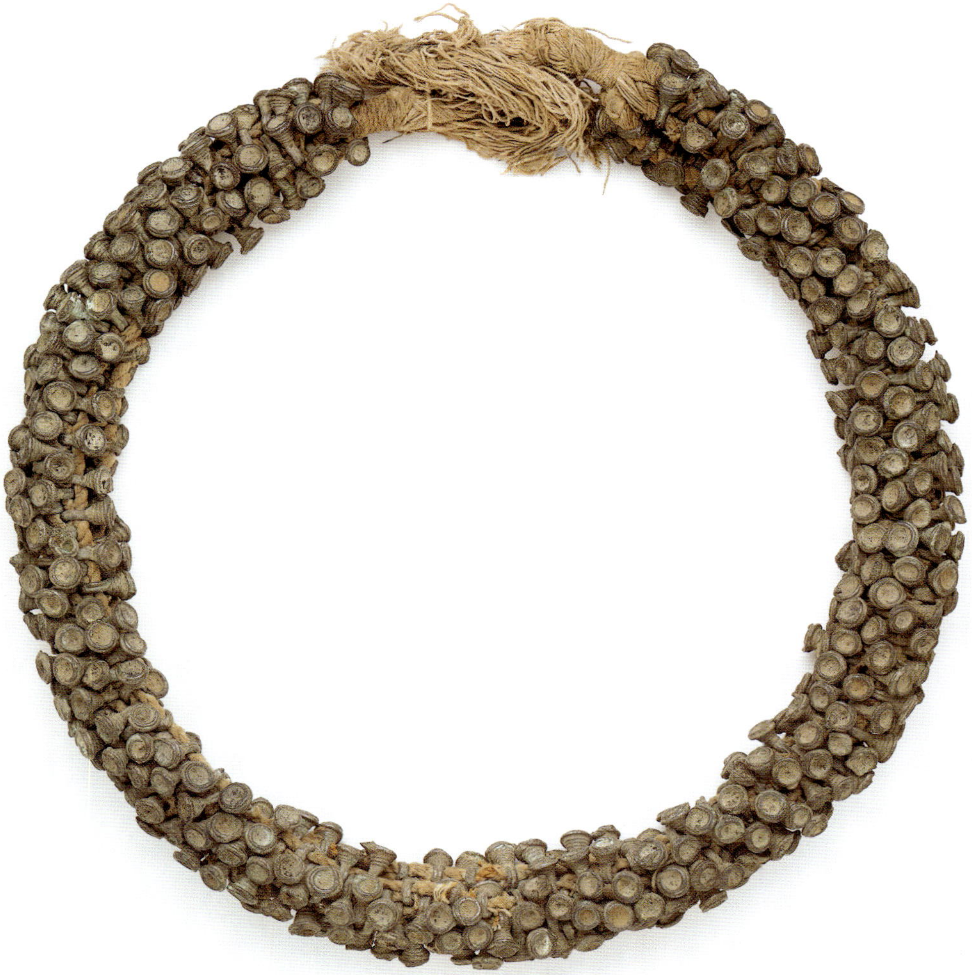

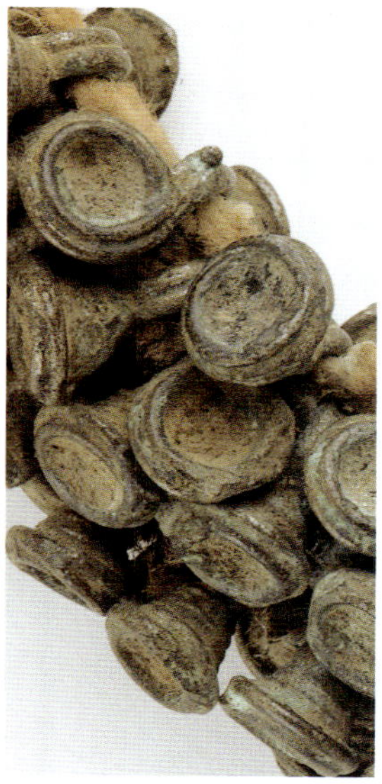

LEFT: 227. *Bronze beads from Burma, possibly modeled to resemble seedpods, may have been derived from motifs used by Chinese craftsmen in the Shang dynasty (1523–1027 B.C.). Collection Colette and Jean-Pierre Ghysels, Brussels*

ABOVE: 227a. *Detail of bronze beads shown in plate 227. Typical bead: diameter, 0.9 cm.*

as well as dowries, ceremonial exchange goods, and sacred altar objects for summoning spirits from the supernatural world. In Indonesia, Malaysia, Sarawak, and the northern Philippines, many layers of social and religious iconography were incorporated into jewelry, which was kept as ancestral treasure and family heirlooms symbolic of their owner's place in the world.[3] Through various designs and colors, jewelry publicly displayed important ideas in the local systems of politics, kinship, and myth. The significant role individual beads (as contrasted with assemblages) had in certain Southeast Asian cultures is striking. On the islands, beads have been used singly in an array of cultural practices, ranging from celebrations of marriage to sanctifying new houses to insuring favorable harvests. Beaded textiles were also accorded high value, although generally not by the same groups.

Beads were important symbols in village life. They were used to strengthen political alliances and to protect warriors from natural and supernatural threats.[4] Today, island tribal people continue to possess a detailed knowledge of each bead they own. A rare, ancient bead has a reputation similar to that of a precious stone or a fine antique

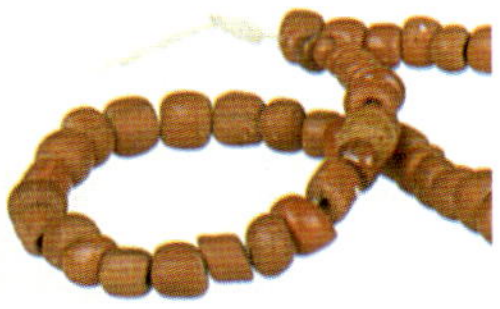

ABOVE: 228. Mutisalah *beads. The famed "Indian reds" are found throughout mainland and island Southeast Asia in archaeological sites of the pre-European era.*

An opaque red glass bead, the mutisalah *is quite identifiable despite the fact that it comes in a great variety of shapes. Scholars agree that the* mutisalahs' *original home was South India, where they are found in large numbers (primarily in Indian megalithic sites dating to about 200 B.C.). The beads were made at a number of locales until at least the sixteenth century.* Mutisalah *are still highly prized in Timor, where in 1965 a twelve-inch-long string equaled the price of a water buffalo.*[1] *Typical bead: diameter, 1.5 cm. Corning Museum of Glass, Corning, New York*

RIGHT: 229. *Rear view of a headdress of a woman from the Akha tribe of Thailand. It was worn in ceremonies as well as in daily field work. The helmet shape identifies its wearer as a member of the Mawn Po clan. The hat is heavily encrusted with silver buttons, coins, and beads. Numerous strands of red glass beads are attached to the sides, falling nearly to the wearer's waist.*[11] *Length (from top of helmet to bottom of long bead strand), 61.6 cm. Collection Ivory Freidus*

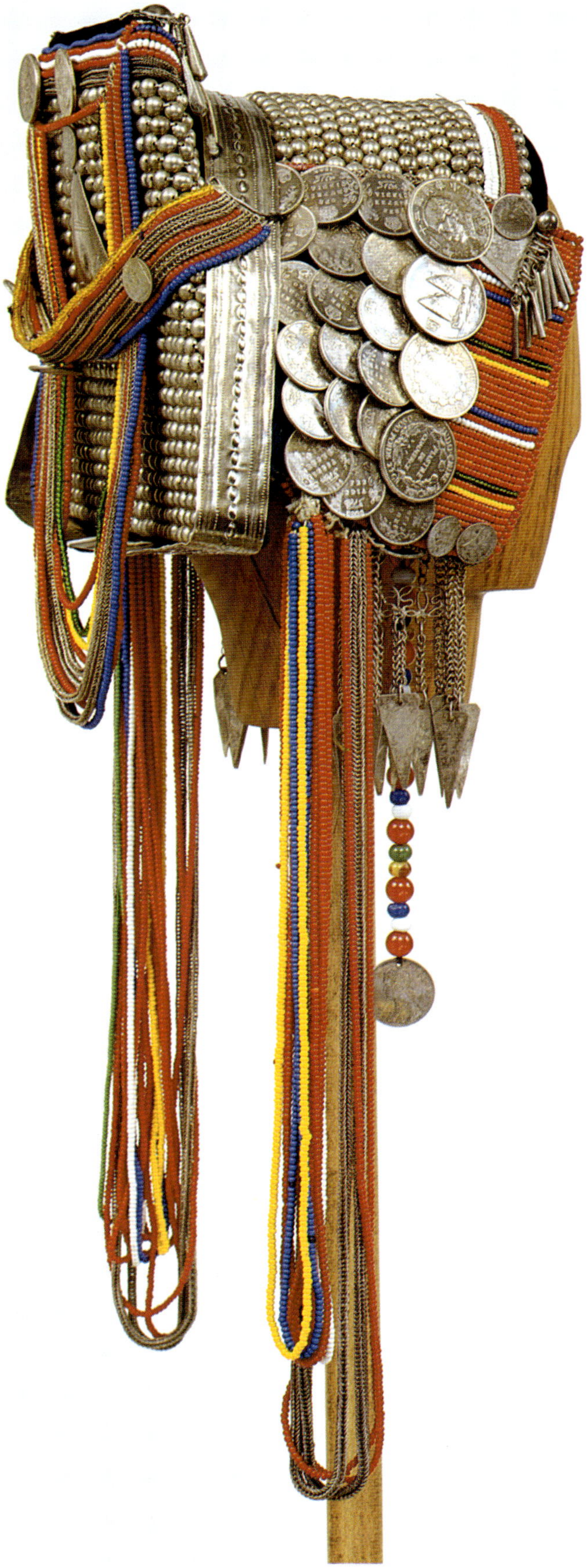

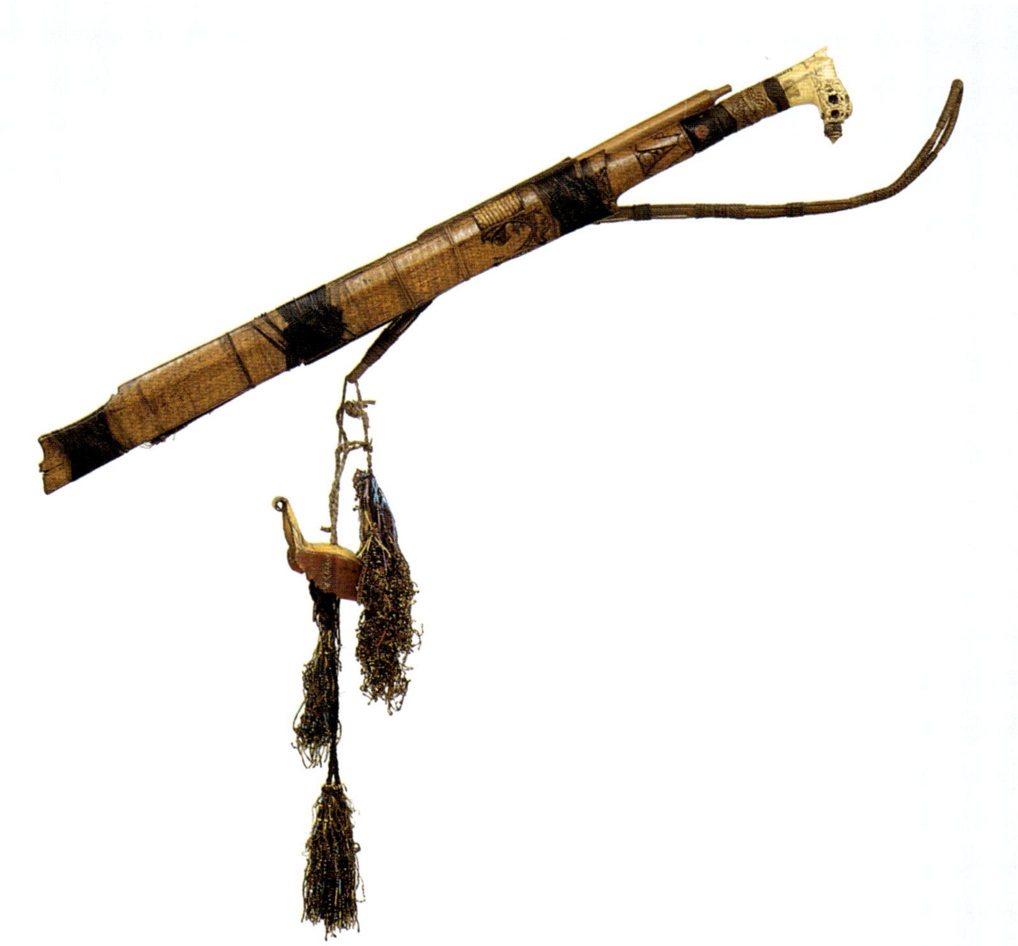

TOP: 230. *Dayak sword, called* mandau *or* pararejo, *with strings of multicolored glass beads and a hornbill skull hanging from the wooden scabbard. Collected in Java in 1902. Sword: length, 72 cm. Private collection*

BOTTOM LEFT: 231. *Detail of tiny glass beads attached to Dayak sword scabbard illustrated in plate 230. Typical bead: length, 1 mm.*

BOTTOM RIGHT: 232. *Glass beads from a Kalimantan necklace. The striped beads are from Venice. The other beads are of unknown origin, although they seem to be somewhat Islamic in style. Top left bead: diameter 1.2 cm. J. Camp Gallery, New York*

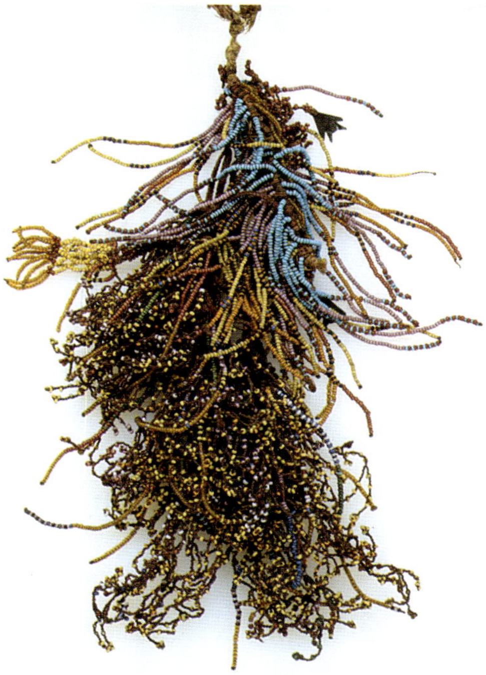

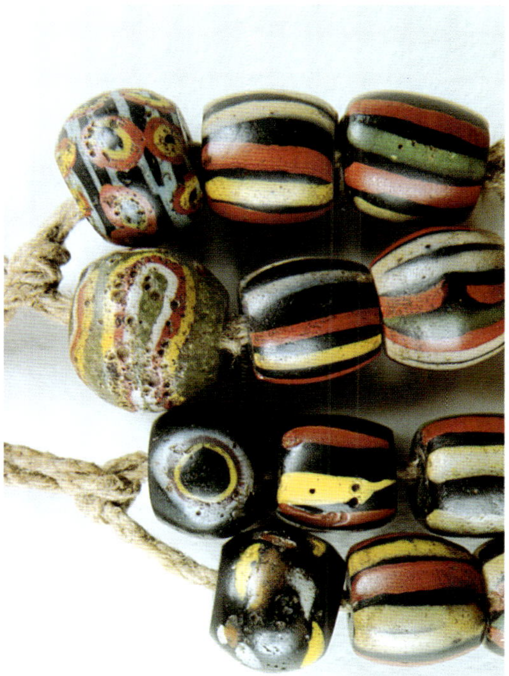

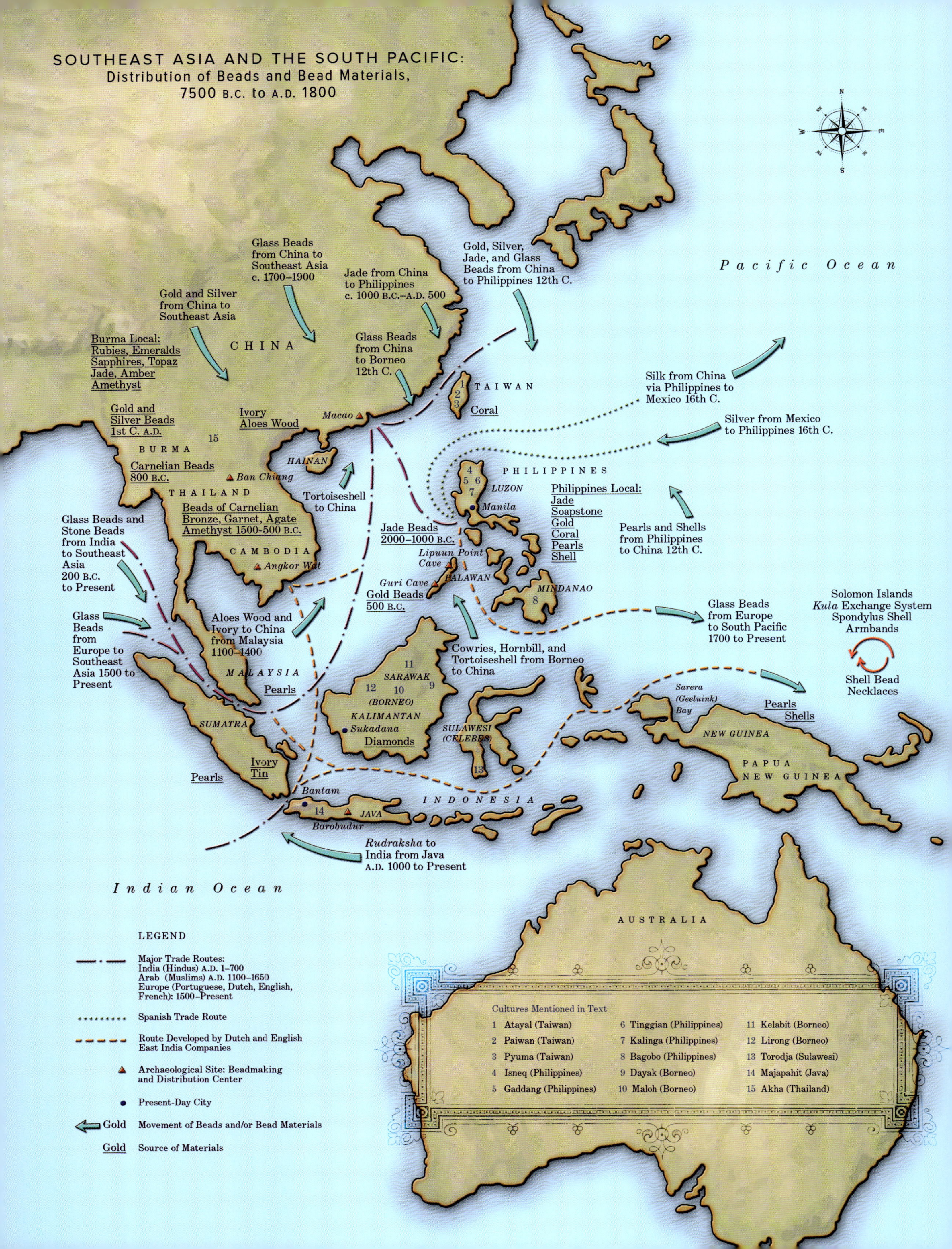
SOUTHEAST ASIA AND THE SOUTH PACIFIC:
Distribution of Beads and Bead Materials,
7500 B.C. to A.D. 1800
Pacific Ocean
Indian Ocean
CHINA
BURMA
THAILAND
CAMBODIA
MALAYSIA
SUMATRA
TAIWAN
PHILIPPINES
LUZON
MINDANAO
PALAWAN
HAINAN
SARAWAK
(BORNEO)
KALIMANTAN
SULAWESI
(CELEBES)
INDONESIA
JAVA
NEW GUINEA
PAPUA
NEW GUINEA
AUSTRALIA
Macao
Ban Chiang
Angkor Wat
Manila
Lipuun Point
Cave
Guri Cave
Sukadana
Bantam
Borobudur
Sarera
(Geeluink)
Bay
Glass Beads
from China to
Southeast Asia
c. 1700–1900
Jade from China
to Philippines
c. 1000 B.C.–A.D. 500
Gold, Silver,
Jade, and Glass
Beads from China
to Philippines 12th C.
Gold and Silver
from China to
Southeast Asia
Burma Local:
Rubies, Emeralds
Sapphires, Topaz
Jade, Amber
Amethyst
Glass Beads
from China
to Borneo
12th C.
Gold and
Silver Beads
1st C. A.D.
Ivory
Aloes Wood
Coral
Silk from China
via Philippines to
Mexico 16th C.
Silver from Mexico
to Philippines 16th C.
Carnelian Beads
800 B.C.
Tortoiseshell
to China
Beads of Carnelian
Bronze, Garnet, Agate
Amethyst 1500-500 B.C.
Philippines Local:
Jade
Soapstone
Gold
Coral
Pearls
Shell
Pearls and Shells
from Philippines
to China 12th C.
Glass Beads and
Stone Beads
from India
to Southeast
Asia
200 B.C.
to Present
Jade Beads
2000–1000 B.C.
Gold Beads
500 B.C.
Glass Beads
from Europe
to South Pacific
1700 to Present
Solomon Islands
Kula Exchange System
Spondylus Shell
Armbands
Shell Bead
Necklaces
Glass
Beads
from
Europe to
Southeast
Asia 1500 to
Present
Aloes Wood and
Ivory to China
from Malaysia
1100–1400
Cowries, Hornbill, and
Tortoiseshell from Borneo
to China
Pearls
Diamonds
Pearls
Shells
Ivory
Tin
Pearls
Rudraksha to
India from Java
A.D. 1000 to Present
1 2 3 4 5 6 7 8 9 10 11 12 13 14 15
LEGEND
Major Trade Routes:
India (Hindus) A.D. 1–700
Arab (Muslims) A.D. 1100–1650
Europe (Portuguese, Dutch, English,
French): 1500–Present
Spanish Trade Route
Route Developed by Dutch and English
East India Companies
Archaeological Site: Beadmaking
and Distribution Center
Present-Day City
Gold Movement of Beads and/or Bead Materials
Gold Source of Materials
Cultures Mentioned in Text
1 Atayal (Taiwan)
2 Paiwan (Taiwan)
3 Pyuma (Taiwan)
4 Isneq (Philippines)
5 Gaddang (Philippines)
6 Tinggian (Philippines)
7 Kalinga (Philippines)
8 Bagobo (Philippines)
9 Dayak (Borneo)
10 Maloh (Borneo)
11 Kelabit (Borneo)
12 Lirong (Borneo)
13 Torodja (Sulawesi)
14 Majapahit (Java)
15 Akha (Thailand)

in other parts of the world. The history of each bead, its name and age, is understood. In Sarawak, older women can easily identify sixty or more different types of scarce, ancient beads.[5]

Various Southeast Asian island cultures valued one bead over another. The Kalinga of the Philippines treasured agates, while some groups in Borneo and Taiwan preferred ancient polychrome glass beads. *Mutisalah* beads were admired everywhere. In the tropical climate of much of Southeast Asia, organic materials, such as seeds or wood, quickly rot; durable stone and glass beads were considered sources of strength and longevity. Among the Maloh tribes in central Kalimantan in Borneo, there were important myths about hazardous journeys embarked on by brave heroes in search of particularly valuable beads. These same people tied beads to the wrists of couples at marriage, and when a new communal dwelling was built, they placed beads in the holes dug for the structure's main posts.[6] The Kelabit of Borneo called the *mutisalah* bead *bau'u si' ada* ("head of the ghost"), affixing two of them to the end of a sharpened stake that was placed in the ground near a rice field to insure a bountiful harvest.[7]

Thailand, on the Southeast Asian mainland, lay far from the Chinese and Indian sea routes and thus remained culturally self-contained. Nonetheless, an enormous variety of beads continues to be excavated from the region's burial sites, indicating the importance of beads to the ancient Thai cultures. Archaeologists have found bronze beads dated between 1500 and 500 B.C., made during the Bronze Age.[8] Stone beads, including carnelian, agate, garnet, and amethyst, were fashionable from very early times until at least the eleventh century A.D. Of particular interest are long, tubular stone beads referred to as "magic beads," which have a long history throughout the area (dating back to about 3400 B.C.) and eventually were copied in glass.[9] While some of the beads were probably imported from India (with which Thailand was then closely associated), others were locally made. Although the extensive looting of archaeological sites has destroyed much information, evidence strongly indicates local stone bead manufacturing existed from a very early date. Etched agate and carnelian beads with patterns far more common in Thailand than India suggest that Thailand may have been another production center for these beads. Clay cylinders with deeply incised designs, rather similar to western Asian seals, were found at the site of Ban Chiang and may have been worn as beads.[10]

Glass beads from Ban Chiang, associated with pottery and iron tools, date to about 300 B.C. Predominantly of opaque orange red (although one burial also contained a few translucent blue and yellow samples), it is unknown whether the beads were locally made or imported. There has been speculation that Thai or Indian craftsmen living in Thailand may have produced some of these beads. Glass beadmaking, under Indian influence, definitely appears to have been under way in parts of Thailand by at least the tenth century A.D., especially along its western coast.[11]

Gold and silver beads from central Thailand date to the first centuries A.D., the period of Indian influence in Southeast Asia. Necklaces of beautifully crafted gold beads in various shapes, including melon and cornerless cube, are associated with Thailand's Mon or Dvaravati period (A.D. 500–1000) as well as the classical age of Khmer art (A.D. 900–1200) in Cambodia, when Indian influence stretched across the sea.[12] Carnelian beads from Vietnam, dating to about 800 B.C., resemble those found in the Philippines. In both instances this may reflect early trade, probably through middlemen, with India.[13]

OVERLEAF TOP: 233. *A netted beadwork skirt from the Maloh tribe in Kalimantan. The beads have been netted into solid panels, as the Maloh may not have actually practiced the weaving of cloth. The ceremonial costume of the Maloh consists of a highly decorated short skirt, jacket, and headcloth.*

Maloh beaded skirts and jackets are decorated with motifs only they can identify. The geometric shapes represent familiar objects from the Maloh natural world translated into designs that were derived from Islamic motifs. In this skirt, the geometric forms represent the "tree of life," a symbol of rebirth popular in Indonesian art. An important motif illustrated here is the squatting human figure, kaletau, *which probably represents a guardian or ancestor spirit.*

Beaded costumes are reserved for ceremonial occasions when the residents of the communal longhouse gather to celebrate marriages, funerals, and successful harvests. The Maloh believe that displaying their finest beaded textiles helps produce a bountiful harvest.[III] Height, 51.9 cm. Private collection

OVERLEAF BOTTOM: 234. *A Dayak beadwork baby carrier* (ba), *which holds the infant during the first months of life. Shells, beads, and the teeth of bears, crocodiles, and pigs—animals with protective spirits—are often suspended from the wooden carrier to make a rattling sound, which frightens away evil spirits. An even number of teeth, in this*

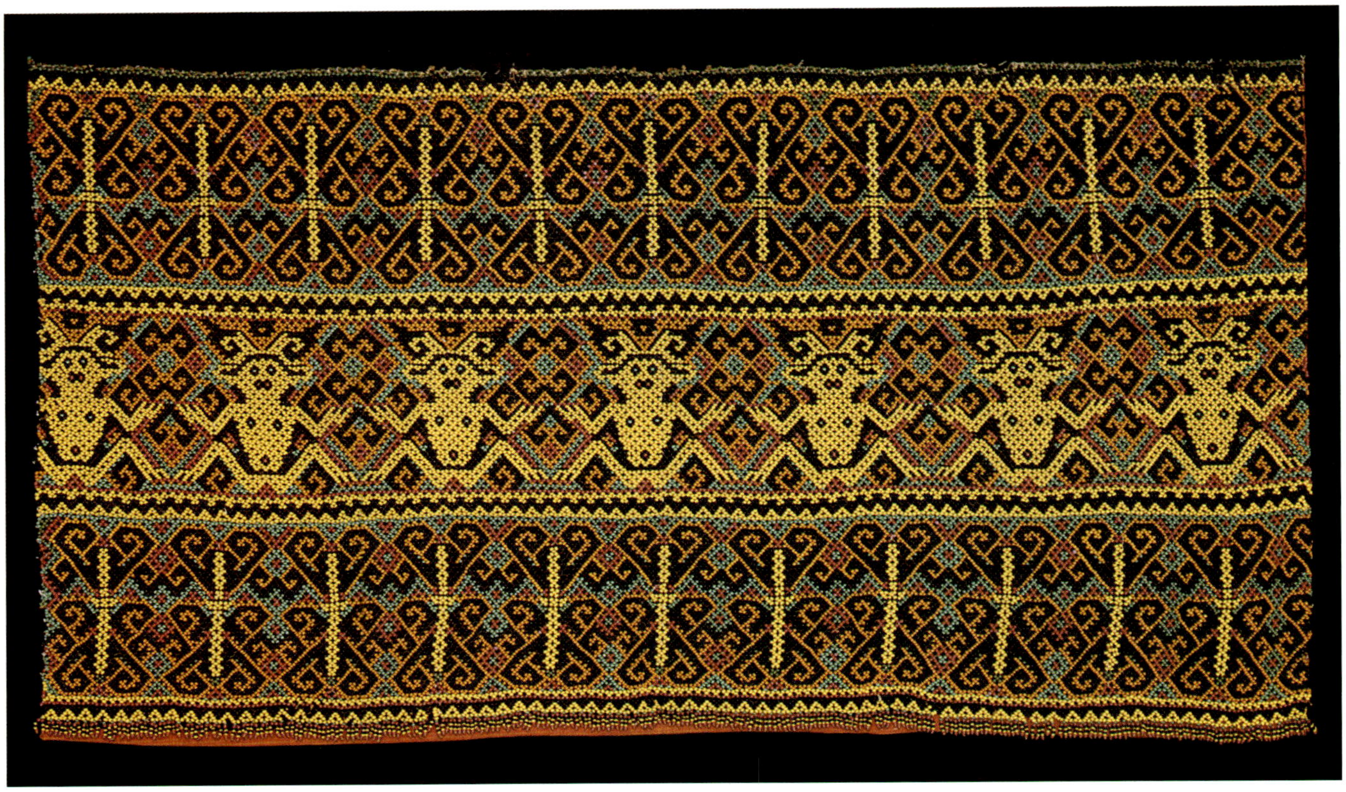

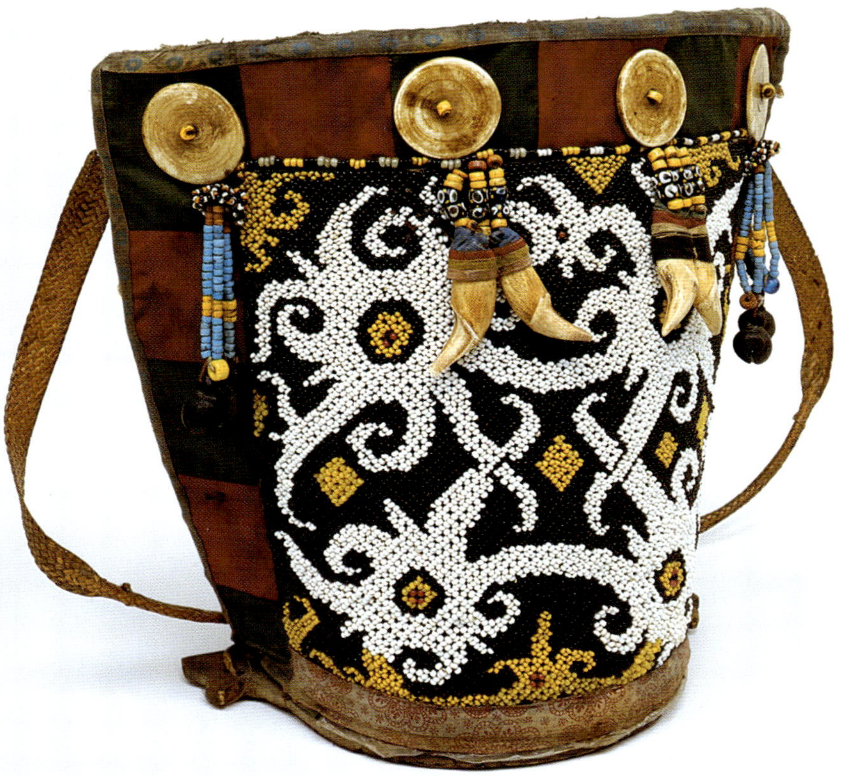

case four, indicates the infant is male. The design of the beaded decoration sewn onto a carrier identifies the owner's social class: the baby carrier of a paran *(leader and aristocrat) may be covered by an entire human figure in beadwork, while that of a* paran iof *(someone of slightly lower rank) will only have a partial figure in a stylized or abstract pattern.*[IV]

The dominant motif in white is an aso, *a stylized open-jawed dragon that frightens away evil spirits. It appears frequently in the art of Borneo.*[V] *Height, 42 cm. Collection Ivory Freidus*

OPPOSITE: 235. *A rare twentieth-century dance cape of netted beadwork and fabric from the Geelvinck Bay region, New Guinea. Length, 55.9 cm. Collection Tambaran Gallery, New York*

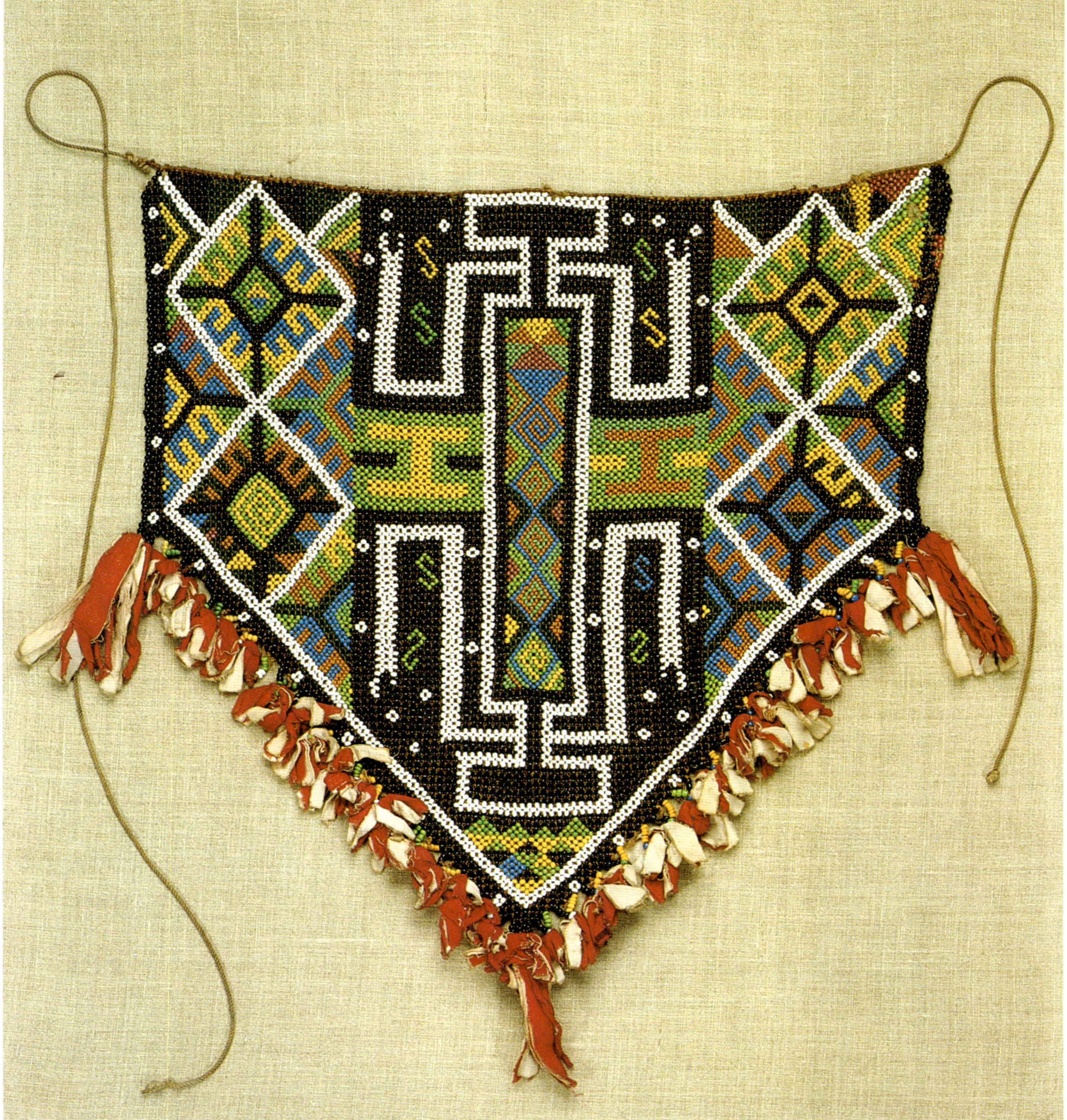

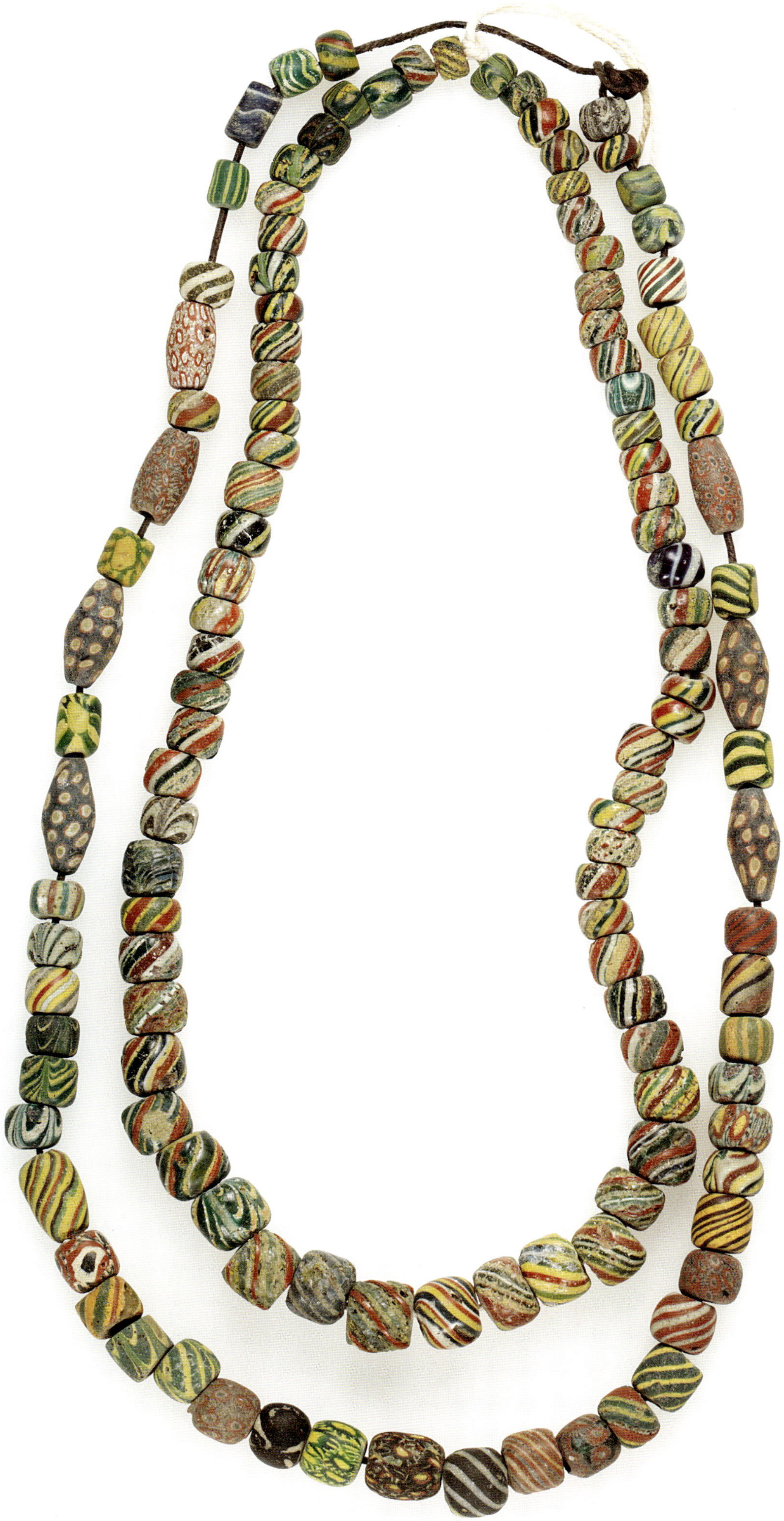

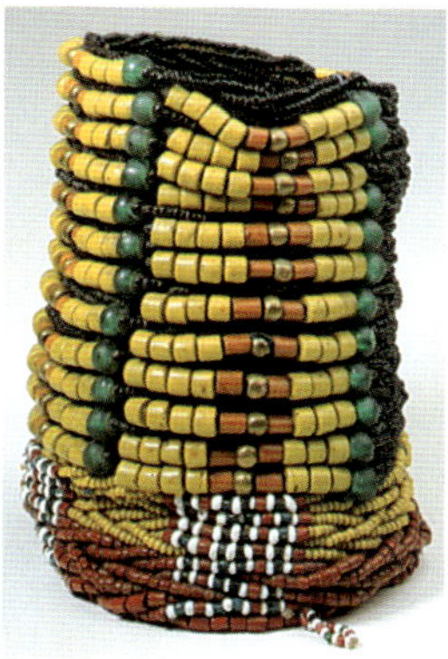

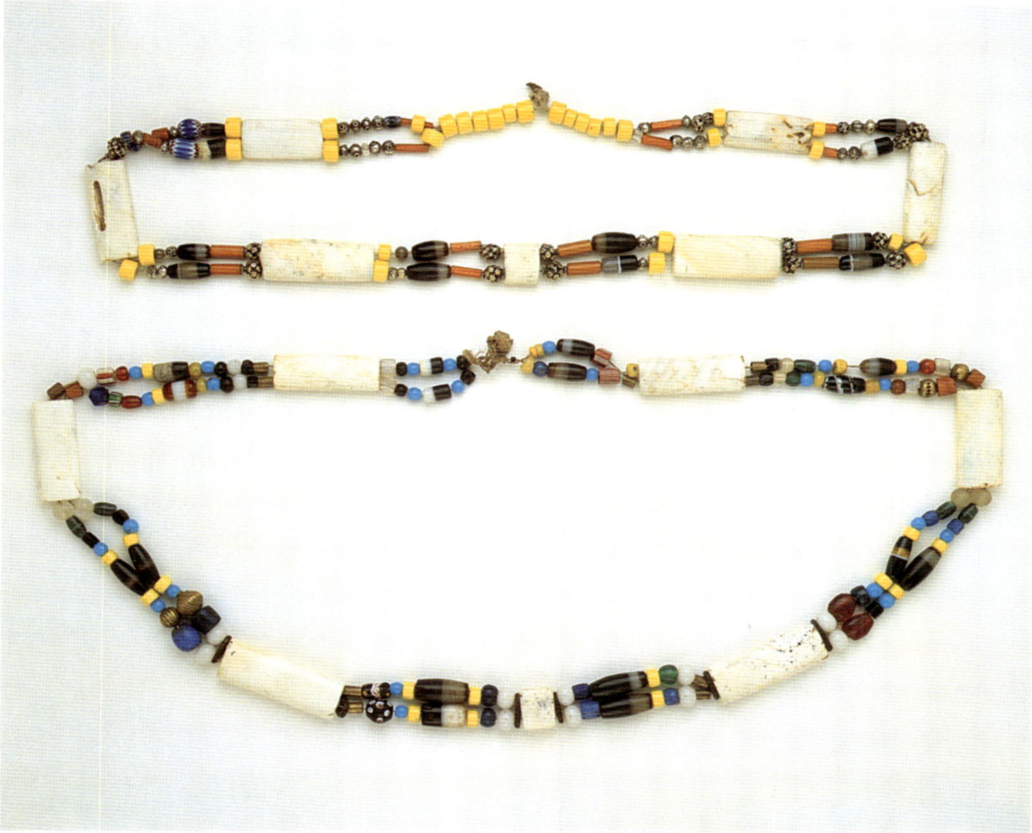

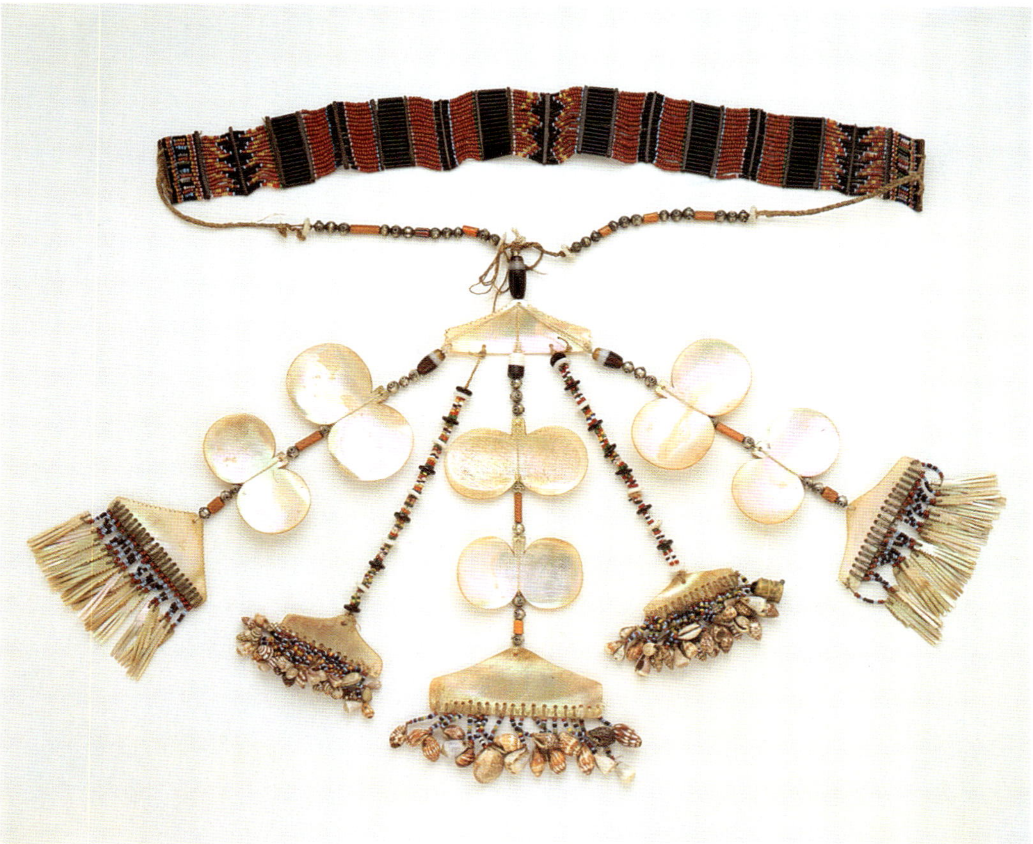

OPPOSITE: 236. *Indonesian glass beads (called "jatim" after Java Timor (East Java), considered its provenance) from southeast Kalimantan, thought to date c.* A.D. *600–800. The beads were most likely inspired by post-Roman, Middle Eastern beads and were created just prior to Islamic times. Made by mosaic and combed techniques, the beads vary in size, typically from .9 to 1.6 cm. The Bead Museum, Glendale, Arizona*

ABOVE: 237. *Glass and brass bead bracelet from the northern Philippines. Length, 15.2 cm. Collection Colette and Jean-Pierre Ghysels, Brussels*

ABOVE LEFT: 238. *Dowry necklaces of shell, agate, and glass beads from the Isneg tribe, northern Luzon, Philippines. Strands of antique beads possess their own genealogies and are heirlooms. Top necklace: length, 34 cm. Collection Colette and Jean-Pierre Ghysels, Brussels*

BOTTOM LEFT: 239. Sipattal, *a chest ornament worn by the Isneg, mountain tribespeople in Luzon. The mother-of-pearl pendants and the shell and glass beads are strung with pineapple fiber. Length (excluding collar),*

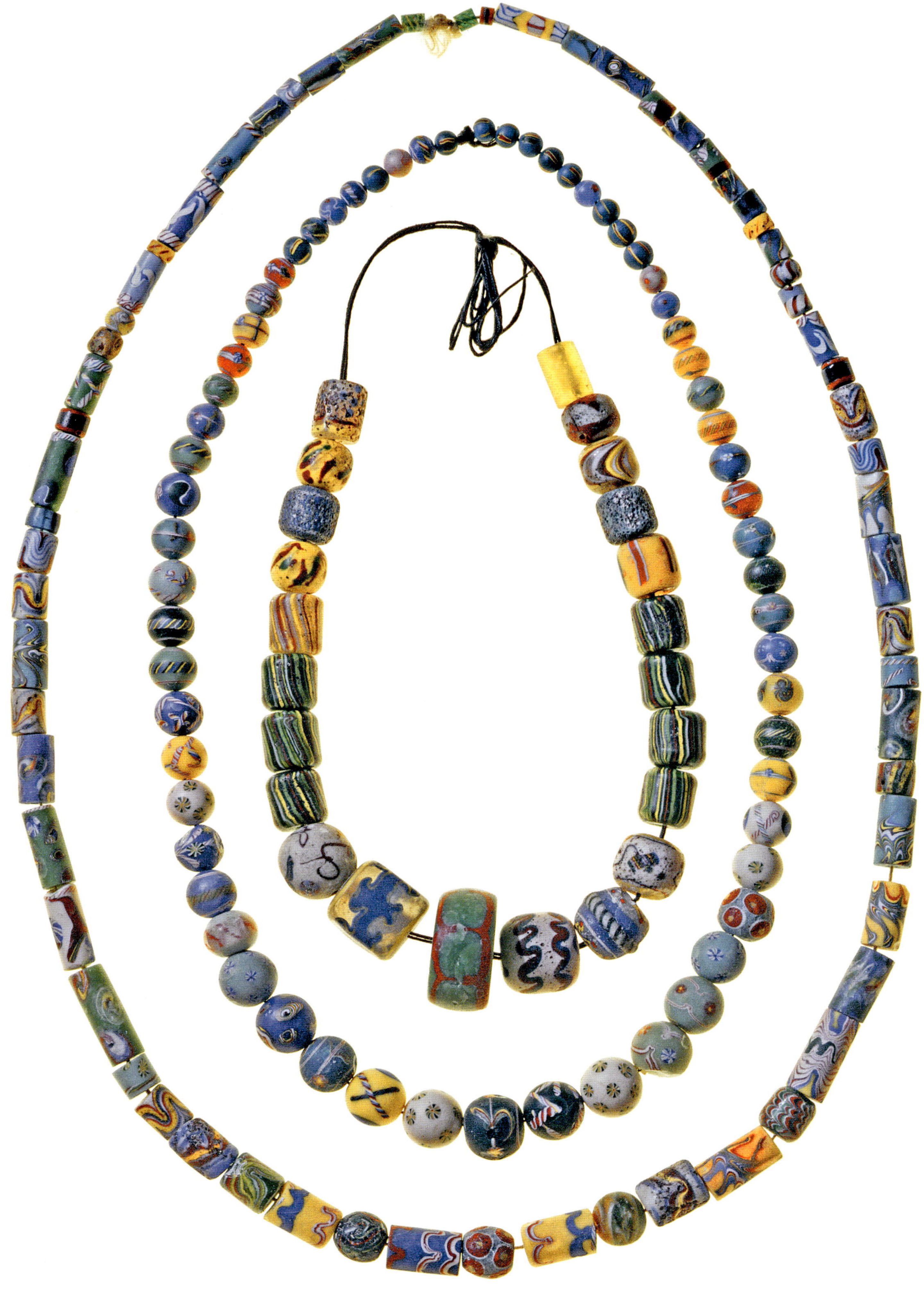

Indonesia

Indonesia, the largest island complex in the world, stretches from the Malaysian peninsula to New Guinea. It includes Sumatra, Borneo, Java, and Sulawesi (formerly Celebes), as well as western New Guinea (West Irian) and thirteen thousand smaller islands. This extensive island chain has been exposed to the almost continuous influences of China, India, and Islam since prehistoric times, yet strong indigenous cultures also developed. Not surprisingly, Indonesia is a complex mixture of peoples, who have produced a rich and varied art.

The archipelago's great natural wealth in spices attracted traders from the mainland Asian powers. Most of the arts of Indonesia show the influence of the Chinese and Bronze Age Dong Son culture (700 B.C.–A.D. 100) of mainland Southeast Asia. Indian traders, acting as middlemen between the Far East and the Mediterranean, entered Indonesia about 300 B.C., while trade with China actually began about 400 B.C. Great Hindu and Buddhist empires thrived in Java, Sumatra, and Bali between the second and fifteenth centuries A.D.[14] By A.D. 100, small colonies of Indian traders were established along the trade routes. They introduced their philosophy, law, literature, and beads to the islands.

The island cultures of Java and Bali were particularly influenced by India and founded Indian-style court cultures. Their art, while inspired by Indian design concepts, has its own distinctive character. The Indianization of Javanese and Balinese cultures is reflected in bas-reliefs and freestanding carvings of male and female deities, which, by at least A.D. 800, are adorned with quantities of beads.

At the site of Borobudur in central Java stands a mountainous Buddhist temple, constructed during the eighth and ninth centuries and composed of a series of terraces that represent levels of existence, ranging from earthly life at the bottom to spiritual enlightenment at the top. Sculptures of people, beautifully dressed in bead jewelry and sitting under trees hung with fruitlike strings of gems and beads, populate the lower levels. The upper terraces contain simple, unadorned, and indistinguishable Buddhas, examples of the rewards accorded the virtuous. The whole complex is designed to link purity with simplicity. At the same time, the human figures on the lower levels show beads are part of a life of sensuality and joy.[15] This is in contrast to their use in Tibet and Nepal, for example, where Buddhist and Hindu religious images wear jewelry and beads to reflect the amuletic properties of adornment.

Islamic influence began to reach Indonesia by A.D. 1200, and today 90 percent of the people are Muslim. Portuguese, English, and Dutch traders first arrived in the 1500s, with the Dutch East India Company forming the basis of the Indonesian colony. The area was not entirely free from European control until 1949, when Indonesia's independence was recognized.

Stone and glass beads were introduced to Indonesia by Indian and Chinese traders. In fact, Indonesian stone beads are identical to those manufactured at Arikamedu in India several centuries before the Christian Era, demonstrating the regions shared both finished beads as well as local craftsmen's interpretations of Indian styles. The earliest glass beads found in Indonesia are monochrome (predominantly yellow, blue, or green hues) and were made by drawn techniques or composed from canes. Opaque red *mutisalah* beads existed in every region of mainland and island Southeast Asia, suggesting *mutisalah* beads were from a common manufacturing tradition but were a broadly shared cultural phenomenon.[16] (The small wound beads that competed with *mutisalah* beads were Chinese-made and introduced much later in time.)[17] Pre-sixteenth-century European polychrome glass beads are extremely rare. Those that have been identified are generally eye and zone beads. Ancient polychrome beads are highly prized by the Dayak

19 cm. Collection Colette and Jean-Pierre Ghysels, Brussels

OPPOSITE: 240. *These three strings of glass beads were owned by a wealthy chief of the Pyuma tribe in southeastern Taiwan. While some of these beads may have come from Dutch traders who traveled the former Indian and Chinese trade routes, the majority are described in Taiwan today as "Osaka-type" beads and are thought to be from eighteenth- or nineteenth-century Japan.[IX] Outside necklace: length, 81 cm. Province and Eleanor Henry Collection, National Museum of Natural History, Smithsonian Institution, Washington, D.C.*

TOP AND MIDDLE: 241–242. *Matching Bagobo jacket and trousers with exquisite ornamentation of glass and shell beads. A fine example of the technique of embroidering and appliquéing beads to textiles (in contrast to netting solid panels, see plate 233). Jacket: length, 44.5 cm.; trousers: length, 64.2 cm. Received at the Smithsonian Institution from E. H. and S. S. Metcalfe in 1915. National Museum of Natural History, Smithsonian Institution, Washington, D.C.*

BOTTOM: 243. *Basketry, as both a craft and an art form, has a long history in the Philippines. This purse or basket was made with a twined weave, then covered with native-made cloth and a heavy beadwork panel.*

The series of connective diamonds in the central panel of this basket are typical, except that the pattern is created with multicolored glass seedbeads and not with the traditional rattan.[VI] This is a Bagobo basket, collected in the Philippines in 1927. Height, 15.2 cm. National Museum of Natural History, Smithsonian Institution, Washington, D.C.

OPPOSITE: 244. *Back side of a garment embroidered with shell beadwork from the Atayal tribe, northern Taiwan. The tiny shell disk beads were strung and then sewn onto the cloth. Most Taiwanese clothes were made by sewing rectangular pieces of cloth together; neck openings and tailoring are rare.[VII] Typical shell disk bead: diameter, 0.25 cm. Collection J. Camp Gallery, New York*

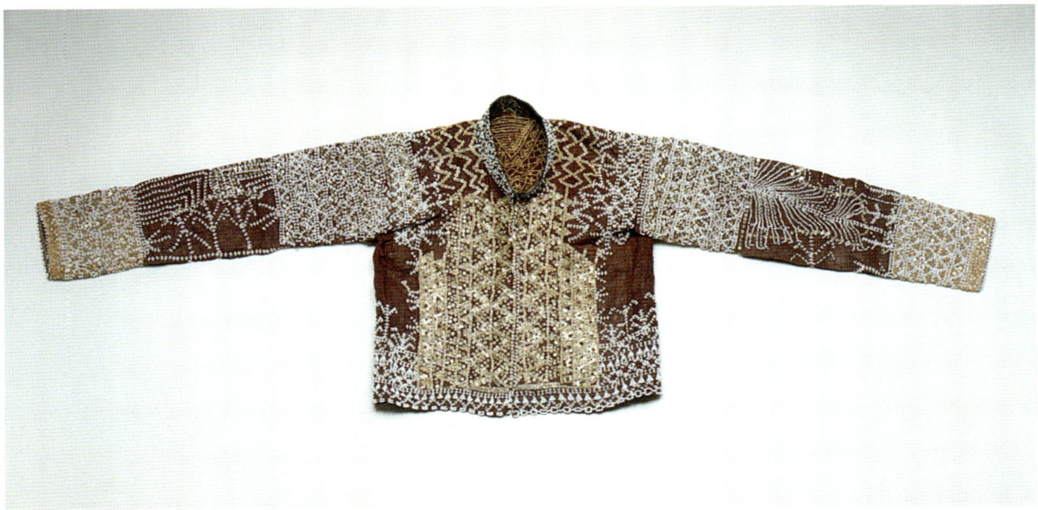

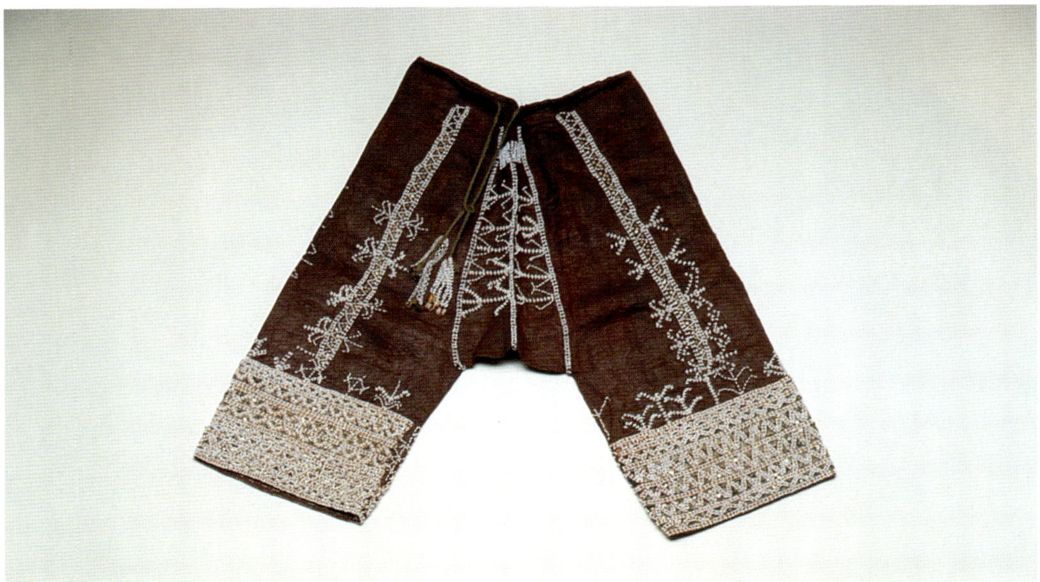

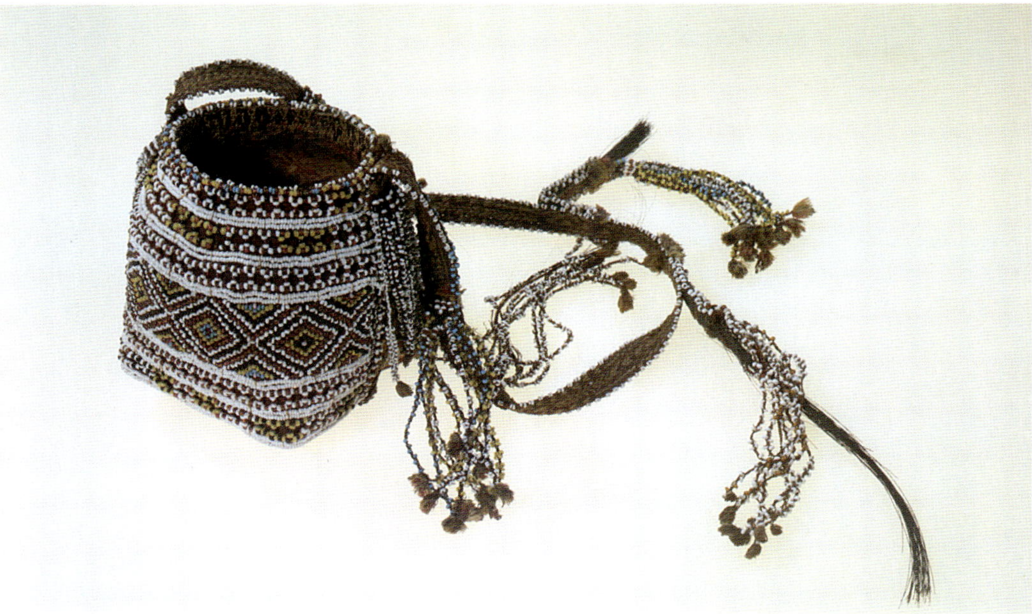

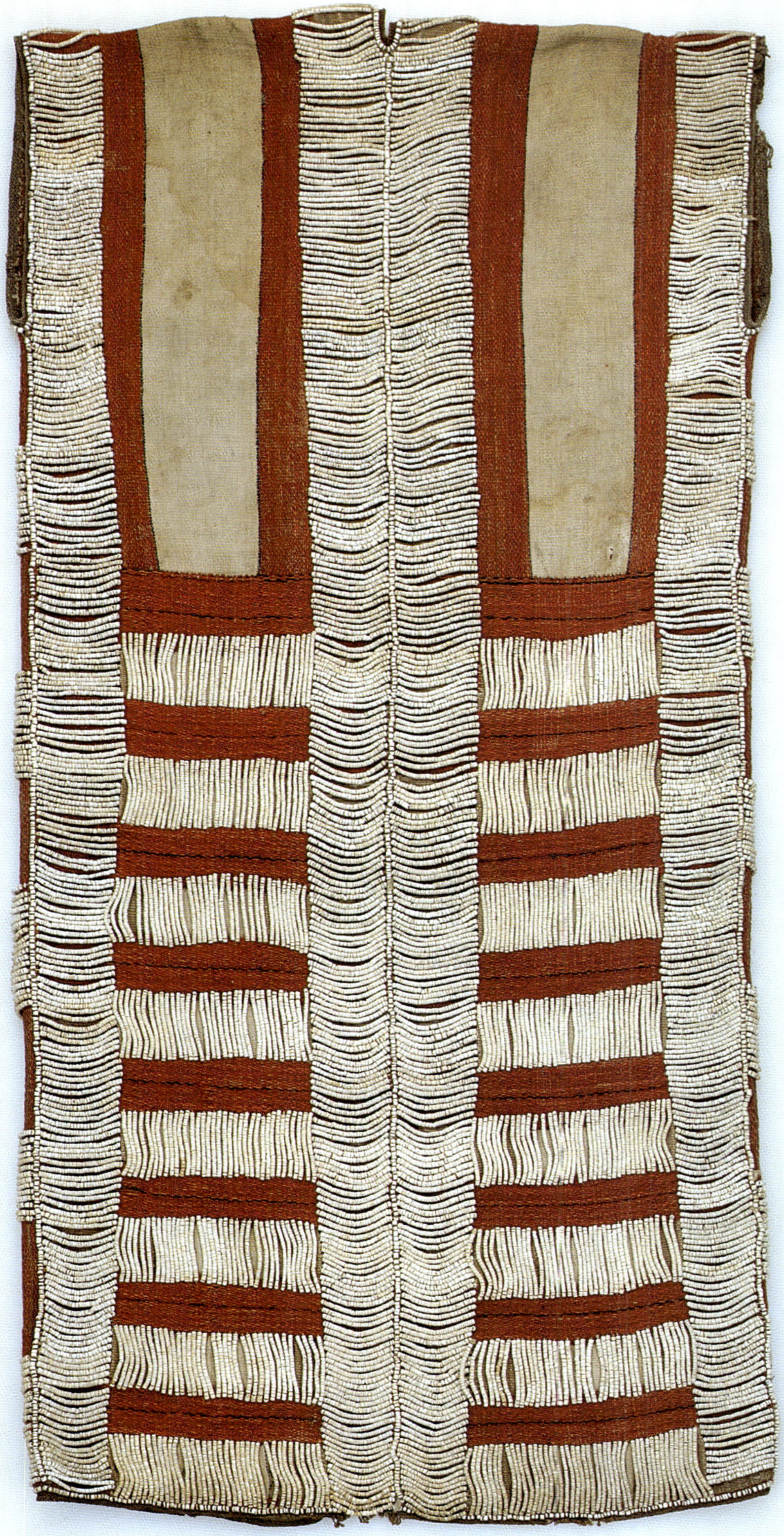

of Borneo, the mountain tribes of the Philippines, and the Paiwan of Taiwan. In early twentieth-century Borneo, a slave could still be bought for a single polychrome bead.[18]

The famous *lukut sekala* beads found in Sarawak, (Timeline 921b), are Islamic or Venetian beads or, proposes Jamey D. Allen, Venetian copies of Islamic period beads. Earlier suggestions that *lukut* were from the Roman era are no longer credible.[19]

Beads were used as amulets throughout Southeast Asia. In Sarawak, *lukut* means both a decorated bead and a design tattooed on the wrist. Rather than fastening one of these beads on a string around his wrist to prevent the soul's departure from the body, a Sarawak would often tattoo the *lukut* design on his wrist, thereby eliminating the risk of loss. As a bead or tattoo, the *lukut* warded off death and disease.[20] Other beads had a value that extended past life: like the ancient Egyptians, the Dayak put beads under a corpse's eyelids, so that the ghost could pay for its passage across the river of death.[21]

The first glass seedbeads were brought to Southeast Asia during the first century A.D. by Indian traders. (There is, however, no evidence that they were used for either woven and netted beadwork or embroidery in Indonesia until the seventeenth century.)[22]

By the sixteenth century, European traders became the main source of seedbeads. Textiles decorated with seedbeads and used for ritual purposes were an important part of Indonesian culture for centuries. Indonesians believed in maintaining harmony between man and the cosmic order by performing sacred rites during most important undertakings, including negotiations for a bride, planning an attack, building a house, or planting crops. These rituals required elaborate music, food, costumes, and gifts, including beaded textiles that protected their owners against evil by pleasing the good spirits. Indonesians had a strong sense of the transformational powers of costume and therefore paid close attention to ritual dress. Beadwork, made of durable glass, was meant to give the wearer strength, especially when it covered the entire body.[23]

In Borneo (Kalimantan and Sarawak), beadwork was particularly important to the Dayak people. A heavily forested island with great rivers, Borneo is situated between mainland Southeast Asia and the Indonesian and Philippine island chains. The island has been exposed to Chinese, Japanese, Celebes, Malay, Dutch, and English influences. As river people, the Dayak maintained contact with the coast and therefore with foreign traders. They made beads of clay, shell, and animal teeth, trading these to the Chinese for glass and porcelain beads. While Dayak art, like that of other tribes in Southeast Asia, adopted motifs from the earlier Dong Son culture, the extensive use of imported colored beads reflects the importance of trade in the creation of their own bead culture.

The Dayak associated fine beaded jewelry with high status and ceremonies honoring ancestors. Glass, porcelain, iron, and clay beads were used to decorate hats, vests, tunics, baby carriers, and ritual objects. Favored patterns included the rhombus and the key spiral, both of which were derived from the Dong Son culture.[24] Dayak religion was based on a complex series of ideas uniting complementary opposites. The weaving of cloth was considered a female activity, while beadwork was associated with men. Beaded textiles were combined male and female efforts and thereby endowed with an extra measure of protective power.[25]

The Philippines

An archipelago of over seven thousand islands, the Philippines were once attached by land bridges to Indonesia on the south and the Asian mainland on the north. Ancestors of modern Filipinos—consisting of more than one hundred distinct groups—appear to have entered the islands over these land bridges.

About 5000 B.C., enterprising people of many different Filipino ethnic groups (who spoke various Austronesian languages) began trading with Celebes, Timor, and Indonesia. They traveled in dugout canoes and outriggers, spreading ideas, skills, and languages along their trade routes, which in part may account for the similarity of cultural patterns in the Philippines despite little evidence of actual migrations.

The earliest beads found in the Philippines came from a small cave at Lipuun Point, on the east coast of Palawan, and date to the second millennium B.C. Made of locally available shell, stone, and jade, these beads were found with some of the earliest known pottery in Southeast Asia.[26]

Between 1000 B.C. and A.D. 500, Philippine culture was virtually free of influences from outside Southeast Asia, although there was limited contact with other societies via trade. Gold, shell, and clay beads were made on the islands; carnelian, agate, black-and-white banded onyx and glass beads were imported from eastern India and jade from China. Burial sites from this period yield numerous monochrome glass beads, including small seedbeads and *mutisalah*, all known to have been manufactured at Arikamedu and other south Indian centers.[27] Large quantities of Indian-made stone and glass beads are found in the Philippines, but there is little evidence that they came through direct Indian-Filipino trade. The beads probably changed hands several times before reaching the Philippines. There was, however, direct Filipino contact with China and Thailand. Since Indo-Pacific beads (the alternate name by which most Asian seedbeads are now known) were made in Thailand or Vietnam, these are also possible bead sources, depending on the times involved.[28]

A succession of traders brought beads into the Philippines, including the Arabs, who dominated commerce in the Pacific from the eleventh to the seventeenth century. They were joined in the tenth century by the Chinese, who, though they had been trading in the region for centuries, greatly increased their activities during the thirteenth century. In exchange for Philippine pearls, the Chinese traded gold, silver, jade, textiles, and porcelain, as well as glass beads. Twelfth- and thirteenth-century archaeological sites have produced a wealth of stone beads, as well as polychrome, melon, and small, monochrome glass beads introduced by Arab and Chinese traders.

Sixteenth-century Spanish explorers reported that beads were a common form of exchange in the Philippines. Wealthy Filipinos wore lavish gold jewelry, including necklaces of gold and glass beads. The earliest gold beads from the Philippines, dating to 500 B.C., have been excavated at Guri Cave on the island of Palawan. Sites dating from A.D. 1000 have yielded skillfully crafted gold beads, including some with granulation. Surprisingly, Philippine goldwork differs from that of other Southeast Asian islands, in contrast to the similarities between other artifacts.[29]

Among the most interesting pre-Hispanic Philippine artifacts are necklaces of gold beads composed of series of small dentate rings with serrated edges that interlock perfectly to form a chain (plate 226). There remain questions as to whether these exquisitely made gold beads, as well as others of glass and stone, were locally crafted or imported. Bands of itinerant craftsmen have been suggested, and a 1568 Spanish account indicates that in Camarines, a province of southern Luzon, "there are many goldsmiths...those men roam the island in order to gain their living."[30] Anthropologist Alastair Lamb postulates that groups of glass and stone beadmakers traveled throughout Southeast Asia, settling temporarily wherever markets existed.[31]

Beads have always been particularly important to the dress and ritual life of ethnic minorities in the Philippines, especially in the highlands. Mountain peoples of northern Luzon boast the greatest variety of beads, while the most elaborate beadwork exists

TOP: 245. *An example of a multistrand assemblage of old, opaque glass beads, separated by metal dividers, used in Paiwan ceremonies. Tribespeople classify beads by their colored patterns and forms, often characterizing them as male and female. Some beads are treated as sacred treasures handed down from the days of the founding ancestors. These beads are similar to ones equally valued by tribes in the Philippines and Indonesia.*[VIII] *Pre-1950s. Length, top to bottom of necklace, 27.9 cm. Height of center area (top row with three beads to bottom row with nine beads) 6.4 cm. Collection Toby Bowlby*

BOTTOM: 246. *These glass beads, similar but older than those of the Paiwan necklace shown in plate 245, probably date to the nineteenth century. National Museum of Natural History, Smithsonian Institution, Washington, D.C.*

OPPOSITE, TOP LEFT: 247. *A money belt of red and black coral and shell beads and dolphin and human teeth, used as a bride-price in Malaita, Solomon Islands. Length, 54.2 cm. Collection Tambaran Gallery, New York*

OPPOSITE, TOP RIGHT: 248. *A crown of porpoise teeth and glass beads from the Marquesa Islands, French Polynesia. Since twenty teeth are currently worth about one U.S. dollar, and the glass trade beads are a valuable cut-glass variety, the crown represents considerable wealth in local terms.*[X] *Outside diameter, 20 cm. Collection Tambaran Gallery, New York*

OPPOSITE BOTTOM: 249. *A shell disk armband* (aba gwaro) *from Malaita, Solomon Islands. This example of the finest shell disk jewelry from Malaita was usually worn by men at feasts and weddings. The pattern is composed of strips of disks set at alternating 45-degree angles. The beadwork demonstrates symmetry, balance, and a sense of restraint, as well as workmanship of extreme precision.*

Strings of shell beads are found throughout the Pacific, but red, white, and black disks woven into patterns are typically Malaitan. The same weaving technique was used for bracelets, anklets, belts, and necklaces.[XI] *Typical bead: diameter, 0.31 cm. Collection Tambaran Gallery, New York*

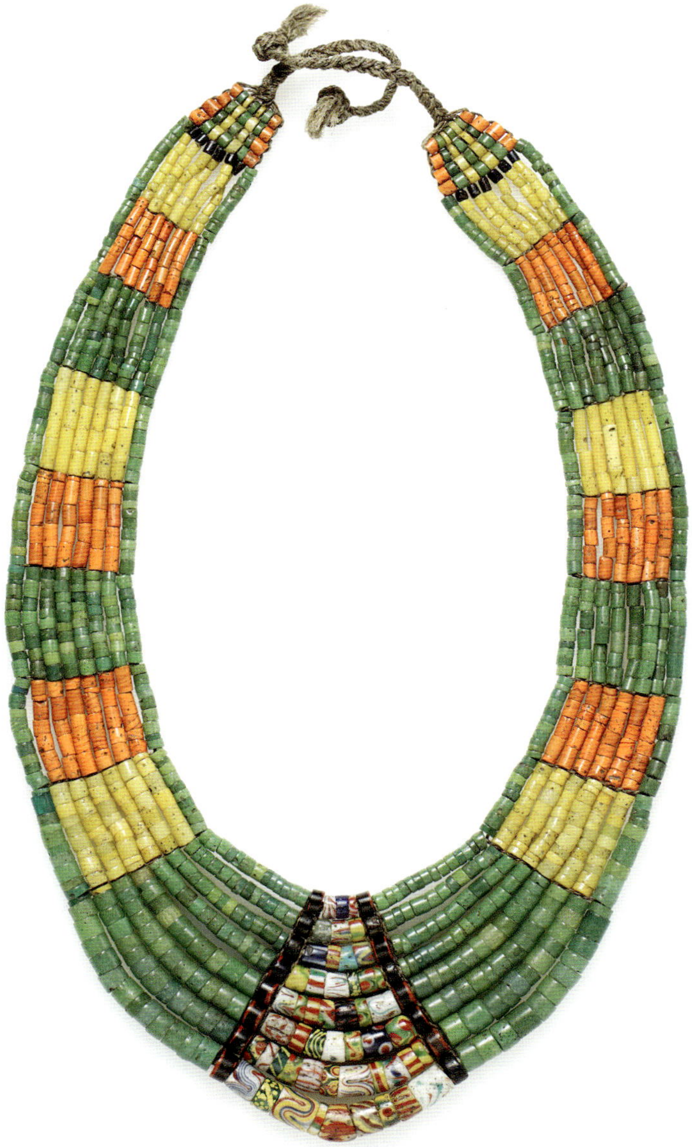

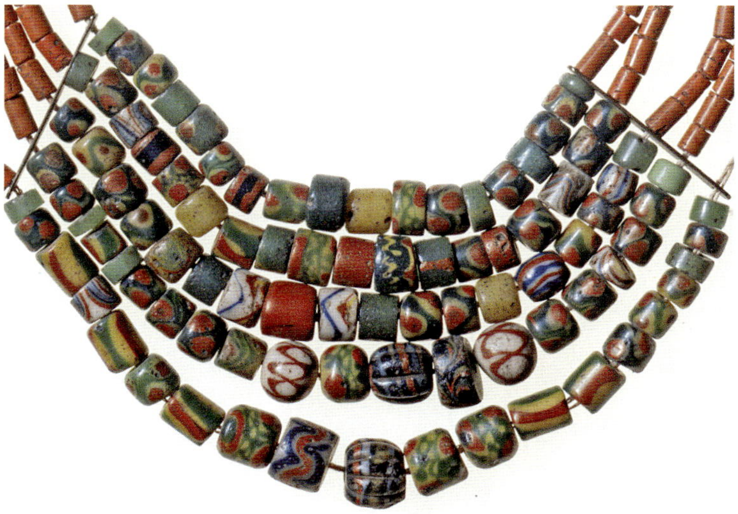

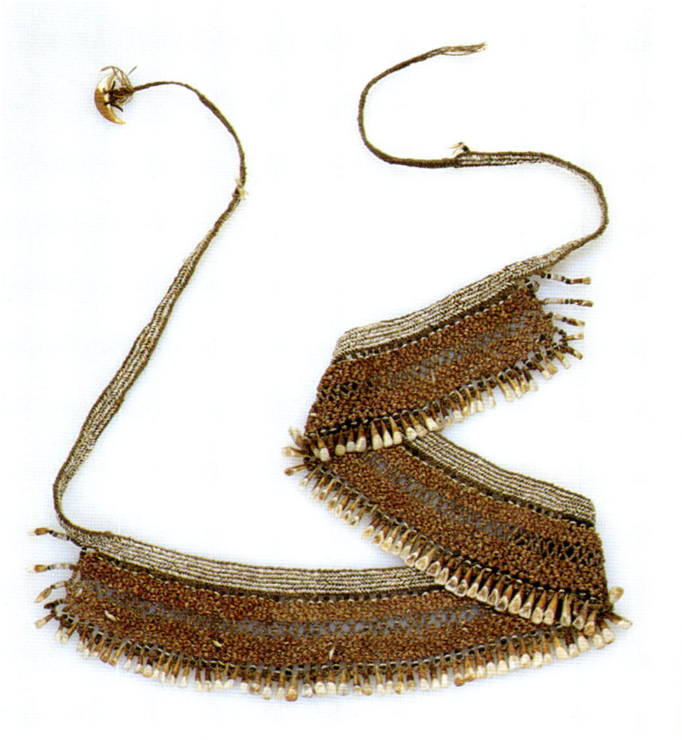

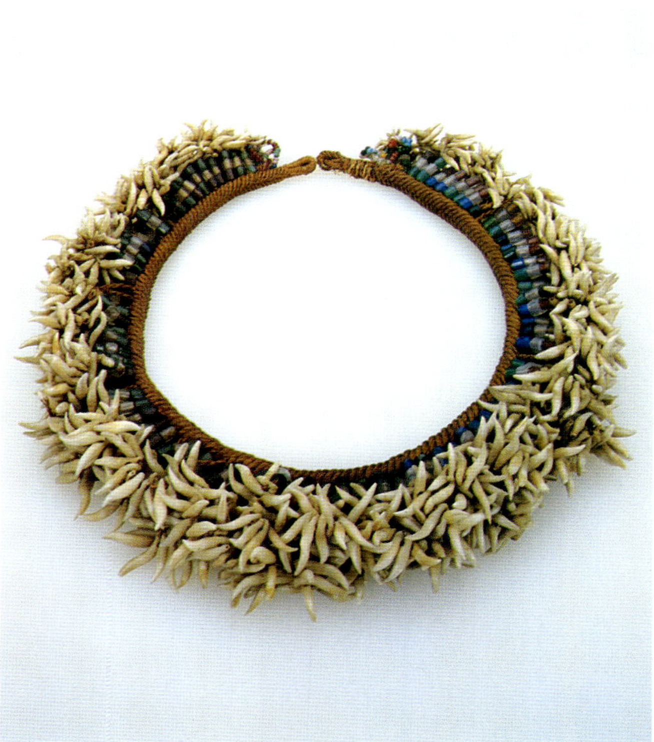

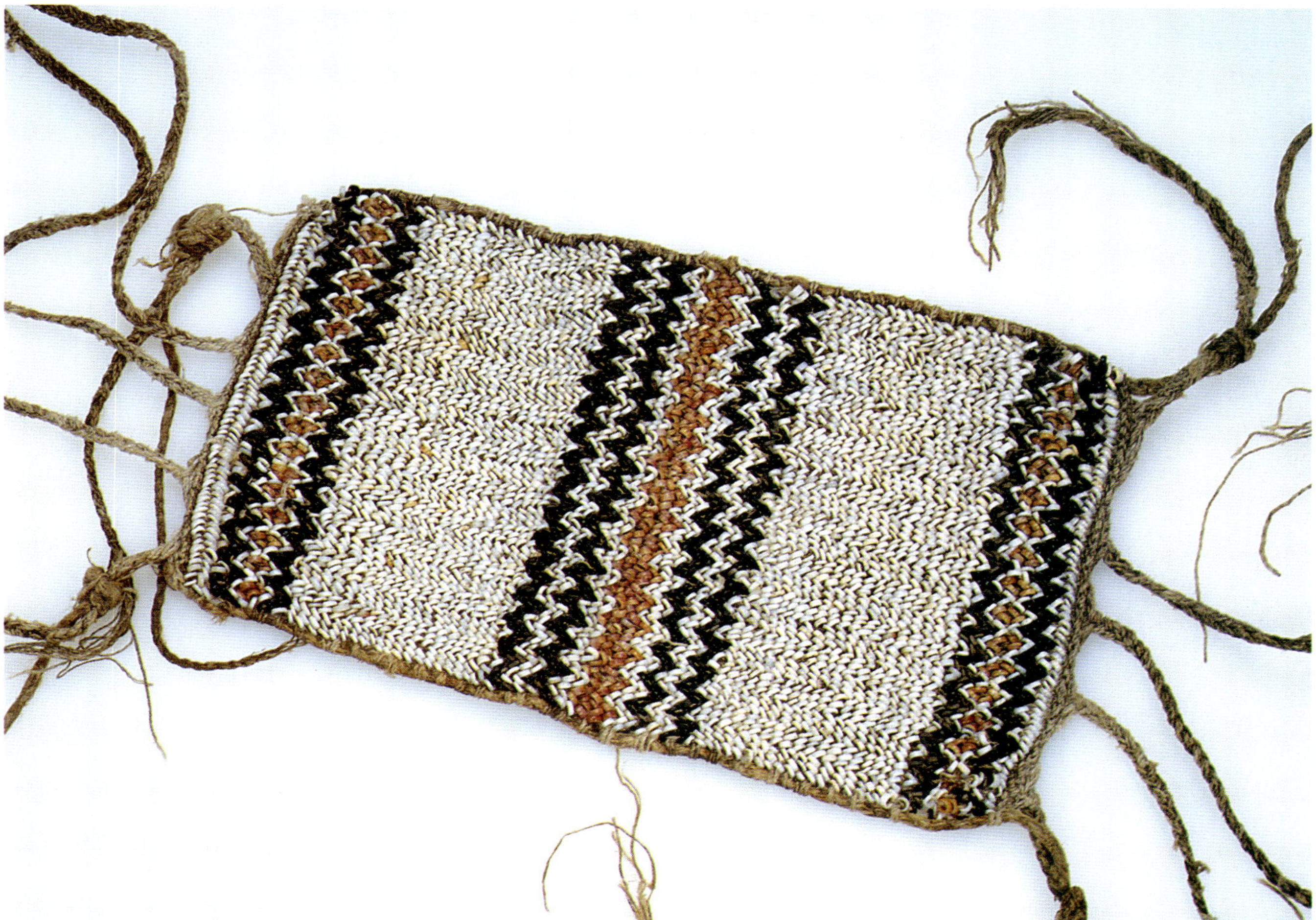

in the southern Philippines, where imaginative designs offset a lack of variety in the beads themselves. Men wore beads as amulets and as part of the ritualistic adornment proclaiming their capacities as warriors and headhunters—activities that transformed an adolescent into an adult. Girls of marrying age wore beads to display family wealth. At mountain tribal weddings, the groom's mother dropped two agate beads into a shell cup from which the bride and groom drank, following the saying "As two beads together at the bottom, so you will go together and not part."[32]

High-ranking families in northern Luzon, like those of Celebes and eastern Indonesia, owned beads of precious metal and stone, while shell and bone beads belonged to the poor. Ranking individuals also claimed certain designs and shapes in jewelry, and carnelian, agate, and old glass beads were important elements of household treasures. These family relics had special names and long histories.

For Luzon highlanders, like the Kalinga, beads were essential articles of clothing and stores of material wealth. They were worn in multiple strands around the head, or in bracelets or armbands. Above the waist, a Kalinga woman wore only multiple strands of beads, with tattoos adorning her arms and shoulders. Her beads were chevrons, *cornaline d'Aleppo*, and monochrome glass in red, white, yellow, and black. Because of their curative powers, Kalinga healers placed beads, especially those of carnelian, beside the sick, reciting incantations over them. Some of the most valuable beads were large, oblong banded-onyx or agate forms called *kalngiking*.[33] Kalinga beads of agate, carnelian, glass, and coral are so numerous and varied that some villages have their own bead terms.

Heirloom beads were greatly treasured by the Kalinga, deriving their value from their nonutilitarian function, their family history, and their local reputation. As a result, it has been observed that "it would be futile for anyone to cast a new gold earring or [make a stone] bead, however closely the color and form of the old one might be imitated in it...and try to get a high price for it, for every Kalinga knows all the old beads in his community or neighboring one."[34]

Other Filipino mountain groups, including the Tinggian, wore ceremonial dress with masses of beads. A French surgeon traveling in Tinggian territory about 1820 saw women wearing "sleeve-like bracelets of beads and head ornaments of pearls, coral beads, and pieces of gold."[35] Among the Gaddang of northern Luzon, the would-be groom's family offered a valuable "marriage bead" (*kiring*), worth up to three water buffalo, to the family of the prospective bride. If her parents accepted the bead, it was considered the beginning of the young man's service to his future wife's family.[36]

For the Gaddang, beads were a medium of exchange and an indicator of family wealth, as well as an important component of religion. Male ritual costume included bead necklaces. Women's ceremonial dress consisted of beaded textiles and masses of heavy beads used as necklaces and head ornaments. Weighed down with many strings of beads, woman mediums went into trances to contact the spirit world, sometimes asking for a bead.[37]

Taiwan

Taiwan's population is composed of both Chinese immigrants and indigenous tribal people whose culture resembles those of highland tribes in the Philippines, Indonesia, and Malaysia. The Atayal tribes occupy northern Taiwan, while the Paiwan live in the south. As with other island cultures, the beads of Taiwan are often made of teeth, bone, or marine shell. Shell of the giant clam was used for disk beads and for spacers in multistrand glass and stone bead necklaces. The Paiwan tribes, with the most sophisticated social system and most elaborate personal adornment, wore complex necklaces of multicolored glass beads and used glass seedbeads extensively on clothing and accessories.[38]

Polychrome glass beads found in Taiwan resemble those associated with other island tribes throughout Southeast Asia (plates 245–6). The far-flung activities of traders throughout the islands of Southeast Asia may explain the strong similarities between Taiwanese beads and those found in the Philippines, Indonesia, and Malaysia. Presently, it is not clear who manufactured these glass beads, although it is known that Chinese glassmakers settled in Java during the early seventeenth century, exporting their beads to Borneo and possibly other islands. The polychrome beads may therefore be the work of Southeast Asian Chinese, although other candidates include the Chinese mainlanders, Indians, Arabs, and even Europeans.[39] Recently, Paiwan-like beads have been coming out of Thailand, and from the Chinese minority tribes.[40]

South Pacific

The small, self-contained island societies of the South Pacific used outrigger canoes in sophisticated interisland trading networks. Beads were an important component of these systems. Ceremonial gift exchanges cemented relationships between island populations. For example, the *Kula* ring, created by the Trobriand Islanders on the eastern edge of New Guinea, combined ethnically diverse and geographically distant peoples into an effective exchange system. Spondylus shell armbands circulated from man to man and from island to island in a counterclockwise direction, while necklaces of shell beads circulated in the opposite direction. Incentive to participate in the system was heightened by the possibility of temporarily possessing one of the more famous *Kula* necklaces or armbands.[41] The *Kula* ring functioned as a network for trading food and raw materials, and the amount and sophistication of gifts demonstrated the donor's wealth and greatness, while placing the recipient in his debt.

The shell beads from Malaita Island in the Solomon chain, southeast of New Guinea, were among the most famous and beautiful in the South Pacific. To gain respect and influence in his community, a man accumulated wealth in the form of shell beads, which were especially valuable because so much work went into grinding and drilling them. A man gave many strings of shell beads as a bride-price to his intended's family. By lending shell beads to relatives who wanted to marry, a man placed them in his debt, assuring similar assistance when needed. A bead lender thus became a leader in his community.[42] Although strings of shells occur in other parts of the Pacific, weaving the disks into patterns is typically Malaitan. Made from shell, teeth, and fiber, this jewelry was worn during feasts, weddings, and other special events to display wealth and social position. Glass beads, introduced through late eighteenth-century explorers, were never as coveted as those of locally made shell (plate 249).

Throughout the mainland and islands of Southeast Asia, there is a great similarity in beads from the most ancient times to the early twentieth century. These beads in turn have counterparts in south India, Africa, the Middle East, Japan, eastern Europe, and the Mediterranean. Despite this objective evidence of a complex relationship between diverse manufacturing locations and widely scattered Southeast Asian cultures, there is little precise dating and documentation of manufacturing locations for many Southeast Asian beads, reflecting the dearth of controlled archaeological field research in this area and in some of the source areas as well. Although some important bead research has been started in the Philippines, Thailand, and Indonesia, Southeast Asia offers significant potential for future investigations.

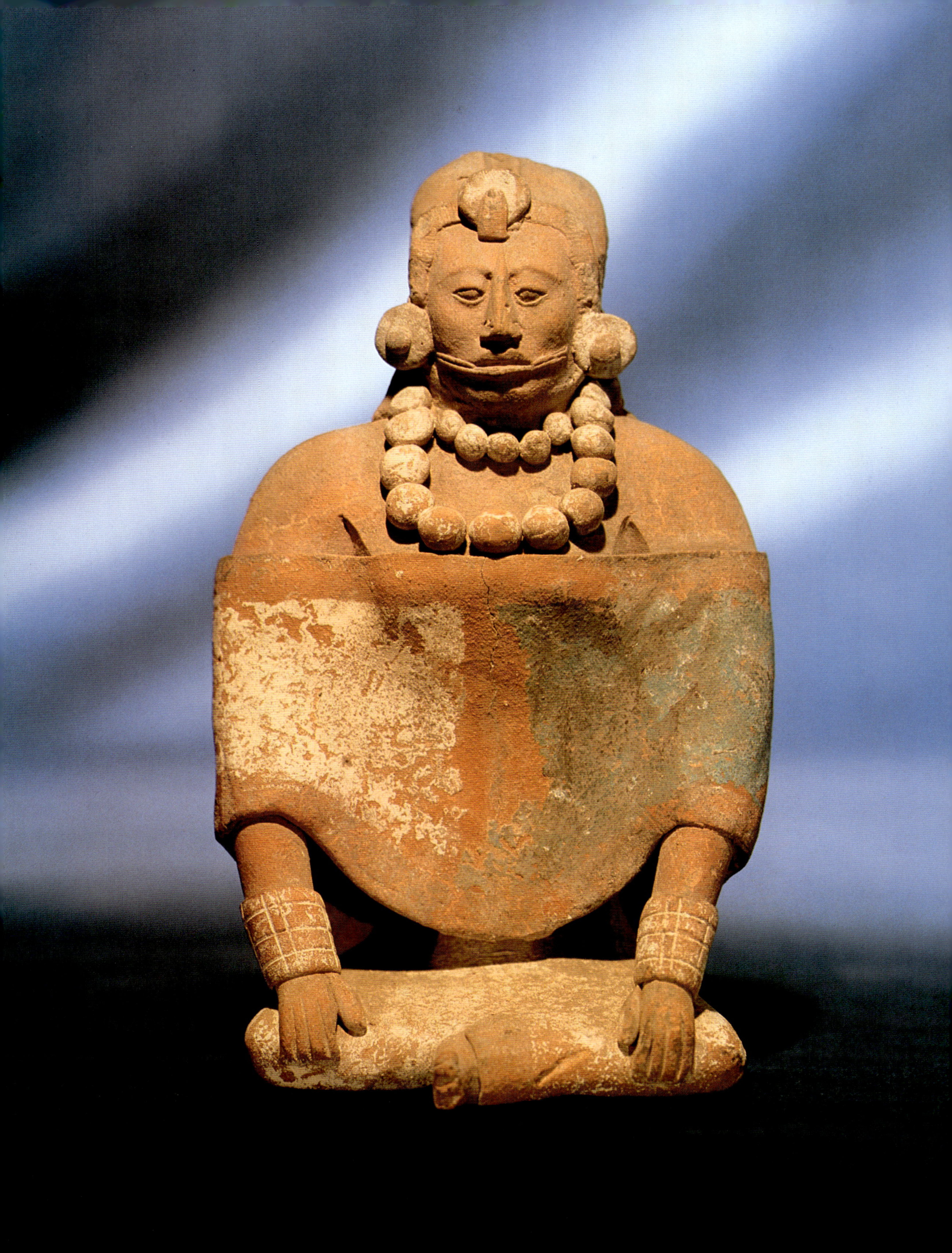

Middle and South America

Ever since their Asiatic ancestors crossed the Bering Strait into what is today Alaska, at least fifteen thousand and perhaps as many as thirty-five thousand years ago, American Indians have been developing and adapting their cultures to the myriad environments of North, Middle, and South America. By the time the Spanish arrived almost five hundred years ago, a wide range of Indian cultures of varying complexity existed between the Arctic Sea and the Strait of Magellan. Most of the Americas was occupied by various forms of village-farming societies, but there were also simple hunting-and-gathering societies, which stood in stark contrast to the great civilizations of the Maya, Aztec, and Inca. Despite the cultural sophistication of the notable Middle and South American civilizations, they lacked important technological assets, including gunpowder, and they were highly vulnerable to European diseases, which prevented them from warding off the Spanish conquest of the New World. From 1519 to 1533, the conquistadors defeated both the Aztec and Inca empires and profoundly changed the customs of their people. Prehistoric Middle and South American peoples had produced a variety of beautiful beads, but the most valued were those of jade and gold. Important symbolic reinforcements of the status structure, beads were significant features of Indian societies, and their manufacture and distribution was carefully controlled. With the breakdown of Indian civilizations and the elimination of the elite, jade and gold beads disappeared.

250. *Maya pottery figurine from the Island of Jaina, Campeche, dating to about* A.D. *800. Note the necklace of large jade beads and the jade ear flares. Height, 17.2 cm. University Museum, University of Pennsylvania, Philadelphia*

Beads appear early in the history of Middle and South American cultures. Snail shell beads from southern Mexico date to 7500 B.C., and a stone discoidal bead from the Mexican Valley of Tehuacán dates to about 3000 B.C.[1] Beadmaking in Middle America developed as farming societies were established and ceremonialism and increasingly complex social and political relationships evolved as part of village life. Much of the evidence for the Middle American beadmaking tradition is found in archaeological sites. Beads appear in substantial numbers beginning with the Pre-Classic period (1500 B.C.) and continuing through the late Post-Classic civilizations of the Mixtec and Toltec up to A.D. 1500. These beads (and their counterparts in South America) are well preserved, for they were buried prior to the arrival of the Spanish. Bead evidence after 1519 is scanty because the products of major jewelry-making cultures like the Aztec and Inca were largely destroyed by the Spanish during or soon after the conquest.

Until the Spanish arrived, beadmaking was a flourishing industry, particularly among the more complex Middle and South American societies. From the emergence of the Olmec civilization in the thirteenth century B.C. to the collapse of the Aztec and Inca empires twenty-seven centuries later, native craftsmen wrought exquisite gold and jade bead necklaces throughout Middle and South America. Located on the Gulf Coast (present-day Veracruz and Tabasco), the Olmecs (1250–400 B.C.) created the first great civilization in Middle America. They produced beautiful beads, particularly of jade, that used motifs similar to the articulation of their stone sculpture (plate 253). Mayan (A.D. 1–900) craftsmen of southern Mexico and Guatemala also made elaborate beads. Ceramic figurines, painted scenes on pottery, and limestone carvings show Mayan gods and rulers wearing large beads (the latters' crown jewels). Carved Mayan beads often incorporated motifs identical to those seen on buildings, pottery, sculpture, and paintings (plates 254–6). In Peru, the Chavin civilization (1200–300 B.C.) produced elaborate stone sculpture, monumental architecture, and new techniques for textile manufacturing, as well as beads made from hammered sheet gold (plate 257). Highly artistic and technically superb beads of stone, shell, and metal, dating to c. A.D. 300–600, were crafted by the Moche people of Sipan in northern Peru (plates 270–271).

As cultures grew more complex throughout Middle and South America, the need to identify rank and social position increased. In the early civilizations of Mexico, Guatemala, and Peru, elaborately carved stone (especially jade) and fabricated or cast gold beads became hallmarks of elite status. Their size, quantity, quality of design and workmanship, made them effective devices for communicating social distinctions. The unusually large size of Middle American Mayan jade beads, for example, reflects their role as repositories of wealth and symbols of status. Quantities of scarce (although locally available) materials, like jade, were concentrated in the hands of the elite, who retained these valuable substances in the form of oversize beads. Farther south, however, cultures such as the Peruvian Chimu in the Andes Mountains did not have jade, and they lived a considerable distance from the sources of most other coveted materials such as turquoise, spondylus shell, and malachite. Consequently, their beads tended to be smaller in scale, made from a wider range of raw materials, and used in more intricately designed assemblages. At the same time, since the Chimu were near sources of gold, their gold beads tended to be oversized.[2]

Jade Beads

In Middle America, jade beads were made primarily by the Olmecs, the Maya, and the peoples of Costa Rica between 100 B.C. and A.D. 600. South of Costa Rica, beadmakers used other hard stones. This may reflect the proximity of the Mexican, Guatemalan, and Costa Rican groups to jade sources. Jade beads first appear in Pre-Classic Olmec tombs about 1000 B.C. made of a distinctive blue-green stone (plate 253). It was during the Classic period (A.D. 1–900) that apple-green jade, probably found in the Guatemalan highlands, began to appear in Mayan and Teotihuacán bead offerings. In the Post-Classic period, the supply of jade seems to have diminished, and later Mixtec and Aztec offerings often disclose less brilliantly colored jade. As a result, earlier Olmec and Mayan jade beads and pendants were sometimes reworked.[3]

Jade was very rare in Europe before the Spanish conquest of the New World in

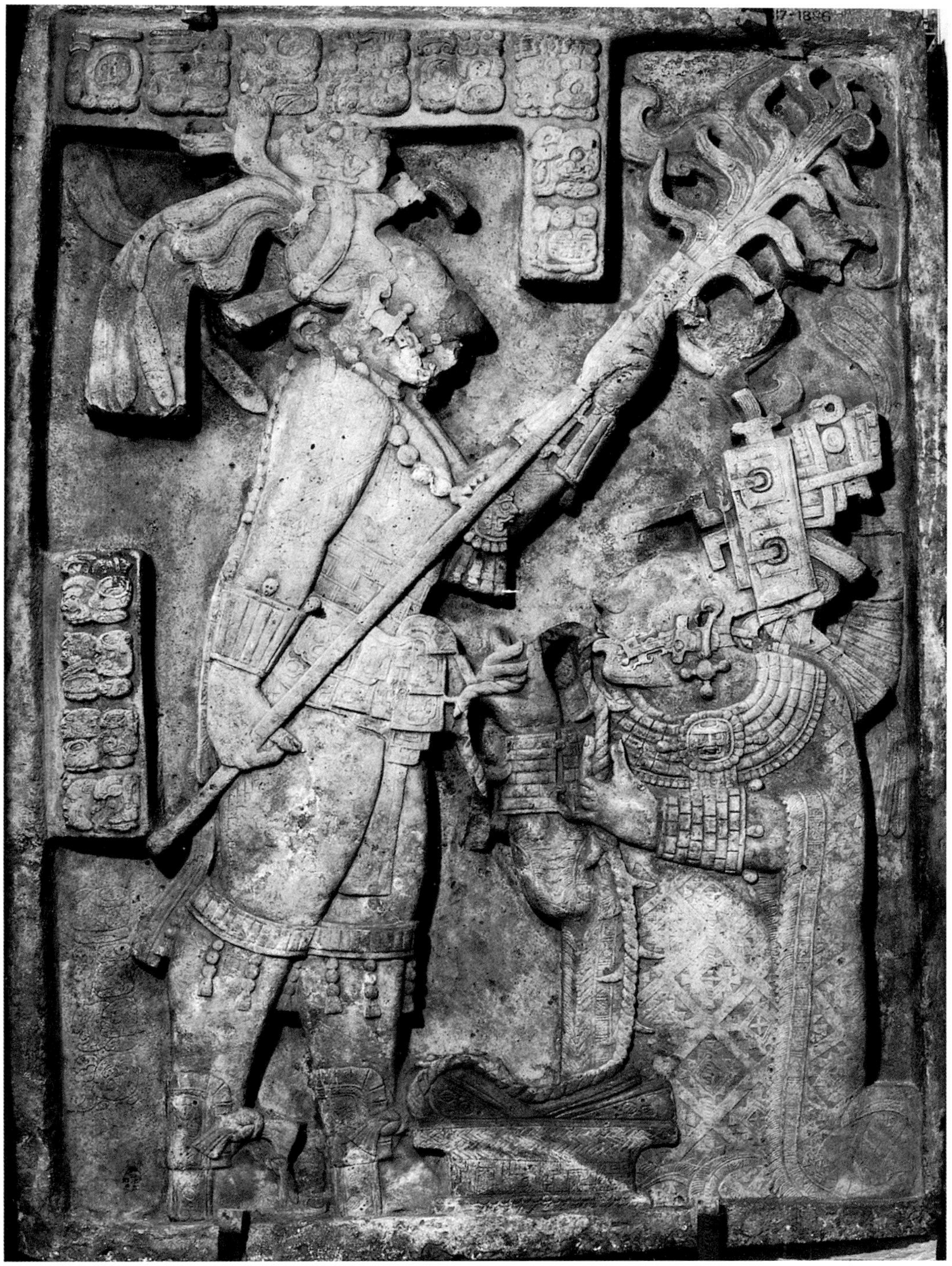

251. *Since many Middle and South American beads have not been recovered under controlled conditions, our knowledge of how they were worn on the human body comes primarily from depictions on pottery and architectural panels.*

This limestone lintel panel from the Palace at Yaxchilán, Chiapas, Mexico—considered one of the masterpieces of Mayan art—depicts a bloodletting scene. The importance of the king (standing) and his wife (kneeling) is indicated by the massive—presumably jade—beads they are wearing. The king's beaded necklace, with a design of the sun god on the pectoral, is counterbalanced by a long strand falling down his back. Late Classic period, A.D. *725. Height, 110.5 cm. British Museum, London*

OVERLEAF: 252. *Two alligator effigy beads from Costa Rica's Atlantic Watershed region dating between* A.D. *1 and 500. The combination of human and alligator forms had symbolic importance in prehistoric Costa Rica. These beads are unusual in that they have been carved and perforated to hang vertically.*[1] *Left bead: height, 15 cm. Instituto Nacional de Seguros, San José, Costa Rica*

the sixteenth century. Although preoccupied with the search for gold, the Spaniards did notice that the Indians held this beautiful green stone in high esteem. To the Aztecs, green, symbolizing water and vegetation, was an ideal color. The Aztec Emperor Montezuma, presenting the Spanish explorer Hernán Cortés with a gift of jade for Charles V, told the astonished Spaniard that "a fine piece of jade was worth two loads of gold."[4] Shortly thereafter, jade beads saved the life of the conquistador Bernal Diaz del Castillo. When the Spanish explorers were forced to flee from the Aztec capital, Tenochtitlán, Castillo traded his captured booty of gold and silver for a few jade beads, which did not weigh him down when he swam to safety and later were exchanged for food.[5]

OPPOSITE, TOP LEFT: 253. *A superb Olmec crescent-shaped jade pectoral bead from the first millennium* B.C.

The Olmec were skilled stone carvers. Their jade carvings exhibit the monumentality of their stone sculpture.

The incised design represents a stylized crocodile deity in profile. It was probably cut into the stone with a cactus spine using pumice abrasive. Red cinnabar fills the incisions. The soft, glossy finish was achieved by polishing with sand and water, a technique requiring great persistence.

The use of cinnabar with burial objects considered precious (gold, silver, and jade) was widespread throughout Middle and South America. The custom was also common in China during the first millennium B.C., *a point frequently mentioned as evidence of ancient trans-Pacific contact. Length, 19 cm. Private Collection*

OPPOSITE, TOP RIGHT: 254. *The mat motif incised on this jade bead and inlaid with red cinnabar has a long and important history in Mayan art. A mat was the Mayan equivalent of the royal throne. Only rulers had the right to sit on the mat and use its symbol.*[IV] *This bead dates to the first century* A.D. *and is from Izapa on the Mexico-Guatemala border. Length, 12.7 cm. Collection Edward Merrin Gallery, New York*

OPPOSITE, BOTTOM LEFT: 255. *A Mayan jade bead,* A.D. *200–500, carved from a water-worn pebble that has been slightly modified, perforated, and polished. The surface of many beads are water-worn, indicating that jade pebbles from river gravels were the source of the raw material. The exact location of jade-yielding alluvial gravels was a carefully guarded secret.*[V] *Diameter, 3.8 cm. Collection Edward Merrin Gallery, New York*

OPPOSITE: 256. *Mayan jade beads dating from* A.D. *300 to 700. Jade lapidaries repeated in miniature many of the symbols that Mayan sculptors carved on their massive stelae and temples. Back row, left to right: flower design; gourd effigy bead; incised snake design; carved acrobatic figure. Middle row: tubular bead. Front row: bar bead; alligator effigy from Uxmal. Back row, left bead: diameter, 1.9 cm. Back row, right bead: collection Andre Emmerich; Front row, left bead: collection Constance Emmerich. All other beads: collection Edward Merrin Gallery, New York*

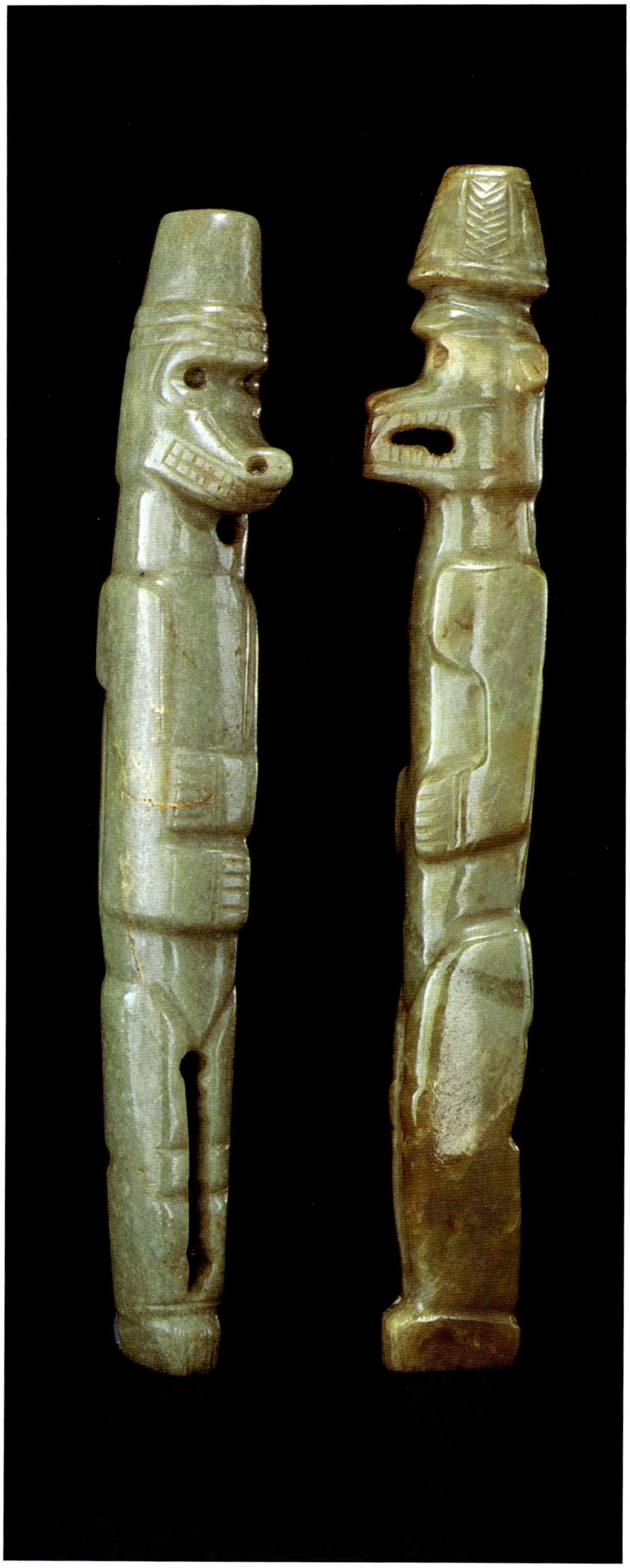

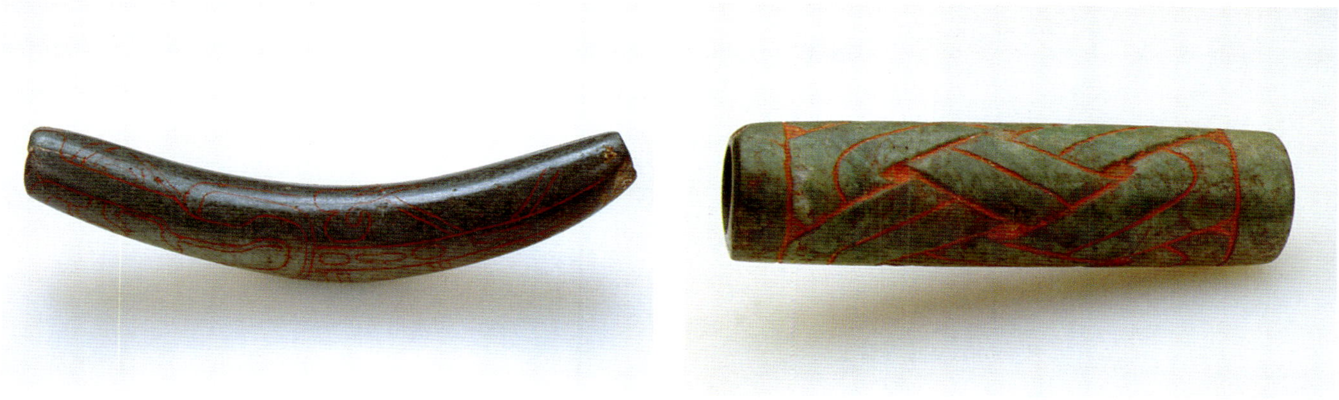

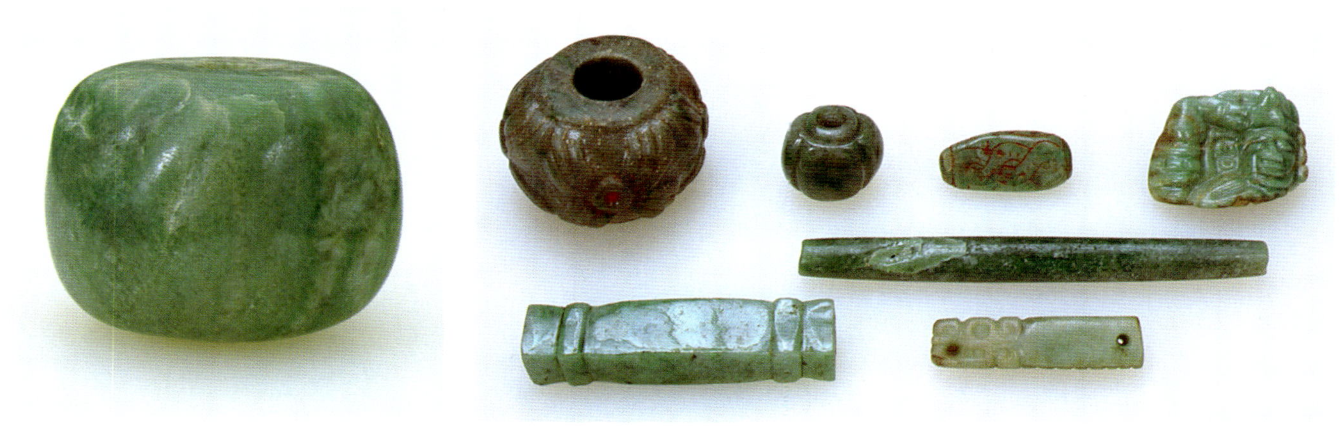

Mayan Jade Beads

Like the Olmecs and the Aztecs later, the Maya considered jade more precious than gold. Mayan nobility wore quantities of jade beads, and jade objects frequently accompanied elite individuals to the grave. All Mayan jade was imported, primarily from the region that today is Guatemala.

Although Mayan craftsmen were capable of creating precise and complex forms, their beads are rarely geometrically perfect, a fact that reflects both the stone's scarcity and its hardness. In order to lose minimal amounts of the precious material, a stone's irregularities and surface blemishes were incorporated into the finished design.

The Mayans preferred apple-colored and emerald green jade to the gray and blue green shades favored by the Olmecs. When carving jade, Mayans attempted to work around the green layers of the stone, further contributing to the uneven shape of the finished bead. Jade does not flake like flint or obsidian, and it must be ground and polished, another reason why the finished object conforms to the stone's natural shape. The acceptance of these irregularities is additional evidence of the scarcity and high value placed on this stone.[II]

Mayan beads were generally treated as single objects, whether in adornment or as mediums of exchange. With the exception of an elaborate burial at Tikal, Guatemala, where a large collar of graduated jade beads was found on a skeleton, most perfectly matched sets of beads only occur as representations on carvings, pottery, and stelae. In reality, various sizes of tubular and spherical beads were combined in an irregular order.[III]

OVERLEAF: 257. *Complex, cut-out beads made from hammered gold sheets by Peruvian Chavin craftsmen about 500 B.C. This is the earliest metalworking technique practiced in South America.*

The earliest known gold objects in Middle and South America are associated with the Chavin cultures (1200–300 B.C.) located on the Pacific coast of Peru.

Goldworking flourished in Peru, and by the Chimu period (A.D. 1000–1470), with the emergence of cities in the Andes, large quantities of beautifully crafted gold beads were made.

Although the art of casting and other complex techniques were executed by master Peruvian goldsmiths, including the Chimu,

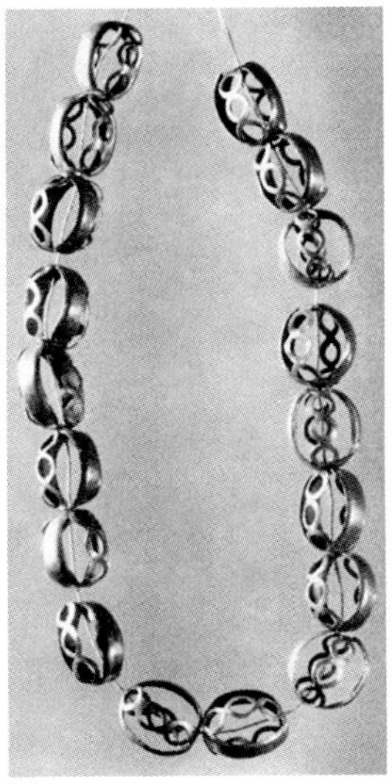

Peruvian metallurgy always used hammered sheetmetal. Using gold in sheets allowed craftsmen to stretch the available supply of metal.[VI] *One of the most interesting aspects of Peruvian (and particularly Chimu) goldwork is its relationship to textiles. Chimu craftsmen developed the technique for joining two pieces of metal together by observing similar techniques in the textiles of the earlier Parcas, Nazca, and Mochica cultures.*[VII] *Photograph courtesy of the Taft Museum, Cincinnati, Ohio*

OPPOSITE: 258. *Two rows of small gold beads joined by mask-shaped and cushion-shaped beads. Found in a Chimu grave (A.D. 1000–1470) at Eten Chiclayo in northern Peru. Necklace: length, 35.6 cm. British Museum, London*

The Codex Mendoza, an Aztec document containing ideographic writing and dating to the Post-Classic time, describes the use of jade beads as tribute, trade items, and currency. The codex also helps us to understand how raw jade was located and mined.[6] The term *jade* describes two distinct minerals, jadeite and nephrite, which vary greatly in quality and color. Ancient Middle American cultures generally worked with jadeite, while nephrite was used in early Chinese carvings and beads.[7] The term *jade* comes from the Spanish *piedra de ijada*, which means "loinstone." By the year 1600, the Spaniards, apparently influenced by Indian folk medicine, believed that wearing jade would cure kidney ailments.[8]

Jade is harder than steel; therefore carving it without metal tools was a masterful achievement. Because of its mineralogical structure, jade cannot be chipped like flint, but has to be worked by slow grinding and polishing. Techniques for shaping jade probably developed from those used earlier on other stones, once the potential of stone and bamboo abrasives was recognized. While pre-Hispanic jadeite beads are often quite large, their drilling and cutting may not have been as time-consuming as we imagine. It is possible, using ancient methods, to saw through one inch of jade in four hours.[9]

Gold Beads

Gold was available to pre-Hispanic Middle and South Americans in metallic nuggets largely found in riverbeds. Because the metal is scarce, readily identifiable, preservable, and not easily altered, it is an ideal repository of value. Its softness also makes it an excellent medium for creating valued jewelry.

In ancient America, both gold and silver were sacred materials closely connected with the sun god. Aztecs called gold "excrement of the gods," and silver, "white gold." Inca legend declares gold to be the "sweat of the sun," and silver, "the tears of the moon."[10] Gold is the one metal made into beads in all three regions of pre-Hispanic Middle and South America, and in each region a distinctive style emerged. The earliest known gold artifacts, thin, hammered sheets of the metal, are associated with the Chavin culture of coastal Peru and date to 500 B.C. (plate 257). Even in later times, when goldsmiths of the Peruvian Chimu and Inca cultures employed more complex casting techniques, there was still a preference for working in sheet gold. A second region in which gold was worked extended from Colombia through Panama and into Costa Rica. Gold ornaments from this area in the form of small sculptures were generally cast rather than hammered.[11] Goldworking also appears in Mexico with the Mixtees of Oaxaca (A.D. 720–1580) during the Post-Classic period (A.D. 900 and after). The Mixtecs' delicate gold beads, often combined in necklaces with multicolored stone beads, contrasted sharply with the Peruvian use of sheet gold.[12]

Pre-Hispanic Middle and South American goldsmiths were remarkably skillful. At the Panamanian site of Code, several strands of beads were found, each nine feet long and containing approximately twelve hundred identical cast gold beads. These beads have thin gold exteriors cast over inner cores that have disintegrated with time. Although Middle and South American beads are generally characterized by their large size, necklaces of miniature gold beads, each only one-sixteenth of an inch long, have been discovered, dating between A.D. 500 and the Spanish conquest.[13]

Lacking iron tools, the Indians created gold beads and intricate gold jewelry and sculpture with stone hammers and chisels, obsidian and copper knives, bone drills, and copper tubes. By the sixteenth century, some of the Indian craftsmanship rivaled that of ancient Egypt or Greece. Montezuma's craftsmen, for example, used gold and precious stones to produce lifelike effigies of all the animals found in the Aztec empire. When Spanish goldsmiths examined Aztec pieces sent home by Cortés, they were unable to understand how they had been made. Although sixteenth-century European documents

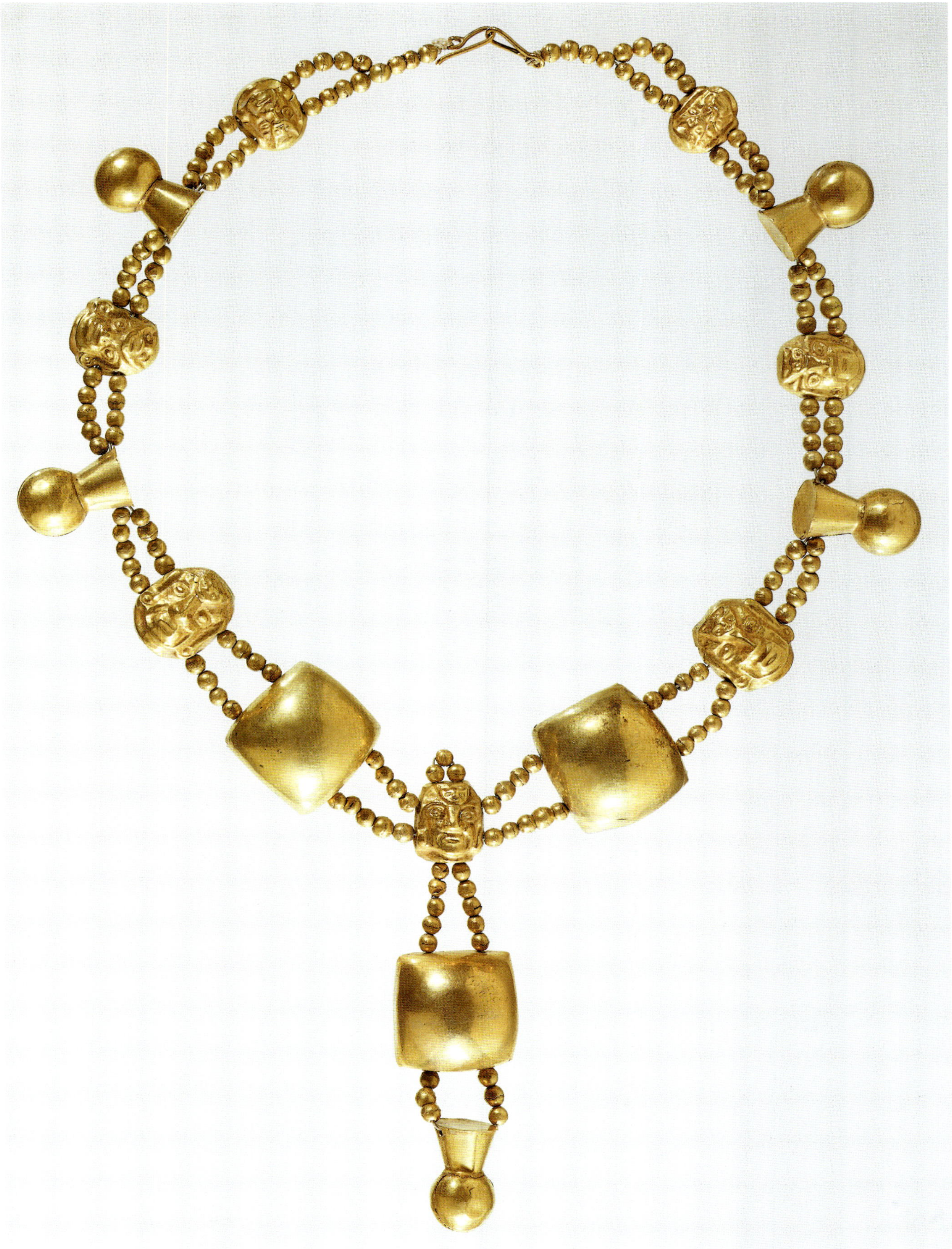

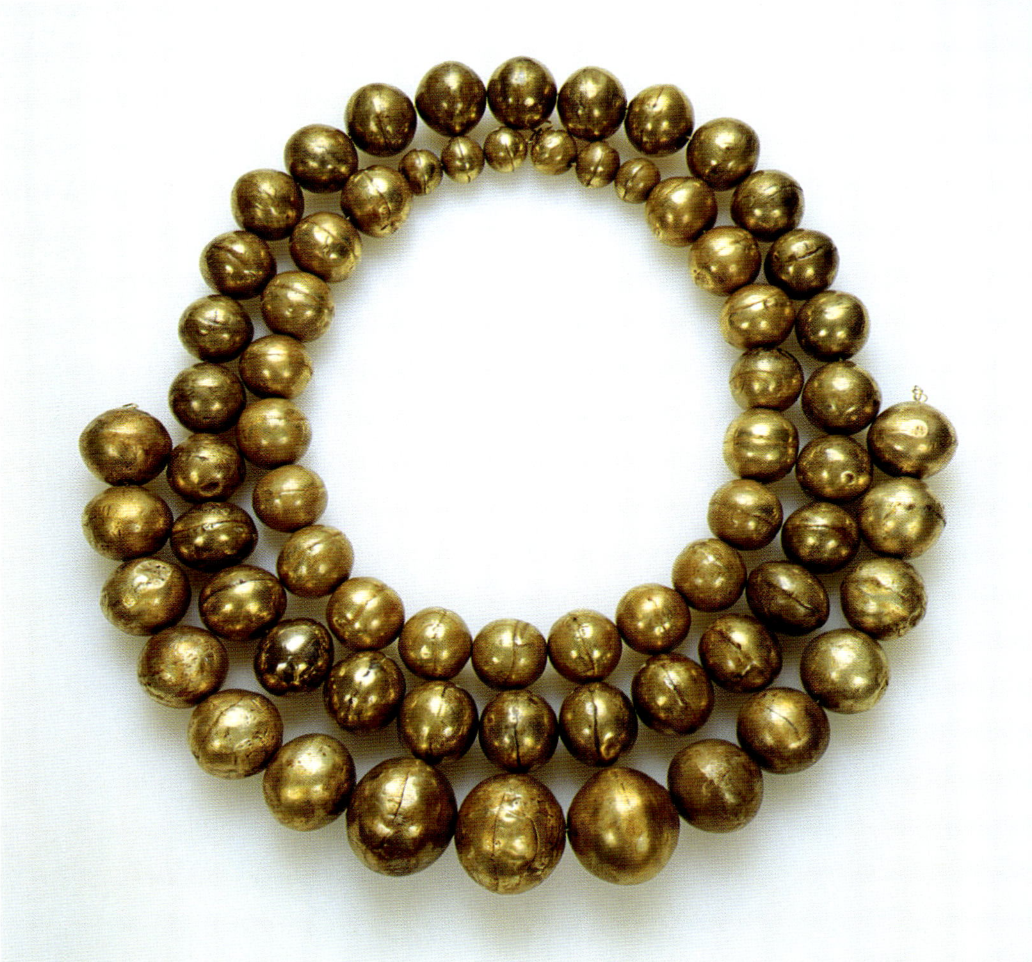

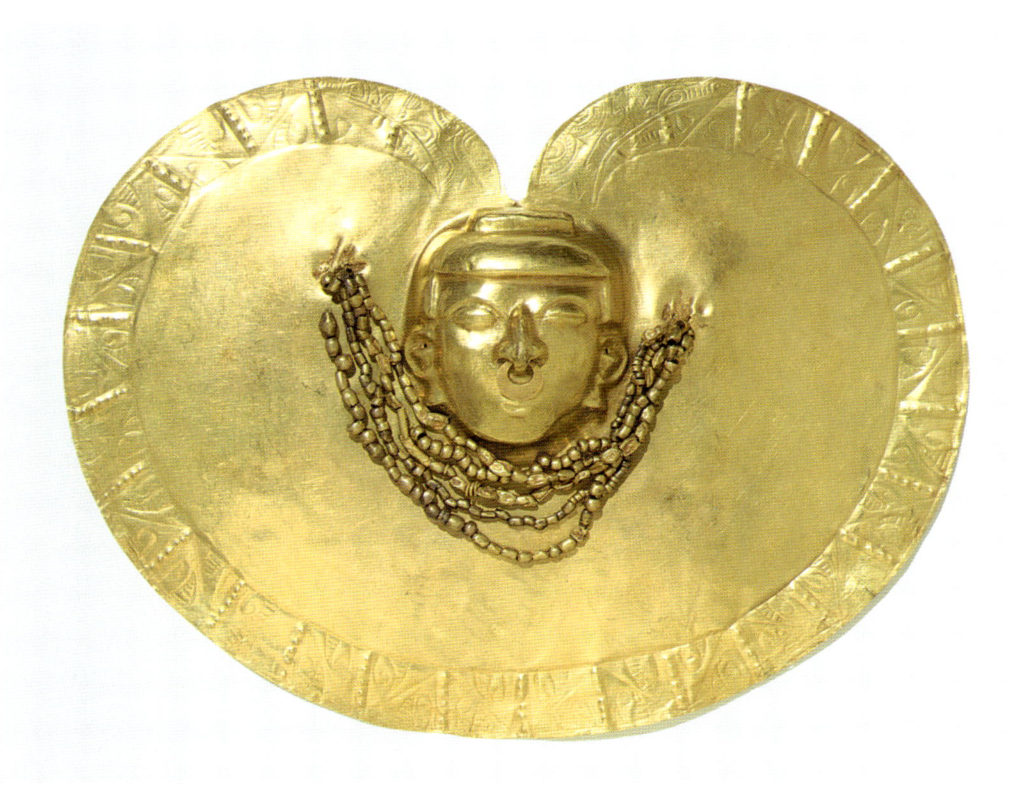

TOP: 259. *Beads made of hollow gold balls by Chimu craftsmen. Two identical hemispheres were created by tapping a gold sheet into a deep die or by shaping the beads over a domed wooden form. The two halves were then affixed with an organic glue; there is no evidence of soldering.*[VIII] *Bottom necklace, largest center bead: diameter, 5 cm. Collections of Andre Emmerich Gallery and Edward Merrin Gallery, New York*

BOTTOM: 260. *A gold breastplate with a bold relief mask in the center, excavated in the Calima region of Colombia. This kidney-shaped pectoral, formed from a hammered sheet of gold, has repoussé patterns along its rim, adding both decoration and strength to the edge. Five strands of gold beads, some cast and some made of rolled strip, are attached to the breastplate. When the wearer of this armor moved, the metal flashed in the sun and the beads rattled—a dramatic accompaniment to any costume.*

The Upper Calima Valley is famous for its rich grave sites. Because this piece comes from uncontrolled excavations, its age and cultural context are uncertain. It is dated between A.D. *500 and 1500. Pectoral: length, 35.5 cm. British Museum, London*

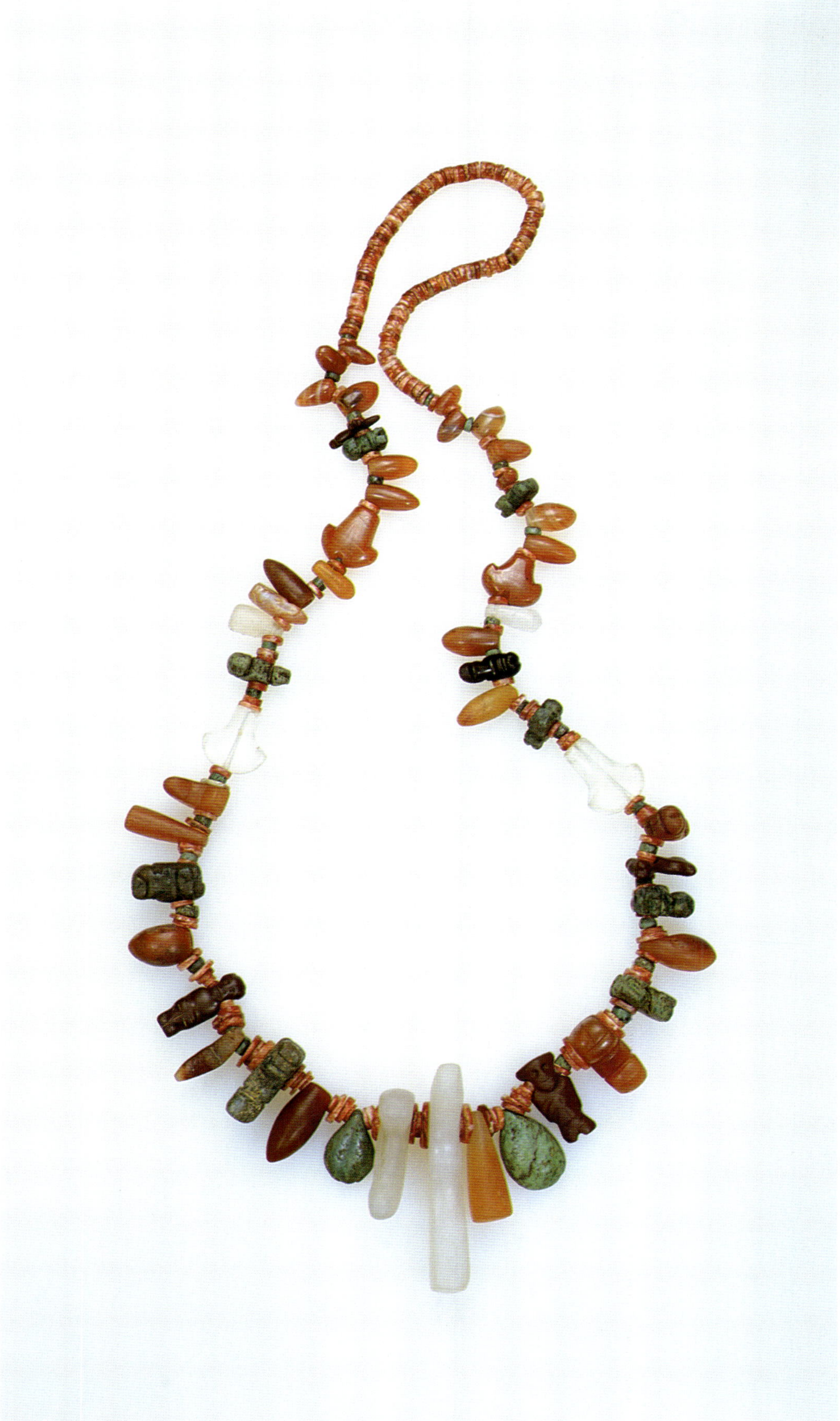

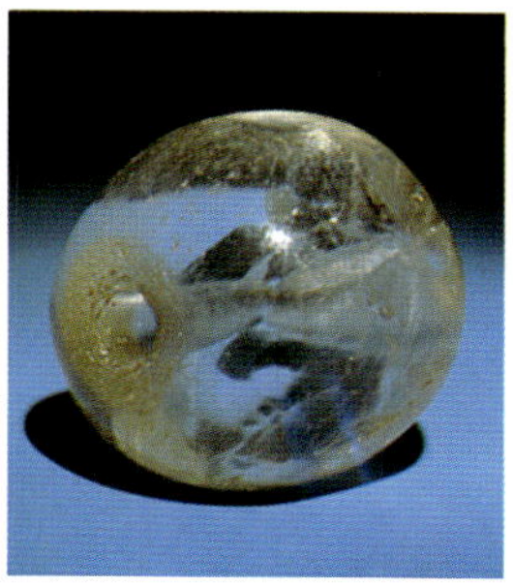

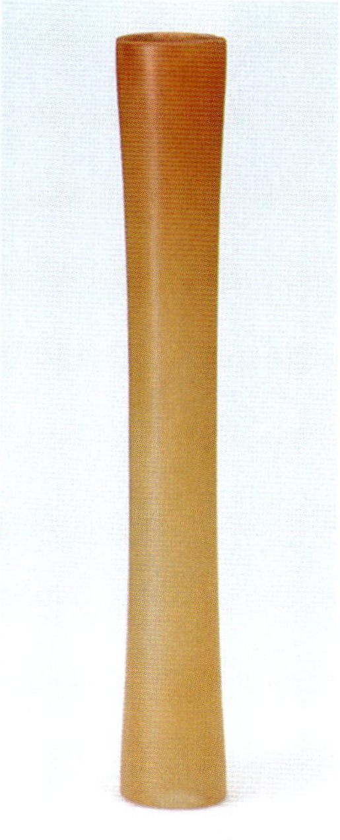

TOP: 261. *Like most early stone beads, the cone-shaped perforations in this Chavin quartz crystal bead (c. 1000 B.C.) are broad at the opening but contract to a much smaller diameter at the center, where the drill holes meet. Diameter, 5 cm. Collection Suzanne Donnelly Jenkins, New York*

ABOVE: 262. *A typical Tairona flared-tubular bead. The bead was formed by a craftsman who utilized the subtle color changes of the quartz or carnelian stone to its best design advantage. Length, 8.1 cm. Private collection. Courtesy Andre Emmerich Gallery, New York*

LEFT: 263. *The beads and amulets in this Tairona necklace from*

*northern Colombia (A.D. 800–1500) represent birds, spread-winged bats, frogs, grub (*guzano*, a rich food source), and quadripeds, inhabitants of the local Tairona environment. The stylized image of a chief appears on the lower left of the necklace in jasper; four Y-shaped frog beads, two each of carnelian and rock crystal, are in the center.*

Occupying the Caribbean coastal plain and foothills of the Sierra Nevada de Santa Marta, the Tairona produced quantities of finely made gold, shell, and stone beads. Although the name Tairona means "gold-worker," these people are equally famous for their stone beads.[IX]

The stones used in these beads came from the streams and valleys of the neighboring Sierra Nevada range. They include rock crystal, agate, chalcedony, carnelian, and jasper. The predominance of carnelian reflects the local abundance of this material. The red shell disks are from the spondylus ("thorny oyster").

A bead's color and depth of polish was important. Polished beads were called "live beads"; those with duller surfaces and softer colors were considered "dead beads."[X] Center bead: length, 7.8 cm. Collection Ivory Freidus

are filled with descriptions of extraordinary indigenous New World gold jewelry, nearly every piece collected by the Spaniards was melted down. Only a few Aztec artifacts survived. Nothing remains of the Inca treasure.

Mixtec and Tairona Beads

While the Olmecs and Maya treasured jade, the Mixtecs prized turquoise, which they associated with the color of the sky and sea. It has been suggested that turquoise may have replaced a decreasing supply of jade.[14] The Mixtecs excelled in making delicate polychrome necklaces by combining beads of gold, amber, jade, amethyst, shell, pearls, and turquoise. They also produced fine necklaces of rock crystal.

Some of the most exceptional beads excavated in ancient Middle America were found in a royal or aristocratic Mixtec burial in Tomb 7 at the Oaxacan site of Monte Albán, dating to the end of the fifteenth or early sixteenth century. Included were necklaces of jet, jade, pearl, amber, coral, shell, and rock crystal beads. One spectacular necklace consisted of thirty-nine gold beads cast as replicas of jaguar molar teeth, with a long bell suspended from each tooth. Another necklace was made of gold beads cast as miniature turtle shells (plate 269). Most Mixtec bead necklaces have a row of gold bells.[15]

Well-crafted stone beads of carnelian and rock crystal were made between A.D. 800 and 1500 by the Tairona (which means "goldworker"), who lived along the Caribbean coast and neighboring foothills of the Sierra Nevada de Santa Marta of northern Colombia. Through this region passed the trade routes linking Middle America with the Andes. The Tairona produced quantities of finely made gold, stone, and shell beads (plates 262–263).[16]

Beads and Pre-Hispanic Trade

The Olmecs were responsible for creating a trading system that extended over much of Middle America. Jade was an important commodity in their commerce. Eventually, complex trading networks were established all across Middle and South America, involving the exchange of agricultural products for scarce mineral and marine resources. Many items of jewelry, especially beads, were traded through this network and have been excavated hundreds of miles from their place of manufacture or the sources of their raw materials. For example, turquoise and sodalite used in beadmaking were exported from Bolivia to neighboring southern regions.[17] Farther north, most of the turquoise used for beads and inlay work by Middle Americans was obtained from sources in present-day Arizona and New Mexico.

Middle and South American cultures are particularly noted for their exquisitely carved beads from jade, rock crystal, onyx, carnelian, and other semiprecious stones. Elaborate jade and serpentine beads, some with likenesses of animal or human deities, are unique to Middle American pre-Hispanic sites.[18] Since Middle and South American beads were largely elite commodities, it is not surprising that they are generally of large size and made of scarce materials—jade, gold, and rock crystal—whose sources were frequently controlled by individuals of rank. Costa Rica is particularly famous for unusually long tubular beads, including a jade bead dating between A.D. 300 and 700 that is sixty-one centimeters long—the longest perforated stone object known.[19]

Glass Beads

Although glass trade beads were never as important in Middle and South America as they were in North America, they were still treasured by the indigenous cultures. Historical accounts and several archaeological excavations document the introduction of glass beads into the Caribbean, Mexico,

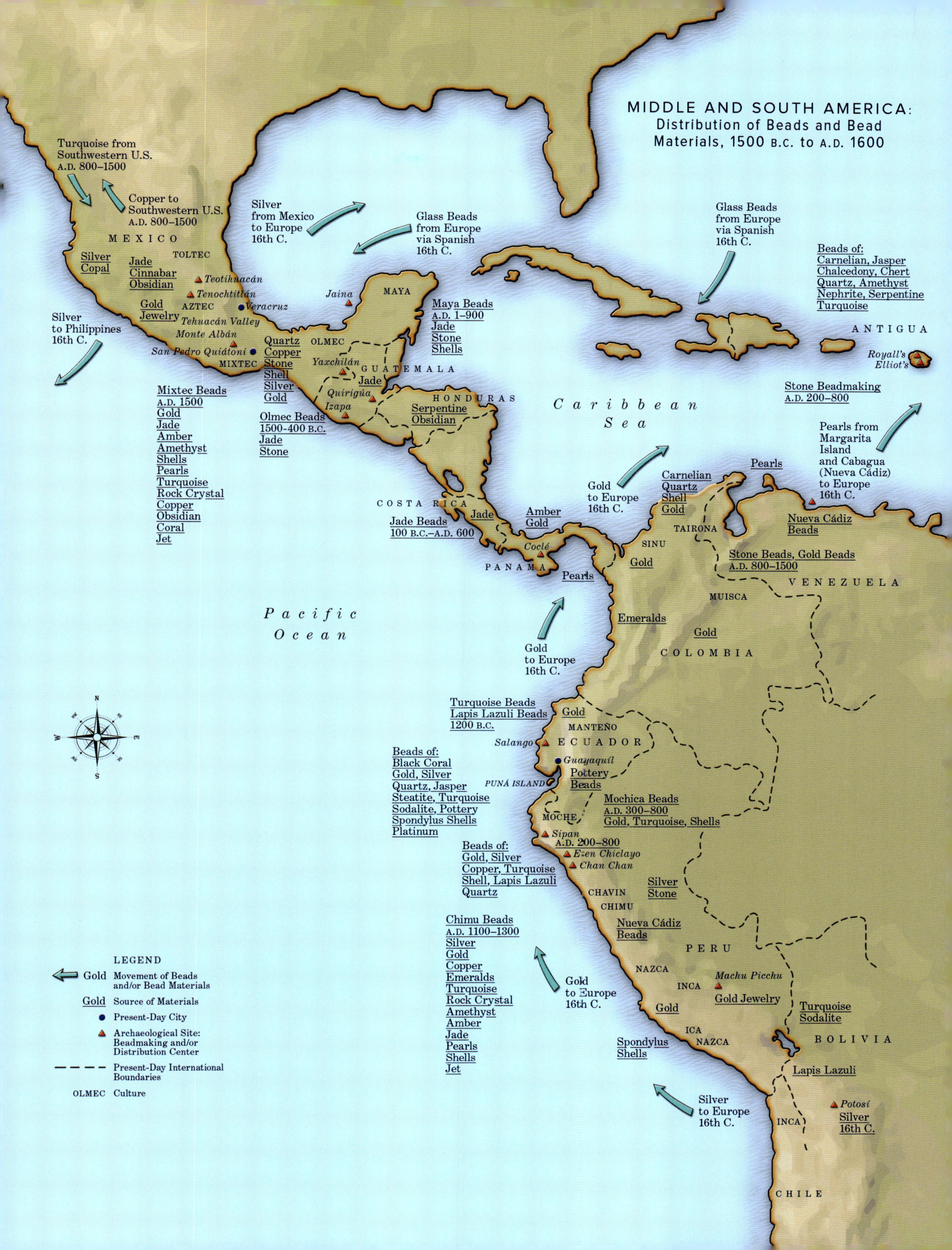
MIDDLE AND SOUTH AMERICA:
Distribution of Beads and Bead Materials, 1500 B.C. to A.D. 1600
Turquoise from Southwestern U.S. A.D. 800–1500
Copper to Southwestern U.S. A.D. 800–1500
MEXICO
Silver Copal
Jade Cinnabar Obsidian
TOLTEC
Teotihuacán
Tenochtitlán
Gold Jewelry
AZTEC
Veracruz
Tehuacán Valley
Monte Albán
San Pedro Quiátoni
MIXTEC
Silver to Philippines 16th C.
Silver from Mexico to Europe 16th C.
Glass Beads from Europe via Spanish 16th C.
Jaina
MAYA
Maya Beads A.D. 1–900 Jade Stone Shells
OLMEC
Quartz Copper Stone Shell Silver Gold
Yaxchilán
GUATEMALA
Jade
Quiriguá
Izapa
HONDURAS
Serpentine Obsidian
Mixtec Beads A.D. 1500 Gold Jade Amber Amethyst Shells Pearls Turquoise Rock Crystal Copper Obsidian Coral Jet
Olmec Beads 1500-400 B.C. Jade Stone
Glass Beads from Europe via Spanish 16th C.
Beads of: Carnelian, Jasper Chalcedony, Chert Quartz, Amethyst Nephrite, Serpentine Turquoise
ANTIGUA
Royall's Elliot's
Stone Beadmaking A.D. 200–800
Caribbean Sea
Pearls from Margarita Island and Cabagua (Nueva Cádiz) to Europe 16th C.
Pearls
Gold to Europe 16th C.
Carnelian Quartz Shell Gold
COSTA RICA
Jade
Jade Beads 100 B.C.–A.D. 600
Amber Gold
Coclé
PANAMA
Pearls
TAIRONA
Nueva Cádiz Beads
SINU
Gold
Stone Beads, Gold Beads A.D. 800–1500
VENEZUELA
MUISCA
Pacific Ocean
Gold to Europe 16th C.
Emeralds
Gold
COLOMBIA
Turquoise Beads Lapis Lazuli Beads 1200 B.C.
Gold
MANTEÑO
Salango
ECUADOR
Guayaquil
Beads of: Black Coral Gold, Silver Quartz, Jasper Steatite, Turquoise Sodalite, Pottery Spondylus Shells Platinum
PUNÁ ISLAND
Pottery Beads
Mochica Beads A.D. 300–800 Gold, Turquoise, Shells
MOCHE
Sipan A.D. 200–800
Eten Chiclayo
Chan Chan
Beads of: Gold, Silver Copper, Turquoise Shell, Lapis Lazuli Quartz
CHAVIN
CHIMU
Silver Stone
Chimu Beads A.D. 1100–1300 Silver Gold Copper Emeralds Turquoise Rock Crystal Amethyst Amber Jade Pearls Shells Jet
Nueva Cádiz Beads
PERU
Gold to Europe 16th C.
NAZCA
INCA
Machu Picchu
Gold Jewelry
Gold
Turquoise Sodalite
ICA
NAZCA
BOLIVIA
Spondylus Shells
Lapis Lazuli
Silver to Europe 16th C.
Potosí
INCA
Silver 16th C.
CHILE
LEGEND
Gold Movement of Beads and/or Bead Materials
Gold Source of Materials
Present-Day City
Archaeological Site: Beadmaking and/or Distribution Center
Present-Day International Boundaries
OLMEC Culture
N E S W

TOP: 264. *Spondylus shell bead necklace (top row) attributed to the Ica culture (c. A.D. 1100) from the south coast of Peru. Red spondylus was obtained from coastal Ecuador by long-distance trade.*

The single spondylus shell beads are Inca, c. A.D. 1500. Among the Maya, red shell beads (probably spondylus) were a medium of exchange. Ica bead: length, 2.7 cm. Ica beads: collection Andre Emmerich Gallery. Inca beads: collection Edward Merrin Gallery

BOTTOM: 265. *The artistry of the Maya also appears in their shell and bone beads. They created highly original beads while working within the constraints of the materials. These beads are from the Guatemalan highlands, c. A.D. 600–900. Top tubular bead: length, 7.2 cm. Collection Andre Emmerich Gallery*

OPPOSITE: 266. *Bib of shell and stone beads from Chan Chan, capital city of the Peruvian Chimu culture (A.D. 1000–1470). The richly colored disk beads, made from orange and purple spondylus shell, white shells, and green malachite, have been used to create human and bird figures similar in style to those found on ancient Peruvian textiles.*

To fully appreciate the bib, it should be understood it was worn in Chan Chan, where the houses were carved with fantastic animals and birds and painted in brilliant colors. Width, 43 cm. American Museum of Natural History, New York

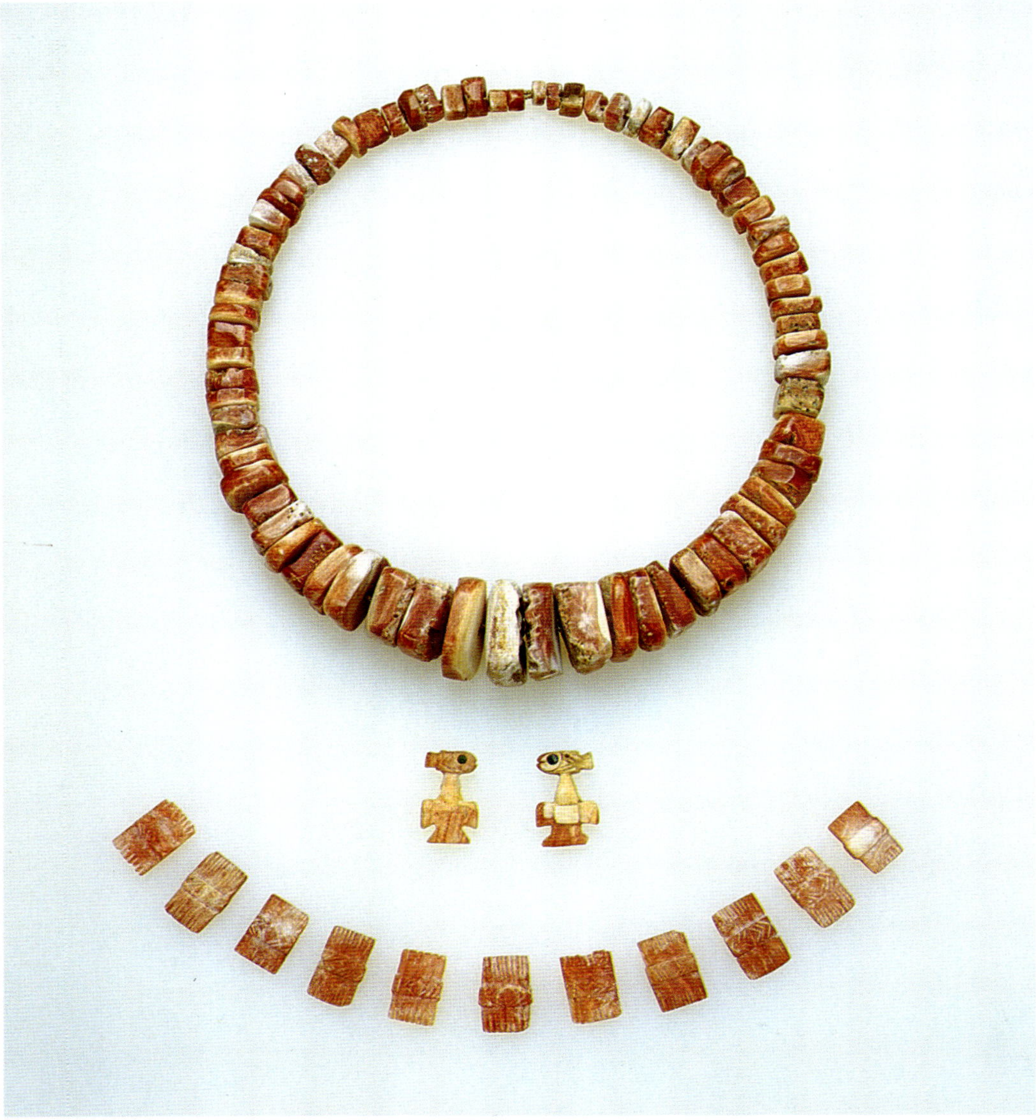

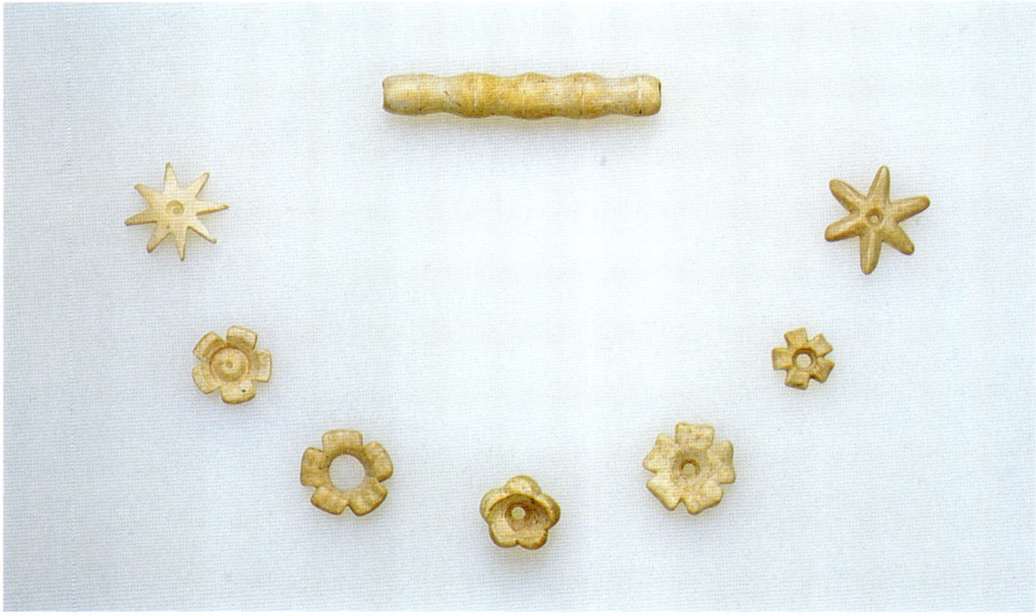

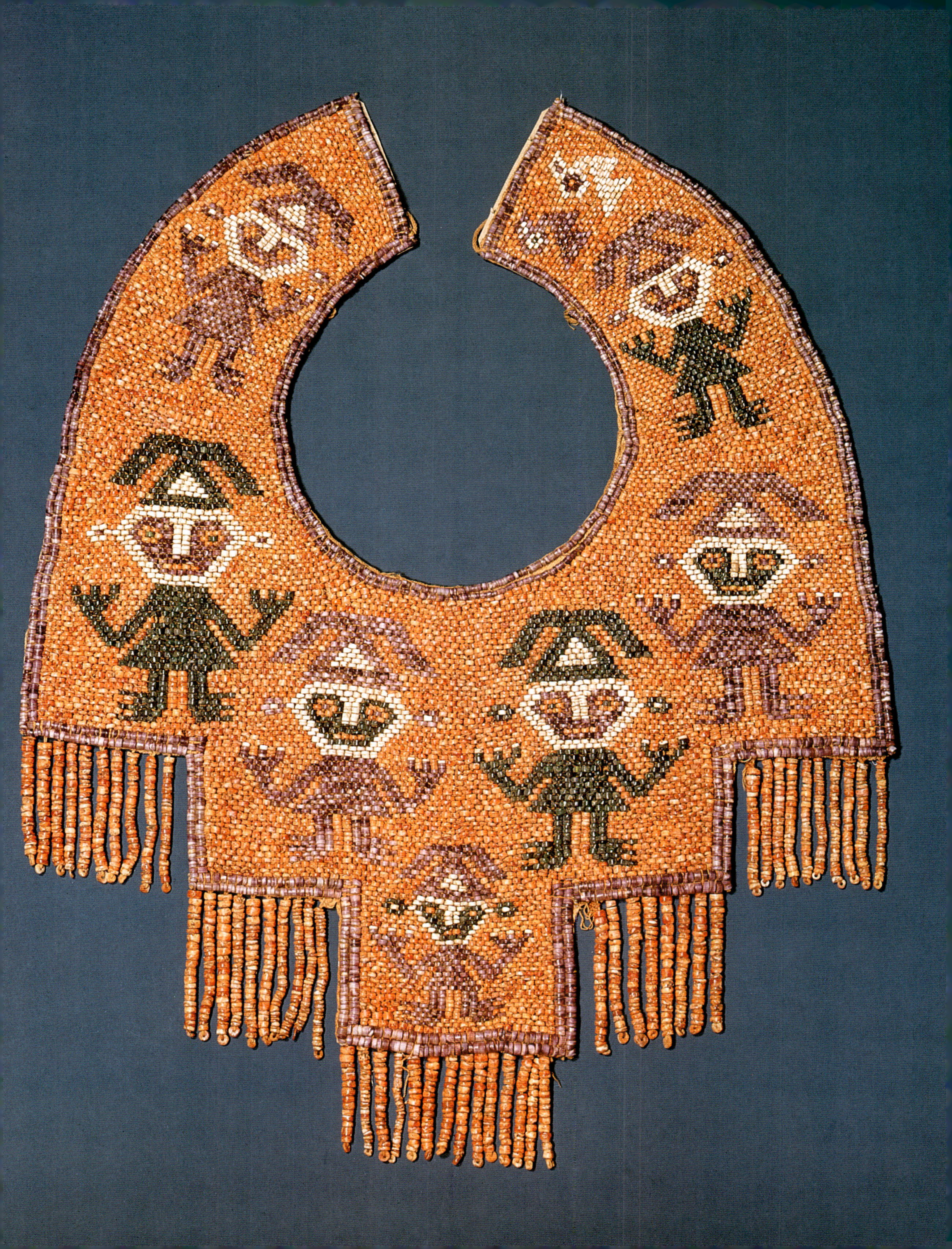

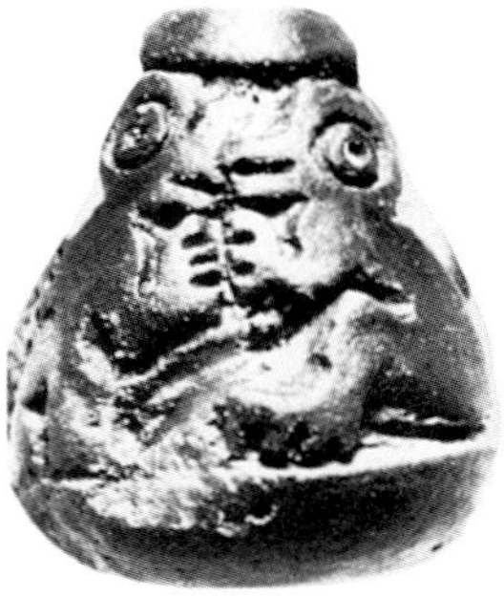

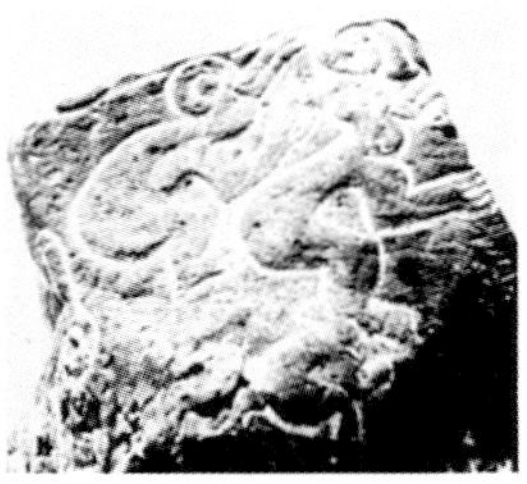

267. *In 1965, in Guayaquil, Ecuador, an American couple from Wyoming bought several strings of pottery beads that were reputedly found on Puna Island. One of the beads, attributed to the Manteno culture (A.D. 500–1500), was carved with two bird-men figures stylistically similar to rock carvings from Easter Island. The similarity between the Ecuadorian and Easter Island figures has led to the suggestion that there was prehistoric contact between the island and the South American mainland. Length, 1.6 cm. Kon-Tiki Museum, Oslo*[XI]

267a. *Drawing of bird-man figures in pottery bead*

and South America by the early Spanish explorers, including Columbus, Cortés, and Francisco Pizarro. Many of these beads were gifts, and others served as important trade items during the sixteenth century.[20]

It also appears that since glass was unknown to the Indian populations, the Spanish were not adverse to treating glass beads as if they were made of precious stones. In 1518, Diaz del Castillo entered the Río de Tabasco in Mexico, where he encountered canoes full of Indian warriors, who did not welcome the party until "we showed them strings of green beads and small mirrors and blue cut-glass beads, and as soon as they saw them they assumed a more friendly manner, for they thought they were [jadeite] which they valued greatly."[21] He also recorded other episodes in which glass beads were exchanged with the Aztecs for gold and precious stones. When Cortés entered the Aztec city of Tenochtitlán, Montezuma awaited him "under a canopy of brilliant green feathers, bordered with gold and silver embroidery and hung with pearls. He was richly attired—even his sandals were of gold trimmed with precious stones. Cortés, dismounting from his horse, himself an impressive figure with his steel armour and red beard, presented the gift he had brought, a necklace of glass beads strung on a gold cord scented with musk. With great ceremony, the necklace was placed around Montezuma's neck. A reciprocal gift to Cortés was a necklace of hand-wrought gold crabs set with shells."[22]

The majority of glass beads distributed in Middle and South America during the sixteenth century were monochrome drawn-cane beads (Bead Chart 38). By the seventeenth century, faceted, multilayered chevron beads and striped beads, similar to those manufactured by the Dutch, are also documented. Of particular interest is the Nueva Cádiz bead, named for an archaeological site on an island off the coast of Venezuela occupied by the Spanish from 1498 to 1545 (Timeline 1135 a–g).

The Nueva Cádiz, generally a long, tube-drawn bead with a square cross section and three-layer construction, is closely related to the chevron bead in its manufacturing technique. A major difference is that Nueva Cádiz beads were sometimes "twisted" and generally consisted of three layers of glass—chevron beads from the same period have seven layers—and their distribution was primarily limited to the Spanish New World, particularly Peru, between the late 1400s and 1560. Small quantities of Nueva Cádiz beads have been found in Africa, but they do not appear to be contemporaneous with New World examples.[23]

The Nueva Cádiz bead is a very sophisticated bead, the product of advanced glassmaking technology. After the first Venetian-made beads of the sixteenth century, the Dutch made similar beads in the seventeenth century. Then in the mid-nineteenth century, at least two late editions of these beads were possibly made by either the Venetians or the Bohemians.[24] Nontheless, Nueva Cádiz beads disappeared from South America after 1560, perhaps as a result of the Spaniards' newly achieved control of trade and goods production in the New World. The beads recovered from the Nueva Cádiz site, for example, were undoubtedly part of the pearl trade centered in Cabagua and Margarita Island. When the pearl beds were depleted, these expensive beads were replaced by cheaper, less complex styles.[25]

Glass beads traded into Middle and South America following the initial period of Spanish settlement include many of the well-known Venetian polychrome and eye beads. The popularity of red *cornaline d'Aleppo* beads (Timeline 68) in Guatemala, even today, has been attributed to their similarity to coral, a highly valued material introduced by the Spaniards.[26] In San Pedro Quiátoni, a small town in Oaxaca, heirloom necklaces

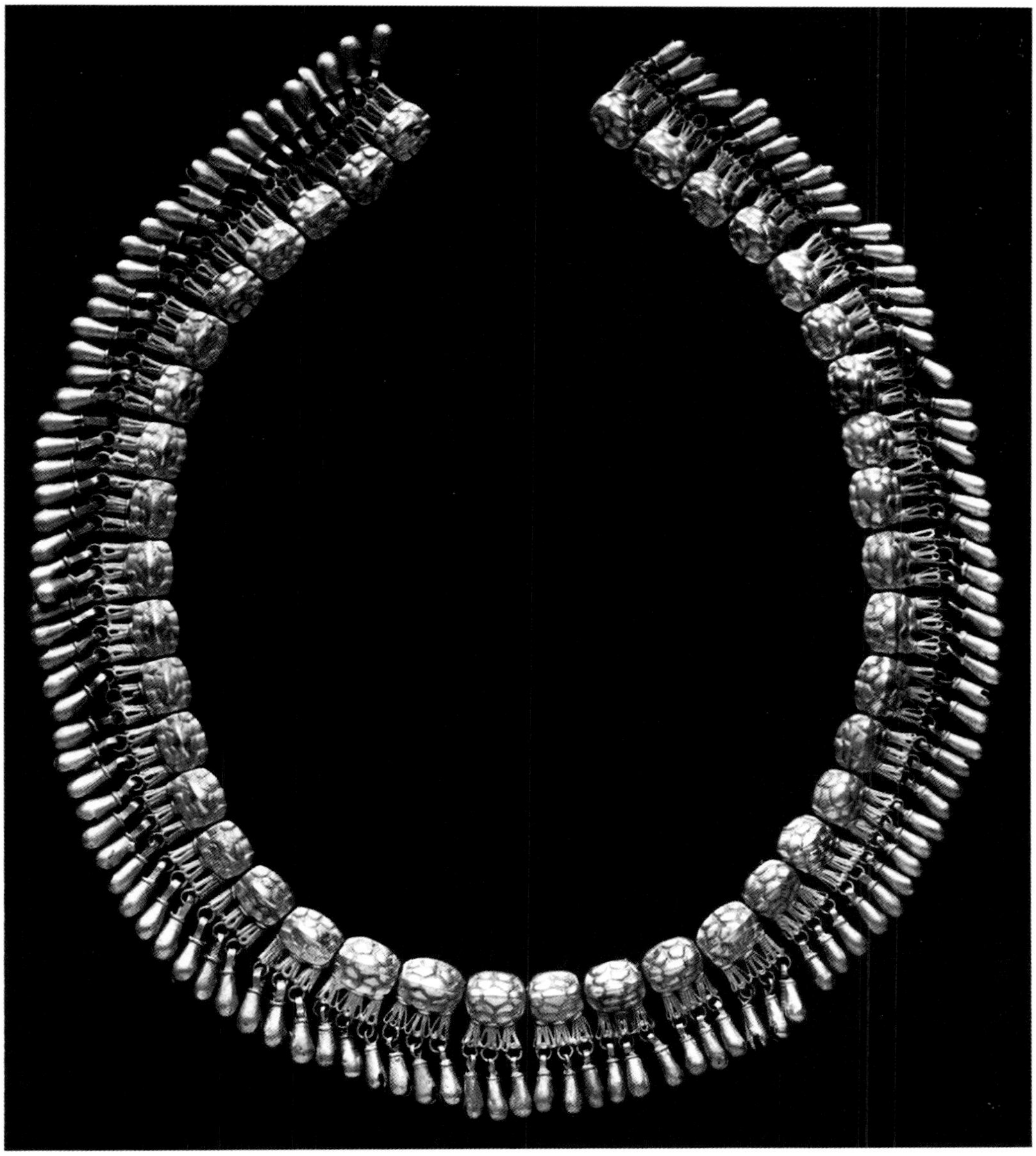

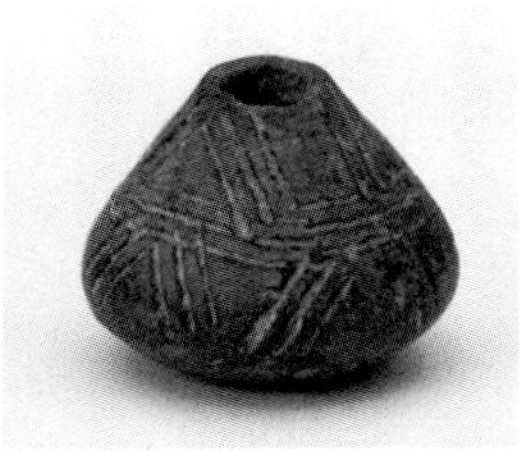

ABOVE: 268. *Pottery bead (or spindle whorl) from Ecuador, found by a collector on an embankment near a stream north of Guayaquil. Possibly Manteno culture,* A.D. *500–1500. Length, 1.5 cm. Collection Phyllis and Peter Mroczkowski, New York*

LEFT: 269. *A Mixtec gold necklace with turtle effigy beads and bells. The beads contain pellets that rattle when the necklace was worn. Dating to the late fifteenth or the early sixteenth century, the beads were found at Oaxaca, Mexico. Length, 50.2 cm. National Museum of the American Indian, Smithsonian Institution, New York, 163451*

include unusual pendant beads formed of glass rods, looped at one end and averaging about six centimeters in length (Timeline 1137). Of unknown origin, these beads were probably made in Europe and date between the sixteenth and eighteenth century.

Jewelry and beads created in Middle and South America since the European conquest exhibit varying degrees of influence from both the prehistoric and Spanish cultures. The craftsmen of Mexico, for example, where mineral wealth was such an integral part of the country's history, continue to produce large quantities of beads from silver, gold, and semiprecious stones, including amethyst, garnet, opal, crystal, and onyx. Jewelry designs frequently incorporate ancient Mayan, Aztec, or Mixtec motifs, or use gold-filigree techniques derived from eighteenth-century Spanish styles. This blend of native and Spanish heritage, using ancient and contemporary techniques, is characteristic of jewelry throughout Latin America.

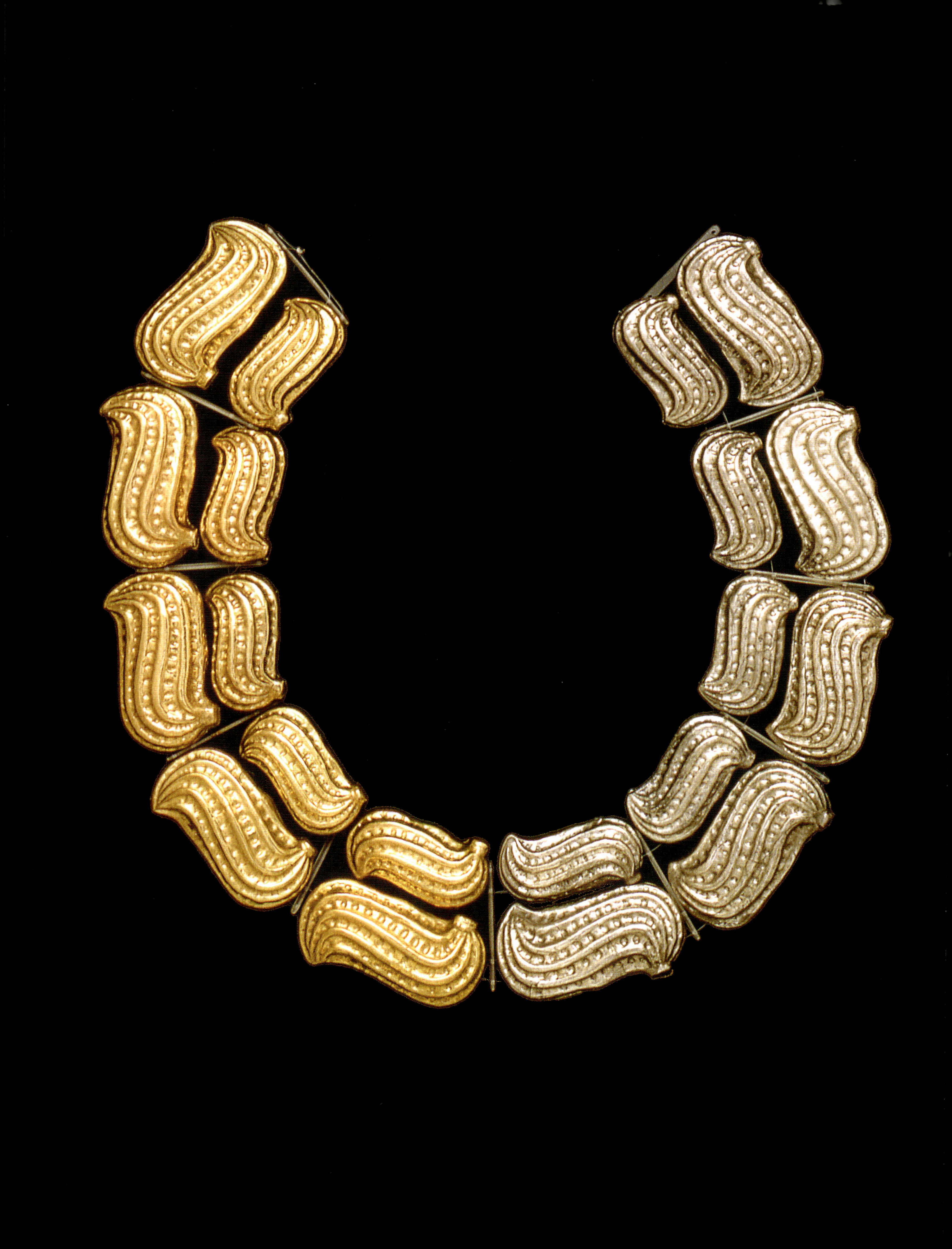

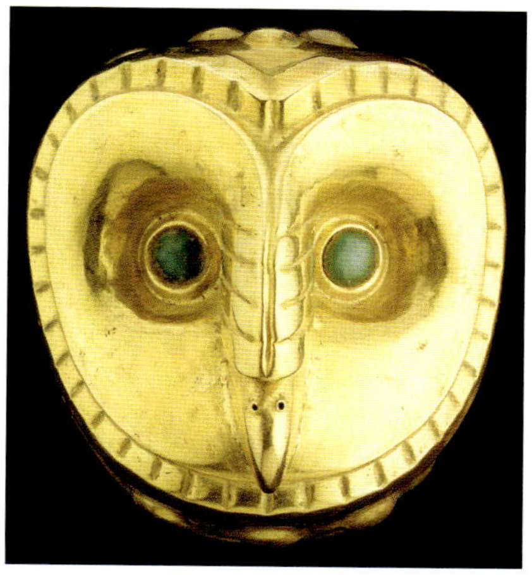

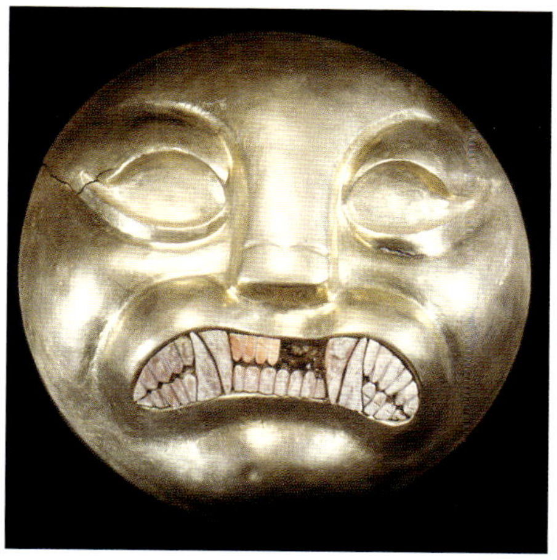

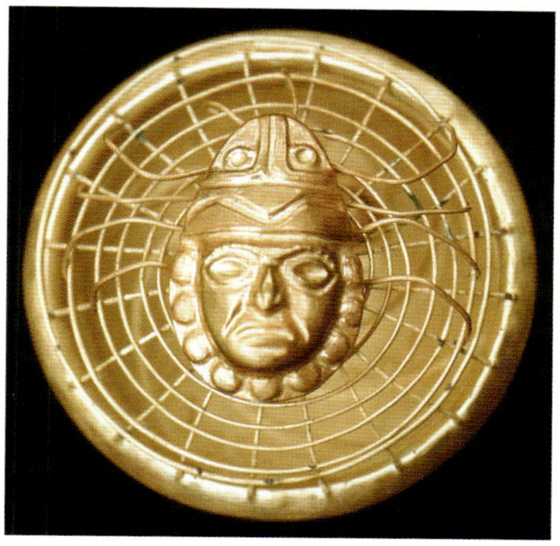

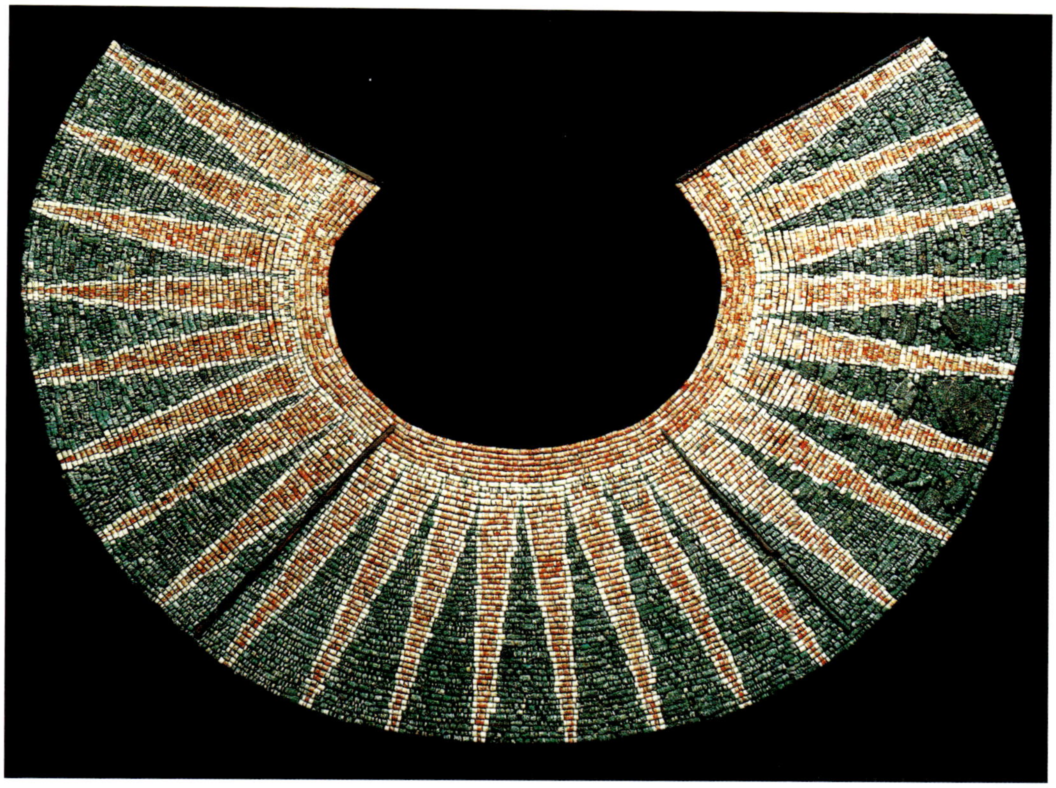

OPPOSITE: 270. *A gold and silver peanut necklace displays an intriguing gold/silver duality. Height, 41 cm. Length of largest bead, 9 cm. Collection Museo Tumbas Royales de Sipán*

TOP LEFT: 271a. *Gold owl head bead with eyes inlaid with green stone. Height, 3.2 cm. Private collection*

TOP MIDDLE: 271b. *Gilded copper feline head bead with shell teeth. Height, 16 cm. Museo Tumbas Royales de Sipán*

TOP RIGHT: 271c. *Gold spider bead. Height, 8.3 cm. Museo Tumbas Royales de Sipán*

LEFT: 271d. *A pectoral composed of white, pink, and green shell beads. Width, 60 cm. Museo Tumbas Royales de Sipán*

Moche Culture Beads

Beads c. A.D. *300–600 from the Moche Culture of Sipán. Located in northern Peru, the site of Sipan was scientifically excavated from 1987–90 when archaeologists discovered three intact tombs of the ruling elite. Among the recovered artifacts was a remarkable array of objects of adornment including beads in stone, shell, and metal that had been assembled into necklaces, pectorals, and bracelets. The beads seen here, though only a tiny sample of what was found, convey the artistic excellence and skilled technology of the Moche artisans.*

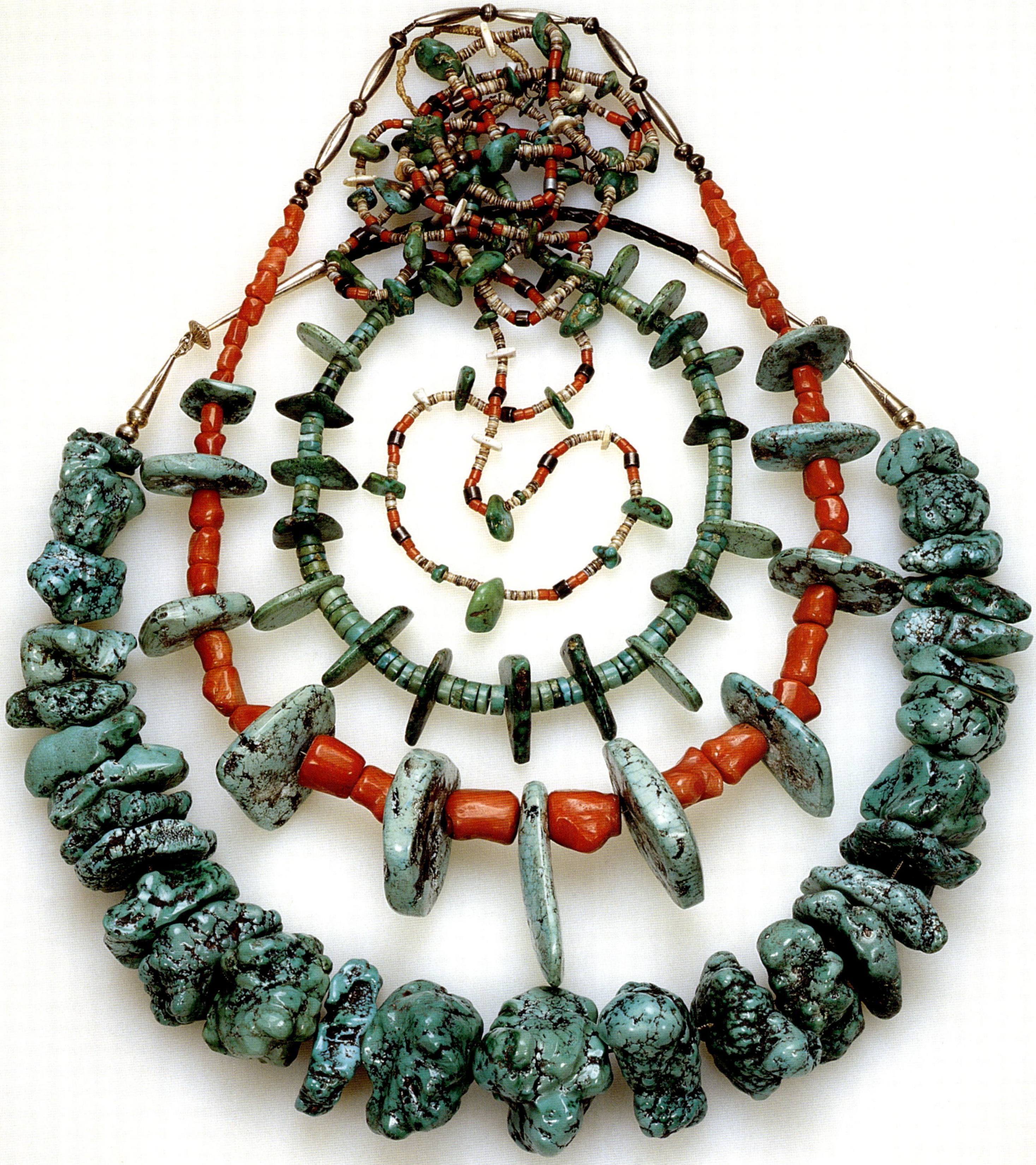

North America

For thousands of years prior to European colonization, Indian civilizations made the North American continent their home Anthropologists place the more than three hundred North American Indian tribes into broad cultural groups, organized by geographic areas: Arctic, Subarctic, Woodland (southeastern and northeastern), Great Lakes, Plains, Plateau, Basin, Northwest Coast, Southwest, and California. The linking of cultural characteristics with environments developed as an aid to interpreting the diverse lifestyles and material cultures of a wide range of tribes.

North American Indian languages appear to have no word for art; artistic expression was fully integrated into many aspects of life and not treated as a separate activity. Objects were crafted to serve a host of functions, both secular and sacred. The extent of their complexity and that of the overall artifact assemblage depended on the lifestyle of the group and the resources available to them.

Although each group of Indians produced objects specific to their customs and beliefs, all North American Indians seem to have shared an appreciation for beads. At least eight thousand years before Europeans crossed the Atlantic, Indians were making, wearing, and trading beads of shell, pearl, bone, teeth, stone, and fossil crinoid stems.[1]

Imported glass beads, first introduced to North American native populations by Christopher Columbus in 1492, had a significant economic and aesthetic impact on Indian material culture. The earliest glass beads were gifts from explorers and missionaries, but in the sixteenth century the small glass seedbeads became an important medium of exchange in the expanding North American fur trade. The availability of these small beads, along with the introduction of trade cloth and thin steel needles, led to the decline of age-old decorative techniques, including quillwork, and the rise of beadwork as the

272. *Typical Southwestern jewelry assembly of turquoise, coral, bone, shell, and silver beads. Southwestern tribes valued shell beads over those of glass. Shells symbolize water to a people for whom rainfall is crucial to survival. Among the southwestern Indians, turquoise and silver jewelry became an important repository of wealth.*[1]

These necklaces were probably made between 1920 and 1950, but the disk and flat, tabular-like beads are ancient forms. Center turquoise flat bead, second necklace from top: length, 3.5 cm. Bottom two necklaces: collection Ivory Freidus

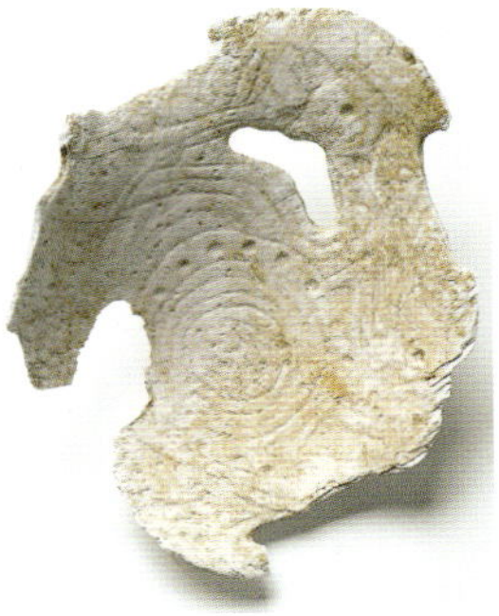

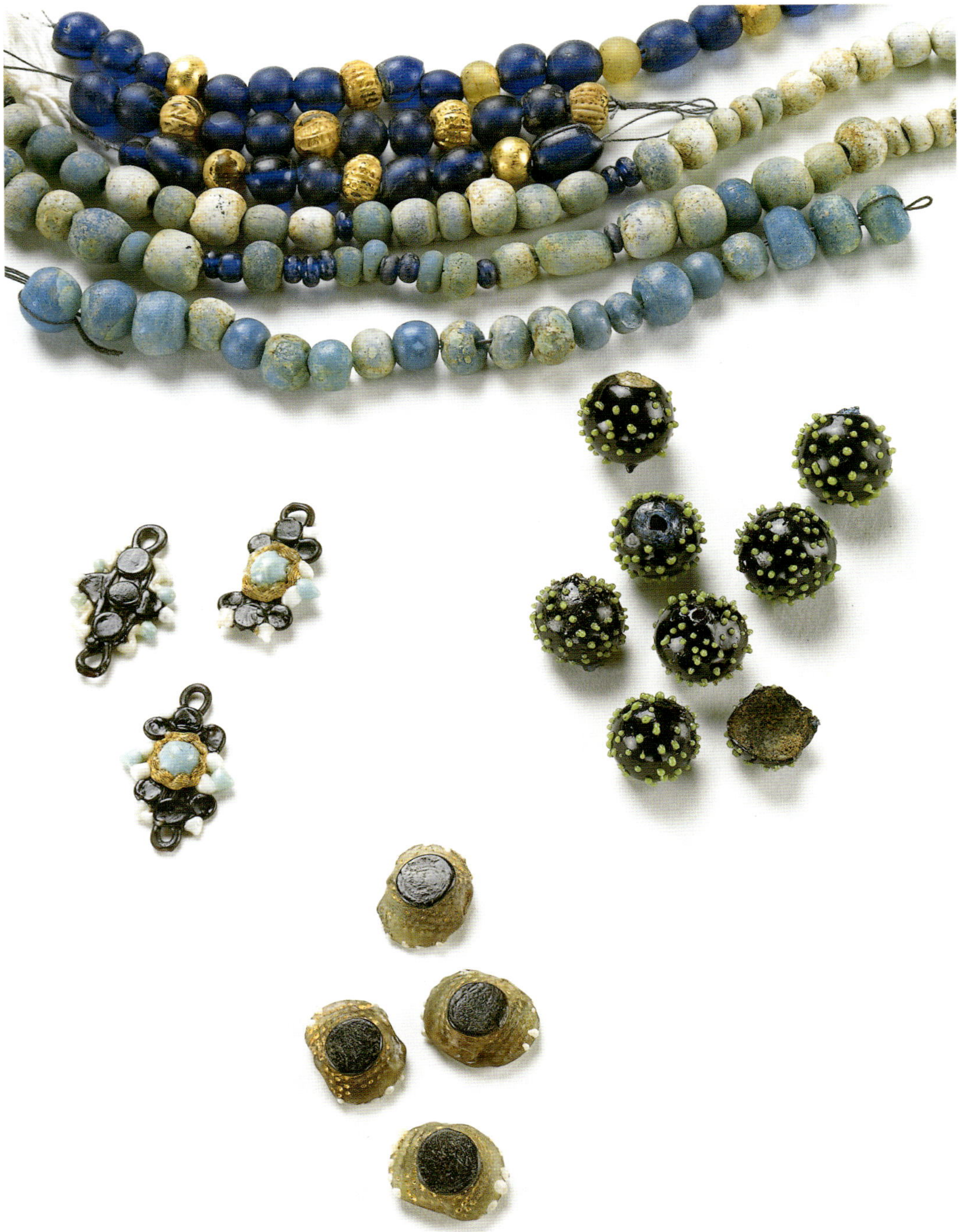

273–274. *The Beads from Mission Santa Catalina de Guale, St. Catherine's Island, Georgia, 1566–1680*

ABOVE: 273. *Guale Indians were traditionally buried with an array of treasured items, including this late Mississippian culture rattlesnake shell gorget, found around the neck of an adolescent. 1566–1680*

RIGHT: 274. *A selection of beads recovered as grave goods from Mission Santa Catalina de Guale. The nearly 70,000 excavated beads include rare glass beads imported by the Spanish from beadmaking centers in Spain, Venice, France, Holland, and Bohemia. Although it is unclear if the beads were obtained by the Guale as secular gifts, payment of labor, or for rosaries, the archaeologist David Hurst Thomas believes that their high quality and inclusion as grave goods may reflect the importance placed upon Guale conversion by the Franciscans.*

Top: Blue glass beads and gold leaf over clear glass beads, shown in the original stringing pattern. Middle left: Glass cross pendants. Middle right: Blown glass beads with raised dots. Bottom: Clear glass beads with black (jet) center dot and gold-leaf and raised white dots. Bead with raised dots: 10.9 mm diameter. All: Collection the Fernbank Museum of Natural History, Atlanta, Georgia

predominant Indian craft. While some beadworkers followed earlier geometric quillwork patterns, many Indian women borrowed heavily from European motifs. Embroidery, needlepoint, lacework, and even Oriental Caucasian rugs, brought to the New World by immigrants and carried across the continent by settlers, provided designs that were translated into beadwork. An unforgettable Cree bag decorated with beads in a flame-stitch pattern to resemble an eighteenth-century Hungarian needlework pocketbook (plate 297) is one example of the widespread European influence.

The blend of Indian imagination and European designs and materials reached a particularly successful synthesis on the Plains in about 1870. The Crow and other tribes created beautiful beaded adornment for themselves and their horses. In the East, however, many tribes were no longer making beadwork for their own use by this time. They had long since depleted their beaver supply and were reduced to earning money by making beaded souvenirs of "authentic Indian clothing," often to European specifications of design and color and for shipment to European markets.

The intermingling of Indian and European beadmaking concepts is perhaps best exemplified in the story of wampum—the most important shell bead in North American history. Although wampum existed before the arrival of Europeans, it was the introduction of steel tools by the Dutch that greatly expanded wampum production into an industry that had broad political and economic ramifications for both Indians and colonists.

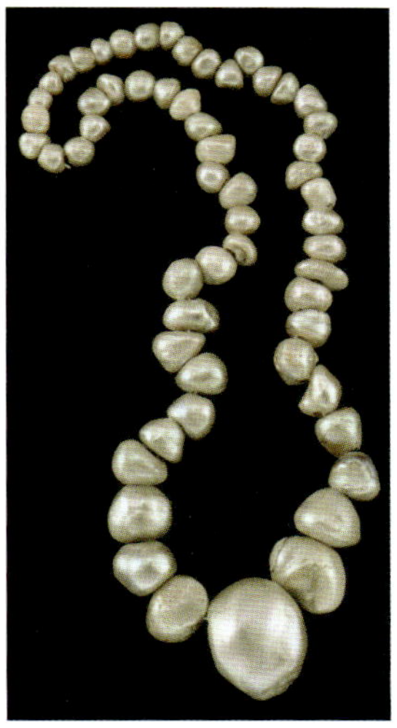

275. *A pre-European contact pearl necklace attributed to the Gabrielino people was collected at San Nicholas Island, California. Largest pearl diameter, 2.2 cm. Natural History Museum of Los Angeles County*

Beads of Indigenous Materials

While North American Indians typically made beads from local materials, they eagerly sought imported stones, shells, and metals to make rare beads that would be prestigious. Extensive trade networks crisscrossed North America. Native copper from Lake Superior, sometimes in the form of rolled tubular or rounded beads, was traded several hundred miles away in the Midwest and Woodlands from as early as 3000 B.C.[2] (plate 290). Prehistoric Southwestern cultures traded turquoise throughout the western regions and into Mexico. Marine shells from the Florida coasts were traded north, made into beads in Illinois, then distributed to the agricultural societies of the Mississippi, Ohio, and Illinois river valleys about A.D. 1100. Dentalium shells from the Pacific Northwest were traded throughout the Plains, and Minnesota pipestone (catlinite) was widely traded through the Great Lakes and Plains regions for more than two thousand years.

Beads made from locally available freshwater pearls were popular among prehistoric cultures of the Mississippi and other major river valleys of the Midwest. Both marine and freshwater pearls were reportedly seen by early European explorers in many parts of the New World, including Virginia, Maine, and California (plate 275).[3] Archaeologist Stuart Struever, in his book *Koster*, describes the discovery near St. Louis of a first-century A.D. grave in which a high-ranking member of the Hopewell culture was buried in a log tomb with armlets and necklaces of freshwater pearls:

> The chest of one woman was covered with quantities of freshwater pearls and cut-shell beads. The way these were arranged suggests that they had been attached to a garment, now deteriorated. As I looked at the carefully placed pearls and beads, I experienced one of those moments that occasionally come over every archaeologist of feeling intensely the common humanity we share with the people whose past we have discovered. The woman apparently was among the elite in her society. Her garment must have been made very painstakingly to achieve that effect and I suspect it was a sign of her rank or wealth or both. Pearls are very rare in freshwater clams, and it would have taken an incredible amount of human energy to gather that many.[4]

We must rely on the observations of early travelers and explorers for our knowledge of beads made of perishable materials. It has been recorded that Pocahontas wore a necklace she made of rose hips. Along the eastern coast of North America, the seeds of chinquapins were frequently worn and eaten right off the string.[5]

Indians used and esteemed beads made of shell above all others, and the raw materials often traveled great distances. Shell of the *Busycon*, a species of conch found along the Florida coast, was traded north on the Mississippi River into the Midwest. Pacific coast shells, particularly *haliotis* (abalone), are commonly discovered in prehistoric sites in New Mexico and Arizona. A string of fifty beads made of *olivella* shells originating on the California coast was excavated from a Nevada site dating to 6000 B.C.[6]

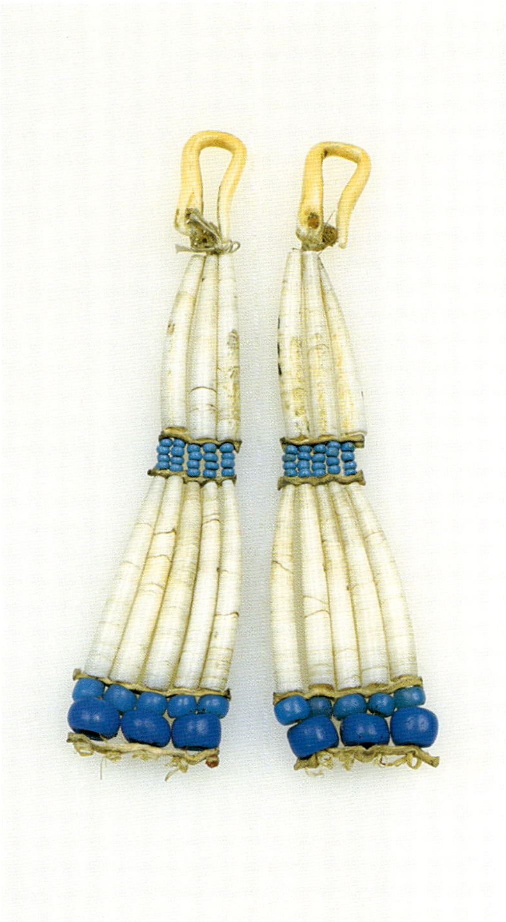

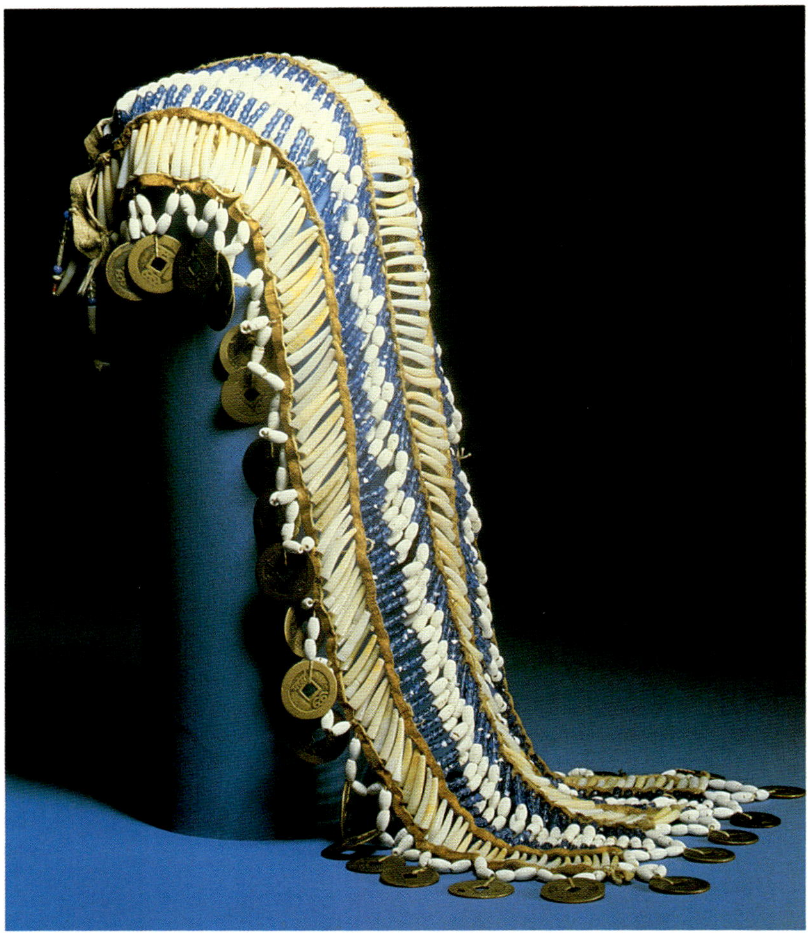

TOP LEFT: 276. *Earrings of* Dentalium pretiosum *shells and glass trade beads, worn by an Inuit girl. They were collected at Hershell Island. Dentalium shell had both monetary and decorative value. The shell was distributed through intertribal barter from the Pacific to the Arctic. Length, 6.7 cm. McCord Museum, McGill University, Montreal*

TOP RIGHT: 277. *A Yakima bridal headdress. The bride's wealth is reflected in the use of highly valued dentalium shells. The Chinese coins and imported blue glass beads came into the Northwest with the trans-Pacific fur trade during the mid-nineteenth century.*[11] *Length, 32 cm. Denver Art Museum*

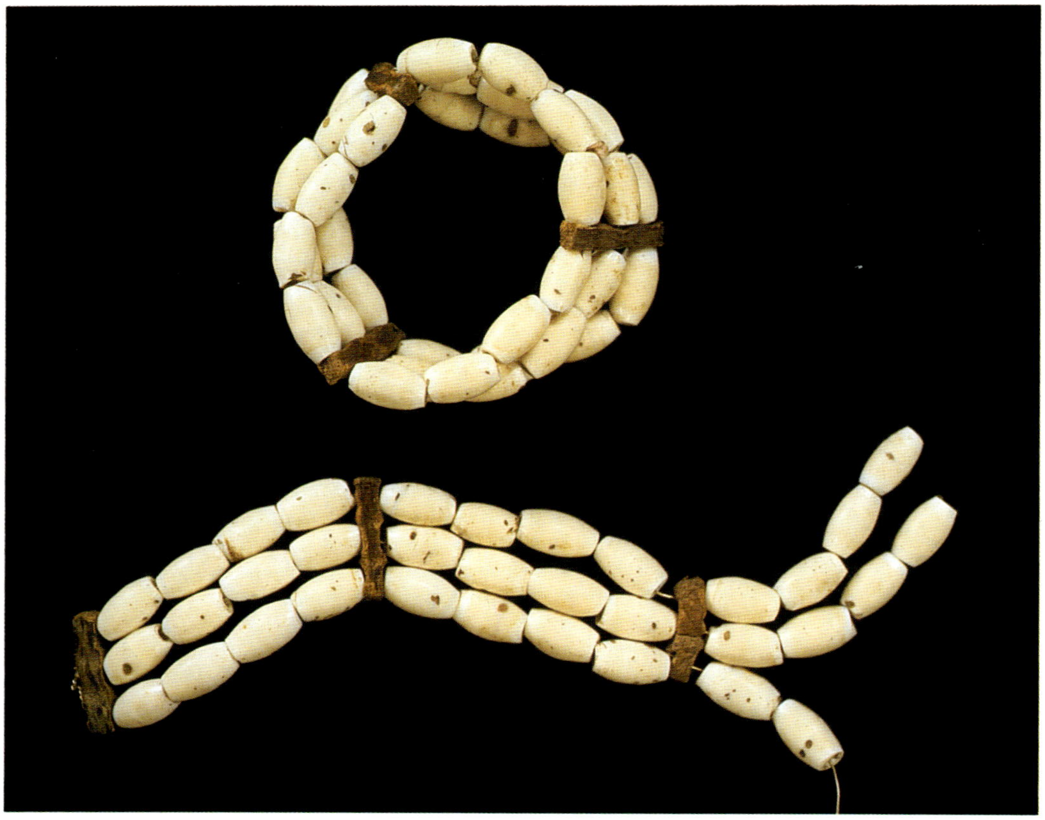

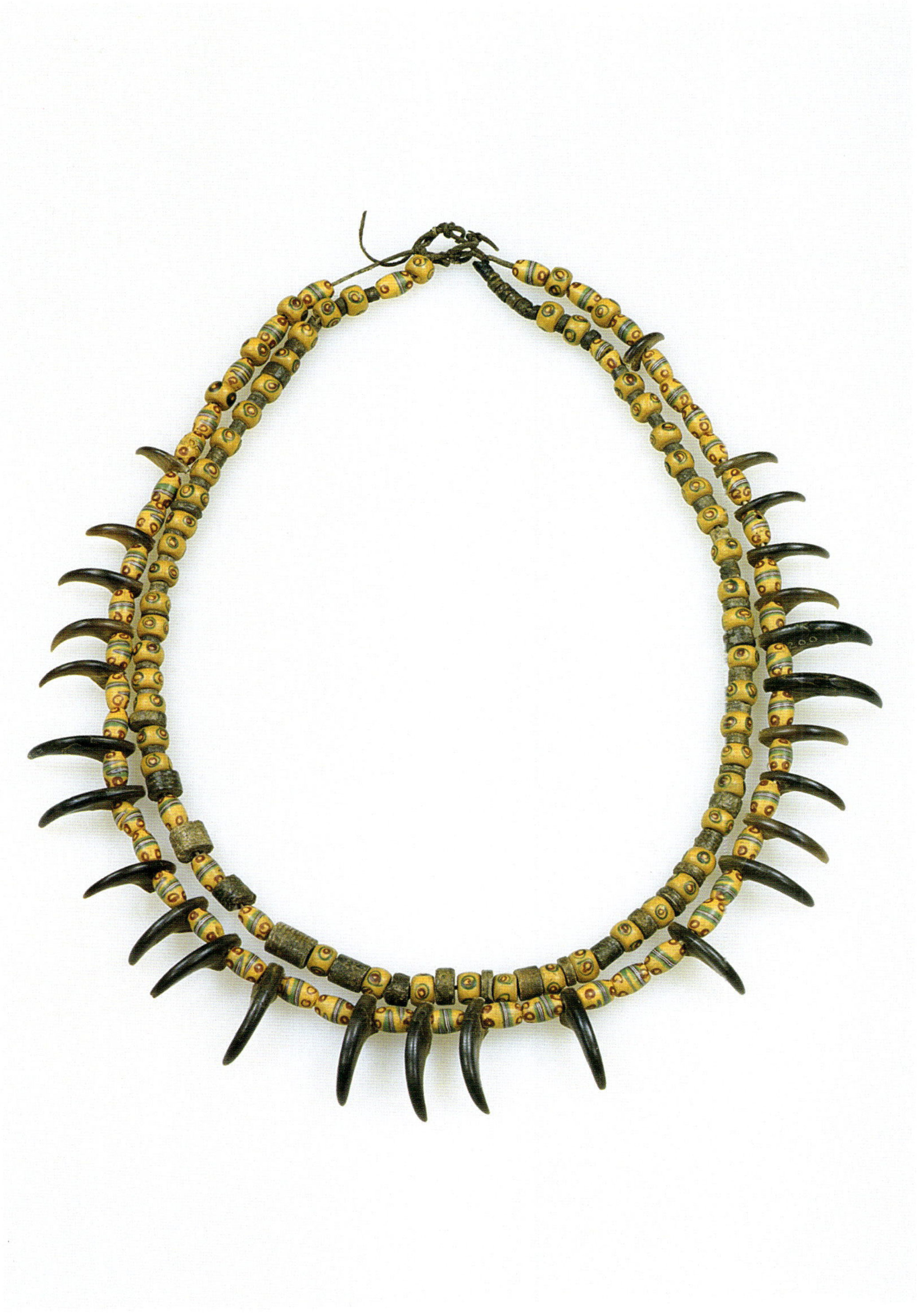

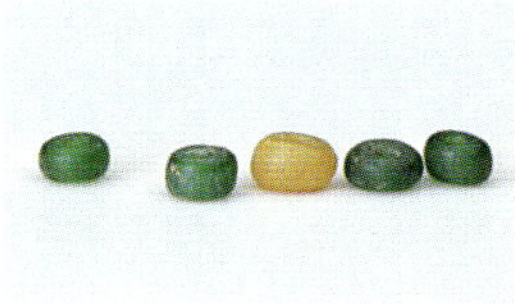

OPPOSITE BOTTOM: 278. *Three-string bracelet of white, opaque, wound-glass trade beads, collected in the Upper Missouri Valley in the 1850s. They are typical of the large, coarse beads carried by early Plains traders. Length, 25.4 cm. Smithsonian Institution, Washington, D.C.*

ABOVE: 279. *Glass beads dating to the early Spanish exploration of the New World, similar to those mentioned in Columbus's log entry of December 3, 1492: "The admiral caused them [the Arawak Indians of Watling Island in the Bahamas] to be given hawks bells and brass rings, and small green and yellow glass beads with which they were well content."*[III] *Typical beads: diameters from 0.3 to 0.45 cm. Private collection*

LEFT: 280. *Dakota (Sioux) necklace of Venetian beads, fossil crinoid stems, and bear claws strung on leather thongs, c. 1850. Grizzly bear claws were highly prized and worn only by leaders. Length, 49 cm. McCord Museum, McGill University, Montreal*

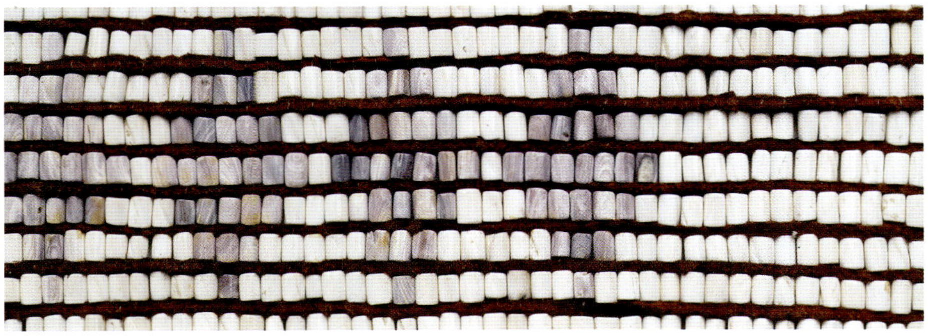

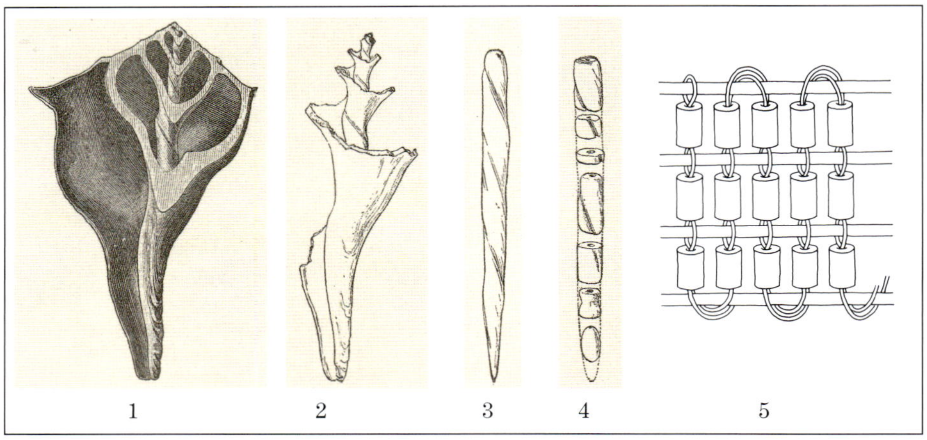

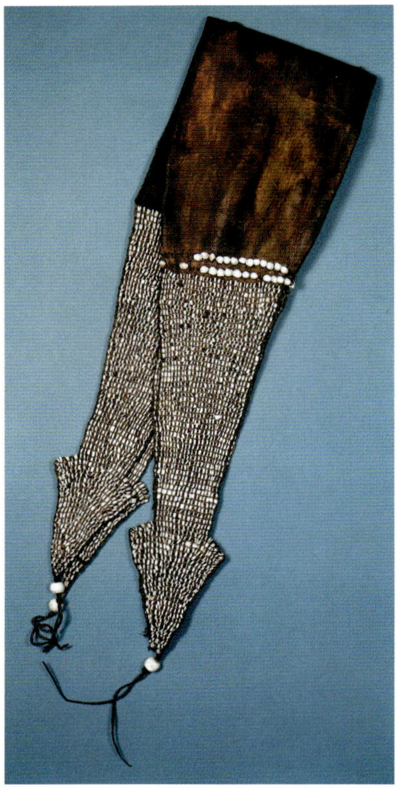

TOP: 281. *Among the most important items of North American Indian lifeways was wampum—small, cylindrical, centrally drilled purple and white shell beads. Considered a sacred material in precontact Indian times, the beads' continuing value was undoubtedly connected to belief in the sacredness of shell. Seen here is a detail of a Seneca white and purple wampum belt woven on leather. Typical bead length, 6 cm. c. 1640–60. Rochester Museum and Science Center, New York.*

BOTTOM: 282. *Wampum Bead Production. (1) Whelk (Busycom) shell. (2) Roughly trimmed whelk columella (central column) cylinder. (3) Finely trimmed columella. (4) Columella cut into sections for beads. (5) Woven Beadwork: cylindrical shell beads on double weft and single-warp threads. This was the technique generally used for making wampum belts, as seen in plate 281.*

The best-known shell bead was wampum: small, cylindrical, centrally drilled white and purple beads made primarily of the quahog clamshell. Strung on leather thongs or woven into belts with sinew thread, wampum was sometimes worn as decoration but developed far greater significance as currency and was used for objects commemorating major political and ceremonial events.

Averaging six millimeters in length and three millimeters in diameter, the white beads were made from the columnella of univalves, periwinkles, or conchs, while white and purple beads came from the Atlantic Ocean clamshell. Although the introduction of European steel tools facilitated the manufacture of large quantities of wampum, the bead appears to have already occupied an important place in pre-European East Coast Indian life. In 1497, Jacques Cartier, a French explorer, encountered shell beads he called "esurgny" near present-day Montreal. "The thing most precious that they have in all the world, they call it esurgny; it is as white as any snow: they take [the shells] in the [St. Lawrence River]....Of them they make beads and wear them about their necks as we do gold, accounting it the most precious thing in the world." Esurgny was possibly wampum. After Cartier, wampum is not mentioned for over a hundred years. Later, the Dutch recognized its economic, social, and political importance to the Indians and introduced the concept to English settlers in 1628.[7]

North American Indians had no written languages, therefore messages were transmitted through symbolic designs. Woven wampum belts developed as a device for recording important events. Signaling peaceful, warlike, or other intentions between tribes (or between tribes and the colonists), the belts were manufactured using beads of one color, with symbolic designs in another color. White represented peace, promise, and good intentions, whereas purple conveyed hostility, sadness, or death. A white belt might therefore express an alliance or peace; a purple one announced war.

Although no Indian culture developed a universally recognized series of hieroglyphics, the wampum patterns were known by most tribes of the region. A few images were almost immediately recognizable: a hatchet design woven into a belt meant war, while

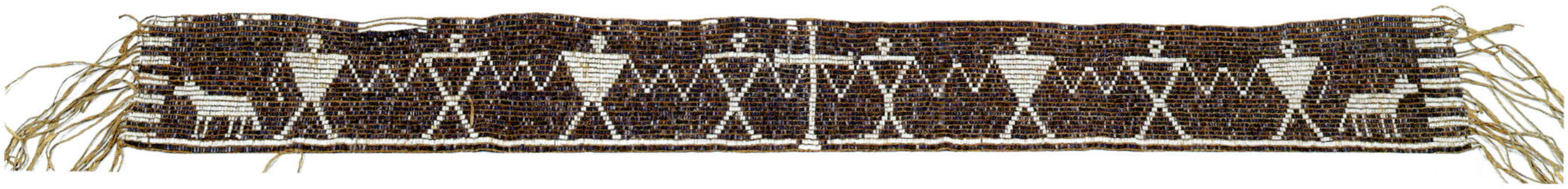

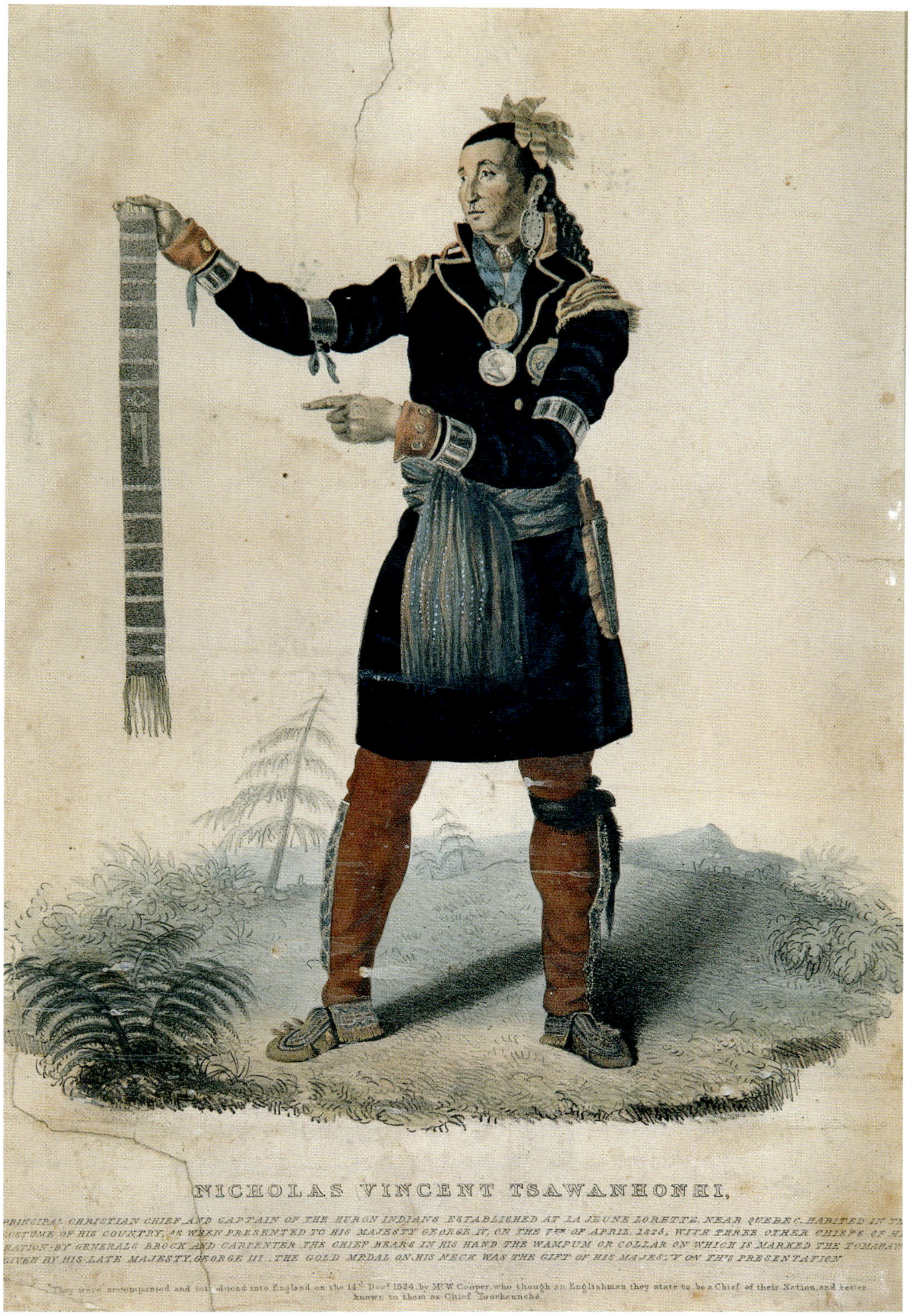

OPPOSITE, RIGHT: 283. *Tanned buckskin purse embroidered with* Marginella nivosa *shells. The Native tendency to adorn surfaces with a repetitive unit such as shells was a precedent for embroidered beadwork. Roanoke, Virginia. Powatan, c. 1656. Length, 77 cm. Ashmolean Museum, Oxford, 1685 B370*

ABOVE: 284. *Wampum was most meaningful to Native Americans in the form of commemoration belts. Because North American Indians recorded information in pictorial rather than written languages, woven wampum became a device for documenting important events regarding peace, war, or other intentions between tribes or between tribes and colonists. Belts were manufactured with background beads of one color and symbolic motifs in a second contrasting color. Patterns were a constant reminder of the message.*

This Kanesatake (Lake of Two Mountains) Mohawk wampum belt commemorates the community's founding. This late seventeenth century belt, which is twenty-seven rows wide, and has nearly 10,000 beads, also certifies the conversion of the tribe or the village to Christianity. The white beads symbolize the pascal lamb, Christian cross and the white man, while the darker ones represent the Native American. 1788. Length, 153.7 cm. McCord Museum of Canadian History, Montreal

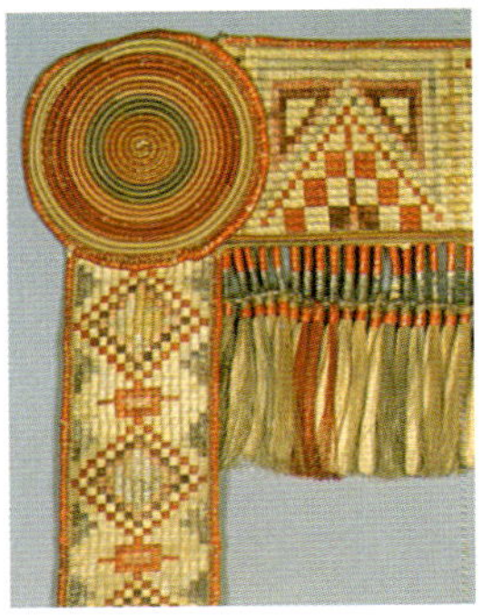

PREVIOUS PAGE, BOTTOM: 285. *A lithograph published in 1825 depicting Nicholas Vincent Tsawanhonei, chief of the Huron, holding the wampum belt commemorating the Treaty of Montreal, an agreement reached between the French and Huron allies and the English. It was recorded in wampum in 1701. McCord Museum, McGill University, Montreal*

ABOVE: 286. *Detail of a quilled bridle cover. Quillwork, a decorative technique created by North American Indians, became the prototype for much native woven and embroidered beadwork. Denver Art Museum*

RIGHT: 287. *A Cheyenne pipebag, c. 1880, that combines beadwork with quilling. Small glass seedbeads are used here to reproduce drawings of men's war exploits. The subject matter is unusual. Beadwork was made by Plains women, who typically created abstract geometric designs, leaving it to the men to paint naturalistic forms.*

In most tribes, tobacco was cultivated and smoked by men only. The tobacco plant had a sacred character and was invariably used on solemn occasions, accompanied by prayers. This finely beaded bag depicts the "awe and respect with

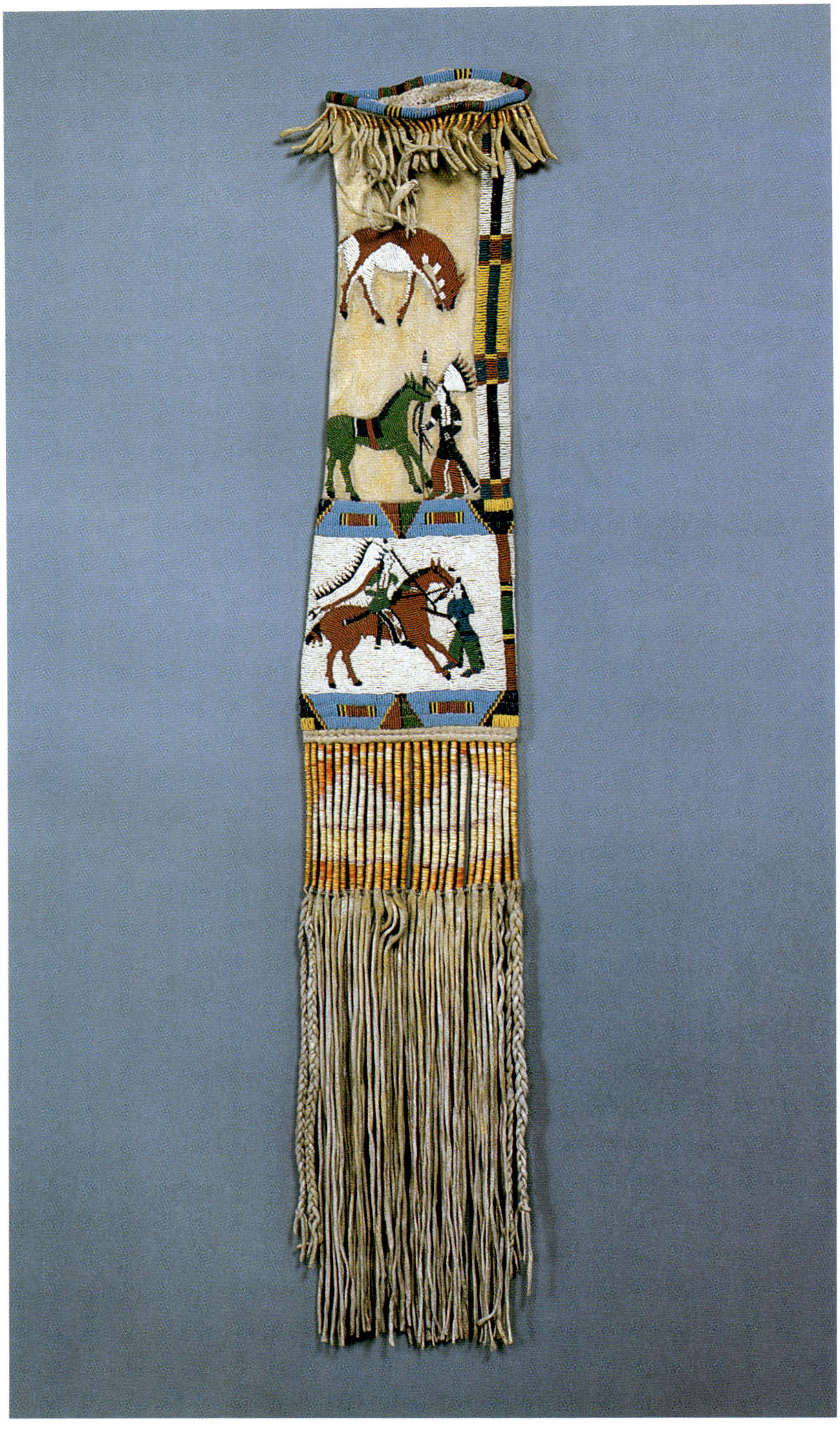

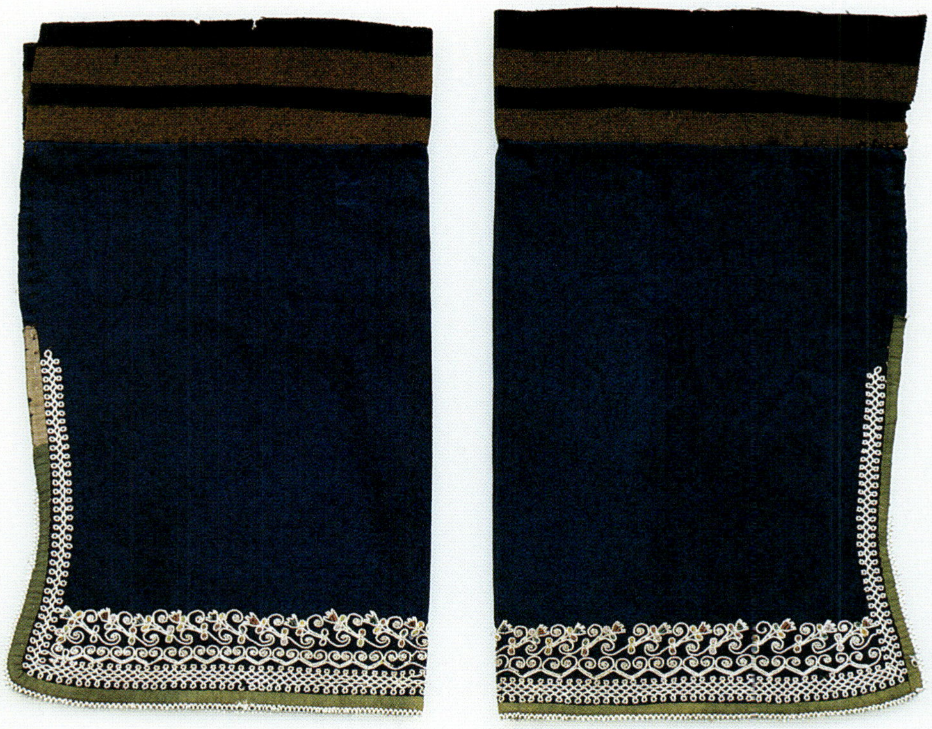

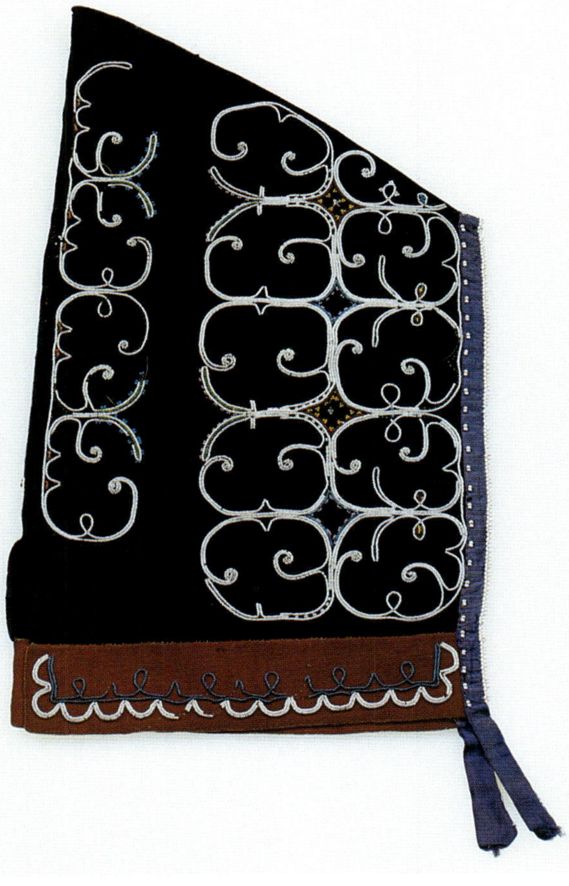

which the ceremonial pipe and tobacco were treated. When not in ceremonial use, the pipe bowl and stem were taken apart and stored separately in the bag; only when they were united did the pipe actually become charged with supernatural power."[V] Length, 99 cm. Denver Art Museum

TOP: 288. *Iroquois (Mohawk) womens' half-leggings of fine blue trade cloth with white, yellow, red, and green beadwork. The beadwork design is adapted from ribbon-work appliqué, a European style taught to young Huron and Iroquois girls in French mission schools. Made in 1894. Length, 42.5 cm. McCord Museum, McGill University, Montreal*

BOTTOM: 289. *Micmac female headdress of blue black trade cloth, with double-curve design and rows of scallops, created in fine seedbeads and sewn with moose hair. These floral patterns, typical of prevailing French neoclassical taste, merged neatly with curvilinear forms used by Woodland Indians for centuries. Bilaterally symmetrical patterns, such as this double curve, may originally have been made by Indian women literally biting patterns into folded sheets of birchbark. Length, 39.3 cm. McCord Museum, McGill University, Montreal*

NORTH AMERICA: Distribution of Beads and Bead Materials, Prehistory to Early 20th Century A.D.

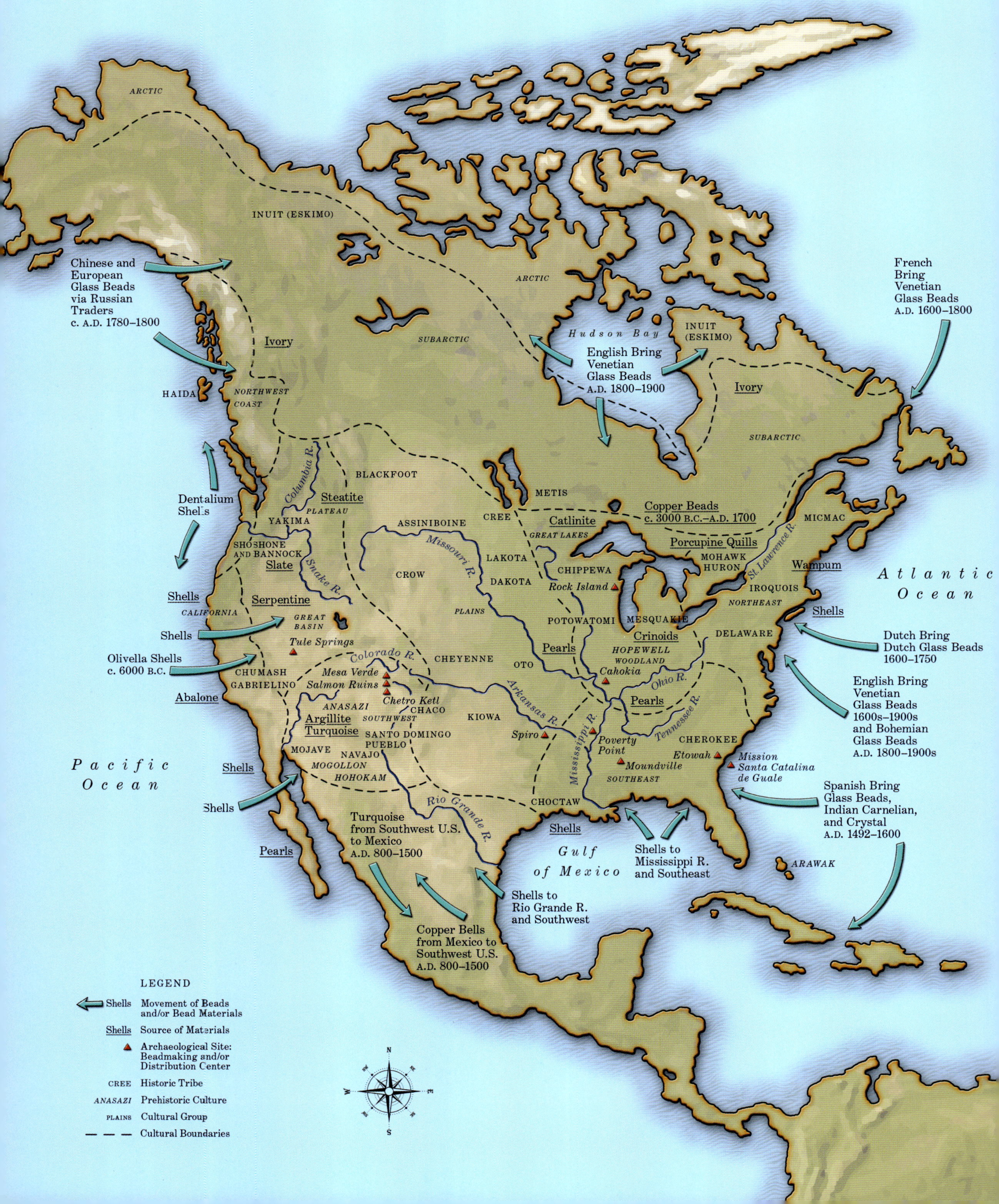

figures of two or more people holding hands meant peace and friendship. The width and length of the belt corresponded to the importance of the event.[8]

A simple square weave was used to make wampum belts. The warp threads consisted of either leather or fiber cords, while the weft elements were made of vegetal fibers or sinew threads (plate 282.5). The first officially recorded wampum belts were made by the Pennsylvania Susquehannock Indians in the 1620s.[9] Twenty years later, wampum belts were reported among the Iroquois, who eventually dominated their manufacture and trade among Indian groups. European colonists employed wampum in transactions with the Indians and among themselves. All thirteen original colonies used wampum as currency. Massachusetts made it legal tender in November 1637. New York was still fixing the exchange rate in 1701.[10]

The use of wampum spread throughout North America in the seventeenth and eighteenth centuries. It is found in Rock Island, Wisconsin, about 1675–1700, and as far south as the mouth of the Mississippi River by 1762. Lewis and Clark gave it to the Sioux and Arikara on the Missouri River.[11] Eventually, the demand for the bead exceeded the capacity of East Coast Indians to provide it. As a result, European colonists in New York and New Jersey started manufacturing wampum in the 1740s for use in the Indian trade. A wampum factory established in the mid-eighteenth century by John Campbell of Passaic, New Jersey, was operated by his descendants until 1917. In addition to the manufacture of wampum, some tubular glass beads seem to have been made to imitate wampum as well.

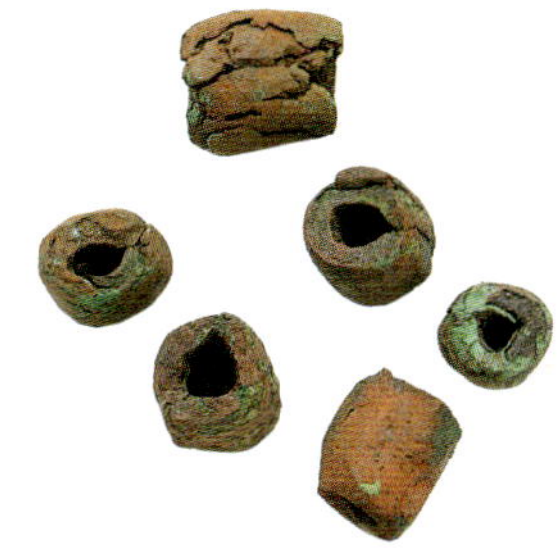

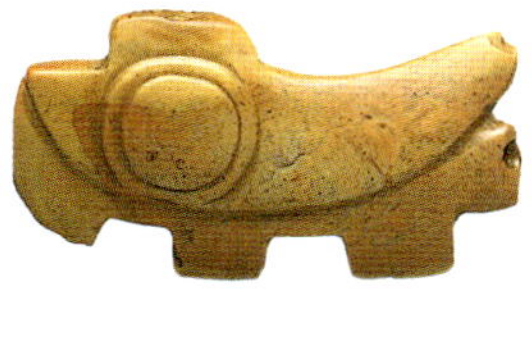

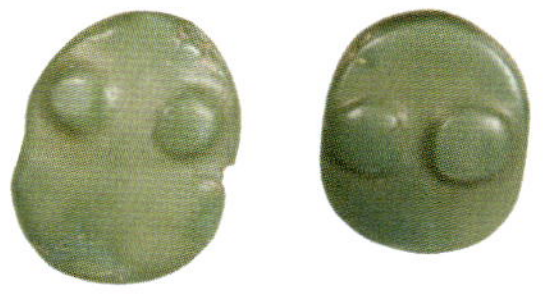

290. *Copper beads characteristic of the Glacial Kame phase in southern Ontario. c. 300 B.C. Length of top bead, 1.27 cm. Rochester Museum and Science Center, New York*

291. *Locust-shaped red jasper bead. Poverty Point–culture carvers used sophisticated techniques to produce tiny stone effigy pendants and beads. Lafayette County, Arkansas. c. 1500–700 B.C. Length, 5.7 cm. Gilcrease Museum, Tulsa. 6123.2964*

292. *Turquoise frog beads from excavations at Salmon Ruin, New Mexico. Salmon was a site of the ancestral Puebloan (Anasazi) culture and dates to the late eleventh century A.D. Frogs were a symbol of water and fertility to the ancestral Puebloans. Right bead: length, 0.9 cm. San Juan Archaeological Research Center and Library, Bloomfield, New Mexico*

The Glass Bead Trade

Most of the beads introduced to the New World by Europeans were made of glass, a material unknown to the native cultures.[12] The first documented glass bead in North America was excavated from the site of Vinland, the short-lived Viking colony situated in what is now Newfoundland and abandoned about 1347. The Vikings traded extensively with northeastern Indian groups, so it is not certain whether this first clear and spherical glass bead was a personal ornament or imported for trade.[13]

Prehistoric North Americans' appreciation for beads helped the Spanish explore and colonize the New World. One of Christopher Columbus's first acts upon reaching the Bahamas in 1492 was to offer glass beads to the Arawak Indians. His October 12 log entry is the earliest record of glass beads in America:

> A large crowd of natives gathered there.... In order to win the friendship and affection of that people and because I was convinced that their conversion to our Holy Faith would be better promoted through love than through force, I placed some of them with red caps and have some strings of beads which they placed around their necks, and with other trifles of insignificant worth that delighted them and by which we have got a wonderful hold on their affections.[14]

Using glass beads to win Indian friendship was a prevalent custom in the days when Spain, Holland, England, France, and Sweden all vied for control of North American territories. The practice lasted through the American Revolution, when gift-giving gradually gave way to trading beads for fur.

Through the fur trade, glass beads had a significant effect on North American Indian life. Early explorers found the American continent teeming with wildlife and soon established a system in which horses, guns, alcohol, and other items were exchanged for the fur pelts so coveted in Europe. When glass beads were introduced as a trade item,

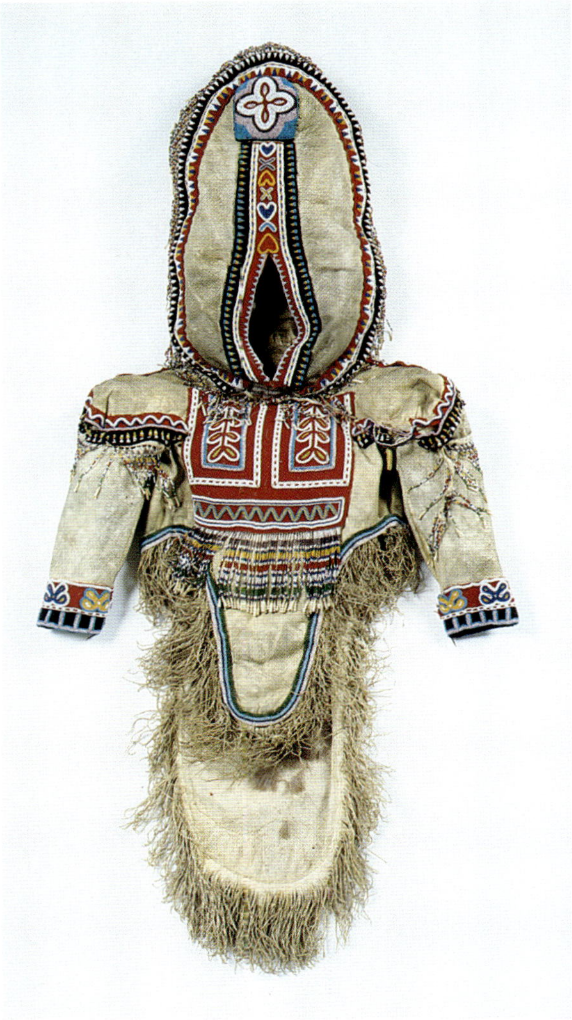

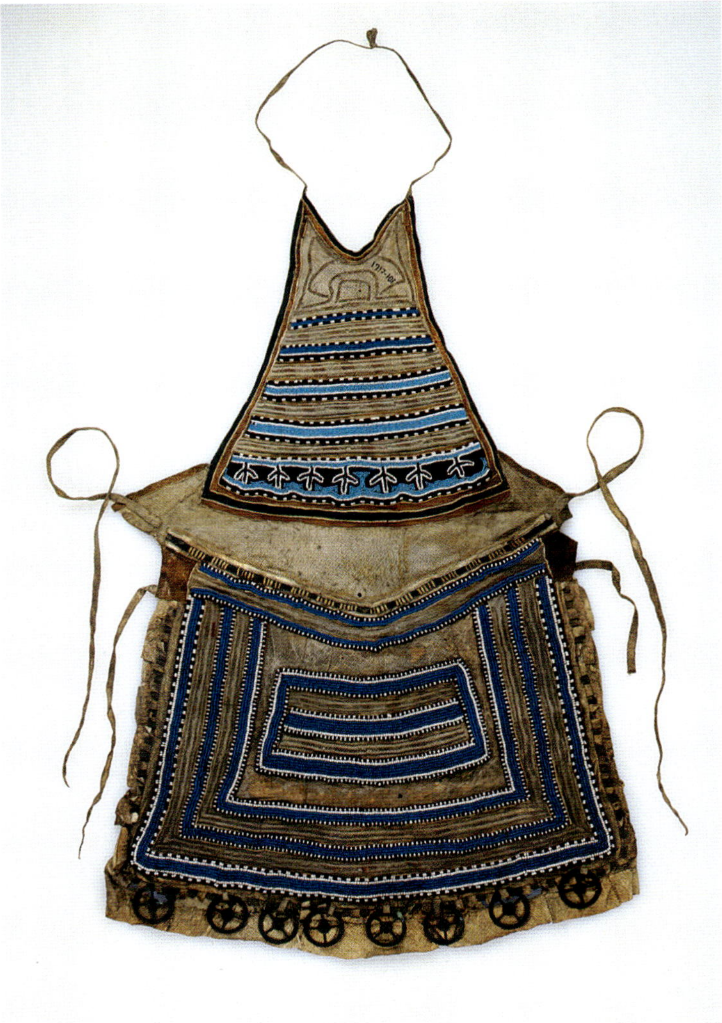

TOP LEFT: 293. *The beadwork designs on this early twentieth-century Inuit woman's parka (amautik) reflect two important eras of Eskimo history. The tiered geometric designs and triangular forms recall patterns of skin tattooing, a traditional ritual practiced by Inuit women. The use of glass beads and the decorative floral motifs show the influence of trade with foreign whalers.*[VI] *Length, 124 cm. McCord Museum, McGill University, Montreal*

TOP RIGHT: 294. *An Inuit dance apron (probably early twentieth century). Length, 51 cm. Collection Tambaran Gallery, New York*

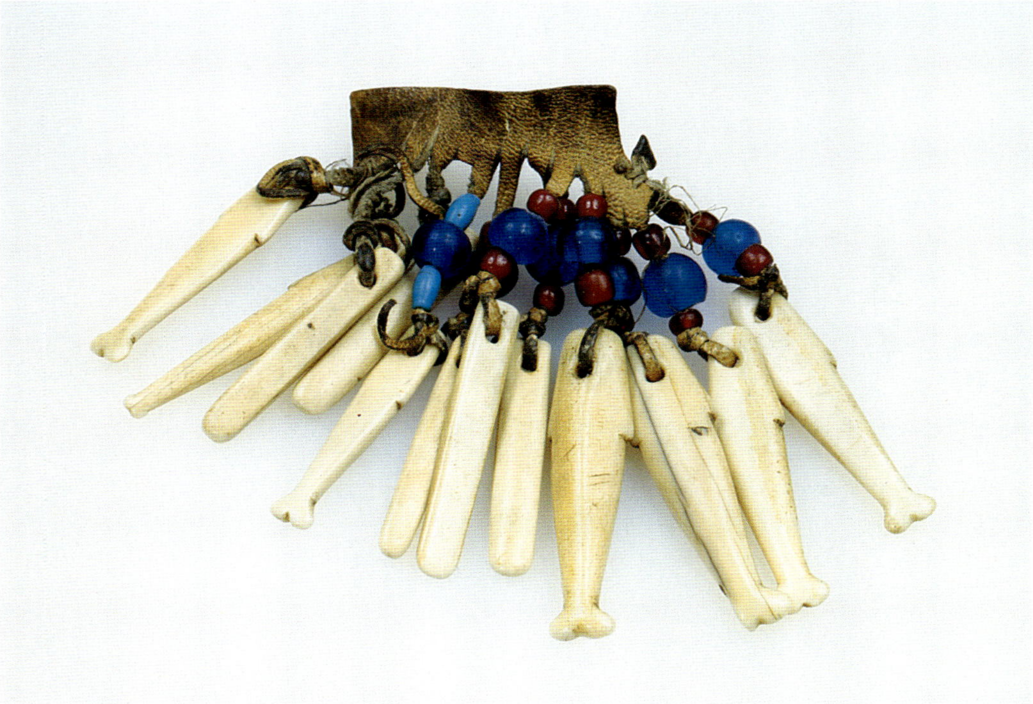

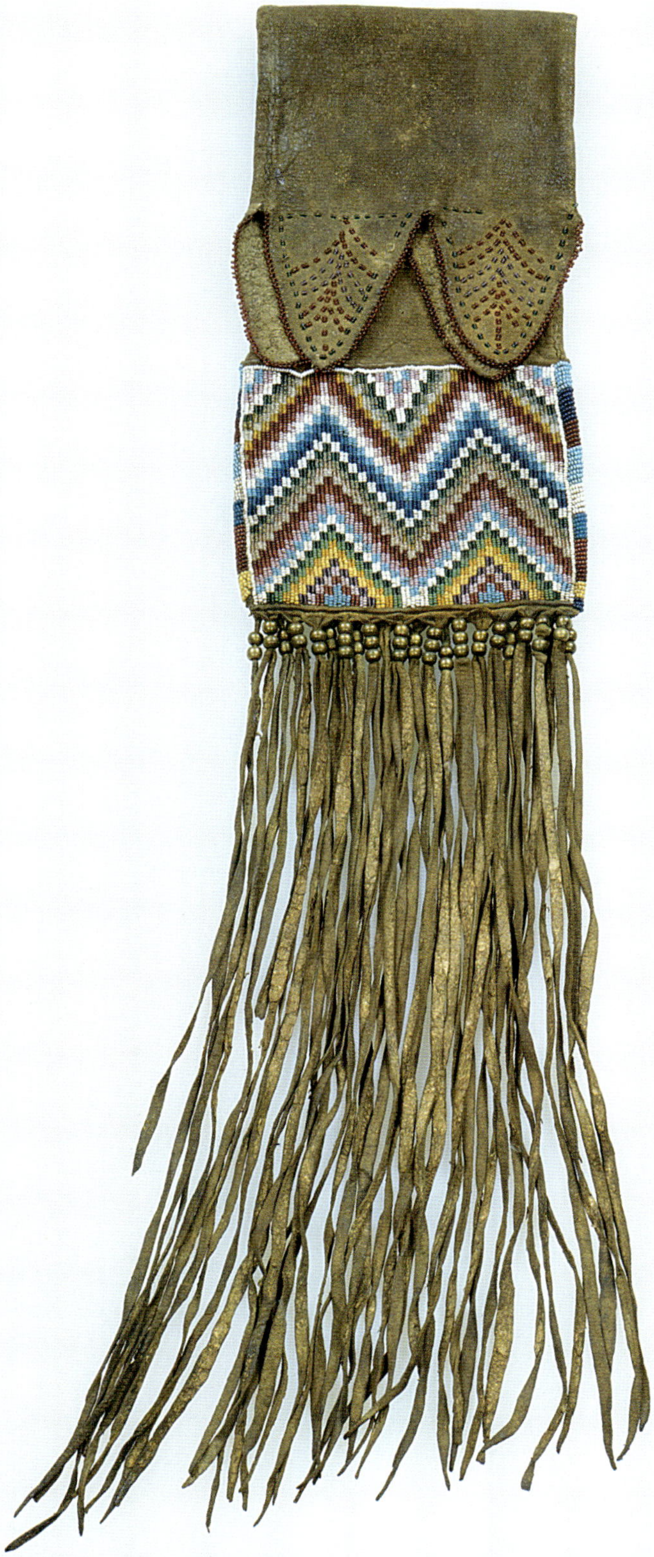

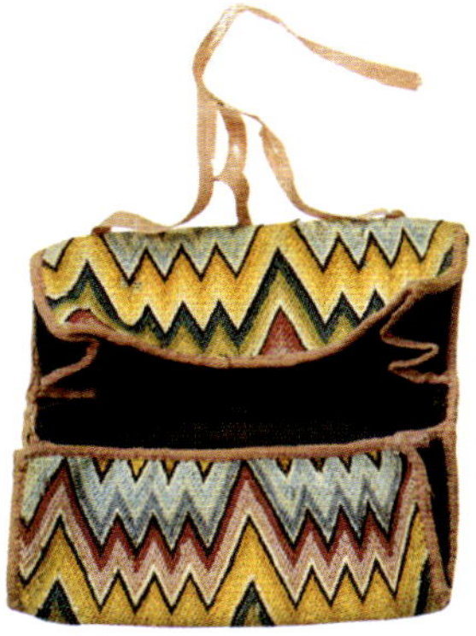

OPPOSITE BOTTOM: 295. *Inuit amulets from Koopuck, c. 1875. Ivory fetishes or charms in the form of fish, seals, and whales were combined with glass trade beads and attached to pieces of skin. The red glass beads are Venetian; the deep blue and turquoise wound-glass beads are possibly of Chinese manufacture.*

Fetishes were used as aids in capturing animals and in appeasing their spirits. Length, 10 cm. McCord Museum, McGill University, Montreal

ABOVE: 296. *An early eighteenth-century European pocketbook, decorated with flame-stitch needlework. Width, 21.7 cm. McCord Museum, McGill University, Montreal*

LEFT: 297. *This Cree firebag belonged to Chief Bear. A slender hide bag with a long fringe incorporating brass beads, it has fine solid beadwork in a diamond design on one side and a serrated design on the other. The beadwork is obviously influenced by the flame stitch, a Hungarian needlework technique of the kind used on the European pocketbook in plate 296. Length (including fringe), 93.9 cm. McCord Museum, McGill University, Montreal*

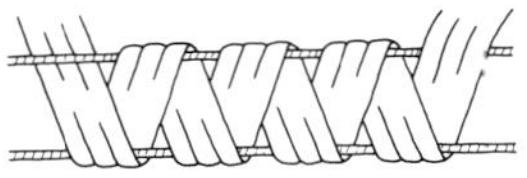

FIG. 2. *Appliqué Quillwork: quills are folded between two rows of stitches.*

they were widely sought after by Indians for their colors and ease of use. They often replaced Indian-made beads of bone, shell, copper, and stone.

Beads were important to the early fur trade because they were compact and easily transportable. One beaver skin was worth a six-foot string of small blue beads in Sault Sainte Marie in 1860, or one "bunch" of seedbeads at Fort McPherson in the Canadian Northwest. The red bead known as *cornaline d'Aleppo*, or "Hudson Bay beads" to traders in the north, carried an exchange value of six beads to one beaver skin.[15]

Lewis and Clark found the so-called Russian (a typically drawn dark blue and faceted glass) bead to be especially valued by the Indians on the Columbia River in the Pacific Northwest (Timeline 132). They noted that:

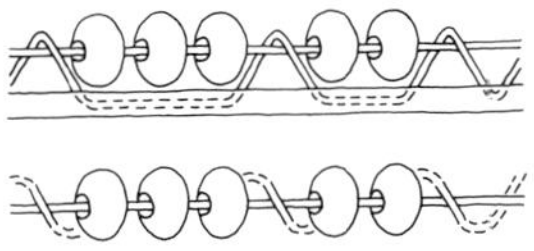

FIG. 3. *Appliqué Beadwork: overlay or spot stitch, also called "couching."*

> In the evening seven Indians of the Clot Sop nation came over in a canoe; they brought with them two sea-otter skins for which they asked blue beads and such high prices that [we] were unable to purchase them without reducing our small stock of merchandise. Merely to try the Indian who had one of these skins, I offered him my watch, handkerchief, a bunch of red beads, and a dollar of the American coin, all of which he refused and demanded '*tia-co-mo-shack*' which is chief's beads and the most common blue beads, but few of which we have at this time.[16]

Catholic missionaries in North America regularly gave beads as gifts to potential Indian converts (plate 274). Writing from the Illinois country in 1694, Father Gravier noted that: "It is true that the hope of getting a red bead—which is a fruit the size of a small bean, which has been sent to us from Martinique or other Islands (Oh, that I had a bushel of them!)...incites the children to answer well; but they must answer very well for several days to obtain either the rosary, the red bead, or the cross."[17]

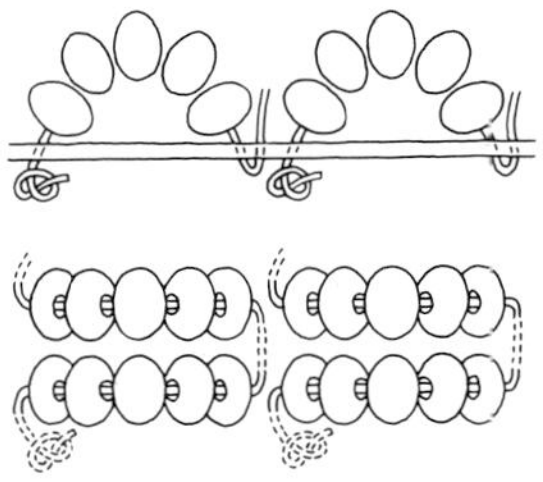

FIG. 4. *Appliqué Beadwork: "lane" stitch.*

The first glass beads traded in quantity were for necklaces that were, for the most part, available in white, blue, and black (plate 278). These colors were cheaper to produce than red or yellow beads, thus providing a greater margin of profit to the trader. Indians may also have requested beads in white, blue, and black because they suggested the white and purple shades so treasured in shell wampum. Blue beads were particularly popular in the Plains, possibly because that color was rare in Indian dye sources.[18] In the western Great Lakes region about 1675, the French introduced smaller "pony beads," thus named because they were transported by traders on ponies. Beginning about 1840, colorful, tiny seedbeads, usually two millimeters or less in diameter, were traded in bulk, the result of the standardization of manufacturing techniques in Venice and Bohemia, which made it possible to produce beads of uniform size, shape, and color.

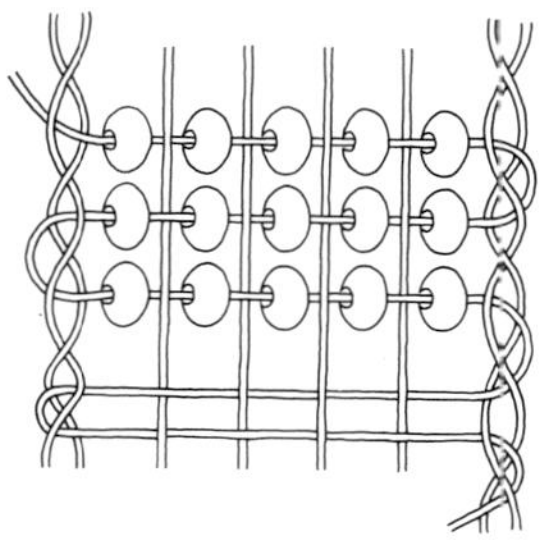

FIG. 5. *Woven Beadwork: single-thread weft and warp.*

Polychrome glass beads were particularly prized by Plains tribes and were used as offerings to the spirits (plate 304). These complex glass beads, of Venetian or occasionally Bohemian manufacture, were not as widely distributed as glass seedbeads. Probably due to their greater cost, polychrome glass beads are found sparingly in archaeological sites throughout most of the continent.

There is much confusion over how glass beads were introduced to Arctic peoples. It is likely that "Russian" or "Siberian" beads were not made in Russia, but were carried by Russian traders to the west coast of North America, subsequently moving eastward via intertribal trade. These beads may have been acquired by the Russians in China (where they had been imported from Europe) and brought to the Northwest coast as part of the fur trade. Alternatively, the beads were made in Venice or Bohemia, shipped to Hong Kong by English trading companies, and traded to Russians who brought them to the Northwest coast; or they may have come directly from Europe, brought by English merchants to the Hudson Bay Company posts in Canada.[19]

There is, incidentally, no evidence for the legend that tells of the Dutchman Peter Minuit purchasing Manhattan for twenty-four dollars worth of glass beads. This colorful story was first mentioned by historian Martha J. Lamb in 1877 and subsequently repeated in numerous books as well as a famous painting by Alfred Frederick.[20]

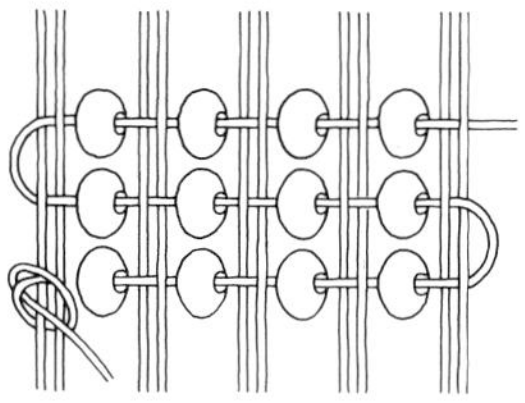

FIG. 6. *Woven Beadwork: single-thread weft and double warp.*

The Impact of Imported Glass Seedbeads

American Indians used beads in three basic ways: stringing, beadwork, and a netting technique. Beadwork involved appliqué (embroidery) on a piece of animal skin or cloth, or the creation of a fabric of beads by weaving them on a loom. With the introduction of seedbeads, the ways of decorating clothing and objects changed dramatically. Whereas large beads were strung and pony beads used sparingly to outline areas and edges, glass seedbeads, aided by the availability of thin steel needles, covered entire surfaces.

Traditional decorative methods were influenced significantly by the introduction of seedbeads. Large necklace and pony beads did not supplant the indigenous practice of quilling and painting. However, with the appearance of quantities of inexpensive seedbeads, women began to sew, embroider, net, and weave beadwork equal in quality to the finest quillwork and paintings.

Quillwork was a unique American Indian technique. Each region had its own styles, colors, and sewing methods; it was developed to perfection by tribes of the Pacific Northwest, Great Lakes, and eastern Plains before the first European beads entered the New World. Whitish porcupine quills were softened in water, flattened, colored with vegetable dyes, and fastened to skins in patterns resembling embroidery (fig. 2).

Appliquéd glass beadwork developed from this earlier quillwork. Indian women, who had previously decorated objects by the time-consuming technique of quilling, quickly realized that many familiar patterns could be executed more easily in beads, especially when cloth fabrics replaced buckskin. By 1800, quillwork appears to have been generally abandoned, although in a few areas, such as the Plains, Canadian Subarctic, and the Warm Springs Reservation in the Great Basin, quillwork continued long after beads were available and is still being made.

Woven beadwork produced in the Woodlands, Great Lakes, and eastern Plains was significantly influenced by quilling. At first sight, the ribbed surface of quillwork can be mistaken for small cylindrical beads strung on the weft. A variety of weaving techniques, usually based on the square weave, was used for making beaded wampum belts, sashes, and bags.

In glass beadwork appliqué, two basic stitches are encountered: the "overlaid" or "spot" stitch (also called "couching") and the "lane" stitch (figs. 3 and 4). The sewing technique of the overlaid stitch is like that of quillwork: several beads on a sinew thread are attached to buckskin or cloth by another sinew thread sewn across it. This stitch is ideal for the floral and other curvilinear patterns favored by the Woodland Indians.

The "lane" stitch was primarily used by Plains tribes for geometric patterns not requiring the intricacy of the overlaid stitch. It consisted of rows of beads sewn only at the ends, creating the ridged or scalloped effect distinct to the central and western Plains. The lane stitch (formerly known as lazy stitch—nicknamed for the ease with which it could be used to cover large areas) was an ideal technique for geometric and abstract forms characteristic of Plains art. It is also a perfect example of the type of beadwork that derived from designs previously done in quillwork.[21]

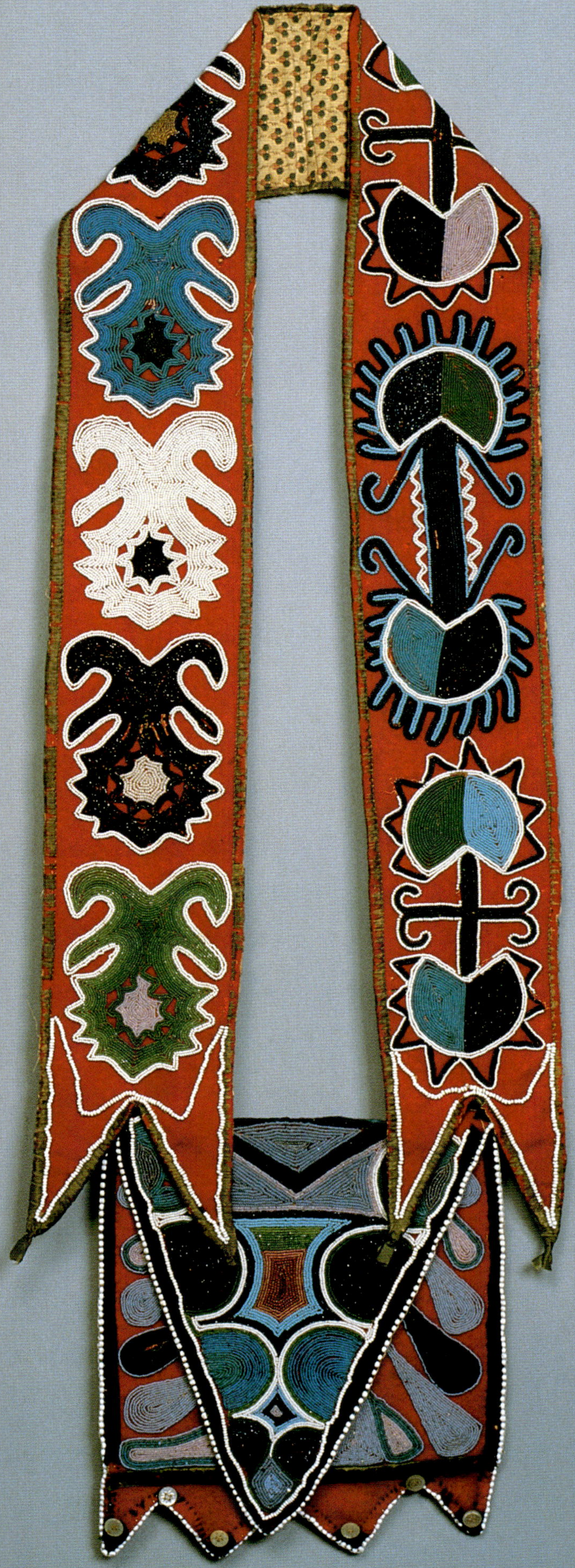

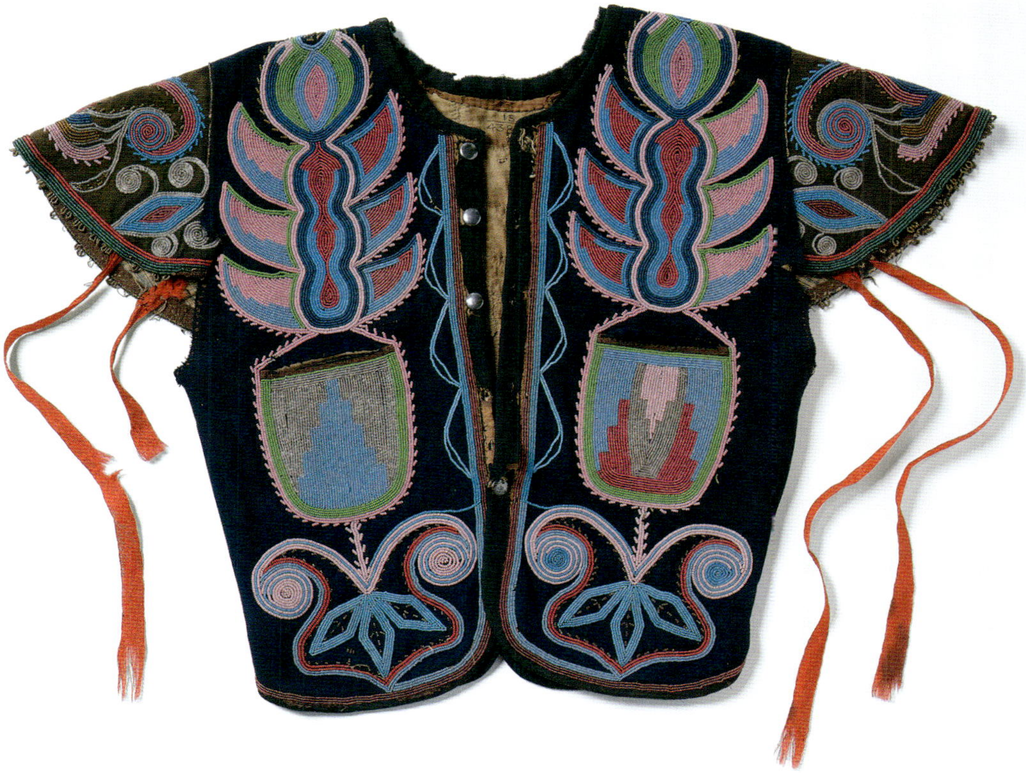

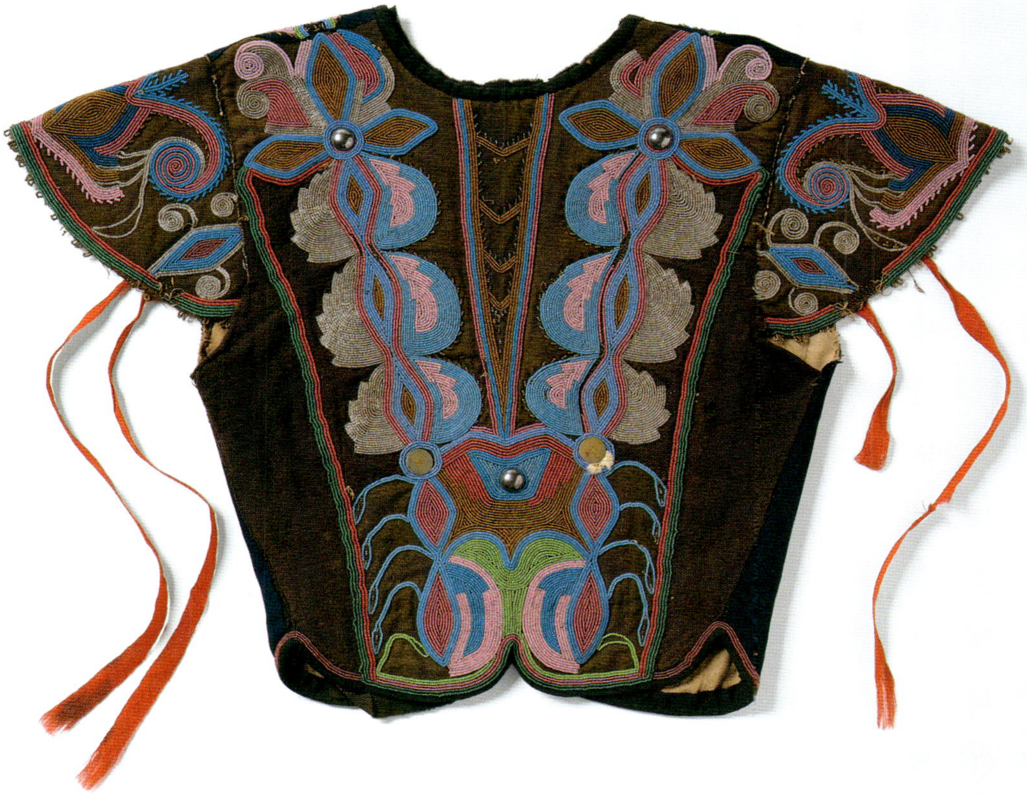

OPPOSITE: 298. *A Cherokee shoulder bag. The ammunition pouch carried by eighteenth-century British soldiers became the prototype for the shoulder bags worn as part of men's dress clothing among tribes in the southeastern U.S.*

Although the bilateral figures on the lower left strap resemble prehistoric Southeastern symbols engraved on shell and stone disks, the designs on this pouch were probably invented by the beadmaker.[VII] Pouch: width, 20.3 cm. Denver Art Museum

LEFT: 299a–b. *A Prairie-style Potawatomi beaded-cloth shirt (front and back views) illustrates the blending of stylistic motifs among several Prairie tribes: Oto, Winnebago, Prairie Potawatomi, and Omaha. The bilaterally symmetrical double curve and radial structures of ancestral embroidery traditions from the Eastern and Southeastern Woodlands (seen in plate 298) are extended with multiple volutes and ambiguous floral or their pictorial references. The approach is the first far-reaching intertribal design synthesis of the nineteenth century. Length, 50.8 cm. National Museum of the American Indian, 15/4383*

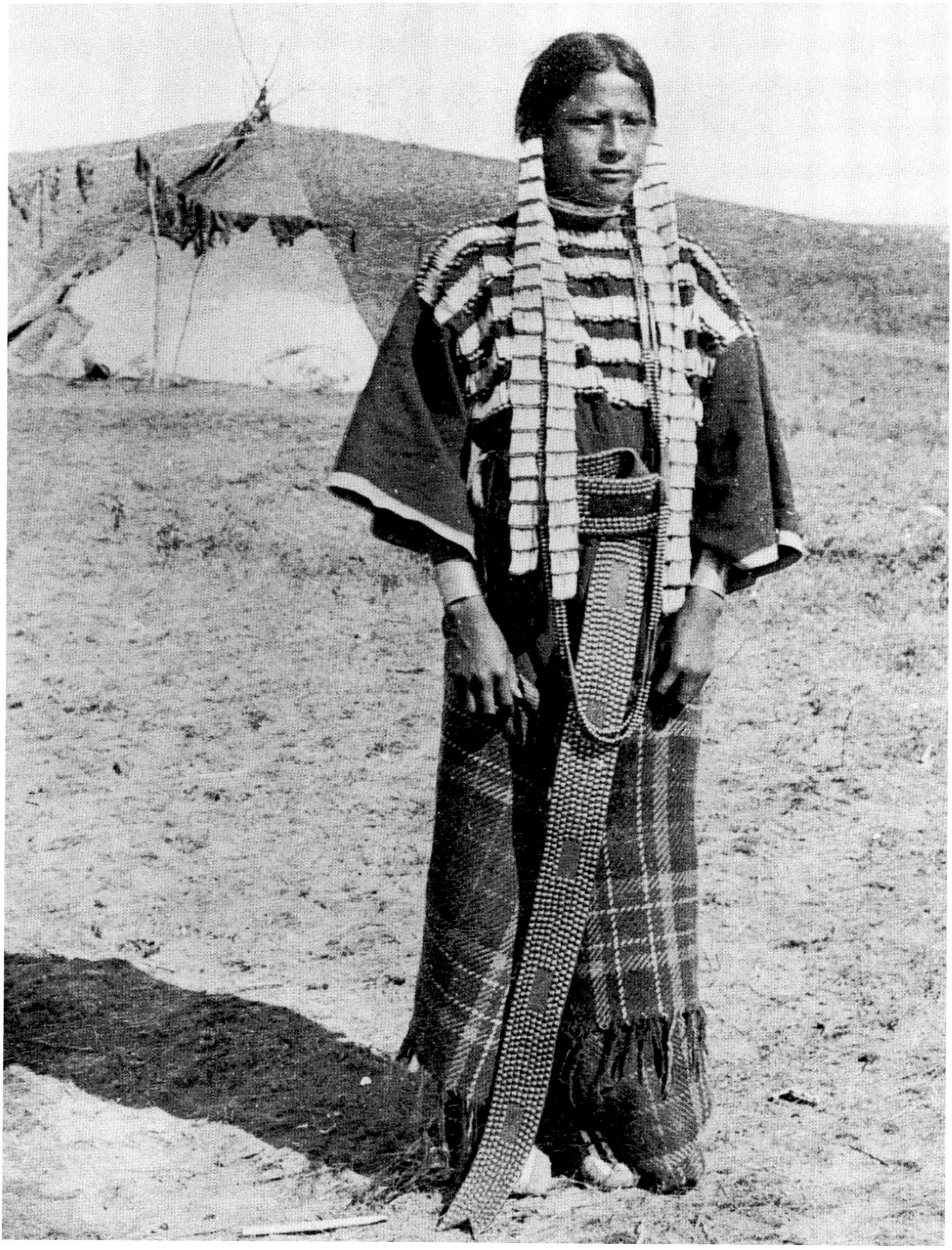

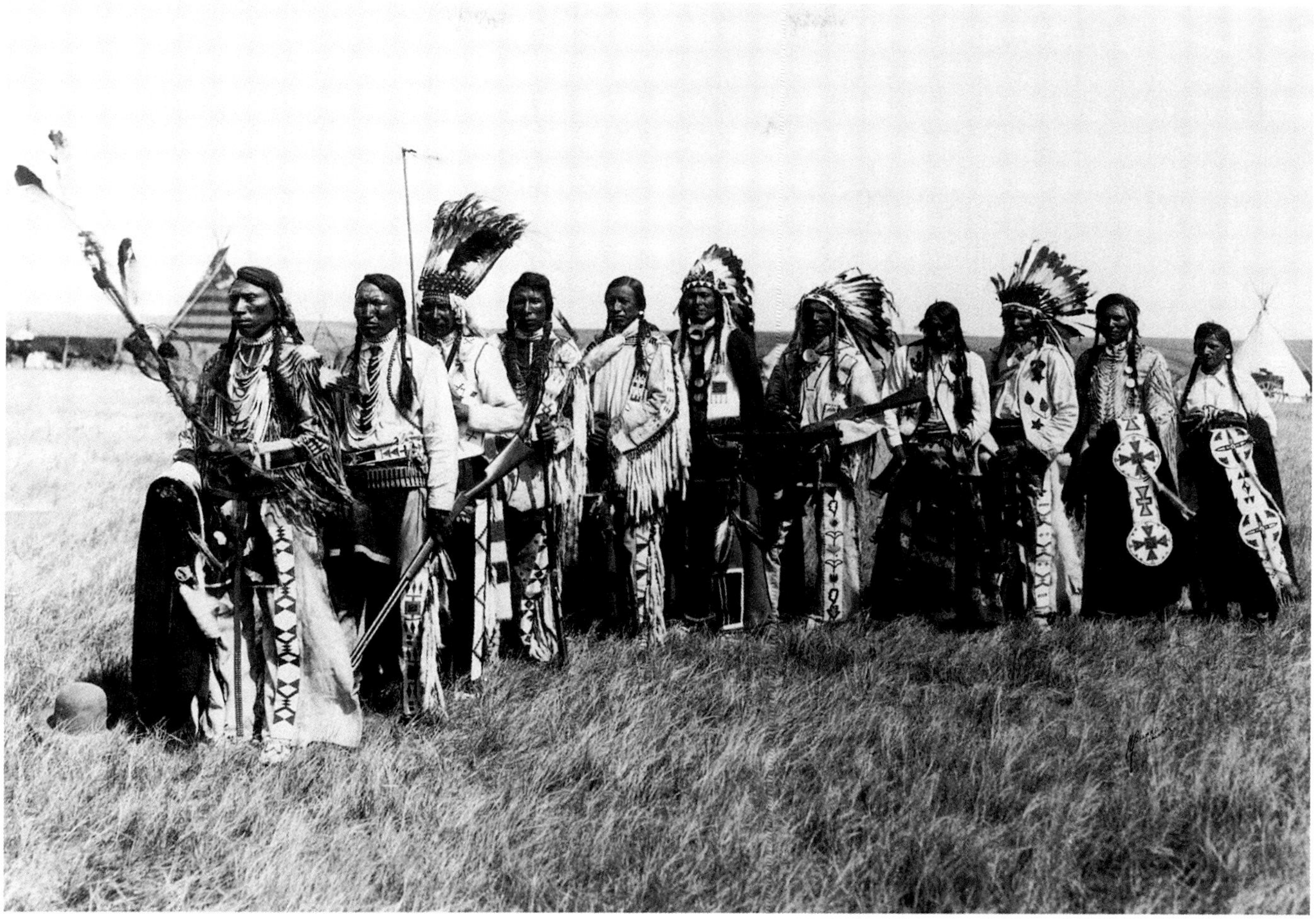

Beadwork of the Plains Tribes

Indian cultures developed in ways that reflect their natural environment. Thus, the Haida of the Pacific Northwest, who lived in immense spruce and redwood forests, were prolific woodcarvers; the Pueblo people, whose lives were organized by mythology and rituals tied to maize agriculture, symbolized this ideology in much of their pottery; and the Plains people adorned their abundant supply of animal hides with paint, quills, and eventually beads. Frederick Dockstader explains in *Indian Art in America*: "Their work revolved and grew out of the natural resources provided by their Creator. In turning these resources into artistic objects, they returned the compliment."[22]

The people of the Plains, a vast grassland stretching from the Great Lakes to the Rocky Mountains, depended almost entirely on the buffalo for food, clothing, shelter, and most of their raw materials. Their nomadic existence, intimately tied to the seasonal movements of the buffalo herds, precluded many material possessions. Consequently they wore small, easily transportable objects that served several functions. A beaded bag of soft leather could be worn, hung in the tent as decoration, and rolled up for removal to a new campsite at a more promising hunting ground.

Although personal possessions were few, Plains Indians fashioned garments from animal skins and elaborately decorated them with beadwork. Each tribe employed its own distinctive designs and techniques. The care devoted to adornment reflected their views of the spiritual world. Respect for the buffalo was paramount, for this animal alone supplied all the basic needs of the community. The relationship was refined:

OPPOSITE: 300. *A Dakota (Sioux) woman with a beaded dentalium shell shirt and long dentalium shell and leather earrings—typical adornment for Plains women in the latter half of the nineteenth century. Photograph taken c. 1886. Smithsonian Office of Anthropology, Bureau of American Ethnology Collection*

301. *Blackfoot Indians in full beaded regalia, Calgary, Alberta. Photograph taken about 1920. Notman Photographic Archives, McCord Museum, McGill University, Montreal*

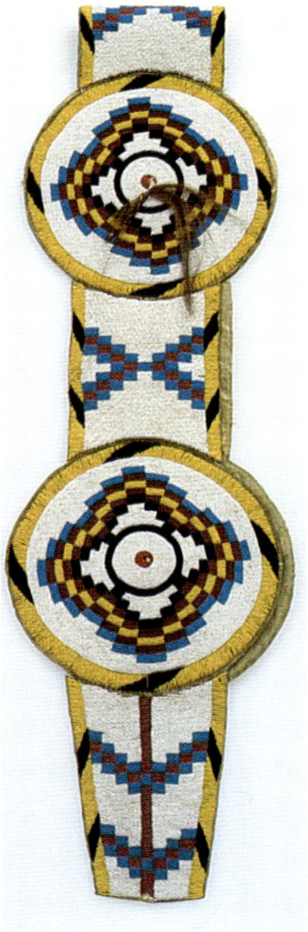

ABOVE: 302. *Beadwork blanket strip used to cover the seams of the buffalo robe of an Assiniboine Indian. Similar objects are held by two Blackfoot men (far right) in plate 301. Rondel: diameter, 24.5 cm. McCord Museum, McGill University, Montreal*

RIGHT: 303. *Blackfoot loop necklace from the Canadian Plains. This is a man's necklace of brass and colored glass trade beads strung on rawhide. Length: 63.5 cm. McCord Museum, McGill University, Montreal*

OPPOSITE: 304. *A string of three hundred and twenty "fancy" glass beads, predominantly Venetian-made. Collected among the Lakota in the Dakotas, c. 1890. Longest bead, 3.8 cm. U.S. Department of the Interior, Indian Arts and Crafts Board, Sioux Indian Museum, Rapid City*

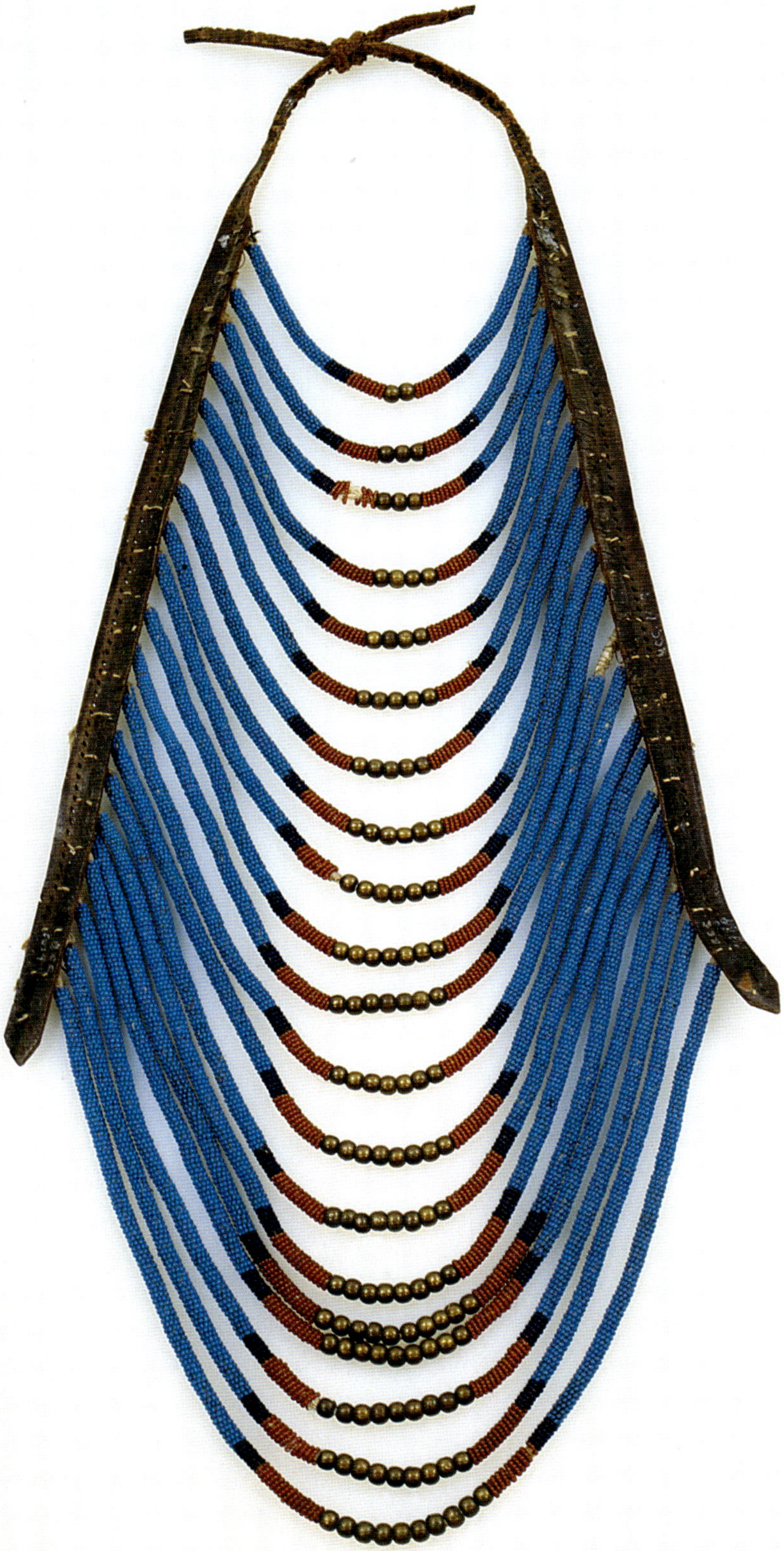

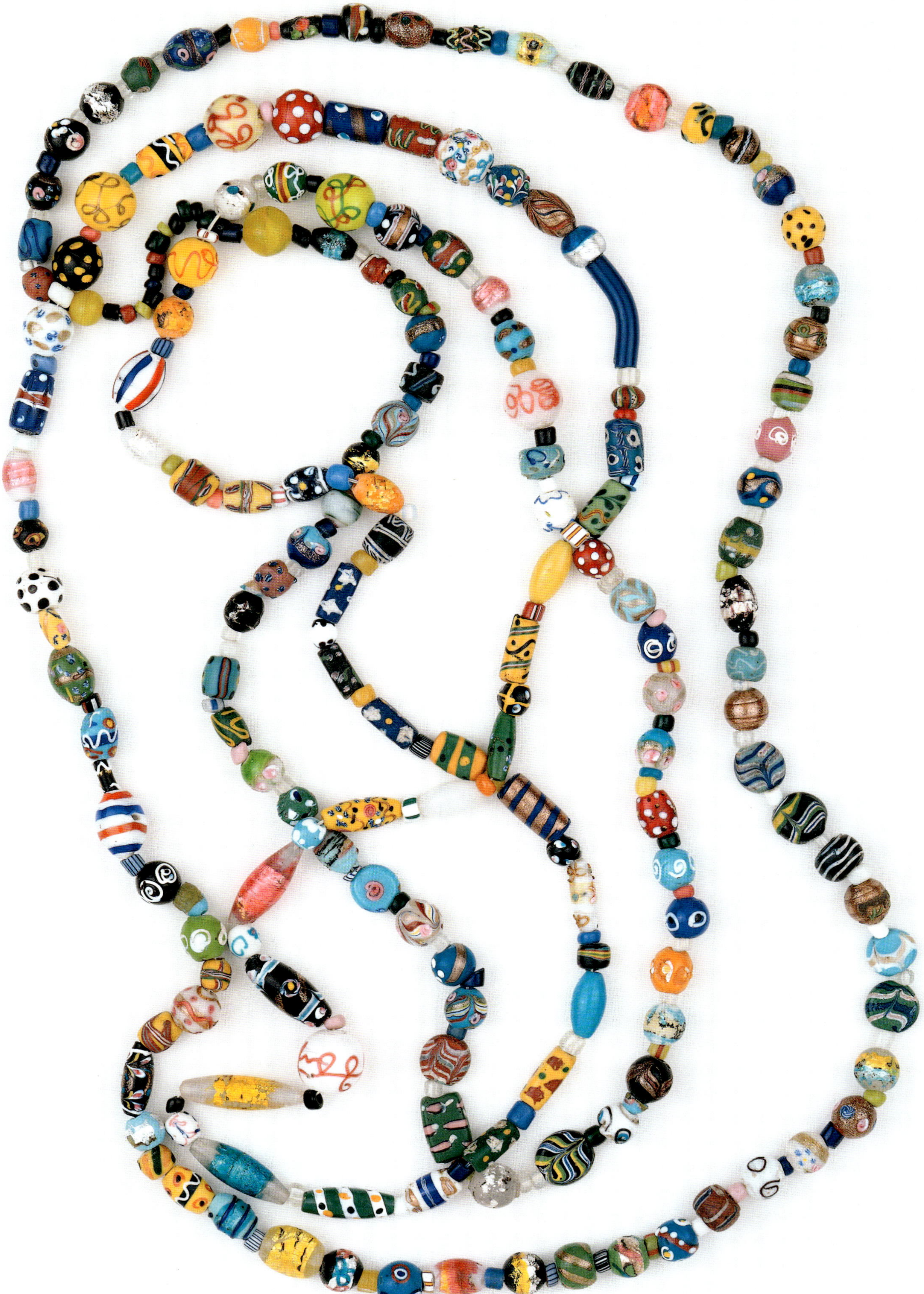

TOP: 305. *The red ochre backing identifies these as the moccasins of a shaman. The circle is a recurring (Blackfoot) Plains motif; it has neither beginning nor end and symbolizes the sun, the moon, the calendar year, and life itself.*[VIII] *Length, 26.7 cm. McCord Museum, McGill University, Montreal*

BOTTOM: 306. *This Mesquakie beaded and twined bag (shown front and back) was carried by a young man. The rich iconography on the bag and strap includes fragments of abstract images. On the front (right) Underwater Panther is surrounded by horizontal zigzags representing water, and elongated hexagon ("otter-tail") shapes further symbolizing Underwater Panther. The back of the bag (left) features a highly abstracted Thunderbird or, possibly, a Thunderbird colony. Designs joining the two opposing images appear on side bands. Collected in Iowa in 1903. Glass beads, cotton wefts, wool warps. Pouch width, 7.8 cm. American Museum of Natural History, 50/4888*

OPPOSITE: 307. *A Midewinin song "reminder" panel. The Midewinin, or Grand Medicine Society, of the Great Lakes region was an institution that cured the sick and functioned on behalf of the tribe's welfare. Since ceremonies were lengthy, there were memory aids to help recall the correct sequence of prayer and song. Members carried cloth plaques like this one to help them remember the magic songs. Length, 31.8 cm. Denver Art Museum*

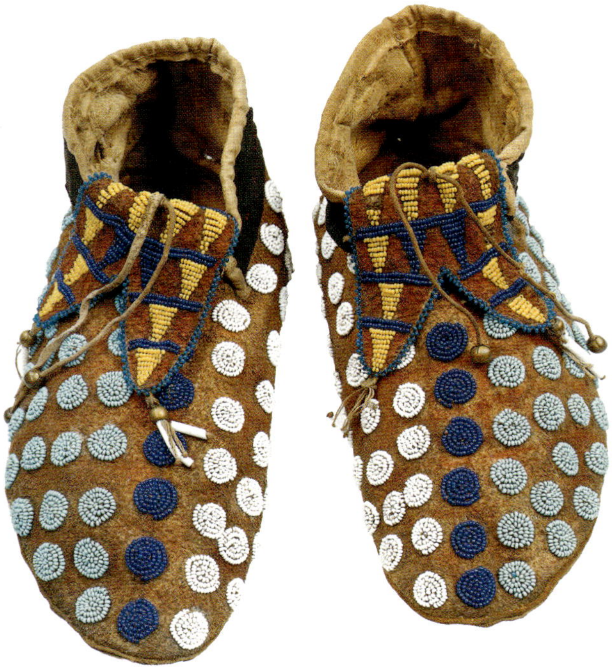

The Cosmos and the Pouch

(Plate 306) All Native North Americans believed in a similar cosmology: the universe was divided into an interrelated and layered world of Sky World, Under World, and This (Earth) World. The zones of the universe are replicated within this Mesquakie beaded bag. On opposite sides, Thunderbird and Underwater Panther represent opposing cosmological powers and regions, Sky World and Under World, respectively. Thunderbirds and Underwater Horned Panthers fought constantly. Maintaining the balance was humankind's overriding responsibility. As a container for This World medicines—roots, herbs, and leaves—the bag is a metaphor, a "cosmic diagram" of the multilayered universe, in which the human who carries the bag participates.[IX]

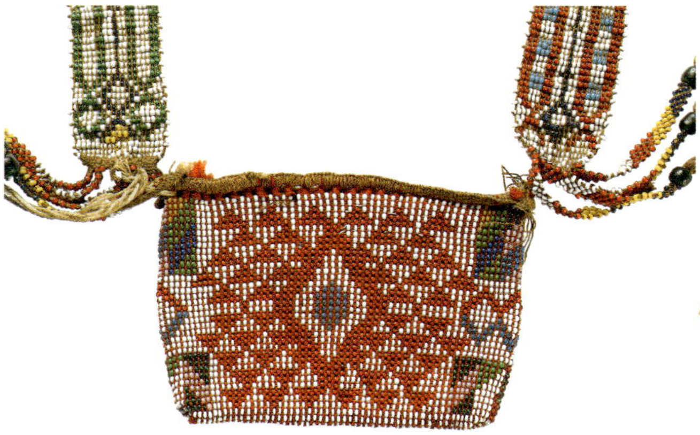

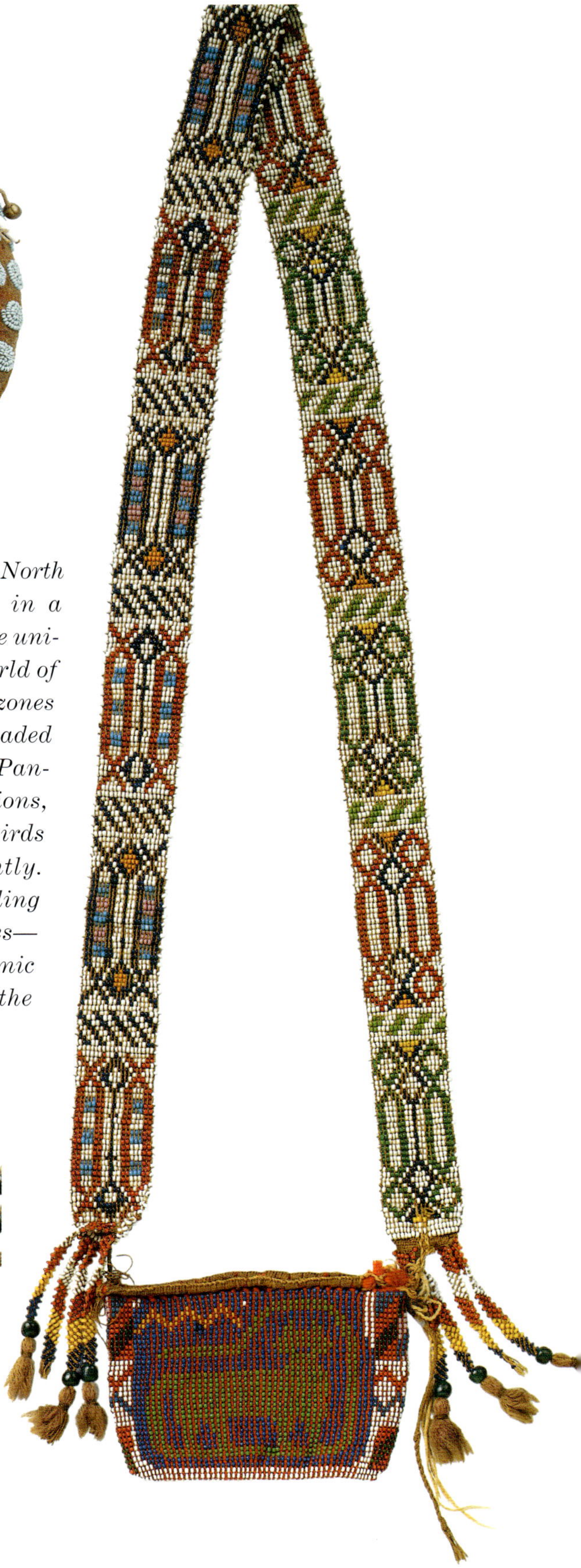

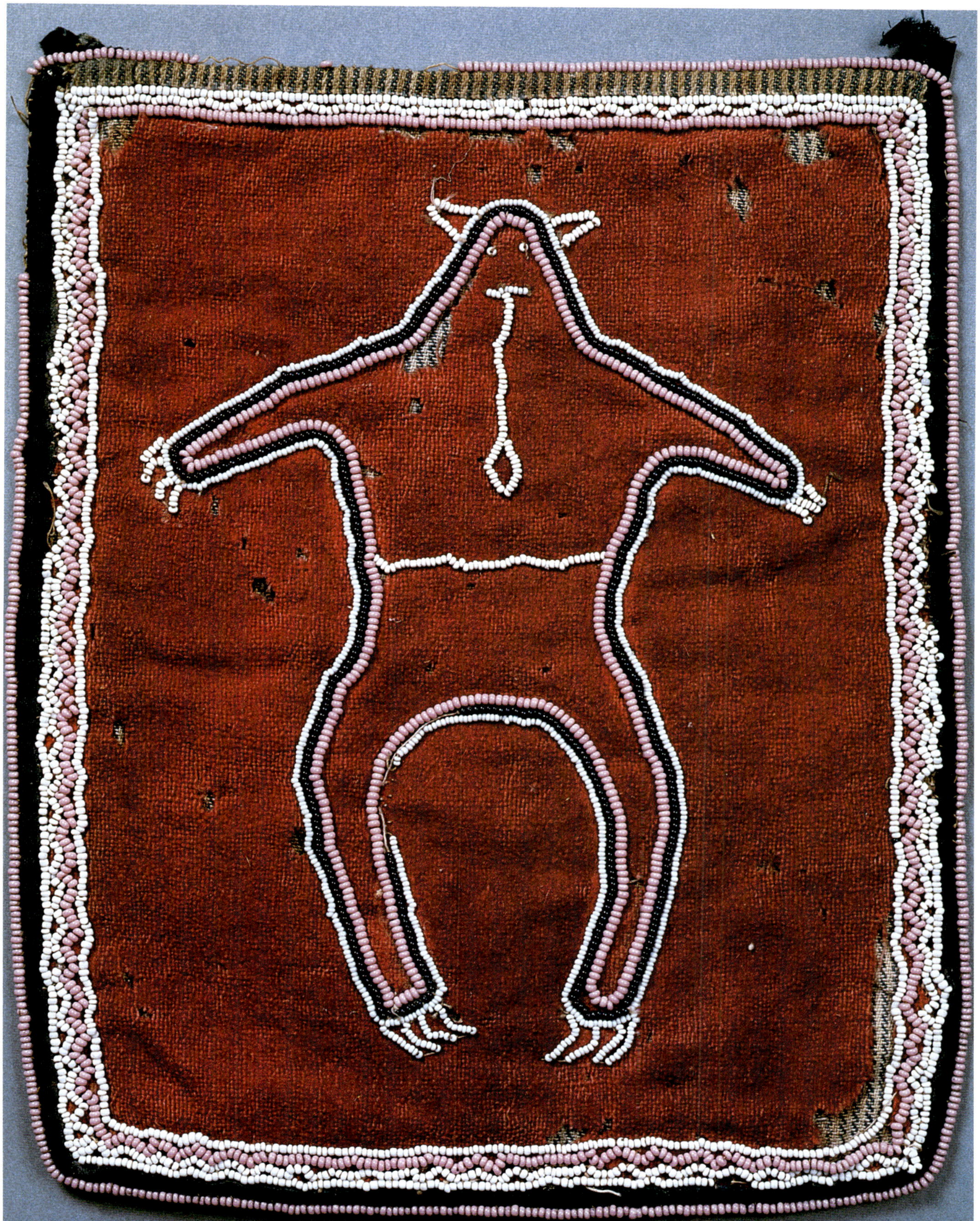

> The skins of game were more than just practical, everyday material for clothing and shelter for they contained some of the spiritual power of the animals from which they had been taken. In life the skin had given the animal its form. Wearing it, or resting in its shelter, symbolized and reinforced the constant and powerful spiritual bond between game and the people whose survival depended on the continued generosity of animals in surrendering their lives. Beautifying a dressed skin not only benefited its human owner but also did honor to the spirit of the animal. Art was part of the customary, indeed obligatory, propitiation of the slain animal to obtain its good will and prevent its wrath and revenge.[23]

Plains Indians believed, as did all Native North Americans, the world was filled with power that resided in objects, animals, or even people. Many tribes employed beads and beadwork to depict the imagery that was sacred to their particular culture (plates 305–7). A beautiful example of the blending of technique and iconography accomplished through beadwork is seen in the Mesquakie medicine pouch (plate 306)

The Plains people decorated themselves, their homes, and their possessions; above all, they ornamented and honored their horses. Horses, introduced in the Southwest by the early Spanish explorers, gave the Plains Indians much greater mobility. With the horse, buffalo hunting shifted from drive-and-ambush techniques to collective hunting, resulting in a dramatic increase in the number of buffalo killed.

The Crow of the upper Missouri River were among the richest and most beautifully adorned Plains tribes. Charles Larpenteur, who traded with the Crow in 1833, described the visible results of their abstinence: "As they do not drink, their trade was all in substantial goods, which kept them well dressed, and extremely rich in horses; so it really was a beautiful sight to see that tribe on the move."[24] Crow beadworkers lavished care and skill on paraphernalia that was visible when the camp was on the march; special emphasis was given to the accoutrements of the horses.

Much of the Plains Indians' decoration was created specifically to be viewed in motion. The Indian craftsman had the "movement of the body, the graceful motion of the horse, and the wafting of the Plains breeze in mind when he developed the corona of feathers, the elaborate fringe, and the many pendants of cloth, leather and beadwork."[25]

Beadworkers took pride in their ability to do fine work. If a man wished to compete with a neighbor who owned a pair of fully beaded moccasins, he could have his wife bead his moccasins on the soles as well as on the tops. (However, moccasins beaded on the soles, known as "spirit moccasins," were designed primarily for burials.) A competitive woman might bead her dress all the way to the bottom edge instead of restricting her beads to the yoke.

Intertribal trade and gift-giving often involved objects of beadwork, resulting in the frequent merging and reinterpretation of styles. For example, the iconography and floral motifs of the eastern Delaware and the southeastern woodland Cherokee were transformed into stylized motifs and floral patterns of the prairie Potawatomi (plates 298, 299). As tribes moved west either through force or in search of game and fur in the nineteenth century, artisans of different tribes were often in contact.

Exposure to European styles directly affected Indian creativity. Along the colonial frontier, Indians observed the floral motifs on furniture and clothing of the Dutch, German, English, Swedish, and French settlers. Religious orders in French Quebec established mission schools where the local Huron and Iroquois girls were taught embroidery, mainly in the floral designs of the French Renaissance. Substituting dyed moose hair for silk thread, eighteenth-century Indian girls in eastern Canada developed an elaborate floral style that was also incorporated into beadwork.

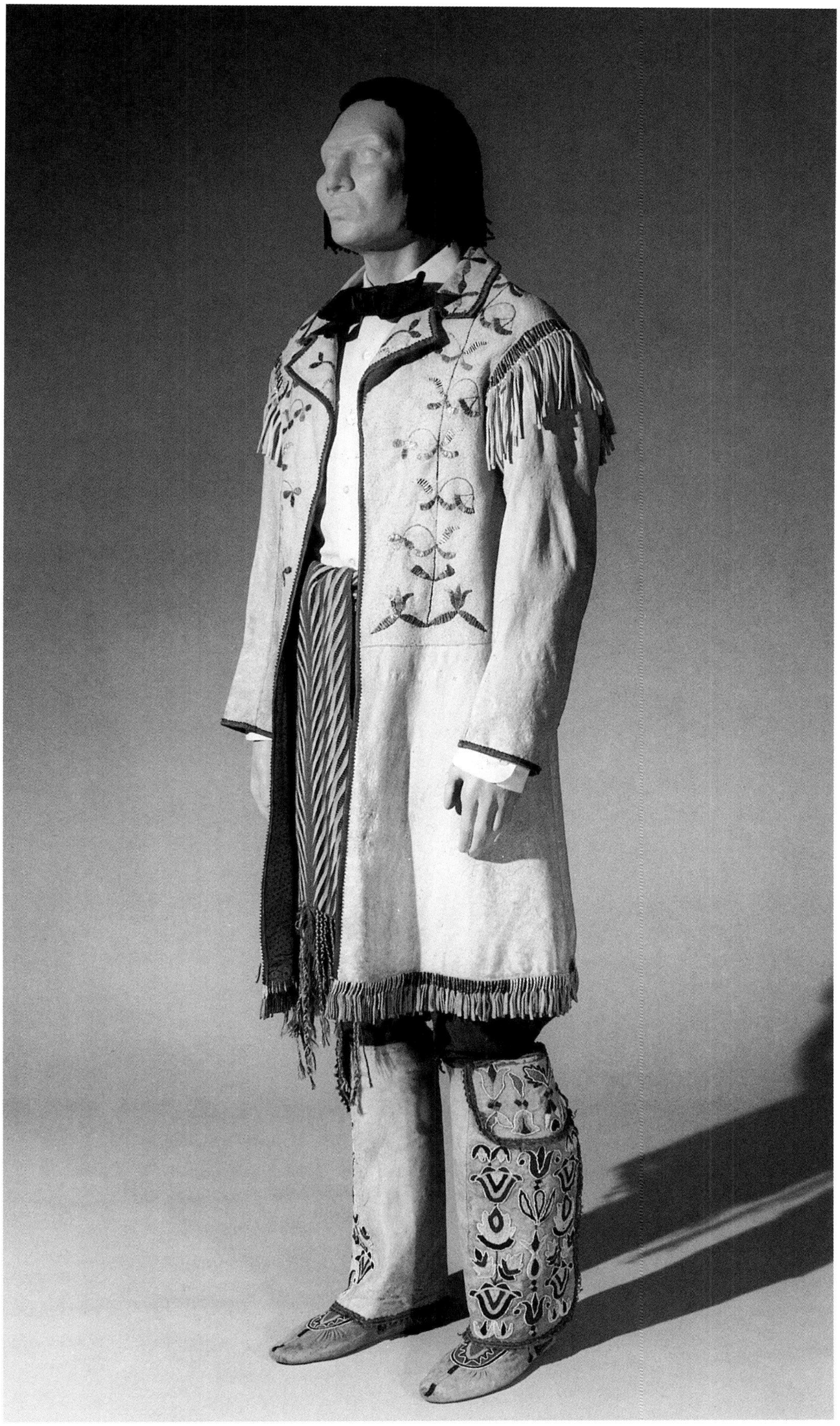

308. *The Metis of southern Canada are people of mixed Indian and European ancestry who built a distinct intermediate culture. This mid-nineteenth century costume combines native and foreign elements. The coat is an exact copy of a Prince Albert jacket, although it is made of leather and decorated with Indian porcupine quill embroidery. The half-leggings have typical Metis beaded floral patterns. Denver Art Museum*

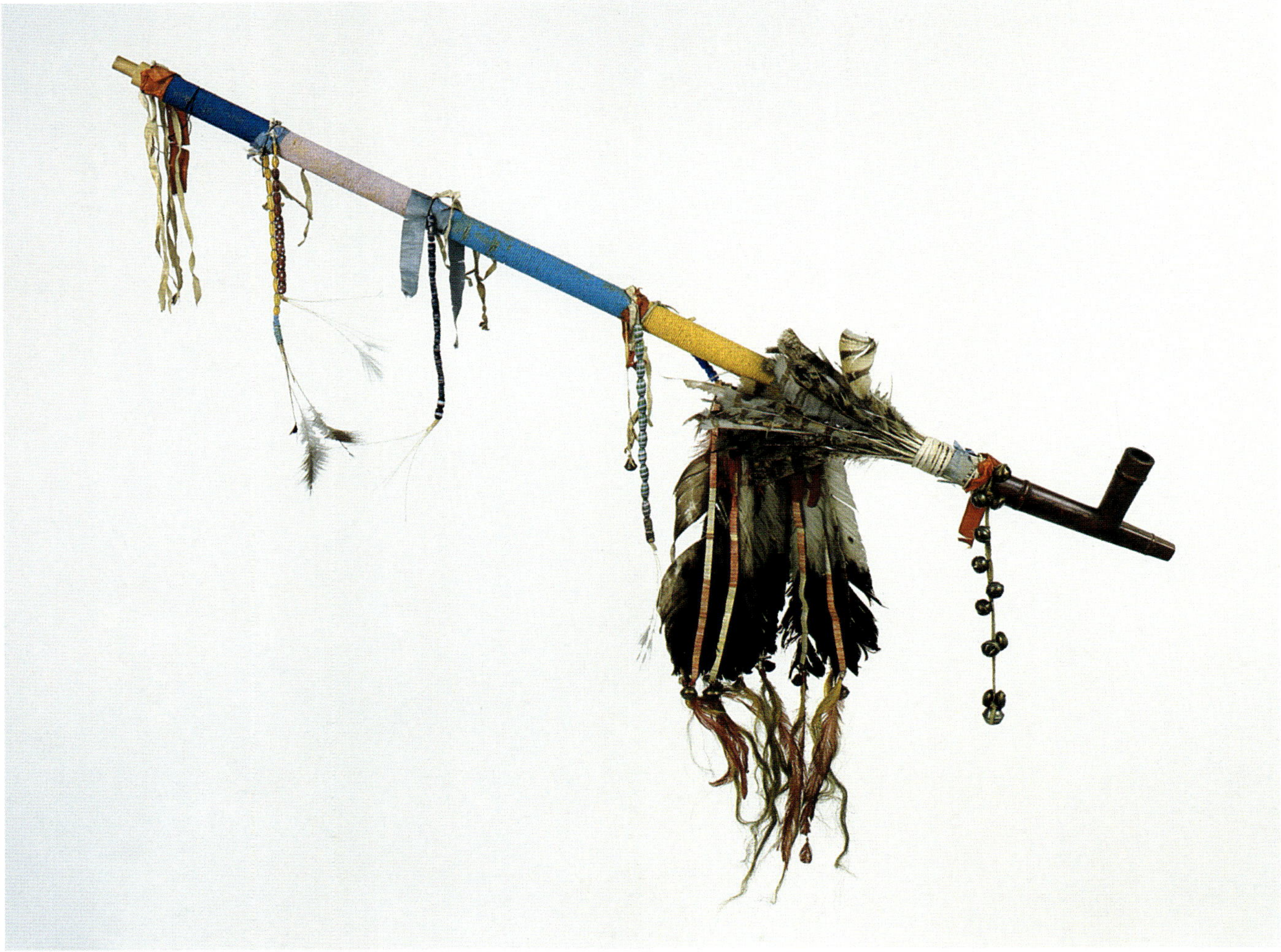

ABOVE: 309. *Blackfoot ceremonial "medicine pipe." Pipes of this kind, with long, elaborate stems, were used for formal smoking at important meetings, including religious ceremonies to summon divine help in various undertakings. This pipe is decorated with an unusually large number of beads. Length, 95.2 cm. Plates 309–10: McCord Museum, McGill University, Montreal*

RIGHT: 310. *Blackfoot stone and leather war clubs of various types were used in hand-to-hand combat. This aggressive, beaded image was intended to be seen by the enemy in the last flash of his life. Length, 50.8 cm.*

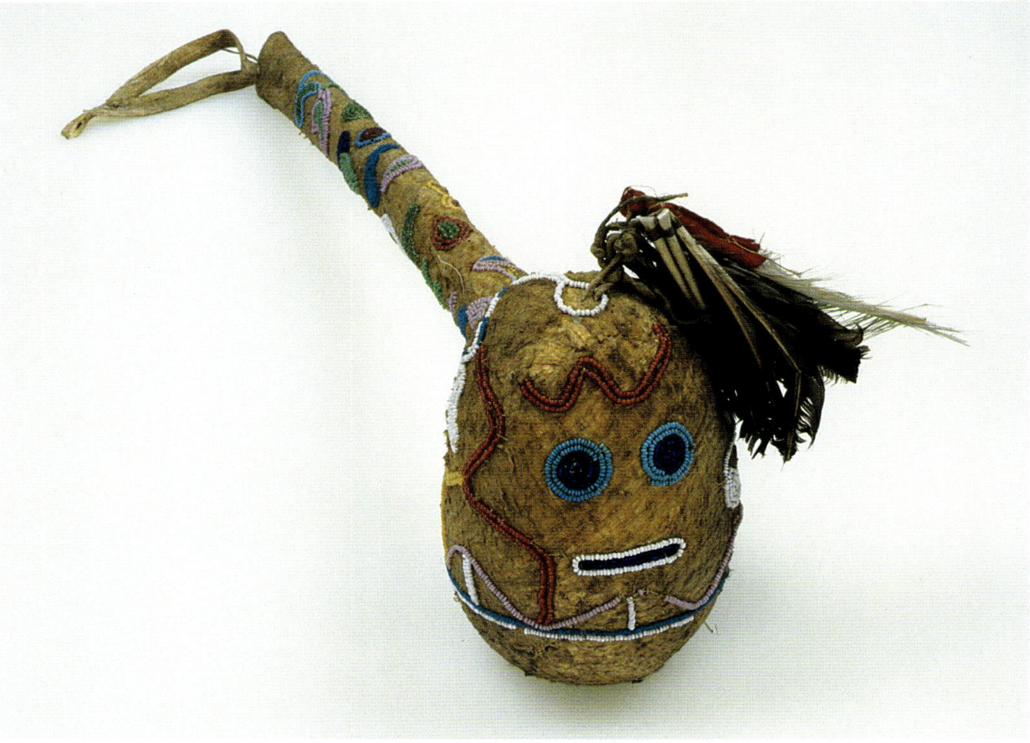

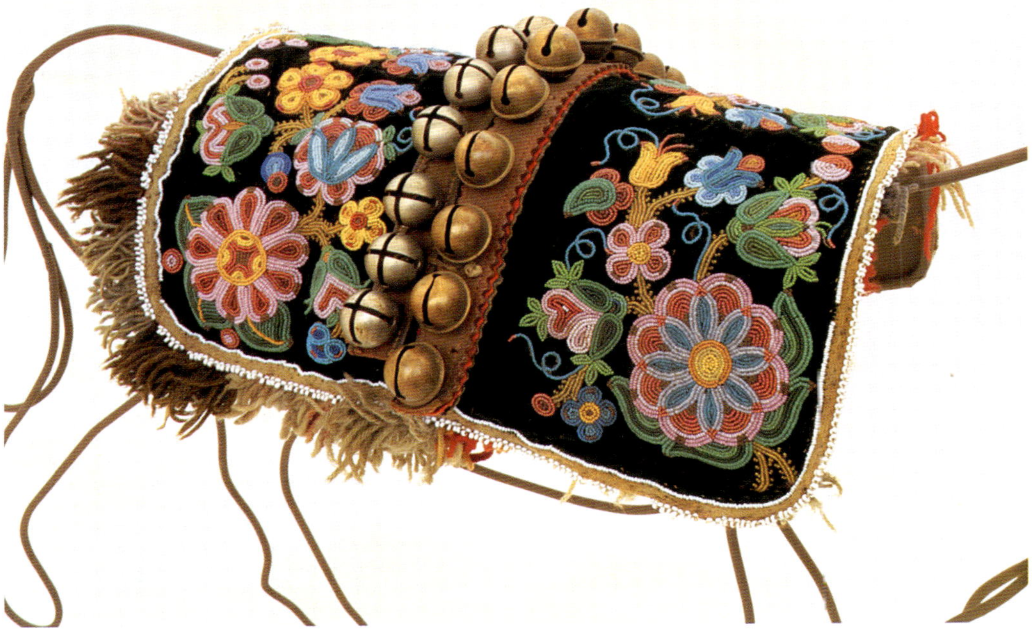

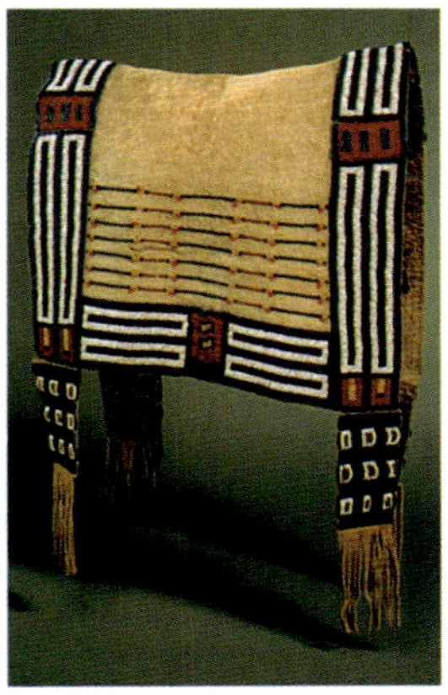

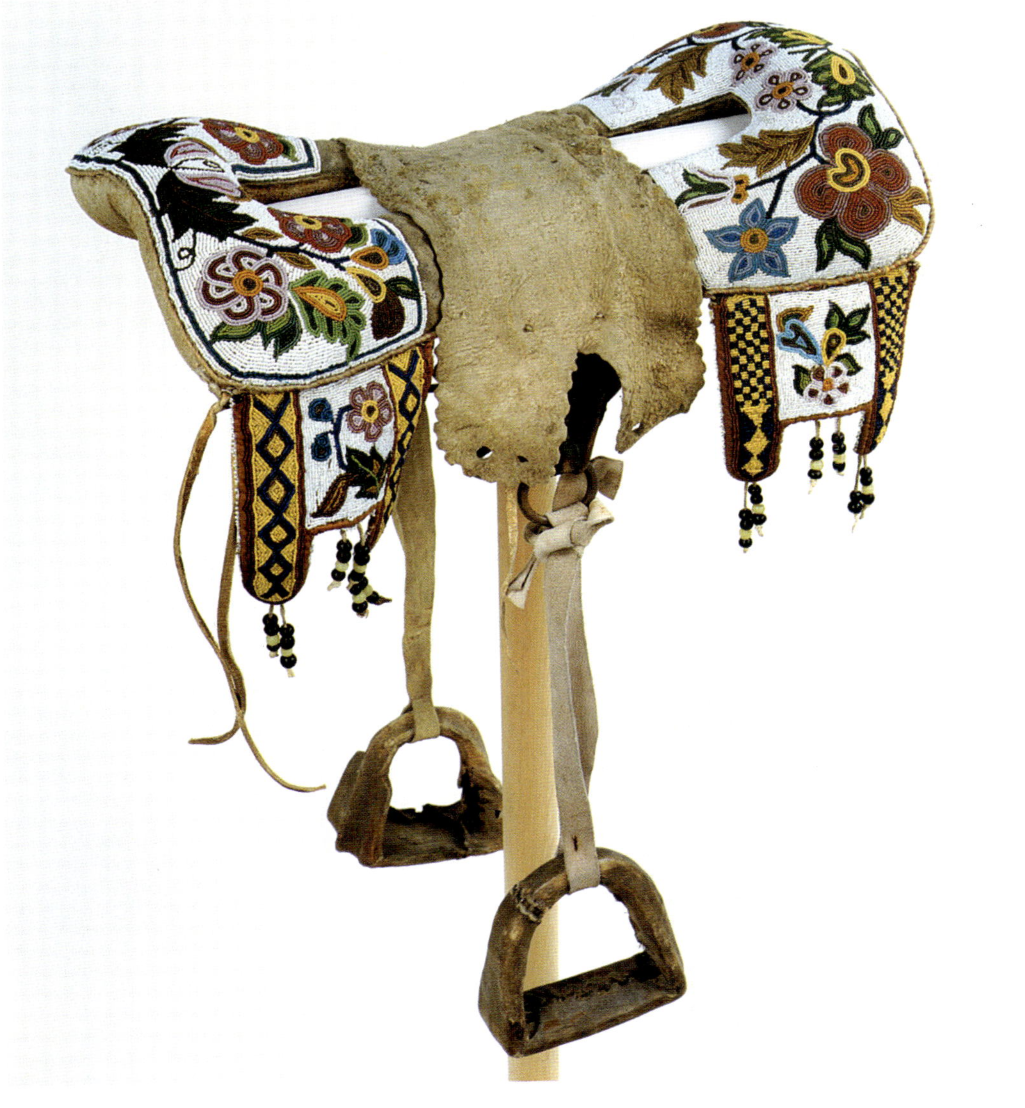

ABOVE: 311. *Cheyenne saddle blanket from the 1840s decorated in typical western Plains beadwork. The availability of large "pony" beads led to the design of bold, geometric patterns. Length, 178 cm. Denver Art Museum*

TOP LEFT: 312. *A late nineteenth-century Metis dog blanket and bell harness from the MacKenzie River basin. The Metis traded their craftwork throughout the northern and central Plains and into the Northwest Territories.*

The western Sioux referred to the Red River Metis in Minnesota as the "flower beadwork people," and throughout the Northwest many Indians confirm the Metis origin of their own floral designs. These artifacts reflect the Indians' encounter with European culture on the American frontier.[X] *McCord Museum, McGill University, Montreal*

BOTTOM LEFT: 313. *A Cree ceremonial saddle from the early 1900s owned by Yellow Horse. The form of the saddle shows early Spanish influence, yet it has the Woodland style of floral decoration, which had spread to the Plains. Length, 48.2 cm. McCord Museum, McGill University, Montreal*

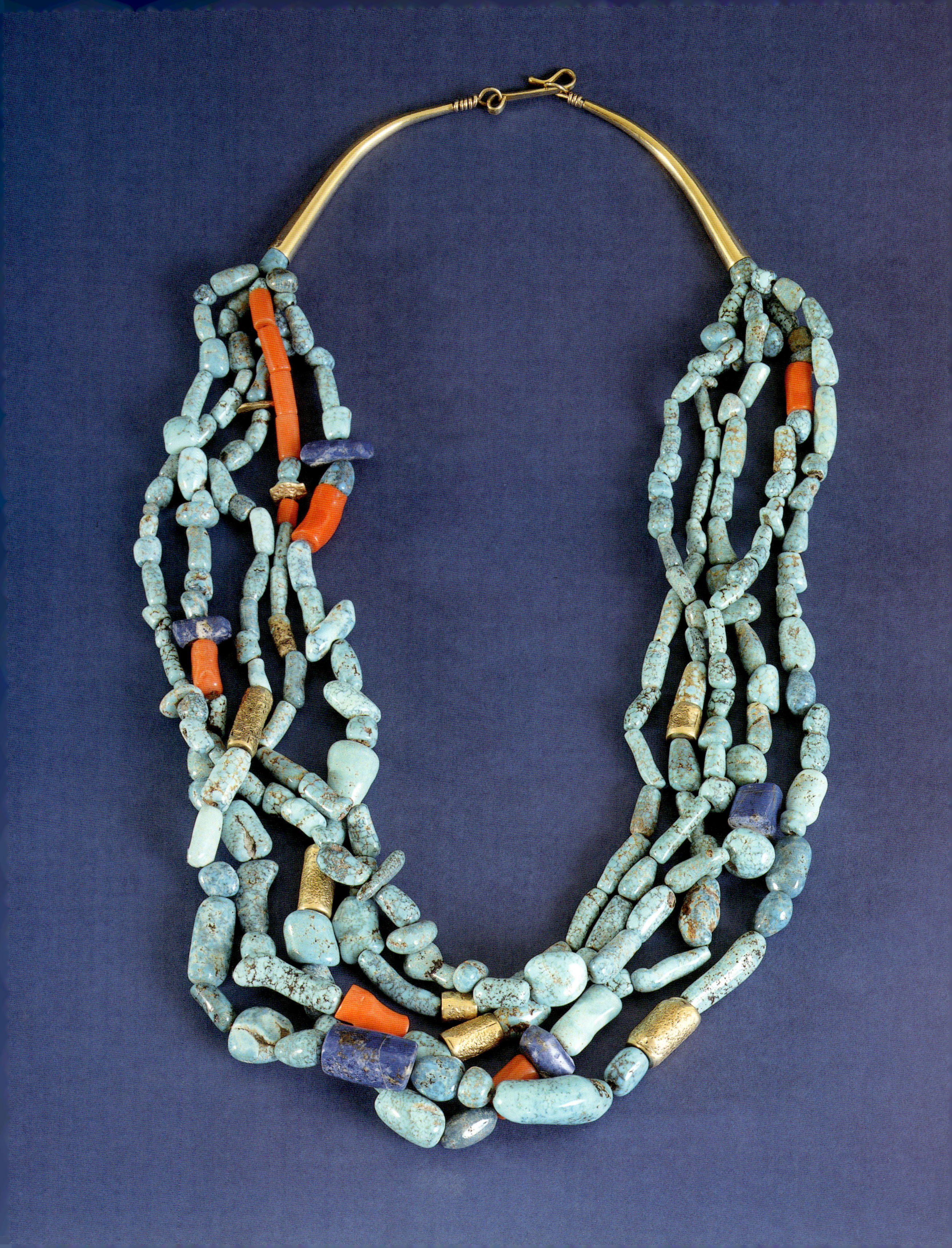

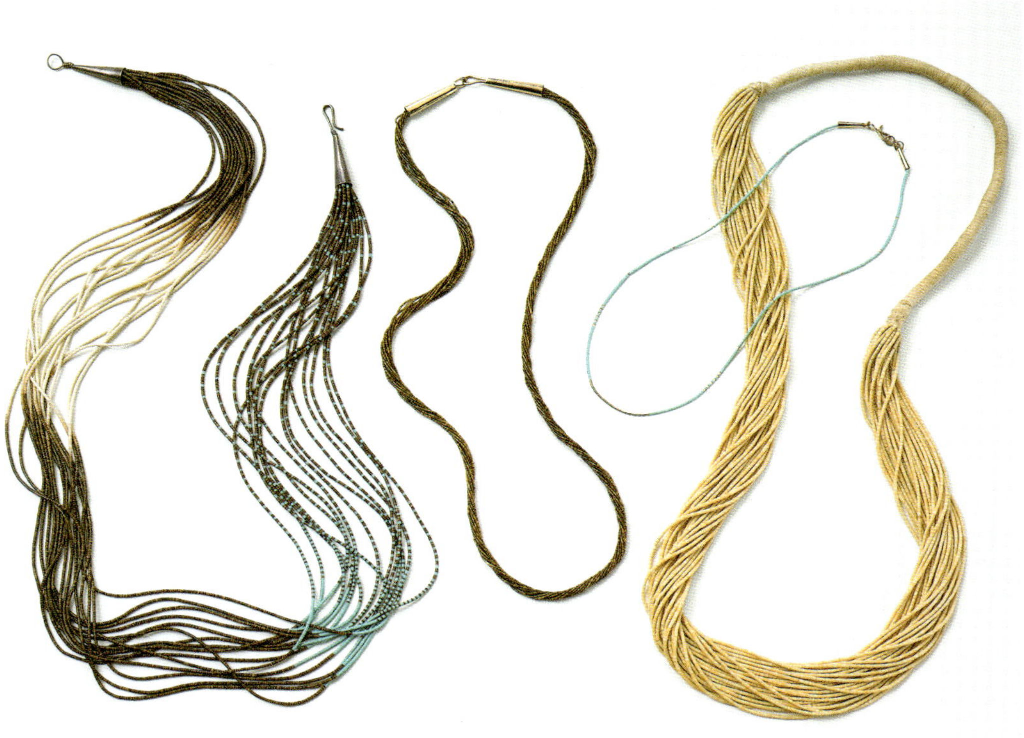

OPPOSITE: 314. *Pieces of gold, which appear to have been placed at random, balance perfectly with the coveted fossilized Spider Web Mountain turquoise beads in this necklace, made by master Hopi jeweler Charles Loloma. 1983. Turquoise, lapis lazuli, gold, coral. Length, 37 cm. Millicent Rogers Museum of Northern New Mexico, 1983-52*

315. *Heishi necklaces so fine that they look like hair and feel like silk. Heishi (from the Santo Domingo word meaning "shell") traditionally referred to necklace shell beds. Today, however, it describes tiny handmade beads of any materials. The Santo Domingo Pueblo carvers are the most proficient heishi producers. All of these necklaces were made at Santo Domingo Pueblo. From left: (1) Rosetta family. 1988. Shell and turquoise. (2) 1970s. Shell, aguilarite, strung thirty-two beads per inch. Length, 31.8 cm. (3) Bernice Reano. Turquoise and gold. (4) Melon shell. 1988. (1, 3, and 4) Collection Lynn Sherr; (2) Collection Tanner*

Eventually, beaded artifacts were produced by the Indians specifically for European tastes. Many of the early explorers and traders collected examples of native arts and crafts and sent them home. A strong interest in these articles developed among the European elite, and this stimulated production of highly decorated objects for export. The gradual shift from products made for tribal use to mass-produced beadwork souvenirs reflected the Indians' absorption into the modern American economic system. Simultaneously, many tribes retained their traditional bead adornment as symbols of identity and pride. The Choctaw of Mississippi, the Bannock and Shoshone of Warm Springs, the Crow, Lakota, and Blackfoot are just a few examples of the many native North American people who consciously maintained a beadwork tradition during economic hardship and stressful periods of change.[26]

American Indians have never ceased to love beads and beadwork. Today, beautiful traditional beading continues. It has experienced a rebirth that can be seen across the North American continent at any powwow. At the same time, contemporary Native beadworkers, such as Marcus Amerman, are producing highly innovative beadwork art (plates 364–365).[27]

Throughout the Southwest, Navajo, Pueblo, and other artisans create well-crafted bead jewelry that also blends ancestral past with the present. Working in turquoise, jet, stone, and shell—the same materials used for thousands of years—as well as a wide variety of introduced exotic stones and metals, Indians of the Southwest retain a vital bead industry. At the same time, innovative Navajo use contemporary glass seedbeads in designs reflecting their timeless beliefs about light and color in nature.[28] Above all, maintaining the balance and achieving harmony remains paramount within Native North American life and art.

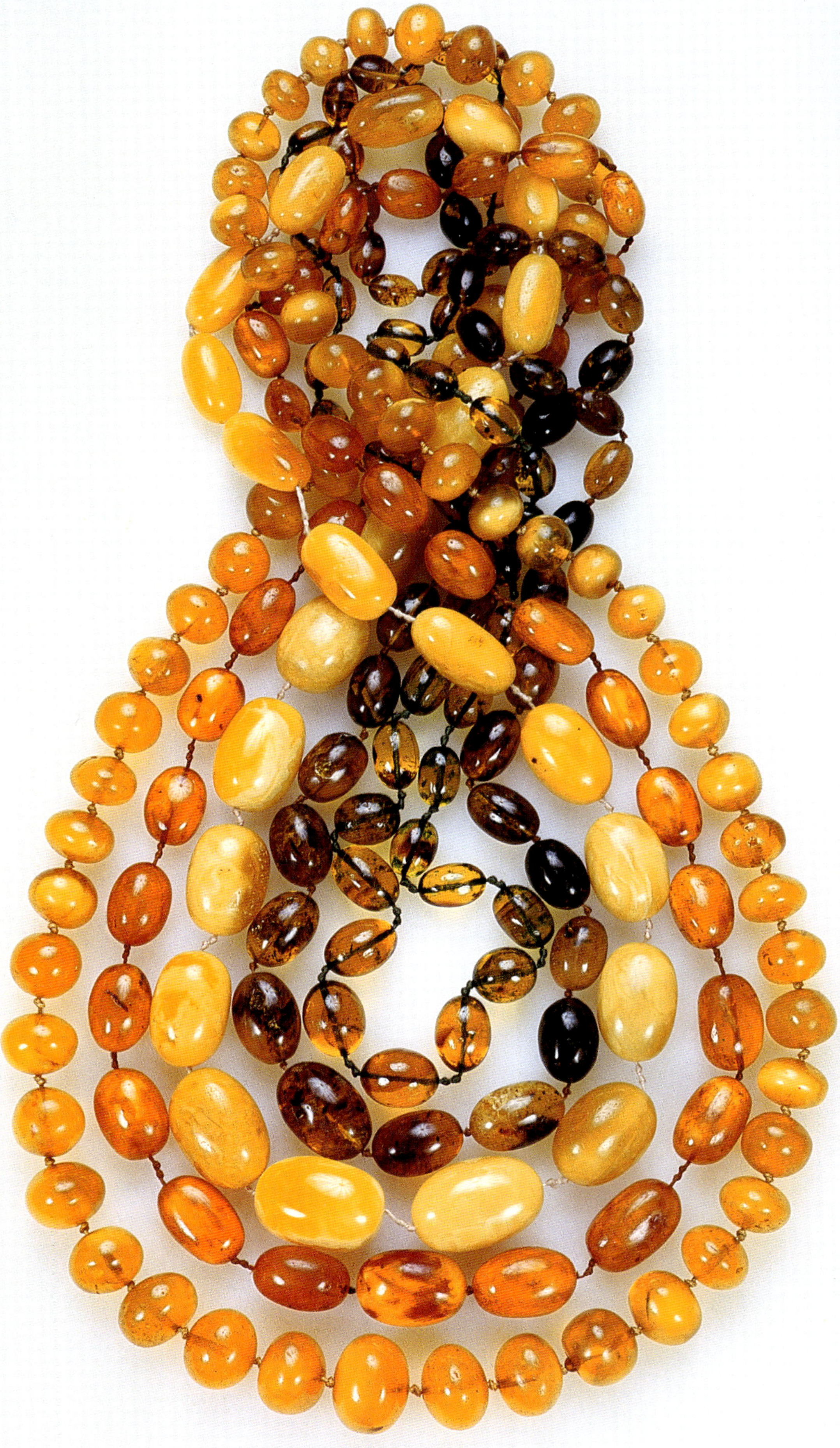

The Special Beads: Amber and Pearls

In the sea of changeable winds, his
  merchants fished for pearls;
In the sea where the North Star culminates,
  they fished for yellow amber.[1]

Over the centuries, the beauty, scarcity, and durability of several natural substances have captured people's attention, and certain ones of these, particularly amber and pearls, have become the subjects of an entire culture of adornment.

316. *A grouping of amber necklaces probably dating to the nineteenth century. From the outside: (1) Baltic amber (succinite); (2) Persian amber or copal; (3) a variety of Baltic amber, "Butter Amber"; (4) Romanian amber (Rumanite); (5) Sicilian amber (Simetite). Necklace, center bead: length, 4.4 cm. Private collection*

Amber

Amber is the fossilized sap of extinct trees that lived in temperate and subtropical forests during the Eocene period, sixty million to forty million years ago.[2] Warm to the touch and light in weight, amber exists primarily in yellow and golden honey tones and in a variety of less common opaque and translucent colors, ranging from ruby red to iridescent greens and blues.

The most significant amber deposits are on or near the coasts of Sweden, Denmark, northern Germany, Poland, and the Soviet Union, buried under 100 to 130 feet of sand and marl in a layer of clay called "blue earth." Today, most of the world's amber comes from the blue earth stratum in the Samland district of Poland, but only about 15 percent of it is of gem quality and suitable for jewelry. Important deposits also occur in a bed that extends fifty miles into the Baltic Sea. Following heavy storms, amber is often retrieved on the beaches and in the shallow waters of the Baltic countries, and it can even be found as far away as the French and English coastlines.

Amber was probably the first gemlike material ever used for personal adornment. Beads and pendants of amber were found in Upper Paleolithic sites of Magdalenian

France and Spain, dating from 15,000 to 10,000 B.C. At Mezhirichi, overlooking the Dnieper River southeast of Kiev, Soviet archaeologists have uncovered amber from a hundred miles away, which was probably traded to the local residents in about 13,000 B.C.[3]

Baltic amber's golden color and pliable nature made it a favorite trade item beginning at least in Neolithic times. Tribes of the Baltic area, central Russia, western Norway, and Finland traded both the raw material and finished beads as early as 3000 B.C.[4] Amber is found in Neolithic and second-millennium B.C. Bronze Age graves in nearly every European country.

By the Bronze Age, Baltic amber was traded along north-south routes that followed major European rivers. One of the most important of these started in Jutland (Denmark), crossed central Germany via the Weser and Elbe valleys, followed the Moldau through Moravia and Austria, crossed the Alps by the Brenner Pass, and met the Po River and the north coast of the Adriatic Sea before descending to the Peloponnisos and traveling on to Crete by sea. A secondary land route followed the Danube and went to the Balkans, while a third began in Germany at Saxe-Thuringia and turned west into Brittany and the English kingdom of Wessex. About 600 B.C., another route followed the Netherlands coast to the Rhine, and then went down the Rhone and terminated at the Mediterranean port of Massilia (Marseilles).[5] Quantities of amber beads have been excavated from sites on all of these routes. (Heinrich Schliemann, for example, found four hundred Baltic amber beads at Mycenae.) Generally, amber was transported as raw material and then worked into beads and pendants by its recipients (see map, page 50).

The Baltic Bronze Age trade in tin and copper (used to manufacture a bronze alloy) evolved simultaneously with the transcontinental amber trade.[6] From about 1600 B.C., amber and tin were Baltic commodities traded to the south, both in exchange for finished bronze weapons and various tools of the more sophisticated Mediterranean cultures.

During the mid- to late second millennium B.C., with central Europeans serving as middlemen, Mycenaean, Phoenician, and Etruscan traders were the focus of a wide-ranging amber network. Striking similarities exist between amber bead necklaces found in Jutland, Wessex, Mycenae, and the Rhine Valley. At the same time, Baltic amber was traded from the Aegean into the eastern Mediterranean countries: a Mycenaean pot that contained Baltic amber beads was excavated at Ras Shamra in Syria.[7]

The earliest literary references to the uses of amber appear in Book XVIII of Homer's *Odyssey*. Written about 700 B.C., it is set in the period after the fall of Mycenae (1100–900 B.C.). Odysseus's wife, Penelope, receives from a suitor, Eurymachus, "an elaborate chain strung with beads of amber like golden sunshine."[8] Also, the narrator, Eumaeus, describes his experiences in Syria: "The Phoenicians...sent a messenger.... The crafty fellow came to my father's house hawking a golden collar beaded here and there with amber...the serving women in the hall and my lady mother were offering him bids for it and devouring it with their eyes."[9]

The word *electricity* comes from *elektron*, the Greek name for amber.[10] When rubbed, amber develops negative electrical static and can pick up small pieces of paper or lint. This phenomenon, observed by Plato and Aristotle during the fourth century B.C., probably increased the esteem and mystery of the gem in the eyes of ancient people.[11] Certainly, amber's electrical properties and golden color underlie the many curative properties ascribed to it over the millennia.

In ancient Greek mythology, amber was believed to be the solidified tears that were shed annually by the Heliades mourning the death of their brother. To the Greek statesman Nicias, it was the essence of sunrays "congealed in the sea and then cast upon the shore." One legend describes amber as the solidified urine of the lynx (one of its names is *lyncurius*).[12] It was even thought to be petrified dolphin or seal sperm.[13] These myths notwithstanding, both the Greeks and Romans knew that amber was tree resin, and it was described with remarkable accuracy by the Roman historian Pliny.

The Phoenicians, either ignorant of amber sources or shrewd merchants seeking to protect their sources, began a strategy of concealing the location of the raw gem from their rivals. The Etruscans, however, learned of the Baltic source and became amber importers, as did the Romans, who sent expeditions to the region during the second century A.D.[14]

Following the collapse of the Roman Empire, the amber trade declined, a casualty of the Teutonic migrations. By the late Middle Ages, however, Baltic amber was once again actively collected and traded, its traffic strictly controlled by German merchants' monopolies for the next several hundred years. From the 1300s to the 1800s, members of established central European guilds manufactured amber beads primarily for Catholic, Buddhist, and Muslim rosaries. Apprentices desiring to join guilds were required "to prove their proficiency by cutting a quarter of a pound of perfectly round, evenly drilled beads by eye, without the aid of a compass."[15]

Amber was also regarded with esteem in the East. The Persians, Turks, Arabs, and Chinese were especially fond of it. A remarkable eighteenth-century Chinese amber necklace was owned by Englishman Thomas Kinton in the twentieth century. Each bead was finely carved into the shape of a Mandarin's head, "every face having a different expression. Some were smiling, some grimacing, others wore a solemn look."[16]

In addition to the Baltic, important amber sources included Sicily, Romania, and Burma, where the amber-bearing trees were concentrated in prehistoric times. However, the quantity of the gem obtained from these regions was comparatively small. Baltic amber ranges from pale yellowish white to reddish brown to almost black, although tones of yellow are most common.[17] Sicilian amber is also yellow, but occurs in a rare ruby red hue as well as green, brown, blue, and purple; furthermore, it often has a luminescence, possibly due to its origins in volcanic soil near Mount Etna. Dark colors typify Romanian amber, including rose red, smoky gray, dark garnet, brownish red, and a greenish blue, green, and brownish green variety with agate like patterns (called "Amber of Piatra"; plate 316). Deep red, highly fluorescent Burmese amber is one of the rarest and most beautiful types known (plate 318).[18]

Variations in the color of amber are due to the presence of foreign matter encountered by the sap after it was secreted. Dark amber, for example, may result from the presence of wood ash or iron pyrites. Blue amber contains carbonate of lime, while several colors reflect the presence of sulfuric acid from decomposing humus.[19] As amber ages it darkens, often obtaining a dark patina. It may change from yellow to reddish brown in as little as one hundred years,[20] although there is speculation that some amber discovered in Greek tombs by archaeologists may be a dark red Sicilian variety. It is argued that much amber used in the classical world came from Sicily.[21] This has not been proved, however, since analysis discloses that most ancient amber has a yellow core and traces of succinic acid, which are features characteristic of the Baltic variety.[22]

Amber may be transparent or opaque. The resin is cloudy or clear due to the presence or absence of masses of minute air bubbles. As amber resin ran down the tree, it frequently engulfed insects, twigs, and leaves, and acted as an embalming agent. Millions of years later, these inclusions have supplied valuable information about the flora and fauna of the prehistoric amber forests.[23]

TOP: 317. *A bronze bracelet with a finely crafted biconical oblate amber bead. This typical piece of Hallstatt or early Celtic jewelry displays the ancient affection for amber. Fifth to fourth century* B.C. *Diameter, 7.1 cm. British Museum, London*

BOTTOM: 318. *A necklace purportedly of Burmese amber (Burmite) that was possibly cut in nineteenth-century Egypt. Largest bead: length, 5.7 cm. Collection Wolf Hunger, London*

OPPOSITE: 319. *Faceted Baltic amber (succinite) said to have belonged to a member of the Russian imperial court. The amber was cut in the Baltic at Königsberg. Center bead: length, 3.1 cm. Collection Wolf Hunger, London*

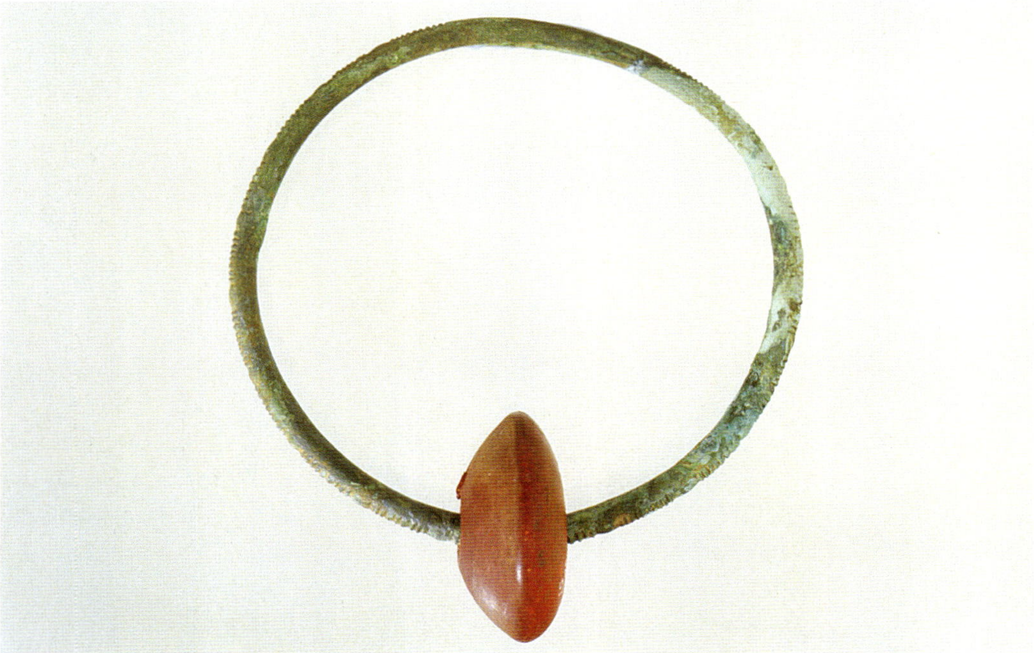

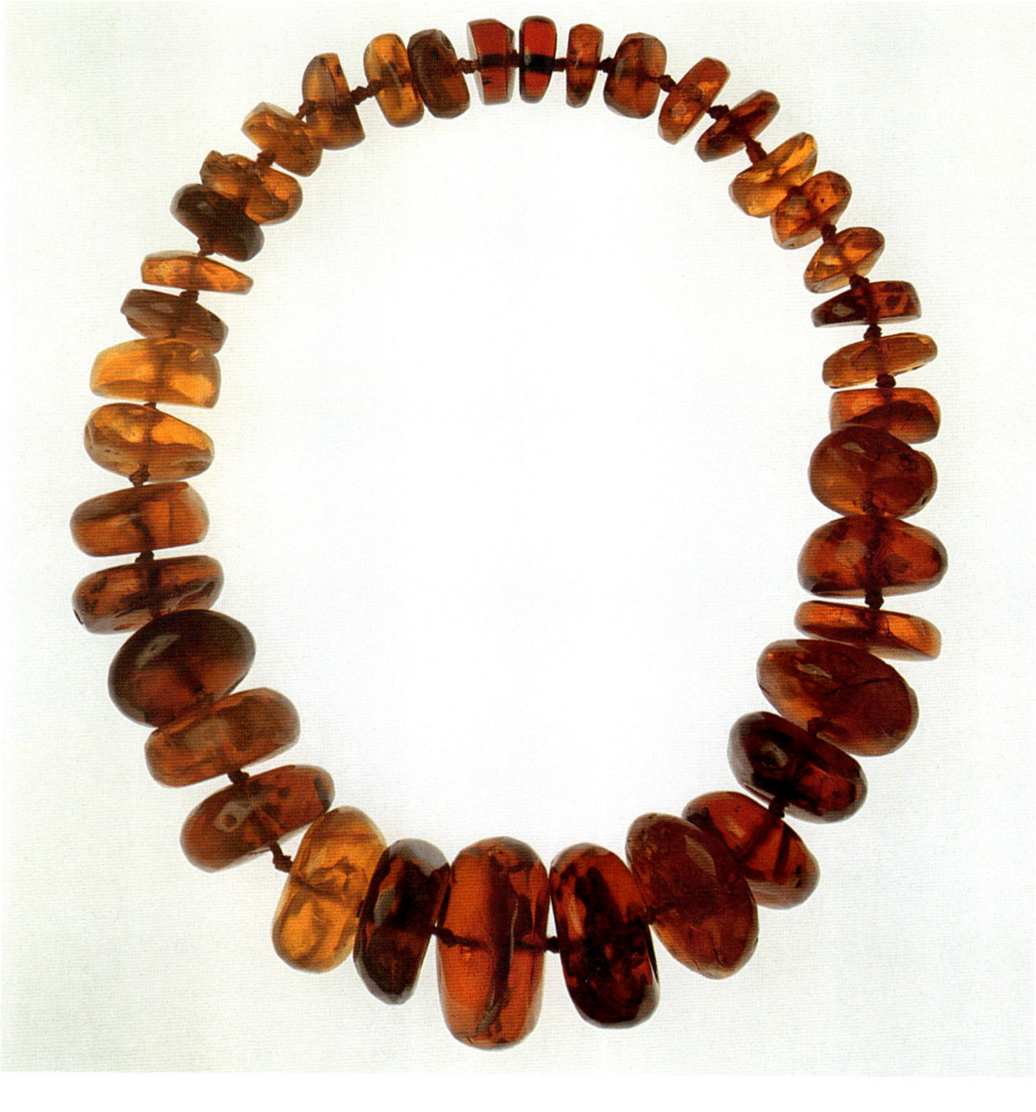

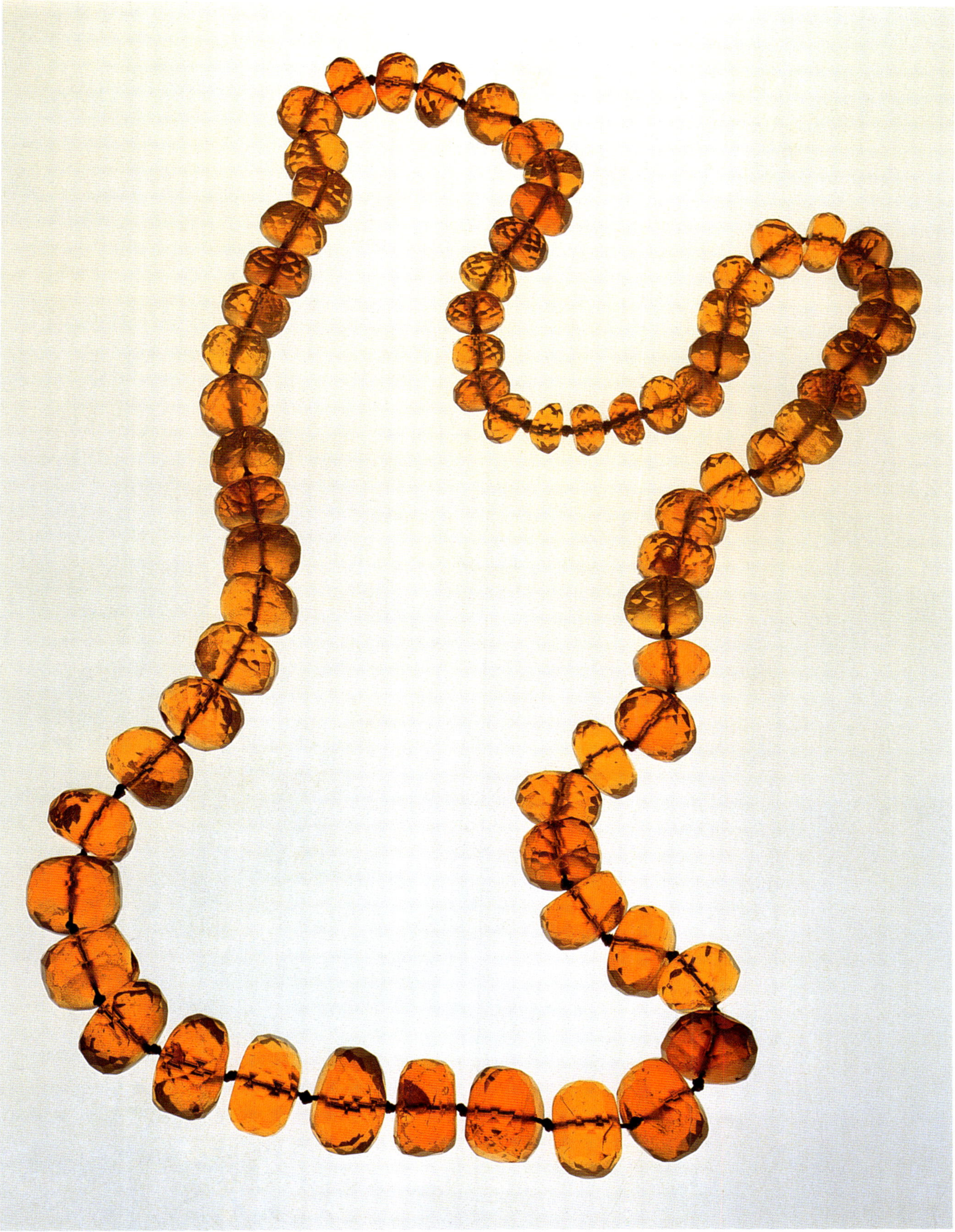

Substances frequently confused with amber include copal, ambroid, and Bakelite.[24] Copal, a natural resin, exists in a semifossilized state ("true copal") and as resin taken directly from living trees ("raw copal"). It is believed that in earlier times copal was used to make beads. However, most beads called copal are, in fact, amber or plastic.

True copal is found in large quantities on the island of Zanzibar, off the coast of Tanzania, where it is mined from shallow deposits during the rainy season, when the ground is soft. Raw copal is also collected in Zanzibar as gum from a tree resembling birch. Both are also found on the west coast of Africa and in New Zealand, Brazil, and Malaysia.[25] It has been suggested that true copal may be a million years old and is undergoing complex chemical changes that would lead eventually to the formation of true amber.[26] Ambroid, or "pressed amber," is formed by compressing small pieces of amber together. Although genuine amber, it lacks the subtle beauty of natural amber.[27]

It has long been thought that Bakelite, a hard thermoset plastic invented in 1909 by Leo Hendrik Backelund, is the artificial material used to imitate amber, generally in jewelry of the 1920s and 1930s. In reality, most plastics resembling amber are varieties of cast-phenolic resins, distinguished by their intense color and translucence, whereas Bakelite is opaque and usually dark.[28]

Today, true amber and ambroid beads continue to be made in the Baltic nations of Russia, primarily for export. Although available in various colors and shapes, most beads are tumble-polished and free-formed.

Pearls

Like amber, pearls are an organic substance, the product of a living organism. Whereas amber is a multimillion-year-old fossilized plant resin, most pearls are formed by glandular secretions of certain living oysters and mussels. Pearls are found in both sea and freshwater mollusks all over the world.

Pearls are nature's ultimate gift to the bead world. Perfected by natural processes, they differ from other gems in requiring no additional cutting and polishing to enhance their beauty. Pearls need only to be set or pierced and strung.

Over the centuries, fantastic theories were created to explain the origin of pearls. Chinese myths suggest they were conceived in the brains of dragons, while Indian writers placed their origins in clouds, elephants, boars, conchs, fish, serpents, bamboo, and oysters—albeit the latter was thought to be the most important source.[29]

That pearls occur in oysters was known by at least ancient Greek and Roman times. Until the sixteenth century, however, little was understood about the actual pearl-formation process. Fascinated by their luminescence and subdued beauty, various ancient poets wrote that pearls were the solidified tears of angels or water nymphs. The most popular explanation was that pearls were formed when drops of dew or rain fell into the open shells of oysters at breeding time. At certain seasons of the year, the oysters would rise to the surface of the ocean in the morning, open their shells, and, aided by the warmth of sunlight, become impregnated with dewdrops that in time were transformed into lustrous pearls. Without the right mixture of light and air, faulty pearls resulted. Pliny, the astute Roman scientific writer and historian, observed in his first-century A.D. *Historia naturalis* that the fruit of the shells were pearls, whose luster and size varied according to the quality and quantity of dew they received.[30]

Challenges to the dew-formation theory began in Renaissance Europe. By 1608, Pedro Teixeira of Portugal noted the similarity between pearls and the interior of the shells in which they were formed. Scientists confirmed this observation by discovering that irritating the soft body of a mollusk with a grain of sand or a piece of seaweed, for example, caused the mollusk to surround the foreign matter with a secretion. While all mollusks coat the intrusion, the general understanding is that all pearls are produced from the mother-of-pearl (nacre) lining of bivalve oyster shells. However, not all pearls are nacreous or come from oysters. Pearls are also produced by univalve mollusks such as the conch and abalone.[31] The image of this lowly creature responding to a bodily intrusion by transforming it into a beautiful gem symbolic of all that is pure and beautiful has stimulated poets for centuries. As the Persian poet Hafez said: "Learn from yon orient shell to love thy foe / And store with pearls the wound that brings thee woe."

The iridescent pearly luster, called "orient," gives pearls their value as gems. This luster is an optical phenomenon caused by light refracting off the nacre, which is 90 percent calcium carbonate and 10 percent conchiolin, a gluelike protein that binds together the calcium carbonate crystals. Nacre is deposited on the surface of the pearl in overlapping platelets that cause waves of light to be reflected from different surface levels. The color of pearls varies with the nacre's thickness and with the color of the upper conchiolin layer, depending on water conditions, the type of mollusk, and the mollusk's diet. Different regions produce pearls of different tints. The shape of the intrusive nucleus and its position within the mollusk result in pearls of various forms and sizes. The Romans believed that no two pearls were ever exactly alike, thus they named them *unio* ("unique").[32]

Pearls are widely discussed in historical and religious writings. The high esteem accorded them by the ancient Hebrews is illustrated in various references in the Talmud and in the Old Testament. (In the story of Abraham and Sarah, only Sarah's beauty is ranked above pearls.) Classic Indian Sanskrit literature (A.D. 1–100) also frequently refers to pearls. Arab writings often relate pearls to paradise: each person admitted to the celestial kingdom is provided with a tent of pearls and attended by beautiful maidens resembling "hidden pearls."[33]

Among the earliest surviving examples of pearl jewelry is a three-strand necklace of an Achaemenid princess of about 350 B.C., found at the site of Susa, the ancient royal Persian winter residence.[34] Another early pearl necklace fragment was found in a large hoard of jewelry at Pasargadae, probably hidden about 330 B.C. from Alexander the Great's advancing army (plate 320).

By Ptolemaic, Hellenistic, and Roman times, pearls had become an important part of adornment, the wearing of which reached excessive proportions with the Romans. Seneca, writing about A.D. 50, commented: "Pearls offer themselves to my view. Simply one for each ear? No! The lobes of our ladies have attained a special capacity for supporting a great number. Two pearls alongside of each other, with a third suspended above, now form a single earring. The crazy fools seem to think that their husbands are not sufficiently tormented unless they wear the value of an inheritance in each ear."[35] The dresses of Roman women were so laden with pearls, Pliny noted with irony, that the wealthy must "trample and walk over them." He further added that pearls adorned rich ladies not only in the daytime, but also at night, "so that in their sleep, they might be conscious of possessing beautiful gems."[36]

The Romans ranked pearls among the most precious of gems and paid exorbitant prices for ones of exceptional importance. Single pearls worth over a million dollars were recorded, such as the one presented by Julius Caesar to Brutus's mother, Servilia.[37] As Roman court behavior degenerated, so their use of pearls increased. It is said that the Emperor Caligula not only wore pearl-encrusted slippers, but after appointing his favorite horse, Incitatus, to the governing council, he also gave him a pearl necklace.[38]

Pearls continued to be esteemed after the establishment of Constantinople as the capital of the eastern Roman Empire. The famous mosaics at San Vitale in Ravenna depict Emperor Justinian in a pearl-encrusted helmet and Empress Theodora in a pearl tiara with numerous strings of pearls descending to her waist.[39]

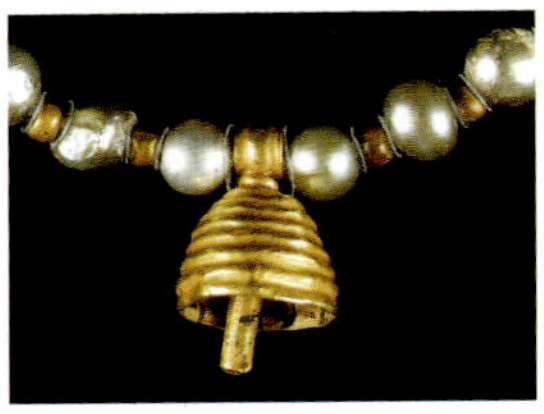

ABOVE: 320. *Part of a necklace of gold and pearl beads, with one gold bell-shaped pendant from Pasargadae (Persia). These beads, dating from the Persian Empire (c. fourth century B.C.) came from a large hoard of jewelry, which was probably hidden around 330 B.C. when Alexander's Greek army was advancing thorugh the region. Among the earliest surviving examples of pearls, presumably from the Persian Gulf. Largest pearl diameter, 5 cm. British Museum, London*

OPPOSITE: 321. *Pearl-diving in Sri Lanka, about 1870. The primitive techniques shown here continued through the 1930s. Divers (mainly Indians and Arabs) were lowered from a boat to pearl beds approximately forty to fifty feet underwater. After collecting as many oysters as possible in a basket, the diver jerked the rope, signaling an attendant to haul him up. After a brief rest, he descended again, averaging thirty to forty dives per day, each lasting slightly more than a minute.*

During the Middle Ages, when jewelry was discouraged by the church, gems enriched European ecclesiastical art. Pearls were sometimes used in rosaries. In addition, from the ninth to the fourteenth century, medicine frequently employed remedies made of pulverized gems, including pearls. While small, inexpensive pearls were used for the most part, those who could afford them consumed larger ones.[40]

By the fourteenth century, pearls had become fashionable again throughout Europe. Both men's and women's clothing was pearl-embroidered at most important festive occasions.[41] Fifteenth-century women wore hairnets (called "frets") of gold threads adorned with pearls. A fret of pearls was considered a sufficient legacy for a duchess to leave her daughter.[42] By the late Renaissance and Baroque periods, paintings portray pearls sewn onto dresses, with multistrand pearl necklaces displaying power and wealth. A sixteenth-century English portrait of Queen Elizabeth I shows her massive assemblage of pearls and aptly symbolizes the materialism that was so much a part of the era of European expansion. (Elizabeth, in fact, loved pearls so much she did not hesitate to add hundreds of fake ones to her dress too.[43]) The importance of pearls in sixteenth- and seventeenth-century Europe is also expressed in the literature of the period. Pearls form a frequent metaphor in many Shakespearean plays. Antony proclaims his love for Cleopatra with an offer of jewelry: "I'll set thee in a shower of gold, and hail / Rich pearls upon thee." The extravagant use of pearls during the sixteenth and seventeenth centuries was in part due to a greatly expanded supply. New trade routes to the East had increased supplies from the Persian Gulf and Sri Lanka (Ceylon), the richest pearl fisheries in the world, while newly acquired territories in the Americas provided quantities of the gem from temperate coastal waters off Venezuela, Panama, and Mexico. These marine sources were supplemented by pearls from freshwater mussels available in mountain streams throughout Europe, particularly in Bohemia, Bavaria, Saxony, Russia, and Scotland.[44] River pearls had been abundant in Europe since ancient times. British river mussel pearls, described as basically of golden brown tones, were highly valued by the Britons and may have been part of the bounty Julius Caesar was seeking when he invaded Britain in 55 B.C.[45]

Even in antiquity, the princes of India and Persia were known to have had first choice of the finest pearls due to their proximity to the Persian Gulf and Sri Lanka, where pearl-producing saltwater oysters were found. Legendary pearl collections were accumulated by Indian royalty. Perhaps the most renowned belonged to one of the nineteenth-century Gaikwars of Baroda, in northwestern India. His treasures included a sash of one hundred rows of pearls with a pearl and emerald tassel that had an estimated value in 1908 of half a million dollars. He also had a carpet of solid pearls with a central panel of diamonds.[46]

Records indicate that both the Persian Gulf and the Gulf of Mannar were fished for pearls in antiquity. Not only the Phoenicians, but the ancient Greeks, Romans, Arabs, and Chinese traded in Sri Lanka for pearls. Marco Polo visited and described this pearl industry in the late thirteenth century.[47] Most Chinese pearls were apparently from freshwater sources, and a pearl fishery at Hepu was first recorded in 111 B.C.[48]

The Russians wore quantities of pearl jewelry, which were not the exclusive property of the rich; indeed, freshwater pearls were widely available to the general populace. Jewish women of humble background in southern Russia, for example, owned black velvet caps embroidered with pearls. They wore their caps all day while working and placed them under their pillows at night. These highly valued caps were passed down to their children.[49]

With the colonization of the Americas, the focus of the pearl industry switched to the New World. The Spaniards noted the South American Indians' pearl ornaments and soon found the oyster beds. On his third and fourth voyages to America, Columbus repeatedly

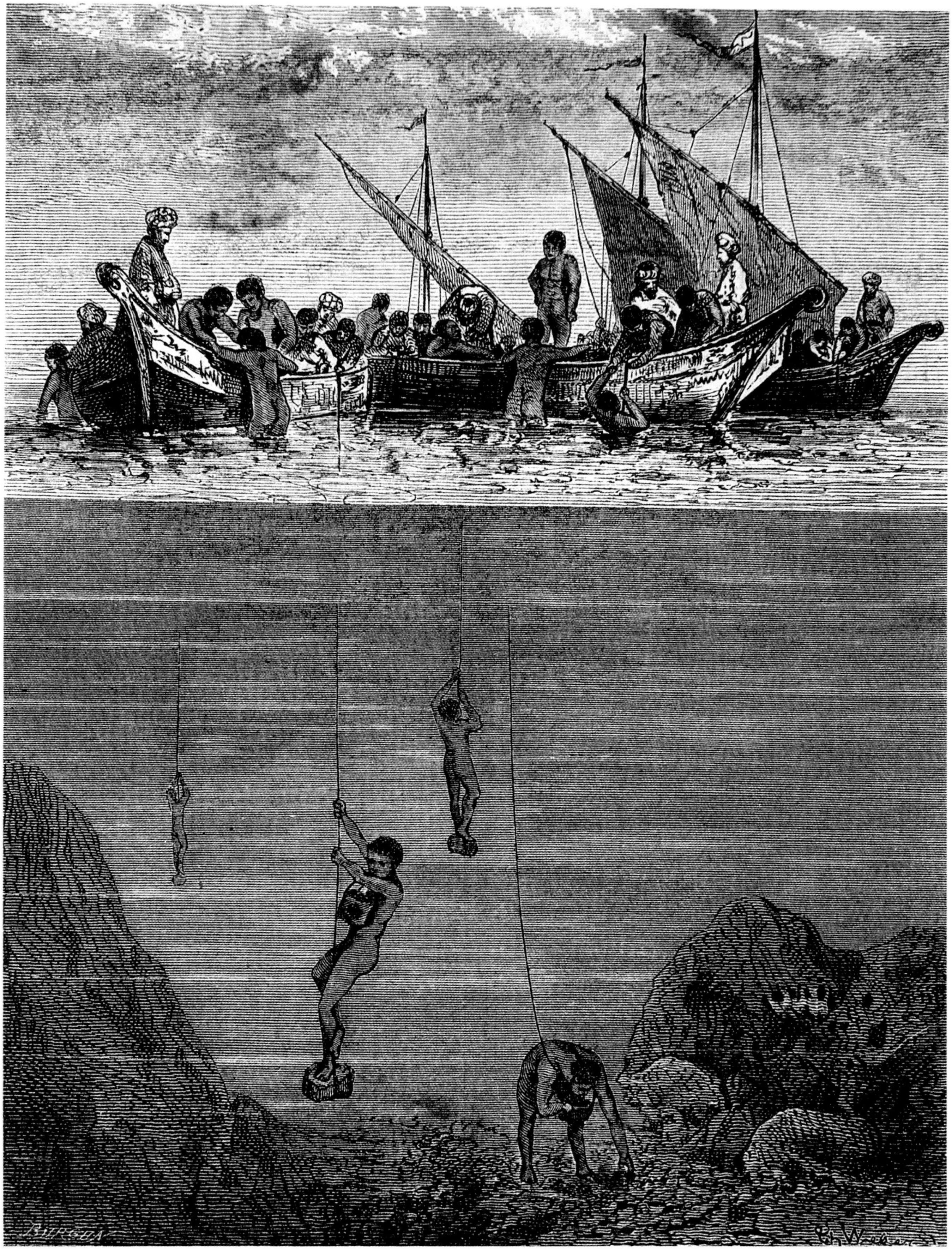

322. *The "Prince of Pearls," the Rana of Dholpur, India, in his pearl regalia, about 1900.*

OPPOSITE: 323. *The Duchess of Marlborough, the former Consuela Vanderbilt, c. 1906. A newly affluent American, she married into the English aristocracy and acquired pearl necklaces with historical pedigree. The long strands shown on the Duchess had reputedly belonged to Catherine the Great and Empress Eugénie. The use of a choker was a fashion inspired by the pearl jewelry of Queen Alexandra, Queen Victoria's daughter-in-law.*[1]

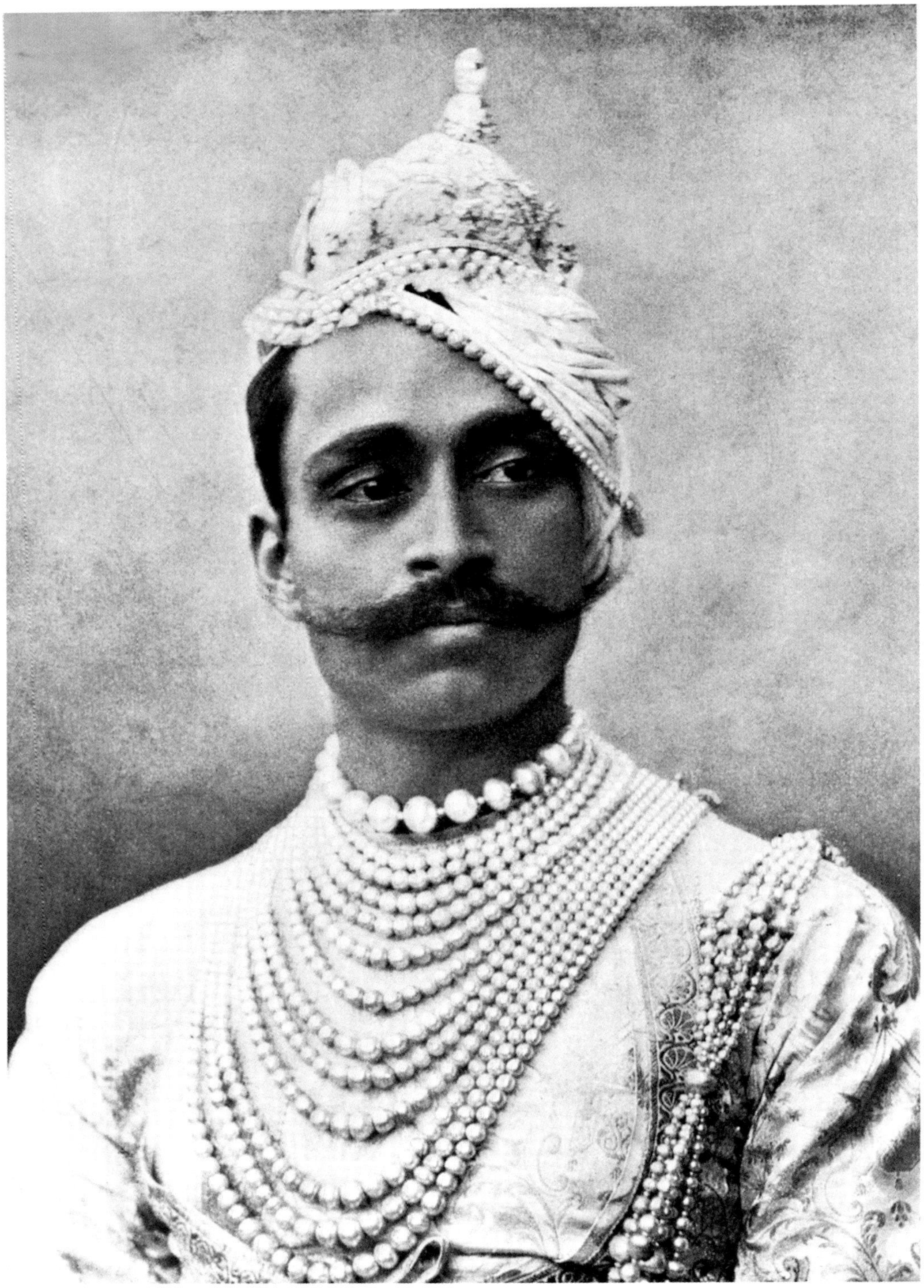

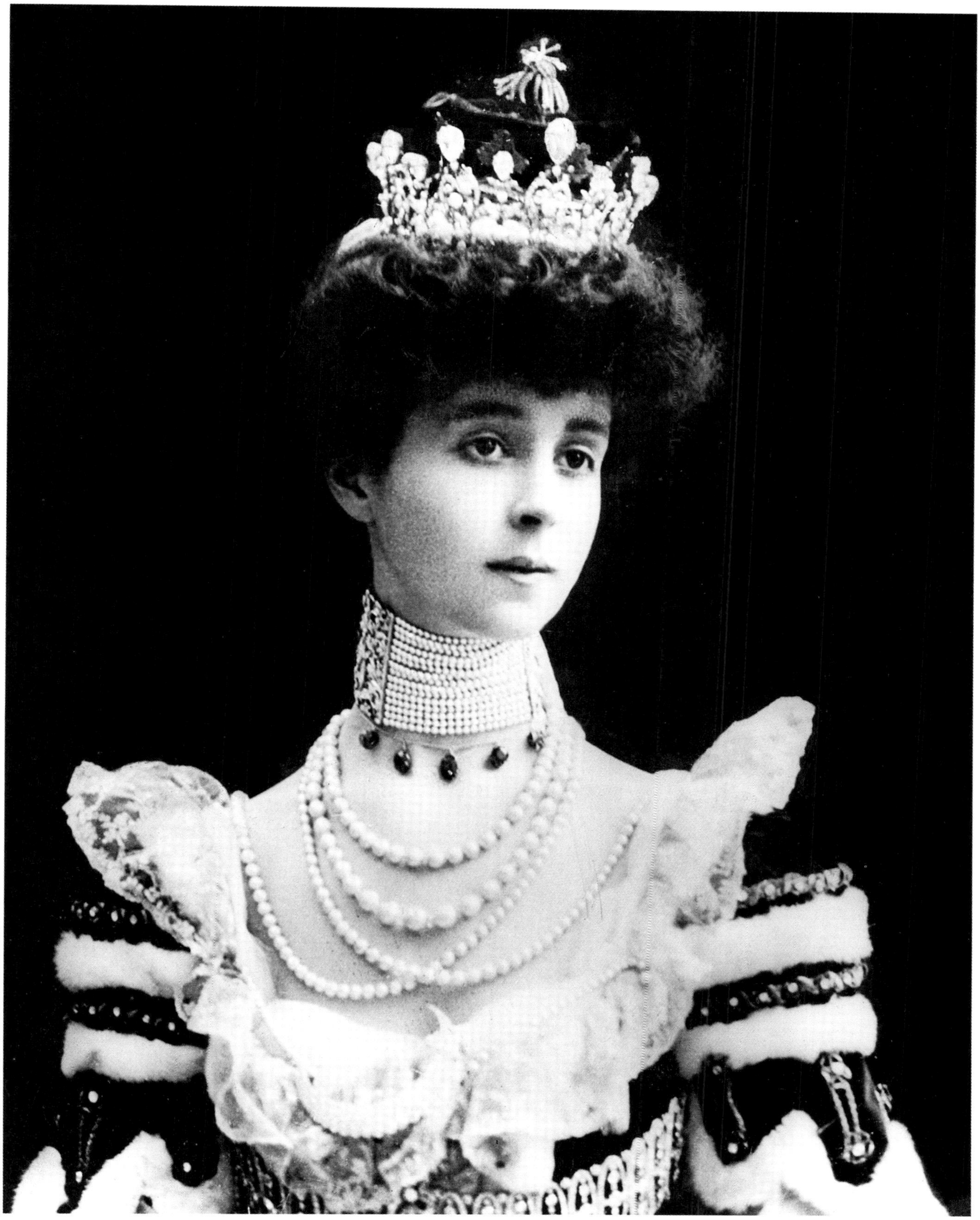

recorded the abundance of pearls.[50] The richest pearl beds at Margarita ("Pearl Island"), in the Caribbean Sea, and at Cabagua, off the coast of Venezuela, were controlled by the Spanish, who sent home great quantities of the gem. Garcilaso de la Vega reports in his Commentaries that in 1564 the American fisheries were so prolific that pearls were sold in heaps at public auction in Seville.[51] By the end of the seventeenth century, however, the beds were largely depleted.

A love of pearls was not confined to the Old World; prehistoric American Indians wore pearls long before the arrival of Europeans. Pearl jewelry has been recovered from the Mexican site of Monte Alban, dating to about A.D. 500–600. The Aztec treasures also contained pearls. After the explorer Cortés's Mexican conquests, the Spanish marched north to the Gulf of California in search of more gold and pearls. Between 1580 and 1857, it is recorded that nearly three thousand pounds of pearls came from the gulf.[52]

Due to the wealth of pearls uncovered in Panama, Venezuela, and Mexico, Europeans searched for the gem in North America. Pearls were reportedly seen by early explorers among tribes from Virginia to Florida. In 1772, Daniel Coxe, son of a pearl trader in America, wrote, "Pearls are found to be in great abundance in this country; the Indians put some value upon them, but not so much as on the colored beads we bring them."[53]

While freshwater pearls were found in numerous rivers throughout the country, few were of gem quality. Although American pearl resources were greatly diminished by the late 1700s, some pearls were obtained from the Lehigh River near Bethlehem, Pennsylvania, by Moravian immigrants familiar with pearl fishing from European streams.[54]

In the eighteenth and early nineteenth centuries, almost the entire world's pearl crop came from the Persian Gulf and a few European and Chinese rivers. Pearls were out of fashion at this time. About 1845, however, they began appearing on the market from the South Seas, and the industry revived along the Mexican coast. Around 1880, quantities of fine "baroque" (irregularly shaped) pearls were rediscovered in the Mississippi River valley.[55]

By the last quarter of the nineteenth century, pearl jewelry was enormously coveted in both Europe and the United States. Americans wore relatively few jewels prior to the Civil War, reflecting both a lack of great wealth and a general simplicity in taste. After the war, however, vast fortunes were accumulated in the industrial North, and one manner of legitimizing social status was for the newly rich to buy jewels with history and provenance. The greatest demand was for pearl necklaces with historical background, no matter how questionable. This was not a short-lived fashion; a necklace valued at half a million dollars, for example, was sold to Barbara Hutton in 1933 by Cartier with the claim that it had once belonged to Marie Antoinette.[56]

To supply increasing demand, pearl fever swept the United States at the turn of the century. Swarms of prospectors raced to a creek or river whenever news of another valuable find surfaced. While most pearls came from the Mississippi River valley, they were also gathered from the headwaters of the Schuylkill River in the coal regions of Pennsylvania, from brooks at the head of Chesapeake Bay in Maryland, and from Adirondack streams in New York. Over twenty thousand pearls were fished in Colorado waters in one year. They were occasionally found in Canadian river mussels, especially in the provinces of Quebec, Prince Edward Island, New Brunswick, and Nova Scotia. While American freshwater pearls were rarely worth as much as saltwater pearls, their value in 1906 is recorded as exceeding that of pearls from any other world region except the Persian Gulf and Sri Lanka.[57]

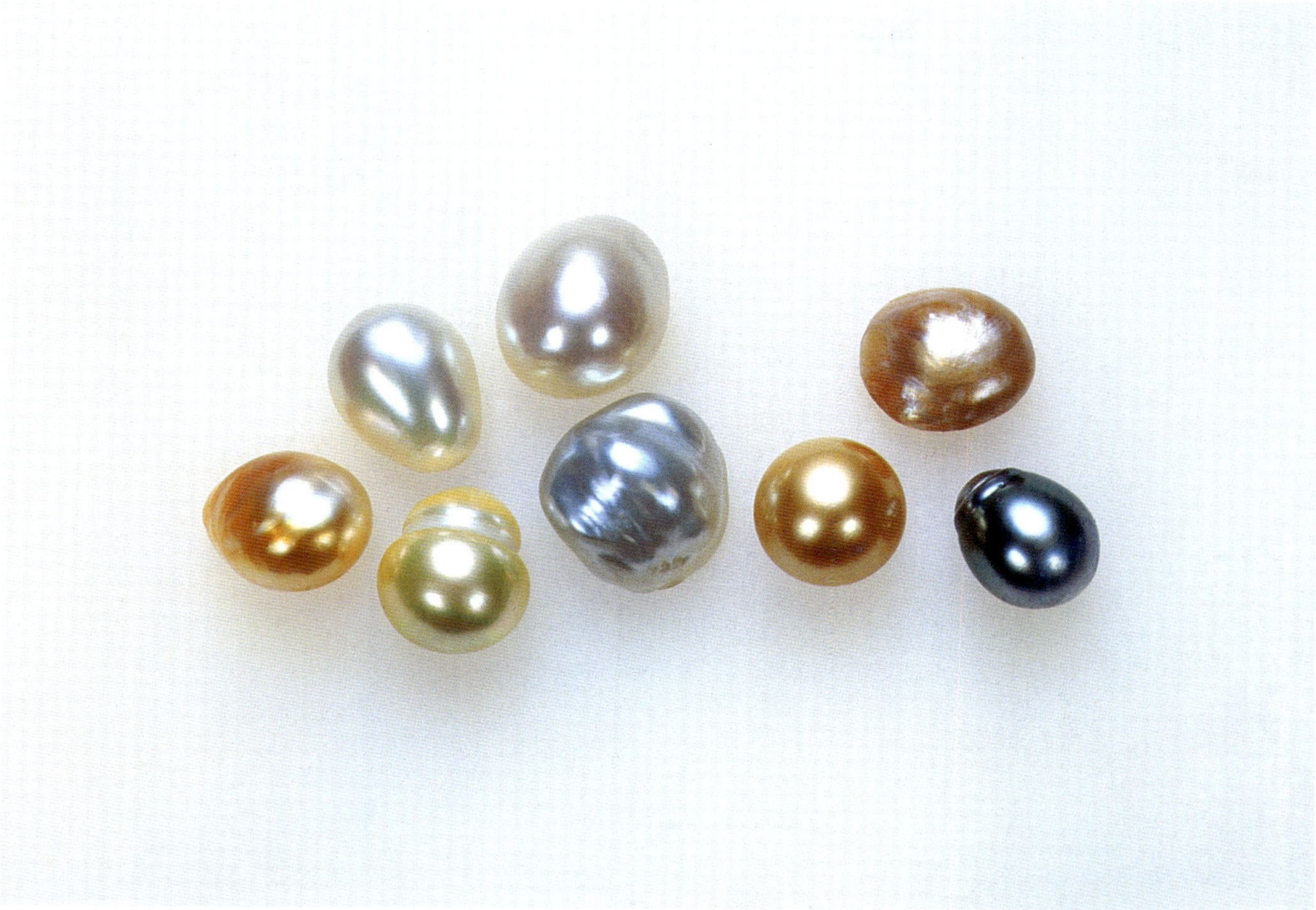

324. *A South Pacific cultured pearl group, including black Tahiti, rainbow drop, white oval, gray baroque, round gold, green baroque, and peach baroque examples. In the upper right corner is a freshwater pink pearl from North America. All 1980s. Round gold pearl: diameter, 1.45 cm. Collection Arthur King, New York*

The most famous and valuable pearl ever found within North America was undoubtedly the "Queen Pearl," discovered by a carpenter, Jacob Quackenbush, about 1857 in a freshwater mussel from Notch Brook near Paterson, New Jersey. A round, magnificent pink pearl weighing ninety-three grams, it was bought by Tiffany and Company in New York and sold to the Empress Eugenie of France. The pearl was worth at least ten thousand dollars in 1906.[58]

The extraordinary value of pearls in the early years of the twentieth century ended with the Depression and has never really recovered. In many instances, enormously expensive pearl necklaces fell to fractions of their former value. There is a famous story of a two-strand pearl necklace owned by May C. Plant, a New York socialite. In 1917, Mrs. Plant traded her six-story, Renaissance-style Manhattan house to the jeweler Pierre Cartier for his most valued pearl necklace, worth one million dollars. Following Mrs. Plant's death, the pearls were auctioned at Parke-Bernet Gallery in 1957 for only $151,000. By that time, however, the house (still the location of Cartier's store) was worth millions.[59]

It was not only the Wall Street crash that reduced the value of pearls, but also the appearance of cultured pearls. Pearl prices had always reflected supply and demand. With the ability to cultivate pearls, the unpredictable search for the gems was replaced by an industry in which pearls were harvested in relatively predictable quantities.

Obtaining pearls had usually been a risky business, generally controlled by assorted cutthroats and adventurers. Pearl divers, the workhorses of the undertaking, were paid

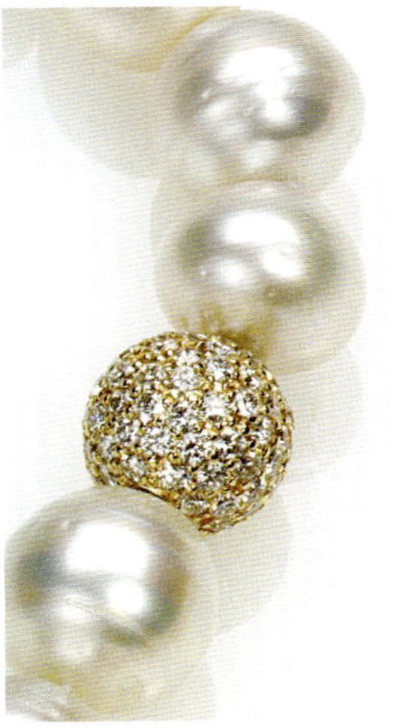

ABOVE: 325. *Detail of an Australian baroque cultured pearl and diamond pavé bead necklace. 2008. Designed by Barbara Bady and Ian Ionescu. Pearl sizes range from 16.7 to 10.3 millimeters.*

OPPOSITE: 326. *Mrs. George Gould, a New York society matron in her famous pearl necklace and pearl-embroidered dress, c. 1910. The wearing of this necklace and dress, each valued at one million dollars, did not escape criticism. In 1908, the magazine Femina noted that "the extravagance of the garment in no way increased its attractiveness...and it tied up vast sums of money that could have been spent in much more useful ways."[1]*

so poorly that they inevitably became enslaved to their masters. Lowered by ropes often to depths of forty to fifty feet, many divers were killed, maimed by sharks, or blinded from the saline waters (plate 321).[60]

It was primarily through the efforts of Japan's Kokichi Mikimoto that a controlled approach to growing pearls was developed in 1913, and the hazardous methods of natural pearl fishing declined in importance. It is not surprising that it was in Japan, where nature is revered in its purest forms, that man and nature jointly created such perfection as the pearl.[61]

The only difference between natural and cultured pearls is that in natural pearls the foreign object (the nucleus around which the oyster secretes nacre) enters the mollusk accidentally, while in cultured pearls it is usually larger, spherical, and deliberately inserted by a technician. Thereafter, the mollusk takes over.

When Mikimoto introduced his cultured pearls in London in 1919, at prices considerably below those of natural pearls, dealers tried hard to discredit the gems as simulations or imitations. Mikimoto had to prove in courts of law around the world that his cultured pearls were genuine, identical to natural ones except that the nucleus had been inserted. Without X rays, even experts are not able to distinguish between cultured and natural pearls.

The culturing of pearls was actually known to the Chinese in the thirteenth century, and to the Swedish naturalist Carolus Linnaeus by the eighteenth. Several Japanese also had early successes, but it was Mikimoto who developed the techniques for creating round pearls and fought the battles in the pearl market to establish their legitimacy. Called the "pearl king," he was the main force behind contemporary Japan's billion-dollar pearl-farming industry.

Today most of the world's pearls are cultured, and the main production center has shifted from Japan to China. This is a radical change from the 1970s and 80s when about 70 percent of pearls come from Japan.[62] Pearls are produced in other regions, such as the South Pacific and Australia, frequently in close association with the Japanese. An exception is Burmese pearls, considered among the finest in the world. Burma farms and auctions off its own pearl crop. In the United States, a company that supplied the mussel-shell nuclei from the Mississippi to the Japanese for over thirty years started growing its own cultured pearls in Tennessee, Louisiana, and Texas in the 1980s. The first major harvest occurred in the spring of 1987.[63]

Pearls are organic and therefore tend to disintegrate if improperly worn or stored. Claude Arpels, founder of the jewelry firm Van Cleef and Arpels, has related an experience in India shortly after the country's independence in 1947:

> A chest of pearls from the estate of one of India's richest maharajahs was available to me. When the coffer was opened, it brimmed with pearls, like a prop from *The Arabian Nights*. Everyone imagined himself a millionaire until I touched them and my hand was white with powder. Pearls come from nature, the sea. Luster is said to be the life of a pearl. It was a bitter disappointment to us all when I announced "They're worthless." The cache had been in a vault for years, locked away from light, air, and moisture. They were dehydrated and dead as ancient bones.[64]

It is fitting that to prolong the life of pearls they must be kept in regular physical contact with their owners—an expression of the intimate ties between people and nature.

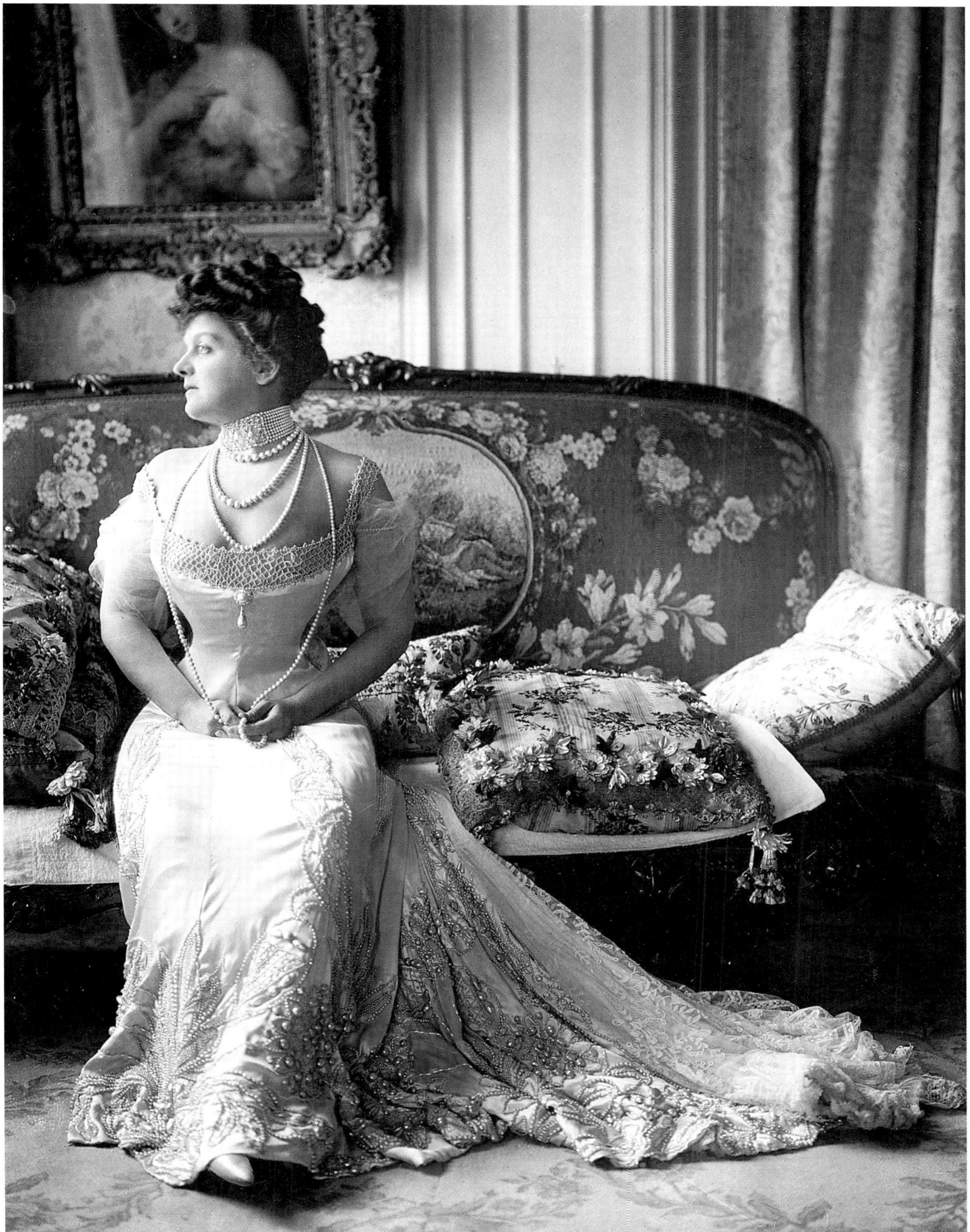

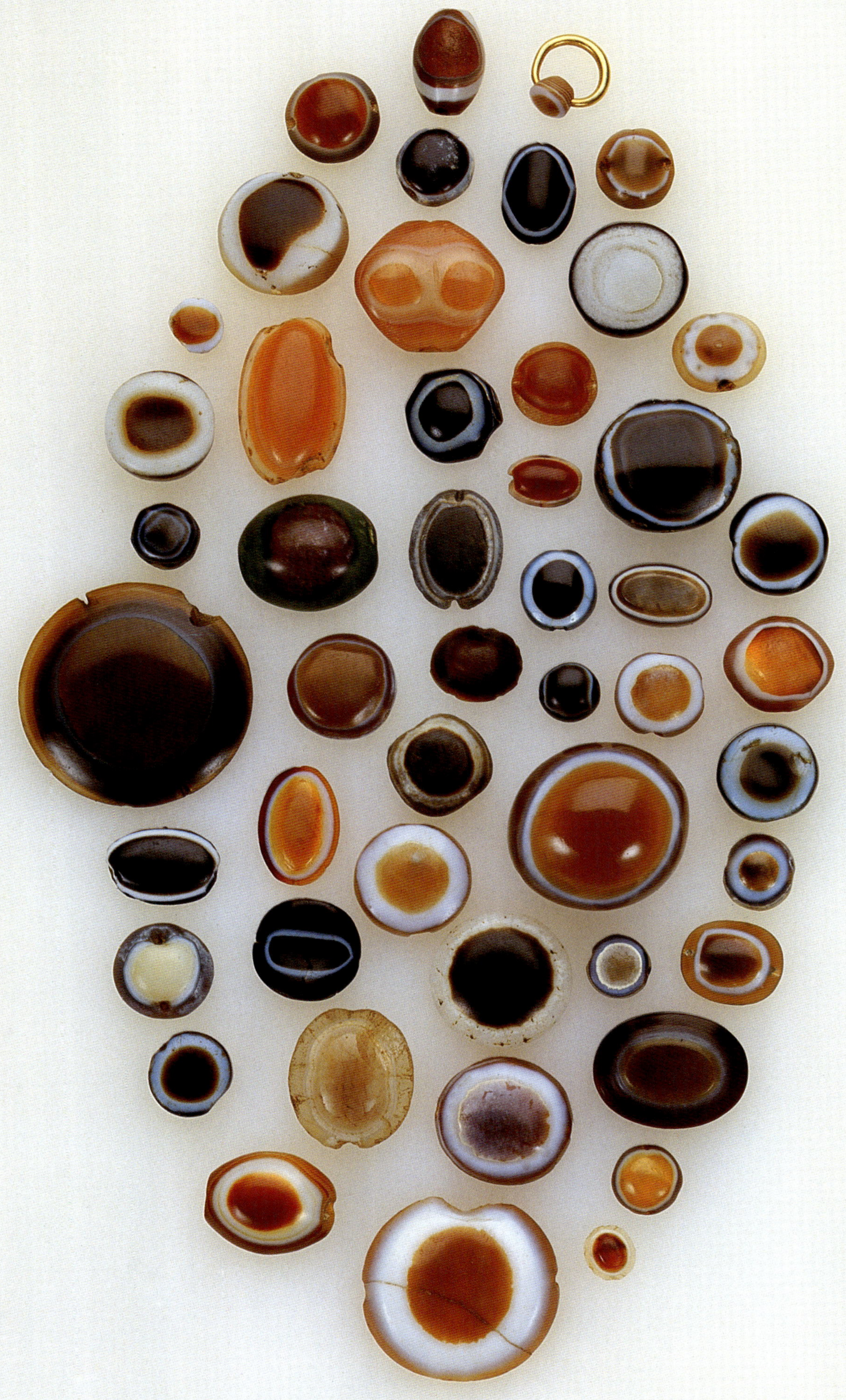

The Magical Eye Bead

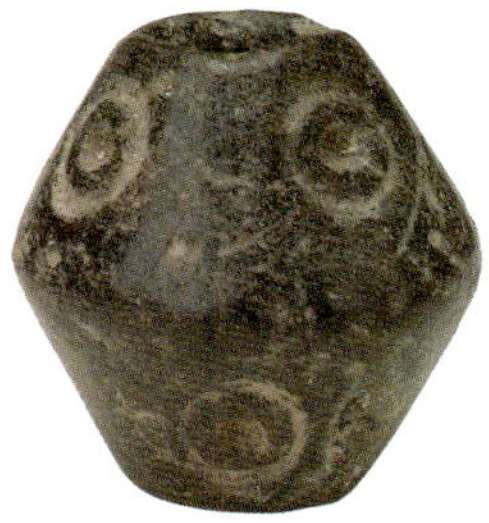

Among the most compelling beads are those with eye imagery. Eye beads have a long history, broad geographic spread, mysterious attraction, and a central place within the context of evil eye beliefs.

Evil eye ideology is complex. The evil eye represents a belief that the gaze from an individual—thought to be motivated by envy—can bring misfortune or death to a person or object envied. Yet although envy is an important part of this phenomenon, the evil eye is more broadly about human distress and power. It is a balance between fear of who has the power (expressed through the eyes) to cause damage and hope that one can protect oneself from it. To combat the feeling of helplessness and to have some control over the evil eye, people align themselves with the seeming protection of prayers, rituals, imagery, gestures, colors, and amulets.

Preventive measures vary from one culture to another. In parts of India and Africa, the cowrie shell is believed to represent the human eye and therefore valued as protection against the evil eye. Throughout Western Asia and the Mediterranean, eyes are painted on buildings, tombs, and boats, or placed on amulets and beads. The protective eye image serves as an intermediary by catching the evil eyes' negative forces and diverting it from the wearer. It counteracts the fatal glance and neutralizes the look.

In addition to eye imagery, there is a range of gestures, objects, and materials used as protection from the evil eye. For some, the hand may be more important than the eye. A hand is first of all a symbol of power; the hand held forward is a gesture of throwing off something. When one encounters an individual who is believed to have the evil eye, one gives him an open hand or two fingers that evoke the idea of blinding the eye. Two fingers also recalls horns. Coral, amber, crystal, and agate have also long been considered powerful materials for protection.

OPPOSITE: 327. *This remarkable collection of Western Asian onyx, chalcedony, and banded-agate beads were made for the most part between the third and first millennium B.C. Each has been cut and polished to look like an eye. Most of these beads were acquired in the Middle East as bakshesh, gifts exchanged at the consummation of a business deal. Collection Derek Content*

ABOVE: 328. *A Western Asian stone bead with incised dot-in-circle motifs, possibly a reference to eyes. c. late fourth millennium B.C. Height, 3.2 cm. Private collection*

Not all people, however, believe in the evil eye, and therefore while eye beads have traditionally been associated with the evil eye, not all beads with eye imagery relate to evil. The evil eye had no place in the earliest hunting and gathering societies, nor among animists, Buddhists, or Hindus. Eye motifs on Himalayan area *dZi* beads symbolize a connection to spirituality rather than protection from evil (plates 216–17). It is also questionable whether the ancient polytheist cultures of Mesopotamia, Persia, Egypt, Phoenicia, Greece, Rome, and the Celts believed in the absolutism of evil, which would have included the evil eye. Therefore, the large quantities of eye beads from all of these cultures were possibly used for an array of issues ranging from holiness to quasi-magic—reasons other than protection from evil.

It is probable that the evil eye emerged at the same time as the concept of absolute evil in western religious thought—sometime between the second and third century B.C. and the third century A.D. This is also when beads with eye motifs most likely began to be used for protection from the evil eye.[1]

While Jewish doctrine clearly disavows folk beliefs based on magic, the ancient Hebrews feared the evil eye and employed protective measures against it. During the third century B.C., Abba Arika, founder of the Rabbinic Academy at Sura, a city in Babylonia, claimed that ninety-nine out of one hundred human deaths were the work of the evil eye.[2] To protect buildings, particularly houses of worship, a symbol known as the "much-enduring eye" was painted on buildings. A third-century A.D. synagogue excavated at the Syrian town of Dura-Europos has such a painting on its ceiling. Christian churches were similarly safeguarded, as demonstrated by a mural in a sixth-century A.D. monastery at Bawit in Egypt.[3]

It is within the Islamic faith, however, that belief in the evil eye and the wearing of protective eye bead amulets has the strongest representation. In all periods of history, Arabs have had a profound fear of the evil eye, even to the point of calling it "the beautiful eye" to avoid its damaging effects.[4] Muslims say that "the evil eye empties the castles and fills the graves."[5] They believe that no one, rich or poor, is safe from its wrathful stare. To counter the evil eye, most Muslims wear some form of protective amulet from birth, including eye beads. In November 2007, a friend was driven to Istanbul's international airport in a taxi with a strand of eye beads prominently dangling on the rearview mirror.[6]

Early Eye Beads

The earliest and greatest quantities of eye beads appear in Western Asia, India, and Egypt. By the middle of the first millennium B.C., they occur in Europe and in certain localities within China, presumably reflecting Western influences, although there was a close association between the words of "eye pupil" and "bead" in the Chinese language.[7]

Stone and shell beads decorated with dot-in-circle motifs (possibly a reference to eyes) are found in Western Asia dating to at least the late sixth millennium B.C. Stone beads with obvious eye imagery appear in the region by 3000 B.C. (Timeline 237). Stone beads with incised eye designs and banded agates cut to produce an eye effect are known from Mesopotamian sites of this period, as are etched carnelians with eye patterns. The latter also occur in mid to late third millennium B.C. sites in the Indus Valley and Afghanistan. Identical polyhedral beads with eyelike dots on each facet were recovered from Lothal and Kalibangan in the Indus Valley.[8]

That eye imagery was significant in ancient Western Asia is evidenced by the plethora of exquisite stone eye beads of onyx, chalcedony, and banded agate dating from the third to first millennium B.C. (plate 327). Precious and semiprecious stones were in

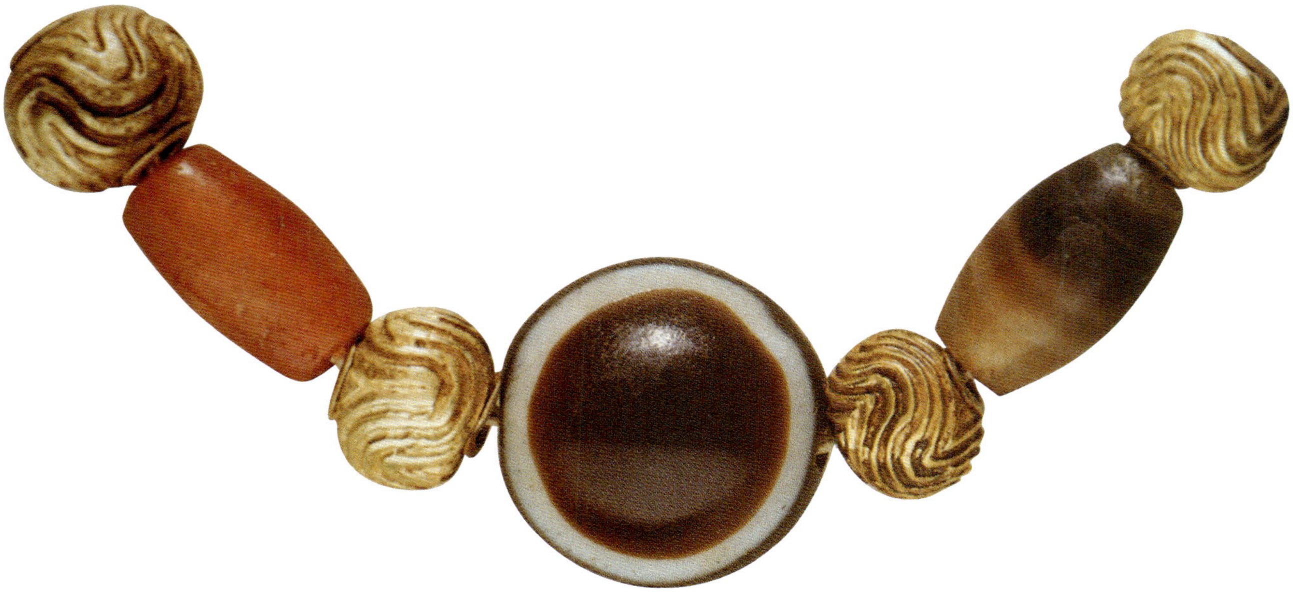

329. *Gold and carnelian beads and a banded-agate eye bead from the royal Sumerian graves of Ur, in Mesopotamia, 2200–2000 B.C. Length, 9 cm. British Museum, London*

general considered protective. Beads and amulets made of precious materials are thought to be more effective than those made of commoner materials. A pragmatic explanation is that those who could afford costly, rare materials had more wealth and hence more power, protective or otherwise.

No more significant symbol existed in ancient Egypt than the eye of the God Horus. Two eyes—the sun and the moon—of the god Ra or Horus gazed down upon the civilization of the Nile. Eye bead amulets called *wedjat*—the eyes of Horus—were widely used in ancient Egypt from early Dynastic times through the Roman era, 2494 B.C.–A.D. 364. (plates 25a–d) .[9] Produced in a wide range of materials, the enormous quantities of *wedjat* within Egyptian burials indicates that they must have been of great importance. Glass eye beads also appear in large numbers from New Kingdom times up to the Ptolemaic and Romano-Egyptian periods.

Glass Eye Beads

With the invention or introduction of glass into western Asia (c. 2500 B.C.), Egypt, and Europe, one of the first objects created was the eye bead. This is not surprising given the visual similarity between the rounded, shining eye and most glass beads. Although there are some stylistic variations between glass eye beads, many similar forms were produced over long periods of time. To assign correct dates and places of manufacture to specific varieties of eye beads, it is necessary to identify the manufacturing techniques employed in each case.

In his 1916 study, Gustavus Eisen used the technical principals of how Egyptian and Western Asian beads were made to generally divide the beads into categories of eye spot (dot or spot of a different color than the bead matrix), rings and rings with dots, spirals, stratified (layered dots), and compound eyes (smaller stratified eyes or layered and inlaid preformed eyes that included mosaic-glass or millefiori). Eisen believed that the complexity of technical processes reflected cultural development: simple to complex.[10]

Eye-spot beads were the earliest type made in most regions. They appear as glass drops or rings impressed into the bead matrix in New Kingdom Egypt (Eighteenth and Nineteenth dynasties, 1567–1200 B.C.). Stratified eyes were popular with the Egyptians, Phoenicians, and Chinese through at least the first millennium B.C. (plates 332, 8–17). The eyes were produced by a drop of glass placed on a base. The glass was then pressed in while the base was still soft. Another drop was placed on the first drop. By this layering technique, the eye was built up. One way of recognizing this technique is that eyes made of transparent glass are thick and dark in their centers. In some instances, multilayered eyes were made separately, then pressed into the base. New Kingdom Egyptian glassmakers of the Eighteenth and Nineteenth dynasties made distinctive and beautifully complex eye beads using a combination of stratified-eye and inlaid-coil techniques (plate 334.11).

Mosaic rod eyes appeared by the fifth century B.C., but were not common until about 300 B.C. when they began to replace stratified eyes, a process completed by Roman times. Mosaic rods were made from layered glass canes of alternating colors, a technique that produced compound glass. When cool, the multilayered rods were cut into sections or disks, each disk representing a ready-made eye with rings. These eyes were then attached to a base, or fused together, so that the eye pattern ran though the entire bead (plate 334.32). In both the stratified and mosaic varieties, patterns ranged from simple spots to more intricate designs composed of multiple eyes surrounded by additional dots, rings, and bars.

Multilayered eye beads of remarkable complexity were made by the Chinese from 400 to 200 B.C. (plate 334.24–334.26). In the latter half of the first millennium B.C., many types of glass beads were both imported into and manufactured within various centers in the Mediterranean, central Europe, and Russia. These included beads with raised spiral eyes, presumably produced in Celtic workshops between 200 and 1 B.C. (plate 334.28). With the decline of the Celts and the collapse of the Roman Empire in the fifth century A.D., European glassmaking shifted to the Rhineland, an era known as "The Migration Period."[11]

Migrations Period eye beads evolved from many cultures. Before A.D. 480, beads were closer to Roman Period designs. After that date, they develop their own styles.

Frankish glassmakers, for example, although basically inspired by earlier Middle Eastern designs, created their own fashions while imitating Celtic beads known from the La Tene and Hallstatt fifteen hundred years earlier. The Franks both copied Celtic patterns and wore Celtic beads with spiral patterns on their own necklaces, perhaps regarding them as protective amulets. Many European beads of this time actually include those imported and grave-robbed from the Middle East.[12]

Technically, available data shows a gradual change of beads with stratified eyes. Earlier beads of the period have a greater number of eyes and layers; beads of the later periods have simpler monochrome eye designs.

The final phase of European migrations involved the Vikings. By A.D. 800, the Vikings were a seafaring people who raided and traded in northern, western, and eastern Europe, including the rivers of France and the British Isles. Glass beadmaking occurred in most of the regions in which they traveled. Workshops were established in Scandinavia where unique local glass beads were produced and worn by Viking women. Glass eye beads found in Scandinavian Viking sites display many origins, which is not unexpected given the far-ranging activities of Viking warriors and traders.

Islamic Beads

The Islamic world included many regions in which significant eye beads evolved, notably Egypt, Mesopotamia, Syria, the Levant, and Iran. Eye beads continued as a major bead type in all of these areas, as well as with several sub-Saharan African Islamic groups in Mali and Mauritania. Islamic Period beads eventually lead into the contemporary European Period of glass bead manufacture (beginning in the late Medieval times) where eye spot motifs became a staple of Venetian bead production for trade and export. Of greater importance, however, are the revivals

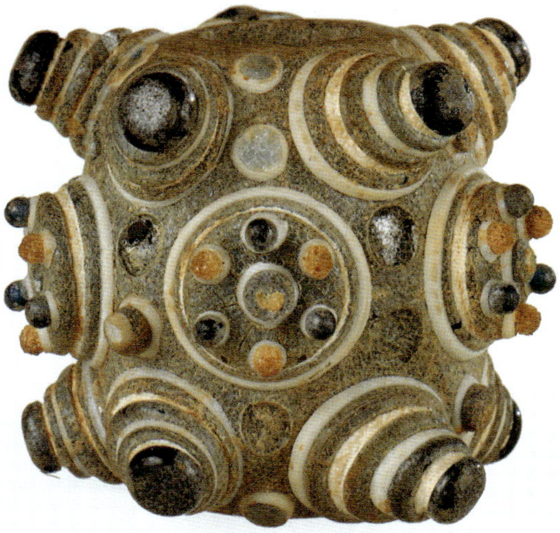

LEFT: 330. *An exceptionally beautiful Chinese glass eye bead from the "Warring States" period (481–221 B.C.) featuring five blue-and-white layered, horned eyes encircling each end and flanking a ring of raised circles, each with seven smaller, simpler eyes set in a dark blue glass background. Diameter 2.54 cm. Corning Museum of Glass, Corning, New York*

BOTTOM: 331. *A Phoenician-made necklace with glass eye beads and a central mask or head pendant, recovered from Grave 1 at Tharros, Sardinia, 600–300 B.C. Necklace: length, 31.5 cm. British Museum, London*[1]

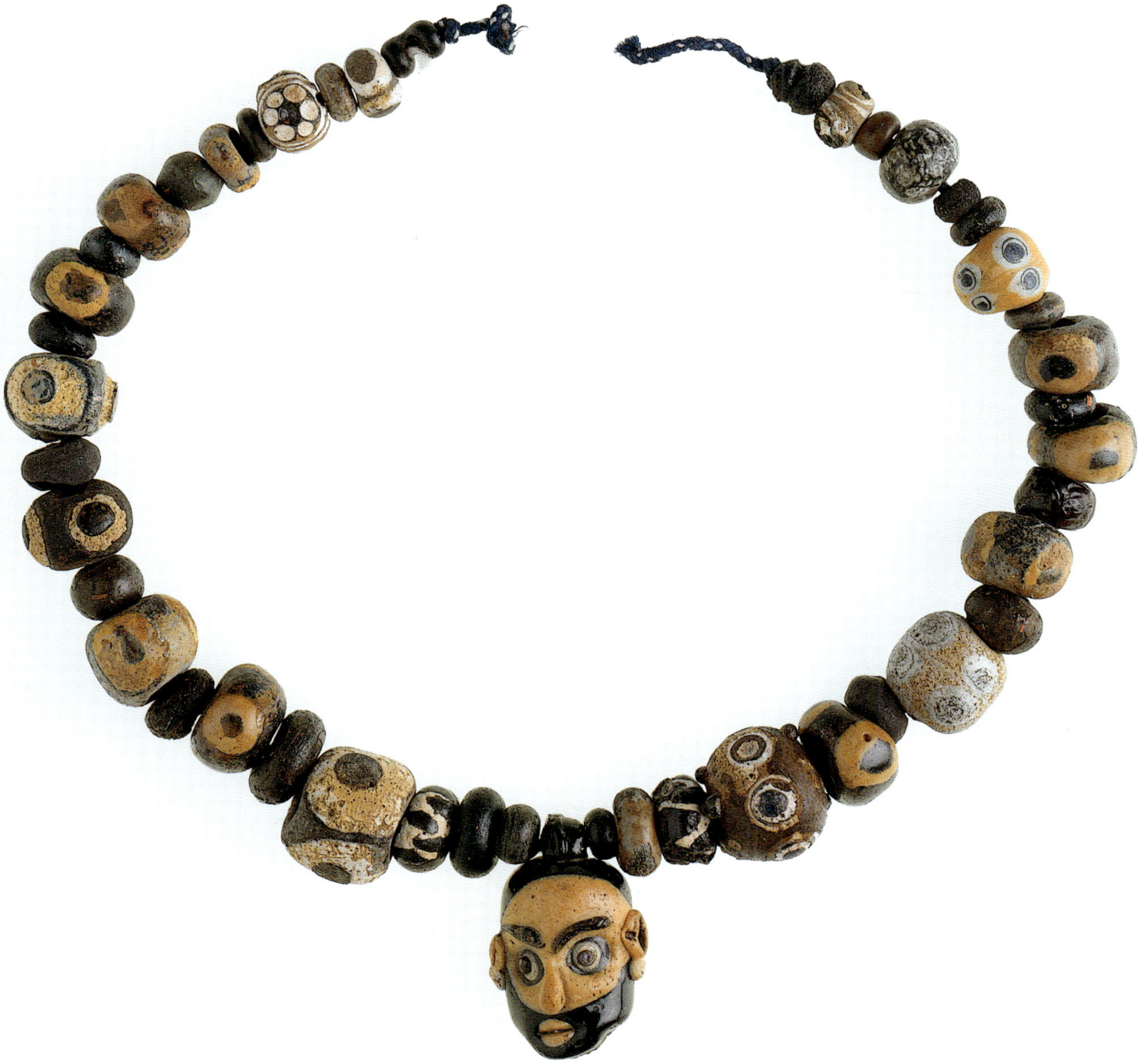

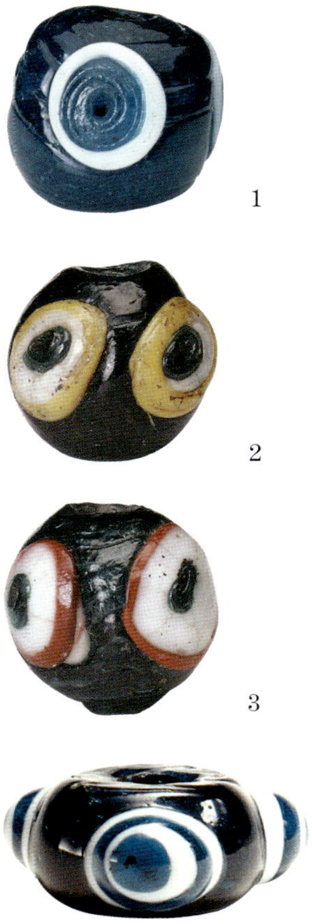

1

2

3

4

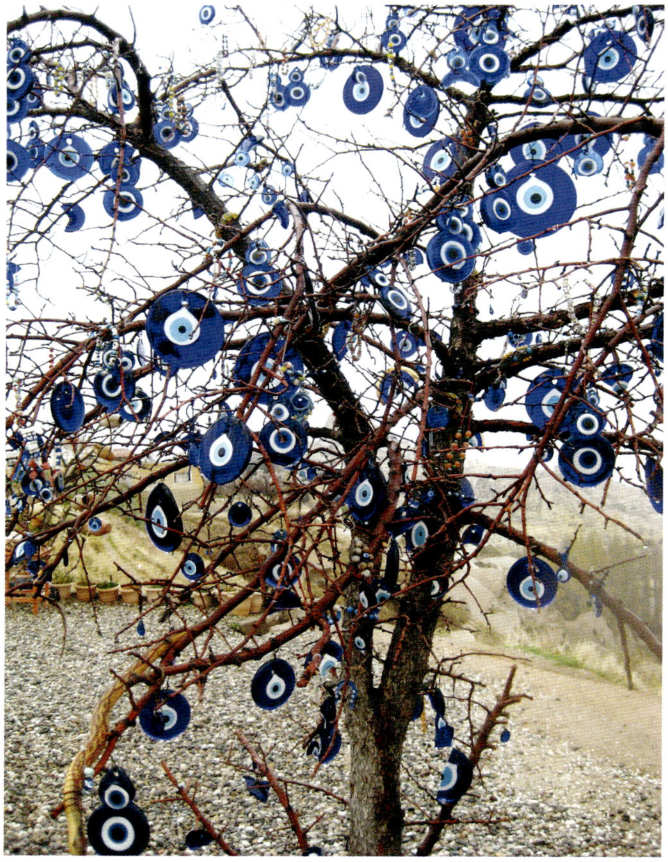

ABOVE LEFT: 332. *figs. 1–4. Eye beads and amulets continue to reach across a broad range of cultures and great span of time, as seen in these contemporary examples. Egypt, Turkey, Tashkent, and Jordan are today's major producers of evil eye beads. (1) Turkey, c. 1990s; (2), (3) Hebron, Jordan, c. 1961; (4) Egypt, c. 2002.*

ABOVE RIGHT: 333. *Cappadochia, Turkey. 2007*

OPPOSITE: 334. *figs. 1–45. A cross-cultural grouping of stone, bone, and glass eye beads dating from the fourth millennium* B.C. *to the present. All beads are shown actual size. For further description, see note II.*

in the Eastern Mediterranean (Turkey, Tashkent, Hebron, and Egypt) where evil eye beads have recently been produced.[13]

A preference for blue beads, particularly blue eye beads to avert evil spirits, appears to be of historical and cross-cultural significance. An often-repeated story is that the wearing of blue beads in the Middle East arose as an antidote to the blue-eyed, blond-haired crusaders or the even earlier Indo-European invaders (c. 4400–2800 B.C.). Blue glass eye beads were produced in Western Asia, the Mediterranean, and Europe at much earlier dates than the medieval crusades. The majority of ancient glass eye beads have a blue matrix with white, yellow, or blue eyes. Perhaps the early appeal of the color lies in the association of the color blue with moisture. Blue was the color of the sky and water, of prime importance in the arid lands where the evil eye emerged as a concept. Blue was also treasured as the color of protection and royalty—blue is a rare color in nature, rare as a dye in Europe and the Mediterranean region until trade with Asia brought indigo to the area. Thus anything of blue indicates power and prestige.[14]

Today, in Greece, donkeys, mules, and cows often have protective blue beads and tassels on their bridles or across their foreheads. Blue beads of turquoise, glass, faience, or plastic are still pinned to children's clothing in Turkey and Greece. By far the majority of contemporary evil eye beads are of blue glass (plates 332).

Eye beads reach across a broad range of cultures and great spans of time. Their history as well as their pervasiveness reminds us once again that beads have always functioned as more than adornment. An insightful observation by Jamey D. Allen helps explain the continuing relevance of eye beads: "I think the mere act of placing an eye onto an apparently inanimate object (a ship, a house, a bead) is the essence of animism. It is an expression that that thing is 'alive.'"[15] A belief in the power of eye beads remains vibrant.

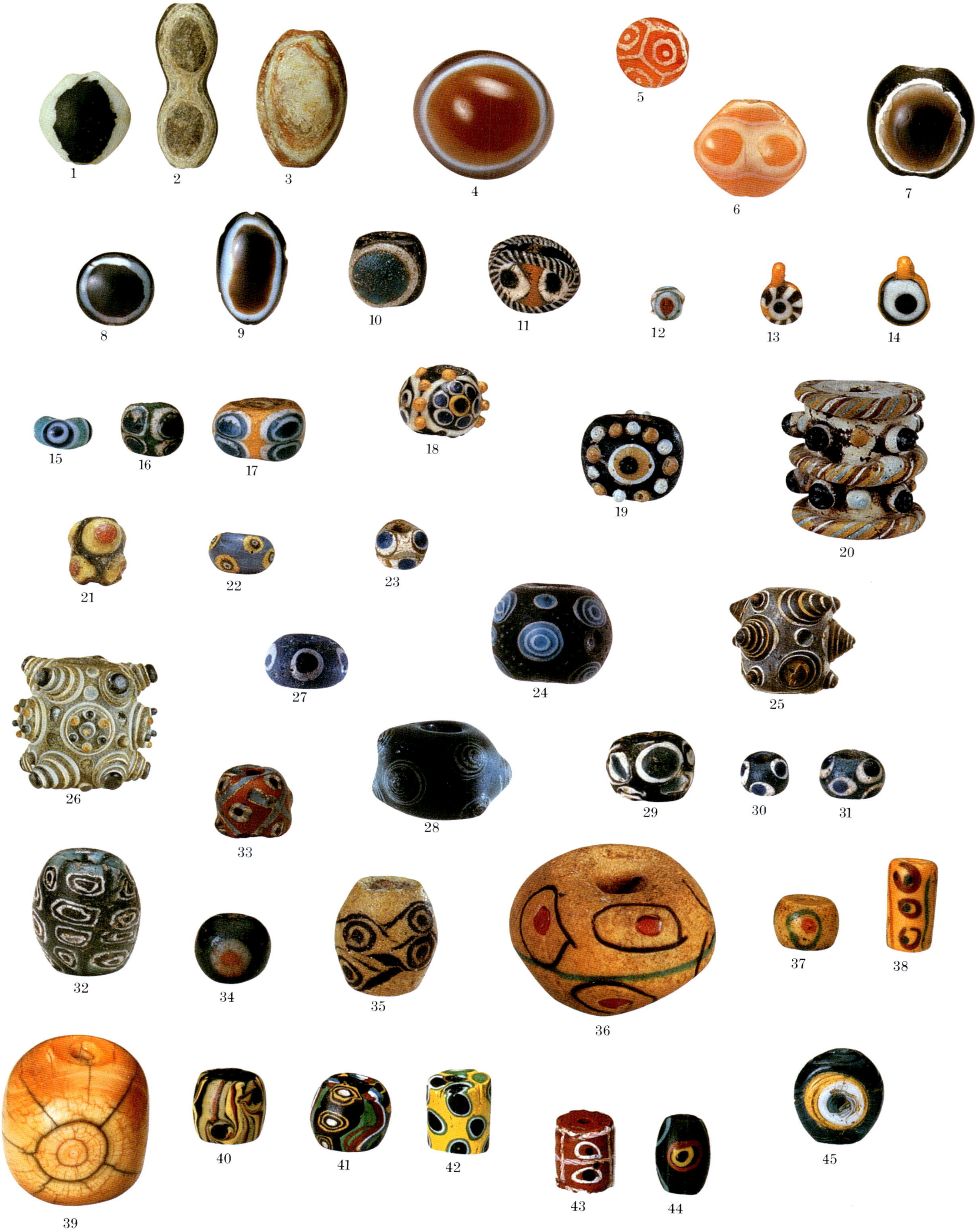
1
2
3
4
5
6
7
8
9
10
11
12
13
14
15
16
17
18
19
20
21
22
23
24
25
26
27
28
29
30
31
32
33
34
35
36
37
38
39
40
41
42
43
44
45

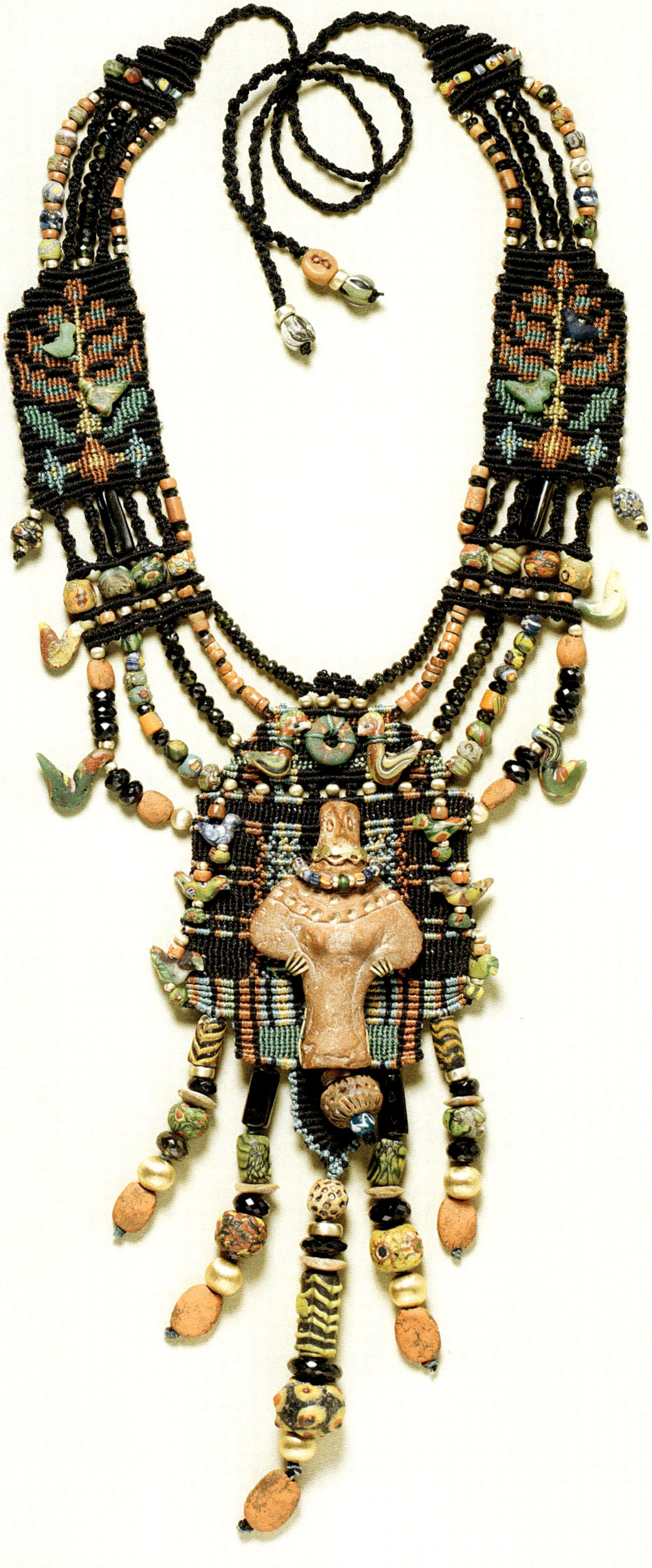

Contemporary: Europe and North America

Contemporary beads from Europe and North America display a great diversity of materials and techniques and reflect widely varying lifestyles. In previous eras, one type of jewelry often remained in use for prolonged spans of time. During the past century, however, profound changes in technology, communications, and economic structures have altered every aspect of life. It is, therefore, not surprising that the making and wearing of jewelry would be affected along with so much else. Perhaps the one theme linking these last eleven decades has been change, clearly operative in all forms of adornment, including beads. At the same time necklaces of round beads made in traditional materials—stone, glass, metal, amber, and pearls—continue to have a timeless appeal.

The story of contemporary Western beads begins in late nineteenth to early twentieth century Europe with examples of elegance and luxurious ostentation. The royal houses still in power provided the focus for most social life. Gemstones, particularly diamonds and pearls, were especially fashionable and were used in matching sets (parures) of earrings, necklaces, chokers, pins, bracelets, and hair ornaments. Clothing and jewelry were lavish but conservative, and they were generally adaptations of styles first designed in the eighteenth century, when large and resplendent jewels conveyed status and wealth. Across the Atlantic, American moneyed aristocrats, whose fortunes were amassed after the Industrial Revolution, were equally inclined to displays of elaborate jewelry. European trends were followed in America, and jewels were purchased from the great London and Paris firms, including Cartier and Bulgari, where work was produced with fine technical skill but limited artistic originality. In these decades, beads, except for pearls and occasionally jade and coral, were not part of the adornment of the wealthy.

OPPOSITE: 335. *A macramé silken thread bib combines a terra cotta Bird Goddess from the Indus Valley (c. 1600 B.C.), Roman era (or earlier) and Islamic terra cotta and glass beads—including many with eye motifs—and modern 14-karat gold beads. Glass bird beads, carved by contemporary Afghan artisans from the broken shards of ancient glass bangles, sit on the branches of two trees of life—an important Indus cultural motif. Artist Barbara Natoli Witt of Oakland, California, is inspired by an array of cultures and weaves a story into each of her tapestry neckpieces. 2008. Bird Goddess: length, 7.3 cm. Private collection.*

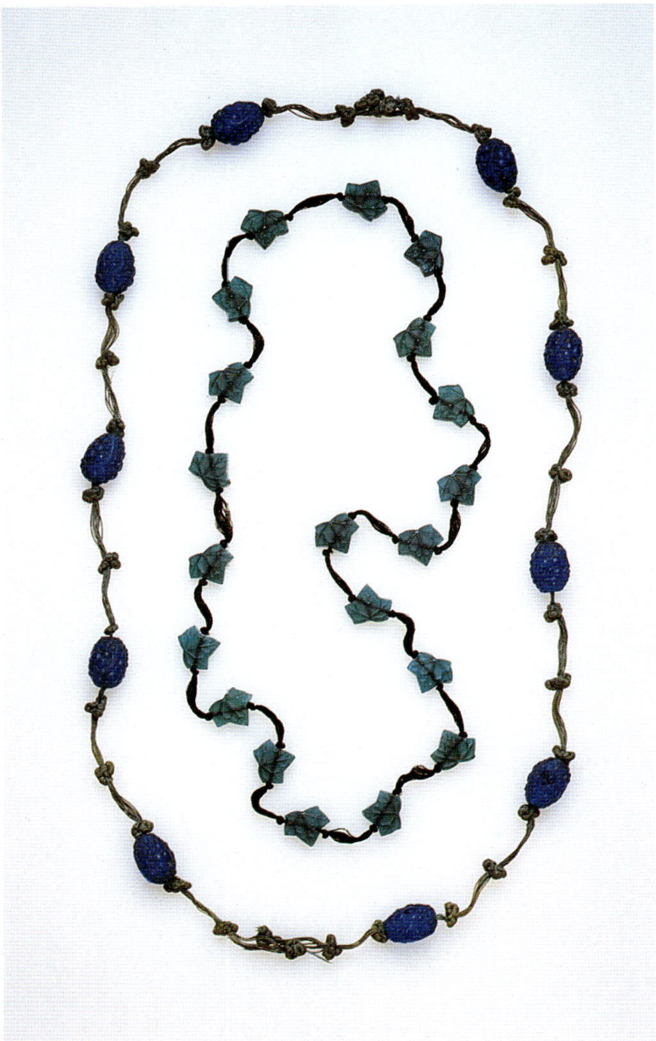

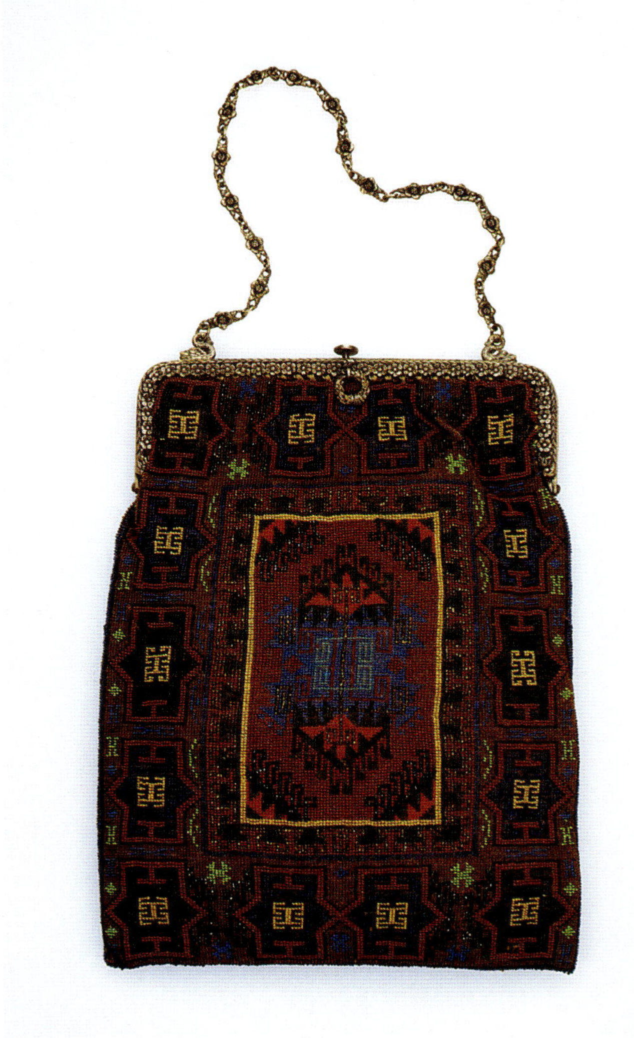

TOP LEFT: 336. *These mold-pressed glass beads were produced in the 1920s by the famed Art Nouveau jeweler René Jules Lalique. The blue grape clusters and green ivy leaves, strung and knotted on silk, were motifs typical of the period's art. Typical ivy leaf bead: diameter, 3 cm. Collection Primavera Gallery, New York*

TOP RIGHT: 337. *An Art Deco beaded bag, 1930, in the pattern of an Oriental rug, woven on a loom with glass and cut-steel beads. Length, 27 cm. Private collection*

OPPOSITE: 338. *A necklace created in 1982 by Austrian jeweler Jacqueline Little uses one*

Not everyone was satisfied with the prevailing conservative styles. By 1900, several groups of artists and designers, including the founders of the Arts and Crafts movement and Art Nouveau style, had profoundly altered tastes. Indeed, Art Nouveau jewelry, although a radical departure in design and philosophy from establishment aesthetics, was very popular with the elite. The great political revolutions of the eighteenth and nineteenth centuries had been followed by periods of austerity as a result of the populace's reaction to the past excesses of the ruling classes. In the latter half of the nineteenth century, however, there was a tendency to revive the styles of earlier eras. Stimulated primarily by hostility to the evolving industrial age and its machine-made, impersonal products, everything from home furnishings to jewelry was inspired by ancient or bygone examples. Archaeologically excavated Etruscan gold beads, for instance, were copied by the Italian jewelers Alessandro and Auguste Castellani. If individuality seemed to have been lost to mass production, a return to past, familiar styles offered psychological security, and appeared to guarantee fine handcraftsmanship by requiring the use of intricate details (such as Etruscan-style granulation).

At the same time, a few designers rejected historical mannerisms. They preferred to search for new forms more appropriate to modern society. Englishman William Morris (1834–1896) was among those interested in combining functional and aesthetic considerations in design. The English Arts and Crafts movement, led by Morris, not only

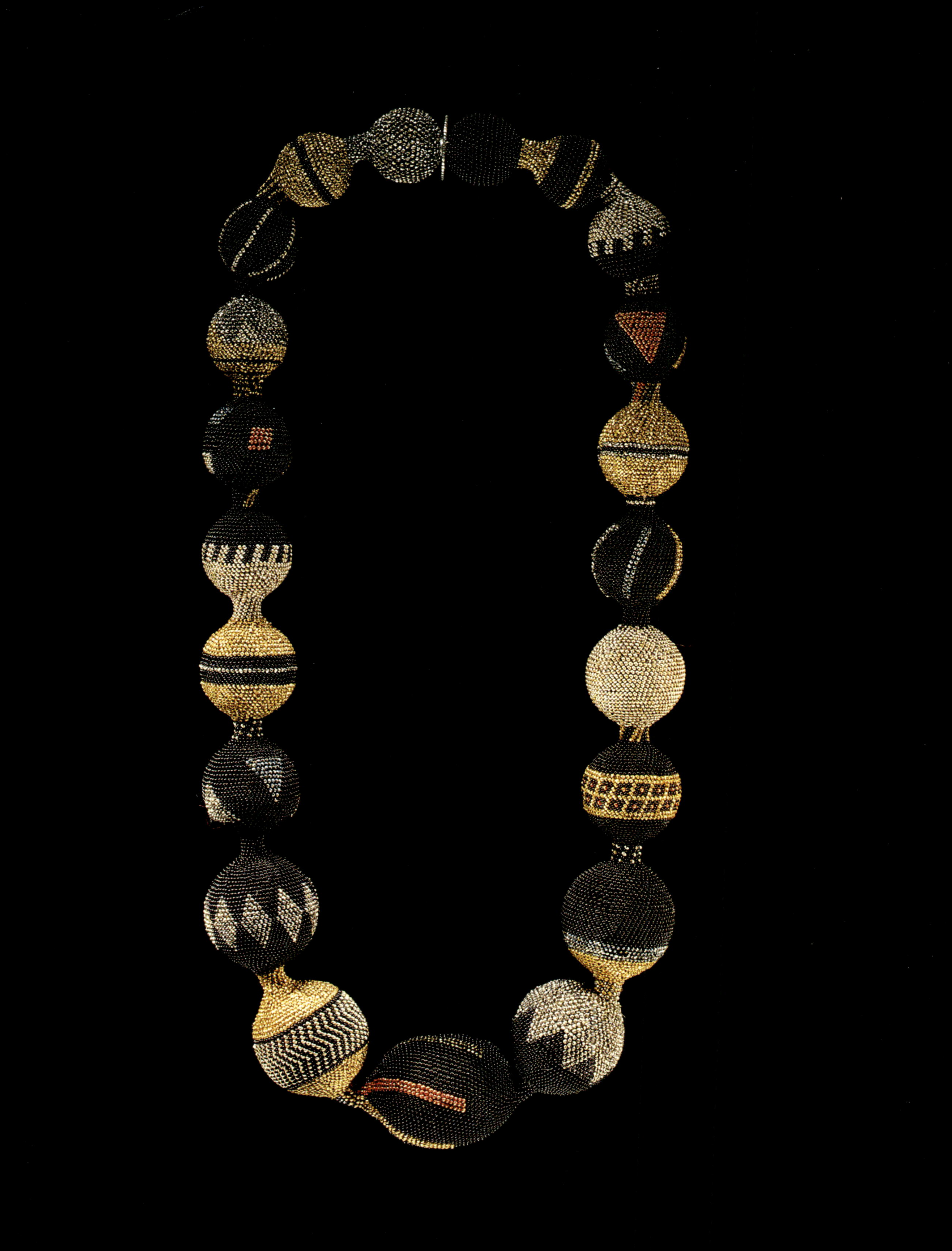

millimeter (or smaller) glass beads and faceted steel beads that date from the late nineteenth century. Each bead is individually knotted, a method insuring the necklace has a high degree of flexibility and suppleness. Length, 47 cm. Private collection

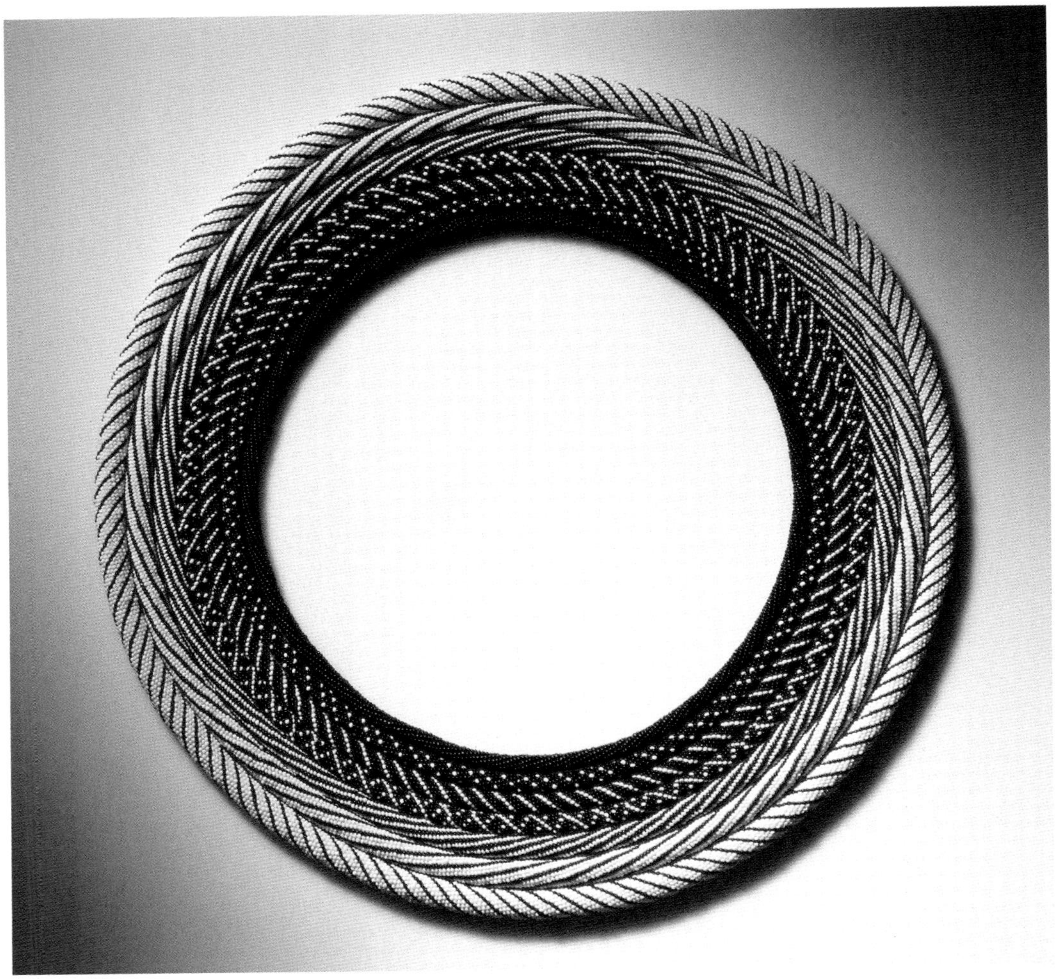

RIGHT: 339. *Working in Switzerland, a country noted for its textile arts, Verena Sieber-Fuchs has developed a unique approach to crocheting with beads. This group of black-and-white necklaces incorporates yarn and glass beads, 1976. Necklace: diameter, 30.3 cm. Collection Verena Sieber-Fuchs, Zurich*

attempted to revive handicraft traditions (in the belief that machines put artisans out of work) but promoted socialism and stressed the moral obligation of integrating beauty with the accessories of daily life. Their efforts to elevate social standards by offering good design to a mass audience was a revolutionary phenomenon. In France, a similar philosophy emerged with a group that adhered to a style called Art Nouveau, the French name for certain new developments in architecture and the decorative arts. Unlike Morris, however, Art Nouveau craftsmen were not as antagonistic toward mechanization. Instead, they hoped to make the machine their servant in art. While this was not a time of prolific beadmaking, the attitudes that evolved were very conducive to the rise of the egalitarian bead as a fashionable item shortly thereafter.

One of the most successful manifestations of Art Nouveau was its jewelry, and its most outstanding practitioner and designer was a jeweler, René Jules Lalique (1860–1945). Lalique achieved fame in two separate areas: jewelry and glass, both of which included beads. Instrumental in ending the materialistic attitudes that had governed jewelers for centuries, Lalique believed the monetary value of materials was irrelevant. He chose substances not for their rarity, size, or value, but for their soft, subdued colors and textures. Lalique employed a mixture of precious and nonprecious materials in his work. He experimented with moonstones, chrysoprase, opals, ivory, bone, baroque pearls, molded glass, enameling, silver, and gold. His jewelry was valued for its imagination and craftsmanship rather than the intrinsic worth of its materials. Eventually, he chose to work entirely in glass. It was in the latter phase of his long career that he made exquisite mold-pressed glass beads (plate 336).

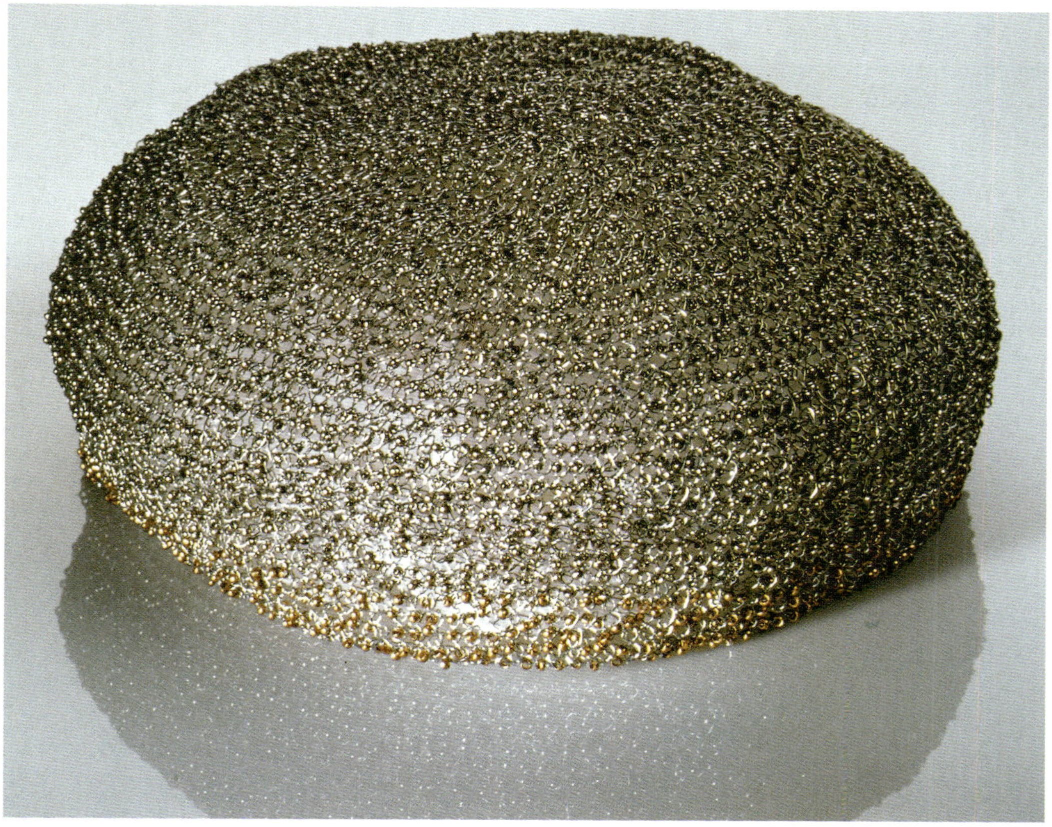

340. *Silver and gold metallic beads crocheted with silver wire to form a gossamer-like net beret, 1982. Diameter, 20 cm. Collection Verena Sieber-Fuchs, Zurich*

Americans, too, were influenced by the new European developments. The most important American Art Nouveau designer was Louis Comfort Tiffany (1848–1933). Although influenced by Lalique, Tiffany developed his own artistic style, which was particularly effective in glass. His important contributions included the invention of fumed glass, a technique developed to simulate ancient iridescent glass. This was achieved by spraying hot glass with a liquid coating that devitrifies the glass surface and produces a luminous rainbow effect.[1] While Tiffany created only a few (primarily gold) beads, his fumed-glass technique has been revived by contemporary glass beadmakers and is an important influence on their work (plate 389).

The Arts and Crafts movement and Art Nouveau style were short-lived but had long-term effects on craftsmen and jewelers. The merger of artist and craftsman, the responsible awareness of social issues, and the obligation to bring good design within the reach of ordinary people inspired future generations of artists and designers. The practice of combining materials according to their aesthetic value rather than material worth continues today among a large and talented group of jewelers and beadmakers.

The era of the Arts and Crafts movement and Art Nouveau style ended by 1914, and World War I virtually halted jewelry production for four years. In many countries, the imperial courts and their supporting nobility disappeared, and the clientele for jewelry shifted from wealthy segments of the population to the emerging middle class. A taste for luxury items again developed among the elite, but it was modified somewhat by the increasingly influential middle class, whose limited resources and restrained attitudes toward flamboyance established the standards of clothes and jewelry. Moreover, the outcome of the war profoundly altered the structure of society. The arrival of women at the workplace—they had been conscripted to fill the jobs of men in the services—meant a different type of jewelry was required, adornment that could move freely on the body and would be equally appropriate at work and social events.[2]

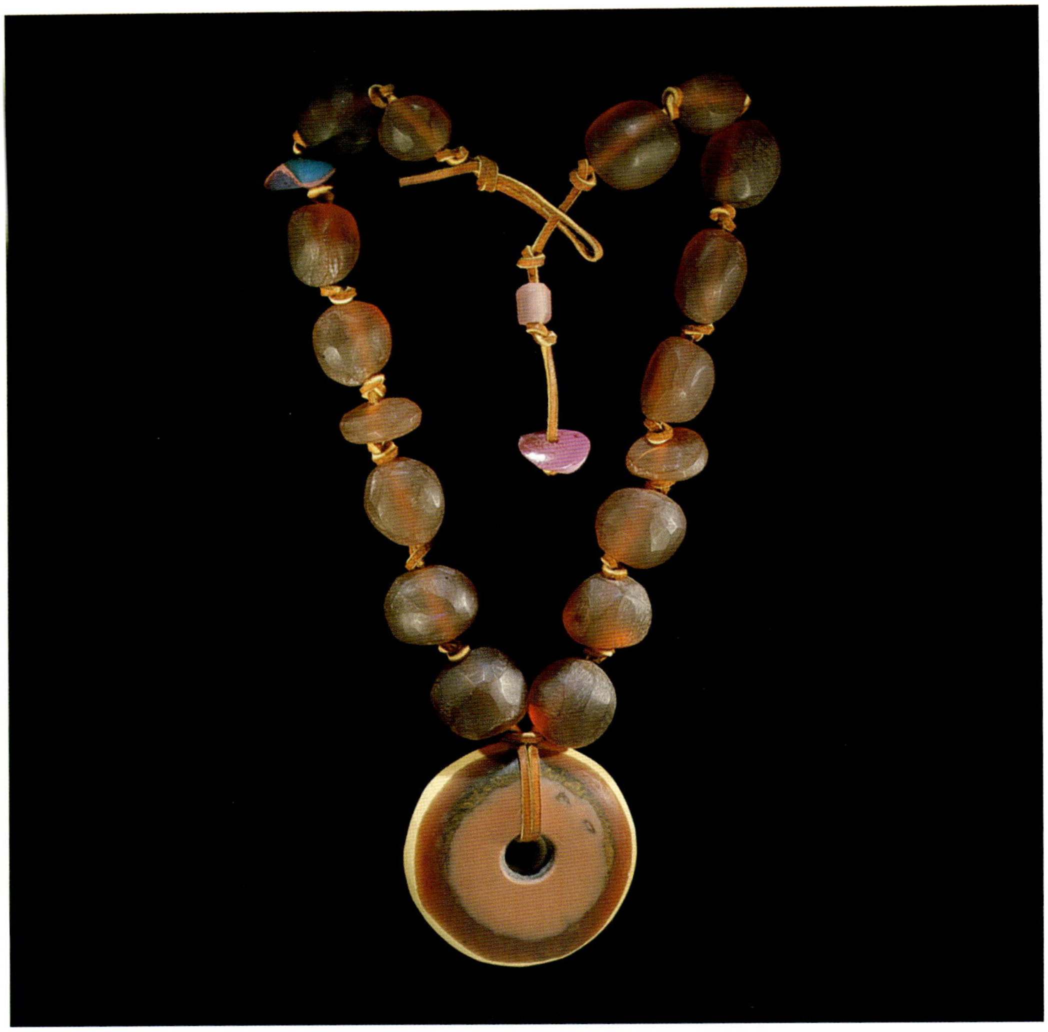

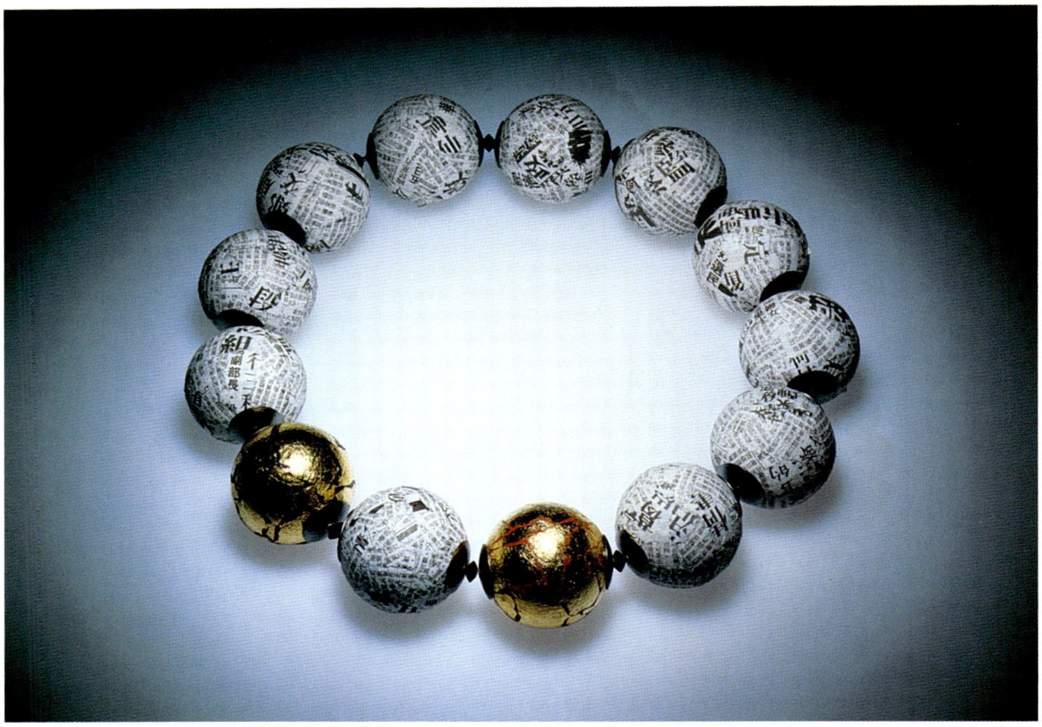

TOP: 341. *One-of-a-kind poured and carved plastic resin beads made by New York designer Cara Croninger in 1983. A pioneer in working this material into jewelry, Croninger has mastered transforming the liquid resin into imitations of almost any conceivable material, including amber, ivory, marble, crystal, emeralds, and granite.*

Although made of plastics, her jewelry's strong and attractive primitive qualities are the result of both her search for universal imagery as well as her ingenious production methods. Liquid resins with added pigments or dyes are poured into molds (frequently receptacles from the week's grocery supplies—orange juice bottles, sardine cans, and cookie tins). The material hardens into blocks in the molds, which are then sawed into cubes and carved into beads. Drilling, frequently the most hazardous phase as the beads can easily fracture (a problem experienced by beadmakers since at least the third millennium B.C.*), is done with an electric drill before the bead is completed, enabling the design to be balanced around the perforation. Necklace: length, 70 cm. Mingei International Museum, San Diego*

RIGHT: 342. *Robert Ebendorf created this necklace with beads made from Chinese newspaper. Two beads are covered with lacquer and 24-karat gold foil, separated by silver, copper, and ebony components. Typical bead: diameter, 5 cm. Victoria and Albert Museum, London*

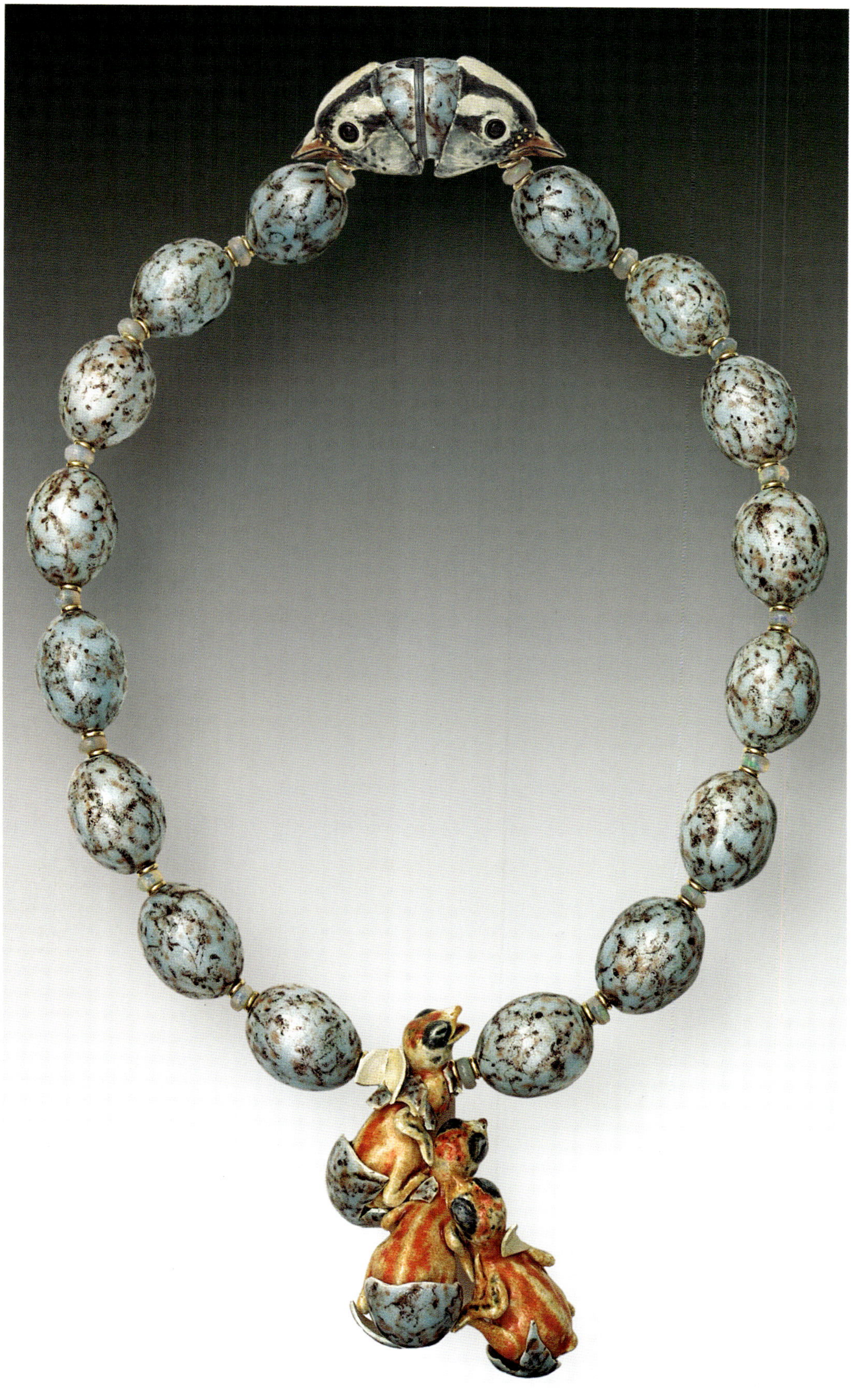

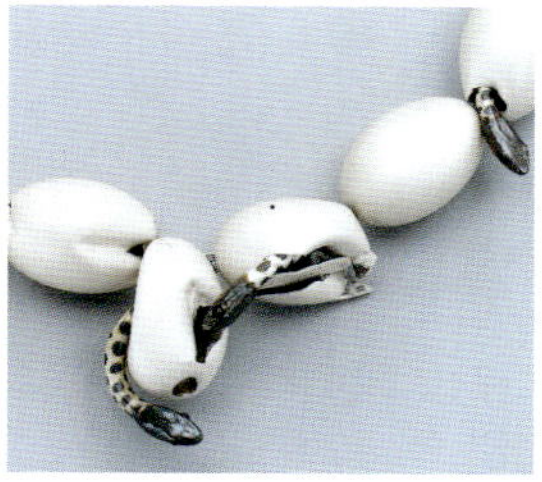

ABOVE: 343. *Detail of a necklace of fine silver eggs with enameled black rat snakes by David C. Freda, who was a taxidermist and illustrator before becoming a jeweler. While living in the Catskill Mountains in New York State, Freda found a clutch of twenty-three hatched snake eggs. Feeling their lightness, he immediately thought to use them as beads and subsequently reproduced the forms in silver, heat-treating and polishing the material to give it an iridescent, pearl-like effect. He also studied a live snake so as to portray its striations properly. 1983. Typical bead diameter, 2.8 cm. Collection Estate of Barbara Rockefeller, New York*

LEFT: 344. *An enameled gold and silver neckpiece entitled "Study of Newborn White Crown Sparrows, Eggs, and Adults." David C. Freda, 2001. 24k and 18k yellow gold, fine sterling silver, opal, and glass enamels. 22.9 × 14 × 3.8 cm. Length of centerpiece, 6.4 cm. Private collection*

RIGHT: 345. *Necklace of intricately constructed, wood laminate beads that were colored with injected vegetal dyes in the mid-1990s. Peter Chatwin and Pamela Martin. Overall circumference length, 76 cm. Typical bead: 2.54 × 2.54 × 1.3 cm. The Bead Museum, Glendale, Arizona*

BELOW LEFT: 346. *Silver hand brooch set with beads of amber, coral, bone, and stone by Kiff Slemmons for Ramona Solberg. 1991. Kiff relates: "Ramona was a great spirit: generous in every way, a wonderful jeweler, and a great lover of beads. Around 1987 I began a series of pieces called Hands of the Heroes as an inquiry into the concept of hero and its possible demise in our culture. I worked on the hands for several years and eventually made one to honor Ramona which I gave to her on her 70th birthday."[1] Length, 8.2 cm. Tacoma Art Museum, Tacoma, Washington*

BELOW RIGHT: 347. *Mixed Media Necklace, 1988. Robert W. Ebendorf. Seashells, bone, gold foil, blue cut glass, beach pebbles, slate, old photographs, postage stamps, ColorCore, Japanese handmade paper, niobium. Average bead diameter, 5 cm. Collection Boston Museum of Fine Arts*

OPPOSITE TOP: 348. *A group of the wound and dyed paper beads created by the Arte Papel beadmakers. 2007*

OPPOSITE BOTTOM: 349. *The Arte Papel beadmakers—from top, clockwise: Carolina Morga Copar, Evelina Marquez Morga, Maribel Chavez Gonzalez, Heidy Enriques Lara, Lucia Ruiz Torres, and Kiff Slemmons—sit at a bead- and jewelry-laden table in October 2007 to admire the "feast" they have prepared for an upcoming exhibition in Oaxaca.*

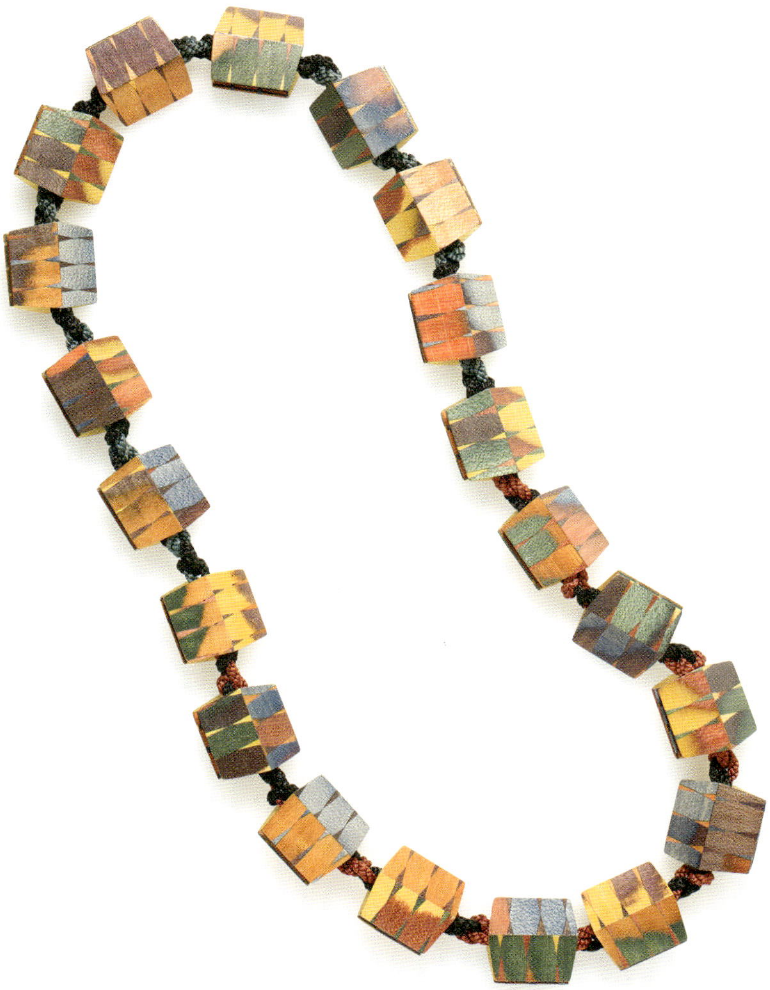

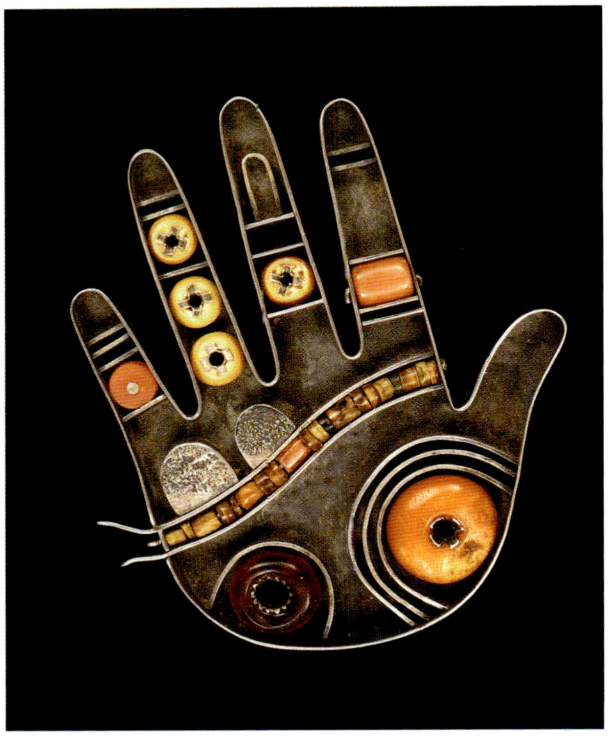

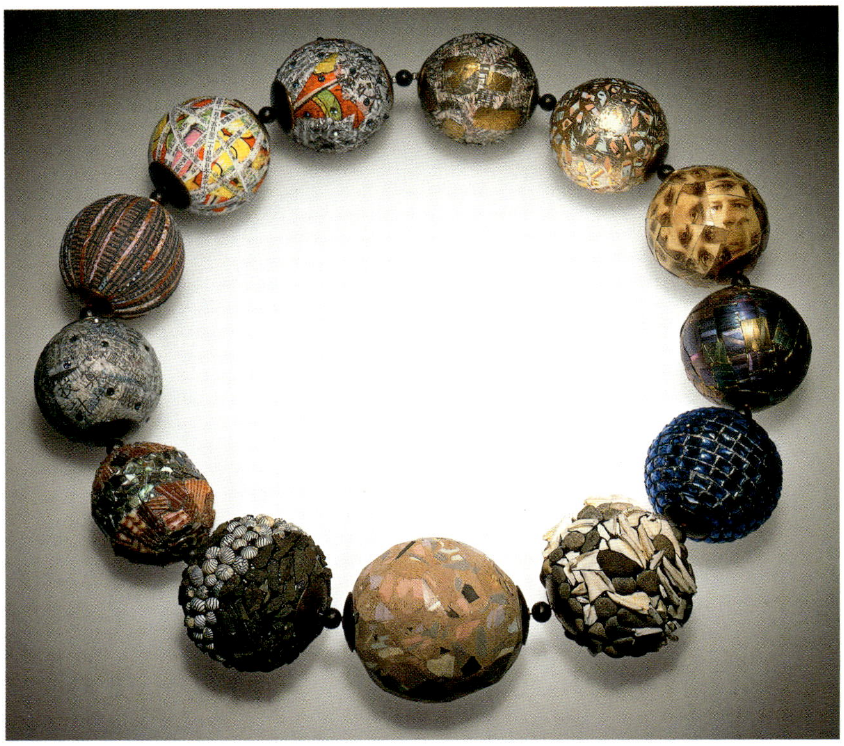

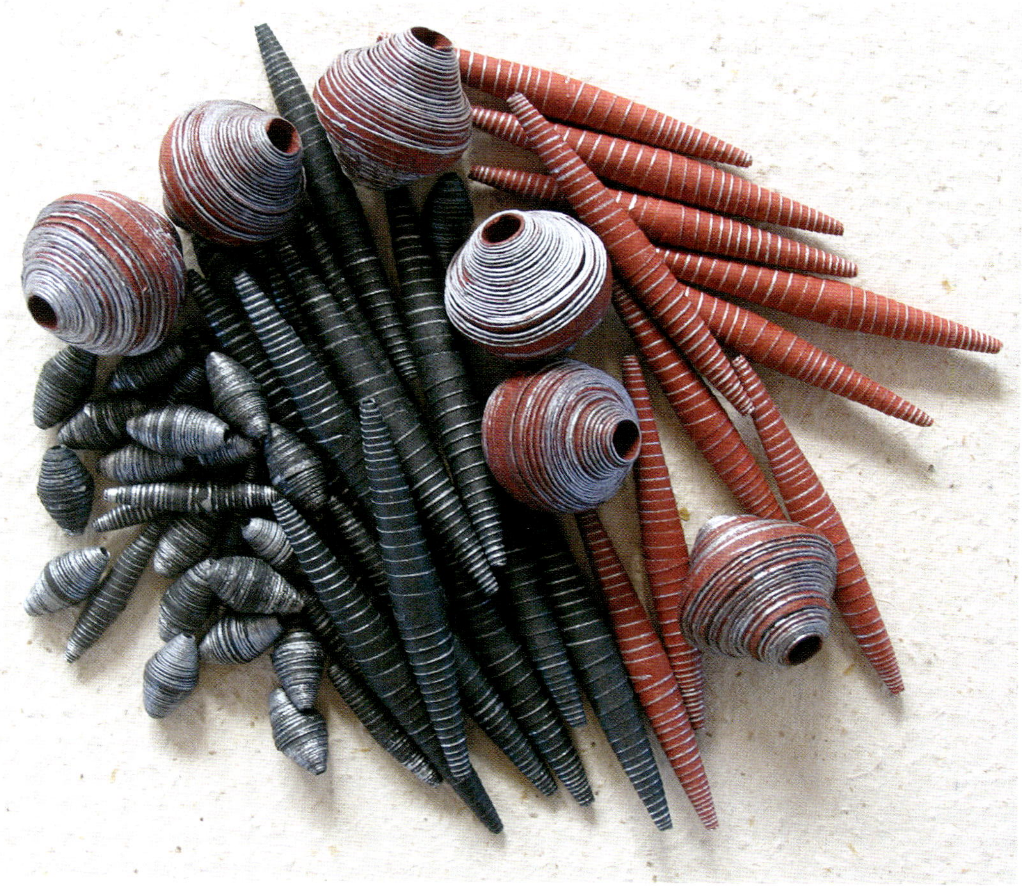

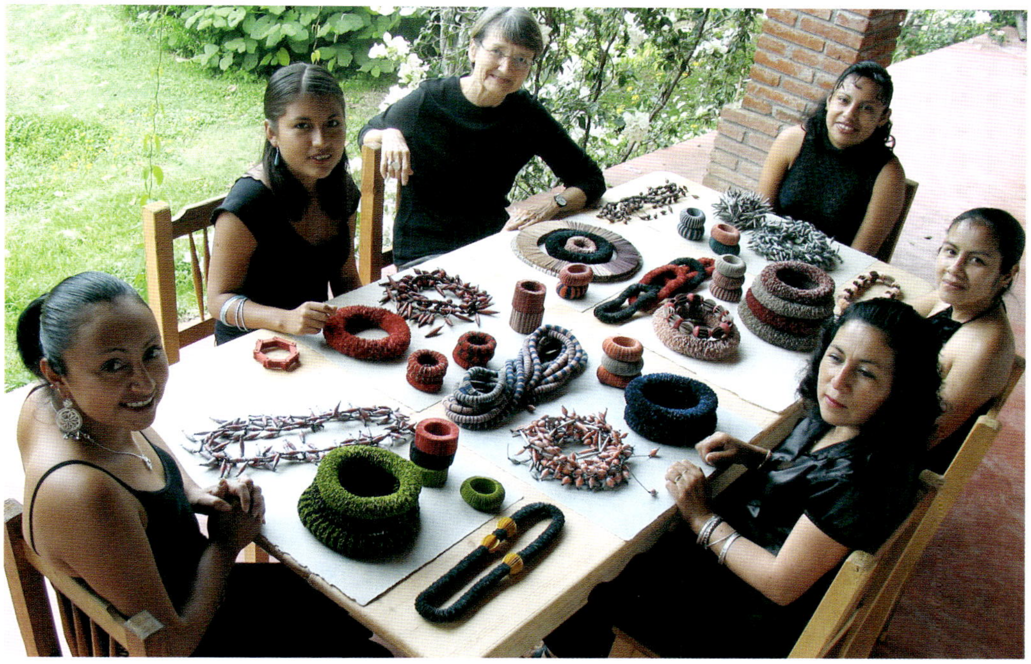

The Beads of Arte Papel Oaxaca

Arte Papel Oaxaca was founded in 1999 by painter and printmaker Francisco Toledo, to revive types of paper made from natural fibers in pre-Columbian times. Working out of a small, refurbished factory in the mountain village of San Augustin Etla, in south-central Mexico, the technology used is contemporary. The fibers, however, are obtained from seedpods, shrubs, and cacti growing in the region, such as majahua, chichicatzli, and pochote. Coloring dyes are derived from peppers, cochineal, indigo, and other local vegetable and mineral sources.

In February 2000, American jeweler Kiff Slemmons was invited to be an artist in residence at the atelier. Over the next eight years, Kiff worked with local artisans to develop designs for beads that could be produced by folding, cutting, hollow-punching, and rolling the paper, "a seemingly fragile but surprisingly strong material" says Kiff. The beads, which are strung into necklaces and bracelets, are now sold in Mexico and the United States. All proceeds from the sales support the workshop and its staff.[11]

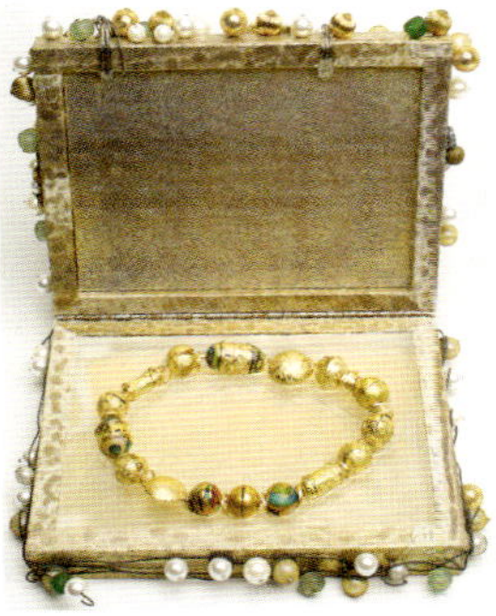

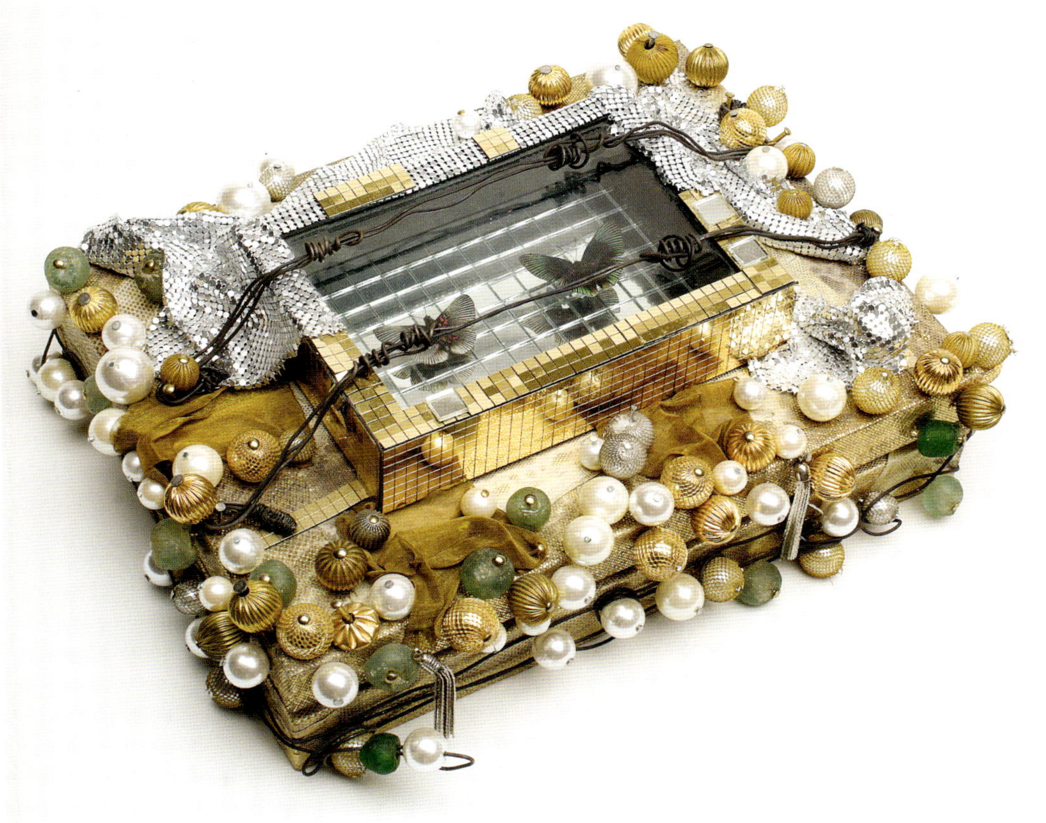

350. Psyche's Beads. William Harper. 2003–2004. Within this jewelry cask or box (one of a series he has created over the years), Bill Harper juxtaposes a range of "noble" materials—beads of gold, precious and semiprecious stones, pearls, and the jewels of nature (butterflies)—with the fragmented pieces of everyday life: mirror, mesh, acrylic. He believes that these combinations inspire new perceptions about the qualities of materials, a philosophy shared by Art Nouveau jewelers. Harper's work also incorporates a rich variety of amuletic symbols, a result of his profound interest in tribal and ethnic art.[111]

The box, rich in texture and meaning, opens to reveal a secret, hidden jewel—the gold and enameled necklace (below right); box open (above); box closed (top right). Necklace of 18k and 24k gold and enameled beads. Box: wood, beads of antique glass, pearls and brass, mirror, mesh, wire, carved acrylic, butterflies, and assorted mixed media. Box: 35.8 × 30 cm. Overall necklace length: 57.8 cm; enameled and gold bead (center right): length, 4.4 cm. Collection Norma and William Roth

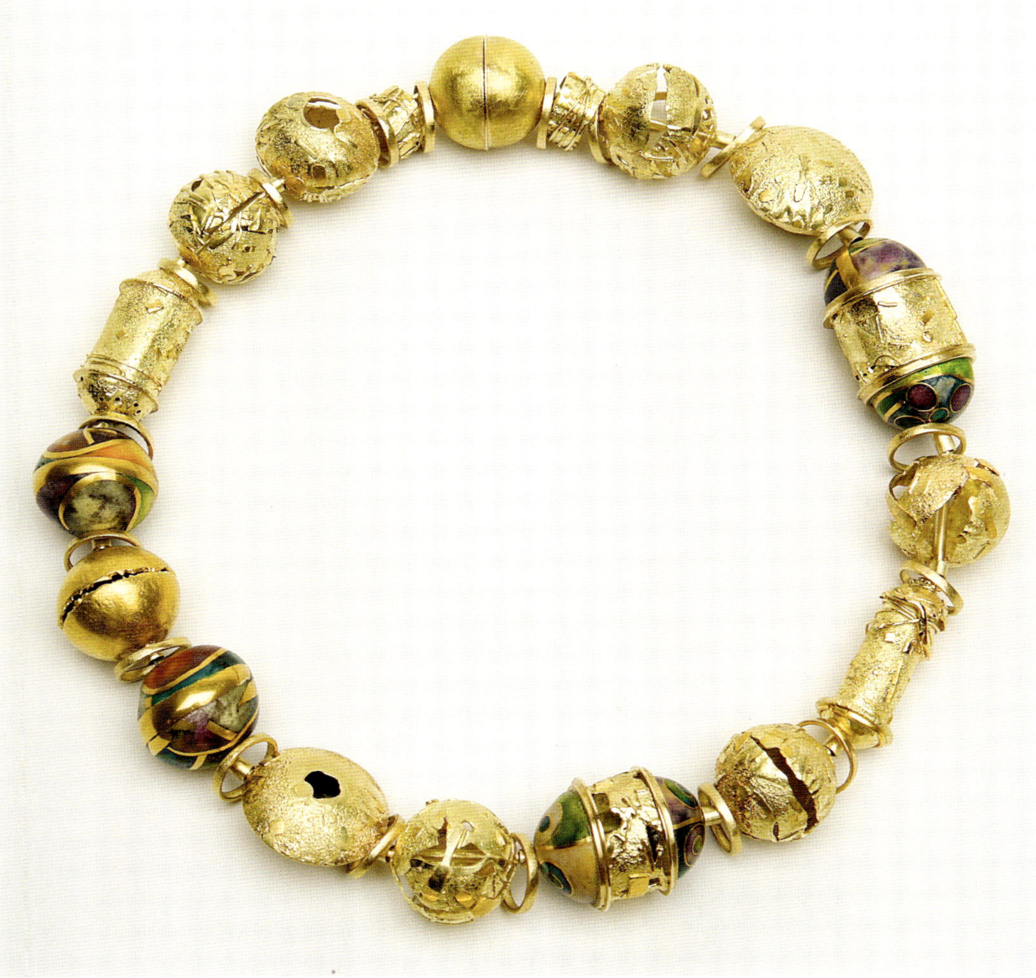

OPPOSITE: 351. *Fabergé's Ashanti Beads. 1994. William Harper. Gold cloisonné enamel on fine gold and fine silver with 24k, 22k, 18k,*

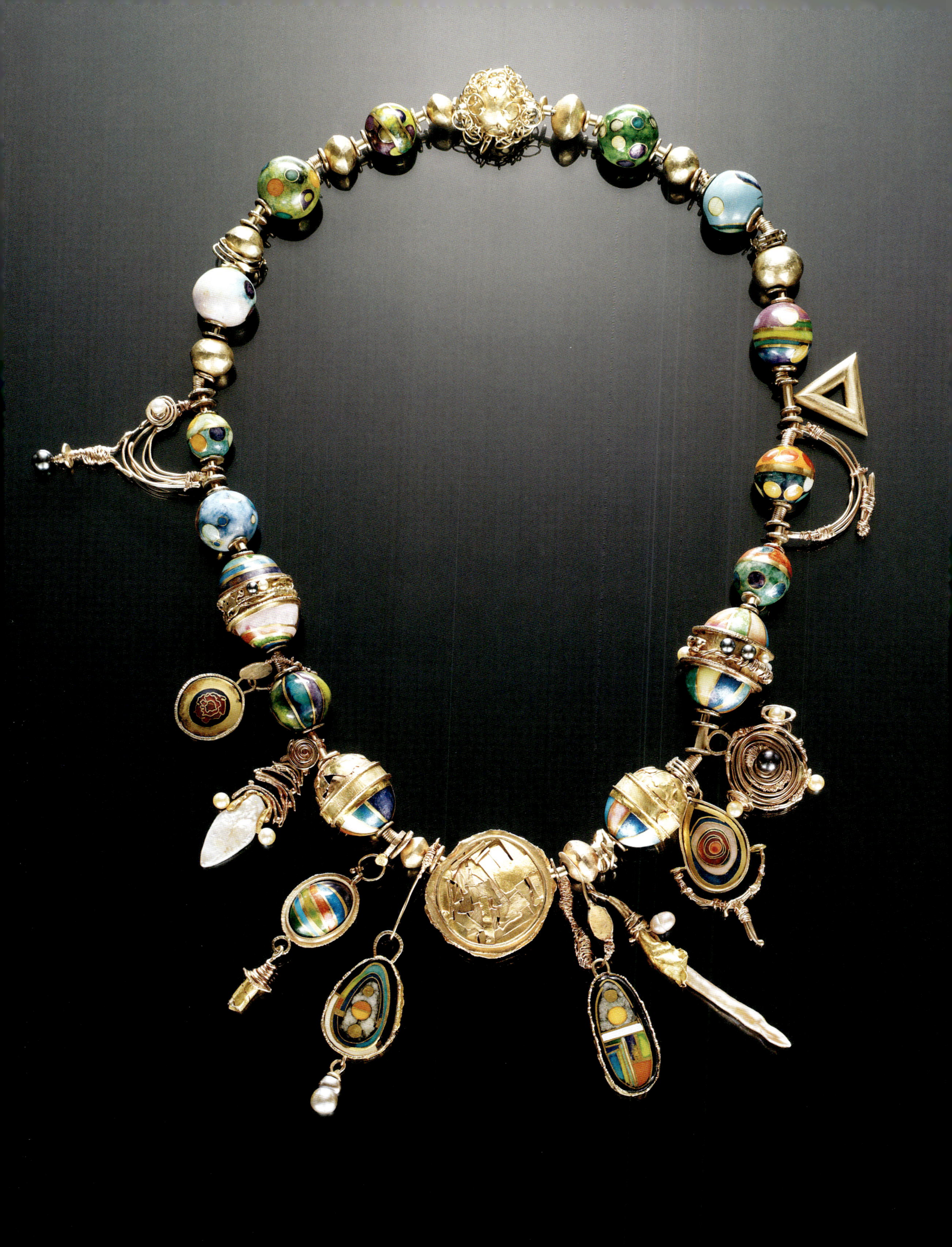

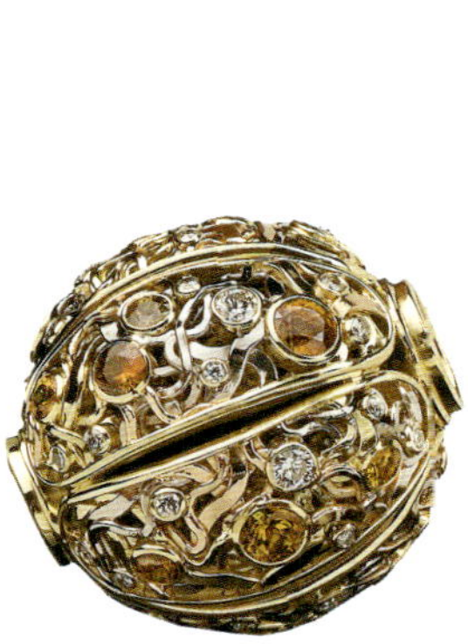

and 14k gold, pearls, tourmaline, glass. 84 cm circumference with variable units. Collection of the artist

ABOVE: 352. *Melon Bead with sphenes and diamonds, fabricated using 18k white, pink, yellow, and green gold loom woven wiggle wire weaving. 2005. 2 cm. Stuart Golder*

TOP RIGHT: 353. *Five Patchy Puffy Cubes Necklace. 1998. Stuart Golder. Fabricated using loom woven white, pink, yellow, and green 18k gold wires in various weaves and set with opals and diamonds. Center bead: 1.9 cm cubed*

MIDDLE RIGHT: 354. *Gurhan Orhan's beads combine contemporary 24k gold and ancient glass. Turkish-born Gurhan, a master goldsmith who lives and works in both New York City and Istanbul, is frequently inspired by the timeless jewelry of his Anatolian and Byzantium ancestors; as seen, for example, in these late third millennium* B.C. *quadruple disk bead designs (Timeline 273). To work with the extremely soft but lustrous 24k gold, typical of ancient goldwork, Gurhan has modified several wood and bone tool types used thousands of years ago. Quadruple disk beads: 1 cm × 1 cm. 2008*

BOTTOM RIGHT: 355. *Archeologia Mundi Vol III, Necklace. Suzan Rezac. 2002. Beads representing broken pottery shards (though fabricated with inlay metal technique rather than clay or porcelain)*

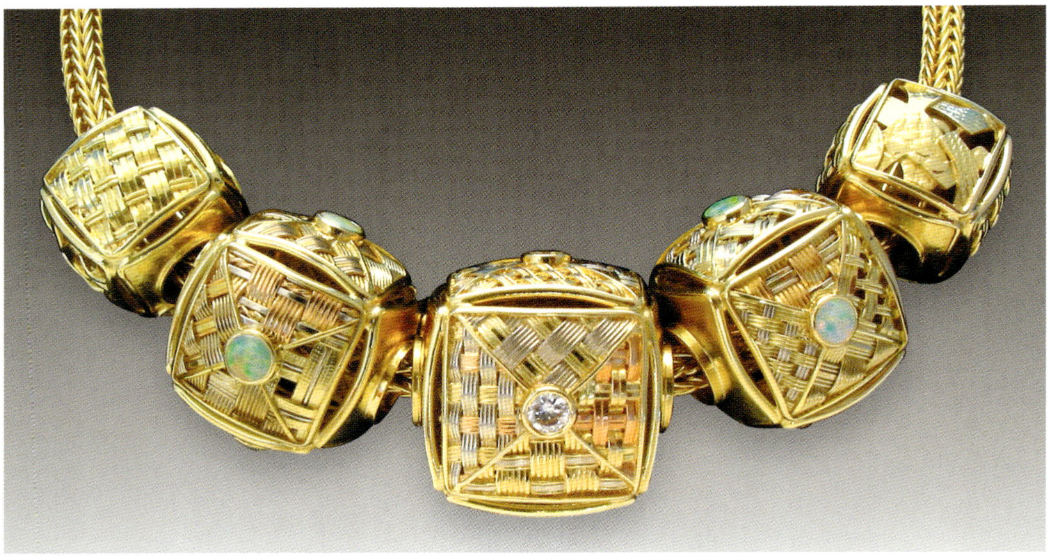

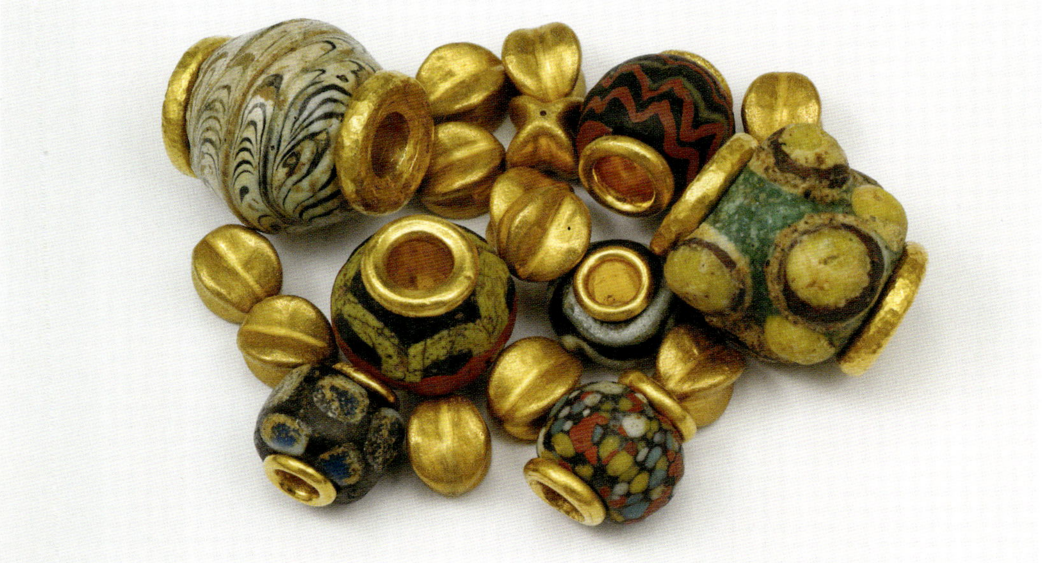

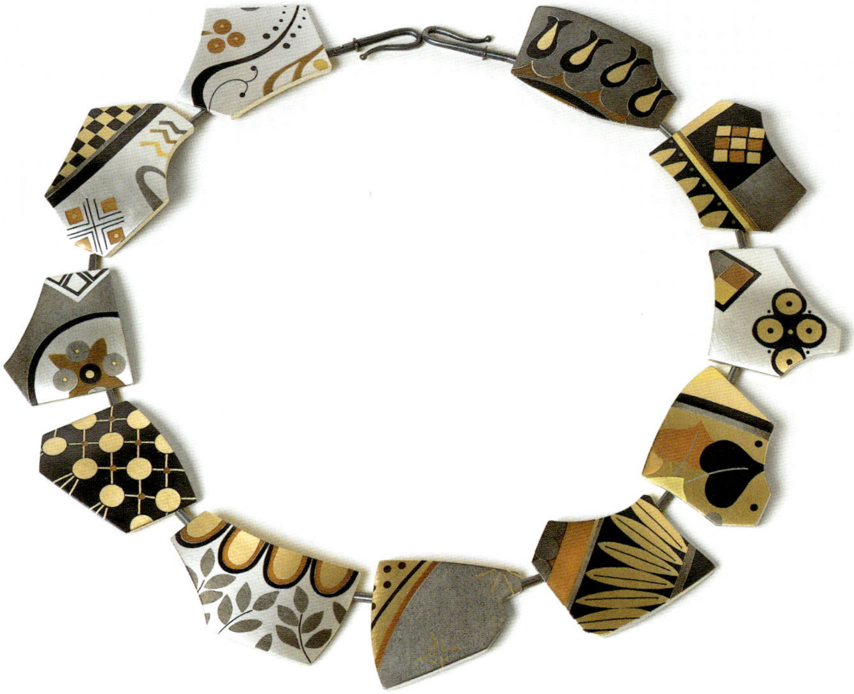

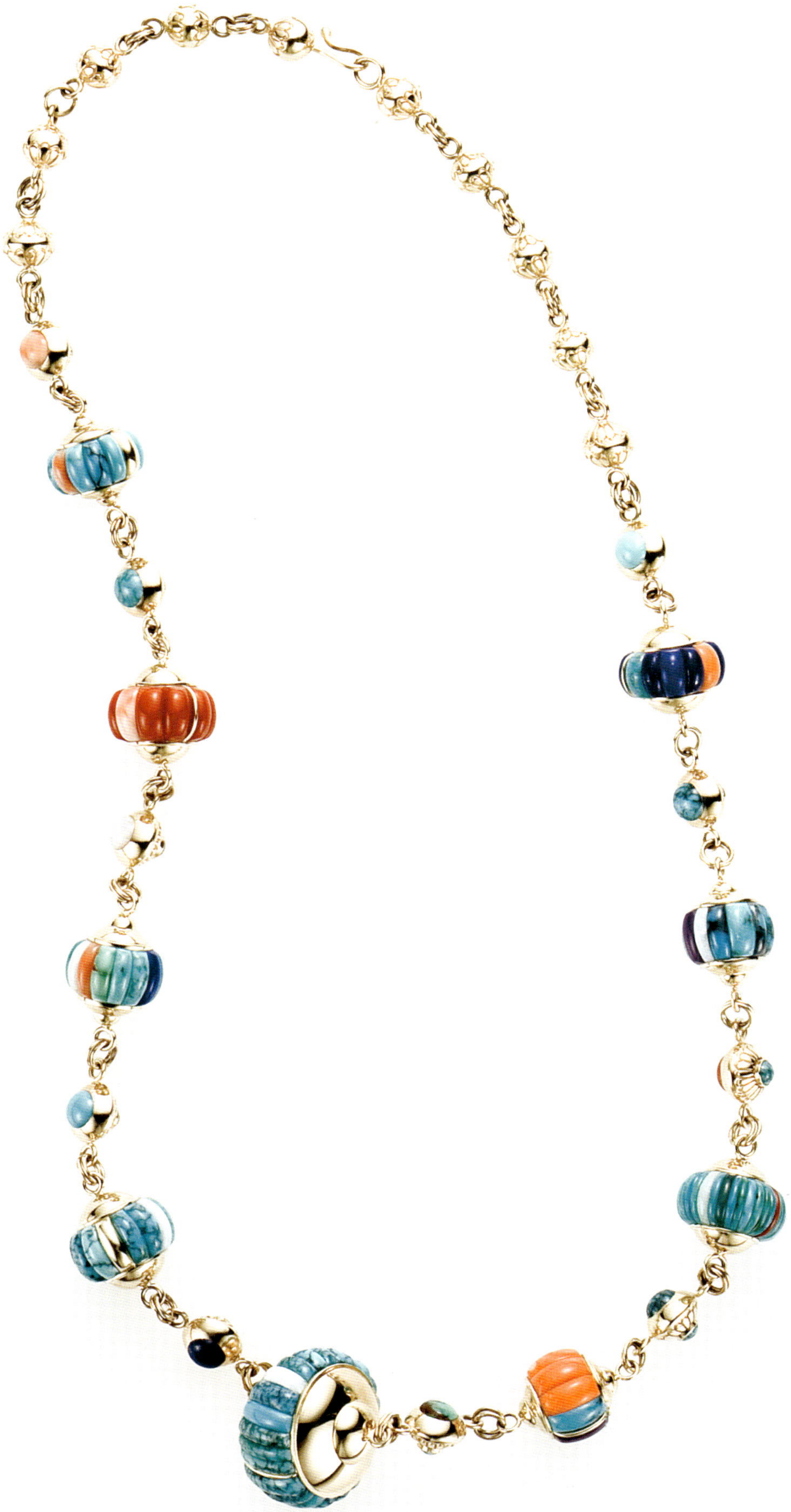

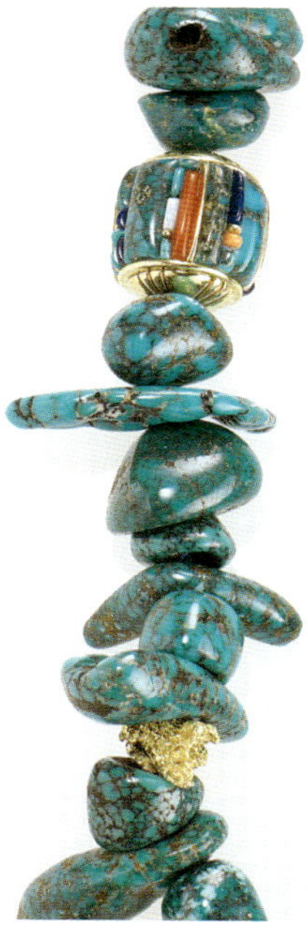

are brought together in a neckpiece that can be read as a metaphor for relating parts and the whole, destruction and construction, past and present. Each piece, in addition to being combined with others of like concept, is a completed design in itself. By creating each fragment, rather than using found objects (actual archaeological shards), the imagery shifts from sentimental to contemporary.[IV] *Silver,* shakudo, *18k gold,* shibuichi, *copper, brass, bronze. Constructed and inlaid. 50.8 × 3.17 cm. Private collection*

LEFT: 356. *Beads of 14k gold inlaid with coral, lapis lazuli, opal, and Lone Mountain, Bisbee, Blue Gem, Morenci, and Royston turquoise were commissioned from Navajo master goldsmith Lee Yazzie by collector Michael Bernstein as a surprise gift for his wife, Helen Geer. 2007–2008. Center bead diameter, 2.54 cm*

ABOVE: 357. *Detail of a "fossil" Lone Mountain turquoise and inlaid bead necklace. 14k gold, coral, lapis, opal. 2003. Raymond C. Yazzie. Private collection*

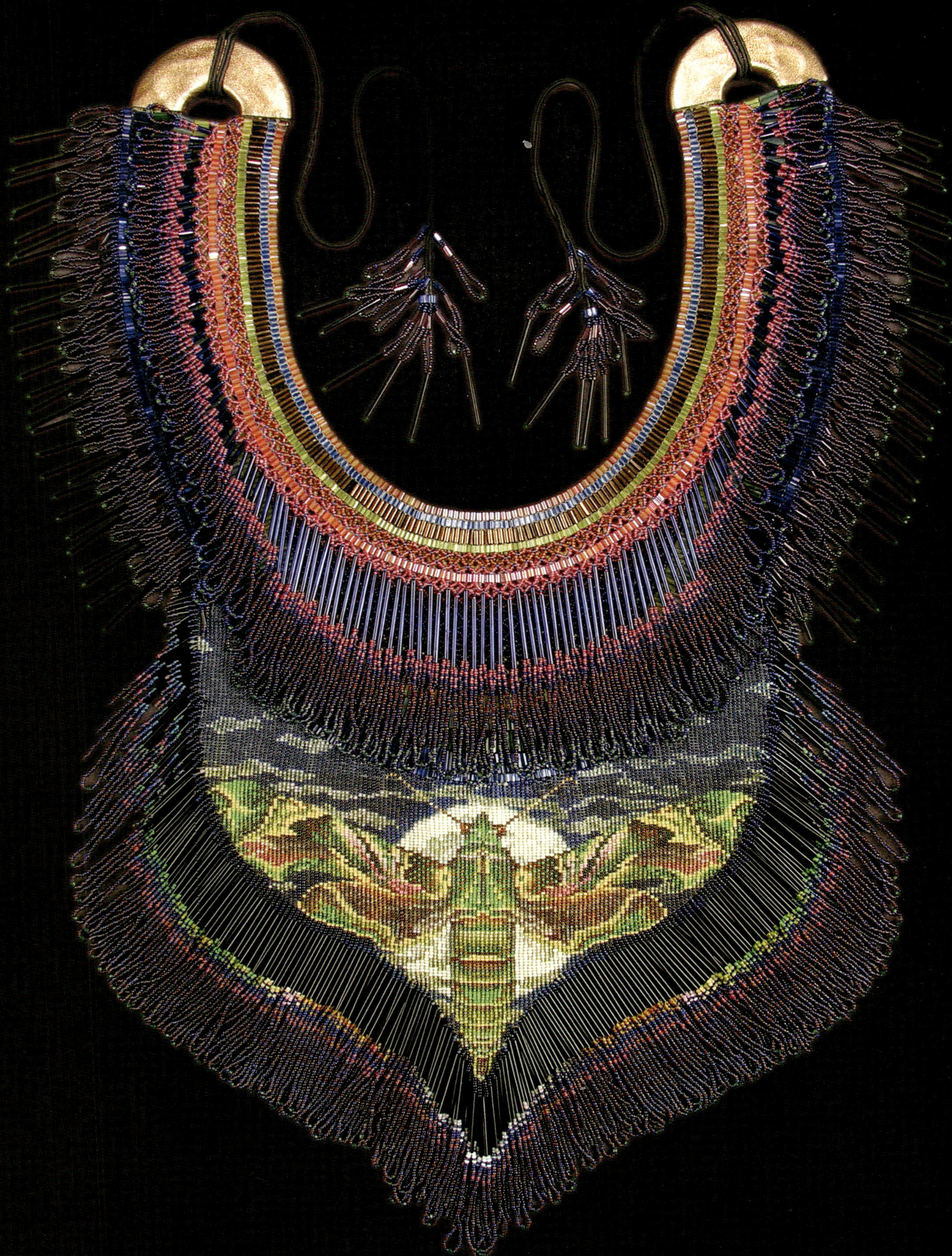

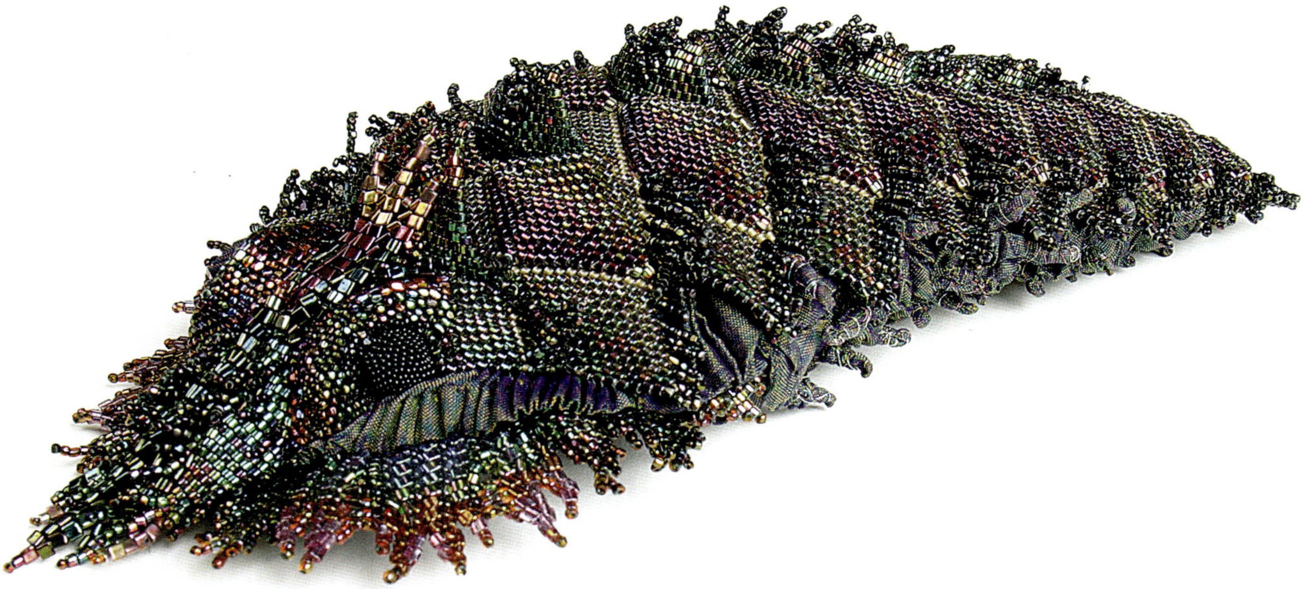

Perhaps the most significant change in the jewelry industry after 1920 was the development of mass-produced costume or fashion jewelry. To meet the demands of the rapidly growing middle-class clientele, who requested low- to medium-priced jewelry (of which beads were a major component), both old and new materials and techniques were employed. Although shoddy and unimaginative work was produced, it was balanced by a wide range of well-made, exciting new designs. Whereas the jewelry industry had traditionally been extremely conservative (precious metals and stones were too expensive an acquisition for much experimentation), costume-jewelry makers could afford to take risks and use bold shapes and colors. Glass beads of great originality were made in Jablonec, in the Czech Republic, for example. While some Czech glass beads imitated precious stones, including ruby, carnelian, and turquoise, many were highly artistic creations in their own right. In Japan, during the first quarter of the twentieth century, Kokichi Mikimoto (1858–1954) discovered methods for mass-producing cultured pearls that revolutionized the pearl industry. As a result, larger numbers of less wealthy women could afford to wear pearl jewelry, a luxury formerly reserved for the world's elite.

New materials—particularly plastic—were light in weight, inexpensive, and could be worked by relatively unskilled labor into a variety of shapes and designs. The thermoset plastics (Bakelite and phenolic resins) were used for making beads that imitated ivory, jet, and amber. Hard plastics, they could be cast and then cut and carved like gems. As each bead was made separately, it was possible to give each an individual design.[3] Beads of German silver (an alloy of copper, nickel, and zinc) became quite popular and were frequently used in the Indian jewelry of the American Southwest. It was, however, when fashion designers (such as Coco Chanel) draped necklaces of glass beads and artificial pearls around haute couture outfits that costume jewelry became truly acceptable.

OPPOSITE: 358. Daphnis nerii *(Oleander Hawk Moth). A loomed beadwork necklace by Virginia Blakelock. 1985. Virginia Blakelock's remarkable beaded art—and most significantly this necklace—has inspired many contemporary beadworkers. 40.6 × 22.9 cm. Collection of the artist*[V]

ABOVE: 359. *Trilobite. 2005. Virginia Blakelock. Trilobite began as an evening bag, but ended up as a "creature," relates Blakelock. Length, 23.4 cm. Collection of the artist*[VI]

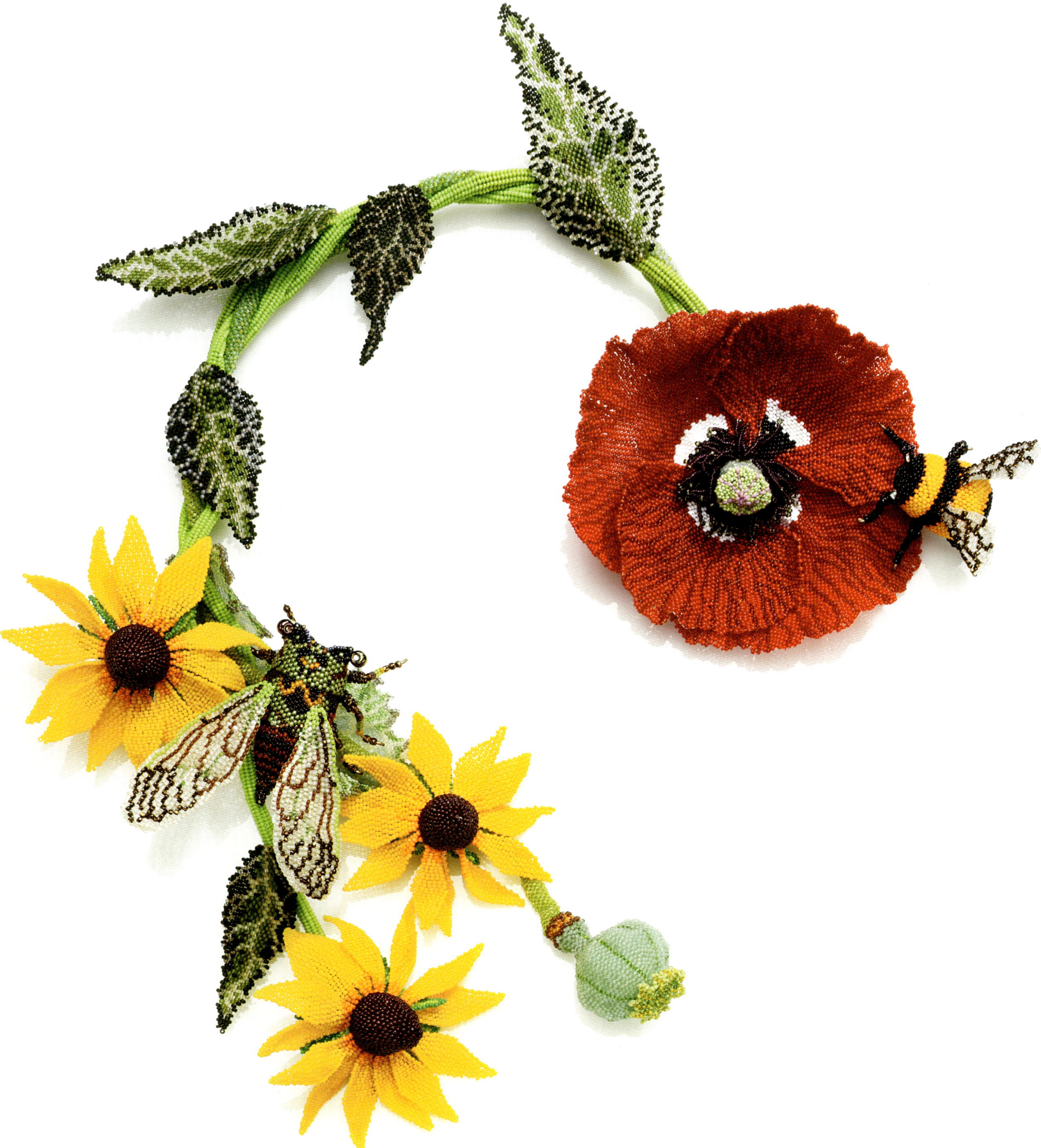

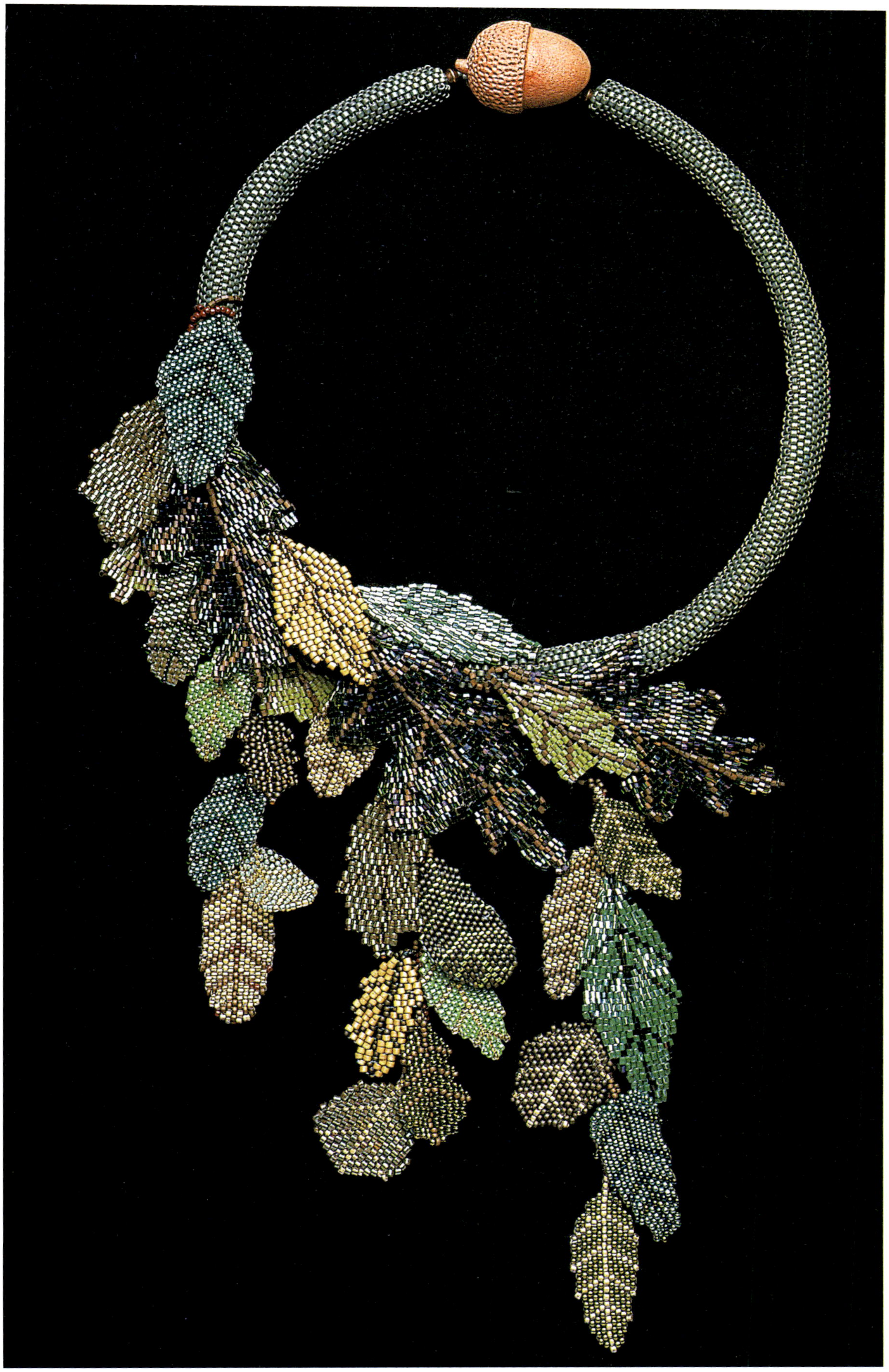

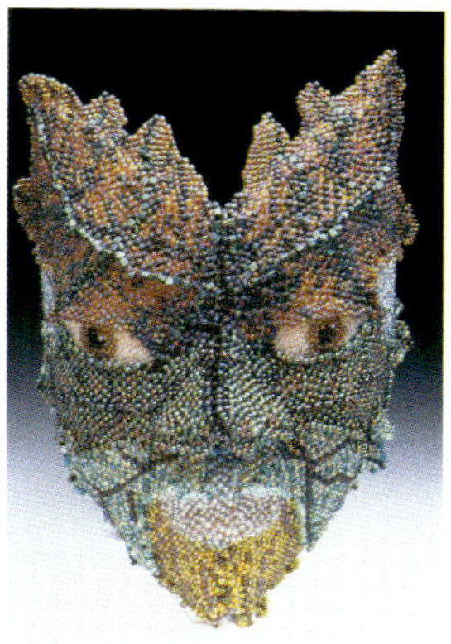

OPPOSITE: 360. *Meadow. Karen Paust, a painter and beadworker with deep interests in botany and gardening, created this beaded masterwork from the wildlife—black-eyed Susans, a poppy, cicada, and a bumble bee—found in the rural landscape surrounding her Pennsylvania home. 2008. Circumference, 48.2 cm. Poppy diameter, approximately 10 cm. Private collection*[VII]

LEFT: 361. *Summer Forest. 1999. Kathy Seely. Woven neckpiece with a carved wooden clasp in the form of an acorn. The woven leaves are attached to the front and fall down in lush tendrils. This piece is from the Four Seasons collection. The size of the flexible circular tube is approximately 40.7 cm.*

ABOVE: 362. *King of Summer mask. 1998. Kathy Seely. The image of a human face made of leaves is a very old one in European myth. This piece is a reminder that human beings are a part of nature. Carved wood covered in beadwork and sewn embellishment. 20.5 × 12.7 cm. Collection of the artist*

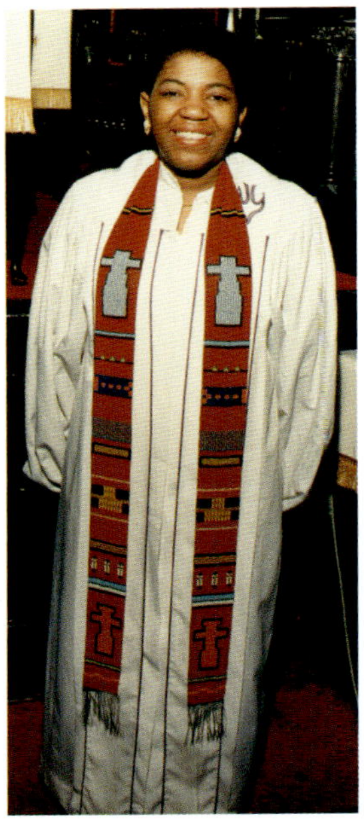

ABOVE: 363. *Reverend Dr. Barbara Austin Lucus wears a loom-beaded shawl made in 1994 by Larry Brown. The shawl, with patterns derived from West African beadwork, was commissioned for Reverend Lucas by members of the Bridge Street A.M.E. Church in Brooklyn, New York, where she ministered as an Assistant Pastor from 1986 to 1996*

RIGHT: 364. *Floral Vest, created between 2004 and 2007 by Marcus Amerman, who works with size 13 glass seed or microbeads, interspersing faceted beads for sparkle. 53 × 66 cm. Collection of the artist*

OPPOSITE: 365. *Hopi Snake Priest wall hanging of seedbeads. 1996. Marcus Amerman. 24.5 × 24.5 cm. Private collection*

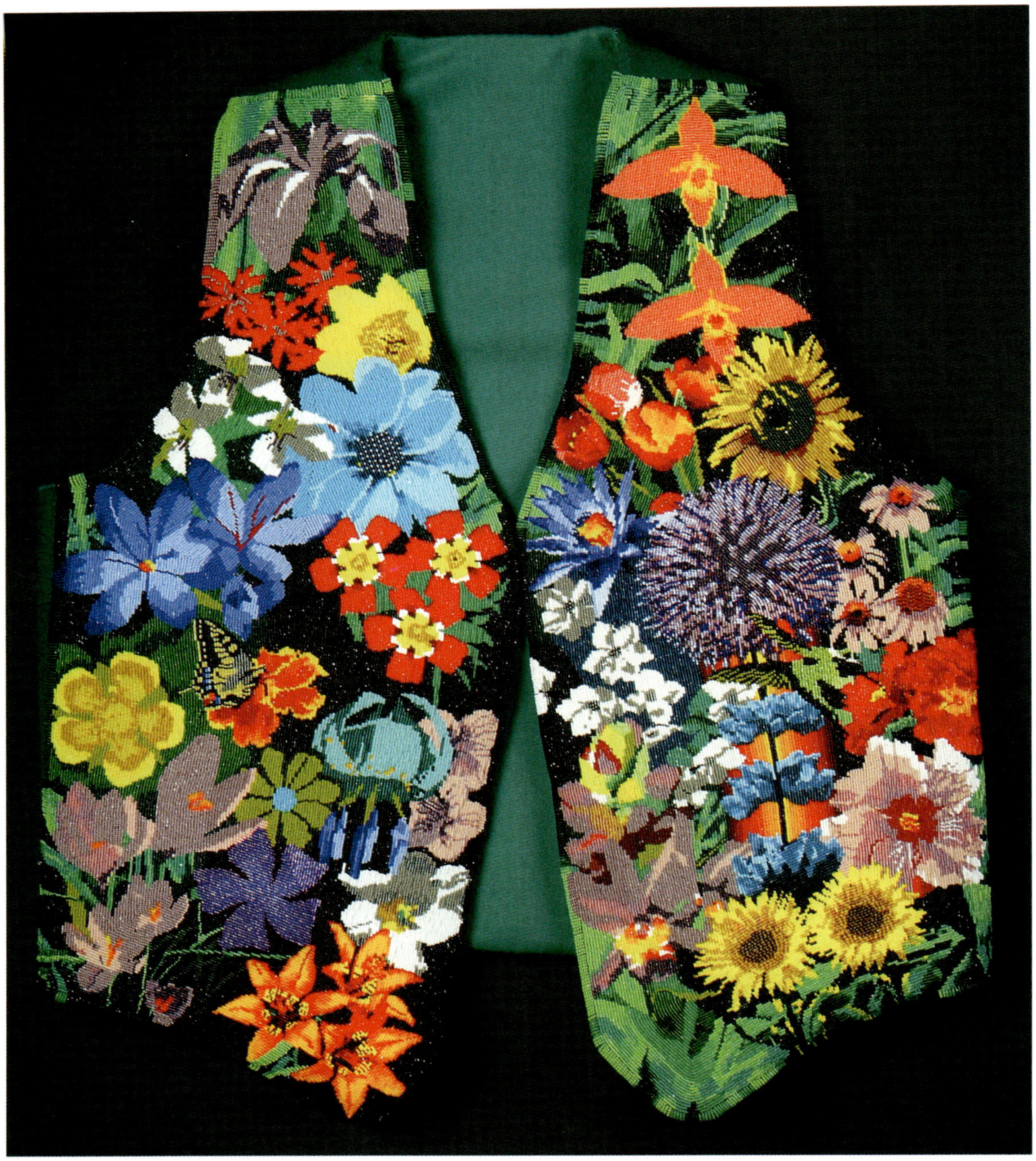

Converging Cultural Traditions

Marcus Amerman, of Choctaw and Hopi heritage, is a painter, sculptor, performance artist, and exceptionally gifted bead artist. His pictorial-style beadwork is a mixture of traditional Native North American subject matter and technique with contemporary elements, as seen in both the floral vest and the Hopi Snake Priest panel (plates 364–5). He has been doing beadwork since a young boy, "as a response to growing up in a very creative family environment…almost everyone in my family did beadwork for our own personal use…and I quite naturally adopted and adapted this family tradition."[VIII]

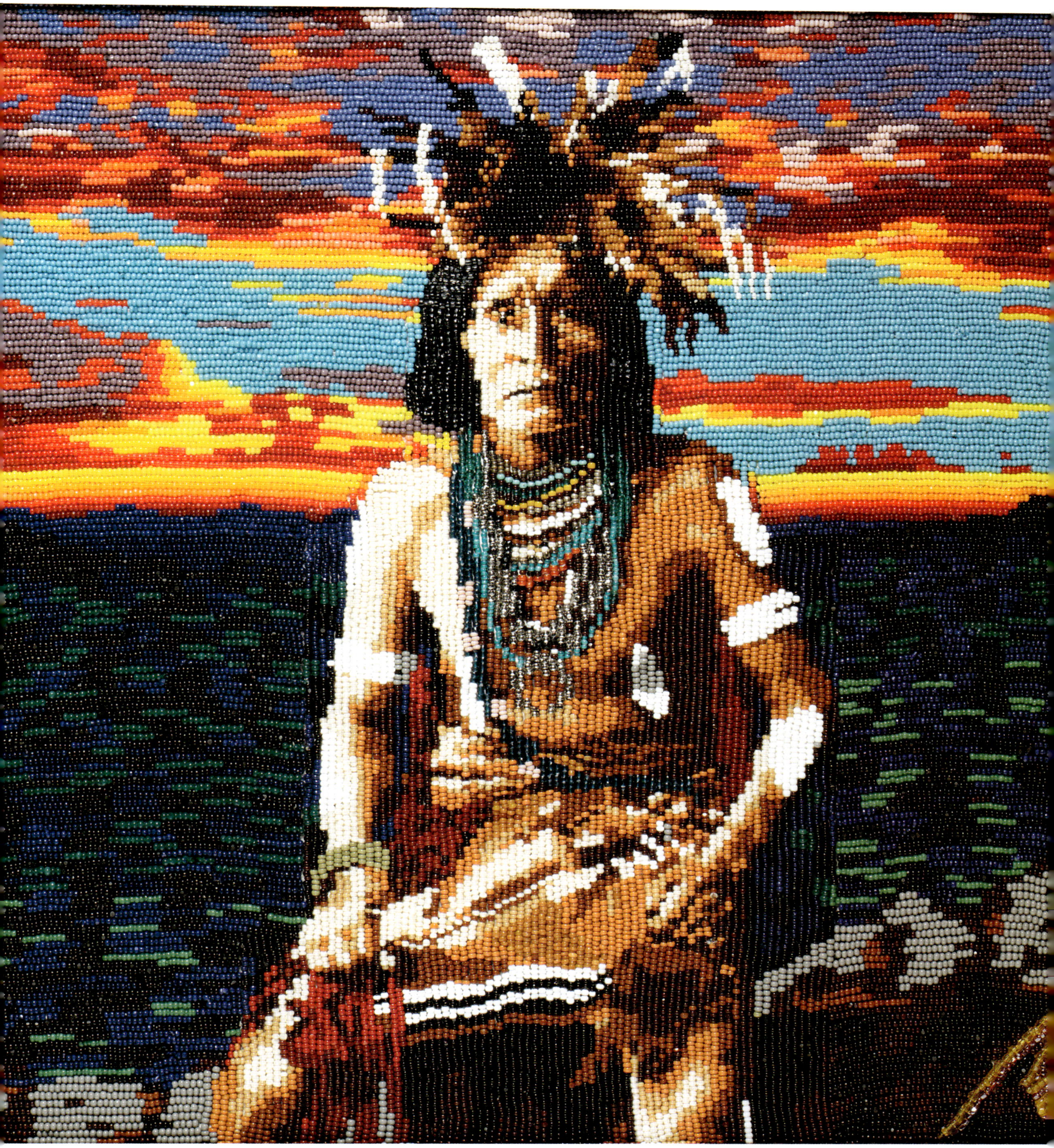

366. *"Virgin of Guadeloupe Redux" necklace. 2008. Joyce Scott. This piece, says the artist, "is about how choosing of, or being chosen by, a saint brings hope to the chosen. It's about putting the weight on the shoulders of those spirits who are dedicated to your wellbeing through faith. The word redux speaks to my redoing this necklace until it was right!"[XI] Length, 33 cm; width, 21.6 cm. Wire and glass beads.*

Joyce Scott is a prime mover behind the revolution in contemporary beadwork that took place in the 1990s. Friend and fellow beadworker Valerie Hector relates: "She went around the country teaching her way of making armatureless human figures in peyote stitch, and giving her pieces liberating and provocative names, and soon everyone was following suit."[XII]

OPPOSITE TOP: 367. *"Hanging on By a Thread." 1998. David K. Chatt. The concept of this piece—a man losing his marbles from the top of the bag (as if it were the top of his head)—displays David's wit and describes "the questionable sanity of someone working in an art form which requires so much time and patience" but is not financially renumerative.[XIII] Glass seedbeads, thread, glass marbles. 20.3 × 20.3 × 23 cm*

OPPOSITE BELOW, LEFT AND RIGHT: 368. *"Private Eye" (open and closed views), 1999. David K. Chatt. Glass seedbeads, thread, glass eye. 10.8 × 13.3 × 5 cm*

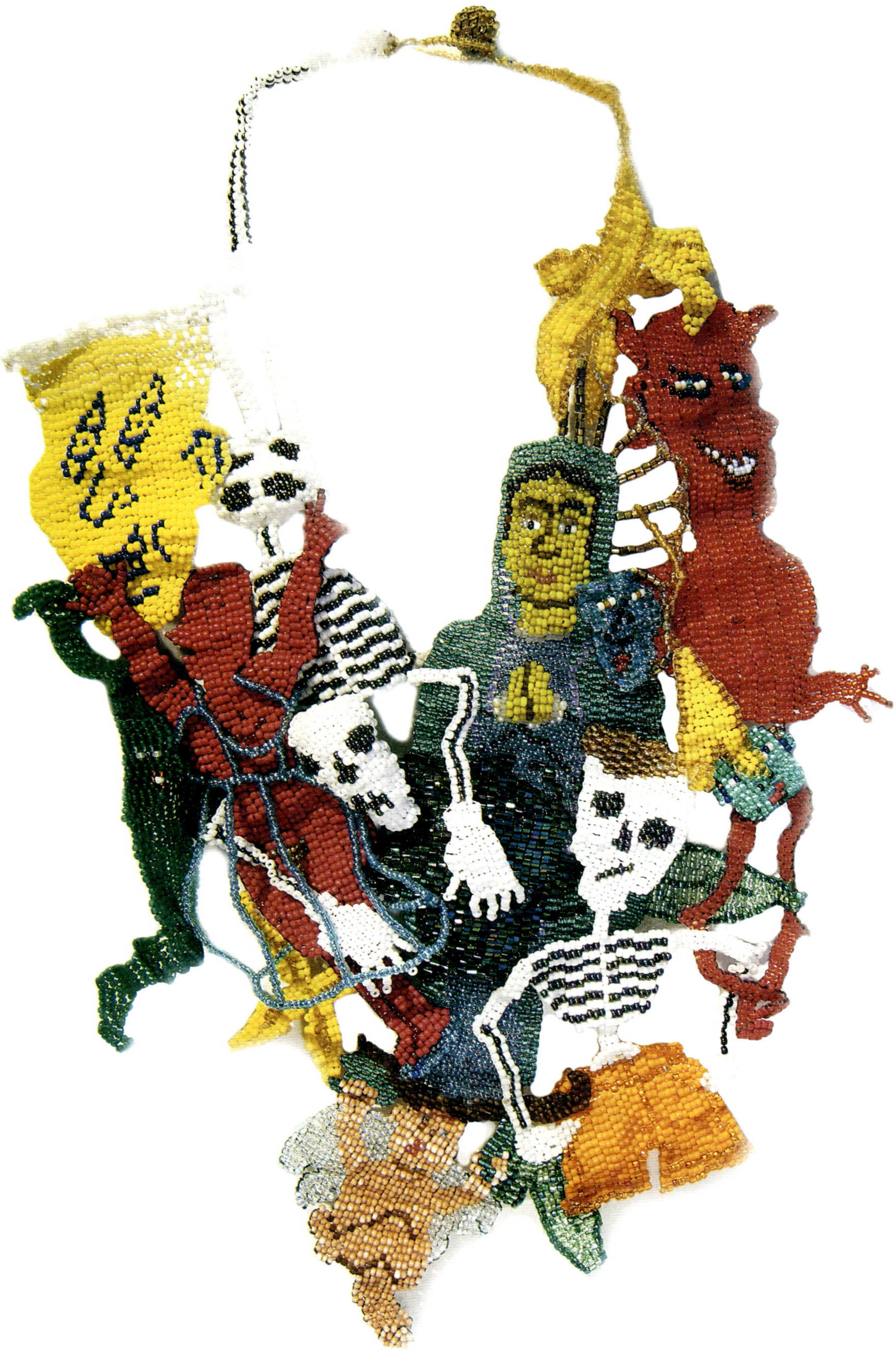

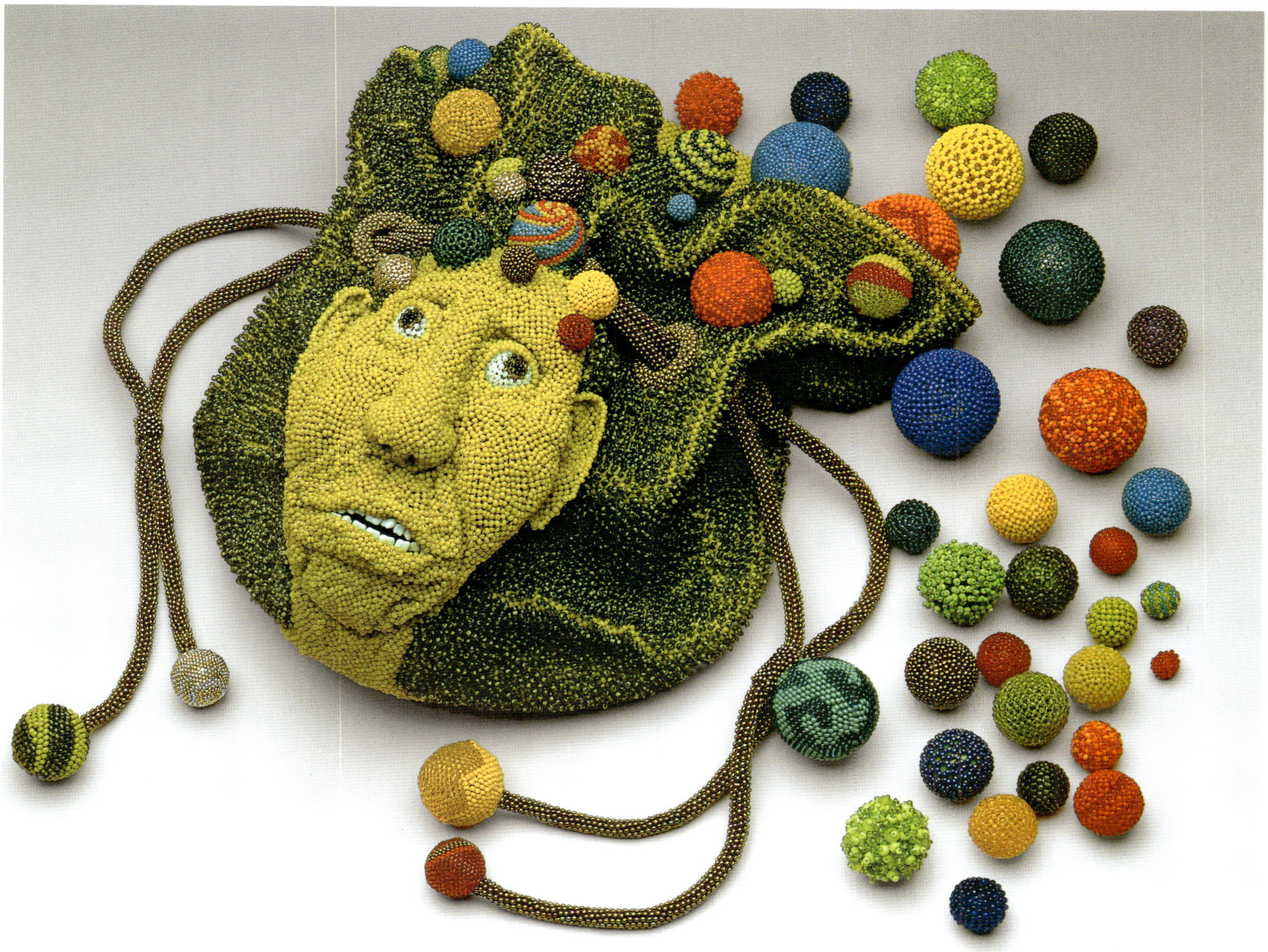

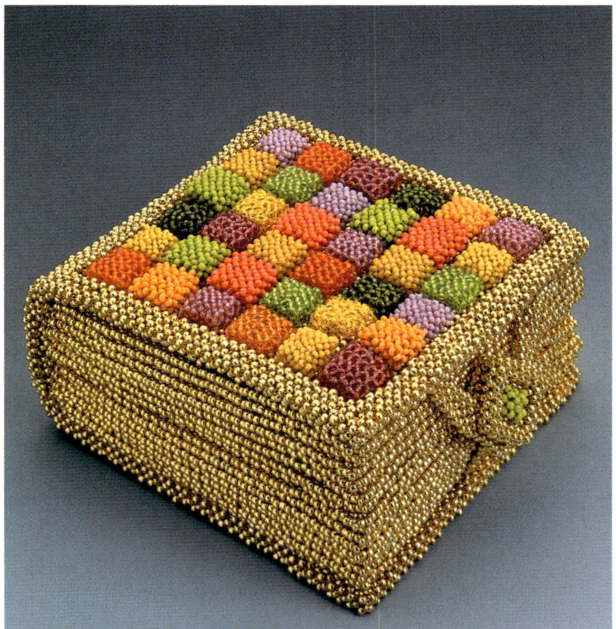

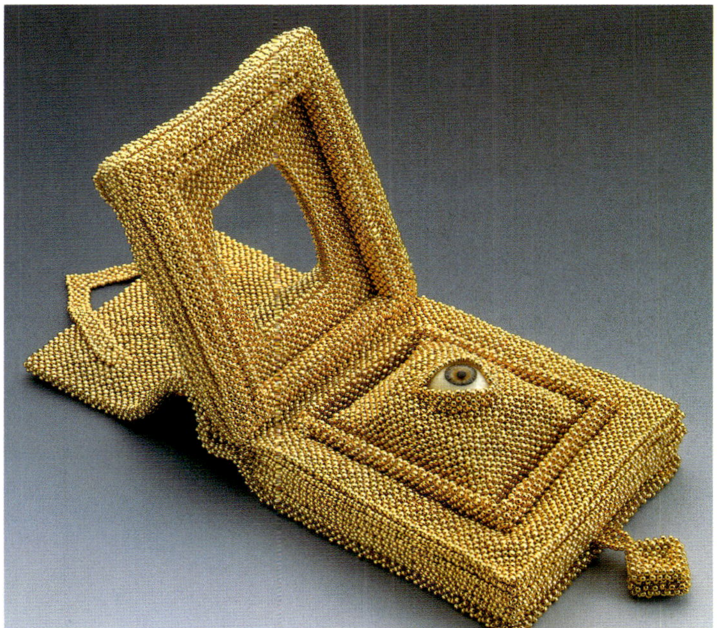

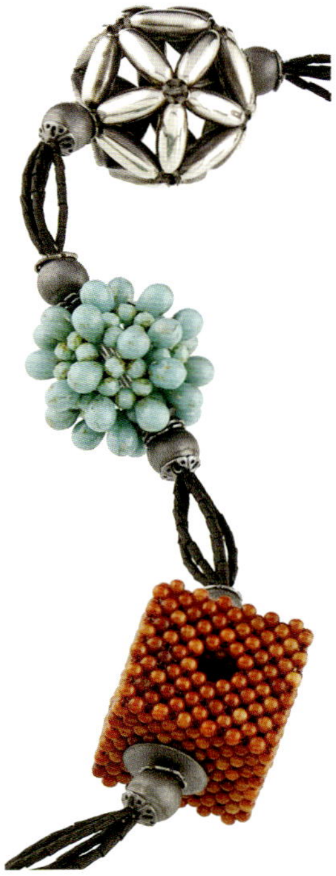

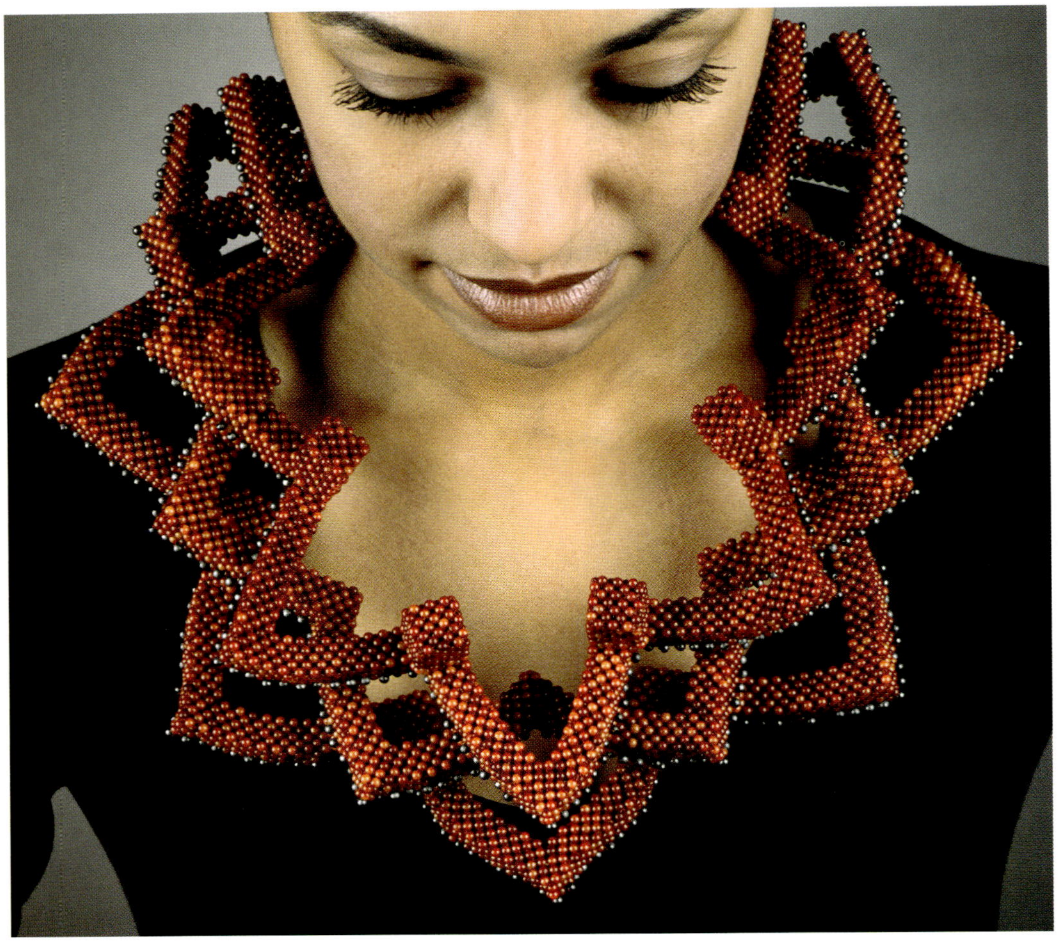

ABOVE: 369. *Three beads from the Elements Necklace. 2008. All of the bead-netted structures in this remarkable necklace are inspired by the "sumptuous universe of Chinese beaded polyedra," says its creator, Valerie Hector. Since the structures are so highly symmetrical, they have been strung asymmetrically for balance. For detailed bead descriptions see note IX. Red cube bead, c. 3.1 × 3.1 cm. Glass, sterling silver, synthetic resin. Collection of the artist*

RIGHT: 370. *Red Lotus Neckpiece. 2003. Valerie Hector. The influences for this elegant architectural neckpiece came from a variety of sources: the work of Floral Book (plates 371–72), David K. Chatt (plates 367–8), Chinese lotus motifs, and a three-tiered Bahai temple near Hector's Chicago home. The technique is a cubic right angle weave worked in Japanese-made synthetic resin beads from the 1960s. Diameter, 31.8 × 6.7 cm high. Collection Rebecca Klemm*

In high design, the romantic and idealistic Art Nouveau jewelry, which utilized heavy glass and metals articulated with motifs from nature and stylized sinuous lines, was replaced by lighter weight materials and more abstract geometric forms. During the 1920s, the Art Deco style emerged, characterized by simple studied compositions of squares, circles, and triangles. Jewelry and beads produced during this period show the influence of Cubist painting as well as the clean and simple design standards of Germany's Bauhaus, the foremost academy of modern design and architecture in pre–World War II times. In Copenhagen, the metal jewelry and beads of designer Georg Jensen (1866–1935) in the 1920s and 1930s symbolized the pleasing, clear designs that today are described as modern.[4]

The period we designate "contemporary" began after World War II when a series of events strongly influenced the direction jewelry continues to take. Following the war, the rising affluence of the West continued to expand the large market for medium-priced jewelry. At the same time, the development of inexpensive commercial air transportation made international travel accessible to everyone. Trips to Asia, Africa, Middle and South America, and the American Southwest, exposed tourists to exotic ethnic groups and their colorful and appealing, handcrafted (frequently bead) jewelry. Furthermore, due to the speed of travel and communications, it became possible to keep up with the latest ideas. As a result, contemporary jewelry and beads rarely exhibit national characteristics, and works of highly diverse cultures show a decided kinship in the use of forms, materials, concepts, and techniques. A massive international exchange of information truly has created a world jewelry community. This is particularly evident in the glass beads produced during the past few years by American, Japanese, and Turkish artists (plates 387–432).

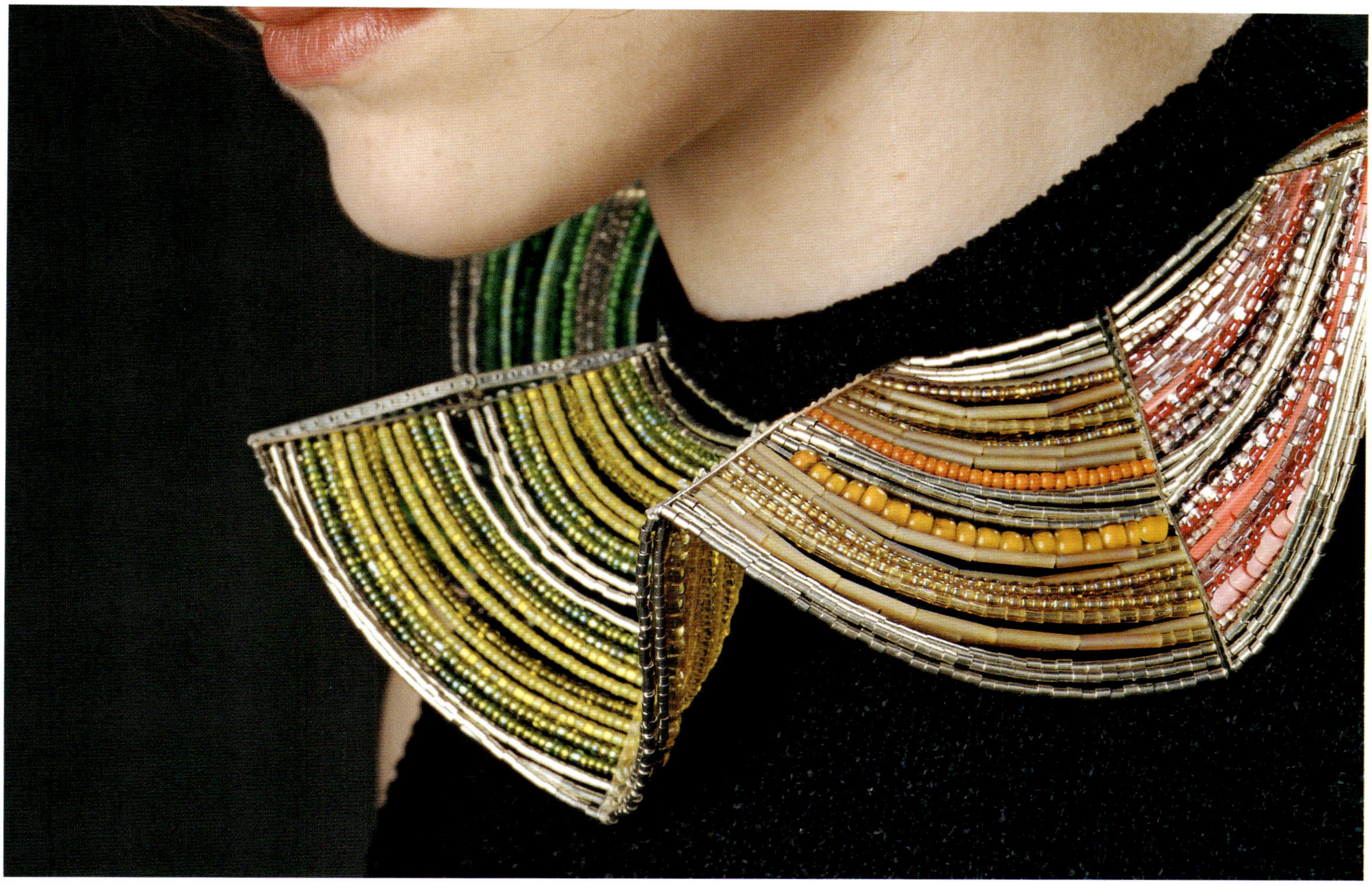

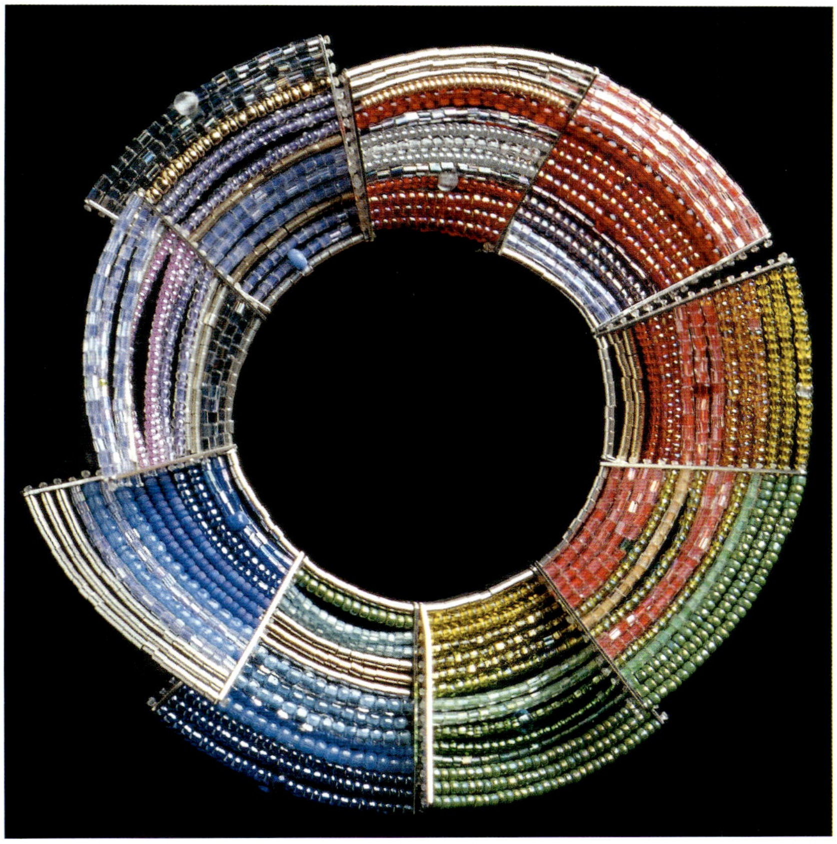

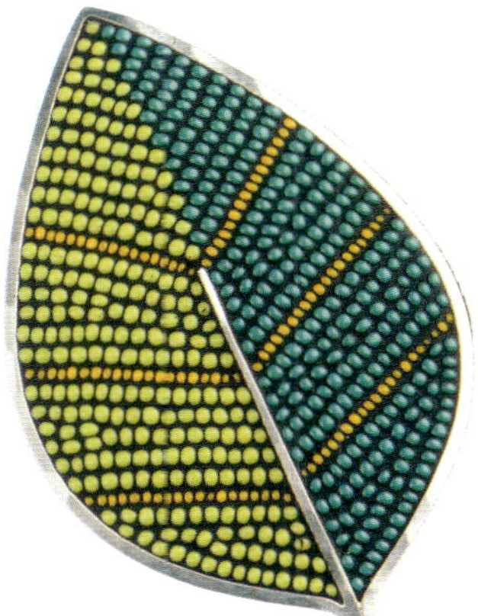

TOP: 371. *Ruffle collar. 2003. In this highly original, three-dimensional structure, artist Flora Book uses only nylon monofilament and glass beads. 26.7 cm diameter, 7.7 cm high. Collection of the artist*[X]

BOTTOM LEFT: 372. *Spectrum necklace. 2004. Flora Book. 26.7 cm diameter*

BOTTOM RIGHT: 373. *Beech Leaf Brooch. 2008. Mary Kanda. A silver frame contains an innovative mosaic inlay of glass beads bonded in a matrix of grout. Length, 7.7 cm. Private collection*

TOP: 374. *Three Rock Necklaces. Jan Yager. A Rhode Island beach provided the rocks and Jan Yager combined them with embossed and fabricated hollow silver forms. 1990. Hanging lengths of the necklaces vary from 30 to 45 cm. Drilled beach rock (center right) length, 5 cm. Collection Toby Bowlby*

BOTTOM LEFT: 375. *Shells and Pebbles. Jan Yager. Brass spent bullet casings, black river pebbles, 18k gold tire tread texture cast bead, gold-filled segmented chain. 1999. Hanging length, 45 cm. Collection of the artist*

BOTTOM RIGHT: 376. *Sidewalk Necklace. 2008. This necklace represents many of the things and plants found on city sidewalks. It describes and is evidence of human activity. The necklace is composed of two tire tread texture beads in the shape of crack cocaine vial caps, two paper clips, two Bic pen tops, two bullets, three tires, eight purslane stems, four cast pebbles, a purslane leaf, a mold used for casting pebbles, and twenty-four oxidized sterling silver beads on a segmented chain. Length, 33 cm. Collection of the artist*

OPPOSITE TOP: 377. *The American Rainbow Collar IV is made with used plastic crack vial caps found on the sidewalk around Jan Yager's inner city studio, and insulin syringes given to her by an artist living with diabetes. It is modeled after the beaded collars associated with contemporary East African Maasai people. 2005. The materials used include: 1431 plastic crack vial caps, ten used insulin syringes, two sterling silver cast crack caps, and steel music wire. Diameter, 46.5 cm. Collection of the artist*

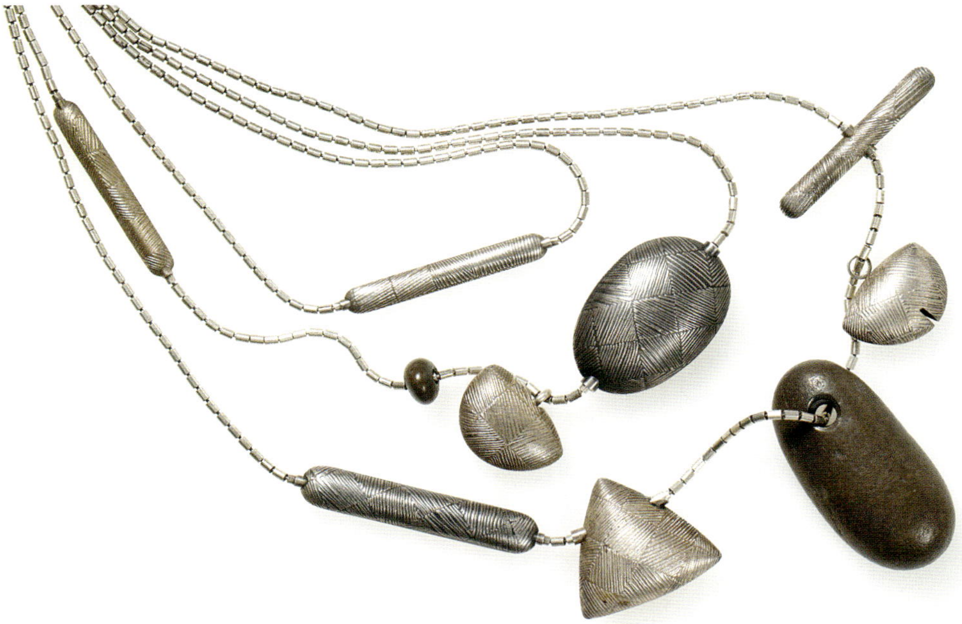

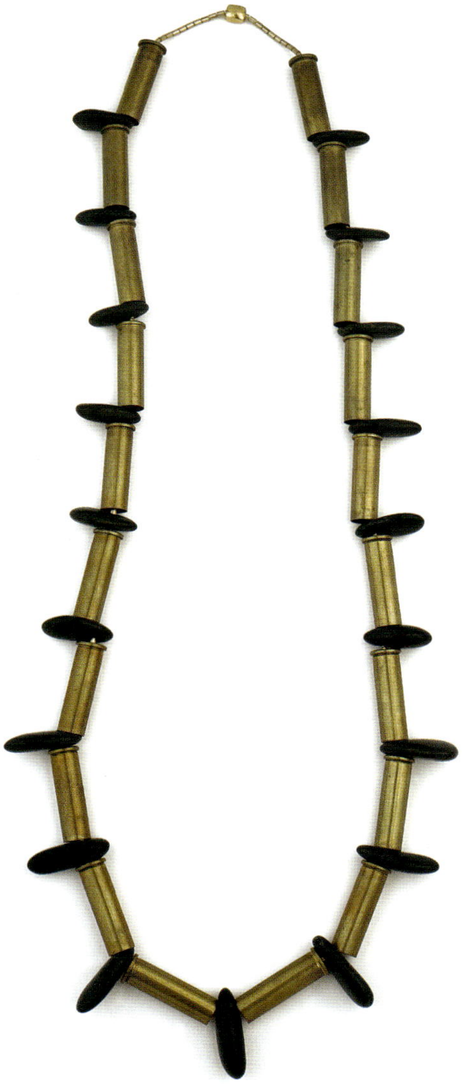

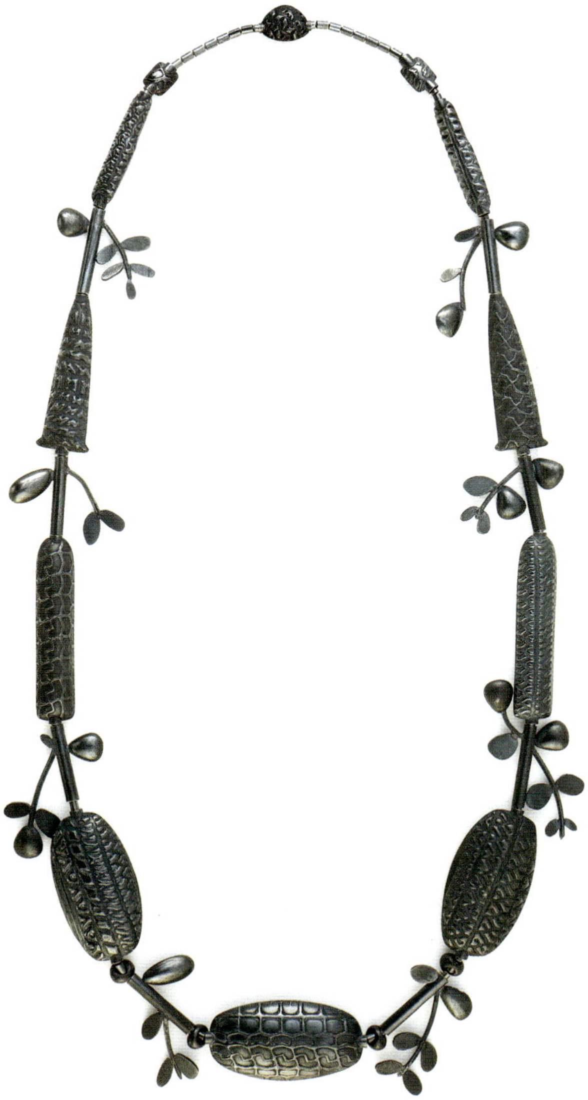

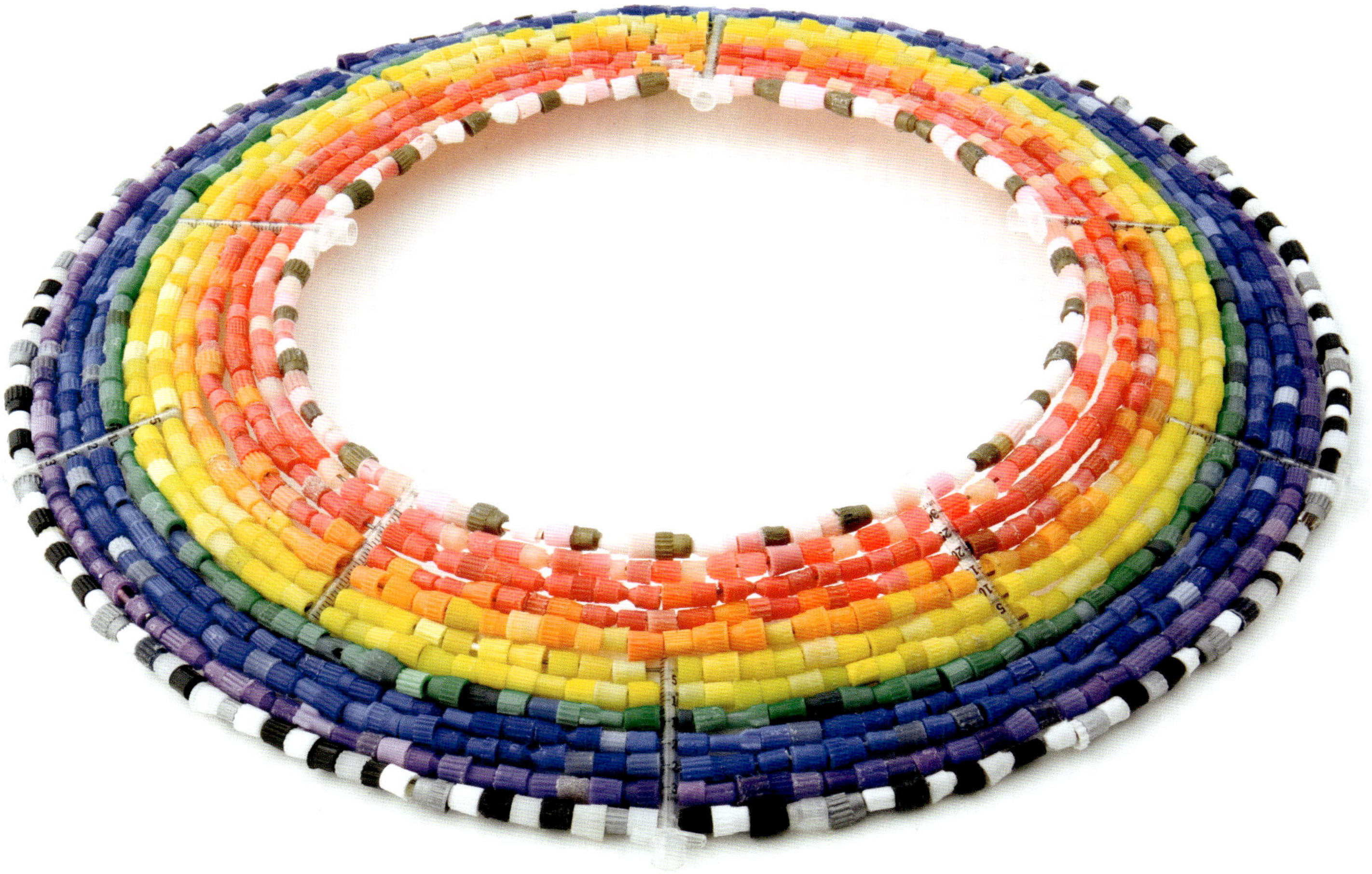

City Flora, City Flotsam

Jewelry emerging from a study of one inner city abandoned lot in Philadelphia, Pennsylvania, from 1990 to 2007 by Jan Yager. One of Jan Yager's missions is to create jewelry that reflects its time and place. The artist states: "When I moved to Rhode Island from Michigan, I beach-combed to gain an understanding of my new surroundings. Those pebbles and shells began the Rock Necklace Series (plate 374). Now I live and work in Philadelphia. When I applied the beach combing idea to my urban landscape, I found crack vials, paper clips, spent bullet casings, cigarette butts, Bic pen caps, and gathered weeds from the block around my studio. Though some of these things are repellent, they are also seductively colorful and endlessly varied in form. Most importantly, it was truthful and spoke undeniably of its place and time—this area."[IXV]

In addition to each piece standing alone with its own intrinsic beauty, the entire body of work forms a story. The necklaces represent the triad of colonialism that tied together Africa, Europe, and the Americas. Yager's botanicals (she is a master metalsmith) represent further evidence of displacement, resilence, and hope of life, as plants grow in abandoned lots and through the cracks of sidewalks. At the same time, the urban landscape leaves its mark and Yager represents this by embossing some of the pieces with tire-tread patterns that she describes as "a kind of modern geometry" (plate 376).[XV]

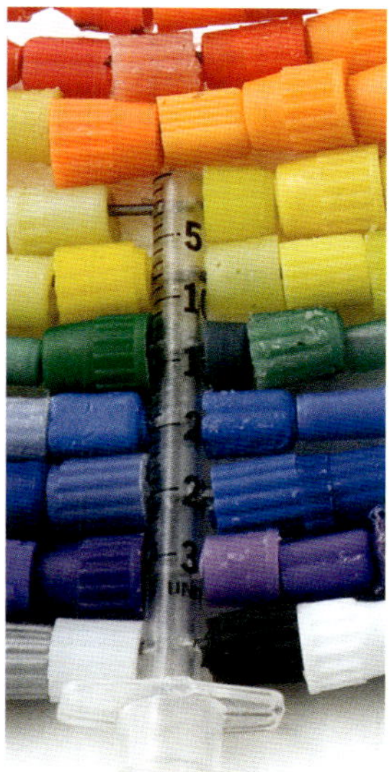

377a. *Detail of the American Rainbow Collar*

RIGHT TOP: 378. *Necklace of Women. Kathleen Dustin, 1999. These fourteen one-of-a-kind polymer clay beads use a translucent layering technique that Dustin developed in the mid-1990s, which allows a rich depth of surface. Because polymer clay is a late twentieth-century medium, it does not have a history of technique. Consequently, techniques were borrowed from other media. This translucent layering technique does make use of hand-sculpting (as in ceramics) and millefiori (as in hot glass) but is otherwise completely unique to polymer clay. The back of each bead includes handwritten quotes from proverbs in the Hebrew Bible that deal with women and/or life.[XVI] Necklace length, 51 cm; length of center bead, 9.5 cm*

RIGHT BOTTOM: 378a. *Detail of top bead of Necklace of Women*

BELOW: 379. *"Flattened Big Bead Necklace." Steven Ford/David Forlano. 2001. Steven Ford and David Forlano are noted for their sophisticated polymer clay jewelry featuring different textures and a nuance of colors. Length, 53.2 cm*

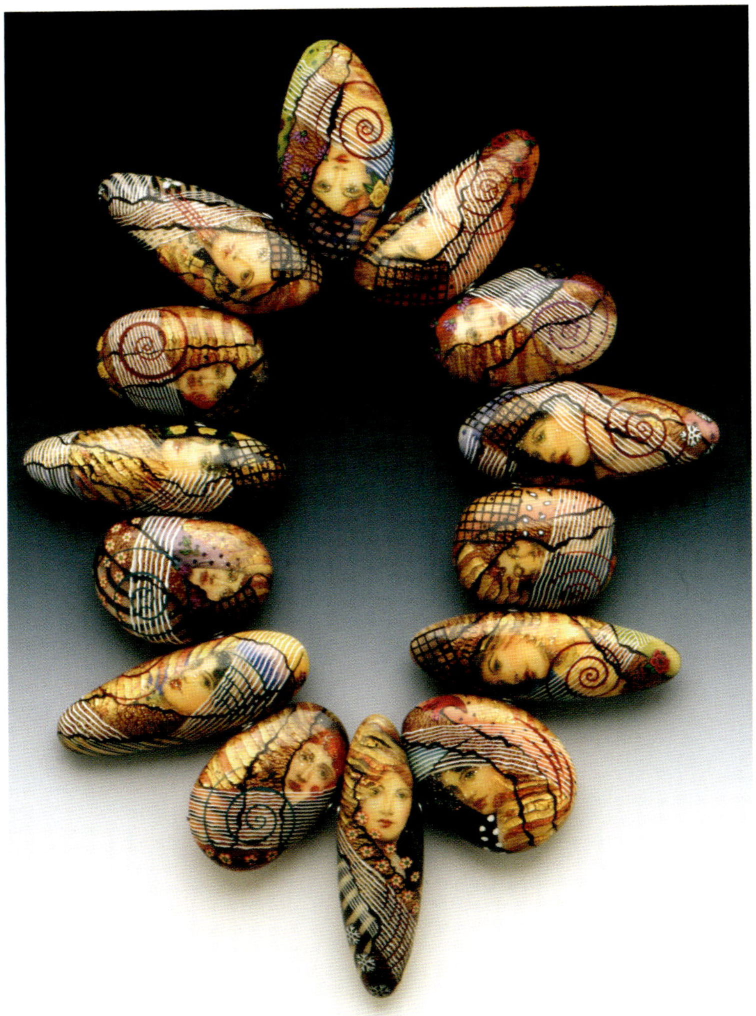

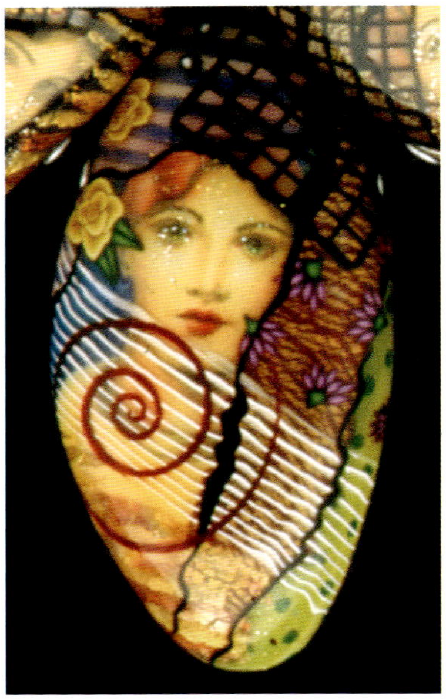

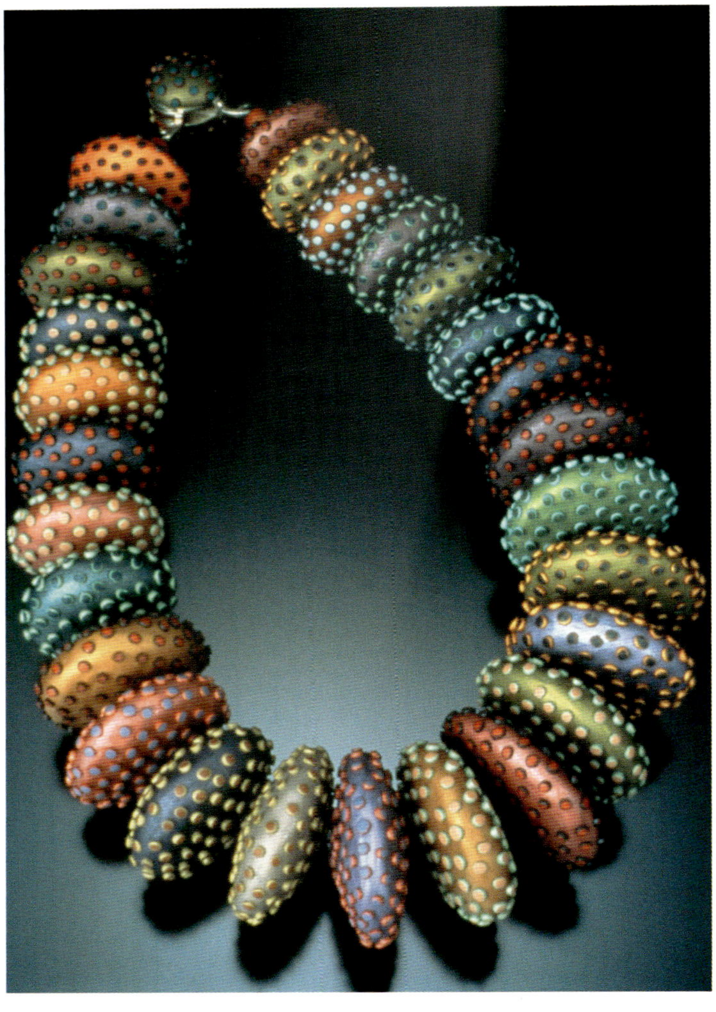

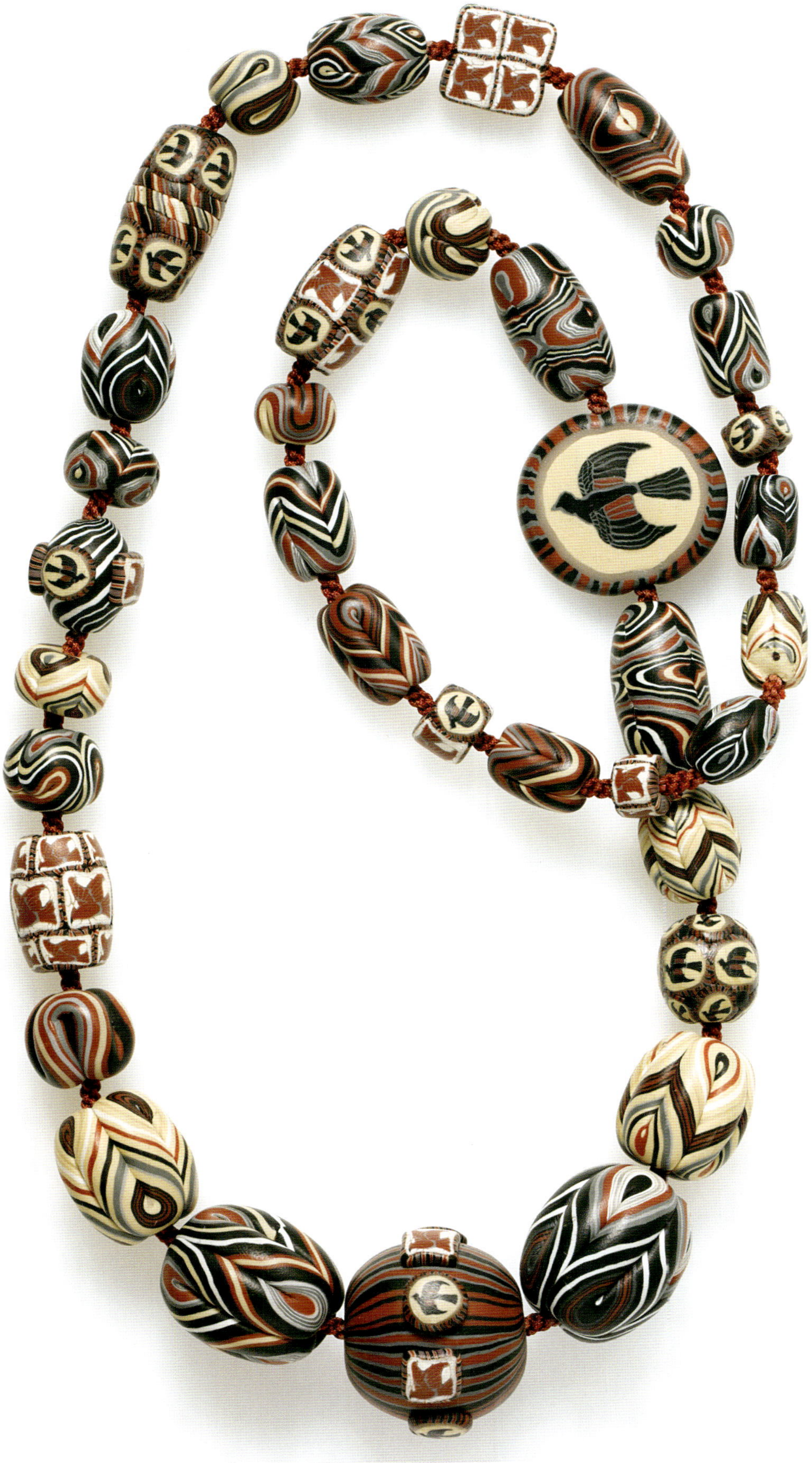

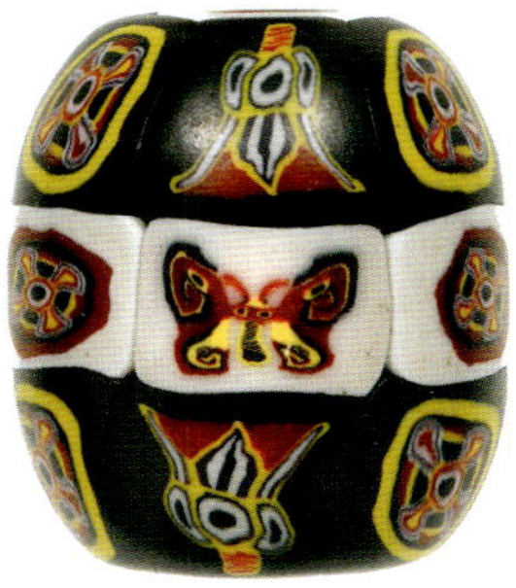

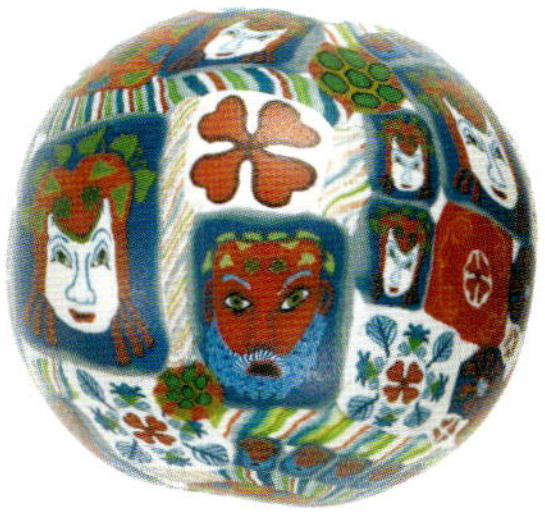

ABOVE: 380. *Polymer clay (Fimo) bead. The canes are authentic reproductions of Roman Period face canes though made with polymer. Jamey D. Allen. Early 1990s. Length, 3.3 cm. Private collection*

ABOVE TOP: 381. *A polymer clay (Fimo) bead inspired by the complex Egypto-Roman Period mosaic-glass bead (c. 300* B.C.*) seen in plate 51 in the original edition of this book. Jamey D. Allen. Early 1990s. Height, 3 cm. Private collection*

LEFT: 382. *A necklace of polymer clay (Fimo) beads, styled after Roman and Islamic Period millefiori, combed, and folded beads. Jamey D. Allen. Early-1990s. Overall circumference length, 97 cm. Central bead width, 3.4 cm. Private collection*

TOP: 383. *A polymer clay bead bracelet with individual units evoking snail shells. Pier Voulkos, 1995. Typical bead length, 1.8 cm. The Bead Museum, Glendale, Arizona*

MIDDLE: 384. *Four Little People polymer clay beads made by Cynthia Toops, mid to late 1990s Far left, height: 1.8 cm. Far left, private collection; numbers two to four, The Bead Museum, Glendale, Arizona*

BOTTOM: 385. *A polymer clay bead necklace in the shape of barnacles. Cynthia Toops. 1997. Circumference length, 102 cm. Individual bead lengths range from 2.54 cm to less than 1.2 cm. The Bead Museum, Glendale, Arizona*

OPPOSITE: 386. *This "sampler" necklace made by the husband-and-wife team of Cynthia Toops and Dan Adams combines Cynthia's polymer clay beads and Dan's lampworked glass beads with those of nineteenth century Czechoslovakian glass and African-made stone. The long polymer clay beads are capped at the ends with glass. The bead with the dog has a bull's eye on the other side. Eye motifs predominate on the necklace. 1999. Overall circumference length, 97 cm, not including the rear counterweight strand. Checkered polymer bead length, 8.9 cm. The Bead Museum, Glendale, Arizona*

OPPOSITE INSET: 386a. *Detail of the dog bead on left side of necklace showing Cynthia Toop's unique micromosaic style. Overall dog bead length, 4.8 cm. Area shown, approximately 2.2 cm*[XVII]

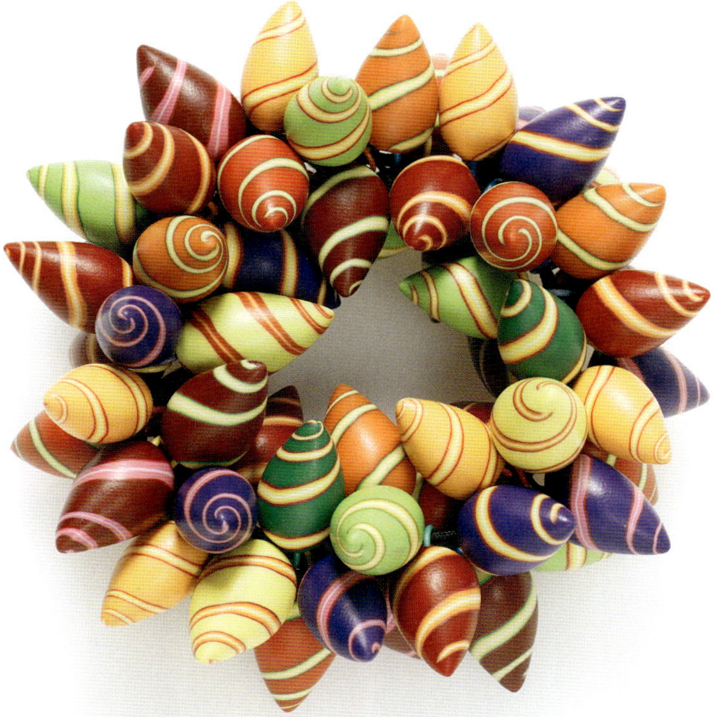

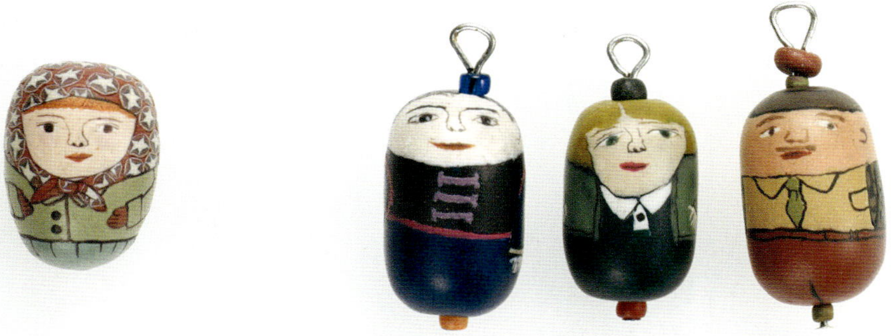

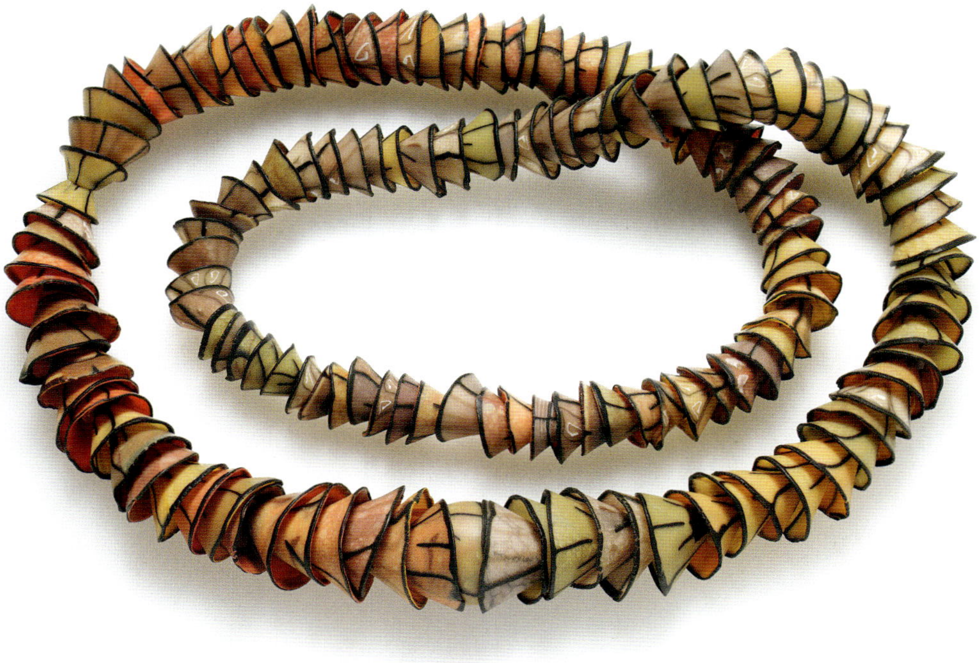

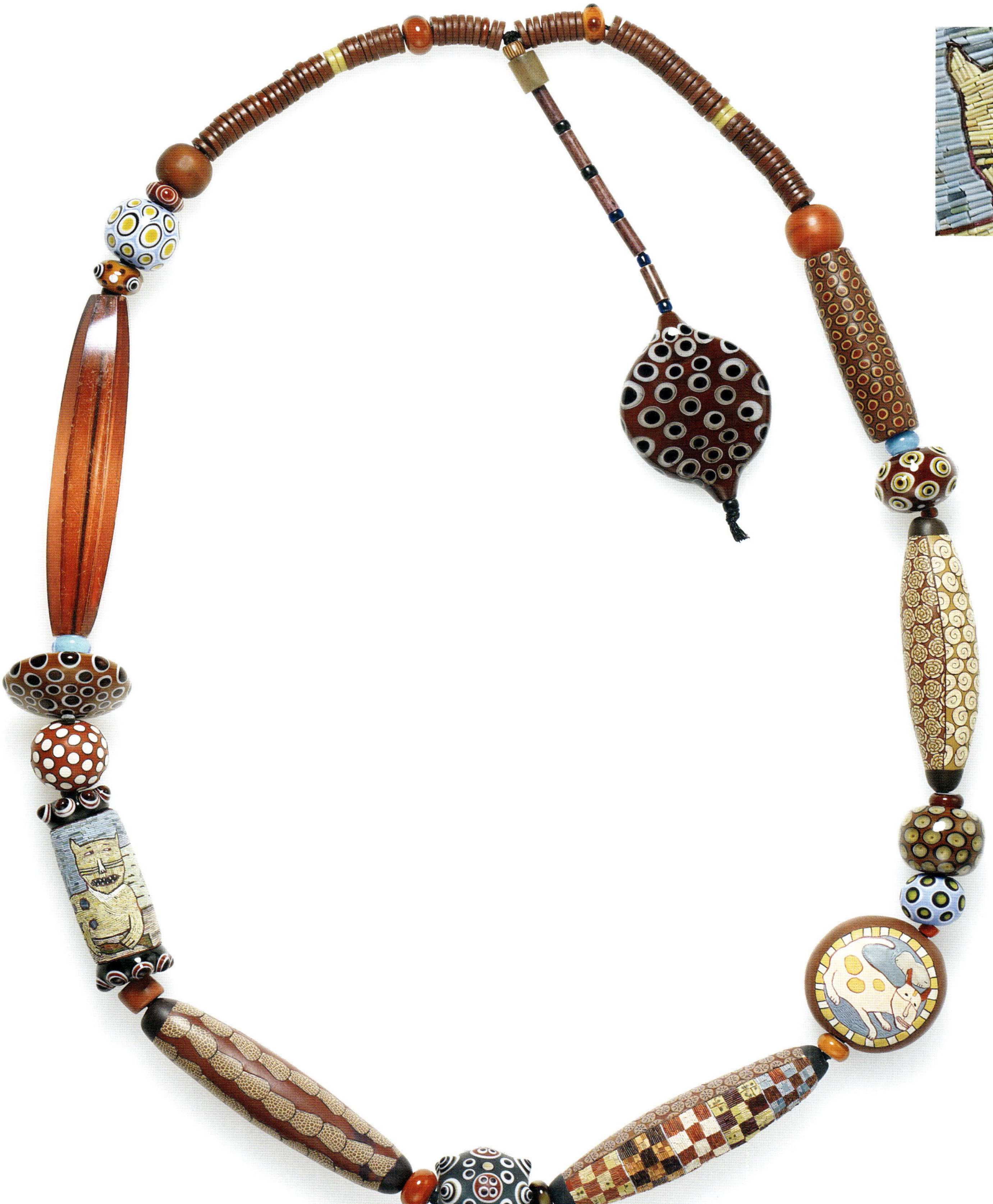
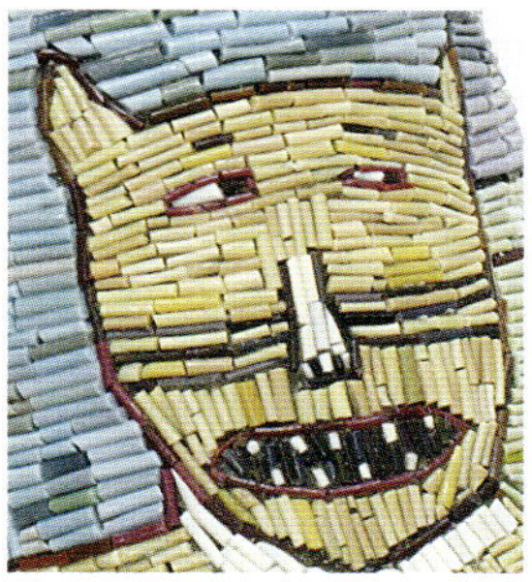

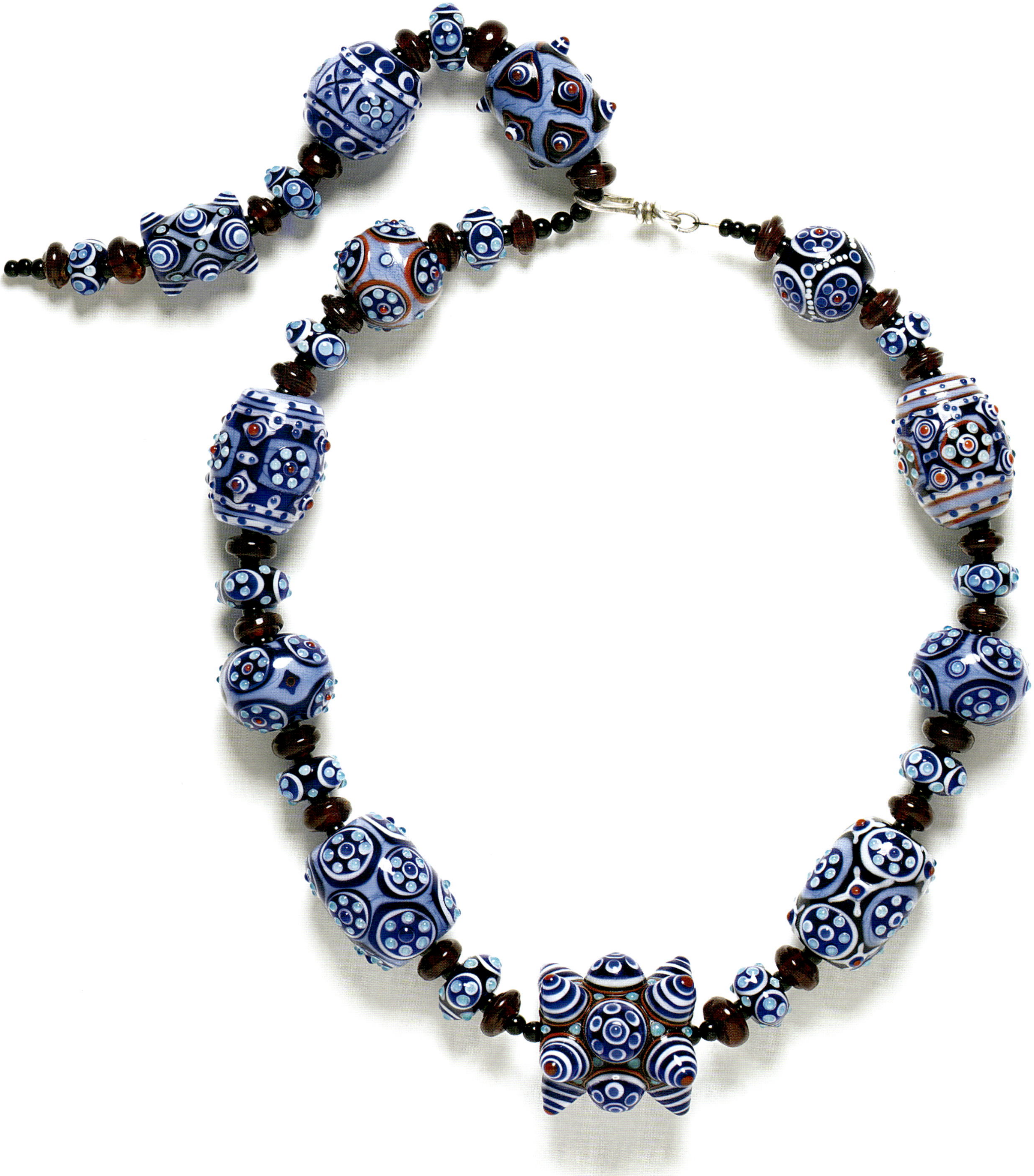

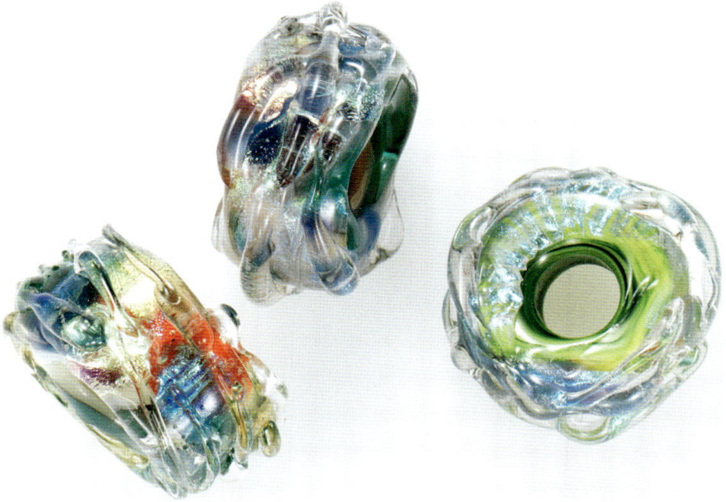

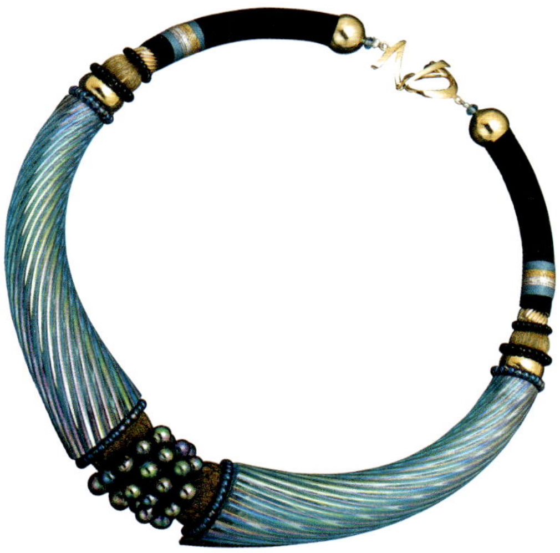

Contemporary jewelry can be classified into three branches: precious one-of-a-kind jewelry from traditional firms, including Cartier, Tiffany, and Bulgari; costume or fashion jewelry, usually of mass-produced, inexpensive materials; and artist-craftsman jewelry, frequently produced in small workshops, where innovative designs and combinations of materials are used.[5]

The great jewelry houses such as Cartier and Tiffany have enjoyed commercial success for decades. They have always adapted to the new demands of a changing clientele. When royal and aristocratic European patronage disappeared, it was replaced by a new elite of wealthy Americans and Middle Eastern potentates. There appears to be no lack of interest in owning large and resplendent jewelry.[6] Contemporary fine jewelry continues to emphasize precious materials. Items of jewelry are often considered investments, and except for pearls and an occasional use of gemstones as beads (plate 198), gems are typically set rather than pierced for beads. While the craftsmanship is generally exquisite, traditional designs are the rule.

Costume jewelry, however, frequently incorporates beads. Trendy necklaces and bracelets, which are intended to last no longer than the dresses they adorn, express the very essence of our time. While often only a thin line divides fine costume from artist-craftsman jewelry, the main difference is that costume jewelry is mass-produced by machines, while artist-craftsman work is handcrafted.

Contemporary artist-craftsmen are currently creating the most innovative beads and beadwork, and it is their art that is the focus of the illustrations in this chapter. Most reject the notions of jewelry being investments or short-lived fashion. Value is related to the craftsmanship and the expression of ideas rather than the monetary worth of rare and precious materials. There is no limit to forms and materials used. Gold, silver, and other precious and semiprecious materials are frequently employed in combinations with wood, glass, bone, stainless steel, paper, brass, copper, acrylic, fabric, and assorted found materials. A shared sensibility seems to be the reevaluation of how materials could and should be used. Artists who have made this philosophy a foundation of their work include Robert Ebendorf (plate 342, 347), William Harper (plates 350, 351) and Jan Yager (plates 374–377).

It is interesting to note that most jewelry techniques and materials used today were known by Roman and possibly earlier times. With the exception of help from recent centrifugal-casting, vacuum-forming, drawplating, and electroplating techniques, almost every piece of jewelry made today could have been produced two thousand years ago. The technical and chemical knowledge is now greater, but the techniques were known.

OPPOSITE: 387. *Warring States Necklace. 1995. Glass. Tom Holland uses techniques of lampworking, double folding, furrowing, and twisted cane to create his masterful beads. Length of center horned eye bead, 2.8 cm. The Bead Museum, Glendale, Arizona*

ABOVE LEFT: 388. *Three lampworked glass beads. Lisa St. Martins. Far left, length, 6.8 cm. Collection Toby Bowlby*

ABOVE RIGHT: 389. *A choker of fumed (iridescent) glass beads—a technique developed by Louis Comfort Tiffany to simulate ancient iridescent glass—combined with metallic thread-wrapped wood beads, silk ribbon, brass beads, and an antique glass bead cluster. The curved tubular beads are drawn-glass canes; the ribbing was formed in a patterned mold.[XVIII] Norman Courtney and Jane Nyhus. 1986. Necklace: diameter, 17.7 cm. Jane Nyhus Designs, Seattle. Private collection*

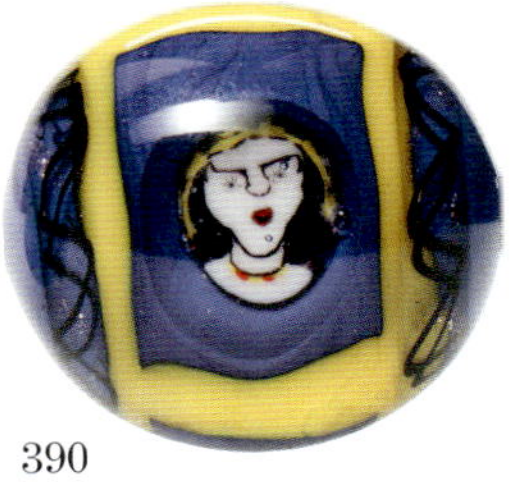

390

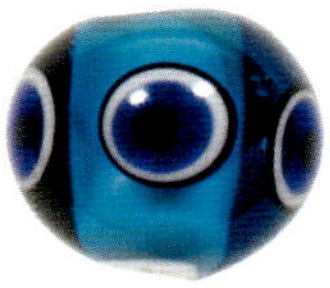

392a

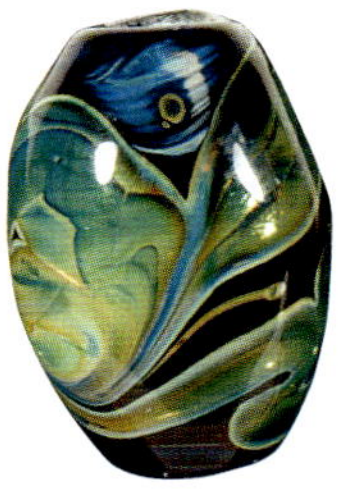

392b

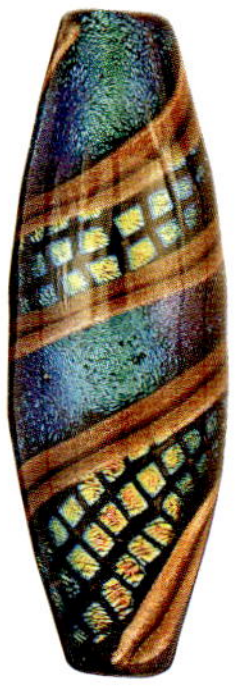

392c

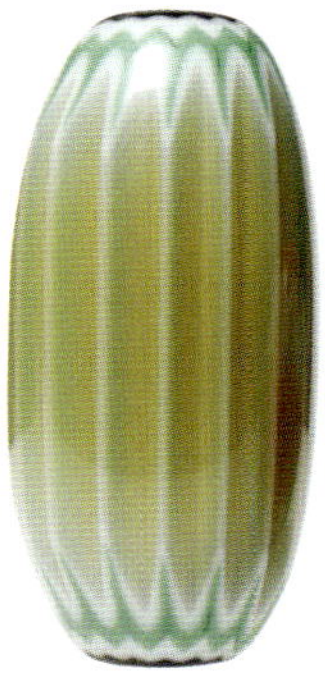

393a

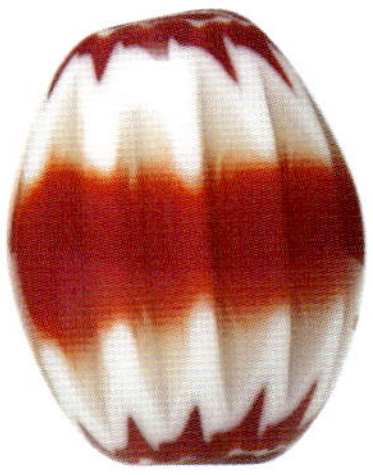

393b

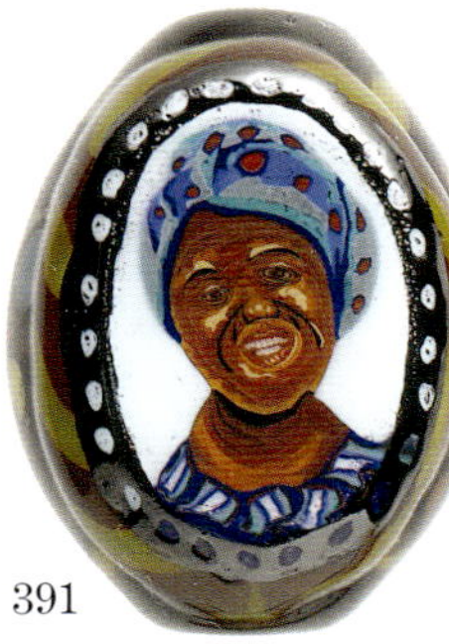

391

390. *A contemporary glass face beads with mosaic insets by Brian Kerkvliet, the first American glassmaker to revive mosaic face cane techniques. 1990. Length of 391a, 2.8 cm. Private collection*

391. *Glass millefiori bead made by Isis Rey in 2008 depicting Wangahi Mugthal, winner of the Nobel Peace Prize in 2002. Length, 2.9 cm. Collection Rachel Fox*

392 a–c. *Three glass beads by Patricia Frantz. a. Eye spot bead. 1989. Lampworked, applied dots, soda-lime glass. Diameter, 1.4 cm. Private collection. (b.) "Oval Bead with Organic Decorations." 2008. Triton glass. Length, 1.9 cm (c.) "Dichroic Bicone Bead with Goldstone detail". 2008. Length, 4.5 cm. b, c. Collection of the artist*

393 a–b. *Chevron Beads. Art Seymour. (a) 1991. Length, 3.1 cm. The Bead Museum, Glendale, Arizona. (b) Early 1990s. Private collection*

The few new bead materials used by craftspeople are plastics, including polymer clay, (the latest generation of plastics seen in plates 378–386); Precious Metals Clay (PMC); and metals connected with the aerospace industry, such as titanium, tantalum, and niobium (Timeline 1304). There is also much experimentation with joining metal alloys of different compositions—"married metals" (plate 355). Since the 1980s, the Japanese have manufactured a new type of glass micro or "seed" beads, known as "Delica," that is considered to be a prime reason for the current renaissance of beadwork.

Divisions between craftsmen, jewelers, and beadmakers continue to disappear, a trend started in the early 1900s. Barbara Natoli Witt has been creating macramé and bead neckpieces of astonishing presence, for over forty years. Her work bridges fiber art and jewelry (plate 335). Jewelry forms are now closely merged with garments, seen, for example, in the beadwork of Verena Sieber-Fuchs (plates 339–40) and Larry Brown (plate 363).

Virginia Blakelock's splendid necklace, "Daphnis Nerii" (plate 358), is considered by many to be the pivotal piece that influenced contemporary beadworkers. At the same time, tribal beadwork has remained an important cultural form among indigenous peoples—most notably in North America, Africa, and Indonesia. For native groups, cultural identity is intimately connected with finely beaded regalia. Tribal continuums are maintained through passing on traditional colors and motifs. Attend any North American powwow or ceremonial to see how native beadworkers brilliantly juxtapose modern and traditional motifs so that symbols from the past are celebrated in the present. Marcus Amerman, of Choctaw and Hopi heritage, is notable for his ability to adapt outside influences while still remaining grounded in history and tradition (plates 364, 365).

Indigenous beadwork has inspired many contemporary non-Native artists, who blend tribal imagery with their own meaningful values and artistry. Joyce Scott's sculptural forms, while recalling West African beadwork, are her own provocative conceptions that frequently address political and social issues (plate 366). Valerie Hector, who acknowledges the influences of a Bahai temple, Chinese mathematics, and other artists upon her art, has invented a totally original body of work including "beaded beads" (plates 369, 370).[7]

The emergence of art glass beadmaking among a rapidly expanding, international group of deeply talented glass bead artisans is the main bead story of the past twenty years. Whereas in the past, glass beadmaking was produced primarily within workshops, factories, and cottage industries, many of today's finest beadmakers are individual artists working within their own home-based studios. Most contemporary glass beads are made by lampworked techniques incorporating trailed and/or drawn cane (millefiori) elements, or lampworking with borosilicate (hard glass) as these methods allow for a wide variety of designs, patterns, and colors.[8] The contemporary glass bead movement owes much to the

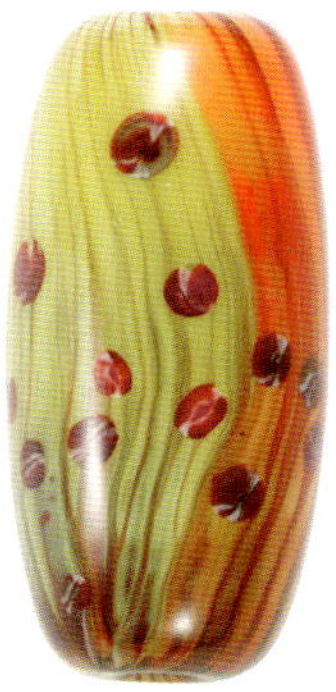

394

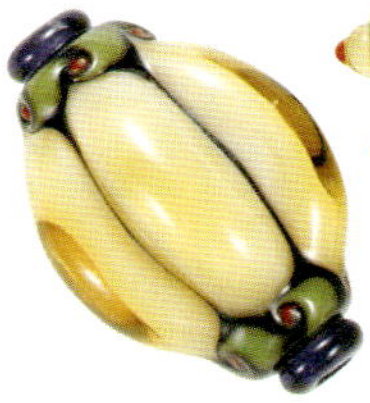

395a

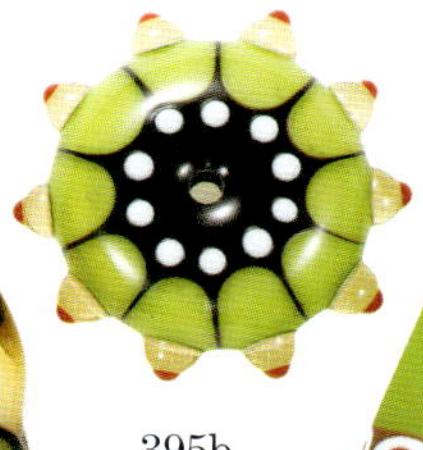

395b

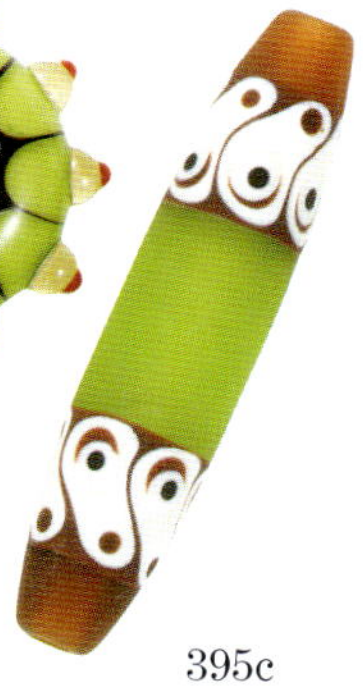

395c

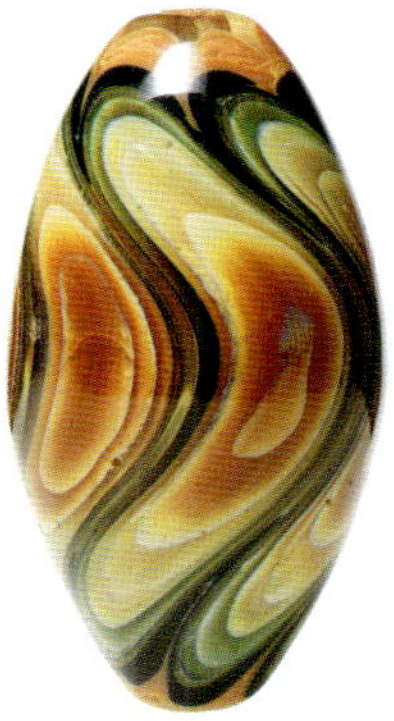

396

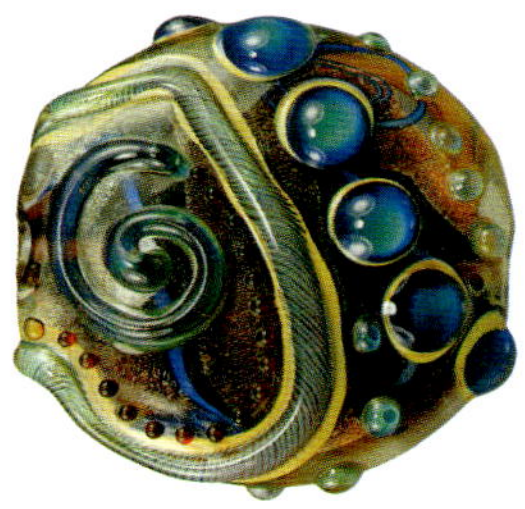

397

confluence of several artists, a magazine, a museum, and an organization. In the late 1980s, four Pacific Northwest glass bead artists from Seattle (Brian Kerkvliet, William Stokes, Julie Clinton, and Patricia Sage) formed a beadmaking cooperative (The Ring of Fire) to share information and the costs for importing high quality, brilliantly colored Moretti glass rods from Italy. (Moretti glass is difficult and expensive to obtain in the United States.) Working with this fine material enabled the beadworkers to expand their art technically and artistically.[9] Shortly thereafter, the influential *Ornament Magazine* began featuring the art of these and other new glass beadmakers. In 1993, Gabrielle Liese, founder of the Bead Museum (originally located in Prescott, Arizona, and now in Glendale, Arizona) organized a groundbreaking exhibition entitled "Contemporary Glass Beadmakers," which was juried by artists Jamey D. Allen, Brian Kerkvliet, and gallery owner Joanne Rapp. The excitement generated by both the exhibition and the gathering of artists (many have their work represented in this chapter) led to the forming of the Society of Glass Beadmakers, which in 1998 became the International Society of Glass Beadmakers.[10]

The proliferation of glass beadworkers these past two decades makes the role of the International Society of Glass Beadmakers particularly important. The Society, established by some of the same members and with a similar spirit of exchange that characterized The Ring of Fire, provides an open, information-sharing forum for its members and the public. Annual gatherings and publications extend their mission, which differs profoundly from the historic secretive Venetian beadmaking guilds. At the same time, the Society encourages high quality work, and the conscious need to synthesize economics and aesthetics, thus providing artisans with the means for a viable livelihood.[11]

Since the beginning of time, jewelry has never functioned on its own: it has always communicated all themes of human behavior. Beads continue to have personal connotations for the wearer, expressing personal tastes, status, and (directly or indirectly) political affiliation. For example, during the 1960s beads (popularly called "love beads") were worn by American and Western European men and women as an antiestablishment statement. Dressed in colorful ethnic garb and beads, counterculture people were sending out visual as well as symbolic messages. By substituting the dress and adornment of Third World countries for business suits and military uniforms, they not only conveyed their rejection of American military policies in Vietnam, but showed yearnings for what were perceived to be the gentler, more humane lifestyles of other societies. The "flower children" were advocating universal love and the communal family. Tribal and ethnic beads were an important part of their image. Unfortunately, in a startling reversal of imagery, instead of symbolizing love and peace, beads are today, some forty years later, frequently worn by members of notorious gangs in many North American inner-city neighborhoods to communicate group identity.[12]

394. *Glass bead. 2003. Nicole Zumkeller and Eric Seydoux. Switzerland. Heat and gravity shaped; soda-lime glass. Length, 4.4 cm. Collection Toby Bowlby*

395 a–c. *Glass beads. 2003. Terri Caspari-Schmidt. Lampworked, heat and gravity shaped, layered; soda-lime glass. (c) Length, 5.7 cm. The bead is called "tomato worm." Collection Toby Bowlby*

396. *Borosilicate glass bead Kevin O'Grady. 2001. Length, 5.6 cm. Collection Toby Bowlby*

397. *Sea Garden 10. 2007. Andrea Guarino-Slemmons. Lampworked and marvered soda-lime glass, with silver added in order to obtain different reactions and colors in the bead. Diameter, 3.9 cm. Collection of the artist*

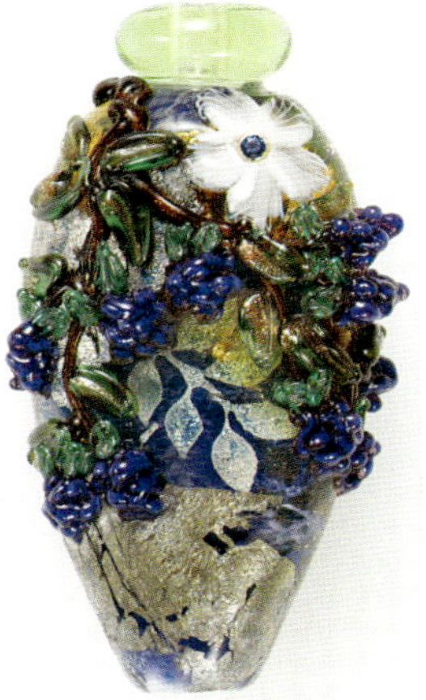

ABOVE: 398. *Glass bead. Lampwork effetre glass. 2003. Leah Fairbanks. Actual size of bead, seen here, is 5.3 cm. in length. Lampworked, heat and paddle shaped, cased canes, dichroic and soda-lime glass, glass powders, 18k gold foil. Collection Toby Bowlby*

RIGHT: 399. *Blown and painted borosilicate glass beads with sterling silver overlay. 1997. Shari Maxson Hopper. Overall circumference length, 53 cm. Center bead length, 4 cm. Collection Toby Bowlby. This necklace was awarded the Best of Show at the International Glass Beadmaker's Show in Albuquerque, 1997*

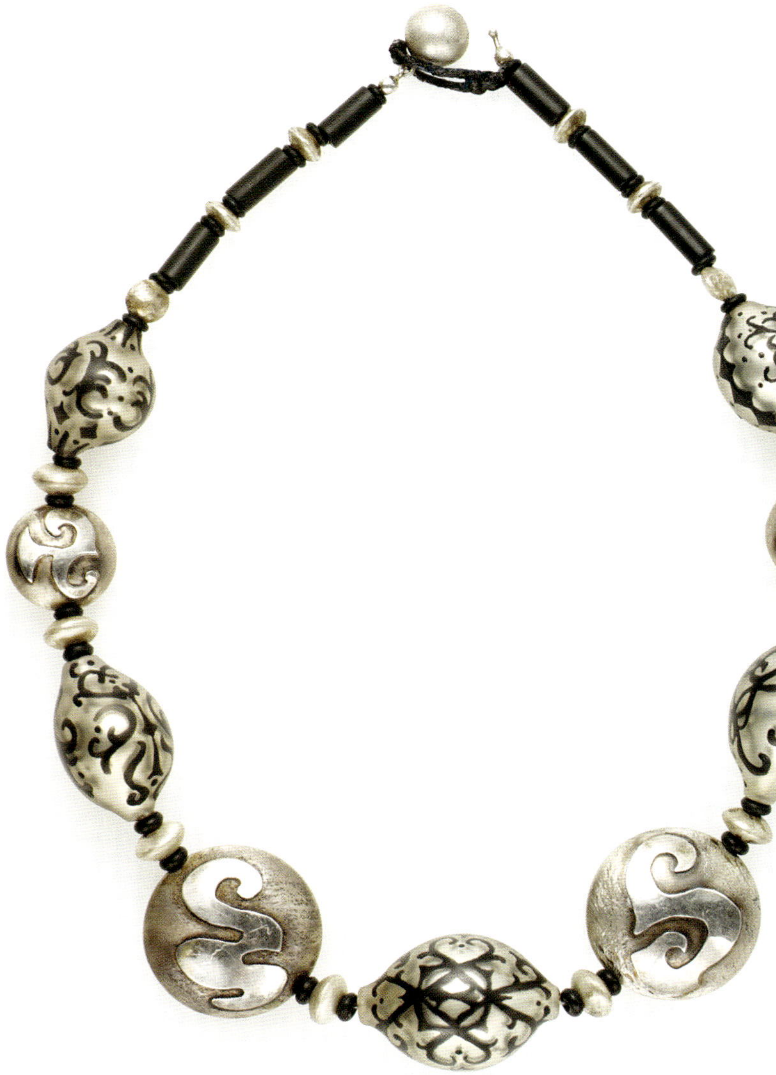

A historical overview of beads from early people to our own age reveals the extraordinary breadth of human creativity. At the same time, it indicates the basic, almost primitive qualities that have been consistent factors throughout the centuries. The purposes for which people adorn themselves may vary, but the underlying aims are constant—be they amuletic, political, or sexual. For adornment, even in our changing and frenetic age, we continue to use and feel comfortable with forms that go back to prehistory—in particular, the simple bead.[13] Tastes and materials may change but the bead endures. Strung on necklaces, serial images encircle the body, giving us the same pleasure our Ice Age ancestors had. In one form or another, people are deeply attached to beads: they create a bridge of continuity between the past, the present, and the future. Although a necklace may be exotic and from a distant culture, one feels a sense of continuity, of unity despite diversity. And in wearing it, we connect ourselves to its makers, to their remote culture, and to the substances of the earth—stone, amber, shells, and metals. We experience the universe in a bead.

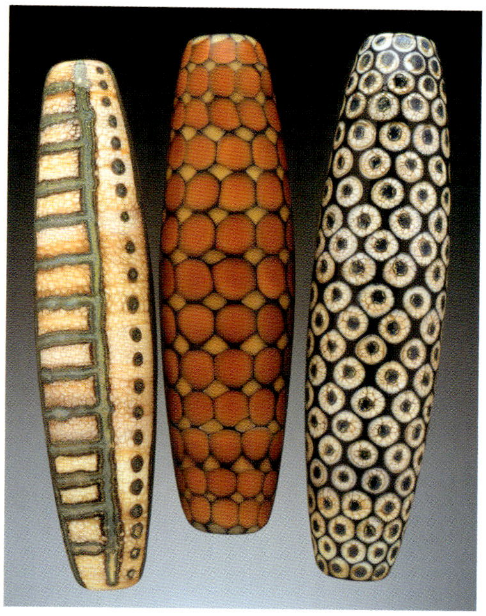
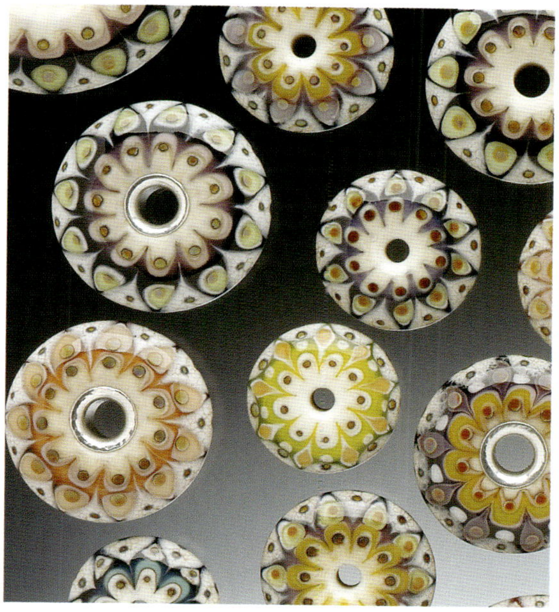
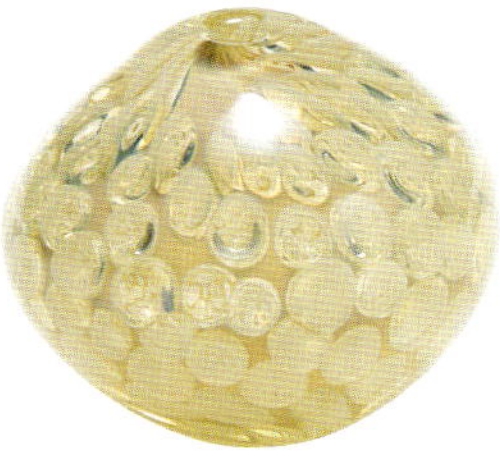
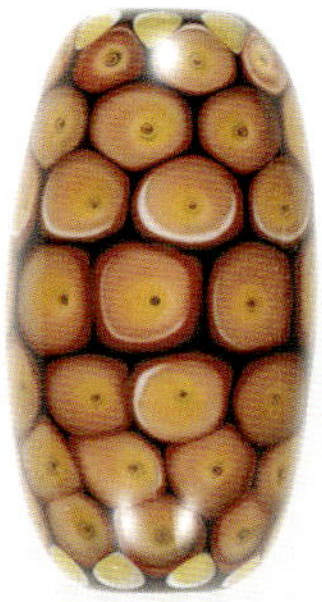
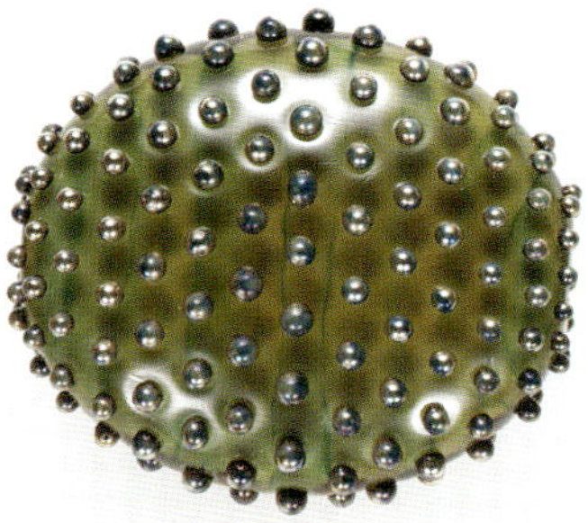
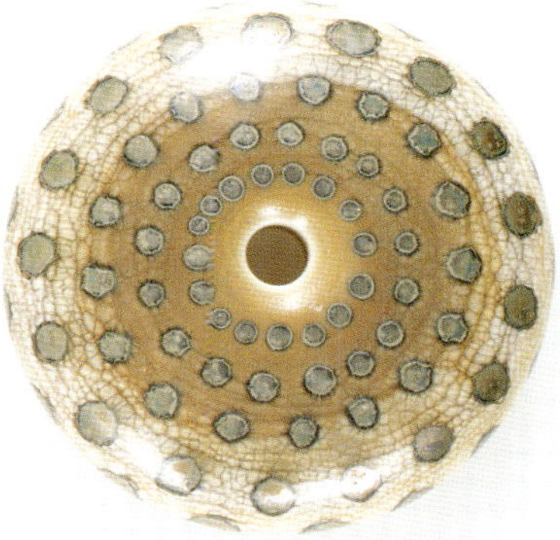
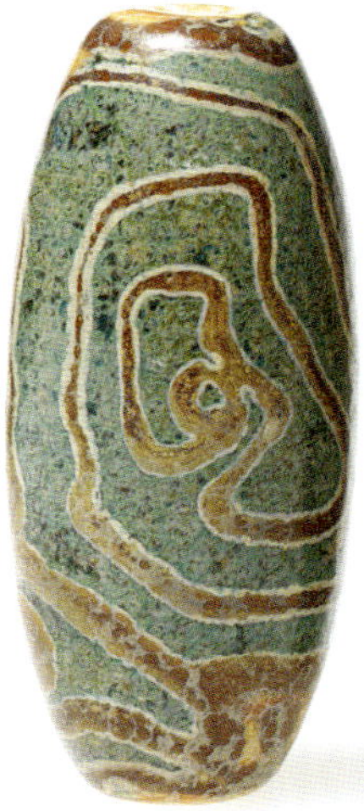
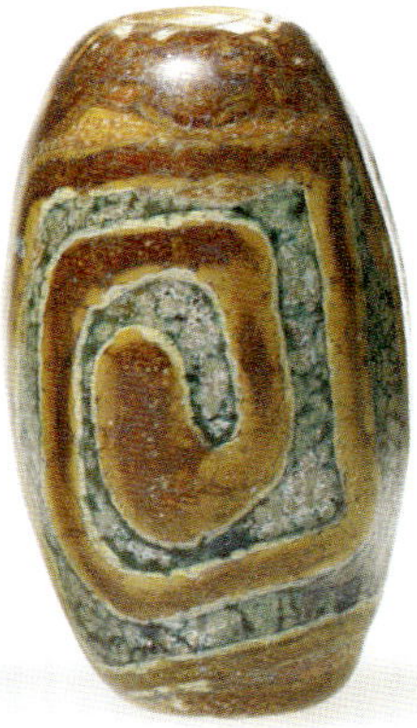
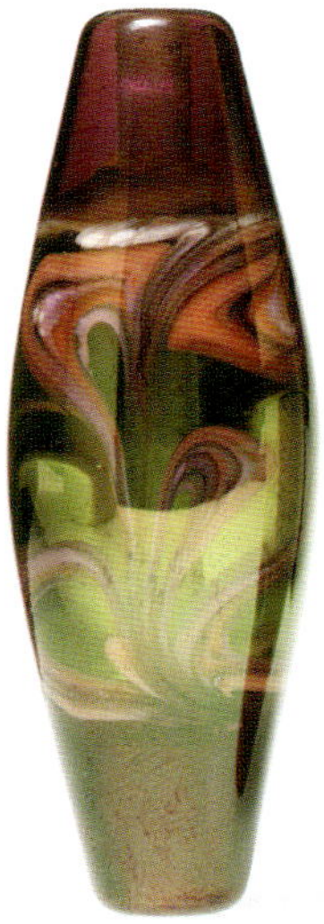
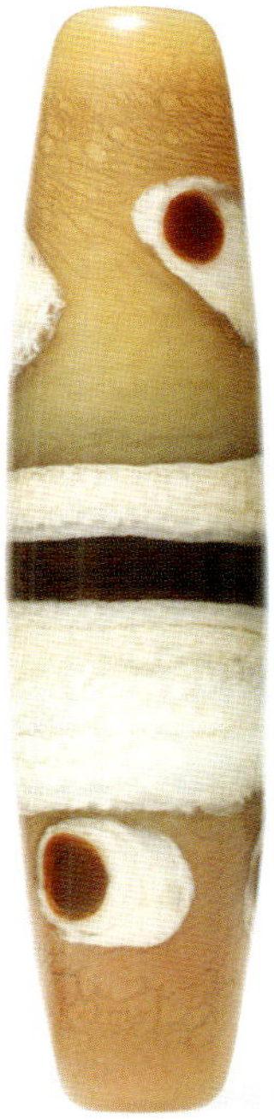

TOP AND MIDDLE ROW: 400. *Beads by Kristina Logan. 1996–2008. Lampworked, surface decorated; soda-lime glass. Top row, left: Three totem beads. Beads one, length 10 cm. Right, constellation beads. All collection of the artist. Middle row: Beads one and two, collection Toby Bowlby. Bead three, diameter 5 cm, The Bead Museum, Glendale, Arizona*

BOTTOM ROW, LEFT: 401. *Two glass beads by Rene Roberts. 2003. Left: length, 4.5 cm. Flameworked, press moulded, etched, tumbled; copper and silver leaf, iron oxide, soda-lime glass. Collection Toby Bowlby*

BOTTOM ROW, RIGHT: 402. *Two glass beads by James Smircich. 2003. Right: length, 6.7 cm. Lampworked, heat and gravity shaped, combed, tumbled: soda-lime glass. The bead on the right in Jim's homage to dZi beads. Collection Toby Bowlby*

ABOVE: 403. *Glass bead of blown hollow borosilicate tubing. 2005. John Olson. John works in a technique that he calls "inside out," as the beads are decorated on the inside and seem to glow with an inner radiance. 3.2 × 2.8 cm. Collection Toby Bowlby*

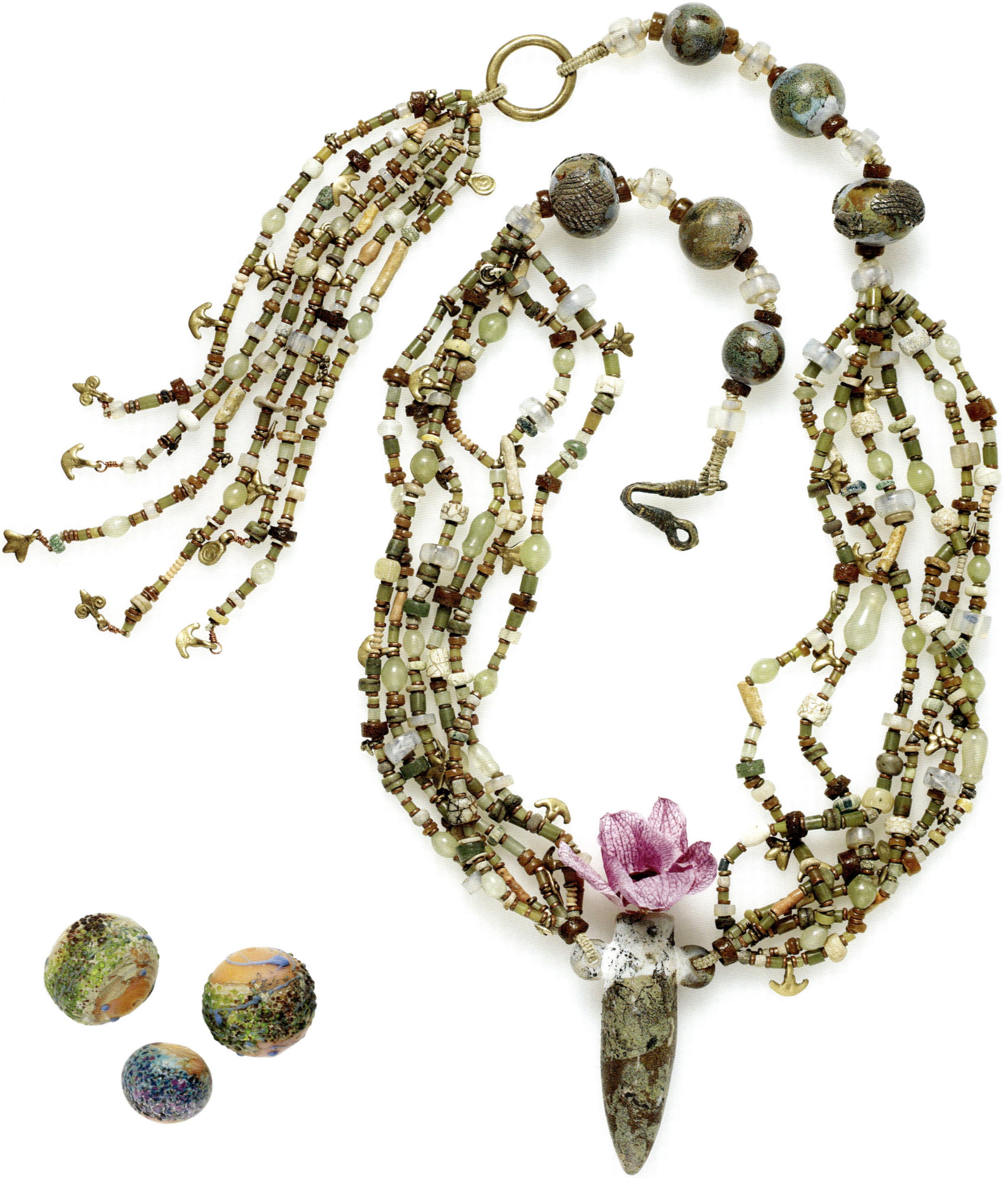

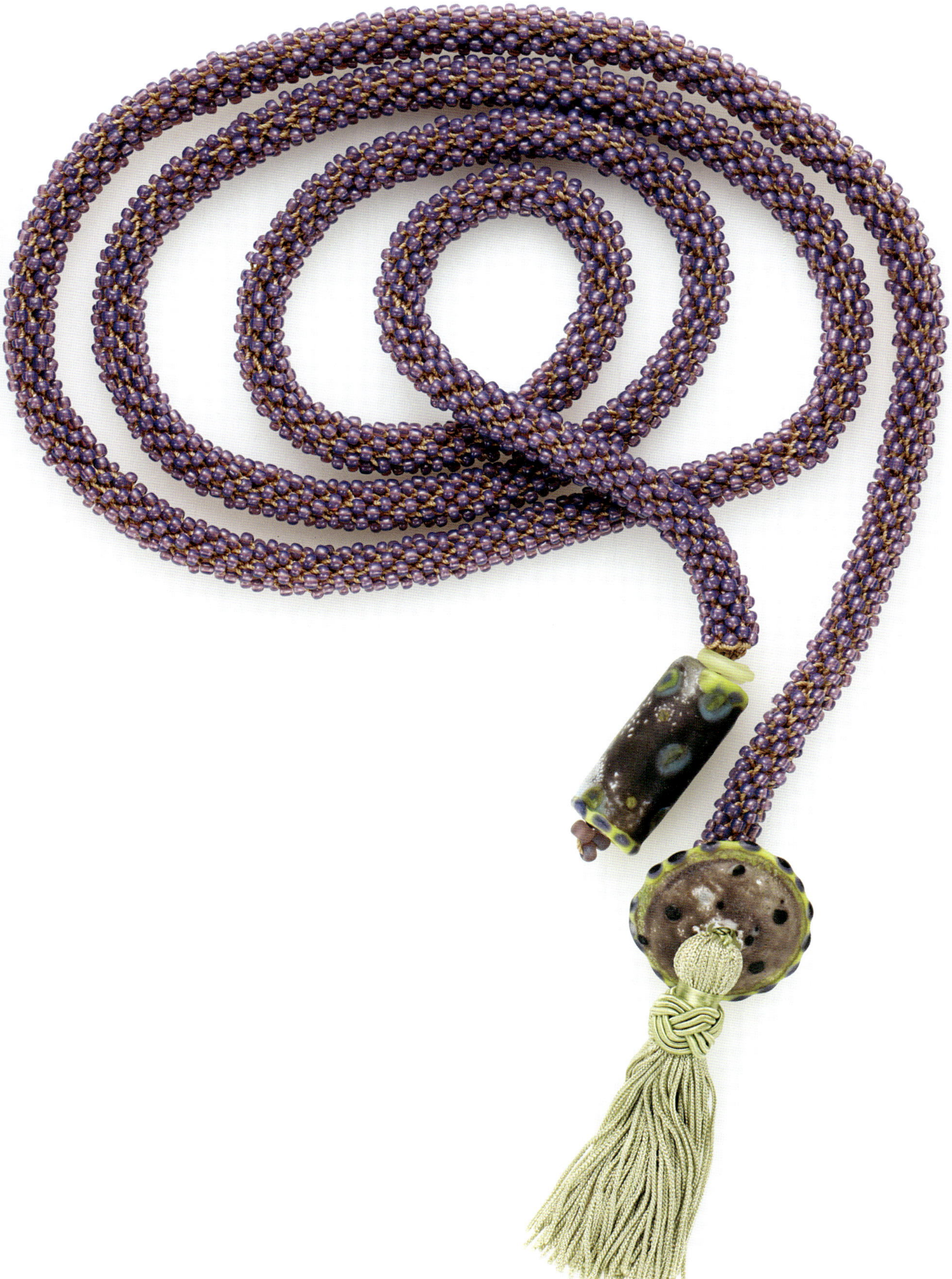

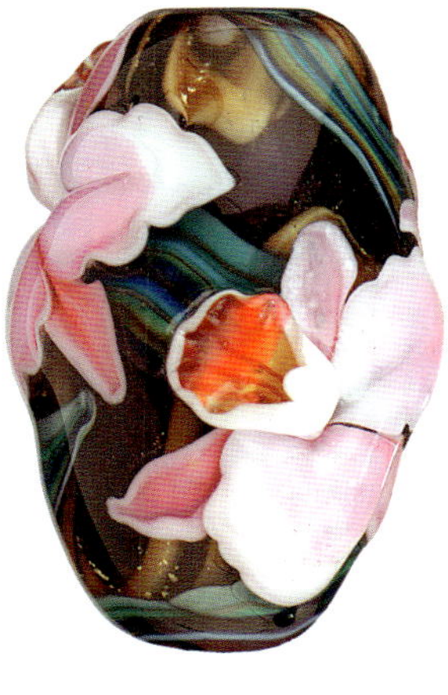

OPPOSITE CENTER: 404. *Necklace by Stevi Belle. 1996. Lampworked hollow beads with surface treatment of frits over soda-lime glass. Strung with a mélange of old and contemporary glass, stone and brass beads, and findings. The center perfume vial holds a fresh anemone. Length of necklace from top of ring to bottom of vial: 91.4 cm. Length of vial, 7.4 cm. Length of tassels, 17.8 cm. Collection Toby Bowlby*

OPPOSITE, BOTTOM LEFT: 405. *Lampworked glass beads with a surface treatment of powders and frit (ground glass), 1990s. Stevi Belle. Top bead, 3.8 × 3.6 cm. Collection Toby Bowlby*

LEFT: 406. *Glass and silk thread beaded rope necklace. 2003. Karen Ovington. Lampworked, heat and gravity shaped, etched; enamels, soda-lime glass. Overall length, 127 cm. Length of terminal bead, left side: 3.6cm. Collection Toby Bowlby*

ABOVE: 407. *Cattleya. Pink cattleya orchids bloom on the outside of a bead, while the roots and leaves are encased within. Ayuko Shiroshita. 2005. Length, 3.3 cm. Collection of the artist*

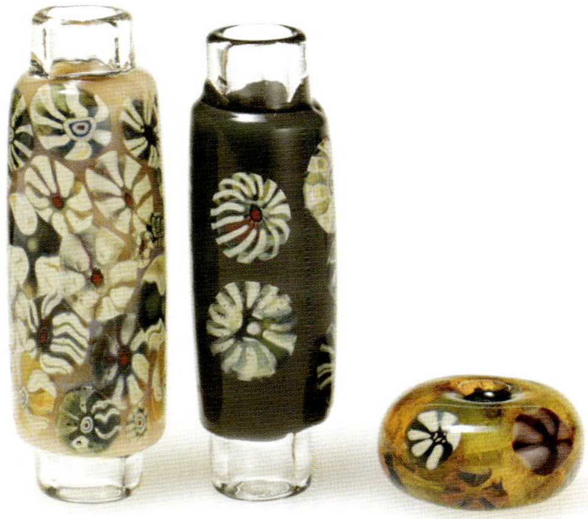

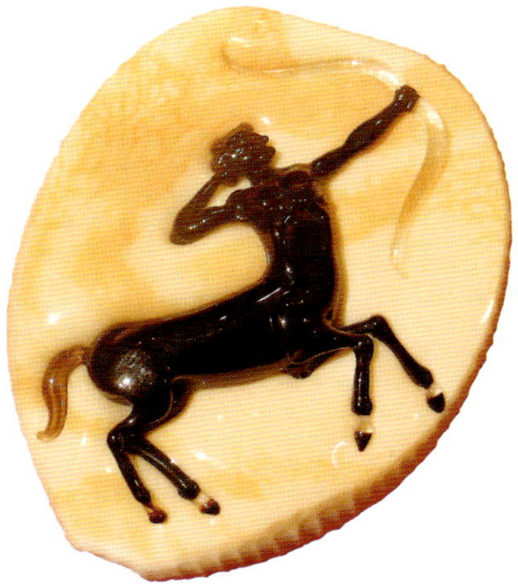

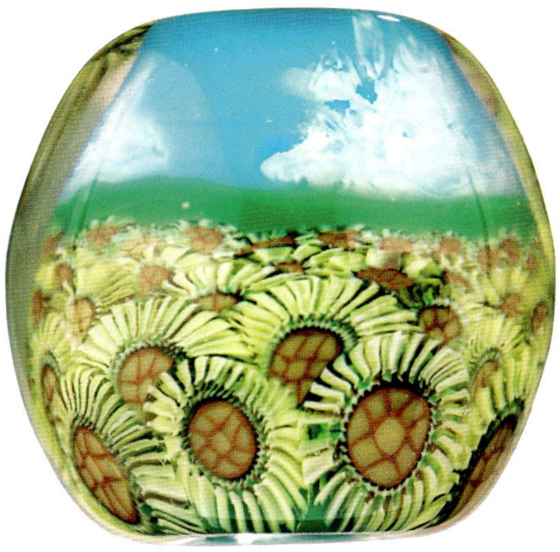

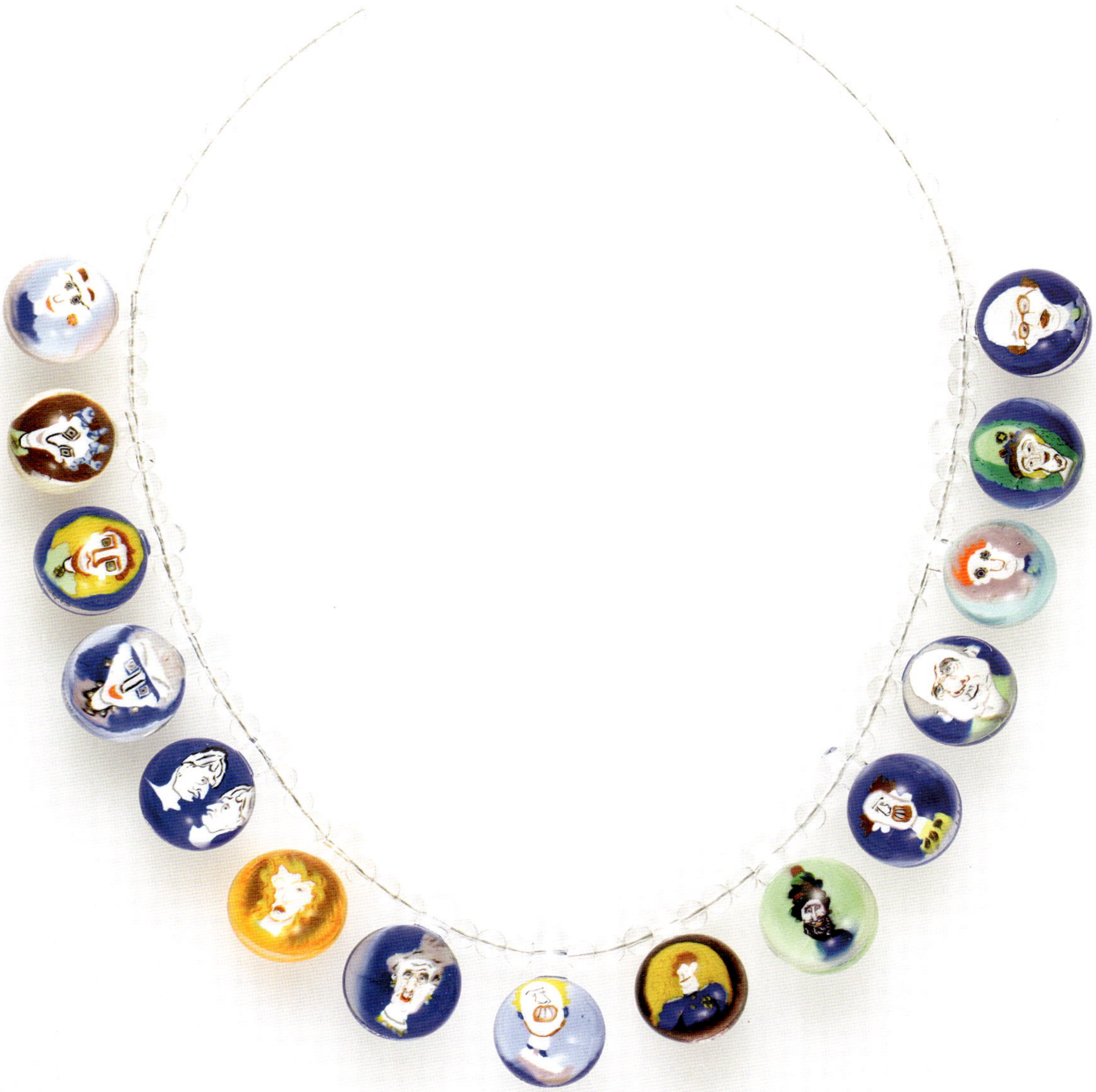

TOP LEFT: 408. *Three glass beads. 1993–2000. Donald Jay Schneider. Borosilicate glass, tubing, and rods, trailing and feathering millefiori, thermally active glasses, and clear glass "lenses" over millefiori and twisted rods. Left: length, 5.3 cm. Collection Toby Bowlby*

TOP MIDDLE: 409. *Centaur Cameo (III) 2004. Lucio Bubacco. A hand-molded Venetian glass bead with a bas-relief Venetian glass overlay. Diameter, 7 cm. Courtesy CFM Gallery, New York*

TOP RIGHT: 410. *Sunflower Field. 2005. The artist Miki Yoshida "intended to express a sunflower field spread limitlessly in a small glass bead."*[XIX] *Soda lime glass. Length, 2.2 cm. Collection the artist*

RIGHT: 411. *"Family Affair" Face Necklace made in early 1990s by Patty and Dinah Hulet of Hulet Glass of northern California; lampwork glass beads. Typical bead diameter, 2.2 cm. The Bead Museum, Glendale, Arizona*

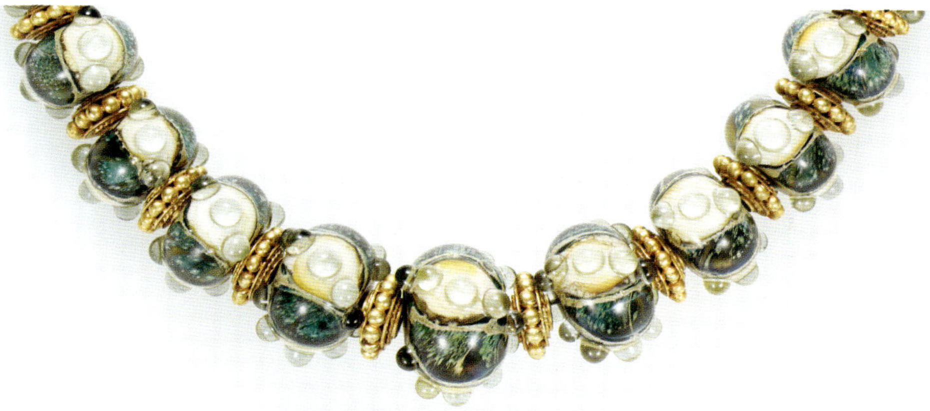

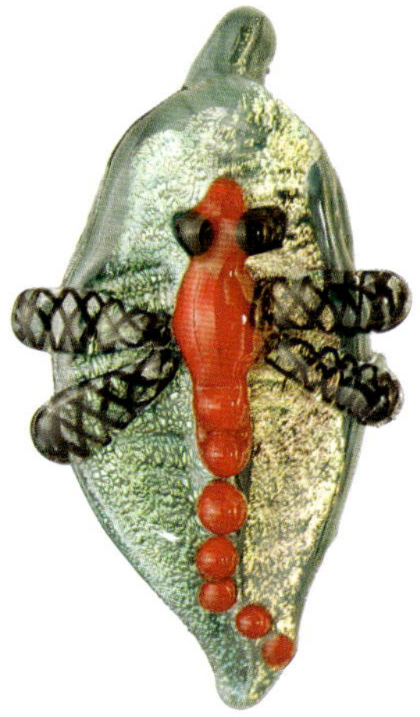

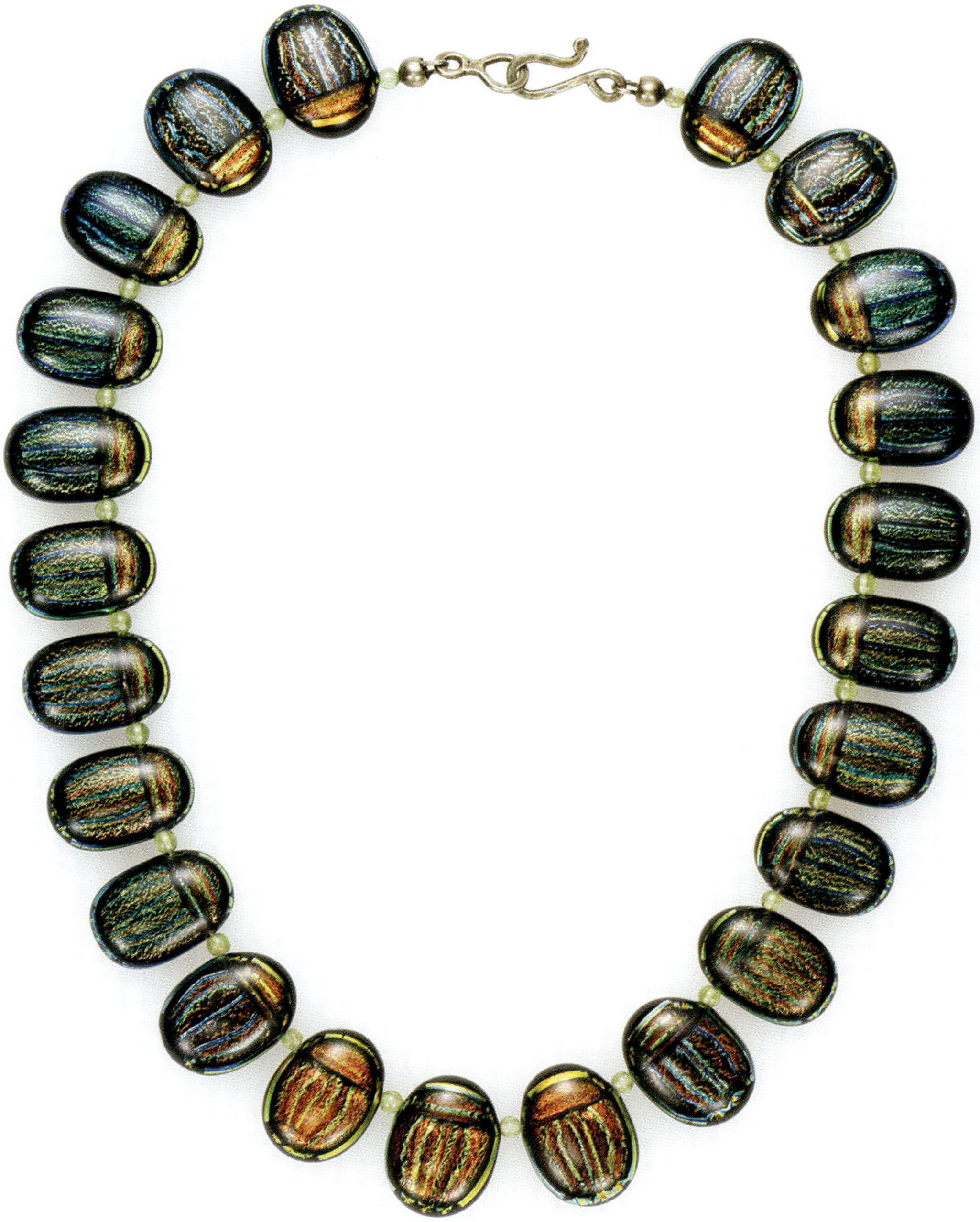

TOP LEFT: 412. *Glass beads, gold-wash spacers, and findings. 2005. Virginia Flowers. Typical glass bead, 2.2 × 1.5 cm. Collection Toby Bowlby*

BOTTOM LEFT: 413. *Glass scarab bead necklace. Bruce St. John Maher. Mid 1990s. Fused and painted. Overall circumference length, 41.9 cm. Typical scarab: 2.2 × 1.5 cm. Private collection*

ABOVE: 414. *Dragonfly Pendant Bead. 2008. Patricia Frantz. The red and black glass dragonfly with wings of effetre glass sits on a leaf crafted of several shades of dichroic glass. Length, 5 cm. Collection of the artist*

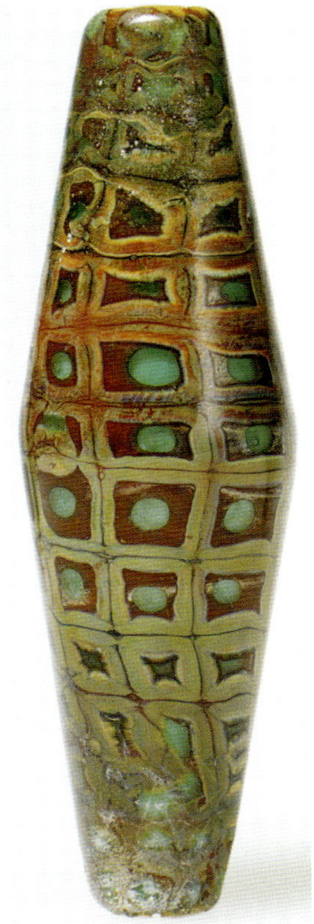

ABOVE: 415. *Checkmates. 2005. Carter Seibels. Lampwork bicone bead made from ivory effetre glass. Gridwork pattern using thin stringer with silver leaf to create an organic surface. Length, 5.8 cm. Collection of the artist*

RIGHT: 416. *Necklace and single beads. Tom Holland. Necklace: 1998. Mosaic murrini and foil. Top: circumference overall length, 46 cm. Center bead length, 3 cm. Collection Toby Bowlby. Bottom beads: 2007. Center bead length, 5 cm. Private collection. Lampworked, silver foil, murrini, coldworked, soda-lime glass. The necklace won Best of Show at the Corning, New York, gathering in 1998*

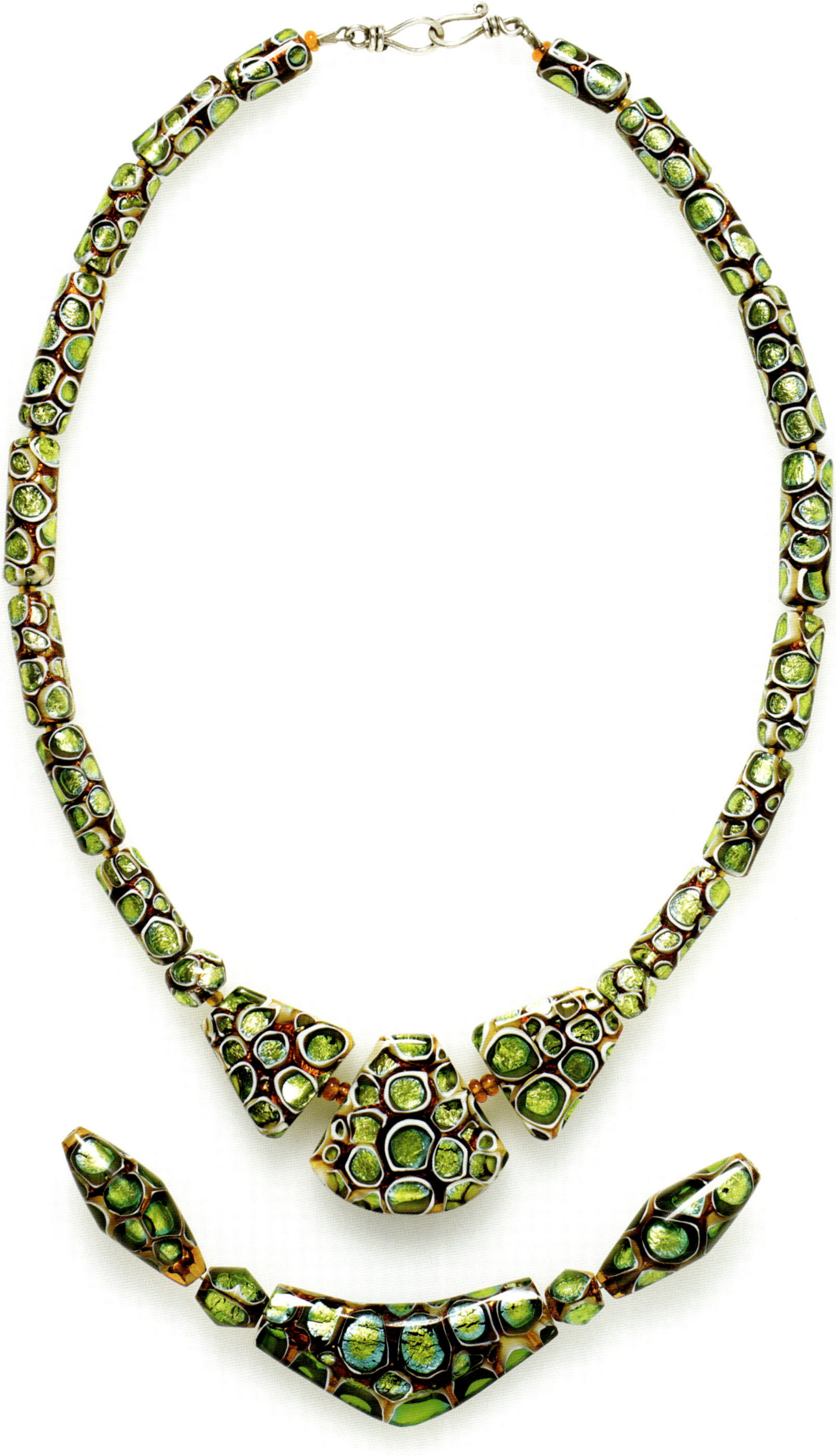

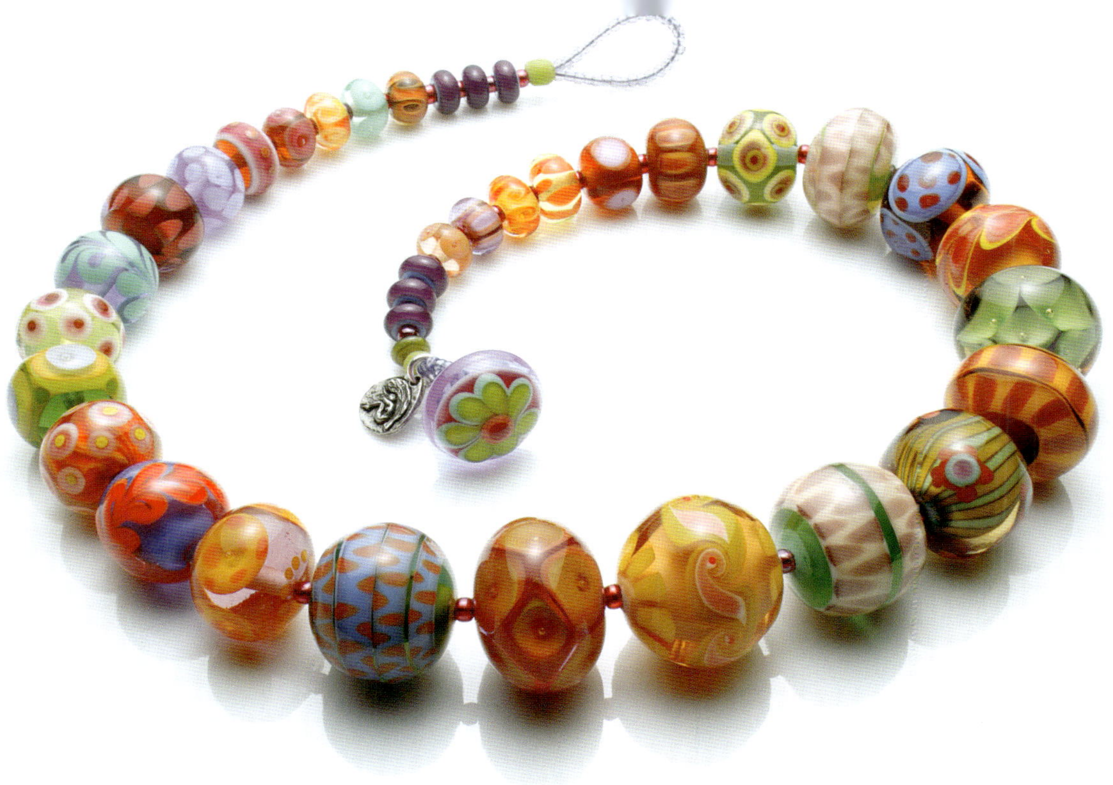

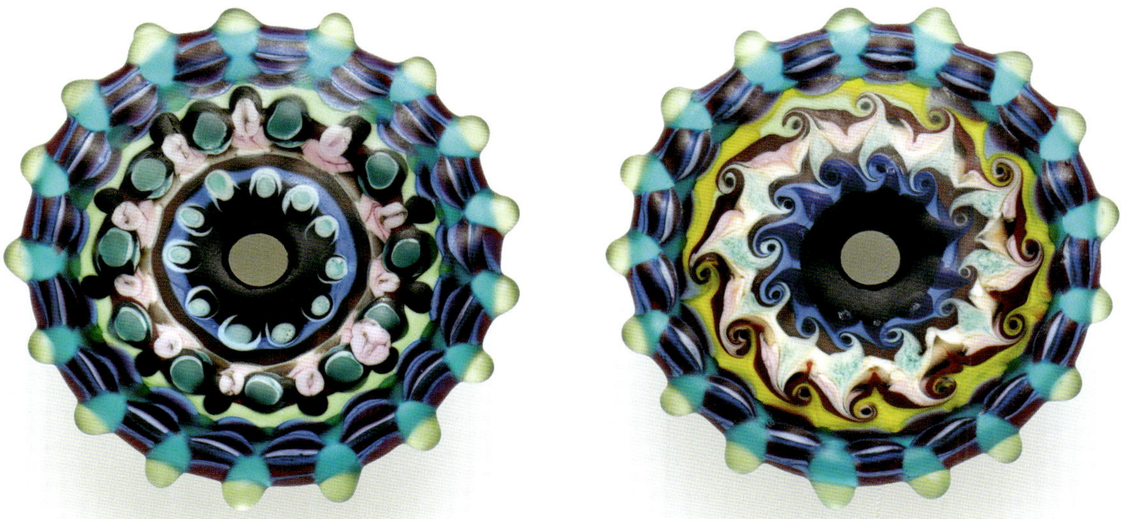

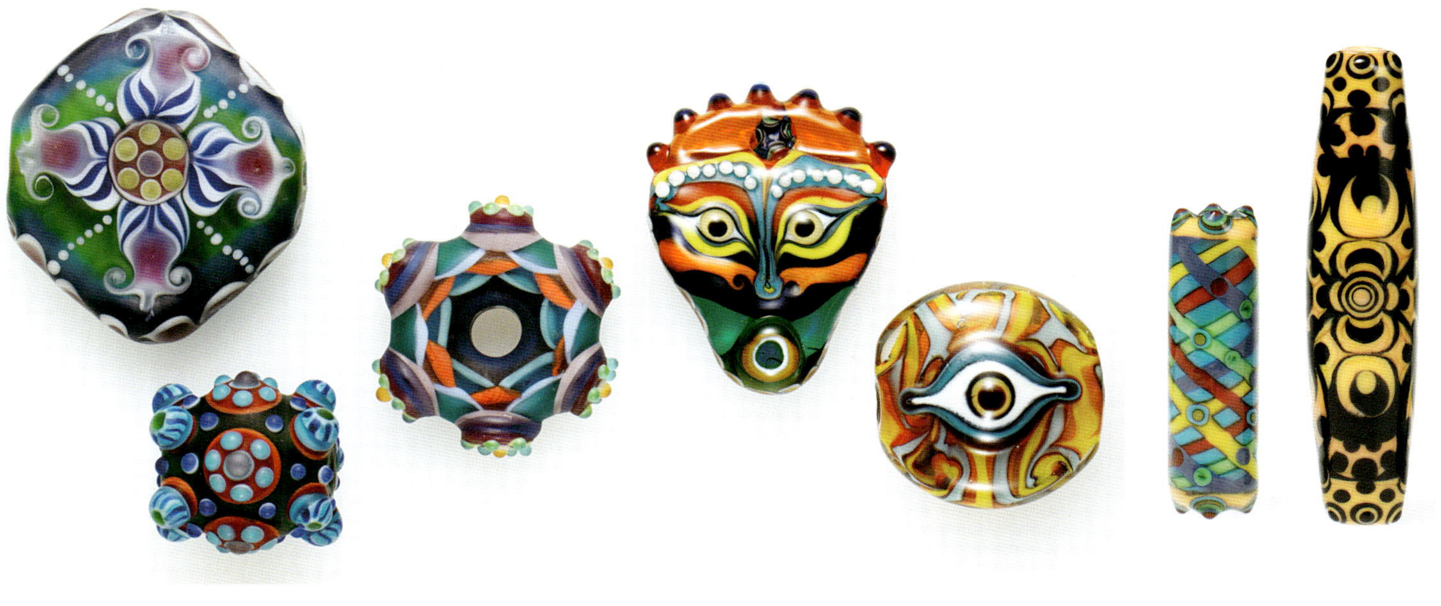

TOP: 417. *Bauble Necklace. 2007. Stephanie Sersich. 46 cm long. Center bead diameter: 2.4 cm. Effetre glass. Lampwork*

MIDDLE: 418. *Two views of one bead. A tour de force of glass beadmaking showing the differing patterns on the two sides. 2007. Patricia Sage Holland. Diameter, 6.5 cm. Collection of the artist*

BOTTOM LEFT: 419. *Beads by Patricia Sage Holland. Glass. Far left: 2007, all others, mid 1990s. Lampworked, feathered, twisted cane, flattened, and decorated; soft glass. Far left, length, 4.35 cm. All private collections*

BOTTOM RIGHT: 420. *Two glass beads. 2007. Beau Anderson. Far right bead length, 5.6 cm. Bead one and three, collection of the artist. Middle bead, Collection* Bead and Button Magazine

421. *Glass bead. 2007. Heather Trimlett. Lampworked and polished. Diameter, 5 cm. Collection of the artist*

422. *Three glass beads. 1993. Molly Haskins. Bullseye and Wasser glass. Fused glass. Far left, length, 2.4 cm. Collection Toby Bowlby*

423. *Glass bead. 2003. Doni Hatz. Length, 7.4 cm. Flameworked, twisted, blown, borosilicate glass tubing/rods. Collection Toby Bowlby*

424. *Geometry. 2004. Akihiro Ohkama. Lampwork with stringer and gold leaf. Lampworked, scratched, Satake glass, gold foil. Length, 2.4 cm. The Bead Museum, Glendale, Arizona*

425. *Flower Garden. 2005. Pati Walton. Glass bead. Lampworked, encased, dichroic glass, murrini. Length, 4.3 cm. The Bead Museum, Glendale, Arizona*

426. *Quilt. 2005. Jennifer Geldard. Enamels, reactive glass and metals, silvered and ivory dotted lentils with tie-dye spirals. Width, 3.8 cm. The Bead Museum, Glendale, Arizona*

427. *Contemporary glass chevrons by Heron Glass (Mary Mullaney and Ralph Mossman) Driggs, Idaho. Furnace worked, blown and drawn, coldworked, cut, hand-ground, tumbler polished; soda-lime glass. Far left: Triangular chevron. 1994. Length, 3 cm. The Bead Museum. Middle: Peach and Burgundy Chevron. Length, 3.8 cm. Far right: Rasta Chevron. Middle and right, 2005, Collection of the artists*

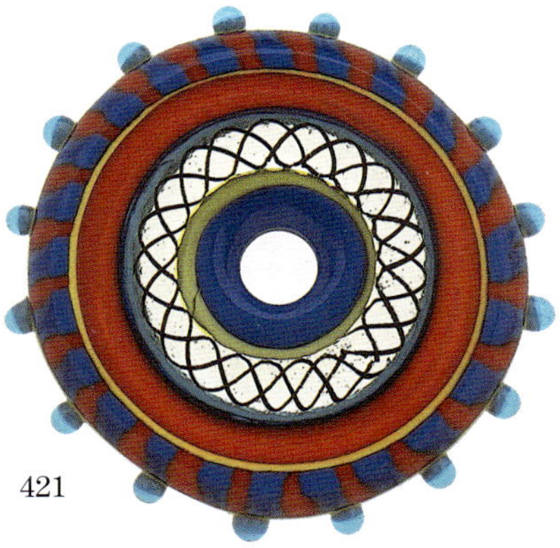

421

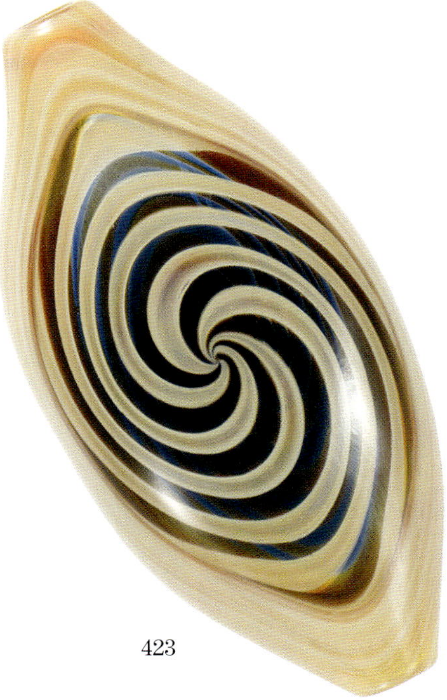

423

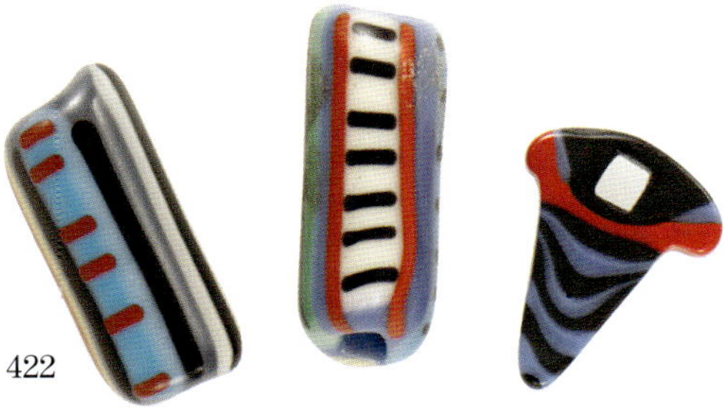

422

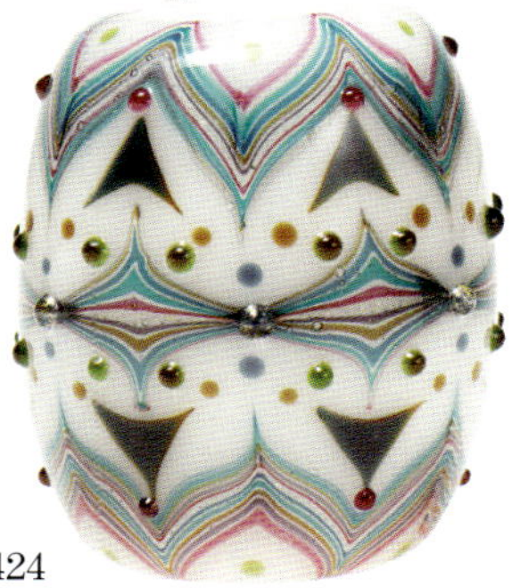

424

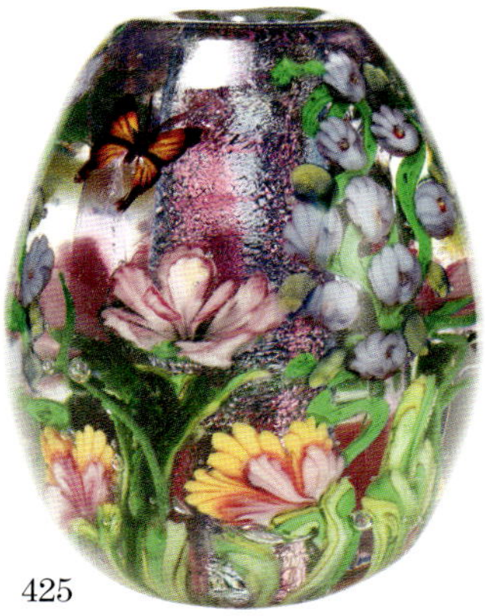

425

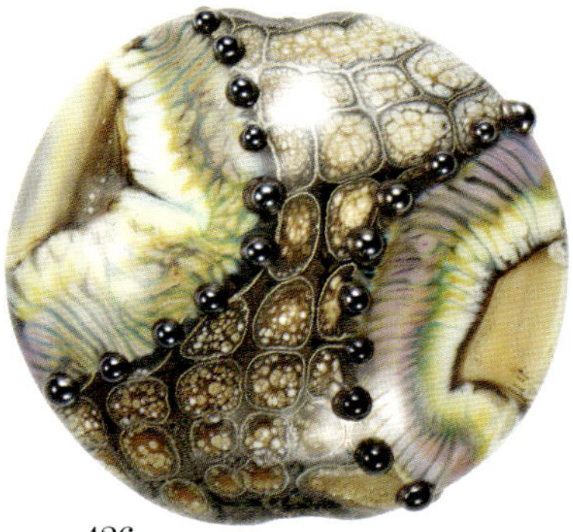

426

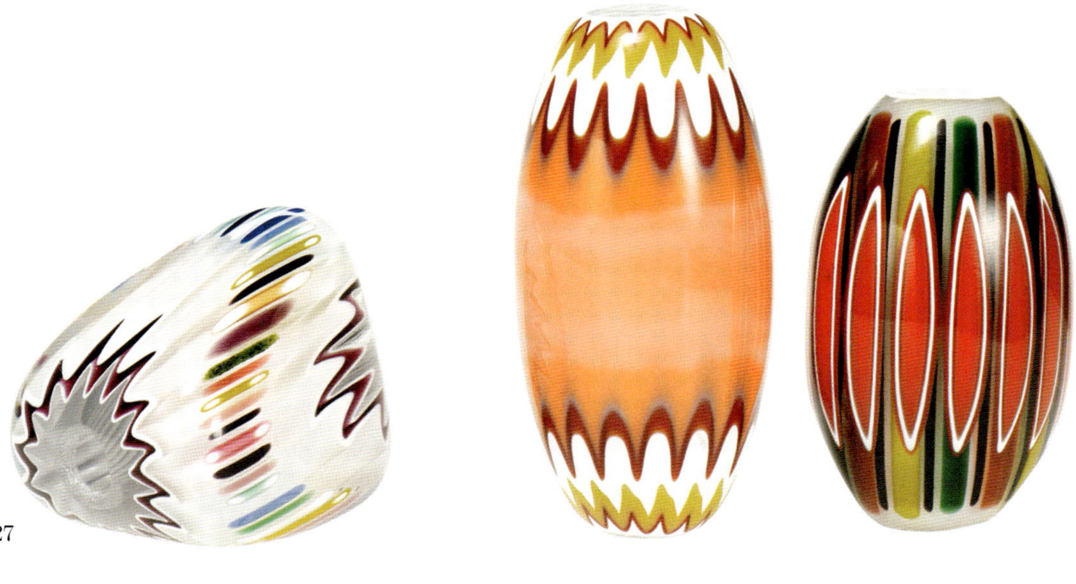

427

428

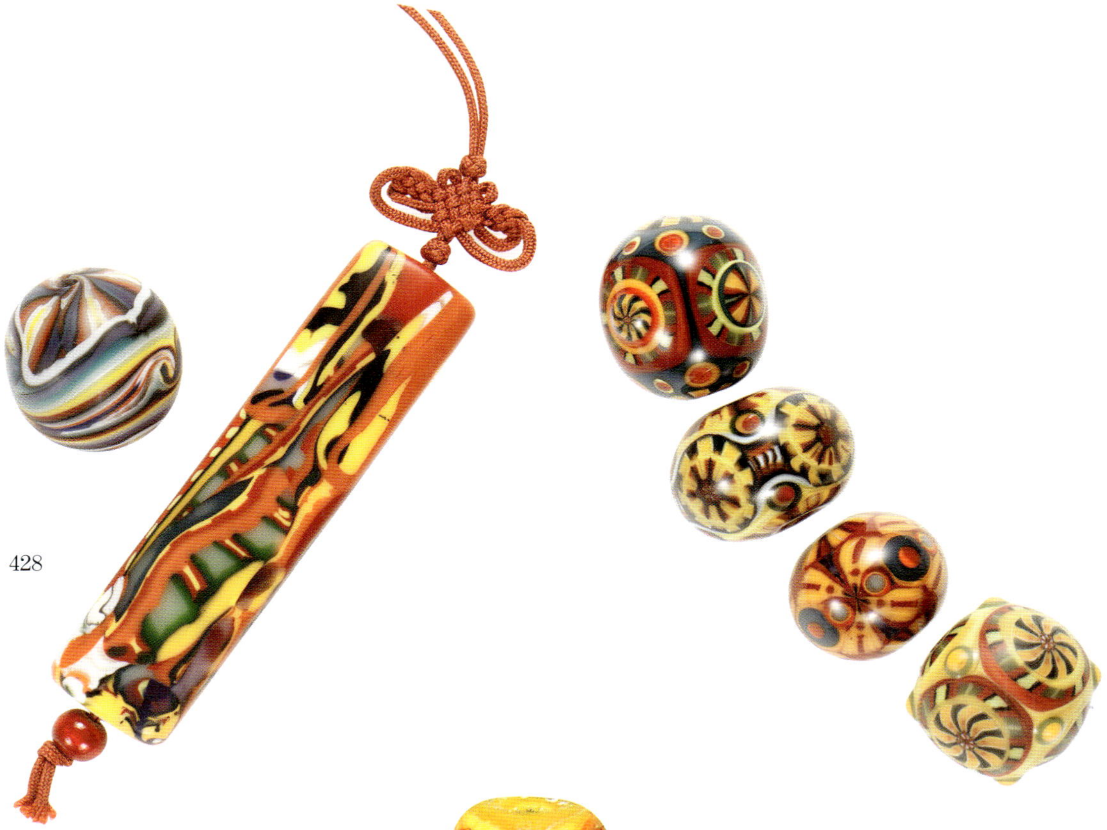

429

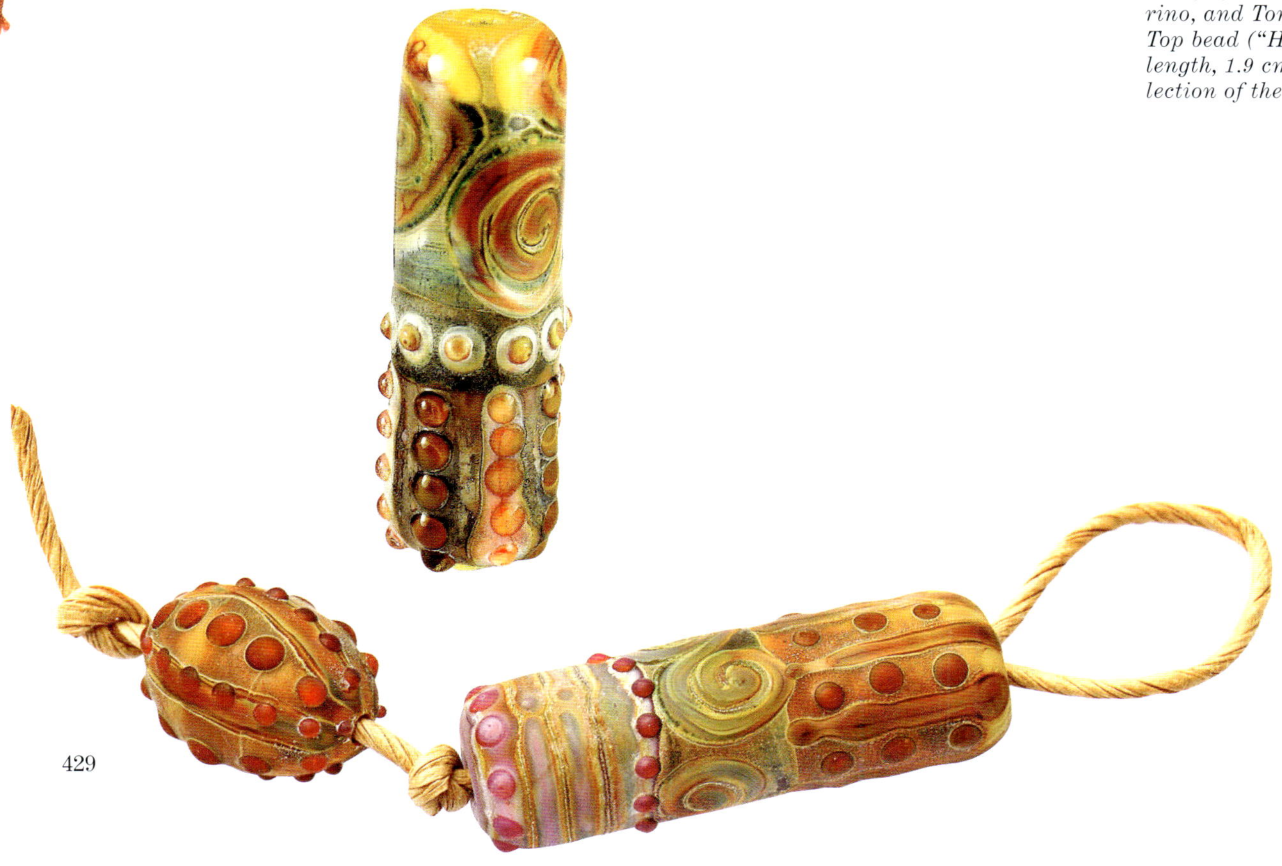

428. *Mosaic-glass beads by James Allan Jones. Lampworked, cold-bundled murrini and endcaps, marvered, soda-lime glass. Second from left: length, 8.3 cm. Third from left: diameter, 2.6 cm. Beads one and two, collection Toby Bowlby. Beads three to six, 2002. Collection of the artist*

429. *"Justinianus" and "Helena." 2007. Lampworked glass beads by Pinar Hakim. Istanbul, Turkey. Pinar, though educated as an archaeologist, has followed her passion for glass beadmaking. She started with classes at the Glass Furnace in Istanbul, and has attended numerous international workshops, including those directed by Kristina Logan, Marie-Odile Savigny, Andrea Guarino, and Tom Holland. Top bead ("Helena") length, 1.9 cm. All: Collection of the artist*

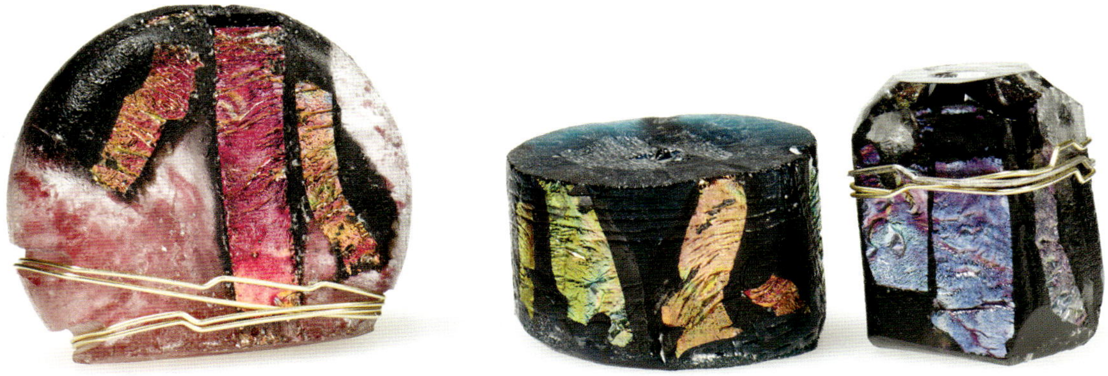

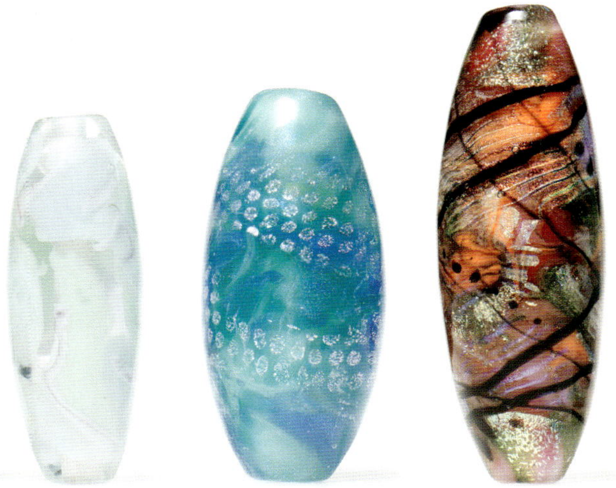

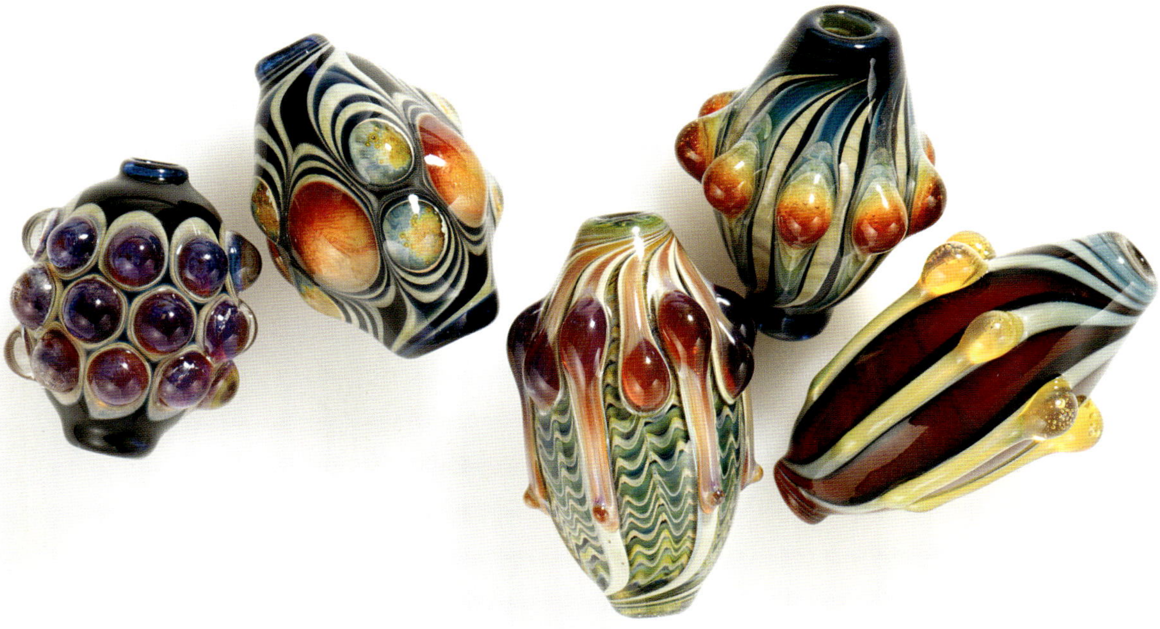

TOP ROW: 430. *Three pâte de verre, shaped and faceted dichroic glass beads by Donna Milliron combine translucent and matte surfaces and niobium wire. 1993. These beads were part of the first Contemporary Glass Beadmakers exhibition held in 1993 at the Bead Museum in Prescott, Arizona. Left: length, 3.8 cm. Collection Toby Bowlby*

MIDDLE ROW: 431. *Three lampworked glass beads of soda-lime (soft) dichroic glass with inclusions of fine silver and gold leaf. 1993. Inara Knight. Far right: 2.9 × 5.2 cm. All collection Toby Bowlby*

BOTTOM ROW: 432. *Glass beads. Late 1980s to 2008. Tom Boylan. Far right: Length, 4.8 cm. The beads are lampworked and blown, heat and gravity shaped of borosilicate glass. The repeated heating produces the different shades of color and levels of opacity. Collection of the artist*

OPPOSITE: 433. *"Beaded Sky Curtain," an architectural sculpture commissioned for the public atrium of the William A. Egan Civic and Convention Center in Anchorage, Alaska. Inspired by the Northern Lights (Aurora Borealis), approximately five million glass seedbeads (six miles of beads!) were hand-strung on polyester multifilament thread by the artist, Jeanne Leffingwell, and seven assistants during a ten-month period in 1985.*[XX] *Approximately 9 × 9 × 9 meters*

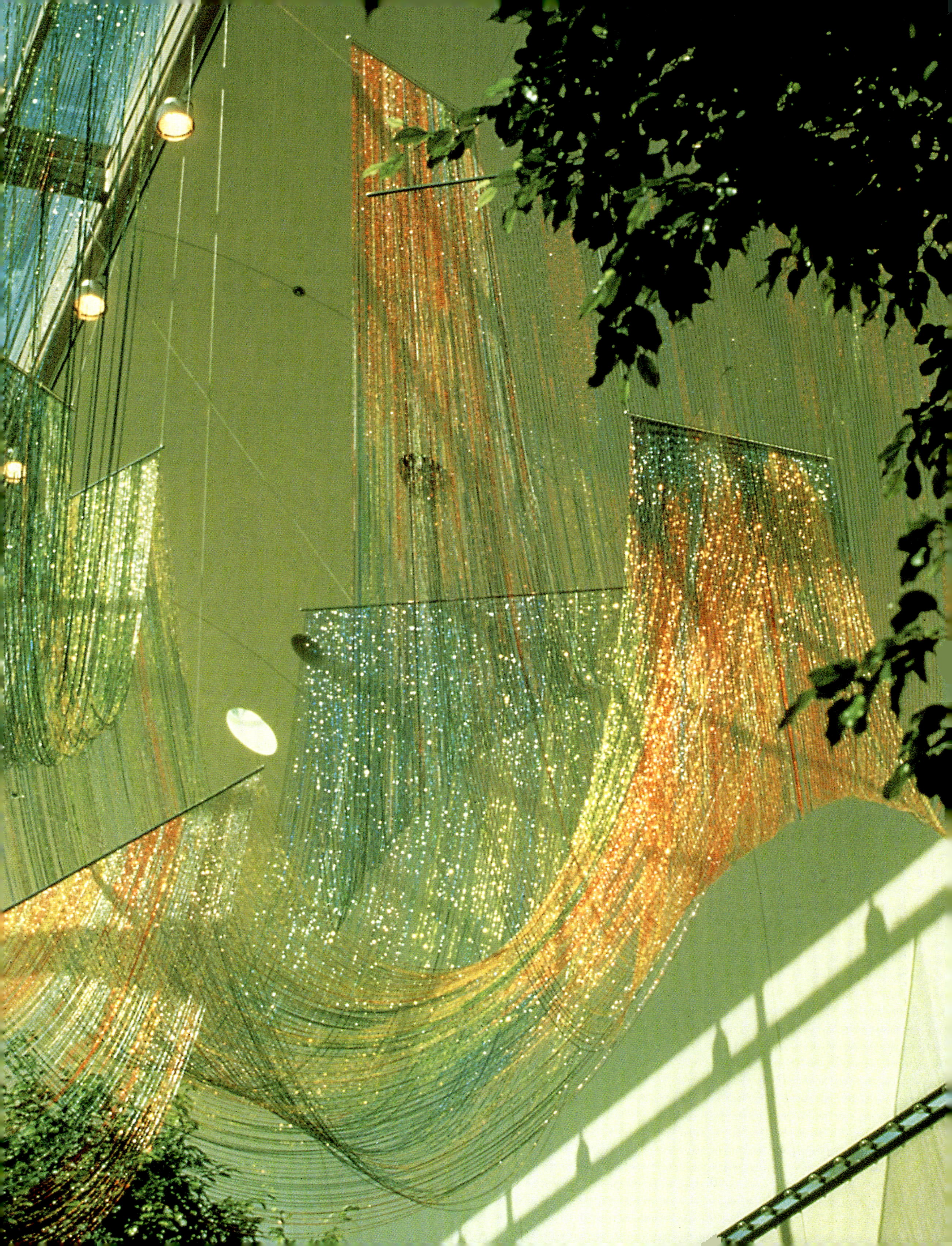

Bead Shape Table

TYPICAL BEAD SHAPES THROUGOUT THE WORLD

The name for each bead shape is from *Classification and Nomenclature of Beads and Pendants* by Horace C. Beck, which remains the classic bead shape reference guide. The shapes depicted on this chart are those most commonly found in stone and glass.

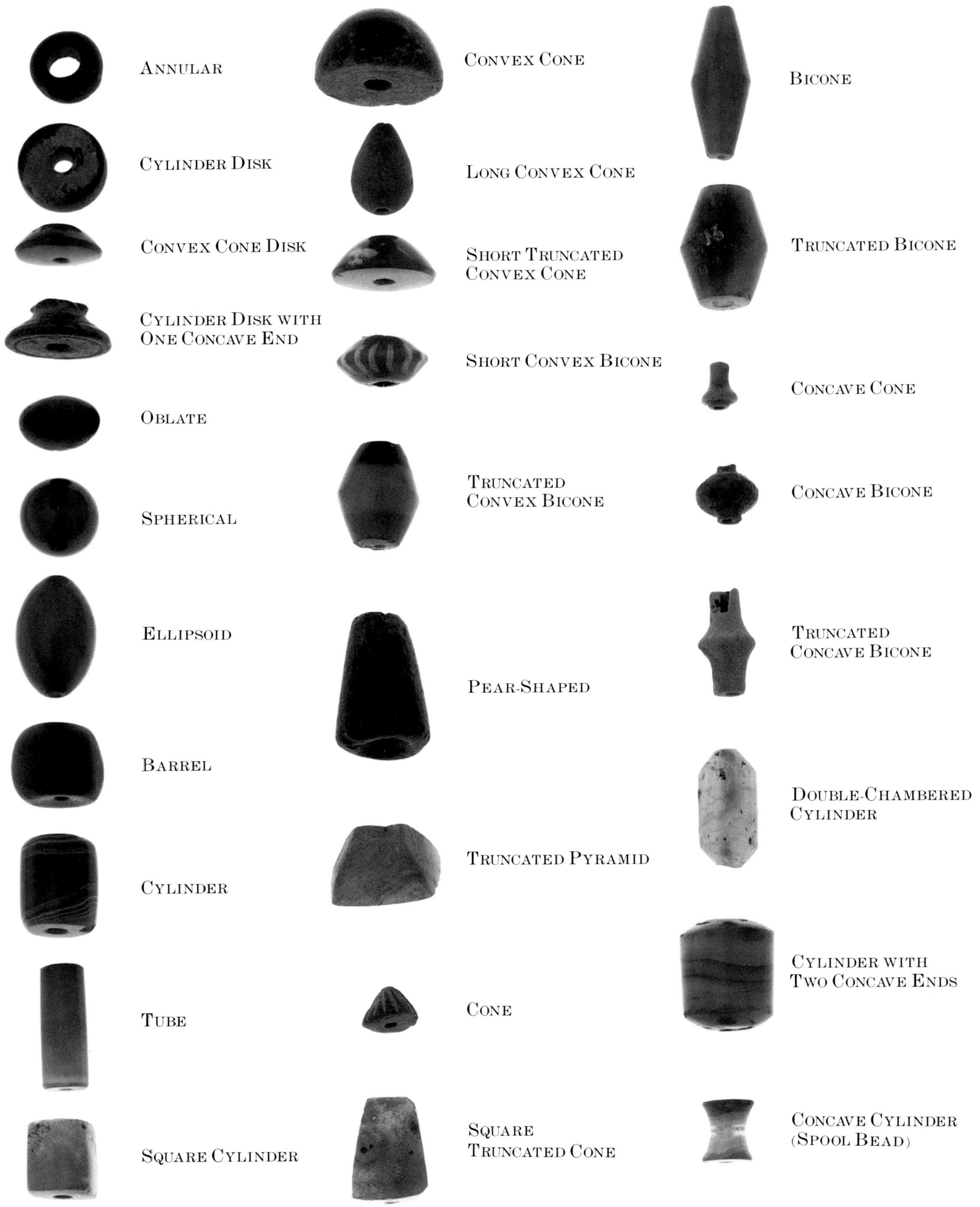

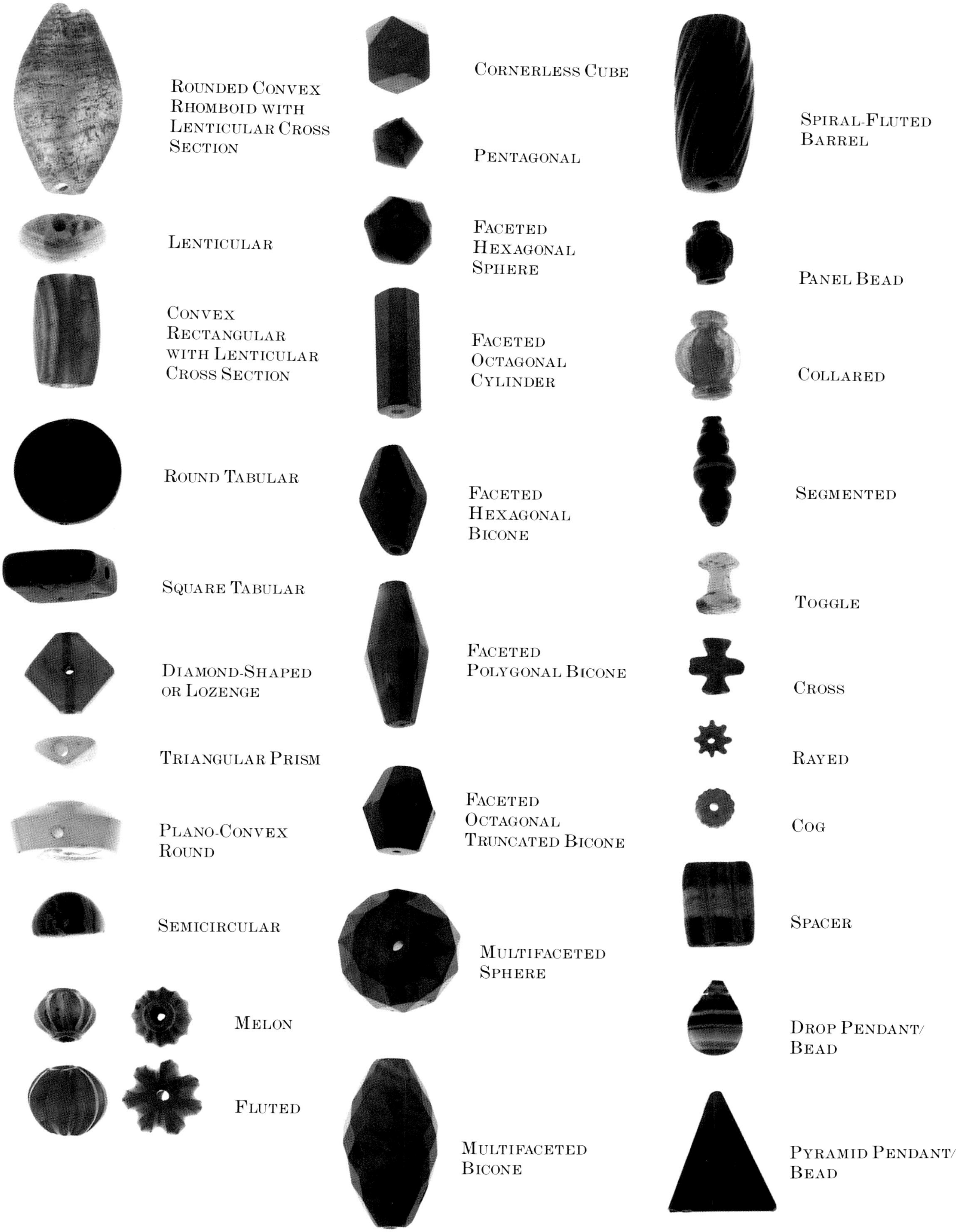
Rounded Convex Rhomboid with Lenticular Cross Section
Lenticular
Convex Rectangular with Lenticular Cross Section
Round Tabular
Square Tabular
Diamond-Shaped or Lozenge
Triangular Prism
Plano-Convex Round
Semicircular
Melon
Fluted
Cornerless Cube
Pentagonal
Faceted Hexagonal Sphere
Faceted Octagonal Cylinder
Faceted Hexagonal Bicone
Faceted Polygonal Bicone
Faceted Octagonal Truncated Bicone
Multifaceted Sphere
Multifaceted Bicone
Spiral-Fluted Barrel
Panel Bead
Collared
Segmented
Toggle
Cross
Rayed
Cog
Spacer
Drop Pendant/Bead
Pyramid Pendant/Bead

A Timeline of Bead History

1. The timeline shows every major bead type in the world and communicates three levels of information:

(A) Archaeological sites with important bead finds. Example:
▲Kostienki 17, Russia. Fox canine and belemnite beads, 35,000 B.C.

(B) Historical events that are part of bead history. Example:
Columbus gives glass beads to Arawak Indians in the Bahamas, 1492.

The historical and archaeological information is supplementary. It was not always possible to show relevant beads as well (or immediately adjacent to the information).

(C) Cultural and chronological groupings of beads coordinated by numbers. To help the reader understand these groupings, the numbering of the beads is in general cultural divisions.

2. Wherever possible, beads have been located on the timeline according to known manufacturing sources. Some beads, however, have unknown sources and/or wide-ranging distribution and are located according to where they have been found. These include: 13–30, 33a–e, 41–44, 333 a–b, 617, 629, 700, 701, 708, 711–716, 909a–e, 916, 919-922, 927, 1135a–g, 1136a–d, 1137.

3. Beads have been placed on the timeline at either their earliest known dates or, if they were manufactured over a long period, within their most representative phase.

4. All ancient beads either have an archaeological provenance (as noted) or usually can be dated by comparison with similar beads from a known archaeological site.

5. Beads 114a–c, although listed as Dutch, are nearly identical to Venetian beads of the same period.

6. Beads 132a–c and 133, although listed as Bohemian, could also be Venetian.

7. Indian drawn-glass "Indo-Pacific" beads, 625a–f, (previously called "trade wind" beads) were identified by W. G. N. van der Sleen as similar to excavated specimens from Kolhapur, India, Bahmani layer, fifteenth century A.D. The examples are from the Corning Museum of Glass, no. 57.1.3.

8. The current lack of a sufficient number of controlled excavation reports makes it difficult to assign Early and Middle Islamic period beads precise dates. Although they are located on the chart from about A.D. 550 to 1300, some may be earlier.

9. The *dZi* bead, 701, is one of the mysteries of the bead world. There is no known method of dating these beads, which are believed to be ancient. The *dZi* bead has been assigned to a pre-Buddhist date in Tibet.

10. All references for the timeline are credited in the bibliography and notes.

11. All beads shown in the chart are 40 percent of their original size unless otherwise noted, or designated without size (ns).

12. This version of the Time Line chart and key has been renumbered from the original version in order to incorporate two hundred additional beads.

HOW TO USE THE TIMELINE

Example 1. Bead 257 is located on the timeline in Mesopotamia, typically dating 2100–2000 B.C. For additional information, refer to the Timeline Key, page 367. This tells us that the bead is a gold-capped agate and has been archaeologically excavated from Uruk (Warka), Sumer. It is dated c. 2000 B.C. on the chart. The bead is 6.04 cm in length.

Example 2. Bead 1324 is located in contemporary Europe and North America, c. 2008. For additional information, refer to the Timeline Key, page 373. This tells us that the bead is made of woven 18-karat gold, sphenes, and diamonds. The artist is Stuart Golder. The bead's actual size is 2 cm in diameter.

Timeline KEY

EUROPE

PREHISTORY TO THE RENAISSANCE (NOS. 1–45)

1. Soapstone or talc. Isturitz, France. 36,000 B.C.
2. Amber. Isturitz. 34,000 B.C.
3. Perforated bear canine. Isturitz. 31,000 B.C.
4. Ivory. Basket-shape. Abri Blanchard, Dordogne, France. 31,000 B.C.
5. Ivory beads and pierced fox teeth. Sungir, Russia. 22,000 B.C.
6. Bone. Animal pendant. Sungir, Russia. 22,000 B.C.
7. Fossil shell. East Gravettian culture, Upper Paleolithic period, Pavlov, the Czech Republic. 28,000 B.C.
8. Ivory. Breast form, East Gravettian culture, Upper Paleolithic period, Dolni Vestonice, the Czech Republic. 28,000 B.C.
9. Jet. Female torso form, Magdalenian culture, Upper Paleolithic period, Petersfels, Germany. 13,000 B.C.
10. Bone. Horse's head, Magdalenian culture, Upper Paleolithic period, Espélugues, France. 10,000 B.C.
11. Bone. Horse's head, Magdalenian culture, Upper Paleolithic period, Le Portal, France. 10,000 B.C.
12. Shale. Nab Head, Pembrokshire, Wales. 9200–7500 B.C. (ns)
13. Amber. Feltwell Fen, Norfolk, England
14. Jet. Yorkshire, England
15. Segmented faience. Wessex culture grave, Wiltshire, England
16. Amber. Norfolk, England
17. Bronze. Kent, England
18. Bronze, amber, and glass. Hallstatt-type beads, Castaneda Misox, Grave 1, Switzerland
19. Wound glass with zigzag trail. Celtic, La Tène (?), France
20. Wound glass with four stratified eyes. England
21. Wound glass with trailed spiral. England
22. Twisted bicolor glass annular. England
23. Wound glass with trailed spiral upon vestigial horn. Celtic, England
24. Wound glass. England
25. Amber. Roman period, British Isles
26. Faience. Melon form, Roman period, British Isles
27. Jet. Half-melon form, Roman period, British Isles
28. Wound glass with zigzag trail. Celtic/Roman period, British Isles
29. Faience. Roman period, British Isles
30a–b. Wound-glass annular. Roman period, British Isles
31–35. Granulated and filigree gold. Denmark
36. Gold inlaid with garnet and lapis lazuli. Anglo-Saxon, England
37. Gold and garnet. Olbia, Russia
38. Wound glass with trailed and dragged design. Frankish, Rhine Valley
39. Glass. Frankish
40. Glass. Frankish
41. Glass. Viking, Eidem, Norway
a–b. Wound glass with trailed decoration
c–e. Mosaic glass
42–43. Wound glass with trailed decoration and mosaic glass inset. Viking, possibly made in eastern Europe
44. Wound glass with mosaic glass insets. Viking, possibly made in eastern Europe
45. Boxwood paternoster bead. Flemish (diameter, 5.7 cm)

VENICE (NOS.46–113)

46. Wound and drawn glass. "Seed," "pony," and tubular beads
47. Glass. Seven-layer faceted chevron
48a–d. Millefiori glass
49. Glass. Seven-layer, twisted-stripe star bead
50. Glass. Seven-layer chevron
51. Glass. Six-layer chevron
52a–b. Drawn glass. Brick red over dark green core
53. Glass paternoster bead
54a–c. Drawn glass. White stripes on light green core, "gooseberry" bead
55. Wound polychrome glass
56. Wound polychrome glass
57. Drawn-glass "seed" beads
58. Glass. Five-layer chevron
59. Wound glass with polychrome dots. Alta Verapaz bead
60a–b. Flattened and drawn glass rosetta beads
61. Drawn(?) glass with polychrome decoration
62a–d. Wound glass with polychrome trailed and dragged decoration
63a–i. Mosaic (millefiori) glass
64a–b. Mosaic (millefiori) glass
65. Wound glass with compound trailed decoration
66a–b. Glass. Four-layer chevrons
67a–d. Drawn glass with stripes. "Wafer" beads
68a. Wound glass with yellow core.
b. Drawn glass with green core. Cornaline d'Aleppo bead
69. Wound glass with compound trailed decoration
70. Wound glass with polychrome decoration
71a–d. Wound glass with polychrome decoration
72. Wound glass with compound trailed decoration
73. Wound compound glass with trailed and mosaic decoration
74. Wound glass with trailed decoration (imitating native African beads)

75a–e. Wound glass with polychrome and mosaic glass decoration
76. Wound glass with polychrome decoration
77. Wound glass with trailed and combed decoration (imitating folded mosaic beads)
78. Wound glass with polychrome decoration
79. Wound glass with polychrome decoration
80a–d. Wound compound glass with polychrome decoration
81a–b. Wound glass with dragged decoration. "Feather" beads
82. Wound glass with dragged trails
83a–c. Wound glass with polychrome decoration
84a–b. Wound glass with dragged decoration
85. Wound glass with polychrome spiral trail
86. Mosaic glass
87a–c. Mosaic glass
88a–b. Mosaic glass
89a–d. Drawn and compound, hot-pinched glass star bead
90. Drawn and compound, hot-pinched glass star bead
91. Wound glass with goldstone and mosaic glass insets. 1920s
92. Glass chevron
93a–c. Wound glass with raised polychrome decoration
94. Glass. Six-layer chevron
95. Glass. Six-layer chevron
96. Glass. Five-layer chevron
97a–c. Wound glass with polychrome decoration
98. Mosaic glass. Possibly made in Bohemia
99a–b. Wound glass with polychrome decoration
100a–b. Wound glass with foil inclusion
101. Drawn glass with internal aventurine layer
102. Wound glass with gold leaf and polychrome decoration
103. Wound glass with aventurine and dragged polychrome decoration
104a–b. Mosaic glass
105. Mosaic glass
106. Mosaic glass
107a–b. Wound glass. 1920s
108a. Wound glass with goldstone and aventurine. 1930s
b. Wound glass with "peacock eye"
109. Trailed glass over silver foil and glass
110a–b. Wound compound glass with polychrome dots
111. Wound glass with "scrabble" glass. "End-of-the-day" beads
112a–b. "Scrabble" glass. "End-of-the-day" beads
113. Wound glass with goldstone and mosaic glass insets

THE NETHERLANDS (NOS. 114–131)

114a–c. Glass. Striped three-layer star beads, possibly made in Venice
115. Glass. Three-layer drawn twisted-stripe Nueva Cadiz type bead
116. Drawn glass
117a–b. Glass. Striped five-layer star beads
118. Glass. Striped three-layer star bead
119a–c. Drawn glass
120. Drawn glass with stripes
121. Wound glass with enameled decoration, including depiction of Mary and baby Jesus
122a. Glass. Six-layer chevron
b. Glass. Five-layer star bead
c. Glass. Three-layer star bead
123a–c. Glass. Striped four-layer star beads
124. Wound glass. Pentagonal cylinder, "St. Eustace" bead
125. Drawn glass. Corn kernel shapes
126a–b. Wound compound glass with polychrome stripes
127. Wound glass with trailed decoration
128–131. Wound glass

BOHEMIA AND MORAVIA (NOS. 132–150)

132a–c. Drawn and faceted glass. "Russian" bead, possibly made in Venice
133. Wound opaline glass. Possibly made in Venice
134. Molded glass imitating faceted carnelian (length, 12 cm)
135. Molded glass simulating ivory tooth
136a–c. Molded glass
137. Molded glass
138. Molded glass. "Vaseline" or "mossi" bead
139a–c. Molded and faceted glass
140. Molded glass. Art Nouveau style
141. Molded glass simulating turquoise. "Hubbell" beads, made for the southwestern United States trade
142a–b. Molded and etched glass. Art Deco style
143, 144. Molded glass. Art Deco motifs. 1920s
145. Plastic. Imitation *dZi* bead, made for Himalayan regions trade
146. Molded glass with metallic coating
147a–g. Molded glass
148a–b. Molded glass
149. Molded glass. "Chain" or "snake" beads
150. Molded glass

BALTIC

151. Amber
a. Romania (Rumanite)
b. Baltic (succinite)
c. Baltic or Iran (succinite?)
d. Baltic (succinite)
152. Faceted Baltic amber (succinite)

GERMANY (153–157)

153a–m. Agate and carnelian (Idar Oberstein)
154. Marble glass. Hot-pinched
155a–d. Wound-glass annulars (German)
156, 157. Wound glass

FRANCE

158–162. Pressed or molded glass. Art Nouveau style, made by René Jules Lalique

WESTERN ASIA

EARLY WESTERN ASIA (NOS. 200–227)

200. Shell. Natufian culture, Eynan, Israel. 10,000–8000 B.C.
201. Nassus shell. Natufian culture, Gilgal II, Israel. 9000–8000 B.C.
202. Dentalium shell. Natufian culture, Eynan, Israel. 10,000–8000 B.C.
203. Bone. Natufian culture, HaNahal Cave, Israel. 10,000–8000 B.C.
204. Stone. Natufian culture, HaNahal Cave, Israel. 10,000–8000 B.C.
205. Bone (breast forms) and dentalium shell. Natufian culture, El Wad, Israel. 10,000–8000 B.C.
206a-c. Stone butterfly or double-axe beads. Tel Abu Hureyra, Syria. c. 7700-5500 B.C.
a. obsidian
b. steatite
c. serpentine
207. Amazonite
208. Calcite
209–211. Shell
212. Calcite
213. Steatite
214. Steatite
215a–b. Shell
216. Shell
217a–b. Shell
218. Shell
219. Animal tooth
220. Shell

221. Alabaster
222. Alabaster
223a–b. Calcified coral
224. Calcified coral
225–227. Shell

MESOPOTAMIA (NOS. 228–257)

228a–b. Stone. Arpachiyah
229. Steatite with linear markings. Arpachiyah
230a-d. Early sealstones with linear markings. Arpachiyah
231. Stone
232. Alabaster
233. Fossil coral
234. Agate
235. Stone
236a–b. Stone
237a–c. Stone eye beads
238a–c. Mother-of-pearl. Jemdet Nasr period
239a–c. Mother-of-pearl. Jemdet Nasr period
240. Stone
241. Stone
242. Shell
243a–b. Steatite cylinder seal with plaster impression. Uruk (Warka) (length, 6 cm)
244. Etched lapis lazuli
245a–c. Lapis lazuli, carnelian, and gold
246–247. Lapis lazuli and gold. Ur, Sumer (ns)
248a–c. Lapis lazuli, carnelian, and gold. Ur, Sumer (ns)
249. Etched carnelian. Ur, Sumer (length, 1.65 cm)
250. Gold filigree. Ur, Sumer (length, 3.31 cm)
251. Gold melon form
252. Fluted gold
253. Agate eye bead
254. Banded agate
255. Gold-capped agate. Ur, Sumer (length, 4.5 cm)
256. Gold. Flat-winged disk
257. Gold-capped agate. Uruk (Warka) (length, 6.04 cm)

ANATOLIA (NOS. 258–273, 326)

258–271. Steatite
272. Limestone
273. Gold. Quadruple spiral and quadruple disk beads. Alacahoyuk, Anatolia

AFGHANISTAN (NOS. 274–290)

274. Stone. "Shaft-of-wheat" bead, possibly made in Iran or northern Syria
275a–f. Banded agates
276a–e. Banded agates
277. Banded agate
278. Banded agate eye bead
279. Banded agate
280. Carnelian. Possibly made in Tepe Marlik or Amlash, Iran
281. Gold coiled wire
282. Limestone
283. Lapis lazuli
284. Lapis lazuli. "Spoon" bead
285. Agate bead with concave face and flat back
286. Gold-winged disk. Possibly made in Iran or Troy, Anatolia
287. Gold-winged disk
288. Gold-capped jasper. Possibly made in Afghanistan, Anatolia, or Aegean
289. Etched carnelian
290. Gold, lapis lazuli, carnelian, turquoise, and feldspar

IRAN, SYRIA, AND IRAQ (NOS. 291–315)

291. Banded agate
292. Stone
293a–h. Lapis lazuli
294a–c. Alabaster
295a–f. Alabaster
296a–c. Obsidian
297. Stone
298. Stone
299. Jet
300. Alabaster (?)
301. Stone. Mari, Iran
302. Steatite and shell. Mari, Iran
303. Stone spacer
304. Alabaster
305. Jasper. Possibly made in Afghanistan
306. Gold spacer. Iran
307. Gold quadruple-spiral
308a–b. Gold spacers. Iran
309. Faience lion bead. Susa, Iran
310. Silver core covered with gold wire cloisons and inlaid with lapis lazuli and yellow stones. Tell Atchana (Alalakh), Iraq
311. Glass. Mittani culture
312a–f. Glass. Mittani culture
313. Glass
314. Gold quadruple-spiral. Mari, Iran
315. Rock crystal scaraboid. North Syria, Iran, or Anatolia

IRAN (PERSIA): Pre-Achaemenid to Parthian period (NOS. 316–322)

316a–c. Banded agates
317a–c. Amber
318. Banded agate
319. Banded agate. "Spool" bead, Iran or Afghanistan
320. Chalcedony
321. Glass with dragged trail decoration. Tepe Marlik, Iran
322a–d. Wound glass with zigzag trail. Possibly made in Amlash, Iran
323a–e. Granulated gold. Iran
324a–e. Bronze
325. Bronze
326. Glass. Alisar, Anatolia
327a–b. Banded agate spacers
328a–b. Faience (?) Ziwiyeh, Iran
329. Blue chalcedony with gold. Achaemenid period
330. Banded mosaic glass. Possibly made in Iran
331. Banded agate. Possibly made as early as 1000 B.C., Iran or Afghanistan
332. Granulated gold
333a–b. Gold lotus blossom beads. Achaemenid period, Iran or possibly Egypt
334. Coral
335. Gold and pearl beads presumably from the Persian Gulf (diameter of largest pearl, 0.5 cm)
336. Banded agate
337. Wound glass with mosaic glass inset. Gilan, Iran
338. Wound glass with stratified eyes. Persepolis, Iran

IRAN (PERSIA): Parthian/Roman period (NOS. 339–365)

339–342. Banded agate
343. Banded mosaic glass
344. Gold and garnet. Sarmatian culture, Caspian Sea region
345–348. Faience. Iran
349. Lapis lazuli. Panel bead
350a–c. Banded agates
351a–c. Mosaic banded and faceted glass
352. Banded agate
353. Banded mosaic glass
354a-b. Banded agate
355. Banded mosaic glass
356. Banded mosaic glass
357. Agate eye bead
358. Stone
359a–f. Faience. Iran
360. Banded agate
361. Banded agate

362. Banded mosaic glass
363. Banded mosaic glass
364a–d. Banded agate
365a–d. Banded mosaic glass

ROMAN EMPIRE (NOS. 366–391)
366a–c. Banded agates
367a–c. Mosaic glass
368. Wound glass
369. Wound glass melon form
370. Wound glass with pressed facets (cornerless cube)
371a-c. Wound glass with stratified eyes
372. Wound glass with floral and figural mosaic plaques. Possibly made in Egypt
373. Wound glass with mosaic glass insets. Possibly made in Egypt
374a–c. Wound glass
375. Emerald crystal beads on gold wire links
376. Emerald crystal bead
377. Carnelian cornerless cube
378. Garnet
379a. Carnelian
b. Rock crystal
c. Amethyst
d. Carnelian
380a. Drawn and pressed glass tabular
b–d. Wound and pressed glass tabulars
381. "Etched" carnelian. Parthian to Sasanian periods
382. Stone "altar" bead
383. Granulated silver
384. Mosaic glass with floral and checker plaques
385. Wound glass with marvered crumb decoration
386. Wound glass with inlaid eye spots
387. Wound glass with mosaic canes
388a. Wound glass with marvered crumb decoration
b. Wound glass with polychrome crumb and mosaic decoration. Late Roman Egypt
389. Mosaic glass with eye spots
390a–c. Folded mosaic glass
391. Folded mosaic glass

MEDITERRANEAN

CRETE, CYPRUS, AND GREECE (NOS. 392–410)
392. Gold, lapis lazuli, and carnelian breast-shaped beads. Aegina Treasure, Minoan period, Aegina island
393. Gold duck bead. Palace of Knossos, Crete
394. Gold relief shell or flower bead. Mycenae
395–396. Gold. Mycenaean, Enkomi, Cyprus
397. Gold rosettes. Mycenae, Lalysos, Rhodes
398–400. Gold. Mycenaean, Enkomi, Cyprus
401. Mold-cast glass pendant beads. Mycenae
402. Gold. Mycenaean, Enkomi, Cyprus
403. Bronze wine jug bead. Potidaea, Macedonia (length, 3.8 cm)
404. Bronze wine jug bead, Potidaea, Macedonia (length, 2.6 cm)
405. Gold. Ephesus, Turkey
a. Length, 0.8 cm
b. Diameter, 0.6 cm
c. Diameter, 1.5 cm
d. Length, 0.9 cm
406. Gold. Ephesus, Turkey
a. Length, 0.8 cm
b. Length, 0.9 cm
c. Length, 0.8 cm
407. Gold. Ephesus, Turkey
a. Length, 1.2 cm
b. Length, 1 cm
c. Length, 1 cm
408. Gold melon beads
409. Amethyst
410. Rock crystal

PHOENICIA AND ETRURIA (NOS. 411–420)
411. Granulated gold beads with wound-glass stratified eye beads and modeled-glass pendant bead. Pendant, Phoenician; beads, Etruscan (pendant: length, 3.1 cm)
412. Granulated gold. Etruscan
413. Modeled grotesque face pendant bead. Phoenician, North Africa, or Syrian-Palestinian coast
414. Wound glass with modeled polychrome face and raised spots. Phoenician, Carthage, or Syrian-Palestinian coast
415–416. Modeled glass head pendant beads. Phoenician, possibly made in Carthage
417. Modeled glass ram's head pendant bead. Phoenician, Carthage, or Syrian-Palestinian coast
418a–c. Wound glass with stratified eyes. Phoenician
419. Wound glass with composite stratified eyes and raised spots. Phoenician
420. Wound glass with spiral-wound coils and raised stratified eyes. Phoenician, Carthage, or Syrian-Palestinian coast

HELLENISTIC PERIOD (NOS. 421–427)
421. Granulated gold. Greece
422. Gold and garnet spool beads on gold wire links. Crete
423. Garnet spool beads on gold wire links. Probably made in eastern Greece
424. Granulated gold and green glass. Greece
425. Embossed and filigree gold with garnet inlay. Olbia, Sardinia
426a–b. Folded and pressed heart-shaped glass. Rhodes
427. Gold Hercules-knot bead. Eastern Mediterranean, late Hellenistic to Graeco-Roman periods

EGYPT

PREDYNASTIC PERIOD TO ROMAN EGYPT (NOS. 428–513)
428a–d. Shells. Badarian period
429. Bone. Badarian period
430a–b. Ivory. Badarian period
431. Copper. Badarian period
432. Alabaster. Badarian period
433. Stone. Badarian period
434. Glazed steatite. Badarian period
435. Alabaster drop. Nagadah period
436. Stone. Nagadah period
437. Glazed faience. Nagadah period
438. Alabaster. Nagadah period
439. Agate. Early Dynastic period
440. Ivory. "Serekh" bead, Early Dynastic period
441. Glazed faience. Early Dynastic period
442. Cowrie shell. Badarian to Early Dynastic period
443. Copper and carnelian. Early Dynastic period
444. Steatite, lapis lazuli, garnet, and shell. Early Dynastic period
445. Green glazed steatite and shell beads with carnelian pendant. Early Dynastic period
446. Carnelian. Old Kingdom period
447. Stone, faience, and glazed "crumb" bead. Old Kingdom period, Fourth to Fifth dynasty, Mostagadda
448a–b. Faience
449. Carnelian, stone, faience, and shell. Old Kingdom period
450. Electrum, gold, carnelian, and feldspar. Old Kingdom period, Fourth to Fifth dynasty, Mostagadda
451. Carnelian and faience. Old Kingdom period
452. Faience. Old Kingdom period
453. Bead amulets of carnelian, turquoise, and amethyst. First Intermediate period
454. Cigar-shaped faience. Middle Kingdom

455. Faience. Wesekh collar. Deir-el-Bahari, Egypt. Length, outer row: 41.6 cm
456. Carnelian, gold, and feldspar acacia seed beads and gold cowrie shell effigy bead. Lahun, Twelfth dynasty (ns)
457. Garnet. Middle Kingdom
458. Gold-capped carnelian. Middle Kingdom period
459. Gold-capped amethyst. Middle Kingdom period
460. Amethyst. Middle Kingdom period
461. Stone with gold. Middle Kingdom period
462. Amethyst and gold. Middle Kingdom period
463. Wedge-shaped faience spacer. New Kingdom period
464a–e. Faience. New Kingdom period
465. Faience spacer. New Kingdom period
466a–b. Folded and ground (?) glass. New Kingdom period, Eighteenth to Nineteenth dynasty
467. Wound-glass heart amulet bead. New Kingdom period, Eighteenth to Nineteenth dynasty
468. Wound-glass pomegranate. New Kingdom period, Eighteenth to Nineteenth dynasty
469a–c. Faience. New Kingdom period, Eighteenth to Nineteenth dynasty
470. Wound glass with impressed coils and stratified eyes. New Kingdom period, Eighteenth to Nineteenth dynasty
471. Wound- and carved-glass heart amulet bead. New Kingdom period, Eighteenth to Nineteenth dynasty
472. Faience lotus blossom. Amarna, New Kingdom period, Eighteenth to Nineteenth dynasty
473. Wound pear-shaped or fig-shaped bead with zigzag trail. New Kingdom period, Eighteenth to Nineteenth dynasty
474. Faience. Amarna, New Kingdom period, Eighteenth to Nineteenth dynasty
a. Grape cluster
b. Mandrake fruit
475. Carnelian lotus seed pod
476. Amethyst
477. Wound-glass double duck bead. New Kingdom period, Eighteenth to Nineteenth dynasty
478. Faience frog. Amarna, New Kingdom period, Eighteenth dynasty
479. Faience. Amarna, New Kingdom period, Eighteenth dynasty
a. Petal
b–c. Seed pods
d. Daisy
480a–e. Wound glass with stratified eyes. New Kingdom period, Eighteenth to Nineteenth dynasty
481. Wound glass with flush, stratified eyes and raised dots. Ramesside period, Nineteenth to Twentieth dynasty. 1320–1085 B.C.
482. Wound glass with flush, stratified eyes. Ramesside period, Nineteenth to Twentieth dynasty. 1320–1085 B.C.
483. Wound glass with flush, stratified eyes and raised dots. Ramesside period, Nineteenth to Twentieth dynasty. 1320–1085 B.C.
484. Wound glass with flush, stratified eyes. Ramesside period, Nineteenth to Twentieth dynasty. 1320-1085 B.C.
485. Wound glass with flush, stratified eyes. Ramesside Period, Nineteenth to Twentieth dynasty. 1320-1085 B.C.
486. Faience wedjat (Eye of Horus). Ramesside Period, Nineteenth to Twentieth dynasty. 1320–1085 B.C.
487. Faience wedjat. Ramesside Period, Nineteenth to Twentieth dynasty. 1320–1085 B.C.
488. Faience spacer bead depicting figures of the god Horus as a child and as a warrior with prisoners (length, 4.5 cm)
489. Faience bead with multiple eye motif. Twenty-second to Twenty-third dynasty. 818–656 B.C.
490. Wedjet. Wood, glass, plaster, gold, copper, or copper alloy. Ptolemaic to Early Roman period. 664–30 B.C.
491. Faience disk beadwork
492. Granulated gold. Twenty-sixth to Twenty-ninth dynasty. 664–380 B.C.
493. Wound glass with eye spots
494. Wound glass with raised eye spots
495. Wound glass with stratified eyes
496. Faience scarab. Ptolemaic period
497. Faience wedjat. Ptolemaic to Early Roman. 664–30 B.C.
498a–b. Banded mosaic glass. Ptolemaic period
499. Mosaic glass. Ptolemaic period
500. Wound glass with impressed stratified eyes. Late Dynastic to Early Ptolemaic. Sixth to fourth centuries B.C.
501. Faience openwork with Eye of Horus. Ptolemaic to Early Roman. 664-30 B.C.
502. Drawn, clear, hot-pinched glass with gold foil and impressed design
503–504. Mosaic glass with checkerboard pattern. Roman Egypt
505. Tabular glass with mosaic plaques. Roman Egypt
506. Figural mosaic glass. Roman Egypt
507a–c. Sandwich gold-in-glass. Hellenistic or Roman periods
508. Mosaic glass. Roman Egypt
509. Floral mosaic glass square tabular. Roman Empire, Egypt, or Rome
510. Faceted mosaic glass. Roman Egypt
511. Wound glass with floral mosaic plaques. Roman Egypt
512. Mosaic glass tabular. Roman Egypt
513. Rolled pad millefiori bead

BYZANTINE
(NOS. 514–519)
514. Wound glass with trailed decoration
515. Amethyst
516. Emeralds, pearls, and sapphires with gold wire links. Piazza della Consolazione Treasure, Rome
517. Sapphire with gold chain
518. Gold filigree
519. Wound glass with dragged trails

ISLAM
(NOS.520- 582)
520. Folded mosaic glass
521. Molded glass amulet case form with marvered crumbs
522. Wound glass with dragged trails
523. Folded mosaic glass tabular with stratified layers
524. Mosaic glass melon-form collared bead
525. Wound-glass melon-form collared bead
526a–b. Folded mosaic glass dove beads
527–528. Wound glass with dragged trails
529. Folded mosaic glass
530. Rolled pad millefiori
531. Rolled pad millefiori
532. Wound-glass pendant bead with trails
533. Wound-glass pendant bead with dragged trails
534. Rock crystal amulet case pendant bead
535. Folded mosaic glass tabular pendant beads
536–537. Wound glass with dragged trails
538. Wound (?) glass with dragged trails
539a–c. Wound glass with zigzag trails
540. Wound and faceted (cut) glass. “Cornerless cube” bead

541. Faceted lapis lazuli. "Cornerless cube" bead
542. Folded mosaic glass with equatorial band
543. Wound glass trailed with mosaic band
544. Wound glass with zigzag trails
545. Wound glass with dragged trails
546–547. Filigree and granulated gold. Syria
548. Wound glass with spiral trails
549–550. Wound-glass pendant bead with trails
551. Wound glass with trails
552. Wound glass with dragged trails
553a–c. Glazed quartz
554. Wound glass with dragged indented trails
555. Lapis lazuli inlaid with turquoise
556. Faceted lapis lazuli without its inlay (probably gold)
557. Collared lapis lazuli inlaid with turquoise
558. Faceted carnelian
559. Rock crystal
560. Folded mosaic glass spacer bead
561. Rock crystal amulet case pendant bead
562. Wound glass with mosaic canes. Made in western Asia
563. Gold. Iran. Seljuk period
564. Mosaic glass canes, no core. Made in western Asia
565. Wound-glass melon form
566. Glazed quartz figas ("clutched fist")
567. Glazed faience. Gorgan, Naispur, Iran
568. Hollow cassolette filigree gold bead of enamel cloisonné set with emeralds and rubies. Moorish Spain
569. Gold inlaid with emeralds, rubies, and/or garnets. Morocco
570a–c. Wound glass with dragged trails. (b–c possibly made in Venice)
571. Wound glass with dragged trails
572. Amber or copal. Iran
573. Granulated silver. Yemen
574–575. Silver. Yemen
576–577. Silver. Turkoman
578a–b. Wound glass with stratified eyes. Hebron, Jordan
579. Wound glass with stratified eyes. Goerce, Turkey
580a–c. Wound glass. Hebron or Turkey
581. Silver and bronze. Kazakh
582. Wound glass with stratified eyes. Turkey

INDIA
(NOS. 600–661)

600. Steatite. Ravi phase
601. Terra cotta. Ravi phase
602. Terra cotta. Ravi phase
603. Carnelian. Ravi phase
604. Lapis lazuli. Ravi phase
605a–c. "Etched" carnelian. Indus Valley manufacture. c. 2600–1600 B.C.
606. Agate
607. Etched carnelian
608. Etched carnelian
609. Etched carnelian
610. Carnelian
611a–c. Banded agate. Pakistan region
612. Collared beads. Taxila
a. stone
b–g. glass
h–i. stone
613a–b. "Etched" agate. Kushan period
614. Drawn glass. "Mutisalah" bead
615a–c. "Etched" carnelian. Kushan to Gandra periods, Pakistan region
616. Collared carnelian
617. Stratified mosaic glass. Possibly made in India, Pakistan, or Afghanistan
618. Folded and pinched mosaic glass. Possibly made in Afghanistan or Pakistan region
619. Wound glass with dragged trails. Northern Pakistan region
620. Rudraksha bead (*Eleaocarpus ganitrus* seed)
621. Folded mosaic glass. Possibly made in Afghanistan or Pakistan region
622a–b. Carnelian
623. Banded mosaic glass. Possibly made in Pakistan region
624a–d. Stone
625a–f. Drawn-glass Indo-Pacific beads. Possibly made in Brahmapuri, India
626. Stone
627a–d. Stone
628. Carnelian
629. Drawn-glass "seed" beads collected in Indonesia. Possibly made later in India or Venice
630a–e. Stone
631. Carnelian
632a–b. Carnelian
633. Emeralds. Mogul period
634–640. Silver
641. Ivory
642. Ivory and silver
643. Silver chain bead
644. Glazed ceramic. "Donkey" bead
645. Gold-plated silver melon form
646. Wound glass with powdered-glass decoration
647. Wound mosaic glass
648. Wound glass with trail
649. Wound glass with bicolor spiral trail
650. Wound glass with mosaic decoration
651. Wound glass with mosaic decoration
652. Compound wound glass with trails
653. Wound glass with spiral trail
654. Wound glass with spiral trail
655a–c. Wound glass with trails
656. Wound glass with spiral trail and pressed melon form
657. Wound glass with spiral trail and pressed melon form
658. Mosaic glass face bead. Probably made in India or Pakistan region
659. Mosaic glass face bead. Probably made in India or Pakistan region
660. Silver set with amethyst
661. Brass inlaid with turquoise

CENTRAL ASIA

HIMALAYAN REGION (NOS. 700–722)

700. "Etched" agate. Date unknown
701. "Etched" agate. Nine-eyed *dZi* bead, Date unknown
702. Carnelian, silver. Pema Raka bead. Tibet
703. Carnelian. Pema Raka bead. Tibet
704a–f. All beads shown at 25 percent of actual size
a. Amber
b. Turquoise
c. Coral
d. Gold-capped amber
e. Coral with turquoise inlay
f. Coral
705. Gold-capped amber inlaid with turquoise (diameter, 9.5 cm)
706. Turquoise
707a–b. Shell
708. Carnelian
709. Carnelian
710. Rock crystal
711–714. Wound glass. Probably made in India
715a–b. Wound glass. Probably made in India
716a–d. Drawn glass. Probably made in India
717. Wound glass. Probably made in India
718. Drawn glass. Probably made in India
719. Opalized palm wood with artificial decoration. Puntek bead, Mizzoram, Burma
720a–c. Opalized palm wood with artificial decoration. Puntek bead, Mizzoram, Burma
721. Wound glass. Probably made in India
722. Pressed amber. Probably made in Europe

FAR EAST

CHINA, KOREA, AND JAPAN (NOS. 800–866)

800. White jade (nephrite) with etched pattern of twisting snakes and traces of red pigment. Western Zhou period, reportedly from Anyang, Shang dynasty, China

801. Etched and cut jade (nephrite) with patterns of dragons in profile and traces of red powder. Late Western Zhou period, China

802. Incised jade (nephrite) with patterns of geometric motifs and eyes and traces of red pigment. Early Eastern Zhou period, China

803. Molded glass with ground hexagonal facets. Probably made in Changsha, Hunan province, Late Zhou period, China

804. Etched jade (nephrite) with patterns of spirals and eyes. Eastern Zhou period, China

805. Etched jade (nephrite) with patterns of diagonally incised, ropelike bands and curvilinear motifs. Eastern Zhou period, China

806. Ground jade (nephrite). Eastern Zhou period, China

807. Wound glass with stratified eyes. Eastern Zhou "Warring States" period, China

808. Wound glass with stratified eyes. Eastern Zhou "Warring States" period, China

809. Kneeling faience attendant. Eastern Zhou "Warring States" period, China

810. Wound glass with stratified and compound eyes. Eastern Zhou "Warring States" period, China

811. Wound glass with raised stratified eyes. Eastern Zhou "Warring States" period, China

812. Glazed pottery (?) with stratified eyes. Eastern Zhou "Warring States" period, China

813. Wound glass with stratified eyes. Eastern Zhou "Warring States" period, China

814. Wound glass with raised stratified and compound eyes. Eastern Zhou "Warring States" period, China

815. Wound glass with trails and raised eyes. Eastern Zhou "Warring States" period, China

816. Cut jade (nephrite). Han dynasty, China

817. Wound glass with trailed designs. Han dynasty, China

818–819. Wound-glass kodama with red pigment. Tomb period, Japan

820. Wound-glass marudama. Tomb period, Japan

821. Jade kogok. Korea

822. Molded, ground, and drilled glass magatama. Japan

823 a–c. Wound glass. Qing dynasty, China

824a–c. Wound glass. Qing dynasty, China

825. Wound glass with applied spots. Qing dynasty, China

826. Wound glass imitating jade. Qing dynasty, China

827a–b. Wound glass melon forms. Qing dynasty, China (827b possibly made in Venice)

828a–b. Wound glass. Qing dynasty, China

829a–c. Wound glass. Qing dynasty, China

830–833. Wound glass. Qing dynasty, China

834. Ivory ojime peony blossom. Edo period, Japan

835. Wound glass with applied spot. Edo period, Japan

836. Wound glass gangidama with zigzag trails. Edo period, Japan

837. Glass tombodama. Edo period, Japan

838. Wound glass with mosaic and filigree glass sarasadama. Edo period, Japan

839. Stained ivory monkey ojime. Edo or Meiji period, Japan

840. Wound-glass melon form. Edo period, Japan

841. Wound glass with mosaic decoration, sarasadama. Edo period, Japan

842. Wound-glass tombodama. Edo period, Japan

843. Lacquer ojime with quail motif. Edo or Meiji period, Japan

844. Chinese millefiori. China

845. Wound glass with encased goldfish. Meiji period, Japan

846. Ivory ojime with shibayama (inlay jewel-work) technique. Meiji period, Japan

847a–c. Wound glass. China

848. Drawn glass. China

849. Drawn glass. China

850. Plique a jour. China

851. Chinese millefiori. Boshan, China

852. Chinese millefiori. Boshan, China

853. Carved coral. China

854a–b. Enameled cloisonné. China

855. Painted porcelain. China

856. Carved wood. China

857. Plique a jour. China

858. Glass chevron. Drawn and folded. China

859. Coral. China

860–862. Wound glass with mosaic inset. Artist: Kyoyu Asao

863. Carved bone. China

864. Turquoise. China

865a-b. Drawn glass with gold foil. Japan

866. "Cattleya." Wound, lampworked, and layered glass. Japan. Artist: Ayuko Shiroshita

SOUTHEAST ASIA

(NOS. 900–937)

900a. Glass. Ban Chiang, Thailand

b. Glass. Possibly Ban Chiang, Thailand

901. Drawn glass. "Mutisalah" bead

902. Agate. Thailand

903. Stone. Thailand

904. Pyu culture, Burma

a. agate

b. quartz crystal

c–d. agate

905. Gold. Jatinou, Java

906. Carnelian. Pyu culture, Burma

907. Drawn, hot-pinched, and enameled glass

908. Drawn and hot-pinched glass. Jatim bead. Similar to a bead found in a royal grave of the Silla Kingdom in Korea, dating to the late fifth to early sixth century A.D.

909. Constricted glass tubes. Possibly Majapahit culture (1293–1400 A.D. or earlier), Java

a. Compound glass with dragged trails

b–e. Applied mosaic decoration

910. Drawn glass cane with millefiori decoration. Jatim

911. Dentate gold disks. Pre-Hispanic period, Philippines

912. Ming porcelain. Indonesia

913a–b. Shell. South Pacific

914. Amber (Burmite). Burma

915. Coconut shell. South Pacific

916. Carnelian, agate, drawn glass, and chevron. Kalinga, Philippines (carnelian, agate, and drawn-glass beads made in India; chevron beads made in Europe)

917a-b. Gold. Philippines

918. Wound with trail decoration

919. Drawn glass. Of unknown origin, Borneo

920. Wound glass with stratified eyes. Of unknown origin, Borneo

921. Wound glass. Of unknown origin, Borneo

a. Double bead with compound stripes

b. Mosaic trails. Lukut sekala bead

c. Trails and spots

922. Wound glass with mosaic decoration. Of unknown origin, Borneo

923. Gilted silver. Sumba
924. Wound polychrome glass. Paiwan, Indonesia
925. Wound polychrome glass. Paiwan, Indonesia
926. Wound with trail decoration. Pyuma tribal beads, Taiwan
927. Drawn-glass seed beads. Probably made in India, Philippines
928–929. Shell. Philippines
930. Ivory. Philippines
931. Baroque South Sea pearl
932. Round South Sea pearl
933. Baroque South Sea pearl
934. Shell mosaic. Philippines
935a–e. Granulated silver. Bali
936a–b. Fossil palm wood. Puntuk beads. Burma
937. Lapidary-worked glass

NORTH AMERICA
(NOS. 1000–1046)

1000. Red jasper. Locust effigy bead. Poverty Point culture, Late Archaic period, Lafayette County, Arkansas. c. 1500–700 B.C.
1001. Abalone shell. Hidden Cave, Nevada. 1350–1300 B.C.
1002. Juniper berry beads. (Juniperus osteosperma). Hidden Cave, Nevada. 1350–1300 B.C.
1003. Stone. Ovoid eye form. Nisga'a cultural area, British Columbia
1004. Stone. Raven image. Boardwalk site, British Columbia. c. 1000 B.C.
1005a–f. Rolled copper. Montgomery Co., Ohio
1006. Copper. Montgomery Co., Ohio
1007. Copper. Adena/Hopewell culture. Recovered near Columbus, Ohio
1008. Copper. Glacial Kame phase. Southern Ontario
1009. Freshwater pearl. Dickison site, Peoria Co., Illinois
1010. Freshwater mussel shell. Dickison site, Peoria Co., Illinois
1011. Rolled copper bead. Wilson site, White Co., Illinois
1012. Copper. Wilson site, White Co., Illinois
1013. Freshwater pearls. Arkansas
1014. Turquoise. Pueblo Bonito, Chaco Canyon, Anasazi Pueblo I–III, New Mexico
1015. Turquoise frog beads. Salmon Ruin, New Mexico
1016. Abalone shell and turquoise strung on Yucca fiber cord. Ancestral Pueblo. Apache Co., Arizona
1017. Turquoise. Pueblo Bonito, Chaco Canyon, Anasazi Pueblo II, New Mexico
1018. Turquoise duck. Pueblo Bonito, Chaco Canyon, Anasazi Pueblo II–III, New Mexico
1019. Abalaone shell. Hohokam depiction of an Aztec Cicactli figure. Snaketown. A.D. 850–1100
1020. Turquoise. Chaco Canyon, Anasazi Pueblo III, New Mexico
1021. Bird bone. Ohio
1022. Shell. Arkansas
1023. Conch shell. Madisonvale, Ohio
1024. Columella shell
1025. Dentalium shell. Washington
1026a–f. Shell. Prehistoric Iroquois
1027. Steatite, argillite, and turquoise disk beads. Typical size: 1 mm. Ancestral Pueblo. A.D. 1225–1300
1028. Ricolite (banded serpentine) stone. Big-horn sheep pendant. Casas Grandes, Chihuahua, Mexico. A.D. 1150–1450
1029. Conus shell tinklers. Casas Grandes, Chihuahua, Mexico. A.D. 1150–1450
1030a–c. Claystone
1031. Abalone shell. Northwest Pacific coast
1032. Black stone with shell inlay and asphaltum adhesive. Chumash culture, Santa Barbara coast, California
1033. Wampum, purple and white clamshell. Iroquois
1034. Detail of sewn shell wampum. Seneca, Iroquois
1035. Wound glass. "Padre" bead, possibly made in China
1036. Turquoise disks and tabulars. Navajo culture, Southwest
1037. Silver beads of coin silver, 1870s. Navajo
1038. Turquoise nuggets. Navajo culture, Southwest
1039. Silver, shell, coral, and glass. Southwest
1040. Claystone with turquoise fetishes. Zuni Pueblo, Southwest
1041. Indian Mountain Nevada turquoise, coral. Artist: Cheryl Yestewa (Hopi)
1042. Stamped silver. Navajo culture, Southwest
1043. Claystone, onyx, turquoise, and tortoiseshell heishi. Santo Domingo Pueblo, Southwest
1044. Shell heishi with turquoise fetishes. Santo Domingo Pueblo, Southwest
1045. Dentalium shell with etched patterns. Northern California. Artist: Richard McClellan (Hupa-Karuk). Early 1990s
1046. Inlaid bead of 14k gold, Lone Mountain "fossil" turquoise, coral, lapis lazuli, opal. 2003. Artist: Raymond C. Yazzie (Navajo)

MIDDLE AND SOUTH AMERICA
(NOS. 1100–1137)

1100. Crystal with cinnabar. Chavin culture, Peru
1101. Jadeite. Olmec culture, Mexico
1102. Rock crystal. Chavin culture, Peru (diameter, 5 cm)
1103. Etched jadeite pectoral bead with cinnabar. Olmec culture, Mexico
1104. Carved stone. Late Olmec culture, Guerrero, Mexico
1105. Jade alligator effigy bead. Costa Rica
1106. Gold owl's head bead. Eyes inlaid with greenstone. Moche Culture, Sipan, Peru
1107. Gold bead. Peanut shape. Moche Culture, Sipan, Peru
1108. Jadeite. Maya culture
1109–1110. Carved jadeite. Maya culture
1111–1112. Jadeite with cinnabar. Maya culture
1113. Etched jadeite with cinnabar. Maya culture
1114. Carved jadeite parrot head bead. Maya culture
1115. Jadeite. Uxmal, Maya culture
1116. Sawn jadeite. Maya culture
1117a–d. Shell. Maya culture
1118–1121. Etched and carved pottery beads or spindle whorls. Manteño culture, Ecuador
1122a–c. Stone. Tairona culture, Colombia
1123. Carnelian. Tairona culture, Colombia
1124. Gold squash bead. Chimu culture, Peru
1125a–b. Gold. Chimu culture, Peru
1126–1127. Gold Janus head. Chimu culture, Peru
1128. Black stone bird bead. Chimu culture, Peru
1129–1130. Shell, black stone, carnelian, turquoise, rock crystal, green stone, jasper, and spondylus shell. Chimu culture, Peru
1131. Rock crystal, shell, and stone. Chimu culture, Peru
1132. Spondylus shell. Ica culture, Peru
1133–1134. Spondylus shell. Inca culture, Peru
1135a–g. Drawn, compound square cross section, straight or twisted glass (c and d are striped). "Nueva Cádiz" bead, Peru
1136a. Drawn, compound, striped, and twisted glass. Peru

b. Drawn, square cross section, faceted chevron. Peru
c. Drawn, faceted seven-layer chevron. Peru
d. Drawn, reheated, and striped star bead. Peru
1137. Glass pendant. San Pedro Quiátoni, Oaxaca, Mexico

AFRICA
(NOS. 1200–1247)

1200. Nassarius shell. Grotte des Pigeons, Taforalt, Eastern Morocco. c. 82,000 B.C.
1201. Stone. Nok culture
1202. Glass beads. Djenne, Mali
a. Wound glass with glass insets
b. Mosaic glass canes, no core
c. Wound glass with mosaic glass canes
1203. Mosaic glass canes, no core. Djenne, Mali
1204. Mosaic glass canes, no core. Djenne, Mali
1205. Bronze. Mali
1206. Bronze. Mali
1207. Bronze. Lost-wax casting technique. Baoule culture
1208. Bronze. Lost-wax casting technique. Baoule culture
1209. Striped powder glass. Bodom bead, West Africa
1210. Swirled powder glass. Bodom bead, West Africa
1211. Spotted powder glass. Bodom bead, West Africa
1212. Powder glass. Akoso. Ghana
1213. Powder glass. Akoso. Ghana
1214. Powder glass. Akoso. Ghana
1215. Scorzalite. Mauritania
1216. Gold, lost-wax casting technique. Asante culture
1217. Gold, lost-wax casting technique. Asante culture
1218. Lapidary-worked dichroic glass. Segi bead, Nigeria
1219. Brass. Ivory Coast
1220. Molded and striped powder glass. West Africa (length, 6.3 cm)
1221. Enameled silver. Berber
1222. Cowrie shell. Eastern Zaire to western Senegal
1223. Ostrich eggshell. East Africa
1224. Bauxite. East Africa
1225. Carved Dhoum palm nut. Kenya
1226. Plant roots. Kenya
1227. Plastic (phenol formaldehyde) simulating amber. Made in Europe
1228. White metal. Tuareg
1229. Shell. "Hippo tooth" bead, Ivory Coast and Nigeria
1230. Striped powder glass. West Africa
1231. Wild seed. Kenya
1232. Pottery. Baoule culture, Ivory Coast, West Africa
1233a–j. Molded and striped powder glass. West Africa
1234a–c. Wound and trailed "Bida" glass. Bida, Nigeria
1235a–c. Silver. Ethiopia
1236. Silver. Mauritania
1237. Silver. Mauritania
1238a–b. Complex powder-glass bead and pendant. Mauritania
1239. Plastic bead with metal inlay
1240–1241. Recycled glass. West Africa
1242. Granulated gold. Mauritania
1243. Powder glass. Ile-Ife. Nigeria
1244. Powder glass with hot worked decoration. Krobo, Ghana
1245a–d. Powder glass. Ghana
1246. Gold straw to resemble gold. Ashanti
1247. Lampworked glass copying traditional patterns. Krobo. Ghana. Artist: Cedi

CONTEMPORARY EUROPE AND NORTH AMERICA
(NOS. 1300–1324)

1300. Pierced silver. Artist: Robert Ebendorf, New York
1301. Oxidized sterling silver with plaid overlay. Artist: Young-Ja Baek, New York and South Korea
1302. Brass bands applied to oxidized silver base. Artist: Young-Ja Baek, New York and South Korea
1303. Silver with 24k gold overlay. Artist: Robert Ebendorf, New York
1304. Acid-treated niobium and gold leaf with ebony wood spacer. Artist: Ivy Ross, New York
1305. Chevron, made from historic canes. Venice. 1987
1306. Lampworked soda-lime glass. Artist: Kristina Logan, 1998
1307. Glass beaded beads. Micro-beads. 2000. Artist: Valerie Hector
1308. Glass micro-beads. An embellished and truncated icosidodecahedron. Artist: Valerie Hector. 2008
1309. Silver and enamel snake's egg bead. Artist: David Freda, New York
1310. Granulated gold. Artist: Jean Reist Stark, Pennsylvania
1311. Drilled acrylic with injected color. Artist: Nina Safdie, Montreal
1312. Knotted antique glass "seed" beads. Artist: Jacqueline Lillie, Vienna
1313. Glass eye bead. Artist: Patricia Sage Holland. 1998
1314. Glass. Warring States bead. Artist: Tom Holland. 2002
1315. Poured and carved resin. Artist: Cara Croninger, New York
1316. Petrified wood. Artist: Neal Dwire, Tucson
1317. Petrified dinosaur bone. Artist: Neal Dwire, Tucson
1318. Inlaid wood and brass. Artist: Dr. Carl G. Becker, New York
1319. Layered Formica. Artist: Robert Ebendorf, New York
1320. Iridescent drawn and twisted glass. Artist: Jane Nyhus Designs, Seattle
1321. Fimo. Millefiori technique. Artist: Jamey D. Allen
1322. Lampworked with trail decoration. Venetian, 1990s
1323. Glass. Lampworked dichroic glass with inclusions of fine silver and gold leaf. 1993. Artist: Inara Knight
1324. Glass. Lampworked and blown borsilicate glass. Artist: Tom Boylan
1325. Woven 18k gold, sphenes, diamonds. Artist: Stuart Golder, 2008

Timeline GLOSSARY

Annular. Disk bead with a large diameter perforation.

Aventurine. (Italian for "by accident") Clear or light-colored glass containing millions of microscopic pyramidal copper crystals, which give it a golden sheen. Aventurine glass is used as the base material for beads and for decorative elements on beads. In addition, it is worked by lapidary techniques and is commonly called "goldstone."

Blown-glass Beads. Although glassblowing is now a common technique, it was only invented about 2,000 years ago, so many previous beads did not depend on this type of work. In modern times, only a few beadmakers exploit glassblowing. In terms of techniques, the worker either blows an individual bead, or manipulates a preformed tube of glass (at the lamp or torch) that is heated and blown. In a factory situation, glass tubes may be mechanically blown in molds to form inexpensive mass-produced beads.

Borosilicate Glass. (Hard glass). Borosilicate glass contains borax as a flux, and has a lower coefficient of expansion. It requires high temperatures to be worked into artifacts, and is often considered a specialty glass.

Chevron. See Rosetta Bead.

Compound. In drawn and wound beads, "compound" means having two or more distinct layers of glass, one upon the other.

Constricted Glass Tubes. See Drawn Glass and Gold-Glass Beads.

Core-Formed Glass. See Wound Glass.

Cornaline d'Aleppo. Compound drawn beads of two-layer construction, the base being opaque white (less often pink), overlaid with translucent red or reddish glass (also orange or yellow). The Italian name means "carnelian of Aleppo," a city in Syria, noted for its magical banded stones thought to heal injuries. Beads are usually heat-rounded like seedbeads, but may be tubular. In the U.S., they are often called "white-heart" beads. The name is often misapplied to other layered beads (i.e. green-heart beads) and to wound beads of similar colors ("Hudson's Bay" beads.) The green-heart beads are older (c. 1600) and the cornaline perhaps from c. 1825.

Crumb Glass. A simple method of decorating glass beads is to roll the softened bead over multicolored small glass pieces, creating the effect of dots and blotches. There are several varieties. The dots may be spaced apart or close together, rounded or angular, and/or raised or flush with the surface of the bead. These varieties have individual names such as "scrabble" glass and "blotched" glass.

Dragged Trail. There are basically two forms of this technique—the "feather" pattern and the "festoon" pattern. In both instances the technique begins similarly. Glass of a contrasting color is trailed onto a base in parallel lines. Then a metal instrument is used to drag the trails in a perpendicular direction. The dragging process has also been called "combing" In festoon, all trails are dragged in one direction. In feather design, the dragging alternates up and down.

Drawn Glass. In the manufacture of glass beads, drawn canes with a central hole are produced as a raw material from which multitudes of nearly identical beads can be created in a short time. In contrast to wound-glass beads, which are individually made and therefore expensive, drawn beads are made in great numbers and are relatively cheap. At the same time, the process allows for a great diversity of pattern, color, and finished shapes. Drawn beads are usually finished by heating techniques that have changed over time ("hot-pinched" beads from antiquity, a speo, and "tumbled"beads) and via lapidary grinding (chevron beads).

***dZi* or *Zi* Bead.** An artificially decorated stone bead of the greatest importance in the Himalayan region. Probably of great antiquity. (See "Etched" Agates.)

"End of the Day" Beads. See Crumb Glass. A popular name given to beads believed to have been assembled from scrap glass left on the factory floor at the end of the day. However, it is more probable that this was a standard production technique.

Equatorial. The middle girth of the bead perpendicular to the perforation, often called "the belt" or "the equator."

"Etched" Agates. The most popular name for a class of treated stone beads with artificial designs. They were first made c. 2500 B.C. in western Asia and appear to have a nearly unbroken chain of production into modern times.

Eye Beads. Beads of any material with circular or spotted decoration may be considered eye beads. They range from very simple to extremely complex crumb beads, mosaic glass beads, and natural and treated stone beads.

Faceted. See Lapidary Techniques.

Faience. Faience can be defined as the direct ancestor of glass, although it has also been perceived as a type of ceramic with a quartz body and glassy glaze. It is composed of partially fused quartz sand, usually with mineral colorants. It is widely believed to be the first artificial material. It was probably devised as a cheaper substitute for rare luxury materials, principally lapis lazuli and turquoise. The major centers of its manufacture were Egypt and western Asia.

Feather. See Dragged Trail.

Filigree. See Mosaic-Glass.

Foil Inclusion. See Gold-Glass Beads.

Frit. Ground glass.

Glass. There are many different types of glass, including soda-lime glass (soft glass) and borosilicate glass (hard glass), with a variety of properties. Glass is composed of quartz sand, soda or potash, and lime. Understanding the constituent parts and the techniques used for manufacture helps identify the approximate time and place of manufacture. The basic ingredient of glass is silica, provided by small crystals of quartz sand. Soda or potash, an alkali, alters the melting point of the silica, while lime is used to strengthen the material. When raw crystalline materials are heated to about 1,200 degrees Celsius, their crystal structures collapse, causing small groups of atoms to assume the random structure of liquid. When cooled at the proper speed, the molecules become "frozen" in a glassy state. Soda is obtained by burning seaweed. Potash is obtained from wood ash. Historically, the character of glass varied with the location of the glass factory. Soda glass was usually produced in areas adjacent to the sea; potash glass in wooded areas.

Gold-Glass Beads. These are created from tubes or canes in which a base layer of clear glass is surrounded by a thin layer of gold foil, which itself is surrounded by a subsequent layer of clear glass. (Hence, they are also called "sandwich" glass.) They derive from late Egyptian and early Roman production. The precise method of manufacture of the beads from the tubes or canes is a matter of speculation and conflicting ideas. It is recognized, however, that the tubes in a heated condition are constricted to form the rounded ends of beads, the segments within segmented beads, and the ends of collared beads.

Formerly, it was assumed that the tubes of glass were drawn. This does not seem likely as the gold foil would not be as ductile as the glass. The processes used for construction are unknown. However, two variations seem likely: (1) The heated cane may be rolled over a sharp tool, and (2) a glass-maker's tool (like a caliper) is used to pinch or constrict the softened cane to form the ends, segments, or collars.

Kiln fusion. Preformed pieces are composed (placed in proximity, often being stacked) in a cold kiln that is then heated until fusion occurs. Kiln fusion should not be confused with furnace work, as a kiln is not a furnace.

Lamp Bead. The product of the cottage industries in Venice and Murano, where the beadmaker sat at a fueled lamp and created beads through the process of heating preformed rods of glass. These rods form the bead itself and any subsequent decoration. See Polychrome and Drawn Glass.

Lapidary Techniques. The lapidary or stonecutter shapes his products with a variety of tools and techniques, several of which remain virtually unchanged since the earliest times; namely, flaking, grinding, cutting, and polishing. Lapidary skills have often been applied to the production of glass beads. This began in ancient times but includes more recent Chinese products too.

Married Metal Technique. The joining of different metals to each other by soldering to form one continuous surface.

Marvering. To shape and consolidate heated glass during its manufacture, it is rolled over a flat marble, stone, or cast-iron surface called a "marvel" or "marvering" board.

Millefiori. See Mosaic-Glass.

Mold-Cast Glass. One of the earliest methods of working with molten glass was to pour it into open forms. Upon cooling, the glass was released from the mold and finished by hand.

Molded Glass. In the manufacture of molded beads, a preformed cane is heated to a softened state and used to fill a (usually) two-part mold. This was the technique of choice of the Bohemian and Germanic glass industries.

Mosaic Glass. In glassmaking, a product created from preformed, multicolored units. Both the units and the finished products are referred to as mosaic glass. There are many varieties of units and categories of finished products, and most of them have individual popular names, including millefiore (medieval Italian for "thousand flowers"), stratified, "ribbon glass" and "filigree glass."

***Pate de Verre* and Powderglass Beads.** *Pate de verre* depends upon glass that has been crushed to a fine consistency, made into a paste using a liquid (often water), and usually used to charge a mold, and then fired to fusion. It is from this technique that some authors get the mistaken "glass paste" that is wrongly applied to many ancient beads that are conventionally hot-worked (usually wound glass beads). The approach has much in common with the glass beadmaking of West Africa, there being both "wet" and "dry" versions. A few contemporary glass beadmakers exploit powdered or crushed glass as a raw material, but very little true *pate de verre* is produced.

Polychrome. "Polychrome" typically means having more than one color. In the context of glass beads, polychrome means individually created beads decorated by hand through the application of molten colored glass. (See Lamp Bead.)

Polymer Clay. A pliable, blendable compound consisting of fine particles of polyvinyl chloride (PVC) suspended in one or more liquid plasticizers (additives that increase the plasticity or fluidity of the material to which they are added). It is called "clay" because its texture and pliability resembles that of mineral clay. Although available in a large variety of colors, pigments may be added to a translucent base. The firing process that fuses the material into a solid requires low temperatures. Finished textures range from shiny and pearly to opaque and stony.

Powderglass. See *pate de verde.*

Precious Metals Clay (PMC). Micro spheres of metal are suspended in a vegetable based (organic) material that gives it a clay-like consistency when moist. When fired, all the organic material burns away, and the resultant material is metal. PMC was invented in Japan about 1996.

Rosetta Bead. Any drawn-glass cane bead with an internal pattern of multiple-layer construction. Star beads, specifically, are rosetta beads with starry patterns. Chevron beads, specifically, are star beads with their ends cut or ground down.

Soda-lime glass. "Soft glass," so called because its melting point is lower than that of borosilicate glass ("hard glass"), is the earliest glass, containing sodium as a flux that lowers the initial melting temperature of the batch. It also uses lime (calcium oxide) as a stabilizer. Soda-lime glass is easily manipulated and readily attenuates or elongates. However, it lacks resistance to high temperatures, is sensitive to sudden temperature changes, and shatters easily.

Star Bead. See Rosetta Bead.

Stratified. See Mosaic-glass. The name is also used for the trailed eye-like decorations of early glass eye beads.

Trailing. The oldest continuing technique of decorating a glass bead is called "trailing," and consists of two distinct approaches (closely related to the distinctions made between furnace work and lampworking or torch work). At the furnace, a trail is a small glob of glass removed from a crucible, which is elongated and applied to a bead. With torch work, the trail is made by heating a small cane (sometimes called a "stringer") until it is malleable, that is likewise applied to the bead. Trails can form lines, zigzags, waves, spirals, and spots. Most famous are stratified "eyes," in which a series of spots are superimposed (like a stack of pancakes, each dot being smaller than the previous). Trails can also be multicolored when derived from mosaic-glass elements, with rather more complicated results. Among multicolored elements, preformed complex canes, such as are made for millefiori work (described above) are a staple and can be bought from a factory or made by the artist who uses them.

Wound Glass. Molten glass is wound around a metallic rod or wire similar to the way thread is wound onto a spool. By forming molten material in this manner, there is no need to drill or perforate the bead as a separate step. Today, we speak of beads from the pre-Christian Era as core-formed beads or pendants. The term "core-formed" is dispensed with in this book to be consistent throughout.

Notes

For complete citations refer to the Bibliography. Short titles are given below only when more than one reference by an author is cited in the Bibliography. Notes designated in the captions are listed by Roman numerals and follow the text notes for each chapter.

INTRODUCTION
1. Erikson, 140. **2.** Ibid.

THE BEGINNINGS
1. Randall White, PC, May 2008. **2.** Bar-Yosef Mayer, 2005. Alexander Marshak, in a letter to the author in February 1983 noted that references to beads and pendants from Lower Paleolithic sites exist. Naturally pierced flakes of flint, shells, and fossils suggest that beads were made in this era but the evidence is inconclusive. **3.** Bar-Yosef Mayer, 2005. **4.** d'Errico, Francesco 2007. Although Nassarius shell beads of possibly similar or even earlier dates have been found in other African sites as well as the Levant, not all of the dates are secure, and whether their perforations were accidental, pierced by a predator, or are human-made remains controversial. **5.** The manufacturing debris included thirteen complete disk-shaped beads, twelve bead preforms, and 593 bead fragments. Hirst, 2008. **6.** Kuhn et al, 2001. **7.** Ibid. **8.** The earliest known beads include twenty-two shell beads made from Conus shell by Aboriginal people found in the Mandu Mandu cave in Western Australia dating c. 32,200. (ref: Nicholls, 2007). Ostrich eggshell beads dating to the Upper Paleolithic, c. 23,000–18,000 B.C., are the earliest known adornment from India (ref: Sali, 1985). Ostrich eggshell beads were found in China and Mongolia, as were some occasional finds of dinosaur eggshell beads. (ref: Branigan, p.193). **9.** See White 1989; 1992, 546; 1997, 95. **10.** Pfeiffer, *The Creative Explosion*, pp. 53–63. **11.** Ibid., pp. 102, 204; See also Pfeiffer, *The Emergence of Man*, pp. 221–27. **12.** See White 1989, 1992, 1993, 1997, 2007. Unlike earlier beads that are scarce, occur in isolation, and are fairly unique, by contrast the Upper Paleolithic beads embody forms that are repeated later at multiple locations and that persisted for thousands of years. This has also been used as an argument to support the hints of an earlier system with shell beads throughout Africa and the Levant. (Kuhn et al, 2001). **13.** Klima, p. 197. **14.** Hiler, pp. 30–33. **15.** Campbell, pp. 427–28. **16.** Ibid. See also White 1993, 296. **17.** Chard, pp. 27, 37; Levin and Potapov, p. 20. **18.** Francis, "The Earliest Beads in India," 1: p. 19; Sali 1985, p.164. **19.** Cheng, p. 35. **20.** Francis, "A Survey of Beads in Korea," pp. 5–6. **21.** Dortch, p. 39. **22.** Jernigan, pp. 10–11. **23.** Pfeiffer, p. 250. **24.** White suggests that the standardization of "basket-shaped" beads (plates 3.5 and 3.6) is related to their use for sewing onto garments as beadwork. (ref: White 1992, 554; White, 1997 105.) **25.** Pfeiffer, Emergence of Man. P. 265; Fagan, p. 74. **26.** White 1989, 98. **27.** Francis, "The Earliest Beads in India,": p. 14. **28.** Fagan, p. 160. **29.** Cheng, p. 37. **30.** National Museums and Galleries of Wale website. **31.** Boric, 2006, pp. 7–13.
I. White; **II.** White 2007: 298; White 1993: 105. **III.** White 2007: 292, fn8, p. 300. **IV.** Randall White, PC, February 16, 2009.

ANTIQUITY
1. Moore, p. 135. **2.** Ogden, p. 17; Tatton-Brown, p. 16; Pierides, p. 1. **3.** Tosi and Piperno, pp. 15–23. **4.** Von Saldern, "Mosaic Glass," pp. 9–25. **5.** Herrmann, p. 21. **6.** Mallowan, p. 159. **7.** Maxwell-Hyslop, *passim*; Higgins, *passim*. **8.** Mellaart, p. 18. **9.** Besborodov and Zadneprovsky, p. 127. **10.** Vandiver, p. 239. **11.** McNeill, p. 71. **12.** Bosse-Griffiths, p. 10. For an illustration, see Vilimkova and Darbois, plate 8. **13.** Andrews, *Egyptian Jewellery*, p. 5. **14.** Aldred, p. 17. **15.** Ibid., pp. 19–21, 30. **16.** Andrews, *Egyptian Jewellery*, p. 7; Aldred, p. 36. **17.** Mellaart, p. 18. Mellaart's dates, however, differ for the Seventh and Eighth dynasties. Using his chronology, these beads are dated 2,387–2,365 B.C. The Egyptian chronologies used for this book are from *Art of Ancient Egypt*, by Kazimierz Michalowski (New York: Harry N. Abrams, Inc., 1968). **18.** For further information, see Chapter 10 and notes of Chapter 11; see also Beck, "Etched Carnelian Beads," pp. 384–98. The term "etched" is not accurate. The word is placed in quotes to indicate that although it is commonly used, it is an endemic error. **19.** Bacon, pp. 251–78. **20.** Jamey D. Allen remains very skeptical that hard stone beads were made in Afghanistan. He believes that most beads credited to Afghanistan manufacture (particularly agate beads) were produced in greater India (including present-day Pakistan) and traded into Afghanistan for lapis lazuli. (Personal Communication, July 2, 2008). **21.** Higgins, pp. 53–71. **22.** Ibid., pp. 72–87. **23.** Taylour, p. 146. **24.** Ibid., pp. 145–146. **25.** Tatton-Brown, pp. 16–17, 29; Pierides, pp. 1–7. **26.** Follett, pp. 64–65. **27.** *Jewellery Through 7,000 Years*, p. 79. **28.** Weinberg, *passim*. **29.** See Ogden for materials traded within the Roman Empire. **30.** Higgins, pp. 175–76. **31.** Jamey D. Allen, telephone conversation with author, November 1986; Von Saldern, *Ancient Glass*, pp. 14–15. **32.** Glumac, pp. 15–17. **33.** Oved, p. 58. **34.** Guido, p. 23. **35.** Oved. p. 58. **36.** Guido. pp. 28–29, 31. **37.** Ibid., *passim*.
I. Some of the beads at the rear of the necklace appear to be pairs of deer teeth. Jamey D. Allen, PC. July 18, 2008. **II.** Bar Yosef Mayer and Porat 2008. **III.** Woolley, pp. 87–88. **IV.** Mallowan and Rose, plate 8; Noveck, p. 16. **V.** Budge, p. 13. **VI.** Liu, "Afghan Stone Beads," p. 34. **VII.** Maxwell-Hyslop, pp. 31, 34–36; Mallowan, "Excavations at Brak," pp. 171–76. **VIII.** Seefried, *passim*. **IX.** Maxwell-Hyslop, pp. 180–197. **X.** Liu, "Iranian Faience," p. 6. Most faience beads were probably glossy when they were manufactured. Many are now "matte" due to the decay of their surfaces. There is a greater tendency for this to happen in Western Asia than Egypt (where many glazes still remain well intact). Egyptian blue (and "frit") are exceptions, since they were not self-glazing, nor glazed materials. Ref: Jamey D. Allen, P.C. July 2, 2008. **XI.** Ogden, pp. 18–19. **XII.** Goldstein, p. 29; Von Saldern, "Mosaic Glass," p. 9. **XIII.** Guido, p. 46.

EUROPE
1. Brown, p. 176. **2.** Randall, pp. 105–6; Kuntzsch, p. 85. **3.** Kuntzsch, p. 86. **4.** See plate 49. **5.** Eisen, *Glass*, II: pp. 550–649. **6.** Peter Francis, letter to author, January 1986. **7.** For information on Byzantine glass beads, see Gregorietti, p. 137. **8.** The "Vision of Constantine" is a large, flat bead with a cross engraved on one side of it and four hosts (religious symbols) on both sides. The "Road to Golgotha" is a flat bead made of yellow and red or brown and white threads inlaid on a dark matrix. Eisen, *Glass*, II: pp. 522–23, 531, 535–36. **9.** Kuntzsch, p. 97. **10.** Randall, pp. 105–6. **11.** Gregorietti, p. 199. **12.** Barraclough, pp. 92–93. **13.** Randall, pp. 87–88. **14.** Gregorietti, pp. 129–32. **15.** *Jewellery Through 7,000 Years*, p. 129. **16.** Kuntzsch, p. 92. **17.** Randall, pp. 87–88. **18.** Haevernick, pp. 180–87. **19.** Oved, pp. 66–67. **20.** Forbes, 197. **21.** This is further complicated for those working in the English language, as most available research is published in German or Russian, or in Scandinavian or central European languages. For references see Callmer and Tempelmann-Maczynska. **22.** Important glass beadmaking industries existed at Starja Ladoga, north of Moscow, from the eighth to the tenth century, in Poland after the first half of the tenth century, and at Kiev by the end of the tenth century. Several of these glassworks produced drawn-glass beads, a technique not produced elsewhere in Europe. Apparently, all of these beadmaking activities ceased by at least the thirteenth century, a casualty of the Mongolian invasions. See Kidd, *Glass Bead-Making*, p. 9; Forbes, pp. 197–98; Peter Francis, letter to author, January 1986. **23.** Forbes, p. 198. **24.** Jamey D. Allen, PC July 2, 2008. **25.** Graham-Campbell and Kidd, pp. 41, 76, 134. **26.** *Jewellery Through 7,000 Years*, p. 138. **27.** Peter Francis, letter to author, January 1986. **28.** Callmer, pp. 7–9. **29.** Graham-Campbell and Kidd, pp. 41, 76, 134; Lundstrom, *passim*. **30.** Callmer, pp. 33–51. **31.** "Seedbead" is the term used throughout the book to designate small, drawn glass beads made primarily for beadwork. This is to differentiate it from a "seed bead"—a bead made from the organic seed of a plant. (PC Jamey D. Allen, July 2, 2008). **32.** Hall, pp. 87–89, 112. **33.** Callmer, *passim*. **34.** It is a largely unrecognized fact that non-glass beads were made at Venice (before glassmaking and working were introduced) that included beads of soft materials and hard stones. These beads were probably made for rosaries as well as for export. Nonetheless, as beads in general were called "perle" (pearls), it is also possible that Venice as a pearl-processing center may be a misinterpretation of some document of that time. PC. Jamey D. Allen, July 2, 2008. **35.** Stout, pp. 58–60, 76; Callmer, plate IV, no. G030. **36.** Peter Francis, letter to author, January 1986.
I. Jamey D. Allen, PC. July 2, 2008. **II.** The production of intricate glass bead making in Northern Europe is somewhat controversial. Viking bead scholar Torben Sode believes that these beads were made by the Scandinavians. Jamey D. Allen is more inclined to think that they were made by Middle Eastern beadmakers who were practicing their craft in Europe. As elsewhere, the Middle Eastern artisans may have initiated this work, and become absorbed into the local culture, as may have happened 1500 years earlier in China with the makers of Warring States beads (plates 154-159). Simultaneously with the appearance of intricate glass beadmaking in Scandinavia, a similar spread of beadmaking may also have occurred in Indonesia, as well as West Africa. Jamey D. Allen, PC July 2, 2008.

THE WORLD OF ISLAM
1. Al-Jadir, p. 13. **2.** Bibby, p. 164. **3.** Peter Francis, letter to author, January 1986. **4.** Many Middle Eastern people believe that Yemen is the source for agate beads. This is very common in Afghanistan, where carnelian is called "Yemini stone." These beads, however, were made in India and traded to Afghanistan via Yemen, which is where men returning from the haj routinely bought them. Jamey D. Allen, PC. July 2, 2008. **5.** Peter Francis, letter to author, January

1986. **6.** Hasson, pp. 109–113. **7.** Al Jadir, pp. 14, 33–34; Jenkins and Keene, p. 9. **8.** Liu, "Beads in the Sudan," p. 27. **9.** Erikson, pp. 164–76. **10.** Budge, p. 325. **11.** Kunz, p. 64. **12.** Jenkins and Keene, p. 27. **13.** Critchlow, p. 8. **14.** Jenkins and Keene, pp. 26, 30. **15.** Ibid., p. 47. **16.** Dr. Carl G. Becker, telephone conversation with author, April 1985. **17.** Al-Jadir, p. 19. **18.** Ibid., p. 31; Hawley, *passim*. **19.** Kolbas, pp. 95–113; Hasson, pp. 109–113.
I. Jamey D. Allen, PC July 2, 2008. **II.** Eisen, *Glass*, II: p. 523. **III.** Muller, p. 23. **IV.** Al-Jadir, p. 108. **V.** Hawley, *passim*.

PRAYER BEADS
1. Wilkins, p. 48. **2.** Pramod Chandra, *Sculpture of India*, 300 B.C.–A.D. 300 (Washington, D.C.: National Gallery of Art, 1985), plate 15. **3.** Edmunds, p. 254. **4.** Wilkins, p. 44. **5.** Hand rosaries or prayer beads have fewer numbers of beads than neck rosaries. Buddist hand rosaries have eighteen beads plus dividers, Muslims have thirty-three plus dividers; Hindus have thirty-two prayer beads. **6.** Ibid, pp. 47, 62; Jamey D. Allen, PC, July 2, 2008. Howe, p. 22. **7.** Wilkins, pp. 80–104. **8.** Ibid. **9.** Ibid. p. 78. **10.** Ibid., p. 50. **11.** Michael Gelber, conversation with author, December 1985. **12.** Casanowicz, p. 34. **13.** Michael Meister, conversation with author, August 1985. **14.** Casanowicz, p. 337. **15.** Ibid. **16.** Francis, *A Survey of Beads in Korea*, p. 29. **17.** All information on Japanese Buddhist prayer beads is from Casanowicz, pp. 341–48. **18.** Casanowicz, p. 349. **19.** Ibid. **20.** Ibid., pp. 349–50; Jenkins and Keene, p. 106. **21.** Budge, p. 81. **22.** Wilkins, p. 30. **23.** Ibid., p. 25. **24.** Ibid., p. 37. **25.** Ibid., p. 34. **26.** Ibid., p. 50. **27.** Ibid., p. 49. **28.** Ibid., p. 60; Casanowicz, p. 354; Evans, p. 118. **29.** Kuntzsch, p. 106. **30.** For a complete history see Wilkins, pp. 105–175. **31.** Ibid., p. 221.
I. *Tibetan Collection*, II: p. 11. **II.** Wilkins, pp. 174, 184, 224.

EUROPEAN EXPANSION
1. McNeill, pp. 565–67. **2.** Harris and Levey, "The Renaissance," in *New Columbia Encyclopedia* (New York: Columbia University Press), pp. 2300–1. **3.** The *Portrait of Simonetta Vespucci* by Botticelli is in the Stadelsches Kunstinstitut, Frankfurt. **4.** Black, p. 156. **5.** Hughes, pp. 81–83. **6.** Muller, p. 13. **7.** Ibid., plate 26. **8.** Gold filigree beads are mentioned in Gregorietti, p. 199; Amber beads in Rowe, p. 51. **9.** Cocks, pp. 41–43; Newman, p. 162. **10.** Black, pp. 209, 234; Kuntzsch, pp. 131–33. **11.** There is a coral parure from the 1830s at the Musée des Arts Decoratifs in Paris reproduced in Gregorietti, p. 225. **12.** Evans, p. 172. **13.** Black, p. 254. **14.** Gregorietti, p. 262. **15.** Kidd, *Glass Bead-Making*, p. 17. Beads made of crystal and carnelian were traded by the early Spanish explorers. The Frenchman Jacques Cartier gave tin beads as gifts to Indians in Montreal, Canada, in 1535. See Francis, *Beads and the Discovery of the New World*, pp. 36–37. **16.** Francis, *Beads and the Discovery of the New World*, p. 26; Karlis Karklins, PC July 24, 2008. **17.** Barraclough, p. 154. **18.** Francis, "Beads and the Discovery of America," pp. 47–50, 53. Handler et al. pp. 15–18. **19.** See writings by Kidd, Karklins, Smith and Good, Allen, Francis, Harris, Liu and Harris, and Hayes. **20.** Kidd, *Glass Bead-Making, passim*. **21.** Jamey D. Allen raises the question of "what happened to all the Indian beads made between A.D. 1400 and 1900? The British destroyed the Indian glass industry during their colonialism in India. It didn't revive itself until the 1970s. But where did all those beads go? I expect that many were used in regional beadwork such as Gujerat and in Afghanistan, and for minority tribes such as the Naga. But this would be a small proportion." PC July 2, 2008. **22.** The Fratesina glassmaking industry greatly predates Venice. And two significant industries—at Pisa and Altare—may have been in competition with and predate Venice. They are not discussed by glass historians, however, since little is known about what they actually produced. Jamey D. Allen, PC, July 2, 2008. **23.** Tait, p. 9–11; Francis, *Venetian Beads*, p. 2. **24.** Francis, *Venetian Beads*, p. 2. **25.** Kidd, *Glass Bead-Making*, p. 18. **26.** Tait, pp. 12, 61–62. **27.** There are apparently two recorded instances of the death penalty having been carried out. Kidd, *Glass Bead-Making*, p. 22. **28.** The Romans made drawn-glass beads by the first century A.D. After the fall of Rome, drawn-glass beads were produced in eastern Europe, western Russia, and Moravia. In western and southern Europe after the fifth century and in eastern Europe after the tenth century, until 1468 there is little evidence of drawn-glass beads. (A good indicator that the drawn process was understood by at least 1468 is the historical document that says that Baroveiros made rosetta beads as early as 1468. ref: Jamey D. Allen, PC, July 2, 2008.) In India, however, drawn-glass beads were probably made from the third century B.C. to the Middle Ages. It is possible the Venetians learned the technique from the Indians, writes Peter Francis, or, more likely, suggests Jamey D. Allen, from the Middle East. Francis, "When India Was Beadmaker," p. 24. Jamey D. Allen, PC, July 18, 2008. **29.** Although the original information was based upon Kidd, *Glass Bead-Making*, pp. 22–28; Francis, *Venetian Beads*, pp. 7–8; Jamey D. Allen, letter to author, October 1986, this information has been updated by Jamey D. Allen, PC, July 2008. See also Carroll, 1917, which was updated by Allen. **30.** Francis, *Venetian Beads*, p. 14. **31.** Ibid., p. 1. **32.** Allen, "The Manufacture of Intricate Glass Canes," p. 191. **33.** Kidd, *Glass Bead-Making*, p. 28. **34.** Ibid., pp. 18–20. **35.** Fuel supplies must always have been of serious concern to the Venetian and Murano industries. Kidd, *Glass Bead-Making*, p. 23. **36.** Ibid., pp. 39–41. **37.** Francis, *Czech Bead Story*, pp. 10–16. Jamey D. Allen, PC, July 2, 2008. **38.** Francis, *Czech Bead Story*, pp. 9–10. **39.** Karklins, "Early Amsterdam Trade Beads," pp. 36–41. **40.** Karklins, "Dutch Trade Beads," p. 114. **41.** Karklins, "Early Amsterdam Trade Beads," p. 41. **42.** Karlis Karklins PC, July 24, 2008. **43.** It is not clear whether these differences, in addition to the composition of the glass, were a function of change over time. Karklins PC. July 24, 2008 relates that "the findings suggest that during the sixteenth through eighteenth centuries, there was an established tradition in Western Europe wherein drawn beads were generally manufactured from soda-lime glass while potash-lime glass was preferred for their wound contemporaries from at least 1687 to 1750. This is possibly because the lower melting point and greater range of plasticity made potash-lime glass more suitable for the smaller scale, wound lamp work. The 1687 date is there because there are no wound beads available for analysis from any context that predated that date, as it appears they were not made for the northeastern North American trade before 1680. Karklins, "Early Amsterdam Trade Beads," p. 41. **44.** Kidd, *Glass Bead-Making*, pp. 33–35, 61, 65. **45.** Feulner. **46.** Trebbins, pp. 3, 8. **47.** Ibid., *passim*. **48.** Ibid., p. 12. **49.** Ibid., pp. 8–12. See Si and Ann Frazier "A history of gem beadmaking in Indar-Oberstein" in Beads: Journal of the Society of Bead Researchers: Ottawa, 10–11, 1998–1999, pp. 35–47), who have done the most extensive research on Idar-Oberstein beads. **50.** Kidd, *Glass Bead-Making*, pp. 29–32. **51.** Jamey D. Allen, PC, July 2, 2008. **52.** Smith, "Chronology from Glass Beads," pp. 147–52. **53.** The "padre" bead may have been made by the Chinese. Liu, "Chinese Glass Beads," p. 14.
I. In that market, yellow and black backgrounds make up well over 80 percent of the beads found of this type. Blue, green, white, and red backgrounds, present in approximately equal quantities, provide most of the balance. Varieties with red backgrounds are often *cornaline d'Aleppo* beads with white or yellow cores. Michael Heide, letter to author, December 1985. **II.** Karklins, *Glass Beads, passim*. **III.** Allen, "Cane Manufacturer for Mosaic Glass Beads," 1: pp. 6–11. **IV.** Liu, "Carnelian Beads and Their Simulations," pp. 14–18. **V.** Allen, "Cane Manufacturer for Mosaic Glass Beads," 1:pp. 6–11. **VI.** Karklins, "Dutch Trade Beads," pp. 59–74. **VII.** "The Manufacture of Intricate Glass. Canes," pp. 173–91. **VIII.** Ibid., "Chevron-Star Rosetta Beads," 1: pp. 19–24; 2: pp. 24–29. **IX.** Smith and Good, passim. **X.** Some elements are similar to earlier Venetian types, particularly the translucent layers. On the other hand, the bead relates to later (1800s) chevrons, especially in its color and layer sequencing, suggesting it should be dated to the 1700s. **XI.** Another example is illustrated in Sorensen, figure CL178. **XII.** The following descriptions, written by the late Michael Heide in 1986, are intended to point out features of various chevrons that are unusual or not clear from the illustration. After examining several million beads from West Africa over the past eighteen years, Heide concluded that all of the beads illustrated here are uncommon. He has utilized the term "scarce" to mean he has seen only six to ten examples of the type. "Rare" means two to five have been found, and "unique" means he has seen only one. During the past twenty-two years, while some of the beads remain "unique," several have since surfaced and are now just "rare." (Jamey D. Allen, PC, July 18, 2008). Unless otherwise mentioned, molded layers have twelve points. (1) Very large (otherwise typical), seven-layer chevron with six facets on each end. First and third layers are a transparent light green color. Length, 7 cm. Rare this large. (2) Same as 1, except first and third layers are black. Length, 2.8 cm. (3) Seven layers with outer layer in translucent green. Length, 3.3 cm. Rare. (4) Seven layers with square cross section. First and seventh layers are transparent and colorless. Two red and two teal blue stripes are embedded in seventh layer. Third layer is translucent teal blue. Related to *Nueva Cádiz* beads. Length 3.5 cm. Rare. (5) Five layers with none of the layers molded into points. Facets at each end yield a "wave" appearance from the side. First layer is transparent and colorless; second layer is a very saturated translucent color: dark red, violet, blue, or green—all typical for this period. Less often, it was a neutral gray. Length, 1.6 cm. Unique. (6) Three layers with seven yellow stripes on outer layer. Length, 1.3 cm. The previous term of "unique" has been deleted from these beads, as they were archaeologically recovered with some frequency in the Northeast. (Jamey D. Allen, PC, July 8, 2008.) (7) Four layers with six red and six blue stripes on outer layer. Length, 1.6 cm. (8) Five layers. Left: first and fifth layers are transparent blue. Length, 1.6 cm. Right: first and fifth layers are transparent and colorless. Length, 1.6 cm. Six red and six blue stripes are embedded in outer layer in each bead. (9) Three layers. First and third layers are black; second layer is gray. Eight red and eight white stripes on outer layer. Length, 0.8 cm. Unique. (10) Three layers. First and third layers are transparent cobalt blue. Twelve white stripes on outer layer. (Bluish "stripes" are points from the second white layer, showing through the third blue layer.) Length, 1.1 cm. (11) Five layers with five flattened surfaces along the sides and faceted at each end. First layer

is translucent cobalt blue. Second and fourth layers are white. Sixteen points. Length, 2.3 cm. Scarce. (12) Four layers. Left: third layer only has twelve points. Length, 1.1 cm., diameter, 1.3 cm. Scarce. Right: first and third layers have twelve points. Length, 1.3 cm. (13) Four layers. Right: fourth layer is black with twelve white stripes. Length, 1.1 cm. Rare. Left: same as first bead, except heat-rounded. Length, 1.1 cm. Scarce. (14) Four layers. Left: fourth layer is black with six yellow stripes. Length, 0.7 cm, diameter, 0.3 cm. Right: fourth layer is translucent green with four compound stripes, black on yellow, alternating with four compound stripes yellow on red. Length, 1.8 cm. Scarce. (15) Two layers. Right: second layer grooves are filled with alternating blue and brick red stripes. A yellow stripe is atop each red stripe. Second layer is ten points. Length, 0.7 cm. Scarce. Left: same as first bead but beveled at both ends. Length, 1.8 cm. Scarce. (16) Six layers, six scooped facets around midline, six facets each end. Length, 2.5 cm. Rare. (17) Four layers. Outer layer blue with four wide green stripes. Length, 2.5 cm. Rare. (18) Six layers. Second and sixth layer dark translucent green, outer layer ground down to appear striped. Length, 2.8 cm. Rare. (19) First layer grayish blue; second layer powder blue; third layer opaque brick-red modulated to a carmine tone; fourth layer translucent blue, appearing purple because of red layer below Length, 1.3 cm. Scarce. (20) First layer red, twelve points. Second layer black, seven petal-shaped lobes. Fourth layer translucent green. Length, 2.5 cm. Scarce. (21) Five layers. First and third layers dark translucent cobalt blue that appear black. Second and fifth layers bright red. Length, 2.0 cm. (Found in the United States, not Africa.) (22) Six layers. Fourth layer yellow Left: length, 2.0 cm., diameter, 1.6 cm. Right: length, 2.8 cm. Each unique. (23) Five layers, six facets each end. Second and fifth layers.translucent madder red appearing as a brownish red or "wine red" tone. Third layer red with no typical white layer between red and brownish red. Length, 2.8 cm. Unique. Jamey D. Allen notes that this bead is not so unusual. Rather, it is more well made than most others. Jamey D. Allen, PC, July 18, 2008. (24) Six layers. First, third, and fifth layers dark brown. Second, fourth, and sixth layers white. Length, 2.3 cm. Unique. (25) Eight layers. First, third, fifth, and seventh layers white. Second layer red. Sixth layer "root-beer" brown with aventurine. Fourth layer translucent teal blue. Third layer twelve points; seventh layer twenty-two points. Length, 3.6 cm. Unique. (26) Six layers. First, third, and fifth layers yellow. Second and sixth layers opaque green. Fourth layer bright opaque red. Length, 2.8 cm. Unique. No longer unique, this cane has been found at Venice and new beads made from it. The red layer is made with selenium/cadmium glass from the 1920s (like number 21). Jamey D. Allen, PC, July 18, 2008.

AFRICA

1. Peter Francis, letter to author, January 1986. **2.** Trebbin, p. 4. Jamey D. Allen, PC, July 2, 2008. **3.** Hodge, p. 65. **4.** Sieber, p. 123. **5.** de Negri, p. 210. **6.** Hodge, p. 65; Roy Sieber, letter to author, March 1986. **7.** Jamey D. Allen, PC, July 2, 2008. **8.** Sieber, p. 123. **9.** Although the Djenne beads were originally given Roman Period dates, they were misidentified. No bead is earlier than Islamic or early European. Jamey D. Allen, PC, July 2, 2008. **10.** Van der Sleen, pp. 79–81; Francis, "The Glass Beads of India", p. 4. **11.** The beadmakers at Oyo and Bida, in Nigeria, and though presently Nupe, claim to have been Egyptian immigrants several generations ago. Jamey D. Allen notes that "it is indeed interesting that these are the only places in West Africa where glass has been hot-worked, and where wound beads are made." Jamey D. Allen, PC, July 2, 2008. **12.** Even at Bida the glass used is largely recycled. The black glass they call "bikini" is collected from the bottom of the furnace where recycled glass has already been dropped. Margaret Carey believes the "gardenroller" beads of South Africa are made of recycled imported glass—possibly Indo-Pacific or Indonesian beads. Jamey D. Allen, PC, July 2, 2008. **13.** Hodge, p. 65. **14.** The Bida create glass beads and bangles with winding and some stretching techniques featuring the traditional bellows-forced draft furnaces. Krobo and Mauritanian glassmakers use an entirely different technique that involves firing powder-glass beads in simple furnaces or ovens without a forced air supply. African powder-glass technology has been divided into two varieties: dry-form and wet-form. Dry-form techniques practiced by the Krobo (plate 112) involve placing finely powdered glass into horizontal or vertical molds. The molds are then heated, and the low-firing temperatures allow the glass particles to fuse without melting. This produces a characteristically soft and grainy matte texture. Wet-form techniques are used to create polychrome beads in Mauritania (plate 109). These beads are made with a wet-inlay technique without a mold. Glass powders made by pulverizing imported monochrome glass beads are mixed with a binder (saliva or gum arabic) to form a moist paste. The colored powder is then spread with a needle over a core bead made from plain bottle glass. Applying the powder glass paste with a needle allows the colors to be treated separately, resulting in a finely detailed bead design. The beads are then heated in a simple oven to create a satinlike finish. This finish probably indicates that wet-form techniques require higher firing temperatures and possibly the beads are polished after being fired. Delaroziere, *passim*; Gumpert, *passim*; Liu, "African-Made Glass Ornaments," pp. 52–53. Powderglass beadmaking is not unique to Africa. It is the basis of "pate de verre," made in France and England since at least the nineteenth century. The monochrome blue glass beads used by the Paiwan in Formosa as well as the biconical blue glass beads thought to be late Ban Chiang beads in Thailand (Timeline 900b). In North America, the Arikara Indians (from Kansas) made powderglass beads in the 1800s by grinding up the glass of trade beads. In any region where there is little or no glass tradition, an easy way to work with glass is to recycle existing glass using powder-glass techniques. In the earliest days of glassmaking, powderglass-working may have been derived from faience-making. Jamey D. Allen, PC, July 2, 2008. **15.** Laidler, p. 2. **16.** Harding, pp. 104–6. **17.** Ibid. **18.** Ibid. **19.** Laidler, p. 3. **20.** For the people of the Kalahari, who tend to feel more comfortable not having conspicuous possessions, beads are used to teach children to give things away. See Pfeiffer, *The Creative Explosion*, p. 65. **21.** For both tribes, beaded jewelry and objects were created to mark courtship and marital status. See Levinsohn, pp. 38–40. **22.** de Negri, pp. 210–16. **23.** Fagg, *Yoruba Sculpture*, p. 88. **24.** Northern, *The Sign of the Beaded Leopard*, pp. 17–23. **25.** Waist beads also played an important role in nineteenth century Asante society: "The most fundamental item of dress for women is a set of waist beads (*toma*)...without them a woman is shamefully naked." McLeod, pp. 143–45. **26.** Fisher, pp. 227–65. **27.** Cole, pp. 29–37. **28.** van der Sleen, *A Handbook on Beads*, p. 85. **29.** Landewijk, pp. 8–14. **30.** Sieber, p. 12. **31.** Cole, p. 30. **32.** Vogel, p. 6.

I. Beckwith and Fisher, 1999. **II.** Lamb, "Krobo Powder-Glass Beads," pp. 23–27. **III.** Michael Heide, letter to author, November 1985. See also Stanfield, 2000–2001. **IV.** Cole, p. 30. **V.** Whereas other East African nomads are hostile to metalsmiths because they do not raise cattle, blacksmiths have become part of Turkana society. They produce, among other things, beads of iron, copper, and aluminum. Fedders and Salvadori, *passim*. **VI.** Cole, p. 30. **VII.** Ibid. **VIII.** Fisher, p. 48. **IX.** All information on the Zulus is from Conner and Pelrine, Levinsohn, and Schoeman. **X.** All information on the Ndebele is from Priebatsch and Knight, and Fisher. **XI.** Fagg, p. 71. **XII.** Ibid, p. 42. **XIII.** Vogel, p. 101. **XIV.** Fisher, pp. 227–65; Suzanne Bach and Albert Gordon, letter to author, September 1984. **XV.** Fisher, p. 265.

THE FAR EAST

1. Current research is beginning to reveal the extensiveness of the Chinese glass bead trade. For further information see Francis, *Chinese Glass Beads*, and Liu, "Asian Glass Ornaments," parts 1 and 2. **2.** Chard, pp. 111, 208. **3.** Lee, p. 9. **4.** "The exchanges between the rulers of Persia and China, for luxury goods that included glass beads, was accomplished in c. 500 B.C. in the form of embassies that traveled back and forth. These were not commercial exchanges, because this sort of trade didn't exist yet, and there was no commercial class nor merchants to facilitate such commerce. Nevertheless, these early exchanges probably instigated the Silk Route and created the need for a merchant class; and made these exotic goods available to people other than the elite. Among the products the Chinese wanted from Persia were multicolored glass beads, as were made in Egypt and Syria/the Fertile Crescent (under Persian domination). Thus, a market for Persian goods developed in China. It was not much later that the Chinese began to make similar glass beads, which quickly evolved into the Warring States group. I believe that a Middle Eastern glassmaker immigrated to China, made beads, developed a unique local style, worked for a few generations, and eventually blended into the local culture ("became Chinese"). Alternately, a Chinese craftsman may have traveled west and learned glassmaking and beadmaking, and brought it home... but the previous seems easier. This idea goes a long way to explaining how Warring States beads came to be made in China—a land that did not previously have glassmaking (though there may have been minor beadmaking from imported glass). By the Han Dynasty, the brilliance of the Warring States glasses was over. The beads then produced were much simpler furnace-wound opaque turquoise blue glass with randomly applied brown threads. (These are recently routinely misidentified as "faience" by Chinese authors and collectors, over the past 15 years.) After this glass-beadmaking all but disappeared from China until the Ming Dynasty, with only the occasional exception—that included lapidary-worked objects made to imitate jade." (Plate 158). Jamey D. Allen, PC, July 2, 2008. **5.** Translation systems used in this book are: Pinyin for Chinese, Hepburn for Japanese, and McCune-Reischauer for Korean. **6.** Cheng, pp. 35–40. **7.** Branigan, p. 193. **8.** Chinese glass beads were not made with soda-lime formulas until the Tang dynasty (A.D. 618–907). **9.** Dohrenwend, *Chinese Jades, passim*; "Glass in China," pp. 426–46. **10.** Francis, *Chinese Glass Beads*, pp. 10, 32. **11.** Francis, "Asian Bead Study Tour II," p. 11. **12.** Nelson Gallery-Atkins Museum, p. 73. **13.** Akiyama, p. 216 and plate 124. The use of amber, coral, and crystal for Tang dynasty beads is noted by Schaefer, pp. 248, 265. **14.** *China, Guide to the Collection of the University Museum*, p. 162. **15.** Francis, *Chinese Glass Beads*, pp. 12–14. **16.** Ibid., pp. 14–15. **17.** Ibid., p. 33. **18.** Ibid., p. 37. **19.** Ibid., pp. 34–37. **20.** Ibid. **21.** Liu, "Chinese Glass Beads,"

p. 14. **22.** Most glass beads in the Qing dynasty were made by a mandrel-winding technique. See Liu, "Chinese Glass Beads," pp. 14–15. Other techniques observed by Francis, Harris, and Liu include: tube-drawing (a technique possibly dating back to the Tang dynasty), molding, pressing, hot-pinching and blowing, and various methods classified as lapidary (grinding and drilling). **23.** All information on Chinese court beads is from Cammann, pp. 341–48. **24.** Ibid. Manchurian Buddhist necklaces had three rather than two counter strings, plus a unique series of pendants that hung down the back. After passing through a flat stone plaque called a "cloud," the cord terminated in a large pendant called a "dewdrop." Dewdrops also terminated the counter strings. The four dewdrops are known as the "disciple beads" or the "regents of the four heavens," representing the emperor, father, mother, and teacher to whom an individual owed reverence and obedience. All these elements differentiated Manchurian beads from Tibetan beads. **25.** Ibid. From the *Huang-ch'ao lichi t'u-shih*, a volume of dynastic law published in 1766, we know that the emperor's court beads were to consist of 108 large freshwater pearls from Manchuria, and all the accessories—the Buddha heads, the memory beads, the black cloud, and the dewdrops—were to be made of precious and semiprecious jewels, including lapis lazuli, amber, coral, and turquoise. **26.** Doris Dohrenwend, letter to author, July 1986; Kunz, p. 83. **27.** Kunz, p. 84. **28.** Nephrite is a silicate of magnesia, while jadeite is a silicate of alumina. Nephrite is fibrous and very tough, jadeite slightly harder but more crystalline and so less tough. **29.** Sullivan, p. 40. **30.** Francis, *A Survey of Beads in Korea*, pp. 5–6, 9. **31.** Kunz, p. 265. The literal translation of *kogok* is "curved jade," and of *magatama*," curved jade" or "curved bead." Several explanations have been advanced for the mysterious shape of the *kogok* and *magatama*, including stylized representations of animal claws or fangs (items frequently associated with medicine bags and shamanism). **32.** Kunz, p. 265. Chard, p. 189. **33.** Blair, p. 356. **34.** Francis, *A Survey of Beads in Korea*, p. 35. **35.** Francis, *A Survey of Beads in Korea*, pp. 10–21. **36.** Yoshimizu, pp. 98–102. **37.** Stout, pp. 58–60. **38.** Francis, *A Survey of Beads in Korea*, pp. 64, 13–16, 27. **39.** Ibid., p. 21. **40.** Chang-su Houchins, letter to author, July 1986. **41.** Francis, *A Survey of Beads in Korea*, pp. 26–28. **42.** Suk, Joo-sun, p. 161, entry no. 47. **43.** Francis, *A Survey of Beads in Korea*, pp. 31–34. **44.** Okamoto, *passim*. **45.** Chard, p. 131. **46.** Blair, pp. 42–45. **47.** Ibid., pp. 51–52, Jamey D. Allen, PC, July 2, 2008. 57. **48.** Ibid., p. 48. **49.** Ibid., pp. 49–51. **50.** Ibid., pp. 67–69. **51.** Included are beads of crystal, glass, amber, agate, gold, silver, gilt copper, jasper, jadeite, obsidian, stone, pearl, coral, ivory, wood, nuts, and seeds. Ibid., pp. 98–103. **52.** Blair, pp. 94–98, 375; plate 77. **53.** Ibid., p. 131. **54.** Ibid., p. 132. **55.** Ibid., p. 152. **56.** Ibid., p. 181. **57.** Arakawa, pp. 187–89. **58.** Arakawa, p. 191. **59.** A journal kept by Matsura Seizan, lord of the Hirado domain in northern Kyushu, is a valuable source of information on the thematic content of late Edo *inro* ensembles. **60.** *Ojime* were also made of porcelain, lacquer, amber, cloisonné, and stones, including jade, carnelian, malachite, and quartz. **61.** Okada, p. 34. **62.** As explained by Mikoshiba and Bushell, p. 60: "The marvel of the sequential portrayal possible in the *ojime* depends not only on fine miniscule craftsmanship, but also on an optical illusion whereby the length of the circumference as a straight line is remarkable as compared with the small bulk of the sphere."

I. For a more complete description of these beads, see Dohrenwend, "Glass in China"; Liu, "Ancient Chinese Glass Beads"; Francis, *Chinese Glass Beads*; and White, *Tombs of Old Lo-Yang*. **II.** Liu, "Glass Ojime," pp. 24–28. The fifth bead from the left (marudama) is a glass imitation of an "ivory" hornbill bead. **III.** The *netsuke-ojime-inro* ensemble in this illustration is somewhat atypical, because the compartments comprising the *inro* have been concealed by a sheath of rich gold lacquer and married metalwork. However, the *ojime* still slides up and down to loosen or tighten the compartments. **IV.** Shogun, p. 80.

INDIA

1. Brijbhushan, p. 3; Latif, p. 42. **2.** Francis, "Minor Indian Beadmakers," p. 18. **3.** Michael Meister, conversation with author, August 1985. **4.** Latif, p. 42. **5.** Brijbhushan, p. 5. **6.** Latif, p. 42. **7.** Francis, "The Earliest Beads in India," 1: pp. 18–19; 2: pp. 14–15. **8.** Kenoyer, pp. 18–19. **9.** Ibid. **10.** Possehl, p. 39. **11.** Chandra, *Studies in the Development of Ornaments*, pp. 57–110. **12.** Ibid. **13.** Ibid., p. 160. **14.** Reade, figure 1; Beck, "Etched Carnelian Beads," pp. 384–98. **15.** Francis, *Indian Agate Beads*, p. 9. **16.** Chandra, *Indo-Greek Jewellery*, pp. 55–58. **17.** Ogden, p. 90. **18.** Ibid., p. 109. **19.** Francis, *Indian Agate Beads*, p. 11. **20.** Ibid. **21.** Ibid. **22.** Francis, *Glass Beads of India*, pp. 2–4. **23.** Ibid. **24.** Ibid., p. 2. **25.** Ibid., p. 3. **26.** Ibid., pp. 3–4. The date of 100 B.C. is supplied by Jamey D. Allen, who also states: "It seems almost self-evident that small seedbeads would have been used in beadwork. However, there is practically no beadwork composed of glass seedbeads anywhere in the world prior to about 300 years ago. Ancient beadwork specimens (as from Egypt and Mesopotamia) were made with faience and stone beads." PC, July 2, 2008. **27.** Ibid., p. 4; Lamb, "A Note on Glass Beads from the Malay Peninsula," *passim*. **28.** van der Sleen, *A Handbook on Beads*, p. 13. **29.** Francis, *Glass Beads of India*, p. 4. **30.** Other countries (Yemen, China, and Iran) have agate and carnelian sources and manufacturers, but neither the size of the stone deposits nor length of their exploitation seriously rivaled the Indian industry. Francis, "When India Was Beadmaker to the World," p. 33. **31.** Ibid. **32.** Handler et al, p. 15. **33.** Brijbhushan. p. 14. **34.** Latif, p. 45. **35.** Brijbhushan, pp. 20–21. **36.** Latif, p. 47. **37.** Brijbhushan, p. 18. **38.** The Venetians made drawn-glass beads as did the Indians. However, there is no evidence that they were using the same techniques. Indeed, the evidence strongly suggests Indians were using their own *tada* technique, similar to a technique used today in Papanaidupet. Francis, "Some Thoughts on Glass Beadmaking," p. 196. **39.** Francis, *Glass Beads of India*, p. 6. In 1879–80, India imported 1,800,000 pounds of foreign glass beads: 78 percent from Venice and 8 percent each from China and Bohemia. **40.** Latif, pp. 88–90. **41.** Francis, *Indian Agate Beads*, p. 35. **42.** Possehl, pp. 40–46. **43.** Carnelian is often not red in color until the material has been heat-treated. At Ratanpur, the iron is natural to the stone; at Idar-Oberstein, the stones were soaked in an iron solution before heat treatment. Peter Francis, Letter to author, January 1986. **44.** Francis, *Glass Beads of India*, pp. 8–20.

I. See Central Asia chapter for further information on etched carnelian beads. **II.** van der Sleen, *A Handbook on Beads*, *passim*. **III.** These beads have been identified through correspondence between the Corning Museum of Glass and van der Sleen, February–March 1957. The beads, according to van der Sleen, are similar to excavated examples from Brahmapuri, Bahmani layer (fifteenth century A.D.). **IV.** Barbier, *passim*. **V.** Ibid. **VI.** Maureen Zarember, conversation with author, December 1982. **VII.** Kanungo, "Impact of Social and Political Change on the use of Beads Among the Konyaks."

CENTRAL ASIA

1. Barraclough, p. 70. **2.** Klimburg-Salter, pp. 112–13. **3.** See The Far East chapter. **4.** Belenitsky, pp. 93–101. Plates 57–58. **5.** Hinduism also spread throughout the region. Subsequently, this period is also referred to as the "Indianization of Asia": it was the time when the religion, culture, and trade goods from India influenced Burma, Cambodia, Laos, Thailand, and Indonesia. Jamey D. Allen, PC, July 16, 2008. **6.** Ref: Tapriza Projects: The History of the Bon Religion, tapriza.org. **7.** Newark Museum, I, pp. 41–42; Newark Museum, II, p. 13. **8.** Jeweled sculptures of Buddha, a form derived from northern India, reflect the influences of the Mahayana sect of Buddhism, which created the Bodhisattvas, the Buddha's earthly representatives worthy of Nirvana who stayed on earth to help mankind. To the Bodhisattva, jewelry denoted his worldly connections. **9.** Klimburg-Salter, *passim*; Reynolds, p. 15; and Zwalf, p. 10. **10.** Zwalf, pp. 9–12. **11.** See Prayer Beads chapter. **12.** The Tibetan trading class was small, but most Tibetans were born traders and engaged in bartering among themselves. The nobility, many of whom owned large provincial farms, had commercial agents who managed the sale of their estate produce and were also sent abroad to buy luxury items. **13.** Most Tibetan villages sported gaily painted wooden doors and window trim. During religious festivals, private homes and monasteries were decked with colorful awnings, banners, and flowers. Reynolds, p. 17. **14.** See Zwalf pp. 79, 137; Newark II, p. 92. **15.** Ebbinghouse, book review of *Himalayan Kingdoms*, 97. Diamonds, rubies, and emeralds were often inexpensively simulated. On the other hand, pearls, strung with large coral and *dZi* beads, were frequently high quality imitations; they used to be sold in Lhasa for nearly the price of real ones. **16.** Pogue, p. 79. **17.** Weinstein, p. 234. **18.** Laufer, p. 5. **19.** Pogue, p. 24. **20.** Thupten Pheloye, conversation with author, November 1983. **21.** Pal, p. 10. This coexistence appears to have ancient origins and ranges from the location of shrines to the portrayal of images. **22.** Waldschmidt, p. 11; Anderson, p. 32. **23.** Gabriel, "Himalayan Portraits," p. 59; Barker, p. 115. **24.** Gabriel, "The Tilari," p. 34. **25.** Masson and Sarianidi, p. 35. **26.** Ibid., p. 58; Bacon, p. 267. **27.** Pogue, p. 75. There are numerous references at this time to children buried with beads. See Masson and Sarianidi, pp. 64–65. **28.** Masson and Sarianidi, pp. 80, 89. **29.** Ibid., pp. 115–16. **30.** Ibid., p. 119. **31.** Ibid., p. 125. **32.** Fitzgibbon and Hale, in "Jewelry of the Ancient Lapis Route," p. 78, postulate that the beads were made in Afghanistan. James Lankton Time Line, p. 36–37 and Jamey D. Allen, PC, July 17, 2008, disagree. **33.** Masson and Sarianidi, pp. 168–69. **34.** Ibid., pp. 145–46. **35.** Barraclough, p. 60; McNeill, p. 104. **36.** Chard, p. 153. **37.** Masson and Sarianidi, p. 151. Mid-second to first millennium B.C. Bronze Age sites, such as Kokcha on the northern steppes of Turkmenistan, yielded beads of bronze, sardonyx, and faience. At Muminabad in the Samarkand oasis, a single burial contained over 1,000 beads. In the Kirghizia Valley, one grave yielded 1,300 bronze, faience, and antimony beads, many of which had been sewn onto clothing. **38.** Chard, p. 152. **39.** Forbes, p. 163. Jamey D. Allen, PC, July 18, 2008 adds: "The La Tene and Celtic beads are Mediterranean, and traded around by the Phoenicians, who were likewise responsible for the same beads that went to China." **40.** Jettmar, p. 97; Levin and Potapov, n.p. **41.** Peter Francis, letter to author, January 1986. **42.** Forbes, p. 163. **43.** Neuburg, p. 29. **44.** Rockhill, p. 24. Jamey D. Allen disagrees. "It is hard to believe Mongolians received much from Tibet. Although they have a lot in common, there are also distinct differences between them—say the turquoise, and metals (mostly silver). Mongolian beads tend to be more refined. They did not seem to like the free-form turquoise nodules used by the Tibetans, but preferred well-cut spherical beads. The coral was much the same in both groups, except for a greater incidence of Chinese coral that is more spherical and tends toward orange. Constructions for the Mongolians were more refined and delicate, and more like those of China"—as shown in plate 222. Jamey D. Allen, PC, July 18, 2008. **45.** Lance, p. 19. **46.** Casady, p. 78; Fitzgibbon and Hale, "Jewelry of the Turkic Tribes," p. 77. **47.** Lance, p. 19.

I. Although originally given to the Ngor Monastery in Tibet, the necklace was retrieved by the Lama Kinga after the Chinese takeover of Tibet and carried out of the country. Ivory Friedus, letter to author, June 1984. **II.** Zwalf, pp. 131, 136; Gabriel, "Himalayan Portraits," *passim*. **III.** Newark Museum, vol. II, p. 11. **IV.** The following descriptions were provided by David Ebbinghouse. Left to right: (1) This is an example of a bead that has been artificially treated to bring out the lines in the stone by the application of white lines that follow the natural banding. (2) White lines do not follow natural lines in the agate, but take forms similar to the previous example. However, the natural eyelike forms in the agate are incorporated into the design and become part of the pattern. (3) The patterns are similar to example 2 but one end of the bead did not take the blackening process and the white line curves around the end of this zone (suggesting that the white lines were applied subsequent to the blackening process). (4) Top: entirely blackened bead with applied white stripes. Bottom: central area blackened and bordered with white stripes. The ends are left untreated. (5) Top: it appears that both light and dark stripes have been applied, but both are very watery and transparent. Bottom: the bead appears to have been completely darkened and white stripes applied, but the blackening is very light brown and the white stripes have taken unevenly. (6) Bead was completely blackened with white lines applied subsequently This very plump shape is similar to natural agate beads from the Namazga culture of about 2000 B.C. (7) These beads have been both blackened and whitened. Beads of this pattern are very highly prized by Tibetans today and are frequently displayed in a traditional ensemble (plates 214 and 220). (8) The steps turn in opposite directions in each bead. A highly prized bead. (9) These are considered more precious than eyed-patterns by Tibetans, possibly because they are rarer than the longer beads. (10) The "Earth-Door, Sky-Door" bead has a square on one side, and a circle on the other. (11) Although not considered to be a pure *dZi*, by most Tibetans, this bead has extremely uncommon markings and a better than usual shape for a *phum dZi*. Tibetans consider it in the *dZi* family, but not nearly as powerful an amulet. The figure and cartouche are puzzling, but suggest connections to ancient Persia during Sasanian times. **V.** The following classification of the *dZi* beads shown in plate 217 follows the system described in note XI: Top to bottom: (1) Nine-eyed "pure" *dZi*. At present, although it is an "etched" bead, none of the existing techniques as originally described by Beck explain its manufacturing process. This bead needs it own technical category (2) Variety A: a combination of types I and II. The end bands are left untreated. Dark bands are applied over a whitened area, leaving narrower white bands. (3) Type II? (4) Natural agate. **VI.** Ebbinghouse and Winsten, "Tibetan *dZi* Beads I," p. 24. **VII.** Ibid. **VIII.** Thupten Pheloye, conversation with, author, November 1983. **IX.** Ebbinghouse and Winsten, "Tibetan *dZi* Beads," vol. I, pp. 24–25. **X.** Similar beads—white chalcedony with dark brown geometric patterns that could be *dZi* predecessors—have been excavated from sites in India, Afghanistan, and Turkmenistan that date back to 1500–1000 B.C. Francis, "Followup: dZi Beads," pp. 55–56. **XI.** The following classification system of "etching" (a misnomer) agate beads is based on the original work of Horace Beck with additions as noted by David Ebbinghouse and Michael Winsten in "Tibetan dZi Beads," vol. I: pp. 19–25; and Jamey D. Allen, conversation with author, October 1986. Type I: white design on natural stone background. An alkali (usually potash or white lead) is painted onto the bead's surface and then the bead is fired. This permanently whitens the area of the bead covered with the alkali. This whitening is not merely a glaze; depending on how porous the stone is, it often penetrates it. Type II: black design on whitened background. The entire bead is whitened, and then a design is painted with another chemical, often copper nitrate. The bead is fired again, producing a dark design on a white background (Timeline 615a–c). Note: There may be no type II. The colors may originally have been carnelian with white patterns that changed color after exposure to fire, (in a cremation, for example.) Type III: black design on natural stone background. Sometimes a dark design is applied to the natural stone. Variety A: a combination of types I and II. Part of the bead is first whitened, leaving part of the bead unwhitened. The black design is etched over the whitened part of the bead. Variety B: a combination of types I and III. Both black and white patterns appear on the same bead, but do not overlap, like variety A. None of these methods appear to describe the manufacture of "pure" *dZi* (see top bead, plate 217). Ebbinghouse and Winsten believe that they were made by black and white being added side by side, and suggest placing pure *dZi* as a subclass of type II. Jamey D. Allen believes the beads are artificially darkened, with the white designs subsquently added. Allen suggests the possibility of type IV or variety C. **XII.** Newark Museum Tibetan Collection, vol. IV: pp. 68–69; Ebbinghouse and Winsten, "Tibetan *dZi* beads," pp. 36–38. Ebbinghouse hypothesizes that the beads might date to between 1500 and 500 B.C., possibly an offshoot of the Harrapan/Sumerian bead tradition. Also, he does not believe that all *dZi* are of the same age or origins, based on the fact that the markings tend to become stylized with a relatively small repertoire of stable design patterns. David Ebbinghouse, letter to author, July 1986. **XIII.** Ebbinghouse and Winsten, "Tibetan *dZi* Beads," vol. I, pp. 19–24. "Pure" *dZi* beads must be made of genuine etched agate with a very shiny or glossy surface free of alkali from the etching process. It should also have a desirable pattern such as the nine-eyed pattern, or a circle and a square, symbolizing "Earth Door and Sky Door." Shape is very important—the bead should be plump and healthy looking. If they are too thin ("anemic looking") or not round in cross section, they are less desirable. Deep colors increase the value of *dZi*; colors should be true black or deep rich brown. Opacity is also a consideration: when the bead is held up to the light, it should not be translucent. Finally, "pure" *dZi* should not have pattern flaws (caused by differences in the underlying agate structure, which results in uneven whitening). The beads should be in good condition with no chips. Note to the author from Jamey D. Allen: "In recent conversations with David Ebbinghouse, he has admitted a change in his perspective. He understands that his informants presented him with a perspective that was true to them, but not necessarily pan-Tibetan. I still think that much of what he wrote is accurate and valid—but I have come to realize that not all Tibetans and Tibetan bead collectors agree about zi [Jamey's revised spelling of *dZi*] and other issues." Jamey D. Allen, PC. July 18, 2008. See Jamey Allen's excellent article, "Tibetan Zi Beads: The Current Fascination with Their Nature and History."

S.E. ASIA AND SOUTH PACIFIC

1. Holt, p. 4; Fraser-Lu, n.p. **2.** Lamb, "Some Observations on Stone and Glass Beads," *passim*. Lamb's theories regarding contact and exchange via the Mediterranean are questioned by, among others, Jamey D. Allen, PC, July 18, 2008. **3.** Rodgers, pp. 21–22. **4.** Ibid., pp. 41–43. **5.** Legarda, p. 64; Dunsmore, Introduction. **6.** Maxwell, p. 136. **7.** Dunsmore, Introduction. **8.** Chongkol, p. 82. **9.** Francis, "Thailand," p. 44. **10.** Ibid. **11.** Ibid.; White p. 76; Francis, p. 44 and letter to author, January 1986. **12.** Chongkol, pp. 82–83. **13.** Casal, p. 46. **14.** Rawson, passim; Rodgers, pp. 32–34. **15.** Rawson, pp. 203–71. **16.** Lamb, "Some Observations on Stone and Glass Beads," pp. 94–98. **17.** Jamey D. Allen, PC, July 18, 2008. **18.** Lamb, "Some Observations on Stone and Glass Beads," pp. 94–98. Dunsmore, p. 5. **19.** Jamey D. Allen, PC, July 18, 2008. **20.** Dunsmore, p. 3. **21.** Ibid, p. 3. **22.** Lamb, "A Note on Glass Beads," p. 84. Jamey D. Allen, PC, July 18, 2008. **23.** Rodgers, pp. 117–21; Adams, passim. **24.** Fraser-Lu, n.p. **25.** Rodgers, p. 121. **26.** Casal, p. 34. **27.** Ibid., p. 52. The earliest glass head excavated in the Philippines was spherical in shape and made of blue glass with many bubbles. It dates to c. 400 B.C. and is of a type found throughout Southeast Asia. **28.** Ibid., p. 71. Jamey D. Allen, PC, July 18, 2008. **29.** Legarda, "Pre-Hispanic Gold," p. 94. **30.** Ibid., p. 96. **31.** Lamb, "Some Observations on Stone and Glass Beads," p. 95. **32.** Legarda, p. 61. **33.** Ibid., pp. 61–70. **34.** Rodgers, p. 243. **35.** Ibid., p. 254. **36.** Ibid. **37.** Ibid., p. 246. **38.** Liu, "Formosan Ornaments," pp. 21–27. **39.** Ibid.; Francis, *Chinese Glass Beads*, p. 33. Large polychrome glass beads with distinctive millefiori and dragged trail decoration (Timeline 909) from Indonesia. Although formerly thought to be from the Majapahit Dynasty (c. 1375–1525) Indonesian beads are now considered earlier. These millefiori beads, while resembling those of the post-Roman Middle-Eastern era, differ considerably. Indonesian millefiori have very thin cane layers fused to a coarse, opaque central glass core, while ancient Roman era beads have canes that typically extend to the perforation. (An exception is some face beads.) Liu, "Asian Glass Ornaments, Part 1." It has been suggested that possibly the cane layers on the Indonesian beads were cut locally from preformed glass ingots manufactured in the Roman Empire. Their thinness may reflect the judicious use of a rare material that came from far away. Derek Content, letter to author, September 1985. **40.** Jamey D. Allen, PC, July 18, 2008. **41.** Rodgers, p. 61; Newton, pp. 4–5. **42.** Ross, pp. 20–26; Burt, pp. 6–7.

I. Lamb, "A Note on Glass Beads," p. 94. **II.** Lewis, pp. 206, 214–16. **III.** Maxwell, pp. 131–40. **IV.** Dunsmore, p. 13; Rodgers, pp. 118–19. **V.** Rodgers, p. 118. **VI.** Casal, pp. 158–59. **VII.** Chen, pp. 163–69, plate 12. **VIII.** Liu, "Formosan Ornaments," pp. 21–27; and "Asian Glass Ornaments Part 1," pp. 28–31; Chen, pp. 357–66; Miyamoto, pp. 89–91. **IX.** This information was obtained from the collector Province M. Henry and submitted to the registrar of the Smithsonian Institution on March 20, 1965, as "General Comments Concerning Formosan Aboriginal Beads." Also see Blair, p. 204. **X.** Ross, pp. 20–36. **XI.** Ibid., p. 23.

MIDDLE AND SOUTH AMERICA

1. Dr. Richard S. MacNeish, letter to author, January 9, 1984. **2.** Robert Liu, conversation with author, November 1986. **3.** Easby, pp. 14–16; Abel-Vidor, pp. 138–39. **4.** Easby, p. 8. **5.** Emmerich, *Sweat of the Sun*, p. 146. **6.** Ibid., pp. 146–49. **7.** Both may be white, various shades of gray, pea-green, grass-green, emerald-green, or blue-green. Both also may be mottled or translucent. The emerald-green and blue-green shades tend to be jadeite, while nephrite also occurs in yellows, oranges, and purples. **8.** Easby, p. 7. **9.** Ibid., pp. 16–26. A weathered jade boulder had to be broken to gain access to the gemlike quality stone within it. The stone was then ground, sawed, grooved, incised, drilled, and polished. The preliminary shaping of the bead depended on fracturing, grinding, and sawing. Some beads, like the bar bead in plate 256 (front left), were shaped entirely by the sawing technique. Cuts were also made with a wooden instrument or with an agave fiber or cord coated with an abrasive, an ancient technique known as "cord sawing." Sawing with a string, a technique apparently invented by the Olmec, enabled craftsmen to make round or angular cuts that could not be made with rigid tools. The drill point, usually a hollow piece of bird bone or bamboo cane, was filled with sand or emery abrasive. Hollow sections of bamboo cane, *Arundinaria*, locally available to Costa Rican lapidaries, were often used for drilling as well as polishing jade, because the plant contains its own abrasive in the form of tiny silica particles. The beads, many of which have an extraordinary soft, almost velvety luster, were finished by being burnished with wood or by polishing with beeswax or jade powder. Easby, pp. 16–26. **10.** Emmerich, *Sweat of the Sun*, p. xix. **11.** Ibid., pp. xxii, 66–68. **12.** Ibid., p. xxii. **13.** Ibid., p. 98; Lothrop, pp. 158–59. **14.** Stierlin, p. 121; Andre Emmerich, conversation with author, December 1985. **15.** Weaver, p. 466. Emmerich, *Sweat of the Sun*, pp. 131–32; Stierlin, pp. 112–20. **16.** Kessler, "Beads of the Tairona," pp. 3–5. **17.** Peter Francis, letter to author, January 1986, and Earl and Shari Kessler, "Ecuadorian Beads," pp. 48–52. **18.** Easby, p. 143. **19.** Liu, "Identification: Smallest and Largest Beads," p. 69. **20.** Smith and Good, *passim*; Liu and Harris, pp. 3–8. **21.** Smith and Good, p. 4; quoted from *The True History of the Conquest of New Spain* by Bernal Diaz del Castillo (vol. 2), edited by Genaro Garcias, (London: Hakluyt Society, 1910), original translation by Albert Percival Maudslay. **22.** Davis and Pack, pp. 20, 35. **23.** Liu and Harris, pp. 5, 7–11; Smith and Good, *passim*. **24.** Jamey D. Allen, PC, July 18, 2008. **25.** Liu and Harris, pp. 3–11. For extensive discussions of *Nueva Cádiz* beads, see Liu and Harris, and Smith and Good. **26.** Johnson, pp. 18–19.

I. Easby, pp. 64–66. Both disk-shaped and elaborately carved bar and tubular jade beads are typical of Costa Rica, while round beads are quite rare. Single, large sculptural beads are believed to have been strung on necklaces of jade disk beads. **II.** Proskouriakoff, p. 18. **III.** Ibid. **IV.** Robicsek, *passim*; Andre Emmerich, conversation with author, December 1985. **V.** Emmerich, *Art Before Columbus*, pp. 59–60. **VI.** Emmerich, *Sweat of the Sun*, pp. xxii, 7–8; Tushingham et al., *passim*; Orchard, pp. 62–63. The technique began in Chavin times. Ancient Peruvian craftsmen cut, embossed, bent, shaped, forged, and punched very thin gold sheets to attain the desired forms. Sheet gold was made by placing melted nuggets between animal hides and beating the hardened metal with a stone hammer. When the process of annealing (reheating metal to restore its ductability) was discovered, it became possible to hammer gold into very thin sheets which were then cut with sharp stone chisels into strips or complex shapes. Beads of clay or charcoal were often covered with a thin layer of gold. **VII.** Tushingham et al., *passim*. Peruvian metallurgists seldom used soldering, preferring methods of joining metal that required only moderate skill and no application of external heat. This meant joining by lacing, stapling, crimping (bending of the edge of one sheet tightly over the edge of another), or inserting the edge of one sheet into slots of another. In joining two pieces of metal together, Chimu metalsmiths expressed an aesthetic observable in the textiles produced by their culture. For example, narrow weavings were joined to form broad textiles without attention to the alignment of design in the attached sections. A similar lack of attention to alignment is seen in the joined sections of Peruvian beads made from thin gold sheets. The gold ball beads in plate 259 show unrefined joints, as does the crimping technique on the mask beads (plate 258). **VIII.** Ibid., p. 14. **IX.** Kessler, "Beads of the Tairona," pp. 3–5. The Tairona wore beads at festivals, and also assigned religious significance to them. The Kogi, modern descendants of the Tairona, recall that their ancestors "danced with objects of red rock to call the summer and green rock to call the rains. Rock crystal beads were used as offerings to the spirits of rain and Water and to Mother Universe." Many Kogi own beads inherited from their Tairona ancestors and still use them for ritual purposes. **X.** Ibid. **XI.** It is possible this, as well as the pottery objects shown in plate 268 are not beads but spindle whorls, weights used in the spinning of fibers into yarn. Rebecca Northern, pp. 14–20.

NORTH AMERICA

1. Jernigan, pp. 10–11. Archaeologists working at Tule Springs, Nevada, have found a bead of white caliche (hardened carbonate) possibly dating to 11,000 B.C.—perhaps the earliest known bead from North America. **2.** Mathews, p. 10. **3.** Francis, *Beads and the Discovery of the New World*, pp. 14–17. **4.** Streuver, p. 62. **5.** Francis, *Beads and the Discovery of the New World*, p. 7. **6.** Jernigan, p. 15. **7.** Francis, *Beads and the Discovery of the New World*, p. 22. **8.** Gillette, *passim*; Orchard, pp. 71–83; Speck and Orchard, *passim*; Grand Rapids Public Museum, pp. 16–22; Brasser, p. 126. **9.** Brasser, p. 26. **10.** Francis, *Beads and the Discovery of the New World*, p. 24. **11.** Ibid., p. 25. **12.** Francis, *Beads and the Discovery of the New World*, p. 33; Smith and Good, *passim*. Other materials were traded in. Carnelian and rock crystal along with glass were brought to the Caribbean and Florida by the Spanish. **13.** Francis, *Beads and the Discovery of the New World*, p. 32. **14.** Orchard, p. 16. **15.** Ibid., p. 102. Jamey D. Allen, PC, July 18, 2008, relates: "One must differentiate between actual *cornaline d'Aleppo* beads which were drawn beads (Timeline 68b) and large wound overlay beads (Timeline 68). It is possible that both were used simultaneously and either might be called 'Hudson's Bay' beads. However, the phrase 'Hudson's Bay beads' is usually taken to indicate the wound beads." **16.** Orchard, pp. 17–18. "It is a popular idea that the Lewis and Clark beads (like Padre beads) may be Chinese. I lean toward the possibility that they similar-looking European wound beads. A primary reason is that they are too well-made (regular), and because they have no mandrel release compound." Jamey D. Allen, PC, July 18, 2008. **17.** Good, p. 16. **18.** Conn, *Circles of the World*, p. 141. **19.** Harris, *The Russian Bead*, pp. 1–9. "Russian" beads were made in Bohemia and probably came to the Russians via the Chinese and British. **20.** Francis, *Beads and the Discovery of the New World*, pp. 41–43. **21.** Orchard, pp. 104–162; Gil, Part 1, pp. 42–51; Part 2, p. 44–49; Lyford, *passim*. **22.** Dockstader, p. 20. **23.** Furst and Furst, p. 165. **24.** Wildschut and Ewers, p. 1. **25.** Dockstader, p. 45. **26.** For an in-depth discussion of this issue, see *North American Indian Jewelry and Adornment*, Lois S. Dubin, 1999. **27.** "A great deal of beadwork is being done to enhance the costumes at the powwows. During the last twenty years, I have seen a change from pieces of beadwork imported from Hong Kong to more traditional designs being beaded by the dancers and their families. Beadwork classes are well attended at Indian centers and other places such as museums.... The Native American Church uses many objects which require beading. Some of the most beautiful beading today is being done on the handles of rattles etc. using size 13 and smaller beads (usually faceted) and the 'peyote stitch.'" Barbara Robertson, letter to author, May 1986. See Dubin, 1999.

I. See Holstein and Erdman; Jacka and Hammack, Pogue, Rosnek and Stacey. Dublin, 1999. **II.** Conn, *Native American Art*, p. 353. **III.** Smith and Good, p. 3. **IV.** The Algonquins, in particular, did not realize that land sales meant they could no longer use their land, one example of the differences between European and Indian concepts of property ownership. **V.** Furst and Furst, pp. 165, 170–172. **VI.** Driscoll, pp. 40–47; Winnipeg Art Gallery, *passim*. **VII.** Conn, p. 141. **VIII.** Conn, *Circles of the World*, pp. 8–9. **X.** King, p. 32; Lenssen, *passim*; Conn, *Native American Art*, p. 139.

THE SPECIAL BEADS

1. Kunz and Stevenson, p. 404. **2.** Poinar, p. 29. Resin from an extinct pine or conifer tree was, for the past hundred years, considered to be the source of amber. More recent studies, however, suggest a species of *Agathis* (the broadleaf Kauri gum of New Zealand is *Aganthis australis*), a genus found in many warm parts of the world. Forty million years ago—the estimated age of most Baltic amber—the climate of the Baltic was subtropical. Today the climate is temperate, and the *aganthis* forests are long gone. **3.** Fagan, p. 160. **4.** Rice, p. 32. **5.** Allen, "Amber and Its Substitutes, Part 1," pp. 18–20; Rice, pp. 35–36; Charles Picard, p. 340. **6.** Rice, p. 36. **7.** Ogden, p. 116. **8.** Shaw, p. 253. **9.** Ibid., p. 219. **10.** *Elektron*, meaning "golden," may derive from a Phoenician word for the sun. **11.** p. 220; Ogden, p. 177. **12.** Kunz, pp. 55–56. **13.** Buffum, p. 77. **14.** Ibid., pp. 17–20. The Etruscans' interest in amber went beyond adornment. Follett mentions that Etruscan goldsmiths, famed for their exquisite filigree and granulated jewelry, ingeniously used amber as flux in the granulation process. Follett, pp. 64–65. Jamey D. Allen disagrees. He believes that the use of amber in granulated goldwork was as a substitute for regular resin—i.e., to hold the granules in place. Any fluxing action was unintentional. Jamey D. Allen, PC, July 18, 2008. **15.** Allen, "Amber and Its Substitutes," p. 16. **16.** Bunger, p. 105. **17.** Baltic amber is called succinite meaning "sap-stone." (The terms "succinite" and "succinic" are both derived from the Latin "succus" meaning juice or sap—the juice of a tree.) A lack of succinic acid usually indicates an origin other than the Baltic formation period. Outside the Baltic, succinite has been found in small quantities at several other locales, including England and Thailand. The ambers from Sicily (simetite), Rumania (rumanite), and Burma (burmite) differ from those of the Baltic as they have little or no succinic acid. In addition, rumanite and burmite are younger than succinite, and were formed during the Miocene period, 10 to 25 million years ago, For further reference, see Allen, "Amber and Its Substitutes," Parts 1 and 2. **18.** Allen, "Amber and Its Substitutes," Part 2,

pp. 12–13. **19.** Ibid., p. 12. **20.** Ibid. **21.** Buffum, pp. 9–28. **22.** Allen, "Amber and Its Substitutes, Part 2," p. 12. **23.** Cloudy amber resin was formed within the trees to heal splits and cracks. Although there has been some discussion about the relationship between resin flows and opaqueness, (see Poinar, p. 29) Jamey D. Allen who has studied amber extensively does not believe there is any validity to the comparison. From his studies, Allen theorizes that resin flows exuded on warm days are thin, runny, and clear, while cool weather causes thick and cloudy resin deposits. Jamey D. Allen, conversation with author, September 1986. **24.** While it is complex to determine the presence or lack of succinite acid, to differentiate between true amber and amberlike objects, Jamey D. Allen has devised a simple test using a hot-point such as a darning needle. The hot-point test indicates the object's composition by the manner in which the specimen burns, as well as by its odor. **25.** Ibid., Part 2, pp. 14–15. **26.** Ibid., Part 1, p. 19. **27.** Ibid., Part 2, p. 15; Part 3, p. 20. **28.** Jamey D. Allen, conversation with author, September 1986. **29.** Kunz and Stevenson, p. 5; Streeter, pp. 57–61. **30.** Kunz and Stevenson, p. 36. **31.** Pearls are best defined as: "a calcareous body, composed of concentric layers around a central nucleus and organically produced by a living mollusk." Landman, et al, 2001, p. 9. **32.** King, p. 267; Kunz and Stevenson, p. 51–53; Sitwell, p. 43. **33.** Kunz and Stevenson, p. 145. **34.** Ibid., p. 5. Also see plate opposite 404. **35.** Ibid., p. 10. **36.** Ibid., p. 9. **37.** Ibid., p. 449. **38.** Ibid., p. 9. **39.** See illustration in Gregorietti on page 128. **40.** Kunz and Stevenson, pp. 16–18. **41.** Ibid., p. 21. **42.** Addison, p. 56. **43.** Gregorietti, p. 192. **44.** Kuntzsch, p. 119. **45.** Ogden, p. 121. **46.** Kunz and Stevenson, p. 460. **47.** Weinstein, p. 79. **48.** Peter Francis, letter to author, January 1986. **49.** Kunz and Stevenson, pp. 184–85. **50.** Ibid., p. 225. **51.** Weinstein, pp. 83–84. **52.** Kunz and Stevenson, p. 251. **53.** Kunz and Stevenson, p. 258. **54.** Ibid., p. 259. **55.** Ibid., pp. 29–31. **56.** Nadelhoffer, pp. 125, 133. **57.** Sitwell, pp. 45–46; Kunz and Stevenson, pp. 266–68, 281–82. **58.** Kunz and Stevenson, p. 261. **59.** Ibid., pp. 130, 297, and Chapter 3, note 13; Sitwell, p. 48. **60.** Birmingham, p. 148; Sitwell, p. 45; Nadelhoffer, p. 136. **61.** Birmingham, p. 196. **62.** Sitwell, p. 48. Natural pearls have not totally disappeared. Most are antiques, but a small quantity of new ones do appear on the market. The chances of finding a round pearl in a cultivated oyster range from one in ten to one in fifty; in natural pearls the odds lengthen to one or two per thousand. **63.** Ibid., p. 50. **64.** Birmingham, p. 198.
I. Nadelhoffer, p. 125. **II.** Ibid., pp. 125, 130.

THE MAGICAL EYE BEAD

1. This concept is currently being developed by Lois S. Dubin and Martine J. Reid for their forthcoming book on the evil eye phenomena. **2.** Maloney, pp. 7–9. **3.** Schienerl, pp. 28, 52. **4.** Budge, p. 359. **5.** Stillman, p. 91. **6.** Budge, pp. 355-59; Alice Scherer, PC, November 2007. **7.** Erikson, p. 176. **8.** Maloney, p. 143. **9.** The Eye of Horus design is shown as a human eye with a cosmetic line extending from the outer corner of the eye, an enhanced eyebrow line, and a stylized marking below the eye evoking the cheek of a falcon. Horus was portrayed as a falcon-headed god, possibly because the bird flew so high, close to the sacred sun. The falcon was also an important royal Egyptian emblem because its gaze was said to paralyze birds, as does the Pharaoh's expression stun his enemies. The noticeable markings in the feathers under the falcon's eye create the impression that they are wide open. Thus Horus' "all-seeing Wedjat eye" (the Eye of Horus) became a symbol for visual acuity and imperviousness to injury as well as a treasured bead and amulet. Ref: Biederman 1994, p. 125. **10.** Eisen, 1916. Eisen studied archaeologically excavated beads from the ancient sites of Lisht and Thebes in the Metropolitan Museum of Art as well as collections in Europe and the Middle East. **11.** Guido 1978; Templemann-Maczlynska 1985. **12.** Jamey D. Allen, PC, November 9, 2007. **13.** Ibid. **14.** James Lankton suggests that a practical explanation for the predominance of blue glass and blue-green faience in early beads, including eye beads, may be due to the fact that with the addition of copper, blue-green glass was an easy color to produce. Lankton 2003. **15.** Jamey D. Allen, PC, November 9, 2007.
I. Eye beads and head pendants are found together in Mediterranean and European sites dating from about 700–200 B.C. **II.** (1–3), Stone from Iran, Syria, or Iraq, late fourth to third millennium B.C. (4) Banded agate from Iran, Syria, or Iraq, third to second millennium B.C. (5) "Etched" carnelian Sassanian to Islamic period (c. A.D. 642–1400) (6) Western Asian double-eye agate, third to first millennium B.C. (7) Western Asian stone base with glass eye top layer, held together by a (probably resin) glue, second to first millennium B.C. (8–9) Western Asian stratified glass imitating banded agate, second to first millennium B.C. (10) Western Asian or Egyptian stratified glass, late second to first millennium B.C. (11) Wound glass with impressed twisted canes and stratified eyes from New Kingdom Egypt, Eighteenth to Nineteenth dynasties (1400–1300 B.C.). (12–14) Wound glass with stratified eyes from New Kingdom Egypt, Eighteenth to Nineteenth dynasties (1400–1300 B.C.). (15–17) Phoenician wound glass with stratified eyes, 700–300 B.C. (18) Phoenician or Egyptian wound glass with composite stratified eyes and raised spots, c. 500 B.C. (19) Egypt wound glass with eye spots, 600–250 B.C. (20) Phoenician wound glass with spirally wound coils and raised stratified eyes from Carthage or Syro-Lebanese coast, 500–300 B.C. (21) Egyptian wound glass with raised stratified eyes, 500–300 B.C. (22) Wound glass with mosaic glass inserts from Gilan, Iran, 300 B.C. (23) Wound glass with stratified eyes from Persepolis, Iran, 300 B.C. (24–26) Chinese wound glass with stratified eyes, 400–200 B.C. (27) Wound glass with stratified eyes from western Asia, Egypt, and Europe, c. 700 B.C.–A.D. 100. (28) Celtic wound glass with trailed spiral eyes upon vestigial horn, 300 B.C.–A.D. 100. (29–31) Roman wound glass with stratified eyes, 100 B.C.–A.D. 200. (32) Islamic or Venetian mosaic-glass canes, no core, from Djenne, Mali. (33) Viking period wound glass with trailed designs and mosaic glass insets, A.D. 800–1000. (34) Wound glass with stratified eyes from Borneo, A.D. 1500 (?). (35) West African powder glass, twentieth century. (36) West African powder-glass bodom bead, early twentieth century. (37) Venetian wound glass with polychrome eye, nineteenth century. (38) Venetian wound glass with polychrome eyes, nineteenth century. (39) Antique ivory from Nepal, nineteenth century. (40) Venetian wound glass with polychrome eyes, nineteenth century. (41) Venetian wound glass with millefiori eyes and designs, nineteenth century. (42) Venetian mosaic-glass canes on center base, nineteenth century. (43–44) Venetian wound glass with polychrome eyes, nineteenth century. (45) Wound glass with stratified eyes from Goerce, Turkey, 1893. (1–46) All private collection except as follows: 1–3, 5, 7–14, 18, collection Henry Anavian, New York; 4, 6, collection Derek Content, Houlton, Maine; 19, 20, 26, 38, Corning Museum of Glass, Corning, New York; 23, British Museum, London. 24, 25, Royal Ontario Museum, Toronto; 36, collection Dr. Michael Heide, Portland; 39, collection Ivory Freidus.

CONTEMPORARY

General note: The technical information for the contemporary glass beads is from Scott, 2008; Finegan, 2005; The Bead Museum, 2007; Toby Bowlby, PC, June 2008 and the artists where credited.

1. Kennedy, S. J. "Nyhus Design Glasswear," p. 16. **2.** Cartlidge, p. 40; Heininger, p. 246. **3.** Gordon and Nerenberg, p. 4. **4.** Black, pp. 278, 287-89. **5.** Cartlidge, p. 75. **6.** Ibid., p. 11. **7.** See Hector 2005, for an in-depth study of the commonalities linking ethnographic and contemporary Western beadworkers. **8.** Kennedy and Liu, pp. 18–19; Liu, 1990, p. 16–17; Jamey D. Allen, PC, July 2008. **9.** Muzzy, 1993, p. 56–59. **10.** Benesh, 1993, p. 31. The artists whose work was represented in the 1993 exhibition, Contemporary Glass Beadworkers, and are illustrated in this book include: Donald Schneider, Tom Boylan, Dinah and Patty Hulet, Kristina Logan, Patricia Frantz, Tom Holland, James Smircich, Art Seymour, Molly Vaughn Haskins, Patricia Sage Holland, James A. Jones, Rene Roberts, Inara Knight and Donna Milliron. **11.** Between 1993 and 1998, the Society of Glass Beadmakers grew from 60 to 500 members. Today, the International Society of Glass Beadmakers has nearly 1600 members. **12.** In a handbook written by the Youth Crime Service Unit of San Antonio, Texas, the police department noted in an article in the *New York Times*: "The use of colored beads is also popular with gang members. The color of the bead is dependent on the color the gang has adopted for their gang. The bead can be made into a necklace…or worn in the shoelaces, made into a key chain, worn in braids in their hair and used in other fashions. Colored rubber bands worn in hair braids or around their wrist can also be indicators of gang membership. The use of colored rosary beads and other religious articles has also been noted. These are subtle indicators of gang membership and are often hard to notice if you are not looking for them. With the introduction of strict dress codes and the use of uniforms in the school sites, these type of indicators seem to be favored by the gangsters." Ref: Tabor, 1994. This information was given to the author by Brian Walls, a New York City police detective, via his sister Jeanette Walls. **13.** Black, Introduction.
I. "Nearly forty years ago, Rod [Slemmons, Kit's husband] and I made our first trip to Oaxaca where I bought in a tiny stall in the market a small strand of beautiful old stone beads. (I was drawn to the beat-up case they were in by the tiny live owl serenely perched on top.) I loved the beads and for a long time they remained as a strand. Several inches of them became part of a necklace for my mother, and it took another thirty years to find just the right moment to use more as the lifeline in Ramona's hand—along with other favorite beads of Ramona's—amber, coral, and bone. Ramona put together two huge bead exhibitions at the Bellevue Art Museum. The Ubiquitous Bead I and II, 1987 and 1991. Ramona's style was inclusive and both these shows were packed. ich and layered and exciting, they had a big impact on many people." Kiff Slemmons, PC, June 2008. **II.** Kiff Slemmons, PC, June 2008. **III.** For an excellent overview of William Harper's work, see Nelson, 2004. **IV.** Brown, 2003, pp. 50–53. **V.** In a letter to the author, Virginia Blakelock wrote: "*Daphis nerii* (Oleander Hawk Moth) represented a culmination of my experience with the loomed [piece called] Galaxy and an off-loom broad collar named Cleopatra. I have always loved butterflies and moths, and when I was in grade school I thought I would become an entomologist. I finally realized that I wasn't into being a scientist; I wanted to be an artist. But bugs and butterflies of all sorts still inspire me. This particular

moth is one of the most colorful Hawk Moths in the world. It lives in North Africa, and its caterpillars feed on oleander, an a highly poisonous, ornamental shrub…Hawk moths are known for their particular wing shape. They are powerful fliers, a little like hummingbirds, and hover in front of flowers to suck nectar with their long, tubular tongues.

So, my first thought was to loom this moth. That's as far as I was thinking when I began. I graphed out the moth, in color, and began looming. Exactly halfway through, I realized that my colors had gotten completely distorted from reality (which I was really trying to copy, because it was so extraordinary), and the aspect ratio of the moth's wings weren't right. So, I set aside that moth, and began again, this time with a black and white pencil graph. I looked again at the photos and paintings I had of the moth, and carefully selected the colors (in size 16° beads this time, because I had the right pinks, lavenders, creams, and greens for the image) that I needed. Then, I essentially "painted in" the moth with my colored beads, using the black and white drawing as a placement guide. It was Gary's [Gary Lee Bett, Virginia's husband] idea to put the moon behind the moth.

The weaving went well, and when the Moth came off the loom, I pinned it to my mannequin and began lamenting over how to turn it into a necklace. I had been so in love with the moth that I couldn't see past it, to a completed piece. We were still living in the cabin (which was only about 200 sq ft.) and when Gary finally got sick of my obsessive whining he said "If it's that bad, let's give it to the cats to play with." Well, that snapped me out of it, and somehow I came up with the off-loom collar that supports the moth. The long cobalt bugle beads I had to actually buy back from a friend. Then, there were so few of them that I had to count them out and plan their use. All the bugle beads are antique, extra thin ones that I got from Wilma Mangum [a bead supplier, in Idaho]." Virginia Blakelock, PC, March 2008. **VI.** "Trilobite was begun as a flat, rectangular peyote stitch panel (for an evening bag) using iridescent 11° Delica beads. The original two-dimensional pattern was overlapping diamonds. I added brick stitch triangles to the long sides of the original panel, to extend the design diamonds past the edges. Then, I made individual brick stitch diamonds, which mimicked the ones in the pattern, and sewed them to the flat panel. For the other half of the bag, I manipulated a piece of silk using a Japanese tie-dying technique called *shibori* taught to me by Darcie Beytebiere (the first non-Japanese to really understand and use *shibori* on fabric). It wasn't until the fabric part and the beaded part came together that Gary and I really decided that it needed to turn into a creature. Gary gave me a book all about trilobites to inspire me. I had the entire piece completed except for the eyes. He and I were on our sailboat, and I made trilobite eyes. All kinds. Finally he said, 'Why don't you try plain black?' As you can see, those are the ones that worked.

Trilobite won the first Toho Delica contest at the end of 2004. The prize was a trip to Japan in April of 2005. I was amazed and delighted. The judges, who know me and know my other work, were stunned to discover that this was my piece. That pleased me, because I definitely like to keep 'em guessing." Virgina Blakelock, PC, March 2008. **VII.** In correspondences with the author on July 16, Virginia Paust wrote: "…I actually have about 6 inches of the stem of the poppy pod finished. I have to bead as much as possible before the chanterelle mushrooms and porcinis start popping out of the ground. This should happen in about one to two weeks…" On July 18: "I want to give you an update. I have started leaves, and will add a black-eyed-susan, and maybe even a purple-cone flower. This is how these necklaces evolve. I start creating pieces, then I can pin them onto my dress-making form and move things around, add elements, and step back and let it tell me what it needs… My husband and I did go out mushroom hunting, and we found about a quart of chanterelles, and ate them for dinner… We also found my favorite, which is called a bi-color bolete. We need more rain before we go out again. I will get beading until the rains come…" **VIII.** School of American Research website. July 16, 2008. **IX.** In a marvelous, informative letter to the author on August 31, 2008, Valerie Hector wrote: "I was really bad at algebra in high school, even though I tried hard, and I liked geometry. It was and still is liberating to make geometric structures in beads!

I am convinced that by 1900 and probably a lot earlier the Chinese had created a large and sumptuous universe of bead polyehdra. Most operate according to the same set of principles. Fabulous examples have no doubt perished in the many upheavals of the twentieth century.

In the last couple of years there has been a huge renaissance in the making of bead polyedra in China, due perhaps largely to the easy availability of colorful and cheap plastic beads being made in China. Also due to the mandatory retirement age of fifty-five, at which time both men and women start looking for new hobbies, and beadwork is one of the hottest hobbies as far as I can tell. These days, new bead polyhedra are being invented all the time in China…some with double- and even triple-layers. The potential to develop new bead polyhedra is infinite, and I think the Chinese are really enjoying exploring the possibilities. It's a kind of play they've been deprived of for too long." Valerie's description of her three complex polyhedra beads from the Elements necklace (plate 369) is as follows: 1) An icosahedron made of thirty sterling silver oval beads measuring 15 mm × 5 mm. An icosahedron is one of the five Platonic solids. A few years ago I found a 100-year-old icosahedron made of brown seed pod beads united with wire in a small curio shop in Beijing…and managed to obtain it from the dealers, who were highly suspicious as to why I wanted it and wondered if they should raise their price. The Chinese used to hold pairs of beaded icosahedrons in their hands and rub them together as "worry" beads. I've also collected 100-year-old octahedrons and other structures used as worry beads. Nowadays the Chinese only use giant walnuts as worry beads (not pierced) and one sees dozens of varieties for sale at local markets. About 1¼ inches in diameter. 2) A sea green sphere worked in 4 mm round Czech glass beads and in 10 × 6 mm Czech teardrop beads. I first found this structure in a small shop in Wenzhou, China during a torrential rainstorm that lasted during my entire stay of three days. The one I found was worked in large plastic beads and was meant to be a hanging ornament. When I got it home and analyzed it I realized it was none other than the truncated icosahedron that Laura Shea analyzed for my book, only the Wenzhou version made brilliant use of teardrop beads to from spiky protrusions. Laura would want me to say that the truncated icosahedron is one of the Archimedean solids. This structure also creates a sense of depth and dual-layering that intrigues all eyes. About 1⅜ inches in diameter. 3) An open cube made of 3 mm mottled rust-colored synthetic resin beads from 1960s Japan. This cube is made of dozens of smaller cubes, each sharing several walls with its neighboring cube. Each of the outer walls of this giant cube extends six cubes across. (In my studio we call it the 6 × 6 × 6 cube to distinguish it from the 5 x 5 x 5, the 4 x 4 x 4, etc.) The Chinese made similar structures in this technique, but David Chatt is the great master, and I am indebted to him for the idea of making solid cubes of beads. I first became aware of how versatile this technique is when I had to write the David Chatt chapter of my book. The name I gave to this technique is "cubic right angle weave," and David approved, but he tends to call it just "right angle weave." This technique can also be worked flat, and the Chinese were making highly complex flat pieces in it by the early Ming Dynasty. About 1¼ by 1¼ inches. This is the same technique I used in the "Rust Lotus" necklace (plate 370). **X.** "I make my jewelry flexible," says Flora Book. "This flexibility refers both to the physical properties of the material as well as to the concept and design. This allows the wearer to interact with the piece, thereby making it their own. I like to think of my work as site-specific installations for the human body." She tries to make hard materials, such as silver and glass flexible by weaving them with nylon. Lately she has begun working with softer materials such as felt that are comfortable and can move with the body. Flora Book has refined her technique to work with minimal equipment and space, essential as she spends much of her time traveling. Floral Book, PC, April 2008; Floral Book website. **XI.** Joyce Scott, PC, May 5, 2008. **XII.** Valerie Hector, PC, March 18, 2008. **XIII.** The unique, three-dimensional figurative beadwork of David K. Chatt is inclusive. Chatt says he believes in engaging everybody. "I believe in art for the masses. Art should be intellectual, but not deliberately intimidating," he says. Beads are "alluring. You can pull people in and they can participate in the message… That's when I feel my medium is at its best." (ref: Phinney 2005.) **IXV.** PC, October 17, 2008. **XV.** Yager, exhibition text, 2001; Brown, 1999. Metalsmith 1995, p. 16; PC, October 17, 2008. **XVI.** Kathleen Dustin describes her technique: "First a base bead shape of white polymer clay is formed by hand and then cured to hardness by baking in an electric oven. It is sanded and then decorated/drawn on with permanent inks and pencils. (Each face is drawn by me based on historic paintings.) Then the entire bead is completely covered with various thin slices of translucent polymer clay that includes millefiori designs, inclusions of 22k gold leaf, or inclusions of glitter powders. The bead is cured again and sanded again. Then lines are carved into the bead and backfilled with layers of polymer clay, most often black, and then cured the third and last time. The bead is then sanded four times with increasingly finer grits, and then polished with a buffing wheel as one polishes a stone." Kathleen Dustin, PC, July 9, 2008. **XVII.** Toop works with tiny polymer clay chips which average less than 2 mm long and ⅓ mm thick. After baking them in a convection oven at 270 degrees for 20 to 30 minutes, she uses tweezers to place each chip into a core of soft unbaked polymer clay upon which the design has been etched. Each bead uses 600 to 1000 chips per square inch and it can take 50 hours to complete the chip placing process. (ref: Lurie, 1999).

Bibliography

Abel-Vidor, Suzanne, et al. "Jade." In Pre-Columbian Art of Costa Rica, edited by Elizabeth Kennedy Easby. Detroit and New York: Detroit Institute of the Arts and Harry N. Abrams, 1981.

Adams, Monni. Threads of Life: A Private Collection of Textiles from Indonesia and Sarawak. Katonah, N.Y.: The Katonah Gallery, 1981.

Addison, Julia de Wolf. *Arts and Crafts in the Middle Ages*. Boston: The Page Company, 1908.

Akiyama, T., et al. *Arts of China, Neolithic Culture to the T'ang Dynasty: Recent Discoveries*. Tokyo: Kodansha International, 1968.

Aldred, Cyril. Jewels of the Pharaohs. London: Thames and Hudson, 1971.

Allen, Jamey D. "Amber and Its Substitutes." Parts 1–3. *The Bead Journal* 2–3, nos. 3, 4, 1 (1976): 15–20, 20–31, 11–22.

———. "Cane Manufacture for Mosaic Glass Beads." Parts 1, 2. Ornament 5, 6, nos. 4, 1 (1982): 6–11, 13.

———. "Chevron-Star Rosetta Beads." Parts 1–4. *Ornament* 7, nos. 1–4 (1983–84): 24–29, 19–24, 24–27 24–26.

———. "Correspondence" *Ornament* 6, no. 2 (1982): 60.

———. "The Manufacture of Intricate Glass Canes and a New Perspective on the Relationship Between Chevron-Star Beads and Mosaic-Millefiore Beads." In *Proceedings of the 1982 Glass Trade Bead Conference*, edited by Charles F. Hayes, III. Rochester, N.Y.: Rochester Museum and Science Center, 1983: 173–191.

———. "Tibetan Zi Beads: The Current Fascination with Their Nature and History." *Arts of Asia*, 32:4, pp. 72–91. 2002.

———. *Five Artists- Five Directions In Polymer Clay*. Gaithersburg, MD: Flower Valley Press, 1995.

Al-Jadir, Saad. Arab and Islamic Silver. London: Stacey International, 1981.

Alva, Walter and Christopher B. Donnan. Royal Tombs Of Sipan. Los Angeles: Fowler Museum of Cultural History, 1993.

Andrews, Carol. *Catalogue of Egyptian Antiquities in the British Museum*. Vol. 6, *Jewellery I: From the Earliest Times to the Seventeenth Dynasty*. London: British Museum Publications, 1981.

———. *Egyptian Jewellery, Predynastic to End of Dynastic Period*. London: British Museum Publications, 1976.

Arakawa, Hirokazu. *The Go Collection of Netsuke*. Tokyo: Kodansha International, 1983.

Arkell, A. J. "Cambay and the Bead Trade." *Antiquity* 10 (1936): 292–305.

The Art of William Harper. New York: Kennedy Galleries, 1981.

Bacon, Edward. *Vanished Civilizations*. London: Thames and Hudson, 1963.

Ballet, Dr. "La paure aux epogues paleolithiques anciennes." *Bulletin de la Societie Prehistorique Française* 7, no. 2 (1915).

Barbier, Jean-Paul. *Art du Nagaland*. Geneva: Musée Barbier-Muller, 1982.

Barker, Evelyn, and David Barker. "Ethnic Jewellery of Nepal." Arts of Asia 14 (1984): n.p.

Barker, Richard, and Lawrence Smith. Netsuke, The Miniature Sculpture of Japan. London: British Museum Publications, 1976.

Barraclough, Geoffrey. *The Times Atlas of World History*. Maplewood, N.J.: Hammond, 1980.

Bar-Yosef Mayer, D.E. "The Exploitation of Shells as Beads in the Palaeolithic and Neolithic of the Levant." *Paléorient*, vol. 31/1, p. 176–185. CNRS Éditions 2005.

Bar-Yosef Mayer, Daniella E. and Naomi Porat. "Greenstone beads at the dawn of agriculture." Proceeding of the National Academy of Sciences of the United States of America, June 24, 2008. Vol. 105, no. 25 8548–8551.

Beads: Their Use by Upper Great Lakes Indians. Grand Rapids, Michigan: Grand Rapids Public Museum, 1977.

Bebbington, Julia M. *Quillwork of the Plains*. Calgary, Alberta: Glenbow Museum, 1982.

Beck, Horace C. "Etched Carnelian Beads." *The Antiquaries Journal* 12 (1933): 384–98.

Beckwith, Carol and Angela Fisher. *African Ceremonies*. 1999. Harry N. Abrams, New York.

Beier, Ulli. *Yoruba Beaded Crown: Sacred Regalia of the Olokuku of Okuku*. London: Ethnographia, 1982.

Belenitsky, Aleksandr. *Central Asia*. London: Barrie and Rockliff, The Cresset Press, 1969.

Benesh, Carolyn L. E. "William Harper." *Ornament* 6, no. 2 (1982): 20–22.

Besborodov, M. A., and J. A. Zadneprovsky. "Early Stages of Glassmaking in the USSR." *Slava Antigua* 12 (1965): n.p.

Bibby, Geoffrey. *Looking for Dilmun*. New York: Alfred A. Knopf, 1970.

Birmingham, Nan. "The Peerless Pearly." *Town and Country* 135 (June 1981): n.p.

Black, J. Anderson. *A History of Jewelry*. New York: Park Lane, 1981.

Blair, Dorothy. *A History of Glass in Japan*. Tokyo and Corning, N.Y.: Kodansha International and the Corning Museum of Glass, 1973.

Boric, Dusan. "New Discoveries at the Mesolithic-Early Neolothic site of Vlasac: Preliminary notes." *Mesolithic Miscellany*. Volume 18, No. 1. December 2006.

Bosse-Griffiths, Kate. *Pictures from the Wellcome Collection*. No. 1, *Beadwork*. Swansea, Wales: University College, 1978.

Branigan, K. *The Atlas of Archaeology*. New York: St. Martin's Press, 1982.

Brasser, Ted J. "Pleasing the Spirits: Indian Art Around the Great Lakes." In *Pleasing the Spirits*, edited by Douglas C. Ewing. New York: Ghylen Press, 1982.

Brijbhushan, Jamila. *Masterpieces of Indian Jewellery*. Bombay: D. B. Taraporevala Sons & Co., 1979.

Brown, Glen R. "Jan Yager: Urban Stigmata." *Ornament* 23.2.1999

———. "Suzan Rezak: Part-to-Whole Relationships." *Ornament* 26.3.2003.

Brown, Peter. *The World of Late Antiquity*. London: Thames and Hudson, 1971.

Brugmann, Birte. *Glass Beads from Early Anglo-Saxon Graves*. Oxford: Oxbow Books, 2004.

Budge, E. A. Wallis. *Amulets and Talismans*. New York: Collier, 1970.

Buffum, W. Arnold. *The Tears of the Heliades*. London: Sampson Low, Marston & Company, 1896.

Burt, Ben. *Solomon Islanders: The Kwara'ae*. London: British Museum Publications, 1981.

Callmer, Johan. *Trade Beads and Bead Trade in Scandinavia c. 800–1000 A.D.*, Bonn West Germany, and Lund, Sweden: Rudolf Habelt and C. W. K. Gleerup, 1977.

Cammann, Schuyler V. R. "Ch'ing Dynasty Mandarin Chains." *Ornament* 4, no. 1 (1979): 25–29.

Campbell, Bernard G. *Humankind Emerging*. 2d ed. Boston: Little, Brown and Company, 1979.

Canton-Thompson, Gertrude. "A Commentary of Dr. Laidler's Article on Beads in Africa South of the Zambesi." *Rhodesia Scientific Association Proceedings and Transactions* 34, Pt. 2 (1936): 10–118.

Cartlidge, Barbara. *Twentieth-Century Jewelry*. New York: Harry N. Abrams, 1985.

Casal, Gabriel, and Regalado Trota José, Jr. *The People and Arts of the Philippines*. Los Angeles: Museum of Cultural History, University of California, 1981.

Casanowicz, Immanuel M. *The Collection of Rosaries in the United States National Museum*. Washington, D.C.: Government Printing Office, 1909.

Chandra, Rai Govind. *Indo-Greek Jewellery*. New Delhi: Abhinav Publications, 1979.

———. *Studies in the Development of Ornaments and Jewellery in Proto-Historic India*. Varranasi, India: The Chowkhamba Sanskrit Series Office, 1964.

Chard, Chester. *Northeast Asia in Prehistory*. Madison: University of Wisconsin Press, 1974.

Charles-Picard, Gilbert. Larousse *Encyclopedia of Archaeology*. London: Hamlyn, 1974.

Chen, C. L. *Material Culture of the Formosan Aborigines*. Taipei, Taiwan: Taiwan Museum, 1968.

Cheng Te-k'un. Archaeology in China. Vol. 1, Prehistoric China. London: W. Heffer & Sons, 1959.

Chetro Ketl. Chaco Canyon, N.M.: Chaco Culture National Historic Park, 1984.

China: Guide to the Collection of The University Museum. Philadelphia: University of Pennsylvania Press, 1965.

Chongkol, Chira. "Jewellery and Other Decorative Arts in Thailand." *Arts of Asia*, November–December, 1982.

Cocks, Anna Somers. *An Introduction to Courtly Jewellery*. London: Victoria and Albert Museum and Compton Press Ltd., 1980.

Cole, Herbert M. "Artistic and Communicative Values of Beads in Kenya and Ghana." *The Bead Journal* 1, no. 3 (1975): 29–37.

Conn, Richard. *Circles of the World*. Denver: Denver Art Museum, 1982.

———. *Native American Art in the Denver Art Museum*. Denver: Denver Art Museum, 1982.

Conner, Michael W, and Diane Pelrine. *The Geometric Vision: Arts of the Zulu*. West Lafayette, Indiana: Purdue University Galleries and Indiana University Press, 1983.

Coomaraswamy, Ananda K. *History of Indian and Indonesian Art*. Reprint. New York: Dover Publications, 1965.

Critchlow, Keith. Islamic Patterns: An Analytical and Cosmological Approach. London: Thames and Hudson, 1976.

Dale, Gloria. "Third Millennium Beads from Euphrates Region." *Ornament* 5, no. 3 (1982): 30–32.

Dance, Peter S. "The Molluscan Fauna." In *Excavation of the Abri Pataud les Eyzies*, edited by H. L. Movius. Cambridge, Mass.: Harvard University Press, 1975.

Davis, Mary L., and Greta Pack. *Mexican Jewelry*. Austin: University of Texas Press, 1963.

Delaroziere, M. F. "Mauritanian Beads." *Ornament* 8, no. 3 (1985): 24–27.

de Negri, Eve. "...The King's Beads." *Nigeria Magazine*, no. 82 (1964): 210–16.

d'Errico, Francesco. "ESF Programme OMLL helps uncover ancient human behavior." European Science Foundation. June 20, 2007.

Digby, Adrian. Maya Jades. London: British Museum Publications, 1972.

Di Stasi, Lawrence. *Mal Occhio: The Underside of Vision*. San Francisco: North Point Press, 1981.

Dockstader, Frederick J. *Indian Art in America*. Greenwich, Conn.: New York Graphic Society, 1966.

Dohrenwend, Doris. *Chinese Jades in the Royal Ontario Museum*. Toronto: The Royal Ontario Museum, 1971.

———. "Glass in China." *Oriental Art* 26, no. 4 (1980–81): 426–46.

Donnen, Dr. Christopher. "Moche Beads from Ancient Peru." The International Bead and Beadwork Conference Proceedings. Kadir Has University, Istanbul. 2007.

Dortch, Charles. "Australia's Oldest Known Ornaments." *Antiquity* 53 (1979): n.p.

Driscoll, Bernadette. "Sapangat: Inuit Beadwork in the Canadian Arctic." *Expedition* 26, no. 2 (1984): 40–46.

Dubin, Lois Sherr. *North American Indian Jewelry and Adornment*. New York: Harry N. Abrams, 1999.

———. "The Good, The Bad and the Evil Eye Bead: A New Look at Eye Beads Throughout History." The International Bead and Beadwork Conference Proceedings. Kadir Has University, Istanbul. 2007.

Dunsmore, Susi. "Beads." Occasional paper, no. 2. Kuching: Sarawak Museum, 1978.

Easby, Elizabeth Kennedy. *Pre-Columbian Jade from Costa Rica*. New York: Andre Emmerich Gallery, 1968.

Ebbinghouse, David. Letter to author, July 1986.

Ebbinghouse, David, and Michael Winsten. " Tibetan dZi Beads." Parts 1, 2. *Ornament* 5, nos. 3, 4 (1982): 19–25, 36–39.

———. Review of *Himalayan Kingdoms: Gods, Peoples, and Art* by Stephanie and G. H. Ghislaine zu Windisch-Graetz. *The Journal of the Tibet Society* 4 (1984): 93–98.

Edmunds, Will H. *Pointers and Clues to the Subjects of Chinese and Japanese Art*. London: Sampson Low, Marston & Co., 1974.

Eisen, Gustavus A." The Characteristics of Eye Beads from the Earliest Times to the Present." *American Journal of Archaeology*, 2d series, no. 20 (1916): n.p.

———. Glass, 2 vols. New York: William Edwin Rudge, 1927.

Emmerich, Andre. *Art Before Columbus*. New York: Simon and Schuster, 1963.

———. *Sweat of the Sun and Tears of the Moon*. Seattle: University of Washington Press, 1965.

Erikson, Joan Mowat. *The Universal Bead*. New York: W. W. Norton, 1969.

Evans, Joan. A History of Jewelry, 1100–1870. Boston: Boston Book and Art, 1970.

Ewing, Douglas C. Pleasing the Spirits. New York: Ghylen Press, 1982.

Eyo, Ekpo, and Frank Willett. *Treasures of Ancient Nigeria*. New York: Alfred A. Knopf, 1980.

Fagan, Brian M. *People of the Earth*. Boston: Little, Brown and Company, 1986.

Fagg, William. *Yoruba Beadwork: Art of Nigeria*. New York: Rizzoli and Pace Editions, 1980.

———. *Yoruba: Sculpture of West Africa*. New York: Alfred A. Knopf, 1982.

Fedders, Andrew, and Cynthia Salvadori. *Turkana Pastoral Craftsmen*. Nairobi, Kenya: Transafrica Publishing, 1977.

Feder, Norman. American Indian Art. New York: Harry N. Abrams, 1969.

Fenstermaker, G. B. Early Susquehanna Iroquois Colored Trade Chart, 1550. Lancaster, Pa.: G. B. Fenstermaker, 1974.

———. *Susquehanna Iroquois Colored Bead Chart 1575–1763*. Lancaster, Pa.: G. B. Fenstermaker, 1974.

Feulner, Erika. "Glass Beadmaking in Franconia." The Bead Society Newsletter (Washington, D.C.) 3, no. 2 (1986): n.p.

Finegan, Cathy. 1000 Glass Beads. New York: Lark Books, 2005.

Fisher, Angela. Africa Adorned. New York: Harry N. Abrams, 1984.

Fitzgibbon, Kate, and Andy Hale. "Jewelry of the Turkic Tribes of Afghanistan, Turkoman, Uzbek, and Kirgiz." In *Bead News: Selections from Ten Years of the Bead Society Newsletter*, edited by Dorthea Casady. Washington, D.C.: Bead News, 1985: 78.

Follett, Thelma. "Amber in Goldworking." *Archaeology* 38, no. 2 (1985): 64–65.

Forbes, R. J. Studies in Ancient Technology 5. Leiden: E. J. Brill, 1966.

Francis, Peter, Jr. *Asia's Maritime Bead Trade. 300 B.C. to the Present*. Honolulu: University of Hawaii Press, 2002.

———. "Bead Report XVI: The Asian Bead Study Tour II, Thailand: Revolution and Ruin, Tradition and Change." *Ornament* 9, no. 2 (1985): 42–48.

———. *Beads of the World*. Atglen, Pa: Schiffer Publishing, Ltd., 1994.

———. "Bead Report XIII: Beads and the Discovery of America, Part III, The Later Bead Trade:" *Ornament* 8, no. 2 (1985): 47–50.

———. "Bead Report VI: The Earliest Beads in India." Parts 1, 2. *Ornament* 5, 6, Nos. 4, 1 (1982): 18–9,14–5.

———. "Bead Report VIII: Minor Indian Beadmakers." *Ornament* 6, no. 3 (1983): 18–21.

———. "Bead Report VII: When India Was Beadmaker to the World." *Ornament* 6, no. 2 (1982): 33–34.

———. *Beads and the Discovery of the New World*. Occasional paper, no. 3. Lake Placid, N.Y.: The Center for Bead Research, 1986.

———. *Chinese Glass Beads: A Review of the Evidence*. Occasional paper, no. 2. Lake Placid, N.Y.: The Center for Bead Research, 1986.

———. *The Czech Bead Story*. The World of Beads Monograph Series, no. 2. Lake Placid, N.Y.: Lapis Route Books, 1979.

———. *The Glass Beads of India*. The World of Beads Monograph Series, no. 7. Lake Placid, N.Y.: Lapis Route Books, 1982.

———. *Indian Agate Beads*. The World of Beads Monograph Series, no. 6. Lake Placid, N.Y.: Lapis Route Books, 1982.

———. "Some Thoughts on Glass Beadmaking." In *Proceedings of the 1982 Glass Trade Bead Conference*, edited by Charles F. Hayes, III. Rochester: Rochester Museum and Science Center, 1983: 193–202.

———. *The Story of Venetian Beads*. The World of Beads Monograph Series, no. 1. Lake Placid, N.Y.: Lapis Route Books, 1979.

———. *A Survey of Beads in Korea*. Occasional paper, no. 1. Lake Placid, N.Y.: Center for Bead Research, 1985.

Fraser-Lu, Sylvia. "The Sarawak Museum." *Arts of Asia*, September–October 1982: n.p.

Frazier, Si and Ann Frazier and Glenn Lehrer. "A History of Gem Beadmaking in Idar-Oberstein." In *Beads* 10–11 (1998–99).

Frobenius, L. The Voice of Africa. London: Hutchinson, 1913.

Furst, Peter T., and Jill Furst. *North American Indian Art*. New York: Rizzoli, 1982.

Gabriel, Hannelore. "Himalayan Portraits." *Ornament* 6, no. 3 (1983): 58–59.

———. "The Tilari, Nepalese Married Woman's Necklace." *Ornament* 5, no. 4 (1982): 34.

Gallo, Miguel. *The Gold of Peru*. English edition. Recklinghausen, Germany: Aurel Bongers, 1959.

Gil, Carol A. Bowdoin. "Native American Seed Beading Techniques: Part 1, Woven Items." *The Bead Journal* 3, no. 2 (1977): 42–51.

Gillette, Charles E. *Wampum Belts and Beads*. Albany: New York State Museum, 1970.

Gilman, Carolyn. *Where Two Worlds Meet: The Great Lakes Fur Trade*. St. Paul: Minnesota Historical Society, 1982.

Glumac, Petar D. "Earliest Known Copper Ornaments from Prehistoric Europe." *Ornament* 8, no. 3 (1985) 15–17.

Goldstein, Sidney M. *Pre-Roman and Early Roman Glass in the Corning Museum of Glass*. Corning, N.Y.: The Corning Museum of Glass, 1979.

Good, Mary Elizabeth. *Guebert Site: An 18th-Century Historic Kaskaskia Indian Village in Randolph County, Illinois*. Memoir no. 2. Wood River, Ill.: Central States Archaeological Societies, 1972.

Gordon, Eleanor, and Jean Nerenberg. "Early Plastic Jewelry: From Imitation to Innovation." *Ornament* 4, no. 3 (1980): 2–6.

Gorelick, Leonard, and A. John Gwinnett. "The Origin and Development of the Ancient Near Eastern Cylinder Seal." *Expedition* 23, no. 4 (1981): 17–30.

Graham-Campbell, James, and Dafydd Kidd. *The Vikings*. London and New York: The British Museum and the Metropolitan Museum of Art, 1980.

Gray, Richard, and David Birmingham, eds. *Pre-Colonial African Trade: Essays on Trade in Central and Eastern Africa Before 1900*. Oxford: Oxford University Press, 1970.

Gregorietti, Guido. *Jewelry Through the Ages*. New York: American Heritage, 1969.

Guido, Margaret. The Glass Beads of the Prehistoric and Roman Periods in Britain and Ireland. Reports of the Research Committee of the Society of Antiquaries of London, no. 35. London: Society of Antiquaries, 1978.

Gumpert, Anita. "Special Beads from Mauritania." The Bead Society Newsletter (Washington, D.C.) 1, no. 4 (1984): 1–2.

———. The Timeless Cowrie. Its Significance the World Over. Washington, DC: Bead Society of Greater Washington, 2007.

Gwinnett, A. John, and Leonard Gorelick. "Beadmaking in Iran in the Early Bronze Age." *Expedition* 24, no. 1 (1981): 10–23.

Haevernick, Thea Elisabeth. Beitrage *zur Glasforschung*. Mainz: Verlag Philipp von Zabern, 1981.

Hall, Richard. *The Viking Dig: The Excavations at York*. London: The Bodley Head, 1984.

Han, Byong-Sam. "Ancient Silla Tumuli Objects." *Arts of Asia* 11, no. 4 (1981): 113–19.

Handler, Jerome S., Frederick W. Lange, and Charles E. Orser. "Carnelian Beads in Necklaces from a Slave Cemetery in Barbados, West Indies." *Ornament* 4, no. 2 (1979): 15–18.

Harden, Donald M. *Catalogue of Greek and Roman Glass in the British Museum*. London: British Museum Publications, 1981.

Harding, J. R. "Nineteenth-Century Trade Beads in Tanganyika." Man 177 (1962): 104–6.

Harris, E. J. *Late Beads in the African Trade*. Lancaster, Pa.: G. B. Fenstermaker, 1984.

Harris, Elizabeth. "More Chinese Glass Beads." *Los Angeles Bead Society Newsletter* 10, no. 5 (1985): 7.

———. The Russian Bead. Northwest *Colored Bead Chart No. 3*. Lancaster, Pa.: G. B. Fenstermaker 1985.

Hasson, Rachel. "Islamic Glass from Excavations in Jerusalem." Journal of Glass Studies 25 (1983): 109–13.

Hawley, Ruth. Omani Silver. London and New York: Longman, 1978.

Hayes, Charles F., ed. *Proceedings of the 1982 Glass Trade Bead Conference*. Rochester, N.Y.: Rochester Museum and Science Center, 1983.

Hector, Valerie. *The Art of Beadwork*. New York: Watson-Guptill Publications, 2005.

Heininger, Ernst, and Jean Heininger. *The Great Book of Jewels*. Boston: New York Graphic Society, 1974.

Herrmann, G. "Lapis Lazuli: The Early Phases of Its Trade." Iraq 30 (1968): 21–67.

Higgins, R. A. Greek and Roman Jewellery. Berkeley and Los Angeles: University of California Press, 1980.

Hiler, Hilaire. From Nudity to Raiment. Paris and New York: Librairie de France and Wehye, 1929.

Hirst, K. Kris. "Enkapune Ya Muto (Kenya)." About.com: Archaeology. 2008.

Hodge, Alison. *Nigeria's Traditional Crafts*. Ethnographic Arts and Culture series, no. 3. London: Ethnographica, 1982.

Hodson, T. C. "Diaries of Two Tours in the Unadministered Area East of the Naga Hills." *Mem. Asiatic Society* (Bengal) 11, no. 1. (n.d.: after 1923).

Holstein, Philip M., and Donnelley Erdman. *Enduring Visions: 1,000 Years of Southwestern Indian Art*. Aspen, Co., and New York: Aspen Center for the Visual Arts and the Publishing Center for Cultural Resources, 1979.

Howe, Michael. Amulets. New York: St. Martin's Press, 1975.

Hughes, Graham. The Art of Jewelry. New York: Viking Press, 1972.

Hunger, Rosa. The Magic of Amber. Radnor, Pa.: Chilton Book Co., 1979.

Hutton, J. H. The Angami Nagas. London: (publisher unknown), 1921.

Jacka, Jerry D., and Nancy S. Hammack. *Indian Jewelry of the Prehistoric Southwest*. Tucson: University of Arizona Press, 1975.

Jenkins, Marilyn, and Manuel Keene. *Islamic Jewelry in The Metropolitan Museum of Art*. New York: The Metropolitan Museum of Art, 1982.

Jenkins, Michael. "Glass Trade Beads in Alaska." *The Bead Journal* 2, no. 1 (1975): 23–26.

Jenyns, Soames. Japanese Porcelain. London: Faber and Faber, 1978.

Jernigan, E. Wesley. *Jewelry of the Prehistoric Southwest*. Santa Fe and Albuquerque, N.M.: School of American Research and University of New Mexico Press, 1978.

Jettmar, K. Art of the Steppes. New York: Crown Publishers, 1964.

Jewellery Through 7000 Years. London: British Museum Publications, 1976.

Johnson, Stephen C. "Living Beads in Guatemala." *The Bead Journal* 2, no. 1 (1975): 18–22.

Kalous, M. "A Propos: Powder-glass Bodom Beads?" *African Arts* 12, no. 3 (1979): n.p.

Kanungo, Dr. Alok Kumar. "Impact of Social and Political Change on the use of Beads Among the Konyaks." In International Bead and Beadwork Conference. Edited by Jamey Allen and Valerie Hector. Istanbul: Rezan Has Museum, 2007.

Karklins, Karlis. "Dutch Trade Beads in North America." In *Proceedings of the 1982 Glass Trade Bead Conference*, edited by Charles F. Hayes, III. Rochester, N.Y.: Rochester Museum and Science Center, 1983: 59–74.

———. "Early Amsterdam Trade Beads." *Ornament* 9, no. 2 (1985): 36–41.

———. *Glass Beads*. History and Archaeology series, no. 59. Ottawa, Canada: National Historic Parks and Sites Branch, 1982.

Keene, Manuel. "The Lapidary Arts in Islam."' *Expedition* 24, no. 1 (1981): 24–39.

Kennedy, Sylvia S. J. "Nyhus Design Glasswear." *Ornament* 9, no. 2 (1985): 12–17.

———. "Some Aspects of Children's Amulets." *Ornament* 9, no. 4 (1986): 50–53.

Kennedy, Sylvia S. J., and Robert K. Liu. "Contemporary Cane Beadmaking." *Ornament* 8, no. 3 (1985): 18–23.

Kenoyer, Jonathan Mark. "The Indus Bead Industry: Contributions to Bead Technology." *Ornament* 10, no. 1 (1986): 18–23.

———. "Stone Beads in Ancient South Asia. 7000–600 BC: A comparative approach to technology, style and ideology." The International Bead and Beadwork Conference Proceedings. Kadir Has University, Istanbul. 2007.

Kessler, Earl, and Shari Kessler. "Beads of the Tairona." *The Bead Journal* 3, no. 3 (1978): 2–5.

———. "Ecuadorian Beads: Ancient to Modern." Ornament 20, no. 2 (1986): 48–52.

Kidd, Kenneth E. *Glass Bead-Making from the Middle Ages to the Early 19th Century*. History and Archaeology series, no. 30. Ottawa, Canada: National Historic Parks and Sites Branch, 1979.

———. "Problems in Glass Trade Bead Research." In *Proceedings of the 1982 Glass Trade Bead Conference*, edited by Charles F. Hayes, III. Rochester, N.Y.: Rochester Museum and Science Center, 1982.

King, C. W. The Natural History of Precious Stones and of the Precious Metals. London: Bell and Daldy, 1870.

Klima, Bohuslav. "The First Ground-Plan of an Upper Paleolithic Loess Settlement in Middle Europe and Its Meaning." In *Courses Toward Urban Life*. Wenner-Gren, N.Y.: Braidwood and Wiley, 1962.

Klimburg-Salter, Deborah. *The Silk Road and the Diamond Path*. Los Angeles: U.C.L.A. Art Council, 1982.

Knight, Natalie, and Suzanne Priebatsch. *Ndebele Images*. Johannesburg: Productions, Ltd., 1983.

Kolbas, Judith G. "A Color Chronology of Islamic Glass." *Journal of Glass Studies* 25 (1983): 95–100.

Kramrisch, Stella. The Art of Nepal. New York: The Asia Society, 1964.

Kuntzsch, Ingrid. *A History of Jewels and Jewelery*. New York: St. Martin's Press, 1981.

Kuhn, Steven L., Mary C. Stiner, David S. Reese and Erksin Gulec. "Ornaments of the earliest Upper Paleolithic: New insights from the Levant." Proceedings of the *Natinal Academy of Sciences*. 2001. June 19; 98 (13): 7641–7646.

Kunz, G. F. The Curious Lore of Precious Stones. New York: Halcyon House, 1913.

Kunz, George Frederick, and Charles Hugh Stevenson. *The Book of the Pearl. The History, Art, Science, and Industry of the Queen of Gems*. New York: The Century Company, 1908.

Laidler, P. W "Beads in Africa South of the Zambesi." *Rhodesia Scientific Association Proceedings and Transactions* 34, no. 1 (1934).

Lamb, Alastair. "Krobo Powder-Glass Beads." *African Arts* 9, no. 3 (1976): 23–27.

———. "A Note on Glass Beads from the Malay Peninsula." *Journal of Glass Studies* 8 (1966): 80–94.

———. "Some Observations on Stone and Glass Beads in Early Southeast Asia." *Journal of Malaysian Branch of the Royal Asiatic Society* 38, no. 2 (1965): 85–124.

———. "Some 17th-Century Glass Beads from Ghana, West Africa." *The Bead Journal* 3, nos. 3, 4 (1978): 23–27.

Lance, Ney Rene. "Ornamentation in Afghanistan." In Bead News: Selection from Ten Years of the Bead Society Newsletter, edited by Dorthea Casady. Los Angeles: The Bead Society, 1982.

Landman, Neil H. Paula M. Mikkelsen, Rudiger Bieler, and Bennet Bronson. Pearls: A Natural History. New York: Harry N. Abrams, Inc. in association with the American Museum of Natural History and The Field Museum, 2001.

Lankton, Dr. James. A Bead TimeLine, Volume 1: Prehistory to 1200 CE. Washington DC: The Bead Society of Greater Washington, 2003.

———. "What Does a Bead Mean? An Archaeologist's perspective." The International Bead and Beadwork Conference Proceedings. Kadir Has University, Istanbul. 2007.

Latif, Momin. Mughul Jewels. Brussels: Societé Generale de Banque, 1982.

Laufer, Berthold. *Notes on Turquoise in the East*. Field Museum of Natural History Anthropological series. Vol. 8, no. 1 (1913).

Lee, Sherman E. *The Genius of Japanese Design*. Tokyo: Kodansha International, 1981.

Legarda, Angelita G. "Antique Beads of the Philippine Islands." *Arts of Asia* 7, no. 5 (1977): 61–70.

———. "Pre-Hispanic Gold in the Philippines." *Arts of Asia* 7, no. 5 (1978): n.p.

Lenssen, Barbara G., Andrew Whiteford, and Susan Brown McGreevey. *Lullabies from the Earth: Cradles of Native North America*. Santa Fe, N.M.: Wheelwright Museum of the American Indian, 1980.

Lesley, Parker. *Renaissance Jewels and Jeweled Objects*. Baltimore: Baltimore Museum of Art, 1968.

Leslie, Mitchell. "Suddenly Smarter." *Stanford Magazine*. July/August, 2002.

Levin, M. G., and L. P. Potapov. *The Peoples of Siberia*. Chicago: University of Chicago Press, 1964.

Levinsohn, Rhoda. "Rural Kwazulu Beadwork." *Ornament* 4, no. 4 (1980): 38–42.

Lewis, Paul, and Elaine Lewis. *Peoples of the Golden Triangle*. London: Thames and Hudson, 1984.

Liu, Robert K. "American Glass Beadmakers. *Ornament* 14 (1) 1990: 16-17.

———. "African-Made Glass Ornaments: Survey and Experimental Results." *Ornament* 8, no. 2 (1984): 52–53.

———. "African Mold-Made Glass Beads." *The Bead Journal* 1, no. 2 (1974): 8–14.

———. "Amira Francoise: Living with Beads in the Sudan." *Ornament* 5, no. 4 (1982): 24–27.

———. "Ancient Chinese Glass Beads." *The Bead Journal* 2, no. 2 (1975): 9–19.

———. "Asian Glass Ornaments." Parts 1, 2. *Ornament* 8, 9, nos. 4, 1 (1985): 28–31.

———. "The Bead in African Assembled Jewelry: Its Multiple Manifestations." In *Beauty by Design: The Aesthetics of African Adornment*, edited by Marie-Therese Brincard. New York: The African-American Institute, 1984.

———. "Chinese Glass Beads and Ornaments." *The Bead Journal* 1, no. 3 (1975): 13–28.

———. Collectible Beads, A Universal Aesthetic. Vista, CA: *Ornament*, Inc., 1995.

———. "Dan Frost Bead Collection." Ornament 6, no. 3 (1983): 25–30.

———. "Formosan Ornaments and Clothing." *Ornament* 6, no. 4 (1983): 21–27.

———. "Glass Ojime." Ornament 6, no. 2 (1982): 24–28.

———. "Identification: Afghani Stone Beads." *Ornament* 7, no. 2 (1983): 34–35.

———. "Identification: Carnelian Beads and Their Simulations." *Ornament* 8, no. 1 (1984): 14–18.

———. "Identification: Smallest and Largest Beads." *Ornament* 9, no. 1 (1985): 69.

———. "Identification: Tzi Beads:" *Ornament* 4, no. 4 (1980): 56–59.

———. "Iranian Faience: Beads/Pendants of Late Periods." *Ornament* 6, no. 2 (1982): 6–7.

———. "Iridescence and Related Phenomena." *Ornament* 9, no. 3 (1986): 31–36.

Liu, Robert K.; and Elizabeth Harris. *Nueva Cádiz and Associated Beads*. Lancaster, Pa.: G. B. Fenstermaker, 1982.
Loring, John. *Tiffany Pearls*. New York: 2006.
Lothrop, Samuel K. *Cocle: An Archaeological Study of Central Panama*. Peabody Museum Memoirs, Vol. 7, Part 1. Cambridge, Mass.: Harvard University Press, 1937.
Lucas, A. *Ancient Egyptian Materials and Industries*. 4th ed. Revised and enlarged by J. R. Harris. London: Edward Arnold, 1962.
Lundstrom, Agneta. "Beadmaking in Scandinavia in the Early Middle Ages." *Antikvarisk Arkiv* (Sweden) 61 (1976): n.p.
Lurie, Mark. "A Blend of Influences-CD Beads." *Lapidary Journal*, October, 1999.
Lyford, Carrie A. *Quill and Beadwork of the Western Sioux*. Boulder, Co.: Johnson Publishing Company, 1982.
Mallowan, M. E. L. "Excavations at Brak and Chagar Bazar." *Iraq* 9 (1947): n.p.
Mallowan, M. E. L., and J. Cruikshank Rose. "Excavations at Tell Arpachiyah, 1933." Iraq 2, Part 1 (1935): 1–178.
Maloney, Clarence, ed. The Evil Eye. New York: Columbia University Press, 1976.
Marshack, Alexander. *Ice Age Art*. New York: American Museum of Natural History, 1978.
Marshall, F. H. *Catalogue of the Jewellery, Greek, Etruscan, and Roman, in the Department of Antiquities, British Museum*. Reprint from 1911 edition. London: The Trustees of the British Museum, 1969.
Mason, Ronald J. Rock Island: Historical Indian Archaeology in the Northern Lake Michigan Basin. Kent, Ohio: Kent State University Press, 1985.
Mason, V. M., and V. I. Sarianidi. *Central Asia: Turkmenia Before the Achaemenids*. London: Thames and Hudson, 1972.
Matheson, Sylvia A. *Persia: An Archaeological Guide*. London: Faber and Faber, 1972.
Mathews, Zena Pearlstone. *Color and Shape in American Indian Art*. New York: The Metropolitan Museum of Art, 1983.
Maxwell, John. "The Beaded Textiles of Maloh." In *Indonesian Textiles*. Washington, D.C.: Textile Museum, 1979.
Maxwell-Hyslop, K. R. *Western Asiatic Jewellery, c. 3000–612 B.C.* London: Methuen & Company, 1971.
McClelland, E. M. The Cult of Ifa Among the Yoruba: Folk Practice and the Art. London: Ethnographica, 1982.
McIntosh, Roderick, and Susan Mc Intosh. "The Inland Niger Delta Before the Empire of Mali: Evidence from Jenne-Jero." *Journal of African History* 22 (1981): 1–22.
McLeod, M. D. The Asante. London: British Museum Publications, 1981.
McNeill, William. *The Rise of the West*. Chicago: University of Chicago Press, 1963.
Mellaart, James. "Egyptian and Near Eastern Chronology: A Dilemma?" *Antiquity* 53 (1979): n.p.
Metalsmith. 1995 Exhibition in Print.
Mikoshiba, Misao, and Raymond Bushell. "The Soken Kisho and Ojime." *Arts of Asia*, July–August 1979: 59–69.
Mille, Polly. "A Historical Explanation of Alaskan Trade Beads." *The Bead Journal* 2, no. 2 (1975): 20–24.
Mills, J. P. The Lhota Nagas. London: Macmillan, 1922.
———. The Ao Nagas. Oxford: Oxford University Press, 1926.
Miyamoto, Nobuto. "Glass Beads of the Formosan Aborigines." Minzoku-Gaku Kenkyu, Japan Journal of Ethnography 21, no. 4 (1957): 89–91.
Moore, Andrew M. T. "A Pre-Neolithic Farmers' Village on the Euphrates." In *Prehistoric Times*, edited by Brian M. Fagan. San Francisco: Freeman and Company, 1979.
Moore, Ellen K. Navajo. *Beadwork: Architectures of Light*. Tucson: University of Arizona Press, 2003.
Moss, Kathleen and Alice Scherer. *The New Beadwork*. New York: Harry N. Abrams, 1992.
Movius, Hallam L., Jr. "The Châtelperronian in French Archaeology: The evidence of Arcy-sur-Cure." *Antiquity* 43 (1969): n.p.
Muller, Priscilla E. *Jewels in Spain: 1500–1800*. New York: The Hispanic Society of America, 1972.
Munan, Heidi. *Beads of Borneo*. Singapore: Editions Didier Millet, 2005.
Muzzy, Shelley. "Glass Beadmaking. The Ring of Fire." *Ornament* 16 (4) 1993, 56–59.
Nadelhoffer, Hans. *Cartier, Jewelers Extraordinary*. New York: Harry N. Abrams, 1984.
National Geographic Society. *Early Civilizations in the Middle East* 154, no. 3 supplement (1978): 326B.
———. *Ethnolinguistic Map of the Peoples of Africa* 140, no. 6 supplement (1971): 737.
———. The Historic Mediterranean 162, no. 6 supplement (1982): 694B.
National Museums of Korea. *Special Exhibition of Relics from Tomb No. 98*. Kyongju, Korea: National Museums of Korea, 1975.
Nelson Gallery-Atkins Museum. *Chinese Exhibition*. Kansas City, Mo.: The Exhibition of Archaeological Finds of the Peoples Republic of China, 1975.
Nelson Harold B. "Interview of William Harper." Smithsonian Archives of American Art, January 12–13, 2004.
Neuberg, F. Glass in Antiquity. London: Art Trade Press, 1949.
Newark Museum. *Tibetan Collection*. 3 vols. Newark, N.J.: Newark Museum, 1983.
Newman, Harold. *An Illustrated Dictionary of Jewelry*. London: Thames and Hudson, 1981.
Newton, Douglas. Massim. New York: Museum of Primitive Art, 1975.
Nicholls, Caroline Jean. "Australian Aboriginal Beads from Around 40,000 B.C. to Pre-European Settlement." The International Bead and Beadwork Conference Proceedings. Kadir Has University, Istanbul. November 22–25, 2007.
Northern, Rebecca. "The Birdman Bead." *Americas* 20, no. 3. Washington, D.C.: Organization of American States, 1968: 14–20.
Northern, Tamara. *The Sign of the Beaded Leopard: Beaded Art of the Cameroon*. Storrs, Conn.: The William Benton Museum of Art, University of Connecticut, 1975.
———. *The Art of Cameroon*. Washington, D.C.: Smithsonian Institution, 1984.
Noveck, Madeline. *The Mark of Ancient Man*. New York: The Brooklyn Museum, 1976.
Ogden, Jack. Jewellery of the Ancient World. London: Trefoil Books, 1982.
Okada, Barbara. *Japanese Netsuke and Ojime*. Newark, N.J.: The Newark Museum Association, 1976.
Okamoto, T. Japanese Arts to Jomon Age. Tokyo: Shibundo, 1983.
Orchard, William C. *Beads and Beadwork of the American Indians*. New York: Museum of the American Indian, Heyes Foundation, 1975.
Oved, Sah. The Book of Necklaces. London: Arthur Barker, 1953.
Pekarik, Andrew J. *Japanese Lacquer 1600–1900*. New York: Metropolitan Museum of Art, 1980.
Pemberton, John III. African Beaded Art, Power and Adornment. Northampton, Mass.: Smith College Museum of Art, 2008.
Penney, David W. *Art of the American Indian Frontier*. Seattle and London: University of Washington Press, 1992.
Pfeiffer, John E. The Creative Explosion. New York: Harper and Row, 1982.
———. The Emergence of Man, 2d ed. New York: Harper and Row, 1972.
Phinney, Susan. "Beadnik." Seattle Post Intelligencer, September 29, 2005.
Pierides, Angeliki. *Jewellery in the Cyprus Museum*. Department of Antiquities. Nicosia: 1971.
Pliny. *Natural History*. 10 vols. Translated and edited by D. E. Eichholz. Loeb Classical Library. Cambridge, Ma.: Harvard University Press, 1962.
Pogue, Joseph E. *Turquoise*. Memoirs of the National Academy of Sciences 12, Part. 2. Reprint from 1915 edition. Glorieta, N.M.: The Rio Grande Press, 1975.
Poinar, George O., Jr. "Sealed in Amber." *Natural History* 92, no. 6. New York: American Museum of Natural History, 1982.
Possehl, Gregory L. "Cambay Beadmaking Expedition 23, no. 4 (1981): 39–47.
Priebatsch, Suzanne, and Nataline White. "Traditional Ndebele Beadwork." *African Arts* 11, no. 2 (1978).
Proskouriakoff, Tatiana. *Jades from the Cenote of Sacrifice, Chichen Itza, Yucatan*. Peabody Museum Memoirs. Vol. 10, no. 1. Cambridge, Mass.: Harvard University Press, 1974.
Randall, Richard H., Jr. *Objects of Adornment*. Baltimore: Walters Art Gallery, 1984.
Rawson, Philip. *The Art of Southeast Asia*. London: Thames and Hudson, 1967.
Reade, Julian. "Early Etched Beads and the Indus-Mesopotamia Trade." Occasional paper, no. 2. London: British Museum, 1979.
Reynolds, Valrae. *Tibet: A Lost World*. New York: The American Federation of the Arts, 1978.
Rice, Patty C. *Amber, The Golden Gem of the Ages*. New York: Van Nostrand Reinhold, 1980.
Richardson, Susan. "Pushing the Envelope." The Beadworkers Guild, September 1999.
Robicsek, Francis. A *Study in Maya Art and History: The Mat Symbol*. New York: Museum of the American Indian, Heye Foundation, 1975.
Rodgers, Susan. *Power and Gold: Jewelry from Indonesia, Malaysia, and the Philippines*. Geneva: Barbier-Muller Museum, 1985.
Rosnek, Carl, and Joseph Stacey. *Sky-stone and Silver*. Englewood Cliffs, N.J.: Prentice-Hall, 1976.
Ross, Kay. "Shell Ornaments of Malaita." Expedition 23, no. 2 (1981).
Rowe, Donald. *The Art of Jewelry 1450–1650*. Chicago: The Martin D'Arcy Gallery of Art, Loyola University, 1975.
Sali, S.A."The Upper Paleolothic Culture at Patne, District Jalgaon, Maharashtra." Recent Advances in Indo-Pacific Prehistory: Proceedings of the International Symposium Poona, 1978. Editors: V. N. Misra, Peter Bellwood, Indo-Pacific Prehistory Association BEILL, 1985.
San Antonio Police Department, Youth Crime Service Unit. GANG AWARENESS. A Handbook for Teachers, Parents and Concerned Citizens. San Antonio. Nd.
Sankalia, H. D. *The Prehistory and Protohistory of India and Pakistan*. Poona, India: Deccan College, 1974.
Schafer, Edward H. *The Golden Peaches of Samarkand, A Study of T'ang Exotics*. Berkeley and Los Angeles: University of California Press, 1963.
Sciama, Lidia D. & Joanne B. Eicher. *Beads and Bead Makers*. Gender, Material Culture and Meaning. Oxford: Berg, 2001 ed.

Schienerl, Peter W. "The Much-Enduring Eye." *Ornament* 7, no. 4 (1984): 27–28.
Schiro, Anne-Marie. "The Return of Pearls: A Guide for Buyers." *The New York Times*. 5 December 1981.
Schoeman, H. "A Preliminary Report on Traditional Beadwork in the Mkhwamazi Area of the Mtunzini District, Zululand." African *Studies* 27, no. 2 (1968).
Schumann, Walter. *Gemstones of the World*. New York and London: Sterling Publishing and NAG Press, 1977.
Scott, Larry. *Masters: Glass Beads*. New York: Lark Books, 2008.
Seefried, Monique. *Les Pendentifs en verre sur noyau*. Farnese: Ecole Française de Rome, 1982.
Seizman, Matsuura. *Kasshi Yawa (Writings Begun on the Night of the First Day of the Rat, 11th Month)*. 6 vols. 1821–41. Edited by Nakamura Yukihiko and Nakano Mitsutoshi. Tokyo: Heibonsha, 1978.
Shaw, T. E. (Colonel T. E. Lawrence), ed. and trans. *The Odyssey of Homer*. Translation 1935. New York: Oxford University Press, 1965.
Shaw, Thurstan. *Igbo-Ukwu*. Evanston, Ill.: Northwestern University Press, 1970.
Sherratt, Andrew. *The Cambridge Encyclopedia of Archaeology*. New York: Crown Publishers, 1980.
The Shogun Age Exhibition. Japan: Tokugawa Art Museum, 1983.
Sieber, Roy. *African Textiles and Decorative Arts*. New York: The Museum of Modern Art, 1972.
Sitwell, Nigel. "Pearls—The Queen of Gems." *Smithsonian* 15, no. 10 (1985): 40.
Smith, Marvin T. "The Chevron Trade Bead in North America." *The Bead Journal* 3, no. 2 (1977): 15–17.
———. "Chronology from Glass Beads: The Spanish Period in the Southeast, c. A.D. 1513–1670." In *Proceedings of the 1982 Glass Trade Bead Conference Research Records* no. 16, edited by Charles F. Hayes, III. Rochester, N.Y.: Rochester Museum and Science Center, 1983.
Smith, Marvin T., and Mary Elizabeth Good. *Early Sixteenth-Century Glass Beads in the Spanish Colonial Trade*. Greenwood, Miss.: Cottonlandia Museum Publications, 1982.
Sorensen, Cloyd. "This Enduring Intrigue of the Glass Bead Trade." *Arizona Highways* 47, no. 7 (1971).
Speck, Frank G., and William C. Orchard. The Penn Wampum Belts. New York: Museum of the American Indian, Heye Foundation, 1925.
Stanfield, Kirk. "The Krobo and Bodom." In *Beads* 12–13 (2000–01).
Stierlin, Henri. Art of the Aztecs. New York: Rizzoli, 1982.
Stout, Ann M. "The Archaeological Context of Late Roman Period Mosaic Glass Face Beads." Ornament 9, no. 4 (1986): 58–61.
Streeter, Edwin W. *Pearls and Pearling Life*. York Street, London: George Bell & Sons, 1886.
Streuver, Stuart, and Felicia Antonelli Holton. *Koster: Americans in Search of Their Prehistoric Past*. Garden City, N.Y.: Anchor Press/Doubleday, 1979.
Suk, Joo-sun. *Personal Ornaments in Yi Dynasty*. Folk Art Research Collection series II. Seoul, Korea: Dankook University Press: The Suk Joo-sun Memorial Museum of Korean Folk Art, 1981.
Sullivan, Michael. *The Arts of China*. Berkeley, Ca.: University of California Press, 1979.
Tabor, Mary B.W. "20 Members of Hispanic Gang Indicted in Multiple Killings." *The New York Times*, June 22, 1994.
Tait, Hugh. *The Golden Age of Venetian Glass*. London: British Museum Publications, 1979.
Tanner, Clara. *Prehistoric Southwestern Craft Art*. Tuscon, Az.: University of Arizona Press, 1976.
Tatton-Brown, Veronica. *Cyprus B.C. 7,000 Years of History*. London: British Museum Publications, 1979.
Taylor, Lord William. The Mycenaeans. London: Thames and Hudson, 1983.
Tempelmann-Maczynska, M. Die Perlen der romischen Kaiserzeit und der fruhen Phasse der Volkerwanderungszeit im Mitteleuropaischen Barbaricum. Mainz: Verlag Philipp von Zabern, 1985.
Thompson, R. Campbell. *A Dictionary of Assyrian Chemistry and Geology*. Oxford: Clarendon Press, 1936.
Tigger, Bruce G., ed. "Northeast." *Handbook of North American Indians*. Vol. 15. Washington, D.C.: Smithsonian Institution, 1978.
Tosi, Maurizio, and Marcello Piperno. "Lithic Technology Behind the Ancient Lapis Lazuli Trade." *Expedition* 16, no. 1. University of Pennsylvania, 1973.
The Bead Museum. *Trajectories: Progressions in contemporary art glass beads*. Glendale, AZ, 2008.
Trebbin, Cornelius. Achate, geschliffen in Idar-Oberstein—Amulette, Schmock und Zahlungsmittel, in Afrika. Idar-Oberstein, West Germany: Museum Idar-Oberstein, 1985.
Tushingham, A. D., et al. *Studies in Ancient Peruvian Metalworking*. Toronto: Royal Ontario Museum, 1979.
Untracht, Oppi. *Jewelry Concepts and Technology*. Garden City, N.Y.: Doubleday, 1982.
van der Sleen, W. G. N. "Ancient Glass Beads, with special reference to the beads of East and Central Africa and the Indian Ocean." *Journal of the Royal Anthropological Institute of Great Britain and Ireland*. (1958): 88.
———. "Beadmaking in 17th-Century Amsterdam." *Archaeology* 16 (1963): 260–63.
———. A Handbook on Beads. Liège, Belgium: Librairie Halbart, 1973.
———. "Trade Wind Beads." Man. 1966.
Vandiver, Pamela. "Glass Technology at the Mid-Second-Millennium B.C. Hurrian Site of Nuzi." *Journal of Glass Studies* 25 (1983): 88–89.
van Landewijk, J.E.J.M. "What Was the Original Aggrey Bead?" Parts 1–3. *Ghana Journal of Sociology* 6, 7, nos. 2, 4, 1 (1970–71): n.p.
van Riet Lowe, C. "The Glass Beads of Mapungubwe." *Archaeological Survey*, no. 9 (1955): 1–21.
Venclova, Natalie. "Prehistoric Eye Beads in Central Europe." *Journal of Glass Studies* 25 (1983): n.p.
Vilimkova, Milada, and Dominique Darbois. *Egyptian Jewellery*. London: Paul Hamlyn, 1969.
Vogel, Susan. *For Spirits and Kings: African Art from the Ruth and Paul Tishman Collection*. New York: Harry N. Abrams and the Metropolitan Museum of Art, 1981.
Volker, T. The Animal in Far Eastern Art. Leiden: E. J. Brill, 1975.
Von Saldern, Axel. Ancient Glass in the Museum of Fine Arts. Boston: Museum of Fine Arts, 1968.
———. "Mosaic Glass from Hasanl, Marlik, and Tell al-Rimah." *The Journal of Glass Studies* 8. Corning, N.Y.: Corning Museum of Glass, 1966.
Waldschmidt, Ernest, and Rose Waldschmidt. *Nepal: Art Treasures from the Himalayas*. New York: Universe Books, 1970.
Warmington, E. H. *The Commerce Between the Roman Empire and India*. Cambridge, England: Cambridge University Press, 1928.
Weaver, Muriel Porter. The Aztecs, Maya, and Their Predecessors. New York: Academic Press, 1981.
Webster, L., ed. *Aspects of Production and Style in Dark Ages Metalwork*. Occasional Paper no. 34. London: British Museum, 1982.
Weinberg, Gladys Davidson. "Glass Manufacture in Hellenistic Rhodes." *Archaiologikon Deltion* 24 (1969): 1971.
Weinstein, Michael. *The World of Jewel Stones*. New York: Sheridan House, 1967.
White, J. C., et al. *Ban Chiang: Discovery of a Lost Bronze Age*. Philadelphia: University Museum, 1982.
White, Randall. "Visual Thinking in the Ice Age." Scientific American, July 1989. pp. 92–99.
———. "Beyond Art: Toward an Understanding of the Origins of Material Representation in Europe." Annual Review of Anthropology. 1992. 21: 537–64
———. "Technological and Social Dimensions of "Aurignacian-Age" Body Ornaments across Europe." Before Lascaux: The Complete Record of the Early Upper Paleolithic. Eds. H. Knecht, A. Pike-Tay, and R. White. Boca Raton: CRC Press. R. 1993. 277–299.
———. "Substantial Acts: From materials to Meaning in Upper Paleolithic Representation. Beyond Art: Pleistocene Imagery and Symbols." Memoirs of the California Academy of Sciences Number 23, 1997. p. 93–121.
———. "Personal Ornaments from the Grotte du Renne at Arcy-sur-Cure." *Athena Review*, Vol. 2, No. 4, 2001. pp. 41–16.
———. "Systems of Personal Ornamentation in the Early Upper Paleolithic: Methodological Challenges and New Observations." In, Mellars, Paul, Boyle, Katie, Bar-Yosef, Ofer and Stringer, Chris (eds.) Rethinking the Human Revolution: New Behavioural and Biological Perspectives on the Origin and Dispersal of Modern Humans. Cambridge, UK, McDonald Institute for Archaeological Research, 2007. pp. 287–302. (McDonald Institute Monographs).
White, William Charles. *Tombs of Old Lo-Yang*. Shanghai: Kelly & Walsh, 1934.
Wild, R. P. "A Method of Beadmaking Practiced in the Gold Coast." *Man* 37 (1937): 96–97.
Wildschut, William, and John C. Ewers. *Crow Indian Beadwork: A Descriptive and Historical Study*. New York: Museum of the American Indian, Heye Foundation, 1959.
Wilkins, Eithene. *The Rose-Garden Game: The Symbolic Background to the European Prayer Beads*. London: Victor Gollancz, 1969.
Willcox, Donald J. *Body Jewelry, International Perspectives*. Chicago: Henry Regnery Company, 1973.
Willett, Frank. *Baubles, Bangles, and Beads: Trade Contacts of Medieval Ifa*. Melville J. Herskovitz Memorial Lecture, no. 13. Edinburgh: Center of African Studies, 1977.
Winnipeg Art Gallery. *The Inuit Amautik: I Like My Hood To Be Full*. Winnipeg, Manitoba: Winnipeg Art Gallery, 1980.
Wooley, Sir Leonard C. *Ur Excavations Vol. 2, The Royal Cemetery*. London and Philadelphia: Publications of the Joint Expedition of the British Museum and of the Museum of the University of Pennsylvania, 1934.
Yager, Jan. *City Flora/City Flotsam*. Design Now, 20th Century Gallery, Victoria and Albert Museum, London, UK. April–August 2001. Exhibition text.
Yoshimizu, T. Eye of the Dragonfly. Tokyo: Heibonsha, 1980.
Zwalf, W. Heritage of Tibet. London: British Museum Publications, 1981.

Index

Page numbers listed in *italics* refer to illustration captions.

A

B

J

K

L

M

U

V

W

Y

Z

PHOTO CREDITS

All photographs were taken by Kiyoshi Togashi or were provided by the museums credited in the captions, unless listed below. Plate numbers follow the photographers' names.

Jamey D. Allen: 100, 171. Noel Allum: 347. Courtesy of Dr. Walter Alva: 271d. Ping Amranand: 206, 219–21, 223, p. 11. Jerry Anthony: 404, 410. Dirk Bakker: 252. Robert Batey: 361, 362. Gary Lee Betts: 358, 359. Barry Blau: 344. Lee Boultin: 21. Larry Brown: 363. Brown Brothers: 323, 325. Mark Carleton and Dr. Michael Heide: 91, 102, 334 (36). Ian R. Cartwright, Institute of Archaeology, Oxford: 2. Michael Cavanagh and Keith Montague: 62–63. Courtesy of CFM Gallery: 409. Amos Chan: 341. Crawley, Wilkinson Associates, Ltd.: 318–19. Robert Diamante: 379, 417. Courtesy of Dr. Christopher Donnan: 270, 271a, c. Lois S. Dubin: 121–22, 315, 333. Courtesy of David Ebbinghouse: 216. Andre Emmerich Gallery: 261. Susan Epstein: 271b. Ray Errett: 31, 33–36, 52, 85, 109 (6), 158, 162–68, 194, 228, 329 (19–20, 26, 35), 330. Mary Evan Picture Library/Photo Researchers, Inc.: 321. Angela Fisher/Carol Beckwith: 103, 106, 111a–b, 114, 120, 149–50. Courtesy of Dr. Melvin Fowler, University of Wisconsin, Milwaukee: 273. Courtesy of Patricia Frantz: 392b–c, 414. Courtesy Ivory Freidus: 213, 218. John Gerrits: 115-117. Michael Ginn: 113. Michael B. Glass: 143, 204, 337, 340. Andrea Guarino-Slemmons: 397. Pinar Hakim: 429. Dennis Hellawell: 433. Gavin Hellier: 118. Melinda Holden: 421. Barry Howard: 7, 145. Eeva Inkeri: 232, 240. Howard Jones: 313. Paul Jones: 304, 314. Courtesy of Mary Kanda: 373. Courtesy of Steven Kossak: 225. Victor Krantz: 241–43, 245–46. Jack Kulawik: 331. Francois LeClair: 311. Alexander Marshack: 1, 4, 5a–d. Michael Meleski: Bead Shape Table (pp. 362–63). Metropolitan Museum of Art: 25c. Mobilia Gallery: 366. Museo Tumbas Reales de Sipán: 271d. National Gallery of Ireland: 101. Jane Nyhus Designs: 389. Gurhan Orhan: 354. Bruno Piazza: 131, 147, 195, 226–27, 237–39. George Post: 378. Dean Powell: 400, top row. Norman Priebatsch: 130. Tom Reid: 144, 350. Jack Ramsdale: 374–77. William Robertson: 152–57, 159, 329 (24–25). Larry Sanders Visual Images: 369, 370. Manu Sassoonian: 197. Heini Schneebeli: 200, 207, 215. Courtesy of Verena Sieber-Fuchs: 339, 340. Michael Schneider: 371, 372. Roger Schreiber: 369, 370. Rod Slemmons: 346, 348, 349. Larry Stesson: 367, 368. Keren Su: 124. Jerry L. Thompson, courtesy of The Metropolitan Museum of Art: 12. Tom Van Eynde: 355. Malcolm Varon: 138. Courtesy of Gene Waddell: 357. Paul Weltchek: 77. Randall White: 3.1–3.10. Art Wolfe: 71, 123. Carolyn Wright: 364.

BEAD SHAPE TABLE
All beads from the collections of Henry Anavian and Lois S. Dubin.

TIMELINE CREDITS
The following museums provided beads and/or photographs for the Timeline. Timeline numbers are listed after each museum.
American Museum of Natural History, New York City: 1001a–f, 1002, 1013–1014, 1017–1018, 1020–1025. Arizona State Museum: 1016, 1019, 1027–1029. Ashmolean Museum, Oxford University, England: 36. The Bead Museum, Glendale, Arizona: 909a, 916, 928–930, 1215. British Museum, London, England: 3–30, 45, 246, 247, 248a–c, 249–250, 255, 310, 355, 375, 392, 394–400, 402–404, 405a–d, 406a–c, 407a–c, 411, 421, 422, 424, 425, 429, 430a–b, 431–437, 439–411, 443–447, 449–454, 457–462, 488–491. Corning Museum of Glass, Corning, New York: 401, 413, 414–420, 465, 625a–f, 803, 814, 818–820, 822, 835–838, 845, 901. Dumbarton Oaks Museum, Washington, D.C.: 516. Gilcrease Museum, Tulsa: 1000. Hegau Museum, Singen, Germany: 9. Herakleion Museum, Crete: 393. Hispanic Society of America, New York City: 568. Illinois State Museum, Springfield: 1009–1012. Indiana University Museum, Bloomington: 422, 428, 517–518. Institute of Archaeology, Oxford University: 1200. Instituto Nacional de Seguros, Costa Rica: 1105. Israel Museum, Jerusalem: 200–205. McCord Museum, McGill University, Montreal: 1033. Metropolitan Museum of Art, New York City: 257, 456, 488, 490, 497, 501, 546–7, 569, 633. Moravske Museum, Brno, the Czech Republic: 7–8. Museum of Anthropology, University of British Columbia, Vancouver: 103, 104. Museo Tumbas Royales de Sipán: 107. National Museum of Copenhagen, Denmark: 31–35. Peabody Museum of Ethnology and Archaeology, Cambridge, Massachusetts: 10, 1007. Rochester Museum and Science Center: 1008, 1034. Royal Ontario Museum, Toronto, Ontario: 800–802, 804–13, 815–16. San Juan Archaeological Research Center and Library, Bloomfield, New Mexico: 1015. Trondheim Royal Norwegian Scientific Society Museum: 41a–e. University Museum, University of Pennsylvania, Philadelphia: 1216–17. Walters Art Gallery, Baltimore, Maryland: 37. Randall White: 1–6.

The following photographers and collectors provided photographs for the Timeline.
Jamey D. Allen: 40, 48a–d, 107, 115–131, 154, 206–208, 212–214, 221–222, 232, 233, 234, 273, 311–313, 513, 530–532, 600, 606–609, 702–703, 817, 850–852, 856–858, 902–904, 906–908, 910, 912, 918, 923, 936–937, 1212–1214, 1218, 1221, 1243, 1246, 1247, 1305, 1322. Birk Bakker: 1105. Mark Carleton and Dr. Michael Heide: 49–51, 94–96, 114a–c, 117, 118, 122a–c, 123a–c, 1209–1211. Michael Cavanagh and Keith Montague: 423, 424, 517–518. Crawley, Wilkinson Associates, Ltd.: 151a–d, 152. Christopher Donnan: 1106, 1107. Andre Emmerich Gallery: 1102. Ray Errett: 401, 413, 414–417, 420, 473, 493, 818–820, 822, 835–838, 845. Michael B. Glass: 1312. Barry Howard: 309, 1005a–f, 1006, 1013–1014, 1017–1025. Eeva Inkeri: 11, 921a–c. Howard Jones: 1015. Paul Jones: 1016, 1019, 1027–1029. Mark Kenoyer: 600–604. Jack Kulawik: 1320. Francois LeClair: 1033. Alexander Marshack: 7–11. Michael Meleski: 1043, 1044, 1103. Dean Powell: 1306. William Robertson: 800–802, 804–13, 815–16. Larry Sanders Visual Images: 1308. Heini Schneebeli: 705. Randall White: 1–6. All other Timeline photographs were taken by Kiyoshi Togashi.

The following collectors and galleries kindly provided beads to be photographed by Kiyoshi Togashi for the Timeline.
Africa Direct; Jamey D. Allen; Henry Anavian, Sumer Gallery; Hermon Baker; Robin Beningson, Antiquarian Gallery; Toby Bowlby; Nico Coppenhagen; Craft Caravan; Derek Content; Nomoda E. Djaba; Lois S. Dubin; Neil Dwire; Edward Merrin Gallery; Bassem Elias; Andre Emmerich; Connie Emmerich; Joan Eppen; Abram Epstein; Ivory Freidus; Audrey Friedman, Primavera Gallery; Cynthia Gofre, Bamboula; Anita Gumpert; Dr. Michael Heide; Wolf Hunger, Sac Frères; J. Camp Gallery; Suzanne Donnelly Jenkins; Arthur King; Margaret and Joe Knopfelmacher; Ravi Kumar; Gabrielle Liese; Naomi Lindstrom; The Bead Museum; Karl Mann; Dave Mort; Peter and Louise Mroczkowski; Rita Okrent; Louise Parrish; Ruth and John Picard; Sylvia Pines, Uniquities; Walter Seifried; Billy Steinberg; Albert Summerfield; Joe Tanner, Tanner's Indian Arts; Abdul Touray; Esther Twersky; Gene Waddell, Waddell Trading Company; Sashi Wagner, Midori Gallery; Charles Whitmore; Maureen Zarember, Tambaran Gallery.